HEALTH CARE LAW:
TEXT AND MATERIALS

AUSTRALIA
Law Book Co.
Sydney

CANADA AND USA
Carswell
Toronto

HONG KONG
Sweet & Maxwell
Asia

NEW ZEALAND
Brookers
Auckland

SINGAPORE AND MALAYSIA
Sweet & Maxwell Asia
Singapore and Kuala Lumpur

HEALTH CARE LAW: TEXT AND MATERIALS

Second Edition

JEAN McHALE

Professor of Law, University of Leicester

MARIE FOX

Professor of Law, University of Keele

MICHAEL GUNN

Pro Vice Chancellor (Learning, Teaching and Scholarship), University of Derby

STEPHEN WILKINSON

Professor of Bioethics, University of Keele

LONDON
SWEET & MAXWELL
2007

Published by
Sweet & Maxwell Limited of
100 Avenue Road,
London NW3 3PF
http://www.smlawpub.co.uk

Typeset by Interactive Sciences Ltd, Gloucester.
Printed and bound in Great Britain by TJ International Ltd,
Padstow, Cornwall

First Edition 1997
Reprinted in 1999, 2001
Second Edition 2007

A CIP catalogue record for this book is available from The British Library.

ISBN–10 0–421–71010–1
ISBN–13 978–0421–71010–8

No natural forests were destroyed to make this product.
Only farmed timber was used and re-planted.

Preface to the Second Edition

Legal issues relating to health care are rarely out of the headlines today. Academic and professional lawyers alike have become increasingly aware of the practical importance and complexity of health care issues. This book focuses upon and reflects the legal, professional and technological developments which have taken place in this area in recent years. It is designed to provide an accessible and stimulating collection of materials with accompanying text.

Health Care Law: Text and Materials is designed to be suitable as a core text for the wide range of undergraduate and postgraduate health care and medical law courses available. It is also intended that this book may be used by health care professionals. This area has moved on considerably since the first edition was published in 1997 and the content of the book reflects the changes. The overall chapter structure remains the same, but the content has been thoroughly revised and updated to reflect the changing dynamic of the law in this area. What is striking over the last decade is the increase in litigation and the willingness of the courts, at least at the rhetorical level, to move away from adherence to the *Bolam* test in a range of areas from the provision of information to patients through to the assessment of best interests in relation to adults without mental capacity. The development of the patient as "consumer" of health care is illustrated through the proliferation of health tourism and the growth in demand for elective surgery.

The drive to regulation as opposed simply to litigation in defining the parameters of the area, which we noted in the introduction to the first edition, is evidenced by, for example, the development of new regulatory frameworks in relation to the use of human material (the Human Tissue Act 2004) and decision-making concerning adults lacking mental capacity (the Mental Capacity Act 2005). A further notable trend is the increasing impact of the European Union on the structure of domestic health care law, as seen in the impact of the Clinical Trials Directive on the conduct of drug trials, the EU Tissue Directive in relation to use of human materials and the free movement principles which underpin *Ex parte Blood* and *Watts*. Finally, the impact of the Human Rights Act 1998 — a piece of legislation which was only a glint in the policy-maker's eye when we were finishing the first edition in 1996 — is considered in a number of areas from reproductive technology to end of life.

The focus of this book is the legal regulation of health care practice in England. We do not attempt to provide detailed descriptions of the approaches adopted in other jurisdictions. Comprehension of comparative approaches may be difficult unless jurisprudential developments are set in the broader context of the structures of health care provision. To attempt such a task alongside our account of English health care law would also have negated one of our aims, which is to produce a book manageable in size for students. Where appropriate, the reader's attention is drawn to a particularly pertinent overseas authority, for example, where this jurisprudence has been considered in the English courts. Some reference is also made to overseas literature as further reading. This area has spawned a vast amount of literature, particularly over the last half-decade. In general, reference to articles on the specific issue under discussion are incorporated within the body of the text, while at the end of each chapter there is a select bibliography indicating useful, although clearly not exhaustive, further reading.

The primary responsibility for the text is that of Jean McHale and Marie Fox. We gratefully acknowledge the contribution in the first edition of Jonathan Montgomery and John Murphy. In this edition, Chapter 2 was written by Stephen Wilkinson and Chapters 5 and 8 by Michael Gunn. For the remainder of the text, primary responsibility for Chapters 1, 3, 4, 9, 10, 14 and 15 was taken by Jean McHale and for Chapters 6, 7, 11, 12 and 13 by Marie Fox.

As always a project such as this would have been impossible without the help and kindness of many people. We gratefully acknowledge the contribution of Jonathan Montgomery and John Murphy in the first edition of this book. In this edition we are indebted for research assistance to Mary Ewert, Arabella Stuart and Jane Wilson.

We all owe considerable debt to our colleagues and students on undergraduate and postgraduate health care law courses in our respective institutions, who acted as sounding boards for some of our ideas and some of whom "road tested" draft chapters.

Special thanks go to Peter Allen, Mark Bell, Margaret Brazier, Emma Cave, Angus Dawson, Veronica English, Ruth Fletcher, Kathy de Gama, Melanie Latham, Julie McCandless, Jose Miola, Nicky Prialux, Sally Sheldon, Michael Thomson, Matthew Weait and Mary Ewert for reading draft chapters.

More generally thanks also to Margaret Brazier, Emma Cave, Ray Geary, Emily Jackson, Bob Lee, Simon Lee and Katherine O'Donovan.

We would also like to thank Kevin Symons, Joe Marriott, Betzy Dinesen and the team at Sweet & Maxwell for their great patience, support and encouragement through the long writing process.

On terminology, for the purposes of this text, health care professionals are referred to as "she" and patients as "he".

The law is as stated at May 1, 2006, although it has been possible to include some more recent developments at proof stage.

Acknowledgments

Grateful acknowledgment is made for permission to reproduce from the undermentioned works:

Blackwell Publishing. David Wong, "Relativism", in Peter Singer (ed.), *A Companion to Ethics*, Oxford: Basil Blackwell Ltd, 1993; and L. W. Sumner, "Rights", in Hugh LaFollette (ed.), *The Blackwell Guide to Ethical Theory*, Malden, Mass: Blackwell Publishers Inc., 2000.

Butterworths Ltd. Extracts from the following reports: *A.G. v Able* [1984] 1 All E.R. 277; *A-G v Guardian Newspapers (No. 2)* [1988] 3 All E.R. 545 at 658; *Airedale NHS Trust v Bland* [1993] 1 All E.R. 521; *Attorney-General's Reference (No. 3)* [1996] 2 All E.R. 10; *B. v Croydon Health Authority* [1995] 1 All E.R. 683; *Barr v Matthews* [1999] 52 B.M.L.R. 217; *Bolam v Friern Hospital Management Committee* [1957] 2 All E.R. 118; *Bravery v Bravery* [1954] 3 All E.R. 59; *C v S* [1987] 1 All E.R. 1230; *Cassidy v Ministry of Health* [1951] 1 All E.R. 574; *Chatterton v Gerson* [1981] 1 All E.R. 257; *Clark v Maclennan* [1983] 1 All E.R. 416; *Doughty v General Dental Council* [1987] 3 All E.R. 843; *Emeh v Chelsea and Kensington Area Health Authority* [1984] 1 All E.R. 1044; *Eyre v Measday* [1986] 1 All E.R. 488; *F v West Berkshire Health Authority* [1989] 2 All E.R. 545; *Freeman v Home Office* [1984] 1 All E.R. 1036; *Frenchay Healthcare National Health Service Trust v S* [1994] 2 All E.R. 403; *Gillick v West Norfolk and Wisbech Area Health Authority* [1985] 3 All E.R. 402; *Gold v Haringey Health Authority* [1987] 2 All E.R. 888; *Health Authority* [1985] 3 All E.R. 402; *Hotson v East Berkshire Area Health Authority* [1987] 2 All E.R. 909; *Hunter v Mann* [1974] 2 All E.R. 414; *Janaway v Salford Area Health Authority* [1988] 3 All E.R. 1079; *Mahon v Osborne* [1939] 1 All E.R. 535; *Maynard v West Midlands Regional Health Authority* [1985] 1 All E.R. 635; *McKay v Essex Area Health Authority* [1982] 2 All E.R. 771; *R. (on the application of the Assisted Reproduction and Gynaecology Centre) and Another v HFEA* [2003] 1 F.C.R. 266, CA; *NHS Trust A v M; NHS Trust B v H* [2001] 1 All E.R. 801; *Paton v Trustees of The British Pregnancy Advisory Service* [1978] 2 All E.R. 987; *R. v Adomako* [1994] 3 All E.R. 79; *R. v Bourne* [1938] 3 All E.R. 615; *R. v Cambridge DHA, Ex p. B* [1995] 2 All E.R. 129; *R. v Cannons Park MHRT, Ex p. A* [1994] 2 All E.R. 659; *R. v. Mental Health Act Commission, Ex p. X* (1988) 9 B.M.L.R. 77; *R. (on the application of DR) v Merseycare NHS Trust* [2002] All E.R. (D) 28; *R. v Mid Glamorgan Family Health Services Authority, Ex p. Martin* [1995] 1 All E.R. 356; *R. v Portsmouth Hospitals NHS Trust, Ex p. Glass* [1999] 50 B.M.L.R. 269; *R. (Quintavalle) v Secretary of State for Health* [2003] 2 All E.R. 113; *R. (on the application of Quintavalle) v HFEA* [2003] 3 All E.R. 257; *Re A* [1992] 3 Med. L.R. 303; *Re B (A Minor) (Wardship: Sterilisation)* [1987]

2 All E.R. 206; *Re B* [1987] 2 All E.R. 206; *Re B* [1990] 3 All E.R. 927; *Re C (Adult: Refusal of Treatment)* [1994] 1 All E.R. 819; *Re C* [1989] 2 All E.R. 782; *Re C (A Minor) (Medical Treatment)* [1998] 1 F.C.R. 1; *Re D* [1976] 1 All E.R. 326; *Re F (In Utero)* [1988] 2 All E.R. 193; *Re J* [1990] 3 All E.R. 930; *Re J* [1992] 4 All E.R. 614; *Re A (A Minor) (Medical Treatment: Court's Jurisdiction)* [1992] 4 All E.R. 627; *Re M (Child: Refusal of Medical Treatment)* [1999] 2 F.C.R. 577; *Re R (A Minor) (Wardship: Medical Treatment)* [1991] 4 All E.R. 177; *Re S (Adult Refusal of Treatment)* [1992] 4 All E.R. 671; *Re S (Hospital Patient: Court's Jurisdiction)* [1995] 3 All E.R. 290; *Re T (Adult: Refusal of Treatment)* [1992] 4 All E.R. 649; *Re T* [1992] 4 All E.R. 649; *Re T* [1992] 4 All E.R. 649; *Re W (A Minor) (Medical Treatment: Court's Jurisdiction)* [1992] 4 All E.R. 627; *Royal College of Nursing v Department of Health and Social Security* [1981] 1 All E.R. 545; *Sidaway v Bethlem RHG* [1985] 1 All E.R. 643; *Tameside and Glossop Acute Services Trust v CH (A Patient)* [1996] 1 F.C.R. 753; *Thake v Maurice* [1986] 1 All E.R. 497; *TP and KM v United Kingdom* [2001] 2 F.C.R. 289; *Vadera v Shaw* (1999) 45 B.M.L.R. 162; *W. v Egdell* [1990] 1 All E.R. 835; *Whitehouse v Jordan* [1981] 1 All E.R. 267; *Wilsher v Essex Area Health Authority* [1986] 3 All E.R. 801; *Wilsher v Essex Area Health Authority* [1988] 1 All E.R. 871; *Wyatt v Portsmouth NHS Trust* [2005] 1 W.L.R. 3995; *X v Y* [1988] 2 All E.R. 648; *X v Bedfordshire CC; M v Newham LBC; E v Dorset CC* [1995] 3 All E.R. 353.

Cambridge University Press. Bernard Williams, *Morality* (1976) and J.J.C. Smart, Bernard Williams, *Utilitarianism* (1973).

Cambridge Quarterly of Healthcare Ethics. Soren Holm, "A Life in the Shadow: One Reason Why We Should Not Clone Humans", 1998, 7.

Human Fertilisation and Embryology Authority: Extracts from HFEA Code of Practice (6th edn) 2003; HFEA, SEED Report: A Report of the Human Fertilisation & Embryology Authority's review of sperm and egg donation in the United Kingdom, London, 2005; HFEA Practice Guidance Note: Egg Sharing (2006); HFEA, *Sex Selection: Options for Regulation. A Report on the HFEA's 2002–03 Review on Sex Selection including a Discussion of Legislative and Regulatory Options*, 2003. HFEA and HGAC, *Cloning Issues in Reproduction, Science and Medicine* (December 1998). Reproduced with kind permission.

Human Tissue Authority: Code of Practice on Consent, published July 2006; Code of Practice on Donation of Organs, Tissues and Cells for Transplantation, published July 2006.

Incorporated Council of Law Reporting. Extracts from the following reports: *Re C (A Child) (HIV Test)* [2000] 2 W.L.R. 270; *R. (Burke) v General Medical Council (Official Solicitor intervening)* [2005] 3 W.L.R. 1132, CA; *U v W (Attorney-General Intervening)* [1997] 3 W.L.R. 739.

John Wiley & Sons. R. Gillon, "Paternalism", in *Philosophical Medical Ethics* (1985).

Jordans Publishing Ltd. Extracts from the following reports: *A v C* [1985] F.L.R. 445; *A v C* [1984] Fam.Law 241; *C v S* [1987] 2 F.L.R. 5; *F v West Berkshire Health Authority* [1989] 2 F.L.R. 476; *Frenchay Healthcare National Health Service Trust v S* [1994] 1 F.L.R. 485; *Gillick v West Norfolk and Wisbech Area Health Authority* [1986] 1 F.L.R. 224; *Glass v UK* [2004] 1 F.L.R. 1019; *Gold v Haringey Health Authority* [1988] 1 F.L.R. 55; *Janaway v Salford Area Health Authority* [1989] 1 F.L.R. 1; *Kelly v Kelly* [1997] 2 F.L.R. 828; *R. v Ethical Committee of St. Mary's Hospital (Manchester), Ex p. Harriott* [1988] F.L.R. 165; *R. v Ethical Committee of St. Mary's Hospital (Manchester), Ex p. Harriott* [1988] 1 F.L.R. 512; *Re R (A Minor) (Blood Transfusion)* [1993] 2 F.L.R. 757; *Re A (medical treatment: male sterilisation)* [2000] 1 F.L.R. 549; *Re B (A Minor) (Wardship: Sterilisation)* [1987] F.L.R. 314; [1985] F.L.R. 846; *Re C (Adult: Refusal of Treatment)* [1994] 1 F.L.R. 31; *Re E (A Minor) (Medical Treatment)* [1991] 2 F.L.R. 585; *Re E (A Minor) (Wardship: Medical Treatment)* [1993] 1 F.L.R. 386; *Re J (A Minor) (Prohibited Steps Order: Circumcision* [2000] 1 F.L.R. 571; *Re K, W and H (Minors) (Medical Treatment)* [1993] 1 F.L.R. 854; *Re L (Medical Treatment: Gillick Competency)* [1998] 2 F.L.R. 810; *Re P (A Minor) (Wardship: Sterilisation)* [1989] 1 F.L.R. 182; *Re P (A Minor) (Wardship: Sterilisation)* [1989] 1 Fam.Law 102; *Re P (Minors) (Wardship: Surrogacy)* [1987] 2 F.L.R. 421; *Re R (A Minor) (Blood Transfusion)* [1993] 2 F.L.R. 757; *Re R (A Minor) (Blood Transfusion)* [1993] Fam.Law 577; *Re R (A Minor) (Wardship: Medical Treatment)* [1992] 1 F.L.R. 190; *Re R* [1996] 2 F.L.R. 99; *Re S (A Minor) (Medical Treatment)* [1994] 2 F.L.R. 1065; *Re T (Adult: Refusal of Treatment)* [1992] 2 F.L.R. 458; *Re T* [1992] 2 F.L.R. 458; *Re (A Minor) (Medical Treatment: Court's Jurisdiction)* [1993] 1 F.L.R. 1, [1992] 2 F.L.R. 785; *Re W (A Minor) (Medical Treatment: Court's Jurisdiction)* Fam.Law 541; *Re Y. (Mental Patient: Bone Marrow Donation)* (1996) F.L.R. 791; *South Glamorgan County Council v W and B* [1993] 1 F.L.R. 574.

New England Journal of Medicine. James Rachels, "Active and Passive Euthanasia" © 1975 Massachusetts Medical Society. All rights reserved.

Nuffield Council on Bioethics. Animal to Human Transplants: The Ethics of Xenotransplantation, London 1996; Human Tissue: Ethical and Legal Issues, 1995; Ethics of Research Involving Animals, 2005. Extracts reproduced with kind permission.

Oxford University Press. Susan Sherwin, "Feminism and Bioethics", in Susan Wolf (ed.), *Feminism and Bioethics* (Oxford: 1996).

Penguin Group UK. Extract from *Causing Deaths and Saving Lives*, Jonathan Glover (Pelican, 1977) © Jonathan Glover, 1977.

Royal College of Obstetricians and Gynaecologists. Extract reproduced from The Care of Women Requesting Induced Abortion. Evidence-based Clinical Guideline Number 7, September 2004, with the permission of the Royal College of Obstetricians and Gynaecologists.

Westview Press. *Morality, Harm, and the Law*, Gerald Dworkin, reprinted by permission of Westview Press, a member of the Perseus Books Group.

Acknowledgment is made for extracts from the following works:

GMC. *Good Medical Practice*, 3rd edn (London: GMC, 2001); *Intimate Examinations* (London: GMC, 2001); and GMC, *Serious Communicable Diseases*, 1997.

King's Fund Institute. B. New, M. Soloman, R. Dingwall, J. McHale "A Question of Give and Take: Improving the Supply of Donor Organs for Transplantation" (London: 1994).

Nursing & Midwifery Council. The NMC Code of Professional Conduct: Standards for Conduct, Performance and Ethics (London: NMC, 2004).

Routledge. Stephen Wilkinson, *Bodies for Sale*, London: Routledge, 2003; D. Lamb, *Organ Transplants and Ethics*, London: Routledge, 1990.

Routledge REP. David McNaughton (1998), "Consequentialism" in E. Craig (ed.), *Routledge Encyclopedia of Philosophy*, London: Routledge; and David McNaughton (1998), "Deontological Ethics" in E. Craig (ed.), *Routledge Encyclopedia of Philosophy*, London: 1998.

The Open University. Eve Garrard and Stephen Wilkinson "The Ethics of Care", Section 4.2 of Workbook 3: Dilemmas and Decisions at the End of Life (Milton Keynes: 2001).

Watts & Co. John Stuart Mill, *On Liberty* (London: 1929).

Contents

Preface   v
Acknowledgments   vii
Table of Cases   xix
Table of Statutes   xxvii
Table of Statutory Instruments   xxxv

PART I

Introduction   3

1.   RIGHTS TO HEALTH AND HEALTH CARE   7
     1.   Introduction   7
     2.   The Scope of Rights to Health and Health Care   8
     3.   Health Promotion and Disease Prevention   11
          (a)   Contagious Disease Control   11
          (b)   Compulsory Care and the Right to be Ill   22
          (c)   Health Promotion   24
     4.   The Provision of NHS Services   30
          (a)   Primary Care   30
          (b)   Secondary Care   33
     5.   Access to Health Services   41
          (a)   Duties to Provide Services   41
          (b)   Enforcement of Duties to Provide Services   45
     Select Bibliography   86

2.   HEALTH CARE ETHICS   87
     1.   Introduction   87
     2.   Is Morality "Relative"?   88
     3.   Law and Morality   92
     4.   Consequentialism   97
     5.   Deontology, Rights and Principalism   102
     6.   Virtue Ethics, Feminist Ethics and Nursing Ethics   111
     7.   Autonomy, Consent and Paternalism   121

8.   Ethical Issues at the Beginning and End of Life   128
Select Bibliography   145

PART II

Introduction   149

3.   PROFESSIONAL ACCOUNTABILITY I   151
     1.   Introduction   151
     2.   The Malpractice Action   152
          (a)   Introduction   152
          (b)   The Duty of Care   153
          (c)   The Standard of Care   157
          (d)   The Burden of Proof   179
          (e)   Causation   183
     3.   Defective Medicinal Products and Drugs   203
     4.   Gross Negligence and Criminal Liability   209
     5.   Reform of Fault-Based Liability   213
          (a)   General Difficulties with the Tort System   213
          (b)   Specific Difficulties with Medical Negligence Litigation   215
          (c)   Reforming the Clinical Negligence System   217
     Select Bibliography   236

4.   PROFESSIONAL ACCOUNTABILITY II   239
     1.   Introduction   239
     2.   Complaints within the NHS   241
          (a)   The Aims of a Complaints Process   241
          (b)   The Complaints Process   243
     3.   Disciplinary Procedures in the NHS in relation to Health Care
          Professionals   258
     4.   Health Service Commissioner   260
     5.   Self-regulation of the Health Care Professions   268
          (a)   Case Study: the Role of the General Medical Council   269
     Select Bibliography   288

PART III

Introduction   291

5.   CAPACITY   295
     1.   Introduction   295

2. The Reform Process 296
3. Principles 298
4. The Challenge of Capacity 302
5. Capacity to Consent at Common Law and under the Mental Capacity Act 2005 307
   (a) The Common Law 307
   (b) The Mental Capacity Act 2005 314
6. Treatment without Consent: Best Interests Test 320
   (a) The Common Law 320
   (b) The Mental Capacity Act 2005 327
Select Bibliography 347

6. CONSENT 349
1. Introduction 349
2. The Need for Consent 351
   (a) The Criminal Law 352
   (b) The Civil Law 358
3. The Meaning of Consent 360
   (a) The Nature of "Real Consent" 360
   (b) Controversies in Relation to Consent 365
   (c) Disclosure and the Quality of Consent 372
4. Vitiation of Consent 379
Select Bibliography 402

7. CHILDREN 405
1. Introduction 405
2. The Legal Position of the Young Child 407
   (a) The Court's Role in Approving the Withdrawal or Withholding of Medical Treatment in the Case of Neonates and Young Children 408
   (b) Cases where Parents Seek to Compel Treatment Contrary to Medical Assessments of Best Interests 423
   (c) The Special Case of Conjoined Twins 434
3. An Older Child's Capacity to Consent to Medical Treatment: Statute and Common Law 439
   (a) The Statutory Power of Consent 439
   (b) The Common Law Power of Consent 440
4. The Retreat from Gillick 451
   (a) Refusal of Treatment by Adolescents 451
   (b) Refusal of Treatment by Adolescents on the Basis of Belief 463
5. Limits to the Parental Power of Consent 470
Select Bibliography 478

8. MENTAL HEALTH 479
1. Introduction 479

	(a)	Reform	479
	(b)	Principles for Mental Health Legislation	482
	(c)	The Significance of Safeguards	488
2.	Admission to Hospital		492
3.	Compulsory Admission to Hospital		502
	(a)	The Main Admission Sections	502
	(b)	Mental Disorder	504
	(c)	Other Criteria for Admission	510
	(d)	Procedural Issues	520
	(e)	Admission for Assessment in Emergency	526
	(f)	Admission of Patents Already in Hospital	526
4.	In Hospital		528
	(a)	Detention	528
	(b)	Leave of Absence	528
	(c)	Discipline and Control of Patient Activity	529
	(d)	Treatment	531
	(e)	Information	547
	(f)	Correspondence	547
	(g)	Mental Health Act Commission	547
5.	Discharge		548
6.	Mental Health Review Tribunals		549
7.	Community Care and Treatment		552
	(a)	Guardianship	553
	(b)	After-Care under Supervision	555
	Select Bibliography		561

9.	HEALTH CARE, PRIVACY AND CONFIDENTIALITY		565
1.	Introduction		565
2.	The Obligation of Confidentiality and Professional Ethical Codes		567
3.	Confidentiality in the Contract of Employment		568
4.	Non-statutory Protection in Law for Confidential Information: Breach of Confidence		571
	(a)	Basis for the Action	571
	(b)	The Relationship between Confidentiality and Privacy	573
	(c)	Confidentiality and Anonymised Information	579
	(d)	Who Can Bring an Action for Breach of Confidence?	581
	(e)	Grounds for Disclosure	596
	(f)	Conflicts of Disclosure where Doctors Have Dual Responsibilities	621
5.	Remedies for Breach of Confidence		622
	(a)	Injunction	622
	(b)	Damages	622
6.	Confidentiality Requirements Imposed by Statute		623
	(a)	Venereal Disease	623
	(b)	Infertility Treatment	623

7. Statutory Exceptions 627
8. Investigation of Crime 633
9. Disclosure and Judicial Proceedings 634
10. Data Protection and Access to Health Records 637
    (a) Data Protection Act 1998 638
    (b) Access to Medical Reports Act 1988 654
    (c) Disclosure of Medical Records as a Preliminary to Legal Proceedings 658
    (d) Access to Health Records at Common Law 660
Select Bibliography 664

10. CLINICAL RESEARCH 667
1. Introduction 667
2. Regulating Research: National Oversight 669
3. Approval of a Clinical Trial: the Research Ethics Committee 670
    (a) The remit of a Research Ethics Committee 670
    (b) Membership of the Committee 673
    (c) Approval of Multi-centred Research 675
    (d) Procedure for Reviewing Trials 676
    (e) Reform of the Research Ethics Committee System 681
4. The Research Subject 682
    (a) Obtaining Consent 682
    (b) Randomised Clinical Trials 686
    (c) Trials Including Child Subjects 688
    (d) Trials Involving Adults without Mental Capacity 692
    (e) Follow-up by Research Ethics Committees 702
5. Trials Concerning Medicinal Products 703
    (a) Scrutiny by Research Ethics Committee of Trials Concerning Medicinal Products 707
6. Confidentiality and Privacy of Research Participants' Information 714
7. Regulating Fraudulent Researchers 717
8. Scrutinising the Approval of Clinical Trials 718
    (a) Challenging the Decision of a Local Research Ethics Committee to Approve a Clinical Trial 718
    (b) Liability of Members of a Research Ethics Committee to a Research Subject Injured in a Clinical Trial 719
9. Compensation for Research Subjects who Suffer Harm through Participation in a Clinical Trial 719
10. Embryo Research 721
    (a) General 721
    (b) Cloning and Stem Cell Research 725
11. Animal Research 737
Select Bibliography 742

PART IV

Introduction   747

11. REPRODUCTIVE CHOICE I: ASSISTED CONCEPTION   751
     1.   Introduction   751
     2.   The Human Fertilisation and Embryology Authority   753
          (a)   Constitution of HFEA   754
          (b)   The Legislative Framework of the Human Fertilisation
                and Embryology Act   755
     3.   Techniques for Alleviating Infertility   758
          (a)   Gamete Donation   759
          (b)   In Vitro Fertilisation (IVF)   777
          (c)   Surrogacy   781
     4.   Access to Reproductive Technologies   802
          (a)   The Welfare of the Child   802
     5.   Conscientious Objection   812
     6.   Allocation of Resources and Treating Infertility   812
     7.   Rights to Reproduce   814
     8.   The Impact of Reproductive Technologies on "the Family" 817
          (a)   Mothers   818
          (b)   Fathers   819
          (c)   Children of the Reproductive Revolution   828
     9.   Donation and Storage of Embryos   835
     10. Reproductive Choices: the Limits of Permissible Choice
          —PGD and the Ethics of Tissue Typing and Sex Selection   841
          (a)   The Selection of Saviour Siblings   841
          (b)   Sex Selection   848
          (c)   Reproductive Cloning   850
     11. Procreative Tourism   853
     12. Liability for Disability   855
     Select Bibliography   856

12. REPRODUCTIVE CHOICE II: CONTRACEPTION AND
     ABORTION   859
     1.   Introduction   859
     2.   Contraception   860
     3.   The Ethics of Abortion   869
          (a)   The Construction of the Ethical Debate   869
          (b)   The Moral Status of the Foetus   870
          (c)   The Relationship between Ethics and Law   872
     4.   The Law of Abortion   874
          (a)   The Criminal Prohibition on Procuring a Miscarriage   874
          (b)   The Statutory Grounds for Lawful Termination   878

(c) Where and How May Lawful Abortion be Performed? 886
(d) Emergency Abortions 898
5. Conflicting Interests at Stake in Abortion Decisions 899
(a) The Pregnant Woman 900
(b) The Incompetent Pregnant Woman 901
(c) The Foetus 902
(d) The Putative Father 912
(e) The Parents of an Under-age Girl 919
6. Conscientious Objection 919
Select Bibliography 923

13. REPRODUCTIVE CHOICE III 925
1. Introduction 925
2. Authorising Sterilisation of the Incompetent Patient 926
(a) General Principles 926
(b) Sterilising the Mentally Incompetent Minor: the Early Case Law 927
(c) Sterilising Mentally Incompetent Adult Patients: the Early Case Law 933
(d) A New Approach to Sterilisation Cases 938
3. Management of Pregnancy 948
4. Childbirth 952
(a) The Choice of Where and How to Give Birth 952
(b) Controlling Childbirth: Enforced Caesarians 954
5. Liability for Injury in Connection with Failed Sterilisation and Childbirth 961
(a) Actions Brought on Behalf of the Child 962
(b) Actions Brought by Parents 971
(c) Claims in Negligence 976
Select Bibliography 988

PART V

Introduction 993

14. END OF LIFE 997
1. Introduction 997
2. Ending the Life of a Patient: Criminal Law 998
(a) Suicide 998
(b) Murder/Manslaughter 1014
3. Judicial Sanctioning of the Approval of Life Support Systems from an Incompetent Patient 1021

(a)   Withdrawal of Treatment from Adult Patients   1021
(b)   Discontinuation of Treatment and the Human Rights
      Act 1998   1037
(c)   Do Not Resuscitate Orders   1044
(d)   Conflicts between Family Members and Clinicians
      Regarding the Continuation of Treatment   1049
(e)   Judicial Sanctioning of Withdrawal of Life-Saving
      Treatment from a Competent Patient   1058
(f)   The Right "to Live"   1060
4.   English Law Reform   1072
(a)   Active Termination of Life   1072
(b)   Defence to those Prosecuted for Active Cessation of Life
      of a Neonate   1076
(c)   Statutory Recognition of Mercy Killing   1077
(d)   Advance Directives   1078
(e)   Power of Attorney   1082
Select Bibliography   1087

15.   DEATH AND LEGAL REGULATION OF THE USE OF LIVE
      AND CADAVER MATERIAL   1089
1.   Introduction   1089
2.   Death   1090
(a)   Diagnosing Death   1092
(b)   Deciding the Point of Death—the Law   1096
(c)   Extending the Definition of Death—Cognitive Death   1099
3.   Legal Regulation of the Use of Human Material   1100
(a)   Introduction   1100
(b)   Human Material from the Living—Common Law   1103
(c)   Organ and Tissue Ownership—Common Law   1112
(d)   Legal Regulation of Human Material: the Human
      Tissue Act 2004   1121
4.   Increasing the Supply of Organs for Transplantation:
      Measures for Reform   1162
(a)   Opting-in Registry   1163
(b)   Altering Clinical Procedures to Facilitate Transplantation 1163
(c)   Presumed Consent   1164
(d)   Required Request and Routine Enquiry   1168
(e)   A Market in Organs   1169
(f)   Xenotransplantation   1170
5.   Accountability for Defective Organs or Tissue   1177
Select Bibliography   1178

Index   1181

Table of Cases

A, Re (1992) 1096, 1097
A v C (1985) 785, 788, 793, 795
A (A Child) v Ministry of Defence (2004) 156
A (Conjoined twins: Surgical Separation), Re (2000) 354, 415, 845, 1017, 1036, 1043
A (Medical Treatment: Male Sterilisation), Re (2000) 326, 433, 931, 938, 941, 947
AB v Glasgow and West of Scotland Blood Transfusion Service (1989) 660
AB v Leeds Teaching Hospital NHS Trust (2004) 1120
AB v National Blood Authority (2001) 204, 208
AK (Adult Patient) (Medical Treatment: Consent), Re (2001) 1033, 1060
Abouzaid v Mothercare (UK) Ltd (2001) 209
Acmanne v Belgium (1985) 17
Addis v Gramaphone Co (1909) 622
Airedale NHS Trust v Bland (1993) 172, 296, 330, 355, 410, 413, 415, 417, 433, 434, 993, 994, 1015,
            1017, 1021, 1022, 1032, 1033, 1034, 1035, 1036, 1037, 1049, 1058, 1072,
            1079, 1097, 1099, 1112, 1164
Al Hamwi v Johnston and Another (2005) 389, 395
Alcock v Chief Constable of South Yorkshire Police (1991) 1120
Allen v Bloomsbury AHA (1993) 978
An Adoption Application, Re (1987) 789
Archer v Williams (2003) 622
Ashingdane v United Kingdom (A/93) (1985) 489
Ashworth HA v Mirror Group Newspapers Ltd (2001) 572
Associated Provincial Picture Houses v Wednesbury Corp (1947) 47
Attorney General v Able (1984) 999
Attorney General v Guardian Newspapers Ltd (No.2) (1990); Attorney General v Observer Ltd (No.2);
    Attorney General v Times Newspapers Ltd (No.2) (1990) 572, 573
Attorney General's Reference (No.6 of 1980), Re (1980) 355
Attorney General's Reference (No.3 of 1994) (1996) 902, 915, 951

B, Re (1987) 748
B v Croydon HA (1995) 314, 460, 543, 545, 546
B v Islington AHA (1992) 962, 967
B (Adult: Refusal of Medical Treatment), Re (2002) 302, 313
B (Consent to Treatment: Capacity), Re (2002) 993, 1058, 1059, 1079
B (A Minor), Re (1990) 409, 410, 413, 415
B (A Minor) (Wardship: Sterilisation), Re (1987) 470, 928, 931, 932, 937
B (Wardship: Abortion), Re (1991) 472
Barnett v Chelsea and Kensington Hospital Management Committee (1968) 153, 183
Barr v Matthews 922
Bartley v Studd (1995) 363
Beloff v Pressdram Ltd (1973) 598
Blythe v Bloomsbury HA (1993) 385, 387, 388, 391, 392, 865
Bolam v Friern Hospital Management Committee (1957) 83, 149, 158, 159, 167, 174, 326, 327, 390
Bolitho (Deceased) v City and Hackney HA (1998) 149, 161, 167, 172, 173, 174, 201, 214, 390, 865, 922,
            977
Bolton Hospitals NHS Trust v O (2003) 961
Bravery v Bravery (1954) 862
Breen v Williams (1996) 664
Briody v St Helens and Knowsley AHA (2000) and (2001) 172, 789, 792, 802
Brooks v Home Office (1999) 179
Bull v Devon AHA (1993) 178, 182
Buzzanca v Buzzanca (1998) 797

C, Re (1994) 295, 313, 314, 397, 956
C v Eisenhower (1983) 354

C v S (1987) 879, 916, 917
C (A Child) (HIV Testing), Re (1999) 473, 474, 475
C (Adult: Refusal of Treatment), Re (1994) 545, 546, 1058
C (Application by Mr and Mrs X under s.30 of the Human Fertilisation and Embryology Act 1990
(2002) 789
C (A Minor) (Medical Treatment), Re [1998] 423, 425, 429, 430
C (A Minor) (Wardship: Medical Treatment) (No.1), Re (1989) 411, 412, 413
C (A Minor) (Wardship: Medical Treatment) (No.2) (1990) 584
C (A Minor) (Wardship: Surrogacy), Re (1985) 786, 790
C (Welfare of Child: immunisation), Re (2003) 477
CH (Contract: Parentage), Re (1996) 827
Campbell v Mirror Group Newspapers Ltd (2004) 293, 566, 573, 581, 622
Cassidy v Ministry of Health (1951) 153, 154, 155, 179, 181, 182
Cattanach v Melchior (2003) 982
Caxton Publishing Co v Sutherland Ltd (1939) 1118
Chappel v Hart (1998) 394
Chatterton v Gerson (1981) 361, 363, 364, 372, 380, 383, 397, 682
Chester v Afshar (2005) 201, 292, 364, 383, 389, 392, 393, 394, 396
Clark v MacLennan (1983) 163
Clements v London & North Western Railway Co (1894) 584
Clunis v Camden and Islington HA (1988) 83
Coker v Richmond, Twickenham and Roehampton AHA (1996) 868
Commission v United Kingdom 204
Cornelius de Taranto (2001) 622
Council for the Regulation of Health Care Professionals v Nursing and Midwifery Council and
Truscott (2004) 240
Council for the Regulation of Health Care Professionals v The General Medical Council and Dr G
Ruscillo (2004) 240
Council for the Regulation of Health Care Professionals v The General Medical Council and Dr
Solanke (2004) 240
Council of Civil Service Unions v Ministers for the Civil Service (1985) 45
Crawford v Board of Governors of Charing Cross Hospital (1953) 160
Curran v Bosze (1990) 1107

D (A Child Appearing by her Guardian ad Litem, Re (2005) 770, 821, 823, 827
D (Medical Treatment), Re (1998) 1035
D (A Minor) v Berkshire County Council (1987) 951
D (A Minor) (Wardship: Sterilisation), Re (1976) 927
D (A Minor) (Wardship: Surrogacy), Re (1976) 747
Defreitas v O'Brien (1993) 166
Department of Health and Social Security v Kinnear (1984) 83, 222
Dickson v United Kingdom (44362/2004) (2006) 748, 815
DPP v Smith (1960) 354
Dobson v North Tyneside HA 1112
Dr Handyside's Case (1749) 1112
Doughty v General Dental Council (1987) 272
Duchess of Kinston's Case (1776) 637
Durant v Financial Services Authority (2003 640

E (A Minor) (Medical Treatment), Re (1991) 937
E (A Minor) (Wardship: Medical Treatment), Re (1993) 463, 471
Emeh v Chelsea and Kensington AHA (1984) 193, 749, 900, 978
Enhorn v Sweden (2005) 18
Evans v Amicus Healthcare Ltd; Hadley v Midland Fertility Services Ltd (2003) and (2004) 764, 836, 840
Eve, Re (1986) 832
Eyre v Measday (1986) 972, 975

F, Re (1989) 295, 308, 320, 321, 326, 327, 330, 333
F (In Utero), Re (1988) 950, 951
F (Mental Patient: Sterilisation), Re. *See* F v West Berkshire HA
F v West Berkshire HA (1989) 172, 292, 320, 359, 397, 498, 546, 592, 692, 693, 931, 933, 936, 937, 994,
1032, 1082, 1105, 1138

Family Planning Association of Northern Ireland v Minister for Health, Social Services and Public
  Safety (2004) 877
Foster v Biosil (2000) 209
Fraser v Evans (1969) 581
Freeman v Home Office (1984) 364, 397, 398, 673
Frenchay Healthcare NHS Trust v S (1994) 1034
Furniss v Fitchett (1958) 572

G (Adult Incompetent: Withdrawal of Treatment), Re (2002) 1044, 1049
GF (Medical Treatment), Re (1992) 937
Gartside v Outram (1857) 598
Geraets-Smits v Stichting Ziekenfonds VGZ (C157/99); Peerbooms v Stichting CZ Groep Zorgverze-
  keringen (C157/99) 70, 77
Gillick v West Norfolk and Wisbech AHA (1985) 292, 308, 405, 406, 407, 440, 443, 444, 445, 450, 451,
                                                       455, 461, 470, 471, 581, 583, 585, 592, 689, 1130
Glass v United Kingdom (2004) 430, 1051, 1071
Gold v Haringey HA (1987) 384, 385, 387, 388, 390, 391, 865, 976
Goodwill v British Pregnancy Advisory Service (1996) 977
Gosai v GMC 280
Grady, Re (1981) 941
Gray v Southampton and South West Hampshire HA (2000) 183
Greenberg v Miami Children's Hospital Research Institute Inc (2003) 1113
Gregg v Scott (2005) 149, 193, 201
Groom v Selby (2001) 984

H (A Health Worker) v Associated Newspapers Ltd (2002) 580, 601
H (A Patient), Re (1998) 1035
HE v Hospital NHS Trust (2003) 1079
HG (Specific Issue: Sterilisation), Re (1993) 471, 931
HIV Haemophiliac Litigation, Re (1990) 81, 84, 659, 1178
HL v United Kingdom (2004) 489, 498
HM v Switzerland (2002) 489
Hall v Wandsworth HA (1985) 659
Hallat v NW Anglia HA (1988) 172
Halushka v University of Saskatchewan (1965) 685
Health and Safety Executive v Southampton NHS Trust, January 11, 2006, unreported 211
Hewer v Bryant (1969) 470
Hotson v East Berkshire HA (1987) 188, 192, 193
Hucks v Cole (1993) 167
Hunter v Mann (1974) 634

Initial Services v Putterill (1967) 598
Inizan v Caisse Primaire d'Assurance Maladie des Hauts de Seine (C56/01)(2003) 71
Irani v Southampton and South West Hampshire HA (1985) 258

J (A Minor) (Child in Care: Medical Treatment), Re (1992) 56, 67, 415
J (A Minor) (Prohibited steps Order: Circumcision, Re (2000) 475
J, Re [1990] 413, 415, 429, 456, 1070
JT v United Kingdom (1997) 490
Janaway v Salford AHA (1988) 919, 921
Janvier v Sweeney (1919) 1120
Jepson v Chief Constable of West Mercia Police Constabulary (2003) 882
Johnson v United Kingdom (1997) 489
Johnstone v Bloomsbury HA (1991) 179
Jones v Manchester Corporation (1957) 155

K (A Child), Re (2006) 433
KW and H (Minors) (Medical Treatment), Re (1993) 456
Kay's Tutor v Ayrshire and Arran Health Board (1987) 183
Kelly v Kelly (1997) 917
Kent v Griffiths (No.3) (2001) 153
Kinnear v Department of Health and Social Security (1989) 86

Knight v Home Office (1990) 179
Kohll v Union des Caisses de Maladie (C158/96) (1998) 70

L (A Child) (Medical Treatment: Benefit), Re (2005) 429
L (Medical Treatment: Gillick Competence), Re (1998) 468
LC, Re 947
Laws Hospital NHS Trust v Lord Advocate (1996) 1036
Lee v South West Thames RHA (1985) 659
Leeds Teaching Hospital NHS Trust v A (2003) 764, 824, 827
Lim Po Chew v Camden Area HA (1989) 970
Lion Laboratories Ltd v Evans (1984) 598
Loveday v Renton (No.1) (1990) 86, 183, 222
Luisi v Ministero del Tesoro (286/82); Carbone v Ministero del Tesoro (1984) 70
Lybert v Warrington HA (1996) 389
Lyhart v Warrington AHA (1995) 977

M v Calderdale and Kirklees HA (formerly West Yorkshire HA) (1998) 155
M (A Child) (Refusal of Medical Treatment), Re (1999) 462, 1110
M (A Minor) (Wardship: Sterilisation), Re (1988) 932, 933, 947
MB (Caesarean Section), Re (1997) 308, 314, 914, 951, 955, 958, 1111
MM (A Child) (Medical Treatment), Re (2000) 474, 475
MS v Sweden (1997) 565, 579
MW (Adoption) (Surrogacy), Re (1995) 789
McAllister v General Medical Council (1993) 272
McAllister v Lewisham and North Southwark HA (1994) 389
McCandless v General Medical Council (1996) 272
McFadden v EE Caledonian (1994) 1120
McFarlane v Tayside Health Board (2000) 749, 978, 982, 985, 988
McGhee v National Coal Board (1972) 186, 188
McInerney v MacDonald (1992) 663
McKay v Essex Area HA (1982) 882, 967, 970, 971
Mahon v Osborne (1939) 180
Malone v United Kingdom (Applications, No.8691/79) (1984) 565
Marriott v West Midlands RHA (1999) 173, 174
Maynard v West Midlands RHA; sub nom. Maynard v West Midlands AHA 160, 163
Moore v University of California (1990) 994, 1112, 1117, 1118
Morrow v DPP (1993) 637
Moyes v Lothian Health Board (1990) 385
Müller-Fauré v Onderlinge Waarborgmaatschappij OZ Zorgverzekeringen UA (C385/99); Van Riet v
     Onderlinge Waarborgmaatschappij OZ Zorgverzekeringen UA (C385/99) (2003) 70, 71, 72, 77

Nancy B. v Hotel-Dieu de Quebec (1992) 1033
National Health Service Trust v D (2000) 425
NHS Trust v I (2003) 1044
NHS Trust v MB (2006) 430, 433
National Health Trust, A v C (2000) 932, 946
NHS Trust A v M; NHS Trust B v H (2000) 994, 1037
Naylor v Preston AHA (1987) 659
Nettleship v Weston (1971) 178
Newham LBC v S (2003) 327
North Western Health Board v W(H) (2001) 475

O (A Minor) (Medical Treatment), Re (1993) 418
Osman v United Kingdom (1999) 64, 1005

P (Medical Treatment: Best Interests), Re (2004) 469
P (A Minor), Re (1981) 471
P (A Minor) (Wardship: Sterilisation), Re (1989) 932, 947
P (Minors) (Wardship: Surrogacy) (1987) 793, 795
P&O Ferries (Dover) Ltd (1991) 212
Palmer v Tees HA (1999) 618
Park, In the Estate of (1954) 313

Parkinson v St James and Seacroft University Hospital NHS Trust (2002) 982, 985, 988
Paton v British Pregnancy Advisory Service (1978) 884, 906, 912, 914
Paton v United Kingdom (1980) 914
Pearce v United Bristol Healthcare NHS Trust (1999) 172, 291, 386, 392, 396, 685, 865
Penney v East Kent HA (2000) 174
Planned Parenthood of S.E. Pennsylvania v Casey (1992) 871, 900
Portsmouth NHS Trust v Wyatt; sub nom. Wyatt (A Child) (Medical Treatment: Continuation of
    Order), Re (2005) 425, 429, 432
Pountney v Griffiths (1976) 530
Powell v Baldaz (1997) 385
Practice Direction (declaratory proceedings: incapacitated adults) (2002) 327
Practice Note (Official Solicitor: Declaratory Proceedings: Medical and Welfare Proceedings for
    Adults Who Lack Capacity) (2001) 940
Pretty v United Kingdom (2002) 993, 1011, 1014

Q (Parental Order), Re (1996) 789, 823, 830
Quinlan, Re (1976) 1033, 1099

R. v Adomako (1994) 210, 212
R. v Arthur (1981) 410, 1014, 1015, 1076
R. v Bateman (1925) 209
R. v Beecham (1988) 998
R. v BHB Community Healthcare NHS Trust Ex p. B (1999) 515
R. v Bingley Magistrates Court Ex p. Morrow (1994) 1034
R. v Bodkin Adams (1957) 1016, 1017, 1033
R. v Bourne (1938) 876, 877, 881, 884
R. v Bournewood Community and Mental Health NHS Trust Ex p. L; sub nom. L, Re (1998) 492
R. v Broadmoor Special Hospital Authority Ex p. S (1998) 531
R. v Brown (1993) 355
R. v Cambridge DHA Ex p. B (No.1)(1995) 51, 56, 68, 419
R. v Canons Park Mental Health Review Tribunal Ex p. A (1994) 515
R. v Canterbury and Thanet DHA South East Thames RHA Ex p. Ford W (1994) 245
R. v Cardiff Crown Court Ex p. Kellam (1994) 633
R. v Carr (1986) 1015
R. v Central Birmingham HA Ex p. Walker (1987) 47
R. v Chan-Fook (1994) 353
R. v Cox (1992) 1015
R. v Crozier (1990) 617
R. v D (1984) 450
R. v Department of Health Ex p. Source Informatics Ltd (No.1) (2001) 579, 580, 598, 645, 716, 1140
R. v Dicca (2004) 358, 620
R. v Dingra (1991) 898
R. v Donovan (1934) 355
R. v Ealing DHA Ex p. Fox (1993) 68
R. v East Berkshire HA Ex p. Walsh (1985) 258
R. v Ethical Committee of St Mary's Hospital Ex p. Harriott (1988) 68
R. v Gelder (1994) 354
R. v Gibbins & Proctor (1918) 1020
R. v Gloucester C.C. Ex p. Barry; R. v Lancashire C.C. Ex p. RADAR (1996) 48
R. v Hallstrom Ex p. W (No.2); R. v Gardner Ex p. L (1986) 511, 529, 552, 555
R. v Hamilton (1983) 885
R. v HFEA Ex p. Blood (1997) 765, 774, 826, 840
R. v Hough (1984) 1001
R. v Ireland; sub nom. R. v Burstow (1998) 353
R. v Kelly (1998) 1112, 1118, 1119
R. v Konzani (2005) 358
R. v Lodwig (1990) 1015
R. v Lowe (1973) 1019
R. v Malcherek and Steel (1981) 1096
R. v Mental Health Act Commission Ex p. X 531, 533, 536, 543
R. v Mental Health Review Tribunal Ex p. Clatworthy (1985) 508
R. v Mental Health Review Tribunal for South Thames Region Ex p. Smith (1999) 517

R. v Mid Glamorgan Family Health Services Authority, Ex p. Martin (1995) 660
R. v Miller (1954) 352
R. v Misra (2004) 211
R. v Morgantaler (1988) 900
R. v Nedrick (1986) 354
R. v North Derbyshire HA Ex p. Fisher (1999) 63
R. v North East Devon HA Ex p. Coughlan (Secretary of State for Health, interveners) (2000) 48, 51
R. v North West Lancashire HA Ex p. A; Same v Same Ex p. D; Same v Same Ex p. G (2000) 4, 57, 65,
                                                                                                                                                68
R. v Portsmouth Hospitals National Health Service Trust Ex p. Glass (1999) 67, 429, 1050, 1057
R. v Price (1968) 898
R. v St Mary's Hospital Manchester Ex p. Harriott (1988) 718, 804, 806
R. v Savage; sub nom DPP v Parmenter R. v Parmenter (No.1) 355
R. v Secretary of State for Health Ex p. Pfizer Ltd (1999) 63
R. v Secretary of State for the Home Department Ex p. Mellor (2001) 748, 793, 814, 815
R. v Secretary of State for Social Services Ex p. Hincks (1980) 45
R. v Senior (1899) 1019
R. v Seymour (1983) 209
R. v Sheffield HA Ex p. Seale (1994) 718, 809
R. v Sheppard (1981) 1019
R. v Smith (1974) 887
R. v South West Hospital Managers Ex p. M (1993) 521, 523
R. v Stone (1977) 1020
R. v Tait (1989) 905
R. v Vantandillo (1815) 22
R. v Welsh (1974) 1112
R. v Wilson Ex p. Williamson (1995) 510
R. v Woolin (1991) 354
R. v Woolin (1999) 1017
R. (on the application of AN) v Mental Health Review Tribunal (Northern Region) (2005) 552
R. (on the application of the Assisted Reproduction and Gynaecology Centre) v HFEA (2003) 780
R. (on the application of Axon) v Secretary of State for Health (2006) 293, 444, 450, 472, 585, 592, 919
R. (on the application of B) v Ashworth Hospital Authority (2005) 546
R. (on the application of B) v Dr Haddock (2005) 490
R. (on the application of B) v Haddock (Responsible Medical Officer) (2005) 538
R. (on the application of Burke) v General Medical Council (2004) 993, 1044, 1060, 1070, 1071
R. (on the application of CS) v MHRT (2004) 515
R. (on the application of D) v Home Secretary (2003) 490
R. (on the application of DR) v Merseycare NHS Trust (1999) 529
R. (on the application of DR) v Merseycare NHS Trust (2002) 514, 515
R. (on the application of E) v Bristol City Council (2005) 490
R. (on the application of H) v Mental Health Review Tribunal (2002) 489
R. (on the application of K) v Camden and Islington HA (2001) 83
R. (on the application of M) v Secretary of State for Health (2003) 490
R. (on the application of MH v Secretary of State for Health (2005) 550
R. (on the application of Munjaz) v Ashworth Hospital Authority (2002); (2005) 530
R. (on the application of Pretty) v DPP (2001) 994, 1001, 1009, 1010, 1011, 1059
R. (on the application of Quintavalle) v Secretary of State for Health (2003) and (2004) (Hashmi
      Case) 726, 842, 845, 847, 848, 851, 852
R. (on the application of Rogers) v Swindon NHS Primary Care Trust (2006) 64
R. (on the application of S) Plymouth City Council (2002) 592
R. (on the application of Smeaton) v SoS for Health (2002) 874, 894, 895, 898
R. (on the application of Wilkinson) v Broadmoor Hospital (2001) 490
R. (on the application of Wooder) v Feggeter and Mental Health Act Commission (2002) 538
R (Adult: Medical Treatment), Re (1996) 1045
R (A Child), Re (2003) 821, 822, 827
R (A Minor), Re (1991) 313
R (A Minor) (Blood Transfusion) (1993) 417, 419, 592
R (A Minor) (Wardship: Medical Treatment), Re (1991) 444, 452, 455, 460
Raj v GMC 279
Rance v Mid Downs HA (1991) 880
Ratcliffe v Plymouth and Torbay HA (1998) 182

Razzel v Snowball (1954) 155
Rees v Darlington Memorial Hospital Trust 985
Rees v United Kingdom (1986) 1005
Reid v United Kingdom (2003) 489, 491
Richardson v LRC Products Ltd (2000) 209
Riverside Mental Health NHS Trust v Fox (1994) 460
Robertson v Nottingham HA (1997) 155
Rodriguez v Attorney-General of Canada (1994) 1009
Roe v Ministry of Health (1954) 155
Roe v Wade (1973) 871
Rogers v Whitaker (1993) 381
Rose v Secretary of State for Health ad Human Fertilisation and Embryology Authority (2002) 832, 834
Royal College of Nursing v Department of Health and Social Security (1981) 878, 888, 891
Royal Wolverhampton Hospitals NHS Trust v B (Medical Treatment) (2000) 424

S v Ireland (application 26499/2002) 911
S (A Minor) (Consent to Medical Treatment), Re (1994) 465
S (A Minor) (Medical Treatment), Re (1993) 419
S (Adult Patient: Sterilisation), Re (2001) 937, 941, 946, 947
S (Adult Patient: Sterilisation: Patient's Best Interests), Re (2000) 292, 326, 748
S (Adult: Refusal of treatment), Re (1992) 955
S (Children) (Specific Issue: Religion: Circumcision), Re (2005) 476
S (Hospital Patient: Court's Jurisdiction) (No.1), Re (1995) 326
S-C (Mental Patient: Habeas Corpus), Re (1996) 523
SG (Adult Mental Patient: Abortion), Re (1991) 902
SL, Re (2000) 692
SS (an adult: medical Treatment), Re (2002) 901
Sadler v General Medical Council (2003) 272
St George's Healthcare NHS Trust v S; R. v Collins (1998) 505, 958, 959
Schloendorff v New York State Hospital (1914) 298
Secretary of State for Health v R. (on the application of Yvonne Watts) (C1–239/2003) (2003) 5, 71, 77, 78
Shakoor (Administratrix of the Estate of Shakoor) v Situ (t/a Eternal Health Co) 160
Sharpe v Southend HA (1997) 172
Sidaway v Board of Governors of the Bethlem Royal Hospital (1985) 162, 291, 351, 363, 364, 366, 372, 381, 382, 384, 385, 386, 387, 385, 390, 391, 396, 664, 685
Sims v Sims and an NHS Trust (2002) 692
Smith v Littlewood (1987) 618
Smith v Salford HA (1994) 389
Smith v Tunbridge Wells HA (1994) 364, 383, 387, 388, 389, 390
South Glamorgan CC v B (1993) 460
Strunk v Strunk (1969) 1105
Sutton v Population Services Family Planning Programme (1981) 192
Swindon & Malborough NHS Trust v S (1995) 1035
Swinnery Chief Constable of the Northumbria Police (1999) 572

T, Re (1992) 295
T v T (1988) 901, 938
T (Adult: Refusal of Treatment) (1992) 310, 360, 397, 400, 401, 900, 364, 1058, 1079, 1111
T (A Minor) (Wardship: Medical Treatment), Re (1997) 419, 420, 475, 477, 1108
TAC, Re (1992) 1112
Tahir v Haringey HA (1995) 192
Tameside and Glossop Acute Services NHS Trust v CH (A Patient) (1996) 544
Tarasoff v Regents of the University of California (1976) 618
Thake v Maurice (1986) 974, 976, 978
Thompson v Sheffield Fertility Clinic (2001) 781
Townley v Rushworth (1963) 524
Tysiac v poland (2006) 911

U v Centre for Reproductive Medicine (2002) 401, 767
U v W (Attorney-General Intervening) (1997) 853
Udale v Bloomsbury AHA (1983) 978

Vadera v Shaw (1999) 866, 868
Venables v News Group Newspapers Ltd (2001) 584
Vo v France 906, 911, 915

W v Egdell (1990) 567, 607, 617, 618, 619, 622, 659
W v L (1974) 506, 508, 521
W (Mental Patient), Re (1993) 937
W (A Minor) (Medical Treatment: Court's Jurisdiction) (1992) 371, 457, 460, 1109, 1110
W (Minors) Surrogacy, Re (1991) 790, 829
W and W v H (Child Abduction: surrogacy) No.2 (2002) 796, 800, 854
W Healthcare Trust v H (2004) 1036
Wainwright v Home Office (2003) 565
Ward of Court, In the matter of (1995) 1036
Watts v Bedford Primary Care Trust (2003) 64
Whitehouse v Jordan (1981) 161, 162
Wilkinson v Downton (1897) 1120
Williams v Williams (1852) 1112
Wilsher v Essex AHA (1986) (1988) 174, 175, 178, 179, 181, 183, 188, 208, 215, 367, 659
Winterwerp v Netherlands (A/33) (1979) 489, 491
Wiszniewski v Central Manchester HA (1998) 172
Woolgar v Chief Constable of Sussex (1999) 618
Worsley v Tambrands Ltd (2000) 209

X v Schering Health Care Ltd; sub nom. XYZ v Schering Health Care Ltd (2002) 207
X v Y (1988) 567, 573, 581, 598
X (Adult Patient: Sterilisation), Re (1998) 937
X (Minors) v Bedfordshire CC; M (A Minor) v Newham LBC; E (A Minor) v Dorset CC (Appeal);
    Christmas v Hampshire CC (Duty of Care); Keating v Bromley LBC (No.2) (1995) 79, 83, 155
XYZ v Schering (2002) 868

Y (Mental Patient: Bone Marrow Donation), Re (1996) 1105, 1136
Yepremian v Scarborough General Hospital (1980) 155
Yeu Keu-yen v Attorney General of Hong Kong (1988) 719

Z v Finland (1998) 565, 579
Z (Local Authority: Duty), Re (2004) 998, 1074
Z (Medical Treatment: Hysterectomy), Re (2000) 946

Table of Statutes

1832 Anatomy Act (2 & 3 Will.4 c.75) 1100
1858 Medical Act (21 & 22 Vict. c.90) 269
    s.29 269
1861 Offences Against the Persons Act (24
    & 25 Vict. c.100) 353, 874, 875,
                     1103
    s.18 .... 353, 354, 355
    s.20 .... 22, 354, 355, 358
    s.23 1016
    s.47 .... 352, 353
    s.58 .... 876, 888, 898, 899
    ss.58–59 874
    s.59 857
1896 Prevention of Cruelty to Children
    Act
    s.1 1019
1929 Infant Life Preservation Act (19 & 20
    Geo.5 c.34) 875, 876, 879, 880, 881,
                     952
    s.1(2) 876
    s.1(1)–(2) 875
1933 Children and Young Persons Act (23
    & 24 Geo.5 c.12) 1019
    s.1 1018
1936 Public Health Act (26 Geo.5 & 1
    Edw.8, c.49)
    s.85 16
    s.85(1)–(4) 16
1938 Infanticide Act (1 & 2 Geo.6 c.36) ... 1018
    s.1(1) 1018
1946 National Health Service Act (9 & 10
    Geo.6 c.81)
    s.6(2) 181
1948 National Assistance Act (11 & 12
    Geo.6 c.29) 24, 553
    s.47 .... 23, 24
    s.47(1)(b) 24
    s.47(1)–(4) 22
    s.47(5) 23
    s.47(6)–(9) 23
    s.47(10) 23
    s.47(11) 23
    s.47(12)–(14) 23
1951 National Assistance (Amendment) Act
    (14 & 15 Geo.6 c.57) 23, 24, 553
    s.191) 24
1952 Corneal Grafting Act (15 & 16 Geo.6
    & 1 Eliz.2 c.28) 1100
1956 Sexual Offences Act (4 & 5 Eliz.2
    c.69)
    s.7 932
1959 Mental Health Act (7 & 8 Eliz c.72) 482,
    491, 508, 531, 549, 554, 555,
                     660
    s.5(1) 498

1959 Mental Health Act—cont.
    s.26 513
    s.60 607
    s.65 607
1961 Human Tissue Act (9 & 10 Eliz.2
    c.54) .. 1100, 1101, 1121, 1122, 1124,
            1128, 1130, 1132, 1134, 1153
    s.1(1) 1100
    s.1(5) 1101
    s.11 1142
1961 Suicide Act (9 & 10 Eliz.2 c.60) .. 998, 1075
    s.1 998
    s.2(1) 999, 1001, 1010
    s.2(1)–(2) 998
    s.2(4) 1010
1967 Misrepresentation Act (c.7)
    s.2(1) 975
1967 Parliamentary Commissioner Act
    (c.13) 264
1967 National Health Service (Family Plan-
    ning) Act (c.39) 860
1967 Abortion Act (c.87) 356, 410, 472, 547,
        634, 637, 859, 872, 873, 877,
        878, 879, 880, 886, 893, 894,
        898, 899, 900, 902, 912, 917,
                  919, 922
    s.1 .... 878, 887, 912
    s.1(1) 886, 921
    s.1(1)(a) 880, 881, 884
    s.1(1)(b) 881, 882, 885
    s.1(1)(b)–(d) 880
    s.1(1)(c) 881, 882
    s.1(1)(d) 881, 882, 885, 911
    s.1(1)–(2) 878
    s.1(2) 885
    s.1(3) 886
    s.1(3A) 886
    s.1(4) 881, 886, 899
    s.2 .... 881, 886
    s.2(1) 886
    s.2(1)–(4) 887
    s.2(2) 886
    s.2(4) 886
    s.3A 886
    s.4(1) 919, 920, 921
    s.4(1)–(2) 919
    s.4(2) 921
    s.5 879
    s.5(1) 880
    s.5(2) 883
    s.6 879
1969 Tattooing of Minors Act (c.24) 356, 455
1969 Family Law Reform Act (c.46) .. 440, 445,
                    1109, 1110
    s.8 .... 440, 457, 464, 1109

1969 Family Law Reform Act—*cont.*
    s.8(1) 440
    s.8(1)–(3) 440
    s.8(2) 440, 1109
    s.8(3) 440, 451, 457, 461
1969 Children and Young Persons Act
    (c.54) 471
1970 Chronically Sick and Disabled Persons
    Act (c.44) 48
    s.2 .... 44, 48
    s.2(1) 44
1972 Road Traffic Act (c.20)
    s.168(3) 634
1973 National Health Service (Reorganisa-
    tion) Act (c.32) 260
1974 Health and Safety at Work Act (c.37)
    s.3 211
1976 Congenital Disabilities (Civil Liabili-
    ty) Act (c.28) 855, 962, 963, 966,
                           967, 970
    s.1(1)–(7) 963
    s.1(2)(b) 965
    s.1(3) 965
    s.1(7) 966
    s.1A 965
    s.1A(1)–(4) 963
    s.2 964
    s.4(1)–(6) 964
    s.4(2) 965
    s.4(2)(a) 962, 966
    s.4(4) 965
    s.4(5) 971
1976 Adoption Act (c.36) 789
1976 Race Relations Act (c.74)
    s.20(1) 1128
    s.31(1) 1128
1977 Patents Act (c.37) 1117
    s.1(3)(a) 1117
    s.1(3)(c) 1117
1977 National Health Service Act (c.49) ... 30, 41,
                           81, 1178
    s.1 1178
    s.1(1) 41
    s.1(2) 41
    s.3 .... 45, 155
    s.3(1) 41
    s.5 .... 41, 42
    s.5(1) 42
    s.5(1)(b) 861
    s.5(1A) 42
    s.5(2) 42
    s.5(2)(b) 42
    ss.11–12 30
    ss.13–17 37
    s.16A 31
    s.16B 31
    s.16CA 33
    s.16CC 32
    s.84A 30
    s.84B 30
    s.85 37
    s.128 41

1979 Vaccine Damage Payments Act
    (c.17) 85
    s.1(1)–(4) 221
    s.1(3) 222
    s.2(1)–(3) 222
    s.3(5) 222
1981 Supreme Court Act (c.54)
    s.31 658
    s.33 658
    s.34 658
    s.34(1)–(4) 658
    s.69(3) 181
1982 Human Tissue and Transplant Act
    (Western Australia)
    s.12 1109
    s.13 1109
1982 Supply of Goods and Services Act
    (c.29)
    s.13 .... 153, 865
1983 Mental Health Act (c.51) ... 24, 41, 292, 371,
              461, 479, 480, 482, 483, 488,
              489, 490, 491, 501, 502, 505,
              506, 509, 520, 526, 528, 532,
              538, 547, 552, 553, 561, 595,
                       617, 901
    Pt IV 491, 511, 529, 530, 531, 533
    Pt IX 342
    s.1(2) 504
    s.1(3) 508, 543
    s.2 .... 504, 510, 513, 526, 531, 550, 557,
                            959
    s.2(1)(b) 483
    s.2(2)–(4) 502
    s.3 .... 503, 504, 510, 511, 512, 514, 515,
       528, 529, 531, 543, 546, 550, 555, 557,
                       558, 561
    s.3(2) 491
    s.3(2)(b) 515
    s.3(2)(c) 483, 517
    s.3(2)–(3) 503
    s.4 .... 526, 531, 557
    s.4(2) 526
    s.4(3) 526
    s.4(4) 526
    s.4(5) 526
    s.5 .... 526, 528
    s.5(1) 526
    s.5(2) 527, 531
    s.5(3) 527
    s.5(4) 527, 528, 531
    s.5(4)–(5) 527
    s.5(6) 526
    s.6(1)–(3) 522
    s.6(3) 523
    s.7 553
    s.7(1)–(2) 553
    s.7(3) 553
    s.7(5) 553
    s.8 .... 554, 555
    s.11 521
    s.11(1) 553
    s.11(2) 521, 553

1983 Mental Health Act—*cont.*
s.11(3) 521
s.11(4) 553
s.11(5) 521, 526
s.12 .... 522, 553
s.13 .... 513, 521
s.14 521
s.15 523
s.17 .... 511, 528
s.17(1) 528
s.17(4) 528
s.17(5) 528
s.18 528
s.18(4) 528
s.20 ... 504, 511, 513, 514, 515, 528, 529
s.20(4) 514
s.21 528
s.21A 528
s.21B 528
s.23 548
s.23(2) 548
s.23(4) 548
s.23(5) 548
s.25 549
s.25(2) 549
s.25A 491
s.25A(1) 555
s.25A(4) 555
s.25A(5) 555
s.25A(6) 556
s.25A(7) 556
s.25A(8) 556
s.25A–25H 555
s.25B(1) 555
s.25B(2) 555
s.25B(3) 555
s.25B(4) 555
s.25B(5) 555
s.25B(8) 556
s.25B(9) 556
s.25B(10) 556
s.25C 556
s.25D(1) 556
s.25D(3)–(4) 556
s.25E(1)–(3) 556
s.25E(4) 556
s.25E(5) 556
s.25E(6) 556
s.25E(7) 556
s.25F 557
s.25G 556
s.25G(1) 556
s.25G(2) 556
s.25G(2)–(10) 556
s.25G(4) 556
s.25H(1)–(3) 557
s.25H(4) 557
s.26 521
s.29 .... 521, 553
s.37 .... 557, 617
s.41 .... 607, 617
s.56 531

1983 Mental Health Act—*cont.*
s.56(1)(a) 531, 532
s.56(1)(b) 532
s.57 .... 531, 532, 533, 535, 542, 543
s.57(1)–(3) 532
s.57(2)(b) 537
s.58 .... 532, 533, 535, 542, 543
s.58(2)(a) 535
s.58(2)(b) 534
s.59 532
s.60 532
s.61 537
s.62 .... 532, 542
s.62(3) 542
s.63 .... 532, 533, 543, 545, 546, 547
s.66 549
s.66(1) 557
s.66(1)(g) 549
s.67 608
s.68 550
s.72 .... 550, 551, 552
s.72(1) 552
s.72(1)(a)(i) 552
s.72(1)(b)(i) 552
s.72(2) 552
s.72(3) 552
s.72(4A) 557
s.115 524
s.117 .... 553, 555, 556
s.117(2) 83
s.120(1) 548
s.120(1)(b) 548
s.129 524
s.131 492
s.131(1) 492, 498
s.131(2) 492
s.132 547
s.132(3) 547
s.132(4) 547
s.134 547
s.135 .... 24, 524, 531
s.136 531
s.145 545
s.145(1) 502, 530
1983 Medical Act (c.54) 269
ss.29A–29 270
s.35C 271
s.35C(2) 270
s.35CC 272
s.35D 272
s.38 275
s.40 276
s.41 277
s.41A 278
s.41C 279
s.49 270
1984 Public Health (Control of Disease) Act
(c.22) 12, 18, 21, 634
s.11 .... 12, 13
s.16 12
s.17 .... 12, 13, 21
s.17(1) 21

1984 Public Health (Control of Disease)
Act—*cont.*
s.17(2) 21
s.19 .... 12, 13, 21
s.35 .... 12, 13, 14
s.35(1) 14
s.35(1)(a)(ii) 13, 14
s.35(3) 14
ss.35–38 13
s.37 .... 12, 13
s.37(1) 15
s 37(2) 15
s.38 .... 12, 13, 14, 15, 16
s.38(1)–(4) 15
s.43 12
ss.43–45 13
s.44 .... 12, 13
s.45 .... 12, 13
1984 Data Protection Act (c.35) ... 566, 638, 647
1984 Police and Criminal Evidence Act
(c.60) 633
s.9 634
s.9(1) 633
ss.9–11 633
s.11 633
s.11(1)–(2) 633
s.12 633
s.19 634
Sch.1 633
1985 Enduring Powers of Attorney Act
(c.29) 330, 1082
1985 Prohibition of Female Circumcision
Act (c.38) 356
s.1 356
s.2 356
1985 Hospital Complaints Act (c.42) ... 240, 569
1985 Surrogacy Arrangements Act (c.49) 788,
789, 791, 797
s.1(1)–(1A) 787
s.1A 788
s.2(1)–(4) 787
s.3 788
1985 Child Abduction and Custody Act
(c.60) 801
1986 Surrogacy Act 797
1986 Animals (Scientific Procedures) Act
(c.14) 668, 738
1986 Public Order Act (c.64) 637
1987 Family Law Reform Act (c.42) 828
s.27 .... 821, 828
1987 Consumer Protection Act (c.43) 204, 225,
719, 855, 868, 966, 1116, 1177,
1178
s.2 204
s.2(3) 207
s.3 205
s.3(1) 208
s.4 .... 205, 208, 1178
s.5 206
s.6(3) 855
s.46 206

1988 Access to Medical Reports Act
(c.28) 654
s.2(1) 654
s.3(1)–(2) 654
s.4(1)–(4) 655
s.5(1)–(2) 655
s.6(1)–(3) 656
s.7(1)–(4) 656
s.8 657
1989 Human Organ Transplants Act (c.31) 274,
1101, 1124, 1143, 1144, 1148,
1150, 1152
1989 Children Act (c.41) 405, 409, 455, 822
s.1 795
s.2 407
s.4 821
s.8 .... 417, 419, 473, 931
s.38(6) 460
s.100(3) 419, 457
s.100(4) 457
1990 National Health Service and Commu-
nity Care Act (c.19) 30, 33, 35
s.4 36
s.4(3) 36
s.5(1) 33
s.10(1)–(2) 34
s.47(1)–(3) 43
s.47(7) 44
Sch.II, para.6(1) 34
Sch.II, para.6(2) 34
Sch.II, para.7(1)–(3) 35
Sch.II, para.8 35
1990 Access to Health Records (c.23) ... 566, 638,
639, 647, 658, 660
s.4(2) 456
1990 Human Fertilisation and Embryology
Act (c.37) 351, 364, 566, 627, 723,
724, 725, 734, 738, 750, 752,
753, 754, 755, 757, 758, 759,
761, 762, 764, 768, 770, 771,
778, 806, 807, 810, 811, 818,
826, 827, 830, 834, 841, 848,
850, 851, 852, 855, 859, 880,
883, 885, 965, 1102, 1124,
1156, 1157, 1161, 1162
s.1(3) 778
ss.1–4 755
s.3 .... 726, 757
s.3(1) 725
s.3(2) 757
s.3(3) 757
s.3A 758
s.4 757
s.4(1) 765
s.4(1)(a) 759
s.4(1)(b) 759, 840
s.5(1)–(3) 754
ss.12–14 763
s.13(5) 767, 806, 807
s.13(6) 764
s.14 836
s.14(1)(b) 840

1990	Human Fertilisation and Embryology Act—*cont.*	
	s.14(1)–(5)	763
	s.15(1)–(4)	724
	s.24(4)	765
	s.27	821
	s.27(1)–(3)	818
	ss.27–29	829
	s.28	821, 827, 830
	s.28(1)–(9)	819
	s.28(2)	821, 826, 830
	s.28(3)	821, 822, 826, 830, 854
	s.28(5)(a)	821
	s.28(6)	821
	s.28(6)(b)	824
	s.29(1)	821
	s.30	789, 790, 797, 828, 829, 830
	s.30(1)–(7)	828
	s.31	965
	s.31(1)–(4)	831
	s.31(4)(a)	834
	s.33	626
	s.33(1)–(7)	623
	s.33(9)(a)	625
	s.36(1)	788
	s.36(2)	788
	s.37	878
	s.37(3)	892
	s.37(4)	880, 886
	s.38	725, 812
	s.41	758
	s.44	855
	s.45(1)–(3)	834
	Sch.1 para.4	754
	Sch.2	757, 842
	Sch.2 para.1	757
	Sch.2 para.3	725
	Sch.2 para.3(1)–(9)	724
	Sch.3	763, 763, 765, 770
1992	Accident Rehabilitation and Compensation Insurance Act (New Zealand)	220
1992	Human Fertilisation and Embryology (Disclosure of Information) Act (c.54)	626
1993	Health Service Commissioners Act (c.46)	260, 263
	s.2(1)	260
	s.2(1A)	263
	s.2(4)–(6)	260
	s.2A(1)	261
	s.2A(4)	261
	s.2B	263
	s.2B(1)	261
	s.2B(4)–(5)	261
	s.3(1)	264
	s.4	261
	s.4(2)	263
	s.4(5)	263
	s.7	262
	s.7(2)	264
	s.7(5)(b)	263

1993	Health Service Commissioners Act—*cont.*	
	s.8	264, 267
	s.9	264
	s.9(1)	267
	s.10	265
	s.11	265
	s.12	266
	s.13	267
	s.14	268
1993	Family Planning (Protection of the Human Foetus and Conditions Permitting Pregnancy Termination) Act (Poland)	911
1994	Criminal Justice and Public Order Act (c.33)	771
	s.156	758
1995	Disability Discrimination Act (c.50)	68, 69
	s.1(1)	68
	Sch.1	69
	Sch.1 para.4(1)	68
1995	Mental Health (Patients in the Community) Act (c.52)	555
1996	Health Service Commissioner (Amendment) Act (c.5)	260, 263, 264, 638
	s.6	263
	s.10	268
1996	Employment Rights Act (c.18)	
	s.43B	570
	s.43B(1)	570
	s.43H	571
	s.43H(2)	571
	s.43K	570
	s.43F	570, 571
	s.43J	571
	s.47B	571
	s.48(2)	571
	s.103	571
1997	Nurses, Midwives and Health Visitors Act (c.24)	
	s.16	953
1998	Public Interest Disclosure Act (c.23)	570, 571
1998	Data Protection Act (c.29)	293, 566, 638, 639, 641, 647, 649, 652, 658, 714
	s.1	639
	s.1(1)	638, 639
	s.2	640
	s.3(1)(f)	639
	s.5(4)	639
	s.7	647
	s.33	644
	s.33(4)	649
	s.35	645
	s.38	649
	s.68(2)	640
	s.69(1)	640
	s.55	641
	Sch.1	641

1998 Data Protection Act—*cont.*
         Sch.2 642
         Sch.3 642
1998 Crime and Disorder Act (c.37)
         s.115 634
1998 Human Rights Act (c.42) 4, 7, 57, 64, 68,
                  211, 292, 425, 438, 489, 538,
                  748, 814, 921, 925, 941, 994,
                  1001, 1009, 1014, 1037, 1070,
                                                  1121
         s.4 489
         Sch.1 1060
1998 Infectious Diseases Act (Sweden) 18
1999 Health Act (c.58)
         s.26 40
2000 Terrorism Act (c.11)
         s.19 634
         s.20 634
2000 Care Standards Act (c.14) 502
2001 Health and Social Care Act (c.15)
         s.12 251
         s.49 51
         s.60 .... 627, 629, 632, 716
         s.61 629
2001 Human Reproductive Cloning Act
         (c.23) 726, 734, 851, 852
2002 National Health Service Reform and
         Health Care Professions Act
         (c.17)
         s.25 240
         s.26 240
2002 Adoption and Children Act (c.38)
         s.1(2) 795
         ss.95–96 788
2003 Human Fertilisation and Embryology
         (Deceased Fathers) Act (c.24) 824
2003 Sexual Offences Act (c.42) 932
2003 Health and Social Care (Community
         Health and Standards) Act (c.43) 32,
                                                  37, 40
         s.1(1) 40
         s.14(2) 40
         s.23 40
2004 Human Tissue Act (c.30) 351, 364, 994,
                  1090, 1098, 1102, 1103, 1108,
                  1110, 1121, 1122, 1130, 1132,
                  1133, 1134, 1135, 1138, 1142,
                                1144, 1156, 1162
         s.1(1)–(6) 1122
         s.1(7) 1139
         s.1(7)–(9) 1139
         s.1(7)–(10) 1139
         s.1(11)–(13) 1123
         s.2 .... 1122, 1129
         s.3 .... 1122, 1130, 1131
         s.3(6) 1132
         s.3(8) 1134
         s.4 .... 1132, 1133, 1134
         s.5 1153
         s.5(4) 1142
         s.6 1135
         s.7 .... 1139, 1140

2004 Human Tissue Act—*cont.*
         s.8 1154
         s.9 1141
         s.10 1139
         s.13 1156
         ss.14–16 1157
         s.26 1162
         s.26(2)(d) 1098
         s.27(4) 1134
         s.27(8) 1135
         s.28 1162
         s.32 1151
         s.32(9) 1153
         s.33 .... 1143, 1144
         s.34 1144
         s.45 1156
         s.45(1) 1155
         s.53 1124
         s.54(7) 1124
         Sch.1 1139
         Sch.2 1156
         Sch.2(1) 1156, 1157
2004 Assisted Human Reproduction Act
         (Canada) 775
2005 Mental Capacity Act (c.30) ... 292, 295, 296,
                  314, 318, 320, 327, 328, 330,
                  333, 342, 346, 347, 397, 479,
                  501, 692, 696, 702, 713, 901,
                  902, 994, 997, 1080, 1081,
                  1082, 1083, 1138, 1175
         s.1 .... 297, 302, 320, 328, 346
         s.1(2) 295
         s.1(3) 297
         s.2 .... 318, 332
         s.3 319
         s.4 328
         s.4(5)(b) 297
         s.5 .... 331, 333, 334
         ss.5–8 297
         s.7 333
         s.8 333
         ss.9–11 1083
         ss.9–14 298
         s.13 1085
         s.14 1085
         s.15 342
         s.16 343
         s.17 343
         s.18 344
         s.19 344
         s.20 344
         s.22 1085
         s.23 1086
         ss.24–26 298
         ss.24–26 1080
         s.27 333
         s.28 334
         s.29 334
         s.30 702
         s.30(3) 699
         ss.30–33 .... 297, 696
         s.34 334

2005	Mental Capacity Act—*cont.*	
	ss.34–38	297
	s.35	335
	s.36	336
	s.37	336
	s.38	337
	s.39	337
	s.43	345
	s.48(1)–(2)	345
	s.48(8)–(9)	346

2005	Mental Capacity Act—*cont.*	
	s.55(1)	346
	s.56(1)	346
	s.58	297
	Sch.1	1086
	Sch.1(4)	1086
	Sch.1(13)	1087
2006	Health Act	28
	s.2	28
	s.3(1)–(7)	28

Table of Statutory Instruments

1968 Abortion Regulations (SI 1968/390) ... 637
1974 National Health Service Venereal Disease Regulations (SI 1974/29) ... 623
1982 Mental Health Review Tribunal Rules (SI 1982/942)
    r.23(2) 552
1983 Mental Health (Hospital, Guardianship and Consent to Treatment) Regulations (SI 1983/893)
    reg.16(1)(a) 533
    reg.16(2) 534
1988 Public Health (Infectious Diseases) Regulations (SI 1988/1546) ... 12, 634
    reg.4 .... 12, 13, 14
    reg.5 .... 12, 16
    Sch.1 12
1991 Abortion Regulations (SI 1991/499) ... 634
1991 Human Fertilisation and Embryology (Statutory Storage Period) Regulations (SI 1991/1540) 770
1992 National Health Service (General Medical Services) Regulations (SI 1992/635) 153
    Sch.2 921
    Sch.2 para.3 922
    Sch.2 para.4(1)(h) 153
1994 Parental Orders (Human Fertilisation and Embryology) Regulations (SI 1994/2767) 829
1996 National Health Service (Clinical Negligence Scheme) Regulations (SI 1996/251) 154
1996 Human Fertilisation and Embryology (Statutory Storage Period for Embryos) Regulations (SI 1996/375) 836
1996 National Health Service Contracts (Dispute Resolution) Regulations (SI 1996/623) 37
1998 Civil Procedure Rules (SI 1998/3132)
    Pt 3 216
    r.26.6(6) 216
    Pt 35 160
2000 Data Protection Subject Access (Modification) (Health) Order (SI 2000/413) 293
    arts 2–8 649
    art.10 652
    art.13 653
    art.14 653
2000 Data Protection (Miscellaneous Subject Access Exemptions) Order (SI 2000/419) 649
2000 Statutory Sum Order (SI 2000/1983)
    art.2 222

2001 Human Fertilisation and Embryology (Research Purposes) Regulations (SI 2001/188) 726
    reg.2 726
2001 Mental Health Act 1983 (Remedial) Order (SI 2001/3712) 490
2002 Health Service (Control of Patient Information) Regulations (SI 2002/1438) 629
2002 National Health Service Act 1977 and National Health Service and Community Care Act 1990 (Amendment) Regulations (SI 2002/2759)
    reg.3(2) 42
2002 Medical Act 1983 (Amendment) Order (SI 2002/3155) 269
    Sch.2 270
2004 National Health Service (General Medical Services Contracts) Regulations (SI 2004/291)
    reg.4 32
2004 National Health Service (Personal Medical Services Agreements) Regulations (SI 2004/627) 32
2004 Medicines for Human Use (Clinical Trials) Regulations (SI 2004/1031) .. 291, 351, 669, 672, 699, 704, 707, 709, 713, 1138
    Pt 2 705
    Pt 4 709
    Pt 5 712
    regs 5–6 669
    reg.11 707
    reg.12 706
    reg.14(3) 707
    reg.14(5) 672
    reg.14(6) 706
    reg.15 707
    Sch.1, Pt 1 para.3(1) 709
2004 HFEA (Disclosure of Information) Regulations (SI 2004/1511) 834
    reg.2(2) 834
    reg.2(3) 834
    reg.3(2)(e) 1138
    reg.5 1138
    reg.8 1138
2004 National Health Service (Complaints) Regulations (SI 2004/1764) 243
    reg.3 244
    reg.4 245

2004   National Health Service (Complaints)
         Regulations—*cont.*
         reg.5 245
         reg.6 246
         reg.7 246
         reg.8 248
         reg.9 249
         reg.10 249
         reg.11 250
         reg.12 251
         reg.13 252
         reg.14 .... 250, 253
         reg.15 253
         reg.16 255
         reg.17 255
         reg.18 256
         reg.19 257
         reg.20 257
         reg.21 257
         reg.22 258
2005   National Blood Authority and UK
         Transplant (Abolition) Order (SI
         2005/2352) 1163

2006   Human Tissue Act 2004 (Ethical Ap-
         proval, Exceptions from Licens-
         ing and Supply of Information
         about Transplants) Regulations
         (SI 2006/1260) 1140
2006   Human Tissue Act 2004 (Persons who
         Lack Capacity to Consent and
         Transplants) Regulations (SI
         2006/1659)
         reg.3 1137
         regs.3–6 1137
         reg.5 1148
         reg.6 1148
         reg.8 1137
         reg.10 1144
         regs.11–14 1145
2006   Mental Capacity Act 2005 (Loss of
         Capacity during Research Pro-
         ject) (England) Regulations
         (Draft)
         reg.2 699
         Sch.1, reg.3 701
         Sch.2, reg.3 701

PART I

INTRODUCTION

The first part of this book introduces the context, institutional and ethical parameters within which health care law operates. Many of the problems explored in the pages that follow raise profound ethical problems and grappling with them requires an awareness of the discipline of ethics. Chapter 2 introduces the main schools of moral thought and explores some of the key concepts and distinctions used by moral philosophers. These include the ideas of justice, paternalism and autonomy and also the role of rights. These issues are discussed in a separate chapter because they are relevant to most of the substantive areas explored later in the book. To deal with them as if they were only relevant to particular areas would obscure the importance of taking a reflective approach to the problems. Thus, Chapter 2 provides some tools to enable you to assess how satisfactory the current law is and considers what reforms might be necessary.

In addition to introducing the main themes of critical thinking in relation to health care ethics, a number of specific debates are considered. Many dilemmas would be quickly resolved if we adopted the principle that life is so sacred that it is never acceptable to cease striving to maintain it whatever the cost. The meaning and the strength of the "sanctity of life" principle is a key question in the ethics of caring for the dying or severely disabled. Its scope may determine the proper approach to abortion and embryo research. The issues that it raises are explored in extracts from the work of ethicists.

Some thinkers suggest that the distinction between acts and omissions can resolve many of the problems that are presented by life and death decisions. They suggest that it is permissible to allow patients to die by letting "nature take its course" but not to take active steps to kill them. This approach may enable decisions to offer only palliative care to patients to be reconciled with a commitment to the sanctity of life. However, the moral significance of this distinction has been rejected by other philosophers. It cannot be accepted without critical consideration, even though the courts have made some use of it.

The possibility that ethics and law may make different use of the same distinctions raises a more general problem in jurisprudence (the philosophy of law). That is the proper relation between law and morality. Although most people would agree that health care gives rise to ethical problems, it is not necessarily right simply to use the law to impose "good ethics" on those involved. Society may not be entitled to force individuals to adopt the morality of others. Thus, we have to ask whether we are entitled to prevent someone who believes that it is acceptable to terminate a pregnancy from doing so merely because we believe that they are undertaking a morally wrong act. We may also believe that there are ethical issues that are specific to the role of the health care professions, including the possibility that they should be given rights of conscientious objection.

One persistent problem that can easily be overlooked is the role of gender in debate about health care law. Many of the most contentious areas of health care law raise issues that cannot be seen as gender neutral. Abortion is clearly a more personal issue for the pregnant woman than for anyone else. Many of the developments in reproductive technology impact more directly on women rather than men. However, gender issues are not confined to questions about the patients involved. Feminist ethics has highlighted the extent to which the dominant traditions of health care ethics have often stressed independence and autonomy at the expense of recognising the social world in which we live. We need to consider how far our approaches to moral thinking have blinkered our understanding of the problems as well as illuminating them.

The ethical dimension of health care is not the only context we need to consider. Health care is not important so much in itself as for what it can achieve. This is not always to make people better; sometimes it may be to prevent people becoming sick, or to help them accept illness and disability and live their lives in spite of them. Sometimes health care may aim to be palliative, caring for patients' needs without trying to cure them. Often, however, health care is aimed at protecting or improving people's health. This wider interest in health is reflected in international law, which sees rights to health care as parts of broader rights to health.

The place of the law in promoting these broader rights to health is explored in Chapter 1. Although this book is mainly about health care law, we must not forget that factors outside the health care system will often have a major impact on the health of citizens. Sometimes these factors are environmental: water and air quality, housing and poverty play important roles. Such issues are regulated by law but are not dealt with in this book. However, some legal interventions are closely related to international rights of citizens to health. A recent notable illustration of the growing concern with public health and with health promotion and health prevention is the proposed ban on smoking in public places in the Health Act 2006, discussed below at pp.28–30. Chapter 1 selects examples to illustrate the role of law and the issues raised. It makes no attempt to be comprehensive in this section but to provide material to enable the potential for the use of the law to be considered.

Health care law itself is more narrowly focused. In the United Kingdom most health care is delivered within the National Health Service. Chapter 1 also sets out the legal entitlements of citizens to access health services. It can be seen that the Secretary of State for Health is obliged to secure a comprehensive range of such services. This provides United Kingdom citizens with health services which go beyond the strict requirements of international law. However, the chapter also shows how difficult it is to enforce claims to the use of such services. The reluctance of the courts to intervene is probably related to a more general reticence on the part of the law to dictate to health professionals. This will be seen elsewhere in the book. Success at challenging access to NHS resources has not notably changed with the advent of the Human Rights Act 1998 (see, for example, *R. v North West Lancashire Health Authority Ex p. A, Same v Same Ex p. D, Same v Same Ex p. G* [2000] 1 W.L.R. 977).

As will be seen in Chapter 1, the courts have been unwilling to uphold claims using the European Convention on Human Rights in the context of claim rights to NHS resources. This is one area, however, where other influences are beginning to be discerned. Patients have for several years been seeking access to treatment services abroad through "health tourism" in areas such as fertility treatment (see Chapter 11)and cosmetic surgery. But the prospect of an individual using their free movement rights under EU law as a means of bypassing NHS waiting lists by obtaining treatment in another EU country and reclaiming the cost from the NHS is a radical new development and one which may have a considerable impact on resource allocation in the future. (See further the discussion of *Secretary of State for Health v R. on the Application of Yvonne Watts*, Case C1-239/2003 at pp.71–79 below.) This is simply one example of a new trend discernable in this book—the growing impact of the EU in health policy and health law in the UK (see further T.K. Hervey and J.V. McHale, *Health Law and the European Union*, Cambridge: CUP, 2004).

The first part of this book thus provides an understanding of many of the broad issues which underpin the debate in subsequent chapters. The dominance of NHS rather than private health care helps to explain judicial attitudes to patients in the past. But a new consumerism in health care through the increased private provision of private health care may lead to changing approaches in the future. Many of the legal questions which are considered later need to be set in the context of the ethical debate which surrounds them. Chapter 2 introduces the main tools that are needed to grapple with these issues. Equipped with an appreciation of these areas, it is much easier to make sense of the body of detailed law that follows.

1

RIGHTS TO HEALTH AND HEALTH CARE

1. INTRODUCTION

Good health is a fundamental precondition of much human activity. It follows that the value of health is rarely challenged. What the importance of health means for governments is more controversial. There is room for considerable disagreement about the definition and level of health that should be used to define what citizens can legitimately expect governments and the law to seek to ensure. Some argue that the role of the state is to ensure that people are as healthy as possible, others that the only concern of the law is with preventing people being or remaining ill (see J. Montgomery, "Recognising a Right to Health" in R. Beddard and D. Hill (eds), *Economic, Social and Cultural Rights, Progress and Achievements*, Basingstoke: Macmillan, 1992). There is also a continuing debate about the relative responsibilities of governments and individuals for taking steps to improve health and health services, and about the relationship between health services, health professionals and market forces. A further aspect of the public health dimension of a right to health is evident today through the involvement of the international community and the European Union. In this chapter, we explore the nature of the "right to health" and the "right to health care" and to what extent actions can be brought based upon such rights in the English courts. There is no specific recognition of a right to health and health care in English law. As we shall see below, while the Human Rights Act 1998 has to date not changed this position, this does not provide a fundamental statement of a right to health. In this chapter we also explore, first, how the right to health in general and health care in particular has been recognised in international statements of human rights. Secondly, we examine the role of the state in facilitating a right to health in the form of measures concerning health promotion and disease prevention, to what extent there is a "right to be ill" and the prospect of compulsory care. Thirdly, we examine the provision of NHS services and legal challenges to NHS resource allocation decisions.

2. The Scope of Rights to Health and Health Care

The international law of human rights includes recognition of health and health care issues, and the relevant provisions can be used to consider the scope of health rights and their place in England and Wales. There is no single source of health rights in international law, but many of the conventions include them (see further, e.g. V. Leary, "The Right to Health in International Human Rights Law" 1 *Journal of Health and Human Rights* (1994) 3; Y. Aria-Takahashi, "The Right to Health in International Law: a Critical Appraisal" in R. Martyn and L. Johnson (eds), *Law and the Public Dimension of Health*, London: Cavendish, 2001). Article 25 of the Universal Declaration of Human Rights, establishes the overarching principle:

> "Everyone has the right to a standard of living adequate for the health and well-being of himself and his family, including food, clothing, housing and medical care and necessary social services . . . ".

This aims to guarantee the preconditions of good health, including the availability of health services.

The International Covenant on Economic, Social and Cultural Rights, Article 12, is concerned with the level of health to which human rights law is committed:

> "the right to enjoyment of the highest attainable standard of physical and mental health".

These two statements provide a general orientation for human rights law. More detail is provided by the European Social Charter of 1961, to which the British government is a signatory. Articles 11 and 13 of Part I establish the following principles:

> "everyone has the right to benefit from any measures enabling him to enjoy the highest standard of health attainable"

and

> "anyone without adequate resources has the right to social and medical assistance".

The meaning of these rights is expanded in Part II of the Convention. Under Article 11 of that Charter, the Government has undertaken:

1. to remove so far as possible the causes of ill-health;
2. to provide advisory and educational facilities for the promotion of health and the encouragement of individual responsibility in matters of health;
3. to prevent as far as possible epidemic, endemic and other diseases.

Under Article 13, the United Kingdom has undertaken to ensure, so that the right to social and medical assistance can be effectively exercised:

"that any person who is without adequate resources and who is unable to secure such resources either by his own efforts or from other sources . . . be granted adequate assistance, and, in the case of sickness, the care necessitated by his condition."

The EU Charter of Fundamental Rights and Freedoms which is now incorporated in the proposed new EU Constitution contains a number of rights which are reflective of those contained in the ECHR, such as Article 2 (the right to life) and Article 4 (the prohibition on inhuman and degrading treatment) (see further T. Hervey, "The Right to Health in EU Law" in T.K. Hervey and J. Kenner, *Economic and Social Rights under the EU Charter of Fundamental Rights*, Oxford: Hart Publishing, 2003).

In addition, Article 35 provides that:

"Everyone has the right of access to preventive health care and the right to benefit from medical treatment under the conditions established by national laws and practices. A high level of human health protection shall be ensured in the definition and implementation of all Union policies and activities."

At present, the Charter of Fundamental Rights and Freedoms is non-binding "soft law", although it is influential. (See further Hervey, *op. cit.*). Its status would change considerably if the new EU constitution is adopted by Member States, though at the moment the fate of that document very much hangs in the balance. Rights to health in the context of public health are also within the concern of the EU, as we shall see below at p.11.

Human rights law has also recognised that the implications of health rights for specific groups often need to be spelt out to ensure that appropriate concrete steps are taken. Thus, the United Nations Convention on the Rights of the Child contains both a general statement of children's health rights and a series of specific commitments. (For full discussion, see G. Van Bueren, *The International Law on the Rights of the Child*, London: Martinus Nijhoff, 1998, Chapter 11.)

UN Convention on the Rights of the Child

Article 24:

(1) States Parties recognise the right of the child to the enjoyment of the highest attainable standard of health and to facilities for the treatment of illness and rehabilitation of health. States Parties shall strive to ensure that no child is deprived of his or her right of access to health services.

(2) States Parties shall pursue full implementation of this right and, in particular, shall take appropriate measures:

(a) to diminish infant and child mortality;
(b) to ensure the provision of necessary medical assistance and health care to all children with emphasis on the development of primary health care;
(c) to combat disease and malnutrition, including within the framework of primary care, through *inter alia*, the application of readily available technology and through

the provision of adequate nutritious foods and clean drinking water, taking into consideration the dangers and risks of environmental pollution;

(d) to ensure appropriate pre-natal and post-natal care for mothers;

(e) to ensure that all segments of society, in particular parents and children, are informed, have access to education and are supported in the use of basic knowledge of child health and nutrition, the advantages of breast-feeding, hygiene and environmental sanitation and the prevention of accidents;

(f) to develop preventive health care, guidance for parents and family planning education and services.

(3) States Parties shall take all effective and appropriate measures with a view to abolishing traditional practices prejudicial to the health of children.

NOTES:

1. Paragraph 4, concerning international co-operation, has been omitted here.
2. Article 4 of the Convention limits the obligations of contracting states by reference to their available resources.

The United Nations Convention on the Elimination of All Forms of Discrimination against Women similarly reaffirms the entitlement of women to benefit from the general right of access to health care (Articles 11(f) and 14(b)) but also recognises the specific problems confronting women (see R.J. Cook, *Woman's Health and Human Rights*, Philadelphia: Philadelphia and Pennsylvania Press, 1994).

Article 12:

(1) States Parties shall take all appropriate measures to eliminate discrimination against women in the field of health care in order to ensure, on a basis of equality of men and women, access to health care services, including those related to family planning.

(2) Notwithstanding the provisions of paragraph 1 of this article, States Parties shall ensure to women appropriate services in connection with pregnancy, confinement and the post-natal period, granting free services where necessary, as well as adequate nutrition during pregnancy and lactation.

QUESTION:

1. Do you think that this provision serves to protect the interests of women or their children?

It is clear from these provisions that the health rights of citizens are concerned with more than merely access to services under a health service. Preventive measures are also required, and citizens should be given the opportunity to improve their own health. The role of the law in removing the causes of ill-health and the issues that are raised are explored in the next section of this chapter. It may be that health rights are actually more valuable than rights to health care. The latter are merely one component of the broader bundle of rights (J. Montgomery, "Recognising a Right to Health" in R. Beddard and D. Hill (eds), *Economic, Social and Cultural Rights: Progress and Achievements*, Basingstoke: Macmillan, 1992). Often, health care will be sought to restore good health, or to reduce the impact of ill-health. It would be preferable to prevent health being impaired in the first place.

Nonetheless there are tensions between health promotion and concerns to safeguard civil liberties. This issue is returned to below.

3. HEALTH PROMOTION AND DISEASE PREVENTION

In this section we explore the role of the state in relation to facilitating the health rights of its citizens through both health promotion and disease prevention. These are issues which are commonly classed under a particular area of health law, that of public health law. (See further L. Gostin, *Public Health Law*, Berkeley and Los Angeles: University of California Press, 2000, p.xix). Public health by its very nature is not simply an issue of national concern. Diseases are no respecters of national borders and this is illustrated only too graphically with conditions such as SARS and the recent international spread of bird flu. Public health is also a major concern of the EU.

Public Health: EC Treaty, Article 152

Article 152 of the EC Treaty makes specific reference to public health. Community action complementing national policies "shall be directed towards improving public health, preventing human illness and obviating sources of danger to public health". The Treaty provides that there is competence to co-ordinate national action in this field under Article 152(2). In addition Article 152(4) provides that the EU institutions have competence to adopt "measures setting high standards of quality and safety of organs and substances of human origin, blood and blood derivatives and measures in the veterinary and phytosanitary fields which have as their direct objective the protection of human health". Although harmonisation of national laws is precluded by this provision, "incentive measures" which are designed to protect and improve human health may be adopted. The EU has been active in public health law and policy in a range of areas including as blood safety following major scandals across the EU concerning infected blood leading to the Blood Safety Directive (Directive 2002/98/EC, setting standards for quality and safety for the collection, testing, processing storage and distribution of human blood and blood components) and in the area of human tissue through the Tissue Directive (Directive 2004/23 of the European Parliament and of the Council of March 31, 2004 on setting standards of quality and safety for the donation, procurement, testing, processing, preservation, storage and distribution of human tissue and cells). They have also played a major role in health promotion for example, in relation to cancer and tobacco (see below at p.28 and see further T.K. Hervey and J.V. McHale, *Health Law and the European Union* (Cambridge: CUP, 2004), chapter 9: T.K. Hervey and J.V. McHale, "Law, Health and the European Union" [2005] 25(2) *Legal Studies* 228).

(a) Contagious Disease Control

We begin by considering the law's contribution to protecting citizens from ill-health. The threat to health may sometimes come from other people rather than impersonal substances or environmental situations. The most obvious example of this is contagious diseases, where one individual may infect another. Clearly, the right to health, and sometimes the right to life, of the "victim" can be called upon to provide a justification for legal measures to prevent such contagion. Equally clearly, limiting the behaviour of people who are already infected raises questions about their own civil rights.

English law uses two main techniques to deal with this area. The first can be described as "control powers". These permit public health officials to take steps to reduce the risk of infection. They operate to identify and segregate those who may infect others. These powers seek to prevent infection by restraining risky behaviour. The second approach operates after infection has occurred, or been irresponsibly risked. Here those who have jeopardised the health of others are made liable to criminal penalties or to compensate those who have been made ill. This approach is principally remedial, compensating for or punishing wrong-doing. However, it is hoped that it would also provide a deterrent effect, which would reduce the incidence of infection. There is a wide range of control powers provided by English law (see J. Montgomery, *Health Care Law* (2nd edn), Oxford: OUP, 2002, Chapter 2, R. Martyn, "Domestic Regulation of Public Health: England and Wales" in R. Martyn and L. Johnson, *Law and the Public Dimension of Health*, London: Cavendish, 2001).

The central piece of legislation is that of the Public Health (Control of Disease) Act 1984. Some of the provisions of that Act are used here to illustrate the issues. The first step in their use is the identification of individuals who are infected by or carry infectious diseases. Sometimes this information is already known, and merely needs to be communicated to the proper authorities. Thus, doctors are obliged to inform public health officials when they know someone has a "notifiable" disease.

The Act specifies five diseases, cholera, plague, relapsing fever, smallpox and typhus, as notifiable. Others have been specified by regulations, and there is provision for diseases to be specified for specific geographical areas where necessary (s.16). While AIDS and tuberculosis come within the Act, they are not strictly notifiable diseases because s.11 does not apply. The Public Health (Infectious Diseases) Regulations 1988 (SI 1988/1546) extend the application of the legislation to a range of other diseases, including leprosy, malaria, meningitis, rabies and yellow fever.

ADAPTED FROM SCHEDULE 1 TO THE PUBLIC HEALTH (INFECTIOUS DISEASES) REGULATIONS 1988 (SI 1988/1546)

Diseases	Enactments applied
Acquired immune deficiency syndrome	ss.35, 37, 38 (as modified by reg.5), 43, 44
Acute encephalitis Acute poliomyelitis Meningitis Meningococcal septicaemia (without meningitis)	ss.11, 17, 19, 35 (as modified by reg.4), 37, 38, 44, 45

Diseases	Enactments applied
Anthrax	ss.11, 17, 19, 35 (as modified by reg.4), 37, 38, 43–45
Diphtheria Dysentery (amoebic or bacillary) Paratyphoid fever Typhoid fever Viral hepatitis	ss.11, 17, 19, 35–38, 44, 45
Leprosy	ss.11, 17, 19, 35 (as modified by reg.4), 37, 38, 44
Leptospirosis Mumps Rubella Whooping cough	ss.11, 17, 19, 35 (as modified by reg.4), 38, 44 and 45
Malaria Tetanus Yellow fever	ss.11 and 35 (as modified by reg.4)
Ophthalmia neonatorum	ss.11, 17
Rabies	ss.11, 17, 19, 38
Scarlet fever	ss.11, 17, 19, 35–38, 44, 45
Tuberculosis	ss.17, 19, 35 (as modified by reg.4), 44, 45; in addition— (a) s.11 shall apply where the opinion of the registered medical practitioner that a person is suffering from tuberculosis is formed from evidence not derived solely from tuberculin tests, and (b) ss.37 and 38 shall apply to tuberculosis of the respiratory tract in an infectious state.
Viral haemorrhagic fever	ss.11, 17, 19, 35–38, 43–45

NOTES:

1. Not all the sections of the Act are applicable in relation to these diseases. This table has been edited to deal only with a selection of these provisions, primarily those which are considered in more detail below. The sections mentioned concern notifiability (s.11), criminal offences of endangerment (ss.17, 19), compulsory examination (ss.35, 36), removal to hospital (s.37), detention in hospital (s.38) and dealings with corpses of those dying while suffering from the disease (ss.43–45).
2. The modification of s.35 made by reg. 4 is to omit s.35(1)(a)(ii) (see below).

QUESTIONS:

1. The Regulations do not define AIDS. Do you think that someone who tested positive for HIV but had no symptoms of AIDS has "AIDS" within the meaning of the regulations? Compare C. d'Ecca, "Medico-legal Aspects of AIDS" in D. Harris and R. Hough, *AIDS: A Guide to the Law*, London: Routledge, 1990 and J. Montgomery, "Victims or Threats? The Framing of HIV" (1992) XII *Liverpool Law Review* 25.

2. Do you agree with the way in which these various diseases are categorised?

It may also be necessary to examine people to see whether they carry a disease within the Act. The main power for this purpose is to be found in s.35. That provides as follows.

Public Health (Control of Disease Act) 1984, s.35(1)(3)

35.—(1) If a justice of the peace (acting, if he deems it necessary, ex parte) is satisfied, on a written certificate issued by a registered medical practitioner nominated by the local authority for a district:

(a) that there is reason to believe that some person in the district:
   (i) is or has been suffering from a notifiable disease, or
   (ii) though not suffering from such a disease, is carrying an organism that is capable of causing it, and
(b) that in his own interest, or in the interest of his family, or in the public interest, it is expedient that he should be medically examined, and
(c) that he is not under the treatment of a registered medical practitioner or that the registered medical practitioner who is treating him consents to the making of an order under this section,

the justice may order him to be medically examined by a registered medical practitioner so nominated . . .

(3) In this section, references to a person's being medically examined shall be construed as including references to his being submitted to bacteriological and radiological tests and similar investigations.

NOTES:

1. For some diseases, s.35(1)(a)(ii) is omitted by reg. 4. See above for the diseases to which this applies.
2. There is a power under s.38 to order the examination of a group of people, where one of them is believed to suffer from a relevant disease.

QUESTION:

1. This provision contains a number of safeguards: the involvement of a magistrate; the need to satisfy the magistrate that there is reason to believe that the person is infected; the need to satisfy the magistrate that a medical examination is required in someone's interests; and the consent of the

person's doctor (if they have one). However, there is no guarantee that the person to be examined will be a party to the application. An order may nevertheless be made in their "own interest". Do you think those safeguards are sufficient?

Once a person has been identified as having a relevant infectious disease, public health officials may have the power to remove them to hospital under s.37.

Public Health (Control of Disease) Act 1984, s.37(1)(2)

37.—(1) Where a justice of the peace (acting, if he deems it necessary, ex parte) is satisfied, on the application of the local authority, that a person is suffering from a notifiable disease and—

(a) that his circumstances are such that proper precautions to prevent the spread of infection cannot be taken, or that such precautions are not being taken, and
(b) that serious risk of infection is thereby caused to other persons, and
(c) that accommodation for him is available in a suitable hospital vested in the Secretary of State or, pursuant to arrangements made by a Health Authority or Primary Care Trust (whether under an NHS contract or otherwise), in a suitable hospital vested in an NHS trust, NHS Foundation Trust, Primary Care Trust or other person,

the justice may, with the consent of the Health Authority in whose area lies the area, or the greater part of the area, of the local authority, order him to be removed to it.

(1A) The consent referred to in subsection (1) above is that of a Primary Care Trust or Health Authority—

(a) any part of whose area falls within that of the local authority and
(b) which appears to the local authority to be an appropriate Primary Care Trust or Health Authority from whom to obtain consent.

(2) An order under this section may be addressed to such officer of the local authority as the justice may think expedient, and that officer and any officer of the hospital may do all acts necessary for giving effect to the order.

QUESTIONS:

1. Are the criteria for making such orders sufficiently precise?
2. Do they give the right weight to the interests of the infected person?
3. Is it right that this power does not apply to those who are carriers of a disease but not suffering from it?

Once a person is in hospital, a magistrate may authorise their detention there under s.38:

Public Health (Control of Disease Act) 1984, s.38(1)–(4)

38.—(1) Where a justice of the peace (acting, if he deems it necessary, ex parte) in and for the place in which a hospital for infectious diseases is situated is satisfied, on the application of any local authority, that an inmate of the hospital who is suffering from a notifiable disease would not on leaving the hospital be provided with lodging or accommodation in which proper precautions could be taken to prevent the spread of the disease by him, the justice may order him to be detained in the hospital.

(2) An order made under subsection (1) above may direct detention for a period specified in the order, but any justice of the peace acting in and for the same place may extend a period so specified as often as it appears to him to be necessary to do so.

(3) Any person who leaves a hospital contrary to an order made under this section for his detention there shall be liable on summary conviction to a fine not exceeding level 1 on the standard scale, and the court may order him to be taken back to the hospital.

(4) An order under this section may be addressed—

(a) in the case of an order for a person's detention, to such officer of the hospital, and

(b) in the case of an order made under subsection (3) above, to such officer of the local authority on whose application the order for detention was made,

as the justice may think expedient, and that officer and any officer of the hospital may do all acts necessary for giving effect to the order.

In relation to AIDS, the wording of s.38 has been amended by reg.5 of the 1988 Regulations.

5.—In its application to acquired immune deficiency syndrome section 38(1) of the Act shall apply so that a justice of the peace (acting if he deems it necessary ex parte) may on the application of any local authority make an order for the detention in hospital of an inmate of that hospital suffering from acquired immune deficiency syndrome, in addition to the circumstances specified in that section, if the justice is satisfied that on his leaving the hospital proper precautions to prevent the spread of that disease would not be taken by him:

(a) in his lodging or accommodation, or

(b) in other places to which he may be expected to go if not detained in the hospital.

QUESTIONS:

1. Why was this amendment made?
2. Does it expose a weakness in the drafting of s.38 that is applicable more widely than just to AIDS?
3. A person suffering from a notifiable disease can be compulsorily tested, removed to hospital against their will, and detained there involuntarily. However, there is no provision for compulsory treatment under the Act. Should there be?

The only example of a power to treat someone without consent in the context of public health seems to be found in s.85 of the Public Health Act 1936.

Public Health Act 1936, s.85(1)–(4)

85.—(1) Upon the application of any person, a county council or a local authority may take such measures as are, in their opinion, necessary to free him and his clothing from vermin.

(2) Where it appears to a county council or a local authority, upon a report from their medical officer of health or, in the case of a local authority, from their sanitary inspector, that any person, or the clothing of any person, is verminous, then, if that person consents to be removed to a cleansing station, they may cause him to be removed to such a station, and, if he does not so consent, they may apply to a court of summary jurisdiction, and the court, if satisfied that it is necessary that he or his clothing should be cleansed, may make an order for his removal to such a station and for his detention therein for such period and subject to such conditions as may be specified in the order.

(3) Where a person has been removed to a cleansing station in pursuance of the last preceding subsection, the county council or local authority shall take such measures as may, in their opinion, be necessary to free him and his clothing from vermin.

(4) The cleansing of females under this section shall be carried out only by a registered medical practitioner, or by a woman duly authorised by the medical officer of health.

QUESTION:

1. Do you think this power is an aberration?

The European Convention on Human Rights and Fundamental Freedoms recognises that it may be legitimate for someone carrying an infections disease to be detained against their will.

European Convention on Human Rights and Fundamental Freedoms 1950

Article 5:

(1) Everyone has the right to liberty and security of the person. No one shall be deprived of this liberty save in the following cases and in accordance with a procedure prescribed by law . . .

(e) the lawful detention for the prevention of the spreading of infectious diseases, of persons of unsound mind, alcoholics or drug addicts or vagrants; . . .

NOTE:

1. This is the most precise example of the fact that public health issues may limit the application of fundamental human rights. However, many of the rights guaranteed by the Convention are limited when they come into conflict with actions that are "necessary in a democratic society in the interests of . . . public safety . . . for the protection of health or morals, or for the protection of the rights and freedoms of others". The rights to privacy, freedom of assembly, expression, thought, conscience and religion are all limited in this way (Articles 8–11 of the Convention).

The extent to which interventions can be justified in the interests of the public health was explored in the following case.

Acmanne v Belgium (1985) 40 D.R. 251

This case concerned a compulsory screening programme for tuberculosis. The applicants had been convicted for refusing to undergo, or permit their children to undergo, tests. They argued that the infringement of their right to privacy under Article 8 of the Convention was not justified as being necessary to protect health. The Commission accepted that compulsory testing was an interference with the right of respect for private life. However, it ruled the complaint inadmissible as being manifestly ill founded. They did so because they considered that the screening programme pursued a legitimate aim, protecting both the public health and the health of the individual applicants. The interference with the applicants' rights that was involved was proportionate to that aim. Finally, the interference was necessary to protect health within a democratic society under Article 8(2) of the Convention.

EUROPEAN COMMISSION OF HUMAN RIGHTS
"According to the Court's case-law a restriction on a Convention right cannot be regarded as necessary in a democratic society two hallmarks of which are tolerance and broadmindedness unless, amongst other things, it is proportionate to the legitimate aim pursued . . . In assessing the necessity of the interference with the applicants' private life, the Commission takes into account the reasoning in the Liege Court of Appeal . . . In particular, it notes that, finding that the applicants had not produced evidence of disadvantages comparable to the former ravages of tuberculosis, particularly among the deprived, the Court held that the individual had a social duty to defer to the general interest and not endanger the health of others where his life was not in danger."

Questions:

1. Do you think that the provisions of the 1984 Act are consistent with human rights law?
2. Do you think that this reasoning would enable compulsory treatment for infectious diseases to be reconciled with human rights law?

Enhorn v Sweden [2005] ECHR 56529

E was 56-year-old man who was HIV positive. He transmitted HIV to a 19-year-old man. The county medical officer instructed him under the Infectious Diseases 1998 Act to comply with various criteria, including informing sexual partners of his HIV status, using a condom, limiting alcohol consumption, and when seeking treatment informing health professionals of his HIV positive status. Following his failure to comply with these requirements, the medical officer obtained an order that the applicant should be subject to compulsory detention in isolation for a period of up to three months. E absconded and was subsequently arrested and obtained. This pattern repeated itself, leading to several periods of detention under a seven-year period. Some evidence was given that due to a personality disorder he was not fully aware of the risks of disease transmission in relation to his behaviour.

An action was brought before the ECHR claiming that the detention was in breach of Article 5(1) of the ECHR.

EUROPEAN COURT OF HUMAN RIGHTS
"41. The Court has only to a very limited extent decided cases where a person has been detained 'for the prevention of the spreading of infectious diseases'. It is therefore called upon to establish which criteria are relevant when assessing whether such a detention is in compliance with the principle of proportionality and the requirement that any detention must be free from arbitrariness.
42. By way of comparison, for the purposes of Article 5 § 1 (e), an individual cannot be deprived of his liberty as being of 'unsound mind' unless the following three minimum conditions are satisfied: firstly, he must reliably be shown to be of unsound mind; secondly, the mental disorder must be of a kind or degree warranting compulsory confinement; and thirdly, the validity of continued confinement depends upon the persistence of such a disorder (see *Winterwerp v. the Netherlands*, judgment of 24 October 1979, Series A no. 33, pp. 17–18, § 39; *Johnson v. the United Kingdom*, judgment of 24 October 1997,

Reports 1997-VII, p. 2409, § 60; and, more recently, *Varbanov v. Bulgaria*, no. 31365/96, § 45, ECHR 2000-X). Furthermore, there must be some relationship between the ground of permitted deprivation of liberty relied on and the place and conditions of detention. In principle, the 'detention' of a person as a mental health patient will only be 'lawful' for the purposes of sub-paragraph (e) of paragraph 1 if effected in a hospital, clinic or other appropriate institution (see *Ashingdane v. the United Kingdom*, judgment of 28 May 1985, Series A no. 93, p. 21, § 44).

Also by way of comparison, for the purposes of Article 5 § 1 (e), an individual cannot be deprived of his liberty for being an 'alcoholic' (within the autonomous meaning of the Convention as set out in *Witold Litwa v. Poland*, §§ 57–63, cited above) unless other, less severe measures have been considered and found to be insufficient to safeguard the individual or public interest which might require that the person concerned be detained. That means that it does not suffice that the deprivation of liberty is executed in conformity with national law; it must also be necessary in the circumstances.

43. Moreover, Article 5 § 1 (e) of the Convention refers to several categories of individuals, namely persons spreading infectious diseases, persons of unsound mind, alcoholics, drug addicts and vagrants. There is a link between all those persons in that they may be deprived of their liberty either in order to be given medical treatment or because of considerations dictated by social policy, or on both medical and social grounds. It is therefore legitimate to conclude from this context that a predominant reason why the Convention allows the persons mentioned in paragraph 1 (e) of Article 5 to be deprived of their liberty is not only that they are dangerous for public safety but also that their own interests may necessitate their detention (see *Guzzardi v. Italy*, judgment of 6 November 1980, Series A no. 39, pp. 36–37, and *Witold Litwa*, cited above).

44. Taking the above principles into account, the Court finds that the essential criteria when assessing the 'lawfulness' of the detention of a person 'for the prevention of the spreading of infectious diseases' are whether the spreading of the infectious disease is dangerous for public health or safety, and whether detention of the person infected is the last resort in order to prevent the spreading of the disease, because less severe measures have been considered and found to be insufficient to safeguard the public interest. When these criteria are no longer fulfilled, the basis for the deprivation of liberty ceases to exist.

45. Turning to the instant case, it is undisputed that the first criterion was fulfilled, in that the HIV virus was and is dangerous for public health and safety.

46. It thus remains to be examined whether the applicant's detention could be said to be the last resort in order to prevent the spreading of the virus, because less severe measures had been considered and found to be insufficient to safeguard the public interest.

47. In a judgment of 16 February 1995, the County Administrative Court ordered that the applicant should be kept in compulsory isolation for up to three months under section 38 of the 1988 Act. Thereafter, orders to prolong his deprivation of liberty were continuously issued every six months until 12 December 2001, when the County Administrative Court turned down the county medical officer's application for an extension of the detention order. Accordingly, the order to deprive the applicant of his liberty was in force for almost seven years.

Admittedly, since the applicant absconded several times, his actual deprivation of liberty lasted from 16 March 1995 until 25 April 1995, 11 June 1995 until 27 September 1995, 28 May 1996 until 6 November 1996, 16 November 1996 until 26 February 1997, and 26 February 1999 until 12 June 1999—almost one and a half years altogether.

48. The Government submitted that a number of voluntary measures had been attempted in vain during the period between September 1994 and February 1995 to ensure that the applicant's behaviour would not contribute to the spread of the HIV infection. Also, they noted the particular circumstances of the case, notably as to the applicant's personality and behaviour, as described by various physicians and psychiatrists; his preference for teenage boys; the fact that he had transmitted the HIV virus to a young man; and the fact that he had absconded several times and refused to cooperate with the staff at

the hospital. Thus, the Government found that the involuntary placement of the applicant in hospital had been proportionate to the purpose of the measure, namely to prevent him from spreading the infectious disease.

49. The Court notes that the Government have not provided any examples of less severe measures which might have been considered for the applicant in the period from 16 February 1995 until 12 December 2001, but were apparently found to be insufficient to safeguard the public interest.

50. It is undisputed that the applicant failed to comply with the instruction issued by the county medical officer on 1 September 1994, which stated that he should visit his consulting physician again and keep to appointments set up by the county medical officer. Although he kept to three appointments with the county medical officer in September 1994 and one in November 1994, and received two home visits by the latter, on five occasions during October and November 1994 the applicant failed to appear as summoned.

51. Another of the practical instructions issued by the council medical officer on 1 September 1994 was that, if the applicant was to have a physical examination, an operation, a vaccination or a blood test or was bleeding for any reason, he was obliged to tell the relevant medical staff about his infection. Also, he was to inform his dentist about his HIV infection. In April 1999, before the County Administrative Court, the county medical officer stated that during the last two years, while on the run, the applicant had sought medical treatment twice and that it had been established that both times he had said that he had the HIV virus, as opposed to the period when he had absconded between September 1995 and May 1996, during which the applicant had failed on three occasions to inform medical staff about his virus.

52. Yet another of the practical instructions issued by the county medical officer on 1 September 1994 required the applicant to abstain from consuming such an amount of alcohol that his judgment would thereby be impaired and others put at risk of being infected with HIV. However, there were no instructions to abstain from alcohol altogether or to undergo treatment against alcoholism. Nor did the domestic courts justify the deprivation of the applicant's liberty with reference to his being an 'alcoholic' within the meaning of Article 5 § 1 (e) and the requirements deriving from that provision.

53. Moreover, although the county medical officer stated before the County Administrative Court in February 1995 that, in his opinion, it was necessary for the applicant to consult a psychiatrist in order to alter his behaviour, undergoing psychiatric treatment was not among the practical instructions issued by the county medical officer on 1 September 1994. Nor did the domestic courts during the proceedings justify the deprivation of the applicant's liberty with reference to his being of 'unsound mind' within the meaning of Article 5 § 1 (e) and the requirements deriving from that provision.

54. The instructions issued on 1 September 1994 prohibited the applicant from having sexual intercourse without first having informed his partner about his HIV infection. Also, he was to use a condom. The Court notes in this connection that, despite his being at large for most of the period from 16 February 1995 until 12 December 2001, there is no evidence or indication that during that period the applicant transmitted the HIV virus to anybody, or that he had sexual intercourse without first informing his partner about his HIV infection, or that he did not use a condom, or that he had any sexual relationship at all for that matter. It is true that the applicant infected the 19-year-old man with whom he had first had sexual contact in 1990. This was discovered in 1994, when the applicant himself became aware of his infection. However, there is no indication that the applicant transmitted the HIV virus to the young man as a result of intent or gross neglect, which in many of the Contracting States, including Sweden, would have been considered a criminal offence under the Criminal Code.

55. In these circumstances, the Court finds that the compulsory isolation of the applicant was not a last resort in order to prevent him from spreading the HIV virus because less severe measures had been considered and found to be insufficient to safeguard the public interest. Moreover, the Court considers that by extending over a period of almost seven years the order for the applicant's compulsory isolation, with the result that he was placed involuntarily in a hospital for almost one and a half years in total, the authorities failed to

strike a fair balance between the need to ensure that the HIV virus did not spread and the applicant's right to liberty.

56. There has accordingly been a violation of Article 5 § 1 of the Convention."

QUESTIONS:

1. Could the powers under the Public Health Act 1984 be subject to a similar human rights challenge? (See further A. Harris and R. Martyn, "The Exercise of Public Health Powers in an Era of Human Rights: the Particular Problem of Tuberculosis" (2004) 118 *Public Health* 312.)

2. Is it possible to prioritise individual autonomy rights in a situation of a major public risk such as a possible SARS, bird flu or TB epidemic? (See further R. Martyn, "The Exercise of Public Health Powers in Cases of Infectious Disease: Human Rights Implications" (2006) 14 *Medical Law Review* 132.)

The Public Health (Control of Disease) Act 1984 also provides examples of the use of the law to deter people from taking risks with the health of others. There are criminal offences of knowingly exposing others to the risk of infections from a notifiable disease under ss.17 and 19 of the 1984 Act.

Public Health (Control of Disease) Act 1984, ss.17(1)(2), 19

17.—(1) A person who:

(a) knowing that he is suffering from a notifiable disease, exposes other persons to the risk of infection by his presence or conduct in any street, public place, place of entertainment or assembly, club, hotel, inn or shop,

(b) having the care of a person whom he knows to be suffering from a notifiable disease, causes or permits that person to expose other persons to the risk of infection by his presence or conduct in any such place as aforesaid, or

(c) gives, lends, sells, transmits or exposes, without previous disinfection, any clothing, bedding or rags which he knows to have been exposed to infection from any such disease, or any other article which he knows to have been so exposed and which is liable to carry such infection, shall be liable on summary conviction to a fine not exceeding level 1 on the standard scale.

(2) A person shall not incur any liability under this section by transmitting with proper precautions any article for the purpose of having it disinfected.

. . .

19. A person who, knowing that he is suffering from a notifiable disease, engages in or carries on any trade, business or occupation which he cannot engage in or carry on without risk of spreading the disease shall be liable on summary conviction to a fine not exceeding level 1 on the standard scale.

NOTES:

1. It is possible that even without these specific offences, a prosecution could be brought where one person knowingly infected another. Public nuisance may also provide a duty to take steps to protect those at risk from infection (see M. Mulholland, "Public Nuisance—a New Use for an Old Tool"

(1995) 11 *Professional Negligence* 70). In *R. v Vantandillo* (1815) 4 M. & S. 73, 105 E.R. 762, an infected child was carried through the streets. Le Blanc J. found that an offence had been committed, and defined it in these terms:

> "if a person unlawfully, injuriously and with full knowledge of the fact, exposes in a public highway a person infected with a contagious disorder, it is a common nuisance to all the subjects, and indictable as such."

He also found that there was no need to show that there was any intention to infect. It is also possible in principle that a civil action might lie for compensation against a person who negligently infected another, or failed to take steps to protect them.

2. Section 20 of the Offences Against the Person Act 1861 has been used to prosecute those who have transmitted HIV to sexual partners. See further the discussion of this in Chapter 6 below.

QUESTIONS:

1. Would you support the creation of a general offence of endangerment in relation to infectious diseases, as proposed by K.J.M. Smith, "Risking Death by Dangerous Sexual Behaviour and the Criminal Law" in D. Morgan and R. Lee (eds), *Death Rites: Law and Ethics and the End of Life*, London: Routledge, 1994.
2. Should there be specific offences of deliberately transmitting a serious disease? (see S. Bronitt, "Spreading Disease and the Criminal Law" [1994] Crim.L.R. 21 and M. Brazier and J. Harris, "Public Health and Private Lives" (1996) 4 *Medical Law Review* 171 and Chapter 6 below).
3. What are the advantages and disadvantages of using criminal and civil liability to deter people from infecting others? (See P. Old and J. Montgomery, "Law Coercion and Public Health" (1992) 304 B.M.J. 891.)

(b) Compulsory Care and the Right to be Ill

Rather than criminalisation a further approach to facilitate health care in the community as a whole is through the use of compulsion in care through the use of the civil law. One notable illustration of this is in the context of mental health and we explore this later in this book at Chapter 8. A further illustration is through the application of the National Assistance Acts.

National Assistance Act 1948, s.47(1)–(4) (6)–(9), (11)

47.—(1) The following provisions of this section shall have effect for the purposes of securing the necessary care and attention for persons who—

(a) are suffering from grave chronic disease or, being aged, infirm or physically incapacitated, are living in insanitary conditions, and
(b) are unable to devote to themselves, and are not receiving from other persons, proper care and attention.

(2) If the medical officer of health certifies in writing to the appropriate authority that he is satisfied after thorough inquiry and consideration that in the interests of any such person as aforesaid residing in the area of the authority, or for preventing injury to the health of, or serious nuisance to, other persons, it is necessary to remove any such person as aforesaid from the premises in which he is residing, the appropriate authority may apply to a court of summary jurisdiction having jurisdiction in the place where the premises are situated for an order under the next following subsection.

(3) On any such application the court may, if satisfied on oral evidence of the allegations in the certificate, and that it is expedient so to do, order the removal of the person to whom the application relates, by such officer of the appropriate authority as may be specified in the order, to a suitable hospital or other place in, or within convenient distance of, the area of the appropriate authority, and his detention and maintenance therein:

Provided that the court shall not order the removal of a person to any premises, unless either the person managing the premises has been heard in the proceedings or seven clear days' notice has been given to him of the intended application and of the time and place at which it is proposed to be made.

(4) An order under the last foregoing subsection may be made so as to authorise a person's detention for any period not exceeding three months, and the court may from time to time by order extend that period for such further period, not exceeding three months, as the court may determine . . .

(6) At any time after the expiration of six clear weeks from the making of an order under subsection (3) or (4) of this section an application may be made to the court by or on behalf of the person in respect of whom the order was made, and on any such application the court may, if in the circumstances it appears expedient so to do, revoke the order.

(7) No application under this section shall be entertained by the court unless, seven clear days before the making of the application, notice has been given of the intended application and of the time and place at which it is proposed to be made:

(a)   where the application is for an order under subsection (3) or (4) of this section, to the person in respect of whom the application is made or to some person in charge of him;

(b)   where the application is for the revocation of such an order, to the medical officer of health.

(8) Where in pursuance of an order under this section a person is maintained neither in hospital accommodation provided by the Minister of Health under the National Health Service Act 1977 . . . nor in premises where accommodation is provided by, or by arrangement with, a local authority under Part III of this Act, the cost of his maintenance shall be borne by the appropriate authority.

(9) Any expenditure incurred under the last foregoing subsection shall be recoverable from the person maintained or from any person who for the purposes of this Act is liable to maintain that person; and any expenditure incurred by virtue of this section in connection with the maintenance of a person in premises where accommodation is provided under Part III of this Act shall be recoverable in like manner as expenditure incurred in providing accommodation under the said Part III. . . .

(11) Any person who wilfully disobeys, or obstructs the execution of, an order under this section shall be guilty of an offence and liable on summary conviction to a fine not exceeding level 1 on the standard scale.

NOTES:

1. Subsection 10 has been repealed, subss.5, 12–14 have been omitted.
2. Under s.47, the person to be removed must be given notice of the application. In 1951, the National Assistance (Amendment) Act 1951 introduced an ex parte procedure where the medical officer of health and

another doctor certify that "in their opinion it is necessary in the interest of that person to remove him without delay" (s.1(1)). Orders made under this statute last only three weeks, and must be extended under the provisions of s.47 if this is necessary.

3. A study published in 1981 indicated that about 200 people were compulsorily removed under these provisions each year (J. Muir Gray, "Section 47" (1981) 7 *Journal of Medical Ethics* 146). Almost all (94 per cent) of these were removed under the emergency powers in the 1951 Act. The provisions of the National Assistance Act 1948 were considered by the Law Commission in their report *Mental Incapacity* (London: HMSO, 1995). They noted the responses to their earlier consultation paper to the effect that there was need for reform of the 1948 Act, stating that "The existing law was said to be ineffective in protecting elderly, disabled and other vulnerable people from abuse and neglect and inadquate in its approach to autonomy and individual rights. It appeared to be counter-productive being so draconian that it was rarely used." (para.9.1).

4. Other powers do exist enabling the removal of vulnerable persons. Section 135 of the Mental Health Act 1983 enables an approved social worker to obtain a warrant from a magistrate to remove a person suffering from a mental disorder to a place of safety. Muir Gray pointed out that these powers of compulsion under the 1948 Act differed from those under the Mental Health Act 1983 in that the person to be removed was recognised to be competent to decide whether they wished to leave. In contrast mental health patients are declared unable to recognise what was good for them, and treated in their interests.

QUESTIONS:

1. Who determines whether care and attention is "necessary"? The person concerned, the doctor, or the court?
2. Are the provisions for applications to have the order revoked sufficient? Is it right that an application may not be brought for six weeks?
3. Is it right that a person's vulnerability to being forcibly removed depends on the availability of others to care for them (s.47(1)(b))?
4. Can people effectively force their relatives to go to hospital by refusing to care for them?
5. Muir Gray suggested that the National Assistance Acts needed amending, but not repealing. Do you agree? What amendments might be made? (See further Law Commission, *Mental Incapacity*, London: HMSO, 1995, para. 9.12 onwards.)

(c) Health Promotion

Health promotion is an increasingly important part of health care delivery (see further Department of Health, *Choosing Health: a Consultation on Action to*

Improve the Public's Health", London: DOH, 2004). Individuals are being encouraged to take responsibility for their own health. Increasingly the Government are promoting the benefits of low-fat diets and exercise. This also includes promotion of healthy behaviour during pregnancy. Health promotion is linked with controls. In other jurisdictions, notably the USA, health promotion has become proscriptive, as for example in relation to the criminalisation of behaviour during pregnancy likely to harm the foetus (see further Chapter 13). In the UK health promotion is still primarily seen in terms of persuasion as opposed to coercion. But in addition some strategies have been used as a means of reducing the prospect of harm resulting from unhealthy activities rather than explicit criminalisation such as the recent ban on smoking in pubs and restaurants (see below at p.28). Nonetheless there have been calls for this approach to be taken one stage further. Some suggest that individuals' access to NHS health care to be linked to their lifestyle. Thus there have been suggestions that alcoholics, such as the late footballer George Best, should not receive access to transplantation procedures (see generally W. Glannon, "Responsibility, Alcoholism and Liver Transplantation" (1998) 23 *Journal of Medical Philosophy* 31), that the over-weight should be refused surgery and/or required to radically lose weight before they are allowed surgery and that access to treatment by smokers should be limited. The National Institute for Clinical Excellence announced in 2006 that it would in the future apply the following principle

"NICE and its advisory bodies should avoid denying care to patients with conditions that are or may be self-inflicted (in part or whole). If however self-inflicted cause(s) of the condition influence the clinical or cost-effectiveness of the use of an intervention it may be appropriate to take this into account."

(National Institute for Clinical Excellence, "Social Value Judgements: Principles for the Development of NHS Guidance" (2005) and see S. Holm, "Self-Inflicted Harm: NICE in Ethical Self-Destruct Mode" (2006) 32 *Journal of Medical Ethics* 125).

But to what extent are such restrictions legitimate? Do health rights also require health obligations/duties placed upon the individual citizen?

Article 11(2) of the European Social Charter implies that the proper way to deal with many health issues is to enable people to take decisions for themselves. It obliges governments to provide advice and information on health matters and to encourage people to take responsibility for themselves, rather than require them to be healthy.

Enabling people to make informed choices also involves some regulation. Foods must be properly labelled so that consumers can take decisions on the basis of their true constituents. Sometimes, however, the government pursues policies which are designed to influence choice without removing it. Examples of these, which are underpinned by legislation, are the licensing of outlets, restriction on their opening and taxation.

The ethical issues concerning limitations on one activity, namely smoking, which may have adverse health consequences are explored by the Nuffield Council on Bioethics in the following extract.

Nuffield Council on Bioethics, *Public Health: Ethical Issues* (2006)

Smoking as a public health risk

Issues for public health are also raised by products that, in dietary terms, are completely unnecessary. These include alcohol, tobacco and a range of recreational drugs that have been classified as illegal. The health risks of smoking have been known for several decades and are well documented. Smoking is associated with increased morbidity and mortality and is linked to more than 20 different causes of death, including certain cancers, respiratory diseases and circulatory diseases. Some of the health effects are experienced not only by smokers themselves, but also, to a lesser extent, by those around them who breathe in their smoke (passive smoking).

Facts and figures

- In 2004, around 23% of both men and women aged 16 and over in the UK were regular smokers. These levels have declined from the highest recorded prevalences of around 80% for men, during the late 1940s and 1950s, and around 45% for women, during the 1960s.
- Since the early 1990s, the highest prevalence of smoking has been seen in the 20–24 age group.
- Data for 12–15 year olds from 2000 show that 10% of boys and 14% of girls in England, and 9% of boys and 15% of girls in Scotland, were regular smokers.
- An estimate of dependence on cigarettes can be obtained from statistics on when a smoker has their first cigarette each day. In 2004, 17% of smokers had their first cigarette within five minutes of waking, indicating high dependence.
- Smoking is most common in the manual occupations sector, in which 29% of people smoke regularly, and least common in the managerial and professional sector, in which 17% of people smoke regularly.
- Each year, over 120,000 deaths in the UK and more than 225,000 hospital admissions can be attributed to smoking.
- Smoking is estimated to cost the NHS up to £1,700 million each year in terms of GP visits, prescriptions, treatment and operations.
- There are also costs arising from those incapacitated by smoking-related diseases, and costs of fires caused by careless smokers.
- In the case of passive smoking, the effects are more difficult to quantify:
  - It is thought that several hundred people each year die from lung cancer as a result of passive smoking, and slightly more from heart disease.
  - The most vulnerable group exposed to other people's smoke is children. It has been estimated that 17,000 hospital admissions each year in children under five years of age are caused by their parents' smoking. Lung illnesses, glue ear, cot death and asthma are all more likely to occur in children whose parents smoke than in those whose parents do not.
- Women who smoke during pregnancy may harm their unborn child. The risks include reduced birth weight and certain health problems. Carcinogens (cancer-causing substances) have also been found to pass to the unborn child. In 2000 19% of women smoked throughout pregnancy.
- In the 2004–2005 financial year, the UK Treasury earned £8,103 million in revenue from tobacco, excluding VAT. This constitutes around 2% of the total income from taxes, duties and other revenue in that year.

Public health measures

There are two main strategies for addressing public health issues relating to smoking, based on somewhat different ethical principles:

☐ Strategies that target smokers or potential smokers include educational campaigns and financial disincentives. Regulations can also be put into place that prohibit smoking in general, or in particular places. The aim is to discourage individuals from pursuing activities that may harm their health and/or impose costs on healthcare systems.

☐ Strategies that target passive smoking aim to reduce exposure of nonsmokers to other people's smoke. The rationale here is that although smokers might be free to harm their own health, this freedom does not extend to harming others. Some measures pursue both strategies.

Measures that have been implemented in the UK include: increased taxes on cigarettes; education and advertising programmes warning of the dangers of smoking; restrictions on advertising and sponsorship by the tobacco industry; health warnings on cigarette packets; and greater provision and promotion of programmes to help people to stop smoking. While it is attractive to assume causal correlations between decreasing numbers of smokers and the individual or cumulative effect of these measures, such attributions are far from straightforward.

Measures to curb smoking have often been controversial. Increased taxes have been criticised because the majority of the people who smoke are in lower income groups and/or receiving benefits. Concern has also arisen over whether the large financial benefit gained by governments on taxes from cigarettes may lead to a half-hearted stance by the state against smoking. There are several consumer groups on both sides of the debate who actively campaign on issues relating to smoking, in particular Action on Smoking and Health (ASH) and the Freedom Organisation for the Right to Enjoy Smoking Tobacco (FOREST). The tobacco industry is also a powerful contributor to the debate and actively lobbies against anti-smoking legislation In 2004, Ireland introduced a smoking ban in enclosed workplaces, including restaurants and pubs. Similar bans have been implemented in Italy and Norway. In the UK, MPs debated the provisions on smoking in the Health Bill in February 2006 and voted by a margin of 200 in favour of imposing a ban on smoking in enclosed public spaces, including all pubs and private members' clubs in England. A total ban on smoking in enclosed public places was introduced in Scotland in March 2006, and Northern Ireland is expected to follow suit in April 2007. The Health Bill gives the Welsh Assembly the right to decide whether to implement a ban it has already approved in principle.

Questions on smoking

• The effects of smoking on health have been known for a very long time. Comprehensive measures by governments to prevent harm to the population are relatively recent. In your view, what are the reasons for this delayed response? Are there any lessons that can be learned from other countries, or from strategies pursued in other areas of public health?

• What are the responsibilities of companies that make or sell products containing hazardous substances, such as nicotine, that can be addictive? Should they be prosecuted for damaging public health or required to contribute to costs for treatments?

• Should smokers be entitled to higher than average resources from the public healthcare system, or should they be asked for increased contributions? Would similar charges be justified for other groups of people who deliberately or negligently increase their chances of requiring public health resources, such as people engaging in adventure sports?

• Smokers argue that they choose to smoke. What rights does the state have to impose sanctions to prevent them from smoking? Does the state have the right to prevent the sale of tobacco, which is known to be addictive and highly dangerous? How vigorously is it reasonable for the state to act to prevent children and teenagers from smoking?

NOTE:

1. Concerns over the detrimental effect to health of tobacco have led to recent controls. There has been regulation of tobacco advertising. A notable illustration is that of the EU Tobacco Advertising Directive prohibiting tobacco advertising in press, printed media and by internet and email— Directive 2003/33 [2003] O.J. L152/16 (it excludes publications aimed exclusively at the tobacco industry). (See generally regarding the involvement of the EU in tobacco advertising, T.K. Hervey and J.V. McHale, *Health Law and the EU*, Cambridge: CUP, 2004, pp.379–384. and I. Hervey, "Up in Smoke! Community Anti-Tobacco Law and Policy" (2001) 26 *European Law Review* 101).

As noted in the Nuffield Report, the Health Bill 2005 targets smoking in a range of public places.

Health Act 2006

CHAPTER 1—SMOKE-FREE PREMISES, PLACES AND VEHICLES

Smoke-free premises

2.—(1) Premises are smoke-free if they are open to the public.
But unless the premises also fall within subsection (2), they are smoke-free only when open to the public.
(2) Premises are smoke-free if they are used as a place of work—

(a) by more than one person (even if the persons who work there do so at different times, or only intermittently), or
(b) where members of the public might attend for the purpose of seeking or receiving goods or services from the person or persons working there (even if members of the public are not always present).

They are smoke-free all the time.
(3) If only part of the premises is open to the public or (as the case may be) used as a place of work mentioned in subsection (2), the premises are smoke-free only to that extent.
(4) In any case, premises are smoke-free only in those areas which are enclosed or substantially enclosed.
(5) The appropriate national authority may specify in regulations what "enclosed" and "substantially enclosed" mean.
(6) Section 3 provides for some premises, or areas of premises, not to be smoke-free despite this section.
(7) Premises are "open to the public" if the public or a section of the public has access to them, whether by invitation or not, and whether on payment or not.
(8) "Work", in subsection (2), includes voluntary work.

Smoke-free premises: exemptions

3.—(1) The appropriate national authority may make regulations providing for specified descriptions of premises, or specified areas within specified descriptions of premises, not to be smoke-free despite section 2.

(2) Descriptions of premises which may be specified under subsection (1) include, in particular, any premises where a person has his home, or is living whether permanently or temporarily (including hotels, care homes, and prisons and other places where a person may be detained).

(3) The power to make regulations under subsection (1) is not exercisable so as to specify any description of—

(a) premises in respect of which a premises licence under the Licensing Act 2003 (c. 17) authorising the consumption of alcohol on the premises has effect,

(b) premises in respect of which a club premises certificate (within the meaning of section 60 of that Act) has effect.

(4) But subsection (3) does not prevent the exercise of that power so as to specify any area, within a specified description of premises mentioned in subsection (3), where a person has his home, or is living whether permanently or temporarily.

(5) For the purpose of making provision for those participating as performers in a performance or in a performance of a specified description not to be prevented from smoking if the artistic integrity of the performance makes it appropriate for them to smoke—

(a) the power in subsection (1) also includes the power to provide for specified descriptions of premises or specified areas within such premises not to be smoke free in relation only to such performers, and

(b) subsection (3) does not prevent the exercise of that power as so extended.

(6) The regulations may provide, in relation to any description of premises or areas of premises specified in the regulations, that the premises or areas are not smoke-free—

(a) in specified circumstances,

(b) if specified conditions are satisfied, or

(c) at specified times, or any combination of those.

(7) The conditions may include conditions requiring the designation in accordance with the regulations, by the person in charge of the premises, of any rooms in which smoking is to be permitted.

NOTES:

1. Section 2 of the Act provides for the Secretary of State to make regulations including other places as "smoke free" within the Act. In addition s.5 makes provision for the Secretary of State to make regulations providing that vehicles are to be smoke free.

2. The Act makes further provision for criminal offences including smoking in a public place (s.7) and failing to prevent smoking in a public place (s.8).

3. The above sections of the Health Act 2006 proved to be very controversial. Initially the Government proposed a compromise position following a public split among the Cabinet as to the appropriate response to take to this issue. The Bill had originally excluded private clubs and non-food clubs following a Labour Manifesto pledge. However, the amendments to the Bill were passed after a free vote was allowed on the Bill following concern as to the prospect of a revolt by rebel Labour MPs. In addition there were concerns expressed by a consultation that the original proposals of a partial ban would be unworkable. The Commons agreed to the ban on February 14, 2006.

4. Note that some premises will be excluded under s.3(2), including private homes and those premises described by the Secretary of State Patricia Hewitt as being "like homes", including care institutions and prisons.

5. It is anticipated that the ban will come into force in summer 2007.

4. THE PROVISION OF NHS SERVICES

Since the National Health Service and Community Care Act 1990, the provision of NHS care has been under a continual degree of evolution. The organisation of the NHS is divided into primary and secondary care. At primary care level, health care is provided through primary care trusts. These comprise general practitioners and may also include nurses, dentists and pharmacists. Provision of secondary care—hospital and NHS community care—is generally through NHS trusts and NHS foundation hospitals.

The NHS is overseen by the Secretary of State for Health. The obligations of the Secretary of State under the National Health Service Act 1977 are considered below on p.41. Below the Secretary of State there are strategic health authorities which are accountable to the Secretary of State (established under ss.11–12 of the National Health Service Act 1977, as amended). The number of these bodies has recently been reduced to ten. Their tasks include monitoring and advising primary care trusts and NHS trusts. They have the power to intervene and to deal with failures in primary care trusts and NHS trusts on behalf of the Secretary of State (see ss.84A and 84B of the National Health Service Act 1977).

A number of other bodies provide general oversight in the NHS. Some of this oversight was triggered by concerns regarding standards of quality and safety in the NHS following Professor Ian Kennedy's Inquiry Report into the deaths in the cardiac paediatric unit at Bristol Royal Infirmary. (See I. Kennedy, R. Howard, B. Jarman and M. McClean, "Learning from Bristol: the Report of the Public Inquiry into Children's Heart Surgery at the Bristol Royal Infirmary 1984–1995" (CM 5207), *http://www.bristol-inquiry.org.uk*); see also O. Quick, "Disaster at Bristol: Explanations and Implications of a Tragedy" (1999) 21 *Journal of Social Welfare and Family Law* 307 and Department of Health, *A First Class Service: Quality in the new NHS*", London: DOH, 1998.) The authorities include the National Institute for Clinical Excellence, the Council for Healthcare Regulatory Excellence and the National Patient Safety Agency. Further oversight and regulation are provided by departmental commissions such as the Healthcare Commission which has a broad remit of oversight and inspection of NHS standards and an involvement in the NHS complaints process (see further Chapter 4 below). The governance of the NHS has been added to piecemeal over the years and this has led to the comment that NHS regulation can be seen as "a distinctly Gothic machinery of accountability, as successive generations of politicians have added new buttresses and spires to the building" (see P. Day and R. Klein, *Auditing the Auditors: Audit in the National Health Service*, Oxford: Nuffield Trust, 2001 and see further C. Newdick, *Who Shall We Treat?* (2nd edn), Oxford: Oxford University Press, 2005, Chapter 8, "NHS Governance and Accountability").

(a) Primary Care

Primary care is provided today through primary care trusts which have the task of managing NHS provision in their area.

National Health Service Act 1977

Primary Care Trusts

16A.—(1) It is the duty of the Secretary of State to establish bodies to be known as Primary Care Trusts for areas in England with a view to their exercising functions in relation to the health service.

(1A) The Secretary of State shall act under this section so as to ensure that the areas for which Primary Care Trusts are at any time established together comprise the whole of England.

(2) Each Primary Care Trust shall be established by an order made by him (referred to in this Act as a PCT order).

(3) A Primary Care Trust shall be established for the area [of England] specified in its PCT order and shall exercise its functions in accordance with any prohibitions or restrictions in the order.

(4) If any consultation requirements apply, they must be complied with before a PCT order is made.

(5) In this section, "consultation requirements" means requirements about consultation contained in regulations (and the regulations must impose requirements where a PCT order establishes a Primary Care Trust).

(6) Schedule 5A to this Act (which makes further provision about Primary Care Trusts) shall have effect.

Exercise of functions by Primary Care Trusts

16B.—(1) This section applies to functions which are exercisable by a Primary Care Trust under or by virtue of this Act (including this section), the National Health Service and Community Care Act 1990 or any prescribed provision of any other Act.

(2) Regulations may provide for any functions to which this section applies to be exercised—

(a) by another Primary Care Trust,
(b) by a Special Health Authority, or
(c) jointly with any one or more of the following: Strategic Health Authorities, Health Authorities, NHS trusts . . . and other Primary Care Trusts.

(3) Regulations may provide—

(a) for any functions to which this section applies to be exercised, on behalf of the Primary Care Trust by whom they are exercisable, by a committee, sub-committee or officer of the trust,
(b) for any functions which, under this section, are exercisable by a Special Health Authority to be exercised, on behalf of that authority, by a committee, sub-committee or officer of the authority,
(c) for any functions which, under this section, are exercisable by a Primary Care Trust jointly with one or more Strategic Health Authorities, Health Authorities or other Primary Care Trusts (but not with any NHS trusts) to be exercised, on behalf of the health service bodies in question, by a joint committee or joint sub-committee.

(4) The Secretary of State may by order make provision for the transfer to a Special Health Authority of the rights and liabilities of a Primary Care Trust under a general dental services contract in a case where the Authority exercises functions of the Trust in relation to the contract by virtue of subsection (2)(b) above (and for their transfer back to the Trust where the Authority ceases to exercise those functions).

Primary medical services

16CC.—(1) Each Primary Care Trust . . . must, to the extent that it considers necessary to meet all reasonable requirements, exercise its powers so as to provide primary medical services within its area, or secure their provision within its area.

(2) A Primary Care Trust . . . may (in addition to any other power conferred on it)—

(a) provide primary medical services itself (whether within or outside its area);

(b) make such arrangements for their provision (whether within or outside its area) as it thinks fit, and may in particular make contractual arrangements with any person.

(3) Each Primary Care Trust . . . must publish information about such matters as may be prescribed in relation to the primary medical services provided under this Part.

(4) A body on which functions are conferred under this section must co-operate with any other such body in the discharge of their respective functions relating to the provision of primary medical services under this Part.

(5) Regulations may provide that services of a prescribed description are, or are not, to be regarded as primary medical services for the purposes of this Part.

(6) Regulations under this section may in particular describe services by reference to the manner or circumstances in which they are provided.

NOTES:

1. One trend is the shift towards more flexible care provision. This includes enhanced provision of "community hospitals", for example for blood tests, diagnostic scans and minor operations (see Department of Health, "Our Health; our Care", London: DOH).

2. The emphasis today is upon practice-based commissioning (see Department of Health, "Health Reform in England Update and Commissioning Framework", London: DOH, 2006, pp.21–22). The aim is that primary care trusts, alongside G.P.s' practices, will have the role of commissioning hospital services, initially with the intention that this will extend to cover such services as "health and well-being", "long-term conditions" and in addition "joint commissioning with local government".

3. Patients are also to have increased "choice" as to health care providers. There is now provision for patients to make a choice of their elective health care provider.

4. Under a new development introduced under the Health and Social Care (Community Health and Standards) Act 2003, PCTs can enter into arrangements with NHS employees and private companies in addition to arrangements with G.P.s. Contractual arrangements may be NHS contracts or standard legal contracts enforceable in the courts.

5. General medical services (GMS) are to be provided in accordance with the NHS General Medical Services Contractual Regulations 2004, SI 2004/291, reg 4. The agreements may relate to "essential", minimal level, additional or enhanced services.

6. Primary care trusts may in addition enter into personal medical services agreements with primary care providers—National Health Service (Personal Medical Services Agreements) Regulations 2004, SI 2004/627).

While these are similar to GMS, a key difference lies in the fact that their precise nature is not stated in regulations, enabling flexibility at the local level.

7. In addition, s.16CA of the National Health Service Act 1977 allows PCTs to provide services themselves by employing their own staff.

8. There is also provision under the Alternative Medical Provider Medical Services Directions 2004 (London: DOH, 2004) for primary care to be provided by other organisations to cover situations in which G.P. provision is difficult to establish or to maintain. It envisages that NHS trusts, foundation trusts or private companies could be involved in providing services in this situation.

(b) Secondary Care

Secondary care is the form of hospital care provided in the NHS through NHS trusts and NHS foundation trusts.

(i) National Health Service Trusts

The functions of NHS hospital trusts are partly determined by the NHS and Community Care Act 1990, and partly by each trust's individual establishment order.

Section 5(1) *et seq.* of the 1990 Act sets out how NHS trusts are established.

5.—(1) "Subject to subsection (2) .... Below the Secretary of State may by order establish bodies, to be known as National Health Service trusts (in this Act referred to as NHS trusts), (to provide goods and services for the purposes of the health services"

(2) No order shall be made under subsection (1) above until after the completion of such consultation as may be prescribed. . . .

(5) Every NHS trust—

(a) shall be a body corporate having a board of directors consisting of a chairman appointed by the Secretary of State and, subject to paragraph 5(2) of Schedule 2 to this Act, executive and non-executive directors (that is to say, directors who, subject to subsection (7) below, respectively are and are not employees of the trust); and

(b) shall have the functions conferred on it by an order under subsection (1) above and by Schedule 2 to this Act.

(6) The functions which may be specified in an order under subsection (1) above include a duty to provide goods or services so specified at or from a hospital or other establishment or facility so specified.

(7) The Secretary of State may by regulations make general provision with respect to—

(a) the qualifications for and the tenure of office of the chairman and directors of an NHS trust (including the circumstances in which they shall cease to hold, or may be removed from, office or may be suspended from performing the functions of the office);

(b) the persons by whom the directors and any of the officers are to be appointed and the manner of their appointment;

(c) the maximum and minimum numbers of the directors;

(d) the circumstances in which a person who is not an employee of the trust is nevertheless, on appointment as a director, to be regarded as an executive rather than a non-executive director;

(e) the proceedings of the trust (including the validation of proceedings in the event of a vacancy or defect in appointment); and

(f) the appointment, constitution and exercise of functions by committees and sub-committees of the trust (whether or not consisting of or including any members of the board) and, without prejudice to the generality of the power, any such regulations, may make provision to deal with cases where the post of any officer of an NHS trust is held jointly by two or more persons or where the functions of such an officer are in any other way performed by more than one person.

(8) Part I of Schedule 2 to this Act shall have effect with respect to orders under subsection (1) above; Part II of that Schedule shall have effect, subject to subsection (9) below, with respect to the general duties and the powers and status of NHS trusts; the supplementary provisions of Part III of that Schedule shall have effect; and Part IV of that Schedule shall have effect with respect to the dissolution of NHS trusts.

(9) A power conferred by paragraph 14 or 15 of Part II of Schedule 2 to this Act may only be exercised—

(a) to the extent that its exercise does not to any significant extent interfere with the performance by the NHS trust of its functions or of its obligations under NHS contracts, and

(b) in circumstances specified in directions under section 17 of the principal Act, with the consent of the Secretary of State.

(10) The Secretary of State may by order made by statutory instrument confer on NHS trusts specific powers additional to those contained in paragraphs 10 to 15 of Schedule 2 to this Act.

All Trusts are required to meet certain statutory financial obligations:

National Health Service and Community Care Act 1990, s.10(1–2)

10.—(1) Every NHS Trust shall ensure that its revenue is not less than sufficient, taking one financial year with another, to meet outgoings properly charged to revenue account.

(2) It shall be the duty of every NHS Trust to achieve such financial objectives as may from time to time be set by the Secretary of State with the consent of the Treasury and as are applicable to it; and any such objectives may be made applicable to NHS Trusts generally, or to a particular NHS Trust or to NHS Trusts of a particular description.

NOTE:

1. Subsection (1) imposes an obligation to break even each year.

The obligations placed upon the NHS trust are set out in further detail in the Schedules to the Act.

National Health Service and Community Care Act 1990, Schedule II, 6(1)(2), 7(1)–(3), 8

6.—(1) An NHS trust shall carry out effectively, efficiently and economically the functions for the time being conferred on it by an order under section 5(1) of this Act and by the provisions of this Schedule and, with respect to the exercise of the powers conferred by section 5(10) of this Act and by the provisions of this Schedule.

7.—(1) For each accounting year an NHS trust shall prepare and send to the Secretary of State an annual report in such form as may be determined by the Secretary of State.

(2) At such time or times as may be prescribed, an NHS trust shall hold a public meeting at which its audited accounts and annual report and any report on the accounts made pursuant to subsection (3) of section 8 of the Audit Commission Act 1998 shall be presented.

(3) In such circumstances and at such time or times as may be prescribed, an NHS trust shall hold a public meeting at which such document as may be prescribed shall be presented.

8. An NHS trust shall furnish to the Secretary of State such reports, returns and other information, including information as to its forward planning, as, and in such form as, he may require.

QUESTIONS:

1. These paragraphs are designed to ensure that NHS trusts are accountable to the Secretary of State. Do you think that they are sufficient?
2. Do you think that the law indicates a greater concern with financial affairs of NHS trusts than with clinical effectiveness or accountability to the public?

(ii) NHS Contracts

The relationship between PCTs and NHS trusts is through "contracts". Initially the National Health Service and Community Care Act 1990 introduced an internal market in health care with a contracting structure. The Labour Government, on taking office in 1997, initially pledged removal of the internal market, but although the nature of some of the health care delivery arrangements have changed, a contractual approach is at the core of health care commissioning. The 1990 Act enables PCTs and NHS trusts to enter into a new type of contract known as NHS Contracts. While in many respects they take the form of contracts as they operate at common law, it was not intended that they would be judicially enforceable.

National Health Service and Community Care Act 1990, s.4

NHS contracts

4.—(1) In this Act the expression "NHS contract" means an arrangement under which one health service body ("the acquirer") arranges for the provision to it by another health service body ("the provider") of goods or services which it reasonably requires for the purposes of its functions. . . .

(3) Whether or not an arrangement which constitutes an NHS contract would, apart from this subsection, be a contract in law, it shall not be regarded for any purpose as giving rise to contractual rights or liabilities, but if any dispute arises with respect to such an arrangement, either party may refer the matter to the Secretary of State for determination under the following provisions of this section.

(4) If, in the course of negotiations intending to lead to an arrangement which will be an NHS contract, it appears to a health service body—

(a) that the terms proposed by another health service body are unfair by reason that the other is seeking to take advantage of its position as the only, or the only practicable, provider of the goods or services concerned or by reason of any other unequal bargaining position as between the prospective parties to the proposed arrangement, or

(b) that for any other reason arising out of the relative bargaining position of the prospective parties any of the terms of the proposed arrangement cannot be agreed,

that health service body may refer the terms of the proposed arrangement to the Secretary of State for determination under the following provisions of this section.

(5) Where a reference is made to the Secretary of State under subsection (3) or subsection (4) above, the Secretary of State may determine the matter himself or, if he considers it appropriate, appoint a person to consider and determine it in accordance with regulations.

(6) By his determination of a reference under subsection (4) above, the Secretary of State or, as the case may be, the person appointed under subsection (5) above may specify terms to be included in the proposed arrangement and may direct that it be proceeded with.

(7) A determination of a reference under subsection (3) above may contain such directions (including directions as to payment) as the Secretary of State or, as the case may be, the person appointed under subsection (5) above considers appropriate to resolve the matter in dispute.

(8) Without prejudice to the generality of his powers on a reference under subsection (3) above, the Secretary of State or, as the case may be, the person appointed under subsection (5) above may be his determination in relation to an arrangement constituting an NHS contract vary the terms of the arrangement or bring it to an end; and where an arrangement is so varied or brought to an end—

(a) subject to paragraph (b) below, the variation or termination shall be treated as being effected by agreement between the parties; and

(b) the directions included in the determination by virtue of subsection (7) above may contain such provisions as the Secretary of State or, as the case may be, the person appointed under subsection (5) above considers appropriate in order satisfactorily to give effect to the variation or to bring the arrangement to an end.

NOTES:

1. It appears that s.4(3) will exclude an action from being brought in contract. There has been some debate as to the possibility of actions being brought in restitution. (See J. Jacob, "Lawyers Go to Hospital" [1991] *Public Law* 255 and K. Barker "NHS Contracts, Restitution and the Internal Market" (1993) 56 *Modern Law Review* 832.)

2. Where disputes arise in relation to NHS contracts a number of mechanisms exist for their resolution. In contrast with private sector contracting, disputes about the formation of contracts (and not just their performance)

can be subject to those processes for dispute resolution. Parties are encouraged by central NHS management to resolve the matter at local level. Where agreement cannot be reached parties are expected to involve a conciliator who will, almost invariably, be an NHS manager. If the dispute cannot be resolved in this manner, then ultimately it may be referred to a special statutory dispute resolution mechanism (NHS Contracts (Dispute Resolution) Regulations 1996 (SI 1996/623)). Disputes are to be referred to an adjudicator. He has the power to find for one party or the other—what is known as "pendulum arbitration". It is not intended that these proceedings will be judicial in nature and there is no right to an oral hearing. There has only been limited use of this procedure. It has been suggested that this may be due to a combination of factors, not least strong encouragement from central NHS management for the contracting parties to settle their disputes on a local basis. (See further J. McHale, D. Hughes and L. Griffiths, "Disputes, Regulation and Relationships" (1996) 2 *Medical Law International* 273, and I. Harden and D. Longley, "NHS Contracts" in J. Birds, J. Bradgate and C. Villiers (eds), *Termination of Contracts*, Law Chancery: Chichester, 1995; and for further discussion see A.C.L. Davies, *Accountability: a Public Law Analysed by Government Contract*, Oxford: OUP, 2001.)

3. The Secretary of State also has "default powers" under s.85 of the NHS Act 1977 which enable him to take over the running of NHS bodies. Powers to direct NHS bodies on how they should operate are provided by ss.13–17 of that Act.

QUESTION:

1. Do these provisions ensure that ultimate control over the NHS rests with the Secretary of State? Are they sufficient?

(iii) NHS Foundation Trust Hospitals

A new type of NHS trust hospital were created by the Health and Social Care (Community Health and Standards) Act 2003.

A Short Guide to Foundation Trusts (London: Department of Health, December 2005)

FOUNDATION HOSPITALS

2.2 NHS Foundation Trusts are a new type of NHS Trust in England. They are part of the Government's plan for creating a patient-led NHS. The aim of these reforms is to provide high quality care, shaped by the needs and wishes of today's patients, in the most efficient way. NHS Foundation Trusts have been created to devolve decision-making from central Government to local organisations and communities so they are more responsive to the needs and wishes of their local people. They are also at the leading edge of many of the other reforms and improvements that are creating a patient-led NHS.

2.3 NHS Foundation Trusts are no longer subject to direction from the Secretary of State for Health. Instead, NHS Foundation Trusts establish stronger connections between themselves and their local communities. Those living in communities served by a hospital of an NHS Foundation Trust can become a member of that organisation. The membership community of each NHS Foundation Trust is made up of local people and staff, with patients and carers also having the option to become a member.

2.4 Members are able to stand and vote to elect representatives, to serve on the Board of Governors. Governors are responsible for representing the interests of the members and partner organisations in the local health economy in the running of the NHS Foundation Trust. Local communities and staff working on the front line can therefore have a bigger say in the management and provision of NHS services in their area. NHS Foundation Trusts can in turn direct their services more closely to their communities, with freedom to develop new ways of working so that hospital services more accurately reflect the needs and expectations of local people.

2.5 Although run locally, NHS Foundation Trusts remain fully part of the NHS. They have been set up in law under the Health and Social Care (Community Health and Standards) Act 2003 as legally independent organisations called Public Benefit Corporations, with a primary purpose to provide NHS services to NHS patients and users according to NHS principles and standards. The public still receive healthcare according to core NHS principles—free care, based on need and not ability to pay.

. . .

3 NHS Foundation Trust core principles

3.1 The first NHS Foundation Trusts were established in 2004. Since then more waves have been established. In addition to acute and specialist Trusts, mental health Trusts are now applying for foundation status. Over time the Government wants all NHS Trusts to be in a position to achieve foundation status so that throughout the country organisations are empowered to deliver high quality services to local people. . . .

3.3 NHS Foundation Trusts are different from existing NHS Trusts in the following ways:

- They are independent legal entities—Public Benefit Corporations.
- They have unique governance arrangements and are accountable to local people, who can become members and governors. Each NHS Foundation Trust has a duty to consult and involve a Board of Governors (comprising patients, staff, members of the public and partner organisations) in the strategic planning of the organisation.
- They are set free from central Government control and are no longer performance managed by Health Authorities. As self-standing, self-governing organisations, NHS Foundation Trusts are free to determine their own future.
- They have new financial freedoms and can raise capital from both the public and private sectors within borrowing limits determined by projected cash flows and therefore based on affordability. They can retain financial surpluses to invest in the delivery of new NHS services.
- They are overseen by Monitor.

3.4 The new set of freedoms gives NHS Foundation Trusts the opportunity to develop new solutions to long-standing problems such as staff shortages and long waits for certain treatments. However, NHS Foundation Trusts cannot work in isolation. They are bound in law to work closely with partner organisations in their local area. Healthcare planning continues to involve the whole NHS community, but with more freedom to set up partnerships between all healthcare providers.

5 Governance arrangements

5.1 NHS Foundation Trusts strengthen local ownership of—and responsibility for—hospital and other health services. Major decisions are informed by active participation from members based in local communities.

5.2 Residents and patients in areas served by an NHS Foundation Trust, with an interest in the wellbeing of their local hospital and health services, can register as members of the organisation.

5.3 NHS Foundation Trusts may also allow for patients who do not live locally, and their carers, to become members.

5.4 Members of NHS Foundation Trusts do not receive any special treatment as NHS patients and users. They have the same access to NHS services as anyone who chooses not to become a member.

5.5 All NHS Foundation Trust members can expect to receive regular information about their local Trust and be consulted on plans for future development.

5.6 Members are able to vote in elections to the Board of Governors of the NHS Foundation Trust. They can also stand for election as governors, and public members are eligible to be appointed as non-executive directors on the Board of Directors.

5.7 The Board of Governors is responsible for representing the interests of the local community in the management and stewardship of the NHS Foundation Trust, and for sharing information about key decisions with other NHS Foundation Trust members.

5.8 The Board of Governors is not responsible for the day to day management of the organisation e.g. setting budgets, staff pay and other operational matters—that is a matter for the Board of Directors. However, the Board of Governors allows local residents, staff and key stakeholders to influence decisions about spending and the development of services. The Board of Governors also appoints the chair and non-executive directors of the Board of Directors.

5.9 It is up to each individual NHS Foundation Trust to determine the detail of the arrangements for the membership and election to the Board of Governors, within certain parameters. In particular, elections must be fair and transparent. Governance arrangements are ultimately tailored to the individual circumstances of each Trust, reflecting the range of diverse relationships with patients, the local community and other stakeholders.

5.10 Foundation Trusts are allowed some local flexibility over the size and composition of their Board of Governors. However, every board must have:

- A majority of governors elected by members in the public constituency;
- At least one governor representing local NHS Primary Care Trusts;
- At least one governor representing Local Authorities in the area;
- At least three governors representing staff;
- A chair;
- At least one governor appointed from the local university (if the trust's hospitals include a medical or dental school).

NOTES:

1. The aim of the introduction of foundation trusts is to encourage competition between hospitals. (See further C. Newdick, *Who Should We Treat?*

(2nd edn), 2005, Oxford: OUP, pp.81–86.) It can also be seen as a fundamental move away from detailed ministerial control of health care provision (see further A.C.L. Davies, "Foundation Hospitals: a New Approach to Accountability and Autonomy in the Public Services" [2004] *Public Law* 808).

2. Foundation trusts are to be public benefit co-operations rooted in local ownership and with the aim of promoting NHS objectives (Health and Social Care (Community Health and Standards) Act 2003, s.1(1)). They are accountable to the Monitor, the Commissions, the Health Care Commission and to the public.

3. Members of the local community can apply to become members of local foundation trusts, as can patients, carers and staff of the trust. There is no fixed limit on the number of members, which is to be determined by the particular trust.

4. The Monitor (the independent regulator) has the task of giving authorisation and is required to determine whether the foundation trust has the purpose of providing goods and services for the health service in England (Health and Social Care (Community Health and Standards) Act 2003, s.14(2)). The Monitor may include specific requirements regarding the delivery of health care services. The Monitor also has the power to intervene if the powers of the foundation trust's authorisation are broken and this is a "significant breach (Health and Social Care (Community Health and Standards) Act 2003, s.23). The Monitor is in theory independent from the Secretary of State and is not subject to the formal direction of the Secretary of State.

5. Application to become a foundation trust can only be made by those trusts which attain a "three-star" rating. As Newdick notes, it is also unclear what the position would be should a hospital lose its three-star ranking. As he notes, there is power placed on the Monitor to ultimately remove directors or transfer property, etc. (see s.26 of the Health Act 1999, as amended by Health and Social Care (Community Health and Standards) Act 2003 and Newdick, 2005, *op. cit.* in note 1, p.85).

6. Unlike NHS trusts, foundation trusts will also have the ability to enter into standard contracts enforceable in the law courts. This is in contrast to the special NHS contracts which applied in relation to NHS trusts.

7. There is also to be a national pricing tariff under which the Government will determine the price for procedures, in contrast to the previous approach under which individual NHS trusts set the cost of services which they provided. Despite the rhetoric of accountability, it has been suggested that this will have the effect of reinforcing governmental control of foundation trusts (see further Davies, *op. cit.* in note 1).

8. How democratic such trusts will be in practice has been questioned. Newdick notes that there is considerable discretion as to how the local interests will be represented and that questions have been raised as to how representative these bodies will be of their locality and of minority interests (see further Newdick, *op. cit.* in note 1).

5. ACCESS TO HEALTH SERVICES

The first element of the framework is the duty to provide services that are imposed under the NHS Act 1977 and related legislation. The second is the ability of patients to enforce their rights to health care services.

(a) Duties to Provide Services

(i) General Obligations

The general obligation that defines the scope of the National Health Service is set out in the NHS Act 1977.

National Health Service Act 1977, s.1(1), (2)

1.—(1) It is the Secretary of State's duty to continue the promotion in England and Wales of a comprehensive health service designed to secure improvement:

(a) in the physical and mental health of the people of these counties, and
(b) in the prevention, diagnosis and treatment of illness,

and for the purpose to provide or secure the effective provision of services in accordance with this Act.

(2) The services so provided shall be free of charge except in so far as the making and recovery of charges is expressly provided for by or under any enactment, whenever passed.

NOTE:

1. Section 128 provides that " 'illness' includes mental disorder within the meaning of the Mental Health Act 1983 and any injury or disability requiring medical or dental treatment or nursing".

Section 3 of the Act further specifies the general duty as follows.

National Health Service Act 1977, s.3(1)

3.—(1) It is the Secretary of State's duty to provide throughout England and Wales, to such extent as he considers necessary to meet all reasonable requirements:

(a) hospital accommodation;
(b) other accommodation for the purpose of any service provided under this Act;
(c) medical, dental, nursing and ambulance services;
(d) such other services and facilities for the care of expectant and nursing mothers and young children as he considers are appropriate as part of the health service;
(e) such other services and facilities for the prevention of illness, the care of persons suffering from illness and the after-care of persons who have suffered from illness as he considers are appropriate as part of the health service;
(f) such other services and facilities as are required for the diagnosis and treatment of illness.

Section 5 contains a number of more detailed duties and powers to provide services. These largely consolidate provisions which were previously scattered among different pieces of NHS legislation. This accounts for the fact that some of the services would already fall within the general duties. The relevant parts of s.5 read as follows.

National Health Service Act 1977, s.5(1)(1A)(2)

5.—(1) It is the Secretary of State's duty:

(a) to provide for the medical inspection at appropriate intervals of pupils in attendance at schools maintained by local education authorities for the medical . . . treatment of such pupils;

(b) to arrange, to such extent as he considers necessary to meet all reasonable requirements in England and Wales, for the giving of advice on contraception, the medical examination of persons seeking advice on contraception, the treatment of such persons and the supply of contraceptive substances and appliances.

(2) The Secretary of State may:

(a) provide invalid carriages for persons appearing to him to be suffering from severe physical defect or disability and, at the request of such a person, may provide for him a vehicle other than an invalid carriage . . .

(c) provide a microbiologies service, which may include the provision of laboratories, for the control of the spread of infectious diseases and carry on such other activities as in his opinion can conveniently be carried on in conjunction with that service;

(d) conduct, or assist by grants or otherwise (without prejudice to the general powers and duties conferred on him under the Ministry of Health Act 1919) any person to conduct, research into any matters relating to the causation, prevention, diagnosis or treatment of illness, and into any such other matters connected with any service provided under this Act as he considers appropriate.

NOTES:

1. Section 5(2)(b) was repealed by SI 2002/2759, reg.3(2).
2. As noted above at p.30, the day to day operation of the NHS is through a wide range of NHS bodies. The performance of the Secretary of State's duties is delegated to NHS bodies such as Strategic Health Authorities and PCT by regulations and also by directions which have mandatory effect and circulars which provide discretion. (See further C. Newdick, "The Organisation of the NHS" in A. Grubb, *Principles of Medical Law* Oxford: OUP (2004) at paras 1.16–1.17.)
3. The National Institute for Health and Clinical Excellence (NICE) provides one way in which treatments are in effect rationed. The body combined with the Health Development Agency from April 1, 2005. It is a special health authority and provides "best practice" guidance to health professionals, patients and the public. It undertakes "technology appraisals" regarding the use of medicines, medical devices, diagnostic devices, surgical techniques and health promotion activities. Economic assessments are involved here: essentially, does the medicine, *etc.* represent "good value for money". NICE is also involved in developing clinical guidelines on appropriate treatment and care of persons with specific diseases. (For criticism of the operation of NICE and its effectiveness, see R. Smith, "The

Failings of NICE", (2000) 321 *B.M.J.* 1261 and J.K. Mason and G. Laurie, *Law and Medical Ethics* (7th edn), Oxford: OUP, 2006 at pp.422–423.)

QUESTIONS:

1. How far are these general duties subject to the political will of the Secretary of State of the day?
2. Do you think any one will be easier to enforce than any other? Compare the requirements of school medical examinations and family planning.

(ii) Community Care

Added to these NHS duties is the area of community care. This refers to a range of services provided by local authorities. They are the provision of accommodation for adults who cannot look after themselves; services for adults who are blind, deaf, dumb or substantially and permanently handicapped by illness, injury or congenital disability, including the adaptation of homes and provision of meals and special equipment; and services promoting the welfare of elderly people. Community care also includes non-residential services for pregnant women and mothers, home help and laundry facilities for households caring for a person who is ill, handicapped or pregnant. With the Secretary of State's approval, local authorities may also provide services for those who are ill, including after-care and preventive care. Finally, community care services cover after-care for those discharged from mental health services.

The primary obligation in relation to these services is to assess the need of individual patients for them.

National Health Service and Community Care Act 1990, s.47(1–3)(7)

47.—(1) Subject to subsections (5) and (6) below, where it appears to a local authority that any person for whom they may provide or arrange for the provision of community care services may be in need of any such services, the authority:

(a) shall carry out an assessment of his needs for those services; and
(b) having regard to the results of that assessment, shall then decide whether his needs call for the provision by them of any such services.

(2) If at any time during the assessment of the needs of any person under subsection (1)(a) above it appears to a local authority that he is a disabled person, the authority:

(a) shall proceed to make such a decision as to the services he requires as is mentioned in section 4 of the Disabled Persons (Services, Consultation and Representation) Act 1986 without his requesting them to do so under that section; and
(b) shall inform him that they will be doing so and of his rights under that Act.

(3) If at any time during the assessment of the needs of any person under subsection (1)(a) above, it appears to a local authority—

(a) that there may be a need for the provision to that person by such Primary Care Trust or Health Authority as may be determined in accordance with regulations of any services under the National Health Service Act 1977, or

    (b)   that there may be a need for the provision to him of any services which fall within the functions of a local housing authority (within the meaning of the Housing Act 1985) which is not the local authority carrying out the assessment,

the local authority shall notify that Primary Care Trust, Health Authority or local housing authority and invite them to assist, to such extent as is reasonable in the circumstances, in the making of the assessment; and, in making their decision as to the provision of the services needed for the person in question, the local authority shall take into account any services which are likely to be made available for him by that Primary Care Trust, Health Authority or local housing authority . . .

    (7) This section is without prejudice to section 3 of the Disabled Persons (Services, Consultation and Representation) Act 1986.

In general, there is no specific obligation actually to provide services. However, it may become easier to show that authorities have acted unlawfully if they refuse to offer services that patients have been identified as needing (see below). In certain circumstances the law does go further. Thus the Chronically Sick and Disabled Persons Act 1970, s.2, imposes a duty to actually provide services.

Chronically Sick and Disabled Persons Act 1970, s.2(1)

    2(1) Where a local authority having functions under section 29 of the National Assistance Act 1948 are satisfied in the case of any person to whom that section applies who is ordinarily resident in their area that it is necessary in order to meet the needs of that person for that authority to make arrangements for all or any of the following matters, namely—

    (a)   the provision of practical assistance for that person in his home;

    (b)   the provision for that person of, or assistance to that person in obtaining, wireless, television, library or similar recreational facilities;

    (c)   the provision for that person of lectures, games, outings or other recreational facilities outside his home or assistance to that person in taking advantage of educational facilities available to him;

    (d)   the provision for that person of facilities for, or assistance in, travelling to and from his home for the purpose of participating in any services provided under arrangements made by the authority under the said section 29 or, with the approval of the authority, in any services provided otherwise than as aforesaid which are similar to services which could be provided under such arrangements;

    (e)   the provision of assistance for that person in arranging for the carrying out of any works of adaptation in his home or the provision of any additional facilities designed to secure his greater safety, comfort or convenience;

    (f)   facilitating the taking of holidays by that person, whether at holiday homes or otherwise and whether provided under arrangements made by the authority or otherwise;

    (g)   the provision of meals for that person whether in his home or elsewhere;

    (h)   the provision for that person of, or assistance to that person in obtaining, a telephone and any special equipment necessary to enable him to use a telephone . . . then, . . . subject . . . to the provisions of section 7(1) of the Local Authority Social Services Act 1970 (which requires local authorities in the exercise of certain functions, including functions under the said section 29, to act under the general guidance of the Secretary of State) and to the provisions of section 7A of that Act (which requires local authorities to exercise their social services functions in accordance with directions given by the Secretary of State),

it shall be the duty of that authority to make those arrangements in exercise of their functions under the said section 29.

(b) Enforcement of Duties to Provide Services

This section considers the role of the courts in enforcing the duties to provide health care examined in the preceding section. It can be argued that the Government is meeting its international obligations to provide health services without giving aggrieved patients the possibility of bringing legal actions to enforce their rights. However, to many patients, unless they can personally bring redress in the courts, their so-called rights are worth little. Two main options are available. The first is the public law action for judicial review. This enables the decisions of public bodies to be challenged on the basis that they have been taken irrationally, illegally or were undermined by serious procedural irregularities (*Council of Civil Service Unions v Minister for the Civil Service* [1985] 1 A.C. 374, 410 *per* Lord Diplock). This type of action can be used when services are refused to try to force the relevant health service body to provide them.

The second type of legal action available for patients claiming that their rights to receive health care have been breached is a claim for compensation. This will be available to those who have suffered damage because of a failure to provide the services to which they claim they were entitled. Clearly, it relates to past failures, and will not usually lead to the desired services actually being provided. Rather, the existence of this type of claim provides health care providers with an incentive to provide appropriate services in order to avoid being sued.

The cases reviewed in the following pages show how reluctant the courts have proved to scrutinise the decisions of health service bodies who deny patients access to services they want. In practice, they may prefer to use the NHS complaints procedures to put pressure on the health service to deliver the care they need. Those procedures are considered in Chapter 4. In relation to service failures by a general medical practitioner, the NHS body may bring proceedings before a disciplinary committee because there will have been a breach of the G.P.'s contract.

(i) Judicial Review: the Early Years

R. v Secretary of State for Social Services, Ex p. Hincks (1980) 1 B.M.L.R. 93

In 1971, plans were made to expand a hospital in Staffordshire. The expansion would have improved facilities for orthopaedic surgery. In 1978, the expansion was postponed for ten years, and virtually abandoned, because it was found to be too expensive. It was acknowledged that there was a need to improve services, but the scheme was not regarded as having sufficient priority for funding. Four patients who were awaiting orthopaedic surgery brought proceedings for judicial review, alleging that the Secretary of State was in breach of his duties under s.3 of the 1977 Act (see above). They argued (as summarised by Lord Denning) that there was no limitation on those duties in respect of available resources:

> "that duty must be fulfilled. If the Secretary of State needs money to do it, then he must see that Parliament gives it to him. Alternatively if Parliament does not give it to him, then a provision should be put in the statute to excuse him from

his duty. Mr Blom-Cooper [for the patients] says that that duty is plain and imperative, and it ought to be fulfilled by the Secretary of State."

All three judges in the Court of Appeal rejected the patients' case. Their reasons are explained by Lord Denning:

LORD DENNING M.R.

" . . . That is an attractive argument, because there is no express limitation on the duty of the Secretary of State in the statute. But, in the course of the argument, many illustrations have been taken showing how necessary it is for a Secretary of State to have regard to forward planning (as it is called), to estimated changes in the population, for instance — or maybe the ageing population. He has to estimate for the future. For instance, when in 1971 the Good Hope Hospital scheme was approved, it was necessarily contemplated that it would be possible within the resources available. Indeed, as the discussion proceeded, it seemed to me inevitable that this provision had to be implied into section 3, 'to such extent as he considers necessary to meet all reasonable requirements such as can be provided within the resources available'. That seems to me to be a very necessary implication to put on that section, in accordance with the general legislative purpose. It cannot be supposed that the Secretary of State has to provide all the latest equipment. As Oliver L.J. said in the course of argument, it cannot be supposed that the Secretary of State has to provide all the kidney machines which are asked for, or for all the new developments such as heart transplants in every case where people would benefit from them. It cannot be that the Secretary of State has a duty to benefit from them. It cannot be that the Secretary of State has a duty to provide everything that is asked for in the changed circumstances which have come about. That includes the numerous pills that people take nowadays: it cannot be said that he has to provide all these free for everybody.

I would like to read a few words from the judgment of Wien J., who gave a very comprehensive and good judgment in this matter. He said:

'The question remains: has there been a breach of duty? Counsel for the [Secretary of State] submits that section 3 does not impose an absolute duty. I agree. He further submits it does, by virtue of the discretion given, include an evaluation of financial resources or the lack of them is at the root of the whole problem in this case. If funds were unlimited, then of course regions and areas could go ahead and provide all sorts of services. But funds are not unlimited. The funds are voted by Parliament, and the health service has to do the best it can with the total allocation of financial resources.'

I agree with that approach of the judge in this case. But there is a further aspect which he dealt with. He said, instead of looking at the health service as a whole, could you pinpoint a particular hospital or a particular area like the Good Hope Hospital in Birmingham, and say, 'That does require an extension, and it is a breach of duty for the Secretary of State not to provide for that hospital and that area'? It seems to me — as, indeed, Mr Richard Moyle said in the course of his letter — that you cannot pinpoint any particular hospital or any particular area. The Secretary of State has to do his best having regard to his wide responsibilities. For instance, there are 12 hospitals in this particular area. The service has to be provided over the whole country. Upon that point, the judge said:

'I have come to the conclusion that it is impossible to pinpoint any breach of statutory duty on the part of the Secretary of State. If he is entitled to take into account financial resources, as in my judgment he is, then it follows that every thing that can be done within the limit of the financial resources available has been done in the region and in the area. I doubt very much whether under section 3(1) it is permissible to put the spotlight, as it were, upon one particular department of one particular hospital and to say that conditions there are unsatisfactory.'

It seems to me that those two paragraphs in the judge's judgment express the position very accurately. It is an interesting point, and it is important from the public point of view because of the grievances which many people feel nowadays about the long waiting list to get into hospital. So be it. The Secretary of State says that he is doing the best he can with the financial resources available to him: and I do not think that he can be faulted in the matter."

QUESTION:

1. Do you think that it would be lawful under this decision for the Secretary of State to decide that there should be no provision of kidney dialysis at all under the NHS?

If it is very difficult to challenge the global allocation of NHS resources, it might nevertheless be open to patients to use judicial review to complain that local managerial decisions, within services that have been funded, are in breach of the statutory duties.

R. v Central Birmingham H.A., Ex p. Walker (1987) 3 B.M.L.R. 32

In 1987 the parents of a baby were told that he would not receive heart surgery because there were insufficient nurses available to look after him. They sought leave to bring judicial review against the health authority. The authority accepted that they were subject to judicial review, but argued that this was not a case that should be examined by the courts. The Court of Appeal agreed and refused to grant leave.

SIR JOHN DONALDSON M.R.
" . . . It is not for this court, or indeed any court, to substitute its own judgment for the judgment of those who are responsible for the allocation of resources. This court could only intervene where it was satisfied that there was a prima facie case, not only of failing to allocate resources in the way in which others would think that resources should be allocated, but of a failure to allocate resources to an extent which was *Wednesbury* unreasonable, if one likes to use the lawyers' jargon, or, in simpler words, which involves a breach of a public law duty (see *Associated Provincial Picture Houses v Wednesbury Corp* [1947] 2 All E.R. 680). Even then, of course, the court has to exercise a judicial discretion. It has to take account of all the circumstances of the particular case with which it is concerned.
    Taking account of the evidence which has been put before us and all the circumstances, it seems to me that this would be an inappropriate case in which to give leave. If other circumstances arose in this case or another case it might be different, because the jurisdiction does exist. But we have to remember, as I think I have already indicated, that if the court is prepared to grant leave in all or even most cases where patients are, from their points of view, very reasonably disturbed at what is going on, we should ourselves be using up National Health Service resources by requiring the authority to stop doing the work for which they were appointed and to meet the complaints of their patients. It is a very delicate balance. As I have made clear and as Mr Bailey has made clear, the jurisdiction does exist. But it has to be used extremely sparingly."

NOTES:

1. In the *Wednesbury* case, to which Lord Donaldson refers, the court identified a type of "unreasonableness" which would permit them to quash decisions. This would be present when the decision was one that no

reasonable public body of the type in question could have reached. There can be a variety of decisions in any particular case, a number of which may be reasonable, but that does not prevent the court criticising those which are not within that range. However, it is not enough to persuade the judge that a better decision could have been made.

2. Contrast this case with a case in which there was judicial indication that courts might be prepared to strike down decisions about resource allocation in the context of community care in *R. v Gloucester CC, Ex p Barry; R. v Lancashire CC, Ex p. RADAR, The Times*, July 12, 1996. Challenges were brought regarding withdrawal of services with the aim of reducing expenditure. There were existing duties to provide services under the Chronically Sick and Disabled Persons Act 1970 s.2 see above. Gloucestershire CC was held to have failed to give individual attention to the specific needs of clients by withdrawing services from a whole class of persons. However while the Court of Appeal held that here there was a procedural impropriety they distinguished the 1970 Act provisions from those under the NHS Act. In relation to the latter they held that resources still remained a relevant consideration.

(ii) Legitimate Expectation

R. v North East Devon Health Authority, Ex p. Coughlan (Secretary of State for Health and Another, interveners) [2000] 3 All E.R. 850

Ms Couglan was a patient at Mardon House, a facility which had been purpose-built for the disabled. She moved there in 1993, following the closure of the hospital where she previously lived. At that time she was promised that she would have a home for life. In April 1998 the health authority (HA) decided to close the house. Judicial proceedings were instigated and at that point the HA decided to undertake a further consultation. It then confirmed in October 1998 that it intended to close Mardon House. Judicial review was sought. In December 1998 Hidden J. quashed the closure decision. This was upheld in the Court of Appeal. The issue the court considered is summarised by Lord Woolf.

LORD WOOLF M.R.

"56. What is still the subject of some controversy is the court's role when a member of the public, as a result of a promise or other conduct, has a legitimate expectation that he will be treated in one way and the public body wishes to treat him or her in a different way. Here the starting point has to be to ask what in the circumstances the member of the public could legitimately expect. In the words of Lord Scarman in *Findlay v Secretary of State for the Home Dept* [1984] 3 All ER 801 at 830, [1985] 1 AC 318 at 338, 'But what was their legitimate expectation?' Where there is a dispute as to this, the dispute has to be determined by the court, as happened in *Findlay*. This can involve a detailed examination of the precise terms of the promise or representation made, the circumstances in which the promise was made and the nature of the statutory or other discretion.

57. There are at least three possible outcomes: (a) The court may decide that the public authority is only required to bear in mind its previous policy or other representation,

giving it the weight it thinks right, but no more, before deciding whether to change course. Here the court is confined to reviewing the decision on *Wednesbury* grounds. This has been held to be the effect of changes of policy in cases involving the early release of prisoners (see *Re Findlay* [1984] 3 All ER 801, [1985] AC 318; *R v Secretary of State for the Home Dept, ex p Hargreaves* [1997] 1 All ER 397, [1997] 1 WLR 906. (b) On the other hand, the court may decide that the promise or practice induces a legitimate expectation of, for example, being consulted before a particular decision is taken. Here it is uncontentious that the court itself will require the opportunity for consultation to be given unless there is an overriding reason to resile from it (see *A-G for Hong Kong v Ng Yuen Shiu* [1983] 2 All ER 346, [1983] 2 AC 629) in which case the court will itself judge the adequacy of the reason advanced for the change of policy, taking into account what fairness requires. (c) Where the court considers that a lawful promise or practice has induced a legitimate expectation of a benefit which is substantive, not simply procedural, authority now establishes that here too the court will in a proper case decide whether to frustrate the expectation is so unfair that to take a new and different course will amount to an abuse of power. Here, once the legitimacy of the expectation is established, the court will have the task of weighing the requirements of fairness against any overriding interest relied upon for the change of policy.

58. The court having decided which of the categories is appropriate, the court's role in the case of the second and third categories is different from that in the first. In the case of the first, the court is restricted to reviewing the decision on conventional grounds. The test will be rationality and whether the public body has given proper weight to the implications of not fulfilling the promise. In the case of the second category, the court's task is the conventional one of determining whether the decision was procedurally fair. In the case of the third, the court has when necessary to determine whether there is a sufficient overriding interest to justify a departure from what has been previously promised . . . .

83. How are fairness and the overriding public interest in this particular context to be judged? The question arises concretely in the present case. Mr Goudie argued, with detailed references, that all the indicators, apart from the promise itself, pointed to an overriding public interest, so that the court ought to endorse the health authority's decision. Mr Gordon contended, likewise with detailed references, that the data before the health authority were far from uniform. But this is not what matters. What matters is that, having taken it all into account, the health authority voted for closure in spite of the promise. The propriety of such an exercise of power should be tested by asking whether the need which the health authority judged to exist to move Miss Coughlan to a local authority facility was such as to outweigh its promise that Mardon House would be her home for life.

84. That a promise was made is confirmed by the evidence of the health authority that:

'. . . the Applicant and her fellow residents were justified in treating certain statements made by the Authority's predecessor, coupled with the way in which the Authority's predecessor conducted itself at the time of the residents' move from Newcourt Hospital, as amounting to an assurance that, having moved to Mardon House, Mardon House would be a permanent home for them.'

And the letter of 7 June 1994 sent to the residents by Mr Peter Jackson, the then general manager of the predecessor of the health authority, following the withdrawal of John Grooms stated:

'During the course of a meeting yesterday with Ross Bentley's father, it was suggested that each of the former Newcourt residents now living at Mardon House would appreciate a further letter of reassurance from me. I am writing to confirm therefore, that the health authority has made it clear to the Community Trust that it expects the Trust to continue to provide good quality care for you at Mardon House for as long as you choose to live there. I hope that this will dispel any anxieties you may have arising from the forthcoming change in management arrangements, about which I wrote to you recently.'

As has been pointed out by the health authority, the letter did not actually use the expression 'home for life'.

85. The health authority had, according to its evidence, formed the view that it should give considerable weight to the assurances given to Miss Coughlan; that those assurances had given rise to expectations which should not, in the ordinary course of things, be disappointed; but that it should not treat those assurances as giving rise to an absolute and unqualified entitlement on the part of the Miss Coughlan and her co-residents, since that would be unreasonable and unrealistic; and that—

'if there were compelling reasons which indicated overwhelmingly that closure was the reasonable and—other things being equal—the right course to take, provided that steps could be taken to meet the Applicant's (and her fellow residents') expectations to the greatest degree possible following closure, it was open to the Authority, weighing up all these matters with care and sensitivity, to decide in favour of the option of closure.'

Although the first consultation paper made no reference to the 'home for life' promise, it was referred to in the second consultation paper as set out above.

86. It is denied in the health authority's evidence that there was any misrepresentation at the meeting of the board on 7 October 1998 of the terms of the 'home for life' promise. It is asserted that the board had taken the promise into account; that members of the board had previously seen a copy of Mr Jackson's letter of 7 June 1994, which, they were reminded, had not used the word 'home'; and that every board member was well aware that, in terms of its fresh decision-making, the starting point was that the Newcourt patients had moved to Mardon on the strength of an assurance that Mardon would be their home as long as they chose to live there. This was an express promise or representation made on a number of occasions in precise terms. It was made to a small group of severely disabled individuals who had been housed and cared for over a substantial period in the health authority's predecessor's premises at Newcourt. It specifically related to identified premises which, it was represented, would be their home for as long as they chose. It was in unqualified terms. It was repeated and confirmed to reassure the residents. It was made by the health authority's predecessor for its own purposes, namely to encourage Miss Coughlan and her fellow residents to move out of Newcourt and into Mardon House, a specially built substitute home in which they would continue to receive nursing care. The promise was relied on by Miss Coughlan. Strong reasons are required to justify resiling from a promise given in those circumstances. This is not a case where the health authority would, in keeping the promise, be acting inconsistently with its statutory or other public law duties. A decision not to honour it would be equivalent to a breach of contract in private law.

87. The health authority treated the promise as the 'starting point' from which the consultation process and the deliberations proceeded. It was a factor which should be given 'considerable weight', but it could be outweighed by 'compelling reasons which indicated overwhelmingly that closure was the reasonable and the right course to take'. The health authority, though 'mindful of the history behind the residents' move to Mardon House and their understandable expectation that it would be their permanent home', formed the view that there were 'overriding reasons' why closure should none the less proceed. The health authority wanted to improve the provision of reablement services and considered that the mix of a long-stay residential service and a reablement service at Mardon House was inappropriate and detrimental to the interests of both users of the service. The acute reablement service could not be supported there without an uneconomic investment which would have produced a second class reablement service. It was argued that there was a compelling public interest which justified the health authority's prioritisation of the reablement service.

88. It is, however, clear from the health authority's evidence and submissions that it did not consider that it had a legal responsibility or commitment to provide a home, as distinct from care or funding of care, for the applicant and her fellow residents. It considered that, following the withdrawal of the John Grooms Association, the provision of care services to the current residents had become 'excessively expensive', having regard to the needs of the majority of disabled people in the authority's area and the 'insuperable problems' involved in the mix of long-term residential care and reablement services at Mardon House . . . .

. . . But the cheaper option favoured by the health authority misses the essential point of the promise which had been given. The fact is that the health authority has not offered to the applicant an equivalent facility to replace what was promised to her. The health authority's undertaking to fund her care for the remainder of her life is substantially different in nature and effect from the earlier promise that care for her would be provided at Mardon House. That place would be her home for as long as she chose to live there.

89. We have no hesitation in concluding that the decision to move Miss Coughlan against her will and in breach of the health authority's own promise was in the circumstances unfair. It was unfair because it frustrated her legitimate expectation of having a home for life in Mardon House. There was no overriding public interest which justified it. In drawing the balance of conflicting interests the court will not only accept the policy change without demur but will pay the closest attention to the assessment made by the public body itself. Here, however, as we have already indicated, the health authority failed to weigh the conflicting interests correctly.

NOTES:

1. In another case decided in the Court of Appeal in 2001 the issues to be considered in a case concerning legitimate expectation were outlined as follows: "The first question is to what has the public authority, whether by practice or by promise committed itself; the second is whether the authority has acted or proposes to act unlawfully in relation to its ommitment; the third is what the court should do." (See *R. (on the application of Bibi) v Newham LBC* [2002] 1 W.L.R. 237.) *Coughlan* indicates the different types of approaches which may be taken to ligitimate expectation: procedural or substantive. In *Coughlan* the Court of Appeal outlined broad alternative approaches: first, that the legitimate expectation could be limited to whatever policy was in force at the time it could be applied to them, or alternatively that it may extend to an expectation of the outcome which has been promised to them (see further I. Steele, "Substantive Legitimate Expectations: Striking the Right Balance" [2005] L.Q.R. 300). As we have already seen, one of the problems with judicial review is that it constitutes review of a decision rather than an appeal, with the prospect of the decision being overturned but then remitted to the original decision-maker to redetermine. If the circumstances give rise to substantive legitimate expectation, then it can be argued that judicial review becomes almost aligned with appeal.

2. There has been considerable criticism as to the extent to which there has been compliance with the *Coughlan* judgment by the Health Service Ombudsman, *NHS Funding for Long Term Care of Older and Disabled People* (HC 399, 2nd Report, Session 2002–3).

(iii) Resources and Clinical Judgment

Where decisions have to be taken about the provisions of services to individuals, resource issues are likely to be closely linked to questions of clinical judgment. This can be seen in a highly controversial case from 1995.

R. v Cambridge DHA, Ex p. B [1995] 2 All E.R. 129, [1995] 1 W.L.R. 898

The father of a 10-year-old girl brought a judicial review of the decision of Cambridge DHA not to fund further treatment for her. She had leukemia, and had previously had a bone marrow transplant and chemotherapy. Her doctors in Cambridge, reinforced by a second opinion from the Royal Marsden Hospital in London, believed that it would be inappropriate to offer a further course of chemotherapy and, if this was successful, a second bone marrow transplant. The father found other doctors in London who believed that further treatment should be given. When the health authority declined to pay for it, he sought to use the courts to force them to do so. He was successful in the High Court, but lost in the Court of Appeal. The arguments used by each court are instructive.

JOHN LAWS J.
" . . . I entertained the greatest doubt whether the decisive touchstone for the legality of the responents' decision was the crude *Wednesbury* bludgeon. It seemed to me that the fundamental right, the right to life, was engaged in the case . . .
. . . the law requires that where a public body enjoys a discretion whose exercise may infringe such a right, it is not to be permitted to perpetrate any such infringement unless it can show a substantial objective justification on public interest grounds. The public body itself is the first judge of the question whether such a justification exists. The court's role is secondary as Lord Bridge said. Such a distribution of authority is required by the nature of the judicial review jurisdiction, and the respect which the courts are certainly obliged to pay to the powers conferred by Parliament upon bodies other than themselves. But the decision-maker has to recognise that he can only infringe such a fundamental right by virtue of an objection of substance put forward in the public interest . . .
In the light of these materials the first two questions I must decide, it seems to me, are whether the respondents in the present case have: (a) taken a decision which interferes with the applicant's right to life; and (b) if they have, whether they have offered a substantial public interest justification for doing so. Mr Pitt much pressed the submission that his clients had done no positive act to threaten anyone's life; they had done nothing whatever to violate the applicant's right to life; all they had done was to arrive at a decision about the use of public funds. But the fact is that without funding for Dr Gravett's treatment, the applicant will soon certainly die. If the funding is made available, she might not. As things stand at present, the respondents are the only apparent source of the necessary funds. I do not consider that, in the relation to the putative infringement of a fundamental right, there is as regards the obligation of a public body a difference of principle between act and omission. In other areas of law, notably the criminal law, such a distinction may possess a high importance. But in a public law case like the present the question is whether a distinct administrative decision is lawful. The decision-maker is answerable to the court whether the decision is in negative or affirmative form. The decision in this case has, to the knowledge of the decision-maker, materially affected for the worse the applicant's chances of life. I hold that the applicant's right to life is assaulted by it, and accordingly the decision can only be justified on substantial public interest grounds.
It follows that the next question for my determination is whether the reasons for the decision put forward by the respondents, which I have described, may reasonably constitute such justification.

The first reason, namely that the proposed treatment would not be in B's best interests, requires some little analysis. I entirely accept these submissions put forward by Mr Pitt:

(a) there are no perceptible circumstances in which a doctor might properly be ordered to administer treatment contrary to his own clinical judgment or his professional conscience: see *Re J (A Minor) (Child in Care: Medical Treatment)* [1992] 2 FLR 165. But there is no question of such an order being made in this case. The doctor who would treat B, Dr Gravatt, is entirely willing to do so;

(b) it is reasonable and proper for the respondents, in making a decision whether to fund a particular course of treatment, to give determinative weight to the views of the specialist doctors whom they consult (here, essentially, Dr Broadbent and Dr Pinkerton) upon the medical issues arising in the case; and there is no whisper of a suggestion that the high competence of the doctors on whose opinions Dr Zimmern relied should be called in question. The difficulty, however, is as to the nature of the issue upon which their opinion was given and in due course acted upon.

The expertise of Dr Broadbent and Dr Pinkerton was rightly deployed by the respondents, as it seems to me, in relation to two questions: (1) What chances of success, in terms first of a remission after chemotherapy, and secondly as to the results of a further transplant, might be expected from Dr Gravett's proposed treatment? As to that, there is no significant difference between them and Dr Gravatt. (2) What are the objective disadvantages of the treatment, in terms of the suffering the patient would be likely to endure, and the risks to life which the treatment itself would involve, when set against the quality of life which the applicant might enjoy in the short time left to her if she were treated palliatively? Those are the objective questions which in essence only the medical experts can answer. But there is a third question: given authoritative advice as to these first two issues, is it in the best interests of the patient to undergo the treatment or decline it? In the present case, Dr Broadbent and Dr Pinkerton have put forward their own views in answer to this third question. Their advice has not been limited to the first two. But in my judgment the third question is not one upon which the doctors possess an authoritative voice. At least in a case like the present it is not, in the end, a medical question at all. Test it by supposing that the patient was not a little girl, but a grown adult of sound understanding. The options would surely be put to him. The pros and cons would be explained. Upon the question what course of action was in his best interests, his views would be respected. I apprehend they would be treated as determinative. If he decided not to undergo the treatment, that would be the end of the matter. If he decided that he wished to take his chance with it, neither the doctors nor the health authority would turn round and say, it is against his best interests, and of those interests they are the sole judges. The treatment might perhaps still be refused as an unjustifiable use of scarce resources; but that engages the respondents' second reason for their decision, with which I am not presently dealing.

Mr Pitt was at pains to submit that I an not here concerned with a case of an adult, so that such an analogy is of no assistance. I disagree. Of course it may readily be assumed that a 10-year-old child, in circumstances like those of this case, cannot make for herself an informed decision upon the question which course of action is in her best interests. That being so, someone else must take the decision for her. But it should not be the doctors; it should be her family, here—her father. He has duties and responsibilities to her shared by no one else. The doctors' obligation is to ascertain and explain all the medical facts, and in the light of them articulate the choice that must be faced. Their expert views on the medical issues, however, do not constitute the premises of a syllogism from which an inevitable conclusion as to what is in the best interests of the patient may be deduced. It is not at all a matter of deduction from the medical facts. It is a personal question which the patient, if he is of full age and capacity, will decide in the light of medical advice. In the case of a little child, others must decide it—not the experts, but those having, legally and morally, overall care of the patient. I do not consider that *Re J* (to which I have already referred) is inconsistent with this result. There, the patient was in a permanent vegetative state. The views of the medical experts as to how his condition should be administered occupied quite a different, and larger, place than is necessarily possessed by the doctors upon the wholly different facts of the present case.

The difficulty in this case does not merely consist in the fact the doctors, on whose opinion Dr Zimmern relied, purported to decide what was in B.'s best interests. It is also clear (though Mr Pitt vehemently submitted to the contrary) that Zimmern did not regard the father's wish that the treatment be carried out as a relevant circumstance for the purpose of his decision whether to authorise funding. First, Dr Zimmern told the father (by his letter of February 21, 1995) that he had 'a policy of not speaking or corresponding directly with patients or their relatives about extra-contractual referrals'. I am at a loss to understand what rational justification might exist for such a policy, but the point was exposed only in Mr McIntyre's reply and I heard no distinct argument about it from Mr Pitt. I shall therefore assume nothing against the respondents arising solely from this policy. And it is right to say that on February 22, 1995 Dr Zimmern sent a reasoned letter to B's father. However, the policy provides the backdrop for the next, and much more important, point which is this: it is plain in particular from paragraph 5 of Dr Zimmern's affidavit that his careful consideration of the case took into account only the medical opinions put before him. That paragraph deals with what in his view was 'clinically appropriate' for B. In deciding that question he had no regard to the father's views as a material factor concerning the question what was in B's best interests. He supposed, wrongly, that the child's best interests engaged only a medical question.

In these circumstances the first reason put forward for the respondents' decision cannot amount to a substantial justification for their depriving B of such chance of life as Dr Gravett's proposed treatment would offer. But in my judgment this conclusion does not depend only on the jurisprudence which I have sought to outline concerning fundamental rights. The ordinary *Wednesbury* principle produces the result, on the facts here, that the respondents have at the least failed to have regard to a relevant consideration, namely B's family's views—which are the legitimate surrogate for her own—as to whether the proposed treatment would be in her best interests . . .

But the real argument as to the respondents' second justification for their decision depends, I think, in considerable measure upon Dr Zimmern's evidence about the deployment of resources. As I have recorded, he says 'the extra-contractual referral budget is finite'. The proposed treatment 'would not be an effective use of resources. The amount of funds available for health care are not limitless'. He had to bear in mind 'the present and future needs of other patients'.

On February 21, 1995, in a letter to which I have referred earlier, Dr Zimmern said to B's father:

'Should there be any misunderstanding I should state quite clearly that any decision taken by the Commission will be made taking all clinical and other relevant matters into consideration and not on financial grounds.'

His affidavit was sworn precisely a fortnight later. The father might, I think, be forgiven for reflecting that it amounted to something of a volte-face; however, it is no doubt self-evident that funds available for health care are indeed not limitless. And of course it is the respondents, not I, who must decide how they are to be distributed. But merely to point to the fact that resources are finite tells one nothing about the wisdom or, what is relevant for my purposes, the legality of a decision to withhold funding in a particular case, if any, might be prejudiced if the respondents were to fund B's treatment. I have no idea where in the order of things the respondents place a modest chance of saving the life of a 10-year-old girl. I have no evidence about the respondents' budget either generally or in relation to the 'extra-contractual referrals'. Dr Zimmern's evidence about money consists only in grave and well-rounded generalities. I quite accept, as *Re J* enjoins me, that the court should not make orders with consequences for the use of health service funds in ignorance of the knock-on effect on other patients. But where the question is whether the life of a 10-year-old child might be saved, by however slim a chance, the responsible authority must in my judgment do more than toll the bell of tight resources. They must explain the priorities that have led them to decline to fund the treatment. They have not adequately done so here."

John Laws J. quashed the health authority's decision, and required it to re-examine the question, although he did not order the treatment to be funded. The authority appealed to the Court of Appeal.

SIR THOMAS BINGHAM M.R.

" . . . [T]his is a case involving the life of a young patient and that that is a fact which must dominate all consideration of all aspects of the case. Our society is one in which a very high value is put on human life. No decision affecting human life is one that can be regarded with other than the greatest seriousness.

The second general comment which should be made is that the courts are not, contrary to what is sometimes believed, arbiters as to the merits of cases of this kind. Were we to express opinions as to the likelihood of the effectiveness of medical treatment, or as to the merits of medical judgment, then we should be straying far from the sphere which under our constitution is accorded to us. We have one function only, which is to rule upon the lawfulness of decisions. That is a function to which we should strictly confine ourselves.

The four criticisms made by the learned judge of the authority's decision were these. First, he took the view that Dr Zimmern as the decision-maker had wrongly failed to have regard to the wishes of the patient, as expressed on behalf of the patient by her family, and in particular by her father. Our attention was directed to the affidavits that I have mentioned. The point was made that nowhere does one see an express statement that among the factors that led Dr Zimmern to his decision was a consideration of the wishes of the family. In that situation, the learned judge held that the authority had failed to take a vitally important factor into consideration and that the decision was accordingly flawed.

I feel bound for my part to differ from the judge. It seems to me that the learned judge's criticism entirely fails to recognise the realities of this situation. When the case was first presented to the authority, it was presented on behalf of the patient, B, as a case calling for the co-operation and funding of the authority. At all times Dr Zimmern was as vividly aware as he could have been of the fact that the family, represented by B's father, were urgently wishing the authority to undertake this treatment; by 'undertake' I of course mean provide the funding for it. He was placed under considerable pressure by the family and, in the first instance, perhaps unfortunately, made reference to his policy of not corresponding directly with patients or their relatives about what he called 'extra-contractual referrals', meaning requests for the purchase of medical services outside the health authority.

The inescapable fact is, however, that he was put under perfectly legitimate, but very obvious, pressure by the family to procure this treatment and he was responding to that pressure. It was because he was conscious of that pressure that he obviously found the decision which he had to make such an agonizing one and one calling for such careful consideration. To complain that he did not in terms say that he had regard to the wishes of the patient as expressed by the family is to shut one's eyes to the reality of the situation with which he was confronted. It is also worthy of note, and there is no hint of criticism in this, that the accusation that he did not take the patient's wishes into account was not made in the grounds annexed to Form 86A. It was not, therefore, recognised as an accusation calling for a specific rebuttal.

The second criticism that is made is of the use of the expression 'experimental' to describe this treatment. The learned judge took the view, and Mr McIntyre on behalf of B urges, that that is not a fair or accurate description given the estimates of success which have been put by reputable practitioners, and given the willingness of Dr Gravett to accept that there was a worthwhile chance of success. The fact, however, is that even the first course of treatment had a chance of success of something between 10 and 20%. It was only if, contrary to the probabilities, that was totally successful, that it would be possible to embark on the second phase of the treatment which itself had a similar chance of success.

The plain fact is that, unlike many courses of medical treatment, this was not one that had a well-tried track record of success. It was, on any showing, at the frontier of medical science. That being so, it does not, in my judgment, carry weight to describe this decision as flawed because of the use of this expression.

The third criticism that is made by the judge is of the reference to resources. The learned judge held that Dr Zimmern's evidence about money consisted only of grave and well-rounded generalities. The judge acknowledged that the court should not make orders with consequences for the use of health service funds in ignorance of the knock-on effect on other patients. He went on to say that 'where the question is whether the life of a 10-year-old child might be saved by however slim a chance, the responsible authority . . . must do more than toll the bell of tight resources'. The learned judge said: 'They must explain the priorities that have led them to decline to fund the treatment', and he found they had not adequately done so here.

I have no doubt that in a perfect world any treatment which a patient, or a patient's family, sought would be provided if doctors were willing to give it, no matter how much it cost, particularly when a life was potentially at stake. It would however, in my view, be shutting one's eyes to the real world if the court were to proceed on the basis that we do live in such a world. It is common knowledge that health authorities of all kinds are constantly pressed to make ends meet. They cannot pay their nurses as much as they would like; they cannot provide all the treatments they would like; they cannot purchase all the extremely expensive medical equipment they would like; they cannot carry out all the research they would like; they cannot build all the hospitals and specialist units they would like. Difficult and agonizing judgments have to be made as to how a limited budget is best allocated to the maximum advantage of the maximum number of patients. That is not a judgment which the court can make. In my judgment, it is not something that a health authority such as this authority can be fairly criticised for not advancing before the court.

Mr McIntyre went so far as to say that if the authority has money in the bank which it has not spent, then they would be acting in plain breach of their statutory duty if they did not procure this treatment. I am bound to say that I regard that submission as manifestly incorrect. Unless the health authority had sufficient money to purchase everything which in the interests of patients it would wish to do, then that situation would never ever be reached. I venture to say that no real evidence is needed to satisfy the court that no health authority is in that position.

I furthermore think, differing I regret from the judge, that it would be totally unrealistic to require the authority to come to the court with its accounts and seek to demonstrate that if this treatment were provided for B then there would be a patient, C, who would have to go without treatment. No major authority could run its financial affairs in a way which would permit such a demonstration."

NOTES:

1. It is unclear how far the Court of Appeal was prepared to disentangle issues related to funding from those concerning the conflict of medical opinion. It may be that medical judgment is almost impossible to override. In *Re J (a minor)* [1992] 4 All E.R. 614 the court went so far as to say that it would be an abuse of the powers of the court to order a doctor to treat a patient in a manner contrary to her clinical judgment. Possibly, if all the doctors available to treat a patient refuse to do so on clinical grounds, the courts would hold themselves powerless to intervene. In the *Ex p. B* case, however, there was a doctor prepared to treat the patient.

2. With hindsight, it has become clear that the doctors' original assessment of the child's likely survival was inaccurate. The medical advice to the health authority had suggested that she would live beyond March of 1995. In fact she lived until May 1996. (See generally concerning the background to this case C. Ham, "Tragic Choices in Healthcare: Implications of the Child B case" (1999) BMJ 1258 and C. Ham and S. Pickard, *Tragic Choices in Health Care*, London: King's Fund, 1998.)

3. One notable aspect of the judgment of Laws J. was the use of human rights arguments (the case was decided prior to the Human Rights Act 1998).
4. It had been thought that the advent of the NHS internal market in health care might have led to an increase in successful judicial review challenges with the judiciary being less inhibited to challenge resource allocation decisions; this, however, did not ultimately prove to be the case (see further N. Whitty in S. Sheldon and M. Thomson (eds), *Feminist Perspectives on Health Care Law*, London: Cavendish, 1998).

QUESTIONS:

1. Do you prefer the approach of John Laws J. or Sir Thomas Bingham M.R.?
2. Which factors were more important, those relating to clinical judgment or those concerning resource allocation?
3. Will a challenge of a health authority decision be possible in the future in cases where it has not acted wholly unreasonably? (See P. Wilson, case note (1995) *Journal of Social Welfare and Family Law*, 359.)

(iii) Resource Allocation, Application of Policies and Human Rights

The decisions considered above pre-date the Human Rights Act 1998. The issue arises to what extent that legislation will impact upon the original jurisprudence.

R. v North West Lancashire Health Authority Ex p. A, Same v Same Ex p. D, Same v Same Ex p. G [2000] 1 W.L.R. 977

The applicants sought access to gender reassignment surgery. Two of them had a diagnosed clinical need and a third was awaiting his classification. The health authority (HA) had adopted a policy in 1998 in relation to such surgery. Gender reassignment surgery was classed as a procedure where the effectiveness was unclear, it had not been tested by scientific research and it should be only commissioned where there was a formal evaluation as to whether it was cost-effective. Exceptions to the policy could be considered where there was an overriding clinical needs. The policy provided that "such exceptions will be rare, unpredictable and will usually be based on circumstances that could not have been predicted at the time when the policy was adopted". At that time the only specialist clinic concerned with this surgery was in London and the HA refused to refer the applicants to this clinic. The applicants brought proceedings for judicial review. At first instance the decision of the HA was quashed. On appeal to the Court of Appeal, the first instance decision was upheld.

AULD L.J.

GENERAL PRINCIPLES

"As illustrated in the *Cambridge Health Authority* case [1999] 1 W.L.R. 898 and *Coughlan's* case [2000] 2 W.L.R. 622, it is an unhappy but unavoidable feature of state funded health care that regional health authorities have to establish certain priorities in funding different treatments from their finite resources. It is natural that each authority, in establishing its own priorities, will give greater priority to life-threatening and other grave illnesses than to others obviously less demanding of medical intervention. The precise allocation and weighting of priorities is clearly a matter of judgment for each authority, keeping well in mind its statutory obligations to meet the reasonable requirements of all those within its area for which it is responsible. It makes sense to have a policy for the purpose—indeed, it might well be irrational not to have one—and it makes sense too that, in settling on such a policy, an authority would normally place treatment of transsexualism lower in its scale of priorities than, say, cancer or heart disease or kidney failure. Authorities might reasonably differ as to precisely where in the scale transsexualism should be placed and as to the criteria for determining the appropriateness and need for treatment of it in individual cases. It is proper for an authority to adopt a general policy for the exercise of such an administrative discretion, to allow for exceptions from it in 'exceptional circumstances' and to leave those circumstances undefined: see *In re Findlay* [1985] A.C. 318, 335–336, per Lord Scarman. In my view, a policy to place transsexualism low in an order of priorities of illnesses for treatment and to deny it treatment save in exceptional circumstances such as overriding clinical need is not in principle irrational, provided that the policy genuinely recognises the possibility of there being an overriding clinical need and requires each request for treatment to be considered on its individual merits.

However, in establishing priorities—comparing the respective needs of patients suffering from different illnesses and determining the respective strengths of their claims to treatment—it is vital for an authority: (1) accurately to assess the nature and seriousness of each type of illness; (2) to determine the effectiveness of various forms of treatment for it; and (3) to give proper effect to that assessment and that determination in the formulation and individual application of its policy. . . .

As I have said, the authority has acknowledged in its evidence before Hidden J. and in its stance on this appeal that transsexualism is an illness. But its recognition of it in its two policies is at best oblique and lacks conviction. Indeed, both policies, read together and as a whole, and Dr. Sudell's elaboration of them strongly indicate that the authority does not really believe it. The inclusion of transsexualism in the 1995 policy, which was concerned only with medical procedures which the authority regarded as of '[no] beneficial health gain or no proven benefit,' and bracketing it with cosmetic plastic surgery and the like are testament to that. The same attitude is evident in the 1998 policy in its introductory references in paragraph 2, under the heading of 'Appropriate, effective and cost effective health care,' to 'interventions on the human body . . . not always related to ill health,' and again bracketing it with cosmetic surgery and other comparable treatments as '[health] care that will not be commissioned, or . . . only with restrictions.' If there were any doubt about the authority's true attitude to the condition, it is removed by paragraphs 42 to 44 of Dr. Sudell's affidavit, which I have set out, clearly evidencing its scepticism of the notion that transsexualism is an illness worthy of medical attention beyond psychiatric reassurance. Where evidence from the policy maker is of a piece with and has as its purpose elaboration of the policy under challenge, it is clearly relevant and capable of throwing light on the true nature of the policy (cf. *Reg. v. Westminster City Council, Ex parte Ermakov* [1996] 2 All E.R. 302, C.A., where the court regarded as exceptional recourse to evidence the purpose of which was to rescue a flawed decision).

It may be that there is some medical support for such scepticism, despite the apparently overwhelming evidence before Hidden J. that transsexualism is an illness which requires treatment. I say nothing about the scope for debate between doctors on the matter. I do not need to do so because the authority accepts in these proceedings that it is an illness. It follows that its policies should, but do not, properly reflect that medical judgment and accord the condition a place somewhere in the scale of its priorities for illnesses instead of relegating it to the outer regions of conditions which it plainly does not so regard.

That basic error, one of failure properly to evaluate such a condition as an illness suitable and appropriate for treatment, is not mitigated by the allowance in both policies for the possibility of an exception in the case of overriding clinical need or other exceptional circumstances. As I have said, such a provision is not objectionable, but it is important that the starting point against which the exceptional circumstances have to be rated is properly evaluated and that each case is considered on its individual merits: see per Bankes L.J. in *Rex v. Port of London Authority, Ex parte Kynoch Ltd.* [1919] 1 K.B. 176;

per Lord Reid in *British Oxygen Co. Ltd. v. Board of Trade* [1971] A.C. 610, 624–625; and per Lord Scarman in *In re Findlay* [1985] A.C. 318, 335–336. The authority's relegation of what was notionally regarded as an illness to something less, in respect of which an applicant for treatment had to demonstrate an overriding clinical need for treatment, confronted each applicant with a very high and uncertain threshold.

The 1995 policy gave no indication of what might amount to an overriding clinical need or other exceptional circumstances; nor did the 1998 policy, save in paragraph 5.1 in which it emphasised the likely rarity and unpredictability of such circumstances, and instanced as a possibility when 'the problem' was the cause of serious mental illness. Expert assessment that a patient needs the treatment would not do; demonstration of the existence of some other illness was a necessary condition for consideration for treatment. The authority gave a hint in its consideration of the case of A. that epilepsy caused by her untreated transsexualism, if established, might have qualified. But, given the authority's reluctance to accept gender reassignment as an effective treatment for transsexualism—and it would follow logically any condition caused by it—the provision for an exception in a case of 'overriding clinical need' was in practice meaningless, as Mr. Blake observed. It was as objectionable as a policy which effectively excluded the exercise by the authority of a medical judgment in the individual circumstances of each case; cf. *Reg. v. Secretary of State for Health, Ex parte Pfizer Ltd.*, *The Times*, 17 June 1999, per Collins J. Looked at in that light, Dr. Sudell's observation in paragraph 31 of his first affidavit that it was 'difficult to imagine what an exceptional clinical need for' gender reassignment might be, is understandable.

I accept, of course, that it is a matter for the medical judgment of the authority, not the court, what, if any, effective medical treatment there might be for transsexualism and any sequelae. As Sir Thomas Bingham M.R. said in the *Cambridge Health Authority* case [1995] 1 W.L.R. 898, 905:

> 'the courts are not, contrary to what is sometimes believed, arbiters as to the merits of cases of this kind. Were we to express opinions as to the likelihood of the effectiveness of medical treatment, or as to the merits of medical judgment, then we should be straying far from the sphere which under our constitution is accorded to us. We have one function only, which is to rule upon the lawfulness of decisions. That is a function to which we should strictly confine ourselves.'

However, if a regional health authority devises a policy not to provide treatment save in cases of overriding clinical need, it makes a nonsense of the policy if, as a matter of its medical judgment, there is no effective treatment for it for which there could be an overriding clinical need. The same applies to any other condition caused by transsexualism such as a mental illness of the seriousness described by Dr. Sudell. If the authority considers the cause of such a condition to be untreatable by hormonal treatment and surgery, it is hard to see how it could regard the condition itself as an overriding need for such treatment.

In my view, the stance of the authority, coupled with the near uniformity of its reasons for rejecting each of the applicant's requests for funding was not a genuine application of a policy subject to individually determined exceptions of the sort considered acceptable by Lord Scarman in *In re Findlay* [1985] A.C. 318. It is similar to the over-rigid application of the near 'blanket policy' questioned by Judge J. in *Reg. v. Warwickshire County Council, Ex parte Collymore* [1995] E.L.R. 217, 224–226, 'which while in theory admitting of exceptions, may not, in reality, result in the proper consideration of each individual case on its merits.' In that case the implementation of the policy, not the policy itself, was quashed, Judge J. considering it unnecessary to decide whether the latter was unlawful. The policy there and that in this case are not so obviously unlawful as that in *Reg. v. Bexley London Borough Council, Ex parte Jones* [1995] E.L.R. 42, where it effectively admitted no exceptions by reference to individual circumstances. Nevertheless, it has the same basic flaw both in form and application. Leggatt L.J. said, at p. 55:

'It is . . . legitimate for a statutory body . . . to adopt a policy designed to ensure a rational and consistent approach to the exercise of a statutory discretion in particular types of case. But it can only do so provided that the policy fairly admits of exceptions to it. In my judgment, the respondents effectually disabled themselves from considering individual cases and there has been no convincing evidence that at any material time they had an exceptions procedure worth the name. There is no indication that there was a genuine willingness to consider individual cases.'

Accordingly, given the authority's acknowledgement that transsexualism is an illness, its policy, in my view, is flawed in two important respects. First, it does not in truth treat transsexualism as an illness, but as an attitude or state of mind which does not warrant medical treatment. Second, the ostensible provision that it makes for exceptions in individual cases and its manner of considering them amount effectively to the operation of a 'blanket policy' against funding treatment for the condition because it does not believe in such treatment.

I was at first attracted to Mr. Pannick's alternative submission that, even if the authority had not properly evaluated the condition of transsexualism, it could, in its allocation of priorities of funding from its finite resources, have lawfully assessed it as not normally worthy of funding and not an exceptional case for treatment in any of the applicant's cases. He suggested that even if the authority were to reformulate its policy to meet the concerns that I have indicated, there is an inherent unlikelihood of a different result. In such a circumstance, he submitted, the court should not interfere with the decisions. He relied upon Sir Thomas Bingham M.R's additional reason in *Reg. v. Cambridge Health Authority, Ex parte B.* [1995] 1 W.L.R. 898, 907c–d, for not disturbing its refusal to fund treatment, that it 'could, on a proper review of all the relevant material, reach the same decision that it had already reached'.

As Mr. Pannick also submitted, the fact that each of the applicants may have had a clinical need for treatment would not render unlawful the application of a properly formulated policy refusing them treatment if they could not show some additional element in the form of 'an overriding clinical need' or otherwise. However, my view is that, as the authority has not genuinely taken as its starting point in the case of each applicant that her condition is or may be an illness worthy and capable of effective treatment, it would be wrong for the court to assume the authority's task. That must remain a matter for it both as a matter of medical judgment in the setting of priorities, the allocation of funds to those priorities having regard to its finite resources and in its provision for exceptions in individual cases.

For those reasons I would quash the authority's 1995 and 1998 policies in so far as they concern gender reassignment treatment and the decisions the subjects of this appeal based on them, and remit the matter to the authority for reconsideration of its policy and the decisions on their individual merits. The authority should reformulate its policy to give proper weight to its acknowledgement that transsexualism is an illness, apply that weighting when setting its level of priority for treatment and make effective provision for exceptions in individual cases from any general policy restricting the funding of treatment for it.

. . . .

As to the European Convention for the Protection of Human Rights and Fundamental Freedoms, it is not yet part of our domestic law and is relevant only, in an appropriate case, to the court's consideration of rationality. Mr. Blake indicated that the purpose of his fairly detailed submissions and references to Strasbourg jurisprudence was merely to show that transsexualism is a sufficiently serious condition 'to raise human rights problems.' Such an unfocused recourse to that jurisdiction, whether before or after the statutory absorption of part of the Convention into the law of England and Wales, is not helpful to the court. Indeed, it is positively unhelpful, cluttering up its consideration of adequate and more precise domestic principles and authorities governing the issues in play. Thus, the deployment of generalised propositions from the European Court of Human Rights ('E.C.H.R.') that a person's sexual identity is of sufficient importance to attract the protection of the right to respect for private and family life under article 8, or that a denial of medical treatment may, if sufficiently serious, amount to 'inhuman or degrading treatment' under article 3, contributes nothing to resolution of the issues here: see, e.g., *Rees v. United Kingdom* (1986) 9 E.H.R.R. 56; *Cossey v. United Kingdom* (1990) 13 E.H.R.R. 622; and the dissenting opinion of Judge Pettiti in *B. v. France* (1992) 16 E.H.R.R. 1, 40–41. It is common ground in this case that transsexualism is an illness; the issues are whether the authority's policy for the public funding of treatment of it properly reflects that and whether it makes proper provision for consideration of each application for treatment on its individual merits.

In any event, article 8 imposes no positive obligations to provide treatment. The E.C.H.R. in *Sheffield and Horsham v. United Kingdom* (1998) 27 E.H.R.R. 163, which concerned post-operative refusal to accord legal status as a woman, said, at p. 191, para. 52:

'The court reiterates that the notion of "respect" is not clear-cut, especially as far as the positive obligations inherent in that concept are concerned: having regard to the diversity of the practices followed and the situation obtaining in the contracting states, the notion's requirements will vary considerably from case to case. In determining whether or not a positive obligation exists, regard must be had to the fair balance that has to be struck between the general interest of the community and the interests of the individual, the search for which balance is inherent in the whole of the Convention.'

Interestingly, the court added, at p. 193, para. 58: 'For the court, it continues to be the case that transsexualism raises complex scientific, legal, moral and social issues, in respect of which there is no generally shared approach among the contracting states'.

As Mr. Pannick observed, if the applicants have no case under article 8 of failure to respect their private and family life, they could not, a fortiori, establish that they were victims of inhuman or degrading treatment under article 3 since the same essential issues arise: see *Olsson v. Sweden* (1988) 11 E.H.R.R. 259, 292, paras. 85–87. And, as he also observed, a breach of the article requires 'a particular level' of severity which, of course depends on the circumstances of the case. It is plain, in my view, that article 3 was not designed for circumstances of this sort of case where the challenge is as to a health authority's allocation of finite funds between competing demands. As Hidden J. observed, in rejecting similar submissions below:

'The Convention does not give the applicants rights to free healthcare in general or to gender reassignment surgery in particular. Even if the applicants had such a right it would be qualified by the authority's right to determine healthcare priorities in the light of its limited resources.'

Similarly, Mr. Blake's somewhat irresolute resort to the notion of discrimination in the context of the Convention and Union law is also misconceived. It was that discrimination between those suffering from transsexualism and other illnesses is contrary to article 14 in that it amounts to discrimination 'on the ground of their sex or other status,' and contrary to article 3(1) of Council Directive (79/7/E.E.C.) providing for equal treatment in matters of social security. He relied on *Reg. v. Secretary of State for Health, Ex parte Richardson* (Case C-137/94) [1996] I.C.R. 471 for the proposition that medical treatment is part of social security. In fact it is an authority for a much narrower point, namely that a scheme for exemption from prescription charges falls within the Directive. As Mr. Pannick observed, the court did not hold that the provision of medical treatment, as an aspect of policies on public health, amounts to the provision of social security. Article 129 of the E.C. Treaty leaves the provision of public health services to member states.

Mr. Blake also referred to a passage from the opinion of the *Advocate-General in P. v. S. (Case C-13/94)* [1996] I.C.R. 795, 808, stating that there is unlawful discrimination on grounds of sex where, as a result of 'a change of sex' a person is discriminated against on the grounds of sex. Clearly, that blindingly obvious and general proposition has nothing to do with the issue in this case which is as to provision of treatment for transsexualism along with other competing demands on finite resources. When pressed as to what form of discrimination he had in mind, Mr. Blake conceded that it was not a difference between the treatment of male and female transsexuals or between transsexuals and anyone else or in any respect other than the necessary difference in provision of treatment for their condition from that of other ill persons for their conditions. That is not a matter of sexual or any other discrimination against which the law provides protection; it is a matter of different priorities for different illnesses, a matter of medical judgment. Accordingly, I would dismiss the appeals and make the order I have already indicated."

BUXTON L.J.
"Article 3 of the E.C.H.R. addresses positive conduct by public officials of a high degree of seriousness and opprobrium. It has never been applied to merely policy decisions on the allocation of resources, such as the present case is concerned with. That is clear not only from the terms of article 3 itself, and the lack of any suggestion in any of the authorities that it could apply in a case even remotely like the present, but also from the explanation of the reach of article 3 that has been given by the Convention organs. Thus in *Tyrer v. United Kingdom* (1978) 2 E.H.H.R. 1, a case concerned with corporal punishment, the Strasbourg Court held, at paragraphs 30 and 35 of its judgment that

'in order for a punishment to be "degrading" and in breach of article 3, the humiliation or debasement involved must attain a particular level . . . the court finds that the applicant was subjected to a punishment in which the element of humiliation attained the level inherent in the notion of "degrading punishment" . . . '

More generally, the Strasbourg Commission has on a number of occasions stressed the degree of seriousness of the conduct that article 3 addresses. For instance, the Commission said in *East African Asians v. United Kingdom* (1973) 3 E.H.R.R. 76, 81, para. 195,

'The Commission finally recalls its own statement in the first Greek Case (1969) 12 Y.B. Eur. Con v. H.R. 1 that treatment of an individual may be said to be "degrading" in the sense of article 3 "if it grossly humiliates him before others or drives him to act against his will or conscience" . . . the word "grossly" indicates that article 3 is only concerned with "degrading treatment" which reaches a certain level of severity'.

These strong statements clearly demonstrate, if demonstration were needed, that to attempt to bring the present case under article 3 not only strains language and commonsense, but also and even more seriously trivialises that article in relation to the very important values that it in truth protects.

The situation is less straightforward with regard to article 8 of the E.C.H.R. There is no doubt that a person's sexual behaviour is an important element in his private life, respect for which is guaranteed by article 8 of the E.C.H.R. It is, however, less easy to see that a person's sexuality is, in itself, an aspect of his private life, as that concept is understood in the context of article 8; as opposed to being an evidently important, possibly even overriding, aspect of his personality and personal integrity. That difficult question does not, however, need to be pursued, because it is plain that in this case there has occurred no interference with either the applicant's private life or with their sexuality.

The E.C.H.R. jurisprudence demonstrates that a state can be guilty of such interference simply by inaction, though the cases in which that has been found do not seem to go beyond an obligation to adopt measures to prevent serious infractions of private or family life by subjects of the state: see *X and Y v. The Netherlands* (1985) 8 E.H.R.R. 235, para. 23 and, more generally, Harris et al., *Law of the European Convention on Human Rights* (1995), pp. 320–324. Such an interference could hardly be founded on a refusal to fund medical treatment. And in any event this case plainly falls under the reiterated guidance given by the Strasbourg court in *Cossey v. United Kingdom* (1990) 13 E.H.R.R. 622, para. 37 and *Sheffield and Horsham v. United Kingdom* (1998) 27 E.H.R.R. 163, para. 52:

'the notion of "respect" is not clear-cut, especially as far as the positive obligations inherent in that concept are concerned: having regard to the diversity of the practices followed and the situations obtaining in the contracting states, the notion's requirements will vary considerably from case to case. In determining whether or not a positive obligation exists, regard must be had to the fair balance that has to be struck between the general interest of the community and the interests of the individual, the search for which balance is inherent in the whole of the Convention.'

It is therefore clear that the facts of this case come nowhere near to the type of factual situations addressed by either article 3 or article 8 of the E.C.H.R. Mr. Blake however said that his reason for not directly relying on the E.C.H.R. was not that, but rather that the Human Rights Act 1998 had not yet come into operation. That argument was however unpersuasive because, as I have demonstrated above, a direct claim under that Act, were it in force, would be bound to fail."

Notes:

1. May L.J. agreed with Auld and Buxton L.JJ. Fundamentally, this case can be seen as a traditional judicial review case concerning review of a binding policy.

2. In *R v North Derbyshire HA Ex p. Fisher* (1997) 38 B.M.L.R. 76, the applicants successfully challenged the refusal by North Derbyshire HA to fund the drug Betainferon. The HA had a blanket policy not to fund this drug unless there were clinical trials being undertaken. No trials were taking place. This also went against existing Department of Health guidance.

3. In *R v Secretary of State for Health Ex p. Pfizer Ltd* [1999] Lloyd's Med. Rep. 289 the Secretary of State issued a Health Service circular with the aim of limiting the prescription of Viagra by G.P.s. This was challenged by the drug company Pfizer. The NHS terms and conditions of service for G.P.s provided that:

   "a doctor shall order any drugs or appliances which are needed for the treatment of any patient to whom he is providing treatment under these terms of service by issuing to that patient a prescription form."

   The action for judicial review succeeded and it was held that the doctor was entitled to give such treatment as was "necessary and appropriate". Regulations were then issued by the Secretary of State which confirmed the restrictions placed on the prescription of Viagra. Such restrictions were justified on the basis that the cost of unrestricted prescribing would lead to an estimated annual increase of £100 million. Pfizer challenged the circular, claiming that this infringed the EU Transparency Directive (Council Directive 89/105) which provides that decisions "to exclude an individual medicinal product from the coverage of the national health insurance system shall contain a statement of reasons based on objective and verifiable criteria". This challenge failed. In the Court of Appeal it was held that the regulations complied with the circular because they were verifiable in that they were published and they were objective because they were based upon the legitimate aim of improving the economic situation of the health system. Syrett suggests that this can be seen as in line with the range of judicial review actions. (See further K. Syrett, "Impotence or Importance? Judicial Review in an Era of Explicit NHS Rationing" (2004) 67 M.L.R. 289.)

4. Human rights were extensively considered in this case. One possibility is that the Human Rights Act 1998 will lead to challenges under Article 2 of the ECHR in relation to resource allocation where there has been refusal of life-saving treatment. However, it has been suggested by O'Sullivan that the courts would replace the doctrine of non-justiciability, instead affording the Government a "margin of appreciation". (See further D. O'Sullivan, "The Allocation of Scarce Resources and the Right to Life under the European Convention of Human Rights" [1998] *Public Law* 389). Certainly it is the case that the ECHR has indicated that in interpreting obligations under Article 2, resources may be seen as a limitation. In *Osman v UK* (1998) 29 EHRR 245 at 116, the European Court of Human Rights commented that, "Bearing in mind the difficulties involved in policing modern societies, the unpredictability of human conduct and operational choices which must be made in terms of priorities and resources, such an obligation must be interpreted in a way which does not impose an impossible or disproportionate burden on the authorities. Accordingly not every claimed risk to life can entail for the Authorities a Convention requirement to take operational measures to prevent that risk from materialising". (See generally A. Maclean, "The Individual's Right to Treatment under the HRA 1998" in A. Garwood Gowers, J. Tingle and T. Lewis (eds), *Health Care Law: the Impact of the Human Rights Act*, London: Cavendish, 2002.) It should be noted that in *Scialaqua v Italy* (1998) 26 EHRR CD164, a claim that refusal of access to medication infringed the claimant's Article 2 rights was unsuccessful.

5. In the *Watts* case at first instance (*Watts v Bedford PCT* [2003] EWHC 2228, discussed below at p.71), Mumby J. equally dismissed the human rights as a basis for litigation here. On the Article 3 point he commented that:

> "Article 3 is not engaged unless the 'ill treatment' in question attains a minimal level of severity and involves actual bodily injury or intense physical or mental suffering. However that is not this case. Making every allowance for the constant pain and suffering that the claimant had to endure—[consequent upon waiting for her hip operation] and I do not see anyway to minimise it—the simple fact in my judgement is that nothing she had to endure was so severe or so humiliating as to engage article 3."

The application of a PCT policy concerning the availability of the drug Herceptin for breast cancer was recently considered in the following case.

R (on the application of Rogers) v Swindon NHS Primary Care Trust and Another [2006] EWCA Civ 392

In February 2006, a 53-year-old woman, Ann Marie Rogers, challenged Swindon PCT's refusal to pay for the drug Herceptin to treat her early-stage breast cancer.

The drug was not licensed for early-stage breast cancer, only for late-stage breast cancer. Although some PCTs were funding the drug for early-stage breast cancers others, such as Swindon, were waiting for regulatory approval and treatment was only paid for in exceptional cases. At first instance, Bean J. found that the policy was not arbitrary nor was it irrational. In addition he held that the refusal did not contravene Article 2 and/or Article 14 of the ECHR because it did not amount to denial of health care which the state had undertaken to make available to the public itself. Ms Rogers then took her case to the Court of Appeal. In the Court of Appeal it was argued that the policy was arbitrary and irrational because there was no basis as to which it could provide funding for some women but not for others. Counsel for Mrs Rogers accepted that it could be lawful to refuse funding in all but undefined circumstances

SIR ANTHONY CLARKE M.R.
The judge referred to the *North West Lancashire* case and continued that in the case.

"Auld LJ stresses that a policy which allows for exceptions in undefined exceptional circumstances is not unlawful 'provided that the policy genuinely recognises the possibility of there being an overriding clinical need and requires each request for treatment to be considered on its individual merits.' As we see it, that means that a policy of withholding assistance save in unstated exceptional circumstances (in the case addressed by Auld LJ, and no doubt in this case also, overriding clinical need) will be rational in the legal sense provided that it is possible to envisage, and the decision-maker does envisage, what such exceptional circumstances might be. If it is not possible to envisage any such circumstances, then the policy will be in practice a complete refusal of assistance: and irrational as such because it is sought to be justified not as a complete refusal but as a policy of exceptionality.

[63] Thus we would not hold that the policy was arbitrary because it refers to unidentified exceptional circumstances. The essential question is whether the policy was rational; and, in deciding whether it is rational or not, the court must consider whether there are any relevant exceptional circumstances which could justify the PCT refusing treatment to one woman within the eligible group but granting it to another. And to anticipate, the difficulty that the PCT encounters in the present case is that while the policy is stated to be one of exceptionality, no persuasive grounds can be identified, at least in clinical terms, for treating one patient who fulfils the clinical requirements for Herceptin treatment differently from others in that cohort . . .

. . . If that policy had involved a balance of financial considerations against a general policy not to fund off-licence drugs not approved by NICE and the healthcare needs of the particular patient in an exceptional case, we do not think that such a policy would have been irrational. However, it was not that policy that the PCT followed. The PCT did not adopt a policy of refusing to fund Herceptin treatment on the ground that it was not licensed by the EMEA or approved by NICE, and thus did not adopt the reasoning in the passage from the statement of Ms Lee quoted above. Contrary to that statement, the PCT did not conclude that it would be irresponsible to introduce this drug in advance of licensing and NICE appraisal. If it had, it would not have admitted the possibility of funding Herceptin treatment for a woman in exceptional personal or clinical circumstances. It would simply have refused to do so on the ground that, if it did, it would be acting irresponsibly. It was influenced in not doing that by the Secretary of State's guidance, to which we now turn. . . .

[74] We have already set out the elements of the guidance. A fair reading of the guidance does provide some encouragement to trusts to fund Herceptin. It emphasises the role of the individual clinician by saying that it is down to him or her to decide whether to prescribe Herceptin after discussions with the patient about potential risks and taking into account

her medical history. In addition to saying that trusts should not refuse funding solely on the ground of cost, it expressly provides that trusts should not rule out treatment in principle but should consider individual circumstances. Thus a trust which complies with the guidance (as the PCT sought to do) cannot refuse to fund treatment simply on the basis that Herceptin is unlicensed and unapproved by NICE.

[75] Mr Havers submits that the Secretary of State did not say that Herceptin should be routinely prescribed and that she could easily have done so if that was what she had intended. There is some forensic force in this point but it seems to us to overlook the relevance or potential relevance of funding considerations. As already stated, the Secretary of State indicated that an application for funding should not be refused solely on the ground of cost but she did not say (or in our view mean to say) that considerations of cost were irrelevant. In these circumstances the Secretary of State was not saying that Herceptin prescribed by a clinician should be routinely funded.

[76] As we see it, she was stressing the potential value of Herceptin while recognising its possible risks and emphasising that it was down to the clinician to decide whether to prescribe Herceptin in consultation with the patient. It was then for the trust to decide whether to fund the treatment, its decision to be taken, not solely on the basis of cost or by ruling it out in principle, but having regard to individual circumstances. This left the trust to take account of the fact that the clinician had prescribed Herceptin notwithstanding that it was off-licence and not approved by NICE, and to balance cost considerations against the individual circumstances of the patient.

[77] We see nothing arbitrary or irrational about that approach. It could properly involve a decision by a trust which was subject to financial constraints and which decided that it could not fund all the patients who applied for funding for Herceptin treatment, to make the difficult choice to fund treatment for a woman with, say, a disabled child and not for a woman in different personal circumstances.

[78] That is not however this case because the PCT developed a policy which treated financial considerations as irrelevant. It thus had funds available for all women within the eligible group whose clinician prescribed Herceptin. Yet its policy is to refuse funding save where exceptional personal or clinical circumstances can be shown.

[79] Mr Havers was naturally asked to give examples of personal circumstances which might justify funding one woman rather than another within the eligible group. He submitted that it was not necessary for the PCT to identify possible examples and relied upon the *North West Lancashire Health Authority* case. The only positive example he gave was that of a woman with a child with a life-limiting condition. For our part, we cannot see how that fact can possibly justify providing funding for that woman but not another when each falls within the eligible group and there are available funds for both. After all, once financial considerations are ruled out, and it has been decided not to rely on NICE without exception, then the only concern which the PCT can have must relate to the legitimate clinical needs of the patient. The non-medical personal situation of a particular patient cannot in these circumstances be relevant to the question whether Herceptin prescribed by the patient's clinician should be funded for the benefit of the patient. Where the clinical needs are equal, and resources are not an issue, discrimination between patients in the same eligible group cannot be justified on the basis of personal characteristics not based on healthcare.

[80] As to clinical characteristics, it was suggested in argument that one woman in the eligible group might have a greater clinical need for Herceptin than another. We can see that that might be theoretically possible but there is no indication that any such possibility in fact exists. The PCT rejected the suggestion that a distinction might be made between one person within the group and another on the ground that the prognosis of each was different. As we understand it, that was on the basis that the research does not support such an approach. It was also suggested that one patient within the group might be unable for medical reasons to take another drug such as tamoxifen, whereas the rest of the group might be able to take it, and that such a case would be an example of an exceptional circumstance upon which a decision to fund Herceptin treatment for the former patient and not for the rest could be justified. There is, however, no evidence which supports such

a possibility. In any event we accept Mr Pannick's submission that it could not be reasonable or rational to deny a patient Herceptin treatment because she can tolerate tamoxifen, where there is no evidence that tamoxifen, or any other drug, is an alternative to Herceptin.

[81] All the clinical evidence is to the same effect. The PCT has not put any clinical or medical evidence before the court to suggest any such clinical distinction could be made. In these circumstances there is no rational basis for distinguishing between patients within the eligible group on the basis of exceptional clinical circumstances any more than on the basis of personal, let alone social, circumstances. In short, we accept Mr Pannick's submission that once the PCT decided (as it did) that it would fund Herceptin for some patients and that cost was irrelevant, the only reasonable approach was to focus on the patient's clinical needs and fund patients within the eligible group who were properly prescribed Herceptin by their physician. This would not open the floodgates to those suffering from breast cancer because only comparatively few satisfy the criteria so as to qualify for the eligible group.

[82] For these reasons we have reached the conclusion that the policy of the PCT is irrational, unless it can properly be said that it is not necessary to identify individual characteristics which might justify distinguishing between one patient within the eligible group and another. In our judgement, that cannot properly be said and the *North West Lancashire Hospital Authority* case is not authority to the contrary. In that case the court emphasised the importance of the policy genuinely recognising the possibility of there being an overriding clinical need. Here the evidence does not establish the possibility of there being relevant clinical circumstances relating to one patient and not another and, in the case of personal characteristics, there is no rational basis for preferring one patient to another.

NOTES:

1. Note that while the Court of Appeal in this case held that this particular policy was irrational this does not mean that primary care trusts will be required to fund the drug. As in earlier cases the Court of Appeal does indicate that budgetary costs will be relevant in determining which patients will receive funded treatment (see further C. Dyer, "Trusts can take costs into account when deciding drug treatment" (2006) 332 B.M.J. 928).

2. In May 2006 the National Institute for Clinical Excellence produced draft guidance approving the use of herceptin for early stage breast cancer. (See further S. Mayor, "NICE approves trastuzumab for early stage breast cancer" (2006) 332 B.M.J. 1409).

3. While the courts have struck down certain decisions to refuse treatment through judicial review they have in the past indicated that they would not order treatment in the face of clinical opposition. So, for example, in *Re J*, Balcombe L.J. emphasised that the courts would not compel medical treatment:

   "I would stress the absolute undesirability of the court making an order which may have the effect of compelling a doctor or health authority to make available scarce resources (both human and material) to a particular child without knowing whethere there are not patients to whom the resources might more advantageously be devoted . . . "

   In the later case of *R. v Portsmouth NHS Trust Ex p. Glass* [1999] Lloyd's Rep Med 367, Lord Woolf indicated obiter that the court may be prepared to order medical treatment in the face of professional opposition. See further discussion of this case in Court of Appeal and in the ECHR in Chapter 7 and Chapter 14 below.

QUESTION:

1. The court did not see it necessary to consider the claims under Articles 2 and 14. Does this mean that in relation to resource allocation claims following earlier cases such as *North West Lancashire* that the Human Rights Act 1998 is effectively redundant?

(iv) Challenges to Resource Allocation Decisions on the Basis of Procedural Irregularities

It may also be possible to challenge decisions on the basis of procedural defects. In one case, the failure to probe the reluctance of doctors to provide services to see whether another source of care could be identified was such a defect (see *R. v Ealing DHA, Ex p. Fox* [1993] 3 All E.R. 170, considered in Chapter 8). It is usually necessary for decision-makers to give those adversely affected an opportunity to put their case. The issue was raised in the *Cambridge* case, but the Court of Appeal rejected the suggestion that the views of the girl's father had not been considered. This problem was also discussed in the case of *R. v Ethical Committee of St Mary's Hospital (Manchester), Ex p. Harriott* [1988] 1 F.L.R. 512, which concerned access to infertility treatment and is extracted in Chapter 11.

More importantly, for this chapter, the *Harriott* case also suggested that decisions could be attacked for being based on improper reasons. The judge gave race, as an example, referring to the illegality of denying treatment to Jews or those with different coloured skin. These are areas where discrimination is prohibited by law. Presumably unjustifiable sex discrimination would also constitute an unlawful basis for determining access to health care.

(v) Disability Discrimination and Resource Allocation

It is possible that the Disability Discrimination Act 1995 will introduce important considerations here. That Act prohibits discrimination on the basis of disability, which is defined in terms that would include some groups with health problems. However, it may be that the type of discrimination prohibited by the Act would be deemed irrelevant to treatment decisions because it would cover almost all patients and not give rise to any usable distinctions between them. If so, the distinctions made when deciding who to treat would have to be made on other grounds which would fall outside the Act.

Disability Discrimination Act 1995, s.1(1), Sch.1, para.4(1)

1(1) Subject to the provisions of Schedule 1, a person has a disability for the purposes of this Act . . . if he has a physical or mental impairment which has a substantial and long-term adverse effect on his ability to carry out normal day-to-day activities.

Schedule 1, paragraph 4(1). An impairment is to be taken to affect the ability of the person concerned to carry out normal day-to-day activities only if it affects one of the following:

(a) mobility;
(b) manual dexterity;
(c) physical co-ordination;
(d) continence;
(e) ability to lift, carry or otherwise move everyday objects;
(f) speech, hearing or eyesight;
(g) memory or ability to concentrate, learn or understand; or
(h) perception of the risk of physical danger.

6A. (1) Subject to sub-paragraph (2), a person who has cancer, HIV infection or multiple sclerosis is to be deemed to have a disability, and hence to be a disabled person.

(2) Regulations may provide for sub-paragraph (1) not to apply in the case of a person who has cancer if he has cancer of a prescribed description.

(3) A description of cancer prescribed under sub-paragraph (2) may (in particular) be framed by reference to consequences for a person of his having it.

NOTE:

1. Schedule 1 also states that mental impairment includes an impairment resulting from mental illness only if the illness is clinically well recognised. It defines long-term as being at least a year (with special provisions for some circumstances). It also provides for regulations to further define the meaning of disability. (See further K. Monaghan, *Blackstone's Guide to the Disability Dicrimination Legislation*, Oxford: OUP, 2005; B. Doyle, *Disability Discrimination Law and Practice* (5th edn) British: Jordans, 2005).
2. Paragraph 6A was inserted by the Disability Discrimination Act 1995.

QUESTIONS:

1. Could a patient with a learning difficulty who was denied an operation because his quality of life was too poor claim that the decision was based on factors that are prohibited by the Disability Discrimination Act 1995?
2. In the light of the case law that has now been considered, do you think that it would be possible to persuade a court to strike down a decision by a health authority not to fund either of the following procedures?
     (i) heart operations for those who refuse to give up smoking;
     (ii) kidney transplants for those over 70 years of age.

(vi) EU Law, Principles of Free Movement and NHS Resource Allocation Decisions

NHS resource allocation decisions must today be seen in the context of European Union law. Article 35 of the Charter of Fundamental Rights and Freedoms, noted above at p.9, provides that there is a right of access to preventative health care. This is still, however, "soft law" and thus, while influential, is not binding on Member States, although it is included in the proposed new EU constitution. Individual litigants may seek to use their free movement rights under EU law, specifically Article 49 of the EC Treaty, as a means of accessing treatment services in another EU Member State and then claiming the cost of reimbursement of that service from their home Member State. Article 49 of the EC Treaty provides that:

"Restrictions on the freedom to provide services within the Community shall be prohibited in respect of nationals of Member States who are established in a State of the Community other than that of the person for whom the services are intended."

Article 50 further provides that:

"Services shall be considered to be 'services' within the meaning of this Treaty where they are normally provided for remuneration . . .
    'Services' shall in particular include . . . (d) activities of the professions."

Medical treatment has long been regarded by the ECJ as a "service". *Luisi and Carbone v Ministero del Tesoro* (joined cases 286/82 and 26/83) [1984] ECR 377. Litigants have sought to combine their claims under Article 49 with Article 22 of Regulation 1408/71 which concerns social security provisions. EU citizens can seek to access medical treatment in another Member State using these provisions. But the rights to obtain reciprocal treatment are not unlimited. Although Article 22 provides states with the discretion to determine whether treatment is reimbursed, it also provides that this authorisation:

"may not be refused where the treatment in question is among the benefits provided for by the legislation of the Member State on whose territory the person concerned resides and where he cannot be given such treatment within the time normally necessary for obtaining the treatment in question in the Member State of residence, taking account of his current state of health and the probable course of the disease".

(See further T.K. Hervey and J.V. McHale, *Health Law and the European Union*, Cambridge: CUP, 2004, Chapter 4; P. Cabral, "The Internal Market and the Right to Cross-Border Medical Care" (2004) 29(5) *European Law Review* 673; P. Koutrakos, "Healthcare as an Economic Service under EC Law" in M. Dougan and E. Spaventa (eds), *Social Welfare and EU Law*, Oxford: Hart Publishing, 2005).

Over a number of years the refusal to reimburse costs of treatment in another Member State by a national social insurance system has been subject to challenge. The ECJ has used free movement principles to interpret the principles concerning social security. So, for example, a refusal by the Luxembourg social insurance scheme to refund the cost of orthodontic treatment in Germany was held to be contrary to free movement principles and not objectively justifiable (*Kohll* (Case C158-96) [1998] ECR I-1931).

These issues were further explored in *Geraet Smits and Peerbooms* (Case C-157/99, judgment of July 21, 2001). The ECJ held that medical services fell within the EC Treaty and this applied to hospital services which had been paid for. Furthermore although it was the case that Member States could impose limitations on the ability of individuals to access services in another Member State these must be proportionate and supported by reference to the overriding public interest. In

Müller-Fauré the ECJ went further and drew a distinction between extra-mural and hospital care (*Müller-Fauré and van Riet*, Case C-385/99 [2003] ECR I-6447). In the former it was suggested that there was no requirement for a prior authorisation rule, whereas in the situation of hospital services it was suggested that without such authorisation there was the danger that this would fundamentally undermine the planning of hospital services. However, the ECJ indicated that it would be prepared to scrutinise what amounted to "undue delay" and this must relate to the condition of the individual patient rather than to the fact that there were waiting lists. This line of cases was subsequently confirmed by the ECJ in *Inizan* (*Inizan v Caisse primaire d'assurance maladie des Hauts de Seine*, Case C-56/01 [2003] ECR I). The ECJ has also confirmed that Member States can impose some restrictions in situations in which, without those restrictions, there may be consequent instability to the operation of national health systems. Without this, there is a risk that resource allocation decisions regarding health care made by individual Member States would be undermined. Restrictions such as waiting lists may be justifiable as long as these restrictions were necessary and proportionate (*Müller-Fauré and Van Riet, op. cit.* at 4509).

Uncertainties, however, remained as to the extent to which these principles were applicable in the context of a state national health service, such as the UK NHS. In the *Müller-Fauré* case, the UK Government sought to argue that this did not apply to the UK as the NHS did not provide services for "remuneration" and in addition to sanction reimbursement in this way would be economically damaging for the UK. This was rejected by the ECJ in that case. However, until 2003 no case had arisen before the courts where this was directly an issue. This has now changed, with the decision in the *Watts* case discussed below.

Secretary of State for Health v R on the application of Yvonne Watts Case C1-239/2003 [2004] EWCA Civ 166

Mrs Watts, a 72-year-old woman, had osteoarthritis in both her hips. She sought a hip-replacement operation. There was a standard NHS waiting time of 12 months. Her case was not classed as urgent and she was placed on the waiting list. Mrs Watts was in severe pain. Her daughter contacted Bedford PCT to authorise her treatment overseas under the E112 scheme, which is based upon Article 22 of Regulation 1408/71. The trust refused, taking the approach that Mrs Watts's case was not specifically supported by the consultant orthopaedic surgeon, was one which was routine in nature and that the standard 12-month waiting time for such an operation did not amount to "undue delay". Judicial review proceedings were launched and in the meantime, in January 2003, Mrs Watts travelled to Lille in France. She was seen by a surgeon and an anaethetist. The latter was concerned by the fact that she was suffering continuing weight loss and that as a result there could come a point where she was not suitable for surgery. The orthopaedic surgeon in France recommended as a result that the operation should be undertaken by March 2003.

In preliminary judicial review proceedings later in January 2003, it was recommended that she should be re-examined. As a consequence she was seen again by a consultant in the UK. Her condition was consequently reclassified as "soon" which meant that she should be seen within three to four months. The NHS operation date was therefore April or May 2003. Mrs Watts did not wish to delay her operation further. She returned to France where the operation was performed in Abbeyville on March 7, 2003. She then claimed the cost of the operation from Bedford PCT: some £3,900. The trust rejected her claim.

At first instance Mumby J. held that the principles of free movement were applicable in relation to the NHS, although on the facts of the case Mrs Watts failed as it was held that she had not been subject to "undue delay". Mumby J. suggested that "considerations of a purely economic nature" do not justify restrictions being imposed upon a patient from receiving treatment in a different Member State earlier than the time stated in the NHS waiting lists. Thus, in the case of Mrs Watts, 12 months would be an undue delay. However, on the facts of the case, because Mrs Watts had been reclassified due to the deterioration of her condition and the operation was now to be undertaken within three to four months, Mumby J. held that she herself had not suffered undue delay and thus her claim failed. This is something which may be criticised, given that Mrs Watts had suffered delay between October 2002 and February 2003, but this was not taken into account in ascertaining whether she had suffered undue delay.

The case was then referred to the Court of Appeal. May L.J. delivering the opinion of the Court of Appeal in this case held that it was clear that in *Müller-Fauré* the ECJ had rejected the argument that Article 49 did not apply to a national health service such as the UK NHS. When interpreting Article 22 of Regulation 1408/71 and ascertaining what time would be normally necessary for this treatment, this was something to be ascertainable by reference to clinical judgment and the impact of the delay upon this patient. It was not something which would require consideration of what otherwise were normal waiting times. Nonetheless, the Court of Appeal were also of the view that, given the wide-ranging policy implications of this issue, there was need for a preliminary ruling from the ECJ to clarify the application of both Article 49 and of Article 22 of Regulation 1408/71 in this case. The Court of Appeal therefore made a reference to the ECJ.

EUROPEAN COURT OF JUSTICE
"The first four questions

"80 By the first four questions, which it is convenient to consider together, the referring court asks essentially whether and in what circumstances an NHS patient is entitled under Article 49 EC to receive hospital treatment in another Member State at the expense of that national service . . .

85 In order to answer those questions, it is first necessary to determine whether Article 49 EC applies to facts such as those in issue in the main proceedings . . .

89 The fact that reimbursement of the hospital treatment in question is subsequently sought from a national health service such as that in question in the main proceedings does not mean that the rules on the freedom to provide services guaranteed by the Treaty do not apply (see to that effect *Smits and Peerbooms*, paragraph 55, and *Müller-Fauré and van Riet*, paragraph 39). It has already been held that a supply of medical services does not cease to be a supply of services within the meaning of Article 49 EC on the ground that the patient, after paying the foreign supplier for the treatment received, subsequently seeks the reimbursement of that treatment from a national health service (see *Müller-Fauré and van Riet*, paragraph 103).

90 It must therefore be found that Article 49 EC applies where a patient such as Mrs Watts receives medical services in a hospital environment for consideration in a Member State other than her State of residence, regardless of the way in which the national system with which that person is registered and from which reimbursement of the cost of those services is subsequently sought operates.

91 It must therefore be found that a situation such as that which gave rise to the dispute in the main proceedings, in which a person whose state of health necessitates hospital treatment goes to another Member State and there receives the treatment in question for consideration, falls within the scope of the Treaty provisions on the freedom to provide services, there being no need in the present case to determine whether the provision of hospital treatment in the context of a national health service such as the NHS is in itself a service within the meaning of those provisions.

92 Whilst it is not in dispute that Community law does not detract from the power of the Member States to organise their social security systems, and that, in the absence of harmonisation at Community level, it is for the legislation of each Member State to determine the conditions in which social security benefits are granted, when exercising that power Member States must comply with Community law, in particular the provisions on the freedom to provide services (see, inter alia, *Smits and Peerbooms*, paragraphs 44 to 46; *Müller-Fauré and van Riet*, paragraph 100; and *Inizan*, paragraph 17). Those provisions prohibit the Member States from introducing or maintaining unjustified restrictions on the exercise of that freedom in the healthcare sector.

93 It is therefore necessary to ascertain whether there is any such restriction in a case such as that in issue in the main proceedings.

94 It should be noted in this connection that according to well-established case-law, Article 49 EC precludes the application of any national rules which have the effect of making the provision of services between Member States more difficult than the provision of services purely within a Member State (Case C-381/93 *Commission* v *France* [1994] ECR I-5145, paragraph 17; *Kohll*, paragraph 33; and *Smits and Peerbooms*, paragraph 61).

95 In the present case it is clear from the decision of 20 February 2004 of the referring court and from the order for reference, in particular the third question, that, whilst NHS patients are free to go to a hospital in another Member State, they cannot have treatment in such an establishment at the NHS's expense without prior authorisation.

96 It is true, as the United Kingdom, Spanish, Maltese and Finnish Governments and Ireland submit, that an NHS patient cannot choose when and where the hospital treatment required by his state of health will be provided under the NHS. However, it is not in dispute that the corollary of the Secretary of State's duty under sections 1 and 3 of the NHS Act (see paragraph 6 of the present judgment) is the right to obtain treatment available under the NHS free of charge in NHS hospitals without having to seek prior authorisation.

97 Thus whereas according to the decision of 20 February 2004 and the order for reference prior authorisation is a prerequisite for the NHS to assume the costs of hospital treatment available in another Member State, the receipt of free NHS treatment does not depend on such authorisation, only the means of receiving that treatment being subject to a prior decision by the national competent authorities.

98 It must therefore be found that the system of prior authorisation referred to in paragraph 95 of the present judgment deters, or even prevents, the patients concerned from applying to providers of hospital services established in another Member State and constitutes, both for those patients and for service providers, an obstacle to the freedom to provide services (see to that effect *Smits and Peerbooms*, paragraph 69, and *Müller-Fauré and van Riet*, paragraph 44).

99 That conclusion is not undermined by the fact, referred to in Question 1(b), that the NHS is not obliged to authorise and assume the cost of hospital treatment provided to patients in private non-NHS hospitals in England and Wales.

100 In applying the case-law set out in paragraph 94 of the present judgment, the conditions for the NHS's assuming the cost of hospital treatment to be obtained in another

Member State should not be compared to the situation in national law of hospital treatment received by patients in private local hospitals. On the contrary, the comparison should be made with the conditions in which the NHS provides such services in its hospitals.

101 Since the existence of a restriction on the freedom to provide services has been established, and before ruling on whether an NHS patient is entitled under Article 49 EC to receive hospital medical treatment in another Member State at the expense of the national service concerned without such a restriction, it is necessary to examine whether that restriction can be objectively justified.

102 As was done in a large number of the observations submitted to the Court, it is necessary to recall in this regard the overriding considerations capable of justifying obstacles to the freedom to provide hospital medical services.

103 The Court has already held that it is possible for the risk of seriously undermining the financial balance of a social security system to constitute an overriding reason in the general interest capable of justifying an obstacle to the freedom to provide services (*Kohll*, paragraph 41; *Smits and Peerbooms*, paragraph 72; and *Müller-Fauré and van Riet*, paragraph 73).

104 The Court has likewise acknowledged that the objective of maintaining a balanced medical and hospital service open to all may also fall within the derogations on grounds of public health under Article 46 EC in so far as it contributes to the attainment of a high level of health protection (*Kohll*, paragraph 50; *Smits and Peerbooms*, paragraph 73; and *Müller-Fauré and van Riet*, paragraph 67).

105 The Court has also held that Article 46 EC permits Member States to restrict the freedom to provide medical and hospital services in so far as the maintenance of treatment capacity or medical competence on national territory is essential for the public health, and even the survival, of the population (*Kohll*, paragraph 51; *Smits and Peerbooms*, paragraph 74; and *Müller-Fauré and van Riet*, paragraph 67).

106 It is therefore necessary to determine whether the restriction at issue can in fact be justified in the light of such overriding reasons, and if such is the case to make sure, in accordance with settled case-law, that it does not exceed what is objectively necessary for that purpose and that the same result cannot be achieved by less restrictive rules (see *Smits and Peerbooms*, paragraph 75, and the case-law cited).

107 As regards hospital medical services, the Court has already made the following observations in paragraphs 76 to 80 of *Smits and Peerbooms*.

108 It is well known that the number of hospitals, their geographical distribution, the way in which they are organised and the facilities with which they are provided, and even the nature of the medical services which they are able to offer, are all matters for which planning, generally designed to satisfy various needs, must be possible.

109 For one thing, such planning seeks to ensure that there is sufficient and permanent access to a balanced range of high-quality hospital treatment in the State concerned. For another thing, it assists in meeting a desire to control costs and to prevent, as far as possible, any wastage of financial, technical and human resources. Such wastage would be all the more damaging because it is generally recognised that the hospital care sector generates considerable costs and must satisfy increasing needs, while the financial resources which may be made available for healthcare are not unlimited, whatever the mode of funding applied.

110 From those two points of view, the requirement that the assumption of costs by the national system of hospital treatment provided in another Member State be subject to prior authorisation appears to be a measure which is both necessary and reasonable.

111 As regards specifically the Netherlands system of health insurance, in issue in the cases giving rise to the *Smits and Peerbooms* judgment, the Court acknowledged in paragraph 81 thereof that, if patients were at liberty, regardless of the circumstances, to use the services of hospitals with which their health insurance fund had no agreement, whether those hospitals were situated in the Netherlands or in another Member State, all the planning which goes into the system of agreements in an effort to guarantee a rationalised,

stable, balanced and accessible supply of hospital services would be jeopardised at a stroke.

112 Those observations, expressed in relation to a system of social security based on a system of agreements between the public health insurance funds and the suppliers of hospital services, which permit, in the name of overriding planning objectives, limits to be placed on the right of patients to resort at the expense of the national system with which they are registered to hospital treatment not provided by that system, may be adopted in respect of a national health system such as the NHS.

113 In the light of the foregoing, and in answer to Question 1(c), Community law, in particular Article 49 EC, does not therefore preclude the right of a patient to receive hospital treatment in another Member State at the expense of the system with which he is registered from being subject to prior authorisation.

114 Nevertheless, the conditions attached to the grant of such authorisation must be justified in the light of the overriding considerations mentioned above and must satisfy the requirement of proportionality referred to in paragraph 106 of the present judgment (see to that effect *Smits and Peerbooms*, paragraph 82, and *Müller-Fauré and van Riet*, paragraph 83).

115 It is settled case-law that a system of prior authorisation cannot legitimise discretionary decisions taken by the national authorities which are liable to negate the effectiveness of provisions of Community law, in particular those relating to a fundamental freedom such as that at issue in the main proceedings (see *Smits and Peerbooms*, paragraph 90, and *Müller-Fauré and van Riet*, paragraph 84, and the case-law cited in those paragraphs).

116 Thus, in order for a system of prior authorisation to be justified even though it derogates from a fundamental freedom of that kind, it must in any event be based on objective, non-discriminatory criteria which are known in advance, in such a way as to circumscribe the exercise of the national authorities' discretion, so that it is not used arbitrarily. Such a system must furthermore be based on a procedural system which is easily accessible and capable of ensuring that a request for authorisation will be dealt with objectively and impartially within a reasonable time and refusals to grant authorisation must also be capable of being challenged in judicial or quasi-judicial proceedings (*Smits and Peerbooms*, paragraph 90, and *Müller-Fauré and van Riet*, paragraph 85).

117 To that end, refusals to grant authorisation, or the advice on which such refusals may be based, must refer to the specific provisions on which they are based and be properly reasoned in accordance with them. Likewise, courts or tribunals hearing actions against such refusals must be able, if they consider it necessary for the purpose of carrying out the review which it is incumbent on them to make, to seek the advice of wholly objective and impartial independent experts (see to that effect *Inizan*, paragraph 49).

118 In relation to the dispute in the main proceedings, it should be noted, as does the Commission, that the regulations on the NHS do not set out the criteria for the grant or refusal of the prior authorisation necessary for reimbursement of the cost of hospital treatment provided in another Member State, and therefore do not circumscribe the exercise of the national competent authorities' discretionary power in that context. The lack of a legal framework in that regard also makes it difficult to exercise judicial review of decisions refusing to grant authorisation.

119 It should be noted with regard to the circumstances and factors referred to in the third and fourth questions that, given the findings set out in paragraphs 59 to 77 of the present judgment, a refusal to grant prior authorisation cannot be based merely on the existence of waiting lists enabling the supply of hospital care to be planned and managed on the basis of predetermined general clinical priorities, without carrying out in the individual case in question an objective medical assessment of the patient's medical condition, the history and probable course of his illness, the degree of pain he is in and/or the nature of his disability at the time when the request for authorisation was made or renewed.

120 It follows that, where the delay arising from such waiting lists appears to exceed in the individual case concerned an acceptable period having regard to an objective medical

assessment of all the circumstances of the situation and the clinical needs of the person concerned, the competent institution may not refuse the authorisation sought on the grounds of the existence of those waiting lists, an alleged distortion of the normal order of priorities linked to the relative urgency of the cases to be treated, the fact that the hospital treatment provided under the national system in question is free of charge, the duty to make available specific funds to reimburse the cost of treatment provided in another Member State and/or a comparison between the cost of that treatment and that of equivalent treatment in the competent Member State.

121 As regards the factors mentioned in Questions 1(a) and 3(d), to the findings set out in paragraphs 59 to 77 of the present judgment should be added the point that, although Community law does not detract from the power of the Member States to organise their social security systems and decide the level of resources to be allocated to their operation, the achievement of the fundamental freedoms guaranteed by the Treaty nevertheless inevitably requires Member States to make adjustments to those systems. It does not follow that this undermines their sovereign powers in the field (see *Müller-Fauré and van Riet*, paragraphs 100 and 102).

122 As Advocate General Geelhoed observed in point 88 of his Opinion, it must therefore be found that the need for the Member States to reconcile the principles and broad scheme of their healthcare system with the requirements arising from the Community freedoms entails, on the same basis as the requirements arising from Article 22 of Regulation No 1408/71, a duty on the part of the competent authorities of a national health service, such as the NHS, to provide mechanisms for the reimbursement of the cost of hospital treatment in another Member State to patients to whom that service is not able to provide the treatment required within a medically acceptable period as defined in paragraph 68 of the present judgment . . .

The seventh question

144 By this question, the referring court asks whether Article 49 EC and Article 22 of Regulation No 1408/71 must be interpreted as imposing an obligation on Member States to fund hospital treatment in other Member States without reference to budgetary constraints and, if so, whether such an obligation is compatible with Article 152(5) EC.

145 It should, first of all, be noted in this regard that, as is clear from the findings set out in relation to the answers to the first six questions, the requirements arising from Article 49 EC and Article 22 of Regulation No 1408/71 are not to be interpreted as imposing on the Member States an obligation to reimburse the cost of hospital treatment in other Member States without reference to any budgetary consideration but, on the contrary, are based on the need to balance the objective of the free movement of patients against overriding national objectives relating to management of the available hospital capacity, control of health expenditure and financial balance of social security systems.

146 Next, it should be noted that, according to Article 152(5) EC, Community action in the field of public health is to fully respect the responsibilities of the Member States for the organisation and delivery of health services and medical care.

147 That provision does not, however, exclude the possibility that the Member States may be required under other Treaty provisions, such as Article 49 EC, or Community measures adopted on the basis of other Treaty provisions, such as Article 22 of Regulation No 1408/71, to make adjustments to their national systems of social security. It does not follow that this undermines their sovereign powers in the field (see to that effect *Müller-Fauré and van Riet*, paragraph 102, and, by analogy, Case C-376/98 *Germany v Parliament and Council* [2000] ECR I-8419, paragraph 78).

148 In the light of the foregoing, the answer to the seventh question must be that the obligation of the competent institution under both Article 22 of Regulation No 1408/71 and Article 49 EC to authorise a patient registered with a national health service to obtain, at that institution's expense, hospital treatment in another Member State where the waiting time exceeds an acceptable period having regard to an objective medical assessment of the

condition and clinical requirements of the patient concerned does not contravene Article 152(5) EC.

NOTES:

1. The impact of the ECJ decision is that NHS bodies will need to establish a system of prior authorisation which is non-discriminatory, easily accessible, capable of being dealt with impartially and in a reasonable time, caapable of being challenged by judicial review. In addition it will be necessary to provide a clear reasoned explanation to the patient and there will also need to be a mechanism for the reimbursement of costs.

2. In the future, following the ECJ judgment, authorisation for going abroad can only be refused if the waiting list time is medically acceptable and the PCT will need to consider the medical condition, the history/probable course of their illness, the degree of pain they are in and the nature of the disability at the time authorisation has been sought.

3. Concerns were expressed prior to the ruling by the ECJ as to the implications of the decision. In the Court of Appeal in *Watts*, May L.J. expressed his concerns regarding this prospect stating that:

> "We consider that the court should proceed on the assumption that, if the NHS were required to pay the cost of some of its patients having treatment abroad earlier than they would receive it in the United Kingdom, this would require additional resources. In theory this could only be avoided if those who did not have treatment abroad received their treatment at a later time than they otherwise would or if the NHS ceased to provide some treatment that it currently does." (para 122).

4. One possibility is that this case may have the effect that attempting to bypass NHS waiting lists will become a "middle-class" solution, as potential litigants will require sufficient capital upfront to pay for the treatment before they can seek reimbursement.

5. One interesting related development prior to this case and following *Geraets Smits* was that it led to the UK Government commissioning delivery of health care service through arrangements with other Member States (see further Department of Health, *Treating More Patients and Extending Choice: Overseas Treatment for NHS patients*, London: Department of Health, 2002).

6. Newdick has questioned the role of EU law in such cases. He asks, "Should EU law seek to undermine national policy by encouraging 'low priority' patients to obtain treatment abroad. Given the need to make difficult choices, surely national governments are best placed to determine national health priorities?" (C. Newdick, *Who Shall we Treat?* (2nd edn), Oxford: Oxford University Press, 2005, p.244).

7. Montgomery, discussing the earlier ECJ judgment in *Müller-Fauré* in a comment now applicable to the ECJ in *Watts*, states that, "From an English perspective what this does is to disregard the fact that choice of provider is not a component of all health systems. To create such a choice is to alter fundamentally the nature of the relationship between the patient

and the health service." (See further J. Montgomery, "The Impact of EU Law on English Healthcare Law" in M. Dougan and E. Spaventa (eds), *Social Welfare and EU Law*, Oxford: Hart Publishing, 2005, p.153).

8. The prospect of patients being treated abroad may bypass waiting lists but may give rise to difficulties if something goes wrong in the context of the treatment provided in the other jurisdiction. Litigants may face enhanced difficulties in litigating where negligence arises in treatment provided in another jurisdiction. Recently there have been moves to try to co-ordinate standards in health care across the EU (see discussion in J.V. McHale and M. Bell, "Traveller's Checks" (2002) *Health Service Journal* 39).

9. One incidental effect of the judgment is almost certain to be the enhanced importance of information regarding treatment becoming available on a cross-EU basis. The European Commission has been invited to develop a framework for health information in Europe (*Follow-up to the High Level Reflection Process on Patient Mobility and Healthcare Developments in the EU*, Com (2004) 301 final and see discussion in A. Kaczorowska, "A Review of the Creation by the European Court of Justice of the Right to Effective and Speedy Medical Treatment and its Outcomes" (2006) 12 *European Law Journal* 345 at p.365). The Commission are concerned to identify differing information needs of patients, policy-makers and professionals and the provision of such information. In addition they are to take into account the work undertaken by relevant organisations in healthcare matters. Finally they are to share information relating to health care supply and available treatments; the procedures for obtaining care and its costs and in addition its quality.

10. In November 2005 the High Level Group on health service and medical care published a document regarding their work in 2005 ("Work of the High Level Group on Health Services and Medical Care in 2005", HLG/2005/16). These include suggested guidelines for commissioners of health care involved in cross-border purchasing and provision of health care. They include suggestions such as malpractice liability in relation to the patient and provider should be determined by reference to private international law or any public law. In addition health care commissioners should ensure that liability insurance is in place for all health services provided under the contract. Further provisions relate to pricing and sharing of information. At the time of writing, proposals on health legislation regarding patient mobility are expected to be published in September 2006. It is suggested that this may include information for patients, reimbursement and also the transparency of regulation.

QUESTIONS:

1. Can free movement principles be used to circumvent restrictions at Member State level upon the provision of certain controversial health services? See further Chapter 11.

2. How realistic is the fear that the *Watts* judgment may result in a flood of patients seeking treatment abroad? At first instance in *Watts*, Mumby J.

commented that, "There is nothing to suggest that huge numbers of NHS patients will, if only given the chance, be clamouring to travel, whether by Eurostar or cross-channel ferry, for treatment in another member state" at para.148. Is he right?

3. Will the ECJ judgment fundamentally undermine the moral choices which form part of resource allocation decisions made by clinicians and undermine the prospect for ethical decision making? (See further the discussion in J. Montgomery, "Law and the Demoralisation of Medicine" (2006) 26(2) *Legal Studies* 185 at p.198).

4. Is this a further step towards a "European health law"? (See further discussion in T.K. Hervey and J.V. McHale, *Health Law and the EU*, Cambridge: CUP, 2004, Chapters 1 and 10 and T.K. Hervey and J.V. McHale, "Law, Health and the European Union" [2005] 25(2) *Legal Studies* 228.)

(vii) Actions for Compensation

A second way in which patients may seek to enforce their rights to services is to sue for compensation when they have been injured by the failure to provide proper care. The leading case in this area is a House of Lords decision in relation to the responsibilities of local authorities in relation to child protection and education. The facts of the cases are not relevant here, but Lord Browne-Wilkinson explained the principles of law, which would also be applied in the health context, in the extracts set out below.

X v Bedfordshire C.C.; M. v Newham L.B.C.; E. v Dorset C.C. [1995] 3 All E.R. 353

LORD BROWNE-WILKINSON
" . . . I am seeking to set out a logical approach to the wide ranging arguments advanced . . .

(a) BREACH OF STATUTORY DUTY SIMPLICITER

This category comprises those cases where the statement of claim alleges simply (i) the statutory duty, (ii) a breach of that duty, causing (iii) damage to the plaintiff. The cause of action depends neither on proof of any breach of the plaintiffs' common law rights nor on any allegation of carelessness by the defendant.

The principles applicable in determining whether such statutory cause of action exists are now well established, although the application of those principles in any particular case remains difficult. The basic proposition is that in the ordinary case a breach of statutory duty does not, by itself, give rise to any private law cause of action. However, a private law cause of action will arise if it can be shown, as a matter of construction of the statute, that the statutory duty was imposed for the protection of a limited class of the public and that Parliament intended to confer on members of that class a private right of action for breach of the duty. There is no general rule by reference to which it can be decided whether a statute does create such a right of action but there are a number of indicators. If the statute provides no other remedy for its breach and the Parliamentary intention to protect a limited class is shown, that indicates that there may be a private right of action since otherwise there is no method of securing the protection the statute was intended to confer.

If the statute does provide some other means of enforcing the duty that will normally indicate that the statutory right was intended to be enforceable by those means and not by private right of action: see *Cutler v. Wandsworth Stadium Ltd* [1949] 1 All E.R. 544 and *Lonrho Ltd v. Shell Petroleum Co. Ltd* [1981] 2 All E.R. 456. However, the mere existence of some other statutory remedy is not necessarily decisive. It is still possible to show that on the true construction of the statute the protected class was intended by Parliament to have a private remedy . . .

Although the question is one of statutory construction and therefore each case turns on the provisions in the relevant statute, it is significant that your Lordships were not referred to any case where it had been held that statutory provisions establishing a regulatory system or a scheme of social welfare for the benefit of the public at large had been held to give rise to a private right of action for damages for breach of statutory duty. Although regulatory or welfare legislation affecting a particular area of activity does in fact provide protection to those individuals particularly affected by that activity, the legislation is not to be treated as being passed for the benefit of those individuals but for the benefit of society in general. Thus legislation regulating the conduct of betting or prisons did not give rise to a statutory right of action vested in those adversely affected by the breach of the statutory provisions, i.e. bookmakers and prisoners: see *Cutler v. Wandsworth Stadium Ltd* and *Hague v. Deputy Governor of Parkhurst Prison* [1991] 3 All E.R. 733. The cases where a private right of action for breach of statutory duty have been held to arise are all cases in which the statutory duty has been very limited and specific as opposed to general administrative functions imposed on public bodies and involving the exercise of administrative discretions . . .

(c) THE COMMON LAW DUTY OF CARE

In this category, the claim alleges either that a statutory duty gives rise to a common law duty of care owed to the plaintiff by the defendant to do or refrain from doing a particular act, or (more often) that in the course of carrying out a statutory duty the defendant has brought about such a relationship between himself and the plaintiff as to give rise to a duty of care at common law . . .

(1) Co-existence of statutory duty and common law duty of care

It is clear that a common law duty of care may arise in the performance of statutory functions. But a broad distinction has to be drawn between: (a) cases in which it is alleged that the authority owes a duty of care in the manner in which it exercises a statutory discretion; and (b) cases in which a duty of care is alleged to arise from the manner in which the statutory duty has been implemented in practice.

An example of (a) in the educational field would be a decision whether or not to exercise a statutory discretion to close a school, being a decision which necessarily involves the exercise of a discretion. An example of (b) would be the actual running of a school pursuant to the statutory duties. In such latter case a common law duty to take reasonable care for the physical safety of the pupils will arise. The fact that the school is being run pursuant to a statutory duty is not necessarily incompatible with a common law duty of care arising from the proximate relationship between a school and the pupils it has agreed to accept. The distinction is between (a) taking care in exercising a statutory discretion whether or not to do an act and (b) having decided to do that act, taking care in the manner in which you do it.

(2) Discretion, justiciability and the policy/operational test

(a) Discretion

Most statutes which impose a statutory duty on local authorities confer on the authority a discretion as to the extent to which, and the methods by which, such statutory duty is to be performed. It is clear both in principle and from the decided cases that the local authority cannot be liable in damages for doing that which Parliament has authorised. Therefore if the decisions complained of fall within the ambit of such statutory discretion they cannot be actionable in common law. However, if the decision complained of is so unreasonable that it falls outside the ambit of the discretion conferred upon the local authority, there is no priori reason for excluding all common law liability . . . "

Lord Browne-Wilkinson reviewed the authorities and concluded:

" . . . From these authorities I understand the applicable principles to be as follows. Where Parliament has conferred a statutory discretion on a public authority, it is for that authority, not for the courts, to exercise the discretion: nothing which the authority does within the ambit of the discretion can be actionable at common law. If the decision complained of falls outside the statutory discretion, it can (but not necessarily will) give rise to common law liability. However, if the factors relevant to the exercise of the discretion include matters of policy, the court cannot adjudicate on such policy matters and therefore cannot reach the conclusion that the decision was outside the ambit of the statutory discretion. Therefore a common law duty of care in relation to the taking of decisions involving policy matters cannot exist.

(3) If justiciable, the ordinary principles of negligence apply. If the plaintiff's complaint alleges carelessness, not in the taking of a discretionary decision to do some act, but in the practical manner in which that act has been performed (e.g. the running of a school) the question whether or not there is a common law duty of care falls to be decided by applying the usual principles, i.e. those laid down in *Caparo Industries plc v. Dickman* [1990] 1 All E.R. 568 at 573–574. Was the damage to the plaintiff reasonably foreseeable? Was the relationship between the plaintiff and the defendant sufficiently proximate? Is it just and reasonable to impose a duty of care? See *Rowling v. Takaro Properties Ltd* and *Hill v. Chief Constable of West Yorkshire* [1988] 2 All E.R. 238.

However, the question whether there is such a common law duty and if so its ambit, must be profoundly influenced by the statutory framework within which the acts complained of were done. The position is directly analogous to that in which a tortious duty of care owed by A to C can arise out of the performance by A of a contract between A and B. In *Henderson v. Merrett Syndicates Ltd* [1994] 3 All E.R. 506 your Lordships held that A (the managing agent) who had contracted with B (the members' agent) to render certain services for C (the names) came under a duty of care to C in the performance of those services. It is clear that any tortious duty of care owed to C in those circumstances could not be inconsistent with the duty owed in contract by A to B. Similarly, in my judgment, a common law duty of care cannot be imposed on a statutory duty if the observance of such common law duty of care would be inconsistent with, or have a tendency to discourage, the due performance by the local authority of its statutory duties."

These principles of law provide severe restrictions upon the scope of actions for breach of statutory duty in the context of welfare agencies. The House of Lords noted that there was no case in which it had been held that the general duties of such agencies gave rise to rights of individual enforcement. The fullest discussion of the scope for bringing an action for breach of statutory duty in respect of the NHS Act 1977 is to be found in the following case.

Re HIV Haemophiliac Litigation, The Independent, October 2, 1990

The issue arose in the course of a preliminary action for discovery of documents in relation to a case in which haemophiliacs who had contracted HIV from contaminated blood transfusions were suing the Department of Health. The plaintiffs based their claim on two alternative arguments. The first was that the Department was in breach of its statutory duties, and that this gave them a right to compensation. The second was that the general law of negligence permitted them to sue. One of the grounds on which the Department resisted disclosure was that the actions were doomed to failure because the law did not permit such actions to be brought.

In relation to the suggestion that an action might be brought on the basis of breach of statutory duty, Gibson L.J. found that:

> "the duties imposed by the 1977 Act [the plaintiffs relied upon subsections 1, 3(1), and 5(2), see above] . . . do not clearly demonstrate the intention of Parliament to impose a duty which is to be enforced by civil action."

Both the other judges in the Court of Appeal expressed their agreement with this assessment. However, in part the Court of Appeal's view was based on their belief that the law of negligence already provided a remedy. If that were not the case they would have found the argument from breach of statutory duty more plausible. This implies that where a negligence action would not be permitted, then an action for breach of statutory duty might have more chance of success. Although Gibson L.J. doubted whether an action would be brought for breach of statutory duty, he did not regard the matter as so far beyond argument that the claim should be struck out. His comment does not, therefore preclude such a claim in the future.

In relation to possibility of liability in negligence, the Department of Health argued against the imposition of a duty of care on the Secretary of State for decisions about the way in which blood products were provided and screened to avoid contamination in the following terms:

> "The nature of the relationship between the plaintiffs [i.e. patients] and the Central Defendants [i.e. the Department of Health, the Welsh Office, the Committee of Safety of Medicines and the licensing authority under the Medicines Act 1968] is such that it is not just and reasonable to impose a duty of care directly enforceable by any member of the public. His protection should be by an action for negligence, if there is a breach of duty, against those who directly provide care and treatment to him; and the remedy for imperfections in the performance of duties imposed by the 1977 Act should be within Parliament or through the ballot box. All the alleged duties upon which the plaintiffs rely contain elements of discretion."

Gibson L.J. accepted that the court hearing the full case might reach the conclusion that a duty of care existed, and concentrated on the problems of proving that there has been a breach of that duty:

> "It is obvious that it would be rare for a case on negligence to be proved having regard to the nature of the duties under the 1977 Act, and to the fact that, in the law of negligence, it is difficult to prove a negligent breach of duty when the party charged with negligence is required to exercise discretion and to form judgments upon the allocation of public resources. That, however, is not sufficient, in my judgment, to make it clear, for the purposes of these proceedings, that there can in law be no claim in negligence."

NOTE:

1. There is a specific statutory duty under s.117(2) of the Mental Health Act 1983 which provides that there is a duty on the NHS body to provide "after-care services for any person to whom this section applies" until they are "satisfied that the person concerned is no longer in need of such services". In practice, however, the courts have indicated that this is not intended to give rise to liability in negligence (see further *Clunis v Camden and Islington HA* [1998] QB 978, and for confirmation that the obligation under this section is not absolute but is subject to budgetary demands see *R(K) v Camden and Islington HA* [2001] EWCA Civ 240).

QUESTIONS:

1. Today resource allocation is delegated to NHS bodies by the Secretary of State. However, the Secretary of State would almost certainly not regard himself as answerable in Parliament for the purchasing decisions of individual authorities. If the ballot box and Parliament can no longer provide a method to challenge decisions, how does this affect the arguments put forward by the Department of Health?
2. Do you think it would be easier to bring an action against a PCT alleging that they negligently purchased services than against the Department in this case?

Even if it is possible to show that a negligence action may be brought, because there is a duty of care, many NHS cases will come up against the argument that they concern non-justiciable policy decisions. In the *Bedfordshire* case, the House of Lords pointed out that there was no rigid distinction between policy and operational decisions, but held that the policy aspects of decisions would only be justiciable in the most extreme case. Resource allocation decisions will almost always involve policy considerations, and will therefore be unlikely to give rise to compensation unless they are wholly unreasonable, in the public law sense discussed above. Clinical decisions are also regarded by the courts as largely non-justiciable, to be judged against reasonable professional practice rather than the views of the judge (see the test established in *Bolam v Friern HMC* [1957] 2 All E.R. 118, discussed in Chapter 3). The prospects for success of compensation claims for failure to provide services will therefore depend on how the courts define what constitutes a policy consideration in the context of health care. This issue was examined in a case concerning the mass vaccination of young children.

D.H.S.S. v Kinnear (1984) 134 N.L.J. 886

The plaintiffs alleged that they had suffered injuries as a result of receiving whooping cough vaccine. They sued the Department of Health and Social Security, alleging that they had been negligent in promoting, on expert advice, a widespread policy of vaccination. The Department of Health applied to have the writ against them struck out as disclosing no cause of action. They accepted that there was sufficient proximity between the plaintiff and the Department to raise a duty of care in negligence; note that this concession was not made in the later *HIV Haemophiliac* case, above. They also accepted that the damage caused was of a kind that was foreseeable. However, they argued that the action could not succeed because it challenged a decision that was within the limits of a bona fide exercise of discretion under their statutory powers. Stuart Smith J. considered that he should strike out the application so far as it related to policy decisions, but that he should not prevent the challenges to operational matters going ahead. Thus, in relation to one plaintiff, he said:

STUART SMITH J.
" . . . Her case is that, between the first and second vaccination, she suffered from a respiratory disease; that, although the plaintiff's mother told the doctor administering the vaccination this, he nevertheless administered the dose. The gravamen of the case against the D.H.S.S. is that, by the circulars which they issued to Health Authorities and general practitioners, they advised how and in what circumstances the treatment should be administered, but that this advice was misleading and negligent because it did not indicate that a respiratory disease was a contra indication for vaccination. Mr. Prynne submits that, in giving advice on these matters, the D.H.S.S. were acting in the operational sphere and were no longer protected by the limits of discretion. His particular complaint was that, while in the earlier editions (i.e. those of 1963 and 1968) of the D.H.S.S. document entitled 'Active Immunisation against Infectious Disease' it was stated that 'no prophylactic should be given routinely to the individual in poor health or one suffering from intercurrent illness', this warning was omitted from the editions current at the time of Naomi Finn's vaccination . . .
   In my view, [the circulars] clearly give advice on procedure of vaccination, dealing amongst other things with the time when it should take place, how the vaccine should be stored, what to do in the event of adverse reactions, and what matters contra indicate its use. To my mind, it is at least arguable, in giving such advice, that the D.H.S.S. had entered the operational area."

The judge's understanding of the distinction between policy and operational issues can perhaps best be seen by looking at those allegations which he struck out. These were that the DHSS:

- failed to heed early enough or in time the numerous published articles indicating that neurological damage was a side effect of the pertussis vaccine;
- failed to take any or sufficient heed of the investigation and report of the Medical Research Council carried out between 1952 and 1957;
- failed to carry out, or initiate the carrying out of, any adequate investigation following the report of the Medical Research Council;
- failed to give any or adequate warnings to the parents and/or guardians of infants being vaccinated with pertussis vaccine of the risks to which they were exposing the child under their care;
- failed to have any or any sufficient regard to the opinion of the parents of children to be vaccinated which expressed itself by the refusal of parents to permit their child to be immunised with pertussis vaccine from 1972 onwards;
- failed to give any or any proper regard to the risk to which the individual child was being exposed;
- failed to give any or any proper regard to the possibility that either the pertussis vaccine should be discontinued in general use; alternatively, that it should be used on a selective basis, to be administered to children at special risk;

- failed to require the manufacturers of the vaccine, the second defendants, to make proper investigations as to the extent of the risk of side effects;
- failed to require the manufacturers to investigate the risk of side effects and to investigate what contra indications there were in its use;
- if the vaccine was supplied in multi-dose use, failed to require the manufacturers to supply it in single dose units.

Stuart Smith J. regarded the following two allegations as more difficult to classify. These were that the DHSS had:

"failed to publish guidelines as a consequence of the failure to carry out research as aforesaid, in any sufficient detail before 1974 (it not being thereby admitted that these were either adequate or exhaustive)";

and that the Department had:

"failed to give any proper supervision and/or instructions to the servants or agents of the third defendants, who were the local Health Authority, in the respects as set forth hereinafter under the particulars of negligence of the third defendants."

Considering them Stuart Smith J. said:

"If and insofar as those sub-paragraphs allege that the D.H.S.S. gave misleading and negligent advice to the second defendants and their employees [i.e. the health authority and medical staff] as to the contra indications to the administration of the vaccine, they are relevant and should not be struck out. Otherwise, they are not relevant and do not disclose a cause of action."

NOTES:

1. The European Commission of Human Rights has rejected the suggestion that there was insufficient respect for the right to life of recipients of the vaccine in the decision to promote mass vaccination.
2. The Vaccine Damage Payments Act 1979 was passed to provide compensation for the victims of the whooping cough vaccine, on a no-fault basis; see Chapter 3 below.
3. In subsequent litigation for negligence against the health authority and doctors who were responsible for vaccinating Kinnear, the case was dismissed; see *Kinnear v DHSS* [1989] Fam. Law 146. A plaintiff in a similar position failed to prove a causal link between the vaccine and the injuries suffered in *Loveday v Renton* [1990] 1 Med. L.R. 117.

SELECT BIBLIOGRAPHY

M. Brazier, "Rights and Health Care" in R. Blackburn (ed.), *Rights of Citizenship*, London: Mansell, 1993.

M. Brazier and J. Harris, "Public Health and Private Lives" (1996) 4 *Medical Law Review* 165.

L. Gostin, *Public Health Law: Power, Duty and Restraint*, Los Angeles: University of California Press, 2000.

C. Ham and S. Pickard, *Tragic Choices in Health Care: The Case of Child B*, London: King's Fund, 1998.

J. Jacob, "Lawyers Go to Hospital" [1991] *Public Law* 255.

D. Longley, *Health Care Constitutions*, London: Cavendish Publishing, 1996.

D. Longley, *Public Law and Health Service Accountability*, Buckingham: Open University Press, 1993.

R. Martyn and L. Johnson, *Law and the Public Dimension of Health*, London: Cavendish, 2001.

J. Montgomery, "Recognising a Right to Health" in R. Beddard and D. Hill (eds), *Economic, Social and Cultural Rights: Progress and Achievement*, Basingstoke: Macmillan, 1992.

J. Montgomery, "Rights to Health and Health Care" in A. Coote (ed.), *The Welfare of Citizens: Developing New Social Rights*, London: Institute for Public Policy Research, 1992.

C. Newdick, "The Organisation of the NHS" in A. Grubb (ed.), *Principles of Medical Law* (2nd edn), Oxford: Oxford University Press, 2004.

C. Newdick, "The Positive Side of Healthcare Rights" in S. McLean (ed.), *First Do No Harm: Law, Ethics and Healthcare*, Aldershot: Ashgate, 2006.

C. Newdick, *Who Shall We Treat?* (2nd edn), Oxford: Oxford University Press, 2005.

Nuffield Council on Bioethics, *Public Health: Ethical Issues*, London: Nuffield Council on Bioethics, 2006.

P. Old and J. Montgomery, "Law, Coercion and the Public Health" (1992) 304 *BMJ* 891.

K. Syrett, "Impotence or Importance? Judicial Review in an Era of Explicit NHS Rationing" (2004) 67 *Modern Law Review* 289.

2

HEALTH CARE ETHICS

1. INTRODUCTION

This chapter provides a brief overview of a number of issues in health care ethics. There are three main reasons for considering ethics separately from and prior to examining the law in depth. First, many of the legal principles considered later purport to be based on ethical foundations. For example, it is often claimed that our law on consent to treatment is based on the moral principle of respect for autonomy. Similarly, the existence of law and regulation governing reproductive technologies and abortion seems to be based partly on moral views about these matters—such as concerns about giving adequate respect to the human foetus, and about the welfare and rights of children. Secondly, on many of the topics we will consider, law is insufficiently developed to provide detailed guidance for health care professionals. This is true, for instance, of the equitable remedy of breach of confidentiality. Thirdly, there may be ethical reasons for not attempting to extend law into certain areas: for example, some would argue that this is the case with attempts to regulate the behaviour of pregnant women, which may be better influenced by education and provision of information, rather than law.

Chapter 2 starts by considering two foundational issues about the status of ethics and its relationship with law. To what extent is morality "relative" or "subjective"? And to what extent should law seek to enforce morality?

We then consider a number of different general ethical theories. These include consequentialism, deontology, the "four principles" approach to biomedical ethics, virtue ethics and feminist ethics (all terms which will be explained later). Each of these competing approaches to ethics offers a different framework within which to think about moral issues, including importantly, ethical questions about what the content of health care law should be.

Finally, we look at some more practical issues in health care ethics: in particular, the concepts of autonomy and consent, and ethical issues at the beginning and end of life (including questions about assisted reproduction and euthanasia).

2. Is Morality "Relative"?

The extracts in this section are about moral relativism: more specifically, *meta-ethical* relativism, which says that there is no single true or most justified morality and that moral propositions are true (in so far as they are true at all) just in virtue of their conforming to the relevant society's attitudes or conventions. This view should be carefully distinguished from (and is definitely not entailed by) *descriptive* relativism, the view that there is, as a matter of fact, extensive cross-cultural and inter-personal diversity in moral attitudes and opinions.

According to moral relativism, then, all moral statements are "relative", dependent for their truth upon the society in which they are uttered. So a particular practice—for example, treating women as slaves—may be "wrong-for-us" (e.g. the population of England) because we generally have negative attitudes to such behaviour, but could at the same time be "right-for-them" (some other society) because, in "their" society, enslaving women is generally approved of. As we will see, this relativist view is more believable for some examples (e.g. norms of politeness) than for others (e.g. cases where serious issues of justice are involved).

David Wong, "Relativism" in Peter Singer (ed.), *A Companion to Ethics*, Oxford: Basil Blackwell, 1993, pp.442–447

i INTRODUCTION

Moral relativism is a common response to the deepest conflicts we face in our ethical lives. Some of these conflicts are quite public and political, such as the apparently intractable disagreement in the United States over the moral and legal permissibility of abortion. Other conflicts inviting the relativistic response are of a less dramatic but more recurrent nature. This author's experience as a first generation Chinese American exemplifies a kind of conflict that others have faced: that between inherited values and the values of the adopted country. As a child I had to grapple with the differences between what was expected of me as a good Chinese son and what was expected of my non-Chinese friends. Not only did they seem bound by duties that were much less rigorous in the matter of honouring parents and upholding the family name, but I was supposed to feel superior to them because of that. It added to my confusion that I sometimes felt envy at their freedom.

Moral relativism, as a common response to such conflicts, often takes the form of a denial that any single moral code has universal validity, and an assertion that moral truth and justifiability, if there are any such things, are in some way relative to factors that are culturally and historically contingent. This doctrine is *meta-ethical* relativism, because it is about the relativity of moral truth and justifiability. Another kind of moral relativism, also a common response to deep moral conflict, is a doctrine about how one ought to act toward those who accept values very different from one's own. This *normative* moral relativism holds that it is wrong to pass judgement on others who have substantially different values, or to try to make them conform to one's values, for the reason that their values are as valid as one's own. Another common response to deep moral conflict, however, contradicts moral relativism in its two major forms. It is the universalist or absolutist position that both sides of a moral conflict cannot be equally right, that there can be only one truth about the matter at issue. This position is so common, in fact, that William James was led to call us "absolutists by instinct". The term "universalism" will be used hereafter, because "absolutism" is used not only to refer to the denial of moral relativism, but also to the view that some moral rules or duties are absolutely without exception.

ii META-ETHICAL RELATIVISM

The debate between moral relativism and universalism accounts for a significant proportion of philosophical reflection in ethics. In ancient Greece at least some of the "Sophists" defended a version of moral relativism, which Plato attempted to refute. Plato attributes to the first great Sophist, Protagoras, the argument that human custom determines what is fine and ugly, just and unjust. Whatever is communally judged to be the case, the argument goes, actually comes to be the case (*Theaetetus*, 172 AB; it is unclear, however, whether the real Protagoras actually argued in this manner). Now the Greeks, through trade, travel, and war, were fully aware of wide variation in customs, and so the argument concludes with the relativity of morality. The question with this argument, however, is whether we can accept that custom determines in a strong sense what is fine and ugly, just and unjust. It may influence what people *think* is fine and just. But it is quite another thing for custom to determine what *is* fine and just. Customs sometimes change under the pressure of moral criticism, and the argument seems to rely on a premise that contradicts this phenomenon.

Another kind of argument given for relativism is premised on the view that the customary ethical beliefs in any given society are functionally necessary for that society. Therefore, the argument concludes, the beliefs are true for that society, but not necessarily in another. The sixteenth-century essayist, Michel de Montaigne, sometimes makes this argument ("Of custom, and not easily changing an accepted law", in Montaigne, 1595), but it has had its greatest acceptance among anthropologists of the twentieth century who emphasize the importance of studying societies as organic wholes of which the parts are functionally interdependent. The problem with the functional argument, however, is that moral beliefs are not justified merely on the grounds that they are necessary for a society's existence in anything like its present form. Even if a society's institutions and practices crucially depend on the acceptance of certain beliefs, the justifiability of those beliefs depends on the moral acceptability of the institutions and practices. To show that certain beliefs are necessary for maintaining a fascist society, for instance, is not to justify those beliefs.

Despite the weaknesses of these arguments for moral relativism, the doctrine has always had its adherents. Its continuing strength has always been rooted in the impressiveness of the variation in ethical belief to be found across human history and culture. In an ancient text (*Dissoi Logoi* or the *Contrasting Arguments*) associated with the Sophists, it is pointed out that for the Lacedaemonians, it was fine for girls to exercise without tunics, and for children not to learn music and letters, while for the Ionians, these things were foul. Montaigne assembled a catalogue of exotic customs, such as male prostitution, cannibalism, women warriors, killing one's father at a certain age as an act of piety, and recites from the Greek historian Herodotus the experiment of Darius. Darius asked Greeks how much they would have to be paid before they would eat the bodies of their deceased fathers. They replied that no sum of money could get them to do such a thing. He then asked certain Indians who customarily ate the bodies of their deceased fathers what they would have to be paid to burn the bodies of their fathers. Amidst loud exclamations, they bade him not to speak of such a thing (Montaigne's "Of custom" (1595), and Herodotus, *Persian Wars*, Book III, 38).

But while many have been moved by such examples to adopt moral relativism, the argument from diversity does not support relativism in any simple or direct way. As the Socrates of Plato's dialogues observed, we have reason to listen only to the wise among us (*Crito*, 44CD). The simple fact of diversity in belief is no disproof of the possibility that there are some beliefs better to have than the others because they are truer or more justified than the rest. If half the world still believed that the sun, the moon, and the planets revolved around the earth, that would be no disproof of the possibility of a unique truth about the structure of the universe. Diversity in belief, after all, may result from varying degrees of wisdom. Or it may be that different people have their own limited perspectives of the truth, each perspective being distorted in its own way.

It is sometimes thought that the extent and depth of disagreement in ethics indicates that moral judgements are simply not judgements about facts, that they assert nothing true or false about the world but straightforwardly express our own subjective reactions to certain facts and happenings, whether these be collective or individual reactions. A more complicated view is that moral judgements purport to report objective matters of fact, but that there are no such matters of fact. The success of modern science in producing a remarkable degree of convergence of belief about the basic structure of the physical world probably reinforces these varieties of scepticism about the objectivity of moral judgements. It is hard to deny that there is a significant difference in the degree of convergence of belief in ethics and in science. Yet there are possible explanations for that difference that are compatible with claiming that moral judgements are ultimately about facts in the world. These explanations might stress, for instance, the special difficulties of acquiring knowledge of subjects that pertain to moral knowledge.

An understanding of human nature and human affairs is necessary for formulating an adequate moral code. The enormously difficult and complex task of reaching such an understanding could be a major reason for differences in moral belief. Furthermore, the subject matter of ethics is such that people have the most intense practical interest in what is established as truth about it, and surely this interest engenders the passions that becloud judgement. Universalists could point out that many apparently exotic moral beliefs presuppose certain religious and metaphysical beliefs, and that these beliefs, rather than any difference in fundamental values, explain the apparent strangeness. Consider, for example, the way our view of Darius' Indians would change if we were to attribute to them the belief that eating the body of one's deceased father is a way of preserving his spiritual substance. Finally, some of the striking differences in moral belief across societies may not be rooted in differences in fundamental values but in the fact that these values may have to be implemented in different ways given the varying conditions that obtain across societies. If one society contains many more women than men (say, because men are killing each other off in warfare), it would not be surprising if polygamy were acceptable there, while in another society, where the proportion of women to men is equal, monogamy is required. The difference in accepted marriage practice may come down to that difference in the proportion of women to men, and not to any difference in basic moral ideals of marriage or of the proper relationships between women and men.

The mere existence of deep and wide disagreements in ethics, therefore, does not disprove the possibility that moral judgements can be objectively correct or incorrect judgements about certain facts. Moral relativists must chart some other more complicated path from the existence of diversity to the conclusion that there is no single true or most justified morality. I believe that the relativist argument is best conducted by pointing to particular kinds of differences in moral belief, and then by claiming that these particular differences are best explained under a theory that denies the existence of a single true morality. This would involve denying that the various ways that universalists have for explaining ethical disagreement are sufficient for explaining the particular differences in question.

One apparent and striking ethical difference that would be a good candidate for this sort of argument concerns the emphasis on individual rights that is embodied in the ethical culture of the modern West and that seems absent in traditional cultures found in Africa, China, Japan and India. The content of duties in such traditional cultures instead seems organized around the central value of a common good that consists in a certain sort of ideal community life, a network of relationships, partially defined by social roles, again, ideal, but imperfectly embodied in ongoing existing practice. The ideal for members is composed of various virtues that enable them, given their place in the network of relationships, to promote and sustain the common good.

Confucianism, for instance, makes the family and kinship groups the models for the common good, with larger social and political units taking on certain of their features, such as benevolent leaders who rule with the aim of cultivating virtue and harmony among their subjects. Moralities centred on such values would seem to differ significantly from ones centred on individual rights to liberty and to other goods, if the basis for attributing such rights to persons does not seem to lie in their conduciveness to the common good of a shared life, but in a moral worth independently attributed to each individual. By contrast a theme frequently found in ethics of the common good is that individuals find their realization as human beings in promoting and sustaining the common good. Given this assumption of the fundamental harmony between the highest good of individuals and the common good, one might expect the constraints on freedom to have greater scope and to be more pervasive when compared to a tradition in which no such fundamental harmony between individual and common goods is assumed.

If the contrast between the two types of morality is real, it raises the question of whether one or the other type is truer or more justified than the other. The argument for a relativistic answer may start with the claim that each type focuses on a good that may reasonably occupy the centre of an ethical ideal for human life. On the one hand, there is the good of belonging to and contributing to a community; on the other, there is the good of respect for the individual apart from any potential contribution to community. It would be surprising, the argument goes, if there were just one justifiable way of setting a priority with respect to the two goods. It should not be surprising, after all, if the range of human goods is simply too rich and diverse to be reconciled in just a single moral ideal.

Such an argument could be supplemented by an explanation of why human beings have such a thing as a morality. Morality serves two universal human needs. It regulates conflicts of interest between people, and it regulates conflicts of interest within the individual born of different desires and drives that cannot all be satisfied at the same time. Ways of dealing with those two kinds of conflict develop in anything recognizable as human society. To the extent that these ways crystallize in the form of rules for conduct and ideals for persons, we have the core of a morality. Now in order to perform its practical functions adequately, it may be that a morality will have to possess certain general features. A relatively enduring and stable system for the resolution of conflict between people, for instance, will not permit the torture of persons at whim.

But given this picture of the origin and functions of morality, it would not be surprising if significantly different moralities were to perform the practical functions equally well, at least according to standards of performance that were common to these moralities. Moralities, on this picture, are social creations that evolve to meet certain needs. The needs place conditions on what could be an adequate morality, and if human nature has a definite structure, one would expect further constraining conditions on an adequate morality to derive from our nature. But the complexity of our nature makes it possible for us to prize a variety of goods and to order them in different ways, and this opens the way for a substantial relativism to be true.

The picture sketched above has the advantage of leaving it open as to how strong a version of relativism is true. That is, it holds that there is no single true morality, yet does not deny that some moralities might be false and inadequate for the functions they all must perform. Almost all polemics against moral relativism are directed at its most extreme versions: those holding that all moralities are equally true (or equally false, or equally lacking in cognitive content). Yet a substantial relativism need not be so radically egalitarian. Besides ruling out moralities that would aggravate interpersonal conflict, such as the one described above, relativists could also recognize that adequate moralities must promote the production of persons capable of considering the interests of others. Such persons would need to have received a certain kind of nurturing and care from others. An adequate morality, then, whatever else its content, would have to prescribe and promote the sorts of upbringing and continuing interpersonal relationships that produce such persons.

A moral relativism that would allow for this kind of constraint on what could be a true or most justified morality might not fit the stereotype of relativism, but would be a reasonable position to hold. One reason, in fact, that not much progress has been made in the debate between relativists and universalists is that each side has tended to define the opponent as holding the most extreme position possible. While this makes the debating easier, it does nothing to shed light on the vast middle ground where the truth indeed may lie.

Bernard Williams, "Interlude: Relativism" in *Morality: An Introduction to Ethics*, Cambridge: Cambridge University Press, 1972, pp.34–35

Let us at this stage of the argument about subjectivism take a brief rest and look round a special view or assemblage of views which has been built on the site of moral disagreements between societies. This is *relativism*, the anthropologist's heresy, possibly the most absurd view to have been advanced even in moral philosophy. In its vulgar and unregenerate form (which I shall consider, since it is both the most distinctive and the most influential form) it consists of three propositions: that "right" means (can only be coherently understood as meaning) "right for a given society"; that "right for a given society" is to be understood in a functionalist sense; and that (therefore) it is wrong for people in one society to condemn, interfere with, etc., the values of another society. A view with a long history, it was popular with some liberal colonialists, notably British administrators in places (such as West Africa) in which white men held no land. In that historical role, it may have had, like some other muddled doctrines, a beneficent influence, though modern African nationalism may well deplore its tribalist and conservative implications.

　　Whatever its results, the view is clearly inconsistent, since it makes a claim in its third proposition, about what is right and wrong in one's dealings with other societies, which uses a *nonrelative* sense of "right" not allowed for in the first proposition. The claim that human sacrifice, for instance, was "right for" the Ashanti comes to be taken as saying that human sacrifice was right among the Ashanti, and this in turn as saying that human sacrifice among the Ashanti was right; i.e., we had no business to interfere with it. But this last is certainly not the sort of claim allowed by the theory. The most the theory can allow is the claim that it was right for (i.e., functionally valuable for) our society not to interfere with Ashanti society, and, first, this is certainly not all that was meant, and, second, is very dubiously true.

QUESTIONS:

1. Can you think of any moral principles or values which ought to be *universally* accepted and applied (i.e. ought to be accepted and applied by all cultures at all times)?
2. Do you agree with Williams (above) that moral relativism is an "absurd" view? If so, why? If not, why not?

3. LAW AND MORALITY

The extracts in this section discuss the relationship between law and morality and, in particular, the question of to what extent the law should be used as a means of enforcing morality. In legal and political philosophy, a great deal of the debate about law and morality has been based around Mill's *Harm Principle*, according to which law may only be used to restrict people's freedom if their behaviour would be harmful to innocent third parties. Take, for example, smoking. According to the *Harm Principle*, while it may be acceptable to ban smoking in certain enclosed public places, because of the risk of fire and the dangers of passive smoking, any attempt to prohibit it altogether in order to protect the health of smokers would be quite wrong because it is not the law's business to save us from ourselves, only to stop us from hurting others. Much of the "law and morality" debate, then, is concerned with the question: is Mill's *Harm Principle* true, or are there other legitimate reasons to restrict people's liberty? Also, what counts as harm for the purposes of the *Harm Principle*? For example, does disgusting and offending people count as harming them and would disgusting and offensive behaviour be permitted under the *Harm Principle*?

Finally, it is worth noting (as Dworkin does) that even banning something because it is harmful has a moral dimension, because it seems to be underpinned by a commitment to the *ethical* view that harming innocent third parties is wrong and ought to be prevented.

John Stuart Mill, *On Liberty*, London: Watts & Co., 1929 (first published 1859), pp.11–15

The object of this Essay is to assert one very simple principle, as entitled to govern absolutely the dealings of society with the individual in the way of compulsion and control, whether the means used be physical force in the form of legal penalties, or the moral coercion of public opinion. That principle is, that the sole end for which mankind are warranted, individually or collectively, in interfering with the liberty of action of any of their number, is self-protection. That the only purpose for which power can be rightfully exercised over any member of a civilized community, against his will, is to prevent harm to others. His own good, either physical or moral, is not a sufficient warrant. He cannot rightfully be compelled to do or forbear because it will be better for him to do so, because it will make him happier, because, in the opinions of others, to do so would be wise, or even right. There are good reasons for remonstrating with him, or reasoning with him, or persuading him, or entreating him, but not for compelling him, or visiting him with any evil, in case he do otherwise. To justify that, the conduct from which it is desired to deter him must be calculated to produce evil to some one else. The only part of the conduct of any one, for which he is amenable to society, is that which concerns others. In the part which merely concerns himself, his independence is, of right, absolute. Over himself, over his own body and mind, the individual is sovereign.

It is, perhaps, hardly necessary to say that this doctrine is meant to apply only to human beings in the maturity of their faculties. We are not speaking of children, or of young persons below the age which the law may fix as that of manhood or womanhood. Those who are still in a state to require being taken care of by others, must be protected against their own actions as well as against external injury...

... It is proper to state that I forego any advantage which could be derived to my argument from the idea of abstract right, as a thing independent of utility. I regard utility as the ultimate appeal on all ethical questions; but it must be utility in the largest sense, grounded on the permanent interests of man as a progressive being. Those interests, I contend, authorize the subjection of individual spontaneity to external control, only in respect to those actions of each, which concern the interest of other people. If any one does an act hurtful to others, there is a prima facie case for punishing him, by law, or, where legal penalties are not safely applicable, by general disapprobation. There are also many positive acts for the benefit of others, which he may rightfully be compelled to perform; such as, to give evidence in a court of justice; to bear his fair share in the common defence, or in any other joint work necessary to the interest of the society of which he enjoys the protection; and to perform certain acts of individual beneficence, such as saving a fellow creature's life, or interposing to protect the defenceless against ill usage, things which whenever it is obviously a man's duty to do, he may rightfully be made responsible to society for not doing. A person may cause evil to others not only by his actions but by his inaction...

... But there is a sphere of action in which society as distinguished from the individual, has, if any, only an indirect interest—comprehending all that portion of a person's life and conduct which affects only himself, or, if it also affects others, only with their free, voluntary, and undeceived consent and participation. When I say only himself, I mean directly, and in the first instance, for whatever affects himself, may affect others through himself; and the objection which may be grounded on this contingency, will receive consideration in the sequel. This, then, is the appropriate region of human liberty. It comprises, first, the inward domain of consciousness; demanding liberty of conscience, in the most comprehensive sense; liberty of thought and feeling; absolute freedom of opinion and sentiment on all subjects, practical or speculative, scientific, moral, or theological. The liberty of expressing and publishing opinions may seem to fall under a different principle, since it belongs to that part of the conduct of an individual which concerns other people; but, being almost of as much importance as the liberty of thought itself, and resting in great part on the same reasons, is practically inseparable from it. Secondly, the principle requires liberty of tastes and pursuits; of framing the plan of our life to suit our own character; of doing as we like, subject to such consequence as may follow—without impediment from our fellow-creatures, so long as what we do does not harm them, even though they should think our conduct foolish, perverse, or wrong. Thirdly, from this liberty of each individual, follows the liberty, within the same limits, of combination among individuals; freedom to unite, for any purpose not involving harm to others: the persons combining being supposed to be of full age, and not forced or deceived.

No society in which these liberties are not, on the whole, respected, is free, whatever may be its form of government; and none is completely free in which they do not exist absolute and unqualified. The only freedom which deserves the name, is that of pursuing our own good in our own way, so long as we do not attempt to deprive others of theirs, or impede their efforts to obtain it. Each is the proper guardian of his own health, whether bodily, or mental and spiritual. Mankind are greater gainers by suffering each other to live as seems good to themselves, than by compelling each to live as seems good to the rest.

Gerald Dworkin, "Introduction" to Gerald Dworkin (ed.), *Morality, Harm, and the Law*, Boulder: Westview Press, 1994, pp.1–4

But knowing what the law says does not answer the question of whether the state has a *right* to enforce a standard of morality...

. . . One or another claim about the legitimacy or illegitimacy of the enforcement of morality has attracted much attention in the philosophy of law and political philosophy ever since the publication in 1859 of John Stuart Mill's classical defense of liberalism, *On Liberty*. One finds such statements in the philosophical literature as the following:

The only purpose for which power can be rightfully exercised over any member of a civilized society against his will is to prevent harm to others. (J. S. Mill, *On Liberty*, (London: n.p., 1859), Chapter 1).

It is not the duty of the law to concern itself with immorality as such. It should confine itself to those activities which offend against public order and decency or expose the ordinary citizen to what is offensive or injurious. (Report of the Committee on Homosexual Offenses and Prostitution (CMD 247), 1957 (Wolfenden Report) (New York: Stein and Day, 1963), para 257).

The harm principle is a principle of toleration. The common way of stating its point is to regard it as excluding consideration of private morality from politics. It restrains both individuals and the state from coercing people . . . on the ground that those activities are morally either repugnant or desirable. (J. Raz, "Autonomy, Toleration, and the Harm Principle," in R. Gavison, *Issues in Contemporary Legal Philosophy* (Oxford: Clarendon Press, 1987) p. 327).

Is the fact that certain conduct is by common standards immoral sufficient to justify making that conduct punishable by law? Is it morally permissible to enforce morality as such? Ought immorality as such be a crime? . . . To this question John Stuart Mill gave an emphatic answer in his essay *On Liberty* one hundred years ago. (H. L. A. Hart, *Law, Liberty and Morality* (Stanford, Calif.: Stanford University Press, 1986)).

Much ink, and perhaps even some blood, has been spilled in debates concerning the views expressed in these propositions. But a clear formulation of the intuitive idea underlying these claims is not easy. As usually stated, either the claims fail to express any precise thesis, or the thesis expressed is so clearly false that it could not plausibly be defended.

To understand in an intuitive way what the controversy is about it is useful to set out specific laws that are favored or opposed by the contending parties. Consider the following legal restrictions that are very likely to be favored by all parties to the debate (category A):

Laws against murder
Laws against theft
Laws against income tax evasion
Laws against public sex
Laws against sexual abuse of children
Laws against perjury

The following are legal restrictions likely to be opposed by all parties to the debate (category B):

Laws forbidding members of racial minorities from living in geographical proximity to racial majorities
Laws regulating the type of music that people can listen to in their homes
Laws restricting the type of religion one may profess

Perhaps the most crucial category is of laws that are often favored by those wishing to enforce morality and rejected by their opponents. Examples include (category C):

Laws against the private consumption of pornography
Laws against consensual homosexual acts between adults
Laws forbidding defacement of the flag
Laws against bigamy
Laws forbidding the sale of bodily organs such as kidneys
Laws forbidding the use of racial or sexual epithets

Over some laws, even within each camp there will be variations of opinion as to their legitimacy. These laws will include various paternalistic laws (laws against suicide), laws where it is not clear if there is harm (laws forbidding brother–sister incest), laws that require forms of positive aid to others (good Samaritan laws), and so forth. Even within the category of laws favored by all, or the category of laws that is supposed to define the dispute (category C), there may be variations of opinion produced by something other than the question of the legitimacy of state power. For example, even someone who favors the enforcement of morality may think, like Devlin, that the costs of enforcing, say, laws about the consumption of pornography in the home may make it unwise to have such laws. The difference then could be expressed in terms of why one favors or opposes a given law. Is the objection to a particular law that it is merely unwise or that it violates some principled restriction on the powers of the state? The latter point is the one at issue, and I shall begin by supposing that those who oppose the enforcement of morality are prepared to produce a plausible principle that would justify passing the laws in category A and that would forbid passing the laws in category C.

However, it is not obvious how they will do this. Consider how opponents of the enforcement of morality might try to distinguish between the laws they defend and those they consider illegitimate. Suppose the thesis is stated as follows: The law ought not to enforce moral values. Then, since they believe that the law ought to prohibit murder and theft, they must claim that in doing so the law is not enforcing moral values. But if, say, murder is not forbidden because, at least in part, it is regarded as wrong or unjust or wicked, then what justifies its being made illegal?

One response is to assert that *another* reason can be used to justify such laws; one that does not rely on a moral judgment about the conduct in question. The most prominent candidate for such a reason is that the conduct is harmful to the interests of others. Murder and theft are legitimately made illegal because they are harmful, not because they are wrong.

If, however, one examines the concept of *harm* it is obvious that this notion is itself, directly or indirectly, linked to a judgment about the wrongness of the conduct in question. The most thoughtful and developed notion of harm, that of Joel Feinberg, explicitly distinguishes between a "non-normative sense of 'harm' as set-back to interest, and a normative sense of 'harm' as a *wrong*, that is a violation of a person's rights." It is only the latter sense of harm that figures in the harm principle as developed and clarified by Feinberg.

It is fairly clear that there is no way to avoid this interjection of normative content into the analysis of harm. For if the idea is that harm is merely a setback to interest, and if interest is purely a descriptive notion, such as that which a person has, or takes, an interest in, then those who propose to prohibit, say, the private consumption of pornography may, correctly, claim that they have an interest in not living in a society that allows such consumption and, hence, that such behavior harms them. For that matter, as Mill pointed out, do not the rejected applicants for a job have an interest that is damaged? The argument against criminalization in these cases must take the form of arguing that the mere setback to interests, or harm in its nonnormative sense, is not something that individuals ought to be protected against.

That individuals do not deserve such protection is a moral judgment, and when we decide the other way—to protect certain interests against invasion—that is equally a moral decision.

There is another line of argument in support of the same conclusion. Consider laws against theft. Are such laws justified by reference to a nonnormative sense of harm or are values built in here as well?

The concept of theft presupposes a definition of property. Protecting against theft assumes certain views about exclusive rights to ownership. In the absence, for example, of copyright and patent laws one cannot be accused of stealing someone's ideas. Recently, in the *Winans* decision the courts had to decide when a reporter's information could be considered to belong to the newspaper and hence be misappropriated. These definitions, and conceptions of ownership are conventions of the society and differ from one society to another. Although they are conventional they are not arbitrary and are defended or opposed in terms of moral and political (as well as economic) arguments. Consider, for example, recent legal discussion about whether living organisms may be patented. Laws against theft, therefore, presuppose prior moral determinations and are another way in which moral values are enforced.

So the nonenforcement thesis cannot be formulated in terms of a simple distinction between laws designed to prevent harm and those used to enforce moral values. Some other way of making the distinction must be found. At the very least one would want to distinguish between the moral judgments involved in making assertions about harm and other moral judgements.

One way to clarify the thesis is to distinguish between that part of morality having to do with rights and that having to do with ideals. This is the tack that Joel Feinberg takes in his book, *Harmless Wrongdoing*. For Feinberg the law should be limited to the protection of *particular values*, namely personal autonomy and respect for persons.

The harm principle mediated by the *Volenti* maxim protects personal autonomy and the moral value of "respect for persons" at is associated with it. . . . But there are other moral principles, other normative judgments, other ideals, other values—some well-founded, some not—that the harm principle does not enforce, since its aim is only to protect personal autonomy and protect human rights, not to vindicate correct evaluative judgments of any and all kinds. (J. Feinberg, *Harmless Wrongdoing* (New York: Oxford University Press, 1988) p. 12).

This, in essence, is Feinberg's solution to the definitional problem. Of course the law enforces morality: The interesting question is what parts of morality it ought to enforce. Now we have a substantive claim that needs be argued. Feinberg's solution is that the law should protect only rights. This contention, however, requires some justification. Why should we protect rights and not ideals? Why should we protect personal and not group autonomy? Why shouldn't a community be able to use the law to defend its moral ideals?

QUESTIONS:

1. Can you think of any activities which should be banned even though they are not harmful to anyone, apart from (possibly) to the people doing them?
2. Is Mill's *Harm Principle* consistent with his view (above) that people may be compelled to give evidence in court, or to contribute to "the common defence".
3. Are our legal prohibitions on theft and murder examples of society using law to enforce its moral values?

4. CONSEQUENTIALISM

Consequentialism (of which utilitarianism is a prominent example) is the view that the right action, the action that we are always morally obliged to do, is the one that will produce (overall, and in the long run) the most good. Most moral theories (including deontology and virtue ethics) take *some* account of consequences, but what marks a person out as a consequentialist is that, for him or her, *nothing but* consequences matter. Initially, this view of ethics might seem very attractive. After all, what could be better than producing the most good possible? However, as we shall see, there are problems. In particular, consequentialism seems to overlook a number of important non-consequence-based moral phenomena such as personal integrity, justice, keeping promises, obligations to family and friends, and even people's basic rights including the right to life. Also, it is a very demanding approach to ethics because it obliges us *always* to do as much good as we can, which does not allow much (if any) scope for personal projects.

David McNaughton, "Consequentialism" in E. Craig (ed.), *Routledge Encyclopedia of Philosophy*, London: Routledge, 1998; retrieved April 12, 2004, from http://www.rep.routledge.com/article/L013

Consequentialism assesses the rightness or wrongness of actions in terms of the value of their consequences. The most popular version is act-consequentialism, which states that, of all the actions open to the agent, the right one is that which produces the most good.

Act-consequentialism is at odds with ordinary moral thinking in three respects. First, it seems excessively onerous, because the requirement to make the world a better place would demand all our time and effort; second, it leaves no room for the special duties which we take ourselves to have to those close to us: family, friends and fellow citizens; and third, it might require us, on occasion, to do dreadful things in order to bring about a good result.

Consequentialists standardly try to bring their theory more into line with common thinking by amending the theory in one of two ways. Indirect act-consequentialism holds that we should not necessarily aim to do what is right. We may get closer to making the world the best possible place by behaviour which accords more with ordinary moral thought. Rule-consequentialism holds that an action is right if it is in accordance with a set of rules whose general acceptance would best promote the good. Such rules will bear a fairly close resemblance to the moral rules with which we now operate.

1 ACT-CONSEQUENTIALISM

Although the term "consequentialism" is a recent coinage—it appears to have first been used in its present sense by Anscombe (1958)—it refers to a type of theory which has a long history. Consequentialism builds on what may seem to be the merest truism, namely that morality is concerned with making the world a better place for all. Consequentialist considerations certainly figure importantly in issues of public policy. Penal, economic or educational programmes are standardly judged by the goodness or badness of their results.

All moral theories offer an account both of the right and of the good. They all tell us, that is, both what makes an action right or wrong, and what kinds of thing are good or valuable. It is characteristic of consequentialist theories to assess whether an action is right in terms of the amount of good it produces (see Section 4, below). Deontological ethical theories, by contrast, hold that the right is independent of the good: certain kinds of action are wrong, and others right, independently of the goodness or badness of their consequences.

Act-consequentialism, the simplest form of the theory, holds that the right action—the one you should do—is the one which would produce the greatest balance of good over bad consequences; that is, the one which would maximize the good. (Where two or more actions come out equal best, then it is right to do any one of them.) Which action is in fact the right one will depend on what account of the good any particular act-consequentialist theory offers.

A theory of the good is an account of those things which are intrinsically good, good in themselves, and not merely good as a means to something else which is good. A visit to the dentist is only extrinsically good, because it leads to healthy teeth and the avoidance of toothache, but it is not in itself a good thing; it is a necessary evil. By far the most popular and influential account of the good within the consequentialist camp is that offered by utilitarianism. On this view, usually known as hedonism or welfarism, the good is pleasure, happiness or wellbeing. The act-utilitarian holds, therefore, that the right action is the one which maximizes happiness.

  . . . Among the [other] things which have been held to be intrinsically good are knowledge, virtue, beauty, justice, and the flourishing of the environment as a whole. Many of these alternative accounts of the good are pluralist: that is, they claim that there are several different kinds of good thing which cannot all be brought under one head. Pluralist act-consequentialism faces a difficulty. In order to determine which of the possible actions is the right one, agents must be able to rank the outcomes of each action, from the worst to the best. But if there are several distinct values which cannot be reduced to a common measure, how can one kind of value be compared with another in order to produce a definitive ranking? This is the problem of incommensurability of value.

The term "consequentialism", though hallowed by frequent philosophical use, may be misleading since it might naturally be taken to imply that an action itself can have no intrinsic value; its value is all to be found in its consequences. Utilitarianism is indeed committed to this view—for what matters on the utilitarian account is not the nature of the act itself but the pleasure which it produces in anyone affected by it—but it is not an essential feature of consequentialism as such. Some consequentialists wish to leave room for the thought that certain kinds of action, such as lying, cheating, and killing the innocent, are intrinsically bad, while other kinds of act, such as generous, loyal, or just ones, are intrinsically good. Consequentialism can take such values into account in calculating which course of action produces the best results. In deciding whether one course of action is preferable to another, a consequentialist needs to know the total value that would be produced by taking each course of action, and that will include not only the value of the consequences but the value, if any, which attaches to the action itself.

Consequentialism is sometimes described as a teleological theory, because it conceives of a moral theory as setting a goal which we should strive to achieve. The goal which consequentialism sets is to bring about a world containing the greatest balance of good over bad. Such a classification risks confusion, however, since a virtue ethics, such as Aristotle's, is also usually classified as teleological, yet Aristotle's theory differs from consequentialism in at least two crucial respects. First, the good at which agents aim, on Aristotle's view (outlined in *Nicomachean Ethics*), is not the best state of the world, but the good life for humans; agents are to seek to realize distinctively human goods in their own lives. Second, Aristotle's theory, unlike consequentialism, does not define the right in terms of the good. On the contrary, a full understanding of the good life rests on a prior conception of the right, for an important part of the good life consists in acting rightly.

We also need to distinguish the kind of consequentialism with which we are here concerned from ethical egoism, which is sometimes classified as a consequentialist theory. Ethical egoism, which holds that the right action is the one which would best promote the agent's own interests, is structurally similar to consequentialism in that the right action is the one which maximizes a good, in this case, the agent's own good. What distinguishes egoism from the sort of consequentialism discussed here is that the latter is an impartial theory, giving equal weight to each person's good.

2 CRITICISMS OF ACT-CONSEQUENTIALISM

How should consequentialists set about deciding what to do? A natural answer is: by calculating, as best they may, what would produce the most good on any particular occasion when they are called upon to act. Of course, lack of time and knowledge limit what they can do by way of calculation, but they must do the best they can. So interpreted, however, act-consequentialism can be criticized for running counter to our intuitive moral convictions in a number of ways.

First, it seems excessively demanding; I shall only be acting rightly in so far as I maximize the good. Given all the bad things in the world, and the fact that few of us do much to improve them, it is clear that, in order to do what act-consequentialism requires, I would have to devote virtually all my energy and resources to making the world a better place. This would give me no time or money to pursue my own interests, or even to relax, except to refresh me ready to redouble my moral efforts on the morrow. The degree of self-sacrifice required would make the lives of the saints look self-indulgent. Ordinary morality is surely not as demanding as this; it gives us permission to pursue our own goals, provided that we are not in breach of any of our fundamental duties. Some have proposed, in order to meet this point, that the theory be modified so that an act is right if its consequences are good, or good enough, even if they are not the best. This suggestion has not been widely adopted, for it is usually held that a rational agent will always prefer the greater good to the less.

Second, act-consequentialism appears to leave no place for the duties we take ourselves to have to our family and friends. Such duties are often classified as agent-relative: each of us should help their own family and friends, so that the persons to whom the duties are owed vary from agent to agent. Act-consequentialism, however, is an agent-neutral moral theory; the goal at which we should aim does not depend on who the agent is. I should direct my efforts towards those for whom I can do the most good; their relationship to me is irrelevant. Even if act-consequentialism places special value on the cultivation of certain relationships, such as friendship, this will still not yield a duty of friendship, as traditionally understood. If friendship is a great good, then my duty as a consequentialist is to promote friendship in general between all persons; that will not necessarily require me to give special attention to my friends, as distinct from helping others to give special attention to their friends.

Third, if act-consequentialism is too demanding in one respect it seems too permissive in another. For it leaves no room for the thought, central to much ordinary moral thinking, that there are certain constraints on our action, certain kinds of act, such as cheating, torturing and killing, which we ought not to contemplate, even if acting in one of these forbidden ways would maximize the good. The end, as we often say, does not justify the means. Once again, constraints seem to be agent-relative. Each of us is required not to kill or torture the innocent ourselves even if, by doing so, we could prevent two such tortures or killings.

3 INDIRECT ACT-CONSEQUENTIALISM

Because it generates these counter-intuitive results, few consequentialists hold that agents should decide what to do by asking what will produce the best results. There are two theories which offer a less direct link between the overall goal of making things go as well as possible and how one should decide to act on any particular occasion. The first of these is known as indirect act-consequentialism. It retains the claim that the right action is the one with the best consequences, but denies that the virtuous agent need be guided directly by consequentialist thoughts when deciding how to act.

Indirect act-consequentialism builds on the thought that we do not necessarily hit the target if we aim directly at it. The gunner must make allowances for wind, gravity and poorly aligned sights; the moralist may have to direct our thoughts away from the goal if we are to achieve it. Act-consequentialism, on this view, tells us what the target is, but not how to hit it. It is not itself a good guide to action for a number of reasons: the calculations are tricky and time-consuming; we may be tempted to skew the results in our favour; doing the right action may require us to go against dispositions which are both deeply rooted and generally useful. So we may actually do better, in terms of achieving the goals which consequentialism sets us, if we do not aim to do what is right, but follow a few fairly simple moral rules of the traditional type, or encourage within ourselves the development of dispositions, such as kindness and loyalty, which will normally lead us to act in beneficial ways. In adopting such rules, or developing such dispositions, we know that we will sometimes act wrongly when we could, perhaps, have acted rightly. Yet we may still get closer, in the long run, to achieving the consequentialist goal than we would have if we had attempted to aim at it directly.

Some indirect act-consequentialists go further. Since we make better decisions if we eschew consequentialist calculations, it might be best if we rejected consequentialism. It seems possible that agents might behave worse, in consequentialist terms, if they were taught the truth of consequentialism than if they were brought up to believe some other moral theory. In which case consequentialists would do well to prevent its truth being generally known. Opponents see this position as incoherent. If the adoption of consequentialism demands its suppression then in what sense can we adopt it? How could a society be said to be governed by a moral code if no-one in that society believed it?

4 RULE-CONSEQUENTIALISM

The second alternative to direct act-consequentialism is rule-consequentialism, which offers a more substantive role for moral rules or principles. Individual acts are judged right or wrong by reference to the rules; the rules, but not the individual acts, are judged by the results of accepting them. The right action is, roughly, the one that is in conformity with a set of moral rules which, if generally accepted, would tend to produce better results than any other set of viable rules we might accept. Rule-consequentialism differs from indirect act-consequentialism in two ways. It maintains that each decision should be guided by thoughts about which action is the right one, and denies that the right action is necessarily the one with the best results. In deciding which rules to accept we should bear in mind that the rules need to be clear, reasonably simple and not too difficult to comply with, given human nature. If they meet these requirements, it is likely that such rules will not be too dissimilar to our present ones.

Rule-consequentialism might be a plausible moral theory, but should it properly be seen as a form of consequentialism? It apparently abandons a central tenet of consequentialism: the claim that our goal should be to maximize the good. The rule I should follow, on this view, is the one that would have better consequences, if generally accepted, than any other rule. If it is not, in fact, generally accepted, then in following it I may not get as close to maximizing the good as I would if I followed some other policy. For that reason, perhaps, act-consequentialism has remained most popular among defenders of the theory, despite its difficulties.

Bernard Williams, "A Critique of Utilitarianism" in J.J.C. Smart and Bernard Williams, *Utilitarianism: for and against*, Cambridge: Cambridge University Press, 1973, pp.97–100

(1) George, who has just taken his Ph.D. in chemistry, finds it extremely difficult to get a job. He is not very robust in health, which cuts down the number of jobs he might be able to do satisfactorily. His wife has to go out to work to keep them, which itself causes a great deal of strain, since they have small children and there are severe problems about looking after them. The results of all this, especially on the children, are damaging. An older chemist, who knows about this situation, says that he can get George a decently paid job in a certain laboratory, which pursues research into chemical and biological warfare. George says that he cannot accept this, since he is opposed to chemical and biological warfare. The older man replies that he is not too keen on it himself, come to that, but after all George's refusal is not going to make the job or the laboratory go away; what is more, he happens to know that if George refuses they will certainly go to a contemporary of George's who is not inhibited by any such scruples and is likely if appointed to push along the research with greater zeal than George would. Indeed, it is not merely concern for George and his family, but (to speak frankly and in confidence) some alarm about this other man's excess of zeal, which has led the older man to offer to use his influence to get George the job . . . George's wife, to whom he is deeply attached, has views (the details of which need not concern us) from which it follows that at least there is nothing particularly wrong with research into CBW. What should he do?

(2) Jim finds himself in the central square of a small South American town. Tied up against the wall are a row of twenty Indians, most terrified, a few defiant, in front of them several armed men in uniform. A heavy man in a sweat-stained khaki shirt turns out to be the captain in charge and, after a good deal of questioning of Jim which establishes that he got there by accident while on a botanical expedition, explains that the Indians are a random group of the inhabitants who, after recent acts of protest against the government, are just about to be killed to remind other possible protestors of the advantages of not protesting. However, since Jim is an honoured visitor from another land, the captain is happy to offer him a guest's privilege of killing one of the Indians himself. If Jim accepts, then as a special mark of the occasion, the other Indians will be let off. Of course, if Jim refuses, then there is no special occasion, and Pedro here will do what he was about to do when Jim arrived, and kill them all. Jim, with some desperate recollection of schoolboy fiction, wonders whether if he got hold of a gun, he could hold the captain, Pedro and the rest of the soldiers to threat, but it is quite clear from the set-up that nothing of that kind is going to work: any attempt at that sort of thing will mean that all the Indians will be killed, and himself. The men against the wall, and the other villagers, understand the situation, and are obviously begging him to accept. What should he do?

To these dilemmas, it seems to me that utilitarianism replies, in the first case, that George should accept the job, and in the second, that Jim should kill the Indian. Not only does utilitarianism give these answers but, if the situations are essentially as described and there are no further special factors, it regards them, it seems to me, as obviously the right answers. But many of us would certainly wonder whether, in (1), that could possibly be the right answer at all; and in the case of (2), even one who came to think that perhaps that was the answer, might well wonder whether it was obviously the answer. Nor is it just a question of the rightness or obviousness of these answers. It is also a question of what sort of considerations come into finding the answer. A feature of utilitarianism is that it cuts out a kind of consideration which for some others makes a difference to what they feel about such cases: a consideration involving the idea, as we might first and very simply put it, that each of us is specially responsible for what *he* does, rather than for what other people do. This is an idea closely connected with the value of integrity. It is often suspected that utilitarianism, at least in its direct forms, makes integrity as a value more or less unintelligible. I shall try to show that this suspicion is correct. Of course, even if that is correct, it would not necessarily show that we should reject utilitarianism; perhaps, as utilitarians sometimes suggest, we should just forget about integrity, in favour of such things as a concern for the general good. However, if I am right, we cannot merely do that, since the reason why utilitarianism cannot understand integrity is that it cannot coherently describe the relations between a man's projects and his actions.

QUESTIONS:

1. In Williams' examples (George and Jim), do you think that utilitarianism gives the correct answer? If so, why? If not, why not?
2. Have you ever experienced a situation in which producing the best available consequences was *not* the right thing to do?

5. DEONTOLOGY, RIGHTS AND PRINCIPLISM

This section deals with three related approaches to ethics. The first of these is deontology, which is often contrasted with and thought of as a sort of opposite of consequentialism. In fact, deontology is rather hard to characterise and it is sometimes *wrongly* defined as the view that consequences are irrelevant to ethics, something that most deontologists would reject. A better characterisation of deontology would say that deontologists normally believe that there are several distinct types of duty (unlike consequentialists who believe that there is one, to maximise good outcomes), that deontologists believe certain *types* of action to be *intrinsically* wrong (classically, but not necessarily, such things as killing, lying and stealing), and also that deontologists believe in "agent-relative" duties, a concept which is explained below by David McNaughton.

David McNaughton, "Deontological ethics" in E. Craig (ed.), *Routledge Encyclopedia of Philosophy*, London: Routledge, 1998, retrieved April 12, 2004, from http://www.rep.routledge.com/article/L015

Deontology asserts that there are several distinct duties. Certain kinds of act are intrinsically right and other kinds intrinsically wrong. The rightness or wrongness of any particular act is thus not (or not wholly) determined by the goodness or badness of its consequences. Some ways of treating people, such as killing the innocent, are ruled out, even to prevent others doing worse deeds. Many deontologies leave agents considerable scope for developing their own lives in their own way; provided they breach no duty they are free to live as they see fit.

Deontology may not have the theoretical tidiness which many philosophers crave, but has some claim to represent everyday moral thought.

Deontology (the word comes from the Greek *deon* meaning "one must") typically holds that there are several irreducibly distinct duties, such as promise-keeping and refraining from lying. Some deontologists, such as W.D. Ross, maintain that one of these duties is a duty to do as much good as possible. Most deny that there is such a duty, while conceding that there is a limited duty of benevolence, a duty to do *something* for the less fortunate. All agree, however, that there are occasions when it would be wrong for us to act in a way that would maximize the good, because we would be in breach of some (other) duty. In this respect they are opposed to act-consequentialism.

Most deontologies include two important classes of duties. First, there are duties which stem from the social and personal relationships in which we stand to particular people. Parents have duties to children, and children to parents; people have duties in virtue of their jobs and the associations to which they belong; debtors have a duty to repay their creditors, promisors to keep their promises and borrowers to return what has been lent to them. Some of these social relationships are ones we enter voluntarily, but many are not. The second kind take the form of general prohibitions or constraints. We should not lie to, cheat, torture or murder *anyone*, even in the pursuit of good aims.

Deontology is often described as an agent-relative moral theory, in contrast to act-consequentialism, which is an agent-neutral theory. According to act-consequentialism the identity of the agent makes no difference to what their duty is on any particular occasion; that is determined solely by which of the courses of action open to them will produce the best consequences. In deontology, by contrast, a reference to the agent often plays an ineliminable role in the specification of the duty. This is especially clear in the case of duties which stem from social relationships. I have a duty to help *this* person. Why? Because he or she is *my* friend, or *my* child. I have a duty to pay *my* debts and to keep *my* promises.

Constraints also involve agent-relativity, though in a slightly different way. The duty not to murder does not take the form of enjoining us to minimize the number of murders. The rule tells me not to commit murder myself even if I could thereby prevent something worse being done, such as two murders being committed. Proponents of deontology think of this as moral integrity; their opponents refer to it disparagingly as "keeping one's hands clean".

Many deontologists hold that our duties, though sometimes very onerous, are quite limited in scope. Provided I am in breach of no duty, I am morally at liberty to devote quite a large part of my time and effort to pursuing my own projects in whatever way I please. This latitude leaves room for acts of supererogation: heroic or saintly acts that clearly go beyond the call of duty, and deserve high praise.

There is a sharp division in the deontologist camp over the status of constraints. Some, such as Fried, think of them as absolute: they have no exceptions and may not be breached in any circumstances which we are likely to encounter. Others regard the fact that an act would breach a constraint as providing a weighty objection to it, but one which could be overcome if there were a sufficiently pressing duty on the other side. Conflicts between two duties which are not absolute must be settled by determining which duty is the more pressing in the circumstances.

Deontology gains much of its appeal from the fact that it seems to capture the essential outlines of our everyday moral thinking, but it is open to several objections. First, its claim that there is a plurality of distinct duties runs counter to the theoretician's search for simplicity. The deontologist will reply, of course, that a theory must do justice to the complexity of the phenomena. Second, many deontologists further defy the supposed canons of good theorizing by denying that there is any overarching explanation of why there are the duties there are; they record our conviction that there are such duties without seeking to justify them. Others, usually inspired by Kant, do attempt such an explanation based on some broader precept, such as respect for persons. Third, those who hold that some kinds of action, such as lying, are absolutely prohibited have to provide clear and detailed criteria for determining the boundary between lying and some supposedly less nefarious activity, such as "being economical with the truth". Such casuistry can appear both excessively legalistic and incompatible with the spirit of morality. Fourth, deontology provides no procedure to settle conflicts of duty (though some might think that an advantage). Finally, from a consequentialist perspective, the notion of a constraint seems perverse. If what is wrong with murder is that it is a bad thing, how can it be rational to forbid an agent to commit one murder in order to prevent two? If deontology is to answer this challenge, it must show how it can be that one's duty does not rest (wholly) on the goodness or badness of the results of acting in that way.

The next concept discussed in this section is moral rights. It is important to keep in mind that moral rights and legal rights are entirely distinct (just like moral and legal duties). A couple of simple examples will illustrate this point. Suppose that you promise to go to the cinema with your friend on Saturday night. Arguably, your friend (because of the promise) has a moral right to be taken to the cinema (by you) on Saturday night, but she almost certainly does not have any such legal right. Or suppose I have a legal right to drive to my local shop in my enormous "people carrier" if I want to (assuming that I comply with all the relevant road traffic laws), even though the shop is only 300m away. In spite of my having this legal right, it could plausibly be argued that I have no moral right to do this (assuming that I am capable of walking etc), and indeed that it would be wrong of me to do so, because such behaviour is lazy and harms the environment.

But although moral and legal rights are distinct, legal rights are often grounded in ethics. We might for example see the legal right to life as a way of endorsing and enforcing the moral right to life. Alternatively, legal rights can be used to promote more broadly utilitarian ends, e.g. giving people a legal right to free health care could promote public health and the general good.

L.W. Sumner, "Rights" in Hugh LaFollette (ed.), *The Blackwell Guide to Ethical Theory*, Malden, Mass: Blackwell Publishers, 2000, pp.288–293

Of all the moral concepts, rights seem most in tune with the temper of our time. At their best they evoke images of heroic struggles against oppression and discrimination. At their worst they furnish the material for lurid tabloid stories of litigious former spouses and lovers. Whatever the use to which they are put, they are ubiquitous, the global currency of moral/political argument at the end of the millennium. Liberal societies in particular seem replete with conflicts of rights: young against old, ethnic minority against majority, natives against foreigners, rich against poor, women against men, believers against non-believers, children against parents, gays against straights, employees against employers, consumers against producers, students against teachers, cyclists against drivers, pedestrians against cyclists, citizens against the police, and everyone against the state.

Love them or hate them, rights are unavoidable and no modern ethical theory seems complete without taking some account of them. It is therefore important to understand them: what they are, what their distinctive function is in our moral/political thinking, how we might distinguish reasonable from unreasonable claims of rights, and how rights might fit into the larger framework of an ethical theory. The aim of this essay is to help promote this understanding.

We can begin by trying to identify the distinctive kind of normative work rights are best equipped to do. Let us say that one part of our moral thinking has to do with the promotion of collective social goals which we deem to be valuable for their own sake: the general welfare, equality of opportunity, the eradication of poverty, bettering the lot of the worst off, or whatever. It is this part of our thinking which is well captured by the broad family of consequentialist ethical theories. On the other hand, we also tend to think that some means societies might use in order to achieve these goals are unjustifiable because they exploit or victimize particular individuals or groups. One way of expressing this thought is to say that these parties have rights which constrain or limit the pursuit of social goals, rights which must (at least sometimes) be respected even though a valuable goal would be better promoted by ignoring or infringing them. Rights then function morally as safeguards for the position of individuals or particular groups in the face of social endeavors; in the image made famous by Ronald Dworkin, they can be invoked as trumps against the pursuit of collective goals. It is this part of our moral thinking which is well captured by deontological theories, and rights therefore seem most at home in such theories.

Rights impose constraints on the pursuit of collective goals. This very general characterization serves to identify in a preliminary way the moral/political function of rights, and also begins to explain their perennial appeal. But it is not yet sufficient to show how rights are distinctive or unique. Duties and obligations impose similar constraints: if I have an obligation to pay my income tax then that is what I must do even though more good would result from my donating the money to Oxfam. So what is the particular way in which rights limit our promotion of valuable states of affairs? And what exactly is the relationship between rights and duties? We need to look more closely at the anatomy of rights.

HOW RIGHTS WORK

A simple example will serve to get us started. Suppose that Bernard has borrowed Alice's laptop computer with the promise to return it by Tuesday, and Tuesday has arrived. Alice now has the right to have her computer returned by Bernard. Note to begin with that there are three distinct elements to this right. First, it has a *subject*: the holder or bearer of the right (in this case, Alice). Second, it has an *object*: the person against whom the right is held (in this case, Bernard). Third, it has a *content*: what it is the right to do or to have done (in this case, to have the computer returned). Every right has these three elements, though they may not always be spelled out fully in the specification of the right. The paradigm subjects of rights are persons, though nothing so far prevents them from being attributed as well to other beings, such as children, animals, corporations, collectivities, and so on. The object of a right must be an agent capable of having duties or obligations, since Alice's right that Bernard return her computer on Tuesday correlates with Bernard's obligation to return the computer on Tuesday. Since rights can be held only against agents, the class of objects of rights may be much narrower than the class of subjects. The object of Alice's right is a specific assignable person, since it is Bernard who has borrowed her computer and who is duty-bound to return it. However, the objects of a right may also be an unassignable group; some rights, such as the right not to be assaulted or killed, may hold against everyone in general.

Finally, the content of a right is always some action on the part of either the subject or the object of the right. This fact is obscured by the shorthand way in which we refer to many rights, where it may appear that the content of the right is a thing or state of affairs. We may speak, for instance, of the right to an education or to health care or to life itself. But in all such cases the full specification of the right will reveal the actions which constitute its content: that the state provide subsidized public education or health care, or that others not act in such a way as to endanger life, or whatever. The contents of many rights are intricate and complex actions on the part of (assignable or unassignable) others, which must be fully spelled out before we know exactly what the right amounts to. In the case of Alice's right the action in question is simple and specific: having her computer returned by Tuesday. Alice therefore has the right that something be done (by the person against whom her right is held). This kind of normative advantage on Alice's part is usually described as a *claim*: Alice has a claim *against Bernard* that he return her computer, which is equivalent to Bernard's duty *to Alice* to return her computer. In general, A's claim against B that B do X is logically equivalent to B's duty toward A to do X: claims and duties are in this way correlative. Claims are always of the form that something be done: the actions which make up their content must be those of another, never those of the right-holder herself. Since the content of Alice's right against Bernard has the form of a claim, we may call it a *claim-right*. Claim-rights constitute one important class of rights, exemplified

primarily by contractual rights (held against assignable parties) and by rights to security of
the person (held against everyone in general).

However, not all rights are claim-rights. Another example will make this clear. Alice
owns her computer, which implies (among other things) that she has the right to use it
(when she wants to). This right has the same subject (Alice) as her claim-right, but a
different content and a different object. Its content is once again an action, but this time
an action on the part of the right-holder rather than someone else: it is a right to *do* rather
than a right *to have done*. The content of the right therefore does not have the form of a
claim; it is common instead to refer to it as a *liberty*. To say that Alice has the liberty to use
her computer is to say that she is under no obligation not to use it, or that her use of it is
permissible. Actually, it is implicitly to say more than this, since Alice's right to use her
computer (when she wants to) includes her right not to use it (when she doesn't want to).
Alice therefore has two distinct liberties: to use the computer (which means that she has no
duty not to use it) and not to use it (which means that she has no duty to use it). We
normally treat these as the two sides of one (complex) liberty: to use or not to use the
computer, as she wishes. In general, A's liberty to do X (or not) is logically equivalent to
the absence both of A's duty to do X and A's duty not to do X. Alice's ownership right over
the computer therefore entails her freedom to choose whether or not to use the computer;
how this is to go is up to her. Since the content of her right has the form of a liberty, we
may call it a *liberty-right*. Liberty-rights constitute another important class of rights,
exemplified primarily by property rights and by rights to various freedoms (of thought,
belief, conscience, expression, etc.).

So far we have located a subject and a content for Alice's liberty-right, but not an object.
Against whom is this right held? In the case of claim-rights the answer to this question is
straightforward: whoever bears the duty which is equivalent to the claim. Because claim-
rights specify obligations, and because these obligations are assigned to particular parties
(or to everyone in general), claim-rights enable us to easily locate their objects. But Alice's
liberty-right to use her computer involves on the face of it no claim (or duty); the liberty
in question just consists in the absence of duties on Alice's part. It is therefore not so
obviously held against anyone. And indeed if we restrict ourselves just to its stipulated
content, that is true: it is a right which imposes no duties. However, we know that property
rights are typically protected by duties imposed on others: for instance, duties not to
interfere with the use or enjoyment of the property in question. By virtue of her property
right Alice has more than just the bare unprotected liberty to use (or not use) her computer
as she pleases; this liberty is safeguarded by what H. L. A. Hart has usefully called a
"protective perimeter" of duties imposed on others. Bernard therefore (and everyone else)
has the duty not to interfere with Alice's use of her computer (by stealing it, damaging it,
using it without permission, etc.). We learn therefore the lesson that liberty-rights are not
as simple as they seem: they involve a complex bundle of liberties (held by the subject) and
duties (imposed on others). The others who bear these duties are the (implicit) objects of
the right.

Even claim-rights are not as simple as they seem. Let us return to Alice's right that
Bernard return her computer by Tuesday. Alice's claim against Bernard is, as we have seen,
logically equivalent to Bernard's duty toward Alice. But suppose that Bernard needs the
computer for an additional day and asks to return it on Wednesday instead. Alice can, of
course, refuse the request and insist on the performance of Bernard's duty. But she can also
agree to it, in which case she waives her right to have the computer returned by Tuesday
and releases Bernard from his original obligation. She now has a new right (to have the
computer returned by Wednesday) and Bernard has a new correlative obligation. In
waiving her original right Alice has exercised a power which enables her to alter Bernard's
obligation. Indeed, in entering into the agreement about the computer in the first place,
both Alice and Bernard have exercised powers which result in the creation of Alice's claim-
right against Bernard and Bernard's liberty-right to use Alice's computer. Contractual
rights, which constitute one important class of claim-rights, therefore involve more than
just claims; they also involve powers (and liberties to exercise those powers, and duties
imposed on others not to interfere with those liberties, and immunities against being

deprived of the powers, and so on). Even relatively simple-seeming claim-rights are therefore typically quite complex bundles of different elements. The core of the right is still a claim, but this core is surrounded by a periphery made up of other elements (claims, liberties, powers, etc.). This periphery may be quite different for different claim-rights. Contractual rights typically confer on their subjects considerable discretion about the exercise of the right, including the power to waive it or to annul it entirely. Other claim-rights, such as the right not to be harmed or killed, may impose more limits on the subject's liberty (or power) to waive or annul the right. The full specification of a claim-right, including all of its periphery, can therefore be a very complex matter.

The same complexity, and the same relation of core to periphery, can be found in the case of liberty-rights. Alice's liberty-right to use her computer (or not, as she pleases) is not accompanied only by a protective perimeter of duties imposed on others. It also includes her power to annul her liberty to use the computer, either temporarily (by lending the computer to Bernard) or permanently (by selling it), plus her liberty to exercise this power, plus further duties imposed on others not to interfere with her exercise of this power, plus . . . Like claim-rights, liberty-rights are typically complex bundles of different elements. The core of the right (what it is a right to) is still a liberty, but it too is surrounded by a periphery made up of other elements (claims, liberties, powers, etc.)

A full exploration of the intricate anatomy of rights can be a complicated affair. Fortunately, we have revealed enough of this anatomy to be able to answer some of our questions about the distinctive normative function of rights. First, the relationship between rights and duties. Although these two deontological concepts are clearly connected, the connections between them are more complex than they first appear. There is a simple relationship between claims and their correlative duties: A's claim against B that B do X is logically equivalent to B's duty toward A to do X. Exclusive attention to claim-rights might lead one to think that rights are just duties seen, as it were, from the perspective of the patient rather than the agent. But this is not the case. In the first place, not all duties are relational in the sense of being owed to assignable persons. Bernard's duty to return Alice's computer has an obvious object (Alice) but my duty to pay my income tax does not: it is not clear to whom (if anyone) this duty is owed. If there are non-relational duties then they do not correlate with any rights. More importantly, there is more to a right, even a claim-right, than just a claim against some correlative duty-bearer. Claim-rights, like liberty-rights, are typically complex clusters of different kinds of elements (duties, liberties, powers, immunities, etc.). Every such right will include some duties, either in its core or in its periphery (or both). But no right of either kind can just be reduced to a duty, or a set of duties. Rights also contain elements which are not duties, and are not definable in terms of duties. Furthermore, they have a structure, an internal logic, which is distinctively different from that of duties.

This brings us to our other question: how is it that rights impose constraints on our pursuit of goals? The complex structure of rights reveals two answers to this question. First, by containing duties imposed on their objects, rights limit the freedom of others to pursue valuable collective goals; they must (at least sometimes) fulfil their duty even when a worthwhile goal would be better promoted by not doing so. Second, by containing liberties conferred on their subjects, rights secure the freedom of right-holders not to pursue valuable collective goals; they may (at least sometimes) choose to exercise their right even when a worthwhile goal would be better promoted by not doing so. Rights therefore impose restrictions on others (who must not promote the collectively best outcome) and confer prerogatives on their holders (who need not do so). By these means rights define protected spaces in which individuals are able to pursue their own personal projects or have their personal interests safeguarded, free from the demands of larger collective enterprises.

The qualifiers "at least sometimes" in the preceding paragraph deserve some brief attention. They signal that neither the duties which rights impose on others nor the liberties they confer on their holders need be absolute. And this brings us to a fourth dimension of a right (besides its subject, object, and content), namely its *strength*. The strength of a right is its level of resistance to rival normative considerations, such as the promotion of worthwhile goals. A right will insulate its holder to some extent against the necessity of taking these considerations into account, but it will also typically have a threshold above which they dominate or override the right. Should it turn out, for instance, that Bernard needs Alice's computer in order to arrange relief for a large-scale disaster in Africa then his duty to return it on time (and her claim that it be returned) may be overridden even if she wants the computer back. Likewise, the same degree of urgency may override her liberty-right to use the computer when she pleases. Rights raise thresholds against considerations of social utility but these thresholds are seldom insurmountable. Some particularly important rights (against torture, perhaps, or slavery, or genocide) may be absolute, but most are not.

QUESTION:

1. Think of some examples of particular moral rights and try to identify: (a) who (or what) the *subject* is, (b) who (or what) the *object* is, (c) what the *content* is, and (d) whether it is a claim-right, a liberty-right, or some other kind of right.

The final idea discussed in this section is the "four principles" approach to health care ethics, also known as "principlism". This is a widely held view, especially in the US. However, it is by no means universally accepted and has also been extensively criticised in the bioethics literature.

Although the "four principles" approach seems fundamentally deontological, because it posits the existence of four distinct ethical duties (autonomy, benefi-cence, non-maleficence and justice) it can also be defended on consequentialist grounds, if we argue that using the four principles as a guide to decision-making will, in the long run, maximise good outcomes.

R. Gillon, "Medical Ethics: Four Principles Plus Attention to Scope", *British Medical Journal*, 1994; 309:184 (July 16)

The "four principles plus scope" approach provides a simple, accessible, and culturally neutral approach to thinking about ethical issues in health care. The approach, developed in the United States, is based on four common, basic *prima facie* moral commitments— respect for autonomy, beneficence, non-maleficence, and justice—plus concern for their scope of application. It offers a common, basic moral analytical framework and a common, basic moral language. Although they do not provide ordered rules, these principles can help doctors and other health care workers to make decisions when reflecting on moral issues that arise at work.

Nine years ago the BMJ allowed me to introduce to its readers an approach to medical ethics developed by the Americans Beauchamp and Childress, which is based on four *prima facie* moral principles and attention to these principles' scope of application. Since then I have often been asked for a summary of this approach by doctors and other health care workers who find it helpful for organising their thoughts about medical ethics. This paper, based on the preface of a large multiauthor textbook on medical ethics, offers a brief account of this "four principles plus scope" approach.

The four principles plus scope approach claims that whatever our personal philosophy, politics, religion, moral theory, or life stance, we will find no difficulty in committing ourselves to four *prima facie* moral principles plus a reflective concern about their scope of application. Moreover, these four principles, plus attention to their scope of application, encompass most of the moral issues that arise in health care.

The four *prima facie* principles are respect for autonomy, beneficence, non-maleficence, and justice. "*Prima facie*," a term introduced by the English philosopher W D Ross, means that the principle is binding unless it conflicts with another moral principle—if it does we have to choose between them. The four principles approach does not provide a method for choosing, which is a source of dissatisfaction to people who suppose that ethics merely comprises a set of ordered rules and that once the relevant information is fed into an algorithm or computer out will pop the answer. What the principles plus scope approach can provide, however, is a common set of moral commitments, a common moral language, and a common set of moral issues. We should consider these in each case before coming to our own answer using our preferred moral theory or other approach to choose between these principles when they conflict.

RESPECT FOR AUTONOMY

Autonomy—literally, self rule, but probably better described as deliberated self rule—is a special attribute of all moral agents. If we have autonomy we can make our own decisions on the basis of deliberation; sometimes we can intend to do things as a result of those decisions; and sometimes we can do those things to implement the decisions (what I previously described as autonomy of thought, of will or intention, and of action). Respect for autonomy is the moral obligation to respect the autonomy of others in so far as such respect is compatible with equal respect for the autonomy of all potentially affected. Respect for autonomy is also sometimes described, in Kantian terms, as treating others as ends in themselves and never merely as means—one of Kant's formulations of his "categorical imperative."

In health care respecting people's autonomy has many *prima facie* implications. It requires us to consult people and obtain their agreement before we do things to them—hence the obligation to obtain informed consent from patients before we do things to try to help them. Medical confidentiality is another implication of respecting people's autonomy. We do not have any general obligation to keep other people's secrets, but health care workers explicitly or implicitly promise their patients and clients that they will keep confidential the information confided to them. Keeping promises is a way of respecting people's autonomy; an aspect of running our own life depends on being able to rely on the promises made to us by others. Without such promises of confidentiality patients are also far less likely to divulge the often highly private and sensitive information that is needed for their optimal care; thus maintaining confidentiality not only respects patients' autonomy but also increases the likelihood of our being able to help them.

Respect for autonomy also requires us not to deceive each other (except in circumstances in which deceit is agreed to be permissible, such as when playing poker) as the absence of deceit is part of the implicit agreement among moral agents when they communicate with each other. They organise their lives on the assumption that people will not deceive them; their autonomy is infringed if they are deceived. Respect for patients' autonomy *prima facie* requires us, therefore, not to deceive patients, for example, about their diagnosed illness unless they clearly wish to be deceived. Respect for autonomy even requires us to be on time for appointments as an agreed appointment is a kind of mutual promise and if we do not keep an appointment we break the promise.

To exercise respect for autonomy health care workers must be able to communicate well with their patients and clients. Good communication requires, most importantly, listening (and not just with the ears) as well as telling (and not just with the lips or a wordprocessor) and is usually necessary for giving patients adequate information about any proposed intervention and for finding out whether patients want that intervention. Good communication is also usually necessary for finding out when patients do not want a lot of information; some patients do not want to be told about a bad prognosis or to participate in deciding which of several treatments to have, preferring to leave this decision to their doctors. Respecting such attitudes shows just as much respect for a patient's autonomy as does giving patients information that they do want. In my experience, however, most patients want more not less information and want to participate in deciding their medical care.

BENEFICENCE AND NON-MALEFICENCE

Whenever we try to help others we inevitably risk harming them; health care workers, who are committed to helping others, must therefore consider the principles of beneficence and non-maleficence together and aim at producing net benefit over harm. None the less, we must keep the two principles separate for those circumstances in which we have or recognise no obligation of beneficence to others (as we still have an obligation not to harm them). Thus the traditional Hippocratic moral obligation of medicine is to provide net medical benefit to patients with minimal harm—that is, beneficence with non-maleficence. To achieve these moral objectives health care workers are committed to a wide range of *prima facie* obligations.

We need to ensure that we can provide the benefits we profess (thus "professional") to be able to provide. Hence we need rigorous and effective education and training both before and during our professional lives. We also need to make sure that we are offering each patient net benefit. Interestingly, to do this we must respect the patient's autonomy for what constitutes benefit for one patient may be harm for another. For example, a mastectomy may constitute a prospective net benefit for one woman with breast cancer, while for another the destruction of an aspect of her feminine identity may be so harmful that it cannot be outweighed even by the prospect of an extended life expectancy.

The obligation to provide net benefit to patients also requires us to be clear about risk and probability when we make our assessments of harm and benefit. Clearly, a low probability of great harm such as death or severe disability is of less moral importance in the context of non-maleficence than is a high probability of such harm, and a high probability of great benefit such as cure of a life threatening disease is of more moral importance in the context of beneficence than is a low probability of such benefit. We therefore need empirical information about the probabilities of the various harms and benefits that may result from proposed health care interventions. This information has to come from effective medical research, which is also therefore a *prima facie* moral obligation. The obligation to produce net benefit, however, also requires us to define whose benefit and whose harms are likely to result from a proposed intervention. This problem of moral scope is particularly important in medical research and population medicine.

One moral concept that in recent years has become popular in health care is that of empowerment—that is, doing things to help patients and clients to be more in control of their health and health care. Sometimes empowerment is even proposed as a new moral obligation. On reflection I think that empowerment is, however, essentially an action that combines the two moral obligations of beneficence and respect for autonomy to help patients in ways that not only respect but also enhance their autonomy.

JUSTICE

The fourth *prima facie* moral principle is justice. Justice is often regarded as being synonymous with fairness and can be summarised as the moral obligation to act on the basis of fair adjudication between competing claims. In health care ethics I have found it useful to subdivide obligations of justice into three categories: fair distribution of scarce resources (distributive justice), respect for people's rights (rights based justice) and respect for morally acceptable laws (legal justice).

Equality is at the heart of justice, but, as Aristotle argued so long ago, justice is more than mere equality—people can be treated unjustly even if they are treated equally. He argued that it was important to treat equals equally (what health economists are increasingly calling horizontal equity) and to treat unequals unequally in proportion to the morally relevant inequalities (vertical equity). People have argued ever since about the morally relevant criteria for regarding and treating people as equals and those for regarding and treating them as unequals. The debate flourishes in moral, religious, philosophical, and political contexts, and we are no closer to agreement than we were in Aristotle's time.

QUESTION:

1. Do you agree with Gillon's view that we should all find it easy to support the four principles, regardless of "our personal philosophy, politics, religion, moral theory, or life stance"? If so, why? If not, why not?

6. VIRTUE ETHICS, FEMINIST ETHICS AND NURSING ETHICS

The relationship between virtue ethics and feminist ethics is not necessarily a very close one. Many virtue ethics enthusiasts do not consider themselves feminist and conversely many feminists are not supporters of virtue ethics. That said, there are nonetheless some reasons to group them together, as we have here. One is that a lot of feminists have viewed mainstream ethics, particularly consequentialist and deontological approaches, as "male" or "masculine" in some way, and have viewed virtue ethics as an attractive alternative to these, perhaps because it appears less driven by abstract principles and rules. Another is that virtue ethics is sometimes said to be similar to another (arguably feminist) set of views known as the ethics of care (discussed below).

Similar comments can be made about the inclusion of nursing ethics in this section. Clearly, many nurses and nurse-ethicists have no interest either in feminism or in virtue ethics. However, as Geoffrey Hunt explains (below), many writers on nursing ethics have argued that there is a close relationship between nursing ethics and the ethics of care, and that nurses and nurse-ethicists should see their work as inextricably linked to feminist and "gender" issues.

Roger Crisp, "Virtue Ethics" in E. Craig (ed.), *Routledge Encyclopedia of Philosophy*, London: Routledge, 1998, retrieved April 17, 2004, from http://www.rep.routledge.com/article/L111

Virtue ethics has its origin in the ancient world, particularly in the writings of Plato and Aristotle. It has been revived following an article by G.E.M. Anscombe critical of modern ethics and advocating a return to the virtues.

Some have argued that virtue ethics constitutes a third option in moral theory additional to utilitarianism and Kantianism. Utilitarians and Kantians have responded vigorously, plausibly claiming that their views already incorporate many of the theses allegedly peculiar to virtue ethics . . .

. . . Modern virtue ethicists often claim Aristotle as an ancestor. Aristotle, however, was himself working through an agenda laid down by Plato and Socrates. Socrates asked the question at the heart of Greek ethics: "How should one live?" All three of these philosophers believed that the answer to this question is, "Virtuously".

The ancient philosophical task was to show how living virtuously would be best for the virtuous person. Plato's *Republic* attempts to answer Thrasymachus' challenge that rational people will aim to get the most pleasure, honour and power for themselves. His argument is that justice, broadly construed, is to be identified with a rational ordering of one's soul. Once one sees that one identifies oneself with one's reason, one will realize that being just is in fact best for oneself. Thrasymachus, of course, might respond that he identifies himself with his desires.

Aristotle continued the same project, aiming to show that human *eudaimonia*, happiness, consists in the exercise (not the mere possession of) the virtues. The linchpin of his case is his "function" argument that human nature is perfected through virtue, a standard objection to which is that it confuses the notions of a good man and the good for man. Ultimately, Aristotle's method is similar to Plato's. Much of *Nicomachean Ethics* is taken up with portraits of the virtuous man intended to attract one to a life such as his.

For Aristotle, all of the "practical" virtues will be possessed by the truly virtuous person, the man of "practical wisdom" (Aristotle's central "intellectual" virtue). Socrates believed that virtue was a *unity*, that it consisted in knowledge alone. Aristotle's position is one of *reciprocity*: the possession of one virtue implies the possession of all. At this point he joined Socrates and Plato in their opposition to Greek "common sense". This opposition to common sense is not something that characterizes modern virtue ethics . . .

. . . What is virtue ethics? It is tempting to characterize it as a theory advocating acting virtuously, but this is insufficiently precise. Virtue ethics is usually seen as an alternative to utilitarianism or consequentialism in general. To put it roughly, utilitarianism says that we should maximize human welfare or utility. A utilitarian, however, may advocate acting virtuously for reasons of utility. Ethical theories are best understood in terms not of what acts they require, but of the reasons offered for acting in whatever way is in fact required.

Which properties of actions, then, according to virtue ethics, constitute our reason for doing them? The properties of kindness, courage and so on. It is worth noting that there is a difference between acting virtuously and doing a virtuous action. One's doing a virtuous action may be seen as doing the action a virtuous person would do in those circumstances, though one may not oneself be a virtuous person. Virtue ethics, then, concerns itself not only with isolated actions but with the character of the agent. There are reasons for doing certain things (such as kind things), and also for being a certain type of person (a kind person).

This account of virtue ethics enables us to distinguish it from its other main opponent, deontology or Kantianism. A Kantian, for example, might claim that my reason for telling the truth is that to do so would be in accordance with the categorical imperative. That is a property of the action of telling the truth quite different from its being honest.

Susan Sherwin, "Feminism and Bioethics" in Susan Wolf (ed.), *Feminism and Bioethics*, Oxford: Oxford University Press, 1996, pp.47–54

The class of people who consider themselves feminists is large and diverse, representing a broad range of different opinions and perspectives. Despite this rich multiplicity of views, it is possible to identify some common themes. Generally, feminists share a recognition that women are oppressed in our society and an understanding that their oppression takes many different forms, compounded often by other forms of oppression based on features such as race, ethnicity, sexual orientation, and economic class. Because feminists believe that oppression is objectionable on both moral and political grounds, most are committed to transforming society in ways that will ensure the elimination of oppression in all its forms.

Much of the harm of sexism is obvious and thus can be readily challenged. For example, the evidence is overwhelming that women are disproportionately subjected to domestic violence and sexual assault, resulting in undeniable physical and psychological damage to many women and a sense of insecurity and vulnerability in all women. In addition, the economic disadvantage women experience in the work place, where their average earnings are less than two-thirds of the average wages paid to men, is widely condemned as unjust. Further, the predominance of men, especially white, middle-class men, in positions of influence in virtually all segments of society (legal, political, financial, cultural, and military) is inescapable.

Other dimensions of sexism are more subtle, however, and can easily be overlooked unless one makes a conscious effort to identify them. For example, the implicit male bias of ordinary language, such as the tendency to confuse explicitly gendered male forms of expression with supposedly gender-neutral generic forms (such as "chairman," "man-power," and even "mankind"), perpetuates culturally embedded notions of male-defined norms and assumptions of female deviance. The difference in adjectives customarily used to describe men and women (for instance, behavior that is called forceful or aggressive in men is likely to be described as strident or hysterical in women) reflects a rigid, dichotomized view of the world in which gender stereotyping is systematically reinforced. In a different dimension, the prevalence of sexual harassment of women by men and the fact that many people often have difficulty in distinguishing it from ordinary male sexual aggression are evidence of the unbalanced power relations in our society. As well, the degree to which the work and ideas of men dominate the curricula in our schools and universities reveals a culturally widespread dismissal of the accomplishments of women.

Feminists have learned that women are devalued and endangered in many complex ways. They understand that unconscious sexism is at least as common and dangerous as the conscious variety. The roots of sexism are intertwined and deeply embedded in the fabric of our culture. Hence, sexism is unlikely to be eradicated without extensive investigation of the various institutions that shape society. Feminists pursue numerous strategies to identify and uproot the many forms of sexism, including the project of examining the effects of diverse social practices and institutions on the established patterns of oppression in society. They try to evaluate the overall influence of each social practice or institution to determine whether the practice in question helps to perpetuate the dominance of one group over another, is neutral with respect to oppression, or helps to undermine the existing oppressive forces.

When feminists have approached the established academic disciplines with this question in mind, they have found that there are ways in which almost all have helped to maintain existing dominance structures. Most disciplines have, for example, largely ignored or silenced the voices of women and other oppressed groups and have pursued projects that are supportive of oppressive patterns. Feminist critiques of the life, physical, and social sciences find a pervasive anti-female bias in the conceptions and practices of each. In addition, feminist scholars who have examined the particular disciplines categorized under the heading of the "humanities" have found each to be male dominated and supportive of social structures that are oppressive to women. To date, though, bioethics has largely escaped such feminist scrutiny.

For the most part, bioethicists proceed as if bioethics is simply neutral in its effects on oppression, pursuing questions that seem to be separate from those that occupy feminists. With the exception of a few topics that clearly affect women differently from men (particularly abortion and the new reproductive technologies), most bioethicists assume that their work has no impact on questions of gender oppression. Of course, many bioethicists personally oppose sexism and are motivated to try to reverse some of its effects; many make conscious efforts to use gender-neutral language and to challenge traditional gender stereotypes in their examples and case studies, such as by using female pronouns to refer to doctors. These bioethicists likely think of themselves as involved in an activity that helps to undermine some of the subtle effects of sexism. But even among these sympathetic bioethicists, gender is seldom raised as a relevant consideration in the topics explored, or viewed as significant in the contexts addressed. Feminists, however, are unlikely to be comforted by these omissions, having learned elsewhere that invisibility is no assurance of irrelevance in matters of oppression.

The question of whether bioethics has a positive, negative, or neutral effect on existing patterns of oppression becomes especially troublesome when we recognize that philosophy, theology, medicine, and law—the disciplines from which bioethics draws most of its practices and practitioners—have all been shown to be deeply infected with patriarchal values and assumptions. Of particular concern to bioethicists is the fact that several recent feminist critiques suggest that rather than being an instrument for challenging oppression, ethics as it is usually pursued may actually be supportive of the oppressive status quo. Thus, when feminists approach the field of bioethics they have reason to consider carefully what role this newly defined discipline plays in the existing structures of oppression. In this essay, I shall outline some of my explicitly feminist concerns about bioethics and offer some suggestions as to how bioethical practices might be changed to be more compatible with the moral objectives of feminism.

FEMINIST ETHICS

Although many bioethicists balk at the label "applied ethics" and resist the suggestion that their work consists simply of some mechanical application of abstract ethical principles, virtually all believe that a clear understanding of the central principles, values, and debates within the field of philosophical or religious ethics is essential to adequate analysis of the issues that arise in the domain of bioethics. Also, despite the commonplace grumbling among bioethicists about the impracticality of theoretical ethics, most bioethical arguments reflect a belief that the insights of theoretical ethics can be effectively supplemented and modified in the light of actual experience and circumstances.

In addition, many of the debates and disagreements that occupy theoretical ethicists carry over to bioethics. Bioethicists are divided, for instance, about whether the central criteria of ethical analysis are best captured by a finite set of principles or by a broader, more open-ended range of values. They also worry about such classical questions as whether moral claims can be said to be ultimately true or false in any meaningful sense, whether happiness or freedom should be seen as the more fundamental value, and whether ethics should focus on establishing norms for action or for character. Finally, most bioethicists are highly dependent on the work of their colleagues in the realm of theoretical ethics in spelling out the meaning of many key concepts they rely on, especially "autonomy," "welfare," and "justice." Thus, it is appropriate to begin a feminist evaluation of bioethics by reviewing some of the criticisms that feminist theorists have brought to bear on the dominant theories of traditional ethics.

Several feminist critics take their lead from Carol Gilligan's proposal that there exist two distinct patterns of moral decision making. They note that most ethical theory reflects only one of the two important approaches to ethical deliberation that Gilligan found practiced in our culture. Traditional ethics is rooted in the approach Gilligan characterized as the ethic of justice, an ethic defined by its commitment to abstract, universal principles. The alternative approach, which she identified as an ethic of care or responsibility, involves a form of person-specific caring in which contextual details take prominence. The ethic of care differs from the ethic of justice in that it is particular and concrete and it directs agents to place a premium on the avoidance of hurting people. It does not pursue general rules independently of their specific effects, and it permits the modification of existing circumstances or rules when that is necessary to circumvent painful choices. While the ethic of justice focuses on persons only generically and abstractly, the ethic of care is occupied with actual persons and the particularities of their circumstances. An ethic of care is readily adaptable to bioethics, where the importance of considering the particular needs of patients and attending to health professionals' special relationship toward them is already well entrenched in moral deliberations.

In her empirical studies, Gilligan found that women were far more likely than men to adopt an ethic of care, and men were more likely than women to adopt an ethic of justice, but she believed that moral agents should be skilled in pursuing both kinds of ethics, since each is appropriate to specific sorts of problems. Many feminists have observed that most male-defined ethical theories (including virtually all of traditional philosophical ethics) address only the concerns of an ethic of justice. Moreover, most of the familiar ethical theories either dismiss women from consideration altogether or assign to them a subordinate role. For obvious reasons, feminists consider it important to develop a moral theory that speaks to women in ways that do not reflect the dominant group's interests in perpetuating their subordination. Therefore, many feminists welcome the fact that Gilligan offers recognition and validity for the sort of moral reasoning that is commonly associated with women. Most feminists also appreciate her recognition that more than one legitimate approach to ethical reasoning is possible. There is no obvious justification for restricting the definition of "ethics" to the sort of deliberation that is most commonly practiced by men.

Many feminists are, however, wary of uncritically valorizing apparently female approaches to moral reasoning and have expressed reservations about establishing too quickly a caring-based conception of feminist ethics. They recognize the dangers inherent in accepting or legitimating gender patterns that have been established within a sexist society. Therefore, some feminists have argued that if we are to recommend a place for caring in ethics, we do so only in conjunction with a political evaluation of the role of caring in our moral deliberations, and others have rejected caring outright as the central element of feminist ethics. In light of the dangers and complications that have been associated with attempts to endorse stereotypically feminine patterns as the basis of ethics, I do not believe it is appropriate to characterize the ethics of care as specifically feminist. It does not capture the dimensions that I regard as distinctively feminist.

Nevertheless, I do share with many other feminist ethicists an appreciation of Gilligan's emphasis on the importance of attention to concrete narrative details in moral decision making." Interestingly, many bioethicists also agree about the value of the concrete. They understand that contextual details are morally relevant to ethical evaluation and that purely abstract considerations are often inadequate for resolving moral concerns. The question that must be considered, then, is what sorts of contextual details are to be deemed relevant for moral judgments; feminists and bioethicists often differ significantly on this point.

I believe feminism's answer derives from its understanding that oppression is a pervasive and insidious moral wrong, and that conscious attention must be directed to its place in the practices that are being ethically evaluated. Therefore, from a feminist perspective, the relevant concrete details to be considered in our ethical deliberations include the political or power relations of the persons who are involved in or who are affected by the practice or policy being evaluated. Questions about dominance and oppression are essential dimensions of feminist ethical analysis. Thus, when approaching moral dilemmas in feminist ethics, and by extension in feminist bioethics, it is important to understand the actual particulars of the encompassing dominance structures.

In other words, feminist ethics proposes that when we engage in moral deliberation, it is not sufficient just to calculate utilities or to follow a set of moral principles. We must also ask whose happiness is increased, or how the principles in question affect those who are now oppressed in the circumstances at hand. Practices that increase the happiness or protect the rights of the dominant group at the expense of an oppressed group cannot count as morally acceptable. Positive moral value attaches to actions or principles that help relieve oppression, and negative value attaches to those that fail to reduce oppression or actually help to strengthen it. Therefore, when we ethically evaluate a practice, whether it is contractual pregnancy or abortion, or even euthanasia or truth-telling, it is important that our analysis attend to the effects of the practice on existing patterns of oppression.

There are further aspects of feminist ethics that should be carried over into bioethics, including feminist challenges to some of the key concepts of traditional ethics. For example, feminists have questioned the usefulness of the concept of the abstract individual as the fundamental social and moral unit. They have argued that this concept masks particular details about persons that are often relevant to ethical evaluations, such as each individual's actual social and political location. Feminism teaches that moral theories are partial and defective when they speak of the interests, values, and rational choices of individuals as abstract entities, as if the personal histories and social contexts of persons are irrelevant. Feminists are very aware that persons are not all situated so as to be independent and equal; many are disadvantaged, dependent, exploited, responsible for the care of others, or otherwise limited in their ability to assert their rights in competition with the claims of other persons. Feminists recognize that these characteristics are of moral significance.

For related reasons, some feminists object to the privileging that is customarily afforded to the concept of autonomy. Although "autonomy" is a term whose meaning is notoriously hard to fix, it retains a place of prominence in most bioethical writings. In most autonomy based discussions, individuals are envisioned as being fundamentally independent and self-directed, at least ideally. They are seen as somehow prior to and independent of their social circumstances. Many feminists, however, are critical of moral theory's usual treatment of persons as autonomous self-asserters. As Annette Baier has stressed, persons do not emerge fully grown and complete into the world, ready to perform actions and form social contracts as autonomous, self-sufficient beings. Rather, she suggests, persons are better described as "second persons," the product of the physical and emotional labor of other persons who socialize them.

In asserting the theoretical primacy of the individual, autonomy-based theories characterize social and moral obligations as essentially secondary to considerations of self-interest. They treat communities and the ties that bind them as a problem that must be accounted for, while proceeding as if the concept of an individual apart from community were coherent. And they ignore the fact that our sense of ourselves and our preferences is very much a product of our social history and current circumstances.

In addition, many feminists perceive that the concept of autonomy, rather than working to empower the oppressed and exploited among us, in practice often serves to protect the privileges of the most powerful. It is taken as an analytic truth among political theorists that individual autonomy cannot be fully reconciled with the needs of the community. Indeed, autonomy provides the most convincing rationale for resisting the intrusion of claims of equality on the privileges of advantaged individuals. Yet greater equality is a precondition for any meaningful exercise of autonomy by seriously disadvantaged members of society. Therefore, theories that place priority on autonomy—at least as the concept is commonly interpreted—must be understood as primarily protecting the autonomy of those who are already well situated, while sacrificing the necessary prerequisites for autonomy for others.

The concept of autonomy is also exclusionary, in that it is generally ascribed only to those persons who are recognized as rational. As Genevieve Lloyd and others have shown, however, rationality has historically been constructed in ways that exclude not only children, but also women and members of other oppressed groups. Those who are declared or perceived to be nonrational are simply beyond the scope and protection of autonomy talk.

Many feminists favor a more community-based conception of the self as the basis for moral value than what is assumed in traditional ethical theorizing. They seek a conception of self in which individuals strive to determine norms for themselves within their communities. In feminist theories, it is usually explicitly acknowledged and made a subject of direct moral interest that all persons do not have equal power or opportunity to do so . . .

. . . feminist critiques of both the methodology and tools of ethics suggest that an underlying gender bias is implicit in the existing ethical theories. Insofar as bioethics is built on the foundations offered by various ethical theories, its own validity and credibility are also suspect. We must, then, be careful in developing bioethics to try to ensure that we do not build into our theoretical framework the sorts of assumptions that may foster continued oppression under the legitimizing label of "ethics".

QUESTIONS:

1. What are the central features of feminist ethics?
2. Is feminist ethics an attractive alternative to "mainstream" or "traditional" ethics? If so, why? If not, why not?

Eve Garrard and Stephen Wilkinson, "The Ethics of Care", Section 4.2 of *Workbook 3: Dilemmas and Decisions at the End of Life*, Milton Keynes: Open University, 2001, pp.44–46

. . . we are first going to introduce you to a set of views called the *ethics of care*. These views constitute both a critique of and an alternative to the "traditional" four principles approach, and have become quite fashionable during the last two or three decades, especially among writers on nursing (as opposed to medical) ethics . . .

According to [many] supporters of the ethics of care . . . the four principles (and, more generally, the whole idea of basing ethics on principles) are problematic for a number of reasons. These include:

(1) Ethical principles do not take account of the complexity and "particularity" of actual situations.

(2) Multi-principled approaches are unhelpful because, very often, one principle clashes with another. For example, it might be impossible both to respect someone's autonomy and to benefit her (if, say, she refuses beneficial treatment).

(3) The four principles approach is, in some sense, male or masculine and may therefore disadvantage and marginalize women and women's views and/or be otherwise unsuitable for women.

(4) The ethical principles approach is, to a large extent, designed for and by doctors and is not appropriate for nurses.

Points (1) and (2) have been debated at great length by moral philosophers for many centuries. Some philosophers (particularists) take the view that there are not really any moral principles, while others (principlists) believe in moral principles. We won't be looking at this debate in any detail because to do so would take us too far away from the ethics of health care and into complex and difficult areas of moral theory. It is however worth noting here that the assertion contained in (1)—that ethical principles cannot take account of the complexity and "particularity" of actual situations—is questionable, since ethical principles can be more, or less, complex and sensitive. Compare, for example, these two principles:

(A) Never lie, no matter what the consequences.

(B) Don't lie unless doing so is necessary in order to prevent extreme suffering, or to preserve patient confidentiality, or to keep an important promise.

Both (A) and (B) are principles, but (B) is much more flexible and sensitive to the "particularities" of the case in hand. What this illustrates is that even if some actual moral principles are in fact too rigid and insensitive, it is far from clear that all moral principles are necessarily like this—since we can always reformulate them in order to make them more complex and subtle.

In the rest of this section we will examine points (3) and (4) in a little more detail, since these specifically concern health care and, in particular, nursing ethics.

Let's start with point (3). At first glance, the claim that the four principles are "gendered" and/or "sexist" seems rather surprising, since they don't mention gender or sex. Furthermore, the inclusion of *justice* suggests that the four principles could be used in arguments *against* sex discrimination. Indeed, the main argument against both racial and sexual discrimination is that they are incompatible with a *principle of justice*. So what reason might there be for believing that the use of ethical principles, such as the four principles, is—in some sense—male or masculine?

The reason normally offered is that men and women (so it is claimed) tend to think about moral issues in different ways. Men's moral thinking, it is argued, is best characterized in terms of *justice/rights, abstraction/rationality* and *impartiality,* whereas women's moral thinking is best characterized in terms of *care, particularity* (i.e. focusing on particular cases, rather than on abstract general principles) and *relationships.* In support of this kind of claim, Carol Gilligan's book *In a Different Voice* (1982) is often cited. In this book Gilligan claims to have shown (by the use of various social-scientific studies) that men are more likely to adopt a "justice-based" approach to ethics than women, who are instead more likely to adopt a "care-based" approach. (However, it should be noted that she does not claim that all men think in one way, while all women think in another.) The general idea, then, is that men's "natural" ways of thinking about ethics (the perspective of justice) may have been unfairly prioritized, excluding the "voice" of women (the perspective of care).

Later on in this section we will examine some problems with this view, but first let us take a look at point (4)—the claim that the ethical principles approach is, to a large extent, designed for and by doctors and is not appropriate for nursing. Nursing ethics, as a distinct academic sub-discipline, is a relatively new phenomenon and, partly for this reason, it is certainly true that the four principles first became popular within *biomedical* ethics, not nursing ethics. But that said, is there any reason to suppose that the four principles approach is not appropriate for nursing, and—more generally—for the whole of health care?

One reason (relating to point (3)) is simply that most nurses are women, and so in so far as the principled approach is inappropriate for women, then it is inappropriate for nurses. However, there are also supposed to be other (i.e. not gender-based) reasons for thinking of nursing and medicine as different in important ways. These include (a) the idea that nursing focuses on care, while medicine focuses on cure, and (b) the idea that nursing focuses on "treating the whole person", while medicine focuses on eliminating particular diseases, or repairing particular body parts or systems.

Both (a) and (b), though, are problematic. For a start, the idea that nursing focuses on care while medicine focuses on cure seems on the face of it to be false. Many nursing interventions (such as the work of intensive care nurses) are curative. And conversely, many medical interventions (such as the work of palliative care consultants) are not curative, but much more to do with general care.

Perhaps this misses the point, however. Noddings, a defender of the ethics of care, suggests that the "caring approach" has much more to do with *attitude* than with the distinction between care and cure, and that to care (in the relevant sense) is to adopt an attitude of what Noddings calls "affective receptivity and engrossment". However, Noddings' idea seems not to be terribly helpful. There are at least two reasons for this. First, maybe (though *only* maybe!) becoming "engrossed" by one's child, spouse or lover is desirable—but ought nurses really to become engrossed by their patients? Is this really an appropriate way for a professional to think about her clients or patients? And wouldn't becoming engrossed by all one's patients take a terrible emotional and psychological toll on busy nurse practitioners? Second, it seems reasonable to suppose that health carers should only become engrossed by their patients in so far as this benefits the patient— otherwise what would be the point of it? But if the reason that engrossment is advocated is that it is good for patients, then it would fall under the principle of beneficence. In other words, either engrossment is good for patients or it isn't. If it isn't, then we shouldn't be adopting such an attitude. But if it is, then engrossment can and should be part of the traditional four principles approach—because (according to that approach) we ought to act beneficently, that is, do things which benefit patients.

Turning now to (b), the idea that nursing is based round treating the whole person while medicine is to do with eliminating diseases or repairing body parts or systems, is equally problematic. Again, it is worth pointing out that some nursing interventions are curative and technical, whereas some medical interventions are non-curative and more focused on general care. Also, we need to ask what "treating the whole person" (sometimes called the holistic approach) means. If it only means treating people with dignity and respect, not just as bodies or cases, then the *holistic approach* is something that traditional ethics would endorse (because of the principles of autonomy and beneficence). But if it means doing things which go substantially beyond the health care needs of the person in question, then it is not clear why, or whether, health care professionals should be doing such things at all—especially given that health care resources are in short supply.

We end this section by returning to the question of ethics and gender. In what sense, if any, is the traditional four principles approach male or masculine? Let's start with a question: if we were to assume that Gilligan's claim (that the women she surveyed were more likely to think in terms of care, rather than in terms of justice) were true, what would follow from that? Well, one thing that Gilligan's study certainly does *not* establish is that women are *naturally* more likely to think in terms of care than men are. This is because there are (at least) two different explanations for the (alleged) differences between men and women. One is that men and women have different "ethical natures" determined by their biology, perhaps. The other is that these differences are caused by their different experience and social roles: for example, women are more likely to act as carers in the home and do more child rearing. This issue, part of what is sometimes called the "nature–nurture debate", isn't something we can explore in detail. However, its existence shows that

Gilligan's study and other similar studies are not sufficient to show that there are any *natural* (such as biological) differences between men's and women's approaches to ethics, since such differences may simply be the effects of social forces.

If you're not convinced, consider this analogy. Some sociologists do a study that shows that men enjoy football more than women do. Some people read this study and conclude that men are naturally (i.e. biologically) more inclined to enjoy and play ball games. Would this be a valid conclusion to draw? Probably not. Why? Because, for all we know, these differences between men and women might be due to social forces (boys are encouraged to play football at school, while girls are encouraged to do other things) and nothing to do with innate differences between the sexes.

This point relates to another objection to the ethics of care suggested by some writers on feminist ethics. The objection is that promoting the idea that women are natural carers may actually contribute to the oppression of women, by reinforcing negative sexist stereotypes such as the idea that women are and/or should be caring, emotional, non-rational and selfless, whereas men are and/or should be ambitious, detached, unfeeling, rational and selfish. So rather than asserting women's "voices", the ethics of care should instead be seen as reinforcing men's dominance by focusing women's attention on the "feminine virtues" such as selflessly caring for others.

This feminist argument, combined with the fact that there is—as yet—very little (if any) evidence for the view that men and women possess naturally (as opposed to merely socially constructed) different attitudes to ethics, leads us to conclude that there is no reason to think that the four principles approach to ethics is specifically male or masculine. Similarly, we conclude that there is little (or no) argument or evidence for the claim that the "principled" approach to ethics is unsuitable for nurses. And finally, we should point out that ethical principles are a vitally important way of (a) understanding and analysing moral problems, (b) resolving such problems, and (c) ensuring consistency across diverse cases . . .

QUESTIONS:

1. Do you think that the "four principles" approach (discussed in Section 5 above) is in some way biased in favour of either: (a) men, or (b) doctors (as opposed to other health care professionals such as nurses)?
2. Is the "ethics of care" an attractive alternative to the "four principles" approach? If so, why? If not, why not?

Most of the material presented so far has either been general (i.e. supposed to apply to all persons, or to all health care professionals) or medical (meant primarily for doctors). So it is important to raise at this point the question of whether nursing ethics might be importantly different from medical ethics. This is one of the issues that Geoffrey Hunt explores below.

Geoffrey Hunt, "Nursing ethics" in E. Craig (ed.), *Routledge Encyclopedia of Philosophy*, London: Routledge, 1998, retrieved April 26, 2004, from http://www.rep.routledge.com/article/L124

Nursing ethics may be defined simply in relation to what nurses do that doctors and others do not characteristically do; or in relation to the nursing perspective on any issues in health care and medicine. More radically, it claims to employ a distinctive conceptual framework, regarding care, rather than cure, as fundamental. Nursing ethics concerns itself with the relationship between "carer" and "cared for" and the meanings embedded in that relationship. It is the moral exploration of an illness or disability as a personal life crisis rather than an instance of a biomedical generalization.

The divergence of medical and nursing ethics took its cue from a distinction between curing and caring. Curing, involving diagnosis, treatment and prognosis, was taken to be characteristic of medicine (with surgery as the paradigm), while caring, involving preparation for treatment, maintenance, and recuperation, was characteristic of nursing (with, perhaps, palliative or domiciliary care as paradigmatic). These were soon taken to be more than just two aspects of physical management of patients but conceptually distinct kinds of activity, one directed to a "distanced" biology-based approach to dysfunctional specimens, or even parts of specimens, of *Homo sapiens*, and the other a humanities-based intimate approach to individual persons with unique life crises. Whereas this distinction is not sustainable as an absolute it does provide enlightening analytic comparisons of emphasis or tendency.

The distinction has continued to develop as a philosophical one and has merged with gender debates. Nursing ethics has taken up the notion of "care" formulated by Carol Gilligan and Nel Noddings. The debate is largely an engagement with the "principlism" founded by Beauchamp and Childress. Some nursing ethicists have developed the idea that the "ethics of care", rooted in a feminine response to life, is a superior alternative to a masculine "ethics of justice". Certainly the overwhelming majority of nurses are female, but while some take this as evidence of an advantageous feminine moral attitude others have thought it reflects only political contingencies.

Some insist that rationalistic, abstract and liberal "impartiality" and "distance" lead to indifference and unresponsiveness in modern medicine, and expound a contrasting "partialist" nursing ethics of context, personal engagement and unique human relationships. Nursing theorists influenced by Gilligan, such as Fry and Watson, take up her suggestion that whereas a principles approach seeks agreement, the caring approach seeks mutual understanding through an exploration of the meaning of a personal crisis (illness, disability, infirmity). Gadow has a distinctively nursing notion of care in her concept of "existential advocacy": a true nursing relationship involves helping patients make sense of their life experiences so as to regain some control, clarifying the patients' values so as authentically to exercise their freedom of self-determination. The emphasis on the "carer/cared for" relationship has led one stream of nursing ethics, influenced by Benner, into phenomenological methods.

Other writers have attempted to integrate principles-based approaches with "caring relationship" approaches. Beauchamp and Childress, admitting that principles may be insufficient for health care ethics, have responded with a clarification of "mutual interdependence" and "emotional response" in the "ethics of care" and still regard the notion of caring as too undeveloped to be integrated coherently. One empirical study finds no significant difference in the distribution of "impartialist" and "partialist" modes of thinking among doctors and nurses and suggests the modes really operate together but at different levels.

The question of a difference between medical and nursing ethics, whether a sharp one or merely one of emphasis and tendency, is carried into questions about which health care issues nurses identify as ethically problematic and how they approach them. Nurse ethicists often do, and *qua* nurses arguably should, select issues which concern nursing activity (the assessment, planning, implementation and evaluation of care) as opposed to medical activity (diagnosis, treatment, prognosis). Such issues would be found in, for example, health promotion and preventative nursing, continuing care of the elderly, and residential and hospice care. Given the intimate and ongoing nature of the nursing process (as opposed to the transitory medical intervention) ethical issues are identified in everyday and routine issues, such as incontinence and toileting, falls among the elderly, and choice of clothing and sleep periods.

Ethically aware nurses may more readily see the human, personal, cultural and social aspects of any issue, whether medical or nursing, such as patient self-esteem and privacy, pain alleviation and comfort, empowering and encouraging self-care, security and general wellbeing. Ethical issues in nursing research may relate in content to clinical nursing (such as wound or bed sore management) or may, in form, approach issues through meanings and relationships employing the methods of ethnography or "action theory".

The considerations above also apply to ethical issues in the organization and professional development of nursing. The themes of "nurse autonomy" and "advocacy" are
particularly strong. The first concerns the degree to which nurses can exercise moral choice
as employees and as the subordinates of doctors. Thus, professional and contractual
obligations may come into conflict, for example, over informing the patient in their interest
about a matter the employer may regard as commercially confidential; and medical
judgment and nursing judgment may conflict, for example, over when to discharge a
patient. In these contexts the rights and wrongs of "blowing the whistle" may arise. This
may even be entailed by the demand that the nurse act as "advocate" of the patient. The
interpretation of this notion is controversial. While it requires that the nurse plead the
cause of the patient, it is not always clear whether this is to be given the "banal"
interpretation that the patient by definition is someone who needs another to do what they
would do if able, or the "radical" interpretation that the nurse must challenge and speak
up to defend the patient against any obstacle whatsoever to their autonomy.

"Nursing ethics" may be taken as a generic term to cover the concerns of all the
professions allied to medicine. In midwifery ethical issues emerge from maternal choice,
the professional autonomy of the midwife *vis-à-vis* obstetrics, and "natural childbirth". In
physiotherapy there are questions around delimiting potentially coercive or unavoidably
uncomfortable or even futile procedures, such as chest physiotherapy on terminally ill
patients.

QUESTION:

1. Are there any fundamental differences between medical ethics and nursing
   ethics? If so, what are they?

7. AUTONOMY, CONSENT AND PATERNALISM

The concept of autonomy occupies such a prominent position in contemporary
health care ethics that it stands in need of further examination. In the next
extract, Gillon puts forward what might be described as "the case in favour of"
autonomy, particularly as part of the "four principles" approach introduced
earlier. He then (in the second passage) gives an explanation of the closely related
concept of paternalism.

R. Gillon, "Ethics Needs Principles—Four Can Encompass the Rest—and
Respect for Autonomy Should Be 'First Among Equals' ", *Journal of Medical
Ethics*, 2003; 29: 310–312

... let me reiterate that the actual use made of the four principles approach can
legitimately vary from person to person, culture to culture. Those who like Dan Callahan
want less emphasis on respect for autonomy can advocate a different balance, or harmony,
between the principles. His communitarian approach to ethics is entirely compatible with
a four principles approach. I recall being assured in Beijing that Chinese people—ethicists
and others—certainly do accept the principle of respect for autonomy; they simply give it
less weight when it competes with concerns of beneficence for the whole group. While I
suspect that Dan would not wish to go so far as the Chinese do in prioritising the provision
of communitarian benefit over respect for individuals' autonomy it is entirely consistent
with the use of a four principles approach to seek to do so more than is currently done in
the USA under either of its political parties. To give but one example, the nonprovision of
a universal health service in the richest country in the world (in contrast to its acceptance
of what seems to be a universal gun service) is in my view too, an example of a political

infrastructure that gives excessive weight to respect for individual autonomy over concerns to benefit the sick. It also manifests what to many of us in Europe (and I know to many in the USA also) seems a wrongly skewed approach to distributive justice. But that is not to show that the four principles approach is wrong; it is to argue against the way those principles are being prioritised within a particular social system, and perhaps also to argue against the substantive interpretation of distributive justice within that social system.

That said, let me reiterate why I personally believe that emphasis on respect for autonomy is in many circumstances morally desirable and why I personally am inclined to see respect for autonomy as *primus inter pares*—first among equals—among the four principles. Firstly, autonomy—by which in summary I simply mean deliberated self rule; the ability and tendency to think for oneself, to make decisions for oneself about the way one wishes to lead one's life based on that thinking, and then to enact those decisions—is what makes morality—any sort of morality—possible. For that reason alone autonomy—free will—is morally very precious and ought not merely to be respected, but its development encouraged and nurtured and the character traits or "habits of the heart" that tend to promote its exercise should indeed be regarded and extolled as virtues.

Secondly, beneficence and non-maleficence to other autonomous agents both require respect for the autonomy of those agents. Although there are some general norms of human needs, benefits and harms, people vary in their individual perceptions and evaluations of their own needs, benefits, and harms. Jehovah's Witness attitudes to blood are simply vivid illustrations of this variability. Thus even to attempt to benefit people with as little harm as possible requires, where possible, discovery of what the proposed beneficiary regards as a benefit, regards as a harm, and regards as the most beneficial and least harmful of the available options. Moreover even if the person agrees that one available intervention would be more beneficial than another, he or she may simply wish to reject the beneficial intervention. It may be because of an idiosyncratic basis of assessment of harm—for example, the autonomous belief that a blood transfusion will lead to eternal damnation or some equivalently massive harm. Or it may be a relatively trivial assessment.

Take my own case as an example of a relatively trivial assessment. I know it would be beneficial for me to do more exercise and eat less animal fats—less crispy bacon fat, roast duck, and roast pork with all the cracklings, foie gras, butter in my baked potatoes, and butter for sautéing the left over boiled potatoes, less Stilton, Roquefort, Camembert, Mont D'Or, and all the other delicious and wicked cheeses. Now of course I know that I would benefit from stopping—or greatly reducing—my intake of these delectable but oleaginous animal materials. But I have autonomously decided not to do so. Should I be made to do so on the basis that it would be better for me (as I agree it would be)? Would it be a better or happier world, would there be more eudaimonia, human flourishing or agape in a world where I and people like me were *made* to do what we acknowledge to be better for us? I freely acknowledge that avoidance of sufficient harm to others may justify overriding my autonomy (though this should be achieved through a political system that respects the autonomy of the governed through some form of democratic law making system). But when it comes to forcing autonomous agents to do, or have done to them, what is good for them despite their autonomous choices not to do so, my vote will be for respect for autonomy—both for its own sake and because overall I believe such respect will result in greater benefit, however it is to be measured.

When it comes to justice, again, I argue that respect for autonomy must play an important role. First comes the problem, true of all our moral values, but perhaps especially acute in the case of justice, of deciding which substantive account of justice we should adopt in different contexts such as those of distributive justice, rights based justice, and legal justice. But for any substantive theory within each of these contexts it seems morally impossible to avoid a place for respect for autonomy. In distributive justice, for example, while a needs based criterion must surely have a central role, so too must respect for autonomy. Why? Both because, as I've just argued, responding to people's needs justly will require respect for those people's autonomous views, including autonomous rejection of offers to meet their needs; and, more importantly, because providing for people's needs requires resources, including other people's resources. Again it seems reasonable to claim that appropriating those resources without at least a political and law making system that, through a democratic process, respects the autonomy of those people would be unjust. But if this is accepted then respect for people's autonomy must be an integral component of any substantive theory of distributive justice just as meeting people's needs must be an integral component. When it comes to rights based justice, an integral component again must be, it is widely acknowledged, respect for people's autonomy rights. And in the context of legal justice (which I interpret as the *prima facie* moral obligation to respect morally acceptable laws) yet again respect for autonomy must surely play an important role. Why? Because if people are to be morally bound by laws they ought to have some opportunity to autonomously accept or reject being thus bound. Hence the moral need for some sort of democratic law making system that—to the extent possible—respects the autonomy of those governed by the laws it creates. Hence, too, the lack of an even *prima facie* moral obligation for people to obey laws that are not open to democratic revision (revision compatible with the four universal *prima facie* principles!).

So yes, for all these reasons it seems clear to me that respect for autonomy—in so far as such respect is consistent with respect for the autonomy of all potentially affected—should be seen as an integral component of the other three of the four principles and thus should be regarded as first among equals. Yet, perhaps paradoxically, I believe such emphasis on nurturing, encouraging, and respecting people's autonomy is actually the best way of encouraging autonomous acceptance of restrictions on our own autonomy, not only in order to respect the autonomy of others but also in the pursuit of the other moral concerns—benefits to others, avoidance of harm to others, and justice for others.

The centrality of respect for autonomy is, I believe, particularly worth emphasising to two groups who often scorn its importance. Those feminists who are inclined to reject its moral importance should ponder its value as a potentially powerful moral weapon to defend women against subjugation by men. A common methodology for male disrespect for women is to deny the existence—or the adequacy—of women's autonomy and thus of the need to respect it, particularly when those who are regarded as autonomous (typically their fathers, husbands, brothers, and other male authority figures) believe it to be against women's interests to have their autonomy respected. Thus it is surely in women's interests throughout the world both to emphasise respect for autonomy as a core moral obligation (something that powerful men rarely deny in respect of their own autonomy) and to emphasise that once they have matured out of childhood (something that girls typically do earlier than boys) women have as much right to have their autonomy respected as men. And incidentally Amartya Sen points out the great benefits that respect for women's autonomy brings in its wake.

A second group to whom I would recommend the importance of respect for autonomy are those who, like Alastair Campbell, tend to regard the four principles approach as a form of moral imperialism threatening to impose moral hegemony upon other moral perspectives. Two points should reassure them. The first is that the principle of respect for autonomy requires respect for the autonomy of *all* autonomous agents, including of course respect for their moral autonomy, in so far as such respect is compatible with respect for the autonomy of all potentially affected. The second point is the empirical one (which I assume would be widely agreed) that people's cultural environments substantially influence their autonomous beliefs, including their moral stances. Human nature being thus, respect for autonomy contingently builds in a *prima facie* moral requirement to respect both individual and cultural moral variability.

QUESTION:

1. Do you agree with Gillon about the importance that should be attached to autonomy? If so, why? If not, why not?

R. Gillon, "Paternalism" in *Philosophical Medical Ethics*, Chichester: John Wiley, 1985, pp.67–71

Sometimes one has as a doctor to be paternalistic to one's patients—that is, do things against their immediate wishes or without consulting them, indeed perhaps with a measure of deception, to do what is in their best interest . . . Just as parents may sometimes have to make important decisions in a child's best interests against the child's will or by deception or without telling the child, so doctors sometimes have to act on behalf of their patients. As Dr Ingelfinger put it, "If you agree that the physician's primary function is to make the patient feel better, a certain amount of authoritarianism, paternalism and domination are the essence of the physician's effectiveness" . . . Here I shall consider some arguments offered in support of medical paternalism.

ARGUMENTS FOR MEDICAL PATERNALISM

The first such argument is that medical ethics since Hippocratic times has required doctors to do the best for their patients. The Hippocratic oath requires that "I will follow that system or regimen which, according to my ability and judgment I consider for the benefit of my patients." It says nothing about doing what patients wish, explaining likely consequences, good or bad, or describing alternative courses of action.

Put so baldly this way of expressing the duty to do the best for one's patients may not sound attractive. Put in terms of various real life circumstances, however, with patients terrified by their diseases, perhaps suffering great pain and other highly unpleasant symptoms such as breathlessness, intractable itching, disordered sensation, misery and depression, and, often, utter bewilderment, it becomes far more plausible to think, especially if one is that patient's doctor, relative, or friend, that the last thing one should do is add to the misery and worry by passing on the results of the biopsy, the risk of treatment, the unsatisfactory options, or whatever other nasty bits of information the doctor has up his sleeve. More plausible indeed, but how justifiable?

Even if one accepts the claim that the overriding moral requirement is to do one's best to improve one's patients' health, minimise their suffering, and prolong their lives, it is by no means clear that these ends are furthered by, for example, false confidence, paternalistic decision making, evasions, deceit, and downright lies. Of course, such behaviour (the hearty slap on the back, "Well of course we're not magicians old boy but we'll do our best for you, you can rest assured of that, and we've had some excellent results . . . ") greatly reduces the anguish for the doctor: honest discussion with people who, for example, have a fatal disease concerning their condition and prospect are emotionally demanding, as is the necessary follow up; it is far less difficult to "look on the bright side". The assumption, however, that this generally makes such patients happier is highly suspect.

What is more, it is often only the patient who is deceived and treated thus, while a relative or relatives are told the truth; the deceit that this imposes on the family (and also on other medical and nursing staff) may itself provoke considerable distress, not to mention the breaking of normal medical confidentiality and the effects of doing so. Then there is the suffering of the patient who suspects that something nasty is afoot but cannot discover what. Finally, there is the suffering of a fatally ill patient on discovering that he or she has been deceived by his or her doctor and family. What a way to go.

Of course, some patients really do want their doctors to shield them from any unpleasant information and to take over decision making on all fronts concerning their illness. Doing what the patient wants, however, is not (by definition) paternalism. My point is that not all patients want doctors to behave like this, and for those who do not it is highly dubious to suppose that their suffering is reduced by it or their health improved or even their lives prolonged. Still, time, and effort are required to find out what the patient really wants, whereas in practice it is often merely assumed that the patient "doesn't want to know".

A second line of justification of paternalistic behaviour is that patients are not capable of making decisions about medical problems: they are too ignorant medically speaking, and such knowledge as they have is too partial in both senses of the word. Thus they are unlikely to understand the situation even if it is explained to them and so are likely to make worse decisions than the doctor would.

Even if one were to accept that "best decisions" are the primary moral determinant it is worth distinguishing the sorts of decisions that doctors might be expected to make better than their patients from those where little or no reason exists to expect this. In the technical area for which they have been specially and extensively trained there is little doubt that doctors are likely to make more technically or medically correct (and hence in that sense better) decisions than their medically ignorant patients. The doctor who advises his patients that to continue her pregnancy would, because of coexisting medical condition, be from her point of view appreciably more dangerous than to have a termination and that therefore a termination would be better may be giving medically sound advice based on superior medical knowledge. If he insisted or even advised that a termination would be better in some moral sense he would be stepping outside his realm of competence: he is not better trained professionally to make moral assessments than is his patient, and even if he were many would object that it is not the doctor's role even to advise on his patient's moral decisions let alone make them.

DOCTORS AS ASSESSORS OF HAPPINESS

The counterargument just offered meets the paternalist on his own ground by agreeing that there are some areas, notably the technical, in which doctors may be expected to make better decisions than their patients. It points out that in other areas, including the moral sphere, there is little reason to expect them to do so. A further matter on which it is doubtful whether doctors are qualified or likely to make better decisions than their patients concerns what course of action is likely to produce most happiness or least unhappiness for everyone, all things considered (the utilitarian objective).

Some doctors believe, for example, that in perplexing cases such as those of severely handicapped newborn infants it is up to them to "shoulder the burden", assess what course of action will produce the greatest benefit all things considered, and than implement it. As one paediatrician wrote, "In the end it is usually the doctor who has to decide the issue: it is . . . cruel to ask the parents whether they want their child to live or die."

The philosopher Professor Allen Buchanan has pointed out that if a doctor undertakes to assess which of various available courses of action (including informing the parents of the options and asking them which they favour) is most likely to produce the greatest happiness all things considered he must consider an awful lot of factors.

> . . . [T]he physician must first make intrapersonal comparisons of harm and benefit of each member of the family, if the information is divulged. Then he must somehow coalesce these various intrapersonal net harm judgements into an estimate of total net harm which divulging the information will do to the family as a whole. Then he must make similar intrapersonal and interpersonal net harm judgments about the results of not telling the truth. Finally he must compare these totals and determine which course of action will minimise harm to the family as a whole.

Buchanan makes a similar analysis for the doctor who tries seriously to assess whether it would be best, all things considered, to tell a dying patient the truth about his predicament. After showing the complexity of any such analysis and its necessarily morally evaluative components Buchanan concludes:

> Furthermore, once the complexity of these judgments is appreciated and once their evaluative character is understood it is implausible to hold that the physician is in a better position to make them the patient or his family. The failure to ask what sorts of harm/benefit judgments may properly be made by the physician in his capacity as a physician is a fundamental feature of medical paternalism.

Of course, such assessments—moral and preference assessments—are difficult for anyone to make. The point is that there is no *prima facie* reason to suppose that doctors make them better than their patients. Even in the strongest case, that of technical medical assessment, the argument from patient ignorance is suspect for in practice many doctors can explain technical medical issues to their patients' satisfaction. Better postgraduate training in effective communication or delegation to colleagues who have these skills, or both, are alternatives to arguing that such effective communication cannot be achieved.

All the preceding counterarguments meet the defence of paternalism on its own ground by accepting its assumption that the overriding moral objective is to maximise the happiness of the patient alone, of the family, or of society as a whole. Kantians (for whom the principle of respect for autonomy is morally supreme) and pluralist deontologists (who believe that an adequate moral theory requires a variety of potentially conflicting moral principles including that of respect for autonomy) will argue that there are many circumstances in which a person's autonomy must be respected even if to do so will result in an obviously worse decision in terms of the patient's, the family's, or, even, a particular society's happiness. . . . [T]his conclusion is also supported by many utilitarians on the grounds that respect for people's autonomy is required if human welfare really is to be maximised.

Sir Richard Bayliss has movingly described the case of a Christian Scientist whose decision to turn to orthodox medicine for treatment of her thyrotoxicosis came too late to save her life. Few who do not accept Christian Scientism can believe she made a "better" decision in relation to her longevity and health when she rejected the advice of her original doctor in favour of her cult's. Those, however, for whom the principle of respect for autonomy is morally important would not deny her the respect of allowing her to refuse medical help in the first place even though this was highly likely to be fatal and thus cause her family and medical attendant great anguish and even though paternalistic intervention could have saved her life.

QUESTION:

1. Can you think of any cases in which medical paternalism would be justified?

The principle of respect for autonomy is widely believed to be related in important ways to more practical ideas such as consent, confidentiality, and veracity (truthfulness). Hence, we can respect patients' autonomy by seeking their consent, by maintaining confidentiality, and by telling the truth. The rest of this section focuses principally on consent, although this to some extent incorporates veracity because "consent" usually means *informed* consent, and we can only inform patients by telling them the truth. (A more extensive discussion of confidentiality, including a discussion of some ethical issues, can be found in Chapter 9 at p.565.) The next extract, by Wilkinson, offers a basic account of "valid consent".

Stephen Wilkinson, *Bodies for Sale*, London: Routledge, 2003, pp.75–78

. . . [A]s well as the distinction between consensual and non-consensual transactions, there is a further distinction—*within* the consensual—between *valid* and *invalid* consent. Whereas the distinction between consensual and non-consensual is essentially psychological or social, the valid/invalid distinction is moral. Invalid consents are perfectly *real*: for example, if I hand over my money in response to a "Your money or your life!" threat, then I really have agreed to give you the money. But such consents don't have the same moral significance as valid consents. In particular, valid consents (for example, to sexual intercourse, surgery, or the taking of property) can morally justify acts in ways that invalid consents can't. Indeed . . . what it means to say that a consent is valid is precisely that it provides a justification for certain action(s) (sometimes on its own, sometimes in conjunction with other facts). For example, to say that I have *validly* consented to having my tooth removed is to say that my consent is of a sufficiently high quality (in conjunction with other facts) to *justify* my dentist's (tooth-removing) actions . . .

. . . The aim of the next few pages is to say what valid consent is. In areas like medical ethics valid consent is normally called *informed consent*. The expression *valid consent* is preferable, however, because, as we'll see, adequate information is only one part of validity, and consent can be invalidated by factors other than lack of information.

The concept of consent is widely used both in everyday contexts and by moral and political philosophers. One of the places where it has been most heavily employed and analysed in recent times is within healthcare ethics. Consider, for example, these two definitions of "consent", both provided by bioethicists (Gillon, and Faden and Beauchamp respectively):

> consent means a voluntary, uncoerced decision, made by a sufficiently competent or autonomous person on the basis of adequate information and deliberation, to accept rather than reject some proposed course of action. (R. Gillon, *Philosophical Medical Ethics*, Chichester: Wiley, 1986, p. 113).

> an informed consent is an autonomous action by . . . a patient that authorises a professional . . . to initiate a medical plan for the patient . . . an informed consent is given if a patient or subject with (1) substantial understanding and (2) in substantial absence of control by others (3) intentionally (4) authorises a professional. (R. Faden and T. Beauchamp, "The concept of informed consent," in T. Beuachamp and L. Walters (eds), *Contemporary Issues in Bioethics*, Belmont, CA: Wadsworth, 1994 (4th ed) p. 149).

Plausibly, both definitions suggest that in order for a consent to be valid, three main elements must be present (or present in sufficient quantities): information, competence, and voluntariness.

Let's now take a look at these three main elements, starting with information. Medical ethicists have spent a great deal of time on attempts to construct a substantive account of how much information a patient or research subject needs in order for her consent to be valid. I'll not try anything that ambitious here, not least because my concerns are rather more general than theirs. It is, however, worth saying something about why information matters and, schematically, about what sort of information matters and how much there should be. The reason why information matters is simply that in order for A to consent to X, A needs to know what X is and what the likely consequences of X are. Exactly how much A needs to know about X is not something that I'll investigate here. However, it seems fair to say that, at least in the standard case, A needs to know about X's main benefits and drawbacks and about any other factors which one would reasonably expect to affect A's decision about whether or not to accept X.

Two further points about information need to be made before we proceed. Both are fairly obvious but nonetheless important, not least because they are sometimes over-looked . . .

The first is that *full* or *complete* knowledge is not required for validity. The main reason for this is that even if we allow that such a complete knowledge state is a theoretical possibility, it is certainly not a state in which humans very often (if ever) find themselves in practice. Hence, if we decided to make full knowledge a requirement, that would commit us to the (absurd) view that there are virtually no cases of valid consent. The second point (which is in many respects similar) is that *experiential* knowledge is not generally required for validity. Experiential knowledge of X is knowing what it is like to experience X, which normally means having experienced X and being able to remember experiencing X. Experiential knowledge—for example, of the pains or pleasures associated with certain things—can be very important and may well help to validate consents a⌐

more generally, help people to make good decisions. However, it can't be a general requirement because otherwise it would be, at best, difficult for people to consent to things for the first time. Again, sexual consent provides a pretty clear case in point. If experiential knowledge were required then it would be almost impossible for virgins to consent validly to their first sexual encounters. And depending on how finely we individuate items of experiential knowledge it may, similarly, be impossible even for non-virgins validly to consent to their first sexual experience with A, with B, with C, of X, and so on . . .

. . . To turn now to *competence*, this term refers to the consenter's mental capacities. Is she capable of making reasonable decisions? Can she understand relevant information and issues and rationally assess the pros and cons of what is proposed? Examples of consents being invalid because of lack of competence include consents given by young children, consents given by people suffering from mental disabilities or illnesses, and consents given by people whose minds are under the influence of alcohol or other mind-affecting drugs. As I've suggested, people in all three categories can validly consent to *some* things, depending on the degree of mental incapacity. For example, we'd view most contracts between drunks and taxi drivers or bartenders as valid, and many drunken consents to sexual intercourse as valid (except, perhaps, in very extreme cases of intoxication, or where the intoxication is itself involuntary). Given their mental limitations, though, people in the categories just mentioned do, in general, run a substantial risk of providing invalid consent, especially for complex and/or important decisions. After all, we wouldn't, for example, take seriously an extremely drunken consent to organ donation from a prospective live donor.

. . . the third element of valid consent is *voluntariness*. This is not to be confused with what philosophers call *free will*. That is, you don't need to be completely free from all causal determinants in order to act voluntarily. Rather, to act voluntarily is just to be free from certain specific types of influence, notably coercion.

QUESTION:

1. Think of some examples in which a morally *invalid* consent is given. What is it that makes the consent invalid in these cases?

8. ETHICAL ISSUES AT THE BEGINNING AND END OF LIFE

We start this section by looking at some key concepts in practical ethics, in particular the supposed "sanctity" and "value" of human life. We then introduce you to some current debates in reproductive ethics, with a special emphasis on issues that have concerned UK courts, legislators, and regulators in recent years, before turning finally to the euthanasia debate.

J. Glover, *Causing Death and Saving Lives*, Harmondsworth: Penguin 1977, pp.39, 45–46, 50–53

Most of us think it is wrong to kill people. Some think it is wrong in all circumstances, while others think that in special circumstances (say, in a just war or in self-defence) some killing may be justified. But even those who do not think killing is always wrong normally think that a special justification is needed. The assumption is that killing can at best only be justified to avoid a greater evil. It is not obvious to many people what the answer is to the question "*Why* is killing wrong?" It is not clear whether the wrongness of killing should be treated as a kind of moral axiom, or whether it can be explained by appealing to some more fundamental principle or set of principles. One very common view is that some principle of the sanctity of life has to be included among the ultimate principles of any acceptable moral system . . .

Someone who thinks that taking life is intrinsically wrong may explain this by saying that the state of being alive is itself intrinsically valuable. This claim barely rises to the level of an argument for the sanctity of life, for it simply asserts that there is value in what the taking of life takes away.

Against such a view, cases are sometimes cited of people who are either very miserable or in great pain, without any hope of cure. Might such people not be better off dead? But this could be admitted without giving up the view that life is intrinsically valuable. We could say that life has value but that not being desperately miserable can have even more value.

I have no way of refuting someone who holds that being alive, even though unconscious, is intrinsically valuable. But it is a view that will seem unattractive to those of us who, in our own case, see a life of permanent coma as in no way preferable to death. From the subjective point of view, there is nothing to choose between the two. Schopenhauer saw this clearly when he said of the destruction of the body:

> But actually we feel this destruction only in the evils or illness or of old age; on the other hand, for the *subject*, death itself consists merely in the moment when consciousness vanishes, since the activity of the brain ceases. The extension of the stoppage to all the other parts of the organism which follows this is really already an event after death. Therefore, in a subjective respect, death concerns only consciousness.

Those of us who think that the direct objections to killing have to do with death considered from the standpoint of the person killed will find it natural to regard life as being of value only as a necessary condition of consciousness. For permanently comatose existence is subjectively indistinguishable from death, and unlikely often to be thought intrinsically preferable to it by people thinking of their own future . . .

It is worth mentioning that the objection to taking human life should not rest on what is sometimes called "speciesism": human life being treated as having a special priority over animal life *simply because* it is human. The analogy is with racism, in its purest form, according to which people of a certain race ought to be treated differently *simply* because of their membership of that race, without any argument referring to special features of that race being given. This is objectionable partly because of its moral arbitrariness: unless some relevant empirical characteristics can be cited, there can be no argument for such discrimination. Those concerned to reform our treatment of animals point out that speciesism exhibits the same arbitrariness. It is not in itself sufficient argument for treating a creature less well to say simply that it is not a member of our species. An adequate justification must cite relevant differences between the species. We still have the question of what features of a life are of intrinsic value.

I have suggested that in destroying life or mere consciousness, we are not destroying anything intrinsically valuable. These states only matter because they are necessary for other things that matter in themselves. If a list could be made of all the things that are valuable for their own sake, these things would be the ingredients of a "life worth living".

One objection to the idea of judging that a life is worth living is that this seems to imply the possibility of comparing being alive and being dead. And, as Wittgenstein said, "Death is not an event in life: we do not live to experience death."

But we can have a preference for being alive over being dead, or for being conscious over being unconscious, without needing to make any "comparisons" between these states. We prefer to be anaesthetized for a painful operation; queuing for a bus in the rain at midnight, we wish we were at home asleep; but for the most part we prefer to be awake and experience our life as it goes by. These preferences do not depend on any view about "what it is like" being unconscious, and our preference for life does not depend on beliefs about "what it is like" being dead. It is rather that we treat being dead or unconscious as nothing, and then decide whether a stretch of experience is better or worse than nothing.

And this claim, that life of a certain sort is better than nothing, is an expression of our preference.

Any list of the ingredients of a worthwhile life would obviously be disputable. Most people might agree on many items but many others could be endlessly argued over. It might be agreed that a happy life is worth living, but people do not agree on what happiness is. And some things that make life worth living may only debatably be to do with happiness. (Aristotle: "And so they tell us that Anaxagoras answered a man who was raising problems of this sort and asking why one should choose rather to be born than not—'for the sake of viewing the heavens and the whole order of the universe'.")

A life worth living should not be confused with a morally virtuous life. Moral virtues such as honesty or a sense of fairness can belong to someone whose life is relatively bleak and empty. Music may enrich someone's life, or the death of a friend impoverish it, without him growing more or less virtuous.

I shall not try to say what sorts of things do make life worth living. (Temporary loss of a sense of the absurd led me to try to do so. But, apart from the disputability of any such list, I found that the ideal life suggested always sounded ridiculous.) I shall assume that a life worth living has more to it that mere consciousness. It should be possible to explain the wrongness of killing partly in terms of the destruction of life worth living, without presupposing more than minimal agreement as to exactly what makes life worthwhile.

I shall assume that, where someone's life is worth living, this is a good reason for holding that it would be directly wrong to kill him. This is what can be extracted from the doctrine of the sanctity of life by someone who accepts the criticisms made here of that view. If life is worth preserving only because it is the vehicle for consciousness, and consciousness is of value only because it is necessary for something else, then that "something else" is the heart of this particular objection to killing. It is what is meant by a "life worth living" or a "worth while life".

The idea of dividing people's lives into ones that are worth living and ones that are not is likely to seem both presumptuous and dangerous. As well as seeming to indicate an arrogant willingness to pass godlike judgements on other people's lives, it may remind people of the Nazi policy of killing patients in mental hospitals. But there is really nothing godlike in such a judgement. It is not moral judgement we are making, if we think that someone's life is so empty and unhappy as to be not worth living. It results from an attempt (obviously an extremely fallible one) to see his life from his own point of view and to see what he gets out of it. It must also be stressed that no suggestion is being made that it automatically becomes right to kill people whose lives we think are not worth living. It is only being argued that, if someone's life is worth living, this is *one* reason why it is directly wrong to kill him.

QUESTIONS:

1. In what circumstances, if any, is killing another person morally acceptable?
2. Do you think that a distinction can be drawn between lives "that are worth living and ones that are not", and what, if anything, would make a life "not worth living"?

The next few passages deal with issues in reproductive ethics that are relevant to contemporary legal and policy debates. In particular, reproductive cloning was the subject of legislation in 2001 (see Chapter 10, p.727) and the permissibility of selecting "saviour siblings" has been considered in a number of cases (see Chapter 11, pp.841–848).

Soren Holm, "A Life in the Shadow: One Reason Why We Should Not Clone Humans", *Cambridge Quarterly of Healthcare Ethics*, 1998, 7, 160–162

INTRODUCTION

One of the arguments that is often put forward in the discussion of human cloning is that it is in itself wrong to create a copy of a human being.

This argument is usually dismissed by pointing out that a) we do not find anything wrong in the existence of monozygotic twins even though they are genetically identical, and b) the clone would not be an exact copy of the original even in those cases where it is an exact genetic copy, since it would have experienced a different environment that would have modified its biological and psychological development.

In my view both these counterarguments are valid, but nevertheless I think that there is some core of truth in the assertion that it is wrong deliberately to try to create a copy of an already existing human being. It is this idea that I will briefly try to explicate here.

THE LIFE IN THE SHADOW ARGUMENT

When we see a pair of monozygotic twins who are perfectly identically dressed some of us experience a slight sense of unease, especially in the cases where the twins are young children. This unease is exacerbated when people establish competitions where the winners are the most identical pair of twins. The reason for this uneasiness is, I believe, that the identical clothes could signal a reluctance on the part of the parents to let each twin develop his or her individual and separate personality or a reluctance to let each twin lead his or her own life. In the extreme case each twin is constantly compared with the other and any difference is counteracted.

In the case of cloning based on somatic cells we have what is effectively a set of monozygotic twins with a potentially very large age difference. The original may have lived all his or her life and may even have died before the clone is brought into existence. Therefore, there will not be any direct day-by-day comparison and identical clothing, but then a situation that is even worse for the clone is likely to develop. I shall call this situation "a life in the shadow" and I shall develop an argument against human cloning that may be labeled the "life in the shadow argument."

Let us try to imagine what will happen when a clone is born and its social parents have to begin rearing it. Usually when a child is born we ask hypothetical questions like "How will it develop?" or "What kind of person will it become?" and we often answer them with reference to various psychological traits we think we can identify in the biological mother or father or in their families, for instance "I hope that he won't get the kind of temper you had when you were a child!"

In the case of the clone we are, however, likely to give much more specific answers to such questions. Answers that will then go on to affect the way the child is reared. There is no doubt that the common public understanding of the relationship between genetics and psychology contains substantial strands of genetic essentialism, i.e., the idea that the genes determine psychology and personality. This public idea is reinforced every time the media report the finding of new genes for depression, schizophrenia, etc. Therefore, it is likely that the parents of the clone will already have formed in their minds a quite definite picture of how the clone will develop, a picture that is based on the actual development of the original. This picture will control the way they rear the child. They will try to prevent some developments, and try to promote others. Just imagine how a clone of Adolf Hitler or Pol Pot would be reared, or how a clone of Albert Einstein, Ludwig van Beethoven, or Michael Jordan would be brought up. The clone would in a very literal way live his or her life in the shadow of the life of the original. At every point in the clone's life there would be someone who had already lived that life, with whom the clone could be compared and against whom the clone's accomplishments could be measured.

That there would in fact be a strong tendency to make the inference from genotype to phenotype and to let the conclusion of such an inference affect rearing can perhaps be seen more clearly if we imagine the following hypothetical situation:

In the future new genetic research reveals that there are only a limited number of possible human genotypes, and that genotypes are therefore recycled every 300 years (i.e., somebody who died 300 years ago had exactly the same genotype as me). It is further discovered that there is some complicated, but not practically impossible, method whereby it is possible to discover the identity of the persons who 300, 600, 900, etc. years ago instantiated the genotype that a specific fetus now has.

I am absolutely certain that people would split into two sharply disagreeing camps if this became a possibility. One group, perhaps the majority, would try to identify the previous instantiations of their child's genotype. Another group would emphatically not seek this information because they would not want to know and would not want their children to grow up in the shadow of a number of previously led lives with the same genotype. The option to remain in ignorance is, however, not open to social parents of contemporary clones.

If the majority would seek the information in this scenario, firms offering the method of identification would have a very brisk business, and it could perhaps even become usual to expect of prospective parents that they make use of this new possibility. Why would this happen? The only reasonable explanation, apart from initial curiosity, is that people would believe that by identifying the previous instantiation of the genotype they would thereby gain valuable knowledge about their child. But knowledge is in general only valuable if it can be converted into new options for action, and the most likely form of action would be that information about the previous instantiations would be used in deciding how to rear the present child. This again points to the importance of the public perception of genetic essentialism, since the environment must have changed considerably in the 300-year span between each instantiation of the genotype.

WHAT IS WRONG ABOUT A LIFE IN THE SHADOW?

What is wrong with living your life as a clone in the shadow of the life of the original? It diminishes the clone's possibility of living a life that is in a full sense of that word his or her life. The clone is forced to be involved in an attempt to perform a complicated partial re-enactment of the life of somebody else (the original). In our usual arguments for the importance of respect for autonomy or for the value of self-determination we often affirm that it is the final moral basis for these principles that they enable persons to live their lives the way they themselves want to live these lives. If we deny part of this opportunity to clones and force them to live their lives in the shadow of someone else we are violating some of our most fundamental moral principles and intuitions. Therefore, as long as genetic essentialism is a common cultural belief there are good reasons not to allow human cloning.

FINAL QUALIFICATIONS

It is important to note that the "life in the shadow argument" does not rely on the false premise that we can make an inference from genotype to (psychological or personality) phenotype, but only on the true premise that there is a strong public tendency to make such an inference. This means that the conclusions of the argument only follow as long as this empirical premise remains true. If ever the public relinquishes all belief in genetic essentialism the "life in the shadow argument" would fail, but such a development seems highly unlikely.

In conclusion I should perhaps also mention that I am fully aware of two possible counterarguments to the argument presented above. The first points out that even if a life in the shadow of the original is perhaps problematic and not very good, it is the only life the clone can have, and that it is therefore in the clone's interest to have this life as long as it is not worse than having no life at all. The "life in the shadow argument" therefore does not show that cloning should be prohibited. I am unconvinced by this counterargument, just as I am by all arguments involving comparisons between existence and nonexistence, but it is outside the scope of the present short paper to show decisively that the counterargument is wrong.

The second counterargument states that the conclusions of the "life in the shadow argument" can be avoided if all clones are anonymously put up for adoption, so that no knowledge about the original is available to the social parents of the clone. I am happy to accept this counterargument, but I think that a system where I was not allowed to rear the clone of myself would practically annihilate any interest in human cloning. The attraction in cloning for many is exactly in the belief that I can recreate myself. The cases where human cloning solves real medical or reproductive problems are on the fringe of the area of cloning.

QUESTIONS:

1. How convincing is the "life in the shadow" argument?
2. Is human reproductive cloning morally wrong? If so, why? If not, why not?
3. Would the fact that human reproductive cloning was morally wrong be a sufficient reason to ban it? (Think back to the earlier discussion of law and morality in Section 3 when answering this.)

Robert J. Boyle and Julian Savulescu, "Ethics of Using Preimplantation Genetic Diagnosis to Select a Stem Cell Donor for an Existing Person", *British Medical Journal*, 2001; 323; 1240–1243 (24 November)

Preimplantation genetic diagnosis (PGD) involves genetic analysis of artificially fertilised embryos to select an embryo with a desired genotype before it is implanted. Since the 1980s, over 2500 cycles of PGD have been performed worldwide. The technique has been used to test for disorders caused by a single gene (cystic fibrosis, thalassaemia, sickle cell disease, muscular dystrophy) and chromosomal abnormalities (Down's syndrome, trisomy 18). The procedure is regulated in the United Kingdom by the Human Fertilisation and Embryo Authority, which says it should be used only for detecting "very serious, life threatening conditions" and not for minor genetic abnormalities.

The technique has been used to detect genes for adult onset disorders such as Huntington's disease and for familial predisposition to cancer, such as Li-Fraumeni syndrome (which involves mutations in p53 cancer suppressor genes). It has been used in Australia by fertile couples without a history of sex linked disorders to select the sex of their child . . .

PGD FOR THE BENEFIT OF A RELATIVE

Children have been conceived to provide stem cells for their siblings. In the most publicised case, the Ayala case, Marissa Ayala was conceived in 1989 to provide stem cells for her sister Anissa. A later report noted, "Marissa is now a healthy four year old, and, by all accounts, as loved and cherished as her parents said she would be. The bone marrow transplant was a success and Anissa is now a married, leukemia-free bank clerk." Assisted reproduction has been used to conceive children to provide stem cells for siblings.

At the end of 1999, a couple in the United States underwent in vitro fertilisation and for the first time used PGD to screen their embryos for those whose tissue type matched that of their daughter, who had Fanconi's anaemia. Over four treatment cycles, five suitable embryos were implanted; one survived and at birth blood from the umbilical cord was harvested. This blood was used in a successful stem cell transplant for the daughter. In Britain the parents of a 2 year old boy with ß thalassaemia applied in October 2001 to the Human Fertilisation and Embryo Authority for permission to select an embryo, using PGD, that can provide him with a matched stem cell transplant, again through umbilical cord blood taken at birth. These are the first publicly recorded cases of requests for PGD for the benefit of a relative; they are likely to herald further requests.

In both these cases, the technique fulfils two functions. Firstly, it is used to select embryos that do not have the genetic mutation that affects the family (Fanconi's anaemia or thalassaemia). This is a standard indication for PGD. Secondly, it is used to select an HLA compatible stem cell donor from these embryos.

Even more controversially, in both the United States and Australia there have been requests to use PGD to select a HLA compatible embryo to serve as a stem cell donor in the absence of any family history of genetic disease. Recently a British couple went to the United States to have in vitro fertilisation and PGD to select a stem cell donor for their child with relapsed leukaemia. The woman is currently pregnant . . .

ETHICAL ISSUES

Commodification

Lord Winston described creating children to provide stem cells as "using an unborn child as a commodity." The commonest objection to this procedure is that it is wrong to bring children into existence "conditionally." This objection finds its philosophical foundation in Immanuel Kant's famous dictum, "Never use people as a means but always treat them as an end."

Though common, this objection is difficult to sustain. Though we might aspire to a world where parents always dote on their children as unconditional ends, in reality many children are born for a purpose: to care for their parents, as a companion to a sibling, or to run the family business. Actually Kant's dictum was "Never use people solely as a means." Provided that parents love their child, there is little problem with that child benefiting others. And, as the Ayala case illustrates, a child conceived for stem cell donation is likely to be valued as a person . . .

Best interests of the child

What if the stem cell transplant is unsuccessful? Would parents unconsciously blame the donor child? What will life be like for the child conceived to produce stem cells? . . .

Before the birth of Marissa Ayala, grim predictions were made about her prospects, but these proved to be false. Blanket predictions about how parents will treat their children, and defining a set of conditions under which it is appropriate to allow people to parent, are dangerous and liable to be mistaken. Moreover, it is important to remember that the alternative for the child who was conceived to provide stem cells is not another life in which he or she was conceived in another way, but non-existence. If Abe Ayala had not had his vasectomy reversed to conceive Marissa as a stem cell donor, she simply would not have existed. Thus psychological harm to the offspring is unpredictable, unlikely to occur, and, even if it did occur, unlikely to be so severe that it would be better for that particular child never to have existed.

Pareto optimality and rational choice

Economists describe a Pareto optimal state of affairs as one that is at least as good as all alternative states of affairs in all relevant respects and better in some respects. Many would argue that it is rational to bring about a Pareto optimal state of affairs, assuming that resources may not be better used elsewhere. In the case before the Human Fertilisation and

Embryo Authority involving a boy with thalassaemia, the couple would be entitled to use PGD to select an embryo that does not have the thalassaemia genes. Why not let them select one that would also be a compatible stem cell donor? Assuming that the couple can produce sufficient numbers of embryos, using PGD in this circumstance would bring about a Pareto optimal state of affairs: it would produce a child without thalassaemia, and it may save the life of an existing child. All the alternatives are equally likely to produce a new child without thalassaemia but less likely to save the existing child.

If it is rational to allow fertile couples with a history of genetic disease to use PGD in this circumstance, then the same principle of Pareto optimality makes it rational for fertile couples without a history of genetic disease to use in vitro fertilisation and PGD to have a child who will provide stem cells for an existing child. All the alternatives are likely to produce a new child but less likely to save the existing child.

Reduced genetic diversity

Some people might argue that by selecting embryos we risk reducing the genetic diversity of our species and exposing the human race to unforeseen risks. Such arguments are speculative. Moreover, the number of requests for PGD is likely to remain limited given the emotional and financial costs of the procedure.

Destruction of embryos

Another objection to this use of in vitro fertilisation and PGD is that it results in the unnecessary destruction of embryos that are non-compatible tissue donors but likely to be healthy. However, UK legislation allows embryos to be destroyed until 14 days of age. To prohibit couples from rejecting healthy but unwanted embryos in a society that condones the destruction of hundreds of thousands of healthy but unwanted fetuses would be wildly inconsistent. Moreover, couples should be encouraged to donate their healthy but unwanted embryos to other couples who cannot conceive.

Harm to society—"eugenics"

Is it harmful to society if families choose their children on the basis of their genetic makeup? There is opposition to the practice of seeking "designer babies," fuelled by concerns about eugenics at an individual family and societal level. Though a compulsory national screening programme to prevent the implantation of embryos with certain genotypes would be eugenic, discriminatory, and akin to the Nazi eugenic project, the best way to prevent state-sponsored eugenics is to ensure that couples—not the state, professionals or other organisations—retain control over reproduction and the decision of which children to have.

Moreover, selection of children on a much grander scale is already commonplace. An estimated 18 000 amniocenteses take place annually in Britain, mainly to detect chromosomal anomalies such as Down's syndrome. Using PGD to select a stem cell donor will have little if any effect on the gene pool or on society more generally.

Moral disapproval by society

Some people find the use of PGD to select children distasteful and offensive. The Human Fertilisation and Embryology Act has arguably been formed to reflect a dominant Christian morality and to protect against offence to that morality. However, liberal societies have a presumption in favour of individual freedom of action unless there is a clear harm to others. Although the United Kingdom and other democratic countries may have laws that prevent gratuitous offence to others (such as creating earrings from embryos), we should be loath to restrict liberty in the absence of evidence of serious harm to others, especially in private behaviour and especially when the activity in question is potentially life-saving (and life-creating).

The famous legal scholar H L A Hart in the 1960s argued effectively against Lord Devlin in relation to the Wolfenden report on sexual behaviour that there is a sphere of private conduct that should be immune to legislation regardless of popular opinion, and that popular opinion or even morals are not always sufficient grounds for legislation. Such arguments were important in repealing the laws that made homosexuality illegal. Similarly, unless our private reproductive decisions cause harm to others, they should remain immune to legislation even if some people morally disapprove of them.

Rationing of resources

To justify providing these procedures within a public health service such as the NHS, it must be shown that allocation of the necessary resources is appropriate. The lifetime treatment costs for someone with ß thalassaemia in Britain are estimated at close to £200 000 ($295 000). This is likely to be considerably higher than the cost of tissue typing using PGD and subsequent stem cell transplantation, although a precise costing for this procedure is not available. There is clearly no economic justification for restricting this procedure.

For couples with no family history of genetic disease (who would not be entitled under current arrangements to use in vitro fertilisation and PGD within the NHS), in vitro fertilisation could be funded as a part of the cost of the treatment of the sibling (as it provides a stem cell source) or funded by the couple privately.

Conclusions

Who is harmed by allowing PGD to be performed solely for the benefit of a relative? Not the couple who wish to produce an embryo. Nor the child who would not otherwise have existed. Nor the person who receives the stem cell transplant that might save his or her life. We must avoid the trap of interfering with individual liberty by preventing such procedures for no good reason, simply out of the "genophobia" that grips much of society today. Some people object to using PGD along with in vitro fertilisation for any indication. But if these procedures are acceptable, as they are in many countries, it is reasonable to use them to both bring a new person into the world and to help save an existing life.

QUESTION:

1. Is performing PGD solely for the benefit of an existing relative (e.g. to create a "saviour sibling") morally wrong, and ought it to be prohibited? (Again, think back to the earlier discussion of law and morality in Section 3 when answering this.)

The next two passages deal with the acts–omissions doctrine and the doctrine of double effect (which Beauchamp and Childress call the Rule of Double Effect or "RDE"). Both of these are very important for the euthanasia debate and, more generally, for debates about "end of life" issues. Also, English law appears to have been influenced by versions of these doctrines and so some understanding of them, and of the main criticisms that have been levelled at them, will be useful later on. (See Chapter 14.)

The main idea behind the doctrine of double effect is that, if certain conditions are met, one is not fully responsible for all the effects of one's actions, but only for those which are intended. It is normally applied therefore to cases in which an action (e.g. administering a drug) has both a good effect (e.g. pain relief) and a bad effect (e.g. adverse side-effects, including perhaps shortening life). What the doctrine of double effect says about such cases is roughly the following. Provided that the good effect is what was intended and the bad effect is a foreseen but unintended side-effect, then the action is ethically acceptable. Although most commonly discussed in the health care setting, the doctrine is meant to capture a more general ethical truth (one which is applicable to everyone, not just health care workers) and, as such, has been used, for example, in attempts to differentiate the "strategic bombing" of military targets (which is supposed to be acceptable—at least sometimes—because the civilian deaths involved are foreseen but unintended side-effects) from the "terror bombing" of non-combatants (which is supposed to be morally indefensible because the civilian deaths involved are the intended means of achieving political or other objectives).

In its most general and simple form, the acts–omissions doctrine says that, other things being equal, acting so as to produce a particular outcome is more morally significant than producing the same outcome by failing to act. So, according to this doctrine, actively killing someone (e.g. by shooting them) will generally be worse than merely failing to prevent their death (e.g. by not saving them from a burning building or from drowning). Similarly, in medical practice, the acts–omissions doctrine is often taken to support the view that while allowing or even "hastening" death by withdrawing or withholding treatment is acceptable, actively killing patients by lethal injection ("active euthanasia") is not.

Tom L. Beauchamp and James F. Childress, *Principles of Biomedical Ethics*, Oxford, New York: Oxford University Press, 2001, pp.128–132

INTENDED-EFFECTS VS. MERELY FORESEEN EFFECTS

Another venerable attempt to specify the principle of nonmaleficence appears in the rule of double effect (RDE), often called the principle or doctrine of double effect. This rule incorporates a pivotal distinction between intended effects and merely foreseen effects (where effects are consequences of actions).

Functions and conditions of the RDE. The RDE is invoked to justify claims that a single act having two foreseen effects, one good and one harmful (such as death), is not always morally prohibited. As an example of the use of the RDE, consider a patient experiencing terrible pain and suffering who asks a physician for help in ending his life. If the physician directly kills the patient to end the patient's pain and suffering, he or she intentionally causes the patient's death as a means to end pain and suffering. But suppose the physician could provide medication to relieve the patient's pain and suffering at a substantial risk that the patient would die earlier as a result of the medication. If the physician refuses to administer a toxic analgesia, the patient will endure continuing pain and suffering; if the physician provides the medication, it may hasten the patient's death. If the physician's provision of medication were intended to relieve grave pain and suffering and not to cause or hasten death and the physician does not intend the lethal effect, the act of hastening death is not wrong, according to the rule of double effect.

Classic formulations of the RDE identify four conditions or elements that must be satisfied for an act with a double effect to be justified. Each is a necessary condition, and together they form sufficient conditions of morally permissible action:

1. *The nature of the act.* The act must be good, or at least morally neutral (independent of its consequences).
2. *The agent's intention.* The agent intends only the good effect. The bad effect can be foreseen, tolerated, and permitted, but it must not be intended.

3. *The distinction between means and effects.* The bad effect must not be a means to the good effect. If the good effect were the direct causal result of the bad effect, the agent would intend the bad effect in pursuit of the good effect.
4. *Proportionality between the good effect and the bad effect.* The good effect must outweigh the bad effect. That is, the bad effect is permissible only if a proportionate reason compensates for permitting the foreseen bad effect.

We begin to investigate the cogency of the RDE by considering four cases of what many call therapeutic abortion (limited to protecting maternal life in these examples): (A) A pregnant woman has cancer of the cervix; a hysterectomy is needed to save her life, but it will result in the death of the fetus. (B) A pregnant woman has an ectopic pregnancy—the nonviable fetus is in the fallopian tube—and removal of the tube, which will result in the death of the fetus, is medically indicated to prevent hemorrhage. (C) A pregnant woman has a serious heart disease that will probably result in her death if she attempts to carry the pregnancy to term. (D) A pregnant woman in difficult labor will die unless the physician performs a craniotomy (crushing the head of the unborn fetus). Official Roman Catholic teaching and many moral theologians and philosophers hold that actions that produce fetal deaths in cases A and B sometimes satisfy the four conditions of the RDE and, therefore, are morally acceptable, whereas the actions that produce fetal deaths in cases C and D never meet the conditions of the RDE and, therefore, are morally unacceptable.

In the first two cases, according to the RDE, a physician undertakes a legitimate medical procedure aimed at saving the pregnant woman's life with the foreseen, but unintended, result of fetal death. Viewed as side effects that are not intended (rather than as ends or means), these fetal deaths are said to be justified by a proportionately grave reason (saving the pregnant woman). In both cases C and D, the action of killing the fetus is a means to save the pregnant woman's life. As such, it requires intending the fetus's death (even if the death is not desired). Therefore, in those cases criteria 2 and 3 are violated and the act cannot be justified by proportionality.

Critics of the RDE contend that it is difficult and perhaps impossible to establish a morally relevant difference between cases such as A (hysterectomy) and D (craniotomy) in terms of the very abstract conditions that comprise the RDE. In neither case does the agent want or desire the death of the fetus, and the descriptions of the acts in these cases do not indicate morally relevant differences between intending, on the one hand, and foreseeing but not intending, on the other. More specifically, it is not clear why craniotomy is killing the fetus rather than crushing the skull of the fetus with the unintended result that the fetus dies. It is also not clear why, in the hysterectomy case, the fetus' death is foreseen but not intended. Proponents of the RDE must have a practicable way to distinguish the intended from the merely foreseen, but they face major difficulties in developing accounts of intention to draw defensible moral lines between the hysterectomy and craniotomy cases. Some modern reformulations of the RDE (especially those emphasizing the fourth condition) even permit craniotomies to save the pregnant woman because of the proportional value of her life.

Additional problems with the RDE. Adherents of the RDE need an account of intentional actions and intended effects of action that properly distinguishes them from nonintentional actions and unintended effects. The literature on intentional action is itself controversial and focuses on diverse conditions, such as volition, deliberation, willing, reasoning, and planning. One of the few widely shared views in this literature is that intentional actions require that an agent have a plan—a blueprint, map, or representation of the means and ends proposed for the execution of an action. For an action to be intentional, then, it must correspond to the agent's plan for its performance.

Alvin Goldman uses the following example in an attempt to prove that merely foreseen effects are unintentional. Imagine that Mr. G is taking a driver's test to prove competence. He comes to an intersection that requires a right turn and extends his arm to signal for a turn, although he knows it is raining and his hand will become wet. According to Goldman, Mr. G's signaling for a turn is an intentional act. By contrast, his getting a wet hand is an unintended effect or "incidental by-product of his hand-signaling. The defender of the RDE elects a similarly narrow conception of what is intended in order to avoid the conclusion that an agent intentionally brings about all the consequences of an action that the agent foresees. The defender distinguishes between acts and effects, and then between (1) effects that are desired or wanted and (2) effects that are foreseen but not desired or wanted. The RDE views the latter effects as foreseen, but not intended.

However, it is more suitable in these contexts to discard the language of desiring and wanting altogether, and to say that effects that are foreseen but not desired are "tolerated." These effects are not so undesirable that the actor would choose not to perform the act that results in them, and they are a part of the plan of an intentional action. To account for this point, let us use a model of intentionality based on what is *willed* rather than what is *wanted*. On this model, intentional actions and intentional effects include any action and any effect specifically willed in accordance with a plan, including tolerated as well as wanted effects. On this conception, a physician can desire not to do what he intends to do, in the same way that we can be willing to do something but, at the same time, reluctant to do it or even detest doing it.

Under this conception of intentional acts and intended effects, the distinction between what is intended and what is merely foreseen in a planned action is not viable. For example, if a man enters a room and flips a switch that he knows turns on both a light and a fan, but desires only to activate the light, he cannot say that he activates the fan unintentionally. Even if the fan were to make an obnoxious whirring that he knows about and desires to avoid, it would be mistaken to say that he unintentionally brought about the obnoxious sound by flipping the switch. More generally, a person who knowingly and voluntarily acts to bring about an effect brings about that effect intentionally. The effect is intended, although the person did not desire it, did not will it for its own sake, and did not intend it as the goal of the action.

Finally, we must consider the moral relevance of the RDE and its distinctions. Is it plausible to distinguish morally between intentionally causing the death of a fetus by craniotomy and intentionally removing a cancerous uterus that causes the death of a fetus? In both actions, the intention is to save the woman's life with knowledge that the fetus will die. No agent in either scenario desires the bad result (the fetus's death) for its own sake, and none would have tolerated the bad result if its avoidance were morally preferable to the alternative outcome. Each party accepts the bad effect only because it cannot be eliminated without sacrificing the good effect. Accordingly, the agents in our various examples above do not appear to want, will, or intend in ways that make a moral difference.

In the standard interpretation of the RDE, the fetus's death is a *means* to saving a woman's life in the unacceptable case, but it is merely a *side effect* in the acceptable case. That is, an agent intends a means, but need not intend a side effect. However, this approach seems to allow almost anything to be foreseen as a side effect rather than intended as a means (although it does not follow that we can create or direct intentions as we please). For example, in the craniotomy case, the surgeon might not intend the death of the fetus but only intend to remove it from the birth canal. The fetus will die, but is this outcome more than an unwanted and (in double effect theory) unintended consequence?

Defenders of the RDE may eventually find a way out of these puzzles, but they have not found it thus far. One constructive effort to retain an emphasis on intention without entirely abandoning or neglecting the point of the RDE focuses on the way actions display a person's motives and character. From this perspective, the core issue is whether a person's conduct flows from a proper motivational structure and a good character. Often in evaluating persons we are more concerned with their *motivation to* perform an action (why they performed the action) than with their *intention* in performing the action (what they planned to do). The intention to kill another person may be less relevant morally than the motive or doing so—for example, to defend ourself, to defend an innocent third party, or to meet the request of a dying patient.

In the case of performing a craniotomy to save a pregnant woman's life, a physician may not *want* or *desire* the death of the fetus and may regret performing a craniotomy, just as much as in the case of removing a cancerous uterus. Such facts about the physician's motivation and character can make a decisive difference to a moral assessment of the action and the agent. But the RDE is unable to reach this conclusion on its own . . .

QUESTIONS:

1. Can you think of any other (real or fictitious) examples to which the doctrine of double effect could plausibly be applied?
2. Do you think that the doctrine of double effect is as problematic as Beauchamp and Childress suggest? If so, why? If not, why not?

J. Glover, *Causing Death and Saving Lives*, Harmondsworth: Penguin, 1977, pp.92–94

Is it worse to kill someone than not to save his life? What we may call the "acts and omission doctrine" says that, in certain contexts, failure to perform an act, with certain foreseen bad consequences of that failure, is morally less bad than to perform a different act which has the identical foreseen bad consequences.

It is worse to kill someone than to allow them to die. Philippa Foot has discussed a case which illustrates this view. She says, "most of us allow people to die of starvation in India and Africa, and there is surely something wrong with us that we do; it would be nonsense, however, to pretend that it is only in law that we make a distinction between allowing people in the underdeveloped countries to die of starvation and sending them poisoned food."

Another case where our intuitive response to killing differs from our response to not striving to keep alive concerns old-age pensioners. Until the introduction of automatic regular increases, the Chancellor of the Exchequer in his annual budget normally either failed to increase the old-age pension or else put it up by an inadequate amount. In either case, it was predictable that a certain number of old-age pensioners would not be able to afford enough heating in winter, and so would die of cold. We think that the decision of such a Chancellor was not a good one, but we do not think it nearly as bad as if he had decided to take a machine-gun to an old people's home and to kill at once the same number of people.

Apart from this support the acts and omissions doctrine derives from our intuitive responses to such cases, it might be argued that to abandon it would place an intolerable burden on people. For, we may think that, without it, we would have morally to carry the whole world on our shoulders. It is arguable that we would have to give money to fight starvation up to the point where we needed it more than those we were helping: perhaps to the point where we would die without it. For not to do so would be to allow more people to die, and this would be like murder. And, apart from this huge reduction in our standard of living, we should also have to give up our spare time, either to raising money or else to persuading the government to give more money. For, if a few pounds saves a life, not to raise that money would again be like murder.

Finally, it could be said that for us the acts and omissions doctrine is a "natural" one: that it is presupposed by the way in which we use moral language. There is in our vocabulary a distinction between duties and those good acts that go beyond the call of duty. A doctor has no duty to risk his life by going from England to a plague-infested town in an Asian country at war in order to save lives there, and we do not blame him if he does not do so. If he does go, we think of him as a hero. But, if we abandoned the acts and omissions doctrine, we might have to abandon our present distinction between acts of moral duty and supererogation.

It will be argued here [however] that we ought to reject the acts and omission doctrine . . .

As we mentioned earlier, a standard application of the acts–omissions doctrine is the view that (other things being equal) killing patients is morally worse than merely "allowing them to die" by withdrawing or withholding treatment. In the following passage, which comes from possibly the most famous paper in the medical ethics literature, James Rachels criticises the "orthodox" view that killing is worse than letting die.

James Rachels, "Active and Passive Euthanasia", *New England Journal of Medicine,* 1975, 292: 78–80

The distinction between active and passive euthanasia is thought to be crucial for medical ethics. The idea is that it is permissible, at least in some cases, to withhold treatment and allow a patient to die, but it is never permissible to take any direct action designed to kill the patient. This doctrine seems to be accepted by most doctors, and it is endorsed in a statement adopted by the House of Delegates of the American Medical Association on December 4, 1973:

> The intentional termination of the life of one human being by another—mercy killing—is contrary to that for which the medical profession stands and is contrary to the policy of the American Medical Association.
> The cessation of the employment of extraordinary means to prolong the life of the body when there is irrefutable evidence that biological death is imminent is the decision of the patient and/or his immediate family. The advice and judgment of the physician should be freely available to the patient and/or his immediate family.

However, a strong case can be made against this doctrine. In what follows I will set out some of the relevant arguments, and urge doctors to reconsider their views on this matter.

To begin with a familiar type of situation, a patient who is dying of incurable cancer of the throat is in terrible pain, which can no longer be satisfactorily alleviated. He is certain to die within a few days, even if present treatment is continued, but he does not want to go on living for those days since the pain is unbearable. So he asks the doctor for an end to it, and his family joins in the request.

Suppose the doctor agrees to withhold treatment, as the conventional doctrine says he may. The justification for his doing so is that the patient is in terrible agony, and since he is going to die anyway, it would be wrong to prolong his suffering needlessly. But now notice this. If one simply withholds treatment, it may take the patient longer to die, and so he may suffer more than he would if more direct action were taken and a lethal injection given. This fact provides strong reason for thinking that, once the initial decision not to prolong his agony has been made active euthanasia is actually preferable to passive euthanasia, rather than the reverse. To say otherwise is to endorse the option that leads to more suffering rather than less, and is contrary to the humanitarian impulse that prompts the decision not to prolong his life in the first place.

Part of my point is that the process of being "allowed to die" can be relatively slow and painful, whereas being given a lethal injection is relatively quick and painless. Let me give a different sort of example. In the United States about one in 600 babies is born with Down's syndrome. Most of these babies are otherwise healthy—that is, with only the usual pediatric care, they will proceed to an otherwise normal infancy. Some, however, are born with congenital defects such as intestinal obstructions that require operations if they are to live. Sometimes, the parents and the doctor will decide not to operate, and let the infant die. Anthony Shaw describes what happens then:

> . . . When surgery is denied [the doctor] must try to keep the infant from suffering while natural forces sap the baby's life away. As a surgeon whose natural inclination is to use

the scalpel to fight off death, standing by and watching a salvageable baby die is the most emotionally exhausting experience I know. It is easy at a conference, in a theoretical discussion, to decide that such infants should be allowed to die. It is altogether different to stand by in the nursery and watch as dehydration and infection wither a tiny being over hours and days. This is a terrible ordeal for me and the hospital staff—much more so than for the parents who never set foot in the nursery.

I can understand why some people are opposed to all euthanasia, and insist that such infants must be allowed to live. I think I can also understand why other people favor destroying these babies quickly and painlessly. But why should anyone favor letting "dehydration and infection wither a tiny being over hours and days?" The doctrine that says that a baby may be allowed to dehydrate and wither, but may not for given an injection that would end its life without suffering, seems so patently cruel as to require no further refutation. The strong language is not intended to offend, but only to put the point in the clearest possible way.

My second argument is that the conventional doctrine leads to decisions concerning life and death made on irrelevant grounds.

Consider again the case of the infants with Down's syndrome who need operations for congenital defects unrelated to the syndrome to live. Sometimes, there is no operation, and the baby dies, but when there is no such defect, the baby lives on. Now, an operation such as that to remove an intestinal obstruction is not prohibitively difficult. The reason why such operations are not performed in these cases is, clearly, that the child has Down's syndrome and the parents and doctor judge that because of that fact it is better for the child to die.

But notice that this situation is absurd, no matter what view one takes of the lives and potentials of such babies. If the life of such an infant is worth preserving, what does it matter if it needs a simple operation? Or, if one thinks it better that such a baby should not live on, what difference does it make that it happens to have an unobstructed intestinal tract? In either case, the matter of life and death is being decided on irrelevant grounds. It is the Down's syndrome, and not the intestines, that is the issue. The matter should be decided, if at all, on that basis, and not be allowed to depend on the essentially irrelevant question of whether the intestinal tract is blocked.

What makes this situation possible, of course, is the idea that when there is an intestinal blockage, one can "let the baby die," but when there is no such defect there is nothing that can be done, for one must not "kill" it. The fact that this idea leads to such results as deciding life or death on irrelevant grounds is another good reason why the doctrine should be rejected.

One reason why so many people think that there is an important moral difference between active and passive euthanasia is that they think killing someone is morally worse than letting someone die. But is it? Is killing, in itself, worse than letting die? To investigate this issue, two cases may be considered that are exactly alike except that one involves killing whereas the other involves letting someone die. Then, it can be asked whether this difference makes any difference to the moral assessments. It is important that the cases be exactly alike, except for this one difference, since otherwise one cannot be confident that it is this difference and not some other that accounts for any variation in the assessments of the two cases. So, let us consider this pair of cases:

In the first, Smith stands to gain a large inheritance if anything should happen to his six-year-old cousin. One evening while the child is taking his bath, Smith sneaks into the bathroom and drowns the child, and then arranges things so that it will look like an accident.

In the second, Jones also stands to gain if anything should happen to his six-year-old cousin. Like Smith, Jones sneaks in planning to drown the child in his bath. However, just as he enters the bathroom Jones sees the child slip and hit his head, and fall face down in the water. Jones is delighted; he stands by, ready to push the child's head back under if it is necessary, but it is not necessary. With only a little thrashing about, the child drowns all by himself, "accidentally," as Jones watches and does nothing.

Now Smith killed the child, whereas Jones "merely" let the child die. That is the only difference between them. Did either man behave better, from a moral point of view? If the difference between killing and letting die were in itself a morally important matter, one should say that Jones's behavior was less reprehensible than Smith's. But does one really want to say that? I think not. In the first place, both men acted from the same motive, personal gain, and both had exactly the same end in view when they acted. It may be inferred from Smith's conduct that he is a bad man, although that judgment may be withdrawn or modified if certain further facts are learned about him—for example, that he is mentally deranged. But would not the very same thing be inferred about Jones from his conduct? And would not the same further considerations also be relevant to any, modification of this judgment? Moreover, suppose Jones pleaded, in his own defense, "After all, I didn't do anything except just stand there and watch the child drown. I didn't kill him; I only let him die." Again, if letting die were in itself less bad than killing, this defense should have at least some weight. But it does not. Such a "defense" can only be regarded as a grotesque perversion of moral reasoning. Morally speaking, it is no defense at all.

Now, it may be pointed out, quite properly, that the cases of euthanasia with which doctors are concerned are not like this at all. They do not involve personal gain or the destruction of normal healthy children. Doctors are concerned only with cases in which the patient's life is of no further use to him, or in which the patient's life has become or will soon become a terrible burden. However, the point is the same in these cases: the bare difference between killing and letting die does not, in itself, make a moral difference. If a doctor lets a patient die, for humane reasons, he is in the same moral position as if he had given the patient a lethal injection for humane reasons. If his decision was wrong—if, for example, the patient's illness was in fact curable—the decision would be equally regrettable no matter which method was used to carry it out. And if the doctor's decision was the right one, the method used is not in itself important.

The AMA policy statement isolates the crucial issue very well; the crucial issue is "the intentional termination of the life of one human being by another." But after identifying this issue, and forbidding "mercy killing," the statement goes on to deny that the cessation of treatment is the intentional termination of a life. This is where the mistake comes in, for what is the cessation of treatment, in these circumstances, if it is not "the intentional termination of the life of one human being by another?" Of course it is exactly that, and if it were not, there would be no point to it.

Many people will find this judgment hard to accept. One reason, I think, is that it is very easy to conflate the question of whether killing is, in it, worse than letting die, with the very different question of whether most actual cases of killing are more reprehensible than most actual cases of letting die. Most actual cases of killing are clearly terrible (think, for example, of all the murders reported in the newspapers), and one hears of such crises every day. On the other hand, one hardly ever hears of a case of letting die, except for the actions of doctors who are motivated by humanitarian reasons. So one learns to think of killing in a much worse light than of letting die. But this does not mean that there is something about killing that makes it in itself worse than letting die, for it is not the bare difference between killing and letting die that makes the difference in these cases. Rather, the other factors—the murderer's motive of personal gain, for example, contrasted with the doctor's humanitarian motivation—account for different reactions to the different cases.

I have argued that killing is not in itself any worse than letting die; if my contention is right, it follows that active euthanasia is not any worse than passive euthanasia. What arguments can be given on the other side? The most common, I believe, is the following:

The important difference between active and passive euthanasia is that, in passive euthanasia, the doctor does not do anything to bring about the patient's death. The doctor does nothing, and the patient dies of whatever ills already afflict him. In active euthanasia, however, the doctor does something to bring about the patient's death: he kills him. The doctor who gives the patient with cancer a lethal injection has himself caused his patient's death; whereas if he merely ceases treatment, the cancer is the cause of the death.

A number of points need to be made here. The first is that it is not exactly correct to say that in passive euthanasia the doctor does nothing, for he does do one thing that is very important: he lets the patient die. "Letting someone die" is certainly different, in some respects, from other types of action—mainly in that it is a kind of action that one may perform by way of not performing certain other actions. For example, one may let a patient die by way of not giving medication, just as one may insult someone by way of not shaking his hand. But for any purpose of moral assessment, it is a type of action nonetheless. The decision to let a patient die is subject to moral appraisal in the same way that a decision to kill him would be subject to moral appraisal: it may be assessed as wise or unwise, compassionate or sadistic, right or wrong. If a doctor deliberately let a patient die who was suffering from a routinely curable illness, the doctor would certainly be to blame for what he had done, just as he would be to blame if he had needlessly killed the patient. Charges against him would then be appropriate. If so, it would be no defense at all for him to insist that he didn't "do anything." He would have done something very serious indeed, for he let his patient die.

Fixing the cause of death may be very important from a legal point of view, for it may determine whether criminal charges are brought against the doctor. But I do not think that this notion can be used to show a moral difference between active and passive euthanasia. The reason why it is considered bad to be the cause of someone's death is that death is regarded as a great evil—and so it is. However, if it has been decided that euthanasia—even passive euthanasia—is desirable in a given case, it has also been decided that in this instance death is no greater an evil than the patient's continued existence. And if this is true, the usual reason for not wanting to be the cause of someone's death simply does not apply.

Finally, doctors may think that all of this is only of academic interest—the sort of thing that philosophers may worry about but that has no practical bearing on their own work. After all, doctors must be concerned about the legal consequences of what they do, and active euthanasia is clearly forbidden by the law. But even so, doctors should also be concerned with the fact that the law is forcing upon them a moral doctrine that may well be indefensible, and has a considerable effect on their practices. Of course, most doctors are not now in the position of being coerced in this matter, for they do not regard themselves as merely going along with what the law requires. Rather, in statements such as the AMA policy statement that I have quoted, they are endorsing this doctrine as a central point of medical ethics. In that statement, active euthanasia is condemned not merely as illegal but as "contrary to that for which the medical profession stands," whereas passive euthanasia is approved. However, the preceding considerations suggest that there is really no moral difference between the two, considered in themselves (there may be important moral differences in some cases in their consequences, but, as I pointed out, these differences may make active euthanasia, and not passive euthanasia, the morally preferable option). So, whereas doctors may have to discriminate between active and passive euthanasia to satisfy the law, they should not do any more than that. In particular, they should not give the distinction any added authority and weight by writing it into official statements of medical ethics.

QUESTIONS:

1. In Rachels' examples, is there any *moral* difference between Smith and Jones?
2. Is there, in general, any moral difference between killing and "letting die"?
3. Is the distinction between killing and "letting die" one which law ought to recognise and uphold?

SELECT BIBLIOGRAPHY

T. Beauchamp and J. Childress, *Principles of Biomedical Ethics* (5th edn), Oxford: Oxford University Press, 2001.

J. Burley and J. Harris, "Human Cloning and Child Welfare" (1999) 25 *Journal of Medical Ethics*, 108.

P. Devlin, *The Enforcement of Morals*, London: Oxford University Press, 1965.

G. Dworkin, *The Theory and Practice of Autonomy*, Cambridge: Cambridge University Press, 1988.

S. Edwards, *Nursing Ethics: a Principle-Based Approach*, Basingstoke: Palgrave Macmillan, 1996.

R. Gillon, *Philosophical Medical Ethics*, Chichester: John Wiley & Sons, 1986.

J. Glover, *Causing Death and Saving Lives*, Harmondsworth: Penguin, 1977.

W. Grey, "Right to Die or Duty to Live? The Problem of Euthanasia" (1999) 16 *Journal of Applied Philosophy*, 19.

J. Harris (ed.), *Bioethics*, Oxford: Oxford University Press, 2001.

J. Harris, *The Value of Life: an Introduction to Medical Ethics*, London: Routledge, 1985.

H. Kuhse and P. Singer (eds), *A Companion to Bioethics*, Oxford: Blackwell, 1998.

H. Kuhse, *Caring: Nurses, Women and Ethics*, Oxford: Blackwell, 1997.

J. Rachels (ed.), *Ethical Theory* (Vols 1 and 2), Oxford: Oxford University Press, 1998.

J. Savulescu, "Procreative Beneficence: Why We Should Select the Best Possible Children" (2001) 15 *Bioethics*, 413.

S. Sheldon and S. Wilkinson, "Hashmi and Whitaker: an Unjustifiable and Misguided Distinction?" (2004) 12 *Medical Law Review*, 137.

S. Sheldon and S. Wilkinson, "Should Selecting Saviour Siblings Be Banned?" (2004) 30 *Journal of Medical Ethics*, 533.

P. Singer, *Companion to Ethics*, Oxford: Blackwell, 1993. 23.

PART II

Introduction

This part considers the accountability of health professionals for their actions. Over the past decade continuing concern has been evidenced by the health professions, particularly the medical profession, as to the growth of a "malpractice crisis". Individuals dissatisfied with the treatment given are, it is alleged, increasingly likely to take their claims to court. One consequence of the rise in claims is that, in certain areas where litigation is likely due to the type of clinical practice involved, this has led to the practice of defensive medicine. One further dimension is that the cost of litigation has led to funds being diverted from the healthcare budget, with a consequent reduction of what are already limited resources. Concern regarding litigation has led to the growth of what are known as "risk management" practices in an attempt to reduce, where possible, the risk of adverse incidents. (See further Department of Health Expert Group "An Organisation with a Memory London" DOH (2000); National Patient Safety Agency "Building a Memory; Preventing Harm, Reducing Risks and Improving Patients Safety London"; National Patient Safety Agency (2005).)

While the courts may, at first sight, appear to provide the most effective method of ensuring the accountability of professionals, on closer inspection difficulties are apparent. Litigation is expensive and over time state-funded legal assistance has been reduced. Moreover, it is claimed that the scales are weighted in favour of the medical profession. Where it is alleged that conduct is negligent, the standard of care is to be ascertained by reference to what is known as the "professional practice" standard or the *Bolam* test. For many years the courts took the approach that health professionals would not generally be held to be negligent as long as they complied with a standard supported by a responsible body of professional practice, even though other health care practitioners might disagree with that approach. More recently the House of Lords in *Bolitho* (*Bolitho v City and Hackney Health Authority* [1998] A.C. 232) has indicated that they are prepared to critically scrutinise the professional practice approach and ensure that the views advanced are logical supported by expert evidence. Nonetheless the advent of *Bolitho*, although lauded initially as a "new *Bolam*", has had an impact which has been less radical than first envisaged. The majority of clinical negligence claims have not been subject to a different approach and there has been no avalanche of successful actions by litigants (*Bolam v Friern Hospital Management Committee* [1957] 2 All E.R. 118).

Even if the conduct of a health professional can be shown to have fallen short of the standard of care, the litigant may still fall at the hurdle of causation because he cannot establish that it was the negligent conduct of the defendant that caused the harm which he suffered. As we shall see below, establishing causation is problematic, not least because of the prospect of multiple causes which arises in many cases. The English courts have also rejected claims brought on the basis of "loss of chance" in the context of clinical negligence (see *Gregg v Scott* [2005] UKHL 2) and discussion at p.193 below. Chapter 3 examines the clinical negligence action and considers how satisfactory this system is. It explores recent proposals for reform in the Chief Medical Officers Report, *Making Amends* (*Making Amends: a consultation paper setting out the proposals for reforming the approach to clinical negligence in the NHS*, Department of Health, 2003) and in the recent NHS Redress Bill.

The judicial system provides one potential means of ensuring accountability. The primary aim of a tort action is to provide compensation, not to administer punishment. Professional misconduct which is grossly negligent may result in a criminal prosecution and indeed there has been increasing use of the criminal law over the last few years. Nevertheless such prosecutions make up only a tiny fraction of all situations of alleged misconduct by health professionals.

There are, however, many cases in which the misconduct alleged is not grave or where the patient does not have compensation as his primary concern. This does not mean that the health professional should not be held accountable for his actions. In such situations investigating an alleged harm suffered may have a number of perceived advantages. It may provide a patient with an explanation of precisely what happened in that particular situation. It may identify problems in the structure of the provision of care and thus lead to changes in the delivery of care for patients as a whole.

The expectation of accountability in the context of health complaints may be seen as partly the result of the increasing perception of the patient as consumer. Accountability through knowledge is the result of an operational complaints system. But it may also lead to accountability in the context of disciplinary proceedings being brought by the employer if adverse finding are made against a health professional. Health professionals may also be the subject of audit and accreditation.

Further systems of accountability are provided through systems of professional self-regulation. Health professionals are, almost invariably subject to a professional ethical code. In Chapter 2 above we considered the nature of such codes. It is worthy of note that the obligations placed upon health professionals by their ethical codes and those of their employers may diverge, raising difficult issues in relation to the interests of patients. In Chapter 4 below we examine the scope of professional self-regulation and the role of professional discipline where, for instance, codes of conduct are broken, taking the General Medical Council as a case study.

The present system is undergoing considerable change. One catalyst for change was the critical report by Professor Sir Ian Kennedy into the deaths at the cardiac paediatric unit at Bristol Royal Infirmary *(Learning from Bristol: the Report of the Public Inquiry into Children's Heart Surgery at the Bristol Royal Infirmary 1984–1995*, Department of Health, 2002). Another has been the criticisms of professional self-regulation contained in the report by Dame Janet Smith into the deaths caused by the serial killer Dr Harold Shipman (Shipman Inquiry, *"Fifth Report Safeguarding Patients—Lessons from the Past—Proposals for the Future"*, (2004) Cm. 6394 London: HMSO, para. 26.205)). Most recently, as this book has gone into production, the Chief Medical Officer Professor Sir Liam Donaldson has proposed radical reforms of the operation and professional regulatory role of the General Medical Council (*Good Doctors—Safer Patients* (London: CMO, 2006)). The balance seems to be gradually moving away from an acceptance of self-regulation and regulatory structures to the need for more perceived independence in regulation. It remains too early to say as to what extent accountability will be truly facilitated by recent developments in professional practice and NHS structure.

3

PROFESSIONAL ACCOUNTABILITY I

1. Introduction

There has been a rise in "claims consciousness" in the population generally and this is reflected in the provision of health care. There is a heightened public awareness of medical error (see, for example, O. Quick, "Outing Medical Errors: Questions of Trust and Responsibility" (2006) 14 *Medical Law Review* 22). But to what extent has this spilt over into a "malpractice crisis"? Certainly this has been a fear among health professionals and has been the subject of considerable academic debate (see, for example, C. Ham, R. Dingwall, P. Fenn and D. Harris, *Medical Negligence, Compensation and Accountability*, London: King's Fund Institute, 1988; M. Jones, *Medical Negligence*, London: Sweet & Maxwell, 2003, pp.6–16). There are concerns that health professionals working in specialities in which litigation is potentially most likely have "been practising defensive medicine", namely altering their clinical practice to what may be perceived to be the "safest" therapy, even though this may not be the most appropriate or convenient for the patient, on the basis that this will reduce the risk of actions being brought (see M. Jones, *Medical Negligence* (3rd edn), London: Sweet & Maxwell, 2003, pp.18–20). The existence of defensive medicine has, however, been questioned. It has been suggested that the evidence of such practice is "equivocal", that defensive practices have risen in countries where litigation is less common and that some "defensive" practices such as caesarean sections may be undertaken either because they are clinically indicated or because they are actively sought by women (see further discussion in S. Pattinson, *Medical Law and Ethics*, London: Sweet & Maxwell, 2006 at p.86). Nonetheless an identifiable consequence of the increase in litigation has been that practitioners have deserted high risk specialities such as obstetrics (see P. Hoyte, "Unsound Practice: the Epidemiology of Medical Negligence" (1995) 3 *Medical Law Review* 53). In contrast, more lawyers today specialise in medical negligence. Firms of solicitors work in concert in major medical negligence claims, most notably, as we shall see later, in the context of litigation against drug firms. It is undoubtedly true that the number of claims brought are considerable (NHS Litigation Authority Figures in

2006, for example, reported that some 7,500 clinical negligence claims were brought each year in England.

While there are considerable concerns regarding the proliferation of litigation set against this is the fact that bringing a claim may be difficult for a number of reasons. These relate to both the substantive law in this area and also to the mechanics of bringing a claim, such as the difficulties in obtaining funding to bring an action. Jones has commented that "From the patient's perspective it could be argued that a 'malpractice crisis' arises from too few patients being able to litigate, rather than too many doctors becoming defendants." (See Jones, *op. cit.*) The concerns regarding the structure of the clinical negligence litigation process led Professor Ian Kennedy in his report of the Bristol Royal Infirmary Inquiry to state that "The system [of clinical negligence litigation] is now out of alignment with other policy initiatives on quality and safety: in fact it serves to undermine those policies and inhibits the safety of care received by patients . . . We believe that the way forward lies in the abolition of clinical negligence litigation, taking clinical error out of the courts and the tort system." (See *Learning from Bristol: the Report of the Public Inquiry into Children's Heart Surgery at the Bristol Royal Infirmary 1984–1995*, Department of Health, 2002.) Over the last few years various reform proposals for the clinical negligence system have been suggested and these are explored later in this chapter.

In this chapter we consider the basis on which health care professionals may be held accountable in law for careless acts or omissions. In Section 2, the general principles of the law of negligence as it applies to health professionals are examined. Particular problems in establishing liability in the context of medical negligence are considered, notably the reliance on the professional practice standard. A patient will face considerable problems in establishing that there was a breach of duty of care if the health professional can put forward evidence to show that a responsible body of professional opinion would have supported his or her actions. Even if breach of duty can be shown, a patient may experience difficulties in establishing causation, which may frustrate the claim. In Section 3, we consider the issue of statutory liability for defective drugs and appliances, an area in which English law has been strongly influenced by initiatives from the European Union. While medical malpractice may lead to a negligence action, grave instances of malpractice resulting in the death of the patient may result in a criminal prosecution being brought against the health professional. This issue is discussed in Section 4. Finally, we consider the effectiveness of the law of tort as a means of redress for those injured as a consequence of medical malpractice, and proposals which have been advanced for reform of the law in this area in Section 5.

2. THE MALPRACTICE ACTION

(a) Introduction

Where a patient suffers harm through treatment provided by a health professional he may bring an action in negligence for damages. For his action to succeed, the patient must be able to show three things. First, that the doctor or nurse concerned owed him a duty of care; secondly, that she was in breach of that duty (i.e. that she failed to provide care of an adequate standard); thirdly, that he suffered harm in consequence of that breach which was not so unforeseeable as to be regarded in law as too remote.

(b) The Duty of Care

In the absence of an established duty of care, English law does not impose upon doctors (or other health care professionals or institutions) any obligation to provide treatment to those who require it. (See further on the issue of a "duty to rescue" and whether it should apply to health care professionals in K.Williams "Medical Samaritans: Is There a Duty to Treat?" (2001) 21 *Oxford Journal of Legal Studies* 393.) To this rule, however, there are limited exceptions. First, where a patient presents at a hospital casualty department, there is an obligation to provide care (*Barnett v Chelsea and Kensington Hospital Management Committee* [1968] 1 All E.R. 1068). A duty has also been held to apply to the Ambulance Service where they accept a call-out and thus they must respond and provide assistance within a reasonable time (*Kent v Griffiths* [2001] Q.B. 36). Similarly, a duty also arises, under the National Health Service (Choice of Medical Practitioner) Regulations 1992, SI 1992/635, where the patient is treated by a General Practitioner (G.P.) as an emergency patient. Interestingly, the GMC provides in its "Good Medical Practice" document (London: GMC, 2001) that "In an emergency wherever it may arise, you must offer anyone at risk the assistance you could reasonably be expected to provide" (at para.9).

Where a patient cannot bring himself within either of these exceptions, he must be able positively to show that he was owed a duty of care before he can bring a medical negligence action. As to the circumstances in which such a duty arises, it is necessary to distinguish two types of case. First, where the patient seeks care from a G.P. on a non-emergency basis, and secondly, where he seeks hospital care. In the former instance, the obligation to treat the patient only crystallises once (a) he is registered with the G.P. and (b) he has consulted the G.P. on the occasion in question. In the latter, the duty does not arise until the hospital has formally accepted the patient. In either case, the existence of a duty of care is ultimately dependent upon the presence of an express or implied undertaking that he will be treated (*Cassidy v Ministry of Health* [1951] 1 All E.R. 574). Where a negligence action is brought, it is rare for a health care professional to be sued personally. It is more likely that an action will be brought against his employer on the basis that they are vicariously liable.

Where care is provided privately, i.e. outside the NHS, the doctor–patient relationship is governed by a contract for services. One consequence of this is that, in addition to his or her tortious duty of care, the doctor will owe a contemporaneous contractual duty which is almost identical in substance (see A. Grubb, "Duties in Contract and Tort", pp.315–322 in A. Grubb, *Principles of Medical Law* (2nd edn), Oxford: OUP, 2004). Under s.13 of the Supply of Goods and Services Act 1982, the doctor is obliged to exercise reasonable care and skill while discharging his contractual obligations. Where care is provided on a contractual basis, liability may arise not only in connection with the manner in which the care is provided, but also in relation to the quality and suitability of any medicines or surgical appliances that might be supplied (see A. Bell, "The Doctor and the Supply of Goods and Services Act 1982" (1984) 4 *Legal Studies* 175).

As far as the costs of litigation are concerned, these are rarely born by the individual practitioner. Health care practitioners have long carried health insurance. In the case of those who were employed by the NHS, the cost of premiums were paid by the employers. By the late 1980s concern was being expressed over the rise in doctor's insurance premiums. This led to the introduction by the government of a scheme known as "NHS indemnity" in 1991 (see further Jones, *op. cit.*). This has the effect that NHS hospital doctors are directly indemnified by their employers. This scheme did not apply to G.P.s who continue to require insurance. NHS trusts must bear the cost of claims themselves or they may join the clinical negligence scheme for trusts which allows them to spread the cost of claims (established by the NHS (Clinical Negligence Scheme) Regulations, SI 1996/251). Since March 1, 1996 this scheme has been administered by the NHS Litigation Authority for Trusts. In the majority of situations, the NHS employer will be vicariously liable for the actions of health professionals. However, in some circumstances there may also be what is known as "primary" or "direct" liability.

Cassidy v Ministry of Health [1951] 1 All E.R. 574; [1951] 2 K.B. 343; [1951] W.L.R. 147 (for the facts, see p.181 below)

DENNING L.J.
" . . . [W]hen hospital authorities undertake to treat a patient and themselves select and appoint and employ the professional men and women who are to give the treatment, they are responsible for the negligence of those persons in failing to give proper treatment, no matter whether they are doctors, surgeons, nurses, or anyone else. Once hospital authorities are held responsible for the nurses and radiographers as they have been in *Gold's* case (*Gold v. Essex County Council* [1942] 2 All E.R. 237), I can see no possible reason why they should not also be responsible for the house surgeons and resident medical officers on their permanent staff . . . "

After setting out the basis for the vicarious liability of the hospital, his Lordship considered whether there was, in fact, any negligence for which it could be held liable. He continued:

" . . . The hospital authorities accepted the plaintiff as a patient for treatment and it was their duty to treat him with reasonable care. They selected, employed, and paid all the surgeons and nurses who looked after him. He had no say in their selection at all. If those surgeons and nurses did not treat him with proper care and skill, then the hospital authorities must answer for it, for it means that they themselves did not perform their duty to him. I decline to enter into the question whether any of the surgeons were employed only under a contract for services, as distinct from a contract of service. The evidence is meagre enough in all conscience on that point, but the liability of the hospital authorities should not, and does not, depend on nice considerations of that sort. The plaintiff knew nothing of the terms on which they employed their staff. All he knew was that he was treated in the hospital by people whom the hospital authorities appointed, and the hospital authorities must be answerable for the way in which he was treated."

NOTES:

1. Lord Denning cited his statement in *Cassidy* in two subsequent decisions, *Roe v Ministry of Health* [1954] 2 Q.B. 66 and *Jones v Manchester Corporation* [1957] 2 All E.R. 125. In *X (Minors) v Bedfordshire CC* [1995] 2 A.C. 633 Lord Browne Wilkinson stated that "even where there is no allegation of a separate duty of care owed by a servant of the County Council. To the plaintiff, the negligent acts of that servant are capable of constituting a breach of a duty of care (if any owed directly by the authority to the plaintiff". The exact implications of this statement are however unclear as Grubb and Jones note that earlier in the judgment he had indicated that he was not expressing a view as to the extent of the duty of the hospital. Moreover, any statement here would be obiter given that this case concerned the obligations regarding child protection issues (see further A. Grubb and M.A. Jones, "Institutional Liability" in A. Grubb (ed.), *Principles of Medical Law* (2nd edn) Oxford: OUP, 2004 at p. 516). In the later case of *Robertson v Nottingham HA* [1997] 8 Med. L.R. 1 this issue was left open by Brooke L.J. Contrast the criticism of the *Cassidy* approach in a Canadian case *Yepremian v Scarborough General Hospital* (1980) 110 D.L.R. (3d) 513 (Ont. C.A.).

2. There may be a non-delegable duty arising from the statutory obligations imposed by s.3 of the National Health Service Act 1977 (see Chapter 1 above, at pp.41). (See *Razzel v Snowball* [1954] 1 W.L.R. 1382, and M. Jones, *Medical Negligence* (3rd edn), London: Sweet & Maxwell, 2002, para. 7-029.)

3. A breach of a non-delegable duty was established in *Robertson v Nottingham HA* [1997] 8 Med. L.R. 1. Here the facts concerned an unnecessary delay of some six hours in delivering a baby which was suffering from pre-natal stress. This was due to the failure to provide a reliable system of medical notes to facilitate communication between the medical staff.
   In the Court of Appeal it was held that the hospital

   > "has a non-delegable duty to establish a proper system of care just as much as it has a duty to engage competent staff and a duty to provide safe and competent equipment . . . if a patient is injured by reason of a negligent breakdown in the systems for communicating material information to the physicians responsible for her care, she is not to be denied redress merely because no identifiable person or persons are to blame for the deficiencies in setting up and monitoring the effectiveness of the relevant communications systems."

   The claim itself however ultimately failed on causation.

4. The courts have also held that this applies where a patient is being treated in a separate private hospital. So for example, in *M v Calderdale and Kirklees Health Authority* [1998] Lloyd's Rep. Med. 157, a 17-year-old girl was referred for an abortion under the NHS to a private clinic under a contract. The abortion did not succeed and the girl gave birth to a boy. Although a negligence action was successful against the doctor and the private clinic, neither was insured. As a consequence proceedings were brought against the NHS hospital who had made the referral. Garner J.

rejected the argument that as there had been no negligence in the choice of clinic the health authority was not liable. He held that the health authority owed the claimant a non-delegable duty of care. He suggested that without this it was the case that NHS patients treated outside the NHS would be in a worse position than those being treated in NHS facilities.

However doubt was cast on the application of the non-delegable duty in the following case.

A v Ministry of Defence and Guy's and St Thomas's Hospital [2004] EWCA Civ, 641

The action was brought by the family of a British serviceman stationed in Germany. The woman gave birth in a German hospital under an arrangement between the Ministry of Defence and Guy's and St Thomas Hospital in London. Under the arrangement Guy's and St Thomas' arranged the provision of treatment in Germany. Due to negligent conduct of the delivery the child was born with serious brain damage. At first instance Bell J. held that while a non-delegable duty can exist it was dependent upon the hospital accepting the patient for advice or treatment. Here there was not liability since there was no evidence that the hospital had negligently selected the provider and otherwise there was no liability as the treatment was undertaken in a hospital which was outside their control.

LORD PHILLIPS M.R.
"Mr Tattersall's submissions seek to extend the law of negligence beyond any previous decision of the English court, subject to one exception. The exception is the finding of the existence of a non-delegable duty of care made by Judge Garner as one of the grounds of his decision in *Calderdale*. This finding did not represent the current state of English law. It seems to have been based on the observations of Lord Greene, MR in *Gold* and of Denning LJ in *Cassidy*, although in neither instance did these represent the reasons for the decision of the majority of the court.

More significantly, in each of these cases the court was concerned with the duty of the hospital that was actually carrying out the treatment of the patient. The Australian cases postulated the non-delegable duty of a hospital on the basis that the hospital had accepted the patient for treatment. Judge Garner (in *M v Calderdale*) extended the principle beyond this. Thus Mr Tattersall is realistic in accepting, as he did, that, if he is to succeed on his appeal, he must persuade us on policy grounds to expand this area of tortious liability . . .

Even if it were correct to hold that an NHS trust, which sends one of its patients abroad for treatment, owes a non-delegable duty to ensure that the patient receives careful treatment, it would not follow that the same was true of the MoD in this case."

QUESTION:

1. Is the implication of this decision that the English courts will in the future be unwilling to find primary liability?

(c) The Standard of Care

The law of negligence requires only that health care professionals exercise reasonable care in the performance of their particular skills. This raises the issue of what amounts to "reasonable care". It also begs the question of who must prove the absence or observance of this standard. Newdick identifies four approaches to the review of professional practice (C. Newdick, *Who Should We Treat?* (2nd edn), Oxford: OUP, 2005, pp.135–144). First, respect for reflective practice according the greatest clinical freedom for doctors. This is evident in the early years of clinical negligence litigation and also may apply where litigation concerns a new area of medical science where knowledge is still evolving. Secondly, a professional consensus model which develops as doctors possess greater understanding of the variety of medical techniques/approaches, etc. Under this model doctors have to illustrate that they are aware of developments in their practice and are required to keep up to date. Thirdly, there is a model of clinical appraisal which arises where there is a greater availability of information regarding medical practice and more control comes from managers. This is characterised by a greater use of guidelines with managers questioning if there has been a departure from such guidelines. Clinical guidelines are disseminated by bodies such as the National Institute for Clinical Excellence and professionals are required to comply with them. (see further B. Hurwitz, *Clinical Guidelines and the Law: Negligence, Discretion and Judgment*, Oxford: Radcliffe Medical Press, 1998). In addition the Clinical Negligence Scheme for Trusts, which is administered by the NHS litigation authority, has approved a set of standards and assessment procedures. Those bodies who comply with those standards may earn substantial discounts on their contributions to the scheme. Standards include, for example, requirements that patients should be provided with appropriate information as to the risks and benefits of proposed treatments and available alternatives (*CNST Manual of Guidance*, Bristol: CNST, 1996). Finally, Newdick suggests there is a "bureaucratic-scientific" model. This stressed the need for evidence-based medicine: medical practice based upon robust and reliable clinical evidence—so called "evidence-based medicine". An important part of evidence-based medicine is the dissemination of research findings. (See J. Applebey, K. Walsh and C. Ham, "Acting on the Evidence", National Association of Health Authorities and Trusts, 1995.) If a particular approach exists which has received the support of a powerful body of scientific evidence, then acting contrary to this may become increasingly difficult to justify. (See K. Walsh, "Evidence Based Health Care: A Brave New World?" (1996) *Health Care Risk Report* 16; B. Hurwitz, "How Does Evidence Based Guidance Influence Determinations of Medical Negligence" (2004) 329 B.M.J. 1024).

QUESTION:

1. Read through the following cases in this section which consider the standard of care. To what extent is judicial consideration of clinical decision-making today reflected in one or more of these models? (See

further C. Newdick, *Who Should We Treat?* (2nd edn) Oxford: OUP, 2005, pp.135–144.)

Bolam v Friern Hospital Management Committee [1957] 2 All E.R. 118, [1957] 1 W.L.R. 582

The plaintiff, John Bolam, was a psychiatric patient suffering depressive illness. He was advised by Dr de Bastarrechea, a consultant attached to Friern Hospital, to undergo electro-convulsive therapy. He signed a consent form but was not alerted to the risk of fracture that can occur because of fit-like convulsions that such treatment induces. In due course he received this treatment, but he was not given any relaxant drugs. As a consequence, he suffered several injuries. These included dislocation of the hip joints and fractures to the pelvis on both sides caused by the femur on both sides being driven through the cup of the pelvis. Bolam claimed damages from Friern hospital, alleging that the provision of electro-convulsive therapy without the prior administration of relaxant drugs, or without restraining his convulsions manually, amounted to negligence.

MCNAIR J.

" . . . On the evidence it is clear, is it not, that the science of electro-convulsive therapy is a progressive science? Its development has been traced for you over the few years in which it has been used in this country. You may think on this evidence that, even today, there is no standard settled technique to which all competent doctors will agree. The doctors called before you have mentioned in turn different variants of the technique that they use. Some use restraining sheets, some use relaxant drugs, some use manual control; but the final question about which you must make up your minds is this—whether Dr Allfrey, following on the practice that he had learned at Friern Hospital and following on the technique which had been shown to him by Dr De Bastarrechea, was negligent in failing to use relaxant drugs or, if he decided not to use relaxant drugs, that he was negligent in failing to exercise any manual control over the patient beyond merely arranging for his shoulders to be held, the chin supported, a gag used, and a pillow put under his back. No one suggests that there was any negligence in the diagnosis, or in the decision to use electro-convulsive therapy. Furthermore, no one suggests that Dr Allfrey, or anyone at the hospital, was in any way indifferent to the care of their patients. The only question is really a question of professional skill.

Before I turn to that, I must explain what in law we mean by 'negligence'. In the ordinary case which does not involve any special skill, negligence in law means this: some failure to do some act which a reasonable man in the circumstances would do, or doing some act which a reasonable man in the circumstances would not do; and if that failure or doing of that act results in injury, then there is a cause of action. How do you test whether this act or failure is negligent? In an ordinary case it is generally said, that you judge that by the action of the man in the street. He is the ordinary man. In one case it has been said that you judge it by the conduct of the man on the top of a Clapham omnibus. He is the ordinary man. But where you get a situation which involves the use of some special skill or competence, then the test whether there has been negligence or not is not the test of the man on the top of a Clapham omnibus, because he has not got this special skill. The test is the standard of the ordinary skilled man exercising and professing to have that special skill. A man need not possess the highest skill at the risk of being found negligent. It is well established law that it is sufficient if he exercises the ordinary skill of an ordinary competent man exercising that particular art. I do not think that I quarrel much with any of the submissions in law which have been put before you by counsel. Counsel for the plaintiff put it in this way, that in the case of a medical man negligence means failure to act in accordance with the standards of reasonably competent medical men at the time. That is a perfectly accurate statement, as long as it is remembered that there may be one or more perfectly proper standards; and if a medical man conforms with one of those proper standards then he is not negligent. Counsel for the plaintiff was also right, in my judgment, in saying that a mere personal belief that a particular technique is best is no defence unless that belief is based on reasonable grounds. That again is unexceptionable. But the emphasis which is laid by counsel for the defendants is on this aspect of negligence: he submitted to you that the real question on which you have to make up your mind on each of the three major points to be considered is whether the defendants, in acting in the way in which they did, were acting in accordance with a practice of competent respected professional opinion. Counsel for the defendants submitted that if you are satisfied that they were acting in accordance with a practice of a competent body of professional opinion, then it would be wrong for you to hold that negligence was established. I referred, before I started these observations, to a statement which is contained in a recent Scottish case, *Hunter v. Hanley* ([1955] SLT 213 at 217), which dealt with medical matters, where the Lord President said:

'In the realm of diagnosis and treatment there is ample scope for genuine difference of opinion, and one man clearly is not negligent merely because his conclusion differs from that of other professional men, nor because he has displayed less skill or knowledge than others would have shown. The true test for establishing negligence in diagnosis or treatment on the part of a doctor is whether he has been proved to be guilty of such failure as no doctor of ordinary skill would be guilty of if acting with ordinary care.'

If that statement of the true test is qualified by the words 'in all the circumstances', counsel for the plaintiff would not seek to say that that expression of opinion does not accord with English law. It is just a question of expression. I myself would prefer to put it this way. A doctor is not guilty of negligence if he has acted in accordance with a practice accepted as proper by a responsible body of medical men skilled in that particular art. I do not think there is much difference in sense. It is just a different way of expressing the same thought. Putting it the other way round, a doctor is not negligent, if he is acting in accordance with such a practice, merely because there is a body of opinion that takes a contrary view. At the same time, that does not mean that a medical man can obstinately and pig-headedly carry on with some old technique if it has been proved to be contrary to what is really substantially the whole of informed medical opinion. Otherwise you might get men today saying: 'I don't believe in anaesthetics. I don't believe in antiseptics. I am going to continue to do my surgery in the way it was done in the eighteenth century.' That clearly would be wrong.

Before I deal with the details of the case, it is right to say this, that it is not essential for you to decide which of two practices is the better practice, as long as you accept that what Dr Allfrey did was in accordance with a practice accepted by responsible persons; but if the result of the evidence is that you are satisfied that his practice is better than the practice spoken of on the other side, then it is a stronger case. Finally, bear this in mind, that you are now considering whether it was negligent for certain action to be taken in August, 1954, not in February, 1957; and in one of the well-known cases on this topic it has been said you must not look through 1957 spectacles at what happened in 1954."

NOTES:

1. Although *Bolam* was a first instance decision, it has since been expressly approved by the House of Lords.
2. As Newdick, *op. cit.*, illustrates today there are a number of factors which may affect the operation of the *Bolam* test. What constitutes the standard to be expected of a responsible professional practice may be influenced by

elements external to that profession. Audit is routinely undertaken. This involves the systematic analysis of quality of care and includes reviews of diagnosis and treatment processes. Expectations raised by audit may affect what is seen as acceptable professional practice. In addition, a term "evidence-based medicine" has developed. This refers to clinical practice being based upon certain factors ascertained through research with the aim of determining clinical and cost effectiveness. Finally, stipulations in NHS contracts may have an impact upon standards of patient care. (See further K. Barker, "NHS Contracting: Shadows in the Law of Tort" (1995) 3 *Medical Law Review* 161.)

3. In *Crawford v Charing Cross Hospital* (*The Times*, December 8, 1953) the court rejected a claim that an anaesthetist was negligent because he had not read an article published in *The Lancet* six months before. Nevertheless, while the health care professional does not have to read everything on her subject, he or she is expected to keep abreast of important developments. (See McNair J. at p.158 above.)

4. Both parties to the litigation are likely to adduce, if possible, expert medical opinion as to what constitutes a responsible body of professional practice. This may lead to difficulties in ascertaining whether the defendant has been negligent, which we explore further in the context of *Maynard v West Midlands HA*, below. Calling expert evidence increases the costs of the proceedings. The conduct of experts in medical negligence cases came under scrutiny by Lord Woolf in his report on civil justice (Lord Woolf, *Access to Justice*, London: HMSO, 1996). The aim of the civil justice reforms was to streamline civil litigation and one resultant recommendation was the reform of the law concerning expert evidence. This is discussed further below at p.215. The conduct of experts is set out in the Civil Procedure Rules 1998, part 35. This states that:

"The facts used in the expert's report must be true.
    The expert's opinion must be reasonable and based on current experience of the problem in question. When there is a range of reasonable opinion the expert is obliged to consider the extent of that range in the report and to acknowledge any matters that might adversely affect the validity of the opinion provided.
    The expert is obliged to indicate the sources of all the information provided and not to include or exclude anything that has been suggested by others (particularly the instructing lawyers) without forming an independent view.
    The expert must make it clear that the opinions expressed represent his or her true or complete professional opinion."

5. The standard relates to the speciality. In *Shakoor v Situ* [2000] 4 All E.R. 181, a patient suffered an adverse reaction to a herbal medicine prescribed by a practitioner of Chinese herbal medicine, which led to acute liver failure from which the patient subsequently died. The standards of a reasonably competent practitioner of orthodox medicine were rejected, along with a reasonably competent practitioner of Chinese herbal medicine. Instead it was held that the standard of care was that of a reasonably competent practitioner of alternative medicine.

QUESTION:

1. According to McNair J., who sets the standard of care to which doctors must conform: the courts or the doctors themselves? Who should set the standard? (See J. Montgomery, "Medicine, Accountability and Professionalism" (1989) 16 *Journal of Law and Society* 319, and see further *Bolitho v City of Hackney HA* below at p.161.)

Whitehouse v Jordan [1981] 1 All E.R. 267, [1981] 1 W.L.R. 246

The defendant was in charge of the plaintiff's delivery. The plaintiff, Stuart Whitehouse, was born with severe and irreparable brain damage, following a high risk pregnancy. After Stuart's mother had been in labour for 22 hours, the defendant decided to carry out a test to see whether forceps could be used to assist the delivery. He made six attempts to deliver the baby with the forceps before quickly and competently proceeding to a caesarean section. Acting through his mother, as next friend, the plaintiff claimed damages for negligence alleging (i) that the defendant had been negligent in pulling too long and too hard with the forceps—the six attempts with the forceps had taken some 25 minutes—and (ii) that in doing so he had caused the brain damage.

LORD EDMUND-DAVIES
" . . . The principal questions calling for decision are: (a) in what manner did Mr Jordan use the forceps? and (b) was that manner consistent with the degree of skill which a member of his profession is required by law to exercise? Surprising though it is at this late stage in the development of the law of negligence, counsel for Mr Jordan persisted in submitting that his client should be completely exculpated were the answer to question (b), 'Well, at the worst he was guilty of an error of clinical judgment'. My Lords, it is high time that the unacceptability of such an answer be finally exposed. To say that a surgeon committed an error of clinical judgment is wholly ambiguous, for, while some such errors may be completely consistent with the due exercise of professional skill, other acts or omissions in the course of exercising 'clinical judgment' may be so glaringly below proper standards as to make a finding of negligence inevitable. Indeed, I should have regarded this as a truism were it not that, despite the exposure of the 'false antithesis' by Donaldson L.J. in his dissenting judgment in the Court of Appeal, counsel for the defendants adhered to it before your Lordships.

But doctors and surgeons fall into no special category, and, to avoid any future disputation of a similar kind, I would have it accepted that the true doctrine was enunciated, and by no means for the first time, by McNair in *Bolam* v. *Friern Hospital Management Committee* [1957] 2 All E.R. 118 at 121 in the following words, which were applied by the Privy Council in *Chin Keow v. Government of Malaysia* [1967] 1 W.L.R. 813:

' . . . where you get a situation which involves the use of some special skill or competence, then the test as to whether there has been negligence or not is not the test of the man on the top of a Clapham omnibus because he has not got this special skill. The test is the standard of the ordinary skilled man exercising and professing to have that special skill.'

If a surgeon fails to measure up to that standard in any respect ('clinical judgment' or otherwise), he has been negligent and should be so adjudged."

LORD FRASER

"After a long trial, the learned judge held negligence established against the registrar, but the Court of Appeal by a majority (Lord Denning M.R. and Lawton L.J., Donaldson L.J. dissenting) reversed his decision. They did so not because they considered that the learned trial judge had misstated the relevant law. Clearly he did not; he said, rightly in my opinion, that negligence for the purposes of this case meant 'a failure . . . to exercise the standard of skill expected from the ordinary competent specialist having regard to the experience and expertise that specialist holds himself out as possessing'. He added the proviso that the skill and expertise to be considered were those applying in 1969 to 1970. Although that statement was not criticised in the Court of Appeal, Lord Denning M.R. did criticise a later sentence in the judgment because, in his view, it suggested that the law made no allowance for errors of judgment by a professional man. Referring to medical men, Lord Denning M.R. said: [1980] 1 All E.R. 650 at 658 'If they are to be found liable [*sic* for negligence] whenever they do not effect a cure, or whenever anything untoward happens, it would do a great disservice to the profession itself.' That is undoubtedly correct, but he went on to say this: 'We must say, and say firmly, that, in a professional man an error of judgment is not negligent.' Having regard to the context, I think that Lord Denning M.R. must have meant to say that an error of judgment 'is not necessarily negligent'. But in my respectful opinion, the statement as it stands is not an accurate statement of the law. Merely to describe something as an error of judgment tells us nothing about whether it is negligent or not. The true position is that an error of judgment may, or may not, be negligent; it depends on the nature of the error. If it is one that would not have been made by a reasonably competent professional man professing to have the skill that the defendant held himself out as having, and acting with ordinary care, then it is negligent. If, on the other hand, it is an error that a man, acting with ordinary care, might have made, then it is not negligence.

The main reason why the Court of Appeal reversed the judge's decision was that they differed from him on the facts. The question therefore is whether the Court of Appeal was entitled to reverse the judge's decision on a pure question of fact. The view of the judge who saw and heard the witnesses as to the weight to be given to their evidence is always entitled to great respect. We were reminded particularly of dicta to that effect in *The Hontestroom* [1927] A.C. 37 and *Powell v. Streatham Manor Nursing Home* [1935] All E.R. 58, and there is other high authority to the same effect. But in this case, unlike cases such as *Powell* and *The Hontestroom*, no direct issue of credibility arises. It is not suggested that any witness, or body of witnesses, was giving dishonest evidence. The only witness whose reliability is seriously in question is Mrs Whitehouse, the mother of the plaintiff, and I shall refer to the critical part of her evidence in a moment. Apart from her evidence, the important facts are almost entirely inferences from the primary facts, and in determining what inferences should properly be drawn, an appellate court is just as well placed as the trial judge. Accordingly this is a case where the judge's decision on fact is more open to be reassessed by an appellate court that it often is."

QUESTIONS:

1. According to Lord Edmund-Davies: " . . . an error of judgment may, or may not, be negligent; it depends on the nature of the error. If it is one that would not have been made by a reasonably competent professional man . . . acting with ordinary care, then it is negligent". Are you convinced by this reasoning or would you prefer to see some reference to the gravity of the error? (*cf.* the opinion of Lord Bridge in *Sidaway v Board of Governors of the Bethlem Royal Hospital and Maudsley Hospital* [1985] 1 All E.R. 643).

2. Do you think that it was appropriate for their Lordships, in *Whitehouse v Jordan*, to question the facts found at first instance?

(i) Diverging Professional Opinions

Difficulties may arise where there is a divergence of professional opinion. This issue was examined in *Maynard v West Midlands Regional Health Authority*.

Maynard v West Midlands Regional Health Authority [1985] 1 All E.R. 635, [1984] 1 W.L.R. 634

Two consultants, employed by the defendant health authority, were treating the plaintiff for a chest complaint. They believed her to be suffering from tuberculosis but thought there was a possibility that it might be Hodgkin's disease. Since Hodgkin's disease is fatal unless treated in its very early stages, they decided that, rather than wait for the results of a sputum test (designed to ascertain whether she had tuberculosis), it was sensible to conduct an exploratory operation, a mediastinoscopy, to determine whether she had Hodgkin's disease.

The operation, which was carried out properly, showed her to have tuberculosis and not Hodgkin's disease. The plaintiff claimed damages from the defendant health authority, alleging that the decision to carry out the mediastinoscopy rather than await the result of the sputum test had been negligent. At the trial, the judge was impressed by the evidence of an expert witness on behalf of the plaintiff who stated that the case had almost certainly been one of tuberculosis from the outset and that it had been dangerous and wrong to undertake the operation. He gave judgment for the plaintiff. The Court of Appeal reversed his decision. The plaintiff appealed to the House of Lords.

LORD SCARMAN
" . . . The only issue for the House is whether the two medical men, Dr Ross who was the consultant physician and Mr Stephenson the surgeon, were guilty of an error of judgment amounting to a breach of their duty of care to their patient. Both accept that the refusal to make a firm diagnosis until they had available the findings of the diagnostic operation was one for which they were jointly responsible.

The issue is essentially one of fact: but there remains the possibility, which it will be necessary to examine closely, that the judge, although directing himself correctly as to the law, failed to apply it correctly when he came to draw the inferences upon which his conclusion of negligence was based. Should this possibility be established as the true interpretation to be put upon his judgment, he would, of course, be guilty of an error of law.

In English law the appeal process is a rehearing of fact and law. But the limitations upon an appellate court's ability to review findings of fact are severe, and well-established. Lord Thankerton stated the principles in *Watt (or Thomas) v. Thomas* [1947] 1 All E.R. 582; and recently the cases and the principles have been reviewed by this House in *Whitehouse v. Jordan* [1981] 1 All E.R. 267, itself a medical negligence case. It is, therefore, unnecessary now to restate them. I would, however, draw attention to some observations by Lord Bridge of Harwich in the *Whitehouse* case and by Brandon L.J. in a Court of Appeal case, *Joyce v. Yeomans* [1981] 2 All E.R. 21, since they are directly relevant to the problems facing your Lordships in this appeal. Lord Bridge of Harwich said ([1981] 1 All E.R. 267, at 270, 286):

'I recognise that this is a question of pure fact and that in the realm of fact, as the authorities repeatedly emphasise, the advantages which the judge derives from seeing and hearing the witnesses must always be respected by an appellate court. At the same time the importance of the part played by those advantages in assisting the judge to any particular conclusion of fact varies through a wide spectrum from, at one end, a straight conflict of primary fact between witnesses, where credibility is crucial and the appellate court can hardly ever interfere, to, at the other end, an inference from undisputed primary facts, where the appellate court is in just as good a position as the trial judge to make the decision.'

The primary facts in this case are undisputed. But there are gaps in our knowledge of some details of the medical picture due to a loss of hospital notes. These gaps occur in the critical period during which the two doctors made the decision which is said to be negligent. The gaps have to be bridged by inference. In this task, the trial judge, it must be recognised, had the advantage of seeing and hearing the two medical men whose professional judgment, reached during that period, is impugned. We are not, therefore at the extreme end of Lord Bridge's 'wide spectrum', though we are near it. There is room for a judgment on credibility for the reasons given by Brandon L.J. in *Joyce v. Yeomans* [1981] 2 All E.R. 21 at 26–27. Speaking of expert evidence, he made this comment:

'There are various aspects of such evidence in respect of which the trial judge can get the "feeling" of a case in a way in which an appellate court, reading the transcript, cannot. Sometimes expert witnesses display signs of partisanship in a witness box or lack of objectivity. This may or may not be obvious from the transcript, yet it may be quite plain to the trial judge. Sometimes an expert witness may refuse to make what a more wise witness would make, namely, proper concessions to the viewpoint of the other side. Here again this may or may not be apparent from the transcript, although plain to the trial judge. I mention only two aspects of the matter, but there are others.'

These are wise words of warning, but they do not modify Lord Thankerton's statement of principle nor were they intended to do so. The relevant principle remains, namely that an appellate court, if disposed to come to a different conclusion from the trial judge on the printed evidence, should not do so unless satisfied that the advantage enjoyed by him of seeing and hearing the witnesses is not sufficient to explain or justify his conclusion. But if the appellate court is satisfied that he has not made a proper use of his advantage, 'the matter will then become at large for the appellate court' (see [1947] 1 All E.R. 582 at 587).

The only other question of law in the appeal is as to the nature of the duty owed by a doctor to his patient. The most recent authoritative formulation is that by Lord Edmund-Davies in the *Whitehouse* case. Quoting from the judgment of McNair J. in *Bolam v. Friern Hospital Management Committee* [1957] 2 All E.R. 118 he said, at [1981] 1 All E.R. 267 at 277:

' "The test is the standard of the ordinary skilled man exercising and professing to have that special skill." If a surgeon fails to measure up to that standard in *any respect* ("clinical judgment" or otherwise), he has been negligent . . . ' (Lord Edmund-Davies's emphasis.)

The present case may be classified as one of clinical judgment. Two distinguished consultants, a physician and a surgeon experienced in the treatment of chest diseases, formed a judgment as to what was, in their opinion, in the best interests of their patient. They recognised that tuberculosis was the most likely diagnosis. But, in their opinion, there was an unusual factor, *viz* swollen glands in the mediastinum unaccompanied by any evidence of lesion in the lungs. Hodgkin's disease, carcinoma and sarcoidosis were, therefore, possibilities. The danger they thought was Hodgkin's disease; though unlikely, it was, if present, a killer (as treatment was understood in 1970) unless remedial steps were taken in its early stage. They, therefore, decided on mediastinoscopy, an operative procedure which would provide them with a biopsy from the swollen glands which could be subjected to immediate microscopic examination. It is said that the evidence of tuberculosis was so strong that it was unreasonable and wrong to defer diagnosis and to put their patient to the risks of the operation. The case against them is not mistake or carelessness in performing the operation, which it is admitted was properly carried out, but an error of judgment in requiring the operation to be undertaken.

A case which is based on an allegation that a fully considered decision of two consultants in the field of their special skill was negligent clearly presents certain difficulties of proof. It is not enough to show that there is a body of competent professional opinion which considers that there was a wrong decision, if there also exists a body of professional opinion, equally competent, which supports the decision as reasonable in the circumstances. It is not enough to show that subsequent events show that the operation need never have been performed, if at the time the decision to operate was taken it was reasonable in the sense that a responsible body of medical opinion would have accepted it as proper. I do not think that the words of Lord President Clyde in *Hunter v. Hanley* (1955) SLT 213 at 217 can be bettered:

'In the realm of diagnosis and treatment there is ample scope for genuine difference of opinion and one man clearly is not negligent merely because his conclusion differs from that of other professional men . . . The true test for establishing negligence in diagnosis or treatment on the part of a doctor is whether he has been proved to be guilty of such failure as no doctor of ordinary skill would be guilty of if acting with ordinary care . . .'

I would only add that a doctor who professes to exercise a special skill must exercise the ordinary skill of his speciality. Differences of opinion and practice exist, and will always exist, in the medical as in other professions. There is seldom any one answer exclusive of all others to problems of professional judgment. A court may prefer one body of opinion to the other: but that is no basis for a conclusion of negligence."

His Lordship stated the facts and evidence in detail, and continued:

"At the trial and in the Court of Appeal there were two issues—causation and negligence. The judge decided both in favour of the plaintiff appellant. The Court of Appeal had no hesitation in upholding the judge on causation but reversed him on negligence. Thus it is that the only issue now is negligence. On this the judge's conclusions were that the operation was unnecessary, wrong, and in the circumstances unreasonable and a breach of the duty of care. He found that Dr Ross instigated the operation and that Mr Stephenson in failing to object to it and in sharing the decision was also in breach of his duty of care. The learned judge accepted the evidence of Dr Hugh-Jones, the appellant's principal expert witness, that it was almost certainly a case of tuberculosis from the outset and should have been so diagnosed, and that it was wrong and dangerous to undertake the operation. His detailed findings against Dr Ross were that he should not have used the operation where the right diagnosis was almost certainly tuberculosis, and that he should at the very least have waited for the pathological reports on the sputum, which in fact turned out to be positive. Dr Ross's defence that because of the risk of Hodgkin's disease he could not delay was rejected by the judge on the grounds that a delay of four to six weeks, up to 10 at maximum, would not have mattered and that the fear of Hodgkin's disease being present was not a reasonable fear in the circumstances. The judge recognised that the defence had called a formidable number of distinguished experts, amongst whom it was legitimate to include Dr Ross and Mr Stephenson themselves, all of whom expressed a contrary view to his and approved the course of action taken in deferring diagnosis and performing the operation. The judge accepted not only the expertise of all the medical witnesses called before him but also their truthfulness and honesty. But he found Dr Hugh-Jones 'an outstanding witness; clear, definite, logical and persuasive'. The judge continued:

'I have weighed his evidence against that of the distinguished contrary experts. I do not intend or wish to take away from their distinction by holding that in the particular circumstances of this particular case I prefer his opinions and his evidence to theirs.'

My Lords, even before considering the reasons given by the majority of the Court of Appeal for reversing the findings of negligence, I have to say that a judge's 'preference' for one body of distinguished professional opinion to another also professionally distinguished is not sufficient to establish negligence in a practitioner whose actions have received the seal of approval of those whose opinions, truthfully expressed, honestly held, were not preferred. If this was the real reason for the judge's finding, he erred in law even though elsewhere in his judgment he stated the law correctly. For in the realm of diagnosis and treatment, negligence is not established by preferring one respectable body of professional opinion to another. Failure to exercise the ordinary skill of a doctor (in the appropriate speciality, if he be a specialist) is necessary.

My Lords, it would be doing an injustice to the careful and detailed reasoning elsewhere evident in the judgment of the trial judge to dismiss this appeal upon the basis of this one passage. But, to borrow a telling phrase from Cumming-Bruce L.J. in the Court of Appeal, it certainly suggests that his finding of negligence is 'vulnerable to attack'. It gives rise to doubt whether he succeeded in making proper use of his advantage of seeing and hearing the witnesses who gave oral evidence."

His Lordship considered the Court of Appeal's criticisms of certain parts of the trial judge's judgment, which he found to be justified, and stated that the Court of Appeal had, therefore, been justified in treating the issue of negligence as being at large for them to draw the appropriate inferences and to reach their own conclusion. He also stated that the final conclusion, as expressed by Cumming-Bruce L.J., that the judge's finding that the decision to operate was unreasonable, could not be supported. He then concluded:

"The judge thought that Dr Ross might have had an 'idée fixe' about the possibility of Hodgkin's disease. This, with respect, is not a possible view of his evidence read as a whole, especially in the light of the judge's own appraisal of him as a witness. Nor is it consistent with the existence of a strong body of evidence given by distinguished medical men supporting and approving of what he did in the circumstances of this case as they presented themselves to him at the time when he made his decision.

My Lords, the House in this case has reviewed the evidence. The review has led me to the clear conclusion that the Court of Appeal was right to reverse the judge's finding of negligence. I would dismiss the appeal."

NOTES:

1. The other four Law Lords who heard the case, Lords Elwyn-Jones, Fraser, Roskill and Templeman, delivered short opinions expressing their agreement with Lord Scarman. Lord Scarman stated, "in the realm of diagnosis and treatment negligence is not established by preferring one respectable body of professional opinion to another".

2. In *De Freitas v O'Brien* [1993] 4 Med. L.R. 281, the court again illustrated its unwillingness to question a body of professional medical opinion. Here the claimant underwent an operation on her spine. The procedure was one which only a very small number of doctors would undertake (in this case four or five out of some 250 neurosurgeons countrywide), although the neurosurgeons claimed that they had a very high degree of expertise. The

surgeon was held not to be negligent, even though the exploratory surgery which had been undertaken carried an unavoidable risk of infection. Nevertheless, the judge in this case did state that the view of a body of medical opinion could be scrutinised by the court following the approach of Dillon L.J. in the Court of Appeal in *Bolitho* (see I. Kennedy, "Medical Negligence: *Bolam* and Professional Practice" (1994) 2 *Medical Law Review* 210) and see *Bolitho* below).

3. There was criticism of the body of professional medical opinion in *Hucks v Cole* [1993] 4 Med. L.R. 393. Here a pathology report indicated that Mrs Hucks should have been given penicillin. The doctors treating her did not take on board this report. Medical evidence was presented to the effect that other clinicians would have taken the same approach as Dr Cole; however, the Court of Appeal was prepared to find him liable in negligence. Sachs L.J. held that a practice could be held to be negligent in a situation in which it was "definitely not reasonable" to take this risk. The judgment was critical of the evidence presented by the medical experts in support of the doctor in this case. He held that the doctor's failure to prescribe penicillin "was not merely wrong but clearly unreasonable". He went on to say that this concerned "doctors who said in one form or another that they would have acted or might have acted in the same way as the defendant did, for reasons which on examination do not really stand up to analysis".

(ii) Revisiting Bolam

The application of the professional practice standard in *Bolam*, while it did allow for scrutiny of clinical judgment, was clearly problematic for litigants. This is one reason why further consideration of the professional practice standard in the House of Lords in the later case of *Bolitho v City of Hackney HA* gave rise to much interest. Below we consider *Bolitho* and its aftermath.

Bolitho v City and Hackney Health Authority [1998] AC 232

A two-year-old child was admitted to hospital suffering from respiratory difficulties. At 12.40 p.m. on the following day, his breathing suddenly deteriorated and a nurse summoned the doctor in charge of the child's care by telephone. The doctor did not attend and in the event the child recovered. At 2 p.m. he suffered a second episode of acute respiratory difficulty which the nurse again reported to the doctor by telephone but the child apparently recovered without the doctor having attended. At 2.30 p.m. the child collapsed owing to failure of his respiratory system, as a result of which he suffered a cardiac arrest. By the time his respiratory and cardiac functions were restored he had sustained severe brain damage. A claim for damages in negligence was brought by the child's parents on behalf of the child and his parents in their own right. Expert evidence stated that a competent doctor who attended the patient after the second period of breathing difficulties would have undertaken prophylactic intubation to provide an airway and that such procedure would have avoided the cardiac arrest and subsequent injury. At first instance it was held that although the doctor was in breach of duty in not attending, if she had attended she would not have arranged for the child to be intubated. The judge noted that an expert in paediatric respiratory medicine called by the defence was of opinion that, on the symptoms presented by the child, intubation would not have been appropriate; thus here the decision by the doctor not to intubate would have been in accordance with a body of responsible professional opinion, and causation had not been proved. The Court of Appeal, by a majority, upheld the judge's decision. The child died during the course of the proceedings. On appeal to the House of Lords by the child's mother, as administratrix of his estate:

LORD BROWNE-WILKINSON
"My Lords, this appeal raises two questions relating to liability for medical negligence. The first, which I believe to be more apparent than real, relates to the proof of causation when the negligent act is one of omission. The second concerns the approach to professional negligence laid down in *Bolam v. Friern Hospital Management Committee* [1957] 1 W.L.R. 583.

Negligence having been established, the question of causation had to be decided: would the cardiac arrest have been avoided if Dr. Horn or some other suitable deputy had attended as they should have done. By the end of the trial it was common ground, first, that intubation so as to provide an airway in any event would have ensured that the respiratory failure which occurred did not lead to cardiac arrest and, secondly, that such intubation would have had to be carried out, if at all, before the final catastrophic episode.

The judge identified the questions he had to answer as follows:

'[Mr. Owen, for the defendants] submitted therefore that (if once it was held that Dr. Horn was negligent in failing to attend at either 12.40 p.m. or 2 p.m.) the sole issue was whether Patrick would on one or other of these occasions have been intubated. In submitting that on this aspect of the case the issue was what would Dr. Horn or another competent doctor sent in her place have done had they attended, Mr. Owen was, I think, accepting that the real question was what would Dr. Horn or that other doctor have done, or *what should they have done*. As it seems to me, if Dr. Horn would have intubated, then the plaintiff succeeds, whether or not that is a course which all reasonably competent practitioners would have followed. If, however, Dr. Horn would not have intubated, then the plaintiff can only succeed if such failure was contrary to accepted medical practice (I am not purporting to consider the legal tests in detail, and merely using shorthand at this stage) . . . Common to both sides is the recognition that I must decide whether Dr. Horn would have intubated (or made preparations for intubation), and, even if she would not, whether such a failure on her part would have been contrary to accepted practice in the profession.' (Emphasis added.)

As to the first of those issues, Dr. Horn's evidence was that, had she come to see Patrick at 2 p.m., she would not have arranged for him to be intubated. The judge accepted this evidence. However, he found that she would have made preparation to ensure that speedy intubation could take place: in the event that proved to be an irrelevant finding since the judge found that such preparations would have made no difference to the outcome. Therefore, the judge answered the first of his two questions by holding that Dr. Horn would not herself have intubated if, contrary to the facts, she had attended.

As to the second of the judge's questions (i.e. whether any competent doctor should have intubated if he had attended Patrick at any time after 2 p.m.), the judge had evidence from no less than eight medical experts, all of them distinguished. Five of them were called on behalf of Patrick and were all of the view that, at least after the second episode, any competent doctor would have intubated. Of these five, the judge was most impressed by Dr. Heaf, a consultant paediatrician in respiratory medicine at the Royal Liverpool

Children's Hospital, which is the largest children's hospital in the United Kingdom. On the other side, the defendants called three experts all of whom said that, on the symptoms presented by Patrick as recounted by Sister Sallabank and Nurse Newbold, intubation would not have been appropriate. Of the defendants' experts, the judge found Dr. Dinwiddie, a consultant paediatrician in respiratory diseases at the Hospital for Sick Children, Great Ormond Street, most impressive.

The views of the plaintiffs' experts were largely based on the premise that over the last two hours before the catastrophe Patrick was in a state of respiratory distress progressing inexorably to hypoxia and respiratory failure. The defendants' experts, on the other hand, considered the facts as recounted by Sister Sallabank indicated that Patrick was quite well apart from the two quite sudden acute episodes at 12.40 p.m. and 2 p.m. The judge held that the evidence of Sister Sallabank and Nurse Newbold as to Patrick's behaviour (which he accepted) was inconsistent with a child passing through the stages of progressive hypoxia.

Having made his findings of fact, the judge directed himself as to the law by reference to the speech of Lord Scarman in *Maynard v. West Midlands Regional Health Authority* [1984] 1 W.L.R. 634, 639:

' . . . I have to say that a judge's "preference" for one body of distinguished professional opinion to another also professionally distinguished is not sufficient to establish negligence in a practitioner whose actions have received the seal of approval of those whose opinions, truthfully expressed, honestly held, were not preferred. If this was the real reason for the judge's finding, he erred in law even though elsewhere in his judgment he stated the law correctly. For in the realm of diagnosis and treatment negligence is not established by preferring one respectable body of professional opinion to another. Failure to exercise the ordinary skill of a doctor (in the appropriate speciality, if he be a specialist) is necessary.'

The judge held that the views of Dr. Heaf and Dr. Dinwiddie, though diametrically opposed, both represented a responsible body of professional opinion espoused by distinguished and truthful experts. Therefore, he held, Dr. Horn, if she had attended and not intubated, would have come up to a proper level of skill and competence, i.e. the standard represented by Dr. Dinwiddie's views. Accordingly he held that it had not been proved that the admitted breach of duty by the defendants had caused the catastrophe which occurred to Patrick.

An appeal to the Court of Appeal was dismissed by Dillon and Farquharson L.JJ., Simon Brown L.J. dissenting. Their decision is reported only in [1993] 4 Med.L.R. 381. I will have to consider some of their reasons hereafter.

The Bolam test—should the judge have accepted Dr. Dinwiddie's evidence?

As I have said, the judge took a very favourable view of Dr. Dinwiddie as an expert. He said:

' . . . I have to say of Dr. Dinwiddie also, that he displayed what seemed to me to be a profound knowledge of paediatric respiratory medicine, coupled with impartiality, and there is no doubt, in my view, of the genuineness of his opinion that intubation was not indicated.'

However, the judge also expressed these doubts:

'Mr. Brennan also advanced a powerful argument—which I have to say, as a layman, appealed to me—to the effect that the views of the defendant's experts simply were not logical or sensible. Given the recent and the more remote history of Patrick's illness, culminating in these two episodes, surely it was unreasonable and illogical not to anticipate the recurrence of a life-threatening event and take the step which it was acknowledged would probably have saved Patrick from harm? This was the safe option, whatever was suspected as the cause, or even if the cause was thought to be a mystery. The difficulty of this approach, as in the end I think Mr. Brennan acknowledged, was that in effect it invited me to substitute my own views for those of the medical experts.'

Mr. Brennan renewed that submission both before the Court of Appeal (who unanimously rejected it) and before your Lordships. He submitted that the judge had wrongly treated the test as requiring him to accept the views of one truthful body of expert professional advice even though he was unpersuaded of its logical force. He submitted that the judge was wrong in law in adopting that approach and that ultimately it was for the court, not for medical opinion, to decide what was the standard of care required of a professional in the circumstances of each particular case.

My Lords, I agree with these submissions to the extent that, in my view, the court is not bound to hold that a defendant doctor escapes liability for negligent treatment or diagnosis just because he leads evidence from a number of medical experts who are genuinely of opinion that the defendant's treatment or diagnosis accorded with sound medical practice. In the case itself, McNair J. [1957] 1 W.L.R. 583, 587 stated that the defendant had to have acted in accordance with the practice accepted as proper by a 'responsible body of medical men.' Later, at p. 588, he referred to 'a standard of practice recognised as proper by a competent reasonable body of opinion.' Again, in the passage which I have cited from [1984] 1 W.L.R.634, 639, Lord Scarman refers to a 'respectable' body of professional opinion. The use of these adjectives—responsible, reasonable and respectable—all show that the court has to be satisfied that the exponents of the body of opinion relied upon can demonstrate that such opinion has a logical basis. In particular in cases involving, as they so often do, the weighing of risks against benefits, the judge before accepting a body of opinion as being responsible, reasonable or respectable, will need to be satisfied that, in forming their views, the experts have directed their minds to the question of comparative risks and benefits and have reached a defensible conclusion on the matter.

There are decisions which demonstrate that the judge is entitled to approach expert professional opinion on this basis. For example, in *Hucks v Cole* (1968) [1993] 4 Med.L.R. 393 (a case from 1968), a doctor failed to treat with penicillin a patient who was suffering from septic spots on her skin though he knew them to contain organisms capable of leading to puerperal fever. A number of distinguished doctors gave evidence that they would not, in the circumstances, have treated with penicillin. The Court of Appeal found the defendant to have been negligent. Sachs L.J. said, at p. 397:

'When the evidence shows that a lacuna in professional practice exists by which risks of grave danger are knowingly taken, then, however small the risk, the court must anxiously examine that lacuna—particularly if the risk can be easily and inexpensively avoided. If the court finds, on an analysis of the reasons given for not taking those precautions that, in the light of current professional knowledge, there is no proper basis for the lacuna, and that it is definitely not reasonable that those risks should have been taken, its function is to state that fact and where necessary to state that it constitutes negligence. In such a case the practice will no doubt thereafter be altered to the benefit of patients. On such occasions the fact that other practitioners would have done the same thing as the defendant practitioner is a very weighty matter to be put on the scales on his behalf; but it is not, as Mr. Webster readily conceded, conclusive. The court must be vigilant to see whether the reasons given for putting a patient at risk are valid in the light of any well-known advance in medical knowledge, or whether they stem from a residual adherence to out-of-date ideas.'

Again, in *Edward Wong Finance Co Ltd v Johston Stoke and Master* [1984] AC 296, the defendant's solicitors had conducted the completion of a mortgage transaction in Hong Kong style rather than in the old fashioned English style. Completion in Hong Kong style provides for money to be paid over against an undertaking by the solicitors for the borrowers subsequently to hand over the executed documents. This practice opened the gateway through which a dishonest solicitor for the borrower absconded with the loan money without providing the security documents for such loan. The Privy Council held that even though completion in Hong Kong style was almost universally adopted in Hong Kong and was therefore in accordance with a body of professional opinion there, the defendant's solicitors were liable for negligence because there was an obvious risk which could have been guarded against. Thus, the body of professional opinion, though almost universally held, was not reasonable or responsible.

These decisions demonstrate that in cases of diagnosis and treatment there are cases where, despite a body of professional opinion sanctioning the defendant's conduct, the defendant can properly be held liable for negligence (I am not here considering questions of disclosure of risk). In my judgment that is because, in some cases, it cannot be demonstrated to the judge's satisfaction that the body of opinion relied upon is reasonable or responsible. In the vast majority of cases the fact that distinguished experts in the field are of a particular opinion will demonstrate the reasonableness of that opinion. In particular, where there are questions of assessment of the relative risks and benefits of adopting a particular medical practice, a reasonable view necessarily presupposes that the relative risks and benefits have been weighed by the experts in forming their opinions. But if, in a rare case, it can be demonstrated that the professional opinion is not capable of withstanding logical analysis, the judge is entitled to hold that the body of opinion is not reasonable or responsible.

I emphasise that in my view it will very seldom be right for a judge to reach the conclusion that views genuinely held by a competent medical expert are unreasonable. The assessment of medical risks and benefits is a matter of clinical judgment which a judge would not normally be able to make without expert evidence. As the quotation from Lord Scarman makes clear, it would be wrong to allow such assessment to deteriorate into seeking to persuade the judge to prefer one of two views both of which are capable of being logically supported. It is only where a judge can be satisfied that the body of expert opinion cannot be logically supported at all that such opinion will not provide the benchmark by reference to which the defendant's conduct falls to be assessed.

I turn to consider whether this is one of those rare cases. Like the Court of Appeal, in my judgment it plainly is not. Although the judge does not in turn say so, it was implicit in his judgment that he accepted that Dr. Dinwiddie's view was a reasonable view for a doctor to hold. As I read his judgment, he was quoting counsel's submission when he described the view that intubation was not the right course as being 'unreasonable and illogical.' The appeal of the argument was to the judge 'as a layman' not a conclusion he had reached on all the medical evidence. He refused to substitute his own views for those of the medical experts. I read him as saying that, without expert evidence he would have thought that the risk involved would have called for intubation, but that he could not dismiss Dr. Dinwiddie's views to the contrary as being illogical.

Even if this is to put too favourable a meaning on the judge's judgment, when the evidence is looked at it is plainly not a case in which Dr. Dinwiddie's views can be dismissed as illogical. According to the accounts of Sister Sallabank and Nurse Newbold, although Patrick had had two severe respiratory crises, he had recovered quickly from both and for the rest presented as a child who was active and running about. Dr. Dinwiddie's view was that these symptoms did not show a progressive respiratory collapse and that there was only a small risk of total respiratory failure. Intubation is not a routine, risk-free process. Dr. Roberton, a consultant paediatrician at Addenbrooke's Hospital, Cambridge, described it as 'a major undertaking—an invasive procedure with mortality and morbidity attached—it was an assault.' It involves anaesthetising and ventilating the child. A young child does not tolerate a tube easily 'at any rate for a day or two' and the child unless sedated tends to remove it. In those circumstances it cannot be suggested that it was illogical for Dr. Dinwiddie, a most distinguished expert, to favour running what, in his view, was a small risk of total respiratory collapse rather than to submit Patrick to the invasive procedure of intubation.

Tragic though this case is for Patrick's mother and much as everyone must sympathise with her, I consider that the judge and the Court of Appeal reached the right conclusions on the evidence in this case. I would dismiss the appeal."

NOTES:

1. Lords Slynn, Nolan, Hoffmann and Clyde agreed with Lord Browne-Wilkinson.
2. It was initially suggested that the judgment in *Bolitho* was the "new *Bolam*"; see the discussion in A. Grubb, "Commentary" (1998) 6 *Medical Law Review* 378. However certain other commentators have questioned the impact of the decision. Brazier and Miola suggest that the effect of the judgment was to return to the original judgment of McNair J. in *Bolam* itself. They go on to comment that:

   > "While the medical experts are still to be required, in rare cases, to justify their opinions on logical grounds, there still appears to be a prima facie presumption that non-doctors will not be able fully to comprehend the evidence. This leads inexorably to a conclusion that the evidence cannot after all be critically evaluated by a judge."

   M. Brazier and J. Miola, "Bye Bye Bolam: a Medical Negligence Revolution?" [2000] 8 *Medical Law Review* 1.
3. The *Bolitho* decision has implications in other areas of health care law. The *Bolam* test was used by the House of Lords in *Re F* in 1990 ([1990] 2 A.C. 1) when ascertaining the basis for providing treatment for adults without capacity (see discussion in Chapter 5 below) and was subsequently utilised in relation to end-of-life decision-making in decisions such as *Airedale NHS Trust v Bland* (see further discussion in Chapter 14 below at p.1021). The case has also impacted upon the courts when considering disclosure of risks in relation to medical treatment—see *Pearce v United Bristol Healthcare NHS Trust* [1999] P.I.Q.R. P53 CA and see Chapter 5 below at p.390.
4. In the years that followed *Bolitho*, the impact of the decision has been mixed. Some cases appear to have taken a *Bolam*-type approach (e.g. *Briody v St Helens and Knowsley AHA* [1999] Lloyd's Rep. Med. 197; *Hallat v NW Anglia HA* [1988] Lloyd's Rep. Med. 197) while other cases seem to have followed a *Bolitho* approach (*Sharpe v Southend HA* [1997] Med. L.R. 299. In *Wisniewski v Central Manchester HA* [1998] Lloyd's Rep. Med. 223, the Court of Appeal refused to find negligence in a situation in which there was a dispute between the experts as to whether the defendant should have undertaken a procedure to ascertain whether the umbilical cord was wrapped around the neck of the foetus during childbirth. They held that the views of the experts were such "as could be logically supported and held by responsible doctors" (*per* Brooke L.J.).

QUESTIONS:

1. Does *Bolitho* indicate a sea-change in judicial approaches to clinical decision-making? (See Lord Woolf, "Are the Courts Excessively Deferential to the Medical Profession?" (2001) 9 *Medical Law Review* 1.)
2. What if the "logic" of the decision is fine but the premise is unsound or not persuasive?

3. What is the impact of the *Bolitho* decision on experimental therapy?

The boundaries of *Bolitho* were explored subsequently in 1999 in the following case.

Marriott v West Midlands Health Authority [1999] Lloyd's Rep. Med. 223 CA

Marriott suffered head injuries after a fall at his home. While initially taken to hospital and X-rayed, he was discharged the next day. However his condition did not improve. Eight days after the discharge, his general practitioner paid a home visit. Neurological tests were undertaken at that stage but no abnormalities were found. A further four days later he was admitted to hospital when his condition worsened. During the operation which was undertaken it was found that he had suffered a fracture of the skull and internal bleeding. Ultimately he suffered paralysis and a speech disorder. An action was brought against the health authority which alleged that the initial discharge was negligent as was the general practitioner who should have referred him back to the hospital during the home visit. On the question of the liability of the general practitioner, the issue was as to whether the tests undertaken by the general practitioner who attended the patient were adequate and would have thus as a consequence have averted the subsequent deterioration in his condition. Should he at that stage have immediately referred the patient back to hospital? At first instance the judge noted that there was a dispute in medical evidence from the experts as to whether the patient should have been referred to the hospital.
   She held that:

"Furthermore, whilst a Court must plainly be reluctant to depart from the opinion of an apparently careful and prudent general practitioner I have concluded that if there is a body of professional opinion which supports the course of leaving a patient who has some 7 days previously sustained a severe head injury at home in circumstances where he continues to complain of headaches drowsiness etc and where there continues to be a risk of an intracranial lesion which could cause a sudden and disastrous collapse, then such an approach is not reasonably prudent. It may very well be that if in the vast majority of cases the risk is very small. Nevertheless, the consequence if things go wrong are disastrous to the patient."

The decision was appealed. One of the defendants' arguments was that the judge had been wrong to discount the evidence adduced by the expert witness for the defence. In the Court of Appeal Beldam L.J. made reference to the words of Lord Browne-Wilkinson in *Bolitho*. He commented that while the risk of a lesion was small, the judge was nonetheless entitled to hold that in these circumstances as she found them it would not be a reasonable exercise of general practitioner's discretion to leave the patient at home rather than to refer the patient to hospital where further diagnostic facilities were available. Interestingly, while another member of the Court of Appeal, Pill L.J., agreed on the facts of the case, he stated that in his view the *Bolitho* point did not actually arise as the medical evidence simply pointed in one direction.
   Nonetheless he went on to say that:

PILL L.J.

"If contrary to my view, it was necessary for the plaintiff to rely on the principle that, in some circumstances, a judge is entitled to form her own view upon the logic of medical evidence introduced to provide a benchmark, I agree with the analysis by Beldam LJ on this issue."

NOTES:

1. This case illustrates the scope for judicial discretion in interpreting the test in *Bolitho*. Commenting on this case, Jones stated that:

   "The importance of *Bolitho* lies in the now explicit requirement to undertake a logical analysis of that evidence before characterising it as responsible, rather than relying upon the eminence or the number of the experts expressing the particular view. But the qualifying comments of Lord Browne-Wilkinson and the actual decision on the facts of *Bolitho* would depend upon how the lower courts and in particular the trial judge, responded to the shift in emphasis that it appeared to herald."

   See further M. Jones, "The Illogical Expert" (1999) *Professional Negligence* 117.

2. Mason and Laurie have commented that here judicial scrutiny was going one step further: "The judge was effectively dismissing the evidence of *both* sides; the court's opinion suggests that the result might have been different had she chosen one expert's evidence in preference to the other rather than substitute her own analysis". They even suggest that *Marriott* may be shifting again the boundaries of judicial scrutiny from a "logic" test to that of "reasonableness"; they note, however, that the situation is still not clear as although the trial judge's approach was supported, the Court of Appeal still used the reasonableness standard (see further J.K. Mason and G. Laurie, *Mason & McCall Smith's Law and Medical Ethics* (7th edn), Oxford: OUP, 2006 at para.9.47).

3. In *Penney v East Kent HA* (2000) 55 B.M.L.R. 63 the case concerned screening for cervical cancer. Three women were wrongly informed that their tests were negative. Although the existence of false positives and negatives is a normal part of the screening process and thus of itself not indicative necessarily of negligence, nonetheless in this case it was held that given this they should not have definitively classed the slides as negative. Pepitt J. at first instance, with whom the Court of Appeal agreed, held that in his opinion it fell outside *Bolam* because all the experts agreed that the screener of the slides was wrong here to class it as negative. But he went on to say that even were *Bolam* to be applicable, the classification as negative was "illogical" applying *Bolitho*.

(iii) The Inexperienced Practitioner

A further question that arises in relation to the standard of care to be observed is whether inexperience has the effect of lowering it. The matter was dealt with by the Court of Appeal in the *Wilsher* case.

Wilsher v Essex Area Health Authority [1986] 3 All E.R. 801, [1987] 1 Q.B. 730, [1987] 2 W.L.R. 425, 3 B.M.L.R. 37, CA

The plaintiff, Martin Wilsher, was an infant who had been born prematurely with various illnesses, one of which was oxygen deficiency. There was a low probability that Martin would survive. He was placed in the hospital's 24-hour special care baby unit. The unit was staffed by a medical team made up of two consultants, a senior registrar and several junior doctors and trained nurses. While Martin was in the unit, an inexperienced junior doctor undertook to monitor the oxygen level in his bloodstream. However, in doing so he inserted a catheter into a vein rather than an artery by mistake. He then requested the senior registrar to check what he had done. The registrar, Dr Kawa, failed to notice his mistake and several hours later, when replacing the catheter made the same mistake himself. In both instances the catheter monitor failed to give an accurate reading of the amount of oxygen in Martin's blood. The result was that he was given an excess of oxygen. He therefore brought an action in negligence against the health authority, alleging that the excess oxygen in his bloodstream had caused an incurable condition of the retina (RLF), resulting in near-blindness. At first instance, the action succeeded. The defendant health authority appealed to the Court of Appeal, contending, inter alia, that there had been no breach of the duty of care owed to the plaintiff because the standard of care required was only that reasonably required of doctors having the same formal qualifications and practical experience as the doctors actually in the unit.

MUSTILL L.J.
" . . . I now turn to the real content of the standard of care. Three propositions were advanced, the first by junior counsel for the plaintiff. It may, I think, be fairly described as setting a 'team' standard of care, whereby each of the persons who formed the staff of the unit held themselves out as capable of undertaking the specialised procedures which that unit set out to perform.

I acknowledge the force of this submission, so far as it calls for recognition of the position which the person said to be negligent held within this specialised unit. But, in so far as the proposition differs from the last of those referred to below, I must dissent, for it is faced with a dilemma. If it seeks to attribute to each individual member of the team a duty to live up to the standards demanded of the unit as a whole, it cannot be right, for it would expose a student nurse to an action in negligence for a failure to possess the skill and experience of a consultant. If, on the other hand, it seeks to fix a standard for the performance of the unit as a whole, this is simply a reformulation of the direct theory of liability which leading counsel for the plaintiff has explicitly disclaimed.

The second proposition (advanced on behalf of the defendants) directs attention to the personal position of the individual member of the staff about whom the complaint is made. What is expected of him is as much as, but no more than, can reasonably be required of a person having his formal qualifications and practical experience. If correct, this proposition entails that the standard of care which the patient is entitled to demand will vary according to the chance of recruitment and rostering. The patient's right to complain of faulty treatment will be more limited if he has been entrusted to the care of a doctor who is a complete novice in the particular field (unless perhaps he can point to some fault of supervision in a person further up the hierarchy) than if he has been in the hands of a doctor who has already spent months on the same ward, and his prospects of holding the health authority vicariously liable for the consequences of any mistreatment will be correspondingly reduced.

To my mind, this notion of a duty tailored to the actor, rather than to the act which he elects to perform, has no place in the law of tort. Indeed, the defendants did not contend that it could be justified by any reported authority on the general law of tort. Instead, it was suggested that the medical profession is a special case. Public hospital medicine has always been organised so that young doctors and nurses learn on the job. If the hospitals abstained from using inexperienced people, they could not staff their wards and theatres, and the junior staff could never learn. The longer-term interests of patients as a whole are best served by maintaining the present system, even if this may diminish the legal rights of the individual patient, for, after all, medicine is about curing, not litigation.

I acknowledge the appeal of this argument, and recognise that a young hospital doctor who must get onto the wards in order to qualify without necessarily being able to decide what kind of patient he is going to meet is not in the same position as another professional man who has a real choice whether or not to practise in a particular field. Nevertheless, I cannot accept that there should be a special rule for doctors in public hospitals, and I emphasise *public*, since presumably those employed in private hospitals would be in a different category. Doctors are not the only people who gain their experience, not only from lectures or from watching others perform, but from tackling live clients or customers, and no case was cited to us which suggested that any such variable duty of care was imposed on others in a similar position. To my mind, it would be a false step to subordinate the legitimate expectation of the patient that he will receive from each person concerned with his care a degree of skill appropriate to the task which he undertakes to an understandable wish to minimise the psychological and financial pressures on hard-pressed young doctors.

For my part, I prefer the third of the propositions which have been canvassed. This relates the duty of care, not to the individual, but to the post which he occupies. I would differentiate 'post' from 'rank' or 'status'. In a case such as the present, the standard is not just that of the averagely competent and well-informed junior houseman (or whatever the position of the doctor) but of such a person who fills a post in a unit offering a highly specialised service. But, even so, it must be recognised that different posts make different demands. If it is borne in mind that the structure of hospital medicine envisages that the lower ranks will be occupied by those of whom it would be wrong to expect too much, the risk of abuse by litigious patients can be mitigated, if not entirely eliminated."

GLIDEWELL L.J.
" . . . I have had the great advantage of reading in draft the judgments of Sir Nicholas Browne-Wilkinson V.-C. and Mustill L.J. I shall comment only about two subjects on which they do not agree. Firstly, what is the proper test to be applied to decide whether a doctor, engaged as were the doctors in this case in a special unit caring for premature babies, has been negligent? The test usually applied is that adopted in his judgment by Peter Pain J. from the charge to a jury by McNair J. in *Bolam* v. *Friern Hospital Management Committee* [1957] 2 All E.R. 118 . . . "

His Lordship set out the *Bolam* test, then continued . . .

"I agree with the judge that this is the correct test by which to weigh the conduct of all the doctors in the present case.

If I understand him correctly, Sir Nicholas Browne-Wilkinson V-C would apply a less stringent test to a newly-qualified practitioner, who has accepted an appointment in order to gain experience. The suggested test would only hold such a doctor liable 'for acts or omissions which a careful doctor with his qualifications and experience would not have done or omitted'. With great respect, I do not believe this is the correct test. In my view, the law requires the trainee or learner to be judged by the same standard as his more experienced colleagues. If it did not, inexperience would frequently be urged as a defence to an action for professional negligence.

If this test appears unduly harsh in relation to the inexperienced, I should add that, in my view, the inexperienced doctor called on to exercise a specialist skill will, as part of that skill, seek the advice and help of his superiors when he does or may need it. If he does seek such help, he will often have satisfied the test, even though he may himself have made a mistake. It is for this reason that I agree that Dr Wiles was not negligent. He made a mistake in inserting the catheter into a vein, and a second mistake in not recognising the signs that he had done so on the X-ray. But, having done what he thought right, he asked Dr Kawa, the senior registrar, to check what he had done, and Dr Kawa did so. Dr Kawa failed to recognise the indication on the X-ray that the catheter was in the vein, and some hours later himself inserted a replacement catheter, again in the vein, and again failed to recognise that it was in the vein. Whichever of the suggested tests of negligence should be applied to Dr Wiles, we are all agreed that Dr Kawa was negligent, and that the defendants must therefore be liable for any damage to the plaintiff proved to have been caused by that negligence."

SIR NICHOLAS BROWNE-WILKINSON V.C. (DISSENTING)
" . . . The first point on which I differ from Mustill L.J. relates to the question of negligence. On this issue I disagree, not with his decision, but with the process whereby he reaches his conclusion. I enter into this field with hesitation since it is one in which I have virtually no experience. But I cannot accept that the standard of care required of an individual doctor holding a post in a hospital is an objective standard to be determined irrespective of his experience or the reason why he is occupying the post in question.

In English law, liability for personal injury requires a finding of personal fault (e.g. negligence) against someone. In cases of vicarious liability such as this, there must have been personal fault by the employee or agent of the defendant for whom the defendant is held vicariously liable. Therefore, even though no claim is made against the individual doctor, the liability of the defendant health authority is dependent on a finding of personal fault by one or more of the individual doctors. The general standard of care required of a doctor is that he would exercise the skill of a skilled doctor in the treatment which he has taken on himself to offer.

Such being the general standard of care required of a doctor, it is normally no answer for him to say the treatment he gave was of a specialist or technical nature in which he was inexperienced. In such a case, the fault of the doctor lies in embarking on giving treatment which he could not skilfully offer: he should not have undertaken the treatment but should have referred the patient to someone possessing the necessary skills.

But the position of the houseman in his first year after qualifying or of someone (like Dr Wiles in this case) who has just started in a specialist field in order to gain the necessary skill in that field is not capable of such analysis. The houseman has to take up his post in order to gain full professional qualification. Anyone who, like Dr Wiles, wishes to obtain specialist skills has to learn those skills by taking a post in a specialist unit. In my judgment, such doctors cannot in fairness be said to be at fault if, at the start of their time, they lack the very skills which they are seeking to acquire.

In my judgment, if the standard of care required of such a doctor is that he should have the skill required of the post he occupies, the young houseman or the doctor seeking to obtain specialist skill in a special unit would be held liable for shortcomings in the treatment without any personal fault on his part at all. Of course, such a doctor would be negligent if he undertook treatment for which he knows he lacks the necessary experience and skill. But one of the chief hazards of inexperience is that one does not always know the risks which exist. In my judgment, so long as the English law rests liability on personal fault, a doctor who has properly accepted a post in a hospital in order to gain necessary experience should only be held liable for acts or omissions which a careful doctor with his qualifications and experience would not have done or omitted. It follows that, in my view, the health authority could not be held vicariously liable (and I stress the word *vicariously*) for the acts of such a learner who has come up to those standards, notwithstanding that the post he held required greater experience than he in fact possessed.

The only argument to the contrary (and it is a formidable one) is that such a standard of care would mean that the rights of a patient entering hospital will depend on the experience of the doctor who treats him. This, I agree, would be wholly unsatisfactory.

But, in my judgment, it is not the law. I agree with the comments of Mustill L.J. as to the confusion which has been caused in this case both by the pleading and by the argument below which blurred the distinction between the vicarious liability of the health authority for the negligence of its doctors and the direct liability of the health authority for negligently failing to provide skilled treatment of the kind that it was offering to the public. In my judgment, a health authority which so conducts its hospital that it fails to provide doctors of sufficient skill and experience to give the treatment offered at the hospital may be directly liable in negligence to the patient. Although we were told in argument that no case has ever been decided on this ground and that it is not the practice to formulate claims in this way, I can see no reason why, in principle, the health authority should not be so liable if its organisation is at fault: *see McDermid v. Nash Dredging and Reclamation Co. Ltd* [1986] 2 All E.R. 676 especially at 684–685 (reported since the conclusion of the argument).

Claims against a health authority that it has itself been directly negligent, as opposed to vicariously liable for the negligence of its doctors, will, of course, raise awkward questions. To what extent should the authority be held liable if (e.g. in the use of junior housemen) it is only adopting a practice hallowed by tradition? Should the authority be liable if it demonstrates that, due to the financial stringency under which it operates, it cannot afford to fill the posts with those possessing the necessary experience? But, in my judgment, the law should not be distorted by making findings of personal fault against individual doctors who are, in truth, not at fault in order to avoid such questions. To do so would be to cloud the real issues which arise. In the modern world with its technological refinements, is it sensible to persist in making compensation for those who suffer from shortcomings in technologically advanced treatment depend on proof of fault, a process which the present case illustrates can consume years in time and huge sums of money in costs? Given limited resources, what balance is to be struck in the allocation of such resources between compensating those whose treatment is not wholly successful and the provision of required treatment for the world at large? These are questions for Parliament, not the courts. But I do not think the courts will do society a favour by distorting the existing law so as to conceal the real social questions which arise."

NOTES:

1. In *Wilsher*, the Court of Appeal made it clear that inexperience on the part of the hospital staff provided no defence to an action in negligence. If *Wilsher* seems unduly harsh on the medical profession, it is perhaps worth noting that inexperience in other contexts is similarly regarded by the courts as providing no excuse for failure to meet the standard of care expected of a more experienced individual. In *Nettleship v Weston* [1971] 3 All E.R. 581, for example, a learner driver, Lavinia Weston, was held liable for failure to attain the standard of care in driving a car expected of someone who had passed their driving test. In the words of Lord Denning M.R., "the law lays down, for all drivers of motor cars, a standard of care to which all must conform . . . even a learner driver, so long as he is the sole driver, must attain the same standard".

2. Browne-Wilkinson L.J. raises the issue as to liability of an NHS body which is subject to financial constraints. This question was explored further by Mustill L.J. in his judgment in *Bull v Devon Area Health Authority* [1993] 4 Med. L.R. 22. He said there that:

   " . . . It is not necessarily an answer to allegations of unsafety that there were insufficient resources to enable administrators to do everything which they would like to do. I do not for a moment suggest that public medicine is precisely analogous to other public services, but there is perhaps a danger in assuming that it is completely sui generis, and that it is necessarily a complete defence to say that even if the system in any hospital was unsatisfactory, it was no more unsatisfactory than those in force elsewhere."

Clearly, then, his Lordship envisages a certain minimal standard of care below which health care providers should not fall, regardless of how (in)adequately they are funded.

3. In *Wilsher*, Browne-Wilkinson L.J. suggests that liability may be imposed directly upon the hospital authorities in such a situation rather than on the health professional. This echoes what was said by Denning in *Cassidy* (see p.154 above).

4. A further issue which arises out of *Wilsher* is the extent to which liability may be imposed where treatment services have been curtailed due to policy decisions at governmental level (see further Chapter 1 at above.)

QUESTIONS:

1. In *Johnstone v Bloomsbury Health Authority* [1991] 2 All E.R. 293 the Court of Appeal recognised the scope for young, overworked doctors bringing actions against health authorities in respect of injury to their health caused by such excessive working hours. Do you think it follows that patients injured by such over-tired doctors, because of their exhaustion, should also be able to sue the health authority?

2. Even if, as we saw above, limited resources do not form a complete defence to a negligence action, is it nonetheless possible that they may have the effect of lowering the standard of care required? (See *Knight v Home Office* [1990] 3 All E.R. 237, 247 on the question of the standard of psychiatric services that can be expected in a prison, as opposed to any other, hospital, *cf. Brooks v Home Office* (1999) 48 B.M.L.R. 109 and see further C. Newdick, *Who Should We Treat?* (2nd edn), Oxford: OUP, 2005, pp.187–188. and C. Witting, "National Health Service Rationing: Implications for the Standards of Care in Negligence" (2001) 21 *Oxford Journal of Legal Studies* 443.)

(d) The Burden of Proof

The burden of proof always rests with the claimant. It is for him to show, on the balance of probabilities, that the defendant has failed to meet the standard of care demanded by the law. In cases where there are very finely balanced views as to whether the doctor in question was negligent, discharging the burden of proof can be extremely problematic. Occasionally, however, a case might occur in which the claimant can plead *res ipsa loquitur*. Literally translated, it means "the thing speaks for itself". The claimant may invoke this rule if he can show three things. First, that he has been injured and that there is no explanation of how the injury arose. Secondly, that his injury arose in circumstances in which such an injury would not normally occur, and thirdly, that the defendant was in control of the situation in which context the injury occurred. There have been differing views expressed as to the impact of *res ipsa loquitur*. One approach is that once *res ipsa* is pleaded, it is for the defendant to explain what has taken place and bring forward some evidence to rebut the allegation. The other is that *res ipsa loquitur* has the effect of reversing the burden of proof. This means that it is for the defendant to prove that he was not negligent.

Res ipsa loquitur has received discussion in only a limited number of medical negligence cases.

Mahon v Osborne [1939] 1 All E.R. 535, [1939] 2 K.B. 14, (1939) 108 L.J.K.B. 567, (1939) L.T. 329

A difficult abdominal operation was performed by the appellant, assisted by a theatre sister and two nurses. At the end of the operation, the number of swabs used and retrieved from the patient's body was counted, and stated to the surgeon to be correct. However, one month later, when the patient underwent a second operation, it was discovered that a swab had been left inside his body. The patient did not survive the second operation.

It was common ground that the patient's death was caused, not by the second operation, but by the swab that had been left in his body. In addition, it was held that the system employed by the hospital for counting swabs—fully described in the evidence laid before the court—was satisfactory. The patient's mother, therefore, brought an action in negligence against the individual surgeon who had performed the operation, contending that the doctrine of *res ipsa loquitur* was applicable.

SCOTT L.J.
" . . . It is difficult to see how the principle of *res ipsa loquitur* can apply generally to actions for negligence against a surgeon for leaving a swab in a patient, even if in certain circumstances the presumption may arise. If it applied generally, plaintiff's counsel, having, by a couple of answers to interrogatories, proved that the defendant performed the operation and that a swab was left in, would be entitled to ask for judgment, unless evidence describing the operation was given by the defendant. Some positive evidence of neglect of duty is surely needed. It may be that a full description of the actual operation will disclose facts sufficiently indicative of want of skill or care to entitle a jury to find neglect of duty to the patient. It may be that expert evidence in addition will be requisite. To treat the maxim as applying in every case where the swab is left in the patient seems to me an error of law. The very essence of the rule, when applied to an action for negligence, is that, upon the mere fact of the event happening, for example, an injury to the plaintiff, there arise two presumptions of fact, (i) that the event was caused by a breach by somebody of the duty of care towards the plaintiff, and (ii) that the defendant was that somebody. The presumption of fact arises only because it is an inference which the reasonable man, knowing the facts, would naturally draw, and that is, in most cases, for two reasons, (i) that the control over the happening of such an event rested solely with the defendant, and (ii) that in the ordinary experience of mankind such an event does not happen unless the person in control has failed to exercise due care. The nature even of abdominal operations varies widely, and many considerations enter into it, the degree of urgency, the state of the patient's inside, the complication of his disorder or injury, the condition of his heart, the effects of the anaesthetic, the degree and kind of help which the surgeon has—for example, whether he is assisted by another surgeon—the efficiency of the team of theatre nurses, the extent of the surgeon's experience and the limits of wise discretion in the particular circumstances—for example, the complications arising out of the operation itself, and the

fear of the patient's collapse. In the present case, all the above considerations combine to present a state of things of which the ordinary experience of mankind knows nothing, and, therefore, to make it unsafe to beg the question of proof."

NOTES:

1. Although there is a discretion to enable a jury to be called, contained in s.69(3) of the Supreme Court Act 1981, juries are today almost never used in negligence suits in this country.
2. Scott L.J. was clearly very sceptical about the ability of patients without medical training to knowledgeably invoke the *res ipsa* principle. Brazier, while perhaps not as sceptical, has also commented: "As most people are not medically qualified, how could they know whether the accident to the patient was one which could or could not happen if proper care was taken" (M. Brazier, *Medicine Patients and the Law*, (3rd edn), Harmondsworth: Penguin, 2002 at p.300).

QUESTION:

1. Do you think that a present-day court would, like Scott L.J., regard "the extent of the surgeon's experience" as a relevant factor in assessing whether he had performed an operation negligently? (Bear in mind the comments of the Court of Appeal on the matter in the *Wilsher* case.)

Cassidy v Ministry of Health [1951] 1 All E.R. 574, [1951] 2 K.B. 343, [1951] W.L.R. 147

The plaintiff in this case underwent an operation on his hand at the defendant's hospital which was performed by Dr Fahrni, a full-time assistant medical officer. After the operation, his hand and forearm were bandaged to a splint in which position they were kept firmly for the next 14 days. Throughout that period, the plaintiff complained of pain but nothing was done by either the doctor who had operated or the house surgeon, except that he was given sedatives. Both Dr Fahrni and the house surgeon were hospital employees. When the bandages were finally removed the plaintiff's hand had become stiff and practically useless for the purposes of his work which involved using a pick and shovel.

By s.6(2) of the National Health Service Act 1946, the hospital was substituted by the Ministry of Health as the defendant, against whom the plaintiff brought an action alleging negligence in relation to the post-operational treatment that he had received.

DENNING L.J.

"If the plaintiff had to prove that some particular doctor or nurse was negligent, he would not be able to do it, but he was not put to that impossible task. He says: 'I went into the hospital to be cured of two stiff fingers. I have come out with four stiff fingers, and my hand is useless. That should not have happened if due care had been used. Explain it, if you can.' I am quite clearly of the opinion that that raises a *prima facie* case against the hospital authorities: see *Mahon* v. *Osborne* [1939] 1 All E.R. 535 at p 561 *per* Goddard L.J. They have nowhere explained how it could have happened without negligence. They have busied themselves in saying that this member or that member of their staff was not negligent, but they have called not a single person to say that the injuries were consistent with due care on the part of all the members of their staff. They called some of the people who actually treated the plaintiff, namely, Dr Fahrni, Dr Ronaldson, and Sister Hall each of whom protested that he was careful in his or her part, but they did not call the senior surgeon, Mr Moroney, or any expert at all, to say that what occurred might happen despite all care. They have not, therefore, displaced the *prima facie* case against them and are liable in damages to the plaintiff."

NOTE:

1. The scope for the invocation of *res ipsa loquitur* in medical negligence cases should not be overestimated. *Cassidy* is an exceptional case. Equally, modern hospital care, which involves the diligent making of notes, means that the chances of an accident occurring without any evidence as to why, are probably very slim. This diminished scope for the *res ipsa* doctrine was recognised judicially in *Bull v Devon Area Health Authority* [1993] 4 Med. L.R. 22, a case in which the first plaintiff, Mrs Bull, alleged that the asphyxia suffered by her son at birth was attributable to the defendant's negligence. There, Mustill L.J. stressed the fact that "[t]he plaintiff's advisers were able to put in evidence from the records as part of their case the outlines of what actually happened". He then added:

   "I do not see how the present situation calls for recourse to an evidentiary presumption applicable in cases where the defendant does, and the plaintiff does not, have within his grasp the means of knowing how the accident took place. Here, all the facts that are ever going to be known are before the court. The judge held that they pointed to liability, and I agree."

This was considered subsequently in *Ratcliffe*.

Ratcliffe v Plymouth and Torbay HA [1998] Lloyd's Rep. Med. 168

HOBHOUSE L.J.
"Res ipsa loquitur is no more than a convenient Latin phrase used to describe the proof of facts which are sufficient to support an inference that the defendant was negligent and therefore to establish a prima-facie case against him.. The burden of proving the negligence of the defendant remains throughout upon the plaintiff. The burden is on the plaintiff at the start of the trial and absent and admission by the defendant is still upon the plaintiff at the conclusion of the trial . . .
   In practice save in the most extreme cases of blatant negligence the plaintiff will still have to adduce at least some expert evidence to get his case on its feet . . .
   Res ipsa loquitur is not a principle of law it does not relate to or raise any presumption. It is merely a guide to help to identify when a prima-facie case is being made out. Where expert and factual evidence has been called on both sides at a trial its usefulness will long since have been exhausted."

NOTE:

1. It has been suggested that this case may have ended the use of the term *res ipsa loquitur*, to be replaced by the words "a prima-facie case" (see J.K. Mason and G. Laurie, *Mason and McCall Smith's Law and Medical Ethics*

(7th edn), 2006, para.9.86) and see *Gray v Southampton and SW Hampshire HA* [2000] 57 B.M.L.R. 148).

(e) Causation

It is insufficient in a malpractice action for the claimant to show merely that he was owed a duty of care and that a breach of that duty took place; he must also be able to show that he has suffered some form of harm or injury that was caused by the defendant's breach of duty. Normally, the claimant endeavours to prove causation, that is, to show that the harm of which he complains was caused by the defendant's breach of duty. To do this, the claimant must, according to *Barnett v Chelsea and Kensington Hospital Management Committee* [1968] 1 All E.R. 1068, demonstrate that but for the defendant's negligence, he would not have suffered the harm in respect of which he seeks damages.

Unfortunately for victims of medical malpractice, proof of causation is not always amenable to a straightforward application of the "but for" test. Four particular problems commonly arise. First, the claimant may have difficulty in proving that any exacerbation of his ill health was attributable to the negligence of the doctor or nurse rather than a simple progression of his illness. Secondly, medical knowledge has its limits, and the aetiology of illness cannot always be understood, even by those with medical expertise (see, for example, *Kay v Ayrshire and Arran Health Board* [1987] 2 All E.R. 417). The claimant may have been treated with drugs, the full range of whose side-effects are not fully known or understood (see, for example, *Loveday v Renton* [1990] 1 Med. L.R. 117).

The third and fourth difficulties, the most problematic by far, can conveniently be taken together. They are, establishing causation where there is more than one causal agent at work, and establishing causation to the requisite standard of proof. (Note that the standard of proof, i.e. the level of certainty with which one must show causation, must be distinguished from the burden of proof, i.e. upon whom the onus of proving their case lies.) Both of these issues have been considered by the House of Lords. The following two cases deal respectively with them.

Wilsher v Essex Area Health Authority [1988] 1 All E.R. 871, [1988] 1 A.C. 1074, (1988) 3 B.M.L.R. 37 HL

The facts of *Wilsher* were set out at p.175 above when we considered the Court of Appeal's discussion of the standard of care required in this case.

LORD BRIDGE
" . . . My Lords, I understand that all your Lordships agree that this appeal has to be allowed and that the inevitable consequence of this is that the outstanding issue of causation must, unless the parties can reach agreement, be retried by another judge. In these circumstances, for obvious reasons, it is undesirable that I should go into the highly complex and technical evidence on which the issue depends any further than is strictly necessary to explain why, in common with all your Lordships, I feel ineluctably driven to the unpalatable conclusion that it is not open to the House to resolve the issue one way or the other, so that a question depending on the consequence of an event occurring in the first two days of Martin's life will now have to be investigated all over again when Martin is

nearly ten years old. On the other hand, the appeal raises a question of law as to the proper approach to issues of causation which is of great importance and of particular concern in medical negligence cases. This must be fully considered . . .

The starting point for any consideration of the relevant law of causation is the decision of this House in *Bonnington Castings Ltd v. Wardlaw* [1956] 1 All E.R. 615. This was the case of a pursuer who, in the course of his employment by the defenders, contracted pneumoconiosis over a period of years by the inhalation of invisible particles of silica dust from two sources. One of these (pneumatic hammers) was an 'innocent' source, in the sense that the pursuer could not complain that his exposure to it involved any breach of duty on the part of his employers. The other source (swing grinders), however, arose from a breach of statutory duty by the employer. Delivering the leading speech in the House Lord Reid said ([1956] 1 All E R at 617–618):

> 'The Lord Ordinary and the majority of the First Division have dealt with this case on the footing that there was an onus on the defenders, the appellants, to prove that the dust from the swing grinders did not cause the respondent's disease. This view was based on a passage in the judgment of the Court of Appeal in *Vyner v. Waldenberg Bros Ltd* [1945] 2 All E.R. 547 at 549 *per* Scott L.J.: 'If there is a definite breach of a safety provision imposed on the occupier of a factory, and a workman is injured in a way which could result from the breach, the onus of proof shifts on to the employer to show that the breach was not the cause. We think that that principle lies at the very basis of statutory rules of absolute duty' . . . Of course the onus was on the defendants to prove delegation (if that was an answer) and to prove contributory negligence, and it may be that that is what the Court of Appeal has in mind. But the passage which I have cited appears to go beyond that and, in so far as it does so, I am of opinion that it is erroneous. It would seem obvious in principle that a pursuer or plaintiff must prove not only negligence or breach of duty but also that such fault caused, or materially contributed to, his injury, and there is ample authority for that proposition both in Scotland and in England. I can find neither reason nor authority for the rule being different where there is breach of a statutory duty. The fact that Parliament imposes a duty for the protection of employees has been held to entitle an employee to sue if he is injured as a result of a breach of that duty, but it would be going a great deal further to hold that it can be inferred from the enactment of a duty that Parliament intended that any employee suffering injury can sue his employer merely because there was a breach of duty and it is shown to be possible that his injury may have been caused by it. In my judgment, the employee must, in all cases, prove his case by the ordinary standard of proof in civil actions he must make it appear at least that, on a balance of probabilities, the breach of duty caused, or materially contributed to, his injury.'

Lord Tucker said of Scott L.J.'s dictum in *Vyner v. Waldenberg Bros Ltd*:

> ' . . . I think it is desirable that your Lordships should take this opportunity to state in plain terms that no such onus exists unless the statute or statutory regulation expressly or impliedly so provides, as in several instances it does. No distinction can be drawn between actions for common law negligence and actions for breach of statutory duty in this respect. In both, the plaintiff or pursuer must prove (a) breach of duty, and (b) that such breach caused the injury complained of (see *Wakelin v. London & South Western Ry Co* (1886) 12 App. Cas. 41), and *Caswell v. Powell Duffryn Associated Collieries* Ltd [1939] 3 All E.R. 722. In each case, it will depend on the particular facts proved, and the proper inferences to be drawn therefrom, whether the respondent has sufficiently discharged the onus that lies on him.' (See [1956] 1 All E.R. 615 at 621.)

Lord Keith said ([1956] 1 All E.R. at 621):

> 'The onus is on the respondent [the pursuer] to prove his case, and I see no reason to depart from this elementary principle by invoking certain rules of onus said to be based

on a correspondence between the injury suffered and the evil guarded against by some statutory regulation. I think most, if not all, of the cases which professed to lay down or to recognise some such rule could have been decided as they were on simple rules of evidence, and I agree that *Vyner v. Waldenberg Bros Ltd* [1945] 2 All E.R. 547, in so far as it professed to enunciate a principle of law inverting the onus of proof, cannot be supported.'

Viscount Simonds and Lord Somervell agreed.

Their Lordships concluded, however, from the evidence that the inhalation of dust to which the pursuer was exposed by the defender's breach of statutory duty had made a material contribution to his pneumoconiosis which was sufficient to discharge the onus on the pursuer of proving that his damage was caused by the defenders' tort. A year later the decision in *Nicholson v. Atlas Steel Foundry and Engineering Co Ltd* [1957] 1 All E.R. 776 followed the decision in *Bonnington Castings Ltd v. Wardlaw* and held, in another case of pneumoconiosis, that the employers were liable for employee's disease arising from the inhalation of dust from two sources, one 'innocent' the other 'guilty', on facts virtually indistinguishable from those in *Bonnington Castings Ltd* v. Wardlaw.

In *McGhee v. National Coal Board* [1972] 3 All E.R. 1008 the pursuer worked in a brick kiln in hot and dusty conditions in which brick dust adhered to his sweaty skin. No breach of duty by his employers, the defenders, was established in respect of his working conditions. However, the employers were held to be at fault in failing to provide adequate washing facilities which resulted in the pursuer having to bicycle home after work with his body still caked in brick dust. The pursuer contracted dermatitis and the evidence that this was caused by the brick dust was accepted. Brick dust adhering to the skin was a recognised cause of industrial dermatitis and the provision of showers to remove it after work was a usual precaution to minimise the risk of the disease. The precise mechanism of causation of the disease however, was not known and the furthest the doctors called for the pursuer were able to go was to say that the provision of showers would have materially reduced the risk of dermatitis. They were unable to say that it would probably have prevented the disease.

The pursuer failed before the Lord Ordinary and the First Division of the Court of Session on the ground that he had not discharged the burden of proof of causation. He succeeded on appeal to the House of Lords. Much of the academic discussion to which this decision has given rise has focused on the speech of Lord Wilberforce, particularly on two paragraphs. He said ([1972] 3 All E.R. 1008 at 1012):

'But the question remains whether a pursuer must necessarily fail if, after he has shown a breach of duty, involving an increase of risk of disease, he cannot positively prove that this increase of risk caused or materially contributed to the disease while his employers cannot positively prove the contrary. In this intermediate case there is an appearance of logic in the view that the pursuer, on whom the onus lies, should fail—a logic which dictated the judgments below. The question is whether we should be satisfied in factual situations like the present, with this logical approach. In my opinion, there are further considerations of importance. First, it is a sound principle that where a person has, by breach of duty of care, created a risk, and injury occurs within the area of that risk, the loss should be borne by him *unless he shows that it had some other cause*. Secondly, from the evidential point of view, one may ask, why should a man who is able to show that his employer should have taken certain precautions, because without them there is a risk, or an added risk, of injury or disease, and who in fact sustains exactly that injury or disease, have to assume the burden of proving more: namely, that it was the addition to the risk, caused by the breach of duty, which caused or materially contributed to the injury? In many cases of which the present is typical, this is impossible to prove, just because honest medical opinion cannot segregate the causes of an illness between compound causes. And if one asks which of the parties, the workman or the employers should suffer from this inherent evidential difficulty, the answer as a matter in policy or justice should be that it is the creator of the risk who, *ex hypothesi*, must be taken to have foreseen the possibility of damage, who should bear its consequences.' (My emphasis.)

He then referred to *Bonnington Castings Ltd v. Wardlaw* and *Nicholson v. Atlas Steel Foundry and Engineering Co. Ltd* and added ([1972] 3 All E.R. 1008 at 1013):

'The present factual situation has its differences: the default here consisted not in adding a material quantity to the accumulation of injurious particles but by failure to take a step which materially increased the risk that the dust already present would cause injury. And I must say that, at least in the present case, to bridge the evidential gap by inference seems to me something of a fiction, since it was precisely this inference which the medical expert declined to make. But I find in the cases quoted an analogy which suggests the conclusion that, *in the absence of proof that the culpable condition had, in the result, no effect*, the employers should be liable for an injury, squarely within the risk which they created and that they, not the pursuer, should suffer the consequence of the impossibility, foreseeably inherent in the nature of his injury, of segregating the precise consequence of their default.' (My emphasis.)

My Lords, it seems to me that both these paragraphs, particularly in the words I have emphasised, amount to saying that, in the circumstances, the burden of proof of causation is reversed and thereby to run counter to the unanimous and emphatic opinions expressed in *Bonnington Castings Ltd v. Wardlaw* [1956] 1 All E.R. 615 to the contrary effect. I find no support in any of the other speeches for the view that the burden of proof is reversed and, in this respect, I think Lord Wilberforce's reasoning must be regarded as expressing a minority opinion.

A distinction is, of course, apparent between the facts of *Bonnington Castings Ltd v. Wardlaw* where the 'innocent' and 'guilty' silica dust particles which together caused the pursuer's lung disease were inhaled concurrently and the facts of *McGhee v. National Coal Board* where the 'innocent' and 'guilty' brick dust was present on the pursuer's body for consecutive periods. In the one case the concurrent inhalation of 'innocent' and 'guilty' dust must both have contributed to the cause of the disease. In the other case the consecutive periods when 'innocent' and 'guilty' brick dust was present on the pursuer's body may both have contributed to the cause of the disease or, theoretically at least, one or other may have been the sole cause. But where the layman is told by the doctors that the longer the brick dust remains on the body, the greater the risk of dermatitis, although the doctors cannot identify the process of causation scientifically, there seems to be nothing irrational in drawing the inference, as a matter of common sense, that the consecutive periods when brick dust remained on the body probably contributed cumulatively to the causation of the dermatitis. I believe that a process of inferential reasoning on these general lines underlies the decision of the majority in *McGhee*'s case."

Lord Bridge sought then to support this view by reference to passages from the speeches of Lords Reid, Simon, Kilbrandon and Salmon in *McGhee*'s case. He then continued:

" . . . *McGhee v. National Coal Board* laid down no new principle of law whatever. On the contrary, it affirmed the principle that the onus of proving causation lies on the pursuer or plaintiff. Adopting a robust and pragmatic approach to the undisputed primary facts of the case, the majority concluded that it was a legitimate inference of fact that the defenders' negligence had materially contributed to the pursuer's injury. The decision, in my opinion, is of no greater significance than that and the attempt to extract from it some esoteric principle which in some way modifies, as a matter of law, the nature of the burden of proof of causation which a plaintiff or pursuer must discharge once he has established a relevant breach of duty is a fruitless one.

In the Court of Appeal in the instant case Sir Nicholas Browne-Wilkinson V-C, being in a minority, expressed his view on causation with understandable caution. But I am quite unable to find any fault with the following passage in his dissenting judgment [1986] 3 All E.R. 801 at 834–835:

'To apply the principle in *McGhee* v. *National Coal Board* [1972] 3 All E.R. 1008 to the present case would constitute an extension of that principle. In *McGhee* there was no doubt that the pursuer's dermatitis was physically caused by brick dust the only question was whether the continued presence of such brick dust on the pursuer's skin after the time when he should have been provided with a shower caused or materially contributed to the dermatitis which he contracted. There was only one possible agent which could have caused the dermatitis, *viz* brick dust, and there was no doubt that the dermatitis from which he suffered was caused by that brick dust. In the present case the question is different. There are a number of different agents which could have caused the RLF. Excess oxygen was one of them. The defendants failed to take reasonable precautions to prevent one of the possible causative agents (e.g. excess oxygen) from causing RLF. But no one can tell in this case whether excess oxygen did or did not cause or contribute to the RLF suffered by the plaintiff. The plaintiff's RLF may have been caused by some completely different agent or agents, e.g. hypercarbia, intraventricular haemorrhage, apnoea or patent ductus arteriosus. In addition to oxygen, each of those conditions has been implicated as a possible cause of RLF. This baby suffered from each of those conditions at various times in the first two months of his life. There is no satisfactory evidence that excess oxygen is more likely than any of those other four candidates to have caused RLF in this baby. To my mind, the occurrence of RLF following a failure to take a necessary precaution to prevent excess oxygen causing RLF provides no evidence and raises no presumption that it was excess oxygen rather than one or more of the four other possible agents which caused or contributed to RLF in this case. The position, to my mind, is wholly different from that in *McGhee*, where there was only one candidate (brick dust) which could have caused the dermatitis, and the failure to take a precaution against brick dust causing dermatitis was followed by dermatitis caused by brick dust. In such a case, I can see the common sense, if not the logic, of holding that, in the absence of any other evidence, the failure to take the precaution caused or contributed to the dermatitis. To the extent that certain members of the House of Lords decided the question on inferences from evidence or presumptions, I do not consider that the present case falls within their reasoning. A failure to take preventive measures against one out of five possible causes is no evidence as to which of those five caused the injury.'

Since, on this view, the appeal must, in any event, be allowed, it is not strictly necessary to decide whether it was open to the Court of Appeal to resolve one of the conflicts between the experts which the judge left unresolved and to find that the oxygen administered to Martin in consequence of the misleading Po_2 levels derived from the misplaced catheter was capable of having caused or materially contributed to his RLF. I very well understand the anxiety of the majority to avoid the necessity for ordering a retrial if that was at all possible. But, having accepted, as your Lordships and counsel have had to accept, that the primary conflict of opinion between the experts whether excessive oxygen in the first two days of life probably did cause or materially contribute to Martin's RLF cannot be resolved by reading the transcript, I doubt, with all respect, if the Court of Appeal was entitled to try to resolve the secondary conflict whether it could have done so. Where expert witnesses are radically at issue about complex technical questions within their own field and are examined and cross-examined at length about their conflicting theories, I believe that the judge's advantage in seeing them and hearing them is scarcely less important than when he has to resolve some conflict of primary fact between lay witnesses in purely mundane matters. So here, in the absence of relevant findings of fact by the judge, there was really no alternative to a retrial."

NOTES:

1. The remaining four Law Lords in *Wilsher* delivered short speeches expressing their agreement with Lord Bridge.
2. *Wilsher* graphically illustrates the difficulty in establishing causation. In this case there were five separate possible causes. In that respect it can be contrasted with the decision in *McGhee*, in that case the causes were cumulative.

QUESTION:

1. What constitutes a "material contribution" to the damage caused?

The House of Lords have also considered the standard of proof required in order to satisfy the court that the defendant's culpable act or omission was the factual cause of the plaintiff's injury.

Hotson v East Berkshire Area Health Authority [1987] 2 All E.R. 909, [1987] 1 A.C. 750

In 1977, when the plaintiff was 13, he fell from a tree and injured his hip. He was taken to the defendant's hospital where his injury was incorrectly diagnosed. He was sent back home where, for the following five days, he remained in severe pain. After this time he was taken back to the defendant's hospital where X-rays revealed that he had suffered an acute traumatic fracture of the left femoral epiphysis. On the next day he underwent an operation to pin the joint but it did not prevent him suffering avascular necrosis of the epiphysis which led to a deformity of the hip joint and, by the time he was 20 years old, left him with a permanent disability.

The defendant health authority admitted negligence in respect of the delay in diagnosis but denied that the delay had caused the plaintiff's long-term condition. At first instance, the trial judge found that even if the defendant's staff had correctly diagnosed his condition when he was first seen at the hospital, there was still a 75 per cent chance that the disability would have developed in any case. He then held that the defendant's breach of duty had resulted in a loss of a 25 per cent chance of recovery and made an award of damages which reflected this. The defendant authority appealed first, and unsuccessfully, to the Court of Appeal, and then to the House of Lords.

LORD BRIDGE
" . . . The plaintiff sued the authority, who admitted negligence in failing to diagnose the injury on April 26, 1977. Simon Brown J., in a judgment delivered on March 15, 1985, *sub nom. Hotson* v. *Fitzgerald* [1985] 3 All E.R. 167, awarded £150 damages for the pain suffered by the plaintiff from April 26 to May 1, 1977 which he would have been spared by prompt diagnosis and treatment. This element of the damages is not in dispute. The authority denied liability for any other element of damages. The judge expressed his findings of fact as follows [1985] 3 All E.R. 167 at 171:

'1. Even had the defendants correctly diagnosed and treated the plaintiff on 26 April there is a high probability, which I assess as a 75 per cent risk, that the plaintiff's injury would have followed the same course as it in fact has, i.e. he would have developed avascular necrosis of the whole femoral head with all the same adverse consequences as have already ensued and with all the same adverse future prospects. 2. That 75 per cent risk was translated by the defendants' admitted breach of duty into inevitability. Putting it the other way, the defendants' delay in diagnosis denied the plaintiff the 25 per cent chance that, given immediate treatment, avascular necrosis would not have developed. 3. Had avascular necrosis not developed, the plaintiff would have made a very nearly full recovery. 4. The reason why the delay sealed the plaintiff's fate was because it followed the pressure caused by haemarthrosis (the bleeding of ruptured blood vessels into the joint) to compress and thus block the intact but distorted remaining vessels with the result that even had the fall left intact sufficient vessels to keep the epiphysis alive (which, as finding no 1 makes plain, I think possible but improbable) such vessels would have become occluded and ineffective for this purpose.'

On the basis of these findings he held, as a matter of law, that the plaintiff was entitled to damages for the loss of the 25 per cent chance that, if the injury had been promptly diagnosed and treated, it would not have resulted in avascular necrosis of the epiphysis and the plaintiff would have made a very nearly full recovery. He proceeded to assess the damages attributable to the consequences of the avascular necrosis at £46,000. Discounting this by 75 per cent, he awarded the plaintiff £11,500 for the lost chance of recovery. The authority's appeal against this element in the award of damages was dismissed by the Court of Appeal (Sir John Donaldson M.R., Dillon and Croom-Johnson L.JJ., [1987] 1 All E.R. 210). The authority now appeal by leave of your Lordships' House.

I would observe at the outset that the damages referable to the plaintiff's pain during the five days by which treatment was delayed in consequence of failure to diagnose the injury correctly, although sufficient to establish the authority's liability for the tort of negligence, have no relevance to their liability in respect of the avascular necrosis. There was no causal connection between the plaintiff's physical pain and the development of the necrosis. If the injury had been painless, the plaintiff would have to establish the necessary causal link between the necrosis and the authority's breach of duty in order to succeed. It makes no difference that the five days' pain gave him a cause of action in respect of an unrelated element of damage . . .

In analysing the issue of law arising from his findings the judge said [1985] 3 All E.R. 167 at 175:

'In the end the problem comes down to one of classification. Is this on true analysis a case where the plaintiff is concerned to establish causative negligence or is it rather a case where the real question is the proper quantum of damage? Clearly the case hovers near the border. Its proper solution in my judgment depends on categorising it correctly between the two. If the issue is one of causation then the defendants succeed since the plaintiff will have failed to prove his claim on the balance of probabilities. He will be lacking an essential ingredient of his cause of action. If, however, the issue is one of quantification then the plaintiff succeeds because it is trite law that the quantum of a recognised head of damage must be evaluated according to the chances of the loss occurring.'

He reached the conclusion that the question was one of quantification and thus arrived at his award to the plaintiff of one quarter of the damages appropriate to compensate him for the consequences of the avascular necrosis.

It is here, with respect, that I part company with the judge. The plaintiff's claim was for damages for physical injury and consequential loss alleged to have been caused by the authority's breach of their duty of care. In some cases, perhaps particularly medical negligence cases, causation may be so shrouded in mystery that the court can only measure statistical chances. But that was not so here. On the evidence there was a clear conflict as to what had caused the avascular necrosis. The authority's evidence was that the sole cause was the original traumatic injury to the hip. The plaintiff's evidence, as its highest, was that the delay in treatment was a material contributory cause. This was a conflict, like any other about some relevant past event, which the judge could not avoid resolving on a balance of probabilities. Unless the plaintiff proved on a balance of probabilities that the delayed treatment was at least a material contributory cause of the avascular necrosis he failed on the issue of causation and no question of quantification could arise. But the judge's findings of fact, as stated in the numbered paragraphs (1) and (4) which I have set out earlier in this opinion, are unmistakably to the effect that on a balance of probabilities the injury caused by the plaintiff's fall left insufficient blood vessels intact to keep the epiphysis alive. This amounts to a finding of fact that the fall was the sole cause of the avascular necrosis . . .

There is a superficially attractive analogy between the principle applied in such cases as *Chaplin v. Hicks* [1911–13] All E.R. 224 (award of damages for breach of contract assessed by reference to the lost chance of securing valuable employment if the contract had been performed) and *Kitchen v. Royal Air Forces Association* [1958] 2 All E.R. 241 (damages for solicitors' negligence assessed by reference to the lost chance of prosecuting a successful civil action) and the principle of awarding damages for the lost chance of avoiding personal injury or, in medical negligence cases, for the lost chance of a better medical result which might have been achieved by prompt diagnosis and correct treatment. I think there are formidable difficulties in the way of accepting the analogy. But I do not see this appeal as a suitable occasion for reaching a settled conclusion as to whether the analogy can ever be applied.

As I have said, there was in this case an inescapable issue of causation first to be resolved. But if the plaintiff had proved on a balance of probabilities that the authority's negligent failure to diagnose and treat his injury promptly had materially contributed to the development of avascular necrosis, I know of no principle of English law which would have entitled the authority to a discount from the full measure of damage to reflect the chance that, even given prompt treatment, avascular necrosis might well still have developed. The decisions of this House in Bonnington *Castings Ltd v. Wardlaw* [1956] 1 All E.R. 615 and *McGhee* v. *National Coal Board* give no support to such a view.

I would allow the appeal to the extent of reducing the damages awarded to the plaintiff by £11,500 and the amount of any interest on that sum which is included in the award."

LORD MACKAY

" . . . In their printed case the health authority first took the position that they were entitled to succeed in this appeal because the plaintiff had not proved that any loss or damage (other than five days' pain and suffering) had been caused by the authority's breach of duty. They also submitted that damages for loss of a chance were not recoverable in tort and at the close of the hearing counsel for the authority invited your Lordships to decide this case not only on the ground of fact which he submitted was available but also on the more general ground that damages for loss of a chance could not be awarded. This latter submission has been discussed in the course of the hearing very fully and I wish to add some observations, particularly on that aspect of the case.

When counsel for the plaintiff was invited to say what he meant by a chance he said that in relation to the facts of this case as found by the judge what was meant by a chance was that if 100 people had suffered the same injury as the plaintiff 75 of them would have developed avascular necrosis of the whole femoral head and 25 would not. This, he said, was an asset possessed by the plaintiff when he arrived at the authority's hospital on April 26, 1977. It was this asset which counsel submits the plaintiff lost in consequence of the negligent failure of the authority to diagnose his injury properly until May 1, 1977.

The case closest on its facts to the present from the United Kingdom, cited at the hearing before your Lordships, is *Kenyon v. Bell* (1953) S.C. 125. In that case the lower lid of a child's eye was cut as a result of an accident and subsequently the eye had to be removed by operation. An action for damages was raised against the medical practitioner who had first treated the injury, alleging that he had failed to exercise reasonable care and ordinary professional skill in carrying out his examination and treatment of the injury and that as a result the child had not been given certain treatment which 'would have made the saving of the eye a certainty or alternatively . . . would have materially increased the chance of saving the eye'. The medical practitioner contended that since all that was being offered to be proved was the weaker of the two alternative statements the case should not be allowed to proceed to proof since the weaker alternative alleging that the treatment would materially have increased the chance of saving the eye did not justify a claim for damages. Lord Guthrie held that the loss of a chance of saving the eye was not of itself a matter which would entitle the claim to succeed but founding particularly on the use of the word 'material' in the pleadings to qualify the chance of saving the eye by proper treatment Lord Guthrie held that on the evidence the chance of saving the eye by proper treatment might be proved to be so material that the natural and reasonable inference to draw from the evidence would be that the loss of the eye was due to the absence of such treatment. In that event, the claim would succeed. Accordingly he allowed it to go to proof. This illustrates that where what is at issue is a patient's condition on being presented to a medical practitioner the question whether the condition was such that proper treatment could effect a particular result is to be determined on the balance of probabilities and that one way of describing that balance is to say that there was at that time a sufficient chance that the particular result could be attained to justify holding that the loss of that result was caused by the absence of proper treatment. On the other hand, Lord Guthrie made it clear that, in his opinion, while the fault could be charged against the doctor as being failure to give the child the opportunity of having an eye preserved by proper treatment, unless the eye would have been saved by such treatment no loss would have been established and no claim for damages justified in respect thereof.

After the proof, Lord Strachan in a decision (9 April, 1954, unreported) held that the defender had established that the boy's eye was irreparably injured on 15 March, 1951 and that no treatment could have made any difference because the initial injury involved a perforating wound of the sclera with consequent haemorrhaging into the interior of the eye . . .

As I have said, the fundamental question of fact to be answered in this case related to a point in time before the negligent failure to treat began. It must, therefore, be a matter of past fact. It did not raise any question of what might have been the situation in a hypothetical state of facts. To this problem the words of Lord Diplock in *Mallett v. McMonagle* [1969] 2 All E.R. 178 at 191 apply:

'In determining what did happen in the past a court decides on the balance of probabilities. Anything that is more probable than not it treats as certain.'

In this respect this case is the same, in principle, as any other in which the state of facts existing before alleged negligence came into play has to be determined. For example, if a claimant alleges that he sustained a certain fracture in a fall at work and there is evidence that he had indeed fallen at work, but that shortly before he had fallen at home and sustained the fracture, the court would have to determine where the truth lay. If the claimant denied the previous fall, there would be evidence, both for and against the allegation, that he had so fallen. The issue would be resolved on the balance of probabilities. If the court held on that balance that the fracture was sustained at home, there could be no question of saying that since all that had been established was that it was more probable than not that the injury was not work-related, there was a possibility that it was work-related and that this possibility or chance was a proper subject of compensation.

I should add in this context that where on disputed evidence a judge reaches a conclusion on the balance of probabilities it will not usually be easy to assess a specific measure of probability for the conclusion at which he has arrived. As my noble and learned friend Lord Bridge observed in the course of the hearing, a judge deciding disputed questions of fact will not ordinarily do it by use of a calculator.

On the other hand, I consider that it would be unwise in the present case to lay it down as a rule that a plaintiff could never succeed by proving loss of a chance in a medical negligence case. In *McGhee v. National Coal Board* [1972] 3 All E.R. 1008 this House held that where it was proved that the failure to provide washing facilities for the pursuer at the end of his shift had materially increased the risk that he would contract dermatitis it was proper to hold that the failure to provide such facilities was a cause to a material extent of his contracting dermatitis and thus entitled him to damages from his employers for their negligent failure measured by his loss resulting from dermatitis. Material increase of the risk of contraction of dermatitis is equivalent to material decrease in the chance of escaping dermatitis. Although no precise figures could be given in that case for the purpose of illustration and comparison with this case one might, for example, say that it was established that of 100 people working under the same conditions as the pursuer and without facilities for washing at the end of their shift 70 contracted dermatitis: of 100 people working in the same conditions as the pursuer when washing facilities were provided for them at the end of the shift 30 contracted dermatitis. Assuming nothing more were known about the matter than that, the decision of this House may be taken as holding that in the circumstances of that case it was reasonable to infer that there was a relationship between contraction of dermatitis in these conditions and the absence of washing facilities and therefore it was reasonable to hold that absence of washing facilities was likely to have made a material contribution to the causation of the dermatitis. Although neither party in the present appeal placed particular reliance on the decision in *McGhee* since it was recognised that *McGhee* is far removed on its facts from the circumstances of the present appeal your Lordships were also informed that cases are likely soon to come before the House in which the decision in *McGhee* will be subjected to close analysis. Obviously in approaching the matter on the basis adopted in *McGhee* much will depend on what is known of the reasons for the differences in the figures which I have used to illustrate the position. In these circumstances I think it unwise to do more than say that unless and until this House departs from the decision in *McGhee* your Lordships cannot affirm the proposition that in no circumstances can evidence of loss of a chance resulting from the breach of a duty of care found a successful claim of damages, although there was no suggestion that the House regarded such a chance as an asset in any sense."

NOTES:

1. Lord Brandon, Lord Goff and Lord Ackner agreed with Lords Bridge and Mackay.
2. The House of Lords in *Hotson* do not totally reject the possibility of a successful action for loss of a chance. Nevertheless the claimant would have to adduce weighty expert evidence to the effect that the mismanagement/delay had reduced the prospect of recovery, and attempt to identify a specific percentage. In the subsequent case of *Tahir v. Haringey HA* (1995), Otton L.J. speaking obiter, expressed the view that there was no action for loss of a chance in English law. (See A. Grubb, "Medical Negligence: Causation" (1996) 1 *Medical Law Review* 92.)
3. In some circumstances there may be recovery for loss if this is more than loss of a chance of recovery. In *Sutton v. Population Services Family Planning Programme Ltd, The Times*, November 7, 1981 the plaintiff's cancer was not diagnosed sufficiently early. She suffered a premature onset of the menopause as a consequence and also lost an additional four years of life because she was denied care which would have postponed the onset of the cancer. She recovered damages.
4. On occasions the claimant's conduct will be held to break the chain of causation. Generally refusal of an abortion in a situation in which a claimant becomes pregnant due to the negligence of the defendant will not break the chain of causation, although there may be some exceptional

circumstances in which this does occur. (See *Emeh v Chelsea and Kensington AHA* [1984] 3 All E.R. 1044 and Chapter 13 below.) The claimant generally is also under an obligation to mitigate his loss and this may include seeking appropriate further medical care.

QUESTION:

1. In the context of medical negligence, how satisfactory is it to treat "causation on the balance of probabilities" as the relevant threshold requirement given the scope for significant differences of expert opinion as to the precise aetiology of a particular disease or illness?

There was further consideration of the issue of loss of a chance of recovery in the following case.

Gregg v Scott [2005] UKHL 2

Here the claimant went to his doctor with a lump under the left arm. The doctor diagnosed the lump as being benign. This was a misdiagnosis as the lump was in fact a malignant tumour. Treatment was needed immediately. Due to the misdiagnosis there was a resultant delay in treatment for some 14 months. By that point cancer had spread to the patient's chest. Had the tumour been diagnosed correctly from the outset there was evidence that the patient would have had a 42 per cent chance of being alive after 10 years. The misdiagnosis meant that this was a 25 per cent chance. The claimant fell outside *Hotson* as there was not a 51 per cent or greater chance of survival.

The House of Lords rejected the claim.

LORD PHILLIPS OF WORTH MATRAVERS
"170. My Lords, these reflections on the present case demonstrate, so it seems to me, that the exercise of assessing the loss of a chance in clinical negligence cases is not an easy one. Deductions cannot safely be drawn from statistics without expert assistance. I am all too well aware that I have drawn a number of deductions from the evidence in this case without expert assistance and that these are at odds with those that have been drawn by others. Even if some of my deductions can be shown to be unsound, I hope that I have demonstrated that analysis of the evidence in this case is no easy task. In contrast, the task of determining the effect of Dr Scott's negligence on a balance of probabilities was very much easier. It is always likely to be much easier to resolve issues of causation on balance of probabilities than to identify in terms of percentage the effect that clinical negligence had on the chances of a favourable outcome. This reality is a policy factor that weighs against the introduction into this area of a right to compensation for the loss of a chance. A robust test which produces rough justice may be preferable to a test that on occasion will be difficult, if not impossible, to apply with confidence in practice.

171. On the other hand it is hard to justify a test which results in substantial injustice simply on the ground that it is easier to apply. I have given careful consideration to the reasoning of my noble and learned friends Lord Nicholls of Birkenhead and Lord Hope of Craighead but I am not persuaded that the injustice that they identify is as cogent as they suggest or that it justifies the change to our law that Lord Nicholls of Birkenhead proposes. While Lord Hope of Craighead has endorsed Lord Nicholls of Birkenhead's conclusions he has added reasons of his own for allowing this appeal which I have difficulty in reconciling with Lord Nicholls of Birkenhead's approach.

172. In *Fairchild v Glenhaven Funeral Services Ltd* [2003] 1 AC 32 this House made a change in the law of negligence in the interests of justice. The change benefits a workman who has contracted a mesothelioma after being exposed to asbestos fibres by a series of employers. An employer who has contributed 20% of that exposure and thus 20% to the employee's risk of contracting the disease will be liable in full to the employee, albeit that the chances are 5 to 1 that he is not in fact responsible for causing the disease. In this case Lord Nicholls of Birkenhead proposes a different approach in the case of a doctor whose negligence has decreased the chance that a patient will be cured of a disease. Under that proposal the doctor will be liable to the extent that his negligence has reduced the chance of a cure. My Lords it seems to me that there is a danger, if special tests of causation are developed piecemeal to deal with perceived injustices in particular factual situations, that the coherence of our common law will be destroyed

173. In enquiring whether justice requires a change to our law, I propose to consider four different heads of claim that may be brought by a living claimant. These are:

   i) A claim that negligence has caused a discrete injury;
   ii) A claim that the injury so caused may, in the future, cause further injury;
   iii) A claim that the injury so caused has reduced the claimant's expectation of life;
   iv) A claim that negligence has reduced the prospect of cure of a fatal illness.

I shall, in discussing these heads, refer to the facts of the present case for purposes of illustration.

A claim that negligence has caused a discrete injury

174. Under our law as it is at present, and subject to the exception in Fairchild, a claimant will only succeed if, on balance of probability the negligence is the cause of the injury. If there is a possibility, but not a probability, that the negligence caused the injury, the claimant will recover nothing in respect of the breach of duty: *Hotson v East Berkshire Health Authority* [1987] AC 750; *Wilsher v Essex Area Health Authority* [1988] AC 1074. There is an argument that justice would be better served if, in such a situation, damages were recoverable for the chance that the negligence may have caused the injury. Neither Lord Nicholls of Birkenhead nor Lord Hope of Craighead considers that in this case we should hold that those two decisions of this House are no longer good law. I agree. So to hold would have implications for the balance of probability test of causation in other areas of our law. That consideration could better be given by the Law Commission than this House and it certainly has not been given in the present case.

175. As I understand the speech of Lord Hope of Craighead, he would hold the normal rule applicable in the present case. His analysis is that, on balance of probability, Dr Scott's negligence caused the enlargement of Mr Gregg's cancer with consequent pain and suffering and that Mr Gregg is entitled to general damages for this head of damage in full. If so, I believe that he differs from Lord Nicholls of Birkenhead, as I shall show when I come to consider the fourth head of claim.

A claim that injury caused by negligence may cause further injury

176. It is commonplace for an injury caused by negligence to carry with it the chance that it may lead to further injury, such as arthritis or epilepsy. The usual approach of the English court is to make a single award of damages which has regard to this chance of future injury. In some circumstances, however, it is more satisfactory for a claimant to recover damages in respect of injury actually sustained and to have the right to claim further damages if and when that injury is shown to have led to further injury. In such circumstances, the court can make an order for provisional damages—see section 32A of the Supreme Court Act 1981. The test of causation in relation to both the original injury and a subsequent injury alleged to be consequent upon the original injury is balance of probability.

A claim that injury caused by negligence has reduced the claimant's expectation of life

177. I agree with Lord Hope of Craighead that this case has been made peculiarly difficult to analyse by reason of the fact that, at least before this House, the only claim advanced has been a claim for loss of expectation of life. English law in relation to personal injury has yet to recognise a claim for the loss of a future prospect that is not consequent upon an established injury. It does, however, recognise that a claimant who has sustained such an injury can recover damages for loss of expectation of life, or 'lost years'. Such a head of claim has been established by decisions of this House, and is something of an oddity.

178. Most of us, if asked why we would not wish to die prematurely, would respond that we would not wish to be deprived of the pleasures of a full life including the enjoyment of the company of those we love. The law, however, gives only token compensation for such loss. What it does give is compensation for the earnings that the claimant will be unable to achieve once he is dead. There is a reason for this.

179. Section 1(1) of the Fatal Accidents Act 1976, as amended, provides:

'If death is caused by any wrongful act, neglect or default which is such as would (if death had not ensued) have entitled the person injured to maintain an action and recover damages in respect thereof, the person who would have been liable if death had not ensued shall be liable to an action for damages, notwithstanding the death of the person injured.'

Those who can bring the action are the dependants of the deceased and the damages that they can claim represent the loss of the dependency. They have, of course, to prove that the death was caused by negligence on balance of probability.

180. In *Pickett v British Rail Engineering Ltd* [1980] AC 136 a claimant suffering from mesothelioma had brought a claim against his employers and won, but his claim for loss of earnings consequent upon his anticipated premature death was not allowed. He appealed and then died. His personal representatives pursued the appeal to this House. The House proceeded on the assumption that, because the claimant had brought a successful claim for his personal injury, a claim by his dependants under the Fatal Accidents Act was precluded, although Lord Salmon emphasised that he expressed no concluded opinion about the correctness of that assumption. In these circumstances the House held that damages could be recovered for loss of earnings in the claimant's lost years. Only in this way could provision be made for the loss to be suffered by the dependants.

181. It was soon recognised that this decision gave rise to problems where the heirs of the deceased were not his dependants—see *Gammell v Wilson* [1982] AC 27. These problems were, to a degree, remedied by section 4 of the Administration of Justice Act 1982, which provided that the damages recoverable for the benefit of a deceased person in a survival action should not include 'any damages for loss of income in respect of any period after that person's death'. It remains the position, however, that a living claimant, who proves that he has been caused a personal injury by negligence, can include in the damages recovered compensation for lost earnings in the 'lost years'.

182. It seems to me that this right is a poor substitute for the right of the claimant's dependants to make full recovery for loss of dependency if and when the claimant dies prematurely. It would be much better if the claimant had no right to recover for such loss of earnings and the dependants' right to claim under section 1(1) of the Fatal Accidents Act 1976 subsisted despite the claimant's recovery of damages for his injury. I am not persuaded that this result could not be achieved by a purposive construction of that section.

183. Meanwhile, so long as the dependants' rights under the Fatal Accidents Act only arise where death is proved, on balance of probability, to have resulted from negligence, I do not see that there is a strong case for changing the law so as to enable a claimant to recover for loss of the chance of achieving earnings in the lost years.

184. I would like, now, to turn to the claim for lost years in the present case. *Pickett v British Rail Engineering* establishes that, where a claimant proves on balance of

probability that an injury has been caused by negligence, and that such injury has shortened his life, he can recover damages in respect of the earnings lost in the 'lost years'. The lost years are calculated by comparing the age at which the claimant would have expected to die had he not been injured with the age at which he is expected to die in consequence of his injury. Statistics will normally be used to calculate the former and, save where death is imminent, the latter. The expected age at death will be the age to which the claimant will live on balance of probability. His chances of reaching a greater age will be less than 50%. His chances of reaching a lesser age will be more than 50%. In so far as calculations are based on statistics the exercise is, of course, a somewhat artificial one.

185. In the present case the claimant has not adopted a conventional manner of advancing his claim for lost years. Insofar as the statistical evidence established that his prospects of surviving had been reduced by Dr Scott's negligence, it should have been possible, by use of statistical evidence, to show that, on balance of probabilities, his life expectancy had been reduced by a specific number of years. It should, with the use of statistics, have been possible to calculate a single life expectancy for all in Professor Goldstone's model. A comparison of that life expectancy with Mr Gregg's life expectancy at the date of trial would have produced a specific number of lost years. On the premise (I believe a false premise) that these years were lost as a consequence of the spread of the cancer, damages should have included any earnings lost in those years.

186. Instead of advancing his claim in this conventional way, Mr Gregg has claimed for the reduction in his chance of surviving for ten years. He has then equated this with his chance of surviving to the age of 65. This has enabled him to claim a proportion of what he would have earned in the rest of his working life. The result may be more satisfactory to him than the result of the conventional approach, but no challenge has been made to the unconventional approach to claiming damages for earnings lost in the lost years.

187. Lord Hope of Craighead has concluded that Dr Scott's negligence caused the spread of Mr Gregg's cancer and that he can recover for the effect that the spread of his cancer had on his life expectancy. That conclusion is not, as a matter of principle, in any way at odds with the current law. It is, I think, the approach adopted by Latham LJ in the Court of Appeal. It involves starting the calculation by considering what Mr Gregg's prospects of surviving would have been had he been treated promptly and achieved complete remission, rather than suffered the spread of the cancer. On Professor Goldsone's model these prospects would have been, not 42 out of 100 but between 38 and 42 out of 55. It seems to me that Lord Hope of Craighead's approach will produce a different result to that of Lord Nicholls of Birkenhead, to which I now turn.

A claim that negligence has reduced the prospect of the cure of a fatal illness

188. Mr Gregg was suffering from a progressive disease which, if not treated, was almost certain to result in the spread of cancer leading to premature death. Delay in commencing the treatment in such a case tends to reduce the prospects of a cure, but whether, and to what extent it will do so in the individual case depends on factors unascertainable by the court. It is in these circumstances that Lord Nicholls of Birkenhead postulates that a claimant should recover damages for the reduction in his prospects of a cure, whether those prospects would have been more or less than 50% in the absence of the negligence. I can envisage the application of this approach once the adverse outcome, which the exercise of due care might have averted, has occurred. I find it less easy to see the basis on which the claim is established where the adverse outcome is still prospective. Does the claimant have to show that the negligence has had some adverse physical impact in order to establish his cause of action? If so, is liability for that adverse impact also to be assessed on a loss of a chance basis, rather than on balance of probability? I suspect that my noble and learned friend would answer yes to each question. If so, it is apparent that his approach will produce a different outcome from that of Lord Hope of Craighead.

189. There are no doubt cases where it is possible to adopt the simple approach of asking to what extent the negligent treatment has reduced the prospects of curing the patient. There are other cases, and this is one, where that simple question is almost

impossible to answer. On the facts known to him at the time of the trial it was possible for the judge to lump together the five adverse events that Mr Gregg had experienced and the prospect of Mr Gregg dying of his cancer and to say that the delay in his treatment had increased the chances of all of these occurring by the same 20%. On the facts known today, that is no longer possible. The likelihood seems to be that Dr Scott's negligence has not prevented Mr Gregg's cure, but has made that cure more painful.

190. The complications of this case have persuaded me that it is not a suitable vehicle for introducing into the law of clinical negligence the right to recover damages for the loss of a chance of a cure. Awarding damages for the reduction of the prospect of a cure, when the long term result of treatment is still uncertain, is not a satisfactory exercise. Where medical treatment has resulted in an adverse outcome and negligence has increased the chance of that outcome, there may be a case for permitting a recovery of damages that is proportionate to the increase in the chance of the adverse outcome. That is not a case that has been made out on the present appeal. I would uphold the conventional approach to causation that was applied by Judge Inglis.

Conclusion

191. The judge concluded, on the data before him, that on balance of probabilities the delay in commencing Mr Gregg's treatment that was attributable to Dr Scott's negligence had not affected the course of his illness or his prospects of survival, which had never been as good as even. The data have now changed and Mr Gregg's prospects of survival, despite the delay in commencing his treatment, seem good. The delay may well, however, have meant that his path to what seems a likely cure has involved more intrusive treatment, and more pain, suffering and distress than would have been experienced had treatment commenced promptly. Those acting for Mr Gregg have, however, not sought to re-open the facts but have relied on the facts as found by the judge. On those facts I agree with Lord Hoffmann and Baroness Hale that this appeal must be dismissed."

BARONESS HALE OF RICHMOND
"My Lords,

The loss of a chance argument

209. The second, and more radical, way of redefining the claimant's damage is in terms of the loss of a chance. Put this way, his claim is not for the loss of an outcome, in this case the cure of his disease, which he would have enjoyed but for the negligence. His claim is for the reduced chance of achieving that outcome. As Jane Stapleton explained (by reference to the argument accepted by the Court of Appeal in *Hotson v East Berkshire Area Health Authority* [1987] AC 750) in 'The Gist of Negligence' (1988) 104 LQR 389, 391–2:

'Clearly, if the gist of the complaint were traditionally formulated in terms of contraction of necrosis, the plaintiff would fail to establish the requisite causal link on the balance of probability. The novelty of the case was that the plaintiff attempted to circumvent this result by choosing to formulate the gist of his action, not in terms of the necrosis outcome, but in terms of the lost chance of avoiding that outcome. In other words, although the plaintiff fails to establish causation on the balance of probabilities to one formulation of the damage forming the gist, he seeks to succeed in doing so to an alternative formulation based on loss of a chance. Importantly, the *Hotson* argument retains the traditional form of the causation test . . . '

210. In that case, the claimant had actually suffered the adverse outcome, avascular necrosis. The risk of suffering that outcome as a result of falling from the tree was 75%. The defendant's negligent failure to detect the injury to his hip took away the remaining 25% chance of avoiding it. Clearly he could not prove that the negligence had caused the

outcome. It was more likely than not that it had made no difference. But might he have proved that it was more likely than not that the negligence had reduced his chance of avoiding that outcome?

211. The House of Lords treated this as a case in which the die was already cast by the time the claimant got to the hospital (or at least the claimant could not prove otherwise). The defendant had not even caused the loss of the chance of saving the situation, because by the time the claimant got to them there was no chance. The coin had already been tossed, and had come down heads or tails. But there must be many cases in which that is not so. The coin is in the air. The claimant does have a chance of a favourable outcome which chance is wiped out or significantly reduced by the negligence. The coin is whipped out of the air before it has been able to land.

212. This is, therefore, a new case, not covered precisely by previous authority. The appellant himself describes his argument as the 'policy approach'. He recognises that it is a question of legal policy whether the law should be developed as he argues it should be. The wide version of the argument would allow recovery for any reduction in the chance of a better physical outcome, or any increase in the chance of an adverse physical outcome, even if this cannot be linked to any physiological changes caused by the defendant. A defendant who has negligently increased the risk that the claimant will suffer harm in future (for example from exposure to asbestos or cigarette smoke) would be liable even though no harm had yet been suffered. This would be difficult to reconcile with our once and for all approach to establishing liability and assessing damage. Unless damages were limited to a modest sum for anxiety and distress about the future, sensible quantification would have to 'wait and see'. The narrower version of the argument would require that there be some physiological change caused by the defendant's negligence, bringing with it a reduced prospect of a favourable outcome.

213. The attractions of adopting this reformulation of the gist of the action are many (see, for example, the discussion by Joseph H King, 'Causation, Valuation, and Chance in Personal Injury Torts Involving Preexisting Conditions and Future Consequences' (1981) 90 *Yale LJ* 1353). First, the conventional approach to causation is, in theory at least, retained. The claimant still has to prove that it is more likely than not that the negligence led to the damage. But the damage is no longer defined in terms of the outcome—saving the leg or achieving disease free survival. It is defined in terms of the loss or diminution of the chance of saving the leg or achieving disease free survival.

214. Against that, although the conventional approach to proof of causation may be retained in theory, in practice it will be far from straightforward to apply. It may be, as my noble and learned friend Lord Phillips of Worth Matravers has demonstrated on the facts of this case, difficult to show that the reduction in the prospects of survival is caused by the delay in treatment rather than the underlying disease. On the other hand, once a breach of duty has been shown, the recent decision of the New South Wales Court of Appeal in *Rufo v Hosking* [2004] NSWCA 391 illustrates how easy it may be to conclude that this has led to a reduction in the patient's prospects of a favourable outcome. A specialist paediatrician treating a patient with lupus had changed from one corticosteroid to another and had failed to introduce a steroid sparer when he should have done. The patient suffered microfractures in her spine. It could not be shown that she would not have suffered these in any event. The negligent treatment had not caused the fractures. But Campbell AJA, giving the leading judgment in the Court of Appeal, held (at para 405) that

'adopting a robust and pragmatic approach to the primary facts of this case . . . it seems to me that more probably than not the excess of corticosteroid consumed after 10 June 1992 in the context of the osteoporotic and vulnerable state of the appellant's spine caused the loss of a chance that the appellant would have suffered less spinal damage than she in fact did.'

215. This conclusion comes after many paragraphs of dense and careful analysis of the evidence before the trial judge. But in the end the appeal is to common sense. And common sense will often suggest that the chances of a better outcome would have been better if the

doctor had done what he should have done: for why else should he have done it but to improve the patient's chances? Reformulating the damage in this way could lead to some liability in almost every case.

216. Second, however, many would argue that this is a good thing. One of the objects of the law of negligence is to maintain proper standards, in the workplace, on the roads, in professional conduct, or whatever. If an employer, or a driver, or a professional person can be shown to have taken less care than he should have taken, then he should have to pay damages of some sort. As Lord Hope of Craighead said in *Chester v Afshar*, para 87, 'The function of the law is to enable rights to be vindicated and to provide remedies when duties have been breached.' In a case such as this, if there is only ever a less than evens chance of a cure (or avoiding an adverse outcome) what incentive is there for the doctor to take proper care of his patient?

217. But of course doctors and other health care professionals are not solely, or even mainly, motivated by the fear of adverse legal consequences. They are motivated by their natural desire and their professional duty to do their best for their patients. Tort law is not criminal law. The criminal law is there to punish and deter those who do not behave as they should. Tort law is there to compensate those who have been wronged. Some wrongs are actionable whether or not the claimant has been damaged. But damage is the gist of negligence. So it can never be enough to show that the defendant has been negligent. The question is still whether his negligence has caused actionable damage. There was no doubt about the damage in *Chester v Afshar*; the only question was whether the doctor who had failed to warn the patient of a small risk of serious harm should have to pay for the consequences when that very risk eventuated. In this case we are back to square one: what is actionable damage?

218. Third, it can be argued that some kinds of negligence do result in liability for loss of a chance. It has long been established that a solicitor whose negligence deprives the client of a viable claim is liable for damages even though the chances of succeeding in the claim were never better than evens: see *Kitchen v Royal Air Force Association* [1958] 1 WLR 563. The court simply asks what his claim was worth, assesses his chances of success, and discounts the full value by reference to the degree to which those chances were less than 100%. So why should my solicitor be liable for negligently depriving me of the chance of winning my action, even if I never had a better than evens chance of success, when my doctor is not liable for negligently depriving me of the chance of getting better, even if I never had a better than evens chance of getting better? Is this another example of the law being kinder to the medical profession than to other professionals?

219. One counter-argument is that, in this as in many other respects, there is a real difference between personal injury and financial loss. As Tony Weir (at p 76) puts it:

'. . . where the claimant is suing in respect of personal injury or property damage, he must persuade the judge that that injury or damage was probably due to the defendant's tort, whereas in cases of financial harm it is enough to show that the claimant had a chance of gain which the defendant has probably caused him to lose. There is nothing irrational in this, unless one supposes it is sensible to speak of "loss of a chance" without saying what the chance is of. Losing a chance of gain is a loss like the loss of the gain itself, alike in quality, just less in quantity: losing a chance of not losing a leg is not at all the same kind of thing as losing the leg.'

220. It is unfashionable these days to distinguish between financial loss and personal injury. Losing the money one has may not be so different from losing the leg one has. But many claims for financial loss do not relate to the money one has but to the money one expected to have—a prospective financial gain. There is not much difference between the money one expected to have and the money one expected to have a chance of having: it is all money. There is a difference between the leg one ought to have and the chance of keeping a leg which one ought to have. There is perhaps an even greater difference between the disease free state one ought to have and the chance of having a disease free state which

one ought to have. (A further answer may lie in the subtle distinction between deterministic events in the natural world and indeterministic events involving the unfathomable actions of human agents, discussed by Helen Reece in 'Losses of Chances in the Law' (1996) 59 MLR 188.)

221. Fourth, it can be argued that an all or nothing approach to outcome based losses is unjust. If it is shown on the balance of probabilities that my doctor caused or failed to prevent my injury or disease, he has to pay 100% of what that injury or uncured disease is worth. But, as Joseph H King argues at (1981) 90 Yale LJ 1353, 1387,

> 'by compensating the 95% chance as though it were 100%, courts overcompensate the plaintiff. Both types of chance should be valued in a way that reflects their probability of occurrence. Such an approach would also promote a more accurate loss allocation.'

222. The logic of this argument, however, is that personal injury law should transform itself. It should never be about outcomes but only about chances. It seems to me that this is the real problem we face in this case. How can the two live together?

223. Until now, the gist of the action for personal injuries has been damage to the person. My negligence probably caused the loss of your leg: I pay you the full value of the loss of the leg (say £100,000). My negligence probably did not cause the loss of your leg. I do not pay you anything. Compare the loss of a chance approach: my negligence probably caused a reduction in the chance of your keeping that leg: I pay you the value of the loss of your leg, discounted by the chance that it would have happened anyway. If the chance of saving the leg was very good, say 90%, the claimant still gets only 90% of his damages, say £90,000. But if the chance of saving the leg was comparatively poor, say 20%, the claimant still gets £20,000. So the claimant ends up with less than full compensation even though his chances of a more favourable outcome were good. And the defendant ends up paying substantial sums even though the outcome is one for which by definition he cannot be shown to be responsible.

224. Almost any claim for loss of an outcome could be reformulated as a claim for loss of a chance of that outcome. The implications of retaining them both as alternatives would be substantial. That is, the claimant still has the prospect of 100% recovery if he can show that it is more likely than not that the doctor's negligence caused the adverse outcome. But if he cannot show that, he also has the prospect of lesser recovery for loss of a chance. If (for the reasons given earlier) it would in practice always be tempting to conclude that the doctor's negligence had affected his chances to some extent, the claimant would almost always get something. It would be a 'heads you lose everything, tails I win something' situation. But why should the defendant not also be able to redefine the gist of the action if it suits him better?

225. The appellant in this case accepts that the proportionate recovery effect must cut both ways. If the claim is characterised as loss of a chance, those with a better than evens chance would still only get a proportion of the full value of their claim. But I do not think that he accepts that the same would apply in cases where the claim is characterised as loss of an outcome. In that case there is no basis for calculating the odds. If the two are alternatives available in every case, the defendant will almost always be liable for something. He will have lost the benefit of the 50% chance that causation cannot be proved. But if the two approaches cannot sensibly live together, the claimants who currently obtain full recovery on an adverse outcome basis might in future only achieve a proportionate recovery. This would surely be a case of two steps forward, three steps back for the great majority of straightforward personal injury cases. In either event, the expert evidence would have to be far more complex than it is at present. Negotiations and trials would be a great deal more difficult. Recovery would be much less predictable both for claimants and for defendants' liability insurers. There is no reason in principle why the change in approach should be limited to medical negligence. Whether or not the policy choice is between retaining the present definition of personal injury in outcome terms and

redefining it in loss of opportunity terms, introducing the latter would cause far more problems in the general run of personal injury claims than the policy benefits are worth.

226. Much of the discussion in the cases and literature has centred round cases where the adverse outcome has already happened. The patient has lost his leg. Did the doctor's negligence cause him to lose the leg? If not, did it reduce the chances of saving the leg? But in this case the most serious of the adverse outcomes has not yet happened, and (it is to be hoped) may never happen. The approach to causation should be the same for both past and future events. What, if anything, has the doctor's negligence caused in this case? We certainly do not know whether it has caused this outcome, because happily Mr Gregg has survived each of the significant milestones along the way. Can we even say that it reduced the chances of a successful outcome, given that Mr Gregg has turned out to be one of the successful minority at each milestone? This is quite different from the situation in *Hotson*, where the avascular necrosis had already happened, or in *Rufo v Hosking*, where the fractures had already happened. Mr Gregg faced a risk of an adverse outcome which happily has not so far materialised, serious though the effects of his illness, treatment and prognosis have been. The complexities of attempting to introduce liability for the loss of a chance of a more favourable outcome in personal injury claims have driven me, not without regret, to conclude that it should not be done."

NOTES:

1. Lord Hoffman agreed with Baroness Hale and Lord Phillips.
2. Dissenting judgments were given by Lords Nicholls and Hope. Lord Nicholls for example saw the decision as unjust in that the decision had the consequence that "a patient with a 60% of recovery reduced to a 40% prospect by medical negligence and obtain compensation. But he can obtain nothing if his prospects were reduced from 40% to nil".

QUESTIONS:

1. Contrast the judgments of the House of Lords in *Chester v Afshar* (see Chapter 6 above), a causation case concerning consent to treatment where the litigant succeeded, and *Gregg v Scott*. Why do you think that the claimant in the first case succeeded and the second did not? See further J.R. Spencer "Damages for Lost Chances: Lost for Good?" [2005] *Cambridge Law Journal* 282 at pp.284–285.
2. Should the House of Lords have accepted an action for "loss of chance" in this situation?

(i) Causation and Failure to Act: the Impact of the Bolam Test on Causation

A final issue concerns the relevance of the *Bolam* standard of "responsible medical opinion" in establishing whether the defendant's breach of duty caused the claimant's injury or illness in the case of litigation concerning failure to act. This issue arose in the case of *Bolitho*.

Bolitho v City of Hackney Health Authority [1998] A.C. 232

For discussion of the facts of this case see above at p.167.

LORD BROWNE-WILKINSON

The Bolam Test and Causation

" . . . Before your Lordships, Mr. Brennan, for the appellant, submitted, first, that the [*Bolam*] test has no application in deciding questions of causation and, secondly, that the judge misdirected himself by treating it as being so relevant. This argument, which was raised for the first time by amendment to the notice of appeal in the Court of Appeal, commended itself to Simon Brown L.J. and was the basis on which he dissented. I have no doubt that, in the generality of cases, the proposition of law is correct but equally have no doubt that the judge in the circumstances of the present case was not guilty of any self-misdirection.

Where, as in the present case, a breach of a duty of care is proved or admitted, the burden still lies on the plaintiff to prove that such breach caused the injury suffered: *Bonnington Castings Ltd. v. Wardlaw* [1956] A.C. 613; *Wilsher v. Essex Area Health Authority* [1988] A.C. 1074. In all cases the primary question is one of fact: did the wrongful act cause the injury? But in cases where the breach of duty consists of an omission to do an act which ought to be done (e.g. the failure by a doctor to attend) that factual inquiry is, by definition, in the realms of hypothesis. The question is what would have happened if an event which by definition did not occur had occurred. In a case of non-attendance by a doctor, there may be cases in which there is a doubt as to which doctor would have attended if the duty had been fulfilled. But in this case there was no doubt: if the duty had been carried out it would have either been Dr. Horn or Dr. Rodger, the only two doctors at St. Bartholomew's who had responsibility for Patrick and were on duty. Therefore in the present case, the first relevant question is 'What would Dr. Horn or Dr. Rodger have done if they had attended?' As to Dr. Horn, the judge accepted her evidence that she would not have intubated. By inference, although not expressly, the judge must have accepted that Dr. Rodger also would not have intubated: as a senior house officer she would not have intubated without the approval of her senior registrar, Dr. Horn.

Therefore the test had no part to play in determining the first question, viz. what would have happened? Nor can I see any circumstances in which the test could be relevant to such a question.

However in the present case the answer to the question 'What would have happened?' is not determinative of the issue of causation. At the trial the defendants accepted that if the professional standard of care required any doctor who attended to intubate Patrick, Patrick's claim must succeed. Dr. Horn could not escape liability by proving that she would have failed to take the course which any competent doctor would have adopted. A defendant cannot escape liability by saying that the damage would have occurred in any event because he would have committed some other breach of duty thereafter. I have no doubt that this concession was rightly made by the defendants. But there is some difficulty in analysing why it was correct. I adopt the analysis of Hobhouse L.J. . . . In commenting on the decision of the Court of Appeal in the present case, he said, at p. 20:

'Thus a plaintiff can discharge the burden of proof on causation by satisfying the court either that the relevant person would in fact have taken the requisite action (although she would not have been at fault if she had not) or that the proper discharge of the relevant person's duty towards the plaintiff required that she take that action. The former alternative calls for no explanation since it is simply the factual proof of the causative effect of the original fault. The latter is slightly more sophisticated: it involves the factual situation that the original fault did not itself cause the injury but that this was because there would have been some further fault on the part of the defendants; the plaintiff proves his case by proving that his injuries would have been avoided if proper care had continued to be taken. In the *Bolitho* case the plaintiff had to prove that the continuing exercise of proper care would have resulted in his being intubated.'

There were, therefore, two questions for the judge to decide on causation. (1) What would Dr. Horn have done, or authorised to be done, if she had attended Patrick? and (2) if she would not have intubated, would that have been negligent? The test has no relevance to the first of those questions but is central to the second.

There can be no doubt that, as the majority of the Court of Appeal held, the judge directed himself correctly in accordance with that approach. The passages from his judgment which I have quoted (and in particular those that I have emphasised) demonstrate this. The dissenting judgment of Simon Brown L.J. in the Court of Appeal is based on a misreading of the judge's judgment. He treats the judge as having only asked himself one question, namely, the second question. To the extent that the Lord Justice noticed the first question—would Dr. Horn have intubated—he said that the judge was wrong to accept Dr. Horn's evidence that she would not have intubated. In my judgment it was for the judge to assess the truth of her evidence on this issue.

Accordingly the judge asked himself the right questions and answered them on the right basis."

NOTE:

1. The approach here by the House of Lords has been subject to criticism. It has been argued that the decision here is a radical departure from legal principle. Historically, determinations of causation have been rooted in factual issues and now it is suggested "in cases in which the breach of duty alleged is an omission to act, the legal enquiry into causation, which is represented as factual, will be converted into a normative investigation as to what the defendant should have done." See A. Grubb and M.A. Jones, "Causation and Defences" in A. Grubb (ed.), *Principles of Medical Law* (2nd edn), Oxford: OUP, 2004 at para. 7.45.

3. DEFECTIVE MEDICINAL PRODUCTS AND DRUGS

The most common form of medical treatment is the administration of drugs. Thus if there is negligence in development, manufacture or supply, the number of potential claimants is considerable. There have been a number of notable instances of legal proceedings being brought in relation to defective drug products.

Concern over the use of the tort system as a means of redress for harm caused by defective drugs was illustrated by the Thalidomide case (H. Teff and C. Munro, *Thalidomide: the Legal Aftermath*, Farnborough: Saxon House, 1976). A number of women were given the drug Thalidomide during pregnancy. When born, the children were discovered to be suffering from multiple handicaps. The litigation continued over a number of years, with the claims being eventually settled. Despite a number of other high-profile cases involving what were alleged to be defective drug products, for instance the actions brought in relation to the anti-arthritis drug Opren, such claims have not led to findings being made in court against the drug manufacturers in the court room. Instead, either settlements have been reached or the claim has failed because causation could not be established (see P.R. Ferguson, *Drug Injuries and the Pursuit of Compensation*, London: Sweet & Maxwell, 1996, pp.10–15).

The difficulties in bringing actions in relation to drug products are in establishing who is responsible for the injury caused and in ascertaining whether the defect caused the harm suffered. A further problem relates to the fact that drug-related injuries may involve a large number of claimants which makes it difficult to co-ordinate such claims.

Before drugs are allowed to be marketed, they are subject to a statutory scheme requiring testing to take place (see H. Teff, "The Regulation of Medicinal Products and Devices" in A. Grubb (ed.), *Principles of Medical Law* (2nd edn), Oxford: OUP, 2004). The drug safety scandals such as Thalidomide led to regulation of medicinal products across the European Union (see further T.K. Hervey and J.V. McHale, *Health Law and the European Union*, Cambridge: CUP, 2004, Chapter 8 and A. Cullvier, "The Role of the European Medicines Agency" in R. Goldberg and J. Lonbay (eds). New drugs are required to be licensed by the Medicines and Health Care Products Regulatory Agency. There is a reporting system where defects in drugs are detected, although the efficacy of this system has been questioned. (See P. R. Ferguson, *Drug Injuries and the Pursuit of Compensation*, London: Sweet & Maxwell, 1996 at p.34.) Nevertheless despite this, problems may arise.

A statutory scheme is now in existence which imposes strict liability on defective products, including defective drugs. Legislation was passed providing strict liability in relation to pharmaceutical products in 1987: the Consumer Protection Act 1987. This statute was enacted as a result of the EC Product Liability Directive (95/374). Although the language of the statute differs in some respect to the Directive, the Act has been upheld by the European Court of Justice (*Commission v UK*). In interpreting the statute the English courts have been prepared to go back to the Directive itself (see, for example, *AB v National Blood Authority* [2001] 3 All E.R. 289).

Consumer Protection Act 1987

2.—(1) Subject to the following provisions of this Part, where any damage is caused wholly or partly by a defect in a product, every person to whom subsection(2) below applies shall be liable for the damage.
    (2) This subsection applies to:

(a) The producer of the product;
(b) any person who, by putting his name on the product or by using a trade mark or other distinguishing mark in relation to the product, has held himself out to be the producer of the product;
(c) any person who has imported the product into a member State from a place outside the Member States in order, in the course of any business of his, to supply it to another.

(3) Subject as aforesaid, where any damage is caused wholly or partly by a defect in a product, any person who supplied the product (whether to the person who suffered the damage, to the producer of any product in which the product in question is comprised or to any other person) shall be liable for the damage if—

(a) the person who suffered the damage requests the supplier to identify one or more of the persons (whether still in existence or not) to whom subsection (2) above applies in relation to the product;

(b) that request is made within a reasonable period after the damage occurs and at a time when it is not reasonably practicable for the person making the request to identify all those persons; and

(c) the supplier fails, within a reasonable period after receiving the request, either to comply with the request or to identify the person who supplied the product to him.

. . .

(5) Where two or more persons are liable by virtue of this Part for the same damage, their liability shall be joint and several.

(6) This section shall be without prejudice to any liability arising otherwise than by virtue of this Part.

3.—(1) Subject to the following provisions of this section, there is a defect in a product for the purposes of this Part if the safety of the product is not such as persons generally are entitled to expect; and for those purposes "safety", in relation to a product, shall include safety with respect to products comprised in that product and safety in the context of risks of damage to property, as well as in the context of risks of death or personal injury.

(2) In determining for the purpose of subsection (1) above what persons generally are entitled to expect in relation to a product all circumstances shall be taken into account including:

(a) the manner in which, and purposes for which, the product has been marketed, its get-up, the use of any mark in relation to the product and any instructions for, or warnings with respect to, doing or refraining from doing anything with or in relation to the product;

(b) what might reasonably be expected to be done with or in relation to the product; and

(c) the time when the product was supplied by its producer to another;
and nothing in this section shall require a defect to be inferred from the fact alone that the safety of a product which is supplied after that time is greater than the safety of the product in question.

4.—(1) In any civil proceedings by virtue of this Part against any person ("the person proceeded against") in respect of a defect in a product it shall be a defence for him to show—

(a) that the defect is attributable to compliance with any requirement imposed by or under any enactment or with any Community obligation; or

(b) that the person proceeded against did not at any time supply the product to another; or

(c) that the following conditions are satisfied, that is to say—
  (i) that the only supply of the product to another by the person proceeded against was otherwise than in the course of business of that person's; and
  (ii) that section 2(2) above does not apply to that person or applies to him by virtue only of things done by virtue only of things done otherwise than with a view to profit; or

(d) that the defect did not exist in the product at the relevant time; or

(e) that the state of scientific and technical knowledge at the relevant time was not such that a producer of products of the same description as the product in question might be expected to discover the defect, if it had existed in his products while they were under his control; or

(f) that the defect—
  (i) constituted a defect in a product ("the subsequent product") in which the product in question had been comprised; and

(ii) was wholly attributable to the design of the subsequent product or to compliance by the producer of the product in question with instructions given by the producer of the product in question with instructions given by the producer of the subsequent product.

(2) In this section "the relevant time", in relation to electricity means the time at which it was generated, being a time before it was transmitted or distributed, and in relation to any other product, means—

(a) if the person proceeded against us a person to whom subsection(2) of section 2 above applies in relation to the product, the time when he supplied the product to another;

(b) if that subsection does not apply to that person in relation to the product, the time when the product was last supplied by a person to whom that subsection does apply in relation to the product.

5.—(1) Subject to the following provisions of this section, in this Part "damage" means death or personal injury or any loss of or damage to any property (including land).

(2) A person shall not be liable under section 2 above in respect of any defect in a product for loss of or damage to the product itself or for the loss of or damage to the whole or any part of a product which has been supplied with the product in question comprised in it.

(3) A person shall not be liable under section 2 above for any loss or damage to property which at the time it is lost or damaged is not—

(a) a description of property ordinarily intended for private use, occupation or consumption; and

(b) intended by the person suffering the loss or damage mainly for his own private use, occupation or consumption.

(4) No damages shall be awarded to any person by virtue of this Part in respect of any loss of or damage to any property if the amount which would fall to be so awarded to that person, apart from this subsection and any liability for interest, does not exceed £275.

(5) In determining for the purposes of this Part who has suffered loss or damage to property and whether any such loss or damage occurred, the loss or damage shall be regarded as having occurred at the earliest time at which a person with an interest in the property had knowledge of the material facts about loss or damage.

(6) For the purposes of subsection (5) above the material facts about any loss of or damage to property are such facts about the loss and damage as would lead a reasonable person with an interest in the property to consider the loss sufficiently serious to justify him instituting proceedings for damages against a defendant who did not dispute liability and who was thus able to satisfy a judgment.

(7) For the purpose of subsection (5) above a person's knowledge includes knowledge which he might reasonably have been expected to acquire:

(a) from facts observable or ascertainable by him; or

(b) from facts ascertainable by him with the help of appropriate expert advice which it is reasonable for him to seek;

but a person shall not be taken by virtue of this subsection to have knowledge of a fact ascertainable by him only with the help of expert advice unless he has failed to take all reasonable steps to obtain and (where appropriate, to act on) that advice. . . .

46.—(1) Subject to the following provisions of this section, references in this Act to supplying goods shall be construed as references to doing any of the following, whether as principal or agent, that is to say—

(a) selling, hiring out or lending the goods;

(b) entering into a hire purchase agreement to furnish the goods;
(c) the performance or any contract of work and materials to furnish the goods;
(d) providing the goods in exchange for any consideration other than money;
(e) providing the goods in or in connection with the performance of any statutory function; or
(f) giving the goods as a prize or otherwise making a gift of the goods;
      and in relation to gas or water, those references shall be construed as including references to providing the service by which the gas or water is made available for use.

(2) For the purposes of any reference to this Act to supplying goods, where a person ("the ostensible supplier") supplies goods to another person ("the customer") under a hire-purchase agreement, conditional sale agreement or credit-sale agreement or under an agreement for the hiring of goods (other than a hire purchase agreement) and the ostensible supplier:

(a) carries on the business of financing the provision of goods for others by means of such agreement; and
(b) in the course of that business acquired his interest in the goods supplied to the customer as a means of financing the provision of them for the customer by a further person ("the effective supplier"),

the effective supplier and not the ostensible supplier shall be treated as supplying the goods to the customer.

NOTES:

1. Actions can only be brought under the legislation in relation to drug products manufactured after March 1, 1988. Where a person is injured by a defective product manufactured before that date, they must bring their action at common law. It is notable that few claims have been brought under the legislation to date and few have proceeded beyond the preliminary stages of litigation (see, for example, *XYZ and Others v Schering Health Care Ltd* [2002] EWHC 1420 QB).
2. While proceedings under the Act will usually be brought against producers of defective products, suppliers may also be held liable. The supplier will be liable where the patient asks her to identify the producer of the product and she is unable to do so (s.2(3)). This may include pharmacists or doctors who dispense their own drugs.
3. There may be difficulties in establishing liability where the company who produced the drug cannot be identified. This issue arose in the United States in the 1950s when a drug, Debendox, was distributed with the aim of reducing miscarriages in pregnant women. This drug was supplied by many firms under a generic name. Certain US courts were prepared to impose liability collectively on the manufacturers by ascertaining their liability in relation to their proportion of the market share. However this approach was not uniformly accepted in the United States and it may be questioned whether such an argument would be accepted by an English court (see C. Newdick, "Special Problems of Compensating Those Damaged by Medicinal Products" in S. McLean (ed.), *Compensation for Damage: an International Perspective*, Aldershot: Dartmouth, 1993).

4. What constitutes a "product" for the purpose of the legislation is undefined. So. for example. this led to some discussion as to whether defects in bodily products such as blood or organs are included within the scope of the legislation. The Pearson Commission were in favour of such an inclusion and this approach has received the support of some commentators and the Nuffield Council on Bioethics (see *Human Tissue: Legal and Ethical Issues*, London: Nuffield Council on Bioethics, 1995). This issue was explored further in *AB v National Blood Authority* [2001] 3 All E.R. 389 where the court accepted that blood fell within the legislative provision.

5. A defect is likely to become evident in the early years of the use of a product such as a drug if it is not uncovered in the course of a clinical trial. The Act requires the court to consider whether the product is safe (s.3(1)). Drugs and other products are not expected to be absolutely safe. The test embodied in the statute is objective. Issues such as side effects require consideration and need to be assessed against the potential benefit from the drug/product. A relevant factor may be approval given to the drug by the Medicines and Healthcare Products Regulatory Agency. A further factor is whether the manufacturer has given warnings as to the use of the product, for instance whether an information sheet has been enclosed with the drug/product.

6. One major difficulty in establishing liability under this Act is likely to be causation. The House of Lords in *Wilsher* confirmed that the claimant must establish causation and it is not sufficient to establish liability that the defendant's conduct was one of a number of factors contributing to the harm suffered.

7. Section 4 provides a "developmental risk defence". The introduction of such a defence was opposed both by the Law Commission and by the Pearson Commission. The defence itself is derived from the European Directive. Jones has noted that the definition contained in the Directive is narrower than that provided in s.4. Article 7(e) of the Directive states that there is a defence "where the state of scientific and technical knowledge at the time when he put the product into circulation was not such as to enable the existence of the defect to be discovered." (See M. Jones, *Medical Negligence* (3rd edn), London: Sweet & Maxwell, 2002, at p.452 and C. Newdick, "The Development Risk Defence of the Consumer Protection Act 1987" (1988) 47 C.L.J. 455.) However, in *AB v National Blood Authority* [2001] 3 All E.R. 389, Burton J. interpreted s.4 of the Consumer Protection Act consistent with the wording in the Directive. Where litigation over a defective product does take place, a question may arise as to whether it is a manufacturing defect rather than a design defect. The distinction between such defects may be crucial. This is because the s.4 defence would not apply if it is shown that a defect is caused by failure to adhere to manufacturing standards as opposed to a defect in product design. In addition it appears that the developmental risk defence will not apply in a situation in which, although some loss was foreseeable, the precise extent of that loss was not. This provision has been subject to

criticism as it can fundamentally undermine the impact of strict liability in relation to medicinal products where risks are currently unknown (see further C. Newdick, "Strict Liability for Defective Drugs in the Pharmaceutical Industry" (1985) LQR 405 at p.408).

8. The approach in the case can be contrasted with that taken in a number of earlier cases in which the test was cast more generally in terms of "reasonableness", aligning this more closely with negligence (see further *Richardson v LRC* [2000] P.I.Q.R., P164; *Worsley v Tambrands* [2000] P.I.Q.R., P95; *Foster v Biosil* [2000] B.M.L.R. 178; *Abouzaid v Mothercare* [2001] 3 All E.R. 289).

QUESTION:

1. Where a patient is harmed through a defective drug, can an action be brought against the Medicines and Health Care Regulatory Agency? (See M. Brazier, *Medicines, Patients and the Law* (2nd edn), Harmondsworth: Penguin, 2002.)

4. GROSS NEGLIGENCE AND CRIMINAL LIABILITY

In most situations a malpractice action brought against a health professional is unlikely to also give rise to liability in criminal law. Nevertheless there is the possibility that a criminal prosecution may be brought in certain situations. We explore certain aspects of the scope of criminal liability in relation to issues consequent upon failure to obtain consent to treatment in Chapter 6 below. Prosecutions have been brought in recent times against health care professionals where a patient had died allegedly as a consequence of a gravely negligent action by the doctor. While the courts in earlier centuries were prepared to impose liability in manslaughter for mere carelessness, this was later limited to conduct amounting to gross negligence. In *R. v Bateman* (1925) 19 Cr.App.R. 8, the court laid down the basis for liability for gross negligence manslaughter. It must be shown that the defendant owed the deceased a duty to take care, he was in breach of that duty and this breach caused the deceased's death. Finally, it is necessary to show that the negligence was gross; namely that it showed such a disregard for the life and safety of other persons as to constitute a crime and be worthy of punishment. This approach has been criticised. In the later case of *R. v Seymour* [1983] 2 A.C. 493, the court took a different approach, requiring it to be established that the conduct of the defendant amounted to an "obvious and serious" risk of death. Some commentators were of the view that the offence of gross negligence manslaughter was redundant. However, its existence was confirmed by the House of Lords in the later case of *R v Adomako*, where the judgment in *Seymour* was disapproved.

R v Adomako [1994] 3 All E.R. 79; [1995] 1 A.C. 624

An anaesthetist in the course of an eye operation failed to notice that the endotracheal tube used to assist the patient's breathing had become disconnected.

After nine minutes, the patient suffered a heart attack and died. Expert evidence described his failure to identify the problem and remedy it as "abysmal" and as a "gross dereliction of care".

LORD MACKAY L.C.

" . . . [I]n my opinion the principles of the law of negligence apply to ascertain whether or not the defendant has been in breach of a duty of care towards the victim who has died. If such breach of duty is established the next question is whether that breach of duty caused the death of the victim. If so, the jury must go on to consider whether that breach of duty should be characterised as gross negligence and therefore as a crime. This will depend on the seriousness of the breach of duty committed by the defendant in all the circumstances in which the defendant was placed when it occurred. The jury will have to consider whether the extent to which the defendant's conduct departed from the proper standard of care incumbent upon him, involving as it must have done a risk of death to the patient, was such that it should be judged criminal.

It is true that to a certain extent this involves an element of circularity, but in this branch of the law I do not believe that is fatal to its being correct as a test of how far conduct must depart from accepted standards to be characterised as criminal. This is necessarily a question of degree and an attempt to specify that degree more closely is I think likely to achieve only a spurious precision. The essence of the matter, which is supremely a jury question, is whether, having regard to the risk of death involved, the conduct of the defendant was so bad in all the circumstances to amount in their judgment to a criminal act or omission . . .

I consider it perfectly appropriate that the word 'reckless' should be used in cases of involuntary manslaughter, but as Lord Atkin put it 'in the ordinary connotation of that word'. Examples in which this was done, to my mind, with complete accuracy are *R v. Stone, R v. Dobinson* [1977] 2 All E.R. 341 and *R v. West London Coroner, ex p. Gray* [1987] 2 All E.R. 129.

In my opinion it is quite unnecessary in the context of gross negligence to give the detailed directions with regard to the meaning of the word 'reckless' associated with *R v. Lawrence* [1981] 1 All E.R. 974. The decision of the Court of Appeal, Criminal Division, in the other cases with which they were concerned at the same time as they heard the appeal in this case indicates that the circumstances in which involuntary manslaughter has to be considered may make the somewhat elaborate and rather rigid directions inappropriate. I entirely agree with the view that the circumstances to which a charge of involuntary manslaughter may apply are so various that it is unwise to attempt to categorise or detail specimen directions. For my part I would not wish to go beyond the description of the basis in law which I have already given."

NOTES:

1. The only full judgment was that of Lord Mackay with whom the other members of the House of Lords Keith, Goff, Browne-Wilkinson and Woolf agreed.
2. The return to a *Bateman* type test has been criticised. For example, Virgo has argued that the reasoning is circular "gross negligence and consequent criminal liability will exist whenever the jury considers that the defendant has departed to such an extent from the proper standards of care that it should be judged criminal". He is of the view that without considerable judicial guidance the case could result in uncertainty and unpredictability (see G. Virgo, "Reconstructing Manslaughter on Defective Foundation" [1995] *Cambridge Law Journal* 14).

3. In *R v Misra* [2004] EWCA 2375 two senior house doctors were convicted of gross negligence manslaughter in connection with the mismanagement of a 31-year-old man who died of toxic shock syndrome following what was a routine operation. Here the Court of Appeal confirmed that the crime of gross negligence manslaughter is compliant with the Human Rights Act 1998 in that it complies with both Article 6, the right to a fair trial, and Article 7 which prevents criminal conviction save where there is a pre-existing criminal offence. The claim that the scope of the offence of gross negligence manslaughter was too vague to comply with the need for a criminal offence to be sufficiently certain was rejected. Subsequently, following this case, the NHS trust in Southampton for whom the doctors worked was convicted under Health and Safety at Work Act 1974, s.3 because of inadequate supervision of the doctors (*Health and Safety Executive v Southampton NHS Trust*, January 11, 2006, unreported). For criticism of the decision in this case and for the discussion of the subsequent prosecution of the NHS trust, see O. Quick, "Prosecuting Medical Mishaps" (2006) 156 *New Law Journal* 394).

4. It has been suggested that in addition to an action for gross negligence manslaughter, a manslaughter prosecution may also be brought on the basis of subjective recklessness (see J.C. Smith, "Manslaughter" [1994] Crim L.R. 758). That is to say that liability will arise for conduct in a situation which includes "Causing death by an act done being aware that it is highly probable that it will cause serious bodily harm". A prosecution may be appropriate if, for example, a surgeon operates while under the influence of drugs or drink. Note that such conduct is likely to lead to action being taken against the health professional by his or her professional disciplinary body (see Chapter 4 below.)

5. The Law Commission has suggested various reforms in this area (*Involuntary Manslaughter: Legislating the Criminal Code*, Law Com. Rep. 231, London: HMSO, 1996.) It proposed that there should be a new offence of reckless killing (paras 5.12–5.13). This would be committed if:

> "(1) a person by his or her conduct causes the death of another;
>   (2) he or she is aware of a risk that his or her conduct will cause death or serious injury: and
>   (3) it is unreasonable for him or her to take that risk, having regard to all the circumstances as he or she knows or believes them to be."

The Law Commission notes that this offence would be committed even in a situation in which the deceased consented to the risk for instance, in consenting to a highly risky surgical operation (para. 5.12). This obviously raises the issue of what precisely an individual may or may not consent to. (This issue is explored fully in Chapter 6 below at p.355.)

It also recommends that there should be a new offence of "killing by gross carelessness" (para.5.34). This would apply if

> "(1) a person by his or her conduct will cause the death of another;
>   (2) a risk that his or her conduct will cause death or serious injury would be obvious to a reasonable person in his or her position;

(3) he or she is capable of appreciating that risk at the material time; and

(4) either

(a) his or her conduct falls far below what can reasonably be expected of him or her in the circumstances, or

(b) he or she intends by his or her conduct to cause some injury, or is aware of, and unreasonably takes, the risk that it may do so, and the conduct causing (or intended to cause) the injury constitutes an offence" (para. 5.34).

The Law Commission suggests that obvious in this context means "immediately apparent", "striking" or "glaring".

6. Whether a health care professional would be held liable in gross negligence manslaughter for an omission such as a failure to treat a patient who subsequently dies is unclear (see Law Commission, *Involuntary Manslaughter: Legislating the Criminal Code*, London: HMSO, 1996, paras 3.13–3.14 and for further discussion of cases in relation to liability for omissions where death results see Chapter 14 below).

7. The decision in *R v Adomako* focuses upon the liability of the individual health professional. But what there are situations in which the standard of care provided has fallen to what may be regarded as unacceptable levels and it is claimed that mistakes by junior staff flow from constraints and pressures resulting from underfunding by hospital management, then where should liability lie? One argument is that in such a situation an action may be brought for what is known as "corporate manslaughter". This involves prosecuting the officers of a company and holding them liable for the conduct of the organisation rather than imposing liability on an individual employee (see *P&O Ferries (Dover) Ltd* (1991) 93 Cr.App.R. 72). Bringing an action for corporate manslaughter is fraught with difficulties. In the past the courts have indicated that it is necessary to show a "controlling mind" which, while feasible in a small company, may pose considerable difficulties in the context of a large organisation (see C. Wells, *Corporations and Criminal Responsibility*, Oxford: Clarendon Press, 1993). The Law Commission, *op. cit.* in note 5, has proposed reforms in this area. It recommends a new offence of "corporate killing, broadly corresponding to the individual offence of killing by gross carelessness" (para. 8.35). In 2005 the Government introduced a draft Bill on corporate manslaughter ("Corporate Manslaughter: The Government's Draft Bill for Reform"). The Bill proposed that an organisation should be guilty of the offence of corporate manslaughter in a situation in which any of the organisation's activities managed or organised by the senior managers first, causes a person's death and secondly amounts to a gross breach of a relevant duty of care owed by the organisation. "Senior managers" of organisations are those who play a significant role in making of decisions about how the whole or a substantial part of the activities of the company are managed or organised; or who are the actual manager or organiser of the whole or a substantial part of those activities. The Bill defined a "gross breach" as a breach of a duty of care by an organisation that falls far below what can reasonably be expected of the organisation in

the circumstances. In considering whether there has been a gross breach of care the jury would need to consider whether the evidence shows that the organisation failed to comply with any relevant health and safety legislation or guidance. Further issues which the jury would consider included whether or not senior managers sought to cause the organisation to profit from its failure, i.e. that they deliberately cut corners to reduce costs or boost profits. The Bill was considered by the Home Affairs and Work and Pensions Joint Select Committee who reported in November 2005 ("Draft Corporate Manslaughter Bill HC 40-i"). They were critical of the Draft Bill and recommended that the Government should return to the recommendations made by the Law Commission. They recommended that the offence should not be based upon the tort of negligence and also that there should be a wider range of sanctions devised.

8. One further issue is this: what should the appropriate penalty be in such a situation if liability cannot be imposed on a particular individual? If a fine is imposed in the context of a public organisation such as the NHS, as Newdick comments, this may have adverse consequences since the fine will have to be taken from funds which would otherwise be used for patient care and thus this could lead to reduced rather than improved standards of care (C. Newdick *Who Should We Treat?* (2nd edn), Oxford: OUP, 2005, p.191).

QUESTION:

1. Is gross negligence a sufficient basis on which to convict a doctor of manslaughter? (For one view, see A. McCall-Smith, "Criminal Negligence and the Incompetent Doctor" (1993) 1 *Medical Law Review* 33.)

5. REFORM OF FAULT-BASED LIABILITY

As may be seen from the discussion in this chapter, bringing an action in the law of tort for compensation where malpractice has occurred is fraught with difficulties. Some of the general difficulties with the tort system as a mechanism for compensation and accountability were explored in a report published by the Kings Fund Institute in 1988.

(a) General Difficulties with the Tort System

C. Ham, R. Dingwall, P. Fenn and D. Harris, *Medical Negligence Compensation and Accountability*, Oxford: King's Fund Institute, 1988

In parallel with the concern of health authorities and of the medical profession, organisations representing patients and their relatives have drawn attention to the shortcomings of the tort system. First, there is the lengthy and expensive procedure involved in pursuing a claim for damages. This means that cases are often brought only by the rich or those able to obtain legal aid. Cases take a considerable time to work their way through the courts: the average time for settling a claim is four years.

Second, the legal process is by definition adversarial. As such, it may cause doctors and health authorities to close ranks and not offer an adequate explanation to patients and their relatives when things go wrong. In addition, the legal process may itself be distressing in providing a constant reminder of painful or unhappy events.

Third, the emphasis on establishing fault and cause and effect in injury cases turns the tort system into a lottery. Compensation is based not on need but on the ability to prove that somebody was at fault. The rules of the legal process which put the burden of proof on those bringing a claim may create significant difficulties for plaintiffs. As a consequence, similar cases of injury may be compensated quite differently. For example, a child suffering brain damage after contracting encephalitis will receive no compensation, a child suffering brain damage as a result of vaccine damage will receive £20,000, and a child suffering brain damage following traumatic birth injury may receive hundreds of thousands of pounds compensation.

Fourth, only a small proportion of people suffering medical injuries are compensated through the tort system. This may mean that the losses incurred as a result of injury are inadequately compensated, although other sources of compensation are available.

Underlying these criticisms is a concern that maintaining high standards of medical practice and holding doctors to account for unacceptable standards of practice are inadequate. Action for the Victims of Medical Accidents (AVMA), established in 1982, has highlighted these issues, and has argued for much greater openness and accountability on the part of the medical profession in dealing with the consequences of accidents. One of the points emphasised by AVMA is that most people who suffer medical injuries are not seeking compensation but want an explanation of what went wrong. An adequate system for dealing with injuries needs to provide for this as well as to offer financial compensation.

Before considering these points more fully, it is worth noting a number of other criticisms levelled at the tort system as it applies to medical injury cases.
These are:

- those making a claim may find it difficult to obtain the services of a solicitor with relevant expertise
- there may be difficulty in obtaining the services of doctors willing to act as expert witnesses for patients
- the legal process causes distress and expense to doctors and health authorities as well as to patients
- the availability of legal aid may result in legal action being initiated in inappropriate cases, that is cases where those making a claim have little chance of success.

It is against this background that alternatives to existing arrangements come under scrutiny. One widely canvassed option is a no-fault compensation scheme. This has found favour with the British Medical Association (BMA) and the Association of CHC's in England and Wales (ACHCEW). Other possibilities include the introduction of differential premiums for doctors to reflect the risks involved in their work: shifting the cost of providing compensation to the NHS: reforming the tort law to overcome some of the shortcomings identified: providing more support to medical injury cases through the social security system: and extending first party insurance cover.

NOTE:

1. The points made regarding the difficulty of establishing fault and causation remain. Although *Bolitho* has provided a different slant on these issues in practice, as research into cases decided post *Bolitho* indicates, establishing

medical negligence is in practice still very difficult (see, for example, A. Maclean, "Beyond Bolam and Bolitho" (2002) 5 *Medical Law International* 205.)

(b) Specific Difficulties with Medical Negligence Litigation

The whole system of medical negligence was considered as part of a wider study undertaken into the civil justice system by Lord Woolf. Lord Woolf consulted widely, holding seminars to which persons including lawyers, health professionals and representatives from patient organisations were invited. In July 1996 Lord Woolf published his report, *Access to Justice* (London: HMSO, 1996).

Access to Justice, HMSO, London, 1996

"1. Why have I singled out medical negligence for the most intensive examination during Stage 2 of my Inquiry? (I am using the term 'medical negligence' in this report to refer to any litigation involving allegations of negligence in the delivery of health care, whether by doctors, nurses or other health professionals.) It may appear a surprising choice, because medical negligence cases have no special procedures or rules of court. They are a sub-species of professional negligence actions, and they also belong to what is numerically the largest category of cases proceeding to trial, personal injury. Neither of these is singled out for special attention.

2. The answer is that early in the Inquiry it became increasingly obvious that it was in the area of medical negligence that the civil justice system was failing most conspicuously to meet the needs of litigants in a number of respects.

(a) The disproportion between costs and damages in medical negligence is particularly excessive, especially in lower value cases.
(b) The delay in resolving claims is more often unacceptable.
(c) Unmeritorious cases are often pursued, and clear-cut claims defended, for too long.
(d) The success rate is lower than in other personal injury litigation.
(e) The suspicion between the parties is more intense and the lack of co-operation frequently greater than in many other areas of litigation."

NOTE:

1. In the report it was stated that there is an average delay from the commencement of legal proceedings to the ultimate hearing of three years in relation to county court hearings and five years for High Court hearings (at para. 421). The appellate process may further lengthen delays. A notable example is that of the *Wilsher* litigation, discussed above, which commenced in 1978 and reached a final resolution of the matter a decade later in 1988. The reform of the civil justice system, introduced by Lord Woolf and which came into operation in 1999, was intended to reduce this delay. Civil proceedings today fall into three broad categories. The first is the *small claims* track. There is a limit of £5,000 on such cases and £1,000 in personal injury cases. These cases are allocated to what were known as the small claims courts. This referred to the procedure used in county courts for claims of low value. Cases regarded as suitable for such hearings are consumer disputes, accident claims, disputes regarding the ownership

of goods and most landlord and tenant disputes other than those for possession. Secondly, there is what is known as the *fast track*, where there is a limit of cases of value of up to £15,000. Such cases will usually be heard in the county court. Here, claims will be subject to a fixed timetable, judicial monitoring and only limited use of oral evidence. Failure to comply with case management directions will be the subject of sanctions. Cases involving claims of larger value and greater complexity are dealt with under the *multi-track* where these are cases not on another track (CPR rule 26. 6(6)). Here there is greater flexibility given to the court in the way in which a case will be managed appropriate to the particular needs of that case. A major feature of the reforms is the role of the procedural judge in "managing" the case—guiding the proceedings through the court (CPR Pt 3). Timetables are used and costs controlled. Failure to comply with the rules/protocols may result in the parties being subject to sanctions so for example, the defence may be struck out or this may have an impact upon the costs to be awarded.

2. The Woolf Report identified the pre-litigation stage as a major source of cost and delay. As a consequence, the conduct of civil litigation is today subject to Pre-Action Protocols and in particular the Pre-Action Protocol for Clinical Disputes. The aim of protocols is to maintain or restore the patient/health care provider relationship and to resolve as many disputes as possible without litigation. Parties must ensure that sufficient information is disclosed. The protocols suggest that NHS bodies should establish clinical risk management but the conduct of such procedures is left to the bodies themselves. In addition, they also suggested that that key staff are trained in an appropriate manner with some knowledge of health care law and of complaints procedures (for further discussion of these procedures, see Chapter 4 below). Information regarding adverse incidents and complaints should be used in a positive manner. In addition patients are to be advised as to an adverse outcome and should be given on request information on what actually happened and also information on other steps which could be taken.

3. Concerns as to the cost of expert evidence were identified in the Woolf Report (see *Access to Justice*, Chapter 13 and Chapter 15, paras 63 onwards). Calling expert evidence now requires permission of the court. There is greater use of written evidence and pre-trial meetings are encouraged to reduce differences.

4. *Access to Justice* also encouraged diverting cases from litigation through the use of alternative dispute resolution (ADR). Alternative dispute resolution has become increasingly popular in recent years in areas such as commercial and family disputes. The practice involves resolution of legal matters by reference to procedures such as conciliation and arbitration as opposed to reference to the courts. In 1991 the Department of Health published a consultation document outlining proposals for a voluntary arbitration scheme (see M. Jones, "Arbitration for Medical Claims in the NHS" (1992) 8 *Professional Negligence* 142). Such a scheme was regarded as having considerable advantages in the reduction of costs. An arbitration

panel would be established, consisting of two doctors (one chosen by each disputing party) and a lawyer specialising in medical negligence. The panel would operate largely applying the same tests as used by the courts in ascertaining negligence and in the award of damages. Pilot schemes into another form of alternative dispute resolution, mediation, were undertaken in the NHS. Mediation involves one person, who may be legally qualified, attempting to bring the parties to an agreement. Unlike an arbitrator, a mediator has no power to impose a solution. A two-year pilot study which began in October 1995 was undertaken in Oxford and Anglia, and Northern and Yorkshire areas. The first mediation case concerned Ruth McCall, who lost her foetus during pregnancy due to the negligence of the consultant caring for her. A settlement was reached in one day between Mrs McCall and the hospital representative in a case that Mrs McCall's solicitor estimated that, had it gone to litigation, would have normally taken three to four years to resolve. Two subsequent cases referred to mediation were also resolved in only one day (see J. Easterbrook, "Resolving Health Care Disputes" (1996) *Solicitors Journal* 140).

(c) Reforming the Clinical Negligence System

A number of options for reform of the existing system have been proposed.

(i) No-fault Compensation

The first and arguably most radical option would be to replace the tort action with a system of "no-fault compensation" (see generally M. Jones, *Medical Negligence* (3rd edn), London: Sweet & Maxwell, 2003, pp.20–40). This was considered in the Chief Medical Officer's Report, *Making Amends*.

Making Amends: a consultation paper setting out the proposals for reforming the approach to clinical negligence in the NHS, Department of Health 2003

1. No fault compensation schemes provide an alternative to tort litigation as a way of providing financial compensation for injuries. They generally remove the need to prove negligence as a criterion for making payments, although most schemes retain a test of causation and many also have tests of avoidability. Advocates of no-fault compensation argue that it provides compensation for harm suffered during medical care faster and more fairly than tort litigation and helps greater numbers of victims. Under no-fault compensation schemes, it is suggested, there is scope for proper investigation of what went wrong and why without the defensiveness inevitable in an adversarial system of litigation. Others, however, argue that medical accountability may be reduced in a no fault system.

2. A number of countries and jurisdictions have introduced no fault compensation schemes for medical injuries. They differ in their scope and in the eligibility criteria used. These existing schemes are reviewed in this section.
. . .

ANALYSIS—KEY FEATURES OF NO-FAULT COMPENSATION

49. The possibility of introducing a no-fault scheme to settle personal injury cases and clinical negligence has been considered a number of times over the years. In 1978 it was the

subject of a Royal Commission Review, led by Lord Pearson. This review rejected the use of no-fault compensation for medical negligence cases on the grounds that it would still be necessary, and difficult, to establish causation; it would be difficult to decide between injury caused by negligence and the natural progression of the disease or the foreseeable side effects of the treatment; if the focus of the scheme was on negligent injury, it would be no clearer who should receive compensation; the use of adjudication procedures would continue to place burdens on the medical manpower available; if no-fault compensation were introduced in medical negligence, there would be a knock-on effect to other areas of personal injury.

50. However, the Pearson Commission recognised that the case for no-fault compensation for medical injury was strong enough to make it likely that the issue would need to be reviewed again in time.

51. The no-fault schemes for medical injury around the world reviewed here have a number of features in common:

- all have tests of causation or avoidability. New Zealand and Sweden include a test of negligence akin to the Bolam test used in tort in the UK;
- a patient must suffer a minimum level of severity of injury to qualify for compensation (this is often set with reference to days of disability or days in hospital);
- there are limits on the types of compensation which can be awarded, for example compensation may not be available for pain and suffering and the levels of compensation may be capped;
- the primary source of compensation is insurance payments, benefits or state funded care—the "no-fault" scheme acts as a "top-up";
- in Scandinavia and New Zealand there are high levels of claims relative to the UK;
- compensation payments are lower than those typically awarded by courts in the UK;
- the New Zealand scheme and to some extent the Virginia and Florida scheme restrict access to the courts.

52. The more comprehensive system of social welfare and social insurance support available in New Zealand and the Scandinavian countries may affect the acceptability of the schemes in those countries. In Scandinavia, in particular, the compensation awards are low relative to UK tort awards because they are topping up already generous social insurance payments for income replacement.

53. England has fewer clinical negligence claims per 100,000 population, and the proportion of successful claims is lower. However, the average compensation award in England is far higher than the average in the New Zealand and Sweden schemes.

54. The advantages of no-fault compensation schemes appear to be:

- speedier resolution of cases by removing the need to dispute negligence in court;
- lower administrative and legal costs per case;
- increased certainty for claimants of the circumstances when they will receive compensation;
- reduced conflict between clinicians and claimants;
- greater willingness by clinicians to report adverse events.

55. The following disadvantages have also been suggested:

- overall costs would be higher than under a tort system because of the increased numbers likely to claim;
- or there would be an unacceptable reduction in the level of compensation awarded to keep costs within affordable levels (and if under-compensated, individuals would fall back on the state);
- disputes about causation would continue even if negligence were removed;
- it would be difficult to distinguish the natural progression of a disease from an error in treatment;

- a tariff-based system of compensation may not be sufficiently responsive to individuals' needs;
- a lack of medical accountability for standards of care;
- a no-fault scheme does not of itself guarantee that claimants receive an explanation or apology.

56. In addition concerns have been expressed about the implications under the Human Rights Act 1998, if restricted access to the courts was a feature of the introduction of a no fault compensation scheme.

57. Much of the argument about no fault schemes centres on the assumption that all harm of whatever severity would automatically be compensated.

58. Given the estimated level of adverse events within the healthcare system and the number of complaints relating to clinical treatment, such a comprehensive no-fault scheme, where payment was automatically available for injury resulting from treatment or missed diagnosis would open up the potential for tens of thousands of claims per year. The no fault schemes in Sweden and New Zealand receive between two and four times more claims than the tort system in England and make payments between three-and-a-half and five times more often. However, in the New Zealand scheme it appears that only about one in 20 potential claims are actually made, 60% of them being successful. A relatively low proportion relate to medical error which raises the question of whether the scheme provides an incentive to prevention.

59. Even with a tariff system limiting the amount of compensation there is the potential for a greatly increased compensation bill. Average payments at 1996 levels were approximately £6,000 per claim in Sweden, £3,000 in New Zealand and £46,000 in Great Britain. For a comprehensive no fault system to be affordable, awards would have to be significantly reduced from current levels. For the more serious injuries and higher levels of awards this is unlikely to be acceptable. The alternative of limiting eligibility according to the degree of disability suffered appears fairer as it is based on need. However, in the schemes examined the thresholds of disability are set quite high—either at a percentage of reduced capacity or length of hospitalisation. If the threshold is set too high few claimants are likely to benefit leading to concerns about a two-tier system and denial of redress to many harmed patients. Many schemes also cap compensation for pain and suffering and for loss of earnings.

60. As the schemes examined have shown, it is possible to construct a scheme which compensates patients for long-term harm suffered as a result of sub-standard care, through an administrative process. Such a process enables claimants to have faster access to compensation, with more certainty about the level of payment they are likely to receive. It also allows the money to be directed to patients rather than the legal process. Minimising adversarial proceedings also avoids diverting the time and efforts of clinicians away from providing patient care. Simpler compensation schemes for straightforward, relatively low value claims would take many claimants out of the tort system. The alternative of faster, more certain, but possibly lower compensation might prove attractive to many people. And while no fault schemes are often criticised for failing to provide the explanations and apologies which claimants seek there is no reason why these cannot be built into a compensation system.

61. While concerns have been raised that the tort system gives rise to defensive medicine, the alternative concern has been raised that no fault schemes reduce clinical accountability and reduce incentives for health professionals to pay attention to the quality of care they provide. Research carried out for this report did suggest some evidence of these incentive effects, as has previous research in America and elsewhere. However it is hard to quantify these effects, and clearly the majority of health professionals strive to offer high quality care, not because of the impending threat of litigation but because of their professionalism and training. However, as we have seen errors do occur. The tort system appears to have provided little incentive for prevention of errors or for putting right the mistakes that are made.

62. The potential of a less adversarial system to help the NHS develop a more open approach to the reporting of error has been described by Sir Ian Kennedy in his *Learning from Bristol* report. In addition, instituting a more direct link between harm and compensation through an administrative system could provide an added incentive to invest in the prevention of adverse events—something which the remote and lengthy litigation process does not currently deliver.

63. There have been a variety of reforms of the tort system in recent years, most significantly those following on from proposals made by Lord Woolf in 1996. These have been set out in more detail in the preceding Chapters. In summary, they were designed to improve access to justice, speed up the judicial process and to reduce the number and cost of experts involved in a case. They were also designed to encourage alternatives to court action to resolve disputes and facilitate agreement on compensation. Many of those commenting to the review suggested that these and other initiatives currently in the pipeline, for example, the legislation to allow courts to order periodical payments to settle claims rather than a lump sum, would in themselves be sufficient to address problems and concerns relating to the legal process for resolving medical disputes.

NOTE:

1. *Making Amends* comprehensively sets out the systems operating in other jurisdictions. No-fault schemes operate in New Zealand and Scandinavia. The operation of no-fault schemes in New Zealand have been controversial due to the cost of the system, and the definition of "medical misadventure" under the legislation has led to difficulties in practice and inhibited claims (see further K. Oliphant, "Defining Medical Misadventure: Lessons from New Zealand" (1996) 4 *Medical Law Review* 1). One problem with no-fault schemes is, clearly, their cost. This was one reason for the legislative reform of the New Zealand scheme in 1992. The Accident Rehabilitation and Compensation Insurance Act 1992 provides that compensation may only be claimed where disability is severe and a rare occurence.

Causation can be a considerable obstacle within a no-fault system. This was considered further by the Pearson Commission in their earlier report in 1978.

Royal Commission on Civil Liability and Compensation for Personal Injury (Pearson Commission) 1978, Cmnd. 7054, paras 1363–1369

ESTABLISHING CAUSATION

1364 The main problem with a no-fault scheme is how to establish causation, since the cause of many injuries cannot be identified. The Medical Research Council said that while future research was likely to establish more causal relationships it would also reveal increasingly complex interactions which would heighten the problems of proving causation in the individual case.

1365 Even with our definition of medical injury we were forced to conclude that in practice there would be difficulty in distinguishing medical accident from the natural progression of a disease or injury, and from a foreseeable side effect of treatment. It is quite normal for a patient not to recover completely for several weeks or months after a major operation: for complications to ensue after operations: and for a patient to find that the drugs prescribed cause serious side effects.

1366 How should words like "expected" or "foreseeable" be interpreted? Even rare side effects such as vaccine damage not caused by medical negligence are often foreseeable in the sense that they are well known to medical science. If such injuries were to be included in a no-fault scheme, where would the line be drawn between them and accepted risks of treatment? If they were to be excluded, the scheme would do little more than convert the negligence test of tort into a statutory formula, thereby making it easier for the victims of negligence to obtain compensation, but doing nothing for those suffering medical injury from other causes.

1367 In establishing causation, who should take the decision? We envisage that a no-fault scheme would be the responsibility of the DHSS. The use of its adjudication procedures however, would either place more burdens on the medical manpower available, or would put the onus of making the initial decision on the shoulders of junior officials who have neither the experience or training to determine those issues.

1368 To establish causation would involve deciding whether the condition was the result of the treatment and, if so, whether it was the result that might have been expected. This would have to be disentangled from the conditions resulting from the progress of the disease or advancing age or from some other purely fortutious cicumstances.

1369 It is easy to distinguish the completely unexpected result from that which was expected. The gray areas in between pose serious difficulties in knowing where to draw the line.

NOTE:

1. Though the Pearson Commission rejected the adoption of a comprehensive system of liability for medical injuries, it did recommend a limited scheme of this kind in relation to persons suffering vaccine damage (para. 1407).

Vaccine Damage Payments Act 1979, s.1(1–4), s.2(1–3)

1.—(1) If, on consideration of a claim, the Secretary of State is satisfied:

(a) that a person is, or was immediately before his death, severely disabled as a result of vaccination against any of the diseases to which this Act applies; and
(b) that the conditions of entitlement which are applicable in accordance with section 2 below are fulfilled,

he shall in accordance with this Act make a payment of the relevant statutory sum to or for the benefit of that person or to his personal representatives.

(1A) In subsection (1) above "statutory sum" means [£100,000] or such other sum as is specified by the Secretary of State for the purposes of this Act by order made by statutory instrument with the consent of the Treasury: and the relevant statutory sum for the purposes of that subsection is the statutory sum at the time when a claim for payment is first made.

(2) The diseases to which this Act applies are:

(a) diphtheria,
(b) tetanus,
(c) whooping cough,
(d) poliomyelitis,
(e) measles,
(f) rubella,
(g) tuberculosis,
(h) smallpox, and
(i) any other disease which is specified by the Secretary of State for the purposes of this Act by order made by statutory instrument.

(3) Subject to section 2(3) below, this Act has effect with respect to a person who is severely disabled as a result of a vaccination given to his mother before he was born as if the vaccination had been given directly to him and, in such circumstances, as may be prescribed by regulations under this Act, this Act has effect with respect to a person who is severely disabled as a result of contracting a disease through contact with a third person who was vaccinated against it as if the vaccination had been given to him and the disablement resulted from it.

(4) For the purposes of this Act a person is severely disabled if he suffers disablement to the extent of 60 per cent., or more, . . .

2.—(1) Subject to the provisions of this section, the conditions of entitlement referred to in section 1(1)(b) above are:

(a) that the vaccination in question was carried out:
     (i) in the United Kingdom or the Isle of Man, and
     (ii) on or after 5th July 1948, and
     (iii) in the case of vaccination against smallpox, before 1st August, 1971;
(b) except in the case of vaccination against poliomyelitis or rubella, that the vaccination was carried out either at a time when the person to whom it was given was under the age of eighteen or at the time of the outbreak within the United Kingdom or Isle of Man of the disease against which the vaccination was given; and
(c) that the disabled person was over the age of two on the date when the claim was made or, if he died before that date, that he died after 9th May 1978 and was over the age of two when he died.

(2) An order under section 1(2)(i) above specifying a disease for the purposes of this Act may provide that, in relation to vaccination against that disease, the conditions of entitlement specified in subsection (1) above shall have effect subject to such modifications as may be specified in the order.

(3) In a case where this Act has effect by virtue of section 1(3) above, the reference in subsection 1(b) above to the person to whom a vaccination was given is a reference to the person to whom it was actually given and not the disabled person.

NOTES:

1. Section 1(3) extends the compensation entitlement to two classes of person who have not themselves been vaccinated: those affected by the vaccination of their mother prior to their birth and those who contract one of the specified diseases by virtue of contact with someone who has been vaccinated.
2. The Act embodies a causation requirement that the disease must be contracted "as a result" of vaccination. Under s.3(5) of the Act, the causal link, in common with the law of negligence, must be established on the balance of probabilities. This can be problematic, as illustrated by *Loveday v Renton* [1990] 1 Med. L.R. 117 where the plaintiff failed to satisfy the court that pertussis vaccine was the cause of brain damage suffered. The effect of the decision in *Loveday* was dramatic. Following the case, the number of successful claims plummeted to almost nil. A further problem facing potential claimants under the scheme is that it was held in *DHSS v Kinnear* (1984) 134 N.L.J. 886 that a policy decision of the Department of Health to promote vaccination is non-justiciable.
3. The "statutory sum" is currently fixed at £100,000 for claims made on or after July 22, 2000 (Statutory Sum Order 2000, SI 2000/1983, art 2).

4. One aspect of a no-fault scheme is that it may not provide a sufficient deterrent for health professionals to avoid negligent conduct in the future (see further Royal Commission on Civil Liability and Compensation for Personal Injury (1978) Cmnd. 7054). It may be the case that an effective no-fault scheme needs to be accompanied by a revision of the system of professional discipline and accountability (see further on this issue Chapter 4 below).

QUESTION:

1. Would it be fair to grant compensation to patients regardless of whether their injury was caused by careless treatment, while others—for example, those injured in road accidents—would still need to prove negligence?

Ultimately the Chief Medical Officer's report, *Making Amends*, rejected the introduction of such a general no-fault scheme at the present time, fundamentally on the basis of cost.

Making Amends: a consultation paper setting out the proposals for reforming the approach to clinical negligence in the NHS, Department of Health, 2003

In summary, the advantages of a comprehensive no fault compensation system are said to be that: claims are settled more quickly (months rather than years for many no-fault schemes);

- administrative and legal costs per claim are lower (for example, tort costs in Florida can account for up to 40% of the award, yet the no-fault scheme spends less than 5% of its expenditure on legal advice);
- patients are clearer about the circumstances when they will receive compensation;
- there is reduced conflict between clinicians and claimants; because of the removal of "blame", clinicians are more willing to report adverse events and repetition can be avoided.

9. However, there are also potential disadvantages:

- overall costs are far higher than under equivalent tort systems because of a lower threshold for claiming (i.e. no need to prove negligence) and increased numbers of claims;
- for a no-fault scheme to be affordable compensation would need to be at substantially lower levels than tort awards currently, which would not necessarily meet the needs of the harmed patient (for example, average tort payments in the UK (1996 prices) were £45,957 whilst those in Sweden and
- New Zealand were only £6,107 and £3,115 respectively (1996 prices));
- on a technical level, it would be difficult to distinguish harm from the natural progression of a disease.

OVERALL COSTS OF NO-FAULT BASED SCHEMES.

10. Although not the sole factor, the costs of any no-fault based scheme are important for the NHS. Every penny spent on compensation is money that could otherwise be spent providing health care. Costs are also a concern for the no-fault schemes already established and it is informative to see how the schemes have responded to this. Each scheme includes

tests to limit access to compensation or caps on the compensation that can be awarded. For example, the scheme in New Zealand incorporates tests of "medical mishap" and "medical error"; these re-introduce concepts similar to Bolam around "reasonable standard of care and skill" as well as a rarity test.

11. Research was commissioned to assess the cost of a comprehensive no-fault based compensation scheme in the NHS. Two types of scheme were tested. First a scheme based on causation alone, which would be most like "true" no fault, as to obtain compensation the injured patient would only have to demonstrate that their treatment caused the injury leading to their claim. Second, a scheme similar to that in Sweden was modelled, based on the concept of "preventability". Compensation would be paid only where the injury might have been prevented (whilst still providing treatment). Administration costs were estimated using a range of values reflecting the costs of different levels of investigation (range £350 per case to £4,100 per case).

12. The percentage of cases to be compensated was estimated using information from the Swedish scheme. The number of likely applicants was estimated from information from the MORI survey of those who believed that they had been injured as a result of medical treatment in recent years (which gave an estimate of just over 800,000 preventable adverse events per year). Finally, the level of compensation awarded was estimated using the present level of damages (it was assumed that the same type of injuries would occur under a no-fault scheme as occur under tort). Assumed damages payments were reduced by 25% and 50% from present levels to reflect the restrictions in other no-fault schemes which result in compensation at levels much lower than English tort claims.

13. I have concluded that in addition to the disadvantages set out above, a comprehensive no-fault scheme was unaffordable for the NHS. Estimates suggest that even with a 25% reduction in the current level of compensation the cost of a true no-fault scheme would vary between £1.6bn per year (if 19% of eligible claimants claimed) to almost £4bn (if 28% of eligible claimants claimed). This compares with the £400 million spent on clinical negligence in 2000/01.

NOTE:

1. The Report also commented that consequent upon Article 6 of the ECHR it would be necessary to have some form of hearing allowing both parties the right to present their case which would also give rise to enhanced costs (paras 14–15).

QUESTION:

1. Do you agree with the conclusions of *Making Amends*?
2. To what extent do no-fault schemes provide an effective response to the problems of the medical negligence system? (See further S. McClean, "Can No Fault Analysis Ease the Problems of Medical Injury Litigation" and M. Brazier, "The Case for a No-Fault Scheme for Medical Accidents" in S. McLean (ed.), *Compensation for Damage: an International Perspective*, Aldershot: Dartmouth, 1993).

(ii) Strict Liability

Closely related to a system of no-fault compensation is one based on strict liability. The fact of having suffered harm, together with the ability to establish causation, would be the only pre-requisites to compensation. Such a scheme was considered in the Pearson Report 1978.

Report of the Royal Commission on Civil Liability and Compensation for Personal Injury (Pearson Commission), 1978, Cmnd. 7054, paras 1337–1338

1337 We also considered whether strict liability should be introduced. Whilst this would avoid the difficulties of proving or disproving negligence, there would remain the difficulty of proving that the injury was a medical accident, that is to say that it would not have occurred in any event. It would be necessary to define the area to be covered. For example, the foreseeable result of medical treatment such as amputation of a limb in a case of gangrene would not be included. The problems in defining the scope of medical injuries to be included would be the same as those we consider later in connection with the possibility of introducing a no-fault scheme.

1338 Even if it were possible to limit the scope satisfactorily, the imposition of strict liability, as with reversing the burden of proof, might well lead to an increase in defensive medicine. It would tend to imply rigid standards of professional skill beyond those which the present law requires to be exhibited, and beyond those which (in our view) can fairly be expected. We decided not to recommend that strict liability should be introduced.

NOTE:

1. Today, as we saw above at p.203, a limited strict liability scheme operates under the auspices of the Consumer Protection Act 1987.

(iii) Reforming the System: a Combination of Approaches

Making Amends: a consultation paper setting out the proposals for reforming the approach to clinical negligence in the NHS, Department of Health, 2003—Recommendations

. . . the recommendations which follow are aimed at fundamental reform. They do not propose removing the patient's right to sue an NHS doctor or provider of care, but they move the role of tort from its current central position to the outer perimeter of the NHS. All of the recommendations will be the subject of detailed consultation and in particular, consideration of their potential impact on policies on a range of benefits and the way in which these are delivered. The recommendations apply to England only.

Recommendation 1: An NHS Redress Scheme should be introduced to provide investigations when things go wrong; remedial treatment, rehabilitation and care where needed; explanations and apologies; and financial compensation in certain circumstances.

Harm to a patient may come to light as the result of an adverse event, a complaint, or a claim from a solicitor. In all cases, the response should be:

- an investigation of the incident which is alleged to have caused harm and of the harm that has resulted;
- provision of an explanation to the patient of what has happened and why and the action proposed to prevent repetition;
- the development and delivery of a package of care, providing remedial treatment, therapy and arrangements for continuing care where needed.

The proposed NHS Redress Scheme would provide a mechanism for organising this response and in suitable cases considering whether payment for pain and suffering, for out of pocket expenses and for care or treatment which the NHS could not provide should be made. The requirement would be to reach a decision on the case within six months from the initial approach from the patient. The new NHS Redress Scheme is centred on the needs of NHS patients, initially those treated in hospital and community health settings. Further consideration will be given to redress for patients treated under NHS funding arrangements but by independent or voluntary sector providers in the United Kingdom or abroad.

Routes of access to the Scheme

Access to the Scheme and to the package of care and possible financial compensation for an adverse outcome of NHS care would be:

- following a local investigation of the adverse event or of a complaint;
- following an independent review of a complaint by the Commission for Healthcare Audit and Inspection (this body is a new health inspectorate which it is proposed, subject to Parliamentary approval, will inspect the quality of local NHS services as well as investigate NHS complaints not resolved at local level);
- following a recommendation by the Health Services Commissioner (who will investigate complaints not resolved by the Commission for Healthcare Audit and Inspection);
- following investigation of a claim made directly by a patient or relatives to the NHSLA.

Criteria for payment

The criteria for receiving payment would be that:

- there were serious shortcomings in the standards of care;
- the harm could have been avoided;
- the adverse outcome was not the result of the natural progression of the illness.

Elements of compensation package

In the short-term, the capacity of the NHS to provide packages of care may be limited and financial recompense may be offered as an alternative. However, the Scheme should encourage the development of this capacity over time. It is envisaged that case managers would be needed under the auspices of the successor body to the NHSLA, to develop care packages and monitor their implementation.

The financial element of the compensation would be limited to:

- the notional cost of the episode of care or other amount as appropriate, at the discretion of the local NHS Trust;
- up to £30,000 where authorised by the national body managing the new scheme (i.e. a successor to the NHSLA—see recommendation 3).

The advantages of the proposed scheme over the current arrangements are that there would be a full investigation of the complaint or claim; development of a package of the remedial care and rehabilitation where required; faster resolution and an offer of compensation where due; and reduction in legal costs as it would not be necessary for lawyers routinely to be involved. The scheme should be piloted within the scope of existing legislation to help with framing the detail of new primary legislation. This will build on earlier "fast-track" scheme pilots and allow the logistics and acceptability of the scheme to be assessed. Under current legislation the pilot will need to be based on a "*Bolam*" test of clinical negligence. However, the pool of cases submitted in the pilot will also be assessed against alternative tests by a medico-legal panel. This will both inform the exact phrasing of the test and also help gauge in more detail the potential impact on the likely number of successful claims and their costs of using a lower qualifying threshold of "sub-standard care".

Recommendation 2: The NHS Redress Scheme should encompass care and compensation for severely neurologically impaired babies, including those with severe cerebral palsy.

Cerebral palsy and birth-related neurological injury are amongst the most complex claims currently handled by the NHSLA and receive some of the largest compensation payments. However, because of the difficulty in proving both causation and negligence, one small group receives compensation while another larger cohort does not. Boundaries are always difficult to draw, as some hard cases will fall the wrong side of the line. However, it is proposed that the remit of the new NHS Redress Scheme should better meet the needs of more of these severely neurologically impaired children and their families.

Eligibility criteria

The following eligibility criteria to qualify for inclusion in the Scheme would apply:

- birth under NHS care;
- severe neurological impairment (including cerebral palsy) related to or resulting from the birth;
- a claim made to the Scheme within eight years of the birth;
- the care package and compensation would be based on a severity index judged according to the ability to perform the activities of daily living;
- genetic or chromosomal abnormality would be excluded.

The package of compensation

Redress would be provided in cash and in kind, according to the needs of the child for assistance with the tasks of daily living resulting from the severity of impairment and would comprise:

- a managed care package;
- a monthly payment for the costs of care which cannot be provided through a care package (in the most severe cases this could be up to £100,000 per annum);
- lump sum payments for home adaptations and equipment at intervals throughout the child's life (in the most severe cases this could be up to £50,000);
- an initial payment in compensation for pain, suffering and loss of amenity capped at £50,000.

Assessment under the Scheme

The scheme would be administered by a national body building on the work of the NHSLA, on application from the parents. A national panel of experts would review the severity of impairment and causation (i.e. whether the impairment related to or resulted from the birth). The advantages of such a scheme would be to make compensation and support available to a wider range of severely disabled babies and children without the need to establish negligence or fault. It would also control costs to the NHS by meeting the actual care needs as they arose. During the consultation period the Department of Health will be working with families with children suffering from severe neurological impairment and their representatives and with expert clinicians and care workers in this field to develop the basis of the severity index for assessing the care package.

Recommendation 3: A national body building on the work of the NHS Litigation Authority should oversee the NHS Redress Scheme and manage the financial compensation element at national level.

The role of the NHSLA since it was established in 1995 has been impressive. It is proposed that a national authority be established with a widened remit to manage the new scheme. The name of the Authority should be changed to reflect the new emphasis of the scheme.

The role of the national body should encompass eight main functions:

- assessing claims or recommendations for NHS compensation payments from patients or families, NHS service providers, the Commission for Healthcare Audit and Inspection, and the Health Service Commissioner;
- allocating compensation payments based on the merits of the claim or recommendation up to a maximum of £30,000 (except for neurologically impaired babies);
- assessing claims and developing packages of care and compensation under the scheme for severely neurologically impaired babies;
- levying "insurance" payments from NHS service providers to fund the new schemes;
- monitoring the provision of care and rehabilitation packages under the scheme at local level;
- monitoring the local and national compensation payments made and publishing annual listings by NHS providers to act as an incentive to reduce risk and improve patient safety at local level;
- assessing and managing claims for care (other than neurologically impaired babies) where damages of greater than £30,000 are progressing under the tort system;
- continuing to manage older medical negligence claims for care given prior to the date of introduction of the new scheme.

Recommendation 4: Subject to evaluation after a reasonable period consideration should be given to extending the scheme to a higher monetary threshold and to primary care settings.

Bringing claims against general practitioners and other primary care professionals within the scheme would extend the benefits of a faster, less litigious process to general practitioners' patients. It would also ensure that provision of care and levels of compensation were equitable between hospital and primary care patients.

Recommendation 5: The right to pursue litigation would not be removed for patients or families who chose not to apply for packages of care and payment under the NHS Redress Scheme. However, patients accepting a package under the Scheme would not subsequently be able to litigate for the same injury through the courts.

Patients or families would retain the right to pursue litigation for clinical negligence under the tort system instead of applying to the NHS Redress Scheme and for claims above the limit of the scheme. However, where a patient enters into the NHS Redress Scheme and accepts a Redress package, they should not subsequently be able to litigate on the same case. The faster decision, care and compensation package together with an explanation and apology should offer a fairer alternative to those harmed than an uncertain litigation process. It is envisaged that before accepting an offer under the NHS Redress Scheme, a small amount of money would be made available to patients to allow them to seek independent advice on the fairness of the offer.

Recommendation 6: A new standard of care should be set for after event/after-complaint management by local NHS providers.

Despite NHSLA guidance to NHS Trusts (most recently in 2002) to encourage apologies being offered at a senior level, claimants and patient groups are still not receiving what they regard as genuine apologies or full explanations in all cases. Each adverse event or complaint should have a full and objective investigation of the facts of the case, commensurate with the severity of the harm, so that patients or their families are provided with a full explanation of what has happened, an apology where something has gone wrong, and a specification of the action (local and national) being taken to reduce the risk of a similar event happening to future patients.

The explanation should be written in simple non-technical terms and should be given to the patient or family with an offer for follow-up discussion if they wish it. Where a service improvement is being implemented, the patient or family should be invited back to the hospital to see or hear about it when implementation is complete. In addition, under the proposed NHS Redress Scheme, NHS Trusts should take early action to offer any remedial treatment or rehabilitation measures that may be indicated to counteract the harm suffered. A senior level member of staff should take responsibility for co-ordinating the immediate response, communicating with the patient or family and liaising with case managers for the development of more complex packages of care and rehabilitation. The benefits of such an approach will be improved "after care" of those receiving a very bad outcome of care. The provision of remedial treatment at an early stage should reduce suffering and the long-term effects of any harm, with obvious benefits to the patient and savings to the NHS. Each NHS Trust would be required to publish information annually on the payments made under the new scheme.

A new standard should be set covering these areas and the new Commission for Healthcare Audit and Inspection should assess compliance with it in inspections.

Recommendation 7: Within each NHS Trust, an individual at Board level should be identified to take overall responsibility for the investigation of and learning from adverse events, complaints and claims.

The techniques of root cause analysis, for which training is being developed by the NPSA in the context of adverse events, are equally applicable to complaints. In essence, the aim is to look for the reasons why an event happened, along a causal chain, rather than seek to allocate blame to a single individual. A full investigation of this kind not only allows for a full explanation to be given to the patient but can also identify the action necessary to prevent repetition. Patients should be told what that action is, and where possible and appropriate provided with evidence of the changes made. Bringing together the investigation of problems in service delivery, however identified, at a senior level will facilitate learning and remedial action.

Recommendation 8: The rule in the current NHS Complaints Procedures requiring a complaint to be halted pending resolution of a claim should be removed as part of the reform of the complaints procedure.

An investigation should automatically take place as part of the initial local response to a complaint. This may reveal a situation where development of a package of care or treatment and consideration of financial recompense under the NHS Redress Scheme may be appropriate. However, even in the larger value cases, if patients subsequently decide to pursue the litigation route, the complaints process should continue to provide the explanations which patients and families seek. The anticipated benefit is that this may reduce rather than increase the number of people who pursue a formal litigation process and may reduce the dissatisfaction complainants and claimants currently feel at the end of the process.

Recommendation 9: Training should be provided for NHS staff in communication in the context of complaints, from the initial response to the complaint through to conciliation and providing explanations to patients and families.

While it is easy to say that complaints should be welcomed as a means of improving services, it is a very human response to feel undermined and personally criticised. In addition, many patients and families will be distressed and angry when they or a loved one have been harmed. Training for staff at all levels will help overcome the defensive reaction which most claimants and complainants feel is the current automatic response to their concerns. The introduction of the Patient Advice and Liaison Services are the first stage in this process but it is vital that communications throughout each NHS Trust are focussed on the needs of patients and their families.

Recommendation 10: Effective rehabilitation services for personal injury, including that caused by medical accidents, should be developed.

Dedicated rehabilitation services are not widely available for those injured as a result of treatment or otherwise. Some other countries place far greater emphasis on the state to provide rehabilitation services and on the patient to follow an agreed rehabilitation programme. Research demonstrates that effective rehabilitation can lead to shorter periods of hospitalisation, hasten recovery and help prevent long term disability. In the short-term, the current NHSLA pilot scheme to offer early rehabilitation in suitable clinical negligence cases should proceed and be subject to independent evaluation. In the longer term, the development of rehabilitation packages should form part of the NHS Redress Scheme. In addition, attention should be given to the development of rehabilitation services as part of the Long Term Conditions National Service Framework. There is an ongoing cross-Departmental review of Employers' Liability Insurance. Given the prominence in that review of discussions on rehabilitation, work to support the development of rehabilitation services should be mindful of the outcomes of the review.

Recommendation 11: The Department of Health together with other relevant agencies should consider the scope for providing more accessible high quality but lower cost facilities for severely neurologically impaired and physically disabled children, regardless of cause.

Special care and education facilities for severely brain damaged and physically disabled children are currently provided in the private sector, at high cost. There are a limited number of such facilities and the lack of geographic spread often contributes to the need for families to establish their own facilities at home. The potential for developing a network of high quality but lower cost facilities should be explored with SCOPE and other patient and carer groups.

Recommendation 12: A duty of candour should be introduced together with exemption from disciplinary action when reporting incidents with a view to improving patient safety.

In 1987, Sir John Donaldson, then Master of the Rolls said "I personally think that in professional negligence cases, and in particular in medical negligence cases, there is a duty of candour resting on the professional man". There has however been no binding decision of the courts on whether such a duty exists. The Law Society's code of professional conduct for solicitors requires them to notify their clients if they become aware of a possible negligent act or omission. Such a duty, which would give statutory force to the General Medical Council's Code of Good Medical Practice for doctors, should be introduced in legislation to require all healthcare professionals and managers to inform patients where they become aware of a possible negligent act or omission. The concomitant of the duty of candour should be provisions providing for exemption from disciplinary action by employers or professional regulatory bodies for those reporting adverse events except where the healthcare professional has committed a criminal offence or it would not be safe for the professional to continue to treat patients.

Recommendation 13: Documents and information collected for identifying adverse events should be protected from disclosure in court.

A statutory provision should be introduced to provide legal protection for adverse event reports provided locally or to national bodies such as the NPSA. This would ensure that such documents could not be compelled to be produced in a court and would reduce the disincentive to the reporting of errors. Such a provision would seek to balance competing public interest in encouraging healthcare professionals to report adverse events and the public or individual interest in access to information about those incidents. The protection would only apply to reports of adverse events where full information on the event is also included in the medical record. Information for a court action would have to be gathered afresh, from the medical record and other sources. Such protection for adverse events reports would follow the practice in Canada, some US States and Australia.

Recommendation 14: Where a claimant was seeking Legal Aid to pursue a claim for clinical negligence, the Legal Services Commission should take into account whether or not the case had already been pursued through the NHS Redress Scheme.

The results of the investigation undertaken to inform decisions on eligibility and level of award under the NHS Redress Scheme would provide valuable information to the LSC in deciding whether or not to support an application for Legal Aid to someone pursuing a claim for clinical negligence where they had not accepted a package of care and compensation under the scheme. For the claims eligible for the NHS Redress Scheme, the expectation would be that they would have been pursued through that route, to protect the public purse from the unnecessary expenditure on Legal Aid in lower value cases (this would not apply to cerebral palsy cases). Existing powers should be sufficient to enable the LSC to act on this recommendation but in the longer term the approach should be built into the Commission's Funding Code criteria.

Recommendation 15: Mediation should be seriously considered before litigation for the majority of claims which do not fall within the proposed NHS Redress Scheme.

The successor body to the NHSLA should require their panel solicitor firms to consider every case for mediation and to offer mediation where appropriate. Mediation is not a cheap alternative to litigation. However, it can offer claimants the package of measures they say they seek: apologies, explanations, an opportunity to discuss the issues with the healthcare providers face to face and to explore issues other than financial compensation. It can also be followed by an out-of-court settlement of a large claim.

To encourage increased take-up of mediation, improved information is required for NHS staff, for Patient Advice and Liaison Services and for Independent Complaints Advocacy Services on what mediation entails and the cases for which it may be suitable. The Department of Health and the NHSLA should develop work to provide this.

In addition a larger pool of trained and accredited mediators is necessary to ensure that appropriate expertise is readily available. The Department of Health, the Department for Constitutional Affairs, and the LSC should build on the initial feasibility study work supported by the LSC, NHSLA, AVMA and CEDR to support the establishment of an advanced clinical negligence mediation training and accreditation programme and to test and evaluate a preliminary process review to explore the suitability of mediation or other forms of dispute resolution in particular cases.

Recommendation 16. The expectation in paying damages for future care costs and losses in clinical negligence cases not covered by the new NHS Redress Scheme should be that periodical payments will be used.

The Courts Bill includes provision to give the courts power to make an order for periodical payments without the consent of the parties. Such payments can provide certainty for claimants that future care needs will be met and avoid distressing arguments about the life expectancy of the victim. It will also allow the NHS to spread its expenditure in large value cases. The Government has indicated during passage of the Bill that the circumstances in which periodical payments can be varied will be tightly drawn to avoid frequent return to the courts for reassessment. However, the legislation will only impact directly on cases decided in the courts, which is less than 1% of clinical negligence claims.

Although the NHSLA has no power to impose periodical payments in cases where settlements are negotiated outside the NHS Redress Scheme, the new legislation should help promote the widespread use of periodical payments by the courts so that the expectation in clinical negligence cases will become that these will apply. This will provide the lead for those negotiating settlements and in time lead to acceptance of periodical payments in negotiated cases.

Recommendation 17: The costs of future care included in any award for clinical negligence made by the courts should no longer reflect the cost of private treatment.

Section 2(4) of the Law Reform (Personal Injury) Act 1948 provides for the care costs component of an award for damages to be based on the costs of private rather than NHS treatment. This applies to all personal injury claims. It is recommended that the law should be changed to exempt clinical negligence cases arising from NHS treatment from this provision. Instead, as part of any settlement, the NHS defendant should undertake to fund a specified package of care or treatment to defined timescales. It is envisaged that case managers under the auspices of the national body administering the NHS Redress Scheme would develop care packages and monitor their delivery to avoid patients having to deal with the NHS Trust where they had suffered harm. Initially at least, the costs may be similar to providing a sum of money to purchase private care as the NHS would have to fund elements of the care package privately and from a variety of sources. However, this recommendation fits well with the vision for the future of the NHS which offers and responds to patients' choices by sourcing the necessary care and treatment from a range of providers.

Recommendation 18: Special training should be provided for Judges hearing clinical negligence cases.

The clinical negligence cases that reach court can be highly complex. They are also infrequent, meaning that any one judge will see clinical negligence cases only rarely. If the introduction of the NHS Redress Scheme is successful, this problem will be exacerbated in the future. Although the nature of these cases is such that a diet consisting only of clinical negligence cases is likely to be unpalatable, the provision of specialist training in medical issues as recommended by Lord Woolf would be beneficial.

NOTES:

1. The report also recommended that the Department for Constitutional Affairs and the Legal Services Commission should further consider mechanisms to control claimants' costs in publicly funded clinical negligence cases (recommendation 19).
2. There is generally a heightened awareness that malpractice solutions need to viewed holistically. There has been increasing concentration on reviewing medical errors outside the courtroom with a more pro-active approach to risk management. An important part is played by the National Patient Safety Agency in collating information with the aim of improving safety. Similarly the Healthcare Commission (see Chapter 1) has an important role to play in promoting standards of care.

3. Questions were raised as to how the compensation scheme for neuro-logically impaired babies would operate and, in relation to situations where deaths had resuled, who would select the adjudicators and claim handlers and how would they operate. (See D. Brahams, "The CMO's Report: Making Amends—A Response" (2003) *Medico-Legal Journal* 71.) Brahams also noted that the report left open as to the procedure and questioned whether the procedures should be adversarial, inquisitorial or a hybrid, enabling submissions to be made by claimants but then for the issues to be investigated. In addition there was a need for consideration as to what appeal procedure should be put into place. She also questions how the care packages would work. Would they involve the purchase of services within the NHS or would they allow vouchers to purchase care in the private sector? She suggests that there needs to be an effective system to feed back data to ensure that there can be effective learning from mistakes by the NHS.

Following *Making Amends*, in November 2005 Lord Warner introduced a NHS Redress Bill into the House of Lords, based on the Chief Medical Officer's Report (see M. Rowles, "Does the Redress Bill Make Amends?" (2005) N.L.J. 1918).

NHS Redress Bill 2005

Power to establish redress scheme

1—(1) The Secretary of State may by regulations establish a scheme for the purpose of enabling redress to be provided without recourse to civil proceedings in circumstances in which this section applies.

(2) This section applies where under the law of England and Wales qualifying liability in tort on the part of a body or other person mentioned in subsection (3) arises in connection with the provision, as part of the health service in England, of services in a hospital (in England or elsewhere).

(3) The bodies and other persons referred to are—

(a)   the Secretary of State,
(b)   a Primary Care Trust,
(c)   a designated Strategic Health Authority, and
(d)   a body or other person providing, or arranging for the provision of, services whose provision is the subject of arrangements with a body or other person mentioned in paragraph (a), (b) or (c).

(4) The reference in subsection (2) to qualifying liability in tort is to liability in tort owed—

(a)   in respect of or consequent upon personal injury or loss arising out of or in connection with breach of a duty of care owed to any person in connection with the diagnosis of illness, or the care or treatment of any patient, and
(b)   in consequence of any act or omission by a health care professional.

(5) In subsection (3)(d), the reference to a person providing services does not include a person providing services under a contract of employment.

(6) In subsection (4), the reference to a health care professional is to a member of a profession (whether or not regulated by, or by virtue of, any enactment) which is concerned (wholly or partly) with the physical or mental health of individuals.

(7) The Secretary of State may by regulations specify circumstances in which services that—

(a) are not provided in a hospital, but
(b) are of a kind that are normally so provided, are to be treated for the purposes of this section as provided in a hospital.

Application of scheme

2—(1) Subject to subsection (2), a scheme may make such provision defining its application as the Secretary of State thinks fit.

(2) A scheme must provide that it does not apply in relation to a liability that is or has been the subject of civil proceedings.

Redress under scheme

3—(1) Subject to subsections (2) and (5), a scheme may make such provision as the Secretary of State thinks fit about redress under the scheme.

(2) A scheme must provide for—

(a) the making of an offer of compensation in satisfaction of any right to bring civil proceedings in respect of the liability concerned, and
(b) the giving of an explanation, except in specified circumstances.

(3) A scheme may, in particular—

(a) make provision for the compensation that may be offered to take the form of entry into a contract to provide care or treatment or of financial compensation, or both;
(b) make provision about the circumstances in which different forms of compensation may be offered.

(4) A scheme that provides for financial compensation to be offered may, in particular—

(a) make provision about the matters in respect of which financial compensation may be offered;
(b) make provision with respect to the assessment of the amount of any financial compensation;
(c) specify an upper limit on the amount of financial compensation that may be included in an offer under the scheme;
(d) specify an upper limit on the amount of financial compensation in respect of a particular matter that may be included in an offer under the scheme.

(5) If a scheme that provides for financial compensation to be offered does not specify an upper limit under subsection (4)(c), it must specify an upper limit under subsection (4)(d) on the amount of compensation for pain and suffering.

Commencement of proceedings under scheme

4—(1) A scheme may make such provision as the Secretary of State thinks fit about the commencement of proceedings under the scheme.

(2) A scheme may, in particular, make provision—

(a) about who may commence proceedings under the scheme;
(b) about how proceedings under the scheme may be commenced;

(c) for time limits in relation to the commencement of proceedings under the scheme;
(d) about circumstances in which proceedings under the scheme may not be commenced;
(e) requiring proceedings under the scheme to be commenced in specified circumstances;
(f) for notification of the commencement of proceedings under the scheme in specified circumstances.

Duty to consider potential application of scheme

5—(1) The Secretary of State may by regulations make provision requiring any body or other person mentioned in subsection (2)—

(a) to consider, in such circumstances as the regulations may provide, whether a case that the body or other person is investigating or reviewing involves liability to which a scheme applies, and
(b) if it appears that it does, to take such steps as the regulations may provide.

(2) The bodies and other persons referred to are—

(a) any body or other person to whose liability a scheme applies, and
(b) the Commission for Healthcare Audit and Inspection.

Proceedings under scheme

6—(1) Subject to subsections (3) and (4), a scheme may make such provision as the Secretary of State thinks fit about proceedings under the scheme.
(2) A scheme may, in particular, make provision—

(a) about the investigation of cases under the scheme;
(b) about the making of decisions about the application of the scheme;
(c) for time limits in relation to acceptance of an offer of compensation under the scheme;
(d) about the form and content of settlement agreements under the scheme;
(e) for settlement agreements under the scheme to be subject in cases of a specified description to approval by a court;
(f) about the termination of proceedings under the scheme.

(3) A scheme must provide for a settlement agreement under the scheme to include a waiver of the right to bring civil proceedings in respect of the liability to which the settlement relates.
(4) A scheme must provide for the termination of proceedings under the scheme if the liability to which the proceedings relate becomes the subject of civil proceedings.

NOTES:

1. The Bill is being promoted as a speedy response to medical negligence issues. In introducing the Bill into the House of House of Lords, the Health Minister stated that "it will mean fairness for patients not fees for lawyers". The Bill itself is heavily dependent upon secondary legislation being introduced.
2. What is notable about the Bill is that, as with several other recent regulatory measures in relation to health care law, a considerable amount

of detail is left to regulations, e.g. in relation to members of the scheme (clause 10). This has the advantage of facilitating the speedy passage of the Bill but of course reduces much of the potential for effective Parliamentary scrutiny of the operation of the scheme.

3. Clause 9 provides for the Secretary of State to make arrangements to such extent as he considers necessary for the provision of assistance by way of representation.
4. Clause 11 provides for the scheme to be regulated by a Special Health Authority established for these purposes and cl.13 provides that this body should co-operate with the Commission for Healthcare Audit and Inspection (the Healthcare Commission).
5. Clause 14 also provides for the Secretary of State to make regulations regarding the consideration of complaints regarding the operation of the scheme.

QUESTION:

1. Does this Bill represent a satisfactory solution to the problems of clinical negligence litigation?

SELECT BIBLIOGRAPHY

A. Bell, "The Doctor and the Supply of Goods and Services Act 1982" (1984) 4 *Legal Studies* 175.

M. Brazier and J. Miola, "Bye-bye Bolam: a Medical Litigation Revolution" (2000) 8 *Medical Law Review* 85.

M. Brazier, "The Case for a No-Fault Compensation Scheme for Medical Accidents" in S. McLean (ed.), *Compensation for Damage: an International Perspective*, Aldershot: Dartmouth, 1993.

P. Case, "Secondary Iatrogenic Harm: claims for Psychiatric Damage Following a Death Caused by Medical Error" (2004) 67 *Modern Law Review* 561.

M. Childs, "Medical Manslaughter and Corporate Liability (1999) 19(3) *Legal Studies* 316.

P. F. Ferguson, *Drug Injuries and the Pursuit of Compensation*, London: Sweet & Maxwell, 1996.

C. Ham, R. Dingwall, P. Fenn and D. Harris, *Medical Negligence: Compensation and Accountability*, Oxford: King's Fund Institute, 1988.

P. Hoyte, "Unsound Practice: the Epiderminology of Medical Negligence" (1995) 3 *Medical Law Review* 53.

M. Jones, "Arbitration for Medical Claims in the National Health Service" (1992) 8 *Professional Negligence* 142.

M. Jones, *Medical Negligence* (3rd edn), London: Sweet & Maxwell, 2003.

A. McCall-Smith, "Criminal Negligence and the Incompetent Doctor" (1993) 1 *Medical Law Review* 33.

K. McK. Norrie, "Common Practice and the Standard of Care in Medical Negligence" [1985] *Juridical Review* 145.

A. Merry and R.A. McCall Smith, *Errors Medicine and the Law*, Cambridge: CUP, 2001.

J. Montgomery, "Medicine, Accountability and Professionalism" (1989) 16 *Journal of Law and Society* 319.

K. Oliphant, "Defining 'Medical Misadventure': Lessons from New Zealand" (1996) 4 *Medical Law Review* 1.

M. Stacey, "Medical Accountability: a Background Paper" in A. Grubb (ed.), *Challenges in Medical Care*, Chichester: John Wiley, 1992.

H. Teff, *Reasonable Care*, Oxford: OUP, 1994.

H. Teff, "The Standard of Care in Medical Negligence—Moving on from Bolam?" (1998) 18 *Oxford Journal of Legal Studies* 473.

Lord Woolf, "Are the Courts Excessively Deferential to the Medical Profession?" (2000) 9 *Medical Law Review* 1.

4

PROFESSIONAL ACCOUNTABILITY II

1. INTRODUCTION

Over the last decade the media spotlight has fallen on health professionals and allegations of misconduct, bad practice and even criminal activity. The medical profession in particular has been hit by such scandals (see further M. Davies, *Medical Regulation: Crisis and Change*, Aldershot: Ashgate, 2006 (forthcoming)). Huge media attention surrounded the investigation into infant mortality at Bristol Royal Infirmary Paediatric Cardiac Unit, chaired by Professor Sir Ian Kennedy (*Learning From Bristol: the Report of the Public Inquiry into Children's Heart Surgery at Bristol Royal Infirmary 1984–1995*, Cm 5702, 2001, *http://www.bristol-inquiry.org.uk*). The inquiry report was a damning condemnation of poor medical practice, documenting numerous failings, including the arrogance and a "club culture" which exemplified practice in that hospital. The impact of the Bristol inquiry report has been felt in a number of areas considered in this book, from organ retention (in relation to the interim report of the inquiry) discussed in Chapter 15 below, to consent to treatment, discussed in Chapter 6, and in relation to medical negligence leading to the Chief Medical Officer's Report, *Making Amends*, discussed in Chapter 4 above. Another tragic indictment of failure of mechanisms of clinical governance and medical regulation was documented in the Shipman Inquiry into the activities of serial killer Dr Harold Shipman. (J. Smith, The Fifth Report of the Shipman Inquiry: *Safeguarding Patients: Lessons from the Past, Proposals for the Future*, *http://www.the-shipman-inquiry.org.uk*). One lesson from both these inquiry reports has been the need for improved clinical governance and for better and more effective regulatory processes. The system of professional accountability post Kennedy and Shipman is still, at the time of writing, the subject of continued evolution. Health professionals may be held to be accountable through audit and scrutiny by agencies such as the National Patient Safety Agency which is concerned with recording errors and failures in NHS practice and through inspections undertaken by the Healthcare Commission (formerly known as the Commission for Health Care Improvement), which has wide-ranging statutory powers of investigation and inspection regarding standards in health care.

In the previous chapter we considered the means by which the healthcare professional may be held accountable for his or her behaviour in the courtroom. However, there also are a number of other ways in which a health professional may be held accountable through complaints processes or through professional regulatory structures. A patient may decide to lodge a complaint about the care he has received. Where complaints are made, in some instances the employer may decide to take disciplinary action against the employee. This is separate from the NHS complaints system.

In addition to the internal systems for complaints within hospitals, the Health Service Commissioner acts as an external regulator or Ombudsman. Patients will usually be expected to refer complaints through the established channels before going to the Commissioner. The Commissioner operates alongside the general complaints process.

The tort system is primarily concerned with affording patients compensation. But there may be instances in which the conduct of a health care professional is sufficiently grave to warrant punishment. In the previous chapter we considered the use of the criminal law in the form of a prosecution for manslaughter when death occurs. However, criminal prosecutions against health care practitioners only occur in rare cases. A more realistic deterrent is afforded through the disciplinary powers of the health professions governing bodies, such as the General Medical Council and the Nursing and Midwifery Council.

There is also oversight of the professional governing bodies in the form of the Council for Healthcare Regulatory Excellence (*www.chre.org.uk*) (initially called the Council for the Regulation of the Health Care Professions). It was established following recommendations made by the Bristol Royal Infirmary Inquiry. This body, which has been operational from April 2003, has the task of promoting best practice and consistency of decision-making across the regulatory bodies (NHS Reform and Health Care Professions Act 2002, s.25). Its powers include the ability to undertake "anything which appears to it to be necessary or expedient for the purpose of, or in connection with, the performance of its functions". It has the power to undertake investigations of the regulatory bodies and issue reports (NHS Reform and Health Care Professions Act 2002, s.26). It may also refer decisions by regulatory bodies concerning findings of professional misconduct and fitness to practice to the High Court where these are "unduly lenient" (s.29). The High Court has a range of powers to dismiss an appeal, allow the appeal and decide to quash the decision, decide to replace the decision of the regulatory body with a decision within the scope of powers of the regulatory body. Alternatively the court can refer the matter to the regulatory body and require it to be determined in accordance with directions given by the court. (*See Council for the Regulation of Health Care Professionals v The General Medical Council and Dr G Ruscillo* [2004] EWHC 527 (Admin), para. 15; and for an example of determination of the court not to intervene, see *Council for the Regulation of Health Care Professionals v The General Medical Council and Dr Solanke* [2004] EWHC 944 (Admin); *Council for the Regulation of Health Care Professionals v Nursing and Midwifery Council and Truscott* [2004] EWHC 585(Admin).)

The changing nature of health care can be seen in the passage of legislation regulating other health care practitioners such as osteopaths and chiropractors.

Health care services are also provided by health professionals, who are governed by their peers outside statute, such as psychotherapists. All these bodies possess some form of professional ethical code (for examples of such codes, see Chapter 2 above). There is usually provision for some form of professional sanctions in situations in which a professional infringes the provisions of his or her code. This chapter considers these mechanisms of accountability. In Section 2 we examine the operation of the NHS patient complaint system. In Section 3 the disciplinary procedures for health care professionals within the NHS are considered. Section 4 discusses the role of the health service commissioner. Section 5 considers professional self-regulation focusing on the disciplinary role of the General Medical Council, an area which has been subject to much scrutiny and recent reform (see further M. Davies, *Medical Self Regulation: Crisis and Change*, Aldershot: Ashgate, 2006 (forthcoming).

2. COMPLAINTS WITHIN THE NHS

The NHS complaints system was the subject of a major reconstruction in 1996 and a further review in 2004. Traditionally there has been a division between the complaints systems operational in relation to family practitioners and those in relation to the hospital system. Hospital complaints were placed on a statutory footing by the Hospital Complaints Act in 1985. This Act was not implemented until 1988, when directions were introduced which stated that an officer within each hospital should be designated to receive complaints (H.C.(88)37). This was usually the unit general manager. Nevertheless, while the complaints system was subject to some reform, problems remained. Not least among these was the complexity of the system. There were a number of avenues through which complaints could be channelled. These were family health service procedures, hospital and community unit procedures, ambulance service procedures, parliamentary procedures such as complaints to a member of Parliament or direct to the Department of Health, or the Health Service Commissioner (for further consideration of his role see below at p.261. A separate procedure dealt with complaints concerning the exercise of clinical judgment.

In response to concerns expressed regarding the operation of the system, the government established the Wilson Committee to consider the complaints system and, where appropriate, to recommend reforms. The Committee's report, *Being Heard*, London: DOH, 1994, was published in 1994. The report highlighted the complexity of the existing system which was accompanied by difficulties for complainants such as lack of information about complaints procedures, delays and problems in obtaining a satisfactory response. It suggested radical reforms be introduced.

(a) The Aims of a Complaints Process

Being Heard: Report of a Review Committee on NHS Complaints Procedures (London: DOH, 1994)

163 In the first place, complaints procedures should be responsive and aim to satisfy complainants. This does not mean that all complainants will be satisfied with the outcome

of their complaint, but the procedure should be directed to satisfying their objectives as well as those of the NHS.

164 As seen in both private and public sectors in Chapter V, complaints provide invaluable management information about the quality of services from the perspective of service users and their families and friends. They can help to identify problems and sometimes suggest solutions. The service improvements this can lead to may be to the benefit of all patients and of those involved in providing services for the NHS.

165 Procedures must be cost effective to operate. Although effective in theory, complaints systems which cannot be implemented because resources are not available benefit no one. Where cash limits apply, it is important that investment in complaint handling is not disproportionate to the resources available to improve services. . . .

166 To satisfy complainants and for management information from complaints to be available, it must be as easy as possible for complainants to make their views known. This should include attempts to reduce potential barriers of class, race, language and literacy, and to recognise the needs of vulnerable groups such as children, people with mental health problems, and people with learning difficulties. Procedures must be well-publicised and understandable to all.

167 Once a complaint is made, both complainant and respondent should be able to expect the matter to be considered impartially. This means that procedures should ensure that different points of view are listened to and investigated without prejudice, and that support should be available to both parties involved. . . .

168 A simple complaints procedure is desirable. It is likely to be more accessible for complainants and easier to use by those operating it. The simplicity of procedures may be constrained by other organisational elements (e.g. the independent contactor status of GPs within the NHS) or by the complexity of the issues involved (e.g. in relation to clinical judgment).

169 Complaints procedures should ensure that complaints receive as fast a response as is possible without jeopardising other principles. This can help to prevent dissatisfaction growing or further complaints arising about delays.

170 Complaints systems should encourage people to complain without fear that their current or future care will be compromised. This is of particular relevance to primary care, to priority care services (for people with learning disabilities, mental illness, long term handicap and so on), and for some patients detained under the Mental Health Act, who may receive long term care from certain staff members or from one particular organisation.

NOTES:

1. Research indicates that people may have other goals in complaining, including obtaining information and wanting changes in policy and practice so that problems do not arise in the future. (See S. Lloyd Bostock and L. Mulcahy, "The Social Psychology of Making and Responding to Hospital Complaints: an Account of Model Complaints Processes" (1994) 16 *Law and Policy* 123.)

2. The Wilson Committee was influenced by complaints procedures operating in the private sector. But it has been questioned whether this approach is in fact directly analogous. (see J. Hanna, "Internal Resolution of NHS Complaints" (1993) 3 *Medical Law Review* 177.) The complaints process within the NHS differs from many external complaints processes, because of the heightened degree of public accountability and because the NHS is a public body.

(b) The Complaints Process

After the publication of *Being Heard* there was a period of formal consultation as to the conclusions/recommendations. The Government then produced a document setting out the proposed new complaints procedure, "Acting on Complaints", in March 1995 (EL(95)37). Interim guidance was published in October 1995, followed by the final guidance in April 1996. The revised structure introduced a two-tier complaints process of "local review" and "independent review" (*Complaints, Listening . . . Acting . . . Improving: Guidance on Implementation of the NHS Complaints Procedure*, NHS Executive, March 1996). The emphasis on informal resolution was indicative of the fact that in many situations the primary objective of the complainant was to obtain an apology and explanation rather than compensation. Both clinical and non-clinical complaints were considered under the same system. At the local stage NHS bodies were required to establish operational complaints procedures. Independent review operated as a more formal second stage. Complaints were to be considered by a panel with an independent lay chair. This structure was subject to criticism because it was insufficiently responsive to patients' needs. This led to a subsequent review and the publication of the document *NHS Complaints Reform: Making Things Right* (London: DOH) in 2003. As part of this review an extensive consultation exercise was undertaken.

NHS Complaints Reform, Making Things Right (London: DOH, 2003)

2.7 In a patient-centred NHS, patients should feel able to express their views—positive and negative, complaints and concerns—about the treatment and services they receive, in the knowledge that they will be:

- taken seriously,
- given a speedy and effective response,
- that their views will inform learning and improvements in service delivery, and
- that there is a system for taking action to address the full range of problems which occur—from minor difficulties to major failures in treatment and care.

2.8 Patients and staff alike have told us—informally, and formally through an independent evaluation study and subsequent listening exercise—that this is often not their experience of the NHS approach to complaints at present. More often:

- it is unclear how, and difficult to, pursue complaints and concerns,
- there is often delay in responding when concerns arise,
- too often there is a negative attitude to concerns expressed,
- complaints don't seem to get a fair hearing,
- patients don't get the support they need when they want to complain,
- the Independent Review stage doesn't have the credibility it needs,
- the process doesn't provide the redress patients want, and
- there does not seem to be any systematic processes for using feedback from complaints to drive improvements in services.

In response the Government enacted the National Health Service (Complaints) Regulations 2004, SI 2004/1764, introducing reform. They decided that the revised complaints process would be introduced on a phased basis after there was representation from the Shipman Inquiry (see J. Smith, *op. cit.*). As a consequence these regulations do not apply to the resolution of complaints which concern G.P.s, dentists, opticians and pharmacists at local level and at present have only partial application to foundation trusts. The system is due to be subject to further amended complaints regulations in 2006 but at the time of writing these have not been issued. Support to patients is also provided through the Patient Advisory and Liaison Service (PALS) which was introduced following the Bristol Inquiry Report to provide increased patient representation. PALS are available in all NHS trusts and provide a link channelling patients to the Independent Complaints Advocacy Service, discussed below at p.25). The current system has however still been the subject of criticism. Recently the Health Service Commissioner—currently Ann Abraham—commented in her annual report that the complaints system which is different for health and for social services means that complainants may have to take complaints concerning their care through different complaints procedures ("Making Things Better?" (2005) at *www.ombudsman.org.uk*. Furthermore she suggested that frequently the first person an individual has to approach concerning a complaint is someone involved in their care and this can act as a deterrent against the resolution of a complaint. (See further Z. Kmietowicz, "NHS Complaints System is Letting Patients down" (2005) 330 B.M.J. 618.)

(i) Local Resolution

Arrangements for the handling and consideration of complaints

National Health Service (Complaints) Regulations 2004, SI 2004/1764

3.—(1) Each NHS body must make arrangements in accordance with these Regulations for the handling and consideration of complaints.

(2) The arrangements must be accessible and such as to ensure that complaints are dealt with speedily and efficiently, and that complainants are treated courteously and sympathetically and as far as possible involved in decisions about how their complaints are handled and considered.

(3) The arrangements must be in writing and a copy must be given, free of charge, to any person who makes a request for one.

(4) Where an NHS trust or a Primary Care Trust makes arrangements for the provision of services with an independent provider, it must ensure that the independent provider has in place arrangements for the handling and consideration of complaints about any matter connected with its provision of services as if these Regulations applied to it.

Guidance to Support Implementation of the NHS (Complaints) Regulations 2004

3.1 NHS bodies must have a well-defined procedure in place for investigating and resolving complaints. The procedure should be open, fair, flexible and conciliatory and should encourage communication on all sides. The primary objective is to resolve the complaint satisfactorily.

3.2 Complaints managers should involve the complainant from the outset and seek to determine what they are hoping to achieve from the process. The complainant should be given the opportunity to understand all possible options for pursuing the complaint, and the consequences of following these options. Throughout the process, the complaints manager should assess what further action might best resolve the complaint. The complainant should be kept informed.

NOTES:

1. The complaints procedure operates at two levels (following the Wilson recommendation), local resolution and independent review. The focus on informal resolution is indicative of the fact that in many situations the complainant's primary objective is obtaining an explanation and an apology rather than compensation. The complaints system maintains a separation of complaints from disciplinary processes. A decision to stop the complaints procedure is only likely to be capable of legal challenge where a body can be shown to have acted unreasonably (*R v Canterbury and Thanet DHA South East Thames RHA, Ex p. Ford W* [1994] 5 Med. L.R. 132).

Responsibility for complaints arrangements

National Health Service (Complaints) Regulations 2004, SI 2004/1764

4. Each NHS body must designate one of its members, or in the case of an NHS trust a member of its board of directors, to take responsibility for ensuring compliance with the arrangements made under these Regulations and that action is taken in the light of the outcome of any investigation.

NOTE:

1. The guidance states that it is a requirement to have senior persons—an executive or non-executive member of the Board—with responsibility for compliance with the Regulations and the complaints process (para. 3.5). The guidance also suggests that the complaints procedure can be linked with those for clinical governance (para. 3.6).

Complaints manager

National Health Service (Complaints) Regulations 2004, SI 2004/1764

5.—(1) Each NHS body must designate a person, in these Regulations referred to as a complaints manager, to manage the procedures for handling and considering complaints and in particular—

(a) to perform the functions of the complaints manager under this Part; and
(b) to perform such other functions in relation to complaints as the NHS body may require.

(2) The functions of the complaints manger may be performed by him or by any person authorised by the NHS body to act on his behalf.

Note:

1. The NHS guidance provides that the exact role and job description of the complaints manager is to be determined by the NHS body (para. 38).

Complaints to NHS bodies

National Health Service (Complaints) Regulations 2004, SI 2004/1764

6. Subject to regulation 7, a complaint to an NHS body may be about any matter reasonably connected with the exercise of its functions including in particular, in the case of an NHS trust or Primary Care Trust, any matter reasonably connected with—

(a) its provision of health care or any other services, including in the case of a Primary Care Trust, its provision of primary medical services under section 16CC of the 1977 Act; and
(b) the function of commissioning health care or other services under an NHS contract or making arrangements for the provision of such care or other services with an independent provider or with an NHS foundation trust.

Matters excluded from the complaints process

National Health Service (Complaints) Regulations 2004, SI 2004/1764

7. The following complaints are excluded from the scope of the arrangements required under this Part—

(a) a complaint made by an NHS body which relates to the exercise of its functions by another NHS body;
(b) a complaint made by a primary care provider which relates either to the exercise of its functions by an NHS body or to the contract or arrangements under which it provides primary care services;
(c) a complaint made by an employee of an NHS body about any matter relating to his contract of employment;
(d) a complaint made by an independent provider or an NHS foundation trust about any matter relating to arrangements made by an NHS body with that independent provider or NHS foundation trust;
(e) a complaint which relates to the provision of primary medical services in accordance with arrangements made by a Primary Care Trust with a Strategic Health Authority under section 28C of the 1977 Act or under a transitional agreement;
(f) a complaint which is being or has been investigated by the Health Service Commissioner;
(g) a complaint arising out of an NHS body's alleged failure to comply with a data subject request under the Data Protection Act 1998 or a request for information under the Freedom of Information Act 2000;
(h) a complaint about which the complainant has stated in writing that he intends to take legal proceedings;
(i) a complaint about which an NHS body is taking or is proposing to take disciplinary proceedings in relation to the substance of the complaint against a person who is the subject of the complaint.

Notes:

1. The guidance provides that where the complaint gives rise to a prima facie case of negligence or likelihood of legal action, then complaints managers

should seek advice from those responsible for risk/claims management (para. 3.13). It is noted that it may be the case that an individual is seeking explanation or apology rather than litigation (para. 3.14) and the fact that there is prima facie evidence of negligence should not delay an explanation/ apology, although the guidance does state that "an apology is not an admission of liability". But if the complainant intends or has begun formal legal action, then the complaints process should be stopped and the complainant informed accordingly (para. 3.16).

2. Disciplinary matters are excluded from the complaints process (para. 3.17) and in relation to primary care providers local disciplinary procedures cannot be undertaken until the Healthcare Commission's investigation has been completed (para. 3.20). The only circumstances in which the complaints process would be halted would be a situation in which it was necessary to protect a patient through involvement of the police or a professional regulatory body (para. 3.20).

3. NHS staff may themselves complain as to the action taken under the complaints process and they can refer their own complaint to the Ombudsman (para. 3.18).

4. If NHS bodies decide to take disciplinary action outside the complaints process, information obtained during the complaints process may be used as part of the disciplinary proceedings (para. 3.19).

5. Grievances of individual staff members are to be dealt with by separate local procedures (para. 3.24).

Further detailed guidance is given in relation to dealing with complaints where this may indicate a serious incident.

Guidance to Support Implementation of the NHS (Complaints) Regulations 2004

3.21 If any complaint received by a member or employee of an NHS body indicates a need for referral to any of the following:

 i) An investigation under the disciplinary procedure;
 ii) One of the professional regulatory bodies;
 iii) An independent inquiry into a serious incident under Section 84 of the National Health Service Act 1977; or
 iv) An investigation of a criminal offence the person in receipt of the complaint should at once pass the complaint to the complaints manager, who will ensure that it is passed on to a suitable person who can make a decision as to whether to initiate such action; the complaints manager may be designated such a suitable person by the NHS body. This reference may be made at any point during any stage of the complaints procedure. However, investigation of other aspects of the complaint will only be taken forward if they do not, or will not, compromise or prejudice the concurrent investigation.

3.22 Where it is decided to take action under any of i–iv above before a complaint investigation has been completed, a full report of the investigation thus far should be made available to the complainant. The complainant should be informed of the expected timeframe of the other investigative process and kept informed of progress. When that process is complete a further response should be sent to the complainant, outlining the outcome and any actions to be taken, being mindful of patient and staff confidentiality at all times.

3.23 When any action under i–iv has been concluded, that part of the original complaint which had been referred to a different procedure should only recommence through the NHS complaints procedure where there are outstanding matters in the complaint that have not been resolved.

Persons who may complain

National Health Service (Complaints) Regulations 2004, SI 2004/1764

8.—(1) A complaint may be made by—

(a) a patient; or
(b) any person who is affected by or likely to be affected by the action, omission or decision of the NHS body which is the subject of the complaint.

(2) A complaint may be made by a person (in these Regulations referred to as a representative) acting on behalf of a person mentioned in paragraph (1) in any case where that person—

(a) has died;
(b) is a child;
(c) is unable by reason of physical or mental incapacity to make the complaint himself; or
(d) has requested the representative to act on his behalf.

(3) In the case of a patient or person affected who has died or who is incapable, the representative must be a relative or other person who, in the opinion of the complaints manager, had or has a sufficient interest in his welfare and is a suitable person to act as representative.

(4) If in any case the complaints manager is of the opinion that a representative does or did not have a sufficient interest in the person's welfare or is unsuitable to act as a representative, he must notify that person in writing, stating his reasons.

(5) In the case of a child, the representative must be a parent, guardian or other adult person who has care of the child and where the child is in the care of a local authority or a voluntary organisation, the representative must be a person authorised by the local authority or the voluntary organisation.

(6) In these Regulations any reference to a complainant includes a reference to his representative.

NOTES:

1. Guidance provides that a potential subject of a complaint may extend beyond medical care (para. 3.25).
2. In a situation in which a representative claims on the behalf of the patient guidance provides that the complaints manager is required to ascertain that the representative has acted with consent (para. 3.26).

The guidance makes particular reference to situations in which the person is incapable or deceased.

Guidance to Support Implementation of the NHS (Complaints) Regulations 2004

3.28 It is for the complaints manager, possibly in discussion with the senior person or chief executive, to determine whether the complainant has "sufficient interest" in the deceased or incapable person's welfare to be suitable to act as a representative. The question of whether a complainant is suitable to represent a patient depends, in particular, on the need to respect the confidentiality of the patient. For example, the patient may earlier have made it known that information should not be disclosed to third parties.

3.29 If the complaints manager determines that a person is not suitable to act as representative, they must provide full information outlining the reasons the decision has been taken.

Making a complaint

National Health Service (Complaints) Regulations 2004, SI 2004/1764

9.—(1) Where a person wishes to make a complaint under these Regulations, he may make the complaint to the complaints manager or any other member of the NHS body which is the subject of the complaint.

(2) A complaint may be made orally or in writing (including electronically) and—

(a) where it is made orally the complaints manager must make a written record of the complaint which includes the name of the complainant, the subject matter of the complaint and the date on which it was made; and
(b) where it is made in writing the complaints manager must make a written record of the date on which it was received.

(3) For the purposes of these Regulations where the complaint is made in writing it is treated as being made on the date on which it is received by the complaints manager or as the case may be, other member of the staff of the NHS body.

NOTES:

1. The NHS Guidance emphasises the need to ensure confidentiality and that information concerning patient's personal information should only be disclosed with their written consent (para. 3.30), although written complaints should be immediately referred to the complaints manager (para. 3.31).
2. The guidance provides that there should be clear local guidance and training which would enable determination of which issues are to be dealt with by front line staff or departmental managers. Complainants are also to be made aware of organisations such as the Independent Complaints Advocacy Service (para. 3.32).
3. The guidance also provides that the patient's immediate health care needs are to be given first priority and may mean that "urgent action" is needed before complaints are resolved (para. 3.33).
4. Patients may also not feel comfortable in referring the complaint to a person involved in their care and the guidance suggests that in such situations they should be advised to refer complaint to complaints manager/senior departmental manager or in writing to the chief executive (para. 3.34).

Time limit for making a complaint

National Health Service (Complaints) Regulations 2004, SI 2004/1764

10.—(1) Subject to paragraph (2) a complaint must be made within—

(a) six months of the date on which the matter which is the subject of the complaint occurred; or
(b) six months of the date on which the matter which is the subject of the complaint came to the notice of the complainant.

(2) Where a complaint is made after the expiry of the period mentioned in paragraph (1), the complaints manager may investigate it if he is of the opinion that—

(a) having regard to all the circumstances, the complainant had good reasons for not making the complaint within that period; and
(b) notwithstanding the time that has elapsed it is still possible to investigate the complaint effectively and efficiently.

NOTES:

1. Guidance provides that in a situation in which the complaint is outside the time limit the admissibility is subject to discretion which should be used "flexibly and with sensitivity" (para. 3.37). It suggests that "An example of where discretion might be exercised would be where the complainant has suffered such distress or trauma as to prevent him/her from making their complaint at an earlier stage."
2. Where it is decided not to investigate complaints which fall outside the time-limits then the complainant has the power to ask the Healthcare Commission to investigate it (reg. 14).

Acknowledgment and record of complaint

National Health Service (Complaints) Regulations 2004, SI 2004/1764

11.—(1) The complaints manager must send to the complainant a written acknowledgement of the complaint within 2 working days of the date on which the complaint was made.

(2) Where a complaint was made orally, the acknowledgement must be accompanied by the written record mentioned in regulation 9(2)(a) with an invitation to the complainant to sign and return it.

(3) The complaints manager must send a copy of the complaint and his acknowledgement to any person identified in it as the subject of the complaint.

(4) The acknowledgement sent to the complainant under paragraph (1) must include information about the right to assistance from independent advocacy services provided under section 19A of the 1977 Act.

NOTES:

1. The guidance provides that it is good practice for the acknowledgment to be conciliatory and the response from the chief executive will be within an agreed time-frame (para. 3.39).

2. It is also provided that further information regarding the complaints process may be given at local level and the guidance suggests that:

> "It is advisable to include information about the disclosure of patient information at this stage. Reassurance should be given that any disclosure will be confined to that which is relevant to the investigation of the complaint and only disclosed to those people who have a demonstrable need to know it for the purpose of investigating the complaint (para. 3.40)."

3. Complainants may also receive support through the new Independent Complaints Advisory Service (see Guidance, para. 3.41). This was established under s.12 of the Health and Social Care Act 2001 which provides that the Secretary of State is under a statutory responsibility to make appropriate arrangements for independent advocacy services in the context of NHS complaints. Organisations were selected to run the service by competitive tender and there are now four such organisations across the NHS (*Independent Complaints Advocacy Service*, September 1, 2003–August 31, 2004). This provides a free complaint service, offering information and advice. The staff are given specific training to deal with particular types of clients such as the older person, persons with mental illness and learning disabilities.

Investigation of complaints

National Health Service (Complaints) Regulations 2004, SI 2004/1764

12.—(1) The complaints manager must investigate the complaint to the extent necessary and in the manner which appears to him most appropriate to resolve it speedily and efficiently.

(2) The complaints manager may, in any case where he thinks it would be appropriate to do so and with the agreement of the complainant make arrangements for conciliation, mediation or other assistance for the purposes of resolving the complaint and in any such case the NHS body must ensure that appropriate conciliation or mediation services are available.

(3) The complaints manager must take such steps as are reasonably practicable to keep the complainant informed about the progress of the investigation.

NOTES:

1. The guidance states that there should be clear systems to ensure that complaints go to the appropriate channels (para. 3.42). All relevant information needs to be recorded and kept in the case-file (para. 3.43). The investigation needs to be fair, impartial and not adversarial and there also needs to be consistent treatment of complaints (para. 3.43). Guidance also states that it is important to ensure that the response is "timely and effective" and the complainant is to be informed as to progress of the investigation and of any reason for delay (para. 3.50).
2. Those who are the subject of a complaint must be informed of the allegation and the progress of the investigation and be given the ability to talk to the investigating officer (para. 3.46). It can be undertaken by the

complaints manager or the NHS body may appoint another "suitable person" (para. 3.45).

3. In a situation in which clinical issues arise, the guidance requires that any findings/response be communicated to relevant clinicians to ensure clinical accuracy (para. 3.47).

Response

National Health Service (Complaints) Regulations 2004, SI 2004/1764

13.—(1) The complaints manager must prepare a written response to the complaint which summarises the nature and substance of the complaint, describes the investigation under regulation 12 and summarises its conclusions.

(2) The response must be signed by the chief executive of the NHS body except in cases where for good reason the chief executive is not himself able to sign it, in which case it may be signed by a person acting on his behalf.

(3) Subject to paragraph (4), the response must be sent to the complainant within 20 working days beginning on the date on which the complaint was made or, where that is not possible, as soon as reasonably practicable.

(4) The response must notify the complainant of his right to refer the complaint to Healthcare Commission in accordance with regulation 14.

(5) Copies of the response mentioned in paragraph (1) must be sent to any other person to whom the complaint was sent under regulation 11(3).

NOTES:

1. The guidance states that in a situation in which it appears to be impossible to respond within 20 working days, then this should be discussed with the complainant and a new date for response agreed (para. 3.52).
2. Before responding formally to the complainant the guidance requires the complaint manager to consult with those who have been the subject of a complaint. The response is to include the details of the investigation. It also states that "It is good practice for responses to be as conciliatory as possible, including appropriate apologies" (para. 3.54). In responding, technical language is to be avoided or, where used, the terms should be explained (para. 3.55).

The guidance also goes on to provide further information as to how to deal with the response.

Guidance to Support Implementation of the NHS (Complaints) Regulations 2004

3.56 The response must refer to the complainant's right to take the complaint to the Healthcare Commission and advise what they can do if they disagree with the response or would like further explanation (see Regulation 13(4)).

3.57 Once the formal response has been sent, it should be shared with those involved in the investigation and named in the complaint (see Regulation 13(5)). In more serious cases the NHS body may wish to consider a formal debrief for the staff involved in the complaint.

3.58 Arrangements should be made for any outcomes to be monitored to ensure that they are actioned. It is good practice to keep the complainant and those involved in the complaint informed of progress, with a final outcome when all actions have been taken.

(ii) Independent Review

The second stage of the complaints process is that of independent review. This followed the recommendations in *Making Things Right* (London: DOH, 2003). Previously the second stage of the complaints process was undertaken through panels comprising an independent lay chair, a non-executive member of the trust/ health authority (as convenor) and a representative of the purchaser. (*Complaints, Listening... Acting... Improving: Guidance on Implementation of the NHS Complaints Procedure*, London: NHS Executive, 1996). Concerns were expressed that this process was not sufficiently impartial (*Making Things Right*, para. 3.42). The new restructured complaints process now entrusts this stage to the Healthcare Commission.

National Health Service (Complaints) Regulations 2004, SI 2004/1764

14.—(1) In any case where—

(a) a complainant is not satisfied with the result of an investigation—
　　(i) by an NHS body under regulation 12, or
　　(ii) by an independent provider, with whom an NHS trust or Primary Care Trust has made arrangements as mentioned in regulation 6, in accordance with its arrangements for the handling and consideration of complaints;
(b) for any reason an investigation mentioned in paragraph (1)(a) has not been completed within 6 months of the date on which the complaint was made, or
(c) a complaints manager has decided not to investigate a complaint on the grounds that it was not made within the time limit mentioned in regulation 10;

he may request the Healthcare Commission to consider the complaint in accordance with this Part.

(2) In any case where a person has made a complaint to a primary care provider and is not satisfied with the outcome of an investigation of his complaint by the primary care provider, in accordance with its procedures for the handling and investigation of complaints, he, or a person who acted as his representative in accordance with those procedures, may request the Healthcare Commission to consider the complaint in accordance with this Part.

(3) A request under paragraphs (1) or (2) may be made either orally or in writing (including electronically) and must be made within 2 months of, or where that is not possible, as soon as reasonably practicable after, the date on which the response mentioned in regulation 13, or, as the case may be, under the complaints arrangements of the primary care provider, was sent to the complainant.

Remit of Healthcare Commission in relation to complaints about NHS foundation trusts

National Health Service (Complaints) Regulations 2004, SI 2004/1764

15.—(1) Subject to paragraphs (2) to (7), where a person has made a complaint to an NHS foundation trust and either

(a) he is not satisfied with the outcome of any investigation of that complaint by the NHS foundation trust in accordance with any procedures it may have; or
(b) the NHS foundation trust has no complaints procedures,

he may request the Healthcare Commission to consider the complaint in accordance with this Part.

(2) The Healthcare Commission's remit in relation to NHS foundation trusts is limited to consideration only of a complaint which—

(a) is made by a patient; and
(b) is reasonably connected with the provision of health care or other services to patients by or for the NHS foundation trust.

(3) The Healthcare Commission may not consider a complaint made under this regulation where the complaint—

(a) is one about which the complainant has stated in writing that he intends to take legal proceedings;
(b) is one about which the NHS foundation trust has stated in writing that it is taking or is proposing to take disciplinary proceedings in relation to the substance of the complaint against a person who is the subject of the complaint;
(c) arises out of the NHS foundation trust's alleged failure to comply with a data subject request under the Data Protection Act 1998 or a request for information under the Freedom of Information Act 2000; or
(d) which is being or has been investigated by the Health Service Commissioner.

(4) Where the Healthcare Commission consider that a complaint or any part of a complaint made under this regulation does not fall within paragraph (2), it must refer that complaint or part of a complaint to the Independent Regulator.

(5) The provisions in regulation 8(2) to (6) (provision about representatives) apply to complaints made to the Healthcare Commission about NHS foundation trusts as if—

(a) the reference in paragraph (2) to paragraph (1) of that regulation were a reference to paragraph (2) of this regulation; and
(b) the references to the complaints manager in paragraphs (3) and (4) were references to the Healthcare Commission.

(6) A request under paragraph (1) must be made within 2 months of, or where that is not possible, as soon as reasonably practicable after, the date on which a response under the NHS foundation trust's complaints arrangements was sent to the complainant or, where there are no such arrangements, as soon as reasonably practicable.

(7) On receipt of a complaint about an NHS foundation trust, the Healthcare Commission must, within two working days and provided that it has the consent, which may be either express or implied, of the complainant, send a copy of the complaint to the Independent Regulator and invite his views on the complaint.

NOTES:

1. The role of the Healthcare Commission in relation to NHS complaints is separate from its inspectorate role. It has been suggested that there may be the prospect of some conflict here in the future (see further T. Wright, "A Renovated Complaints Process" (2004) 154 N.L.J. 7144).
2. The change to independent review being undertaken through the Healthcare Commission led to a large increase in the number of complaints being considered. In the period August 2000–July 2005 the number of complaints being subject to independent review increased from a figure of

approximately 3,000 to an estimated 9,000–10,000 per annum. Over 25 per cent of these complaints were referred back for local determination because it was believed that they had received insufficient consideration at local level. Issues identified included poor clinical practice, poor communication, staff attitudes and complaints handling. (See further A. Cole "Complaints Handling Must Improve in NHS Trusts" (2005) 331 B.M.J. 11.)

Decision on handling of complaint

National Health Service (Complaints) Regulations 2004, SI 2004/1764

16.—(1) On receipt of the complaint the Healthcare Commission must assess the nature and substance of the complaint and decide how it should be handled having regard to—

(a) the views of the complainant;
(b) the views of the body complained about;
(c) in the case of a complaint about an NHS foundation trust which falls within regulation 15(2), the views of the Independent Regulator;
(d) any investigation of the complaint, whether under Part II or otherwise, and any action taken as a result of such investigation; and
(e) any other relevant circumstances.

(2) As soon as reasonably practicable the Healthcare Commission must notify the complainant as to whether it has decided—

(a) to take no further action;
(b) to make recommendations to the body which is the subject of the complaint as to what action might be taken to resolve it;
(c) to investigate the complaint further in accordance with regulation 17, whether by establishing a panel to consider it or otherwise;
(d) to consider the subject matter of the complaint as part of or in conjunction with any other investigation or review which it is conducting or proposes to conduct in the exercise of its functions under the 2003 Act;
(e) to refer the complaint to a health regulatory body;
(f) in the case of a complaint about an NHS foundation trust which falls within regulation 15(2), to refer the complaint to the Independent Regulator; or
(g) to refer the complaint to the Health Service Commissioner in accordance with section 10 of the Health Service Commissioners Act 1993.

(3) The notice of decision mentioned in paragraph (2)—

(a) must be sent to any person who or body which is the subject of the complaint;
(b) may be sent to any other body which the Healthcare Commission considers has an interest in it;
(c) must include the Healthcare Commission's reasons for its decision; and
(d) in the case of a notification under paragraph (2)(a), must inform the complainant of his right to refer his complaint to the Health Service Commissioner.

(4) For the purposes of its decision under this regulation, the Healthcare Commission may—

(a) distinguish one part of a complaint from another and make different proposals in respect of those different parts; and

(b) take such advice as appears to it to be required.

Investigation by the Healthcare Commission

National Health Service (Complaints) Regulations 2004, SI 2004/1764

17.—(1) Where the Healthcare Commission proposes to investigate a complaint itself, it must, within 10 working days of the date on which it sent the notice mentioned in regulation 16(2), or where that is not possible, as soon as reasonably practicable, send to the complainant and any other person to whom the notice was sent its proposed terms of reference for its investigation.

(2) The complainant and any person or body to whom the terms of reference are sent as mentioned in paragraph (1) may comment in writing on the proposed terms of reference provided that they do so within 10 working days of the date on which they were sent.

(3) The Healthcare Commission may conduct its investigation in any manner which seems to it appropriate, may take such advice as appears to it to be required and, having regard in particular to the views of the complainant and any person who or body which is the subject of the complaint, may appoint a panel to hear and consider the complaint in accordance with regulation 18.

(4) The Healthcare Commission may request any person or body to produce such information and documents as it considers necessary to enable a complaint to be considered properly.

(5) A request under paragraph (4) must be in writing (which may be electronically), must specify what information is requested and state why it is relevant to the consideration of the complaint.

(6) The Healthcare Commission may not make a request under paragraph (4) for information which is confidential and relates to a living individual unless the individual to whom the information relates has consented, such consent may be either express or implied, to its disclosure and use for the purposes of the investigation of the complaint.

Panels

National Health Service (Complaints) Regulations 2004, SI 2004/1764

18.—(1) Subject to paragraph (2), the Healthcare Commission must prepare and keep up to date a list of people who, in its opinion, are suitable to be members of an independent lay panel to hear and consider complaints.

(2) The following persons are not eligible for membership of an independent lay panel—

(a) a member or employee of an NHS body;
(b) any person who is, or who has at any time been, a health care professional or an employee of a health care professional.

(3) Where the Healthcare Commission proposes to refer a complaint to a panel it must make arrangements for the complaint to be considered by a panel of three people selected from the list mentioned in paragraph (1), one of whom must be appointed to be the chairman.

(4) Subject to paragraphs (5) to (7), a panel may consider a complaint in any manner and adopt any procedure which appears to it to be appropriate to resolve the complaint, having regard to any representations to it which may be made by the complainant or by the person who is the subject of the complaint (in this regulation referred to as the participants).

(5) The panel must ensure that the participants are kept informed generally and in particular about—

(a) the composition of the panel;
(b) the date and time of any hearing; and
(c) the names of any person whom the panel proposes to interview or from whom it proposes to take advice or evidence.

(6) A participant before a panel may be accompanied or represented by a friend or advocate but may not be represented by a legal representative acting as such.

(7) In the event of disagreement among members of the panel, the view of the majority shall prevail.

Report of investigation by the Healthcare Commission

National Health Service (Complaints) Regulations 2004, SI 2004/1764

19.—(1) Where the Healthcare Commission investigates a complaint it must, as soon as reasonably practicable, prepare a written report of its investigation which—

(a) summarises the nature and substance of the complaint;
(b) describes the investigation and summarises its conclusions including any findings of fact, the Healthcare Commission's opinion of those findings and its reasons for its opinions;
(c) recommends what action should be taken and by whom to resolve the complaint; and
(d) identifies what other action, if any, should be taken and by whom.

(2) The report may include suggestions which it considers would improve the services of an NHS body, an NHS foundation trust or a primary care provider, or which would otherwise be effective for the purpose of resolving the complaint.

(3) Subject to paragraph (4), the report must be sent to—

(a) the complainant together with a letter explaining to him his right to take his complaint to the Health Service Commissioner;
(b) the body which was the subject of the complaint and, in the case of a complaint arising out of services provided by an independent provider, the body which commissioned those services;
(c) in the case of a complaint involving a primary care provider, to the relevant Primary Care Trust;
(d) any relevant Strategic Health Authority; and
(e) in the case of a complaint involving an NHS foundation trust to the Independent Regulator.

(4) The Healthcare Commission must adapt the report to ensure that confidential information from which the identity of a living individual can be ascertained is not disclosed without the express consent of the individual to whom it relates.

NOTES:

1. The Regulations (reg. 20) and consequent guidance (para. 5) also provide that there should be effective publicity of complaints arrangements and that reasonable steps regarding such arrangements are brought to the attention of patients and their families, NHS staff and independent providers.

Monitoring

National Health Service (Complaints) Regulations 2004, SI 2004/1764

21.—(1) For the purpose of monitoring the arrangements under these Regulations each NHS body must prepare a report for each quarter of the year for consideration by its Board.
(2) The reports mentioned in paragraph (1) must—

(a) specify the numbers of complaints received;
(b) identify the subject matter of those complaints;
(c) summarise how they were handled including the outcome of the investigation; and
(d) identify any complaints where the recommendations of the Healthcare Commission were not acted upon, giving the reasons why not.

NOTES:

1. Guidance requires that the information used in the annual and quarterly reports should be used to identify trends and lessons which may lead to an improvement in NHS services (para. 5.4).

Annual Reports

National Health Service (Complaints) Regulations 2004, SI 2004/1764

22.—Each NHS body must prepare an annual report on its handling and consideration of complaints and send a copy of that report—

(a) in the case of a Strategic Health Authority or Special Health Authority, to the Healthcare Commission.
(b) in the case of an NHS Trust, to its relevant Strategic Health Authority and the Healthcare Commission.
(c) in the case of a Primary Care Trust, to its relevant Strategic Health Authority and the Healthcare Commission.

Guidance to Support Implementation of NHS (Complaints) Regulations 2004

5.5 The information contained in the annual report should summarise information contained in the quarterly reports and identify any progress or areas in need of improvement.
5.6 Strategic health authorities may wish to consider inviting complaints managers or chief executives of NHS bodies to present annual reports personally to them.
5.7 NHS bodies may wish to include information from annual reports in the service improvement section of their annual report and on Freedom of Information web sites.

3. DISCIPLINARY PROCEDURES IN THE NHS IN RELATION TO HEALTH CARE PROFESSIONALS

As noted above, the Wilson Committee and the Government's restructuring of the system provided for a clear separation between complaints and the disciplinary system. These disciplinary procedures operate alongside the usual channels of redress in employment matters in the legal process through actions for unfair dismissal and wrongful dismissal. In some instances NHS employees have also sought to challenge action taken against them by their employer through judicial review (*R. v East Berkshire HA, Ex p. Walsh* [1985] Q.B. 152). Where disciplinary procedures have not been adhered to there is the possibility of a legal challenge as to its validity (see *Irani v Southampton and South-West Hampshire HA* [1985] I.R.L.R. 203).

The previous disciplinary procedures set out in DOH Circular HC90 were subject to review in 2003 following concerns regarding the delay and costs of these procedures. Some concerns were directed at the fact that practitioners may be suspended for long periods pending the resolution of allegations. Average suspensions were usually around two years but on occasions an individual could be suspended for a very lengthy period indeed. In 1982 Dr O'Connell was suspended by North Thames RHA. In 1994 a settlement was finally reached and the health authority withdrew disciplinary proceedings while Dr O'Connell withdrew legal proceedings. The total costs arising out of this suspension totalled £600,000. The case was criticised by the House of Commons Public Accounts Committee (Fortieth Report 1994–5) (HC paper 322, July 10, 1995). There are other drawbacks to suspension in addition to cost. As Samuels has commented the doctor may become "rusty" and need to be retrained (see A. Samuels, "Suspension of Hospital Doctor" (1996) 64 *Medico-Legal Journal* 45).

The perceived problems with the existing system led to the Department of Health publishing a document, "High Professional Standards in the Modern NHS" (2003/012). The new framework was introduced in 2005 (*Maintaining High Professional Standards in the Modern NHS*, London: DOH, 2005). This provides that all NHS bodies are required to have procedures to handle "serious concerns about an individual's conduct and capability" (para. 3). The framework provides for informal resolution if possible, but also provides that:

"5. When serious concerns are raised about a practitioner, the employer must urgently consider whether it is necessary to place temporary restrictions on their practice. This might be to amend or restrict their clinical duties, obtain undertakings or provide for the exclusion of the practitioner from the workplace. Part II of this framework sets out the procedures for this action.

6. The duty to protect patients is paramount. At any point in the process where the case manager has reached the clear judgement that a practitioner is considered to be a serious potential danger to patients or staff, that practitioner must be referred to the regulatory body, whether or not the case has been referred to the NCAA. [Footnote not reproduced here.] . . . ."

To deal with the concerns regarding the previous situation where practitioners were subject to long suspensions, the framework sets out procedures for exclusion from work with provision for review at four-week intervals and with the practitioner being able to return to work if these are not complied with. In addition in relation to more long-term exclusions there is provision for the involvement and scrutiny of the National Clinical Asessment Authority (NCAA) and the Strategic Health Authority.

One notable difference is that the new procedure does not differentiate between personal and professional misconduct. Cases now have to be settled within 13 weeks which is 19 weeks less than that under the previous procedure. A major role is to be played by the NCAA which is a division of the National Patient Safety Agency (see further Chapter 3 above). The NCAA is a body which provides supports to NHS trusts who have concerns regarding the performance of practitioner. The NCAA is to be involved either as an informal sounding board or at a more formal level to undertake clinical assessment of the clinician during an initial assessment period. If these measures are unsuccessful or where doctors fail to comply with them, then their case will be considered by a capability panel. This is a body of three people, at least one of whom will be a medical or dental adviser not employed by the trust. The capability panel has a broad jurisdiction ranging from taking no action to terminating a contract. Provision is also made for an appeal panel.

QUESTION:

1. Given that there is the avenue of redress through the courts or an industrial tribunal in the event of unfair or wrongful dismissal, why should NHS employees be the subject of a complex series of disciplinary processes?

4. HEALTH SERVICE COMMISSIONER

The office of Health Service Commissioner or Ombudsman was originally established under the National Health Service (Reorganisation) Act 1973 (as amended). The current statutory framework establishing the Commissioner is contained in the Health Service Commissioner Act 1993. The Commissioner is the same person who acts as Parliamentary Commissioner for Administration and investigates complaints of maladministration in relation to central government. His functions are to consider complaints made by patients. Since the establishment of the office of Health Service Commissioner the number of complaints referred to him has increased considerably. The Commissioner's role was been expanded by the Health Service Commissioner (Amendment) Act 1996. Today the Commissioner operates alongside the existing complaints procedures described above.

Health Service Commissioner Act 1993 (as amended)

2.—(1) The bodies subject to investigation by the Health Service Commissioner for England are

(a) Strategic Health Authorities,
(c) Special Health Authorities to which this section applies not exercising functions only or mainly in Wales,
(d) National Health Service trusts managing a hospital, or other establishment or facility, in England,

(da) Primary Care Trusts,
(dd) NHS foundation Trusts,
(e) . . .
(f) the Dental Practice Board.

. . .

(4) References in this Act to a "health service body" are to any of the bodies mentioned above.

(5) The Special Health Authorities to which this section applies are those—

(a) established on or before 1st April 1974, or
(b) established after that date and designated . . . as ones to which this section applies.

(6) A designation for the purposes of subsection (5)(b)

(a) in the case of a Special Health Authority exercising functions only or mainly in Wales, by order made by the Assembly by statutory instrument and
(b) in any other case, by Order in Council and a statutory instrument containing an Order in Council made by virtue of paragraph (b)

shall be subject to annulment in pursuance of a resolution of either House of Parliament.

Health service providers subject to investigation

2A.—(1) Persons are subject to investigation by the Commissioner if they are or were at the time of the action complained of—

(a) persons (whether individuals or bodies) providing services under a contract entered into by them with a Primary Care Trust under section 28K or 28Q of the National Health Service Act 1977;
(b) persons (whether individuals or bodies) undertaking to provide in England general ophthalmic services or pharmaceutical services under Part II of that Act;
(c) individuals performing in England primary medical services or primary dental services in accordance with arrangements made under section 28C of that Act (except as employees of, or otherwise on behalf of, a health service body or an independent provider); or
(d) individuals providing in England local pharmaceutical services in accordance with arrangements made under a pilot scheme established under section 28 of the Health and Social Care Act 2001 (except as employees of, or otherwise on behalf of, a health service body or an independent provider).

. . .

(4) In this Act—

(a) references to a family health service provider are to any person mentioned in [subsection (1)]
(b) references to family health services are to any of the services so mentioned.

Independent providers subject to investigation

2B.—(1) Persons are subject to investigation by the Commissioner if—

(a) they are or were at the time of the action complained of persons (whether individuals or bodies) providing services in England under arrangements with health service bodies or family health service providers, and

(b) they are not or were not at the time of the action complained of themselves health service bodies or family health service providers.

(4) The services provided under arrangements mentioned in subsection (1)(a) may be services of any kind.

(5) In this Act references to an independent provider are to any person providing services as mentioned in [subsection (1)].

Availability of other remedy

4.—(1) The Commissioner shall not conduct an investigation in respect of action in relation to which the person aggrieved has or had—

(a) a right of appeal, reference or review to or before a tribunal constituted by or under any enactment or by virtue of Her Majesty's prerogative, or
(b) a remedy by way of proceedings in any court of law, unless the Commissioner is satisfied that in the particular circumstances it is not reasonable to expect that person to resort or have resorted to it.

(2) The Commissioner shall not conduct an investigation in respect of action which has been, or is, the subject of an inquiry under section 84 of the National Health Service Act 1977.

(3) A Commissioner shall not conduct an investigation in respect of action by a health service body other than the Mental Welfare Commission for Scotland if it is action in relation to which the protective functions of the Mental Welfare Commission for Scotland have been, are being or may be exercised under the Mental Health (Scotland) Act 1984.

(4) Subsection (5) applies where—

(a) action by reference to which a complaint is made under section 3(1), (1A) or (1C) is action by reference to which a complaint can be made under section 113(1) or (2) of the Health and Social Care (Community Health and Standards) Act 2003 or under a procedure operated by a health service body, a family health service provider or an independent provider, and
(b) subsection (1), (2) or (3) does not apply as regards the action.

(5) In such a case [the Commissioner] shall not conduct an investigation in respect of the action unless he is satisfied that—

(a) the other procedure has been invoked and exhausted,
(b) or in the particular circumstances it is not reasonable to expect procedure to be invoked or (as the case may be) exhausted.

Personnel, contracts etc.

7.—(1) The Commissioner shall not conduct an investigation in respect of action taken in respect of appointments or removals, pay, discipline, superannuation or other personnel matters in relation to service under the National Health Service Act 1977 or the National Health Service and Community Care Act 1990.

(2) The Commissioner shall not conduct an investigation in respect of action taken in matters relating to contractual or other commercial transactions, except for—

(a) matters relating to NHS contracts (as defined by section 4 of the National Health Service and Community Care Act 1990),
(b) matters arising from arrangements between a health service body and an independent provider for the provision of services by the provider, and
(c) matters arising from arrangements between a family health service provider and an independent provider for the provision of services by the independent provider.

(3) In determining what matters arise from arrangements mentioned in subsection (2)(b) the Commissioner shall disregard any arrangements for the provision of services at an establishment maintained by a Minister of the Crown mainly for patients who are members of the armed forces of the Crown.

(3A) The Commissioner shall not conduct an investigation in pursuance of a complaint if—

(a) the complaint is in respect of action taken in any matter relating to arrangements made by a health service body and a family health service provider for the provision of family health services,

(b) the action is taken by or on behalf of the body or by the provider, and

(c) the complaint is made by the provider or the body.

(3B) Nothing in the preceding provisions of this section prevents [the Commissioner] conducting an investigation in respect of action taken by a health service body in operating a procedure established to examine complaints.

(4) Her Majesty may by Order in Council amend this section so as to permit the investigation by [the Commissioner] of any of the matters mentioned in subsection (1) or (2).

(5) A statutory instrument containing an Order in Council made by virtue of subsection (4) shall be subject to annulment in pursuance of a resolution of either House of Parliament.

NOTES:

1. The Commissioner's role is to operate alongside existing complaints procedures. The legislation requires that complainants should, save in exceptional circumstances, exhaust alternative methods of complaint prior to the Commissioner accepting an investigation (s.4(5)). Nor will the Commissioner usually investigate a complaint where this will be the subject of legal proceedings (s.4(2)).

2. The jurisdiction of the Health Service Commissioner was extended in 1996 by the Health Service Commissioners (Amendment) Act 1996 which inserted provisions into the 1993 Act. Complaints against general practitioners may now be investigated (s.2(1A)) as may also complaints against private health providers providing health services for health service bodies (s.2B). The extension of the jurisdiction to G.P.s follows recommendations in *Being Heard* (London: DOH, 1994, para. 3.22), but does not apply to G.P. disciplinary proceedings (s.7(5)(b)). These complaints are now the main part of the Commissioner's work.

3. Until 1996 there was a ban upon the Commissioner investigating complaints relating to clinical judgment. This resulted in a considerable number of complaints referred for investigation being turned away. For example, in 1992, some 25 per cent of complaints were turned away on this basis (Select Committee on the Parliamentary Commissioner for Administration, "The Powers, Work and Jurisdiction of the Ombudsman" (HC 33-1; para. 101)). Nevertheless, this general exclusion did not mean that a doctor could simply allege that a matter was of a clinical nature and thus avoid investigation. The Commissioner was prepared to look behind this claim to ascertain whether it was truly a clinical matter. Some

complaints with a clinical element were investigated. There was considerable debate as to whether this restriction upon the Commissioner's investigative powers was justifiable. It was finally removed by the Health Service Commissioner (Amendment) Act 1996 (s.6). The Act does not define clinical judgment. The Commissioner is to call upon specialist medical and nursing advice in investigating such complaints. These advisers will not act in a representative role and the advice given will generally only concern their professional discipline. It should be emphasised that the role of these professionals is one of providing advice and the Commissioner will compile the ultimate report. In a paper outlining his new powers (issued prior to the passage of the 1996 Act), the Commissioner stated that "Without seeking in any way to encourage or promote a 'blame culture' it is the ombudsman's responsibility to criticise where in his view the patient does not receive the service he is reasonably entitled to expect" (Office of the Health Service Commissioner, *Responsibilities of the Health Service Commissioner*, 1996).

4. The Commissioner investigates "injustice and hardship" as a result of failures in service and also "maladministration" (s.3(1)). This last term is imported from the earlier legislation setting out the role of the Parliamentary Commissioner for Adminstration. As Richard Crossman, a former minister, stated when the Parliamentary Commissioner Act 1967 was being debated it encompasses "bias, neglect, inattention, delay, incompetence, ineptitude, perversity, turpitude". The Commissioner issues reports consequent upon investigations. In exceptional circumstances the Commissioner may decide to issue a special report about an individual case. For example, in 1996 the Commissioner published his investigation into the handling of complaints by Salford Royal Hospital. The report concerned investigations of 12 separate allegations made to the Commissioner concerning incidents over a four-year period. The report identified poor communication, slow responses to complaints, records which had been mislaid and poor monitoring of procedures (see "Investigation of Complaint Handling by Salford Royal Hospitals NHS Trust", Report of the Health Service Commissioner: HMSO, 1996).

5. The Commissioner provides an outlet through which patients may highlight concerns in relation to NHS contracting (s.7(2)). The Commissioner can consider complaints in relation to both NHS contracts and contracts made by NHS purchasers with private providers. The Commissioner has however been circumspect when investigating such claims (*HSC Annual Report 93–94*, HC 499, para. 3.8).

Individuals and bodies entitled to complain

8.—(1) A complaint under this Act may be made by an individual or a body of persons, whether incorporated or not, other than a public authority.

(2) In subsection (1), "public authority" means—

(a) a local authority or other authority or body constituted for the purposes of the public service or of local government (including the Assembly),

(b) an authority or body constituted for the purposes of carrying on under national ownership any industry or undertaking or part of an industry or undertaking, and

(c) any other authority or body —
    (i) whose members are appointed by Her Majesty or any Minister of the Crown or government department or by the Assembly, or
    (ii) whose revenues consist wholly or mainly of money provided by Parliament or out of the Scottish Consolidated Fund or the Assembly.

Requirements to be complied with

9.—(1) The following requirements apply in relation to a complaint made to the Commissioner.

(2) A complaint must be made in writing.

(3) The complaint shall not be entertained unless it is made —

(a) by the person aggrieved, or
(b) where the person by whom a complaint might have been made has died or is for any reason unable to act for himself, by —
    (i) his personal representative,
    (ii) a member of his family, or
    (iii) some body or individual suitable to represent him.

(4) The Commissioner shall not entertain the complaint if it is made more than a year after the day on which the person aggrieved first had notice of the matters alleged in the complaint, unless he considers it reasonable to do so.

(4A) In the case of a complaint against a person who is no longer of a description set out in section 2A(1), but was of such a description at the time of the action complained of, the Commissioner shall not entertain the complaint if it is made more than three years after the last day on which the person was a family health service provider.

(4B) In the case of a complaint against a person falling within [section 2B(1) in relation to whom there are no longer any such arrangements as are mentioned there, the Commissioner shall not entertain the complaint if it is made more than three years after the last day on which the person was an independent provider.

Referral of complaint by health service body

10.—(1) A health service body may itself refer to a Commissioner a complaint made to that body that a person has, in consequence of a failure or maladministration for which the body is responsible, sustained such injustice or hardship as is mentioned in section 3(1).

(2) A complaint may not be so referred unless it was made —

(a) in writing,
(b) by the person aggrieved or by a person authorised by section 9(3)(b) to complain to the Commissioner on his behalf, and
(c) not more than a year after the person aggrieved first had notice of the matters alleged in the complaint, or such later date as the Commissioner considers appropriate in any particular case.

(3) A health service body may not refer a complaint under this section after the period of one year beginning with the day on which the body received the complaint.

(4) Any question whether a complaint has been duly referred to a Commissioner under this section shall be determined by him.

(5) A complaint referred to a Commissioner under this section shall be deemed to be duly made to him.

Procedure in respect of investigations

11.—(1) Where the Commissioner proposes to conduct an investigation pursuant to a complaint under section 3(1), he shall afford—

(a) to the health service body concerned, and

(b) to any other person who is alleged in the complaint to have taken or authorised the action complained of,

an opportunity to comment on any allegations contained in the complaint.

(1A) Where the Commissioner proposes to conduct an investigation pursuant to a complaint under section 3(1A), he shall afford—

(a) to the family health service provider, and

(b) to any person by reference to whose action the complaint is made (if different from the family health service provider),

an opportunity to comment on any allegations contained in the complaint.

(1B) Where the Commissioner proposes to conduct an investigation pursuant to a complaint under section 3(1C), he shall afford—

(a) to the independent provider concerned, and

(b) to any other person who is alleged in the complaint to have taken or authorised the action complained of,

an opportunity to comment on any allegations contained in the complaint.

(1C) Where the Commissioner proposes to conduct an investigation pursuant to a complaint under section 3(1E), he shall afford to the person or body whose maladministration is complained of an opportunity to comment on any allegations contained in the complaint.

(2) An investigation shall be conducted in private.

(3) In other respects, the procedure for conducting an investigation shall be such as the Commissioner considers appropriate in the circumstances of the case, and in particular—

(a) he may obtain information from such persons and in such manner, and make such inquiries, as he thinks fit, and

(b) he may determine whether any person may be represented, by counsel or solicitor or otherwise, in the investigation.

(4) The Commissioner may, if he thinks fit, pay to the person by whom the complaint was made and to any other person who attends or supplies information for the purposes of an investigation—

(a) sums in respect of expenses properly incurred by them, and

(b) allowances by way of compensation for the loss of their time.

Payments made by [the Commissioner] under this subsection shall be in accordance with such scales and subject to such conditions as may be determined by the Treasury.

(5) The conduct of an investigation pursuant to a complaint under section 3(1) shall not affect any action taken by the health service body concerned, or any power or duty of that body to take further action with respect to any matters subject to the investigation.

(5A) The conduct of an investigation pursuant to a complaint under section 3(1A) or (1C) shall not affect any action taken by the family health service provider or independent provider concerned, or any power or duty of that provider to take further action with respect to any matters subject to the investigation.

(6) Where the person aggrieved has been removed from the United Kingdom under any order in force under the Immigration Act 1971 he shall, if the Commissioner so directs, be

permitted to re-enter and remain in the United Kingdom, subject to such conditions as the Secretary of State may direct, for the purposes of the investigation.

Evidence

12.—(1) For the purposes of an investigation pursuant to a complaint under section 3(1) [the Commissioner] may require any officer or member of the health service body concerned or any other person who in his opinion is able to supply information or produce documents relevant to the investigation to supply any such information or produce any such document.

(1A) For the purposes of an investigation pursuant to a complaint under section 3(1A) or (1C) or (1E) [the Commissioner] may require any person who in his opinion is able to supply information or produce documents relevant to the investigation to supply any such information or produce any such document.

(2) For the purposes of an investigation [the Commissioner] shall have the same powers as the Court in respect of—

(a) the attendance and examination of witnesses (including the administration of oaths and affirmations and the examination of witnesses abroad), and
(b) the production of documents.

(3) No obligation to maintain secrecy or other restriction on the disclosure of information obtained by or supplied to persons in Her Majesty's service, whether imposed by any enactment or by any rule of law, shall apply to the disclosure of information for the purposes of an investigation.

(4) The Crown shall not be entitled in relation to an investigation to any such privilege in respect of the production of documents or the giving of evidence as is allowed by law in legal proceedings.

(5) No person shall be required or authorised by this Act—

(a) to supply any information or answer any question relating to proceedings of the Cabinet or of any Committee of the Cabinet, or
(b) to produce so much of any document as relates to such proceedings;

and for the purposes of this subsection a certificate issued by the Secretary of the Cabinet with the approval of the Prime Minister and certifying that any information, question, document or part of a document relates to such proceedings shall be conclusive.

(6) Subject to subsections (3) and (4), no person shall be compelled for the purposes of an investigation to give any evidence or produce any document which he could not be compelled to give or produce in civil proceedings before the Court.

Obstruction and contempt

13.—(1) [The Commissioner] may certify an offence to the Court where—

(a) a person without lawful excuse obstructs him or any of his officers in the performance of his functions, or
(b) a person is guilty of any act or omission in relation to an investigation which, if that investigation were a proceeding in the Court, would constitute contempt of court.

(2) Where an offence is so certified the Court may inquire into the matter and after hearing—

(a) any witnesses who may be produced against or on behalf of the person charged with the offence, and

(b) any statement that may be offered in defence, the Court may deal with the person charged with the offence in any manner in which it could deal with him if he had committed the like offence in relation to the Court.

(3) Nothing in this section shall be construed as applying to the taking of any such action as is mentioned in section 11(5).

NOTES:

1. The Act sets out who can bring a complaint before the Commissioner in ss.8 and 9(1). Health professionals may bring complaints on behalf of patients. One instance may be where the health professional is of the view that standards of care have fallen to unacceptable levels.
2. Where a Commissioner makes a finding against a health service body he issues a report. He is required to report to the complainant, health service body, family health service provider and any M.P. involved in the complaint (s.14). However, compliance with this report is not compulsory. This lack of mandatory powers is a feature of the office of Commissioners for Administration. There has been discussion in relation to other Commissioners of the need for judicial enforcement, although this has not been a major issue in the context of the NHS. There are a number of instances of authorities disregarding the Commissioners' recommendations. In addition certain authorities appear to be repeatedly the subject of complaints — see J. Allsop and L. Mulcahy, *Regulating Medical Work*, Buckingham: Open UP (1997) at p.70.
3. The Commissioner's decisions are subject to the courts and to judicial review.
4. The Commissioner is now empowered by s.10 of the 1996 Act to lay reports directly before Parliament. Prior to the enactment of this provision he was only under an obligation to report directly to the Secretary of State.

5. SELF-REGULATION OF THE HEALTH CARE PROFESSIONS

Health care professionals are not only accountable through the general law and their contracts of employment, but are also frequently subject to regulation through a governing body of their profession. Common elements of self-regulation are the requirement that practitioners be placed upon a register and that they are bound by a professional ethical code/statement of practice. Failure to comply with this code may lead to disciplinary action being taken by the professional body (see further T. Glynn and D. Gomez, *Fitness to Practise: Health Care Regulatory Law, Principle and Process*, London, Sweet & Maxwell, 2005). There has been an increase in the number of such bodies established under statute over the past two decades, with bodies such as chiropractors and osteopaths now subject to regulation (see J. Stone and J. Matthews, *Complementary Medicine and the Law*, Oxford: OUP, 1996, at p.145 *et seq.*) In some respects statutory regulation can be seen as a sign of the maturity of a profession in the eyes of the public, a sign that it has been accorded general legitimacy.

While professional regulation, whether or not embodied in statute, may facilitate accountability, it may bring certain problems. As was noted in Chapter 2 above and is illustrated later in Chapter 8, when we consider the practice of "whistleblowing" in health care, in some situations the professional's obligations under his or her professional ethical code conflict with requirements set out in the contract of employment. One further problem with reliance upon professional self-regulation is the increasing proliferation of such professional bodies. These all have their own professional standards which do not necessarily correlate with one another. Below we consider accountability through professional self-regulation in the context of the body governing the medical profession the General Medical Council.

(a) Case Study: the Role of the General Medical Council

(i) Introduction: The Regulatory Role

The medical profession has a long history of professional self-regulation. A charter was given to the Royal College of Physicians in 1518. A body of surgeons, the College of Surgeons, split with the Company of Barbers with whom they had been previously associated in 1745. In addition to these two bodies, a Society of Apothecaries was established. These practitioners provided health care to persons who had more limited financial means. Criticisms of the disputes between the three branches of the profession were made in the 19th century and around that time the professions themselves began to take a tougher stance on "quack" practitioners. The Medical Act of 1858 introduced a statutory framework. Section 29 of that Act provided that doctors who were convicted of felonies or misdemeanours could be removed from the register. The GMC was described as having elements of a "gentleman's club" with poor behaviour being censored. Today the GMC is constituted in accordance with the Medical Act 1983, as amended.

The reliance upon self-regulation of the health care professions may be questioned. Stacey has argued that the GMC has consistently favoured the professionals over the public. As she notes, an investigation only results where a complaint has been made, as the GMC does not have its own inspectorate. (See M. Stacey, "Medical Accountability: a Background Paper" in A. Grubb (ed.), *Challenges in Medicine*, Chichester: John Wiley, 1992.) Nor indeed does the GMC have the power to initiate its own investigations, in contrast with other professional bodies such as the pharmaceutical society. While complaints may be made against doctors by members of the public, as Stone and Matthews note, there is little attempt to draw this to individuals' attention (J. Stone and J. Matthews, *Complementary Medicine and the Law,* Oxford: OUP, 1996, at p.51). The role of the NHS complaints system are discussed above (and see J. Allsop and L. Mulcahy, *Regulating Medical Work*, Buckingham: Open UP, 1996, Chapter 4).

The structure of the GMC was amended in 2003. This followed years of criticism that it was inadequately safeguarding patients and health professionals alike. The GMC undertook a consultation exercise (see "Effective, Inclusive and Accountable: Reform of the GMC's Structure, Constitution and Governance", London: GMC, 2001 and "Acting Fairly to Protect Patients: Reform of the Fitness to Practice procedures" London: GMC, 2001). The Government then in turn consulted on reform of the GMC (see "Reform of the General Medical Council: Report of the Consultation", London: DOH, 2002).

The Medical Act (Amendment) Order 2002 reformed the GMC. This reduced the membership from 104 to 35 members. Of these, 19 are registered medical practitioners and are elected by registered medical practitioners who are registered in the UK. Two further medical practitioners are appointed by the Council of the Heads of Medical Schools and by the Academy of Medical Royal Colleges. In addition 14 members are lay members who are nominated by the Privy Council. The Council performs three main functions: it maintains a register of qualified practitioners; it controls medical education and sets the standards for qualification as a doctor in the United Kingdom and it polices professional conduct and fitness to practise. (Medical Act 1983, s.49).

QUESTION:

    1. The reformed GMC is still dominated by medical practitioners. To what extent is this satisfactory and should the membership be amended?

From January 1, 2005 medical practitioners have been required to possess a "licence to practise" (Medical Act 1983, s.29) which they will be given on first registration. In addition doctors will be required to be revalidated every five years with the aim of ensuring that they are fit to practise and that they possess relevant current information regarding their speciality. This has not been uncontroversial and the GMC proposals were subject to criticism in the Shipman Inquiry in that the revalidated assessment is internal as opposed to independent assessment (Shipman Inquiry, *Fifth Report Safeguarding Patients: Lessons from the Past— Proposals for the Future,* Cm. 6394 (2004) London: HMSO, para. 26.205)) Dame Janet Smith also argued that the process could suggest to the public that it was more extensive than in fact it was because in practice a doctor would be revalidated unless it was the case that their standard of practice should be referred to a Fitness to Practise Panel. In addition Dame Janet Smith suggested that the public perception could be that doctors would only be revalidated if they had passed some objective test whereas in fact revalidation would be on the basis of appraisal.

(ii) **Review on the Basis of "Fitness to Practise"**

The medical profession is also subject to review in relation to "fitness to practise". This is a change to the previous position. Originally there were three different ways in which the GMC could consider fitness to practice: conduct and criminal convictions, health and personal performance. Each of these jurisdictions operated through a range of different committees. This was criticised in the Shipman

Inquiry because it led to complexity with a range of different procedures coming into operation at different times and operating independently of each other (J. Smith, Shipman Inquiry, *op. cit.* para. 15.43, and see further on the old procedures J. Glynn and D. Gomez, *Fitness to Practise: Health Care Regulatory Law, Principle and Process*, London: Sweet & Maxwell, 2005 at paras 2–018—2–079; and M. O'Rourke and J. Holl-Allen, "Regulating Health Care Professions" in A. Grubb (ed.), *Principles of Medical Law* (2nd edn), Oxford: OUP 2004). New procedures were introduced through the Medical Act 1983 (Amendment) Order 2002, SI 2002/3155, Sch.2. The main change is that the system has been considerably streamlined. The old Interim Orders Committees, Preliminary Proceedings Committees, Professional Conduct Committee, Assessment Referral Committee, Committee on Professional Performance and Health Committee are abolished. There are now two main stages. First, investigation by the Investigation Committee and secondly, the adjudication by the Fitness to Practise Panels. There is also provision in the Fitness to Practise Rules 2004 for the allegation to be considered initially by the Registrar to ensure that it falls within the categories of s.35C(2). Where it does so, then it may be referred to a lay or medical case examiner for consider (Fitness to Practise, rule 4.2). Cases are then to be considered by a case examiners (medical or lay) (Fitness to Practise, rule 2) and these may decide as to whether an allegation should not go any further, may issue a warning, may refer the issue to the Investigation Committee (on request or where it is appropriate (rule 11(2)) or make a direct reference to the Fitness to Practise Panel. The President of the Council also has a power to review a case where it has been decided to issue a warning, a decision not to refer to the fitness to practise panel or decision to cease consideration of the case where undertakings have been given. His powers are, however, only to be exercised in a situation in which this is necessary for the public protection, necessary for the prevention of injustice to a practitioner or "otherwise necessary in the public interest" (Fitness to Practise, rule 12).

Medical Act 1983

Functions of the Investigation Committee

35C.—(1) This section applies where an allegation is made to the General Council against—

(a) a fully registered person;
(b) a person who is provisionally registered; or
(c) a person who is registered with limited registration,

that his fitness to practise is impaired.

(2) A person's fitness to practise shall be regarded as "impaired" for the purposes of this Act by reason only of—

(a) misconduct;
(b) deficient professional performance;
(c) a conviction or caution in the British Islands for a criminal offence, or a conviction elsewhere for an offence which, if committed in England and Wales, would constitute a criminal offence;

(d) adverse physical or mental health; or
(e) a determination by a body in the United Kingdom responsible under any enactment
     for the regulation of a health or social care profession to the effect that his fitness
     to practise as a member of that profession is impaired, or a determination by a
     regulatory body elsewhere to the same effect.

(3) This section is not prevented from applying because the allegation is based on a
matter alleged to have occurred—

(a) outside the United Kingdom; or
(b) at a time when the person was not registered.

(4) The Investigation Committee shall investigate the allegation and decide whether it
should be considered by a Fitness to Practise Panel.
(5) If the Investigation Committee decide that the allegation ought to be considered by
a Fitness to Practise Panel—

(a) they shall give a direction to that effect to the Registrar;
(b) the Registrar shall refer the allegation to a Fitness to Practise Panel; and
(c) the Registrar shall serve a notification of the Committee's decision on the person
     who is the subject of the allegation and the person making the allegation (if
     any).

(6) If the Investigation Committee decide that the allegation ought not to be considered
by a Fitness to Practise Panel, they may give a warning to the person who is the subject of
the allegation regarding his future conduct or performance.
(7) If the Investigation Committee decide that the allegation ought not to be considered
by a Fitness to Practise Panel, but that no warning should be given under subsection (6)
above—

(a) they shall give a direction to that effect to the Registrar; and
(b) the Registrar shall serve a notification of the Committee's decision on the person
     who is the subject of the allegation and the person making the allegation (if
     any).

NOTES:

1. The test as to whether fitness to practise is impaired is broader than the
   previous position which concerned allegations of serious professional
   misconduct and in the case of professional performance, seriously deficient
   conduct. For consideration of the nature of serious professional misconduct see *Doughty v General Medical Council* [1987] 3 All E.R. 843, and
   David Noel McCandless v GMC [1996] 1 W.L.R. 167. However, it was
   still subject to criticism in the Shipman Inquiry by Dame Janet Smith who
   commented that the new test "means different things in different circumstances, it is almost without meaning" (Shipman Inquiry), *"Fifth Report
   Safeguarding Patients: Lessons from the Past—Proposals for the Future"*
   Cm. 6394, London: HMSO, 2004, para. 26.205)).
2. The legislation does not provide as to what constitutes the standard of
   proof. It was suggested in *McAllister v GMC* [1993] A.C. 339 that the
   applicable standard may be the criminal standard of proof, but this may be
   related to the issue under consideration and obiter in *Sadler v GMC* [2003]
   UKPC 59 the Privy Council have suggested that in a situation in which

conduct was "seriously deficient" a civil standard may apply although they also noted that the criminal standard of proof should be applied in a situation where, for example, allegations which may also constitute serious criminal charges are made.

3. Section 35CC provides that rules may be enacted to enable the Registrar to exercise the functions of the Investigation Committee.

Functions of a Fitness to Practise Panel

35D.—(1) Where an allegation against a person is referred under section 35C above to a Fitness to Practise Panel, subsections (2) and (3) below shall apply.

(2) Where the Panel find that the person's fitness to practise is impaired they may, if they think fit—

(a) except in a health case, direct that the person's name shall be erased from the register;
(b) direct that his registration in the register shall be suspended (that is to say, shall not have effect) during such period not exceeding twelve months as may be specified in the direction; or
(c) direct that his registration shall be conditional on his compliance, during such period not exceeding three years as may be specified in the direction, with such requirements so specified as the Panel think fit to impose for the protection of members of the public or in his interests.

(3) Where the Panel find that the person's fitness to practise is not impaired they may nevertheless give him a warning regarding his future conduct or performance.

(4) Where a Fitness to Practise Panel have given a direction that a person's registration be suspended—

(a) under subsection (2) above;
(b) under subsection (10) or (12) below; or
(c) under rules made by virtue of paragraph 5A(3) of Schedule 4 to this Act, subsection (5) below applies.

(5) In such a case, a Fitness to Practise Panel may, if they think fit—

(a) direct that the current period of suspension shall be extended for such further period from the time when it would otherwise expire as may be specified in the direction;
(b) except in a health case, direct that the person's name shall be erased from the register; or
(c) direct that the person's registration shall, as from the expiry of the current period of suspension, be conditional on his compliance, during such period not exceeding three years as may be specified in the direction, with such requirements so specified as the Panel think fit to impose for the protection of members of the public or in his interests,

but, subject to subsection (6) below, the Panel shall not extend any period of suspension under this section for more than twelve months at a time.

(6) In a health case, a Fitness to Practise Panel may give a direction in relation to a person whose registration has been suspended under this section extending his period of suspension indefinitely where—

(a) the period of suspension will, on the date on which the direction takes effect, have lasted for at least two years; and

(b) the direction is made not more than two months before the date on which the period of suspension would otherwise expire.

(7) Where a Fitness to Practise Panel have given a direction under subsection (6) above for a person's period of suspension to be extended indefinitely, a Fitness to Practise Panel shall review the direction if—

(a) the person requests them to do so;
(b) at least two years have elapsed since the date on which the direction took effect; and
(c) if the direction has previously been reviewed under this subsection, at least two years have elapsed since the date of the previous review.

(8) On such a review the Panel may—

(a) confirm the direction;
(b) direct that the suspension be terminated; or
(c) direct that the person's registration be conditional on his compliance, during such period not exceeding three years as may be specified in the direction, with such requirements so specified as the Panel think fit to impose for the protection of members of the public or in his interests.

(9) Where—

(a) a direction that a person's registration be subject to conditions has been given under—
    (i) subsection (2), (5) or (8) above,
    (ii) subsection (12) below,
    (iii) rules made by virtue of paragraph 5A(3) of Schedule 4 to this Act, or
    (iv) section 41A below; and
(b) that person is judged by a Fitness to Practise Panel to have failed to comply with any requirement imposed on him as such a condition,

subsection (10) below applies.
(10) In such a case, the Panel may, if they think fit—

(a) except in a health case, direct that the person's name shall be erased from the register; or
(b) direct that the person's registration in the register shall be suspended during such period not exceeding twelve months as may be specified in the direction.

(11) Where a direction that a person's registration be subject to conditions has been given under—

(a) subsection (2), (5) or (8) above; or
(b) rules made by virtue of paragraph 5A(3) of Schedule 4 to this Act,

subsection (12) below applies.
(12) In such a case, a Fitness to Practise Panel may, if they think fit—

(a) except in a health case, direct that the person's name shall be erased from the register;
(b) direct that the person's registration in the Register shall be suspended during such period not exceeding twelve months as may be specified in the direction;
(c) direct that the current period of conditional registration shall be extended for such further period from the time when it would otherwise expire as may be specified in the direction; or

(d) revoke the direction, or revoke or vary any of the conditions imposed by the direction, for the remainder of the current period of conditional registration,

but the Panel shall not extend any period of conditional registration under this section for more than three years at a time.

NOTES:

1. The powers of the Fitness to Practise Panel are much more extensive than those of the Investigating Committee and they extend to cover removal from the register.
2. Conduct which may result in removal from the register includes drug and alcohol abuse, improper associations with patients, failures to visit, treat and refer patients. A notable example of the role played by the GMC can be seen in the "kidneys for cash" case. Here doctors involved in transplanting organs from persons from Turkey who were paid to come to England and have their organs removed so that they could be transplanted into patients were disciplined. This case resulted in legislation in the form of the Human Organ Transplants Act 1989 (see below Chapter 15). The GMC have also acted to discipline a doctor for scientific fraud (see S. Lock, "Lessons from the Pearce Affair: Handling Scientific Fraud" (1995) 311 B.M.J. 1547) and for bad clinical practice in the case of operations in relation to Rodney Ledward (see further Department of Health, "An Inquiry into the Quality and Practice within the National Health Service Arising from the Actions of Rodney Ledward", London: DOH, 2000.)
3. The parties have to comply with case management under the new scheme. The case manager may under the Fitness to Practise Rules order a case review (rule 16(1)(2)). Directions can be issued including requirements for witness statements, skeleton arguments and time estimates (see further discussion in J. Glynn and D. Gomez, *Fitness to Practise: Health Care Regulatory Law, Principle and Process* London: Sweet & Maxwell, 2005 paras 2.139–140).

Power to order immediate suspension etc. after a finding of impairment of fitness to practise

38.—(1) On giving a direction for erasure or a direction for suspension under section 35D(2), (10) or (12) above, or under rules made by virtue of paragraph 5A(3) of Schedule 4 to this Act, in respect of any person the Fitness to Practise Panel, if satisfied that to do so is necessary for the protection of members of the public or is otherwise in the public interest, or is in the best interests of that person, may order that his registration in the register shall be suspended forthwith in accordance with this section.

(2) On giving a direction for conditional registration under section 35D(2) above, or under rules made by virtue of paragraph 5A(3) of Schedule 4 to this Act, in respect of any person the Fitness to Practise Panel, if satisfied that to do so is necessary for the protection of members of the public or is otherwise in the public interest, or is in the best interests of that person, may order that his registration be made conditional forthwith in accordance with this section.

(3) Where, on the giving of a direction, an order under subsection (1) or (2) above is made in respect of a person, his registration in the register shall, subject to subsection (4) below, be suspended (that is to say, shall not have effect) or made conditional, as the case may be, from the time when the order is made until the time when—

(a) the direction takes effect in accordance with—
     (i) paragraph 10 of Schedule 4 to this Act; or
     (ii) rules made by virtue of paragraph 5A(3) of that Schedule; or
(b) an appeal against it under section 40 below or paragraph 5A(4) of that Schedule is (otherwise than by the dismissal of the appeal) determined.

(4) Where a Fitness to Practise Panel make an order under subsection (1) or (2) above, the Registrar shall forthwith serve a notification of the order on the person to whom it applies.

(5) If, when an order under subsection (1) or (2) above is made, the person to whom it applies is neither present nor represented at the proceedings, subsection (3) above shall have effect as if, for the reference to the time when the order is made, there were substituted a reference to the time of service of a notification of the order as determined for the purposes of paragraph 8 of Schedule 4 to this Act.

(6) Except as provided in subsection (7) below, while a person's registration in the register is suspended by virtue of subsection (1) above, he shall be treated as not being registered in the register notwithstanding that his name still appears in it.

(7) Notwithstanding subsection (6) above, sections 35C to 35E above shall continue to apply to a person whose registration in the register is suspended.

(8) The relevant court may terminate any suspension of a person's registration in the register imposed under subsection (1) above or any conditional registration imposed under subsection (2) above, and the decision of the court on any application under this subsection shall be final.

(9) In this section "the relevant court" has the same meaning as in section 40(5) below.

. . .

Appeals

40.—(1) The following decisions are appealable decisions for the purposes of this section, that is to say—

(a) a decision of a Fitness to Practise Panel under section 35D above giving a direction for erasure, for suspension or for conditional registration or varying the conditions imposed by a direction for conditional registration;
(b) a decision of a Fitness to Practise Panel under section 41(9) below giving a direction that the right to make further applications under that section shall be suspended indefinitely; or
(c) a decision of the General Council under section 45(6) below giving a direction that the right to make further applications under that section shall be suspended indefinitely.

(2) A decision of the General Council under section 39 above giving a direction for erasure is also an appealable decision for the purposes of this section.

(3) In subsection (1) above—

(a) references to a direction for suspension include a reference to a direction extending a period of suspension; and
(b) references to a direction for conditional registration include a reference to a direction extending a period of conditional registration.

(4) A person in respect of whom an appealable decision falling within subsection (1) has been taken may, before the end of the period of 28 days beginning with the date on which notification of the decision was served under section 35E(1) above, or section 41(10) or 45(7) below, appeal against the decision to the relevant court.

(5) In subsection (4) above, "the relevant court"—

(a) in the case of a person whose address in the register is (or if he were registered would be) in Scotland, means the Court of Session;

(b) in the case of a person whose address in the register is (or if he were registered would be) in Northern Ireland, means the High Court of Justice in Northern Ireland; and

(c) in the case of any other person (including one appealing against a decision falling within subsection (1)(c) above), means the High Court of Justice in England and Wales.

(6) A person in respect of whom an appealable decision falling within subsection (2) above has been taken may, before the end of the period of 28 days beginning with the date on which notification of the decision was served under section 39(2) above, appeal against the decision to a county court or, in Scotland, the sheriff in whose sheriffdom the address in the register is situated.

(7) On an appeal under this section from a Fitness to Practise Panel, the court may—

(a) dismiss the appeal;

(b) allow the appeal and quash the direction or variation appealed against;

(c) substitute for the direction or variation appealed against any other direction or variation which could have been given or made by a Fitness to Practise Panel; or

(d) remit the case to the Registrar for him to refer it to a Fitness to Practise Panel to dispose of the case in accordance with the directions of the court,

and may make such order as to costs (or, in Scotland, expenses) as it thinks fit.

(8) On an appeal under this section from the General Council, the court (or the sheriff) may—

(a) dismiss the appeal;

(b) allow the appeal and quash the direction appealed against; or

(c) remit the case to the General Council to dispose of the case in accordance with the directions of the court (or the sheriff),

and may make such order as to costs (or, in Scotland, expenses) as it (or he) thinks fit.

(9) On an appeal under this section from a Fitness to Practise Panel, the General Council may appear as respondent; and for the purpose of enabling directions to be given as to the costs of any such appeal the Council shall be deemed to be a party thereto, whether they appear on the hearing of the appeal or not.

Restoration of names to the register

41.—(1) Subject to subsections (2) and (6) below, where the name of a person has been erased from the register under section 35D above, a Fitness to Practise Panel may, if they think fit, direct that his name be restored to the register.

(2) No application for the restoration of a name to the register under this section shall be made to a Fitness to Practise Panel—

(a) before the expiration of five years from the date of erasure; or

(b) in any period of twelve months in which an application for the restoration of his name has already been made by or on behalf of the person whose name has been erased.

(3) An application under this section shall be made to the Registrar who shall refer the application to a Fitness to Practise Panel.

(4) In the case of a person who was provisionally registered under section 15, 15A or 21 above before his name was erased, a direction under subsection (1) above shall be a direction that his name be restored by way of provisional registration under section 15, 15A or 21 above, as the case requires.

(5) The requirements of Part II or Part III of this Act as to the experience required for registration as a fully registered medical practitioner shall not apply to registration in pursuance of a direction under subsection (1) above.

(6) Before determining whether to give a direction under subsection (1) above, a Fitness to Practise Panel shall require an applicant for restoration to provide such evidence as they direct as to his fitness to practise; and they shall not give such a direction if that evidence does not satisfy them.

(7) Where the Professional Conduct Committee give a direction under subsection (6), the Registrar shall without delay serve on the person in respect of whom it has been made a notification of the direction and of his right to appeal against it in accordance with section 40.

(8) Any person in respect of whom a direction has been given under subsection (6) may, after the expiration of three years from the date on which the direction was given, apply to the Professional Conduct Committee for that direction to be reviewed by the Committee and, thereafter, may make further applications for review; but no such application may be made before the expiration of three years from the date of the most recent review decision.

(9) Where, during the same period of erasure, a second or subsequent application for the restoration of a name to the register, made by or on behalf of the person whose name has been erased, is unsuccessful, a Fitness to Practise Panel may direct that his right to make any further such applications shall be suspended indefinitely.

(10) Where a Fitness to Practise Panel give a direction under subsection (9) above, the Registrar shall without delay serve on the person in respect of whom it has been made a notification of the direction and of his right to appeal against it in accordance with section 40 above.

(11) Any person in respect of whom a direction has been given under subsection (9) above may, after the expiration of three years from the date on which the direction was given, apply to the Registrar for that direction to be reviewed by a Fitness to Practise Panel and, thereafter, may make further applications for review; but no such application may be made before the expiration of three years from the date of the most recent review decision.

Interim Orders

41A.—(1) Where an Interim Orders Panel or a Fitness to Practise Panel are satisfied that it is necessary for the protection of members of the public or is otherwise in the public interest, or is in the interests of a fully registered person, for the registration of that person to be suspended or to be made subject to conditions, the Panel may make an order—

(a) that his registration in the register shall be suspended (that is to say, shall not have effect) during such period not exceeding eighteen months as may be specified in the order (an "interim suspension order"); or

(b) that his registration shall be conditional on his compliance, during such period not exceeding eighteen months as may be specified in the order, with such requirements so specified as the Panel think fit to impose (an "order for interim conditional registration").

(2) Subject to subsection (9) below, where an Interim Orders Panel or a Fitness to Practise Panel have made an order under subsection (1) above, an Interim Orders Panel or a Fitness to Practise Panel—

(a) shall review it within the period of six months beginning on the date on which the order was made, and shall thereafter, for so long as the order continues in force, further review it—

(i) before the end of the period of six months beginning on the date of the decision of the immediately preceding review; or

    (ii) if after the end of the period of three months beginning on the date of the decision of the immediately preceding review the person concerned requests an earlier review, as soon as practicable after that request; and

  (b) may review it where new evidence relevant to the order has become available after the making of the order.

(3) Where an interim suspension order or an order for interim conditional registration has been made in relation to any person under any provision of this section (including this subsection), an Interim Orders Panel or a Fitness to Practise Panel may, subject to subsection (4) below—

  (a) revoke the order or revoke any condition imposed by the order;

  (b) vary any condition imposed by the order;

  (c) if satisfied that to do so is necessary for the protection of members of the public or is otherwise in the public interest, or is in the interests of the person concerned, replace an order for interim conditional registration with an interim suspension order having effect for the remainder of the term of the former; or

  (d) if satisfied that to do so is necessary for the protection of members of the public, or is otherwise in the public interest, or is in the interests of the person concerned, replace an interim suspension order with an order for interim conditional registration having effect for the remainder of the term of the former.

(4) No order under subsection (1) or (3)(b) to (d) above shall be made by any Panel in respect of any person unless he has been afforded an opportunity of appearing before the Panel and being heard on the question of whether such an order should be made in his case; and for the purposes of this subsection a person may be represented before the Panel by counsel or a solicitor, or (if rules made under paragraph 1 of Schedule 4 to this Act so provide and he so elects) by a person of such other description as may be specified in the rules.

(5) If an order is made under any provision of this section, the Registrar shall without delay serve a notification of the order on the person to whose registration it relates.

(6) The General Council may apply to the relevant court for an order made by an Interim Orders Panel or a Fitness to Practise Panel under subsection (1) or (3) above to be extended, and may apply again for further extensions.

(7) On such an application the relevant court may extend (or further extend) for up to 12 months the period for which the order has effect.

(8) Any reference in this section to an interim suspension order, or to an order for interim conditional registration, includes a reference to such an order as so extended.

(9) For the purposes of subsection (2) above the first review after the relevant court's extension of an order made by an Interim Orders Panel or a Fitness to Practise Panel or after a replacement order made by an Interim Orders Panel or a Fitness to Practise Panel under subsection (3)(c) or (d) above shall take place—

  (a) if the order (or the order which has been replaced) had not been reviewed at all under subsection (2), within the period of six months beginning on the date on which the relevant court ordered the extension or on which a replacement order under subsection (3)(c) or (d) was made; and

  (b) if it had been reviewed under the provision, within the period of three months beginning on that date.

(10) Where an order has effect under any provision of this section, the relevant court may—

  (a) in the case of an interim suspension order, terminate the suspension;

  (b) in the case of an order for interim conditional registration, revoke or vary any condition imposed by the order;

(c) in either case, substitute for the period specified in the order (or in the order extending it) some other period which could have been specified in the order when it was made (or in the order extending it), and the decision of the relevant court under any application under this subsection shall be final.

(11) Except as provided in subsection (12) below, while a person's registration in the register is suspended by virtue of an interim suspension order under this section he shall be treated as not being registered in the register notwithstanding that his name still appears in the register.

(12) Notwithstanding subsection (11) above, sections 35C to 35E above shall continue to apply to a person whose registration in the register is suspended.

(13) This section applies to a provisionally registered person and to a person registered with limited registration whether or not the circumstances are such that he falls within the meaning in this Act of the expression "fully registered person".

(14) In this section "the relevant court" has the same meaning as in section 40(5) above.

. . .

NOTES:

1. The Fitness to Practise Panel has the power under s.41(9) to indefinitely suspend the right to apply for restoration to the Register. (See generally J. Glynn and D. Gomez, *Fitness to Practise: Health Care Regulatory Law, Principle and Process*, London: Sweet & Maxwell, 2005 24–005 – 24–008).

   The procedure to adopt in such cases was considered in *Raji v General Medical Council* [2003] UKPC 204. To ensure fairness it was held that the issue of restoration should be considered first and then subsequently there should be consideration of the issue of the suspension. It has also be confirmed that there is no presumption that the power of restoration should only be undertaken in exceptional circumstances (see further *Gosai v General Medical Council* [2003] UK PC 31).

2. As noted above on p.240, a decision to restore a medical practitioner to the register may also be referred to the Council for the Regulation of Healthcare Professions as unduly lenient.

(iii) Reform of the GMC

In July 2006 Sir Liam Donaldson, the Chief Medical Officer, published *Good Doctors: Safer Patients*, London: CMO, 2006. This report noted that despite the restructuring of the GMC, it still remained subject to considerable criticism. The report contains some proposals for further major reform. Fundamentally, the report proposals, if implemented, will mean that the GMC will lose most of its powers. In relation to fitness to practise cases, it would only be concerned with the initial assessment but the actual determination of fitness to practise is to be referred to an independent tribunal. There will also be a radical re-evaluation of doctors through appraisal. The recommendations are set out below with commentary.

Chief Medical Officer's Report, Good Doctors: Safer Patients, London: CMO, 2006

The General Medical Council: Moving Forward

Recommendation 1:

In adjudicating upon concerns about a doctor's performance, health or conduct, the standard of proof should be the civil standard rather than the criminal standard.

NOTE:

1. This follows the approach taken in the Shipman Report (discussed above). The Donaldson Report states that, "Medical regulation is a protective jurisdiction and the civil standard should apply."

Recommendation 2:

The General Medical Council's role in investigating concerns or complaints about a doctor's standards of care or conduct should be extended to a local level by the creation of medically qualified licensed General Medical Council affiliates within each organisation (or group of organisations) providing healthcare.

NOTE:

1. This recommendation is aimed at dealing with what are at present inconsistencies and overlap in dealing with professional practice issues through employment as well as through the GMC.

Recommendation 3:

General Medical Council affiliates should be authorised to deal with some fitness to practise cases locally (according to detailed guidelines and definitions) and refer cases at the more severe end of the spectrum to the General Medical Council centrally. Affiliates should have the power to agree a "recorded concern" (but not to impose sanctions affecting registration). The affiliate should inform a doctor's employer or contracting organisation and any complainant when a "recorded concern" is accepted. "Recorded concerns" should be reported to the General Medical Council centrally for collation.

NOTE:

1. This is again aimed at aligning the role of the GMC and the employer.

Recommendation 4:

Where a doctor does not accept a recommendation from a General Medical Council affiliate that a "recorded concern" be entered on the Medical Register, they will automatically be referred to the General Medical Council centrally.

NOTE:

1. On this point the Donaldson Report provides that "if the General Medical Council determines that the doctor has a case to answer, it will investigate it afresh and will not be permitted to rely upon any concessions or admissions made to its affiliate."

Recommendation 5:

Each General Medical Council affiliate should be paired with a member of the public, who should be trained in regulatory and disciplinary procedures. Together, they should operate as part of a wider team within each organisation. This team should include existing complaints management staff and should have administrative support.

Recommendation 6:

A national committee should routinely review all "recorded concerns" entered on the Medical Register. This committee should be able to discuss individual cases with the relevant General Medical Council affiliate if necessary and, in exceptional circumstances, may choose to refer a practitioner for further assessment or investigation.

NOTES:

1. The Report states that importantly this "committee will have a lay majority and will be convened solely for this purpose".
2. The Committee will also have a reporting and scrutiny role.

Recommendation 7:

Each healthcare organisation should identify, and bring to the attention of the relevant General Medical Council affiliate, those complaints that raise concerns about the performance or conduct of a specific doctor.

NOTE:

1. The report indicates that the aim of this measure is to enable the affiliate to identify the most serious issues.

Recommendation 8:

Patients and their representatives should be given the option of lodging complaints about services and individuals in primary care, either at the level of the practice, or at the level of the primary care trust. Such arrangements should be publicised widely in surgeries and within patient information resources.

Recommendation 9:

General Medical Council affiliates, together with the complaints management staff of the organisation, should offer to meet with individual complainants (where appropriate) to address their concerns about specific doctors, explaining any actions taken, or the reasons for apparent inaction. Individual doctors may be required to attend such conflict resolution meetings at the discretion of the General Medical Council affiliate.

NOTE:

1. The Donaldson Report sees this as a means of facilitating "a dialogue with complainants and will enable the complainant to learn what action is being taken to prevent similar problems in the future. The meeting will also provide a forum for an apology to be made, where this is appropriate". The report also notes this needs to be aligned with the new NHS redress scheme.

Recommendation 10:

The General Medical Council should establish rigorous training, accreditation and audit for affiliates, along with comprehensive arrangements for their support in carrying out these functions.

Recommendation 11:

In serious fitness to practise cases, which cannot be dealt with by local regulatory action, investigation and assessment should be carried out by the General Medical Council but formal adjudication should be undertaken by a separate and independent tribunal (with legal, medical and lay representation). Doctors and the General Medical Council should have the right of appeal against the decision of the independent tribunal to the High Court.

NOTE:

1. Again, this will align the GMC with the Shipman recommendations.

Recommendation 12:

The Healthcare Commission and the Parliamentary and Health Service Ombudsman should be able to require the General Medical Council to assess or investigate an individual doctor's performance, health or conduct. These bodies should also be authorised to investigate and bring doctors before the independent tribunal in exceptional circumstances.

Recommendation 13:

During its assessment of a practitioner whose fitness to practise has been called into question, the General Medical Council should make full use of the expertise of the National Clinical Assessment Service.

NOTE:

1. This will give a further role to the National Clinical Assessment Service — see discussion earlier.

Recommendation 14:

The National Clinical Assessment Service should further develop methodologies for the assessment of practitioners with mental health and addiction problems. The NHS should commission a specialised addiction treatment service.

NOTES:

1. This recommendation had been included in an earlier report by the Chief Medical Officer in 1999, *Supporting Doctors, Protecting Patients*.
2. The Donaldson Report proposes that doctors using this service will do so under strict conditions, including follow-up drug and alcohol testing once they return to the workplace.

Recommendation 15:

In managing cases where fitness to practise has been called into question but which cannot be dealt with locally through a "recorded concern", the General Medical Council centrally should have the power to specify packages of rehabilitation and conditions on practice, following a comprehensive assessment. Cases should be brought before the independent tribunal only where a practitioner is uncooperative, where such measures have failed to remove serious risk to patients, or where specified serious misconduct has occurred. Arrangements for making interim orders concerning a registrant's practice where urgent action is required should remain in place. The Council for Healthcare Regulatory Excellence should review the handling of such cases, and refer for adjudication before the independent tribunal any for which it is considered that more serious sanctions were appropriate.

NOTES:

1. The report provides that "sanctions should include undertakings to comply with a wider range of practice conditions than at present, rehabilitation and training programmes, and interim suspension. Once this new system is established, it is anticipated that the number of cases reaching the medical tribunal for formal adjudication will fall.
2. The report also comments that certain misconduct offences would go directly to the independent tribunal.

Recommendation 16:

A clear, unambiguous set of standards should be created for generic medical practice, set jointly by the General Medical Council and the (Postgraduate) Medical Education and Training Board, in partnership with patient representatives and the public. These standards should be adopted by the General Medical Council and made widely available. They should incorporate the concept of professionalism and should be placed in the contracts of all doctors.

NOTE:

1. The aim here is to provide "a universal, operational definition of a 'good doctor' " and again align the role of the employment situation with that of the GMC and harmonise the approach to clinical governance.

Recommendation 17:

A clear and unambiguous set of standards should be set for each area of specialist medical practice. This work should be undertaken by the medical Royal Colleges and specialist associations, with the input of patient representatives, led by the Academy of Medical Royal Colleges.

NOTE:

1. This will help to avoid the overlap and duplication between the present situation of a wide range of guidelines produced by different governing bodies.

Recommendation 38:

The Medical Register should be the key national list of doctors entitled to practise in the United Kingdom and should contain tiers of information (some publicly available, others available with restricted access) about each doctor and their standard of practice. The new Medical Register should be a continuously updated electronic document that would over time subsume a number of other lists and registers currently in place, including primary care performers lists, which should cease to be a statutory requirement.

NOTE:

1. The aim here is to ensure the Medical Register becomes "an up-to-date and accurate source of information".

Recommendation 42:

The primary role of the members of the General Medical Council should be the appropriate corporate governance of the organisation. This role is one of accountability for the quality of services delivered by the organisation in respect of: registration functions; the maintenance of accurate, up-to-date information; the investigation and prosecution of fitness to practise cases; the operation of the devolved system of licensed affiliates; the oversight of revalidation, and the effectiveness of working arrangements with partner organisations.

NOTE:

1. The Donaldson Report noted that the role of the members here should be strategic rather than operational.

Recommendation 43:

The composition of the General Medical Council should be changed to reflect its new responsibilities. It should become more "board-like". Its members should be independently appointed by the Public Appointments Commission, and its President elected from amongst those members.

NOTE:

1. One of the aims of this restructuring is to reduce the prospect of claims of "protectionism" and this is a move from "election" to formal appointment.

Revalidating doctors

Following concerns regarding the need to ensure that doctors are up to date in practice, proposals for revalidation had already been advanced—see discussion above at p.270. This issue is addressed further in the CMO's report.

Recommendation 26:

The process of revalidation will have two components: first, for all doctors, the renewal of a doctor's licence to practise and therefore their right to remain on the Medical Register ("re-licensure"); secondly, for those doctors on the specialist or GP registers, "re-certification" and the right to remain on these registers. The emphasis in both elements should be a positive affirmation of the doctor's entitlement to practise, not simply the apparent absence of concerns.

Recommendation 27:

As doctors approach retirement, they should be invited to a review with their General Medical Council affiliate, where registrant and affiliate should decide together whether a further five-year period of re-licensure is desirable and appropriate. The idea of maintaining a register of retired doctors (to extend beyond such a five-year period) should be considered in more depth: a working group should be established to examine this area and to establish which professional privileges should be permissible for those on such a register. In particular, the safety and desirability of the proposal to allow retired doctors to issue private prescriptions for a limited and defined range of medicines should be considered.

NOTE:

1. The Donaldson Report notes that this is intended to address perceived concern about the standard of retired doctors.

Recommendation 28:

The re-licensing process should be based on the revised system of NHS appraisal and any concerns known to the General Medical Council affiliate. Necessary information should be collated by the local General Medical Council affiliate and presented jointly as a confirmatory statement to a statutory clinical governance and patient safety committee by the chief executive officer of the healthcare organisation and the General Medical Council affiliate. The chairman of this committee should then submit a formal list of recommendations to the General Medical Council centrally.

Recommendation 29:

When a practitioner changes employer or contracting organisation between re-licensure cycles, the previous General Medical Council affiliate should provide a standardised record outlining the practitioner's current position in relation to the elements contributing to re-licensure. In addition to any other professional references sought, prospective employers should ensure that such a record is obtained in a timely fashion.

NOTE:

1. This recommendation should ensure consistency and that persons are not practising inappropriately.

Recommendation 31:

Specialist certification should be renewed at regular intervals of no longer than five years. This process should rely upon membership of, or association with, the relevant medical Royal College, and renewal should be based upon a comprehensive assessment against the standards set by that college. Renewal of certification should be contingent upon the submission of a positive statement of assurance by that college. Independent scrutiny will be applied to the processes of specialist re-certification operated, in order to ensure value for money.

Recommendation 32:

Where doctors fail to satisfy the requirements of either element of revalidation, they should spend a period in supervised practice or out of practice, prior to assessment, in order that a tailored plan of remediation and rehabilitation may be put in place.

NOTES:

The report also makes a range of other recommendations, some of the most pertinent are included here in note form.

1. The General Medical Council is to be made accountable to Parliament and required to produce an annual report (recommendation 44).
2. Other recommendations relate to education and cross-European training issues. These include the recommendation that the responsibility for the undergraduate curriculum and inspection and approval of medical schools should be transferred to the Postgraduate Medical Education and Training Board (recommendation 19).
3. Other proposals include a clinical audit advisory group to be established nationally to drive the development of clinical audit programmes.
4. There are to be new iniatives in primary care including "practice profiling" to enable reflective practice and learning within practices, drawing upon a wide range of clinically relevant data, including information about deaths, prescribing habits and data from the quality and outcomes framework (recommendation 34). This draws upon the experience of the Shipman Inquiry, *op cit*.
5. Primary care trusts are to have a statutory obligation to ensure that "lessons are learned from specific medical errors and complaints" (recommendation 35).

6. In addition, the aim is to facilitate greater accountability through standardised contracts and unlimited access to patient records (recommendation 36).
7. In October 2006 the GMC agreed as part of its response to the report *Good Doctors: Safer Patients* that it would recommend that it would get rid of the medical majority on its council (see C. Dyer, "GMC recommends scrapping medical majority on its council" (2006) 333 B.M.J. 719).

QUESTIONS:

1. Do the CMO's recommendations provide the necessary degree of independence?
2. Do these proposals effectively signal the end of professional self-regulation?

SELECT BIBLIOGRAPHY

J. Allsop and L. Mulcahy, *Regulating Medical Work: Formal and Informal Contracts*, Buckingham: Open UP, 1996.
Chief Medical Officer, *Good Doctors: Safer Patients*, London: CMO, 2006.
C. Christensen, "Complaints Procedures in the NHS: All Change" (1996) 2 *Medical Law International* 247.
Mark Davies, *Medical Self-Regulation: Crisis and Change*, Aldershot: Ashgate, 2006 (forthcoming).
J. Glynn and D. Gomez, *Fitness to Practise: Health Care Regulatory Law, Principle and Process*, London: Sweet & Maxwell, 2005.
J. Hanna, "Internal Resolution of NHS Complaints" (1995) 3 *Medical Law Review* 177.
D. Irvine, *The Doctors' Tale*, Oxford: Ratcliffe Medical Press, 2006.
J. Jacob, *Doctors and Rules: a Sociology of Professional Values*, London: Routledge, 1988.
J. Montgomery, "Medicine, Accountability and Professionalism" (1989) 16 (US) *Journal of Law and Society* 319.
M. Moran and B. Wood, *States, Regulation and the Medical Profession*, Buckingham: Open UP, 1993.
L. Mulcahy, *Disputing Doctors*, Maidenhead: Open University Press, 2003.
L. Mulcahy, "From Fear to Fraternity: Doctors' Contract of Accounts of Complaints" (1996) 18 *Journal of Social Welfare and Family Law* 397.
R. Smith, *Medical Discipline: The Professional Conduct Committee Jurisdiction of the General Medical Council, 1858–1990*, Oxford: Clarendon Press, 1994.
M. Stacey, "Medical Accountability: a Background Paper" in A. Grubb (ed.), *Challenges in Medical Care*, Chichester: John Wiley, 1992.
M. Stacey, *Regulating British Medicine: the General Medical Council*, Chichester: John Wiley, 1992.
Wilson Committee, *Being Heard: the Report of the Wilson Committee*, London: Department of Health, 1994.

PART III

Respect for individual autonomy or right to self-determination is a recurrent theme in health care ethics and practice. To exercise autonomy a patient requires knowledge—knowledge about himself, his current state of health and about the clinical options available. A fundamental basis of health care provision is that the patient should consent freely to clinical procedures. Failure to obtain consent may result in civil proceedings, and in some circumstances a criminal prosecution may be brought. It is important to note that the patient's right to determine his own treatment is both facilitated and constrained by the reality of clinical practice. Furthermore the freedom to consent is limited by the choices which the health professional places before the patient. Indeed, as we saw in Chapter 1 above, the patient cannot demand whatever treatment he wishes.

The *Bolam* test, so influential in the area of clinical malpractice litigation, was adopted by the House of Lords in the context of the disclosure of information regarding treatment in *Sidaway v Bethlem Royal Hospital Governors* [1985] 1 All E.R. 643. Thus, information about risks of treatment must be disclosed in accordance with the standard expected of a responsible body of professional practice. The implications of *Sidaway* are explored in Chapter 6 below. However, while the basis of disclosure is the standard accepted by a body of professional practice, this does not mean that in all situations the views of the defendant's experts will be accepted. Recently, judicial willingness to be prepared to question the body of professional opinion in relation to clinical negligence has generally been reflected in the area of information disclosure (*Pearce v United Bristol NHS Trust* [1999] P.I.Q.R. P53, CA). In addition, the courts have openly articulated the view that information disclosure can be seen in terms of the autonomy of the individual in the leading House of Lords judgment on causation in information disclosure cases (*Chester v Afshar* [2005] 1 A.C. 234, see below).

There is some uncertainty as to whether application of the professional practice standard would be recognised in situations in which it is proposed to include persons in innovative therapy or a clinical trial. Clinical trial procedures, including information sheets supplied to patients, are the subject of scrutiny by a research ethics committee (see Chapter 10 below). The whole area of clinical research and the consent process has been considerably impacted by recent developments, notably the EU Clinical Trials Directive (Directive 2001/20 of the European Parliament and of the Council of April 4, 2001 on the approximation of the laws, regulations and administrative provisions of the Member States relating to the implementation of good clinical practice in the conduct of clinical trials on medicinal products for human use), enacted into English law through the Medicines for Human Use (Clinical Trials) Regulations 2004. This has led to new consent procedures in relation to the inclusion of adults lacking mental capacity and children in trials concerning medicinal products (see Chapter 10 below). A further notable development is that in trials such as these, approval by a research ethics committee is now mandatory before they can be commenced.

For various reasons, for instance due to youth, temporary incapacity or mental disability, patients may be unable to consent to treatment. This raises two issues.

First, who should decide on their behalf, and secondly on what basis should the decision to be given treatment be made? Where an adult patient lacks mental capacity, the House of Lords have confirmed that treatment may be given by a health care professional on the basis that it is in the patient's best interest, although no-one has the power to act as a proxy for the patient (*F v West Berkshire HA* [1989] 2 All E.R. 545). Initially, the courts rooted the assessment of best interests in the *Bolam* test of the responsible body of medical practice. However, over time the courts have indicated that they are prepared to take a more expansive approach, looking at a broader range of social and personal considerations, in determining what constitutes "best interests" (*Re S* [2000] 3 W.L.R. 1288). Decision-making concerning adults lacking capacity will be subject to major changes when the Mental Capacity Act 2005 comes into force in 2007 (see Chapter 5 below). This legislation provides for the first time comprehensive regulation of the law concerning adults lacking mental capacity, ranging from health to general welfare issues. It places the test for capacity on a statutory framework and provides a structure for the "best interests" test and specific statutory safeguards for procedures such as the inclusion of adults lacking mental capacity in clinical research (see further Chapter 10). The child patient poses particular problems in that it is recognised that the child's competence to consent to medical procedures is gradually acquired, and a relative test of capacity may prove acutely difficult to apply (*Gillick v West Norfolk and Wisbech AHA* [1985] 3 All E.R. 402).

The right to consent to treatment usually also encompasses the right to refuse treatment. This is the case even if by refusing that treatment the patient is virtually accepting that he will die. This principle is not universally recognised. First, where patients are regarded as mentally ill, then if the Mental Health Act 1983 is used, they may be required to accept certain care and treatment regardless of their wishes (see Chapter 8) . The imposition of compulsory care and treatment needs to be seen in the light of the increasing litigation regarding human rights and mental health following the Human Rights Act 1998 (see below). Mental health is an area which has been the subject of considerable reform proposals over the last few years following the Richardson Report in 1999 (*Report of the Expert Committee: Review of the Mental Health Act 1983* (1999). Notable tensions have arisen between the policy objectives of respecting individual rights and at the same time dealing with calls to regulate on the basis of perceived risk to others. The controversy which this has generated has led to the Government indicating that a new Mental Health Act is now unlikely in the near future.

There are a number of cases in which the patient's refusal has been overridden, albeit controversially, on application to the court. One of the most controversial areas relates to judicial acceptance of the notion that the parental power of consent may trump treatment refusal by a competent minor (see Chapter 7). This provides a stark illustration of how adherence to the rhetoric of autonomy in the case of the adolescent is in practice circumscribed in important decisions by other considerations, notably clinical assessments regarding the appropriate treatment decision.

The need to respect autonomy is also demonstrated in the protection given to patient information by health care professionals. They are required to maintain confidentiality and not to make unauthorised disclosure of patient information. Today the courts have confirmed that confidentiality is bolstered by the human right to privacy (*Campbell v MGN* [2004] 2 A.C. 457, HL). Health care professionals are required to maintain confidentiality and not to make unauthorised disclosures of patient information (see Chapter 9). Nevertheless, confidentiality is not recognised as absolute either in the law or by professional ethical codes. This can lead to a difficult balancing exercise being undertaken. When determining the legitimacy of disclosure, the courts have made reference to guidelines set out by the General Medical Council. Conflicts may arise between the duty of confidentiality owed to the patient and the need to promote effective decision-making. This is illustrated in relation to the child patient, when situations may arise in which a child seeks to withhold from his or her parents information which the parents will require in order to override the child's refusal of treatment—an issue which arose controversially recently in the context of information concerning abortion (see *R (on the application of Axon) v Secretary of State* [2006] EWCA 37 (Admin)). A patient may also have a statutory right of access to his or her personal health information, whether on computerised or manual files, although again this right is not absolute and can be overridden on "therapeutic" grounds where disclosure may cause harm to the patient (see, for example, the Data Protection Act 1998 and the Data Protection Subject Access (Modification) (Health) Order 2000, SI 2000/413). This may be seen as yet another instance where individual autonomy is circumscribed by medical discretion.

5

CAPACITY

1. Introduction

In a health care context, capacity refers to competence to make decisions with respect to medical treatment, usually whether to consent to or refuse treatment. In Chapter 6, we will address the issue of consent. Before anyone can give a valid consent to medical treatment, he or she must possess the requisite capacity. The current law is the common law, but the Mental Capacity Act 2005 comes into force in 2007. To set the scene for subsequent coverage of the law, we first provide a summary of the law reform process. Secondly, we consider the principles that underlie capacity. Thirdly, and in order to gain some insight into this issue and into questions of capacity generally, we examine the case of Miss B. Next we turn to consider the question of what capacity to make a decision is, both at the common law and in the Mental Capacity Act 2005. We look at what may be done if it is the case that a person is not capable of making their own decision at the common law and under the Mental Capacity Act 2005 in terms of the approach to be relied on, that is a "best interests" test, and the procedures available at common law (a declaration from the High Court) and under the 2005 Act.

No English case had dealt with the issue of capacity until *Re T* in 1992 and *Re C* in 1994. The basis upon which decisions could be made for those who lacked capacity only came to the courts in 1987 and reached the House of Lords in *Re F* in 1989. There have been considerable case law developments since then, which have presented a well-developed common law approach to the basis upon which to identify what is in a person's best interests. These developments have advanced the common law far beyond the point to which it had developed when the Law Commission set out on the reform process which has led to the passage of the Mental Capacity Act 2005.

English law presumes (see Mental Capacity Act 2005, s.1(2), which reflects the common law position) that, in the absence of evidence to the contrary, adult patients are capable of giving or withholding consent to treatment. It thus presumes capacity, rationality, autonomy and freedom. Where there is reason to believe that a patient is unable to understand the decision they are being asked to make, it is necessary to consider whether an adult presumption of capacity is rebutted in the particular case.

Issues in relation to capacity are of major relevance to those involved with health care services. People are not competent to make decisions when they have not yet reached maturity; when they lose capacity through, for example, suffering from dementia; when they never achieve capacity through, for example, some forms of intellectual impairment; and when they have their capacity affected by mental illness. Issues of capacity also become keen as more people survive early childhood illnesses but with serious intellectual impairments and physical problems. Issues of capacity are likely to be raised in a particularly acute form at the end of life (see Chapter 15). There has also been a series of cases in relation to the capacity of young people (see Chapter 7), and a line of cases which deals with decisions about sterilising or performing caesarian sections on women who are deemed to be incompetent (see Chapter 13).

2. THE REFORM PROCESS

In 1989, the Law Commission set out on a project to consider the law in relation to incapacity. The journey involved establishing underlying principles, consultation and, ultimately, a report that appeared in 1995 (*Mental Incapacity*, Law Com No. 231). While there have been many detailed changes, that report remains the essential basis upon which the Mental Capacity Act is built. Subsequent to the Law Commission's proposals, the Government took on the project. It took the proposals through two consultation processes, committed itself to legislation "when Parliamentary time allows", and drafted a Mental Incapacity Bill 2002 that went to pre-legislative scrutiny in 2003. As a consequence of the report of that scrutiny, the Government amended its ideas and introduced the Mental Capacity Bill 2004, while also preparing codes of practice (for the 2006 draft, see *www.dca.gov.uk*) which will expand on the legislation. The Bill received the Royal Assent on April 7, 2005, becoming the Mental Capacity Act 2005. It is anticipated that it will come into force in April 2007.

The Government had originally removed a number of what may appear to be key parts of the Law Commission's scheme, noticeably the following:

1. The independent supervision/second opinion procedures. It wished to simplify the procedures and so removed these protections.
2. Withdrawing hydration and nutrition, that is, the statutory format of the *Bland* decision, because it wished to avoid the passage of the Bill being significantly adversely affected by the anti-euthanasia lobby (see Chapter 14).
3. Withdrawing the provisions in relation to research, on the basis that they were unnecessarily controversial and the legal position could be left to the developing common law and to the European Convention on Biomedicine (see Chapter 10).

Otherwise, the Government made a number of important changes in the light of consultation in a desire to improve the effectiveness and simplicity of the Bill. In order to endeavour to ensure that adequate protections are included and that the entire area is properly covered, subject to what can be left to the code of practice, the Act is relatively long and complicated. In itself this is an issue, since most of the users are not likely to be legally trained or qualified, and the level of necessary complexity may be inhibitive of proper usage.

The pre-legislative scrutiny was broadly supportive of the Bill. The most notable areas of concern were: (1) the need to have provisions in relation to medical research; (2) the need to legislate for the withdrawal of nutrition and hydration; (3) the need to recognise that significant work will have to be done in preparing a code of practice to deal with matters that cannot be included in the legislation; and (4) the need to rethink some of the issues in relation to the proposed general authority for carers and others to act without formal procedures, as it had the tendency to be interpreted too widely. Indeed, much of what the Committee did is to reinstitute many of the recommendations of the Law Commission.

Subsequent to the report of the Pre-Legislative Scrutiny Committee, the 2004 Bill was further amended. In addition to making many drafting improvements and drawing on recommendations of the Scrutiny Committee to make many improvements (e.g. the burden of proof provision in s.1(3), the clarification of the importance of beliefs and values of the incapable person in determining best interests (s.4(5)(b)), perhaps the most noticeable changes are as follows:

1. Change to the title of the Act, thereby emphasising the fact that most people are capable of making most decisions, that most people's decision-making skills may be improved and that this legislation is about supporting vulnerable adults.
2. Introduction of a set of principles that underpin the legislation and should operate as a considerable aid to the use of the Act (s.1).
3. Changes to what was the general authority to act so as to endeavour to ensure that it is not used too frequently and for inappropriate purposes (see ss.5–8).
4. Introduction of provisions in relation to research (see ss.30–33). These are dealt with in Chapter 10.
5. Introduction of the independent consultee services, a form of advocacy, that will also be significant in dealing with the *Bournewood* problem (see Chapter 9 on mental health). The relevant provisions are in ss.34–38. What they clearly mean is that there will be independent input into many, but not all, decisions made about a person who lacks capacity. It will be noted that the independent consultee has a right to seek a declaration from the Court of Protection, but only after seeking the leave of the court.
6. Introduction of provisions to endeavour to ensure that life-sustaining treatment is normally, though not always, given priority and that nothing in the Bill affects the law of murder, manslaughter or assisted suicide (s.58). These are considered in Chapter 14.

The Act has been broadly welcomed, though there are still some concerns, not least whether there will be challenges when necessary to ensure protection for vulnerable adults and compliance (when engaged) with Articles 5, 6 and 8 of the Convention.

Further, the general question of whether there was a need for legislation remains, since the basis upon which the need for legislation was identified was very different by the time the legislation had been passed, as will be seen by noting the current state of the developed common law from 1989 onwards.

For a consideration of the provisions of the Mental Capacity Act relating to the lasting powers of attorney, ss.9–14 (which replace continuing powers of attorney as recommended by the Law Commission) and advance decisions to refuse treatment, covered in ss.24–26, see Chapter 14. These means of decision-making are put in place by a competent person and apply when he is no longer competent. Therefore, they take priority over other means of decision-making on behalf of an incompetent adult.

3. PRINCIPLES

Capacity is a prerequisite for participation in our social and legal system. It involves issues central to health care ethics, concerning autonomy, power and choice, and raises important questions about the ability to make and effectuate decisions with regard to health care and treatment (see S. Stefan, "Silencing the Different Voice: Competence, Feminist Theory and Law" (1993) 47 *University of Miami Law Review* 763). Priority is therefore given to the right to self-determination, and if someone is competent, their decision must be accepted. This is not always easy for those providing health care to accept.

The centrality of respect for the principle of autonomy and the right of self-determination is stated by Cardozo J.

Schloendorff v New York State Hospital (1914) 105 NE 92

" . . . every human being of adult years and sound mind has a right to determine what shall be done with his own body; and a surgeon who performs an operation without his patient's consent, commits an assault."

The Law Commission's reform programme commenced by identifying a set of key underlying principles as follows. It commenced this process in its first consultation paper.

Law Commission, Mentally Incapacitated Adults and Decision-Making: an Overview (Consultation Paper No. 119, 1989)

Principles and values

4.17 The philosophies which should underlie legislation for the care and guardianship of mentally incapacitated people have been the subject of much international debate in recent years. Various basic principles have gained widespread recognition as matters to which any modern legislation should have regard. Whilst opinions may legitimately differ upon these principles and values and their application in any particular circumstances, any law reform will need to reflect and, in some instances, to reach a compromise or conclusion upon them. Given the wide variety of situations and issues which can arise, it is unrealistic to expect that it will be possible to apply the same solutions over the whole range of problems. However, the choice between different solutions may be informed by these principles. In the following paragraphs we summarise the position which debate on the main issues now appears to have reached and would welcome views upon the matters raised.

a) Normalisation

4.18 This principle can be expressed in a variety of different ways. Fundamentally, it aims to treat mentally disordered people as much like other people as possible and to integrate them into the mainstream of everyday life. It also encompasses the maximisation of potential by encouraging people who are to some extent mentally disordered or incapacitated to make decisions for themselves, so that they can learn from them and thus attain a greater degree of independence. For example, a person who does not live at home is not necessarily or even probably unable to decide how to spend his pocket money or what time to go to bed. Another aspect of this is the recognition that, taken to its logical conclusion, the maximisation of potential can involve allowing a person to take calculated risks, and to suffer the consequences when things go wrong.

b) The presumption of competence

4.19 This principle requires all dealings with mentally disordered people and all legislation to be based on the premise that every individual is capable of looking after his own affairs until the contrary is proved. It follows that although people may have to be categorised for certain purposes, their general type of disability (mental handicap, senility etc) should not be used as a criterion; otherwise, once the existence of that disability is proved, a finding of incapacity tends to follow almost automatically. This leads, in effect, to a presumption of incompetence rather than a presumption of competence. Emphasis on functional tests of capacity, rather than "labels", can help to avoid this. The standard of proof of incapacity would normally be the balance of probabilities; however, it could be argued that, in view of the drastic consequences of an adverse finding, the criminal standard of proof beyond reasonable doubt would be more appropriate. The presumption of competence needs to operate alongside a clear system for determining incapacity, and, when relevant, degrees of incapacity, and its consequences.

c) The least restrictive alternative

4.20 This principle has two distinct aspects. The first is that treatment or care should be provided in the least restrictive circumstances possible, for example, in an open rather than a locked ward, or in the community rather than in an institution. The second is that "preference must be given to the means of accomplishing an end that least restricts individual rights", so that intervention must be the minimum required to provide adequate protection. This has led, not only to a preference for informality rather than compulsory powers, but also to the development of the concept of limited guardianship, which is tailored to meet the particular needs of the individual concerned. In most countries which have the alternatives of limited or plenary guardianship, the former is generally preferred whenever possible.

d) Providing safeguards without stigma

4.21 Stigma arises when others perceive someone to belong to a particular category (i.e. the incompetent) about which they have negative preconceptions. This can be minimised by well designed procedures framed in a way which, so far as possible, recognises the widespread reluctance of families and professionals to invoke formal provisions. For example, archaic and stigmatising terminology should be abandoned and, when hearings are necessary, they should be conducted in an informal way in an unintimidating atmosphere. This principle also argues for a non-categorising approach.

e) The "substituted judgement" versus the "best interests" test

4.22 Two different tests have been developed for making decisions on behalf of a mentally incapacitated adult. The "best interests" standard is derived principally from child care law and represents the more paternalistic and at times restrictive approach: the decision taken is that which the decision-maker thinks is best for the person concerned. It was adopted in *Re F.* Under the "substituted judgement" standard, decisions made for an incapacitated person attempt to arrive at the choice that particular person would have made had he been competent to do so. This has, for example, been adopted as the correct standard for the execution of a statutory will. In *Re D (J)*, Megarry V.-C. said "it is the actual patient who has to be considered and not a hypothetical patient. One is not concerned with the patient on the Clapham omnibus . . . I do not think that the Court should give effect to antipathies or affections of the patient which are beyond reason. But subject to all due allowances, I think the Court must seek to make the will which the actual patient, acting reasonably, would have made if notionally restored to full mental capacity, memory and foresight." More recently, the "best interests" and "substituted judgement" tests have been combined in deciding whether it would be best for a severely handicapped baby to be allowed to die rather than to be given strenuous life-saving treatment. In *Re J (a minor) (wardship: medical treatment)*, the Court of Appeal adopted the following passage from the judgement of McKenzie J. in *Re Superintendent of Family and Child Service and Dawson*: "It is not appropriate for an external decision-maker to apply his standards of what constitutes a liveable life . . . The decision can only be made in the context of the disabled person viewing the worthwhileness or otherwise of his life in its own context as a disabled person—and in that context he would not compare his life with that of a person enjoying normal advantages. He would know nothing of a normal person's life having never experienced it."

4.23 The substituted judgement standard is generally thought preferable to the best interests test in principle. Attractive though it may be in theory, however, applying it in practice raises problems. It is more difficult to apply in the case of someone who has never had capacity, for example, someone suffering from severe mental handicap. Most significant decisions in such a person's life will invariably have been taken by others and any choices made by him will have been from a very restricted range of options. Consequently, it can be difficult to draw meaningful conclusions about the views or values he would have had if of full capacity. Any decision will inevitably be influenced by the decision-maker's view of what will be best for him, and the distinction between the two tests may be little more than a matter of language. The substituted judgement standard is easier to apply in the case of someone who once had capacity. There is a chosen life-style to refer to and he is likely to have expressed views on a variety of subjects in the past. But even then there are difficulties. What is to be done if the person in question was throughout his earlier life a notoriously bad judge of certain matters?

Although the interpretation put upon the substituted judgement test by Megarry V.-C. above allows for modification of the more fanciful possibilities in such circumstances, the introduction of an element of reasonableness detracts from the very purpose behind adopting this standard. Given that some degree of "censorship" by those applying the test is probably inevitable, it is difficult to know whether it would in the vast majority of cases make much practical difference. The distinction is, perhaps, likely to be more important as an indication of ethos and emphasis: thinking oneself into the shoes of the person concerned and recognising the value we all place on personal preferences (not all decisions are, or should be, taken on reasonable grounds) is a mark of respect for human individuality which may have a value greater than its practical effect.

f) Achieving a balance

4.24 The demarcation between these principles is not always particularly clear, some overlap and others are to some extent pulling in different directions, reflecting the conflict found throughout this subject between self determination and paternalism, rights and welfare, autonomy and protection. However one expresses it, the dilemma remains the same and one of the more difficult and important decisions to be made will be judging the correct point in any new legislation at which to halt the pendulum. There can be little doubt that there are occasions when intervention is justified; the debate concerns the circumstances in which it should take place. Different degrees of intervention will be appropriate in different circumstances, and there are bound to be differing opinions upon the right degree in any particular case. If the intention is to maximise an individual's own decision-making capacity, then the legal system can respond by requiring a comparatively low threshold when determining competence. Nevertheless, whilst lowering this threshold may be good for the welfare of the individual in terms of autonomy and learning to take responsibility for his own actions, it may be positively bad in other respects, such as, financial decision-making or the care of and provision for his dependants.

4.25 However, it would be consistent both with the traditional approach of English law and with the normalisation principles that the threshold of capacity should remain relatively low. It is not easy to see how any legal system which allows one person to take decisions on behalf of another can at the same time preserve that person's ability to make the decision for himself if he can. A distinction should therefore be drawn between mechanisms which are designed to help a vulnerable but capable person to lead as normal a life as possible and those which are designed to ensure that proper decisions are taken on behalf of those who cannot do so for themselves . . .

4.27 The aims of policy in this area may perhaps be summarised thus:

  (i) that people are enabled and encouraged to take for themselves those decisions which they are able to take;

 (ii) that where it is necessary in their own interests or for the protection of others that someone else should take decisions on their behalf, the intervention should be as limited as possible and concerned to achieve what the person himself would have wanted; and

(iii) that proper safeguards be provided against exploitation, neglect, and physical, sexual or psychological abuse.

These principles and values were distilled, with considerable levels of agreement after consultation, into the following aims of policy for law reform.

Law Commission, Mental Incapacity (Law Com Report No. 231, 1995), para. 2.46

Our overview paper suggested that the aims of policy for this project should be:

  (i) that people are enabled and encouraged to take for themselves those decisions which they are able to take;

 (ii) that where it is necessary in their own interests or for the protection of others that someone else should take decisions on their behalf, the intervention should be as limited as possible and should be concerned to achieve what the person himself would have wanted; and

(iii) that proper safeguards should be provided against exploitation and neglect, and against physical, sexual or psychological abuse.

These policy aims have received very broad support throughout the consultation process. We should, however, now stress that there is no place in the scheme we recommend in this report for the making of decisions which would protect other persons but would not be in the best interests of the person without capacity. We have already argued that the protection of others is the proper preserve of the controlling jurisdiction of the Mental Health Act 1983, whether by way of compulsory detention in hospital or compulsory reception into guardianship. Subject to this proviso, however, our original policy aims still govern our present recommendations.

The principles established by the Law Commission see their legislative interpretation in the Act. The new title of the Act, Mental Capacity rather than Mental Incapacity, emphasises that the law is about maximising capacity wherever possible. The Act now commences with a statement of principles. This relatively recent innovation is to be warmly welcomed as it sets out the key factors to be taken into account within the legislation and should assist in its operation.

Mental Capacity Act 2005

The principles

1.—(1) The following principles apply for the purposes of this Act.

(2) A person must be assumed to have capacity unless it is established that he lacks capacity.

(3) A person is not to be treated as unable to make a decision unless all practicable steps to help him to do so have been taken without success.

(4) A person is not to be treated as unable to make a decision merely because he makes an unwise decision.

(5) An act done, or decision made, under this Act for or on behalf of a person who lacks capacity must be done, or made, in his best interests.

(6) Before the act is done, or the decision is made, regard must be had to whether the purpose for which it is needed can be as effectively achieved in a way that is less restrictive of the person's rights and freedom of action.

QUESTIONS:

1. Do you agree with the priority given to the principle of autonomy and the right of self-determination? You will wish to reflect upon this question after reading the next section. You might also wish to return to this question after studying some of the material in the Chapter 9 on mental health law.
2. Was legislation necessary by 2005?
3. Is it a good idea for legislation to commence with a clear statement of underlying principles? What impact do you think this might have on the usage of the Act and on subsequent litigation?

4. THE CHALLENGE OF CAPACITY

Some of the difficulties associated with accepting the proposition that a capable person makes their own decisions are raised in the following case.

Re B (adult: refusal of medical treatment) [2002] EWHC 429 (Fam)

DAME ELIZABETH BUTLER-SLOSS P.

"[1] The claimant, whom I shall call Ms B, seeks declarations from the High Court in its exercise of the inherent jurisdiction. She claims that the invasive treatment which is currently being given by the defendant by way of artificial ventilation is an unlawful trespass.

[2] The defendant is the NHS hospital trust (the trust) responsible for the hospital which is currently caring for Ms B (the hospital) . . . The main issue is whether Ms B has the capacity to make her own decision about her treatment in hospital. Underlying this important issue is the tragic story of an able and talented woman of 43 who has suffered a devastating illness which has caused her to become tetraplegic and whose expressed wish is not to be kept artificially alive by the use of a ventilator.

The history

[3] Ms B . . . had an unhappy childhood but triumphed over many difficulties to achieve a degree in social science and social work, and a Master's degree in public policy and administration. She is a qualified practice teacher for social work, and has a management diploma from a London college. She worked as a social worker for a number of local authorities and became a team manager. She was appointed in that role to a hospital and was promoted to head of department and principal officer for training and staff development. She is unmarried. She has a close circle of friends and a godchild to whom she is devoted.

Medical history

[4] On 26 August 1999, Ms B suffered a haemorrhage of the spinal column in her neck. She was admitted to the hospital and a cavernoma was diagnosed, a condition caused by a malformation of blood vessels in the spinal cord. She was transferred to another hospital where she stayed for five weeks. She was informed by doctors that there was a possibility of a further bleed, or surgical intervention, which would result in severe disability. On the basis of this advice she executed a living will (dated 4 September 1999). The terms of the will stated that, should the time come when Ms B was unable to give instructions, she wished for treatment to be withdrawn if she was suffering from a life-threatening condition, permanent mental impairment or permanent unconsciousness. She was, however, also told that the risk of re-haemorrhage was not particularly great, and so she felt very optimistic about the future. Her condition gradually improved and after leaving hospital and a period of recuperation, she returned to work. Thereafter Ms B was in generally good health although she had some continued weakness in her left arm.

[5] At the beginning of 2001, Ms B began to suffer from general weakening on the left side of her body, and experienced greater numbness in her legs. She felt unwell on 12 February 2001, and was admitted to the hospital in the early hours of 13 February 2001. She had suffered an intramedullary cervical spine cavernoma, as a result of which she became tetraplegic, suffering complete paralysis from the neck down. On 16 February 2001 she was transferred to the Intensive Care Unit (the ICU) of the hospital. She began to experience respiratory problems, and was treated with a ventilator, upon which she has been entirely dependent ever since.

[6] Ms B told Dr R (a consultant anaesthetist in the ICU of the hospital) and another consultant anaesthetist on about 24 February 2001 that she had a living will on file, and did not want to be ventilated. The doctors informed her that the terms of the living will were not specific enough to authorise withdrawal of ventilation. On 23 March 2001 at another hospital she underwent neurological surgery to remove the cavernous haematoma. After the operation, her condition improved slightly. She regained the ability to move her head, and to articulate words. She was however, as she said, bitterly disappointed that the operation had not been more successful. It was at that time that she first asked for the ventilator to be switched off.

[7] On 26 March 2001 she was assessed by Dr RG, a consultant psychiatrist from another hospital. On 28 March 2001 Ms B was returned to the ICU at the hospital where she remains. She made a request to a consultant anaesthetist to have the ventilator switched off. On 5 April 2001, Ms B gave formal instructions to the hospital, via her solicitors, that she wished the artificial ventilation to be removed. The trust got in touch by telephone with its solicitors, Capsticks, who replied by a letter to the head of external relations. I shall return to that letter later in this judgment. A case conference followed and it was arranged that two independent psychiatric assessments would be conducted before any further steps were taken.

[8] On 10 April 2001 she was assessed by Dr L, a consultant psychiatrist at the hospital, who concluded she had capacity. On 11 April 2001 she was assessed by another consultant psychiatrist at the hospital, Dr E, who initially found that Ms B did have capacity. Dr E on 12 April 2001 then amended her report to state that Ms B did *not* have capacity, after which Dr L amended his original assessment so as to agree with Dr E. After Dr E's initial

opinion, preparations had begun to be made for the ventilator to be turned off. Ms B held discussions with one of the doctors and a lead nurse of the hospital, and it was agreed that three days should be allowed for Ms B to say goodbye to her family and friends and to finalise her affairs. However, these preparations were called off after Dr E changed her report.

[9] Ms B was prescribed anti-depressants on 13 April 2001. She was seen by both Dr E and Dr R on 30 April 2001. Both doctors stated that on this occasion Ms B said that she was relieved the ventilator had not been switched off. On 29 May 2001, Ms B participated in assessment for rehabilitation, and agreed to try it. Long-term plans were made for her rehabilitation, with a view to eventually returning home with 24-hour care, or alternatively a residential nursing home. Dr R gave evidence that on 29 May 2001 Ms B, having been visited by the rehabilitation specialists, was 'very cheerful' and 'upbeat'. She was referred to several spinal units. She received help, which is continuing, from a clinical psychologist. She was reassessed on 29 June 2001 by Dr L, and on 4 July 2001 by Dr E. Their assessments did not provide a firm conclusion as to her mental capacity. On 12 July 2001 a bronchoscopy was carried out as part of treatment for a left lung collapse. At her request, an independent reassessment was conducted by Dr RG on 8 August 2001. He indicated that he did not consider her to be suffering from depression and that he considered her competent to make the decision to discontinue her treatment. Thereafter the hospital treated Ms B as having capacity to make decisions.

8 August to the hearing

[10] Ms B made a further living will on 15 August 2001. On 12 and 25 September two further bronchoscopies were performed with Ms B's consent. She was suffering respiratory distress at the time. The medical director considered that there should be involvement from an ethics committee and that assistance should be sought from outside. The trust did not have an ethics committee and the health authority was unable to consider the problem. Between August 2001 and the issue of these proceedings by Ms B on 16 January 2002 the trust sought advice from various outside sources. The possibility of a one-way weaning programme was suggested by Dr S, a consultant in neuroanaesthesia and intensive care from another hospital who was consulted. One-way weaning is a programme whereby over a period of time the number of breaths supplied by the ventilator is gradually reduced and the patient's body is allowed to become used to breathing on its own again. Generally if the patient cannot manage on his/her own then the number of breaths is increased. In a one-way weaning programme it would be reduced without going back on the support. Sedation would be given but not so as to cause respiratory depression unless clinically indicated. The clinicians were not prepared to turn off the ventilator. The one-way weaning programme was agreed by the clinicians but with reluctance as an acceptable compromise. It was also agreed that this could be achieved either by sending Ms B to a weaning centre or carrying it out in the ICU.

[11] On 12 November Ms B was offered referral to a weaning centre which she rejected. In the alternative she was offered the programme in the ICU. This she also rejected for two reasons, being the length of the process (about three weeks), and the omission of painkillers as part of the treatment. Ms B made it clear from September 2001 that she did not want to go to a spinal rehabilitation unit. She refused the possibility of a referral to one clinic when her name was near the top of the waiting list in October. She also refused the possibility of a bed in a hospice in December since the hospice would not accept her wish to have her ventilator withdrawn.

The issues

[12] Mr Havers QC, for Ms B, has not, for the purpose of this hearing, challenged the conclusions of the psychiatrists as to her lack of mental capacity between April and August 2001 and it is not necessary for me to consider her ability to make decisions before 8 August . . . I shall . . . have to consider in some detail her ability [from August] to make decisions and in particular the fundamental decision whether to require the removal of the

artificial ventilation keeping her alive. It is important to underline that I am not asked directly to decide whether Ms B lives or dies but whether she, herself, is legally competent to make that decision. It is also important to recognise that this case is not about the best interests of the patient but about her mental capacity.

[13] The issues are therefore: (a) does the claimant, Ms B, have the mental capacity to choose whether to accept or refuse medical treatment, in circumstances in which her refusal will, almost inevitably, lead to her death? If the answer is Yes, (b) did she have the capacity to choose from August 2001? Ms B seeks declarations from the court in respect of both questions. (c) If the answer to (b) is Yes, then Ms B seeks a declaration from the court that the hospital has been treating her unlawfully from 8 August 2001. (d) If the answer to (b) is Yes, then Ms B also seeks nominal damages to recognise the tort of trespass to the person. (e) It will be necessary to continue injunctions in relation to publicity.

The law on mental capacity

[14] The general law on mental capacity is, in my judgment, clear and easily to be understood by lawyers. Its application to individual cases in the context of a general practitioner's surgery, a hospital ward and especially in an intensive care unit is infinitely more difficult to achieve . . .

. . .

(a) Assessing capacity

[Having drawn on the law relating to mental capacity, Butler-Sloss identified ambivalence, that is Ms B changing her mind and its possible legal significance.]

[35] In my view, ambivalence may be relevant if, and only if, the ambivalence genuinely strikes at the root of the mental capacity of the patient. As I have already said the principles are clear and, in certain cases, their application to the individual case may be extremely difficult. To resolve disputed issues of capacity, as a last resort, there may have to be an application to the High Court for guidance . . .

. . .

Conclusion on mental capacity

[89] As I have already said Ms B was a most impressive witness. I therefore considered with especial care the evidence of the two psychiatrists and the submissions of Mr Francis for the trust. I start with the presumption that Ms B has mental capacity. That presumption was displaced between April and August 2001 in the light of the assessments by Dr E and Dr L, which have not been challenged in this court. Dr LG in August assessed her as mentally competent and the hospital thereafter treated her as such. Nevertheless, Mr Francis has argued that it is legal capacity which I must consider not the assessment of the mental capacity provided by the doctors. That may be so, but, unless it is an exceptional case, the judicial approach to mental capacity must be largely dependent upon the assessments of the medical profession whose task it is on a regular basis to assess the competence of the patient to consent or refuse the medical/surgical treatment recommended to the patient. If, as in the present case, two experienced and distinguished consultant psychiatrists give evidence that Ms B has the mental capacity to make decisions, even grave decisions about her future medical treatment, that is cogent evidence upon which I can and should rely. That evidence supports and reinforces the assessment of Ms B's competence in August 2001. No psychiatrist has suggested since August that Ms B is not competent.

[90] Mr Francis has pointed to a number of temporary factors which might affect Ms B's competence or erode her capacity: possible evidence of psychological regression; the effect of her grave physical disability; the absence of her experience of rehabilitation which was thought likely to be a positive experience; and the effect of her environment in the ICU. Mr Francis also points to concern about Ms B's history of ambivalence about ventilation and her consent to bronchoscopies.

[91] It is important to note from the outset, as Dr Sensky properly emphasised in his evidence to the court, the importance of avoiding generalisations about the possibilities for patients in Ms B's position for capacity to be diminished by one or a number of temporary factors. Rather, the court's task in the instant case is to determine whether *in fact* Ms B's capacity is affected by any of the factors identified by the trust.

[92] I reject any suggestion that Ms B's capacity has been impaired by the advent of psychological regression. There is no evidence to support it. I do not consider that Ms B has been ambivalent in her determination to choose her medical treatment and in her wish to cease to have artificial ventilation. She did look at the alternatives and went down the path of rehabilitation when she was deemed incapable of making her own decision. As soon as she was deemed capable she made it clear that she did not want to go to a spinal rehabilitation unit and turned down the opportunity of a place in October last year. Her relief at not having to say goodbye to her family and friends in April is entirely explicable on two grounds. First, it must not be forgotten that she was deemed not competent at that time so it would be unjust of me to place great weight on her emotions. Second, if, contrary to the psychiatric assessment, she was competent, her explanation of relief in not undergoing painful and distressing final goodbyes to those she loves, does not seem to me to be incompatible with her long term objective of cessation of artificial ventilation. Equally there is no incompatibility in consenting to the bronchoscopies, refusal of which she felt would involve pain and discomfort, which understandably she did not wish to undergo.

[93] Mr G's evidence to the effect that one must experience the advantages of rehabilitation is probably excellent advice for the vast majority of paraplegic and tetraplegic patients. His view that not to have experienced rehabilitation means that the patient lacks informed consent cannot be the basis for the legal concept of mental capacity. If Mr G were correct, the absence of experience in the spinal rehabilitation clinic would deny Ms B or any other similar patient the right to choose whether or not to go to one. It is not possible to experience before choosing in many medical situations. That is not the state of the law nor, I assume, would the medical profession accept it for many fundamental and practical reasons.

[94] . . . Unless the gravity of the illness has affected the patient's capacity, a seriously disabled patient has the same rights as the fit person to respect for personal autonomy. There is a serious danger, exemplified in this case, of a benevolent paternalism which does not embrace recognition of the personal autonomy of the severely disabled patient. I do not consider that either the lack of experience in a spinal rehabilitation unit and thereafter in the community or the unusual situation of being in an ICU for a year has had the effect of eroding Ms B's mental capacity to any degree whatsoever.

[95] I am therefore entirely satisfied that Ms B is competent to make all relevant decisions about her medical treatment including the decision whether to seek to withdraw from artificial ventilation. Her mental competence is commensurate with the gravity of the decision she may wish to make. I find that she has had the mental capacity to make such decisions since 8 August 2001 and that she will remain competent to make such decisions for the foreseeable future. I should however like to underline the wise submission made to me by Mr Jackson that my decision leaves Ms B with a future choice which she can consider freely now that she will be relieved of the burdens of litigation. She is not bound by her past decision and when she goes to the hospital prepared to accept her, she has the right to reflect on what she may wish to do with her life. I would like to add how impressed I am with her as a person, with the great courage, strength of will and determination she has shown in the last year, with her sense of humour, and her understanding of the dilemma she has posed to the hospital. She is clearly a splendid person and it is tragic that someone of her ability has been struck down so cruelly. I hope she will forgive me for saying, diffidently, that if she did reconsider her decision, she would have a lot to offer the community at large.

Remedies

[96] In the light of my decision that the claimant has mental capacity and has had such capacity since August 2001 I shall be prepared to grant the appropriate declarations after

discussions with counsel. I also find that the claimant has been treated unlawfully by the trust since August.

[97] Throughout the sad developments of this case, all those looking after Ms B have cared for her to the highest standards of medical competence and with devotion. They deserve the highest praise. Ironically this excellent care has to some extent contributed to the difficulties for the hospital. Ms B has been treated throughout in the ICU in which the medical and nursing team are dedicated to saving and preserving life, sometimes in adverse medical situations. As Dr C said, they are trained to save life. The request from Ms B, which would have been understood in a palliative care situation, appears to have been outside the experience of the ICU in relation to a mentally-competent patient. It was seen by some as killing the patient or assisting the patient to die and ethically unacceptable. The solicitors to the trust, Capsticks, wrote an excellent letter in April which set out with admirable clarity the legal position. As a result of the assessment of Ms B by Dr L and Dr E, the trust did not have to reconsider the situation until August. At that time it would appear that the letter was not re-read. The solicitors were not asked to advise further and the trust over a period of seven to eight months went down a number of ineffective paths.

. . .

[99] It is important to draw a careful distinction between the duties of the dedicated team in the ICU of the hospital caring for Ms B and the trust responsible for the working of the hospital. In my view, the latter should have taken steps to deal with the issue. The failure to do so has led me to the conclusion that I should mark my finding that the claimant has been treated unlawfully by the NHS hospital trust by a small award of damages. I shall not decide the amount until Mr Francis has had an opportunity to make representations if he wishes to do so."

QUESTIONS:

1. Do you agree that the law is clear and easily understood but its application can be difficult? See M.J. Gunn, J.G. Wong, I.C.H. Clare and A.J. Holland, "Decision-making Capacity" (1999) 7 *Medical Law Review* 269.
2. Did the doctors treating Ms B struggle to accept her decision? Why do you think that was the case? Does this cause you to revisit your views on the priority to be given to respect for the principle of autonomy?
3. Is it difficult to be objective about capacity when its consequences may be the rejection of what appears to the health care providers to be a good treatment offer? Why?
4. If, as Mr G suggested (para. [93]), a patient must have experience of an option before having capacity, what consequences would that have had for decision-making by anyone facing a treatment option for the first time?
5. If Ms B changed her mind, is that evidence of ambivalence or is it evidence of the difficulty the decision? How do you judge?

5. CAPACITY TO CONSENT AT COMMON LAW AND UNDER THE MENTAL CAPACITY ACT 2005

(a) The common law

According to Lord Brandon in *Re F* [1990] 2 A.C. 1 (discussed below at p.321), to be competent to give a legally effective consent the patient must be able to understand the nature and purpose of the treatment, and must be able to weigh the risks and benefits of it. The importance of understanding had also been stressed in *Gillick v West Norfolk and Wisbech AHA* [1985] 3 All E.R. 402 which established that a young person's capacity to consent to treatment is a matter of clinical judgment (see Chapter 7). Focusing on understanding is not the only possible approach to take.

M.J. Gunn, J.G. Wong, I.C.H. Clare and A.J. Holland, "Decision-making Capacity" (1999) 7 Medical Law Review 269

In America it has been made clear [by P.S. Applebaum and T. Grisso] that the functional approach can involve some or all of the following *four* abilities: (1) *Understanding*, which refers "to the ability to comprehend the information provided in the treatment disclosure for informed consent"; (2) *Appreciation*, which refers "to the patient's beliefs about the disorder and potential treatments, especially the ability to apply realistically to one's own situation that which is understood"; (3) *Reasoning*, which refers "to the ability to process treatment information and one's preferences in a logical manner"; (4) *Expressing a choice*, which refers "to the patient's ability to state a preference".

Bearing this in mind, consider the leading case on capacity, which is the following Court of Appeal decision. What follows is the extracts relevant only to the issue of capacity.

Re MB (medical treatment) [1997] 2 F.L.R. 426

Giving the judgment of the court:

BUTLER-SLOSS L.J.

"*General principles*

We start by setting out the basic principles which underpin the proper approach to the issues raised on this appeal.

(1) Subject to (3) below, in general it is a criminal and tortious assault to perform physically invasive medical treatment, however minimal the invasion might be, without the patient's consent, see *Collins v Wilcox* [1984] 1 WLR 1172 per Goff LJ at page 1177, cited with approval in *Re F (Mental Patient: Sterilisation)* [1990] 2 AC 1.
(2) A mentally competent patient has an absolute right to refuse to consent to medical treatment for any reason, rational or irrational, or for no reason at all, even where that decision may lead to his or her own death, see *Sidaway v Board of Governors of the Bethlem Royal Hospital* [1985] AC 871 per Lord Templeman at pages 904–905; see also *Re T (An Adult) (Consent to Medical Treatment)* [1993] Fam 95 per Lord Donaldson MR at page 102.
(3) Medical treatment can be undertaken in an emergency even if, through a lack of capacity, no consent had completely been given, provided the treatment was a necessity and did no more than was reasonably required in the best interests of the patient: *Re F* (supra).

Capacity to decide

Problems can arise on the issue of capacity to consent to or refuse treatment. The starting point for consideration of the test to be applied is the decision of this Court in *Re T* (supra).

Thorpe J, in *Re C (Refusal of Medical Treatment)* [1994] 1 FLR 31, formulated the test to be applied where the issue arose as to capacity to refuse treatment . . . Thorpe J said at page 36:

'I consider helpful Dr E's analysis of the decision-making process into three stages: first, comprehending and retaining treatment information, secondly, believing it, and, thirdly, weighing it in the balance to arrive at choice . . . .'

[Butler-Sloss then referred to the similar approach recommended by the Law Commission. And then turned her attention to some of the caesarian section decision: *Tameside and Glossop Acute Services Trust v CH* [1996] 1 F.L.R. 762; *Norfolk and Norwich HealthCare (NHS) Trust v W* [1996] 2 F.L.R. 613; *Rochdale Healthcare (NHS) Trust v C* (1996) (unreported); *Re L* (1996) (unreported), *Re S (Adult: Surgical Treatment)* [1993] 1 F.L.R. 26.]

Conclusions on capacity to decide

. . . [I]t is important to keep in mind the basic principles we have outlined, and the court should approach the crucial question of competence bearing the following considerations in mind. They are not intended to be determinative in every case, for the decision must inevitable depend upon the particular facts before the court.

1. Every person is presumed to have the capacity to consent to or to refuse medical treatment unless and until that presumption is rebutted.
2. A competent woman who has the capacity to decide may, for religious reasons, other reasons, for rational or irrational reasons or for no reason at all, choose not to have medical intervention, even though the consequence may be the death or serious handicap of the child she bears, or her own death. In that event the courts do not have the jurisdiction to declare medical intervention lawful and the question of her own best interests objectively considered, does not arise.
3. Irrationality is here used to connote a decision which is so outrageous in its defiance of logic or of accepted moral standards that no sensible person who had applied his mind to the question to be decided it could have arrived at it. As Kennedy and Grubb (*Medical Law*, Second Edition 1994) point out, it might be otherwise if a decision is based on a misperception of reality (e.g. the blood is poisoned because it is red). Such a misperception will be more readily accepted to be a disorder of the mind. Although it might be thought that irrationality sits uneasily with competence to decide, panic, indecisiveness and irrationality in themselves do not as such amount to incompetence, but they may be symptoms or evidence of incompetence. The graver the consequences of the decision, the commensurately greater the level of competence is required to take the decision: *Re T* (supra), *Sidaway* (supra) at p. 904 and *Gillick v West Norfolk and Wisbech Area Health Authority* [1986] 1 AC 112, 169 and 186.
4. A person lacks capacity if some impairment or disturbance of mental functioning renders the person unable to make a decision whether to consent to or to refuse treatment. That inability to make a decision will occur when
   a. The patient is unable to comprehend and retain the information which is material to the decision, especially as to the likely consequences of having or not having the treatment in question.
   b. The patient is unable to use the information and weight it in the balance as part of the process of arriving at the decision. If, as Thorpe J observed in *Re C* (supra), a compulsive disorder or phobia from which the patient suffers stifles belief in the information presented to her, then the decision may not be a true one. As Lord Cockburn C.J. put it is *Banks v Goodfellow* (1870) L.R. 5 Q.B. 549 at p. 569:
      'One object may be so forced upon the attention of the invalid as to shut out all others that might require consideration.'

5. The 'temporary factors' mentioned by Lord Donaldson M.R. in *Re T* (supra) (confusion, shock, fatigue, pain or drugs) may completely erode capacity but those concerned must be satisfied that such factors are operating to such a degree that the ability to decide is absent.

6. Another such influence may be panic induced by fear. Again careful scrutiny of the evidence is necessary because hear of an operation may be a rational reasons for refusal to undergo it. Fear may also, however, paralyse the will and thus destroy the capacity to make a decision.

Applying these principles to the facts of this case we find:

1. Miss MB consented to a caesarian section.

2. What she refused to accept was not the incision by the surgeon's scalpel but only the prick of the anaesthetist's needle. Capacity is commensurate with the gravity of the decision to be taken.

3. She could not bring herself to undergo the caesarian section she desired because, as the evidence established, 'a fear of needles . . . has got in the way of proceeding with the operation.' 'At the moment of panic, . . . her fear dominated all.' ' . . . at the actual point she was not capable of making a decision at all . . . at that moment the needle or mask dominated her thinking and made her quite unable to consider anything else.'

On that evidence she was incapable of making a decision at all. She was at that moment suffering an impairment of her mental functioning which disabled her. She was temporarily incompetent . . . ."

Butler-Sloss L.J. then turned to the best interests of Miss MB to decide whether the caesarian section should have taken place and also considered the position of the unborn child and dealt with some procedural matters, which are very important but not covered in any detail in this work.

NOTES:

1. In *Re T (Adult: Refusal of Treatment)* [1993] Fam. 95, the Court of Appeal had to consider the decision of a woman to refuse a blood transfusion. It decided that her refusal was not valid because of the undue influence of her mother, a Jehovah's Witness, and so T's decision did not have the requisite voluntariness. In the course of his judgment, Lord Donaldson M.R. provided the following guidance.

" . . . The law requires that an adult patient who is mentally and physically capable of exercising a choice *must* consent if medical treatment of him is to be lawful, although the consent need not be in writing and may sometimes be inferred from the patient's conduct in the context of the surrounding circumstances. Treating him without his consent or despite a refusal of consent will constitute the civil wrong of trespass to the person and may constitute a crime. If, however, the patient has made no choice and, when the need for treatment arises, is in no position to make one, the classic emergency situation with an unconscious patient, e.g. the practitioner can lawfully treat the patient in accordance with his clinical judgment of what is in the patient's best interest.
There seems to be a view in the medical profession that in such emergency circumstances the next of kin should be asked to consent on behalf of the patient and that, if possible, treatment should be postponed until that consent has been obtained. This is a misconception because the next of kin has no legal right either

to consent or to refuse consent. This is not to say that it is an undesirable practice if the interests of the patient will not be adversely affected by any consequential delay . . .

The right to decide one's own fate presupposes a capacity to do so. Every adult is presumed to have that capacity, but it is a presumption which can be rebutted. This is not a question of the degree of intelligence or education of the adult concerned. However a small minority of the population lack the necessary mental capacity due to mental illness or retarded development . . . This is a permanent or at least a long-term state. Others who would normally have that capacity may be deprived of it or have it reduced by reason of temporary factors, such as unconsciousness or confusion or other effects of shock, severe fatigue, pain or drugs being used in their treatment.

Doctors faced with a refusal of consent have to give very careful and detailed consideration to the patient's capacity to decide at the time when the decision was made. It may not be the simple case of the patient having no capacity because, for example, at that time he had hallucinations. It may be the more difficult case of a temporarily reduced capacity at the time when his decision was made. What matters is that the doctors should consider whether at that time he had a capacity which was commensurate with the gravity of the decision which he purported to make. The more serious the decision, the greater the capacity required. If the patient had the requisite capacity, they are bound by his decision. If not, they are free to treat him in what they believe to be his best interests.

This problem is more likely to arise at a time when the patient is unconscious and cannot be consulted. If he can be consulted, this should be done, but again full account has to be taken of his then capacity to make up his own mind.

As I pointed out at the beginning of this judgment, the patient's right of choice exists whether the reasons for making that choice are rational, irrational, unknown or even non-existent. That his choice is contrary to what is to be expected of the vast majority of adults is only relevant if there are other reasons for doubting his capacity to decide. The nature of his choice or the terms in which it is expressed may then tip the balance.

The vitiating effect of outside influence

A special problem may arise if at the time the decision is made the patient has been subjected to the influence of some third party. This is by no means to say that the patient is not entitled to receive and indeed invite advice and assistance from others in reaching a decision, particularly from members of the family. But the doctors have to consider whether the decision is really that of the patient. It is wholly acceptable that the patient should have been persuaded by others of the merits of such a decision and have decided accordingly. It matters not how strong the persuasion was, so long as it did not overbear the independence of the patient's decision. The real question in each case is 'Does the patient really mean what he says or is he merely saying it for a quiet life, to satisfy someone else or because the advice and persuasion to which he has been subjected is such that he can no longer think and decide for himself?' In other words 'Is it a decision expressed in forma only, not in reality?'

When considering the effect of outside influences, two aspects can be of crucial importance. First, the strength of the will of the patient. One who is very tired, in pain or depressed will be much less able to resist having his will overborne than one who is rested, free from pain and cheerful. Second, the relationship of the 'persuader' to the patient may be of crucial importance. The influence of parents on their children or of one spouse on the other can be, but is by no means necessarily, much stronger than would be the case in other relationships. Persuasion based upon religious belief can also be much more compelling and the fact that arguments based upon religious beliefs are being deployed by someone in a very close relationship with the patient will given them added force and should alert the doctors to the possibility—no more—that the patient's capacity or will to decide has been overborne. On other words the patient may not mean what he says.

The scope and basis of the patient's decision

If the doctors consider that the patient has the capacity to decide and has exercised his right to do so, they still have to consider what was the true scope and basis of that decision. [Where the matter cannot be discussed because of the lack of capacity of the patient, w]hat they *can* do is to consider whether at the time the decision was made it was intended by the patient to apply in the changed situation . . . If the factual situation falls outside the scope of the refusal or if the assumption upon which it is based is falsified, the refusal ceases to be effective . . .

Summary

1. Prima facie every adult has the right and capacity to decide whether or not he will accept medical treatment, even if a refusal may risk permanent injury to his health or even lead to premature death. Furthermore, it matters not what whether the reasons were rational or irrational, unknown or even non-existent. This is so notwithstanding the very strong public interest in preserving the life and health of all citizens. However the presumption of capacity to decide, which stems from the fact that the patient is an adult, is rebuttable.

2. An adult patient may be deprived of his capacity to decide either by long term mental incapacity or retarded development or by temporary factors such as unconsciousness or confusion or the effects of fatigue, shock, pain or drugs . . .

4. Doctors faced with a refusal of consent have to give very careful and detailed consideration to what was the patient's capacity to decide at the time when the decision was made. It may not be a case of capacity or no capacity. It may be a case of reduced capacity. What matters is whether at that time the patient's capacity was reduced below the level needed in the case of a refusal of that importance, for refusals can vary in importance. Some may involve a risk to life or of irreparable damage to health. Others may not.

5. In some cases doctors will not only have to consider the capacity of the patient to refuse treatment, but also whether the refusal has been vitiated because it resulted not from the patient's will, but from the will of others. It matters not that those others sought, however strongly, to persuade the patient to refuse, so long as in the end the refusal represented the patient's independent decision. If, however, his will was overborne, the refusal will not have represented a true decision. In this context the relationship of the persuader to the patient—for example, spouse, parents or religious adviser—will be important, because some relationships more readily lend themselves to overbearing the patient's independent will than do others.

6. In all cases doctors will need to consider what is the true scope and basis of the refusal. Was it intended to apply in the circumstances which have arisen? Was it based upon assumptions which in the event have not been realised? A refusal is only effective within the scope and is vitiated if it is based upon false assumptions."

2. The necessary degree of understanding does not vary with the treatment, but how difficult it is to understand the information does vary. Therefore, more people will lack capacity to make decisions about complex treatments (especially where there is complexity about both the technical aspects and the impact on health and life of the treatment, such as brain or heart surgery) than non-complex treatments (such as a blood test). So,

capacity may vary depending on the gravity of the decision involved. The classic illustration is the case of *In the Estate of Park* [1954] P. 122. In this case Mr Park had suffered a disabling stroke which left his memory and speech impaired. It was held that although he lacked the capacity to make a valid will on May 30, 1945, he retained sufficient understanding to marry validly on that same day. The crucial difference was that, on the facts, the will was much more complicated than the consequences of marriage. It does not follow that marriage is necessarily always an easier matter to understand.

3. A particular difficulty is fluctuating capacity, which may, in some cases, appear as ambivalence. It seems that the law may respond to the issue of fluctuating capacity differently, depending on whether the patient is an adult or a minor. (For the position in relation to minors, see Lord Donaldson's judgment in *Re R (A Minor)* [1991] 4 All E.R. 177, extracted in Chapter 7).

4. For practical guidance on the assessment of capacity, see *Assessment of Mental Capacity: Guidance for Doctors and Lawyers*, Report of the British Medical Association and the Law Society (2nd edn), London: BMA, 2004.

QUESTIONS:

1. What is the role of next of kin in relation to consent? Might some relatives find your conclusions difficult? If so, why?
2. If the law is clear (as stated by Butler-Sloss P. in *Re B*, above), is the real difficulty applying that law to various different situations? Consider the following:

   (a) When does a needle phobia sufficiently interfere with the decision-making process to produce incapacity? How is fear to be distinguished from phobia? Are there implications for the training of doctors, psychologists and others involved in these judgments?
   (b) What if someone has grandiose delusions about being a doctor and refuses an amputation of their gangrenous leg? In *Re C* [1994] 1 All E.R. 819, the court felt that Mr C was, nevertheless, competent to refuse. He was a patient in Broadmoor Hospital with chronic paranoid schizophrenia. He had stated that he would prefer to die with two feet than live with one. He believed that he might survive with the help of God, the doctors and the nurses. Thorpe J. upheld C's anticipated refusal. For consideration of advance directives, see Chapter 14.

3. Why should the patient have to believe the information? Fennell suggests that it does not mean that the patient must accept the medical evaluation of the likely outcome of having the treatment or not having it and of the trade-off between risks and benefits. Thorpe J. clarified the test in his later judgment in *B v Croydon Health Authority* [1995] 1 All E.R. 683 (see

below at pp.543–544) where he differentiated between outright disbelief, which meant being "impervious to reason, divorced from reality, or incapable of judgment after reflection", and "the tendency which most people have when undergoing medical treatment to self assess and then to puzzle over the divergence between medical and self assessment". (See P. Fennell, *Treatment without Consent*, at p.257.)

4. How far, if at all, can a general assessment of capacity help ascertain whether a patient is legally competent to consent to, or refuse, a particular treatment? (For criticism of existing legal definitions of capacity as based on the assumption that competence is an inherent, objective and measurable attribute of an individual, see S. Stefan, "Silencing the Different Voice: Competence, Feminist Theory and Law" (1993) 47 *University of Miami Law Review* 763.)

5. Do you think that the approach in *Re MB* and in *Re C* takes sufficient account of the comment by Lord Donaldson in *Re T* that the patient's capacity must be "commensurate with the gravity of the decision"?

6. Could an anorexic satisfy Thorpe J.'s test of capacity, given that compulsion to refuse treatment (i.e. feeding) is itself the major symptom of the condition?

(b) The Mental Capacity Act 2005

The Mental Capacity Act contains a statutory test for capacity, which commenced life on the basis of the Law Commission's Report.

Law Commission, Mental Incapacity, Law Com. 231, 1995

(Footnotes and references to its draft Bill omitted)

(1) Capacity and Lack of Capacity

3.2 It is presumed at common law that an adult has full legal capacity unless it is shown that he or she does not. If a question of capacity comes before a court the burden of proof will be on the person seeking to establish incapacity, and the matter will be decided according to the usual civil standard, the balance of probabilities. We proposed in Consultation Paper No. 128 that the usual standard should continue to apply and the vast majority of our respondents agreed with this proposal. A number, however, argued that it would be helpful if the new statutory provisions were expressly to include and restate both the presumption of capacity and the relevant standard of proof.

We recommend that there should be a presumption against lack of capacity and that any question whether a person lacks capacity should be decided on the balance of probabilities.

3.3 . . . There are three broad approaches [to capacity]: the "status", "outcome" and "functional" approaches. A "status" test excludes all persons under eighteen from voting and used to exclude all married women from legal ownership of property . . . The status approach is quite out of tune with the policy aim of enabling and encouraging people to take for themselves any decision which they have capacity to take.

3.4 An assessor of capacity using the "outcome" method focuses on the final content of an individual's decision. Any decision which is inconsistent with conventional values, or with which the assessor disagrees, may be classified as incompetent. This penalises individuality and demands conformity at the expense of personal autonomy. A number of our respondents argued that an "outcome" approach is applied by many doctors; if the outcome of the patient's deliberations is to agree with the doctor's recommendations then he or she is taken to have capacity, while if the outcome is to reject a course which the doctor has advised then capacity is found to be absent.

3.5 Most respondents . . . supported the "functional" approach. This also has the merit of being the approach adopted by most of the established tests in English law. In this approach, the assessor asks whether an individual is able, at the time when a particular decision has to be made, to understand its nature and effects. Importantly, both partial and fluctuating capacity can be recognised. Most people, unless in a coma, are able to make at least some decisions for themselves, and many have levels of capacity which vary from week to week or even from hour to hour.

3.6 In view of the ringing endorsement of the "functional" approach given by respondents to the overview paper, we formulated a provisional "functional" test of capacity and set this out in all three of our 1993 consultation papers. This test focused on inability to understand or, in the alternative, inability to choose. We also made specific provision for those unable to communicate a decision they might in fact have made. We were encouraged to find that many respondents approved our draft test, and we have been able to build on it while taking into account suggestions made on consultation. Although one respondent argued that the whole idea of a test of capacity was ill-conceived and unhelpful, many said that it was vital to have a clear test, and one which catered explicitly, for partial and fluctuating capacity. Professor Michael Gunn has referred to "the virtue of certainty" and written that our proposals for a statutory test of capacity will be welcomed, "if for no other reason than introducing certainty and clarity".

3.7 The present law offers a number of tests of capacity depending on the type of decision in issue . . . For the purposes of our new legislative scheme, a single statutory definition should be adopted. We turn now to consider the terms of such a definition.

3.8 In the consultation papers we suggested that a person (other than someone unable to communicate) should not be found to lack capacity unless he or she is first found to be suffering from "mental disorder" as defined in the Mental Health Act 1983. The arguments for and against such a diagnostic hurdle are very finely balanced . . . In the event, most respondents agreed with our preliminary view that a diagnostic hurdle did have a role to play in any definition of incapacity, in particular in ensuring that the test is stringent enough not to catch large numbers of people who make unusual or otherwise unwise decisions . . . Although we gave very careful consideration to the arguments against the inclusion of any diagnostic threshold, we have concluded that such a threshold would provide a significant protection and would in no sense prejudice or stigmatise those who are in need of help with decision-making.

3.9 That said, a significant number of respondents, including many who favoured a diagnostic threshold of some sort, expressed misgivings about the new legislation "coat-tailing" on the statutory shorthand of "mental disorder" and the definition set out in the Mental Health Act 1983 . . . Although this definition is extremely broad and may well cover all the conditions which a diagnostic threshold should cover we no longer favour its incorporation into the new legislation. We learned at first hand in working party meetings how "mental disorder" is equated in many minds, both lay and professional, with the much narrower phenomenon of psychiatric illness or with the criteria for compulsory detention under the Mental Health Act 1983 . . .

3.12 We take the view that (except in cases where the person is unable to communicate) a new test of capacity should require that a person's inability to arrive at a decision should be linked to the existence of a "mental disability". The adoption of the phrase "mental disability" will distinguish this requirement from the language of the Mental Health Act 1983 and will stress the importance of a mental condition which has a disabling effect on the person's capacity.

We recommend that the expression "mental disability" in the new legislation should mean any disability or disorder of the mind or brain, whether permanent or temporary, which results in an impairment or disturbance of mental functioning.

3.13 We took the provisional view in the consultation papers that those who cannot communicate decisions should be included within the scope of the new jurisdiction. We had in mind particularly those who are unconscious. In some rare conditions a conscious patient may be known to retain a level of cognitive functioning but the brain may be completely unable to communicate with the body or with the outside world. In other cases, particularly after a stroke, it may not be possible to say whether or not there is cognitive dysfunction. It can, however, be said that the patient cannot communicate any decision he or she may make. In either case, decisions may have to be made on behalf of such people, and only two respondents expressed the purist view that they should be excluded from our new jurisdiction because they do not suffer from true "mental incapacity". It appears to us appropriate that they should be brought within the scope of our new legislation rather than being left to fend for themselves with the uncertain and inadequate principles of the common law.

The definition of incapacity

3.14 The functional approach means that the new definition of incapacity should emphasize its decision-specific nature. A diagnostic threshold of "mental disability" should be included, except in cases of inability to communicate.

> *We recommend that legislation should provide that a person is without capacity if at the material time he or she is:*
>
> *(1) unable by reason of mental disability to make a decision on the matter in question, or*
> *(2) unable to communicate a decision on that matter because he is unconscious or for any other reason.*

3.15 It would defeat our aim of offering clarity and certainty were no further guidance given as to the meaning of the phrase "unable to make a decision". In the consultation papers we identified two broad sub-sets within this category, one based on inability to understand relevant information and the other based on inability to make a "true choice". Although many respondents expressed disquiet about the elusiveness of the concept of "true choice", there was broad agreement that incapacity cannot in every case be ascribed to an inability to understand information. It may arise from an inability to use or negotiate information which has been understood. In most cases an assessor of capacity will have to consider both the ability to understand information and the ability to use it exercising choice, so that the two "sub-sets" should not be seen as mutually exclusive. This was emphasised by Thorpe J. in the very important High Court case of *Re C (Adult: Refusal of Treatment)* . . . [He] had to make a preliminary finding as to whether the patient concerned had capacity to refuse consent to amputation of his leg. He found it helpful to analyse decision-making capacity in three stages: first, comprehending and retaining information, second, believing it and, third, "weighing it in the balance to arrive at choice . . . "

3.16 Respondents favoured our suggestion that it was more realistic to test whether a person can understand information, than to test whether he or she can understand "the nature of" an action or decision. It was, however, suggested that an ability to "appreciate" information about the likely consequences of a decision might be conceptually different from an ability to understand such information. We prefer to approach this question in a slightly different way, on the basis that information about consequences is one of the sorts of information which a person with capacity understands. Respondents supported the express mention of foreseeable consequences in our draft test, and we still see advantage in drawing attention to the special nature of information about likely consequences, as information which will in every case be relevant to the decision.

> *We recommend that a person should be regarded as unable to make a decision by reason of mental disability if the disability is such that, at the time when the decision needs to be made, he or she is unable to understand or retain the information relevant to the decision, including information about the reasonably foreseeable consequences of deciding one way or another or failing to make the decision.*

3.17 There are cases where the person concerned can understand information but where the effects of a mental disability prevent him or her from using that information in the decision-making process . . . [C]ertain compulsive conditions cause people who are quite able to absorb information to arrive, inevitably, at decisions which are unconnected to the information or their understanding of it. An example is the anorexic who always decides not to eat. There are also some people who, because of a mental disability, are unable to exert their will against some stronger person who wishes to influence their decisions or against some *force majeure* of circumstances. As Thorpe J. said in *Re C*, some people can understand information but are prevented by their disability from being able to believe it. We originally suggested that such cases could be described as cases where incapacity resulted from inability to make a "true choice". Common to all these cases is the fact that the person's eventual decision is divorced from his or her ability to understand the relevant information. Emphasising that the person must be able to use the information which he or she has successfully understood in the decision-making process deflects the complications of asking whether a person needs to "appreciate" information as well as understand it. A decision based on a compulsion, the overpowering will of a third party or any other inability to act on relevant information as a result of mental disability is not a decision made by a person with decision-making capacity.

We recommend that a person should be regarded as unable to make a decision by reason of mental disability if the disability is such that, at the time when the decision needs to be made, he or she is unable to make a decision based on the information relevant to the decision, including information about the reasonably foreseeable consequences of deciding one way or another or failing to make the decision.

3.18 In the draft test of incapacity . . . we suggested that a person should be found to lack capacity if he or she was unable to understand an explanation of the relevant information in broad terms and simple language. Many respondents supported this attempt to ensure that persons should not be found to lack capacity unless and until someone has gone to the trouble to put forward a suitable explanation of the relevant information. This focus requires an assessor to approach any apparent inability as something which may be dynamic and changeable. As one commentator to our original draft test has written, we chose "to import the patient's right to information by implication into the test of capacity". Further guidance on the way the new statutory language may impinge on the methods of assessing capacity in day to day practice should be given in a code of practice accompanying the legislation.

We recommend that a person should not be regarded as unable to understand the information relevant to a decision if he or she is able to understand an explanation of that information in broad terms and simple language.

3.19 Those we consulted, however, overwhelmingly urged upon us the importance of making . . . an express stipulation [a person should not be regarded as lacking capacity because the decision made would not have been made by a person of ordinary prudence]. This would emphasise the fact that the "outcome" approach to capacity has been rejected, while recognising that it is almost certainly in daily use.

We recommend that a person should not be regarded as unable to make a decision by reason of mental disability merely because he or she makes a decision which would not be made by a person of ordinary prudence.

(2) Inability to communicate a decision

3.20 As most of our respondents appreciated, we intend the category of people unable to communicate a decision to be very much a residual category. This test will have no relevance if the person is known to be incapable of deciding (even if also unable to communicate) but will be available if the assessor does not know, one way or the other, whether the person is capable of deciding or not . . . This second category is a fall-back where the assessor cannot say whether any decision has been validly made or made at all but nonetheless can say that the person concerned cannot communicate any decision.

3.21 In relation to persons who are simply unconscious, many respondents made the point that strenuous steps must be taken to assist and facilitate communication before any finding of incapacity is made. Specialists with appropriate skills in verbal and non-verbal communication should be brought in where necessary.

We recommend that a person should not be regarded as unable to communicate his or her decision unless all practicable steps to enable him or her to do so have been taken without success.

The assessment of incapacity: a code of practice

3.22 Many respondents who commented on our provisional tests of incapacity and were content with the broad outlines of the proposed test addressed themselves to technical questions about the methods of assessment and testing which should be applied. Some were insistent that outdated and discredited psychometric testing should not be used. There was grave concern about the concept of "mental age". We found the arguments against the use of any such concept extremely compelling. It is unhelpful to discuss, for example, the merits of sterilisation as opposed to barrier contraception for a mature woman with a learning disability on the basis that she is somehow "equivalent" to a child of three. Particular professional bodies . . . asserted that their members had the relevant skills to assess mental capacity. Others reminded us that cultural, ethnic and religious values should always be respected by any assessor of capacity. These are all very important matters, albeit not apt subjects for primary legislation. One of the matters which should certainly be covered by a code of practice is the way in which any assessment of capacity should be carried out.

We recommend that the Secretary of State should prepare and from time to time revise a code of practice for the guidance of persons assessing whether a person is or is not without capacity to make a decision or decisions on any matters.

It is clear that the Mental Capacity Act 2005 pursues this approach:

People who lack capacity

2.—(1) For the purposes of this Act, a person lacks capacity in relation to a matter if at the material time he is unable to make a decision for himself in relation to the matter because of an impairment of, or a disturbance in the functioning of, the mind or brain.

(2) It does not matter whether the impairment or disturbance is permanent or temporary.

(3) A lack of capacity cannot be established merely by reference to—

(a)   a person's age or appearance, or
(b)   a condition of his, or an aspect of his behaviour, which might lead others to make unjustified assumptions about his capacity.

(4) In proceedings under this Act or any other enactment, any question whether a person lacks capacity within the meaning of this Act must be decided on the balance of probabilities.

(5) No power which a person ("D") may exercise under this Act—

(a)   in relation to a person who lacks capacity, or
(b)   where D reasonably thinks that a person lacks capacity,

is exercisable in relation to a person under 16.

(6) Subsection (5) is subject to section 18(3).

Inability to make decisions

3.—(1) For the purposes of section 2, a person is unable to make a decision for himself if he is unable—

(a) to understand the information relevant to the decision,
(b) to retain that information,
(c) to use or weight that information as part of the process of making the decision, or
(d) to communicate his decision (whether by talking, using sign language or any other means).

(2) A person is not to be regarded as unable to understand the information relevant to a decision if he is able to understand an explanation of it given to him in a way that is appropriate to his circumstances (using simple language, visual aids or any other means).

(3) The fact that a person is able to retain the information relevant to a decision for a short period only does not prevent him from being regarded as able to make the decision.

(4) The information relevant to a decision includes information about the reasonably foreseeable consequences of—

(a) deciding one way or another, or
(b) failing to make the decision.

NOTES:

1. Gunn notes that in formulating a test for capacity the Law Commission is treading a difficult path. On the one hand, the standard chosen must allow as many people as possible to take their own treatment decisions; but, on the other, it must be recognised that paternalism is justifiable up to a point, and that setting the standard too low could be harmful to the individual (see M. Gunn, "The Meaning of Incapacity" (1994) 2 *Medical Law Review* 8).

2. In response to criticism of its earlier proposals, the Law Commission dropped the formulation that an apparent consent may be disregarded if it does not represent a "true choice" (see Consultation Paper 128). Commentators were of the view that this could be invoked to override an irrational decision, thereby effectively reverting to an "outcome" approach to capacity which the Commission had earlier rejected (see for example, P. Fennell, "Statutory Authority to Treat, Relatives and Treatment Proxies" (1994) 2 *Medical Law Review* 30, at page 41).

3. At para 3.21, the Law Commission stresses the importance of communication, and states that all practicable steps should be taken to enable a person to communicate, before she is deemed incompetent. This is also stressed in the guidance for doctors prepared by the BMA and the Law Society. While perhaps not quite so explicit, this approach is confirmed in the Act at s.1, see above.

QUESTIONS:

1. Do you agree that the test proposed by the Law Commission and in the Mental Capacity Act is basically the same as that which exists under the common law?

2. Is it right to have a clear test for capacity in legislation? If so, is it right that it should be a functional approach?
3. Is it justifiable to leave important details, such as the information to be disclosed, to be incorporated in a code of practice, as opposed to spelling out such details in the legislation?

6. TREATMENT WITHOUT CONSENT: BEST INTERESTS TEST

(a) The Common Law

In order for the health care professional to provide treatment, the patient must consent. However, where he is not capable, no one is in a position to consent on another adult's behalf (for the position re children, see Chapter 7). For the incapable adult, treatment will be lawful if it is in his best interests. The House of Lords in *Re F* determined that the crucial issue in making treatment decisions is what is in the "best interests" of the patient. It is widely adopted throughout medical law in relation to the incompetent patient (see Chapters 7 and 15 on children, neonates and those in a persistent vegetative state). It is also used to debar certain would-be parents from access to techniques of assisted conception on the grounds that it would not be in the interests of any resulting child (see Chapter 11). The "best interests" test was also accepted as appropriate by the Law Commission in its consideration of reform of the law on incapacity. Nevertheless, the test has been subjected to criticism. There is a definitional problem. What precisely does the test mean? In particular, how are the best interests of a patient to be defined, given the vagueness of the test. Case law developments since *Re F* have provided much greater clarity, but is it sufficient? The other major issue is whether it is for the doctors (or other health care providers) to determine on the basis that what they propose to do is a reasonable approach, within the guidelines of the *Bolam test*. Case law developments have also been significant in this area.

Re F (mental patient sterilisation) [1990] 2 A.C. 1

F was a woman of 36 with serious learning difficulties. Her mental age was assessed at five, and her verbal capacity at two. She had been a voluntary in-patient at a mental hospital for over 20 years, and had formed a sexual relationship with a male patient. Expert evidence suggested that it would be disastrous for her to become pregnant. Furthermore, both her mother and the professionals caring for her thought it was best for her to be sterilised. As she was unable to consent, a declaration was sought that the operation would be lawful. The House of Lords held that it had no power to consent on her behalf, but considered whether it would be lawful for the operation to be performed without F's consent. Their Lordships also dealt with issues specific to sterilisation, which are discussed in Chapter 13. Their examination of the more general principles which permit certain types of treatment to be given without consent is extracted below.

LORD BRANDON

" . . . At common law a doctor cannot lawfully operate on adult patients of sound mind, or give them any other treatment involving the application of physical force however small (which I shall refer to as 'other treatment'), without their consent. If a doctor were to operate on such patients, or give them other treatment, without their consent, he would commit the actionable tort of trespass to the person. There are, however, cases where adult patients cannot give or refuse their consent to an operation or other treatment. One case is where, as a result of an accident or otherwise, an adult patient is unconscious and an operation or other treatment cannot be safely delayed until he or she recovers consciousness. Another case is where a patient, though adult, cannot by reason of mental disability understand the nature or purpose of an operation or other treatment. The common law would be seriously defective if it failed to provide a solution to the problem created by such inability to consent. In my opinion, however, the common law does not fail. In my opinion, the solution to the problem which the common law provides is that a doctor can lawfully operate on, or give other treatment to, adult patients who are incapable, for one reason or another, of consenting to his doing so, provided that the operation or other treatment concerned is in the best interests of such patients. The operation or other treatment will be in their best interests if, but only if, it is carried out in order either to save their lives or to ensure improvement or prevent deterioration in their physical or mental health.

Different views have been put forward with regard to the principle which makes it lawful for a doctor to operate on or give other treatment to adult patients without their consent . . . The Court of Appeal in the present case regarded the matter as depending on the public interest. I would not disagree with that as a broad proposition, but I think that it is helpful to consider the principle in accordance with which the public interest leads to this result. In my opinion, the principle is that, when persons lack the capacity, for whatever reason, to take decisions about the performance of operations on them, or the giving of other medical treatment to them, it is necessary that some other person or persons, with the appropriate qualifications, should take such decisions for them. Otherwise they would be deprived of medical care which they need and to which they are entitled.

In many cases, however, it will not only be lawful for doctors, on the ground of necessity, to operate on or give other medical treatment to adult patients disabled from giving their consent: it will also be their common law duty to do so.

In the case of adult patients made unconscious by an accident or otherwise, they will normally be received into the casualty department of a hospital, which thereby undertakes the care of them. It will then be the duty of the doctors at that hospital to use their best endeavours to do, by way of either an operation or other treatment, that which is in the best interests of such patients . . .

The application of the principle which I have described means that the lawfulness of a doctor operating on, or giving other treatment to, an adult patient disabled from giving consent will depend not on any approval or sanction of a court but on the question whether the operation or other treatment is in the best interests of the patient concerned. That is, from a practical point of view, just as well, for, if every operation to be performed, or other treatment to be given, required the approval or sanction of the court, the whole process of medical care for such patients would grind to a halt . . .

There is one further matter with which I think that it is necessary to deal. That is the standard which the court should apply in deciding whether a proposed operation is or is not in the best interests of the patient. With regard to this Scott Baker J said:

'I do not think they [the doctors] are liable in battery where they are acting in good faith and reasonably in the best interests of their patients. I doubt whether the test is very different from that for negligence.'

This was a reference to the test laid down in *Bolam* v. *Friern Hospital Management Committee* [1957] 2 All E.R. 118, namely that a doctor will not be negligent if he establishes that he acted in accordance with a practice accepted at the time by a responsible body of medical opinion skilled in the particular form of treatment in question.

All three members of the Court of Appeal considered that the *Bolam* test was insufficiently stringent for deciding whether an operation or other medical treatment was in a patient's best interests. Lord Donaldson M.R. said:

'Just as the law and the courts rightly pay great, but not decisive, regard to accepted professional wisdom in relation to the duty of care in the law of medical negligence (the *Bolam* test), so they equally would have regard to such wisdom in relation to decisions whether or not and how to treat incompetent patients in the context of the law of trespass to the person. However, both the medical profession and the courts have to keep the special status of such a patient in the forefront of their minds. The ability of the ordinary adult patient to exercise a free choice in deciding whether to accept or to refuse medical treatment and to choose between treatments is not to be dismissed as desirable but inessential. It is a crucial factor in relation to all medical treatment. If it is necessarily absent, whether temporarily in an emergency situation or permanently in a case of mental disability, other things being equal there must be greater caution in deciding whether to treat and, if so, how to treat, although I do not agree that this extends to limiting doctors to treatment on the necessity for which there are "no two views" (per Wood J. in *T* v. *T* [1988] 1 All E.R. 613 at 621). There will always or usually be a minority view and this approach, if strictly applied, would often rule out all treatment. On the other hand, the existence of a significant minority view would constitute a serious contra-indication.'

Neill L.J. said:

'I have therefore come to the conclusion that, if the operation is necessary and the proper safeguards are observed, the performance of a serious operation, including an operation for sterilisation, on a person who by reason of a lack of mental capacity is unable to give his or her consent is not a trespass to the person or otherwise unlawful. It therefore becomes necessary to consider what is meant by "a necessary operation". In seeking to define the circumstances in which an operation can properly be carried out Scott Baker J said: "I do not think they are liable in battery where they are acting in good faith and reasonably in the best interests of their patients. I doubt whether the test is very different from that for negligence." With respect, I do not consider that this test is sufficiently stringent. A doctor may defeat a claim in negligence if he establishes that he acted in accordance with a practice accepted at the time as proper by a responsible body of medical opinion skilled in the particular form of treatment in question. This is the test laid down in *Bolam* v. *Friern Hospital Management Committee*. But to say that it is not negligent to carry out a particular form of treatment does not mean that that treatment is necessary. I would define necessary in this context as that which the general body of medical opinion in the particular specialty would consider to be in the best interests of the patient in order to maintain the health and to secure the well-being of the patient. One cannot expect unanimity but it should be possible to say of an operation which is necessary in the relevant sense that it would be unreasonable in the opinion of most experts in the field not to make the operation available to the patient. One must consider the alternatives to an operation and the dangers or disadvantages to which the patient may be exposed if no action is taken. The question becomes: what action does the patient's health and welfare require?'

Butler-Sloss L.J. agreed with Neill L.J.

'With respect to the Court of Appeal, I do not agree that the *Bolam* test is inapplicable to cases of performing operations on, or giving other treatment to, adults incompetent to give consent. In order that the performance of such operations on, and the giving of such other treatment to, such adults should be lawful, they must be in their best interests. If doctors were to be required, in deciding whether an operation or other treatment was in the best interests of adults incompetent to give consent, to apply some test more stringent than the *Bolam* test, the result would be that such adults would, in some circumstances at least, be deprived of the benefit of medical treatment which adults competent to give consent would enjoy. In my opinion it would be wrong for the law, in its concern to protect such adults, to produce such a result . . . '"

LORD GRIFFITHS

" . . . In a civilised society the mentally incompetent must be provided with medical and nursing care and those who look after them must do their best for them. Stated in legal terms the doctor who undertakes responsibility for the treatment of a mental patient who is incapable of giving consent to treatment must give the treatment that he considers to be in the best interests of his patient, and the standard of care required of the doctor will be that laid down in *Bolam* v. *Friern Hospital Management Committee* [1957] 2 All E.R. 118 . . . "

LORD GOFF

" . . . On what principle can medical treatment be justified when given without consent? We are searching for a principle on which, in limited circumstances, recognition may be given to a need, in the interests of the patient, that treatment should be given to him in circumstances where he is (temporarily or permanently) disabled from consenting to it. It is this criterion of a need which points to the principle of necessity as providing justification.

That there exists in the common law a principle of necessity which may justify action which would otherwise be unlawful is not in doubt. But historically the principle has been seen to be restricted to two groups of cases, which have been called cases of public necessity and cases of private necessity. The former occurred when a man interfered with another man's property in the public interest, for example (in the days before we could dial 999 for the fire brigade) the destruction of another man's house to prevent the spread of a catastrophic fire, as indeed occurred in the Great Fire of London in 1666. The latter cases occurred when a man interfered with another's property to save his own person or property from imminent danger, for example when he entered on his neighbour's land without his consent in order to prevent the spread of fire onto his own land.

There is, however, a third group of cases, which is also properly described as founded on the principle of necessity and which is more pertinent to the resolution of the problem in the present case. These cases are concerned with action taken as a matter of necessity to assist another person without his consent. To give a simple example, a man who seizes another and forcibly drags him from the path of an oncoming vehicle, thereby saving him from injury or even death, commits no wrong. But there are many emanations of this principle, to be found scattered through the books. These are concerned not only with the preservation of the life or health of the assisted person, but also with the preservation of his property (sometimes an animal, sometimes an ordinary chattel) and even to certain conduct on his behalf in the administration of his affairs. Where there is a pre-existing relationship between the parties, the intervener is usually said to act as an agent of necessity on behalf of the principal in whose interests he acts, and his action can often, with not too much artificiality, be referred to the pre-existing relationship between them. Whether the intervener may be entitled either to reimbursement or to remuneration raises separate questions which are not relevant to the present case.

We are concerned here with action taken to preserve the life, health or well-being of another who is unable to consent to it. Such action is sometimes said to be justified as arising from an emergency; in Prosser and Keeton *Torts* (5th edn, 1984) page 117 the action is said to be privileged by the emergency. Doubtless, in the case of a person of sound mind, there will ordinarily have to be an emergency before such action taken without consent can be lawful; for otherwise there would be an opportunity to communicate with the assisted person and to seek his consent. But this is not always so; and indeed the historical origins of the principle of necessity do not point to emergency as such as providing the criterion of lawful intervention without consent . . . But, when a person is rendered incapable of communication either permanently or over a considerable period of time (through illness or accident or mental disorder), it would be an unusual use of language to describe the case as one of 'permanent emergency', if indeed such a state of affairs can properly be said to exist. In truth, the relevance of an emergency is that it may give rise to a necessity to act in the interests of the assisted person without first obtaining his consent. Emergency is however not the criterion or even a prerequisite; it is simply a frequent origin of the necessity which impels intervention. The principle is one of necessity, not of emergency.

We can derive some guidance as to the nature of the principle of necessity from the cases on agency of necessity in mercantile law . . . [F]rom them can be derived the basic requirements, applicable in these cases of necessity, that, to fall within the principle, not only (1) must there be a necessity to act when it is not practicable to communicate with the assisted person, but also (2) the action taken must be such as a reasonable person would in all the circumstances take, acting in the best interests of the assisted person.

On this statement of principle, I wish to observe that officious intervention cannot be justified by the principle of necessity. So intervention cannot be justified when another more appropriate person is available and willing to act; nor can it be justified when it is contrary to the known wishes of the assisted person, to the extent that he is capable of rationally forming such a wish. On the second limb of the principle, the introduction of the standard of a reasonable man should not in the present context be regarded as materially different from that of Sir Montague Smith's 'wise and prudent man', because a reasonable man would, in the time available to him, proceed with wisdom and prudence before taking action in relation to another man's person or property without his consent. I shall have more to say on this point later. Subject to that, I hesitate at present to indulge in any greater refinement of the principle, being well aware of many problems which may arise in its application, problems which it is not necessary, for present purposes, to examine. But as a general rule, if the above criteria are fulfilled, interference with the assisted person's person or property (as the case may be) will not be unlawful. Take the example of a railway accident, in which injured passengers are trapped in the wreckage. It is this principle which may render lawful the actions of other citizens, railway staff, passengers or outsiders, who rush to give aid and comfort to the victims: the surgeon who amputates the limb of an unconscious passenger to free him from the wreckage; the ambulance man who conveys him to hospital; the doctors and nurses who treat him and care for him while he is still unconscious. Take the example of an elderly person who suffers a stroke which renders him incapable of speech or movement. It is by virtue of this principle that the doctor who treats him, the nurse who cares for him, even the relative or friend or neighbour who comes in to look after him will commit no wrong when he or she touches his body.

The two examples I have given illustrate, in the one case, an emergency and, in the other, a permanent or semi-permanent state of affairs. Another example of the latter kind is that of a mentally disordered person who is disabled from giving consent. I can see no good reason why the principle of necessity should not be applicable in his case as it is in the case of the victim of a stroke. Furthermore, in the case of a mentally disordered person, as in the case of a stroke victim, the permanent state of affairs calls for a wider range of care than may be requisite in an emergency which arises from accidental injury. When the state of affairs is permanent, or semi-permanent, action properly taken to preserve the life, health or well-being of the assisted person may well transcend such measures as surgical operation or substantial medical treatment and may extend to include such humdrum matters as routine medical or dental treatment, even simple care such as dressing and undressing and putting to bed.

The distinction I have drawn between cases of emergency and cases where the state of affairs is (more or less) permanent is relevant in another respect. We are here concerned with medical treatment, and I limit myself to cases of that kind. Where, for example, a surgeon performs an operation without his consent on a patient temporarily rendered unconscious in an accident, he should do no more than is reasonably required, in the best interests of the patient, before he recovers consciousness. I can see no practical difficulty arising from this requirement, which derives from the fact that the patient is expected before long to regain consciousness and can then be consulted about longer term measures. The point has however arisen in a more acute form where a surgeon, in the course of an operation, discovers some other condition which, in his opinion, requires operative treatment for which he has not received the patient's consent. In what circumstances he should operate forthwith, and in what circumstances he should postpone the further treatment until he has received the patient's consent, is a difficult matter which has troubled the Canadian courts (see *Marshall* v. *Curry* [1933] 3 D.L.R. 260 and *Murray* v. *McMurchy* [1949] 2 D.L.R. 442), but which it is not necessary for your Lordships to consider in the present case.

But where the state of affairs is permanent or semi-permanent, as may be so in the case of a mentally disordered person, there is no point in waiting to obtain the patient's consent. The need to care for him is obvious; and the doctor must then act in the best interests of his patient, just as if he had received his patient's consent so to do. Were this not so, much useful treatment and care could, in theory at least, be denied to the unfortunate. It follows that, on this point, I am unable to accept the view expressed by Neill L.J. in the Court of Appeal, that the treatment must be shown to have been necessary. Moreover, in such a case, as my noble and learned friend Lord Brandon has pointed out, a doctor who has assumed responsibility for the care of a patient may not only be treated as having the patient's consent to act, but also be under a duty so to act. I find myself to be respectfully in agreement with Lord Donaldson M.R. when he said:

'I see nothing incongruous in doctors and others who have a caring responsibility being required, when acting in relation to an adult who is incompetent, to exercise a right of choice in exactly the same way as would the court or reasonable parents in relation to a child, making due allowance, of course, for the fact that the patient is not a child, and I am satisfied that that is what the law does in fact require.'

In these circumstances, it is natural to treat the deemed authority and the duty as interrelated. But I feel bound to express my opinion that, in principle, the lawfulness of the doctor's action is, at least in its origin, to be found in the principle of necessity. This can perhaps be seen most clearly in cases where there is no continuing relationship between doctor and patient. The 'doctor in the house' who volunteers to assist a lady in the audience who, overcome by the drama or by the heat in the theatre, has fainted away is impelled to act by no greater duty than that imposed by his own Hippocratic oath. Furthermore, intervention can be justified in the case of a non-professional, as well as a professional, man or woman who has no pre-existing relationship with the assisted person, as in the case of a stranger who rushes to assist an injured man after an accident. In my opinion, it is the necessity itself which provides the justification for the intervention.

I have said that the doctor has to act in the best interests of the assisted person. In the case of routine treatment of mentally disordered persons, there should be little difficulty in applying this principle. In the case of more serious treatment, I recognise that its application may create problems for the medical profession; however, in making decisions about treatment, the doctor must act in accordance with a responsible and competent body of relevant professional opinion, on the principles set down in *Bolam* v. *Friern Hospital Management Committee* [1957] 2 All E.R. 118. No doubt, in practice, a decision may involve others besides the doctor. It must surely be good practice to consult relatives and others who are concerned with the care of the patient. Sometimes, of course, consultation with a specialist or specialists will be required; and in others, especially where the decision involves more than a purely medical opinion, an inter-disciplinary team will in practice participate in the decision. It is very difficult, and would be unwise, for a court to do more than to stress that, for those who are involved in these important and sometimes difficult decisions, the overriding consideration is that they should act in the best interests of the person who suffers from the misfortune of being prevented by incapacity from deciding for himself what should be done to his own body in his own best interests . . . "

QUESTIONS:

1. When would the declaratory jurisdiction be triggered? Must there be a civil or criminal wrong to which the health care provider requires a defence?
2. What is the basis for making a decision where an adult is incapable?
3. When, on the basis of this decision, would health care providers have to seek the guidance of the courts?

The law has come a long way since *Re F.* It has been developed by the judges, particular Dame Butler-Sloss, President of the Family Division of the High Court. The point of development that it has reached is best illustrated reading her judgment and that of Thorpe L.J. in the later sterilisation case of *Re S* [2001] Fam. 15 which is extracted in Chapter 13. After reading this case, it would be worth reflecting on the answers to the above questions, which will help identify how much the law has changed.

There are two matters that *Re S* did not fully tease out. First, that for the court's jurisdiction to be engaged, there must be a "serious justiciable issue" to be resolved. In *Re S (Hospital Patient: Court's Jurisdiction)* [1995] 3 All E.R. 290, Sir Thomas Bingham M.R. stated that he had "no doubt that the substantial issue in this case is a serious justiciable issue, involving as it potentially does the happiness and welfare of a helpless human being". Secondly, the role of *Bolam* is that any approach to a problem must be compliant with *Bolam*. However, and much more importantly, there can be only one approach that is in the best interests of the incapacitated adult, and this must be selected by the judge, drawing on the medical evidence, but not, necessarily, bound by it. In the earlier decision, *Re A (medical treatment: male sterilisation)* [2000] 1 F.C.R. 193 (see Chapter 13), Thorpe L.J. proposed a checklist approach to the determination of best interests.

THORPE L.J.
"Pending the enactment of a checklist or other statutory direction it seems to me that the first instance judge with the responsibility to make an evaluation of the best interests of a claimant lacking capacity should draw up a balance sheet. The first entry should be of any factor or factors of actual benefit. In the present case the instance would be the acquisition of foolproof contraception. Then on the other sheet the judge should write any counterbalancing dis-benefits to the applicant. An obvious instance in this case would be the apprehension, the risk and the discomfort inherent in the operation. Then the judge should enter on each sheet the potential gains and losses in each instance making some estimate of the extent of the possibility that the gain or loss might accrue. At the end of that exercise the judge should be better placed to strike a balance between the sum of the certain and possible gains against the sum of the certain and possible losses. Obviously only if the account is in relatively significant credit will the judge conclude that the application is likely to advance the best interests of the claimant."

The court determined, adopting the above checklist, that A should not be sterilised. This approach has been utilised subsequently, see, for example, *Newham LBC v S* [2003] EWHC 1909 (Fam).

NOTES:

1. Particularly helpful guidance on procedure is provided by the Official Solicitor in *Practice Direction (declaratory proceedings: incapacitated adults)* [2002] 1 All E.R. 794.

QUESTIONS:

1. Initially, the jurisdiction was triggered, from *Re F*, by the need to provide a defence to assault for a health care provider, so a legal wrong had to be identified. Is "serious justiciable issue" wider? If so, how?

2. What factors are now to be taken into account in deciding what is in a person's best interests, and what is the role of *Bolam*?
3. How does the court (or a health care provider) have to determine what is in a person's best interests?
4. If jurisdiction is wide, because of the breadth of the meaning of the phrase "serious justiciable issue", and the decision-making by the courts takes all relevant matters into account, because of the broad understanding of "best interests", and the courts must decide what option is in the best interests of the patient, is there any need for legislation?

(b) The Mental Capacity Act 2005

Under the Mental Capacity Act 2005, the best interests approach is also adopted. There is, though, a much more extensive and coherent set of procedures to see delivery of that approach in a number of respects, while also paying proper regard to respect for autonomy, where individuals are capable of making their own decision. Indeed, it might be considered that the decision that an individual would have made is the decision that is in their best interests, thus challenging the frequently seen juxtaposition of a best interests and substituted judgment approach.

Law Commission, Mental Incapacity, Law Com. 231, 1995

3.24 We will set out in later Parts of this report a graduated scheme for decision-making, designed to ensure that any substitute decision is taken at the lowest level of formality which is consistent with the protection of the person without capacity, both from the improper usurpation of his or her autonomy and from inadequate or even abusive decision-making. Although decisions are to be taken by a variety of people with varying degrees of formality, a single criterion to govern any substitute decision can be established. Whatever the answer to the question "who decides?", there should only be one answer to the subsequent question "on what basis?".

3.25 ... two criteria ... have been developed in the literature in this field: "best interests" on the one hand and "substituted judgment" on the other. In Consultation Paper No. 128 we argued that the two were not in fact mutually exclusive and we provisionally favoured a "best interests" criterion which would contain a strong element of substituted judgment. It had been widely accepted by respondents to the overview paper that, where a person has never had capacity, there is no viable alternative to the "best interests" criterion. We were pleased to find that our arguments in favour of a "best interests" criterion found favour with almost all our respondents, with the Law Society emphasising that the criterion as defined in the consultation papers was in fact "an excellent compromise" between the best interests and substituted judgment approaches.

We recommend that anything done for, and any decision made on behalf of, a person without capacity should be done or made in the best interests of that person.

3.26 Our recommendation that a "best interests" criterion should apply throughout our scheme cannot be divorced from a recommendation that statute should provide some guidance to every decision-maker about what the criterion requires. No statutory guidance could offer an exhaustive account of what is in a person's best interests, the intention being that the individual person and his or her individual circumstances should always determine the result ...

3.28 In putting forward a "best interests" criterion in our 1993 consultation papers, we linked it to a checklist of factors which should be taken into account by a substitute decision-maker . . . [W]e have now developed a single check list which includes all the elements originally identified as important and commended by consultees. We take this opportunity to repeat some of the general comments made in our report on Guardianship and Custody . . . First, that a checklist must not unduly burden any decision-maker or encourage unnecessary intervention; secondly, that it must not be applied too rigidly and should leave room for all considerations relevant in a particular case; thirdly, that it should be confined to major points, so that it can adapt to changing views and attitudes . . .

We recommend that in deciding what is in a person's best interests regard should be had to:

(1) *the ascertainable past and present wishes and feelings of the person concerned, and the factors that person would consider if able to do so;*

(2) *the need to permit and encourage the person to participate, or to improve his or her ability to participate, as fully as possible in anything done for and any decision affecting him or her;*

(3) *the views of other people whom it is appropriate and practicable to consult about the person's wishes and feelings and what would be in his or her best interests;*

(4) *whether the purpose for which any action or decision is required can be as affectively achieved in a manner less restrictive of the person's freedom of action.*

The Mental Capacity Act broadly confirms this approach to the meaning of "best interests". The following clause, in particular, should be read in conjunction with s.1, above.

Best interests

4.—(1) In determining for the purposes of this Act what is in a person's best interests, the person making the determination must not make it merely on the basis of—

(a) the person's age or appearance, or

(b) a condition of his, or an aspect of his behaviour, which might lead others to make unjustified assumptions about what might be in his best interests.

(2) The person making the determination must consider all the relevant circumstances and, in particular, take the following steps.

(3) He must consider—

(a) whether it is likely that the person will at some time have capacity in relation to the matter in question, and

(b) if it appears likely that he will, when that is likely to be.

(4) He must, so far as is reasonably practicable, permit and encourage the person to participate, or to improve his ability to participate, as fully as possible in any act done for him and any decision affecting him.

(5) Where the determination relates to life-sustaining treatment he must not, in considering whether the treatment is in the best interests of the person concerned, be motivated by a desire to bring about his death.

(6) He must consider, so far as is reasonably ascertainable—

(a) The person's past and present wishes and feelings and in particular any relevant written statement made by him when he had capacity,

(b) The belief's and values that would be likely to influence his decision if he had capacity, and

(c) the other factors that he would be likely to consider if he were able to do so.

(7) He must take into account, if it is practicable and appropriate to consult them, the views of

(a) anyone named by the person as someone to be consulted on the matter in question or on matters of that kind,
(b) anyone engaged in caring for the person or interested in his welfare,
(c) any donee of a lasting power of attorney granted by the person, and
(d) any deputy appointed for the person by the court,

as to what would be in the person's best interests and, in particular, as to the matters mentioned in subsection (6).

(8) The duties imposed by subsections (1) to (7) also apply in relation to the exercise of any powers which—

(a) are exercisable under a lasting power of attorney, or
(b) are exercisable by a person under this Act where he reasonably believes that another person lacks capacity.

(9) In the case of an act done, or a decision made, by a person other than the court, there is sufficient compliance with this section if (having complied with the requirements of subsections (1) to (7)) he reasonably believes that what he does or decides is in the best interests of the person concerned.

(10) "Life-sustaining treatment" means treatment which in the view of a person providing health care for the person concerned is necessary to sustain his life.

(11) "Relevant circumstances" are those—

(a) of which the person making the determination is aware, and
(b) which it would be reasonable to regard as relevant.

NOTES:

1. Under the "substituted judgment" test, the proxy decision-maker is required to try to place himself or herself in the position of the incapacitated patient, and seek to decide on the basis of what the patient himself would have decided if he possessed the requisite capacity. It will only work where the patient has at some time had capacity. Even then, in *Airedale NHS Trust v Bland* [1993] 1 All E.R. 821 the House of Lords rejected the substituted judgment test in favour of the best interests criterion (see Chapter 15).

2. The best interests test suggested by the Law Commission differs markedly from that established in *Re F* (see P. Fennell, *Treatment without Consent* London: Routledge, 1996 at p.259). However, the difference between the current position of the common law and the approach in the Act seems to be far less.

QUESTIONS:

1. Do you agree with the Law Commission in favouring the "best interests" test over that of "substituted judgment" in cases of persons who once were competent? Did the Commission effect an "excellent compromise" between the two competing tests? Is the Government right to pursue this approach in the Act?

2. Is the Law Commission's guidance on assessing the best interests of the patient sufficiently full? How useful is its attempt to draw up a checklist of factors which should be taken into account by the substitute decision-

maker? Does the Bill improve on the original proposals from the Law Commission?

(i) Making Decisions on behalf of an Incapable Adult

Under the common law, as has been seen above, the position is that if a person needs to take action where the adult is incapable and the action is in their best interests, and where there are any concerns, the matter can be resolved by seeking a declaration from the High Court. The concerns about this include (a) the lack of clarity in the procedures for taking action short of going to the High Court, and (b) the expense and complexity of seeking a declaration to resolve issues of contention or dispute.

Of course, an individual may take the matter into their hands if they are able to do so. A capable adult may, under the common law, make an advance decision that is binding in the future. Further, a capable adult may make an enduring power of attorney under the Enduring Powers of Attorney Act 1985 to deal with the management of their own property and affairs that can survive their subsequent incapacity. These procedures are relatively clear, but there is more than one source for them and they are limited in their application (particularly the enduring power of attorney). Under the Mental Capacity Act there are more options for a capable adult to take the matter into their own hands. They may create a lasting power of attorney (which gives to the donee power not only in relation to property and affairs but also to health and welfare matters) or they make an advance refusal of treatment (see Chapter 14). Of course, this approach is only available to those with the capacity to act and with the knowledge and support to do so. Where no such provision exists, the following routes for making decisions and taking action will apply.

(ii) Dealing with Most Matters Concerned with Care and Treatment

For those who have never been competent, or who have failed to make advance provision, the Law Commission suggested that it was necessary to introduce a new mechanism to reach appropriate decisions in such cases. In the extract below, the Commission suggested that certain routine medical treatment could be carried out without formal or juridical approval. Instead, the decision could be made under a general authority conferred upon "treatment providers" by statute.

Law Commission, Mental Incapacity, Law. Com. 231, 1995

4.4 [W]e provisionally proposed a new statutory authority whereby "carers" and "treatment providers" might act reasonably to safeguard and promote the welfare and best interests of a person without capacity. Our original formulation provoked some mis-understanding on consultation, with respondents fearing that disagreement and disputes would arise as to the identity of "the carer" or "the treatment provider" in possession of the authority. In fact, reasonable action at the informal level can be taken by a variety of different people. On any one day it might be reasonable for the primary carer to dress the person concerned in suitable clothes, for the district nurse to give a regular injection and nursing care, for a worker from a voluntary organisation to take the person out on a trip and for another family member to bring round the evening meal and help the person to eat it. Just as the common law affords each person whose actions fall within the principle of necessity a defence to a suit for trespass, so a statutory "general authority" should make the qualifying actions of any such person lawful. It is not, therefore, helpful to suggest that any one person can be defined and identified as the holder of the authority. We consider it preferable to refer to actions which are reasonable for the person doing them to do. This underlines the fact that number of people may have power to act on any one day. It also serves as a reminder that independent restrictions on who should be taking action are not superseded. Such restrictions might be imposed by employment contracts, by professional rules of conduct or by the law of negligence. In the example given, it would not be reasonable for the district nurse to administer treatment which requires prior authorisation from a registered medical practitioner; nor for the voluntary organisation worker to take actions expressly prohibited by the terms and conditions of his or her employment.

We recommend that it should be lawful to do anything for the personal welfare or health care of a person who is, or is reasonably believed to be, without capacity in relation to the matter in question if it is in all the circumstances reasonable for it to be done by the person who does it.

The obligation to act in the best interests of the person without capacity, having regard to the statutory factors, will immediately apply to anyone purporting to exercise this "general authority".

4.5 It would be out of step with our aims of policy, and with the views of the vast majority of the respondents to our overview paper, to have any general system of certifying people as "incapacitated" and then identifying a substitute decision-maker for them, regardless of whether there is any real need for one. In the absence of certifications or authorisations, persons acting informally can only be expected to have reasonable grounds to believe that (1) the other person lacks a capacity in relation to the matter in hand and (2) they are acting in the best interests of that person.

In pre-legislative scrutiny there were deep concerns about what was called, in the Mental Incapacity Bill, the general authority to act reasonably. In part this was to do with the name of the power, as it suggested that a carer could do anything if the person cared for was not capable. This was clearly not what was intended nor achieved by the proposed legislation, but, to endeavour to prevent misunderstanding of the approach, the Bill was significantly redrafted. It now legitimises acts in connection with care and treatment. Further, the provision dealing with payments for necessaries is separated out and clarified.

Mental Capacity Act 2005

Acts in connection with care or treatment

5.—(1) If a person ("D") does an act in connection with the care and treatment of another person ("P"), the act is one to which this section applies if—

(a) before doing the act, D takes reasonable steps to establish whether P lacks capacity in relation to the matter in question, and

(b) when doing the act, D reasonably believes—
    (i) that P lacks capacity in relation to the matter, and
    (ii) that it will be in P's best interests for the act to be done.

(2) D does not incur any liability in relation to the act that he would not have incurred if P—

(a) had had capacity to consent in relation to the matter, and

(b) had consent to D's doing the act.

(3) Nothing in this section excludes a person's civil liability for loss or damage, or his criminal liability, resulting from his negligence in doing the act.

(4) Nothing in this section affects the operation of sections 24 to 26 (advance decisions to refuse treatment).

Section 5 acts: limitations

6.—(1) If D does an act that is intended to restrain P, it is not an act to which section 5 applies unless two further conditions are satisfied.

(2) The first condition is that D reasonably believes that it is necessary to do the act in order to prevent harm to P.

(3) The second is that the act is a proportionate response to—

(a) the likelihood of P's suffering harm, and
(b) the seriousness of that harm.

(4) For purposes of this section D restrains P if he—

(c) uses, or threatens to use, force to secure the doing of an act which P resists, or
(d) restricts P's liberty of movement, whether or not P resists.

(5) But D does more than merely restrain P if he deprives P of his liberty within the meaning of Article 5(1) of the Human Rights Convention (whether or not D is a public authority).

(6) Section 5 does not authorise a person to do an act which conflicts with a decision made, within the scope of his authority and in accordance with this Part, by—

(a) a donee of a lasting power of attorney granted by P, or
(b) a deputy appointed for P by the court.

(7) But nothing in subsection (5) stops a person—

(a) providing life-sustaining treatment, or
(b) doing any act which he reasonably believes to be necessary to prevent a serious deterioration in P's condition,

while a decision as respects any relevant issues is sought from the court.

Payment for necessary goods and services

7.—(1) If necessary goods and services are supplied to a person who lacks capacity to contract for the supply, he must pay a reasonable price for them.

(2) "Necessary" means suitable to a person's condition in life and to his actual requirements at the time when the goods or services are supplied.

Expenditure

8.—(1) If an act to which section 5 applies involved expenditure, it is lawful for D—

(a) to pledge P's credit for the purpose of the expenditure, and
(b) to apply money in P's possession for meeting the expenditure.

(2) If the expenditure is borne for P by D, it is lawful for D—

(a) to reimburse himself out of money in P's possession, or

(b)   to be otherwise indemnified by P.

(3) Subsections (1) and (2) do not affect any power under which (apart from these subsections) a person—

(a)   has lawful control of P's money or other property, and
(b)   has power to spend money for P's benefit.

NOTES:

1. If the decision falls to be made under s.5 of the Act, there is no limit upon who may act. These powers are intended to apply to anyone who may need to act and so includes not only health care providers but also those without medical qualifications, such as relatives, or workers administering prescribed medication. Hence it confers authority much more widely than did the decision in *Re F.* There will be further guidance in the code of practice.
2. The Law Commission went on to propose certain exclusions from the "general authority". This approach is maintained in the Mental Capacity Act. Some specific exclusions are included in the sections above. But also there are exclusions that do not just apply to exercise of power under s.5, but indicate that there is a range of decisions to which the Act does not apply at all.

Family relationships etc.

27.—(1) Nothing in this Act permits a decision on any of the following matters to be made on behalf of a person—

(a)   consenting to marriage or a civil partnership,
(b)   consenting to have sexual relations,
(c)   consenting to a decree of divorce being granted on the basis of two years' separation,
(d)   consenting to a dissolution order being made in relation to a civil partnership on the basis of two years' separation,
(e)   consenting to a child's being placed for adoption by an adoption agency,
(f)   consenting to the making of an adoption order,
(g)   discharging parental responsibilities in matters not relating to a child's property,
(h)   giving a consent under the Human Fertilisation and Embryology Act 1990 . . . .

Mental Health Act matters

28.—(1) Nothing in this Act authorises anyone—

(a)   to give a patient medical treatment for mental disorder, or
(b)   to consent to a patient's being given medical treatment for mental disorder,

if, at the time when it is proposed to treat the patient, his treatment is regulated by Part 4 of the Mental Health Act.
(2) "Medical treatment", "mental disorder" and "patient" have the same meaning as in that Act.

Voting rights

29.—(1) Nothing in this Act permits a decision on voting at an election for any public office, or at a referendum, to be made on behalf of a person . . .

QUESTIONS:

1. Do you support the idea of having such a broad provision as s.5? How, if at all, will it improve on the common law position? Are there sufficient protections for the individual in s.5?
2. Is there any potential for confusion about when and how to apply it? Is it intended to be used for significant bodily intrusions?
3. Must there be an effective means of challenging the application of the general authority on behalf of an incapable adult in order to comply with Article 6 of the ECHR?

(iii) Independent mental capacity advocates

In its report the Law Commission proposed that certain types of treatment and research which raised special concern should not be authorised by a treatment provider but should always be independently approved through either a second opinion procedure or a court approval procedure. This approach was not accepted by the Government, which initially proposed the introduction of independent consultees, who were intended to assist in the decision-making process. However, as a result of considerable lobbying, the Govrnment accepted a significant change to this part of the Act. It accepted the need for advocates to be involved and hence agreed to establish an independent mental capacity advocate service. The primary function of such an advocate is, according to s.35(1), "to be available to represent and support persons to whom acts or decisions proposed under [certain parts of the MCA]." Sections 35 and 36 repay very careful reading. The specific functions of the advocate are the same as those proposed under the original proposals for independent supervision, but the role is more engaged and it should be noted that such advocates could refer any matter about capacity or best interests that they have a concern to the Court of Protection (with the court's leave). Thus, it is now more likely that cases that demand challenge will be so challenged, thus making it more likely that the procedures of the MCA are compliant with Art 6 of the European Convention on Human Rights.

Appointment of independent mental capacity advocates

35.—(1) The appropriate authority must make such arrangements as it considers reasonable to enable persons ("independent mental capacity advocates") to be available to represent and support persons to whom acts or decisions proposed under sections 37, 38 and 39 relate.

(2) The appropriate authority may make regulations as to the appointment of independent mental capacity advocates.

(3) The regulations may, in particular, provide—

(a) that a person may act as an independent mental capacity advocate only in such circumstances, or only subject to such conditions, as may be prescribed;
(b) for the appointment of a person as an independent mental capacity advocate to be subject to approval in accordance with the regulations.

(4) In making arrangements under subsection (1), the appropriate authority must have regard to the principle that a person to whom a proposed act or decision relates should,

so far as practicable, be represented and supported by a person who is independent of any person who will be responsible for the act or decision.

(5) The arrangements may include provision for payments to be made to, or in relation to, persons carrying out functions in accordance with the arrangements.

(6) For the purpose of enabling him to carry out his functions, an independent mental capacity advocate—

(a) may interview in private the person whom he has been instructed to represent, and

(b) may, at all reasonable times, examine and take copies of—
  (i) any health record,
  (ii) any record of, or held by, a local authority and compiled in connection with a social services function, and
  (iii) any record held by a person registered under Part 2 of the Care Standards Act 2000 (c. 14),
which the person holding the record considers may be relevant to the independent mental capacity advocate's investigation.

(7) In this section, section 36 and section 37, "the appropriate authority" means—

(a) in relation to the provision of the services of independent mental capacity advocates in England, the Secretary of State, and

(b) in relation to the provision of the services of independent mental capacity advocates in Wales, the National Assembly for Wales.

Functions of independent mental capacity advocates

36.—(1) The appropriate authority may make regulations as to the functions of independent mental capacity advocates.

(2) The regulations may, in particular, make provision requiring an advocate to take such steps as may be prescribed for the purpose of—

(a) providing support to the person whom he has been instructed to represent ("P") so that P may participate as fully as possible in any relevant decision;

(b) obtaining and evaluating relevant information;

(c) ascertaining what P's wishes and feelings would be likely to be, and the beliefs and values that would be likely to influence P, if he had capacity;

(d) ascertaining what alternative courses of action are available in relation to P;

(e) obtaining a further medical opinion where treatment is proposed and the advocate thinks that one should be obtained.

(3) The regulations may also make provision as to circumstances in which the advocate may challenge, or provide assistance for the purpose of challenging, any relevant decision.

Provision of serious medical treatment by NHS body

37.—(1) This section applies if an NHS body—

(a) is proposing to provide, or secure the provision of, serious medical treatment for a person ("P") who lacks capacity to consent to the treatment, and

(b) is satisfied that there is no person, other than one engaged in providing care or treatment for P in a professional capacity or for remuneration, whom it would be appropriate to consult in determining what would be in P's best interests.

(2) But this section does not apply if P's treatment is regulated by Part 4 of the Mental Health Act.

(3) Before the treatment is provided, the NHS body must instruct an independent mental capacity advocate to represent P.

(4) If the treatment needs to be provided as a matter of urgency, it may be provided even though the NHS body has not been able to comply with subsection (3).

(5) The NHS body must, in providing or securing the provision of treatment for P, take into account any information given, or submissions made, by the independent mental capacity advocate.

(6) "Serious medical treatment" means treatment which involves providing, withholding or withdrawing treatment of a kind prescribed by regulations made by the appropriate authority.

(7) "NHS body" has such meaning as may be prescribed by regulations made for the purposes of this section by-

(a)   the Secretary of State, in relation to bodies in England, or
(b)   the National Assembly for Wales, in relation to bodies in Wales.

Provision of accommodation by NHS body

38.—(1) This section applies if an NHS body proposes to make arrangements—

(a)   for the provision of accommodation in a hospital or care home for a person ("P") who lacks capacity to agree to the arrangements, or
(b)   for a change in P's accommodation to another hospital or care home,

and is satisfied that there is no person, other than one engaged in providing care or treatment for P in a professional capacity or for remuneration, whom it would be appropriate for it to consult in determining what would be in P's best interests.

(2) But this section does not apply if P is accommodated as a result of an obligation imposed on him under the Mental Health Act.

(3) Before making the arrangements, the NHS body must instruct an independent mental capacity advocate to represent P unless it is satisfied that—

(a)   the accommodation is likely to be provided for a continuous period which is less than the applicable period, or
(b)   the arrangements need to be made as a matter of urgency.

(4) If the NHS body—

(a)   did not instruct an independent mental capacity advocate to represent P before making the arrangements because it was satisfied that subsection (3)(a) or (b) applied, but
(b)   subsequently has reason to believe that the accommodation is likely to be provided for a continuous period—
      (i) beginning with the day on which accommodation was first provided in accordance with the arrangements, and
      (ii) ending on or after the expiry of the applicable period,
      it must instruct an independent mental capacity advocate to represent P.

(5) The NHS body must, in deciding what arrangements to make for P, take into account any information given, or submissions made, by the independent mental capacity advocate.

(6) "Care home" has the meaning given in section 3 of the Care Standards Act 2000 (c. 14).

(7) "Hospital" means—

(a)   a health service hospital as defined by section 128 of the National Health Service Act 1977 (c. 49), or

(b) an independent hospital as defined by section 2 of the Care Standards Act 2000.

(8) "NHS body" has such meaning as may be prescribed by regulations made for the purposes of this section by—

(a) the Secretary of State, in relation to bodies in England, or
(b) the National Assembly for Wales, in relation to bodies in Wales.

(9) "Applicable period" means—

(a) in relation to accommodation in a hospital, 28 days, and
(b) in relation to accommodation in a care home, 8 weeks.

Provision of accommodation by local authority

39.—(1) This section applies if a local authority propose to make arrangements—

(a) for the provision of residential accommodation for a person ("P") who lacks capacity to agree to the arrangements, or
(b) for a change in P's residential accommodation, and are satisfied that there is no person, other than one engaged in providing care or treatment for P in a professional capacity or for remuneration, whom it would be appropriate for them to consult in determining what would be in P's best interests.

(2) But this section applies only if the accommodation is to be provided in accordance with—

(a) section 21 or 29 of the National Assistance Act 1948 (c. 29), or
(b) section 117 of the Mental Health Act,

as the result of a decision taken by the local authority under section 47 of the National Health Service and Community Care Act 1990 (c. 19).

(3) This section does not apply if P is accommodated as a result of an obligation imposed on him under the Mental Health Act.

(4) Before making the arrangements, the local authority must instruct an independent mental capacity advocate to represent P unless they are satisfied that-

(a) the accommodation is likely to be provided for a continuous period of less than 8 weeks, or
(b) the arrangements need to be made as a matter of urgency.

(5) If the local authority—

(a) did not instruct an independent mental capacity advocate to represent P before making the arrangements because they were satisfied that subsection (4)(a) or (b) applied, but
(b) subsequently have reason to believe that the accommodation is likely to be provided for a continuous period that will end 8 weeks or more after the day on which accommodation was first provided in accordance with the arrangements,

they must instruct an independent mental capacity advocate to represent P.

(6) The local authority must, in deciding what arrangements to make for P, take into account any information given, or submissions made, by the independent mental capacity advocate.

Exceptions

40.—Sections 37(3), 38(3) and (4) and 39(4) and (5) do not apply if there is—

(a) a person nominated by P (in whatever manner) as a person to be consulted in matters affecting his interests,

(b) a donee of a lasting power of attorney created by P,
(c) a deputy appointed by the court for P, or
(d) a donee of an enduring power of attorney (within the meaning of Schedule 4) created by P.

Power to adjust role of independent mental capacity advocate

41.—(1) The appropriate authority may make regulations—

(a) expanding the role of independent mental capacity advocates in relation to persons who lack capacity, and
(b) adjusting the obligation to make arrangements imposed by section 35.

(2) The regulations may, in particular—

(a) prescribe circumstances (different to those set out in sections 37, 38 and 39) in which an independent mental capacity advocate must, or circumstances in which one may, be instructed by a person of a prescribed description to represent a person who lacks capacity, and
(b) include provision similar to any made by section 37, 38, 39 or 40.

(3) "Appropriate authority" has the same meaning as in section 35.

NOTES:

1. Whilst the explicit function of the IMCA is broadly the same as that of independent supervision, it seems likely that it is the firsat step towards a true advocacy service. For people not able to make choices in advance about how their decisions should be made in the future (because lacking capacity to makee.g., a lasting power of attorney), this is a significant step.
2. The original government proposals dropped any provisions in relation to research and incapable adults as being thought to be politically too sensitive to put to Parliament. However, it has sensibly been persuaded that this is an area in need of better regulation (see Chapter 00).

QUESTIONS:

1. Will the independent mental advocacy service provide an essential and effective mechanism to protect the rights of the incapable adult? Is what the Act provides sufficient?
2. What value do you believe the independent mental capacity advocacy service provides?
3. Would you extend its role beyond serious medical treatment and accommodation?
4. Do you agree that it is important the advocate has a right, with permission, to seek declarations from the Court of Protection? Do you agree that this may make more sure that the Mental Capacity Act 2005 survives any challenge to it under Art. 6 of the European Convention on Human Rights?

(iv) A New Court-Based Jurisdiction

In Part VIII of its Report, the Law Commission recommended the introduction of a court-based jurisdiction to resolve the problems caused for carers where an individual lacks capacity. It would provide a forum for disputes to be resolved. It would be an important element in ensuring that the privacy rights of the incapable adult were adequately protected. It was designed to provide an integrated framework for the making of personal welfare, health care and financial decisions. It would replace the High Court's inherent jurisdiction to grant declarations in medical law cases. It would possess powers to make declarations as to the person's incompetence, the current validity of any earlier expressions of his wishes, and to approve or disapprove medical treatments which fall into one of the special categories. In paragraph 8.9 the Commission recommended that this court should have power to:

> "(1) make any decision on behalf of a person who lacks capacity to make that decision or
> (2) appoint a manager to be responsible for making a decision on behalf of a person who lacks capacity to make it."

It added that:

> "The decisions in question may extend to any matter relating to the personal welfare, health care, property or affairs of the person concerned, including the conduct of legal proceedings."

In relation to managers, the Commission emphasised that a specific decision by the court is preferable to the appointment of a manager, and that powers conferred on a manager should be as limited in scope and duration as possible (paras 8.12—8.13).

The following extract deals with the court's jurisdiction on health care matters.

Law Commission, Mental Incapacity, Law. Com. 231, 1995

Health care matters

8.22 We suggested . . . two kinds of orders would be required in relation to health care, namely an order approving (or not) a particular treatment and an order transferring the care of the patient to another person. Our consultees approved . . . , acknowledging that a power in the court to approve or disapprove proposed actions would be a great advance on the current declaration procedure. Attention could then focus on whether the thing *should* be done, rather than on its legality if it were to be done . . .

> *We recommend that the court's powers in relation to health care matters should cover (1) approving or refusing approval for particular forms of health care (2) appointing a manger to consent or refuse consent to particular forms of health care, (3) requiring a person to allow a different person to take over responsibility for the health care of the person concerned.*

8.23 We provisionally suggested that any proxy with health care powers should be able to exercise the rights of the person without capacity to access personal health records. Respondents agreed with this proposal, pointing out that access to records would often be essential to allow the manager to make a valid informed decision . . .

> *We recommend that the court's powers should cover obtaining access to the health records of the person concerned.*

8.24 It follows from our policy in relation to advance refusals of treatment that neither the court nor a manager may approve any treatment which the patient has already refused. In that connection, however, it should also be made clear that, since no advance refusal of "basic care" by a patient who now lacks capacity can be effective, neither the court nor the manager may authorise the withholding of that type of care.

We recommend that the court may not approve, nor a manager consent to, (1) the withholding of basic care, or (2) any treatment refused by an advance refusal of treatment.

8.25 We have already recommended that certain kinds of medical decision should require independent supervision. In Consultation Paper No. 129 we suggested that no court-appointed manager should ever be able to reach such decisions. We no longer see the need for a blanket restriction of that type. It may be, for example, that the court has been asked whether sterilisation by hysterectomy would be in the patient's best interests, and it is then agreed to attempt a less intrusive method of contraception. Nonetheless, the court feels able to decide that the patient's sister is an appropriate person to make decisions about her health care, including any decision to consent to a sterilisation at a later stage. In such circumstances, there would be little merit in requiring everyone to return to court when that later stage is reached. Equally, the second opinion procedure is intended to ensure some supervision of serious decisions by someone independent of the responsible doctor. The court might sometimes be satisfied that a "health care manager" who was a family member, citizen advocate or friend was quite capable of providing the necessary independent input. Although we would not anticipate power over "court category" or "second opinion category" treatments being granted to managers as a matter of course, we are now persuaded that there could be cases where this was an appropriate step. Any such authority should be expressly granted by the court.

8.26 We have recommended the adoption of special procedures where it is proposed to carry out a procedure or a research project which will not bring direct benefit to the person without capacity. Again, there might be rare circumstances where the court may determine that a manager should in future have power to consent to such matters. Any such authority should, however, be expressly granted by the court. In relation to non-therapeutic research, no decision of the court could ever obviate the need for prior approval of the project by the statutory committee.

We recommend that the court may grant a manager express authority to consent to the carrying out of treatments which would otherwise require court approval or a certificate from an independent medical practitioner; or to consent to the carrying out of non-therapeutic procedures or research.

In the extract above, the Law Commission simply referred to "the court'" which would underpin its suggested framework of decision-making. In the extract which follows it makes it clear what this court or new "judicial forum" might look like.

Law Commission, Mental Incapacity, Law Com. 231, 1995

10.4 Many respondents favoured an informal and inquisitorial approach to the issues which would arise under the new jurisdiction. There was also a very loud and clear call for the jurisdiction to be locally based and easily accessible. A number of respondents favoured tribunals for these reasons . . .

10.5 . . . The perceived advantages of informality and an inquisitorial approach could in fact be worked into a court-based system. It is true that a tribunal can include non lawyers with relevant expertise in the process of adjudication. However, the very wide range of decisions covered by the new "incapacity" jurisdiction would make it very hard to identify which non-legal specialism was relevant in a particular case. Decisions about financial matters, personal and social matters and complex medical decisions will all fall to be made ... [T]here was a widespread view on consultation that certain very serious medical decisions should continue to be taken by senior members of the judiciary. There is, moreover, little doubt that the type of property and finance issues currently being resolved in the Court of Protection will continue to be the major part of the workload. Jurisdiction over new-style Continuing Powers of Attorney should also be integrated with the broad decision-making powers of the judicial forum which is chosen. All these factors make the use of the court system seem increasingly appropriate ...

10.8 We now consider that the use of existing court structures and personnel, albeit arranged so as to meet the needs of those without capacity, is the most responsible and practical way forward. The new statutory jurisdiction to make decisions on behalf of persons lacking capacity and to grant orders for the protection of vulnerable persons should be exercised by courts, both by an expanded and reconstituted Court of Protection and, in relation to the public law powers only, by magistrates courts.

10.9 ... [A] single court should in future exercise jurisdiction in relation to Continuing Powers of Attorney; and in relation to personal, health care and financial decisions for a person who lacks capacity. The expertise of the existing Court of Protection, especially in relation to financial matters and powers of attorney, should be retained and built upon. At the same time, the opportunity should be taken to change the anomalous nature of the present Court of Protection, an 'office' of the Supreme Court with a single location in central London. The types of decisions which the judicial forum will be called upon to make are decisions which should be taken in a properly constituted court, whose decisions can contribute to a body of case-law. We recommend that a new superior court of record called the Court of Protection should be established and that the office of the Supreme Court known as the Court of Protection should be abolished ...

10.12 The new Court of Protection will have jurisdiction to deal with all of the matters with which this Report is concerned, including the same powers as magistrates' courts to issue entry warrants or make other orders for the care and protection of the vulnerable ...

10.13 The Court of Protection should consist of an appropriate number of judges nominated by the Lord Chancellor to exercise the jurisdiction of the Court. These judges will build up special expertise in cases involving people who may lack mental capacity. The availability of a range of judicial personnel should mean that cases, depending on their subject matter or complexity, are heard at the appropriate level by a judge with the appropriate experience and expertise. The range of judges should include district and circuit judges, and judges from the Chancery and Family Divisions of the High Court. Judges of the Chancery Division are currently nominated to deal with cases concerning the property and affairs of patients under Part VII of the Mental Health Act 1983 and their experience in this area should be retained. Judges of the Family Division deal with such cases as arise at present concerning the personal welfare or medical treatment of persons without capacity to consent.

We recommend that the jurisdiction of the Court of Protection should be exercised by judges nominated by the Lord Chancellor, whether Chancery Division or Family Division High Court judges, circuit judges or district judges ...

10.16 ...

We recommend that the Court of Protection should be able to sit at any place in England and Wales designated by the Lord Chancellor ...

10.20 Applications for public law orders may only be made by authorised officers of a local authority. In the consultation papers we suggested that some applicants for private law orders should be able to apply as of right, while others would require leave. Respondents supported the idea of a filtering mechanism, but tended to suggest more and more categories of persons who should be able to apply as of right. It became clear that it would be extremely difficult to create an acceptable list of relatives who should have an automatic right to apply. We have concluded that the category of persons with an automatic right to apply should be restricted to those who have *existing* decision-making powers, or who are mentioned in an *existing* order . . . The leave requirement can then be used in a positive and helpful way, to direct prospective applicants towards the factors which are likely to be relevant to the determination of any application for which leave is given.

> We recommend that leave should be required before an application to the Court of Protection can be made. In granting leave the Court should have regard to:
>   (1) the applicant's connection with the person concerned,
>   (2) the reason for the application,
>   (3) the benefit to the person concerned of any proposed order,
>   (4) whether the benefit can be achieved in any other way.
> No leave should be required for any application to the court by
>   (1) a person who is or is alleged to be without capacity, or, in respect of such a person who is under 18 years old, any person with parental responsibility for that person,
>   (2) a donee of a CPA granted by the person without capacity or a court-appointed manager [continuing Power of Attorney],
>   (3) the Public Trustee as respects any functions exercisable by virtue of an existing order, and
>   (4) any person mentioned in an existing order of the Court. (Draft Bill, clause 47.)

10.21 As in the case of Part VII of the Mental Health Act 1983 we consider that it would be useful for the Court of Protection to be able to make an order or give directions even if it cannot yet determine whether the person concerned actually lacks the capacity to take the decision in question. In exercising this emergency jurisdiction the court would only be able to make the order or give the directions sought if it is of the opinion that the order or direction is in the best interests of the person concerned.

> We recommend that the Court of Protection should have power to make an order or give directions on a matter, pending a decision on whether the person concerned is without capacity in relation to that matter . . .

10.25 Decisions taken by the court on behalf of a person without capacity must be taken in the person's "best interests". The court will be obliged to have regard to the wishes and feelings of the person concerned, and the factors he or she should have considered. It may not always be appropriate for the person concerned to be present in court, whether because of physical or mental frailty. Other parties and witnesses to the proceedings may offer conflicting assessments of the situation. It should be expected that an independent report should be prepared in such circumstances.

> We recommend that, where the person concerned is neither present nor represented, the court should (unless it considers it unnecessary) obtain a report on his or her wishes.

10.26 The decisions which the court is asked to make may not depend purely on legal points.

10.27 Arriving at the solution which is in the best interests of the person concerned might require evidence from expert professionals, and the House of Lords Select Committee particularly urged that "some mechanism must be adopted whereby the new court will make full use of appropriate independent medical and ethical advice." The most appropriate mechanism, adapting existing procedures and personnel, is to involve court welfare officers and local authority officers where necessary.

> We recommend that the Court of Protection should have power to ask a probation officer to report to the court, and power to ask a local authority officer to report or arrange for another person to report, on such matters as the court directs, relating to the person concerned.

The commitment to a new jurisdiction has continued and now finds a place in the Mental Capacity Act with the establishment of a Court of Protection. It bears the same name as an existing organisation. However, the old Court of Protection was not a court but a means of overseeing the management of property and affairs of incapable people under the Mental Health Act 1983, Part IX. The new Court of Protection is a real court with the necessary jurisdiction.

Mental Capacity Act 2005

Power to make declarations

15.—(1) The court may make declarations as to—

(a) whether a person has or lacks capacity to make a decision specified in the declaration;
(b) whether a person has or lacks capacity to make decisions on such matters as are described in the declaration;
(c) the lawfulness or otherwise of an act, omission or course of conduct in relation to that person.

(2) "Act" includes an omission and a course of conduct.

Powers to make decisions and appoint deputies: general

16.—(1) This section applies if a person ("P") lacks capacity in relation to a matter or matters concerning—

(a) P's personal welfare, or
(b) P's property and affairs.

(2) The court may—

(a) by making an order, make the decision or decisions on P's behalf in relation to the matter or matters, or
(b) appoint a person (a "deputy") to make decisions on P's behalf in relation to the matter or matters.

(3) The powers of the court under this section are subject to the provisions of this Act and, in particular, to section 4 (best interests).

(4) When deciding whether it is in P's best interests to appoint a deputy, the court must have regard (in addition to the matters mentioned in section 4) to the principles that—

(a) a decision by the court is to be preferred to the appointment of a deputy to make a decision, and
(b) the powers conferred on a deputy should be as limited in scope and duration as is reasonably practicable in the circumstances.

(5) The court may make such further orders or give such directions, and confer on a deputy such powers, as it thinks necessary or expedient for giving effect to an order or appointment made by it under subsection (2).

(6) Without prejudice to section 4, the court may make the order, give the directions or make the appointment on such terms as it considers are in P's best interests, even though no application is before the court for an order, directions or an appointment on those terms.

(7) An order of the court may be varied or discharged by a subsequent order.

(8) The court may, in particular, revoke the appointment of a deputy or vary the powers conferred on him if it is satisfied that the deputy—

(a) has behaved, or is behaving, in a way that contravenes the authority conferred on him by the court or is not in P's best interests, or

(b) proposes to behave in a way that would contravene that authority or would not be in P's best interests.

Section 16 powers: personal welfare

17.—(1) The powers under section 16 as respects P's personal welfare extend in particular to—

(a) deciding where P is to live;

(b) deciding what contact, if any, P is to have with any specified persons;

(c) making an order prohibiting a named person from having contact with P;

(d) giving or refusing consent to the carrying out or continuation of a treatment by a person providing health care for P;

(e) giving a direction that a person responsible for P's health care allow a different person to take over that responsibility.

(2) Subsection (1) is subject to section 20 (restrictions on deputies).

Section 16 powers: property and affairs

18.—(1) The powers under section 16 as respects P's property and affairs extend in particular to—

(a) the control and management of P's property;

(b) the sale, exchange, charging, gift or other disposition of P's property;

(c) the acquisition of property in P's name or on P's behalf;

(d) the carrying on, on P's behalf, of any profession, trade or business;

(e) the taking of a decision which will have the effect of dissolving a partnership of which P is a member;

(f) the carrying out of any contract entered into by P;

(g) the discharge of P's debts and of any of P's obligations, whether legally enforceable or not;

(h) the settlement of any of P's property, whether for P's benefit or for the benefit of others;

(i) the execution for P of a will;

(j) the exercise of any power (including a power to consent) vested in P whether beneficially or as trustee or otherwise;

(k) the conduct of legal proceedings in P's name or on P's behalf.

(2) No will may be made under subsection (l)(i) at a time when P has not reached 18.

(3) The powers under section 16 as respects any other matter relating to P's property and affairs may be exercised even though P has not reached 16, if the court considers it likely that P will still lack capacity to make decisions in respect of that matter when he reaches 18.

(4) Schedule 2 supplements the provisions of this section.

(5) Section 16(7) (variation and discharge of court orders) is subject to paragraph 6 of Schedule 2.

(6) Subsection (1) is subject to section 20 (restrictions on deputies).

Appointment of deputies

19.—(1) A deputy appointed by the court must be—

(a) an individual who has reached 18, or . . . .

(3) A person must not be appointed as a deputy without his consent . . . .

Restrictions on deputies

20.—(1) A deputy does not have power to make a decision on behalf of P in relation to a matter if he knows or has reasonable grounds for believing that P has recovered capacity in relation to the matter.

(2) Nothing in section 16(5) or 17 permits a deputy to be given power—

(a) to prohibit a named person from having contact with P;
(b) to direct a person responsible for P's health care to allow a different person to take over that responsibility . . .

(4) A deputy may not be given power to make a decision on behalf of P which is inconsistent with a decision made, within the scope of his authority and in accordance with this Act, by the donee of a lasting power of attorney granted by P (or, if there is more than one donee, by any of them).

(5) A deputy may not refuse consent to the carrying out or continuation of life-sustaining treatment in relation to P.

(6) The authority conferred on a deputy is subject to the provisions of this Act and, in particular, section 1 (the principles), section 4 (best interests).

(7) A deputy may not do an act that is intended to restrain P unless four conditions are satisfied.

(8) The first condition is that, in doing the act, the deputy is acting within the scope of an authority expressly conferred on him by the court.

(9) The second is that P lacks, or the deputy reasonably believes that P lacks, capacity in relation to the matter in question.

(10) The third is that the deputy reasonably believes that it is necessary to do the act in order to prevent harm to P.

(11) The fourth is that the act is a proportionate response to—

(a) the likelihood of P's suffering harm, or
(b) the seriousness of that harm.

(12) For the purposes of this section, a deputy restrains P if he—

(a) uses, or threatens to use, force to secure the doing of an act which P resists, or
(b) restricts P's liberty of movement, whether or not P resists,

or if he authorises another person to do any of those things . . . .

[Sections 22–23 deal with the powers of the court in relation to lasting powers of attorney. Clauses 24–26 deal with advance decisions to refuse treatment.]

The Court of Protection

45.—(1) There is to be a superior court of record known as the Court of Protection.

(2) The court may sit at any place in England and Wales, on any day and at any time . . . .

[Sections 44–47 deal with who may be the judges, the general powers of the court, its power to issue interim orders and directions and power to call for reports.]

Applications to the Court of Protection

50.—(1) No permission is required for an application to the Court of Protection for the exercise of any of its powers under this Act—

(a) by a person who lacks, or is alleged to lack, capacity,
(b) if such a person has not reached 18, by anyone with parental responsibility for him,

(c) by the donor or a donee of a lasting power of attorney to which the application relates,

(d) by a deputy appointed by the court for a person to whom the application relates, or

(e) by a person named in an existing order of the court, if the application relates to the order.

(2) But, subject to Court of Protection Rules . . . , permission is required in the case of any other application to the court.

. . .

(3) In deciding whether to grant permission the court must, in particular, have regard to—

(a) the applicant's connection with the person to whom the application relates;
(b) the reasons for the application;
(c) the benefit to the person to whom the application relates of a proposed order or directions;
(d) whether the benefit can be achieved in any other way.

(9) "Parental responsibility" has the same meaning as in the Children Act 1989.

[Section 51 provides for the creation of Court of Protection Rules and s.52 for the ability to make practice directions. Section 53 creates relevant rights of appeal, and ss.54–56 deal with fees and costs.]

The Public Guardian

57.—(1) For the purposes of this Act, there is to be an officer, to be known as the Public Guardian . . .

Functions of the Public Guardian

58.—(1) The Public Guardian has the following functions—

(a) establishing and maintaining a register of lasting powers of attorney;
(b) establishing and maintaining a register of orders appointing deputies;
(c) supervising deputies appointed by the court;
(d) directing a Court of Protection Visitor to visit—
   (i) a donee of a lasting power of attorney, or
   (ii) a deputy appointed by the court, or
   (iii) the person granting the power of attorney or for whom the deputy is appointed ("P"),
   and to make a report to the Public Guardian on such matters as he may direct;
(e) receiving security which the court requires a person to give for the discharge of his functions;
(f) receiving reports from donees of lasting powers of attorney and deputies appointed by the court;
(g) reporting to the court on such matters relating to proceedings under this Act as the court requires;
(h) dealing with representations (including complaints) about the way in which a donee of a lasting power of attorney or a deputy appointed by the court is exercising his powers . . .

[Subsequent sections deal with supplementary provisions. Section 61 allows for the appointment of Court of Protection Visitors, who may be Special Visitors (i.e. doctors) or General Visitors.]

QUESTIONS:

1. Do you think that it is right that it should be possible for a court to appoint a manager (Law Commission) or deputy (Mental Capacity Act)? Do you

agree that this should be avoided where the court can make a decision? Which principle in s.1 of the Act does this underpin?

2. Do you think that the "judicial forum" proposed by the Law Commission should take the form of a court? Would the introduction of a multi-disciplinary tribunal have been a better idea? In your view, who would be appropriate persons to sit on it?

3. How could it be guaranteed that challenges to decisions/actions are made to the Court of Protection on behalf of an incapable adult when they should be? Does compliance with Article 6 of the ECHR require effective court access?

NOTES:

1. The court would have no powers other than those possessed by a competent person. Unlike the current Court of Protection, which is based in London, the new forum would have a base in each judicial circuit.

2. For the recommendations on Lasting Powers of Attorney and advance directives, see pp.1083 *et seq.*

3. The Act is possibly the most consulted upon piece of legislation in Parliament's history. The Law Commission engaged in two large consultation exercises during the course of its work, the Government consulted the public on the first two stages of its work, and the draft Bill was put before pre-legislative scrutiny which involved the Joint Parliamentary committee undertaking its own work and receiving evidence both orally and in person.

QUESTIONS:

1. Reflecting on the Mental Capacity Act, in the light of the work of the Law Commission, do you think it is a valuable piece of legislation?

2. Do you think that the Act ensures an effective means of making decisions on behalf of incapable adults while also providing suitable protection from exploitation and abuse?

3. Having now looked at both the existing common law position and the proposals for reform, will the Act make improvements on the existing position? Has the common law developed to a point where legislation is unnecessary? Could many of the desired improvements be achieved by way of a code of practice?

SELECT BIBLIOGRAPHY

P. Bartlett, "The Consequences of Incapacity" (1997) *Web Journal of Current Legal Issues,* Part 4.

P. Bartlett, *Blackstone's Guide to the Mental Capacity Act,* Oxford: OUP 2005.

P. Bartlett and R. Sandland, *Mental Health Law: Policy and Practice* (2nd edn) Oxford: OUP, 2003, especially Chapters 10 and 11.

M. Brazier and M. Lobjoit (eds), *Protecting the Vulnerable: Autonomy and Consent in Health Care,* London: Routledge, 1991.

A. Buchanan and D. Brock, *Deciding for Others: the Ethics of Surrogate Decision Making*, Cambridge: CUP, 1989, especially Chapter 1.

R. R. Faden and T. Beauchamp, *A History and Theory of Informed Consent*, New York: OUP, 1986.

P. Fennell, "Inscribing Paternalism in the Law: Consent to Treatment and Mental Disorder" (1990) 17 *Journal of Law and Society* 29.

P. Fennell, "Statutory Authority to Treat, Relatives and Treatment Proxies" (1994) 2 *Medical Law Review* 30.

P. Fennell, "The Law Commission Proposals on Mental Incapacity" (1995) *Family Law* 420.

P. Fennell, *Treatment without Consent*, London: Routledge, 1996.

M. Freeman, "Deciding for the Intellectually Impaired" (1994) 2 *Medical Law Review* 77.

N. Glover and M. Brazier, "Ethical Aspects of the Law Commission Report on Mental Incapacity" (1996) 6 *Reviews in Clinical Gerontology* 365.

L. Gostin, "Consent to Treatment: the Incapable Person" in C. Dyer (edn), *Doctors, Patients and the Law*, Oxford: Blackwell, 1992.

A. Grubb, "Treatment Decisions: Keeping it in the Family" in A. Grubb (edn), *Choices and Decisions in Health Care*, Chichester: John Wiley, 1993.

M. Gunn, "Mental Incapacity: the Law Commissioner's Report" (1995) 7 *Child and Family Law Quarterly* 209.

M. Gunn, "The Meaning of Incapacity" (1994) 2 *Medical Law Review*.

M.J. Gunn, J.G. Wong, I.C.H. Clare and A.J. Holland, "Decision-making Capacity" (1999) 7 *Medical Law Review* 269.

M. Gunn, J. Bellhouse, I. Clare, T. Holland and P. Watson, "Families and New Medical Dilemmas: Capacity to Make Decisions" (2001) 13 *Child and Family Law Quarterly* 383.

S. Hirsch and J. Harris (eds), *Consent and the Incompetent Patient: Ethics, Law and Medicine*, London: Gaskell, 1988.

B. Hoggett, "The Royal Prerogative in Relation to the Mentally Disordered: Resurrection, Resuscitation or Rejection" in M. Freeman (edn), *Medicine, Ethics and the Law*, London: Sweet & Maxwell, 1988.

M. Jones and K. Keywood, "Assessing the Patient's Competence to Consent to Medical Treatment" (1996) 2 *Medical Law International* 107.

A. Parkin, "Where Now on Mental Incapacity?" (1995) *Web Journal of Current Legal Issues*, part 2.

P. Skegg, *Law, Ethics and Medicine: Studies in Medical Law*, Oxford: OUP (1984/88) especially Chapters 2 and 3.

S. Stefan, "Silencing the Different Voice: Competence, Feminist Theory and Law" (1993) 47 *University of Miami Law Review* 763.

M. Terrell, P. Letts and L. Oates, *Mental Capacity: The New Law*, Bristol: Jordans, 2006.

A. Ward, *Adult Incapacity* Edinburgh: W. Green, 2003.

P. Wilson, "The Law Commission's Report on Mental Incapacity: Medically Vulnerable Adults or Politically Vulnerable Law?" (1996) 4 *Medical Law Review* 227.

6

CONSENT

1. INTRODUCTION

Consent to medical procedures plays an extremely important role in the context of health care provision. The concept of consent operates as a unifying principle running through health care law. It represents the legal and ethical expression of the human right to have one's autonomy and self-determination respected (see I. Kennedy, "Patients, Doctors and Human Rights" in Kennedy, *Treat Me Right: Essays in Medical Law and Ethics*, Oxford: Clarendon, 1988). O'Nora O'Neill has contended that consent has effectively replaced the notion of trust as the cornerstone of the health professional/patient relationship (see O. O'Neill, *A Question of Trust: the BBC Reith Lectures*, Cambridge: CUP, 2002; and *Autonomy and Trust in Bioethics*, Cambridge: CUP, 2002.) Although, as we have seen in Chapter 2, autonomy is regarded by many ethicists as the fundamental value in health care ethics, it has never been fully recognised as a legally protectable interest. Instead, it has been vindicated as a by-product of two other interests which have been accorded legal protection. The first of these is bodily integrity. This is protected by rules prohibiting bodily contact unless the person consents. The second is bodily well-being, which is protected by rules governing professional competence that prohibit an unqualified person from practising medicine (see M.M. Shultz, "From Informed Consent to Patient Choice: a New Protected Interest" (1985) 95 *Yale Law Journal* 219). However, although respect for the patient's wishes will normally protect his welfare, tensions may arise if concerns for the patient's welfare leads to paternalism, which conflicts with the patient's right to make autonomous decisions (see Chapter 2 at pp.121–123).

The requirement that the patient's consent be obtained thus operates as a constraint on the power of the health care professional. It is particularly important that the law protects this right given that the health care professional, particularly the doctor, is in a powerful position vis-à-vis the patient (see Chapter 2 at pp.119–121), and that his or her role frequently involves touching, examining and operating on patients. Given this power dynamic, control of information becomes a key feature in defining the balance of power between the health professional and the patient. (See J. Montgomery, "Patients First: the Role of Rights" in K.W.M. Fulford, *et al.* (eds), *Essential Practice in Patient-Centred Care*, Oxford: Blackwell Science, 1996.)

However, it should also be noted that certain judges, notably Lord Donaldson in dicta in cases involving adolescent refusal of consent (see Chapter 7 at pp.451–463), have also viewed consent as offering the health professional a shield against litigation.

For a patient to give an informed consent, it is essential that he first have information about the benefits and risks of the proposed course of treatment (see S. McLean, *A Patient's Right to Know: Information Disclosure, the Doctor and the Law*, Aldershot: Dartmouth, 1989). Shultz notes the irony that the most significant threat to patient autonomy comes from doctors themselves, who often pre-empt patient authority because of their greater knowledge and traditional role (*op. cit.* at p. 221). As she points out, attention has also focused upon the issue of patient autonomy because of the changing nature of medicine:

"Medical choice increasingly depends upon factors that transcend professional training and knowledge. As medicine has become able to extend life, delay and redefine death, harvest and transplant organs, correct abnormality within the womb, enable artificial reproduction, and trace genetic defect, questions about values have come to the fore in medical decision making. Health care choices involve profound questions that are not finally referable to professional expertise." (See Shultz, *op. cit.* at p.222.)

English law has focused upon the questions of (i) which risks should be disclosed to the patient, and (ii) according to whose standard should the materiality of risk be assessed? The common law does not appear fully to espouse a right to autonomy, although arguably it has moved in the direction of enhancing patient autonomy since the first edition of this book was published in 1997. The principles which can be derived from the common law establish two requirements. First, that physical contact is permissible only where the health care professional has the patient's consent. This requirement is backed up by liability under both criminal and civil law (see Section 2). Secondly, that health professionals are under a duty to provide patients with information about proposed treatment, and alternatives. The issue of capacity to consent has been considered in the previous Chapter. The need for consent is discussed in Section 2 below, and the meaning of consent in Section 3. Section 3 also explores the duty to inform patients. Finally Section 4 addresses what happens when consent is refused or vitiated.

Because the law of consent, like much of health care law, has been developed by the courts, rather than Parliament, it follows that the rules have emerged in the context of specific disputes, rather than being drafted to deal with general issues. This sometimes makes it difficult to predict how they should be applied in different circumstances. As Tobias has noted (writing in the context of research), notwithstanding the legal emphasis on informed consent, lawyers, ethicists and scientists have failed to agree on precisely what the term actually means" (J.S. Tobias, "BMJ's present policy (sometimes approving research in which patients have not given fully informed consent) is wholly correct" (1997) 314 B.M.J.,

1111). This is now beginning to change as a result of public concern about processes for obtaining consent, especially in the context of research, which were promoted by inquiries into failures to obtain consent at Bristol and Alder Hey hospitals. In turn, this has sparked debates about defining consent and whether it should be generic or specific (see Chapter 10 at pp.682–686 and O. O'Neill, "The Limits of Informed Consent" (2003) 29 *Journal of Medical Ethics* 4. A further problem with judge-made law is that it can be especially difficult to distil the principles on which the rules are based, especially when judges in the same case give different accounts of them. This is particularly problematic in relation to the principal case on disclosing information, *Sidaway v Bethlem RHG* [1985] 1 All E.R. 643 (discussed fully below at pp.372–383), in which it is virtually impossible to establish any clear *ratio*.

Although consent has evolved as a common law doctrine, the concept is also enshrined as a central tenet of some of the most significant legislative inter-ventions in the health care field, notably the Human Fertilisation and Embryology Act 1990 (see Chapter 11) and the Human Tissue Act 2004 (see Chapter 15). Moreover, European Union initiatives, such as Directive 2001/20 of the European Parliament and of the Council of April 4, 2001 on the approximation of the laws regulating clinical trials of medicinal products, which resulted in the Medicines for Human Use (Clinical Trials) Regulations) 2004 in the UK, also enshrine consent as a key principle in the clinical research context (see Chapter 10). However,once again, there is little attempt to engage with what consent means in such legislation (see, for instance, Chapter 15 at pp.1121–1139.) Often, there-fore, important practical guidance for health professionals is contained in professional Codes of Practice, such as those issued by the GMC and the Nursing and Midwifery Council (see pp.396–397 below). These stress the importance of understanding consent as a process involving dialogue, rather than a one-off transaction, and of explaining procedures in a language appropriate to the patient and arranging for interpreters if necessary.

2. THE NEED FOR CONSENT

If medical treatment is provided without consent having been obtained, the health professional is liable to be sued in tort. The patient may sue the health professional in trespass to the person. In certain extreme circumstances there exists the theoretical possibility of a criminal prosecution for assault or battery. Alternatively, the health professional may be sued in negligence. Under this head of action, the patient alleges that the health professional negligently carried out his or her duty to advise him, so that he was not given sufficient information to make a fully informed choice.

Everybody has a right to bodily integrity, which is protected by the criminal and civil law of assault and battery. Medical procedures which involve touching the patient come within the potential scope of the crimes of battery or assault. In the criminal law context, the crimes of assault and battery are now treated as though they are synonymous, though historically at common law the technical meaning of assault was the threat of unlawful battery. The traditional definition of a battery is an act that directly and either intentionally or negligently causes some physical contact with the person of another without that person's consent. If a person has consented to the contact, expressly or impliedly, there is no battery, although it has been argued that battery would be better redefined as "an act that directly and either intentionally or negligently causes some physical contact with the person of another in circumstances in which such contact is not generally acceptable in the ordinary conduct of life" (see H. Brooke, "Consent to Treatment or Research: the Incapable Patient" in S.R. Hirsch and J. Harris (eds), *Consent and the Incompetent Patient*, London: Gaskell, 1988).

Together with false imprisonment, assault and battery comprise what the common law calls trespass to the person, which is any type of activity that infringes the bodily integrity or liberty of another. These actions are condemned by the common law as civil wrongs which are actionable in damages. In this chapter we shall adopt the terminology of "trespass to the person" to refer to civil actions and "assault" to refer to criminal actions, as those are the terms commonly adopted in case law. We deal first with the criminal law.

(a) The Criminal Law

As we shall see, although the actions of health care professionals are always circumscribed by criminal law, it is extremely rare for a doctor or nurse to be charged with a criminal offence. It is much more likely that an aggrieved patient will pursue a civil law action with the aim of obtaining compensation. Criminal law plays only a secondary role in ensuring accountability for medical mal-practice because its main concern is not with compensation but with punishment by the state. As most injuries occasioned in the course of medical treatment will be inflicted inadvertently or negligently (see Chapter 3), criminal sanctions will generally be inappropriate. However, where a health carer deliberately or recklessly causes injury to a patient, a criminal prosecution may be appropriate. In practice, this is most likely to occur where the patient dies and the doctor is charged with manslaughter (see Chapter 14). In this chapter, for the sake of completeness, we consider non-fatal offences against the person which may theoretically be committed by a health care professional.

(i) Assault Occasioning Actual Bodily Harm

The common law offence of assault is the basis of all the criminal law offences against the person.

Offences Against the Person Act 1861, s.47

47.—Whosoever shall be convicted on indictment of any assault occasioning actual bodily harm shall be liable to be imprisoned for any term not exceeding five years.

NOTES:

1. The Act is clear that actual bodily harm is required under s.47. According to Lyndsay J. in *R v Miller* [1954] 2 Q.B. 282, citing Archbold, "actual

bodily" includes "any hurt or injury calculated to interfere with health or comfort". This excludes emotional harm (unless it manifests as a recognisable medical condition, which would include recognisable psychiatric illness: *R. v Chan-Fook* [1994] 2 All E.R. 552; *R. v Ireland; R. v. Burstow* [1998] A.C. 147).

2. Section 47 of the 1861 Act does not require "malice" on the part of the doctor, merely actual bodily harm to which the patient did not consent. So, just as with the civil law, consent will form a defence to any proceedings based on the infliction of actual bodily harm. This means, conceivably, that a health care professional might face prosecution in the following situations: (a) where no consent to the procedure undertaken was provided; (b) where consent has been extracted under duress; (c) where the patient is not competent to give a valid consent to treatment; (d) where the procedure is performed in spite of express refusal of consent; (e) where the patient was inadequately informed about the procedure proposed so as not to be able to provide an effective consent; and (f) where the doctor or nurse mistakes the scope of her authority.

QUESTIONS:

1. Where an interventionist medical procedure is on the whole beneficial to a patient, is it right to construe that procedure as "bodily harm" for the purposes of a s.47 offence?
2. What is the legal position where a nurse, rather than a specific surgeon (Dr X), performs an appendectomy given that when the patient consented to the procedure, he did not intend it to be performed by anyone other than Dr X? (See pp.365–368 below.)

(ii) Offences Involving Grievous Bodily Harm and/or Wounding

Two further provisions of the Offences Against the Person Act 1861 are specifically concerned with causing more serious harm. These sections create very serious offences which, in practice, it would be rare for a doctor or nurse to commit (but which may be committed by a non-registered practitioner who masquerades as a fully qualified registered doctor).

Offences Against the Person Act 1861, s.18

18.—Whosoever shall unlawfully and maliciously by any means whatsoever wound or cause any grievous bodily harm to any person, with intent to do some grievous bodily harm to any person . . . shall be guilty of an offence, and being convicted thereof shall be liable to imprisonment for life.

NOTES:

1. The *actus reus* (or physical element) envisaged by s.18 is that the accused must either "wound" or cause "grievous bodily harm". In *C v Eisenhower*

[1983] 3 All E.R. 230 it was held that, for there to be a wound, both the outer and inner skin must be broken.

In *DPP v Smith* [1960] 3 All E.R. 47 the House of Lords held that the phrase "grievous bodily harm" simply meant "really serious harm". (Whether psychiatric injury may ever amount to grievous bodily harm was mooted in *R. v Gelder*, (1994) *The Times*, December 16.)

2. The *mens rea* required is intention, a concept which has not been clearly defined in the criminal law. However, it seems that if a result is a virtually certain consequence of the defendant's action and the defendant foresees that consequence as virtually certain, then the jury *may* find that the result is intended (see *R. v Nedrick* [1986] 1 W.L.R. 1025; *R. v Woolin* [1991] 1 A.C. 82). Clarkson and Keating suggest that the test allows the jury "flexibility in medical cases where doctors administer drugs or other treatment with lawful motives (for example to relieve pain) but knowing the treatment will kill the patient as in *Re A (conjoined twins: surgical separation)* [2000] 4 All E.R. 961 (C. Clarkson and H. Keating, *Criminal Law: Text and Materials* (5th edn), London: Sweet & Maxwell, 2003 at p.132). (On *Re A* see Chapter 7 at pp.434–439 and Chapter 14 at p.1036; on the "double effect" doctrine which Clarkson and Keating raise in this context, see Chapter 2 at pp.136–141). As Clarkson and Keating note, the judges in *Re A* interpret "intention" in two different ways:

> "Ward LJ and Brooke LJ in effect followed the definitional interpretation. The doctors would foresee death [of the weaker twin] as a virtual certainty and therefore they *would* intend death. However, Robert Walker LJ (implicitly) allowed himself moral elbow-room in holding that the doctors would not intend to kill the weaker twin because that was not 'The purpose or intention of the surgery'." (*op. cit.* at p. 133.)

QUESTION:

1. In what circumstances, if any, would it be possible to charge a doctor or nurse under s.18? Is a medical researcher in a different position? (See Chapter 10.)

Offences Against the Person Act 1861, s.20

20.—Whosoever shall unlawfully and maliciously wound or inflict any grievous bodily harm upon any person, either with or without any weapon or instrument, shall be guilty of an offence, and being convicted thereof shall be liable to a term of imprisonment not exceeding five years.

NOTES:

1. Section 20 resembles s.18 in that both sections are concerned with two types of outcome: wounding and grievous bodily harm. However, it is easier to secure a conviction under s.20 because the *mens rea* requirement is less stringent: there is no need to prove the intention to cause the wound or grievous bodily harm, or even that the defendant foresee actual bodily

harm. In *R. v Savage*; *DPP v Parmenter* [1991] 4 All E.R. 698 Lord Ackner explained the *mens rea* requirement for s.20 thus:

" . . . I am satisfied that the decision in *Mowatt* [[1967] 3 All E.R. 47] was correct and that it is quite unnecessary that the accused should either have intended or have foreseen that his unlawful act might cause physical harm of the gravity described in section 20, *i.e.* a wound or serious physical injury. It is enough that he should have foreseen that some physical harm to some person, albeit of a minor character, might result."

In other words, the *mens rea* for s.20 turns on a test of subjective foresight. This means that a doctor who undertakes a surgical procedure that he or she knows carries a risk of causing some harm, but who does not intend to inflict serious harm, may nonetheless be convicted under this provision. (See Clarkson and Keating, *op. cit.* at pp. 583–7).

2. Section 20 also differs from s.18 in that it stipulates that the wound or grievous bodily harm must be "inflicted" rather than, in the language of s.18, merely "caused". This means that criminal omissions, which seriously harm a patient to whom the accused doctor owed a duty of care, can only be prosecuted under s.18, and not s.20.

The absence of legally effective consent is an essential element of each of these criminal offences. Hence, if a legally effective consent is deemed to have been given, the medical touching will not constitute an assault. However, if the doctor is aware that no effective consent has been given, then even a therapeutic medical touching will amount to assault, unless some statutory or common law justification is available to the doctor (see P.D.G. Skegg, *Law, Ethics and Medicine*, Oxford: Clarendon Press, 1988, Chapter 2). Moreover, there are some forms of touching to which, it has been held, no legally effective consent can be given. In these situations, the law has determined that, for reasons of public policy, a patient is not entitled to give a legally valid consent, even if he wishes to. This means that treatment may be unlawful even if a patient wants it. Consent will not normally render lawful the infliction of physical injury — *R. v Donovan* [1934] 2 K.B. 498. The general position was considered by the Court of Appeal in *A.-G.'s Reference (No. 6 of 1980)* [1981] 2 All E.R. 1057. In this case, Lord Lane C.J. referred to the "accepted legality" of "reasonable surgical interference" and said that this, and other apparent exceptions to otherwise illegal conduct, were "needed in the public interest" (at p.1059). In *R. v Brown* [1993] 2 All E.R. 65, which held that adults could not lawfully consent to the infliction of harm during sado-masochistic sex, it was suggested that consent to "proper medical treatment" is valid, even though the bodily invasion involved may be extreme (*per* Lord Mustill at pp.109–110). In *Airedale NHS Trust v Bland* [1993] 1 All E.R. 821 (see Chapter 14 at pp.1021–1032) Lord Mustill stated that "bodily invasions in the course of proper medical treatment stand completely outside the criminal law" (at p.889). It is unlikely that treatment carried out in good faith, with the patient's consent, would be invalidated by public policy, but this poses the question of what is "proper" medical treatment, or "reasonable" surgery. The issue of whether it is reasonable to consent to one's death or the removal of one's organs is discussed in Chapters 14 and 15. Public policy limitations are sometimes specifically set out in statutes. For instance, the only circumstances in which the law permits the termination of pregnancy are stipulated in the Abortion Act 1967 (see Chapter 12), while non-therapeutic female circumcision is outlawed by the Prohibition of Female Circumcision Act 1985.

Prohibition of Female Circumcision Act 1985

1.—(1) Subject to section 2 below, it shall be an offence for any person—
(a) to excise, infibulate or otherwise mutilate the whole or any part of the labia majora or labia minora or clitoris of another person; or
(b) to aid, abet, counsel or procure the performance by another person of any of those acts on that other person's own body.

(2) A person guilty of an offence under this section shall be liable—
(a) on conviction on indictment, to a fine or to imprisonment for a term not exceeding five years or to both; or
(b) on summary conviction, to a fine not exceeding the statutory maximum (as defined in section 74 of the Criminal Justice Act 1982) or to imprisonment for a term not exceeding six months, or to both.

2.—(1) Subsection (1)(a) of section 1 shall not render unlawful the performance of a surgical operation if that operation—
(a) is necessary for the physical or mental health of the person on whom it is performed and is performed by a registered medical practitioner; or
(b) is performed on a person who is in any stage of labour or has just given birth and is so performed for purposes connected with that labour or birth by—
   (i) a registered medical practitioner or a registered midwife; or
   (ii) a person undergoing a course of training with a view to becoming a registered medical practitioner or a registered midwife.

(2) In determining for the purposes of this section whether an operation is necessary for the mental health of a person, no account shall be taken of the effect on that person of any belief on the part of that or any other person that the operation is required as a matter of custom or ritual.

NOTES:

1. The exemptions for medical practitioners and midwives indicate legal recognition of the need for special provision to be made for the purposes of health care. Similar exemptions for medical practitioners are found in the Tattooing of Minors Act 1969.

2. Female circumcision raises, in acute form, the problem of cultural relativism in judging the acceptability of medical practices (see Chapter 2 at pp.88–92). The procedure is required by certain traditions in order to accord with their ideal of feminine roles. It may be questioned how different this is from cosmetic surgery undergone by Western women in order to conform to our society's ideal of feminine beauty. (See L. Bibbings, "Female Circumcision: Mutilation or Modification?" in J. Bridgeman and S. Millns (eds), *Law and Body Politics*, Aldershot: Dartmouth, 1995; M. Atoki, "Should Female Circumcision Continue to be Banned?" (1995) 3 *Feminist Legal Studies* 223). Note that the criminal law's prohibition of female circumcision contrasts sharply with its tolerance of routine infant male circumcision (see M. Fox and M. Thomson, "Short Changed? The

Law and Ethics of Male Circumcision" (2005) 13 *International Journal of Children's Rights* 161; and discussion of limits to parental consent to this procedure in Chapter 7 at p.475.)

3. More generally, there is an issue as to whether other operations should be outlawed, regardless of whether the patient consents, on the grounds of public policy. Although the Law Commission noted in its report, *Consent in the Criminal Law: a Consultation Paper*, Consultation Paper No. 139, London: HMSO, 1995, that conventional medical and surgical treatment for a therapeutic purpose by qualified practitioners gives rise to no particular difficulties, it did identify some areas related to medical practice which it perceived to be problematic. (For discussion of sterilisation see Chapter 13 at pp.926–947, on abortions see Chapter 12 and on organ transplantation see Chapter 15.) Gender reassignment surgery, which may entail removal of sex organs is carried out on the National Health Service, and it seems accepted that such operations are lawful. (See G. Williams, "Consent and Public Policy" [1962] *Criminal Law Review* 154; D. Meyers, *The Human Body and the Law* (2nd edn), Edinburgh: Edinburgh University Press, 1990, Chapter 9.) Each of these issues may be differently regarded in different cultures.

4. For the purposes of clarifying the existing law, the following provision was proposed by the Law Commission:

> 8.50 We therefore provisionally propose that—
> (1) a person should not be guilty of an offence, notwithstanding that he or she causes injury to another, of whatever degree of seriousness, if such injury is caused during the course of proper medical treatment or care administered with the consent of the other person:
> (2) in this context "medical treatment or care"—
>   (a) should mean medical treatment or care administered by or under the direction of a duly qualified medical practitioner;
>   (b) should include not only surgical and dental treatment or care, but also procedures taken for the purposes of diagnosis, the prevention of disease, the prevention of pregnancy or as ancillary to treatment; and
>   (c) without limiting the meaning of the term, should also include the following:
>   (i) surgical procedures performed for the purposes of rendering a patient sterile;
>   (ii) surgical operations performed for the purposes of enabling a person to change his or her sex;
>   (iii) lawful abortions;
>   (iv) surgical operations performed for cosmetic purposes; and
>   (v) any treatment or procedure to facilitate the donation of regenerative tissue, or the donation of non-regenerative tissue not essential for life.

QUESTIONS:

1. Is proscribing female circumcision to proscribe the best way to eliminate it? What other strategies might be used? (See D. Pearl, "Legal Issues Arising out of Medical Provision for Ethnic Groups" in A. Grubb and M. Mehlman (eds), *Justice and Health Care: Comparative Perspectives*,

Chichester: John Wiley, 1995). Is it an unjustifiable interference with individual liberty to use law to restrain an adult woman from having an abortion or being circumcised on public policy grounds if she wants to consent to the procedure?

2. Should the law deem invalid, on public policy grounds, consent to sexual intercourse with someone who deliberately conceals the fact that they are infected with the HIV virus, thus making it easier to convict a person who intends to infect other people with the virus? According to recent case law, it seems that for a defendant to be able to rely on the defence of consent when charged with transmitting HIV under s.20, he must honestly believe that the person infected consented to the risk of infection. (See *R. v. Dica* [2004] 2 Cr.App.R. 2; *R. v Konzani* (2005) 2 Crim.App.R.; M. Weait, "Criminal Law and the Sexual Transmission of HIV: R v Dica" (2005) 68 *Modern Law Review* 120; M. Weait, "Knowledge, Autonomy and Consent: R v Konzani" [2005] *Criminal Law Review* 763.)

3. Why is consent to the *risk* of bodily harm treated differently in criminal law from consent to bodily harm? Should a specific criminal offence be enacted to cover the issue of transmission of disease? (See K. Smith, "Risking Death by Dangerous Sexual Behaviour and the Criminal Law" in R. Lee and D. Morgan (eds), *Death Rites: Law and Ethics at the End of Life*, London: Routledge, 1994; M.J. Weait, "Taking the Blame: Criminal Law, Social Responsibility and the Sexual Transmission of HIV" (2001) 23 *Journal of Social Welfate and Family Law* 441; J. Chalmers, "Criminalizing HIV Transmission" (2002) 28 *Journal of Medical Ethics* 160; M. Weait, "Harm, Consent and the Limits of Privacy" (2005) 13 *Feminist Legal Studies*, 97.) The legal powers to deal with public health concerns generated by communicable diseases were discussed in Chapter 1 at pp.12–22.)

(b) The Civil Law

In a health care context, it is much more likely that a civil action will be brought for trespass to the person, rather than a criminal action for assault. As Shultz notes, patient autonomy was initially identified with and subsumed under an interest in physical security, protected by the legal rules proscribing touching without consent. However, it eventually became apparent that many aspects of the health care relationship did not fit comfortably into the trespass model. (See M.M. Shultz, "From Informed Consent to Patient Choice: a New Protected Interest" (1985) 95 *Yale Law Journal* 219 at pp.224–225.) For instance, treatments that involved no physical touching received no protection under trespass doctrine. Gradually, therefore, the dominant framework for litigation arising out of claims based in patient autonomy and self-determination has become the negligence action for non-disclosure of information. Nevertheless, as Shultz argues, under negligence doctrine, choice remains encapsulated within the dominant interest in physical well-being (*op. cit.* at p.232.)

As we shall see below, the courts have been reluctant to countenance even civil actions for trespass against health care professionals. However, the availability of these legal provisions means that, in theory at least, patients are entitled to veto the care that health professionals wish to give them. The law only permits treatment to be forced upon patients in narrowly defined circumstances. The principal exception to the requirement that consent must be obtained is where the patient is unconscious and needs emergency treatment (see below, p.328). Other examples are: testing for certain infectious diseases (see Chapter 1 and pp.368–374 below), in the context of mental health (see Chapter 9), and in the case of children and immature young people (see Chapter 7). The focus in this chapter is on the right of competent adult patients to give or refuse consent to medical care and treatment. However, as we shall see, even in the case of competent adults, the courts may readily find justification for overriding a purported refusal of consent.

Re F (Mental Patient: Sterilisation) [1989] 2 All E.R. 545, [1990] 2 A.C. 1, [1989] 2 W.L.R. 938, [1989] 2 F.L.R. 476

The facts of this case have been discussed in the previous chapter at p.321; this extract concerns the legal significance of consent:

LORD GOFF:
" . . . I start with the fundamental principle, now long established, that every person's body is inviolate . . . [T]he effect of this principle is that everybody is protected not only against physical injury but against any form of physical molestation (see *Collins v Wilcock* [1984] 3 All E.R. 374 at 378).

Of course, as a general rule physical interference with another person's body is lawful if he consents to it; though in certain limited circumstances the public interest may require that his consent is not capable of rendering the act lawful. There are also specific cases where physical interference without consent may not be unlawful: chastisement of children, lawful arrest, self-defence, the prevention of crime and so on. As I pointed out in *Collins v Wilcock* [1984] 3 All E.R. 374 at 378, a broader exception has been created to allow for the exigencies of everyday life: jostling in a street or some other crowded place, social contact at parties and such like. This exception has been said to be founded on implied consent, since those who go about in public places, or go to parties, may be taken to have impliedly consented to bodily contact of this kind. Today this rationalisation can be regarded as artificial; and, in particular, it is difficult to impute consent to those who, by reason of their youth or mental disorder, are unable to give their consent. For this reason, I consider it more appropriate to regard such cases as falling within a general exception embracing all physical contact which is generally acceptable in the ordinary conduct of everyday life.

In the old days it used to be said that, for a touching of another's person to amount to a battery, it had to be a touching 'in anger' (see *Cole v Turner* (1704) Holt KB 108 per Holt C.J.) and it has recently been said that the touching must be 'hostile' to have that effect (see *Wilson v Pringle* [1986] 2 All E.R. 440 at 447). I respectfully doubt whether that is correct. A prank that gets out of hand, an over-friendly slap on the back, surgical treatment by a surgeon who mistakenly thinks that the patient has consented to it, all these things may transcend the bounds of lawfulness, without being characterised as hostile. Indeed, the suggested qualification is difficult to reconcile with the principle that any touching of another's body is, in the absence of lawful excuse, capable of amounting to a battery and a trespass. Furthermore, in the case of medical treatment, we have to bear well in mind the libertarian principle of self-determination which, to adopt the words of Cardozo J. (in

Schloendorff v. Society of New York Hospital (1914) 211 N.Y. 125 at 126), recognises that:

> 'Every human being of adult years and sound mind has a right to determine what shall be done with his own body; and a surgeon who performs an operation without his patient's consent, commits an assault . . . ' "

NOTE:

1. Lord Goff's starting point in this extract is similar to the starting point taken by Lord Donaldson in *Re T* [1992] 4 All E.R. 649 (see Chapter 5 at pp.310–313). However, notwithstanding the emphasis placed on autonomy, like Lord Donaldson, he was ultimately prepared to sanction treatment without consent in certain circumstances, by holding that treatment was lawful provided it was judged necessary by doctors. (See I. Kennedy, "Patients, Doctors, and Human Rights" in *Treat Me Right: Essays in Medical Law and Ethics*, Oxford: Clarendon, 1988.)

3. THE MEANING OF CONSENT

We noted above the difficulty in pinning down the meaning of informed consent. However, what is clear is that provided that the patient is capable of consenting, then no care or treatment will be lawful unless he has given a "real consent". This requires the patient to have been informed "in broad terms" of the procedure in question and to have indicated his acceptance of it. The precise form in which consent must be given is not laid down by the law. Written consent is generally no more valid than oral consent or "implied" consent (where it is clear from the actions of the patient that he is consenting, for example rolling up his sleeve to receive an injection). In each of these three situations what matters is that the patient did in fact consent. Consent may also be "imputed", for example where the patient is unconscious, and it is argued that his tacit consent to treatment which is immediately necessary may be assumed. Less artificially, such treatment may be justified on the basis of necessity, as it is clearly in the public interest to come to the aid of a person needing medical treatment in an emergency. (See M. Brazier, *Medicine, Patients and the Law* (3rd edn), Harmondsworth: Penguin, 2003 at pp.112–113.) However, in most situations it is much easier to prove that a patient consented if there is written evidence of consent, and patients are usually asked to sign a consent form for surgical and other major procedures.

(a) The Nature of "Real Consent"

The meaning of "real consent" is discussed in the following case, which considers the respective requirements of the torts of trespass and negligence (the latter is considered more fully later in this chapter).

Chatterton v Gerson [1981] 1 All E.R. 257, [1981] Q.B. 432, [1980] 3 W.L.R. 1003, (1990) 1 B.M.L.R. 80

Miss Chatterton suffered chronic intractable pain following a hernia operation. She was given an injection to block the pain, but it subsequently returned. She then had the procedure repeated, but this time the pain was not relieved and she was left gravely disabled—unable to feel anything in her right leg and foot. She sued Dr Gerson, alleging first that she had not given a valid consent to the procedure because it had not been explained to her and, secondly, that Dr Gerson's explanation had been negligent. The judge considered the most appropriate way to deal with allegations that a doctor has not properly informed her patients:

BRISTOW J.

" . . . It was Dr Gerson's regular practice to explain to patients whom he intended to try to help by intrathecal phenol solution injection all about the process. His practice was to tell them that he hoped to relieve their pain by interrupting the nerve along which it was signalled to the brain, that this would involve numbness in the area from which the pain signals had been transmitted, numbness over an area larger than the pain source itself, and might involve temporary loss of muscle power. Sister Welch who worked with him at the clinic from 1973 says that he was very meticulous about his explanations . . .

I have come to the conclusion that on the balance of probability Dr Gerson did give his usual explanation about the intrathecal phenol solution nerve block and its implications of numbness instead of pain plus a possibility of slight muscle weakness, and that Miss Chatterton's recollection is wrong . . .

The claim

 . . . The claim against [Dr Gerson] is put in two ways; (i) that her consent to operation was vitiated by lack of explanation of what the procedure was and what were its implications, so that she gave no real consent and the operation was in law a trespass to her person, that is, a battery; and (ii) that Dr Gerson was under a duty, as part of his obligation to treat his patient with the degree of professional skill and care to be expected of a reasonably skilled practitioner having regard to the state of the art at the time in question, to give Miss Chatterton such an explanation of the nature and implications of the proposed operation that she could come to an informed decision on whether she wanted to have it, or would prefer to go on living with the pain which it was intended to relieve; that such explanation as he gave was in breach of that duty; that if he had performed that duty she would have chosen not to have the operation; and that therefore the unhappy consequences resulting from the operation, however wisely recommended and skilfully performed it may have been, are damage to Miss Chatterton which flows from Dr Gerson's breach of duty and for which he is responsible . . .

Trespass to the person and consent

It is clear law that in any context in which consent of the injured party is a defence to what would otherwise be a crime or a civil wrong, the consent must be real . . .

In my judgment what the court has to do in each case is to look at all the circumstances and say 'was there a real consent?' I think justice requires that in order to vitiate the reality of consent there must be a greater failure of communication between doctor and patient than that involved in a breach of duty if the claim is based on negligence. When the claim is based on negligence the plaintiff must prove not only the breach of duty to inform but that had the duty not been broken she would not have chosen to have the operation. Where the claim is based on trespass to the person, once it is shown that the consent is unreal, then what the plaintiff would have decided if she had been given the information which would have prevented vitiation of the reality of her consent is irrelevant.

In my judgment once the patient is informed in broad terms of the nature of the procedure which is intended, and gives her consent, that consent is real, and the cause of the action on which to base a claim for failure to go into risks and implications is negligence, not trespass. Of course if information is withheld in bad faith, the consent will be vitiated by fraud. Of course if by some accident, as in a case in the 1940s in the Salford Hundred Court, where a boy was admitted to hospital for tonsillectomy and due to administrative error was circumcised instead, trespass would be the appropriate cause of action against the doctor, though he was as much a victim of the error as the boy. But in my judgment it would be very much against the interests of justice if actions which are really based on a failure by the doctor to perform his duty adequately to inform were pleaded in trespass.

In this case in my judgment even taking Miss Chatterton's evidence at its face value she was under no illusion as to the general nature of what an intrathecal injection of phenol solution nerve block would be, and in the case of each injection her consent was not unreal. I should add that getting the patient to sign a proforma expressing consent to undergo the operation 'the effect and nature of which have been explained to me', as was done here in each case, should be a valuable reminder to everyone of the need for explanation and consent. But it would be no defence to an action based on trespass to the person if no explanation had in fact been given. The consent would have been expressed in form only, not in reality.

Negligence

The duty of the doctor is to explain what he intends to do, and its implications, in the way a careful and responsible doctor in similar circumstances would have done; see *Bolam v Friern Hospital Management Committee* [1957] 2 All E.R. 118.

I am satisfied that Dr Gerson told the plaintiff what an intrathecal phenol solution injection nerve block was all about. I am satisfied that he told her that the concomitant of relief from pain would be numbness not confined to the scar but in the area served by the sensory nerves the injection would be intended to block, and that she might suffer from slight muscle weakness. Ought he to have done more? . . .

In my judgment there is no obligation on the doctor to canvass with the patient anything other than the inherent implications of the particular operation he intends to carry out. He is certainly under no obligation to say that if he operates incompetently he will do damage. The fundamental assumption is that he knows his job and will do it properly. But he ought to warn of what may happen by misfortune however well the operation is done, if there is a real risk of a misfortune inherent in the procedure, as there was in the surgery to the carotid artery in the Canadian case of *Reibl v Hughes* (1978). In what he says any good doctor has to take into account the personality of the patient, the likelihood of the misfortune, and what in the way of warning is for the particular patient's welfare.

I am not satisfied that Dr Gerson fell short of his duty to tell Miss Chatterton of the implications of this operation, properly carried out. At the level at which he gave the injection there was on the evidence no real risk of damage to bladder control, and it is clear that the bladder difficulty of which Miss Chatterton now complains was wholly independent of the injections. There was no risk of significant damage to the motor nerves. There was no foreseeable risk that her leg and foot would be deprived of sensation or control, nor am I satisfied that anything done in the course of the second injection caused that result. In my judgment, on the expert evidence here that may be functional, just as the continuance of her scar pain is functional. The certain and intended result of the injections was to replace the pain at which they were aimed by numbness, numbness over an area larger than the scar area itself. This I am satisfied she was told before the first injection. Before the second injection she knew what to expect and in my judgment there was no need to spell it out again . . . Accordingly the claim of negligence fails.

I should add that if I had thought that Dr Gerson had failed in his duty to inform her of the implications inherent in the second injection, I would not have been satisfied that if properly informed Miss Chatterton would have chosen not to have it. The whole picture on the evidence is of a lady desperate for pain relief, who has just been advised by Mr Crymble to let Dr Gerson try again … "

NOTES:

1. This case illustrates the difficulties which confront a court attempting to assess what really happened. The patient and health professionals may well disagree about the true course of events, and the judge is faced with a choice of whom to believe. Once the judge has made a finding as to what probably happened, then the court treats the case as if those were the true facts, even though it may have been a very contested decision.

2. Since the decision in *Chatterton v Gerson*, English courts have consistently held that trespass actions should play only a very limited role in health care law. (see G. Seaborne, "The Role of the Tort of Battery in Medical Law" (1995) 24 *Anglo-American Law Review* 265–298). Bristow J.'s position was endorsed by the House of Lords in *Sidaway v Bethlem RHG* [1985] 3 All E.R. 643 (below). (See G. Robertson, "Informed Consent to Medical Treatment" (1981) 97 *Law Quarterly Review* 102 for the policy arguments which dictate the limited role of trespass actions.) An example of a successful trespass action is the case of *Bartley v Studd* July 15, 1995 (*Medical Law Monitor* (1995) 2 at p.1). The plaintiff, a 34-year-old woman had consented to a hysterectomy, but when she was under anaesthetic the gynaecologist removed her ovaries for what he considered justifiable clinical reasons. However, generally, as John Harrington notes, "Battery, with its connotations of violence and criminality, is seen as an inappropriately stigmatic label for doctors seeking in good faith to act in their patients' interests" (J. Harrington, "Privileging the Medical Norm: Liberalism, Self-determination and Refusal of Treatment" (1996) 16 *Legal Studies* 348). Moreover, where such cases do occur, as Michael Jones points out, they will almost invariably be settled before reaching court (M. Jones, "Informed Consent and Fairy Stories" (1999) 7 *Medical Law Review* 103–250 at note 9.)

3. Brazier points out that it is difficult to distinguish between actions which do constitute battery and those which does not on the *Chatterton* test (M. Brazier, *Medicine, Patients and the Law* (3rd edn), Harmondsworth: Penguin, 2003 at p.101; and see, for example, its application to the issue of blood tests for the HIV virus at pp.368–370 below).

4. Pursuing his action in trespass as opposed to negligence carries certain advantages for the patient. First, in a trespass claim he need not establish any tangible injury, since the actionable injury is the unpermitted invasion of his body. Thus, the patient can succeed even if the battery actually improves his health, rather than causing him harm. By contrast, in a negligence action the patient must prove that damage resulted from the negligent behaviour of the health professional. Secondly, in the case of trespass all damage flowing from treatment imposed without consent will

be recoverable, whether it was foreseeable or not, whereas in a negligence action unforeseeable damage will not be recoverable. Moreover, in some trespass cases punitive damages may be awarded if the health professional's actions were particularly blameworthy. However, a major drawback is that a trespass claim may only be made where there is actual physical contact between patient and health professional. (See Brazier, *op. cit.* in note 1 at p.91.) Furthermore, in *Freeman v Home Office* [1984] 1 All E.R. 1036 (discussed below at pp.398–399), the Court of Appeal held that where a patient alleges that he did not consent to treatment and sues in trespass, the onus of proof lies on the patient.

5. As far as the negligence action in this case was concerned, the test applied to determine whether Dr Gerson's explanation was negligent or not has now been elaborated by the House of Lords in *Sidaway v Bethlem RHG* [1985] 1 All E.R. 643. Although the *ratio* of the latter case is not entirely clear, *Sidaway* seemed to move away from a simple application of the *Bolam* test, a trend which has been confirmed in subsequent cases—see pp.387–396 below.

6. Note the important point at the end of Bristow J.'s judgment, that in negligence actions even if the doctor is guilty of failure to disclose material risks, the patient will only recover damages if he is able to demonstrate that having considered such risks he would have chosen to forgo the treatment in question.

7. Patients will generally be asked to sign written consent forms, although they are not compulsory and may vary in format, according to whether treatment is private or on the NHS. Moreover, although Bristow J. notes that they are only evidence of consent, in some circumstances written consent is now a statutory requirement, e.g. under the Human Fertilisation and Embryology Act 1990 (see Chapter 11) and the Human Tissue Act 2004 (see Chapter 15).

QUESTIONS:

1. How useful are consent forms? What is their legal effect? (Note the comments of Bristow J. in *Chatterton v Gerson* (at pp.361–363 above) and judicial criticism of their layout by Lord Donaldson in *Re T* (at pp.400–401 below; see also I. Kennedy, "Consent to Treatment: the Capable Person" in C. Dyer (ed.) *Doctors, Patients and the Law*, Oxford: Blackwell, 1992, at p.49.)

2. Consider the difficulties that Bristow J. had in determining what explanation was actually given by Dr Gerson. Do you think that judges are more likely to believe patients or doctors? Are judges entitled to place more reliance on evidence given by a health care professional? (On this point see also the cases of *Smith v Tunbridge Wells* and *Chester v Afshar*, discussed below at pp.393–396.)

3. Would Miss Chatterton have succeeded if Dr Gerson's explanation had been unacceptable?

4. Why did Bristow J. believe that trespass was inappropriate for "informed consent" cases? What types of case does Bristow J. think are appropriate for trespass?
5. Given the considerable advantages to the patient of framing his action in trespass, is the reluctance of the courts to countenance trespass actions justifiable? (See T.K. Feng, "Failure of Medical Advice: Trespass or Negligence?" (1987) 7 *Legal Studies* 149.)
6. In relation to the question of risks which the law requires a health professional to disclose, what does a "real risk of misfortune inherent in the procedure" mean?
7. Will the duty of disclosure be the same if the doctor is carrying out therapeutic research or a form of experimental treatment on the patient, rather than offering a tried and tested treatment? Are the boundarries between these different categories always clear cut? (See Chapter 10.)

(b) Controversies in Relation to Consent

(i) Treatment by Whom?

An issue which has been much debated recently is whether consent is valid when a patient agrees to a particular doctor carrying out treatment or examination, but it is actually performed by another doctor, a nurse or a student doctor. (In the past outrage has been occasioned by reports that a student on work experience at Bradford Hospital stitched a patient's wound, *The Guardian*, November 2, 1995, and by exposure of the fact that a nurse had performed an appendectomy in 1994 "Nurse performs 200 operations", *Sunday Telegraph*, June 23, 1996.) Notwithstanding criticism of the proposals from the BMA, the Department of Health has pressed ahead with plans for nurses and technicians to be trained to carry out certain forms of surgery, such as vasectomies and removing skin lesions, under the supervision of a consultant surgeon (see H. Mulholland, "Nurses 'to carry out routine operations'", *The Guardian*, December 6, 2004; "Unease over plan to train nurses to do surgery", *The Guardian*, March 25, 2005; C. Shannon, "Doctors object to a wider role for surgical care practitioners" (2005) 330 B.M.J. 1103). The Department of Health has recently consulted over the role of such "surgical" or "medical care practitioners" (See *The Curriculum Framework for the Surgical Care Practitioners: a Consultation Document*, London: Department of Health, 2005.)

A further issue has arisen in the wake of the Bristol Inquiry which estimated that between 1984 and 1995 20–30 babies died because of incompetence on the part of two paediatric surgeons in performing new forms of neonatal heart surgery (Bristol Inquiry Interim Report, *Removal and Retention of Human Material*, 2000—see Chapter 15 at pp.1102–1103 for detailed discussion). The revelation of significant variations in success rates of consultants performing surgery focused attention on whether valid consent requires the disclosure of such information before patients or parents decide to go ahead with treatment. Andrew Grubb notes that, currently, a change of doctor cannot affect the consent given, even if the patient expected a particular doctor to carry out the procedure

(A. Grubb, "Consent to Treatment: the Competent Patient" in A. Grubb (ed.), *Principles of Medical Law* (2nd edn) Oxford: OUP, 2004, 131–203 at p.177.) However, as Michael Jones points out, developments in the aftermath of Bristol call into question Brown Wilkinson L.J.' s view in *Sidaway* (see p.372 below) that doctors do not have to disclose their experience in handling similar cases. Jones suggests that such dicta "may in future have to be reconsidered in the light of the Bristol enquiry, thought the limits of such a duty will be difficult to lay down with any precision" M. Jones, "Informed Consent and Fairy Stories" (1999) 7 *Medical Law Review* 103–250 at pp.112–113).

Certainly some commentators take the view that transparency requires the issuance of league tables based on survival rates of patients after surgery (Leader, "The heart of the matter", *The Guardian*, March 16, 2005). Such moves have generated huge opposition by the medical establishment, which claims that they will result in doctors being reluctant to perform surgery in difficult cases or using experimental techniques (see O. Dyer, "Heart surgeons are to be rated according to bypass surgery rates" (2003) 326 B.M.J. 1053; "Doctors attack mortality league tables", *The Guardian*, February 15, 2005).

If the treatment is carried out by an incompetent person the patient may sue in negligence. Moreover, if the patient was not informed that the treatment was to be delivered by a nurse or student, this may give rise to a trespass action. (See M. Brazier, *Medicine, Patients and the Law* (3rd edn), Harmondsworth: Penguin, 2003, pp.110–112.)

The GMC offers the following guidance on this issue:

Good Medical Practice (3rd edn), London: GMC, 2001)

Delegation or referral

46. Delegation involves asking a nurse, doctor, medical student or other health care worker to provide treatment or care on your behalf. When you delegate care or treatment you must be sure that the person to whom you delegate is competent to carry out the procedure or provide the therapy involved. You must always pass on enough information about the patient and the treatment needed. You will still be responsible for the overall management of the patient.

47. Referral involves transferring some or all of the responsibility for the patient's care, usually temporarily and for a particular purpose, such as additional investigation, care or treatment, which falls outside your competence. Usually you will refer patients to another registered medical practitioner. If this is not the case, you must be satisfied that any health care professional to whom you refer a patient is accountable to a statutory regulatory body, and that a registered medical practitioner, usually a general practitioner, retains overall responsibility for the management of the patient.

NOTE:

1. Particular controversy has in the past surrounded the case of vaginal examinations. Traditionally medical students have been taught by examining women who are anaesthetised. Such examinations are performed not for the benefit of that particular patient but for the benefit of students and future patients, and it is often unclear whether the woman in question has

given consent. Again this raises the question of whether she could bring a action in trespass. (See S. Bewley, "The Law, Medical Students and Consent" (1992) 304 B.M.J. 1551.) GMC guidance is as follows:

Intimate Examinations (London: GMC, 2001)

The GMC regularly receives complaints from patients who feel that doctors have behaved inappropriately during an intimate examination. Intimate examinations, that is examinations of the breasts, genitalia or rectum, can be stressful and embarrassing for patients. When conducting intimate examinations you should:

- Explain to the patient why an examination is necessary and give the patient an opportunity to ask questions.
- Explain what the examination will involve, in a way the patient can understand, so that the patient has a clear idea of what to expect, including any potential pain or discomfort . . .
- Obtain the patient's permission before the examination and be prepared to discontinue the examination if the patient asks you to. You should record that permission has been obtained.
- Keep discussion relevant and avoid unnecessary personal comments.
- Offer a chaperon or invite the patient (in advance if possible) to have a relative or friend present. If the patient does not want a chaperon, you should record that the offer was made and declined. If a chaperon is present, you should record that fact and make a note of the chaperon's identity. If for justifiable practical reasons you cannot offer a chaperon, you should explain that to the patient and, if possible, offer to delay the examination to a later date. You should record the discussion and its outcome.
- Give the patient privacy to undress and dress and use drapes to maintain the patient's dignity. Do not assist the patient in removing clothing unless you have clarified with them that your assistance is required.

Anaesthetised patients

You must obtain consent prior to anaesthetisation, usually in writing, for the intimate examination of anaesthetised patients. If you are supervising students you should ensure that valid consent has been obtained before they carry out any intimate examination under anaesthesia.

QUESTIONS:

1. Is an experienced nurse likely to be more or less competent at performing routine operations than a student doctor? (See the discussion in the Court of Appeal in *Wilsher v Essex Area Health Authority* [1986] 3 All E.R. 801, discussed in Chapter 3 at pp.175–179.)
2. Is delegating more power to nurses simply evidence that nurses are becoming increasingly specialised to the point where they are entirely competent to undertake duties traditionally carried out by junior doctors, or is the Government encroaching on the traditional territory of doctors in an effort to cut costs? (See J. Revill, "Why angels must spread their wings", *The Observer*, April 24, 2005.)
3. Should patients have a choice over the surgeon who operates on them? Given some evidence that women prefer to see a female breast surgeon (I. Reid, "Patients' Preference for Male or Female Breast Surgeons: Questionnaire Study" (1998) 317 B.M.J. 1051–60), should patients be offered

a choice of female or male doctors? (See C.W. Martin, "Female surgeons might be preferred but may not be better" (1999) 318 B.M.J. 1213.)

(ii) Consent to HIV Tests

A further controversy pertaining to consent has been raised in the context of testing for the HIV virus (see R. Bennett and C. Erin (eds), *HIV and AIDS: Testing, Screening and Confidentiality*, Oxford: Clarendon, 1999). Debate has centred on situations where a patient consents to giving blood so that tests can be undertaken, but is not specifically told that one test will be to detect the presence of the HIV virus. It is arguable that in this situation the patient broadly understood the nature and purpose of the operation, which would rule out a trespass action under the *Chatterton v Gerson* test (see pp.361–365 above). This issue has never been litigated. In 1987 a majority of BMA members voted in favour of a proposal that non-consensual testing should take place at the discretion of the patient's physician, but the decision was never implemented owing to counsel's opinion that there was a possibility that it would give rise to legal difficulties. More recently, a BMJ editorial proposed that as a result of changing social attitudes and improved drug regimes for treating HIV, HIV testing should be treated as a more routine process. It argued that it was time to dispense with in-depth counselling on the implications of testing (K. Manavi and P. Welsby, "HIV testing should no longer be accorded special status" (2005) 330 B.M.J. 492; see also R. Bayer, "Public Health Policy and the AIDS Epidemic: an End to AIDS Exceptionalism? (1991) 324 *New England Journal of Medicine* 1500; WHO, *The right to Know: New Approaches to HIV Testing and Counselling*, 2003).

The GMC's stance on the matter is as follows:

Serious Communicable Diseases (London: GMC, 1997)

4. You must obtain consent from patients before testing for a serious communicable disease, except in the rare circumstances described in paragraphs 6 [children], 7 [unconscious patients], 9, 11 and 17 below. The information you provide when seeking consent should be appropriate to the circumstances and to the nature of the condition or conditions being tested for. Some conditions, such as HIV, have serious social and financial, as well as medical, implications. In such cases you must make sure that the patient is given appropriate information about the implications of the test, and appropriate time to consider and discuss them . . .

9. If the patient refuses testing, is unable to give or withhold consent because of mental illness or disability, or does not regain full consciousness within 48 hours, you should reconsider the severity of risk to yourself, or another injured health care worker, or to others. You should not arrange testing against the patient's wishes or without consent other than in exceptional circumstances, for example where you have good reason to think that the patient may have a condition such as HIV for which prophylactic treatment is available. In such cases you may test an existing blood sample, taken for other purposes, but you should consult an experienced colleague first. It is possible that a decision to test an existing blood sample without consent could be challenged in the courts, or be the subject of a complaint to your employer or the GMC. You must therefore be prepared to justify your decision . . .

11. If the patient dies you may test for a serious communicable disease if you have good reason to think that the patient may have been infected, and a health care worker has been

exposed to the patient's blood or other body fluid. You should usually seek the agreement of a relative before testing. If the test shows the patient was a carrier of the virus, you should follow the guidance in paragraphs 21–23 of this booklet on giving information to patients' close contacts . . .

You should not routinely test for serious communicable diseases before performing post-mortems; but you should take precautions to protect yourself and other health care workers. If you have reason to believe the deceased person had a serious communicable disease, you should assume the body to be infectious . . .

NOTES:

1. Given that other blood tests, such as that for CD4 cells in blood, are now accepted indicators of HIV status, if HIV tests are subject to special practices, should they apply to these other tests? (See L.A. Jansen, "HIV Exceptionalism, CD4+ Cell Testing, and Conscientious Subversion" (2005) 31 *Journal of Medical Ethics* 322–326.)

2. The general position in relation to consent by children is discussed in Chapter 7. However, particular issues are raised in relation to the testing of children for HIV. As the GMC guidelines make clear, there may be situations where it is in the best interests of the child to test him, but the parents are reluctant to consent.

3. Special issues also arise with testing of pregnant women at the ante-natal stage, especially given evidence that anti-retroviral treatment, avoidance of breastfeeding and the carrying out of an elective Caesarean section can reduce the transmission of HIV from mother to baby from 25 per cent to 5 per cent. The GMC advises doctors as follows:

Ante natal testing for HIV (London: GMC, 2000)

The seriousness of a condition, its treatment, and its possible social consequences, will affect the amount of information patients need to be given, and the time they need to consider whether to agree to be tested. Therefore, pre-test discussions with pregnant women about HIV testing should be:

a. Based on core information and basic advice to all women being asked to consider undergoing testing. Information can be provided in written form . . .

b. Such that where women are assessed as having a medium or high risk of infection, additional information and advice, and arrangements for counselling are available.

c. Clear and comprehensible to a wide range of people. All women should be told how to get access to additional advice, and that they can take as much time as they need to reach an informed decision.

Details of discussions with the pregnant woman, the information given and her decision, should be recorded in her case notes or on a consent form. Recommending HIV testing in pregnancy should be an integral part of antenatal care, which includes providing information and recommending tests for other infections and abnormalities. Whilst still recommending written consent for HIV testing as best medical practice, it is not essential provided the information given and decision made is clearly recorded. It may be appropriate for written consent for all antenatal tests agreed to by the woman to be obtained together.

QUESTIONS:

1. If a doctor suspects that a patient may be HIV+ and wishes to take a sample of blood for testing, does the doctor commit trespass if she merely tells the patient that the blood is required for testing, and does not disclose that she proposes to test it for the HIV virus? (See J. Keown, "The Ashes of AIDS and the Phoenix of Informed Consent" (1989) 52 *Modern Law Review* 790; J. Montgomery, "Victims or Threats? The Framing of HIV [1990] 12 *Liverpool Law Review* 25. Do you agree with Mason and Laurie that "a patient who consults a doctor gives tacit consent to the carrying out of those diagnostic tests that the doctors considers necessary—the patient's consent to each and every test to be performed on a blood sample need not be obtained"? (J.K. Mason and G.T. Laurie, *Mason and McCall Smith's Law and Medical Ethics* (7th edn), Oxford: OUP, 2006, at p.392).)
2. Are there ethical objections to health care professionals simply assuming that all patients are HIV+ and taking the necessary precautions, thus avoiding the need to test anyone?
3. Would it be justifiable for a doctor to test a newly born baby if she suspects his mother is HIV+, but the mother refuses to consent to a HIV test? Is anonymised HIV testing of pregnant women ethical? (See P. De Zuletta, "The Ethics of Anonymised HIV Testing of Pregnant Woman: a Reappraisal" (2006) 26 *Journal of Medical Ethics* 16–21.)
4. Do you accept Lucy Frith's argument that the special practices surrounding consent to HIV testing coupled with an "insistence on pre-test counselling can be seen as a paternalistic response that actually reduces, rather than fosters, a person's autonomy"? (L. Frith, "HIV Testing and Informed Consent" (2005) 31 *Journal of Medical Ethics* 699.)

(iii) Force-feeding of Anorexics and Consent to Cosmetic Surgery

One of the most vexed questions relating to consent concerns the force-feeding of anorexics. Anorexia is an eating disorder. It manifests itself in an obsession with weight, a distorted perception of one's body size and shape and a compulsion to lose weight, resulting in a refusal to eat. The first medical description of anorexia as a discrete disorder dates from an address by W. Gull in 1868, but its incidence has risen dramatically in the last two decades. It disproportionately affects women, although there is now evidence that it is being diagnosed in young men with increasing frequency. (See R. Dresser, "Feeding the Hungry Artist: Legal Issues in Treating Anorexia Nervosa" (1984) 2 *Wisconsin Law Review* 297; J. Bridgeman, "They Gag Women, Don't They?" in J. Bridgeman and S. Millns (eds), *Law and Body Politics: Regulating the Female Body*, Aldershot: Dartmouth, 1995; P. Lewis, "Feeding Anorexic Patients Who Refuse Food" (1999) 7 *Medical Law Review* 21.) Some commentators have posited that, just as anorexia may be a response to societal preoccupations with appearance, so the growing demand for elective cosmetic surgery and the normalisation of "extreme beauty" treatments raise issues about women's ability to choose and freely consent to such surgery (K.P. Morgan, "Women and the Knife: Cosmetic Surgery and the Colonization of Women's Bodies" (1991) 6 *Hypatia* 36; reprinted in S. Sherwin and B. Parish (eds) *Women, Medicine, Ethics and Law*, Aldershot: Dartmouth, 2002.) Parallels have also been drawn between the practices of female circumcision and cosmetic surgery, on the basis that both may be grounded in pressure to conform to dominant societal ideals about appearance (S. Sheldon and S. Wilkinson, "Female Genital Mutilation and Cosmetic Surgery: Regulating Non-therapeutic Body Modification" (1998) 12 *Bioethics* 263–285).

QUESTIONS:

1. If an anorexic patient refuses to eat, is the court justified in authorising health professionals to feed and otherwise treat him against his will? This issue has been considered in cases involving young women (see Chapter 7 at pp.457–462) and women detained under the Mental Health Act 1983 (see Chapter 8 at pp.543–544).

2. Would the reasoning in *Re W (A Minor) (Medical Treatment: Court's Jurisdiction)* [1992] 4 All E.R. 627 (extracted in Chapter 7 at pp.457–462) apply to a person aged over 18? (See J. Bridgeman, "Old Enough to Know Best?" (1993) 13 *Legal Studies* 69.)

3. Do you think that gender has been a factor in the courts' reluctance to accept refusal of consent in cases of anorexia, or is it simply down to the power of the condition to undermine choice?

4. Under what conditions would an individual make a truly voluntary choice to undergo cosmetic surgery? (See K. Davis, *Reshaping the Female Body: the Dilemma of Cosmetic Surgery*, London: Routledge, 1995; H. Wijsbek, "The Pursuit of Beauty: the Enforcement of Aesthetics of a Freely Adopted Lifestyle?" (2000) 26 *Journal of Medical Ethics* 454–458.) Is any societal pressure to undergo surgery to approve appearance comparable to the pressures on women to undergo procedures to alleviate infertility? (See Chapter 11). If so, why is fertility treatment so strictly regulated, whereas cosmetic surgery is not? (In relation to cosmetic surgery on children, see Chapter 7 at p.477.)

5. Would it ever be justifiable for doctor to amputate a healthy limb if requested to do so by a patient? (See R. MacKenzie and S. Cox, "Apotemnophilia: Bodily Alteration, Autonomy and Harm" presented at AHRC Workshop, "Engendering Bioethics: Stigmatised Bodies, Citizenship and Choice", University of Keele, 18 November 2005.)

6. Can you think of other forms of surgery where there may be doubts about whether the patient's consent is truly voluntary? (See R. Kay and A.K. Siriwardena, "The Process of Informed Consent for Urgent Abdominal Surgery" (2001) 27 *Journal of Medical Ethics* 157–161; S.M. White, "Consent for anaesthesia" (2004) 30 *Journal of Medical Ethics* 286–290; and discussion of xenotransplantation in Chapter 15 at pp.1170–1178.)

(c) Disclosure and the Quality of Consent

The obligations of a health professional to counsel his or her patients about decisions that the patient is required to make are governed by the tort of negligence. If a patient is improperly counselled and has suffered loss as a result, he may sue for compensation. To win a negligence case based on a failure to counsel properly, a patient must show that he was not given an explanation that responsible professionals would support; that had he been given a proper explanation he would have refused the care (see *Chatterton v Gerson* (at p.361 above)), and that he has been harmed by giving consent on the basis of improper advice. In effect he is alleging that the *quality* of consent which the health care professional obtained was not good enough. We begin by examining the general rules governing the health professional's obligation to disclose information to patients undergoing treatment for therapeutic reasons. Two special circumstances are then examined: non-therapeutic procedures, and cases where the patient asks questions. Finally, in this section, we address the position of other health care professionals.

(i) The Obligation to Disclose Information to the Patient: Therapeutic Cases

The leading case on the obligation to disclose information to patients as to the risks of a particular course of conduct is the House of Lords decision in *Sidaway v Bethlem RHG* [1985] 1 All E.R. 643. Each of the four speeches in this case contain significant differences of approach. Identifying a majority view in order to provide a coherent statement of the law is therefore difficult.

Sidaway v Bethlem RHG [1985] 1 All E.R. 643, [1985] 1 A.C. 871, [1985] 2 W.L.R. 480, 1 B.M.L.R. 132

Mrs Sidaway had undergone an operation on her spine to relieve pain. That operation involved two specific risks of injury over and above the more general risks of surgery. First, there was a possibility that a nerve root might be damaged in the area of the operation. Secondly, there was a risk that the spinal cord might be damaged. Neither risk was statistically large, estimated at between 1 per cent and 2 per cent by one expert witness. However, the consequences were very serious if either risk was to materialise. In the event, Mrs Sidaway was left severely disabled, with partial paralysis. She sued the doctor who had treated her, alleging that he had failed properly to warn her of the risks inherent in the operation, and that had she been so informed she would not have agreed to the operation. She did not suggest that the operation itself had been carried out negligently. The case was complicated by the fact that the doctor had died by the time it came to trial. He could not, therefore, give evidence about the precise nature of the warning that he had given Mrs Sidaway. Nevertheless, the judge felt able to infer that the doctor probably warned Mrs Sidaway about the risk of damage to the nerve root, but not that of damage to the spinal cord. Further, the judge found that the doctor did not explain to Mrs Sidaway that the operation was not absolutely necessary, but a matter of her choice. The case went to the

House of Lords on appeal, on the basis that those were the true facts. The House of Lords had to decide whether the failure to advise Mrs Sidaway of the risk of injury to the spinal cord was negligent. In order to do so, they had to determine the standard of care that was applicable in this area of negligence.

LORD SCARMAN

" . . . The *Bolam* principle has been accepted by your Lordships' House as applicable to diagnosis and treatment: see *Whitehouse v. Jordan* [1981] 1 All E.R. 267, (treatment) and *Maynard v. West Midlands Regional Health Authority* [1985] 1 All E.R. 635 (diagnosis). It is also recognised in Scots law as applicable to diagnosis and treatment; indeed, McNair J. in the *Bolam* case cited a Scottish decision to that effect, *Hunter v. Hanley* 1955 SLT 213 at 217 per the Lord President (Clyde) . . .

But was the judge correct in treating the 'standard of competent professional opinion' as the criterion in determining whether a doctor is under a duty to warn his patient of the risk, or risks, inherent in the treatment which he recommends? Skinner J. and the Court of Appeal have in the instant case held that he was correct. Bristow J. adopted the same criterion in *Chatterton v. Gerson* [1981] 1 All E.R. 257. The implications of this view of the law are disturbing. It leaves the determination of a legal duty to the judgment of doctors. Responsible medical judgment may, indeed, provide the law with an acceptable standard in determining whether a doctor in diagnosis or treatment has complied with his duty. But is it right that medical judgment should determine whether there exists a duty to warn of risk and its scope? It would be a strange conclusion if the courts should be led to conclude that our law, which undoubtedly recognises a right in the patient to decide whether he will accept or reject the treatment proposed, should permit the doctors to determine whether and in what circumstances a duty arises requiring the doctor to warn his patient of the risks inherent in the treatment which he proposes.

The right of 'self-determination', the description applied by some to what is no more and no less than the right of a patient to determine for himself whether he will or will not accept the doctor's advice, is vividly illustrated where the treatment recommended is surgery. A doctor who operates without the consent of his patient is, save in cases of emergency or mental disability, guilty of the civil wrong of trespass to the person; he is also guilty of the criminal offence of assault. The existence of the patient's right to make his own decision, which may be seen as a basic human right protected by the common law, is the reason why a doctrine embodying a right of the patient to be informed of the risks of surgical treatment has been developed in some jurisdictions in the United States of America and has found favour with the Supreme Court of Canada. Known as the 'doctrine of informed consent', it amounts to this: where there is a 'real' or a 'material' risk inherent in the proposed operation (however competently and skilfully performed) the question whether and to what extent a patient should be warned before he gives his consent is to be answered not by reference to medical practice but by accepting as a matter of law that, subject to all proper exceptions (of which the court, not the profession, is the judge), a patient has a right to be informed of the risks inherent in the treatment which is proposed. The profession, it is said, should not be judge in its own cause; or, less emotively but more correctly, the courts should not allow medical opinion as to what is best for the patient to override the patient's right to decide for himself whether he will submit to the treatment offered him. It will be necessary for the House to consider in this appeal what is involved in the doctrine and whether it, or any modification of it, has any place in English law . . .

It is, I suggest, a sound and reasonable proposition that the doctor should be required to exercise care in respecting the patient's right of decision. He must acknowledge that in very many cases factors other than the purely medical will play a significant part in his patient's decision-making process. The doctor's concern is with health and the relief of pain. These are the medical objectives. But a patient may well have in mind circumstances, objectives and values which he may reasonably not make known to the doctor but which may lead him to a different decision from that suggested by a purely medical opinion. The doctor's duty can be seen, therefore, to be one which requires him not only to advise as to medical treatment but also to provide his patient with the information needed to enable the patient to consider and balance the medical advantages and risks alongside other relevant matters, such as, for example, his family, business or social responsibilities of which the doctor may be only partially, if at all, informed.

I conclude, therefore, that there is room in our law for a legal duty to warn a patient of the risks inherent in the treatment proposed, and that, if such a duty be held to exist, its proper place is as an aspect of the duty of care owed by the doctor to his patient. I turn, therefore, to consider whether a duty to warn does exist in our law and, if it does, its proper formulation and the conditions and exceptions to which it must be subject.

Some American courts have recognised such a duty . . .

It is necessary before discussing the doctrine to bear in mind that it is far from being universally accepted in the United States of America, or indeed elsewhere . . .

In *Canterbury v. Spence* the court enunciated four propositions.

(1) The root premise is the concept that every human being of adult years and of sound mind has a right to determine what shall be done with his own body.

(2) The consent is the informed exercise of a choice, and that entails an opportunity to evaluate knowledgeably the options available and the risks attendant on each.

(3) The doctor must, therefore, disclose all 'material risks'; what risks are 'material' is determined by the 'prudent patient' test, which was formulated by the court (464 F 2d 772 at 787):

> '[a] risk is . . . material when a *reasonable person*, in what the physician knows or should know to be the patient's position, would be likely to attach significance to the risk or cluster of risks in deciding whether or not to forego the proposed therapy.' (My emphasis.)

(4) The doctor, however, has what the court called a 'therapeutic privilege'. This exception enables a doctor to withhold from his patient information as to risk if it can be shown that a reasonable medical assessment of the patient would have indicated to the doctor that disclosure would have posed a serious threat of psychological detriment to the patient.

In Canada, in *Reibl v. Hughes* (1980) 114 D.L.R. (3d) 1, Laskin C.J.C. expressed broad approval of the doctrine as enunciated in *Canterbury v. Spence*, though it would seem that approval of the doctrine was not necessary to a decision in the case. I find no difficulty in accepting the four propositions enunciated in *Canterbury*'s case . . . without excluding medical evidence they set a standard and formulate a test of the doctor's duty the effect of which is that the court determines the scope of the duty and decides whether the doctor has acted in breach of his duty. This result is achieved, first, by emphasis on the patient's 'right of self-determination' and, second, by the 'prudent patient' test. If the doctor omits to warn where the risk is such that in the court's view a prudent person in the patient's situation would have regarded it as significant, the doctor is liable.

The *Canterbury* propositions do indeed attach great importance to medical evidence, though judgment is for the court. First, medical evidence is needed in determining whether the risk is material, *i.e.* one which the doctor should make known to his patient. The two aspects of the risk, namely the degree of likelihood of it occurring and the seriousness of the possible injury if it should occur, can in most, if not all, cases be assessed only with the help of medical evidence. And, second, medical evidence would be needed to assist the court in determining whether the doctor was justified on his assessment of his patient in withholding the warning.

My Lords, I think the *Canterbury* propositions reflect a legal truth which too much judicial reliance on medical judgment tends to obscure. In a medical negligence case where the issue is as to the advice and information given to the patient as to the treatment proposed, the available options and the risk, the court is concerned primarily with a patient's right. The doctor's duty arises from his patient's rights . . .

Ideally, the court should ask itself whether in the particular circumstances the risk was such that this particular patient would think it significant if he was told it existed. I would think that, as a matter of ethics, this is the test of the doctor's duty. The law, however, operates not in Utopia but in the world as it is; and such an inquiry would prove in practice to be frustrated by the subjectivity of its aim and purpose. The law can, however, do the next best thing, and require the court to answer the question, what would a reasonably prudent patient think significant if in the situation of this patient? The 'prudent patient' cannot, however, always provide the answer for the obvious reason that he is a norm (like the man on the Clapham omnibus), not a real person; and certainly not the patient himself. Hence there is the need that the doctor should have the opportunity of proving that he reasonably believed that disclosure of the risk would be damaging to his patient or contrary to his best interest. This is what the Americans call the doctor's 'therapeutic privilege'. Its true analysis is that it is a defence available to the doctor which, if he invokes it, he must prove. On both the test and the defence medical evidence will, of course, be of great importance.

The 'prudent patient' test calls for medical evidence. The materiality of the risk is a question for the court to decide on all the evidence. Many factors call for consideration. The two critically important medical factors are the degree of probability of the risk materialising and the seriousness of possible injury if it does. Medical evidence will be necessary so that the court may assess the degree of probability and the seriousness of possible injury. Another medical factor, on which expert evidence will also be required, is the character of the risk . . . Clearly medical evidence will be of the utmost importance in determining whether such a risk is material; but the question for the court is ultimately legal, not medical, in character . . . "

LORD DIPLOCK

" . . . For the last quarter of a century the test applied in English law whether a doctor has fulfilled his duty of care owed to his patient has been that set out in the summing up to the jury by McNair J. in *Bolam v. Friern Hospital Management Committee* . . .

The merit of the *Bolam* test is that the criterion of the duty of care owed by a doctor to his patient is whether he has acted in accordance with a practice accepted as proper by a body of responsible and skilled medical opinion. There may be a number of different practices which satisfy this criterion at any particular time. These practices are likely to alter with advances in medical knowledge. Experience shows that, to the great benefit of humankind, they have done so, particularly in the recent past. That is why fatal diseases such as smallpox and tuberculosis have within living memory become virtually extinct in countries where modern medical care is generally available.

In English jurisprudence the doctor's relationship with his patient which gives rise to the normal duty of care to exercise his skill and judgment to improve the patient's health in any particular respect in which the patient has sought his aid has hitherto been treated as a single comprehensive duty covering all the ways in which a doctor is called on to exercise his skill and judgment in the improvement of the physical or mental condition of the patient for which his services either as a general practitioner or as a specialist have been engaged. This general duty is not subject to dissection into a number of component parts to which different criteria of what satisfy the duty of care apply, such as diagnosis, treatment and advice (including warning of any risks of something going wrong however skilfully the treatment advised is carried out). The *Bolam* case itself embraced failure to advise the patient of the risk involved in the electric shock treatment as one of the allegations of negligence against the surgeon as well as negligence in the actual carrying out of treatment in which that risk did result in injury to the patient. The same criteria were applied to both these aspects of the surgeon's duty of care. In modern medicine and surgery such dissection of the various things a doctor has to do in the exercise of his whole duty of care owed to his patient is neither legally meaningful nor medically practicable . . .

My Lords, no convincing reason has in my view been advanced before your Lordships that would justify treating the *Bolam* test as doing anything less than laying down a principle of English law that is comprehensive and applicable to every aspect of the duty of care owed by a doctor to his patient in the exercise of his healing functions as respects that patient. What your Lordships have been asked to do, and it is within your power to do so, is to substitute a new and different rule for that part only of the well-established test as comprises a doctor's duty to advise and warn the patient of risks of something going wrong in the surgical or other treatment that he is recommending.

The juristic basis of the proposed substitution, which originates in certain state court jurisdictions of the United States of America and has found some favour in modified form by the Supreme Court of Canada, appears to me, with great respect, to be contrary to English law . . . My Lords, I venture to think that in making this separation between that part of the doctor's duty of care that he owes to each individual patient, which can be described as a duty to advise on treatment and warn of its risks, the courts have misconceived their functions as the finders of fact in cases depending on the negligent exercise of professional skill and judgment. In matters of diagnosis and the carrying out of treatment the court is not tempted to put itself in the surgeon's shoes; it has to rely on and evaluate expert evidence, remembering that it is no part of its task of evaluation to give effect to any preference it may have for one responsible body of professional opinion over another, provided it is satisfied by the expert evidence that both qualify as responsible bodies of medical opinion. But, when it comes to warning about risks, the kind of training and experience that a judge will have undergone at the Bar makes it natural for him to say (correctly) it is my right to decide whether any particular thing is done to my body, and I want to be fully informed of any risks there may be involved of which I am not already aware from my general knowledge as a highly educated man of experience, so that I may form my own judgment whether to refuse the advised treatment or not.

No doubt, if the patient in fact manifested this attitude by means of questioning, the doctor would tell him whatever it was the patient wanted to know but we are concerned here with volunteering unsought information about risks of the proposed treatment failing to achieve the result sought or making the patient's physical or mental condition worse rather than better. The only effect that mention of risks can have on the patient's mind, if it has any at all, can be in the direction of deterring the patient from undergoing the treatment which in the expert opinion of the doctor it is in the patient's interest to undergo. To decide what risks the existence of which a patient should be voluntarily warned and the terms in which such warning, if any, should be given, having regard to the effect that the warning may have, is as much an exercise of professional skill and judgment as any other part of the doctor's comprehensive duty of care to the individual patient, and expert medical evidence on this matter should be treated in just the same way. The *Bolam* test should be applied . . . "

LORD BRIDGE

" . . . Broadly, a doctor's professional functions may be divided into three phases: diagnosis, advice and treatment. In performing his functions of diagnosis and treatment, the standard by which English law measures the doctor's duty of care to his patient is not open to doubt. 'The test is the standard of the ordinary skilled man exercising and professing to have that special skill.' These are the words of McNair J. in *Bolam v. Friern Hospital Management Committee* . . .

In *Maynard v. West Midlands Regional Health Authority* [1985] 1 All E.R. 635 *per* . . . Lord Scarman, with whose speech the other four members of the Appellate Committee agreed, further cited with approval the words of the Lord President (Clyde) in *Hunter v. Hanley* 1955 SLT 213 at 217:

'In the realm of diagnosis and treatment there is ample scope for genuine difference of opinion and one man clearly is not negligent merely because his conclusion differs from that of other professional men . . . The true test for establishing negligence in diagnosis or treatment on the part of a doctor is whether he has been proved to be guilty of such failure as no doctor of ordinary skill would be guilty of if acting with ordinary care . . . '

The important question which this appeal raises is whether the law imposes any, and if so what, different criterion as the measure of the medical man's duty of care to his patient when giving advice with respect to a proposed course of treatment. It is clearly right to recognise that a conscious adult patient of sound mind is entitled to decide for himself whether or not he will submit to a particular course of treatment proposed by the doctor, most significantly surgical treatment under general anaesthesia. This entitlement is the foundation of the doctrine of 'informed consent' which has led in certain American jurisdictions to decisions and, in the Supreme Court of Canada, to dicta on which the appellant relies, which would oust the *Bolam* test and substitute an 'objective' test of a doctor's duty to advise the patient of the advantages and disadvantages of undergoing the treatment proposed and more particularly to advise the patient of the risks involved . . .

I recognise the logical force of the *Canterbury* doctrine, proceeding from the premise that the patient's right to make his own decision must at all costs be safeguarded against the kind of medical paternalism which assumes that 'doctor knows best'. But, with all respect, I regard the doctrine as quite impractical in application for three principal reasons. First, it gives insufficient weight to the realities of the doctor/patient relationship. A very wide variety of factors must enter into a doctor's clinical judgment not only as to what treatment is appropriate for a particular patient, but also as to how best to communicate to the patient the significant factors necessary to enable the patient to make an informed decision whether to undergo the treatment. The doctor cannot set out to educate the patient to his own standard of medical knowledge of all the relevant factors involved. He may take the view, certainly with some patients, that the very fact of his volunteering, without being asked, information of some remote risk involved in the treatment proposed, even though he describes it as remote, may lead to that risk assuming an undue significance in the patient's calculations. Second, it would seem to me quite unrealistic in any medical negligence action to confine the expert medical evidence to an explanation of the primary medical factors involved and to deny the court the benefit of evidence of medical opinion and practice on the particular issue of disclosure which is under consideration. Third, the objective test which *Canterbury* propounds seems to me to be so imprecise as to be almost meaningless. If it is to be left to individual judges to decide for themselves what 'a reasonable person in the patient's position' would consider a risk of sufficient significance that he should be told about it, the outcome of litigation in this field is likely to be quite unpredictable . . .

Having rejected the *Canterbury* doctrine as a solution to the problem of safeguarding the patient's right to decide whether he will undergo a particular treatment advised by his doctor, the question remains whether that right is sufficiently safeguarded by the application of the *Bolam* test without qualification to the determination of the question what risks inherent in a proposed treatment should be disclosed. The case against a simple application of the Bolam test is cogently stated by Laskin C.J.C., giving the judgment of the Supreme Court of Canada in *Reibl v. Hughes* (1980) 114 DLR (3d) 1 at 13:

'To allow expert medical evidence to determine what risks are material and, hence, should be disclosed and, correlatively, what risks are not material is to hand over to the medical profession the entire question of the scope of the duty of disclosure, including the question whether there has been a breach of that duty. Expert medical evidence is, of course, relevant to findings as to the risks that reside in or are a result of recommended surgery or other treatment. It will also have a bearing on their materiality but this is not a question that is to be concluded on the basis of the expert medical evidence alone. The issue under consideration is a different issue from that involved where the question is whether the doctor carried out his professional activities by applicable professional standards. What is under consideration here is the patient's right to know what risks are involved in undergoing or foregoing certain surgery or other treatment.'

I fully appreciate the force of this reasoning, but can only accept it subject to the important qualification that a decision what degree of disclosure of risks is best calculated to assist a particular patient to make a rational choice whether or not to undergo a particular treatment must primarily be a matter of clinical judgment. It would follow from this that the issue whether non-disclosure in a particular case should be condemned as a breach of the doctor's duty of care is an issue to be decided primarily on the basis of expert medical evidence, applying the *Bolam* test. But I do not see that this approach involves the necessity 'to hand over to the medical profession the entire question of the scope of the duty of disclosure, including the question whether there has been a breach of that duty'. Of course, if there is a conflict of evidence whether a responsible body of medical opinion approves of non-disclosure in a particular case, the judge will have to resolve that conflict. But, even in a case where, as here, no expert witness in the relevant medical field condemns the non-disclosure as being in conflict with accepted and responsible medical practice, I am of opinion that the judge might in certain circumstances come to the conclusion that disclosure of a particular risk was so obviously necessary to an informed choice on the part of the patient that no reasonably prudent medical man would fail to make it. The kind of case I have in mind would be an operation involving a substantial risk of grave adverse consequences, as for example the 10 per cent risk of a stroke from the operation which was the subject of the Canadian case of *Reibl v. Hughes* (1980) 114 DLR (3d) 1. In such a case, in the absence of some cogent clinical reason why the patient should not be informed, a doctor, recognising and respecting his patient's right of decision, could hardly fail to appreciate the necessity for an appropriate warning . . . "

LORD TEMPLEMAN

" . . . In my opinion, if a patient knows that a major operation may entail serious consequences, the patient cannot complain of lack of information unless the patient asks in vain for more information or unless there is some danger which by its nature or magnitude or for some other reason requires to be separately taken into account by the patient in order to reach a balanced judgment in deciding whether or not to submit to the operation. To make Mr Falconer liable for damages for negligence, in not expressly drawing Mrs Sidaway's attention to the risk of damage to the spinal cord and its consequences, Mrs Sidaway must show, and fails to show, that Mr Falconer was not entitled to assume, in the absence of questions from Mrs Sidaway, that his explanation of the nature of the operation was sufficient to alert Mrs Sidaway to the general danger of unavoidable and serious damage inherent in the operation but sufficiently remote to justify the operation. There is no reason to think that Mr Falconer was aware that, as Mrs Sidaway deposed, a specific warning and assessment of the risk of spinal cord damage would have influenced Mrs Sidaway to decline the operation although the general explanation which she was given resulted in her consenting to the operation.

There is no doubt that a doctor ought to draw the attention of a patient to a danger which may be special in kind or magnitude or special to the patient. In *Reibl v. Hughes* 114 DLR (3d) 1 a surgeon advised an operation on the brain to avoid a threatened stroke. The surgeon knew or ought to have known that there was a 4 per cent chance that the operation might cause death and a 10 per cent chance that the operation might precipitate the very stroke which the operation was designed to prevent. The patient ought to have been informed of these specific risks in order to be able to form a balanced judgment in deciding whether or not to submit to the operation.

When a patient complains of lack of information, the court must decide whether the patient has suffered harm from a general danger inherent in the operation or from some special danger. In the case of a general danger the court must decide whether the information afforded to the patient was sufficient to alert the patient to the possibility of serious harm of the kind in fact suffered. If the practice of the medical profession is to make express mention of a particular kind of danger, the court will have no difficulty in coming to the conclusion that the doctor ought to have referred expressly to this danger as a special danger unless the doctor can give reasons to justify the form or absence of warning adopted by him. Where the practice of the medical profession is divided or does not include express mention, it will be for the court to determine whether the harm suffered is an example of a general danger inherent in the nature of the operation and if so whether the explanation afforded to the patient was sufficient to alert the patient to the general dangers of which the harm suffered is an example. If a doctor conscientiously endeavours to explain the arguments for and against a major operation and the possibilities of benefiting and the dangers, the court will be slow to conclude that the doctor has been guilty of a breach of duty owed to the patient merely because the doctor omits some specific item of information. It is for the court to decide, after hearing the doctor's explanation, whether the doctor has in fact been guilty of a breach of duty with regard to information.

A doctor offers a patient diagnosis, advice and treatment. The objectives, sometimes conflicting, sometimes unattainable, of the doctor's services are the prolongation of life, the restoration of the patient to full physical and mental health and the alleviation of pain. Where there are dangers that treatment may produce results, direct or indirect, which are harmful to the patient, those dangers must be weighed by the doctor before he recommends the treatment. The patient is entitled to consider and reject the recommended treatment and for that purpose to understand the doctor's advice and the possibility of harm resulting from the treatment.

I do not subscribe to the theory that the patient is entitled to know everything or to the theory that the doctor is entitled to decide everything. The relationship between doctor and patient is contractual in origin, the doctor performing services in consideration for fees payable by the patient. The doctor, obedient to the high standards set by the medical profession, impliedly contracts to act at all times in the best interests of the patient. No doctor in his senses would impliedly contract at the same time to give to the patient all the information available to the doctor as a result of the doctor's training and experience and as a result of the doctor's diagnosis of the patient. An obligation to give a patient all the information available to the doctor would often be inconsistent with the doctor's contractual obligation to have regard to the patient's best interests. Some information might confuse, other information might alarm a particular patient. Whenever the occasion arises for the doctor to tell the patient the results of the doctor's diagnosis, the possible methods of treatment and the advantages and disadvantages of the recommended treatment, the doctor must decide in the light of his training and experience and in the light of his knowledge of the patient what should be said and how it should be said. At the same time the doctor is not entitled to make the final decision with regard to treatment which may have disadvantages or dangers. Where the patient's health and future are at stake, the patient must make the final decision. The patient is free to decide whether or not to submit to treatment recommended by the doctor and therefore the doctor impliedly contracts to provide information which is adequate to enable the patient to reach a balanced judgment, subject always to the doctor's own obligation to say and do nothing which the doctor is satisfied will be harmful to the patient. When the doctor himself is considering the possibility of a major operation the doctor is able, with his medical training, with his knowledge of the patient's medical history and with his objective position, to make a balanced judgment whether the operation should be performed or not. If the doctor making a balanced judgment advises the patient to submit to the operation, the patient is entitled to reject that advice for reasons which are rational or irrational or for no reason. The duty of the doctor in these circumstances, subject to his overriding duty to have regard to the best interests of the patient, is to provide the patient with information which will enable the patient to make a balanced judgment if the patient chooses to make a balanced judgment. A patient may make an unbalanced judgment because he is deprived of adequate information. A patient may also make an unbalanced judgment if he is provided with too much information and is made aware of possibilities which he is not capable of assessing because of his lack of medical training, his prejudices or his personality. Thus the provision of too much information may prejudice the attainment of the objective of restoring the patient's health. The obligation of the doctor to have regard to the best interests of the patient but at the same time to make available to the patient sufficient information to enable the patient to reach a balanced judgment if he chooses to do so has not altered because those obligations have ceased or may have ceased to be contractual and become a matter of duty of care. In order to make a balanced judgment if he chooses to do so, the patient needs to be aware of the general dangers and of any special dangers in each case without exaggeration or concealment. At the end of the day, the doctor, bearing in mind the best interests of the patient and bearing in mind the patient's right to information which will enable the patient to make a balanced judgment, must decide what information should be given to the patient and in what terms that information should be couched. The court will award damages against the doctor if the court is satisfied that the doctor blundered and that the patient was deprived of information which was necessary for the purposes I have outlined. In the present case on the judge's findings I am satisfied that adequate information was made available to Mrs Sidaway and that the appeal should therefore be dismissed."

NOTES:

1. Lord Keith agreed with Lord Bridge.

2. The difficulty of ascertaining the *ratio decidendi*—or binding principle of law—in this case has already been noted. The only points on which all five Law Lords seem to agree are that, first, Mrs Sidaway does not recover because of the difficulties in proving what actually was said; secondly, that the enquiring patient should be given the information which he requests; and thirdly that a subjective test for disclosure is untenable.

3. The major legal issue left to be decided following *Chatterton v Gerson* (above at pp.361–365) was who ascertained the materiality of the risk in order to decide whether it should be disclosed: the doctor according to the professional medical standard, or the patient? All of the Law Lords rejected any suggestion that the test should be the subjective one of what the particular patient actually wanted to know. Lord Scarman was of the view that, in deciding whether something was a material consideration, the court should ask whether a reasonable person in the patient's position would have regarded it as being significant, i.e. he adopted a "prudent patient" test. Note that such a test is subject to the doctor's "therapeutic privilege" to withhold information which she reasonably believes would be detrimental to the patient's health. The other Law Lords adopted the test of professional medical practice, but only Lord Diplock fully endorsed the application of the *Bolam* test in this context. (For examination of the glosses to that test introduced by Lords Bridge and Templeman, see S. Lee, "Towards a Jurisprudence of Consent" in J. Eekelaar and J. Bell (eds), *Oxford Essays in Jurisprudence* (3rd series), Oxford: Oxford University Press, 1987.)

4. Ian Kennedy has criticised the House of Lords' decision on the basis that Lord Scarman was the only Law Lord who showed any awareness that he was dealing with the fundamental human right to control one's destiny by having sufficient information to make an informed choice whether to accept or refuse treatment. The other Law Lords couched their opinions in the discourse of doctor's duties rather than patient rights. This led them to focus on narrower factual issues concerning what precisely was said and

what doctors viewed as good practice. (See I. Kennedy, "Patients, Doctors, and Human Rights" in I. Kennedy, *Treat Me Right: Essays in Medical Law and Ethics*, Oxford: Clarendon, 1988, at p.389.)

5. A further criticism Kennedy makes of the *Sidaway* decision is its failure to explore why doctors should be in a special position compared to other professionals. As he points out, it is unimaginable, for example, that a solicitor should take action without her client's permission and be regarded as legally justified in doing so, on the basis that it saved her client from making hard decisions in times of distress (see I Kennedy, *op. cit.* at p.391).

6. The High Court of Australia adopted a significantly different approach to the issue of informed consent than that taken by the majority in *Sidaway* a few years later. In *Rogers v Whitaker* [1993] 4 Med. L.R. 78 the Australian court, in a joint judgment of five judges, referred to the dangers of applying the *Bolam* principle in the area of advice and information, and took the view that:

> "The law should recognise that a doctor has a duty to warn a patient of the material risk inherent in the proposed treatment. A risk is material if in the circumstances of the particular case a reasonable person in the patient's position if warned of the risk would be likely to attach significance to it; or if the medical practitioner is, or should reasonably be aware, that the particular patient, if warned of the risk, would be likely to attach significance to it."

(See D. Chalmers and R. Schwartz, "*Rogers v. Whitaker* and Informed Consent in Australia: a Fair Dinkum Duty of Disclosure" (1993) 1 *Medical Law Review* 139–159.) As Fennell notes, given the similarities between the Australian and North American approaches, it seems likely that the United Kingdom will be the last bastion of *Bolam* type tests concerning information disclosure. (See P. Fennell, *Treatment without Consent*, London: Routledge, 1996. Generally on comparative legal approaches to this issue see D. Giesen and J. Hayes, "The Patient's Right to Know—A Comparative View" (1992) 21 *Anglo-American Law Review* 101.) In the light of the cases discussed below, you should consider whether English law does now effectively adopt the *Rogers v Whitaker* test (see A.R. Maclean, "The Doctrine of Informed Consent: Does it Exist and Has it Crossed the Atlantic?" (2004) 24 *Legal Studies* 386; J.K. Mason and G.T. Laurie, *Mason & McCall Smith's Law and Medical Ethics* (7th edn, Oxford: OUP at pp.405–406).

7. Sheila McLean has argued that applied to the issue of consent to treatment:

> "the *Bolam* Test sets hurdles for the patient which . . . make it relatively certain that no claim will succeed unless the failure to disclose information is so gross as in any event to merit consideration under assault analysis. If the important issue is patients' rights, however, then the relevant question is not whether or not the doctor is entitled to use the defence of *volenti*. For this to apply, the patient must have been informed of the type of risk(s) to which exposure was possible, and must have agreed to accept them. This is a test much more readily susceptible of

proof, and in a sense much less objectionable, than that of reasonable or accepted medical practice."

(See S. McLean, *A Patient's Right to Know*, Aldershot: Dartmouth, 1989 at p.134.) In assessing this criticism of *Sidaway*, it is again important to take account of subsequent cases discussed below.

8. A further important distinction to bear in mind is that between informed consent and informed *choice*. Even if a greater obligation had been imposed upon doctors to disclose the risks of a particular treatment, this would frequently leave the patient only with a straightforward choice of whether to accept or reject that particular treatment. To make a fully informed choice, the patient must also be aware of a range of alternatives. (This became a crucially important issue in the Court of Appeal decisions subsequent to *Sidaway* which are discussed below). Moreover, as Freedman argues, while health professionals are in a position to quantify the risk of an outcome, they cannot tell the patient what *value* to put on that risk, since the likelihood of it occurring is only one of many factors that will go into a patient's analysis of his or her own situation (see L. Freedman, "Censorship and Manipulation of Reproductive Health Information" in S. Coliver (ed.), *The Right to Know: Human Rights and Access to Reproductive Health Information*, Pittsburg: University of Pennsylvania Press, 1995). For example, it will be the patient's own particular circumstances which dictate whether he would prefer treatment which would offer him a shorter period of high-quality life, or a longer lifetime during which he will suffer pain and have restricted mobility.

9. On the importance of communication between health professional and patient in ensuring that information disclosure is adequate, see W.C. Wu and R.A. Pearlman, "Consent in Medical Decision Making: the Role of Communication" (1988) 3 *Journal of General Internal Medicine* 9. Note the stress on communication in recent professional guidance, notably the GMC's, *Seeking Patients' Consent: the Ethical Considerations* (London: GMC, 1999). As Jones remarks, "It is difficult to envisage any court . . . coming up with such a detailed set of rules by way of guidance" (M. Jones, "Informed Consent and Fairy Stories" (1999) 7 *Medical Law Review* 103–134 at p.133).

10. In *Sidaway* two judges (Browne-Wilkinson L.J. in the Court of Appeal and Lord Scarman in the House of Lords) rejected suggestions that a doctor's obligation to inform a patient of risks in a proposed course of treatment could be derived from any fiduciary duty she owed the patient to act for her benefit. However, Grubb has argued that the doctor–patient relationship displays many characteristics of a fiduciary relationship. He contends that it is likely in the future that the courts will have to re-examine the *Sidaway* decision, and that if the duty to disclose was to be regarded as an aspect of the doctor's fiduciary duty, this could well require the law to "heighten the standard of disclosure to require a doctor to disclose all information that would be material to the patient's decision". (See A. Grubb, "The Doctor as Fiduciary" [1994] *Current Legal Problems* 311 at

p.337; for other situations where this analysis may be applied see Chapter 9 at p.596.)

QUESTIONS:

1. Was there a majority of the House of Lords in favour of any of the following: (i) applying the *Bolam* test without modifications; (ii) using a modified *Bolam* test; or (iii) requiring the disclosure of "material" risks? Do you agree with the outright rejection of a subjective patient test?

2. What objections did their Lordships express to (i) the use of the *Bolam* test, and (ii) the legal doctrine of informed consent, as developed in Canada and the US? How far do you accept their criticisms?

3. Do any of the speeches improve on the test for material risk propounded by Bristow J. in *Chatterton v Gerson*? If so, how?

4. Do you agree with Lord Scarman that it is possible to split the doctor's duty into various component parts—diagnosis, treatment and counselling—and that different considerations apply in the case of disclosure, which may render the *Bolam* test inappropriate to a counselling role?

5. Do you think there is in practice a real difference between the *Bolam* test and the "prudent patient" test? Note John Harrington's point that the latter test "leads to a substantial endorsement of medical decision-making in spite of its pro-patient purpose. The information as to risks required by the truly idiosyncratic patient is not likely to coincide with that demanded by his 'reasonable' counterpart." (J. Harrington, "Privileging the Medical Norm: Liberalism, Self-determination and Refusal of Treatment" (1996) 16 *Legal Studies* 348 at p.354.)

6. Were the Law Lords justified in unanimously ruling out a subjective test of what the actual patient would have wanted to know, given Faulder's contention, that "The 'reasonable person' is you, me and every other adult, autonomous human being who normally expects to make decisions according to our own perceptions of what is reasonable for us"? (See C. Faulder, *Whose Body Is It? The Troubling Issue of Informed Consent*, London: Virago, 1984 at p.37.)

7. In what circumstances did the Law Lords envisage that judges would be entitled to disagree with the views of medical experts as to whether non-disclosure would be legitimate? (See further *Smith v Tunbridge Wells Health Authority* and *Chester v Afshar* below.)

8. In your view, which of the four speeches should be taken as being most representative of the majority view in the case?

9. Does his endorsement of the doctrine of therapeutic privilege undermine even Lord Scarman's framework to vindicate the patient's right to self-determination? (See J. Harrington, "Privileging the Medical Norm: Liberalism, Self-determination and Refusal of Treatment" (1996) 16 *Legal Studies* 348 at p.355; M. Jones, "Informed Consent and Fairy Stories" (1999) 7 *Medical Law Review* 103–134 at p.113.)

(ii) The Obligation to Disclose Information to the Patient: Non-therapeutic Cases

The test for disclosure of information in *Sidaway* was later examined in the Court of Appeal decision of *Gold v Haringey* [1987] 2 All E.R. 888, a case which on the face of it appeared to raise different issues. It was concerned with the provision of contraceptive advice and treatment rather than therapeutic care.

Gold v Haringey Health Authority [1987] 2 All E.R. 888, [1988] 1 Q.B. 481, [1987] 3 W.L.R. 649, [1988] 1 F.L.R. 55

Mrs Gold decided that she wished to have no further children. Her consultant obstetrician suggested that she should be sterilised. The operation went ahead, with Mrs Gold's consent, but was not successful, and she subsequently became pregnant again. It was found that the operation had been properly performed and was not guaranteed to succeed. However, Mrs Gold claimed that the consultant had been negligent in failing to discuss the treatment properly. Two mistakes were alleged: first, that he had failed to explain the risk of failure, and secondly, that he had not discussed any alternative method by which steps could be taken to avoid Mrs Gold becoming pregnant (namely by her husband undergoing a vasectomy). All the medical witnesses said that they would have warned Mrs Gold of the risk of failure, but that a sizeable proportion of doctors (estimated at up to 50 per cent) would not have done so at the time when she had the operation. However, the judge at first instance decided that the existence of this substantial body of medical opinion did not resolve the matter, because *Sidaway* only applied to therapeutic procedures, not to non-therapeutic procedures for contraceptive reasons. Thus, Mrs Gold was awarded £19,000 damages. The health authority appealed and the Court of Appeal offered its interpretation of the rule of law that *Sidaway* had established:

LLOYD L.J.
So I turn to the second question, which assumes, as I have held, that the *Bolam* test applies. Here counsel for the plaintiff acknowledges that he is in some difficulty . . .

Counsel for the plaintiff relies on the documentary evidence, some of which is set out in the judge's judgment. I need not refer to it in detail. As was to be expected, it emphasises the importance of counselling before deciding on an operation, whether for male or female sterilisation. In addition, the documents published by the medical defence bodies, again as was only to be expected, discourage the giving of any sort of guarantee of success. But this evidence does not meet the point made by counsel for the defendants and by all the witnesses, including those called by the plaintiff, who said that though they would themselves have warned the plaintiff of the risk of failure, there was a body of responsible doctors in 1979 who would not have done so. The judge accepted in his judgment that the distinction between advising in a contraceptive and non-contraceptive context was not 'crystal clear' on the evidence. With respect, that is an understatement. The witnesses were never asked to distinguish between the two cases. There was therefore only one finding open on the evidence, namely that there was a body of responsible medical opinion which would not have given any warning as to the failure of female sterilisation, and the possible alternatives, in the circumstances in which the defendants actually found themselves. So I would not accept the second of the two grounds on which the judge decided against the defendants . . .

For the reasons I have given the plaintiff has failed to make good her claim for negligence. Accordingly, I would allow this appeal."

NOTES:

1. Watkins L.J. and Stephen Brown L.J. agreed.
2. The interpretation of *Sidaway* adopted in *Gold* is the most protective of the medical profession and, in Lord Scarman's view, represented an abdication of the court's role to establish the limits of professional judgment. It was followed in *Blyth v Bloomsbury* below; *Moyes v Lothian Health Board* [1990] 1 Med. L.R. 463; *Powell v Baldaz* (1997) 39 B.M.L.R. 35. (See A. Grubb, "Consent to Treatment: the Competent Patient" in A. Grubb (ed.), *Principles of Medical Law* (2nd edn) Oxford: OUP, 2004, 131–203 at p.190.)

QUESTIONS:

1. Was the interpretation of the *Sidaway* decision offered by the Court of Appeal a legitimate one? (See I. Kennedy, "The Patient on the Clapham Omnibus" in *Treat Me Right: Essays in Medical Law and Ethics*, Oxford: Clarendon, at pp.210–212 for a trenchant critique of the way in which the decision undermines patient autonomy.)
2. Do you think that it is possible to draw a distinction between therapeutic and non-therapeutic procedures? (You may like to consider the discussion of this matter in relation to sterilisation procedures, see Chapter 12, or in the context of clinical research, see Chapter 10.)
3. Does the whole tenor of Lloyd L.J.'s judgment undermine the significance of counselling in a contraceptive context? (For further discussion see Chapter 12 at pp.860–869)

(iii) The Obligation to Disclose Information to the Patient: Where the Patient Asks Questions

In *Blyth v Bloomsbury* [1993] Med. L.R. 151 it was argued that the *Sidaway* test should be limited to volunteering information, different rules applying where patients ask questions. Here, too, the Court of Appeal proved resistant to forcing doctors to disclose information against their clinical judgment.

Blyth v Bloomsbury Health Authority [1993] 4 Med. L.R. 151

The plaintiff, a nurse, claimed that she had asked her doctor about the side-effects of the injectable contraceptive drug Depo-Provera. At the time it was generally accepted medical opinion that Depo-Provera was well tolerated, and no significant side-effects had been reported. However, the doctor who treated her was aware that there might be a problem with irregular bleeding; and that another doctor in the hospital had carried out research (which was contained in the hospital files) which indicated that there may be other side-effects. The patient subsequently experienced menstrual irregularity and bleeding. She brought an action for damages, alleging that as she had expressly enquired of the risks inherent in the contraceptive she should have been told of all the risks known to the hospital at that time. At first instance she was awarded £3,500 damages, as the judge held that she was entitled to receive *all* the information known to the hospital about the drug. In the Court of Appeal the judgment in her favour was reversed on the facts because it was found that she had not in fact requested the information. Two judges briefly discussed the law of consent in respect of cases where information has been requested. These dicta are set out below:

KERR L.J.
"The question of what a plaintiff should be told in answer to a general enquiry cannot be divorced from the *Bolam* test, any more than when no such enquiry is made. In both cases the answer must depend upon the circumstances, the nature of the enquiry, the nature of the information which is available, its reliability, relevance, the condition of the patient, and so forth. Any medical evidence directed to what would be the proper answer in the light of responsible medical opinion and practice—that is to say, the *Bolam* test—must in my view equally be placed in the balance in cases where the patient makes some enquiry, in order to decide whether the response was negligent or not . . .

Indeed I am not convinced that the *Bolam* test is irrelevant even in relation to the question of what answers are properly to be given to specific enquiries, or that Lord Diplock or Lord Bridge intended to hold otherwise. It seems to me that there may always be grey areas, with differences of opinion, as to what are the proper answers to be given to any enquiry, even a specific one, in the particular circumstances of any case. However, on the evidence in the present case this point does not arise, since no specific enquiry was found to have been made."

NEILL L.J.
" . . . Furthermore, I do not understand that in the decision of the House of Lords in *Sidaway*, either Lord Diplock or Lord Bridge were laying down any rule of law to the effect there where questions are asked by a patient, or doubts are expressed, a doctor is under an obligation to put the patient in possession of all the information on the subject which may have been available in the files of a consultant, who may have made a special study of the subject. The amount of information to be given must depend upon the circumstances, and as a general proposition it is governed by what is called the *Bolam* test. In 1978 irregular bleeding was the side-effect which was known and recognised. The plaintiff was told about it. In my judgment it was not established, either by means of evidence of some usual system, which broke down in this particular case, or by the application of some rule of law, that the plaintiff would, or should, have been put in possession of the material, or the bulk of the material, then in Dr Law's files."

NOTES:

1. The approach suggested by dicta in this case seems incompatible with the comments in *Sidaway* regarding the proper response to a patient who asked questions. Even Lord Diplock, who came down most strongly in favour of the application of the *Bolam* test, was very clear that the enquiring patient has a right to be given the information which he requests. Fortunately, however, the courts seem have endorsed the rights of the enquiring patient in the case of *Pearce v United Bristol Healthcare Trust* (see p.390 below).

QUESTIONS:

1. Do approaches which would draw a distinction between the silent and enquiring patient discriminate in favour of the better educated patient?
2. Should a distinction be drawn between those cases where the patient asks a specific question, and those where he simply seeks more information in general terms?
3. Should the fact that the patient in this case was a nurse have had any impact on the degree of information which should have been disclosed to her?

(iv) The Obligation to Disclose Information: a New Pro-Patient Trend?

The interpretation of *Sidaway* offered by the Court of Appeal in *Gold* and *Blythe* has been heavily criticised by commentators like Kennedy for entrenching medical paternalism. However, more recent decisions on medical negligence have offered some evidence of the readiness of the English courts' to question medical practice.

Smith v Tunbridge Wells Health Authority [1994] 5 Med. L.R. 334

The plaintiff, Mr Smith, was a 28-year-old married man with two children. His consultant, Mr Cook, had diagnosed a full thickness rectal prolapse, and advised surgery—an ivalon sponge rectopexy (the Wells operation)—which was generally performed on elderly women, and rarely upon men, who generally have a narrower pelvis. The operation was successful in the sense that the rectum was repositioned in its correct anatomical place. However, due to nerve damage during surgery, the plaintiff was rendered impotent and suffered from significant bladder malfunction.

MORLAND J.
" . . . the first issue . . . [is] whether or not Mr Cook [the plaintiff's consultant surgeon] was under a legal duty to inform the plaintiff of, in particular, the risk of impotence when on September 23, 1988, he recommended an ivalon sponge rectopexy . . .
    I accept the defendant's submission that Mr Cook's personal view as to his duty is not definitive evidence that in law he owed that duty. In my judgment it is however cogent evidence that general surgeons in 1988 when faced with a patient with a similar condition and history to this plaintiff's, and recommending an ivalon sponge rectopexy, would have regarded it as the proper and accepted practice to warn such a patient of the risk of impotence . . .
    In Mr Northover's [a distinguished colorectal surgeon called by the plaintiff] experience for ten years the proper practice had demanded warning of the risks about the type of operation recommended to the plaintiff. In his view by 1988 the general body of responsible medical opinion was that the patient had to be fully informed of the risks . . .
    Professor Golligher, the greatest of experts [author of *Surgery of the Anus, Rectum and Colon* (1984)], was called by the defendants. In his evidence in chief he frankly said that, considering his textbook to which I have referred:

'Perhaps we were slow and conservative. I should have been quicker. I was responsible for misleading surgeons. They look at standard text books. I did not then know. I now would definitely insert the risk in my text book.'

In his opinion quite a number of surgeons, because of his text book, would not have given a warning in 1988. He said the risk was not put in his book because he and his collaborators could not be sure that the risk existed. As he put it: "Now I regret to some extent the omission". However, as he made clear, that was hindsight. He said he became convinced of the risk in 1985 or 1986 when a patient was referred to him for a second opinion who was impotent following a rectal prolapse . . . He says that certainly since 1985 or 1986 he would give a warning of the risk of impotence, but he still believed that quite a lot of surgeons would not have adopted the attitude of Mr Cook in 1988—Mr Cook's attitude being, of course, that he considered himself under a duty to give a warning . . .

In my judgment by 1988, although some surgeons may still not have been warning patients similar in situation to the plaintiff of the risk of impotence, that omission was neither reasonable nor responsible.

In my judgment Mr Cook, in stating that he considered that he owed a duty to warn, was reflecting not only the generally accepted standard practice, but also the only reasonable and responsible standard of care to be expected from a consultant in Mr Cook's position faced with the plaintiff's situation.

On this issue in my judgment the plaintiff succeeds applying the *Bolam* test as elucidated in *Sidaway* . . .

I now come to consider the second question: Did Mr Cook give an adequate warning to the plaintiff of the risks of the Wells operation when recommending it in appropriate language for understanding by the plaintiff? . . .

I prefer the evidence of the plaintiff to that of Mr Cook. I found the plaintiff truthful and fair. I have no doubt that Mr Cook, not unnaturally, is now convinced in his own mind that he did specifically mention the risk of impotence because he believes he would have done so as he felt it his duty. I suspect that Mr Cook omitted the mention of bladder damage because he was not clear in his own mind as to how and to what extent he should explain the risks of the surgery to the plaintiff. In human terms this is explicable. The plaintiff was his first sexually active man to whom he recommended rectopexy as a consultant. As Mr Cook was not clear in his own mind, his explanation to the plaintiff was confused, with the result the plaintiff misunderstood the message.

In my judgment the plaintiff has established on the balance of probabilities that Mr Cook failed to explain with sufficient clarity to be expected in 1988 of a consultant general surgeon with his interest in colorectal surgery the risk of impotence, and on this occasion was negligent.

I am entirely satisfied that if the risk of impotence had been explained to the plaintiff, he would have refused the operation.

It is worthwhile to consider the plaintiff and his condition. He was happily married, close to his wife, as he happily still is. His wife was outside in the waiting room. They lived within minutes of the hospital. In my judgment it is unlikely that this plaintiff at the age of 28 would there and then have consented to an operation for a condition which he had lived with for eight years without asking for further details and without asking whether there were any other methods of treatment which did not have this risk of impotence, if impotence had been mentioned.

In my judgment the very fact of consent and the speed of consent are indicative that a clear warning of the risk of impotence was not communicated clearly to the plaintiff . . . "

NOTES:

1. This case does seem to embody a more "pro-patient" attitude than the cases of *Gold* and *Blyth*. However, it is worth noting that in each of those cases the plaintiff had also succeeded at first instance and judgment in her favour was overturned on appeal. Thus the position after this case was that it remained to be seen whether *Smith* represented a move towards stricter

legal requirements for informing patients about their care. This was especially true given that it is an unusual case on the facts, since the doctor admitted that he would normally give warnings and that the risk should have been disclosed in these circumstances.

2. Another case of this era in which it was held that risks should have been disclosed was still more clear cut. In *McAllister v Lewisham and North Southwark HA* [1994] Med. L.R. 343 it was decided that no responsible body of medical opinion could have held that it was reasonable to withhold information about hemiplegia and other risks attendant on brain surgery.

3. Michael Jones notes that an important feature of the *Smith* case is that it stipulates that "risk disclosure is meant to be a process of *communicating* information. Simply telling the patient about the risks without making any attempt to see if the patient has understood the information can be negligent" (M. Jones, "Informed Consent and Fairy Stories" (1999) 7 *Medical Law Review* 103–134 at p.118.). This was re-iterated in subsequent cases. Thus in *Smith v Salford Health Authority* [1994] 5 Med. L.R. 321 it was noted that particular care must be taken in explaining risks where a patient is debilitated due to his underlying condition or the effects of medication. In *Lybert v Warrington Health Authority* [1996] 7 Med. L.R. 71 the Court of Appeal upheld Lachs J.'s view that "the warning [that a hysterectomy might fail to prevent conception] was not of a nature in terms of force and emphasis as to impinge on the plaintiff's thought". Such dicta in the case law also accords with the emphasis in the Report on the Bristol Inquiry (see p.351 above) that consent should be seen as a process rather than a one-off transaction (see J. McHale and A. Gallagher, "After Bristol: the Importance of Informed Consent" (2001) 97 *Nursing Times* 32.) However, in *Al Hamwi v Johnston and Another* [2005] EWHC 206 where a pregnant woman complained that the risks of miscarriage were exaggerated, Simon J. held that it was "too onerous" to impose on the clinician a duty to ensure that the patient understood the information that had been given. As Jose Miola notes, the decision is particularly surprising given the House of Lords decision in *Chester v Afshar,* below, and that "[i]t is difficult to imagine that the majority in *Chester* would agree with the notion that the important aspect of risk disclosure is that the information is imparted rather than understood" (J. Miola, "Autonomy Rued OK? *Al Hamwi v. Johnston and Another*" (2006) 14 *Medical Law Review* 108–114 at p.112).

4. After these cases Newdick took the view that it could only be a matter of time before English law adopted the North American approach, with its presumption of openness and candour between health professional and patient. He suggests that the fact that failure to disclose risks in *Smith* was held to have been negligent on the court's own assessment of the facts may be indicative of an emerging more proactive approach on the part of the courts, rather than simply deferring to medical experts. (See C. Newdick, *Who Should We Treat? Law, Patients and Resources in the NHS*, Oxford:

Oxford University Press, 2005 at p.152; and the following case law seems to bear out his contention.)

QUESTIONS:

1. Do you think that the decision in *Smith v Tunbridge Wells HA* is more in line with the spirit of *Sidaway* than that in *Gold*?
2. What do you think would have happened had the decision been appealed?

The trend in judicial decision-making towards a more "pro-patient" standard, which Newdick predicted, was given particular impetus by the case of *Bolitho v Hackney HA* [1998] A.C. 232 which we considered in detail in Chapter 3 at p.201. There we discuss the general implications of this decision for the *Bolam* test. With regard to its implications in the context of the duty to disclose, Grubb notes that "With the loosening of the court's commitment to *Bolam*, it can only be a matter of time . . . before *Sidaway* is also consigned to history. It was never necessary anyway to derive the rule in *Sidaway* from *Bolam*. With *Bolam* being refashioned, *Sidaway* (apart from Lord Scarman's speech), becomes even less sustainable" (A. Grubb, "Consent to Treatment: the Competent Patient" in A. Grubb (ed.), *Principles of Medical Law* (2nd edn), Oxford: OUP, 2004 at p.195.)

The first significant test of the possible changes wrought by *Bolitho* in the context of information disclosure occurred in the following case:

Pearce v United Bristol Healthcare NHS Trust [1999] P.I.Q.R. 53, (1999) 48 B.M.L.R. 118

Mrs Pearce had been due to give birth two weeks previously when she saw Mr Niven, the consultant responsible for her care, and begged him to induce the birth or perform a Caesarean section. Having formed the view that intervention was undesirable, the consultant explained the risks of induction and of a Caesarean section (i.e the normal risks of major surgery, coupled with the fact that it would delay the plaintiff's recovery (see Chapter 13 at pp.952–961). He failed to warn her of the risk of still birth consequent on doing nothing, which was estimated at 0.1–0.2 per cent. Five days later her baby was delivered still born. Mrs Pearce claimed that she would have opted for a Caesarean if the risk of still birth had been disclosed.

LORD WOOLF M.R.
"In a case where it is being alleged that a plaintiff has been deprived of the opportunity to make a proper decision as to what course he or she should take in relation to treatment, it seems to me to be the law, as indicated in the cases to which I have just referred, that if there is a significant risk which would affect the judgment of a reasonable patient, then in the normal course it is the responsibility of a doctor to inform the patient of that significant risk, if the information is needed so that the patient can determine for him or herself as to what course he or she should adopt.

In the *Sidaway* case Lord Bridge recognises that position. He refers to a 'significant risk' as being a risk of something in the region of 10 per cent. When one refers to a 'significant risk' it is not possible to talk in precise percentages, but I note, and it may be purely coincidental, that one of the expert doctors who gave evidence before the judge gave the following answer in evidence. I refer to the evidence of Mr Pearson:

'A. If she hadn't asked I wouldn't have mentioned the subject as she was already distressed and the risk is excessively small. I generally practise according to the belief that it is not the doctor's duty to warn of very small risks. If the risk, however, was of the order of 10%, for instance, then of course it would be my duty to warn against such a level of risk.'

Obviously the doctor, in determining what to tell a patient, has to take into account all the relevant considerations, which include the ability of the patient to comprehend what he has to say to him or her and the state of the patient at the particular time, both from the physical point of view and an emotional point of view. There can often be situations where a course different from the normal has to be employed. However, where there is what can realistically be called a 'significant risk', then, in the ordinary event, as I have already indicated, the patient is entitled to be informed of that risk. Turning to the facts of this case, the next question is, therefore, 'Was there a significant risk? To what extent was the risk of Jacqueline being a stillborn child increased by delay?' Miss Edwards, on behalf of the respondent, has referred us to the relevant passages in the transcript. They show that, on any basis, the increased risk of the still birth of Jacqueline, as a result of additional delay, was very small indeed. The statistical material which was available can be broken down into different classes. Even looked at comprehensively it comes to something like 0.1 to 0.2 per cent. The doctors called on behalf of the defendants did not regard that risk as significant, nor do I. Indeed, it is right to point out that the operative treatment involved in a Caesarean section would inevitably have had some risk. Miss Edwards also pointed out, rightly, that earlier during the pregnancy the risk of the child being stillborn would have been greater than the figures with which we are concerned after November 13 and November 27, 1991 in this case. Particularly when one bears in mind Mrs Pearce's distressed condition, one cannot criticise Mr Niven's decision not to inform Mrs Pearce of that very, very small additional risk. Mr Niven would know that the baby was not large, which would also mean that the risk would be reduced. This is a case where, in my judgment, it would not be proper for the courts to interfere with the clinical opinion of the expert medical man responsible for treating Mrs Pearce.

As to what would have been the consequence if she had been told of this particularly small risk, it is difficult to envisage. The judge made no clear finding as to this, but my conclusion is that, in so far as it was possible for this court to make an assessment of this, the inference is that if Mrs Pearce had been able to understand what she had been told about the increased risk, her decision would still have been to follow, reluctantly, the advice of the doctor who was treating her, namely Mr Niven. In those circumstances it seems to me that, although one has sympathy for Mr and Mrs Pearce, the only possible result of this appeal is that the appeal should be dismissed.

NOTES:

1. Roch L.J. and Mummery L.J. agreed.
2. Lord Woolf in this case regarded the speech of Lord Templeman in *Sidaway* as "not precisely that of the majority" but noted that it "does reflect the law and does not involve taking a different view from the majority", thus marking a shift from the emphasis in *Gold* and *Blyth* on Lord Diplock's speech (at p.57).
3. Michael Jones argues that the requirement in this case to disclose significant risks "appears to combine a prudent patient standard with a reasonable doctor standard—a significant risk affecting the judgment of a

reasonable patient places the onus upon the doctor to disclose that significant risk by virtue of the *Bolam* test. In other words, no reasonable doctor would fail to disclose a risk regarded as significant by a reasonable patient" (M. Jones, "Informed Consent and Fairy Stories" (1999) 7 *Medical Law Review* 103–134 at p.118.). However, as Andrew Grubb notes, there is little guidance on the notion of when a risk is to be deemed significant, expect that it can not be determined simply in terms of percentages (A. Grubb, "Medical Negligence: Duty to Disclose after *Bolitho*" (1999) 7 *Medical Law Review* 61).

4. Grubb (*op. cit.* in note 3) suggests that as a result of *Pearce*, "the legal standard in all cases, be they concerned with treatment, diagnosis or disclosure of information, is the same and can be derived from a synthesis of *Sidaway* and *Bolitho*".

5. Although he did not directly consider the case of *Blyth*, Lord Woolf appears to regard it as wrongly decided, as he accepted counsel's view that "if a patient asks a doctor about the risk then the doctor is required to given an honest answer" (at p.54). This interpretation has been strongly supported by health care lawyers.

QUESTIONS:

1. Given the severity of the consequences in the *Pearce* case, do you think that the risk of still birth, even if it was statistically very low, was one that was not significant enough to require disclosure? Are statistical analyses useful in such cases, given the inherent uncertainty in such judgments?

2. Do you agree with the Court of Appeal that this was not a proper case to interfere with the doctor's judgment? Do you agree with Shaun Pattinson that "[d]espite the outcome for Mrs Pearce, this judgment is very pro-claimant"? (S. Pattinson, *Medical Law and Ethics*, London: Sweet & Maxwell, 2006 at p.111.)

3. Alistair Maclean suggests that the test adopted in *Pearce*, i.e. that there must be disclosure "of those risks that the reasonable doctor believes the reasonable patient ought to find significant to a decision" is a significantly different test from one that would require disclosure of the information that a reasonable patient would want to be told (A.R. Maclean, "The Doctrine of Informed Consent: Does it Exist and Has It Crossed the Atlantic?" (2004) 24 *Legal Studies* 386.) Do you agree?

In 2005 the issue of the duty to disclose risks in treatment was finally reconsidered by the House of Lords in the case of *Chester v Afshar*. By the time it reached the House of Lords the dispute hinged solely on the question of causation. However, Lord Steyn's opinion contains a lengthy, albeit obiter, consideration of the duty to disclosure, affirming the line taken by the Court of Appeal in *Pearce* as regards the appropriate test of disclosure.

Chester v Afshar [2005] 1 A.C. 134, [2004] 4 All E.R. 587

The claimant was advised by the defendant—a neurosurgeon—to undergo spinal surgery for persistent lower back pain. It was accepted that the surgery carried certain risks of serious complications, including nerve damage and paralysis of the order of 1–2 per cent. Although the surgery was properly carried out, a small risk of cauda equina syndrome materialised, with the result that the claimant suffered significant motor and sensory disturbance. It was accepted that it would be in accordance with good medical practice to warn of the risk, and while the evidence as to whether a warning had been given was disputed, Taylor J. preferred the claimant's evidence and found that the defendant had negligently failed to warn of the risk of the syndrome. The case raised an interesting point about causation, in that the claimant said she would have taken time for reflection had the warning been given, although she may have consented to surgery in the future. The appeal was dismissed unanimously by the Court of Appeal and by a three to two majority of the House of Lords.

LORD STEYN
"14 . . . The starting point is that every individual of adult years and sound mind has a right to decide what may or may not be done with his or her body. Individuals have a right to make important medical decisions affecting their lives for themselves: they have the right to make decisions which doctors regard as ill advised. Surgery performed without the informed consent of the patient is unlawful. The court is the final arbiter of what constitutes informed consent. Usually, informed consent will presuppose a general warning by the surgeon of a significant risk of the surgery.

15 In the case before the House a single cause of action is under consideration, viz the tort of negligence. How a surgeon's duty to warn a patient of a serious risk of injury fits into the tort of negligence was explained by Lord Woolf MR, with the agreement of Roch and Mummery LJJ, in *Pearce v United Bristol Healthcare NHS Trust* . . . Lord Woolf MR observed:

'In a case where it is being alleged that a plaintiff has been deprived of the opportunity to make a proper decision as to what course he or she should take in relation to treatment, it seems to me to be the law, as indicated in the cases to which I have just referred, that if there is a significant risk which would affect the judgment of a reasonable patient, then in the normal course it is the responsibility of a doctor to inform the patient of that significant risk, if the information is needed so that the patient can determine for him or herself as to what course he or she should adopt.'

16 A surgeon owes a legal duty to a patient to warn him or her in general terms of possible serious risks involved in the procedure. The only qualification is that there may be wholly exceptional cases where objectively in the best interests of the patient the surgeon may be excused from giving a warning. This is, however, irrelevant in the present case. In modern law medical paternalism no longer rules and a patient has a prima facie right to be informed by a surgeon of a small, but well established, risk of serious injury as a result of surgery.

17 Secondly, not all rights are equally important. But a patient's right to an appropriate warning from a surgeon when faced with surgery ought normatively to be regarded as an important right which must be given effective protection whenever possible.

18 Thirdly, in the context of attributing legal responsibility, it is necessary to identify precisely the protected legal interests at stake. A rule requiring a doctor to abstain from performing an operation without the informed consent of a patient serves two purposes. It tends to avoid the occurrence of the particular physical injury the risk of which a patient

is not prepared to accept. It also ensures that due respect is given to the autonomy and dignity of each patient . . . Recognising an individual right of autonomy makes self-creation possible. It allows each of us to be responsible for shaping our lives according to our own coherent or incoherent—but, in any case, distinctive—personality. It allows us to lead our lives rather than be led along them, so that each of us can be, to the extent a scheme of rights can make this possible, what we have made of ourselves. We allow someone to choose death over radical amputation or a blood transfusion, if that is his informed wish, because we acknowledge his right to a life structured by his own values.

19 Fourthly, it is a distinctive feature of the present case that but for the surgeon's negligent failure to warn the claimant of the small risk of serious injury the actual injury would not have occurred when it did and the chance of it occurring on a subsequent occasion was very small. It could therefore be said that the breach of the surgeon resulted in the very injury about which the claimant was entitled to be warned.

20 These factors must be considered in combination. But they must also be weighed against the undesirability of departing from established principles of causation, except for good reasons. The collision of competing ideas poses a difficult question of law . . .

[His Lordship proceed to discuss *Chappel v Hart* (see Note 2 below).]

24 Standing back from the detailed arguments, I have come to the conclusion that, as a result of the surgeon's failure to warn the patient, she cannot be said to have given informed consent to the surgery in the full legal sense. Her right of autonomy and dignity can and ought to be vindicated by a narrow and modest departure from traditional causation principles.

25 On a broader basis I am glad to have arrived at the conclusion that the claimant is entitled in law to succeed. This result is in accord with one of the most basic aspirations of the law, namely to right wrongs. Moreover, the decision announced by the House today reflects the reasonable expectations of the public in contemporary society.

26 The result ought to come as no surprise to the medical profession which has to its credit subscribed to the fundamental importance of a surgeon's duty to warn a patient in general terms of significant risks: Royal College of Surgeons, *Good Surgical Practice* (2002), ch 4, guidelines on consent . . . "

Notes:

1. Lords Hope and Walker delivered the other majority speeches, while Lords Bingham and Hoffmann dissented on the issue of causation. Stauch attributes the dissenting opinions to a confusion between legal and factual causation (M. Stauch, "Causation and Confusion in Respect of Medical Non-Disclosure" (2005) 14 *Nottingham Law Journal* 66).

2. The same point on causation had earlier arisen in the Australian case of *Chappel v Hart* [1998] H.C.A. 55; and the majority in *Chester* were strongly influenced by the majority of the Australian High Court in that case (see T. Honore, "Medical Non-disclosure, Causation and Risk: *Chappel v. Hart*" (199) 7 *Torts Law Journal* 1; A. Grubb. "Clinical negligence: Informed Consent and Causation" (2002) 10 *Medical Law Review* 322).

3. In some ways the *Chester* decision is quite remarkable because of the paucity of cases in which the plaintiff succeeds in arguing that a failure to disclose is negligent (M. Jones, "Informed Consent and Fairy Stories" (1999) 7 *Medical Law Review* 103. However, as Stauch notes (*op. cit.* in note 1 at p.68), it is significant that Lord Steyn refers about to the Royal

College of Surgeons guidelines, which recognise the rights of patient to be informed of significant risks in treatment. He suggests that arguably now "the dichotomy . . . between the *Sidaway* 'prudent doctor' and US-style 'informed consent' approaches has disappeared . . . because, on the logic of the *Bolam* test itself, if responsible accepted practice generally is to disclose risks that a reasonable patient would wish to know about, the failure of a particular doctor to do so in a given case will be a straightforward breach of duty."

4. Lord Steyn continues to endorse the doctrine of therapeutic privilege although he does note that it is limited to "wholly exceptional cases".

5. As Miola notes, the Chester decision is as important because of the tone of the majority decision and their readiness to affirm patient autonomy as it is for the content. However, the fact that this tone may not be reflected in all subsequent case law is demonstrated by his discussion of *Al Hamwi v Johnston and Another* (p.389 above; J. Miola, "Autonomy Rued OK? *Al Hamwi v. Johnston and Another*" (2006) 14 *Medical Law Review* 108 at p.113).

QUESTIONS:

1. Notwithstanding claims that the House of Lords reached a "very pro-claimant, patient-centred decision" (S. Pattinson, *Medical Law and Ethics*, London: Sweet & Maxwell, 2001 at p.116; see also S. Devaney, "Autonomy Rules OK" (2005) 13 *Medical Law Review* 102), does the case really represent a sea change or can it be argued that, in practice, the requirement of consent will continue to "privilege the medical norm"? (See J. Harrington, "Privileging the Medical Norm: Liberalism, Self-determination and Refusal of Treatment" (1996) 16 *Legal Studies* 348; E. Jackson, " Informed Consent to Medical Treatment and the Impotence of Tort" in S.A.M. McLean (ed.), *First Do No Harm* (Aldershot: Ashgate, 2006.)

2. Do you agree with finding the doctor liable in negligence if her failure to disclose the risk merely alters the time of the patient's exposure to it? (Note Stauch's point that on the facts of the case, had Miss Chester postponed surgery the risk of harm was 98–99 per cent likely not to materialise (*op. cit.* in note 1 at p.69.)

3. Does English law now differ substantially from Australian law in relation to disclosure of information? It has been argued that in Australia, "there is evidence of a waning commitment to *Rogers v. Whittaker* and a policy inclination to rein in the doctrine of informed consent" (J. Manning, "Informed Consent to Medical Treatment: the Common Law and New Zealand's Code of Patients' Rights" (2004) 12 *Medical Law Review* 181–216 at p.214). Manning suggests that the New Zealand Code of Health and Disability Services Consumers Rights 1996 may offer a more promising model for English law in this area than the Australian or US common law. (See also P.D.G. Skegg, "English Medical Law and 'Informed Consent': an Antipodean Assessment and Alternative" (1999) 7 *Medical Law Review* 135–165.)

4. Is there a duty in English law for the health professional to advise the patient of alternatives to the proposed course of treatment? Should there be?

(v) The Obligation to Disclose Information to the Patient: the Position of Other Health Care Professionals

Sidaway, *Pearce* and *Chester* were all concerned with the doctor's duty to disclose risks, although requirement to disclose significant risks will clearly apply to other professionals involved in the patient's treatment. Not only may nurses or midwives find themselves in a situation where they have to obtain consent but, if a patient is confused or uncertain about the doctor's explanation and his own treatment choice, he may well seek advice or clarification from a nurse or other carer. The relevant professional code contains the following advice on obtaining consent (note that it is currently under review).

Nursing & Midwifery Council, *The NMC Code of Professional Conduct: Standards for Conduct, Performance and Ethics* (London: NMC, 2004)

3.1 All patients and clients have a right to receive information about their condition. You must be sensitive to their needs and respect the wishes of those who refuse or are unable to receive information about their condition. Information should be accurate, truthful and presented in such as way as to make it easily understood. You may need to seek legal or professional advice or guidance from your employer, in relation to the giving or withholding of consent . . .
3.3 When obtaining valid consent, you must be sure that it is:

 – given by a legally competent person
 – given voluntarily
 – informed.

3.4 You should presume that every patient and client is legally competent unless otherwise assessed by a suitably qualified practitioner. A patient or client who is legally competent can understand and retain treatment information and can use it to make an informed choice.
3.5 Those who are legally competent may give consent in writing, orally or by co-operation. They may also refuse consent. You must ensure that all your discussions and associated decisions relating to obtaining consent are documented in the patient's or client's health care records . . .
3.10 Usually the individual performing a procedure should be the person to obtain the patient's or client's consent. In certain circumstances, you may seek consent on behalf of colleagues if you have been specially trained for that specific area of practice.

NOTE:

1. Aveyard has argued that in the nursing literature attention has focused almost exclusively on the nurse's role in facilitating consent prior to treatment or enrolment in research, and that there has been inadequate discussion of the application of principles of informed consent prior to nursing care. Her research into how nurses obtained consent demonstrated that the principles were not always translated into practice. She found that

nurses sometimes applied unacceptable pressure to "persuade" the patient to consent to treatment which she deemed to be in the patient's best interests. (H. Aveyard, "The Patient who Refuses Nursing Care" (2004) 30 *Journal of Medical Ethics* 346–350.)

QUESTIONS:

1. Critically assess this guidance. Does it accord strictly with the legal position? What changes, if any, would you make to it?
2. If a patient is diagnosed as suffering from terminal cancer, and the doctor exercises her therapeutic privilege not to disclose this diagnosis to the patient, does the nurse have a duty to tell the truth if the patient asks her directly? (See J. McHale, "Consent and the Adult Patient: The Legal Perspective" in J. Tingle and A. Cribb (eds), *Nursing Law and Ethics* (3rd edn), Oxford: Blackwell, 2006.)

4. VITIATION OF CONSENT

Even if the patient has full capacity, and has been given adequate information on which to make a choice, this is not the end of the matter. In determining whether the consent was truly voluntary, a number of other factors which may vitiate consent must be taken into account. In some circumstances, an apparently valid consent to or refusal of treatment may be vitiated by the circumstances in which it was given. This might occur where it is obtained fraudulently (see *Chatterton v Gerson* discussed at pp.361–365 above), by force (*Freeman v Home Office* below), or otherwise as a result of undue influence (*Re T*, below). In these very rare circumstances, it may appear that the patient has consented but policy reasons exist for invalidating that apparent consent.

Theoretically it would seem that there should be no difference in the legal analysis of consent and of refusal to consent to health care treatment. In practice, however, the consequences of withholding consent to treatment are usually much more significant and potentially dangerous than simply giving consent; thus it can be argued that refusing to give consent is a higher order of decision-making than merely giving consent. (See J. Pearce, "Consent to Treatment during Childhood: the Assessment of Competence and Avoidance of Conflict" (1994) 165 *British Journal of Psychiatry* 713.) As we shall see in Chapter 7, the different consequences of consenting to and refusing treatment may mean that this is not the case as far as young people are concerned. Even if a young person refuses his consent to treatment, those with parental responsibility or the court may be able to consent. By contrast, if an adult patient refuses his consent to treatment, no one else is in a position to give a proxy consent (*F v West Berkshire Health Authority* [1989] 2 All E.R. 545, unless the Mental Capacity Act 2005 applies). This may pose problems in the situation where the patient is deemed to be competent but makes a decision which most people would judge irrational. (See, for example, the case of *Re C* [1994] All E.R. 819, and the cases on forced caesarean discussed in Chapter 13 at p.954). In these circumstances it has been suggested that judges too readily find excuses to justify vitiating the patient's refusal on the grounds that it is irrational (see M. Brazier, "Patient Autonomy and Consent to Treatment: the Role of Law" (1987) 7 *Legal Studies* 169; C. Faulder, *Whose Body Is It? The Troubling Issue of Informed Consent*, London: Virago, 1985, Chapter 3). Arguably this is what happened in *Re T* (see p.400 below), where the Court of Appeal stressed the importance of patient autonomy, which extended to the right to refuse life-saving treatment, only to find reasons to undercut that autonomy when it conflicted with the views of the doctors and posed a threat to her life. Reasons given for overriding a purported refusal of consent by a competent patient may relate to the public policy factors identified at p.397 above.

One circumstance in which an apparently valid decision may not be effective in law is where, in reality, the consent of the patient was given only because he was under improper pressure to accept or refuse treatment. This possibility has been considered in the following cases:

Freeman v Home Office [1984] 1 All E.R. 1036, [1984] 2 W.L.R. 802

Mr Freeman was a life prisoner. He was given drugs to alleviate a psychiatric condition. He claimed that those drugs had been forcibly administered against his consent. However, the judge found that he had in fact consented. Mr Freeman further contended that he had not given a real consent because the prison officers administering the drug had disciplinary authority over him and, consequently, he could not make a free choice.

SIR JOHN DONALSON M.R.
" . . . Counsel appearing for the plaintiff has sought to argue that (a) his client never in fact consented to being injected (factual absence of consent), (b) his client, being a prisoner serving a life sentence, could not as a matter of law consent to such treatment (legal inability to consent), and (c) even if he could consent in fact and in law, such a consent was no defence to a claim for damages for trespass to the person unless, before he consented, he had been told (i) what he was suffering from, (ii) what was the precise nature of the treatment prescribed, and (iii) what, if any, were the side effects and risks involved in that treatment (uninformed consent). It may be convenient to deal with these contentions in reverse order.

Uninformed consent

If there was real consent to the treatment, it mattered not whether the doctor was in breach of his duty to give the patient the appropriate information before that consent was given. Real consent provides a complete defence to a claim based on the tort of trespass to the person. Consent would not be real if procured by fraud or misrepresentation but, subject to this and subject to the patient having been informed in broad terms of the nature of the treatment, consent in fact amounts to consent in law . . .

Legal inability to consent

Counsel for the plaintiff submitted that such were the pressures of prison life and discipline that a prisoner could not, as a matter of law, give an effective consent to treatment in any circumstances. This is a somewhat surprising proposition since it would mean that, in the absence of statutory authority, no prison medical officer could ever treat a prisoner. The answer of counsel for the plaintiff was in part that outside medical officers could be brought in, but I am not persuaded that this would reduce the pressures, whatever they may be. In support of this proposition, we were referred to the judgment of Scott L.J. in *Bowater v. Rowley Regis BC* [1944] 1 All E.R. 465. Scott L.J. there said:

'In regard to the doctrine *volenti non fit injuria*, I would add one reflection of a general kind. That general maxim has to be applied with especially careful regard to the varying facts of human affairs and human nature in any particular case, just because it is concerned with the intangible factors of mind and will. For the purpose of the rule, if it be a rule, a man cannot be said to be truly "willing", unless he is in a position to choose freely and freedom of choice predicates, not only full knowledge of the circumstances upon which the exercise of choice is conditioned, in order that he may be able to choose wisely, but the absence from his mind of any feeling of constraint, in order that nothing shall interfere with the freedom of his will.'

The maxim *volenti non fit injuria* can be roughly translated as 'You cannot claim damages if you have asked for it', and 'it' is something which is and remains a tort. The maxim, where it applies, provides a bar to enforcing a cause of action. It does not negative the cause of action itself. This is a wholly different concept from consent which, in this context, deprives the act of its tortious character. *Volenti* would be a defence in the unlikely scenario of a patient being held not to have in fact consented to treatment, but having by his conduct caused the doctor to believe that he had consented.

The judge expressed his view on this aspect of the argument by saying ([1983] 3 All E.R. 589 at 597) 'The right approach, in my judgment, is to say that where, in a prison setting, a doctor has the power to influence a prisoner's situation and prospects a court must be alive to the risk that what may appear, on the face of it, to be a real consent is not in fact so.'

I would accept that as a wholly accurate statement of the law. The judge said that he had borne this in mind throughout the case. The sole question is therefore whether, on the evidence, there was a real consent.

Factual absence of consent

The case of counsel for the plaintiff was that he was forcibly restrained from resisting the administration of the injections by no less than four or five prison officers. It was *not* that, due to the constraints of prison life and discipline, his will to refuse the injections was overborne and what appeared to be consent was in reality merely submission. The judge rejected this allegation of forcible restraint. He saw and heard the plaintiff give evidence at length and concluded that if he had not been consenting, it would have been necessary for him physically to be held down and injected by superior force. He had no doubt that this did not happen and he therefore concluded that the plaintiff consented.

There was ample evidence to support this conclusion, the plaintiff having on at least two occasions refused to accept treatment."

QUESTIONS:

1. Can you imagine any circumstances when, following this decision, an apparently valid consent would be vitiated because the patient had no real choice? (See M. Brazier, "Prison Doctors and their Involuntary Patients" [1982] *Public Law* 282.)
2. Does the rule that consent must be freely given, not forcibly extracted, prevent a delirious patient being restrained while being given a sedative? Would such a patient be legally competent?

Re T [1992] 4 All E.R. 649, [1992] 3 W.L.R. 782, [1992] 2 F.L.R. 458

The facts of this case were discussed in the preceding chapter at pp.310–313. In summary, T was rushed to hospital following a car accident and, having talked with her mother who was a devout Jehovah's Witness, indicated for the first time that she did not wish to have a blood transfusion.

SIR JOHN DONALDSON M.R.

" . . . A special problem may arise if at the time the decision is made the patient has been subjected to the influence of some third party. This is by no means to say that the patient is not entitled to receive and indeed invite advice and assistance from others in reaching a decision, particularly from members of the family. But the doctors have to consider whether the decision is really that of the patient. It is wholly acceptable that the patient should have been persuaded by others of the merits of such a decision and have decided accordingly. It matters not how strong the persuasion was, so long as it did not overbear the independence of the patient's decision. The real question in each such case is 'Does the patient really mean what he says or is he merely saying it for a quiet life, to satisfy someone else or because the advice and persuasion to which he has been subjected is such that he can no longer think and decide for himself?' In other words 'Is it a decision expressed in form only, not in reality?'

When considering the effect of outside influences, two aspects can be of crucial importance. First, the strength of the will of the patient. One who is very tired, in pain or depressed will be much less able to resist having his will overborne than one who is rested, free from pain and cheerful. Second, the relationship of the 'persuader' to the patient may be of crucial importance. The influence of parents on their children or of one spouse on the other can be, but is by no means necessarily, much stronger than would be the case in other relationships. Persuasion based upon religious belief can also be much more compelling and the fact that arguments based upon religious beliefs are being deployed by someone in a very close relationship with the patient will give them added force and should alert the doctors to the possibility—no more—that the patient's capacity or will to decide has been overborne. In other words the patient may not mean what he says."

STAUGHTON L.J.

" . . . The first reason [why a consent may be inoperative] is that the apparent consent or refusal was given as a result of undue influence. It is, I think, misleading to ask whether it was made of the patient's own free will, or even whether it was voluntary. Every decision is made of a person's free will, and is voluntary, unless it is effected by compulsion. Likewise, every decision is made as a result of some influence: a patient's decision to consent to an operation will normally be influenced by the surgeon's advice as to what will happen if the operation does not take place. In order for an apparent consent or refusal of consent to be less than a true consent or refusal, there must be such a degree of external influence as to persuade the patient to depart from her own wishes, to an extent that the law regards it as undue. I can suggest no more precise test than that."

NOTE:

1. Butler-Sloss L.J. expressed her agreement with the test for undue influence propounded by Staughton L.J.

QUESTIONS:

1. How can health professionals distinguish the situation where a patient has taken his own decision (having sought the advice of friends and relatives)

from that where his ability to make a choice has been vitiated by undue influence?

2. Do you think that courts too readily categorise a refusal of consent as being not truly voluntary when it diverges from the views of the health professionals treating the patient, and thus appears to them irrational? (See M. Brazier, "Patient Autonomy and Consent to Treatment: the Role of Law" (1987) 7 *Legal Studies* 169; H. Teff, "Consent to Medical Procedures: Paternalism, Self-Determination or Therapeutic Alliance" (1985) 101 *Law Quarterly Review* 432.)

T was distinguished in the following case:

Mrs U v Centre for Reproductive Medicine [2002] EWCA Civ 565

The facts are discussed in Chapter 11 at p.767 but essentially concerned a husband's decision to withdraw his consent to the posthumous use of his stored sperm when a nursing sister at a fertility clinic informed him of the clinic's objection to posthumous use.

HALE L.J.

" . . . [19] The only relevant authority quoted to the President was *Re T (Adult: Refusal of Treatment)* . . . in which it was held that the giving of blood to a pregnant young woman whose life was in danger was justified by the doctrine of necessity as her refusal of consent was not such as to bind the doctors to refuse her treatment. After quoting from the judgments of Lord Donaldson MR and Staughton LJ (but not her own) the President reached her conclusion in this case (Judgment, para 28):

'28. When one stands back and looks at the facts of this case, it seems to me that it is difficult to say that an able, intelligent, educated man of 47, with a responsible job and in good health, could have his will overborne so that the act of altering the form and initialling the alterations was done in circumstances in which Mr U no longer thought and decided for himself. I have no doubt that Mr U did not want a pause in the treatment and did want to go along with the Centre. He did not have the opportunity for consultation with his wife, although he could have asked for it. As Mr Jenkins said, it is likely that he and his wife did not really think that there was any likelihood that this part of the form would ever be necessary. He succumbed to the firmly expressed request of Ms Hinks and under some pressure. But to prove undue influence, Mr U has to show something more than pressure. As Lord Donaldson said in *Re T*, it does not matter how strong the persuasion was so long as it did not overbear the independence of the patient's decision. The case of Miss T. showed the sort of pressure in an emergency which might amount to undue influence. This case is far removed from the case of Miss T. Can it be said that Mr U made the alterations under compulsion? Once one asks the question in this case, the answer has to be no.' . . .

[25] In this context, none of the case law on undue influence in other contexts is particularly helpful . . . Nor, as Mr Moon on behalf of the Centre points out, is it like deciding upon the lawfulness of medical treatment. There are other justifications for performing life-saving medical treatment apart from the possession of an effective consent. There is no other justification for continuing to store human sperm.

[26] Hence a Centre having in their possession a form dealing with the matters with which it is required by Sch 3 to the 1990 Act to deal should be both entitled and expected to rely upon that form according to its letter, unless and until it can clearly be established that the form does not represent a valid decision by the person apparently signing it. The

most obvious examples are forgery, duress or mistake as to the nature of the form being signed (*non est factum*). The equitable concepts of misrepresentation and undue influence may have a part to play but the courts should be slow to find them established in such a way as to supply a centre with a consent which they would not otherwise have.

[27] We do not therefore accept that the President applied too strict a test. Nor do we accept that she should have applied the test differently to the facts of this case. It has frequently been said that undue influence is more easily recognised than defined. The President was much better placed than this court could ever be to decide whether the decision to change the form was valid at the time that it was made. She had the benefit of hearing from two of the three people present. Her judgement of those two people is crucial."

QUESTION:

1. Given the President's finding that the nursing sister in this case was "formidable" and that the issue of posthumous use of sperm was raised only at a very late stage in the proceedings, at which point Mrs U testified that her husband feared it might delay treatment, do you think that Mr U's decision to withdraw his consent was voluntary? Does it take adequate account of power disparities between health professionals and patients? (See S. Pattinson, "Undue Influence in the Context of Medical Treatment" (2002) 5 *Medical Law International* 305–317.)

SELECT BIBLIOGRAPHY

M. Brazier, "Patient Autonomy and Consent to Treatment: the Role of Law" (1987) 7 *Legal Studies* 169.

C. Faulder, *Whose Body Is It? The Troubling Issue of Informed Consent*, London: Virago, 1985.

P. Foster, "Informed Consent in Practice" in S. Sheldon and M. Thomson (eds), *Feminist Perspectives on Health Care Law*, London: Cavendish, 1998.

A. Grubb, "Consent to Treatment: the Competent Patient" in A. Grubb (ed.) *Principles of Medical Law* (2nd edn), Oxford: OUP, 2004, 131–203.

J. Harrington, "Privileging the Medical Norm: Liberalism, Self-determination and Refusal of Treatment" (1996) 16 *Legal Studies* 348.

E. Jackson, " Informed Consent to Medical Treatment and the Impotence of Tort" in S.A.M. McLean (ed.), *First Do No Harm* (Aldershot: Ashgate, 2006).

M. Jones, "Informed Consent and Fairy Stories" (1999) 7 *Medical Law Review* 103–134.

I. Kennedy, "Consent to Treatment: the Capable Person" in C. Dyer (ed.), *Doctors, Patients and the Law*, Oxford: Blackwell, 1992.

I. Kennedy, "The Patient on the Clapham Omnibus" in *Treat Me Right: Law and Medical Ethics*, Oxford: Oxford University Press, 1991.

S. Lee, "Towards a Jurisprudence of Consent" in J. Bell and J. Eekelaar (eds) *Oxford Essays in Jurisprudence* (3rd series), Oxford: OUP 1987.

A.R. Maclean, "The Doctrine of Informed Consent: Does it Exist and has it Crossed the Atlantic?" (2004) 24 *Legal Studies* 386.

S.A. McLean, *A Patient's Right to Know: Information Disclosure, the Doctor and the Law*, Aldershot: Dartmouth, 1989.

J. Montgomery, "Power/Knowledge/Consent: Medical Decisionmaking" (1988) 51 *Modern Law Review* 245.

S. Pattinson, "Undue Influence in the Context of Medical Treatment" (2002) 5 *Medical Law International* 305–317.

G. Robertson, "Informed Consent to Medical Treatment" (1981) 97 *Law Quarterly Review* 102.

M.M. Shultz, "From Informed Consent to Patient Choice: a New Protected Interest" (1985) 92 *Yale Law Journal* 219.

P.D.G. Skegg, *Law, Ethics and Medicine*, Oxford: OUP, 1984 (revised 1988), Pt II.

H. Teff, "Consent to Medical Treatment: Paternalism, Self-determination or Therapeutic Alliance" (1985) 101 *Law Quarterly Review* 432.

C. Wells, "Patients, Consent and Criminal Law" [1994] *Journal of Social Welfare Law* 65.

7

CHILDREN

1. INTRODUCTION

In the previous two chapters we have examined the rights of adults to autonomy and self-determination, their competence to consent to or refuse medical treatment and what should happen in the case of the incapacitated adult. Particularly complex issues concerning capacity for medical decision-making arise in the case of children and adolescents. This issue must be viewed in the context of growing recognition that children have rights. Much of the impetus for a now extensive literature on children's rights derived from the leading case of *Gillick v West Norfolk and Wisbech Area Health Authority and Another* [1985] 3 All E.R. 402, which endorsed the rights of the "mature minor" or "Gillick-competent" child to consent to her own medical treatment, the Cleveland Inquiry into Child Sexual Abuse (Report of the Inquiry into Child Abuse in Cleveland 1987, Cm. 412 (1988)) and the passage of the Children Act 1989 which reflected the changing structure of the family and the philosophy of children's rights. (See, generally, J. Eekelaar, "The Emergence of Children's Rights" (1986) 6 *Oxford Journal of Legal Studies* 161; M. Freeman, "Taking Children's Rights More Seriously" (1992) 6 *International Journal of Law and the Family* 52.) As Jo Bridgeman and Daniel Monk have noted:

"[O]ver the past decade child law has become a discrete category of legal practice and academic study... This development can be understood as a simple process of consolidation of issues relating to children across a number of more established legal categories and... as a reflection of increased specialisation and juridification... [as well] as a reflection of children's rights" (J. Bridgeman and D. Monk, "Introduction" in Bridgeman and Monk (eds) *Feminist Perspectives on Child Law*, London: Cavendish, 2000, at p. 1).

In similar vein, Andrew Bainham suggests that:

"[I]f we were to identify the one feature which best characterises late twentieth century development in the law relating to children, it might well be the shift away from law's almost exclusive concentration on the protection of the individual child to the recognition of the interests, indeed rights, of children as a class or group." (A. Bainham, "Children Law at the Millennium" in S. Cretney (ed.), *Family Law: Essays of the New Millennium*, London: Family Law, 2000 at p. 113.

This ascription of rights to children is important if children are to be treated with equality and as autonomous beings. In 1989 the United Nations framed the International Convention on the Rights of the Child. It advocates the right of every child to self-determination, dignity, respect, non-interference and the right to make informed decisions (see J. Fortin, *Children's Rights and the Developing Law*, Cambridge: CUP, 2003). More specifically, the European Charter for Children in Hospital states that "children and parents have the right to informed participation in all decisions involving their health care. Every child shall be protected from unnecessary medical treatment and investigation" (see P. Alderson, "European Charter of Children's Rights" [1993] *Bulletin of Medical Ethics* 13.) It has been argued that United Kingdom law falls far short of the ideal such Conventions set out. Because children have lacked the moral coinage of rights it has been easy to brush their interests aside in a sweep of consequentialist thinking. As Freeman remarks, in an ideal world children may not need rights, but it is not an ideal world and certainly not for children (see Freeman, *op. cit.*). Nevertheless, the discourse of rights is particularly contentious when it is claimed by or on behalf of children, who historically have been viewed as lacking legal rights. Thus, O'Donovan has argued that the standard legal (rights-bearing) subject is constructed as rational and reasonable and that these are not qualities which law ascribes to children. She suggests that law's "ways of talking about children are paternalistic and predictive: the child's welfare is central to decisions . . . [b]ehind the word 'welfare' lies a claim to knowledge of what is in the child's interests." (See K. O'Donovan, "The Child as Legal Object" in *Family Law Matters*, London: Pluto, 1993, at p.90.) In O'Donovan's view, children constitute a site for struggle between the parents, or between parents and various professional groups, including health care professionals. This is certainly one interpretation of the House of Lords decision in *Gillick*. While the standard reading of the case was to hail it as a vindication of children's autonomy and judicial endorsement of children's rights, as O'Donovan argues, the "doctrine of the 'mature minor' enunciated in the *Gillick* case leaves scope for the assertion of autonomy, . . . [but] it is for adults with parental responsibility initially, and ultimately for the courts, to determine the child's welfare; this decision does not belong to the child" (*op. cit.* at pp.95–96). O'Neill meanwhile has contended that it is more appropriate to talk in terms of parental obligations than of children's rights (see O. O'Neill, "Children's Rights and Children's Lives" (1981) 98 *Ethics* 445).

Given the dominance of autonomy-based reasoning in health care law, the major issue is whether children are really able to exercise a right to autonomy. As was recognised by the majority in *Gillick*, the answer to this question is dependent on the maturity of the individual child—it is impossible to set an age limit at which all children suddenly become capable of autonomous decision-making. If children are accorded rights, this entails being allowed to take risks and make choices. However, as we have seen in relation to case law on the capacity of adults in Chapter 5, the law may circumscribe those rights by questioning competence where a decision appears irrational, especially if persisting in it will result in death. Understandably, law is even more reluctant to countenance risky choices taken by minors. Thus, much of the case law justifies paternalistic decisions by determining that the young person lacks capacity, especially if he is refusing medical treatment. In the reported cases subsequent to *Gillick*, the rhetoric of autonomy has therefore been downplayed. Moreover, the judges have been reluctant to lay down clear guidance as to when a young person is to be deemed sufficiently mature to make his own health care decisions. The issue of what exactly a child must understand in order to be able to exercise choice is not explicitly addressed. As we saw in the case of adults who lack capacity, the question of whether medical treatment can lawfully be administered has been resolved by recourse to the doctrine of necessity. By contrast, in the case of children the law has allowed those with parental responsibility to supply the requisite consent. If no one has parental authority, the court can exercise such power under the Children Act, wardship or its inherent jurisdiction. However, this leaves open the crucial question of how the best interests of the child are to be determined, particularly where the parents wish to make risky choices in relation to their children, or include them in research (see Chapter 10 at pp.688–692).

We begin, however, in Section 2 by considering the position of the younger child who is clearly not in a position to make decisions. Case law pertaining to this issue has arisen out of disputes where parents and health professionals disagree over what is in the best interests of the child, rather than because of any conflict between the child and a third party. In this section we are concerned with disputes over withdrawing or withholding life-saving treatment. In Section 3 we address the older child's capacity to consent to medical treatment, both under statute and at common law, considering the impact of the *Gillick* decision. Section 4 examines the subsequent judicial retreat from the *Gillick* ruling and attempts to circumscribe adolescent autonomy. We conclude in Section 5 by addressing the limits law imposes on the parental power to consent.

2. THE LEGAL POSITION OF THE YOUNG CHILD

It simply is not meaningful to talk of very young children exercising rights to autonomy or self-determination. Brazier has in the past suggested that it could be said with reasonable certainty that a child under 12 years of age has virtually never achieved sufficient maturity to be entrusted with the power to make her own decisions about medical treatment, and that it would be rare for a 12 to 14-year-old to possess the requisite capacity. Hence the grey area revolves largely around the 14 plus age group who are the focus of most of the case law. (See M. Brazier, *Medicine, Patents and the Law* (2nd edn), London: Penguin, 1993, at p.341.) Nevertheless, it is important to remember that there are many different levels of decisions to be made, and thus the requisite capacity will vary. For example, even a very young child may be competent to consent to bandages being applied to a wound, whereas a higher threshold of capacity would be required before he could validly consent to an organ transplant. Moreover, one study found that relevant experience of illness, treatment or disability was a far more salient factor than age for acquiring competence. (See L. Hammond *et al.*, *Children's Decisions in Health Care and Research*, London: Institute of Education, 1993.) This suggests that the crucial factor in assessing competence, as with the incapacitated adult (see Chapter 5) may be the way in which children are informed about their condition and treatments for it and supported in their decision-making. (See P. Alderson and J. Montgomery, "What about Me?" *Health Services Journal*, April 11, 1996 at p.22; P. Alderson, *Young Children's Rights*, London: Jessica Kingsley, 2000.) However, where the child clearly lacks the competence to make choices about his health care, the position is less complex than it has been with adults prior to the coming into force of the Mental Capacity Act 2005, because the parents are in the position to act as proxy decision-makers. Thus, in the straightforward case of a sick child with caring parents, parental consent to treatment which is in the best interests of the child authorises the doctor to proceed without any risk of a trespass action.

However, the courts have, in the past 25 years, been confronted with several particularly intractable cases where parents and doctors have disagreed about treatment decisions. In practice, problems tend to arise in the case of young children, who are clearly too young to consent, where the parents refuse to consent to treatment which the health professionals deem to be in the best interests of the child or where the parents disagree about treatment. More recently, there have also been a significant number of cases where parents have sought to compel doctors to treat, after health professionals have formed the view that treatment is not in the best interests of a child who is too young to consent. As Brazier has noted, such conflicts tend to revolve not around *whether* a child should live or die, but *how* and *when* they should die (M. Brazier, "An Intractable Dispute: When Parents and Professionals Disagree" (2005) 13 *Medical Law Review* 412 at p.413.) In some cases the parents seek to rely on their religious beliefs as the basis for their disagreement with health professionals, raising the issue of whether a religious basis for parental opposition to the views of doctors should be accorded more weight in law than other reasons for parental disagreement.

Of course the most disturbing cases are those where the disagreement concerns potentially life-saving treatment. As Margaret Somerville has observed, there are few more difficult issues in health care law (M. Somerville, *The Ethical Canary: Science, Society and the Human Spirit*, Toronto: Penguin, 2000 at p.177).

(a) The Court's Role in Approving the Withdrawal or Withholding of Medical Treatment in the Case of Neonates and Young Children

The first cases which came before the courts in relation to non-treatment concerned disabled infants. (The subsequent cases relating to adults are discussed in Chapter 14). Where a seriously disabled child is born, some commentators have taken the view that it is better not to pursue aggressive treatment, particularly where life expectancy is short. In the past this perspective was reflected in medical practice in certain hospitals such as in Sheffield in the 1970s under the paediatrician John Lorber, for example. However the legality of withdrawing treatment from a disabled neonate did not reach the courts until the 1980s. The decision whether to continue treatment of a neonate may be brought before the court by use of the inherent jurisdiction or by one of the orders available under the Children Act 1989. In each of the following cases the local authority or NHS trust sought a declaration about the lawfulness of discontinuing treatment in circumstances where the parents either wanted to discontinue treatment or were not in a position to express a view.

Re B [1990] 3 All E.R. 927; [1981] 1 W.L.R. 1421

B was a baby girl born suffering from Down's syndrome and with an intestinal blockage which would be fatal unless operated on. Her parents took the view that it would be better for her not to have the operation and to die within a few days. In the interval before her death she could be kept from pain and suffering by sedation. The doctors informed the local authority of the parents' decision and applied for the child to be made a ward of court. The court authorised the operation, but the child was then moved to another hospital where differences of medical opinion developed. The surgeon who was to carry out the operation declined to operate against the wishes of the parents. On an expedited hearing, the case came before a two-judge Court of Appeal.

TEMPLEMAN L.J.
" . . . The question which this court has to determine is whether it is in the interests of this child to be allowed to die within the next week or to have the operation in which case if she lives she will be a mongoloid child, but no one can say to what extent her mental or physical defects will be apparent. No one can say whether she will suffer or whether she will be happy in part. On the one hand the probability is that she will not be a 'cabbage' as it is called when people's faculties are entirely destroyed. On the other hand it is certain that she will be very severely mentally and physically handicapped.

On behalf of the parents counsel for the parents has submitted very movingly, if I may say so, that this is a case where nature has made its own arrangements to terminate a life which would not be fruitful and nature should not be interfered with. He has also submitted that in this kind of decision the views of responsible and caring parents, as these are, should be respected and that their decision that it is better for the child to be allowed to die should be respected. Fortunately or unfortunately, in this particular case the decision no longer lies with the parents or with the doctors, but lies with the court. It is a decision which of course must be made in the light of the evidence and views expressed by the parents and the doctors, but at the end of the day it devolves on this court in this particular instance to decide whether the life of this child is demonstrably to be so awful that in effect the child must be condemned to die, or whether the life of this child is still so imponderable that it would be wrong for her to be condemned to die. There may be cases, I know not, of severe proved damage where the future is so certain and where the life of the child is so bound to be full of pain and suffering that the court might be driven to a different conclusion, but in the present case the choice which lies before the court is this: whether to allow an operation to take place which may result in the child living for 20 or 30 years as a mongoloid or whether (and I think this must be brutally the result) to terminate the life of a mongoloid child because she also has an intestinal complaint. Faced with that choice I have no doubt that it is the duty of this court to decide that the child must live.

The judge was much affected by the reasons given by the parents and came to the conclusion that their wishes ought to be respected. In my judgment he erred in that the duty of the court is to decide whether it is in the interests of the child that an operation should take place. The evidence in this case only goes to show that if the operation takes place and is successful then the child may live the normal span of a mongoloid child with the handicaps and defects and life of a mongoloid child, and it is not for this court to say that life of that description ought to be extinguished."

NOTES:

1. Dunn L.J. agreed, but used the phrase "intolerable" rather than "demonstrably awful")
2. The trial of Dr Arthur (discussed in Chapter 14 at pp.1016–1017) took place just after this case. As Mason and Laurie note, *Re B* and *Arthur's* case are virtually impossible to reconcile, yet *Re B* was not referred to in the criminal trial. (See J.K. Mason and G. Laurie, *Mason and McCall Smith's Law and Medical Ethics* (7th edn), London: Butterworths, 2006 at p.549).
3. Jo Bridgeman points out that both *Re B* and *Arthur's* case demonstrate the historically and socially specific nature of disability. Current medical and social understandings of Down's syndrome as a chromosomal disorder causing physical abnormalities and learning difficulties which cannot be determined at birth would not now support the conclusion that consent should be withheld for ordinary treatment or "nursing care only" provided. (See J. Bridgeman, "Caring for Children with Severe Disabilities: Boundaries and Relational Rights" (2005) 13 *International Journal of Children's Rights* 99–109 at p.101.)

QUESTIONS:

1. What is the exact *ratio* of this case?
2. Does an assessment of whether the child's life is "intolerable" or "demonstrably awful" provide a workable test for health professionals or judges?
3. How significant is the life expectancy in this case?
4. Would this case be decided the same way today, in view of the fact that the Abortion Act 1967 (as amended), now sanctions termination on the basis of serious foetal handicap up until birth. (See Chapter 12 below at pp.878–886; see also Nuffield Council on Bioethics, *Critical Care Decisions in Fetal and Neonatal Medicine: Ethical Issues*, Public Consultation Document, 2005.)
5. In the *Bland* case Lord Goff talked in terms of "futility" of treatment as a basis for the withdrawal of treatment (see Chapter 14 at pp.1021–1058) Is "futility" a preferable test to that of a "demonstrably awful" or "intolerable" life as proposed by the judges in this case? (See M.B. Zucker and H.D. Zucker (eds), *Medical Futility*, Cambridge: CUP, 1997.)

Re C [1989] 2 All E.R. 782

Baby C was made a ward of court when it was found that her parents would have great difficulty in caring for her. She was born prematurely with severe hydro-cephalus. She was described as having massive "handicaps" as a result of a permanent brain lesion. Her disabilities were apparently a mixture of severe mental disability, blindness, probable deafness and spastic cerebral palsy of all four limbs. She was thin and did not gain weight. Without constant doses of the sedative chloral she cried as if in pain. The medical experts agreed that there was no prospect of improvement. The judge at first instance had referred to *Re B* (above) but stressed the significantly different facts, in particular the fact that C—who at that stage was 16 weeks old—was dying. He therefore, con-troversially, made an order to the effect that:

"Putting the interests of this child first and putting them foremost so that they override all else, and in fulfilment of the awesome responsibility which Parliament has entrusted upon me, I direct that leave be given to the hospital authorities to treat the ward to die; to die with the greatest dignity and the least of pain, suffering and distress."

He later revised this to read:

"I direct that leave be given to the hospital authorities to treat the ward in such a way that she may end her life and die peacefully with the greatest dignity and the least of pain, suffering and distress."

The local authority appealed.

LORD DONALDSON OF LYMINGTON M.R.
" . . . All concerned accept that the judge correctly directed himself that the first and paramount consideration was the well-being, welfare and interests of C as required by the decision of this court in *Re B (a minor) (wardship: medical treatment)* and by the House of Lords in a later and different case with the same name *Re B (a minor) (wardship: sterilisation)* [1987] 2 All E.R. 206 at 211, per Lord Hailsham L.C. [see Chapter 13 at p.928] . . .

The Official Solicitor in bringing this appeal had three objectives. The first was to question the propriety of an order expressed to be 'liberty to treat the minor to die'. As I hope I have made clear, neither Ward J. nor anyone else would uphold such phraseology and he has himself amended it. Secondly, the Official Solicitor wished to question that part of the order of the judge which appeared to provide that in no circumstances should certain treatment be undertaken. To that I will return in a moment. Third, the Official Solicitor wished to allay anxieties in some quarters that the hospital staff were treating C in a way designed to bring about her death. These anxieties, whilst no doubt sincerely felt, were wholly without foundation and, when expressed, were deeply wounding to the dedicated staff caring for C who, as the professor said, were providing C with devoted care which could not be replicated in many children's units.

Let me make it clear that, in my judgment, the Official Solicitor has been quite right to adopt this course. His first objective was achieved by the judge himself, but the Official Solicitor was not to know that this would occur. His third objective has, I hope, now been achieved. There remains only the second objective.

In para. (4) of his order the judge ordered that:

'The hospital authority do continue to treat the minor within the parameters of the opinion expressed by [the professor] in his report of 13.iv.1989 which report is not to be disclosed to any person other than the hospital authority.'

However, in para. (3) he had ordered:

' . . . but it shall not be necessary either, (a) to prescribe and administer antibiotics to treat any serious infection which the minor might contract; or (b) to set up intravenous fusions or nasal gastric feeding regimes for the minor.'

These two parts of the order are inconsistent with one another because the professor did not wholly rule out these steps if the local nurses and carers took a different view when the question arose for decision. He merely said that he did not think that such measures were correct if the object was simply to prolong a life which had no future and appeared to be unhappy for C. I have no doubt that he would have considered revising his opinion, and indeed would have revised it, if the local nurses and carers had thought that such treatment would relieve C's suffering during such life as remained for her.

The second difficulty which arises out of this part of the order is the ban on any publication of the professor's advice. This was one of those comparatively rare cases of special difficulty and sensitivity in which the public interest requires that, subject to maintaining the privacy of those concerned, the courts decision and the reasons for it shall be open to public scrutiny. The formal order itself will not be likely to be very informative, and in any event it would require considerable editing to remove any clues as to the identity of those concerned. What is required in such cases is that the judge should give judgment in open court, taking all appropriate measures to preserve the personal privacy of those concerned. However, such a judgment can set out all the relevant facts and the medical and other considerations of which the judge has taken into account. Thus, in this judgment I have quoted extensively from the professor's advice without I hope, giving any clue as to his identity or that of C, her parents or the authority involved.

No new principle is involved in this appeal. I would allow the appeal to the extent of deleting the whole of paragraph (3) of the judge's order. I do so for two reasons. First, the inclusion of specific instructions as to treatment is potentially inconsistent with paragraph (4) which adopts the professor's advice. Second, paragraph (3) of the order as amended starts with these words:

'The hospital authority be at liberty to treat the minor to allow her life to come to an end peacefully and with dignity and, act pursuant to such leave, it is directed that the hospital authority shall administer such treatment to the minor as might relieve her from pain, suffering and distress inter alia by sedation.'

Now, the specific references to treatment are, of course amply covered by the professor's advice. But the opening words seem to me to have a potential for giving rise to misunderstanding and are, therefore, much better avoided and now deleted. To that extent I would allow the appeal."

Notes:

1. Balcombe and Nicholls L.JJ. agreed with Lord Donaldson M.R.
2. In *Re C* the Court of Appeal made explicit reference to the fact that the decision to withdraw active treatment if necessary had the support of the medical staff, nurses and other carers. This is an important recognition of how health care decisions are made in "teams" composed of a wide variety of personnel, including persons other than medical practitioners. However, should such a decision be left to the treatment team? (Bridgeman, while

applauding the involvement of other carers on the the healthcare team in this case, also suggests that parents should be involved where possible. In this particular case, the father accepted medical advice, while the mother could not cope "with the present dilemma" (J. Bridgeman, "Caring for Children with Severe Disabilities: Boundaries and Relational Rights" (2005) 13 *International Journal of Children's Rights* 99–109 at pp.114–115.) An alternative would be for such decisions to be referred to an institutional ethics committee. (See R. Weir, *Selective Non-Treatment of Severely Damaged Neonates*, Oxford: OUP, 1988) Contrast this with the judgment of Lord Mustill in *Bland*—see Chapter 14 at pp.1021–1032.)

QUESTIONS:

1. On the facts of *Re C*, how useful was *Re B* as a precedent? What are the relevant differences between the cases?
2. What amounts to treatment in the best interests of the child? Is the test subjective or objective? (See C. Wells *et al.*, "An unsuitable case for treatment" [1990] *New L.J.* 1544.)

The following case was to become the leading case on withholding treatment from disabled neonates:

Re J [1990] 3 All E.R. 930; [1991] Fam. 33 (subsequently referred to as *Re J* [1990]

J was born nearly 13 weeks premature, weighing only 1.1kg. He was not breathing, and was immediately placed on a ventilator to assist survival. He was drip fed, and given antibiotics to counteract infection. At four weeks J was removed from the ventilator. However, on several occasions relapses occurred and further use of the ventilator was necessary. The medical evidence showed that J was very severely brain damaged, apparently blind and probably deaf. It was likely that he would be paralysed in all his limbs. However, the evidence suggested that, while he would be unable to communicate or understand what was happening to him, he would experience pain to the same extent as a "normal" child. His life expectancy was uncertain but he was expected to die before late adolescence. The judge at first instance held that if J were to stop breathing he should not be reventilated.

LORD DONALDSON OF LYMINGTON M.R.
" . . . The Official Solicitor submits that there are two justifications for an appeal. (i)*Re C* gives guidance on the approach which it is appropriate to adopt in relation to the medical treatment of children who are dying and whose deaths can only be postponed for a short while *Re B* gives similar guidance in relation to severely but not grossly handicapped children with a shortened, but nevertheless substantial expectation of life. In the Official Solicitor's view, the present case illustrates a different category falling between these two on which guidance should be given. (ii) Whilst Scott Baker rightly directed himself that he must act in what he considered to be the best interests of the child, in the Official Solicitor's submission he erred in that a court is never justified in withholding consent to treatment which could enable a child to survive a life threatening condition, whatever the quality of

life which it would experience thereafter. This is the absolutist approach. Alternatively, he submits that the judge erred in that a court is only justified in withholding consent to such treatment if it is certain that the quality of the child's subsequent life would be 'intolerable' to the child, 'bound to be full of pain and suffering' and 'demonstrably . . . so awful' that in effect the child must be condemned to die (see *Re B*). In this case, in the Official Solicitor's submission, this has not been shown . . .

Re B seems to me to come very near to being a binding authority for the proposition that there is a balancing exercise to be performed in assessing the course to be adopted in the best interests of the child. Even if it is not, I have no doubt that this should be and is the law.

This brings me face to face with the problem of formulating the critical equation. In truth it cannot be done with mathematical or any precision. There is without doubt a very strong presumption in favour of a course of action which will prolong life, but, even excepting the 'cabbage' case to which special considerations may well apply, it is not irrebuttable. As this court recognised in *Re B* account has to be taken of the pain and suffering and quality of life which the child will experience if life is prolonged. Account has also to be taken of the pain and suffering involved in the proposed treatment itself. *Re B* was probably not a borderline case and I do not think that we are bound to, or should, treat Templeman L.J.'s use of the words 'demonstrably so awful' or Dunn L.J.'s use of the word 'intolerable' as providing a quasi-statutory yardstick.

For my part I prefer the formulation of Asch J. in *Re Weberlist* (1974) 360 NYS 2d 783 at 787 as explained by McKenzie J. in the passage from his judgment in Dawson's case (1983) 145 DLR (3d) 610 at 620–621 . . . [Here the judge had said: "There is a strident cry in America to terminate the lives of *other* people deemed physically or mentally defective . . . Assuredly, one test of a civilisation is its concern with the survival of the 'unfittest', a reversal of Darwin's formulation . . . In this case, the court must decide what its ward would choose, if he were in a position to make a sound judgment."] although it is probably merely another way of expressing the same concept. We know that the instinct and desire for survival is very strong. We all believe in and assert the sanctity of human life. As explained, this formulation takes account of this and also underlines the need to avoid looking at the problem from the point of view of the decider, but instead requires him to look at it from the assumed point of view of the patient. This gives effect, as it should, to the fact that even very severely handicapped people find a quality of life rewarding which to the unhandicapped may seem manifestly intolerable. People have an amazing adaptability. But in the end there will be cases in which the answer must be that it is not in the interests of the child to subject it to treatment which will cause increased suffering and produce no commensurate benefit, giving the fullest possible weight to the child's, and mankind's, desire to survive . . .

The issue here is whether it would be in the best interests of the child, to put him on a mechanical ventilator and subject him to all the associated processes of intensive care, if at some future time he could not continue breathing unaided. Let me say at once that I can understand the doctors wishing to ascertain the court's wishes at this stage, because it is an eventuality which could occur at any time and, if it did, an immediate decision might well have to be made. However, the situation is significantly different from being asked whether or not to consent on behalf of the child to particular treatment which is more or less immediately in prospect . . .

The doctors were unanimous in recommending that there should be no mechanical reventilation in the event of his stopping breathing, subject only to the qualifications injected by Dr W and accepted by the judge that in the event of a chest infection short term manual ventilation would be justified and that in the event of the child stopping breathing the provisional decision to abstain from mechanical ventilation could and should be revised, if this seemed appropriate to the doctors caring for him in the then prevailing clinical situation . . .

The basis of the doctors' recommendations, approved by the judge, was that mechanical ventilation is itself an invasive procedure which, together with its essential accompaniments, such as the introduction of a nasogastric tube, drips which have to be resited and constant blood sampling, would cause the child distress. Furthermore, the procedures involve taking active measures which carry their own hazards, not only to life but in terms of causing even greater brain damage. This had to be balanced against what could possibly be achieved by the adoption of such active treatment. The chances of preserving the child's life might be improved, although even this was not certain and account had to be taken of the extremely poor quality of life at present enjoyed by the child, the fact that he had already been ventilated for exceptionally long periods, the unfavourable prognosis with or without ventilation and a recognition that if the question of reventilation ever arose, his situation would have deteriorated still further.

I can detect no error in the judge's approach and in principle would affirm his decision . . . "

NOTES:

1. Taylor L.J. and Balcombe L.J. agreed.
2. The court in this case appeared to support a "substituted" judgment test when considering authorising non-treatment. However, the use of such a test is fraught with its own difficulties, particularly in the case of infants, where obviously the court will not have any previously expressed views. The test was rejected in the *Bland* decision (see Chapter 14), and by the Law Commission when it considered the basis on which the mentally incompetent patient should be given treatment (Law Commission, *Mental Incapacity*, Law Com. No. 231, London: HMSO, 1995) by the Mental Capacity Act 2005 — which has no application in the case of minors under 16. In *Re A (children) (conjoined twins)* (see below at pp.434–439) Ward L.J. doubted whether his dicta remains good law, but, as Bridgeman points out, "what is required here is not determination of what the patient would have wanted (substituted judgment) but assessment of quality of life from the perspective of the child living with the disability" (J. Bridgeman, "Caring for Children with Severe Disabilities: Boundaries and Relational Rights" (2005) 13 *International Journal of Children's Rights* 99–119 at p.117, note 6).
3. Note the emphasis in this case on the invasive nature of the therapy that might be necessary.

QUESTIONS:

1. What is the key factual difference which made *Re J* a more difficult case that *Re C*? Should it be open to a court to sanction non-intervention in relation to cases where the condition, if left untreated, would be life-threatening, but would not automatically lead to the death of the patient? (See R. Thornton, "Wardship — Withholding Medical Treatment" [1991] *Cambridge Law Journal* 38.)
2. Do Lord Donaldson M.R. and Taylor L.J. agree about the weight that should be attached to the dicta in *Re B* regarding the "intolerable" nature of the child's life?

Re J [1992] 4 All E.R. 614

J was 16 months old. He was severely disabled having hit his head after an accidental fall when only one month old. He suffered from cerebral palsy, severe epilepsy and was largely fed by a naso-gastric tube. Medical opinion was that he was unlikely to develop beyond his present level of functioning. The local authority had placed him with foster parents. They sought an order to determine whether life-saving measures should be given to J if he suffered a life-threatening event. At first instance the judge made an interim order granting an injunction requiring the health authority to use intensive therapeutic measures (including artificial ventilation) for so long as such measures were capable of prolonging his life. The health authority, supported by the Official Solicitor, acting as guardian *ad litem*, and the local authority (which had changed its views) appealed against the order. The child's biological mother supported continuing treatment.

LORD DONALDSON M.R.

" . . . The fundamental issue in this appeal is whether the court in the exercise of its inherent power to protect the interests of minors should ever require a medical practitioner or health authority acting by a medical practitioner to adopt a course of treatment which in the bona fide clinical judgement of the practitioner concerned is contra indicated as not being in the best interests of the patient . . .

The order of Waite J. was wholly inconsistent with the law [in *Re J* [1990] and *Re R*—see pp.417–418 below] and cannot be justified on the basis of any authority known to me. Furthermore it was, in my judgement, erroneous on two other substantive grounds, only slightly less fundamental than that to which I have just averted. The first is its lack of certainty as to what was required of the health authority. The second is that it does not adequately take account of the sad fact of life that health authorities may on occasion find that they have too few resources, either human or material or both, to treat all patients whom they would like to treat in the way in which they would like to treat them. It is then their duty to make choices.

The court when considering what course to adopt in relation to a particular child has no knowledge of competing claims to a health authority's resources and is in no position to express any view as to how it should elect to deploy them. Although the order is subject to the condition precedent that the required drugs and equipment are or could reasonably have been made available it makes no reference to the availability of staff and it has to be borne in mind that artificial ventilation of a young child in an intensive care unit is highly intensive of highly skilled staff. It gives no guidance as to what is meant by the concept of being reasonably available, yet it is not difficult to imagine circumstances in which there could be bona fide differences of opinion as to whether equipment or staff was reasonably available. The health authority is entitled to object and does object to being subject to an order of the court with penal consequences in the event of disobedience when it does not know precisely what is required of it . . .

The health authority would have a legitimate interest in the decision in the light of its currrent responsibilities towards J and towards other patients for whose care its necessarily limited resources have to be used. I would hope that each would adopt an understanding attitude towards the other's problems in circumstances in which the checks and balances of consent and willingness and ability to treat of which I spoke in *Re J* [1990] [above] could come under considerable strain.

In announcing the decision of the court at the conclusion of the argument I stressed and I repeat that the effect of setting aside the order leaves the health authority and its medical staff free subject to consent not being withdrawn to treat J in accordance with their best clinical judgment . . . What we were saying is that so long as those with parental responsibilities consent to J being treated by the medical staff of the health authority, he must be treated in accordance with their clinical judgment."

BALCOMBE L.J.

" . . . I can conceive of no situation where it would be a proper exercise of the (inherent) jurisdiction to make such an order as was made in the present case; that is to order a doctor whether directly or indirectly to treat a child in a manner contrary to his or her clinical judgment . . .

The court is not or certainly should not be in the habit of making orders unless it is prepared to enforce them. If the court orders a doctor to treat a child in a manner contrary to his or her clinical judgment it would place a conscientious doctor in an impossible position. To perform the court's order could require a doctor to act in a manner which he genuinely believed not to be in the patient's best interests; to fail to treat the child as ordered would amount to a contempt of court. Any judge would be most reluctant to punish the doctor for such a contempt, which seemed to me to be a very strong indication that such an order could not be made.

I would also stress the absolute undesirability of the court making an order which may have the effect of compelling a doctor or health authority to make available scarce resources (both human and material) to a particular child without knowing whether or not there are other patients to whom those resources might more advantageously be devoted."

NOTES:

1. Leggatt L.J. delivered a concurring judgment.
2. The court recognised that it may not always be in the patient's best interests for aggressive therapy to be pursued. This approach was subsequently followed in the *Bland* case (see Chapter 14 at pp.1021–1032.) Note also that the court ordered that treatment be discontinued in the face of opposition from J's mother.
3. The judicial unwillingness in this case to make statements in relation to medical resources is consistent with other cases involving resource allocation (see Chapter 1 at pp.45–68).

QUESTIONS:

1. Were any new issues raised by this case?
2. Do you agree that a court should never compel a doctor to administer a particular type of treatment?
3. Is it ever possible for a court to judge whether an individual has an adequate quality of life? In any event, should quality of life be the standard that is used when determining whether treatment should be withdrawn? (See J. Keown, "Restoring Intellectual Shape to the Law after *Bland*" (1997) 113 *Law Quarterly Review* 481–503.)
4. To what extent do you think the outcome in such cases is dictated by considerations of scarce resources?

The following case was referred to in Lord Donaldson's judgment:

Re R (A Minor) (Blood Transfusion) [1993] 2 F.L.R. 757, [1993] 2 F.C.R. 544

A 10-month-old girl was suffering from B-cell lymphoblastic leukaemia. The doctor had advised that she would require treatment for two years, which could necessitate the provision of blood transfusions. Her parents, both devout Jehovah's Witnesses, refused to consent to such treatment. The local authority therefore obtained leave to apply for a specific issue order under s.8 of the

Children Act 1989 in order to gain judicial sanction for the use of blood products against the parents' wishes.

BOOTH J.

" . . . The parents are extremely anxious that their daughter should receive the best possible medical care. Their primary objection to the proposed medical procedure is one of scriptural conscience. But the parents are also aware of the known hazards of blood transfusions and are anxious on this account. They further make the telling point that advances in medical science are so rapid that alternative blood management becomes possible in many procedures and as parents they want to be able to argue for their use whenever possible. If the court authorises the use of blood the parents are concerned to ensure that it is not a blanket authority to the doctors to do whatever they wish without consultation with them.

To obtain the court's authorisation for the use of blood products the local authority applied for a specific issue order under section 8 of the Children Act 1989. By definition a specific issue order means an order giving directions for the purpose of determining a specific question which has arisen, or which may arise, in connection with any aspect of parental responsibility for a child.

In the present case I am in no doubt that the application is well-founded under section 8 of the Act. The result which the local authority wishes to achieve, namely, the court's authorisation for the use of blood products, can clearly be achieved by the means of such an order. There is no need for the court otherwise to intervene to safeguard the little girl, so that I am satisfied that it is unnecessary and inappropriate for the court to exercise its inherent jurisdiction.

I therefore turn to consider the application and the matters to which the court must have regard under section 1 of the Act. The welfare of the little girl is the court's paramount consideration. At 10 months of age she is too young to express her wishes and feelings. The evidence is clear, however, that because of her medical condition the opinion of those who are responsible for her treatment supports the use of blood products. Without that treatment, the consensus is that the treatment will be unsuccessful and she will suffer harm. Only because they cannot give their consent to this treatment are her caring parents unable to meet her needs. But so overwhelming is her need for blood and so much is it in her best interests to have it in the light of current medical knowledge that, for her welfare, I am bound to override the parents' wishes and authorise the use of blood products, thus enabling the doctors to give her transfusions.

Mr Daniel, however, makes the powerful submission that such an order should not provide the medical consultants with a blanket authority to carry out such treatments without any further reference to the parents. They wish not only to be involved as far as possible in the care of their daughter but also to be able to draw attention to treatments alternative to the use of blood products and this is a field in which medical science is advancing rapidly and more such treatments are quickly becoming available. I consider this to be a perfectly proper approach. In a life-threatening emergency situation, the doctors clearly could not consult with the parents; but in the normal course of events it is reasonable that they should do so. Mrs Dangor, on behalf of the local authority, has been able to agree this and consequently the order which I made on Friday last provides for such consultation to take place."

NOTES:

1. This issue had been addressed in earlier cases. In *Re O (A Minor) (Medical Treatment)* [1993] 2 F.L.R. 149 a baby was born prematurely, suffering from a respiratory distress syndrome, which would at some stage require a blood transfusion. Her parents were Jehovah's Witnesses, who were torn between their desire to preserve her life while wanting to avoid damaging

her prospects in her next life. Other solutions were attempted, but the consultant paediatrician, who wished to anticipate the necessity for a blood transfusion, applied for an emergency protection order which was granted by the judge on the basis that "there is reasonable cause to suspect that the child is suffering or is likely to suffer significant harm because the parents are withholding their permission to give urgent medical treatment and unless this treatment is received the child may die". The effect of the order was to give the local authority parental responsibility for the baby. After weighing up the various considerations, including the religious principles which underlay the family's decision, Johnson J. concluded that the court's duty, acting as the judicial reasonable parent, was to give directions to ensure that whenever the need arose, the child would receive the blood transfusion that medical advice dictated.

2. In *Re S (a minor) (medical treatment)* [1993] 1 F.L.R. 396 a four-year-old boy suffered from T-cell leukaemia. His consultant paediatrician considered blood transfusion to be an essential supplement to the child's treatment regime of intensified chemotherapy. However, the parents, who were Jehovah's Witnesses, refused consent to the transfusion of blood or blood products. Without the intensified treatment there was no prospect of a cure. In this case the local authority were prepared to invoke the inherent jurisdiction of the High Court under s.100(3) of the Children Act. However, the application was unopposed, and once again the court authorised this treatment in the best interests of the child. Brazier notes the difficulty in reconciling *Re S* with *Re T* at p.420 below (M. Brazier, *Medicine, Patients and the Law* 3rd edn), London: Penguin, 2003 at p.352).

3. *Re R* refers to scientific advances in developing blood substitutes, which may provide an alternative to blood products in many procedures. This offers one example of how scientific developments may alleviate ethical dilemmas rather than exacerbating them. There has also been some softening of the position of the Jehovah's Witness' world governing body on use of blood for medical reasons, provided members afterwards repent (S. Bates, "Transfusion row rocks Jehovah's Witnesses" *The Guardian* June 15, 2000.) However, as we shall see when we examine the position of older children (at pp.439–470 below) some adherents of the faith still choose to die rather than receive blood once they reach adulthood.

4. If parents were to refuse *all* medical treatment for their child, this would amount to a criminal offence, if the child was to suffer harm as a result (see Chapter 14 at pp.1018–1021). After *Re R*, it is likely that the case of a parent refusing only one form of treatment would be dealt with by way of a specific issue order under s.8 of the Children Act 1989.

5. Similar problems may be generated for courts where parents decide that they want to subject their child to a course of innovative medical treatment which may be onerous and which carries no guarantee of a cure. For instance, in a case like *R v. Cambridgeshire Health Authority, Ex p. B* (see Chapter 1 at p.51), the issue arises of whether parents should have the right to submit their children to aggressive invasive therapies which are

likely to ultimately prove futile. The question of subjecting a child to innovative therapy also blurs into the right of parents to consent to the involvement of their child in clinical research programmes (see Chapter 10 at pp.688–692).

QUESTIONS:

1. A major difficulty in such cases is determining where the child's welfare lies if the parents genuinely believe that damage in a future life is likely to be occasioned by the preservation of life. Do you think that the courts are right to consistently assert that the child's welfare is served by preserving life in the face of parental objections? (See C. Bridge, "Parental Beliefs and Medical Treatment of Children" [1994] *Butterworth's Family Law Journal* 131.)
2. Does the welfare of the child require that he receive the most effective and painless course of treatment available, even if other riskier and less effective treatments provide an alternative?

Re T (a minor) (wardship: medical treatment) [1997] 1 All E.R. 906; [1997] 1 W.L.R. 242.

T was an 18-month-old child suffering from the liver defect bilary atresia. At the age of three and half weeks, T had undergone surgery which had failed to correct the defect. The unanimous medical prognosis was now that without a liver transplant he would not live beyond two and a half years and that it was in his best interests to undergo a transplant as soon as a suitable organ became available. However, his parents, who were health professionals with experience in the care of sick children, were strongly opposed to the operation, especially since they lived in New Zealand which lacked the facilities to carry out this transplant procedure.

BUTLER-SLOSS L.J.
" . . . From the decisions to which I have referred which bind this court it is clear that when an application under the inherent jurisdiction is made to the court the welfare of the child is the paramount consideration. The consent or refusal of consent of the parents is an important consideration to weigh in the balancing exercise to be carried out by the judge. In that context the extent to which the court will have regard to the view of the parent will depend upon the court's assessment of that view. But, as Sir Thomas Bingham M.R. said in *In re Z*, the court decides and in doing so may overrule the decision of a reasonable parent.

Applying those principles to the present appeal, the first argument of Mr. Francis that the court should not interfere with the reasonable decision of a parent is not one that we are able to entertain even if we wished to do so . . . It is wholly inapposite to the welfare test . . .

In my view, however, the judge erred in his approach to the issue before the court. He accepted the unchallenged clinical opinion of the three consultants and assessed the reasonableness of the mother's decision against that medical opinion . . . Since he had already decided the mother's approach was unreasonable he did not weigh in the balance reasons against the treatment which might be held by a reasonable parent on much broader grounds than the clinical assessment of the likely success of the proposed treatment. Some of the objections of the mother, such as the difficulties of the operation itself, turned out, from the evidence of Mr. R., to be less important than the mother believed. Underlying those less important objections by the mother was a deep-seated concern of the mother as to the benefits to her son of the major invasive surgery and post-operative treatment, the dangers of failure long term as well as short term, the possibility of the need for further transplants, the likely length of life, and the effect upon her son of all these concerns. The judge did not assess the relevance or the weight of such considerations in his final balancing exercise. In particular he did not consider at that stage the evidence of Dr. P. and his strong reservations to the effect of coercing, as Dr. P. put it, this mother into playing the crucial and irreplaceable part in the aftermath of major invasive surgery not just during the post-operative treatment of an 18-month-old baby but also throughout the childhood of her son . . .

I doubt that he was right to deem the mother to be unreasonable in her assessment of the broader perspective of whether this operation should be carried out. But in any event the reasonableness of the mother was not the primary issue. This mother and this child are one for the purpose of this unusual case and the decision of the court to consent to the operation jointly affects the mother and son and it also affects the father. The welfare of this child depends upon his mother. The practical considerations of her ability to cope with supporting the child in the face of her belief that this course is not right for him, the requirement to return probably for a long period to this country, either to leave the father behind and lose his support or to require him to give up his present job and seek one in England, were not put by the judge into the balance when he made his decision . . .

It falls therefore for this court to make the decision whether to consent to the operation and require the return of the child to the jurisdiction . . . Unlike the intestinal obstruction of the Down's syndrome baby [in *Re B*] which could be cured by a simple operation, T.'s problems require complicated surgery and many years of special care from the mother.

The reservations of Dr. P., to which he held despite concessions he made in his evidence, remain of great significance and importance. His view that the decision of a loving, caring mother should be respected, ought to be given great weight and are reinforced by *Fact Sheet No. 10* provided by hospital X. The alternative of the court giving the consent and passing back the responsibility for the parental care to the mother and expecting her to provide the commitment to the child after the operation is carried out in the face of her opposition is in itself fraught with danger for the child. She will have to comply with the court order; return to this country and present the child to one of the hospitals. She will have to arrange to remain in this country for the foreseeable future. Will the father stay in country AB and work or come with her to England, giving up his job and having to seek another job? If he does not come she will have to manage unaided. How will the mother cope? Can her professionalism overcome her view that her son should not be subjected to this distressing procedure? Will she break down? How will the child be affected by the conflict with which the mother may have to cope? What happens if the treatment is partially successful and another transplant is needed? The mother may not wish to consent to the further surgery. Is the court to be asked again for consent to the next operation?

The welfare of the child is the paramount consideration and I recognise the 'very strong presumption in favour of a course of action which will prolong life' and the inevitable consequences for the child of not giving consent. But to prolong life, as Lord Donaldson of Lymington M.R. recognised in *In re J* [1990] in somewhat different circumstances, is not the sole objective of the court and to require it at the expense of other considerations may not be in a child's best interests. I would stress that, on the most unusual facts of this case with the enormous significance of the close attachment between the mother and baby, the court is not concerned with the reasonableness of the mother's refusal to consent but with the consequences of that refusal and whether it is in the best interests of T. for this court in effect to direct the mother to take on this total commitment where she does not agree with the course proposed . . .

I would allow this appeal . . . ''

WAITE L.J.

"I agree. The law's insistence that the welfare of a child shall be paramount is easily stated and universally applauded, but the present case illustrates, poignantly and dramatically, the difficulties that are encountered when trying to put it into practice . . . [In this case the] parents' opposition is partly instinctive and, being based on their own awareness of the procedures involved, partly practical. It has sufficient cogency to have led one of the principal medical experts in the field of this operation to say that his team would decline to operate without the mother's committed support.

What is the court to do in such a situation? It is not an occasion—even in an age preoccupied with 'rights'—to talk of the rights of a child, or the rights of a parent, or the rights of the court. The cases cited by Butler-Sloss L.J. are uncompromising in their assertion that the sole yardstick must be the need to give effect to the demands of paramountcy for the welfare of the child . . .

All these cases depend on their own facts and render generalisations—tempting though they may be to the legal or social analyst—wholly out of place. It can only be said safely that there is a scale, at one end of which lies the clear case where parental opposition to medical intervention is prompted by scruple or dogma of a kind which is patently irreconcilable with principles of child health and welfare widely accepted by the generality of mankind; and that at the other end lie highly problematic cases where there is genuine scope for a difference of view between parent and judge. In both situations it is the duty of the judge to allow the court's own opinion to prevail in the perceived paramount interests of the child concerned, but in cases at the latter end of the scale, there must be a likelihood (though never of course a certainty) that the greater the scope for genuine debate between one view and another the stronger will be the inclination of the court to be influenced by a reflection that in the last analysis the best interests of every child include an expectation that difficult decisions affecting the length and quality of its life will be taken for it by the parent to whom its care has been entrusted by nature . . . "

NOTE:

1. Roche L.J. also delivered a judgment allowing the appeal.

QUESTIONS:

1. Can this decision be reconciled with the earlier cases cited above? What are the material factual differences?
2. How influential do you think the court found the following facts:

   (a) that the parents were health professionals?
   (b) that the child's earlier operation was unsuccessful?
   (c) that the family lived in New Zealand?

   Do you think that the court overstated how unusual the facts are in this case?
3. In a case such as this, is it possible to separate out the best interests of the child and those who care for him? What did Butler-Sloss L.J. mean by stating that "[t]his mother and this child are one for the purpose of this unusual case"? (See A. Bainham, "Do Babies have Rights?" [1997] C. L. J. 48; M. Fox and Jean McHale, "In Whose Best Interests?" (1997) 60 *Modern Law Review* 700–709; S. Michalowski, "Is it in the Best Interests of a Child to Have a Life-Saving Liver Transplantation?—*Re T (Wardship:*

Medical Treatment" (1997) 9 *Child and Family Law Quarterly* 179–189; K. O'Donovan and R. Gilbar, "The Loved Ones: Families, Intimates and Patient Autonomy" (2003) *Legal Studies* 332.)

4. Why do you think that Waite L.J. sought to distinguish this case from those "prompted by scruple or dogma of a kind which is patently irreconcilable with principles of child health and welfare widely accepted by the generality of mankind"? What sort of cases do you think he had in mind? (See Fox and McHale, *op. cit.* in note 3.)

5. Michael Freeman has described this case as "the nadir of judicial thinking in this area". Do you agree? (See M. Freeman, "Whose Life Is It Anyway?" [2001] *Medical Law Review* 259, at 273; see also "Can We Leave the Best Interests of Very Sick Children to their Parents?" in M.D.A. Freeman and A. Lewis (eds), *Law and Medicine*, Oxford: OUP, 2000).

(b) Cases where Parents Seek to Compel Treatment Contrary to Medical Assessments of Best Interests

Whereas the early case law on withdrawing or withholding treatment from severely disabled infants concerned cases where the parents opposed treatment or failed to express a view, more recently there have been a spate of cases (largely centred on one particular NHS trust) where parents have sought to compel doctors to treat disabled infants in circumstances where doctors believe such treatment is not in the best interests of the infant.

Re C (a minor) (medical treatment) [1998] 1 F.C.R. 1

C was a 16-month-old child who suffered from a fatal disease known as spinal muscular atrophy, type 1 (SMA 1) which usually caused death within a year. Her severe disability meant that she was seriously emaciated with a little movement in her feet, none in her legs and impaired arm movements. She was dependent on intermittent positive pressure ventilation. The doctor responsible for her care described her as in a "no chance" situation. According to the Royal College of Paediatrics and Child Health, *Withholding or Withdrawing Lifesaving Treatment in Children: a Framework for Practice* (1997) (now in a second edition 2004), such a situation is "where the child has such severe disease that life-sustaining treatment simply delays death without significant alleviation of suffering. Medical treatment in this situation may be deemed inappropriate." The doctors wished to take C off the ventilation, which in their view was likely to produce increasing distress. In the event that she suffered respiratory relapse, they thought that it would be against her interests to reventilate her, and sought a declaration that this would be lawful. Her orthodox Jewish parents refused to consent to this proposed course of action.

SIR STEPHEN BROWN P.
"This is a serious situation for doctors to contend with. It is a dreadful situation for the parents to have to face. The parents of C are highly responsible religious orthodox Jews. They love their child. They have other children. They cannot bring themselves to face what seems to be the inevitable future for this little child. They visit her and see a reaction which

is a favourable reaction in her face towards them. They do not believe that it is within their religious tenets to contemplate the possibility of indirectly shortening life, even if that is not the purpose of the course which the doctors believe to be appropriate in order to spare her further suffering. Accordingly, they have not been able to consent to the proposed course of treatment which the doctors have recommended. That is to say that whilst they believe that she should be taken off ventilation as a last attempt, as it were, to see whether she might survive for a time without the intermittent positive pressure ventilation presently being administered, they believe that they should be able to be assured that should she suffer further respiratory relapse or arrest she should be replaced on to ventilation. The doctors are unable to contemplate undertaking such a course of treatment in the best interests of the child . . .

Because the parents were unwilling to consent to such treatment the hospital authority has applied to this court to exercise its inherent jurisdiction and to approve the course which the doctors wish to follow . . .

The order sought would be in these terms:

'There be leave to treat the minor, C, as advised by Dr H, such treatment to include the withdrawal of artificial ventilation and non-resuscitation in the event of a respiratory arrest and palliative care to ease her suffering and permit her life to end peacefully and with dignity, such treatment being in C's best interests . . . '

It is quite clear from the authorities, and is stated perhaps most aptly in the leading case of *Re J (a minor) (medical treatment)* . . .

'No one can dictate the treatment to be given to the child—neither court, parents nor doctors. There are checks and balances. The doctors can recommend treatment A in preference to treatment B. They can also refuse to adopt treatment C on the grounds that it is medically contra-indicated or for some other reason is a treatment which they could not conscientiously administer. The court or parents for their part can refuse to consent to treatment A or B or both, but cannot insist on treatment C . . . ' "

NOTES:

1. Ian Kennedy is critical of the judge's deference to medical opinion and his failure to justify his preference for the medical view over that of the parents. He also argues that, although a court may benefit from referring to professional guidance (such as that published by the Royal College of Paediatrics and Child Health), this particular guidance is unhelpful and has been much criticised by the medical profession for the use of unclear and insensitive language (I. Kennedy, "Child: Terminal Illness: Withdrawal of Treatment" (1998) 6 *Medical Law Review* 99). The guidance was also relied on in the case discussed in note 3 below and subsequent cases.

2. In *Royal Wolverhampton Hospitals NHS Trust v B* [2000] 2 F.C.R. 76, Bodey J. issued a declaration that it would be lawful for doctors not to ventilate E, a five-month-old child who had multi-organ failure and chronic lung disease. Her condition had worsened to the point where it was thought that she might die within a day and the consultant paediatrician's view was that reventilation would only result in distressing prolongation of her life with no real prospect for recovery. The parents' opposition to non-intervention in this case was due to their loss of faith in the doctors who had wrongly predicted that E would never be able to come off a ventilator. Because of the urgency, the health professionals and E's mother gave evidence via telephone. Bridge has noted the very inadequate communication between doctors and the parents in this case (C. Bridge,

"Religion, Culture and the Body of the Child" in A. Bainham *et al.*, *Body Lore and Laws*, Oxford: Hart, 2001 at p.274).

3. Similarly, in *A National Health Service Trust v D* (2000) 55 B.M.L.R. 19 the High Court granted declarations making ID—a 19-month-old child suffering from heat failure, lung disease and renal dysfunction—a ward of court and authorising palliative care only, in the face of parental opposition. Andrew Grubb notes that the striking feature of this case is Cazalet J.'s confidence that the decision would be compatible with the Human Rights Act which was shortly coming into force. The judge considered there was no breach of Article 2 of the ECHR, as non-treatment was in the child's best interests; while the right not to be subject to inhuman or degrading treatment under Article 3, in his view, encompassed a right to die with dignity. (A. Grubb, "Incompetent Patient (Child): Withholding Treatment and Human Rights" (2000) 8 *Medical Law Review* 339 at p.341.) Subsequent cases involving treatment withdrawal from children have paid little heed to human rights arguments, but they have been addressed in cases involving adults discussed in Chapter 14.

QUESTIONS:

1. Given Sir Stephen Brown's conclusion in this case that the law was settled, why do you think that *Re C* was litigated at all?
2. Is there any situation in which a court should be able to compel doctors to undertake treatment? (See Kennedy, *op. cit.* in note 1 at p.102). Should parents' views be given greater weight if they are prepared to bear the costs of treatment?
3. Is it possible in a case such as *Re C* to reconcile the court's assessment of "best interests" and the religious beliefs of the parents?
4. Do you think that *Re C* would qualify as a case "prompted by scruple or dogma" for Waite L.J. (at p.442, above), given that the President described the parents as are highly responsible religious orthodox Jews. How can valid religious beliefs be distinguished from dogma? What is the difference, given Michael Freeman's point that "[s]incerely held religious views are often rooted in dogma"? Freeman goes on to ask "And why should religious views be accorded respect which other sincerely-held and (perhaps) controversial views are not?" (See M. Freeman, "Whose Life Is It Anyway?" [2001] *Medical Law Review* 259, at 264).

Portsmouth Hospitals NHS Trust v Wyatt and another [2005] 1 W.L.R. 3995; [2005] EWCA Civ 1181

The much publicised (and litigated) case of Charlotte Wyatt concerned a particularly embittered conflict between parents, who were described as "devout Christians", and doctors over the treatment of a baby girl born three months prematurely. At birth she weighed 1lb and was suffering from fundamental and probably irreparable damage to her respiratory system and kidney function as well as permanent and irreversible brain damage occasioned by the failure of her head to grow. Medical evidence indicated that she certainly experienced pain, although it was uncertain whether she could, as her parents contended, experience pleasure. Unanimous medical evidence was that if (as she almost certainly would) she required artificial ventilation, it would not be in her best interests or provide it. When she was one year old, in October 2004, Hedley J. issued a declaration, which was not challenged by the parents, that aggressive treatment would not be in her interests and that the consultants responsible for her care would be entrusted with discretion to determine appropriate palliative care in her best interests. Mr and Mrs Wyatt did, however, argue that when the judge came to consider continuation of the declarations in April 2005, Charlotte's condition had radically improved to the point where she was no longer terminally ill. The judge, however, ordered that the declarations should remain in force at that point and also when they later came up for review in October 2005. It was this latter decision that was challenged before the Court of Appeal, with the parents arguing that given Charlotte's defiance of medical prognosis, the judge had misapplied the best interests test.

Wall L.J. delivered the judgment of the court:

WALL L.J.
" . . . [9] We think it very important that at the outset of this judgment, we should make clear both what the case is about, and what it is not about. The case is not, and never has been about the withdrawal of treatment from Charlotte in order to allow her to die. It is not about whether or not Charlotte should be subject to a 'do not resuscitate' (DNR) policy. Nor is it about the level of care provided for her. Charlotte has been profoundly disabled from birth, but she has been kept alive by the devoted care and treatment she has received from the trust's nursing and medical staff. Without that care and treatment she would undoubtedly now be dead . . .

[11] What the case is about is what should happen if Charlotte contracts an infection or suffers some other crisis which is likely to lead to her death, but which cannot be treated by drugs and thus requires her to be ventilated if she is to stand any chance of remaining alive . . .

[19] The order which lies at the heart of the case is that made by the judge on 8 October 2004. That order contains the following declarations in relation to Charlotte:

'1. Charlotte, as a child, lacks capacity to make decisions about medical treatment to be delivered to herself for her physical health care.

2. Having regard to Charlotte's best interests, and in the event that the paediatric medical consultants responsible for Charlotte's case, at [the trust], the Southampton University Hospitals NHS Trust or any NHS Trust treating Charlotte, consider that she is suffering an infection which has or may lead to a collapsed lung, it shall be lawful for the doctors treating Charlotte to provide all suitable medical care including antibiotics.

3. That in the events anticipated in para 2 above, and having regard to Charlotte's best interests:

   (i) in the event that the responsible paediatric medical consultants reach a decision that Charlotte's medical condition shall have deteriorated to such an extent that she is unable to maintain oxygen and carbon dioxide exchange, it shall be lawful for responsible paediatric medical consultants to reach a decision that she should not be intubated and/or ventilated.

   (ii) Whilst the responsible paediatric medical consultants may reach a decision that it is appropriate to administer Continuous Positive Airways Pressure (CPAP) to help keep Charlotte's airways open and to ease Charlotte's breathing, if she is

visibly distressed by CPAP, it shall be lawful for the responsible paediatric medical consultants to reach a decision that CPAP shall be withdrawn.
(iii) The responsible paediatric medical consultants shall be entitled to reach a decision to use symptomatic relief which may be in the form of opiates in the knowledge that this may depress Charlotte's efforts to breathe whilst making her more comfortable.' . . .

[58] If the judge's analysis of the law relating to the 'best interests' question was correct, there was plainly material upon which he could properly both make and continue the declarations. The key question, accordingly, was: is the judge's analysis of the law correct? . . .

[Wall L.J. then analysed Hedley J.'s review of the relevant case law, focusing particularly on *Re B* and *Re J* [1990] above before concluding:]

[85] For all these reasons, we came to the clear conclusion that the judge had approached the best interests question correctly, and that permission to appeal against his decision in principle to make the declarations should be refused. We have taken some considerable time over this part of the case because we think it important that in cases of this sensitivity and difficulty, the guidelines which the experienced judges of the Family Division have to follow should be both as clear and as simple as is consistent with the serious issues which they engage . . .

[87] . . . The judge must decide what is in the child's best interests. In making that decision, the welfare of the child is paramount, and the judge must look at the question from the assumed point of view of the patient (*Re J* [1990]). There is a strong presumption in favour of a course of action which will prolong life, but that presumption is not irrebuttable (*Re J* [1990]). The term 'best interests' encompasses medical, emotional, and all other welfare issues (*Re A* [see Chapter 13 at p.938). The court must conduct a balancing exercise in which all the relevant factors are weighed (*Re J* [1990]) and a helpful way of undertaking this exercise is to draw up a balance sheet (*Re A*).

[88] Inevitably, whilst cases involving the treatment of children will fall into recognised categories, no two cases are the same, and the individual cases will, inevitably, be highly fact specific. In this context, any criteria which seek to circumscribe the best interests tests are, we think, to be avoided. As Thorpe LJ said in *Re S* 'it would be undesirable and probably impossible to set bounds to what is relevant to a welfare determination'.

[89] This is not, of course, to say that the judge has *carte blanche* to do what he or she likes. The judge must in each case perform the balancing exercise identified by the Master of the Rolls in *Re J* [1990], helpfully amplified by the 'balance sheet' approach advocated by Thorpe LJ in *Re A* . . .

[91] We do not, however, dismiss 'intolerability' as a factor altogether. As we have already stated, we agree with Hedley J that whilst 'intolerable to the child' should not be seen either as a gloss on or a supplementary guide to best interests, it is, as he said, a valuable guide in the search for best interests in this kind of case.

[Finally Ward L.J. turned to address the issue of whether the declarations should have been given in such broad terms given the parents' contention that there was a change in Charlotte's condition.]

[111] We have not found this part of the case altogether easy, and it seems to us that the arguments are quite finely balanced. From the perspective of the trust and the guardian, we quite see the advantages, in terms of Charlotte's treatment, of there being in place a treatment plan which can be implemented without further application to the court. On the other hand, we detect a tension between the concept of a declaration, which is designed to state what is lawful in given circumstances, and a situation which is sufficiently fluid to render it likely that the circumstances may change, with the consequence that the lawfulness of the conduct identified in the declaration may be called in question . . .

[114] In our judgment, like so much of the law in this area, the answer has to be fact and case specific. In other words, each case has to be decided on its particular facts. On the facts of this case, which includes the history which we have outlined in [17] to [25] above, and the powerful medical consensus that Charlotte's underlying condition had not

changed, the judge, in our view, was both entitled to continue the declarations, and right to order a review.

[115] We therefore accept the submissions on this part of the case made by the trust and the guardian. Furthermore, although we have made it clear that we are unable to analyse the fresh information put before us on Mr and Mrs Wyatt's behalf, we bear strongly in mind the judge's finding in April 2005 that nothing had changed in Charlotte's underlying condition, even though its consequences had substantially ameliorated.

[116] Whilst, as the trust acknowledges, it may be very difficult for Mr and Mrs Wyatt to accept that Charlotte's underlying condition has not altered, that was clearly the trust's evidence before the judge, which, as we have already made clear, he was entitled to accept . . .

[117] . . . [I]t is, in our view, not the function of the court to oversee the treatment plan for a gravely ill child. That function is for the doctors in consultation with the child's parents. Judges take decisions on the basis of particular factual sub-strata. The court's function is to make a particular decision on a particular issue.

[118] As a general proposition, therefore, we have reservations about judges making open-ended declarations which they may have to re-visit if circumstances change. But all that said, we came to the clear conclusion that Hedley J had indeed thought through the implications of what he was doing, and was entitled both to make and renew the declarations . . .

[120] These, accordingly, are the reasons why we refused Mr and Mrs Wyatt permission to appeal against the judge's application of the best interests test, and dismissed their appeal against the judge's decision to continue the declarations pending their review."

NOTES:

1. Wall L.J. highlighted the unusual nature of this case, which had required Hedley J. to grant a number of different orders relating to Charlotte's treatment. He stressed the willingness of the trust to reconsider the current decision not to reventilate Charlotte in the light of ongoing clinical review.

2. The judge was also critical of the conduct of the parents in this case, particularly the fact that they reported the doctors involved to the police.

3. Two months after the Court of Appeal ruling, in October 2005, Hedley J. decided that in the light of Charlotte's "remarkable progress" the declaration not to reventilate could be rescinded. He stated:

> "I have tried to set out, in a way comprehensible to all, what I understand to be both the duties and also the limits on the duties of the treating clinician. He does not take orders from the family any more than he gives them. He acts in what he sees as the best interests of the child: no more and no less. In doing so, however, parental wishes should be accommodated as far as professional judgment and conscience will permit, but no further." (*per* Hedley J. in *Re Wyatt (A child) (Medical Treatment: Continuation of Order)* [2005] 4 All E.R. 1325; [2005] EWHC 2293.)

However, despite optimistic reports of her prognosis (P. Lewis, "Baby Charlotte could be home for Christmas", *The Guardian*, November 29, 2005), Charlotte's condition worsened and following an emergency application to the High Court in February 2006, the order authorising non-intervention was restored. Noting that he was now delivering his fifth judgment in the case, Hedley J. concluded:

"I am wholly satisfied from my long acquaintance with this case that the circumstances have now arisen where the court should make it clear that in the best interests of Charlotte the medical profession should be free to refrain from intervention by way of intubation and ventilation. I make it clear that this is permissive and not mandatory and, accordingly, at the moment the decision arises to be taken the medical authorities are required to use their best judgment in Charlotte's best interests as to whether they desist. All this court is saying is that a decision to desist would be lawful. As I say, I do that on the basis that CPAP can continue and that the matter can then be dealt with by palliative care." (*per* Hedley J. in *Re Wyatt* [2006] EWHC 319)

(See S. Jones, "Doctors can let girl, 2, die, says judge", *The Guardian*, February 25, 2006.)

4. In the case of *R. v Portsmouth Hospitals NHS Trust, Ex p. Glass* (discussed in Chapter 14 at p.1050) another bitter conflict occurred between the same NHS trust and a mother who wished doctors to pursue aggressive treatment for her severely mentally and physically disabled child. She was ultimately successful in arguing before the European Court of Human Rights that her child's right to respect for his private life had been infringed by UK law.

5. In *Re L (A Minor)* [2005] 1 F.L.R. 491, the High Court granted a declaration that it would be lawful for an NHS trust to withdraw ventilation from a child suffering from trisomy 18 (or "Edward's syndrome") as a result of which he suffered from multiple heart defects, chronic respiratory failure, gastroesophageal reflux, severe developmental delay, epilepsy and hypertonia and had remained in hospital since birth. It was accepted that the condition was incurable and that most children suffering from it died within weeks or months. His mother's position was that mechanical ventilation should not be excluded in the event of an emergency. Having cited *Re J* [1990] (see p.413 above), Dame Butler-Sloss said that taking a broad interpretation of best interests (which should be the focus rather than "intolerability"):

"[E]ven very severely handicapped people find a quality of life rewarding which to the un-handicapped may seem manifestly intolerable. People have an amazing adaptability. But in the end there are cases in which the answer must be that it is not in the interests of the child to subject it to treatment which would cause increased suffering and produce no commensurate benefit, giving the fullest possible weight to the child's and mankind's desire to survive."

QUESTIONS:

1. Do you agree that the decisions in these cases have to be fact and case specific? In the light of *Re J* [1992] and *Re C* [1998] above, was there really any new legal issue in the *Wyatt* or *L* cases?

2. In *Wyatt* did the court pay sufficient regard to the view of some commentators that the parents, who have closest contact with their child, are best placed to assess the interests of their child? (J. Bridgeman, "Caring for Children with Severe Disabilities: Boundaries and Relational Rights" (2005) 13 *International Journal of Children's Rights* 99–119 at p.117,

note 6.) Do the various rulings in this saga accord with the European Court of Human Rights judgment in *Glass v UK*? (see Chapter 14 at p.1051).
3. Notwithstanding Hedley J.'s rejection of "intolerability" as the appropriate test in these cases, might this in fact be the better test? (See M. Brazier, "An Intractable Dispute: When Parents and Professionals Disagree" (2005) 13 *Medical Law Review* 412, at p.415.)

An NHS Trust v MB [2006] EWHC 507

This case, like *Re C* [1998] at p.423 above also involved a child suffering from SMA I. MB, who was 18 months old when the case was heard, was described by one of the expert witnesses as the "the most severely affected child with SMA that I have ever personally seen". MB's condition had deteriorated to the point where he had no movement except for his eyes and barely perceptible movements of his eyebrows, at the corners of his mouth, and of his thumbs, toes and feet. He was unable to communicate. While most SMA babies are congenitally normal, there was some doubt about whether that was true in this case as the infant was also epileptic, possibly due to an episode of oxygen deprivation, the effect of which was unclear. However, the court proceeded on the assumption that MB had the normal thought processes of an 18-month-old child, albeit without normal stimulation, since most of his life had been spent in a paediatric intensive care unit.

The *MB* case differed from *Re C* [1998] as the child in that earlier case had been only on intermittent positive pressure ventilation and the case turned on whether the ventilation should be restarted if she suffered a respiratory arrest. In this case, by contrast, the declaration sought was that it would be lawful to withdraw all forms of ventilation and provide palliative care. The evidence suggested that, given his difficultly in breathing unaided, this would result in death in a very short time. The parents wished a tractracheostomy to be performed in order to continue long-term ventilation.

HOLMAN J.
" . . . 16. . . . [T]he law around this topic is now well established and tolerably clear and can, I believe, be shortly stated in the following propositions without the need for copious reference to authority.

(i) As a dispute has arisen between the treating doctors and the parents, and one, and now both, parties have asked the court to make a decision, it is the role and duty of the court to do so and to exercise its own independent and objective judgment.
(ii) The right and power of the court to do so only arises because the patient, in this case because he is a child, lacks the capacity to make a decision for himself.
(iii) I am not deciding what decision I might make for myself if I was, hypothetically, in the situation of the patient; nor for a child of my own if in that situation; nor whether the respective decisions of the doctors on the one hand or the parents on the other are reasonable decisions.
(iv) The matter must be decided by the application of an objective approach or test.
(v) That test is the best interests of the patient. Best interests are used in the widest sense and include every kind of consideration capable of impacting on the decision. These

include, non-exhaustively, medical, emotional, sensory (pleasure, pain and suffering) and instinctive (the human instinct to survive) considerations.

(vi) It is impossible to weigh such considerations mathematically, but the court must do the best it can to balance all the conflicting considerations in a particular case and see where the final balance of the best interests lies.

(vii) Considerable weight (Lord Donaldson of Lymington MR referred to 'a very strong presumption') must be attached to the prolongation of life because the individual human instinct and desire to survive is strong and must be presumed to be strong in the patient. But it is not absolute, nor necessarily decisive; and may be outweighed if the pleasures and the quality of life are sufficiently small and the pain and suffering or other burdens of living are sufficiently great.

(viii) These considerations remain well expressed in the words as relatively long ago now as 1991 of Lord Donaldson of Lymington in *Re J* [1990] . . . [see p.413 above]

(ix) All these cases are very fact specific, i.e. they depend entirely on the facts of the individual case.

(x) The views and opinions of both the doctors and the parents must be carefully considered. Where, as in this case, the parents spend a great deal of time with their child, their views may have particular value because they know the patient and how he reacts so well; although the court needs to be mindful that the views of any parents may, very understandably, be coloured by their own emotion or sentiment. It is important to stress that the reference is to the views and opinions of the parents. Their own wishes, however understandable in human terms, are wholly irrelevant to consideration of the objective best interests of the child save to the extent in any given case that they may illuminate the quality and value to the child of the child/parent relationship.

17. I avoid reference to the concept of 'intolerability'. It seems to me that it all depends on what one means by 'intolerable' and that use of that word really expresses a conclusion rather than provides a test . . .

[Having detailed the medical evidence and the views of the parents and the guardian in relation to the advantages and disadvantages of the various treatment options, Holman J. concluded:]

89. I am not persuaded, even taking into account predicted future deterioration, that it is currently in the best interests of M to discontinue ventilation with the inevitable result that he will immediately die . . .

90. I actually go further and consider that currently it is positively in his best interests to continue with continuous pressure ventilation and with the nursing and medical care that properly go with it, including suctioning and deep suctioning when required, replacement of the tube as necessary, and chest and lung physiotherapy to clear his secretions. Although that is my opinion, I cannot and do not make an order or declaration to that effect. I merely state it.

91. There are, however, procedures which go beyond maintaining ventilation, which require the positive infliction of pain and which, if required, will, in my view, mean that M has moved naturally towards his death despite the ventilation. If that point is reached, it would be in his best interests then to withhold those procedures even though he would then probably die . . .

94. I now give my reasons why, with great and very genuine respect for all the doctors, and also for the view of the guardian, I can only partially agree with them; and do not agree with them on the central issue of withdrawing ventilation.

95. M is going to die. He will probably die within about a year although I fully accept he may live longer. He may also die much sooner . . .

96. If he should suffer a cardiac failure such that any of the forms of CPR described above are required, then he would at that point definitely be dying, even if he might, by forms of CPR, be saved. But the CPR potentially requires renewed pain, renewed aggressive intervention and potentially distress and little dignity in death. That is not

justified or in his best interests when it is his destiny, even if revived on that occasion, soon to die.

97. So I am clear that the doctors need not resort again to CPR, or any ECG monitoring merely as an indicator for, or adjunct of, CPR.

98. The administration of intravenous antibiotics and blood sampling also requires the infliction of pain (particularly in his case because of the difficulty of getting a vein). They would be indicated by some new and serious infection, not able to be treated via the gastrostomy tube. That, too, may mean that death is near and it would not be in his best interests or justified once again to embark on the infliction of pain . . .

100. I take a different view, however, about deliberate withdrawal of ventilation. I fully accept all the burdens of discomfort, distress and some pain to which M is daily subjected, but from which I would now specifically exclude, if the need arises, CPR and the other treatments I have just described. Even excluding these, I accept that there is almost relentless discomfort, periods of distress and relatively short episodes of pain (deep suctioning). It is indeed a helpless and sad life.

101. But that life does in my view include within it the benefits that I have tried to describe and will not repeat. Within those benefits, and central to them, is my view that on the available evidence I must proceed on the basis that M has age appropriate cognition, and does continue to have a relationship of value to him with his family, and does continue to gain other pleasures from touch, sight and sound. A number of these benefits are expressed in the guardian's list as 'possible/probable' and it may be that doubts in the guardian's mind as to whether he in fact gains these benefits is part of the difference between us . . .

103. I do take into account, and have very anxiously considered, future deterioration. The prospect of it is not, of course, something of which M himself can be aware and cannot of itself cause him anguish or foreboding in the way that it may to an adult, or a much older child. The time may come when he has further deteriorated to such an extent and in certain ways that the balance changes. But I do not consider that the future, however awful it may become, yet justifies that today, tomorrow, or the next day his current burdens outweigh the benefits and that he should be allowed to die . . .

106. I wish to stress that this is a very fact specific decision taken in the actual circumstances as they are for this child and today. These circumstances include, critically, the facts that he already has been and is on ventilation and has already survived to the age of 18 months; is assumed not to be brain damaged; is in a close relationship with a family who have spent and are able to spend very considerable time with him; and does already have an accumulation of experiences and the cognition to gain pleasure from them."

NOTES:

1. In this case, in line with Bridgeman's contention that the views of carers should be taken into account, the judge does attached "considerable weight" to the mother's evidence, while noting that it was "not wholly objectively reliable" (see J. Bridgeman, "Caring for Children with Severe Disabilities: Boundaries and Relational Rights" (2005) 13 *International Journal of Children's Rights* 99–119.)

2. It is also noteworthy, and unusual, in this case that the views of the nurses undertaking the daily care of *Re MB* were explicitly canvassed. (In relation to the *Wyatt* case at p.425 above, Brazier had noted how "the voices of the nurses . . . are barely heard in the courtroom drama" (M. Brazier, "An Intractable Dispute: When Parents and Professionals Disagree" (2005) 13 *Medical Law Review* 412, at p.416.) Their views were split, with the most experienced paediatric intensive care nurses who had prior experience of

SMA agreeing with the trust that ventilation should be withdrawn, while the less experienced staff wanted the status quo to remain.

3. Holman J accepted the controversial view of the majority in *Bland* that discontinuing life support could be characterised as an omission rather than an act.

4. Recently the High Court heard a further case involving the withdrawal of treatment in which *Re MB* was distinguished. *Re K (A Child)* [2006] EWHC 1007 concerned a six-month-old child suffering from congenital myotonica dystrophy, an inherited neuromuscular disorder which caused chronic muscle weakness. At the age of one month, as part of a process known as total parenteral nutrition (TPN), she had a line inserted in her abdomen to enable artificial intravenous feeding. When it became apparent that K's condition was worsening, the trust sought a declaration that the line should be removed and TPN cease, followed by a period of organised palliative care and transfer to a hospice. Sir Mark Potter P. granted a declaration that it would be lawful to discontinue TPN on the grounds that it was "in her best interests to cease to provide CPN which she is still clinically stable, so that she may die in peace and over a comparatively short space of time, relieved by the palliative treatment contemplated, which will cause her neither pain nor discomfort and enable her to live out her short life in relative peace in the close care of parents who love her." Comparing K's situation to that of MB, the President stated that "She has no accumulation of experiences and cognition comparable with that of MB . . . . On the evidence before me there is no realistic sense in which one can assign to her the simple pleasure of being alive or having other than a life dominated by regular pain, distress and discomfort and unrelieved by the pleasures of eating." In fact the case only came to court because parental responsibility lay with the local authority so that the parents could not act alone in consenting to the withdrawal of treatment, which they supported.

QUESTIONS:

1. Was Holman J. justified in reaching his decision in *Re MB*, given that it did not concur with the "very formidable" body of medical evidence of very high quality in this case which is all, without exception, to the same effect" i.e. that ventilation should be discontinued?

2. Do you agree with the judge's recommendation (following the approach of Thorpe L.J. in *Re A (Mental Patient: Sterilisation)* (see Chapter 13 at p.983) that checklists of advantages and disadvantages of the various options should be drawn up by the parties to such cases?

3. The judge concluded that the father's religious beliefs, as a practising Muslim who believed that the decision about when each of us should die should be left to God, were irrelevant, on the grounds that "[a]n objective balancing of [MB's] own best interests cannot be affected by whether a parent happens to adhere to one particular religious belief, or another, or

none" Do you agree? Is this in line with other case law? (See p.425, Note 4 above.)

4. Do you agree with the judge that the concept of an "intolerable" life is meaningless as a legal test?

(c) The Special Case of Conjoined Twins

While the application of the "best interests" test is now well established in health care law, and clearly to be determined on a case-by-case basis, a particularly challenging situation was posed when a hospital in Manchester sought a declaration from the court that it would be lawful to perform surgery to separate a pair of conjoined twins. The parents of the twins had travelled from Gozo to receive specialist treatment in Manchester and the babies were born with their spinal cords fused and sharing a bladder and aorta. Additionally the weaker twin (known in court as "Mary") had heart and lungs which did not function and her blood supply was pumped by the stronger twin ("Jodie"). Medical evidence suggested that, if the twins were not separated, the strain would eventually damage Jodie's heart and lungs and cause her heart to fail, resulting in the death of both twins within two years, or alternatively Mary might die, necessitating an emergency separation procedure to save Jodie's life. However, electing to separate the twins would inevitably cause Mary's death, although it would free Jodie to live a comparatively normal life, albeit with some degree of disability. The parents, who were Catholic, opposed separation surgery. Johnson J. held that, given Mary's condition, the separation would be in her best interests as well as Jodie's, and that, following the *Bland* case (see Chapter 14), the surgery could be deemed an omission rather than an act, on the basis that it simply withdrew the supply of blood received from Jodie. The Court of Appeal unanimously rejected the parents' appeal, but did depart from the reasoning adopted in the High Court. Here we reproduce extracts from the leading judgment by Ward L.J., although it should be noted that the grounds for decisions reached by the other Lord Justices of Appeal were somewhat different.

WARD L.J.
" . . . The fundamental principle, now long established, is that every person's body is inviolate: see, *per* Lord Goff of Chieveley in *In re F (Mental Patient: Sterilisation)* [1990] 2 AC 1, 72e . . .

[T]he crucial questions which arise in this appeal are: (1) is it in Jodie's best interests that she be separated from Mary? (2) Is it in Mary's best interests that she be separated from Jodie? (3) If those interests are in conflict is the court to balance the interests of one against the other and allow one to prevail against the other and how is that to be done? (4) If the prevailing interest is in favour of the operation being performed, can it be lawfully performed? . . .

Johnson J was, in my judgment, plainly right to conclude that the operation would be in Jodie's best interest.

The salient facts are these. The operation itself carries a negligible risk of death or brain damage. On the contrary the operation is overwhelmingly likely to have the consequence that Jodie's life will be extended from the period of three to six months or a little more to one where she may enjoy a normal expectancy of life. Prolonging her life is an obvious benefit to her. In general terms, she will live a normal or fairly normal life . . . [I]n the context of the argument which has dominated this case, namely the sanctity of life and the worthwhileness of life, it seems to me impossible to say that this operation does not offer infinitely greater benefit to Jodie than is offered to her by letting her die if the operation is not performed . . .

The question of Mary's best interests is one of the key and one of the difficult issues in the case . . . That Mary's welfare is paramount is a trite observation for family lawyers . . .

The first step must be to characterise [the proposed] course of action. Here it is proposed to operate to separate Mary from Jodie. So the first question is: what are the gains and losses from that intervention? . . . The only gain I can see is that the operation would, if successful, give Mary the bodily integrity and dignity which is the natural order for all of us. But this is a wholly illusory goal because she will be dead before she can enjoy her independence and she will die because, when she is independent, she has no capacity for life . . .

What the sanctity of life doctrine compels me to accept is that each life has inherent value in itself and the right to life, being universal, is equal for all of us. The sanctity of life doctrine does, however, acknowledge that it may be proper to withhold or withdraw treatment. The Archbishop points out that in Roman Catholic moral theology one is justified in declining 'extraordinary' treatment where the prospective benefits of treatment do not clearly warrant the burdensome consequences it is likely to impose, such as physical pain, psychological stress, social dislocation and financial expenditure. John Keown argues, to my mind very persuasively, 113 LQR 481, 485 that:

'the question is always whether the treatment would be worthwhile, not whether the patient's life would be worthwhile. Were one to engage in judgments of the latter sort, and to conclude that certain lives were not worth living, one would forfeit any principled basis for objecting to intentional killing.'

In my judgment, that is essentially what the court was doing in *In re J* [1990] and what I was trying to do in *In re C* [1990] . . .

Given the international conventions protecting 'the right to life' to which I will return later, I conclude that it is impermissible to deny that every life has an equal inherent value. Life is worthwhile in itself whatever the diminution in one's capacity to enjoy it and however gravely impaired some of one's vital functions of speech, deliberation and choice may be. I agree with the Archbishop that: 'The indispensable foundation of justice is the basic equality in worth of every human being.' This accords with the observation of Lord Mustill in Bland's case [1993] AC 789, 894:

whilst the fact that a patient is in great pain may give him or her a powerful motive for wanting to end [his or her life], to which in certain circumstances it is proper to accede, [that] is not at all the same as the proposition that because of incapacity or infirmity one life is intrinsically worth less than another. This is the first step on a very dangerous road indeed, and one which I am not willing to take.'

Neither am I. In my judgment, Johnson J was wrong to find that Mary's life would be worth nothing to her. I am satisfied that Mary's life, desperate as it is, still has its own ineliminable value and dignity . . .

What is proposed should be done and what the court is being asked to sanction demands that the question be framed in this way: is it in Mary's best interests that an operation be performed to separate her from Jodie when the certain consequence of that operation is that she will die? There is only one answer to that question. It is: "No, that is not in her best interests." . . . It will bring her life to an end before it has run its natural span. It denies her inherent right to life. There is no countervailing advantage for her at all. It is contrary to her best interests. Looking at her position in isolation and ignoring, therefore, the benefit to Jodie, the court should not sanction the operation on her.

On the sharpest horns of dilemma: what does the court do now? . . .

If the duty of the court is to make a decision which puts Jodie's interests paramount and that decision would be contrary to the paramount interests of Mary, then, for my part, I do not see how the court can reconcile the impossibility of properly fulfilling each duty by simply declining to decide the very matter before it. That would be a total abdication of the duty which is imposed upon us. Given the conflict of duty, I can see no other way of dealing with it than by choosing the lesser of the two evils and so finding the least detrimental alternative. A balance has to be struck somehow and I cannot flinch from undertaking that evaluation, horrendously difficult though it is. Before doing so, I must decide what weight to give to the parents' wishes . . .

[I]t is perhaps useful to repeat the passage in the judgment of Sir Thomas Bingham MR in *In re Z (A Minor) (Identification: Restrictions on Publication)* [1997] Fam 1, 32–33, in accordance with which Johnson J approached this part of the case. Sir Thomas Bingham MR said:

'I would for my part accept without reservation that the decision of a devoted and responsible parent should be treated with respect. It should certainly not be disregarded or lightly set aside. But the role of the court is to exercise an independent and objective judgment. If that judgment is in accord with that of the devoted and responsible parent, well and good. If it is not, then it is the duty of the court, after giving due weight to the view of the devoted and responsible parent, to give effect to its own judgment . . . '

I would wish to say emphatically that this is not a case where opposition is 'prompted by scruple or dogma'. The views of the parents will strike a chord of agreement with many who reflect upon their dilemma. I cannot emphasise enough how much I sympathise with them in the cruelty of the agonising choice they had to make. I know because I agonise over the dilemma too. I fear, however, that the parents' wish does not convince me that it is in the children's best interest.

(i) From Jodie's point of view they have taken the worst possible scenario that she would be wheelchair bound, destined for a life of difficulty. They fail to recognise her capacity sufficiently to enjoy the benefits of life that would be available to her were she free and independent.

(ii) She may indeed need special care and attention and that may be very difficult fully to provide in their home country. This is a real and practical problem for the family, the burden of which in ordinary family life should not be underestimated. It may seem unduly harsh on these desperate parents to point out that it is the child's best interests which are paramount, not the parents'. Coping with a disabled child sadly inevitably casts a great burden on parents who have to struggle through those difficulties. There is, I sense, a lack of consistency in their approach to their daughters' welfare. In Mary's case they are overwhelmed by the legitimate, as I have found it to be, need to respect and protect her right to life. They surely cannot so minimise Jodie's rights on the basis that the burden of possible disadvantage for her and the burdens of caring for such a child for them can morally be said to outweigh her claim to the human dignity of independence which only cruel fate has denied her.

(iii) They are fully entitled to recoil at the idea, as they see it, of killing Mary. That is wholly understandable. This lies at the core of their objection. Yet they came to this country for treatment. They were aware of the possibility that Mary might be stillborn and they seemed reconciled to an operation which would separate Jodie from her. They seemed to have been prepared, and presented their case to Johnson J on the basis that they would agree to the operation if Mary predeceased Jodie. The physical problems for Jodie would be the same, perhaps even worse in such an event. The parents appear to have been willing to cope in that event, and the burdens for parents and child cannot have changed. Mary is lost to them anyway.

(iv) In their natural repugnance at the idea of killing Mary they fail to recognise their conflicting duty to save Jodie and they seem to exculpate themselves from, or at least fail fully to face up to, the consequence of the failure to separate the twins, namely death for Jodie. In my judgment, parents who are placed on the horns of

such a terrible dilemma simply have to choose the lesser of their inevitable
loss . . .

The question which the court has to answer is whether or not the proposed treatment,
the operation to separate, is in the best interests of the twins. That enables me to consider
and place in the scales of each twin the worthwhileness of the treatment. That is a quite
different exercise from the proscribed (because it offends the sanctity of life principle)
consideration of the worth of one life compared with the other. When considering the
worthwhileness of the treatment, it is legitimate to have regard to the actual condition of
each twin and hence the actual balance sheet of advantage and disadvantage which flows
from the performance or the non-performance of the proposed treatment. Here it is
legitimate, as John Keown demonstrates, and as the cases show, to bear in mind the actual
quality of life each child enjoys and may be able to enjoy. In summary, the operation will
give Jodie the prospects of a normal expectation of relatively normal life. The operation
will shorten Mary's life but she remains doomed for death . . . Mary may have a right to
life, but she has little right to be alive. She is alive because and only because, to put it
bluntly, but none the less accurately, she sucks the lifeblood of Jodie. She will survive only
so long as Jodie survives. Jodie will not survive long because constitutionally she will not
be able to cope. Mary's parasitic living will be the cause of Jodie's ceasing to live. If Jodie
could speak, she would surely protest, 'Stop it, Mary, you're killing me.' Mary would have
no answer to that. Into my scales of fairness and justice between the children goes the fact
that nobody but the doctors can help Jodie. Mary is beyond help.

Hence I am in no doubt at all that the scales come down heavily in Jodie's favour. The
best interests of the twins is to give the chance of life to the child whose actual bodily
condition is capable of accepting the chance to her advantage even if that has to be at the
cost of the sacrifice of the life which is so unnaturally supported. I am wholly satisfied that
the least detrimental choice, balancing the interests of Mary against Jodie and Jodie against
Mary, is to permit the operation to be performed . . . .

I would grant permission for the operation to take place provided, however, what is
proposed to be done can be lawfully done. That requires a consideration of the criminal
law, to which I now turn . . .

[D]espite several earlier attempts by the House of Lords to clarify the mens rea required
to establish murder, 'The law of murder was in a state of disarray': *per* Lord Steyn in *R v
Woollin* [1999] 1 AC 82, 91a. *Woollin* is binding upon us . . . Law which has long needed
to be settled should be left to settle. The test I have to set myself is that established by that
case. I have to ask myself whether I am satisfied that the doctors recognise that death or
serious harm will be virtually certain, barring some unforeseen intervention, to result from
carrying out this operation. If so, the doctors intend to kill or to do that serious harm even
though they may not have any desire to achieve that result. It is common ground that they
appreciate that death to Mary would result from the severance of the common aorta.
Unpalatable though it may be—and Mr Whitfield contends it is—to stigmatise the doctors
with 'murderous intent', that is what in law they will have if they perform the operation
and Mary dies as a result . . .

The reality here—harsh as it is to state it, and unnatural as it is that it should be
happening—is that Mary is killing Jodie. That is the effect of the incontrovertible medical
evidence and it is common ground in the case. Mary uses Jodie's heart and lungs to receive
and use Jodie's oxygenated blood. This will cause Jodie's heart to fail and cause Jodie's
death as surely as a slow drip of poison. How can it be just that Jodie should be required
to tolerate that state of affairs? One does not need to label Mary with the American
terminology which would paint her to be 'an unjust aggressor', which I feel is wholly
inappropriate language for the sad and helpless position in which Mary finds herself. I
have no difficulty in agreeing that this unique happening cannot be said to be unlawful. But
it does not have to be unlawful. The six-year-old boy indiscriminately shooting all and
sundry in the school playground is not acting unlawfully for he is too young for his acts
to be so classified. But is he 'innocent' within the moral meaning of that word as used by

the Archbishop? I am not qualified to answer that moral question because, despite an assertion — or was it an aspersion? — by a member of the Bar in a letter to 'The Times' that we, the judges, are proclaiming some moral superiority in this case, I for my part would defer any opinion as to a child's innocence to the Archbishop for that is his territory. If I had to hazard a guess, I would venture the tentative view that the child is not morally innocent. What I am, however, competent to say is that in law killing that six-year-old boy in self-defence of others would be fully justified and the killing would not be unlawful. I can see no difference in essence between that resort to legitimate self-defence and the doctors coming to Jodie's defence and removing the threat of fatal harm to her presented by Mary's draining her lifeblood. The availability of such a plea of quasi-self-defence, modified to meet the quite exceptional circumstances nature has inflicted on the twins, makes intervention by the doctors lawful."

NOTES:

1. Walker L.J. and Brooke L.J. agreed that the operation could lawfully be carried out. All three judges thought that nothing in the Human Rights Act 1998 altered their conclusion that the operation to separate the twins was lawful.
2. The judges disagreed on whether separation can be deemed to be in Mary's best interests, with both the first instance judge and Walker L.J. arguing that separation and Mary's death could be in her best interests while Ward L.J. and Brooke L.J. accepted that it was against her best interests. On your reading of the law considered to date, which view do you think is correct?
3. Rather than invoking the doctrine of self-defence or "quasi-self-defence" as a justification for the doctors' actions in killing Mary, the other two judges rely on the doctrine of necessity. However, as Jenny McEwan notes, it is well-settled criminal law that necessity is no defence to murder. Notwithstanding Ward L.J.'s assertion that the case is unique and the court must be wary of upsetting established principles of criminal law, McEwan contends that in this case "we find Family Division judges making a fundamental change to criminal law doctrine". She argues that the Court of Appeal has "opened the door to lawful acquittal where euthanasia is the reason for a killing and that there is now considerable doubt as to how much value the common law attaches the sanctity of life" (J. McEwan, "Murder by Design: the 'Feel-Good Factor' and the Criminal Law" (2001) *Medical Law Review*, 246 at pp.247–248; R. Huxtable, "Separation of Conjoined Twins: Where Next for English Law?" [2002] *Criminal Law Review* 459–470.)

QUESTIONS:

1. Is it possible to draw parallels between the difficulties the courts had in this case with conceptualising conjoined bodies and applying the usual principles of health care law to them, with the difficulties that law has experienced in dealing with the condition of pregnancy? (See Chapters 12 and 13; V. Munro, "Square Pegs and Round Holes: the Dilemma of Conjoined Twins and Individual Rights" (2001) 10 *Social and Legal Studies* 4.

2. Barbra Hewson has argued, following Alice Domurat Dreger, that "attempts to separate conjoined twins are driven largely by a deep-seated concern for cultural norms of individuality" and are rooted in notions of restoring physical normality (B. Hewson, "Killing Off Mary: Ws the Court of Appeal Right?" (2001) 9 *Medical Law Review* 281 at p.282.) Do you agree? (See also M. Shildrick, *Embodying the Monster: Encounters with the Vulnerable Self*, London: Sage, 2001, Chapter 3.)

3. Even if you agree that it was right to separate the twins, should the procedure have been carried out in the face of parental objections? (See J. Harris, "Human Beings, Persons and Conjoined Twins: An Ethical Analysis of the Judgment in *Re A*" (2001) 9 *Medical Law Review* 221; R. Gillon, "Imposed Separation of Conjoined Twins—Moral Hubris by the English Courts?" (2001) 27 *Journal of Medical Ethics* 3.)

4. Is it defensible to draw the distinction which both Ward L.J. and Brook L.J. seek to draw (following the health care lawyer John Keown) between worthwhile treatment and a worthwhile life? (See Harris, *op. cit.* in question 3). Notwithstanding their denials, do the judges effectively treat Jodie's life as being of greater value than Mary's? (See S. Michalowski, "Sanctity of Life — Are Some Lives More Sacred than Others?" (2002) 22 *Legal Studies* 377–397.)

5. The characterisation of Mary in the judgments is particularly interesting. In employing self-defence arguments, Ward L.J. characterises her as an aggressor; in the other judgments she is liked to a parasite. Harris (*op. cit.* in question 3 at p.235) argues that "the judges tacitly assumed that Mary and Jodie were more like fetuses or individuals in PVS than persons". Do you agree? Mason suggests that it is even arguable that Mary could have been deemed a still birth which would have avoided some of the ethical difficulties raised by the case (K. Mason, "Conjoined Twins: A Diagnostic Conundrum" (2001) 5 *Edinburgh Law Review* 226). Should the Official Solicitor have appealed in this case? Do you think there would have been any chance of winning on appeal? (See Hewson, *op. cit.* in question 1).

6. Notwithstanding the attention and critical commentary it has attracted, does *Re A* offer anything worthwhile to health care law doctrine? What implications could it have for other cases if one twin can effectively be sacrificed to save the life of another? (See S. Sheldon and S. Wilkinson, "Conjoined Twins: the Legality and Ethics of Sacrifice" (1997) 5 *Medical Law Review* 150.)

3. AN OLDER CHILD'S CAPACITY TO CONSENT TO MEDICAL TREATMENT: STATUTE AND COMMON LAW

(a) The Statutory Power of Consent

Different problems arise when the question for the court is whether a minor is sufficiently competent to decide upon his own medical treatment. For the purposes of English law, a child is only deemed to reach adulthood at 18 years of age. However, once he reaches the age of 16, the Family Law Reform Act 1969 validates his consent to certain forms of medical procedure, as though he was an adult.

Family Law Reform Act 1969, s.8(1–3)

8.—(1) The consent of a minor who has attained the age of sixteen years to any surgical, medical or dental treatment which, in the absence of consent, would constitute a trespass to his person, shall be as effective as it would be if he were of full age; and where a minor has by virtue of this section given an effective consent to any treatment it shall not be necessary to obtain any consent for it from his parent or guardian.

(2) In this section "surgical, medical or dental treatment" includes any procedure undertaken for the purposes of diagnosis, and this section applies to any procedure (including, in particular, the administration of an anaesthetic) which is ancillary to any treatment as it applies to that treatment.

(3) Nothing in this section shall be construed as making ineffective any consent which would have been effective if this section had not been enacted.

NOTES:

1. Subsection 2 fails to make clear whether the "surgical, medical or dental treatment" envisaged by subs. (1) must be therapeutic. This might place a limit on the medical procedures to which a 16-year-old may give a valid consent under the 1969 Act.
2. Notice that subs.3 clearly preserves someone's power of consent but that it does not make clear whose power of consent that is. It could be the parents' power, the child's power, or both parents' and the child's—the provision is simply not explicit. This is a vital question when confronted with cases in which parents and children or the court disagree about medical procedures. It is explored further at pp.451–463 below.

(b) The Common Law Power of Consent

Section 8 deals only with a minor's power to give consent where he has attained 16 years of age. In relation to the younger child, any power to grant a valid consent to health care provision necessarily emanates from the common law. The leading case concerning a child's capacity to provide a valid consent at common law came before the House of Lords in 1985.

Gillick v. West Norfolk and Wisbech Area Health Authority and Another
[1985] 3 All E.R. 402, [1986] 1 A.C. 112, [1985] 3 W.L.R. 830

The DHSS (as it then was) issued a circular to area health authorities which contained advice effectively stating that if, at a family planning clinic, a doctor was consulted by a girl under 16, she would not be acting unlawfully if she prescribed contraceptives for the girl, as long as she was acting in good faith to protect the girl from the harmful effects of sexual intercourse. The plaintiff, Mrs Gillick, who herself had five daughters under 16, sought an assurance from her local area health authority that her own daughters would not be given any contraceptive advice or treatment without her (Mrs Gillick's) prior knowledge and consent so long as those girls were under 16. The authority refused to provide that assurance. In consequence, Mrs Gillick brought an action seeking, against the area health authority, a declaration that a doctor, or other professional employed by it in its family planning service, could not give advice and treatment on contraception to any of her children under 16 without her consent, because to do so would be unlawful as being inconsistent with the plaintiff's parental rights. At first instance, Woolf J. refused to grant the declaration. Mrs Gillick appealed to the Court of Appeal where she was successful and the judgments emphasised the parental right to control the child. The health authority then appealed to the House of Lords, which allowed the appeal by a 3–2 majority.

LORD FRASER

" . . . The central issue in the appeal is whether a doctor can ever, in any circumstances, lawfully give contraceptive advice or treatment to a girl under the age of 16 without her parents' consent . . .

The first statutory provision for contraceptive advice and treatment in the NHS was made by s.1 of the National Health Service (Family Planning) Act 1967 . . .

These, and other, provisions show that Parliament regarded 'advice' and 'treatment' on contraception and the supply of appliances for contraception as essentially medical matters. So they are, but they may also raise moral and social questions on which many people feel deeply, and in that respect they differ from ordinary medical advice and treatment. None of the provisions to which I have referred placed any limit on the age (or the sex) of the persons to whom such advice or treatment might be supplied . . .

There are some indications in statutory provisions to which we were referred that a girl under 16 years of age in England and Wales does not have the capacity to give valid consent to contraceptive advice and treatment . . . One of those provisions is s.8 of the Family Law Reform Act 1969 [see p.440 above] . . . The contention on behalf of Mrs Gillick was that subs. (1) of s.8 shows that, apart from the subsection, the consent of a minor to such treatment would not be effective. But I do not accept that contention because subs. (3) leaves open the question whether consent by a minor under the age of 16 would have been effective if the section had not been enacted. That question is not answered by the section, and subs. (1) is, in my opinion, merely for the avoidance of doubt.

[Having referred to a number of other statutory provisions his Lordship continued:] . . .

The statutory provisions to which I have referred do not differentiate so far as the capacity of a minor under 16 is concerned between contraceptive advice and treatment and other forms of medical advice and treatment. It would, therefore, appear that, if the inference which Mrs Gillick's advisers seek to draw from the provisions is justified, a minor under the age of 16 has no capacity to authorise any kind of medical advice or treatment or examination of his own body. That seems to me so surprising that I cannot accept it in the absence of clear provisions to that effect. It seems to me verging on the absurd to suggest that a girl or a boy aged 15 could not effectively consent, for example, to have a medical examination of some trivial injury to his body or even to have a broken arm set. Of course the consent of the parents should normally be asked, but they may not be immediately available. Provided the patient, whether a boy or a girl, is capable of understanding what is proposed, and of expressing his or her own wishes, I see no good reason for holding that he or she lacks the capacity to express them validly and effectively and to authorise the medical man to make the examination or give the treatment which he advises. After all, a minor under the age of 16 can, within certain limits, enter into a contract. He or she can also sue and be sued, and can give evidence on oath. Moreover, a girl under 16 can give sufficiently effective consent to sexual intercourse to lead to the legal result that the man involved does not commit the crime of rape: see *R. v. Howard* [1965] 3 All E.R. 684 at 685, when Lord Parker C.J. said:

' . . . in the case of a girl under sixteen, the prosecution, in order to prove rape, must prove either that she physically resisted, or if she did not, that her understanding and knowledge were such that she was not in a position to decide whether to consent or resist . . . there are many girls under sixteen who know full well what it is all about and can properly consent.'

Accordingly, I am not disposed to hold now, for the first time, that a girl aged less than 16 lacks the power to give valid consent to contraceptive advice or treatment, merely on account of her age.

I conclude that there is no statutory provision which compels me to hold that a girl under the age of 16 lacks the legal capacity to consent to contraceptive advice, examination and treatment provided that she has sufficient understanding and intelligence to know what they involve . . . "

LORD SCARMAN

" . . . The modern law governing parental right and a child's capacity to make his own decisions was considered in *R v. D* [1984] 2 All E.R. 449. The House must, in my view, be understood as having in that case accepted that, save where statute otherwise provides, a minor's capacity to make his or her own decision depends on the minor having sufficient understanding and intelligence to make the decision and is not to be determined by reference to any judicially fixed age limit . . . Lord Brandon, with whom their other Lordships agreed, commented that this might well have been the view of the legislature and the courts in the nineteenth century, but had this to say about parental right and a child's capacity in our time to give or withhold a valid consent ([1984] 2 All E.R. 449 at 456):

'This is because in those times both the generally accepted conventions of society and the courts by which such conventions were buttressed and enforced, regarded a father as having absolute and paramount authority, as against all the world, over any children of his who were still under the age of majority (then 21), except for a married daughter. The nature of this view of a father's rights appears clearly from various reported cases, including, as a typical example, *Re Agar-Ellis, Agar-Ellis v. Lascelles* (1883) 24 Ch.D. 317. The common law, however, while generally immutable in its principles, unless different principles are laid down by statute, is not immutable in the way in which it adapts, develops and applies those principles in a radically changing world and against the background of radically changed social conventions and conditions.' . . .

In the light of the foregoing I would hold that as a matter of law the parental right to determine whether or not their minor child below the age of 16 will have medical treatment terminates if and when the child achieves a sufficient understanding and intelligence to enable him or her to understand fully what is proposed. It will be a question of fact whether a child seeking advice has sufficient understanding of what is involved to give a consent valid in law. Until the child achieves the capacity to consent, the parental right to make the decision continues save only in exceptional circumstances. Emergency, parental neglect, abandonment of the child or inability to find the parent are examples of exceptional situations justifying the doctor proceeding to treat the child without parental knowledge and consent; but there will arise, no doubt, other exceptional situations in which it will be reasonable for the doctor to proceed without the parent's consent.

When applying these conclusions to contraceptive advice and treatment it has to be borne in mind that there is much that has to be understood by a girl under the age of 16 if she is to have legal capacity to consent to such treatment. It is not enough that she should understand the nature of the advice which is being given: she must also have a sufficient maturity to understand what is involved. There are moral and family questions, especially her relationship with her parents; long-term problems associated with the emotional impact of pregnancy and its termination; and there are the risks to health of sexual intercourse at her age, risks which contraception may diminish but cannot eliminate. It follows that a doctor will have to satisfy himself that she is able to appraise these factors before he can safely proceed on the basis that she has at law capacity to consent to contraceptive treatment. And it further follows that ordinarily the proper course will be for him, as the guidance lays down, first to seek to persuade the girl to bring her parents into consultation, and, if she refuses, not to prescribe contraceptive treatment unless he is satisfied that her circumstances are such that he ought to proceed without parental knowledge and consent.

Like Woolf J., I find illuminating and helpful the judgment of Addy J. of the Ontario High Court in *Johnston v. Wellesley Hospital* (1970) 17 D.L.R. (3d) 139, a passage from which he quotes in his judgment in this case ([1984] 1 All E.R. 365 at 374). The key passage bears repetition (17 D.L.R. (3d) 139 at 144–145):

> 'But, regardless of modern trend, I can find nothing in any of the old reported cases, except where infants of tender age or young children were involved, where the Courts have found that a person under 21 years of age was legally incapable of consenting to medical treatment. If a person under 21 years were unable to consent to medical treatment, he would also be incapable of consenting to other types of bodily interference. A proposition purporting to establish that any bodily interference acquiesced in by a youth of 20 years would nevertheless constitute an assault would be absurd . . . I am, therefore, satisfied that the department's guidance can be followed without involving the doctor in any infringement of parental right. Unless, therefore, to prescribe contraceptive treatment for a girl under the age of 16 is either a criminal offence or so close to one that to prescribe such treatment is contrary to public policy, the department's appeal must succeed . . . ' "

NOTES:

1. Lord Bridge also delivered a short speech, but he expressly agreed with both Lord Fraser and Lord Scarman, notwithstanding the fact that there are significant differences in their opinions. Both Lord Brandon and Lord Templeman dissented on the question of whether a doctor could ever give contraceptive advice or treatment to a girl under 16 without parental knowledge or consent. It is worth noting that overall a majority of the total of nine judges who heard the case would have found in favour of Mrs Gillick.

2. Various commentators have pointed out that the House of Lords failed to determine what exactly it is that the young person must understand in order to be deemed sufficiently mature to be entrusted with decision-making powers. Lord Fraser simply states without explanation that the girl must understand the doctor's advice. Lord Scarman does attempt to define the requisite capacity (at pp.442–443 above), but this is problematic in that setting the threshold of understanding so high may mean that many adults would fail to satisfy his test. This is particularly evident when he speaks of "the attainment by a child of an age of sufficient discretion to enable him or her to exercise a wise choice in his or her own interests" and of the child achieving "a sufficient intelligence to enable him or her to understand fully what is proposed". (See S. Lee, *Judging Judges*, London: Faber, 1988, Chapter 11; J. Montgomery, "Children as Property?" (1988) 51 M.L.R. 323.)

3. The result of the majority decision in *Gillick* is that no criminal offence is committed by a doctor who gives contraceptive advice or treatment to a

young person under 16 without parental consent. The majority emphasised that criminal liability would depend upon intention, so that a doctor who provided contraceptive advice or treatment to a girl under the age of 16, honestly intending to act in the girl's best interests (by avoiding the consequences of an unwanted pregnancy) rather than with the intention of facilitating unlawful sexual intercourse would incur no criminal liability. (See J. Bridgeman, "Don't Tell the Children: The Department's Guidance on the Provision of Information about Contraception to Individual Pupils" in N. Harris (ed.), *Children, Sex Education and the Law: Examining the Issues*, London: National Children's Bureau, 1996 at p.53.)

4. In *R (on the application of Axon) v SoS for Health* [2006] 2 W.L.R. 1130 the High Court dismissed an application by a mother of teenage girls, who sought judicial review of 2004 Department of Health guidance based on Lord Fraser's guidelines in *Gillick*. Sue Axon maintained that the guidance breached a parent's right to know if health professionals were advising or treating children under 16 in relation to contraception, sexually transmitted diseases or abortion. Although the case is primarily concerned with the young person's right to confidentiality (see Chapter 10), Silber J did affirm the right of a competent young person to medical treatment, as laid down in the majority judgments. He also stressed that the Fraser guidance could have broader application:

> "there is no reason why Lord Fraser's Guidelines and Lord Scarman's criteria should not be adapted and applied to advice and treatment for abortion even though abortions raise, as I have explained, more serious and complex issues than contraception."

Furthermore, he held that the guidance did not breach Article 8 of the European Convention on Human Rights; and noted that children's rights had become increasingly prominent since the *Gillick* decision. There was no mention in the judgment of the retreat from *Gillick* discussed below.

QUESTIONS:

1. To be regarded as competent to consent to treatment, must a young person understand merely in broad medical terms what is proposed, or must he also understand the familial and social implications of what is involved? Contrast the different views expressed by Lords Fraser and Scarman.

2. Is "*Gillick* competence" an absolute concept, representing a watershed beyond which a sufficiently mature minor is capable of consenting to all and any medical procedures? Or is it an incremental concept, allowing a child to consent to simple operations—such as a tonsillectomy—at a relatively early stage in his development and then more complex medical procedures at a later stage, when he has matured even further? Also, can a child have fluctuating capacity (i.e. be "*Gillick* competent" one day but not the next)? (See *Re R* at pp.452–454 below.)

3. Does the *Gillick* decision really emancipate children, or does it simply transfer the right to make paternalistic decisions from parents to doctors? (See J. Montgomery, *op. cit.* in note 2.)
4. Given the difficulties in defining and demonstrating competence, would it be preferable to simply presume that children of compulsory school age (five years old) are presumed competent, so that the onus would lie upon adults to demonstrate the child's incompetence, rather than requiring the child to pass tests of competence which many adults might fail? (See P. Alderson and J. Montgomery, *Health Care Choices: Making Decisions with Children*, London: Institute for Public Policy Research, 1996.)

Though the Family Law Reform Act 1969 confers an unequivocal power to consent to medical treatment upon a child when he reaches 16 years, the legislation does not address the power to refuse such treatment. This is not an academic point for, if a 16-year-old adolescent is incapable of expressing a view or unwilling to grant consent, it raises the question as to whether his parents retain their power of consent (until the child's majority). If they do, then it becomes possible for parents to sanction treatment to which a "*Gillick* competent" child objects.

Whether parents do in fact retain their power to give consent to their child's treatment beyond 16 years of age or the attainment of *Gillick* competence was considered obliquely by their Lordships in the *Gillick* case.

Gillick v West Norfolk and Wisbech Area Health Authority and Another
[1985] 3 All E.R. 402, [1986] 1 A.C. 112, [1985] 3 W.L.R. 830

LORD FRASER
" . . . The amended [DHSS] guidance expressly states that the doctor will proceed from the assumption that it would be 'most unusual' to provide advice about contraception without parental consent. It also refers to certain cases where difficulties might arise if the doctor refused to promise that his advice would remain confidential and it concludes that the department realises that 'in such exceptional cases' the decision whether or not to prescribe contraception must be for the clinical judgment of a doctor. Mrs Gillick's contention that the guidance adversely affects her rights and duties as a parent must, therefore, involve the assertion of an absolute right to be informed of and to veto such advice or treatment being given to her daughters even in the 'most unusual' cases which might arise (subject, no doubt, to the qualifications applying to the case of court order or to abandonment of parents' duties).

It was, I think, accepted both by Mrs Gillick and by the DHSS, and in any event I hold, that parental rights to control a child do not exist for the benefit of the parent. They exist for the benefit of the child and they are justified only in so far as they enable the parent to perform his duties towards the child, and towards other children in the family. If necessary, this proposition can be supported by reference to *Blackstone's Commentaries* (1 Bl Com (17th edn, 1830) 452), where he wrote: 'The power of parents over their children is derived from . . . their duty.' The proposition is also consistent with the provisions of the Guardianship of Minors Act 1971, s.1, as amended, as follows:

'Where in any proceedings before any court . . . (a) the legal custody or upbringing of a minor . . . is in question, the court, in deciding that question, shall regard the welfare of

the minor as the first and paramount consideration, and shall not take into consideration whether from any other point of view the claim of the father in respect of such legal
custody, upbringing, administration or application is superior to that of the mother, or
the claim of the mother is superior to that of the father.'

From the parents' right and duty of custody flows their right and duty of control of the
child, but the fact that custody is its origin throws but little light on the question of the
legal extent of control at any particular age. Counsel for Mrs Gillick placed some reliance
on the Children Act 1975. Section 85(1) provides that in that Act the expression 'the
parental rights and duties' means 'all the rights and duties which by law the mother and
father have in relation to a legitimate child and his property', but the subsection does not
define the extent of the rights and duties which by law the mother and father have. Section
86 of the Act provides:

'In this Act, unless the context otherwise requires, "legal custody" means, as respects a
child, so much of the parental rights and duties as relate to the person of the child
(including the place and manner in which his time is spent) . . . '

In the Court of Appeal Parker L.J. attached much importance to that section, especially to
the words in brackets. He considered that the right relating to the place and manner in
which the child's time is spent included the right, as he put it, 'completely to control the
child' subject of course always to the intervention of the court. Parker L.J. went on thus
([1985] 1 All E.R. 533 at 540):

'Indeed there must, it seems to me, be such a right from birth to a fixed age unless
whenever, short of majority, a question arises it must be determined, in relation to a
particular child and a particular matter, whether he or she is of sufficient understanding
to make a responsible and reasonable decision. This alternative appears to me singularly
unattractive and impracticable, particularly in the context of medical treatment.'

My Lords, I have, with the utmost respect, reached a different conclusion from that of
Parker L.J. It is, in my view, contrary to the ordinary experience of mankind, at least in
Western Europe in the present century, to say that a child or a young person remains in fact
under the complete control of his parents until he attains the definite age of majority, now
18 in the United Kingdom, and that on attaining that age he suddenly acquires
independence. In practice most wise parents relax their control gradually as the child
develops and encourage him or her to become increasingly independent. Moreover, the
degree of parental control actually exercised over a particular child does in practice vary
considerably according to his understanding and intelligence and it would, in my opinion,
be unrealistic for the courts not to recognise these facts. Social customs change, and the law
ought to, and does in fact, have regard to such changes when they are of major
importance . . .
    It is a question of fact for the judge (or jury) to decide whether a particular child can give
effective consent to contraceptive treatment . . . "

LORD SCARMAN
" . . . Mrs Gillick relies on both the statute law and the case law to establish her
proposition that parental consent is in all other circumstances necessary. The only
statutory provision directly in point is s.8 of the Family Law Reform Act 1969 . . .
    I cannot accept the submission made on Mrs Gillick's behalf that sub-s.(1) necessarily
implies that prior to its enactment the consent of a minor to medical treatment could not
be effective in law. Subsection (3) leaves open the question whether the consent of a minor
under 16 could be an effective consent. Like my noble and learned friend Lord Fraser, I
read the section as clarifying the law without conveying any indication as to what the law
was before it was enacted. So far as minors under 16 are concerned, the law today is as it
was before the enactment of the section.

Nor do I find in the provisions of the statute law to which Parker L.J. refers in his judgment in the Court of Appeal (see [1985] 1 All E.R. 533) any encouragement, let alone any compelling reason, for holding that Parliament has accepted that a child under 16 cannot consent to medical treatment. I respectfully agree with the reasoning and conclusion of my noble and learned friend Lord Fraser on this point.

The law has, therefore, to be found by a search in the judge-made law for the true principle. The legal difficulty is that in our search we find ourselves in a field of medical practice where parental right and a doctor's duty may point us in different directions. This is not surprising. Three features have emerged in today's society which were not known to our predecessors: (1) contraception as a subject for medical advice and treatment; (2) the increasing independence of young people; and (3) the changed status of women. In times past contraception was rarely a matter for the doctor but with the development of the contraceptive pill for women it has become part and parcel of every-day medical practice, as is made clear by the department's *Handbook of Contraceptive Practice* (1984 revision) esp para. 1.2. Family planning services are now available under statutory powers to all without any express limitation as to age or marital status. Young people, once they have attained the age of 16, are capable of consenting to contraceptive treatment, since it is medical treatment; and, however extensive be parental right in the care and upbringing of children, it cannot prevail so as to nullify the 16-year-old's capacity to consent which is now conferred by statute. Furthermore, women have obtained by the availability of the pill a choice of life-style with a degree of independence and of opportunity undreamed of until this generation and greater, I would add, than any law of equal opportunity could by itself effect.

The law ignores these developments at its peril. The House's task, therefore, as the supreme court in a legal system largely based on rules of law evolved over the years by the judicial process is to search the overfull and cluttered shelves of the law reports for a principle or set of principles recognised by the judges over the years but stripped of the detail which, however appropriate in their day, would, if applied today, lay the judges open to a justified criticism for failing to keep the law abreast of the society in which they live and work.

... Parental rights clearly do exist, and they do not wholly disappear until the age of majority ... The principle of the law, as I shall endeavour to show, is that parental rights are derived from parental duty and exist only so long as they are needed for the protection of the person and property of the child. The principle has been subjected to certain age limits set by statute for certain purposes; and in some cases the courts have declared an age of discretion at which a child acquires before the age of majority the right to make his (or her) own decision. But these limitations in no way undermine the principle of the law, and should not be allowed to obscure it ...

Although statute has intervened in respect of a child's capacity to consent to medical treatment from the age of 16 onwards, neither statute nor the case law has ruled on the extent and duration of parental right in respect of children under the age of 16. More specifically, there is no rule yet applied to contraceptive treatment, which has special problems of its own and is a late comer in medical practice. It is open, therefore, to the House to formulate a rule. The Court of Appeal favoured a fixed age limit of 16, basing itself on a view of the statute law which I do not share and on its view of the effect of the older case law which for the reasons already given I cannot accept. It sought to justify the limit by the public interest in the law being certain. Certainty is always an advantage in the law, and in some branches of the law it is a necessity. But it brings with it an inflexibility and a rigidity which in some branches of the law can obstruct justice, impede the law's development and stamp on the law the mark of obsolescence where what is needed is the capacity for development. The law relating to parent and child is concerned with the problems of the growth and maturity of the human personality. If the law should impose on the process of 'growing up' fixed limits where nature knows only a continuous process, the price would be artificiality and a lack of realism in an area where the law must be sensitive to human development and social change. If certainty be thought desirable, it is better that the rigid demarcations necessary to achieve it should be laid down by legislation after a full consideration of all the relevant factors than by the courts, confined as they are by the forensic process to the evidence adduced by the parties and to whatever may properly fall within the judicial notice of judges. Unless and until Parliament should think fit to intervene, the courts should establish a principle flexible enough to enable justice to be achieved by its application to the particular circumstances proved by the evidence placed before them.

The underlying principle of the law was exposed by Blackstone and can be seen to have been acknowledged in the case law. It is that parental right yields to the child's right to make his own decisions when he reaches a sufficient understanding and intelligence to be capable of making up his own mind on the matter requiring decision."

LORD TEMPLEMAN (DISSENTING)

" . . . An unmarried girl under the age of 16 does not, in my opinion, possess the power in law to decide for herself to practise contraception. Section 6 of the Sexual Offences Act 1956 makes it an offence for a man to have unlawful sexual intercourse with a girl under the age of 16. Consent by the girl does not afford a defence to the man or constitute an offence by the girl. Parliament has thus indicated that an unmarried girl under the age of 16 is not sufficiently mature to be allowed to decide for herself that she will take part in sexual intercourse. Such a girl cannot therefore be regarded as sufficiently mature to be allowed to decide for herself that she will practise contraception for the purpose of frequent or regular or casual sexual intercourse. Section 6 of the Sexual Offences Act 1956 does not, however, in my view, prevent parent and doctor from deciding that contraceptive facilities shall be made available to an unmarried girl under the age of 16 whose sexual activities are recognised to be uncontrolled and uncontrollable. Section 6 is designed to protect the girl from sexual intercourse. But if the girl cannot be deterred then contraceptive facilities may be provided, not for the purpose of aiding and abetting an offence under s 6 but for the purpose of avoiding the consequences, principally pregnancy, which the girl may suffer from illegal sexual intercourse where sexual intercourse cannot be prevented. In general, where parent and doctor agree that any form of treatment, including contraceptive treatment, is in the best interests of the girl, there is, in my opinion, no legal bar to that treatment.

Difficulties arise when parent and doctor differ. The parent, claiming the right to decide what is in the best interests of a girl in the custody of that parent, may forbid the provision of contraceptive facilities. A doctor, claiming the right to decide what is in the best interests of a patient, may wish to override the parent's objections. A conflict which is express may be resolved by the court, which may accept the view of either parent or doctor or modify the views of both of them as to what is in the best interests of the girl. The present appeal is concerned with a conflict which is known to the doctor but is concealed from the parent and from the court. The girl, aware that the parent will forbid contraception, requests the doctor to provide and the doctor agrees to provide contraceptive facilities and to keep the parent in ignorance.

A parent is the natural and legal guardian of an infant under the age of 18 and is responsible for the upbringing of an infant who is in the custody of that parent. The practical exercise of parental powers varies from control and supervision to guidance and advice depending on the discipline enforced by the parent and the age and temperament of the infant. Parental power must be exercised in the best interests of the infant and the court may intervene in the interests of the infant at the behest of the parent or at the behest of a third party. The court may enforce parental right, control the misuse of parental power or uphold independent views asserted by the infant. The court will be guided by the principle that the welfare of the infant is paramount. But, subject to the discretion of the court to differ from the views of the parent, the court will, in my opinion, uphold the right of the parent having custody of the infant to decide on behalf of the infant all matters which the infant is not competent to decide. The prudent parent will pay attention to the wishes of the infant and will normally accept them as the infant approaches adulthood. The parent is not bound by the infant's wishes, but an infant approaching adulthood may be able to flout the wishes of the parent with ease . . .

I accept . . . that a doctor may lawfully carry out some forms of treatment with the consent of an infant patient and against the opposition of a parent based on religious or any other grounds. The effect of the consent of the infant depends on the nature of the treatment and the age and understanding of the infant. For example, a doctor with the consent of an intelligent boy or girl of 15 could in my opinion safely remove tonsils or a troublesome appendix. But any decision on the part of a girl to practise sex and contraception requires not only knowledge of the facts of life and of the dangers of pregnancy and disease but also an understanding of the emotional and other consequences to her family, her male partner and to herself. I doubt whether a girl under the age of 16 is capable of a balanced judgement to embark on frequent, regular or casual sexual intercourse fortified by the illusion that medical science can protect her in mind and body and ignoring the danger of leaping from childhood to adulthood without the difficult formative transitional experiences of adolescence. There are many things which a girl under 16 needs to practise but sex is not one of them. Parliament could declare this view to be out of date. But in my opinion the statutory provisions discussed in the speech of my noble and learned friend Lord Fraser and the provisions of s.6 of the Sexual Offences Act 1956 indicate that as the law now stands an unmarried girl under 16 is not competent to decide to practise sex and contraception.

There are several objections to [the majority's] approach. The first objection is that a doctor, acting without the views of the parent, cannot form a 'clinical' or any other reliable judgement that the best interests of the girl require the provision of contraceptive facilities. The doctor at the family planning clinic only knows that which the girl chooses to tell him. The family doctor may know some of the circumstances of some of the families who form his registered patients but his information may be incomplete or misleading . . .

The second objection is that a parent will sooner or later find out the truth, probably sooner, and may do so in circumstances which bring about a complete rupture of good relations between members of the family and between the family and the doctor . . .

The third and main objection advanced on behalf of the respondent parent, Mrs Gillick, in this appeal is that the secret provision of contraceptive facilities for a girl under 16 will, it is said, encourage participation by the girl in sexual intercourse and this practice offends basic principles of morality and religion which ought not to be sabotaged in stealth by kind permission of the national health service. The interests of a girl under 16 require her to be protected against sexual intercourse. Such a girl is not sufficiently mature to be allowed to decide to flout the accepted rules of society. The pornographic press and the lascivious film may falsely pretend that sexual intercourse is a form of entertainment available to females on request and to males on demand but the regular, frequent or casual practice of sexual intercourse by a girl or a boy under the age of 16 cannot be beneficial to anybody and may cause harm to character and personality. Before a girl under 16 is supplied with contraceptive facilities, the parent who knows most about the girl and ought to have the most influence with the girl is entitled to exercise parental rights of control, supervision, guidance and advice in order that the girl may, if possible, avoid sexual intercourse until she is older. Contraception should only be considered if and when the combined efforts of parent and doctor fail to prevent the girl from participating in sexual intercourse and there remains only the possibility of protecting the girl against pregnancy resulting from sexual intercourse . . .

This appeal falls to be determined by the existing law . . . The position seems to me to be as follows. A doctor is not entitled to decide whether a girl under the age of 16 shall be provided with contraceptive facilities if a parent who is in charge of the girl is ready and willing to make that decision in exercise of parental rights. The doctor is entitled in exceptional circumstances and in emergencies to make provision, normally temporary provision, for contraception but in most cases would be bound to inform the parent of the treatment. The court would not hold the doctor liable for providing contraceptive facilities if the doctor had reasonable grounds for believing that the parent had abandoned or abused parental rights or that there was no parent immediately available for consultation or that there was no parent who was responsible for the girl. But exceptional circumstances and emergencies cannot be expanded into a general discretion for the doctor to provide contraceptive facilities without the knowledge of the parent because of the possibility that a girl to whom contraceptive facilities are not available may irresponsibly court the risk of pregnancy. Such a discretion would enable any girl to obtain contraception on request by threatening to sleep with a man . . . "

NOTES:

1. The other dissenting Law Lord, Lord Brandon, based his decision on a perusal of statutory provisions governing the situation where a man has sexual intercourse with a girl under the age of 16. As Simon Lee points out, he thus not only evades the majority's search for legal principle, but is also in the curious position of having provided the principal legal authority for the majority judges, *i.e.* his landmark decision in *R v D* [1984] 2 All E.R. 449 (see S. Lee, *Judging Judges*, London: Faber, 1988 at pp. 80–82). Moreover, Lord Brandon actually adopts a position which is more extreme than that advocated by Mrs Gillick in concluding that: " . . . on the view which I take of the law, making contraception available to girls under sixteen is unlawful whether their parents know of and consent to it or not."

2. The standard academic interpretation of Lord Scarman's opinion in the wake of the decision was that once a child has reached capacity there is no room for a parent to impose a contrary view (even if such a view seems to be more in accord with the child's best interests) because the parental right is extinguished once the child has reached full capacity. However, John Eekelaar points out that Lord Fraser's judgment is much less firm on this matter. Whereas Lord Scarman suggests that the child assumes the power both to consent to and refuse treatment, Lord Fraser does not go beyond the issue of competence to assent to treatment and appears to contemplate that, in some situations, parental rights survive the minor's acquisition of capacity (J. Eekelaar, "The Emergence of Children's Rights" (1986) 6 *Oxford Journal of Legal Studies* 161 at pp.180–181). In the recent *Axon* decision (see p.444, Note 4 above) Silber J. does note that:

    "there is nothing in the speeches of the majority in Gillick, which suggests that parental authority has any place in decision-making for a young person, who in the words of Lord Scarman . . . 'achieves a sufficient understanding and intelligence to enable him or her to fully understand what is proposed.' "

QUESTIONS:

1. Lord Fraser states that the solution to the issue in the *Gillick* case "depends upon a judgment of what is best for the child". Who do you think is best placed to make this judgment—the parents or the doctors—and why? (See J. Montgomery, "Children as Property" (1988) 51 *M.L.R.* 323.) Is there a possibility that the decision in *Gillick* may simply store up future problems by suggesting that it is more appropriate for children's interests to be defined by the state, rather than by their parents? On what basis, if any, should the law circumscribe the power of the conscientious parent? (See J.

Roche, "Children's Rights: in the Name of the Child" (1995) 17 *Journal of Social Welfare and Family Law* 281.)

2. Do you agree with Lord Fraser's view that the nature of family structure has radically altered, and that cases decided at a time when the family was controlled by the father are no longer relevant? Does this only apply to the traditional western "nuclear" family? (See Roche, *op. cit.* in question 1.)

3. Note that Lord Templeman would mitigate the practical effects of deeming young persons under 16 incompetent to consent to contraceptive treatment by invoking exceptional circumstances as a ground for dispensing with the requirement of parental consent. What precisely are the circumstances in which the court would sanction a health professional proceeding without parental consent, or at least permit the doctor to act as a proxy in giving consent? (See Lee, *op. cit.* in note 1, at pp.78–79.)

4. The Retreat from Gillick

As we have seen in the *Gillick* case, Lords Fraser and Scarman were equivocal on the question of whether the attainment of "*Gillick* competence" marked the extinction of the parental power to give consent. Instead, they simply refuted the suggestion that parents have *absolute* control over the health of their children until they reach majority. Neither of their Lordships offered a definitive interpretation of the problematic provision in s.8(3) of the Family Law Reform Act 1969 that: "Nothing in this section shall be construed as making ineffective any consent which would have been effective if this section had not been enacted." Two questions therefore remained unanswered. First, did a child's parents retain any power of consent after the child reaches 16 or acquires "*Gillick* competence" and secondly, where (assuming such power is retained), did the balance of power lie as between parents and their mature children, and what was the role of the court? As subsequent cases established, leaving these issues open allowed the judiciary to retreat from the endorsement of adolescent rights which underpinned the majority decisions in *Gillick*. In these later cases courts have intervened to reassert a welfare principle (as opposed to autonomy) in cases involving adolescents who refuse treatment. Here we follow Caroline Bridge who argues that such intervention has been prompted by two categories of cases, (i) where the young person involved has been deemed by the court to be mentally ill or mentally disturbed, thus rendering the objection to treatment invalid, and (ii) where the refusal has been promoted by a religious belief which denounces the specific form of treatment. (C. Bridge, "Religious Beliefs and Teenage Refusal of Medical Treatment" (1999) 62 M.L.R. 585.)

(a) Refusal of Treatment by Adolescents

The questions left open in *Gillick* were addressed first by the then Master of the Rolls, Lord Donaldson, in two cases concerning adolescent girls:

Re R (A Minor) (Wardship: Medical Treatment) [1991] 4 All E.R. 177, [1992] Fam. 11, [1991] 3 W.L.R. 592, [1992] 1 F.L.R. 190

A 15-year-old girl, R, who had been on the local authority's at-risk register, was received into voluntary care and was placed in a children's home after a fight with her father. While there, the state of her mental health grew progressively worse and she began to suffer hallucinations. Her behaviour also became more and more disturbed, to the point of threatening suicide and absconding to her father's house where she attacked him with a hammer. Following these episodes, the local authority obtained place of safety and interim care orders and placed her in an adolescent psychiatric unit. While she was in the unit, her behaviour remained very disturbed and the unit sought the local authority's permission to administer anti-psychotic drugs to her. Her mental state fluctuated but the prognosis was that, despite her periodic lucidity, if the drugs were not provided, her psychotic state would return.

In lucid periods, during which R was capable of understanding the nature and effect of the medication, she objected to taking the drugs. To begin with, the local authority refused to authorise the administration of drugs against her will; but eventually the unit was not prepared to continue caring for her without authorisation to administer the proposed medication. The local authority then commenced wardship proceedings, seeking permission for the unit to give R the anti-psychotic drugs, with or without her consent. The court had to consider, among other things, whether R was "*Gillick* competent", and if so whether, and in what circumstances, her refusal to consent to the drug treatment could be overridden.

LORD DONALDSON M.R.
" . . . It is trite law that in general a doctor is not entitled to treat a patient without the consent of someone who is authorised to give that consent. If he does so, he will be liable in damages for trespass to the person and may be guilty of a criminal assault. This is subject to the necessary exception that in cases of emergency a doctor may treat the patient notwithstanding the absence of consent, if the patient is unconscious or otherwise incapable of giving or refusing consent and there is no one else sufficiently immediately available with authority to consent on behalf of the patient. However consent by itself creates no obligation to treat. It is merely a key which unlocks a door. Furthermore, whilst in the case of an adult of full capacity there will usually only be one keyholder, namely the patient, in the ordinary family unit where a young child is the patient there will be two keyholders, namely the parents, with a several as well as a joint right to turn the key and unlock the door. If the parents disagree, one consenting and the other refusing, the doctor will be presented with a professional and ethical, but not with a legal, problem because, if he has the consent of one authorised person, treatment will not without more constitute a trespass or a criminal assault . . .

In the instant appeal Mr James Munby Q.C., appearing for the Official Solicitor, submits that (a) if the child has the right to give consent to medical treatment, the parents' right to give or refuse consent is terminated and (b) the court in the exercise of its wardship jurisdiction is only entitled to step into the shoes of the parents and thus itself has no right to give or refuse consent. Whilst it is true that he seeks to modify the effect of this rather startling submission by suggesting that, if the child's consent or refusal of consent is irrational or misguided, the court will readily infer that in the particular context that individual child is not competent to give or withhold consent, it is necessary to look very carefully at the *Gillick* decision to see whether it supports his argument and, if it does, whether it is binding upon this court.

The key passages upon which Mr Munby relies are to be found in the speech of Lord Scarman ([1985] 3 All E.R. 402 at 423–424):

' . . . as a matter of law the parental right to determine whether or not their minor child below the age of 16 will have medical treatment terminates if and when the child achieves a sufficient understanding and intelligence to enable him or her to understand fully what is proposed. It will be a question of fact whether a child seeking advice has sufficient understanding of what is involved to give a consent valid in law. Until the child achieves the capacity to consent, the parental right to make the decision continues save only in exceptional circumstances. Emergency, parental neglect, abandonment of the child or inability to find the parent are examples of exceptional situations justifying the doctor proceeding to treat the child without parental knowledge and consent; but there will arise, no doubt, other exceptional situations in which it will be reasonable for the doctor to proceed without the parent's consent.'

And ([1985] 3 All E.R. 402 at 421–422):

'The underlying principle of the law was exposed by Blackstone (1 Bl Com (17th ed, 1830) chs 16 and 17)] and can be seen to have been acknowledged in the case law. It is that parental right yields to the child's right to make his own decisions when he reaches a sufficient understanding and intelligence to be capable of making up his own mind on the matter requiring decision.'

What Mr Munby's argument overlooks is that Lord Scarman was discussing the parents' right 'to *determine* whether or not their minor child below the age of 16 will have medical treatment' (my emphasis) and this is the 'parental right' to which he was referring in the latter passage. A right of determination is wider than a right to consent. The parents can only have a right of determination if *either* the child has no right to consent, *i.e.* is not a keyholder, *or* the parents hold a master key which could nullify the child's consent. I do not understand Lord Scarman to be saying that, if a child was '*Gillick* competent', to adopt the convenient phrase used in argument, the parents ceased to have an independent right of consent as contrasted with ceasing to have a right of determination, *i.e.* a veto. In a case in which the '*Gillick* competent' child refuses treatment, but the parents consent, that consent *enables* treatment to be undertaken lawfully, but in no way determines that the child shall be so treated. In a case in which the positions are reversed, it is the child's consent which is the enabling factor and again the parents' refusal of consent is not determinative. If Lord Scarman intended to go further than this and to say that in the case of a '*Gillick* competent' child, a parent has no right either to consent or to refuse consent, his remarks were obiter, because the only question in issue was Mrs Gillick's alleged right of veto. Furthermore I consider that they would have been wrong.

One glance at the consequences suffices to show that Lord Scarman cannot have been intending to say that the parental right to consent terminates with the achievement by the child of '*Gillick* competence'. It is fundamental to the speeches of the majority that the capacity to consent will vary from child to child and according to the treatment under consideration, depending upon the sufficiency of his or her intelligence and understanding of that treatment. If the position in law is that upon the achievement of '*Gillick* competence' there is a transfer of the right of consent from parents to child and there can never be a concurrent right in both, doctors would be faced with an intolerable dilemma, particularly when the child was nearing the age of 16, if the parents consented, but the child did not. On pain, if they got it wrong, of being sued for trespass to the person or possibly being charged with a criminal assault, they would have to determine as a matter of law in whom the right of consent resided at the particular time in relation to the particular treatment. I do not believe that that is the law . . .

Both in this case and in *Re E* [see p.463 below] the judges treated *Gillick's* case as deciding that a '*Gillick* competent' child has a right to refuse treatment. In this I consider that they were in error. Such a child can consent, but if he or she declines to do so or refuses, consent can be given by someone else who has parental rights or responsibilities. The failure or refusal of the '*Gillick* competent' child is a very important factor in the doctor's decision whether or not to treat, but does not prevent the necessary consent being obtained from another competent source . . .

[After considering the effect of R having been made a ward of court and whether she was *Gillick* competent, Lord Donaldson summed up as follows:]

(1) No doctor can be required to treat a child, whether by the court in the exercise of its wardship jurisdiction, by the parents, by the child or anyone else. The decision whether to treat is dependent upon an exercise of his own professional judgment, subject only to the threshold requirement that, save in exceptional cases usually of emergency, he has the consent of someone who has authority to give that consent. In forming that judgment the views and wishes of the child are a factor whose importance increases with the increase in the child's intelligence and understanding.

(2) There can be concurrent powers to consent. If more than one body or person has a power to consent, only a failure to, or refusal of, consent by all having that power will create a veto.

(3) A '*Gillick* competent' child or one over the age of 16 will have a power to consent, but this will be concurrent with that of a parent or guardian. . . . "

FARQUHARSON L.J.

" . . . It is to be emphasised that *Gillick's* case was not a wardship case and was concerned with mentally normal children. For my part I would find it difficult to import the criteria applied in *Gillick's* case to the facts of the present case. We are not here solely concerned with the developing maturity of a 15-year-old child but with the impact of a mental illness upon her. The *Gillick* test is not apt to a situation where the understanding and capacity of the child varies from day to day according to the effect of her illness. I would reject the application of the *Gillick* test to an on/off situation of that kind. The authority of a High Court judge exercising his jurisdiction in wardship is not constrained in this way. The judge's well-established task in deciding any question concerning the upbringing of the ward is to have regard to the welfare of the ward as the first and paramount consideration. In some cases the decision might well be different if the *Gillick* test were applied. That the two approaches are distinct is vividly illustrated in the dramatic case of *Re E (a minor)* (September 21, 1990, unreported) [see p.463 below] by the decision of Ward J.

It is clear in the present appeal that, whether R's capacity to withhold consent to medication was tested on the *Gillick* criteria or whether the court approached the issue on the basis of her welfare being paramount, the result would have been the same.

I would dismiss the appeal."

NOTES:

1. The opinion expressed by Lord Donaldson in this case that the parents of a "*Gillick* competent" child, or a young person over the age of 16, retain their power of consent until the child reaches majority was, strictly speaking, *obiter*. Because of that Staughton L.J. noted that in this case it was not necessary for him to resolve the apparent difference between Lord Scarman and Donaldson L.J. over whether a doctor could lawfully administer treatment when the parent consented but the competent child did not.

2. As Phil Fennell has pointed out, in this line of cases on adolescent children, wardship and the inherent jurisdiction have been used in much the same way as the jurisdiction to grant declarations (discussed in Chapter 5 at pp.302–307) in order to establish a new body of judicial rules on the rights

and duties of doctors and patients (see P. Fennell, *Treatment without Consent*, London: Routledge, 1996 at p.276).

3. In *Re R* the Court of Appeal were unanimous that the *Gillick* reasoning had no direct application in wardship cases. The court decided that in exercising its wardship jurisdiction it could override the refusal of a minor to consent to medical treatment which was in his best interests, even if he was "*Gillick* competent". Staughton L.J. was prepared to go even further, stating that the wardship court also has the power to veto treatment to which a competent child has consented, although in this situation the parents of a "*Gillick* competent" child would have no right of veto. (See R. Thornton, "Multiple Keyholders — Wardship and Consent to Medical Treatment" [1992] C.L.J. 34; A. Bainham, "The Judge and the Competent Minor" (1992) 108 L.Q.R. 194.)

4. Andrew Grubb has criticised Lord Donaldson's reasoning in *Re R* as disingenuous. He argues that the Master of the Roll's statement that *Gillick* was not concerned with the question of whether a parent could validly consent to treatment in the face of a competent child's refusal is a remarkably narrow interpretation of *Gillick*. Furthermore, he is critical of how the judgment ignores the historical context in which the 1969 Act was passed, since the 1960s was very much the era of parental rights. (See A. Grubb, "Treatment Decisions: Keeping it in the Family" in A. Grubb (ed.), *Choices and Decisions in Health Care*, Chichester: John Wiley, 1993 at pp.60–65.)

5. One problem with the view implicit in Lord Donaldson's judgment that R is to be assessed according to a measurement of her capacity on her bad days, is that it is inconsistent with the law's usual approach to issues of capacity. Generally, the law recognises that it is capacity at the time of the act that is relevant, so that cases on fluctuating capacity recognise the validity of consents given in rational moments (see, for example, Chapter 5 at p.313). Furthermore, the adoption of such a stance entails a refusal to accept the autonomy of those suffering from mental disorders even when they are capable of making certain autonomous decisions. (See J. Montgomery, "Parents and Children in Dispute: Who Has the Final Word?" (1992) 4 *Journal of Child Law* 85, C. Bridge, "Religious Beliefs and Teenage Refusal of Medical Treatment (1999) 62 *Modern Law Review* 585.)

6. Andrew Bainham notes that, unless the administration of sedative drugs can be meaningfully distinguished from other medical or psychiatric procedures, *Re R* appears to conflict with many of the statutory provisions in the Children Act 1989, which would seem to endorse the *Gillick* principle by giving a child a right to refuse medical or psychiatric examination or treatment where he has "sufficient understanding to make an informed decision"; although he does concede that the Act is ambivalent on how decisive the views of a competent child are generally. (See A. Bainham, *op. cit.* in note 3 at p.196: J.A. Devereaux *et al.*, "Can Children withhold Consent to Treatment?" (1993) 306 B.M.J. 1459.) Similarly, in providing that, where child patients are capable of consenting to an application to see their health records parental applications may only be

made with the consent of that child (s.4(2) of the Access to Health Records Act 1990 discussed in Chapter 9 at p.637, Parliament appears to endorse the *Gillick* approach. (See Montgomery, *op. cit.* in note 5.)

7. As to the power to determine health provision, recall that Lord Donaldson himself observed in the earlier case of *Re J* [1991] 3 All E.R. 930 at p.934 (see p.413 above) that:

> "No one can dictate the treatment to be given to any child, neither court, parents nor doctors . . . The doctors can recommend treatment A in preference to treatment B. They can also refuse to adopt treatment C on the grounds that it is medically contra-indicated . . . The court or parents for their part can refuse to consent to treatment A or B or both, but cannot insist on treatment C. The inevitable and desirable result is that choice of treatment is in some measure a joint decision of the doctors and the court or parents." As we saw above this principle has been reaffirmed in a number of subsequent cases. (See also Montgomery, *op. cit*).

8. In *Re K, W and H (Minors) (Medical Treatment)* [1993] 1 F.L.R. 854 an issue arose about whether emergency medication could be given to three young people (aged 14 or 15) who were receiving specialist psychiatric treatment in a secure psychiatric unit. Although the issue was not canvassed in detail, Thorpe J. accepted that none of the adolescents were *Gillick* competent, but went on to add that even if they were:

> "The decision of the Court of Appeal in *Re R* made it plain that a child with *Gillick* competence can consent to treatment, but that if he or she declines to do so, consent can be given by someone else who has parental rights or responsibilities. Where more than one person has power to consent, only a refusal of all having that power will create a veto."

Questions:

1. Do you agree with the Court of Appeal's unanimous conclusion that R was incompetent? Do you think that the doctors involved would have questioned R's competence if she had consented to the administration of the anti-psychotic drugs? (See Grubb, *op. cit.* in note 4 at p.58.) Do you accept Bainham's view that this decision "confirms the suspicion that the acquisition of capacity by children is capable of manipulation by adults"? (See Bainham, *op. cit.* in note 3 at p.200.) For instance, is it significant in this case that the unit was not prepared to allow R to stay unless the anti-psychotic drugs could be administered to her?

2. Do you agree with Staughton L.J. that "the *Gillick* test is not apt to a situation where the understanding and capacity of the child varies from day to day according to the effect of her illness"?

3. Is it tenable to make a distinction, as Lord Donaldson does, between a right to *determine* treatment, and a right to give or withhold consent to treatment? (See Montgomery, *op. cit.* in note 5; Devereaux *et al.*, *op. cit.* in note 6.)

4. Do you concur with Grubb's view that the effect of Lord Donaldson's judgment, by giving the parents a right to veto, or at least to trump, the

young person's refusal of treatment, is giving them the very power to determine treatment which they were denied in *Gillick*? (See Grubb, *op. cit.* in note 4 at p.64.)

5. Is this judgment unduly paternalistic in its emphasis on what others believe to be in the young person's best interests? Even if the court does technically possess the power to override the wishes of a mature adolescent, should it do so? (See Bainham, *op. cit.* in note 3.)

6. How useful is Lord Donaldson's keyholder analogy?

When the Court of Appeal returned to this issue of the balance of power in child health decision-making, closer analysis of the import of s.8(3) of the Family Law Reform Act 1969 was supplied.

Re W (A Minor) (Medical Treatment: Court's Jurisdiction) [1992] 4 All E.R. 627, [1993] Fam. 64, [1992] 3 W.L.R. 758, [1993] 1 F.L.R. 1, [1992] 9 B.M.L.R. 22, Fam. Law 541, [1992] 2 F.C.R. 785

W, a girl of 16, suffered from anorexia. As we have noted in Chapter 6 (at p.370), this condition can pose particular problems in relation to consent. W was admitted to a specialist adolescent residential unit. Her condition was deteriorating and it was proposed that she should be moved to a hospital specialising in the treatment of eating disorders. W wished to remain where she was and therefore objected to this proposal. Accordingly, the local authority applied to invoke the court's inherent jurisdiction under s.100(3), (4) of the Children Act 1989 for a direction that it should be permitted to move her to the specialist institution. At first instance, Thorpe J. held that although W was "*Gillick* competent", the court had inherent jurisdiction to make the order sought. W appealed, contending that under s.8 of the Family Law Reform Act 1969, she had an *exclusive* right to consent to medical treatment or care.

LORD DONALDSON M.R.

The purpose of consent to treatment

There seems to be some confusion in the minds of some as to the purpose of seeking consent from a patient (whether adult or child) or from someone with authority to give that consent on behalf of the patient. It has two purposes, the one clinical and the other legal. The clinical purpose stems from the fact that in many instances the co-operation of the patient and the patient's faith or at least confidence in the efficiency of the treatment is a major factor contributing to the treatment's success. Failure to obtain such consent will not only deprive the patient and the medical staff of this advantage, but will usually make it much more difficult to administer the treatment. I appreciate that this purpose may not be served if consent is given on behalf of, rather than by, the patient. However, in the case of young children knowledge of the fact that the parent has consented may help. The legal purpose is quite different. It is to provide those concerned in the treatment with a defence to a criminal charge of assault or battery or a civil claim for damages for trespass to the person. It does not, however, provide them with any defence to a claim that they negligently advised a particular treatment or negligently carried it out . . . .

The argument that W, or any other 16- or 17-year-old, can by refusing to consent to treatment veto the treatment notwithstanding that the doctor has the consent of someone who has parental responsibilities, involves the proposition that section 8 has the further effect of depriving such a person of the power to consent. It certainly does not say so. Indeed if this were its intended effect, it is difficult to see why the subsection goes on to say that it is not *necessary* to obtain the parents' consent, rather than providing that such consent, if obtained, should be ineffective . . .

On reflection I regret my use in *Re R (a minor) (wardship: medical treatment)* [1991] 4 All E.R. 177 at 184 of the keyholder analogy because keys can lock as well as unlock. I now prefer the analogy of the legal 'flak jacket' which protects the doctor from claims by the litigious whether he acquires it from his patient who may be a minor over the age of 16 or a '*Gillick* competent' child under that age or from another person having parental responsibilities which include a right to consent to treatment of the minor. Anyone who gives him a flak jacket (*i.e.* consent) may take it back, but the doctor only needs one and so long as he continues to have one he has the legal right to proceed . . .

W's case

W is not in fact refusing all treatment. Her attitude is that she wishes to continue with the treatment which she was receiving when the hearing of this appeal began. Her reasons are not to be and were not dismissed lightly, but during the hearing the situation changed dramatically. The hearing began on 29 June at which time, so far as we knew, W's condition was stable or deteriorating only slowly, although there had been some further loss of weight. This accorded with information given to the court when the appeal was first set down. The Registrar of Civil Appeals appreciated that the issue could be one of extreme urgency, but was assured that it was not. Hence the fact that although Thorpe J. gave judgment on 12 May, more than a month elapsed before the appeal hearing began. However, on 30 June we were told in response to inquiries by the court that she had not taken solid food since 21 June and that, although she had maintained a fluid intake of 12 cups of tea a day, her weight had dropped from 39 kg on June 16 to 35.1 kg on 30 June. This represents a loss of weight of 8 lb in 14 days with a final weight of 5 stone 7 lb for a girl 5 feet 7 inches tall. More serious was the agreed medical opinion that should she continue in this way, within a week her capacity to have children in later life would be seriously at risk and a little later her life itself might be in danger.

In these circumstances, as we were agreed that we had power to do so, we made an emergency order enabling her to be taken to and treated at a specialist hospital in London, notwithstanding the lack of consent on her part. Later we were glad to hear that, whilst not consenting, W accepted that the order would have to be complied with. Thereafter we carried on with the hearing of the argument on whether Thorpe J. was or was not right to make the order which he did in the different circumstances which then existed and as to the more general issues raised by this appeal. It was this change of circumstances which led me in announcing the making of the emergency order to say that W's wishes were no longer of weight. At that stage they were completely outweighed by the threat of irreparable damage to her health and risk to her life. I was not purporting to consider, and was not considering, the importance of W's views at an earlier stage in the development of the illness or the importance of the views of patients under the age of 18 generally. They are matters to which I now turn.

As I say, W wished to continue with the same regime . . . it appears from the judgment of Thorpe J., and I do not doubt that he was right, that a dominant factor was W's desire to be in an environment where, as she thought, she was in control and could cure herself if and when she thought it right to do so. That she might leave it too late, does not seem to have occurred to her.

I have no doubt that the wishes of a 16- or 17-year-old child or indeed of a younger child who is '*Gillick* competent' are of the greatest importance both legally and clinically, but I do doubt whether Thorpe J. was right to conclude that W was of sufficient understanding to make an informed decision. I do not say this on the basis that I consider her approach irrational. I personally consider that religious or other beliefs which bar any medical treatment or treatment of particular kinds are irrational, but that does not make minors who hold those beliefs any the less '*Gillick* competent.' They may well have sufficient intelligence and understanding fully to appreciate the treatment proposed and the consequences of their refusal to accept that treatment. What distinguishes W from them, and what with all respect I do not think that Thorpe J. took sufficiently into account (perhaps because the point did not emerge as clearly before him as it did before us), is that it is a feature of anorexia nervosa that it is capable of destroying the ability to make an informed choice. It creates a compulsion to refuse treatment or only to accept treatment which is likely to be ineffective. This attitude is part and parcel of the disease and the more advanced the illness, the more compelling it may become. Where the wishes of the minor are themselves something which the doctors reasonably consider need to be treated in the minor's own best interests, those wishes clearly have a much reduced significance.

There is ample authority for the proposition that the inherent powers of the court under its *parens patriae* jurisdiction are theoretically limitless and that they certainly extend beyond the powers of a natural parent: see for example *Re R (a minor) (wardship: medical treatment)* [1991] 4 All E.R. 177 at 186, 189. There can therefore be no doubt that it has power to override the refusal of a minor, whether over the age of 16 or under that age but '*Gillick* competent.' It does not do so by ordering the doctors to treat, which, even if within the court's powers, would be an abuse of them, or by ordering the minor to accept treatment, but by authorising the doctors to treat the minor in accordance with their clinical judgment, subject to any restrictions which the court may impose . . .

BALCOMBE L.J.
" . . . It will be readily apparent that [section 8] is silent on the question which arises in the present case, namely whether a minor who has attained the age of 16 years has an absolute right to refuse medical treatment. I am quite unable to see how, on any normal reading of the words of the section, it can be construed to confer such a right. The purpose of the section is clear: it is to enable a 16-year-old to consent to medical treatment which, in the absence of consent by the child or its parents, would constitute a trespass to the person. In other words, for this purpose, and for this purpose only, a minor was to be treated as if it were an adult. That the section did not operate to prevent parental consent remaining effective, as well in the case of a child over 16 as in the case of a child under that age, is apparent from the words of sub-s. (3).

If there was any ambiguity as to the meaning of the section—and in my judgment there is not—it would be resolved by a glance at the *Report of the Committee on the Age of Majority* (Cmnd. 3342 (1967)) (the Latey Report) to see what was the mischief which the section was intended to remedy. Paragraphs 474 to 489 of the Latey Report make it clear that doctors felt difficulty in accepting the consent of someone under 21 (the then age of majority) to medical treatment, even though parental consent might be unobtainable or, for reasons of the minor's privacy, undesirable . . .

This interpretation of s.8 was given, *obiter*, by Lord Donaldson of Lymington M.R. in *Re R*. His judgment attracted a considerable degree of academic criticism. I have to say that I find this criticism surprising since, as I have already said, the section is in my judgment clear, unambiguous and limited in its scope . . .

I share the doubts of Lord Donaldson of Lymington M.R. whether Lord Scarman [in *Gillick*] was intending to mean that the parents of a '*Gillick* competent' child had no right at all to consent to medical treatment of the child as opposed to no exclusive right to such consent. If he did so intend then, in the case of a child over the age of 16, his interpretation of the law was inconsistent with the express words of s.8(3) of the Act of 1969. It is also clear that Lord Scarman was only considering the position of the child vis-à-vis its parents: he was not considering the position of the child vis-à-vis the court whose powers, as I have already said, are wider than the parents'.

I am therefore satisfied that there is no interpretation of section 8 of the Act of 1969, and certainly no 'settled' interpretation, which persuades me that my view of the clear meaning of the section is wrong . . . "

Notes:

1. Nolan L.J., who delivered a concurring judgment, did not directly consider whether reaching 16 or the attainment of "*Gillick* competence" extinguished the parental power to consent. He focused simply upon the balance of power between the child and the court in the exercise of its inherent jurisdiction.

2. Lord Donaldson hinted that anorexia nervosa was a condition that could destroy a patient's ability to make an informed choice. On this basis it could be argued that he did not regard W as "*Gillick* competent". (See J. Masson, "Re W: Appealing from the Golden Cage" (1993) 5 *Journal of Child Law* 37.) This also raises the issue of whether the case should have been dealt with under the mental health legislation, as were the cases of *Riverside Mental Health NHS Trust v Fox* [1994] 1 F.L.R. 614 and *B. v Croydon District Health Authority* [1995] 1 All E.R. 683. (See Chapter 8 at p.543; P. Lewis, "Feeding an Anorexic Patient who Refuses Food" (1997) 7 *Medical Law Review* 21).

3. Lord Donaldson expressed the view that no minor, whatever her age, could, by refusing treatment, override a consent to treatment given by someone with parental responsibility. This clearly represents a fundamental incursion into the adolescent's right to self-determination which *Gillick* seemed to establish. (See J. Bridgeman, "Old Enough to Know Best?" (1993) 13 *Legal Studies* 69; S. Elliston, "If You Know What is Good for You: Refusal of Consent to Medical Treatment by Children" in S. McLean (ed) *Contemporary Issues in Law, Medicine and Ethics* Aldershot: Dartmouth, 1996; Lewis, *op. cit.* in note 2).

4. It has been suggested that *Re W* should not be interpreted as being about the right of a teenager aged 16 or 17 to refuse life-saving treatment, but as concerning the right of a competent teenager to determine the medical treatment which she receives, *i.e.* whether to receive one form rather than another (see Bridgeman, *op. cit.* in note 3).

5. Masson notes that, as in the case of *Re R*, the Court of Appeal in this case appeared to be less concerned with producing a clearly reasoned decision on the topic at issue than with pronouncing on the general area of children and consent. Thus, once again, many of the dicta in the judgments are *obiter* (see Masson, *op. cit.* in note 2 at p.37).

6. In *South Glamorgan County Council v W and B* [1993] 1 F.L.R. Douglas Brown J. invoked the inherent jurisdiction of the High Court to compel a reclusive 15-year-old girl who was refusing psychiatric assessment to be moved from her home to an adolescent unit, notwithstanding his view that she was "not *Gillick* incompetent". The case has been criticised for seeming to erode the rights of a *Gillick* competent child to refuse psychiatric assessment under s. 38(6) of the Children Act 1989 (M. Brazier and C. Bridge, "Coercion or Caring: Analysing Adolescent Autonomy" (1996) 16 *Legal Studies* 84). Christina Lyon goes further, arguing that the judgment "conveys to children the message that they cannot trust that the clearly expressed 'rights' given by Parliament will be safe in the hands of

the judges" (see C. Lyon, "What's Happened to the Child's Right to Refuse?" (1994) 6 *Journal of Child Law* 84 at p.87).

QUESTIONS:

1. Even if s.8(3) of the Family Law Reform Act 1969 preserved the common law power of a parent to grant consent, is it not possible that "*Gillick* competent" children have the exclusive right to determine their health care by virtue of the actual *Gillick* decision? (See J. Murphy, "W(h)ither Adolescent Autonomy?" [1992] *Journal of Social Welfare and Family Law* 539; Brazier and Bridge, *op. cit.* in note 5.)

2. In constructing the metaphor of consent as a "flak jacket", Lord Donaldson appears to have been more concerned with doctors' liberties (to undertake medical procedures immune from a trespass suit) than with adolescents' rights. Is this a proper way to approach such cases?

3. Lord Donaldson briefly considered the applicability of the Mental Health Act 1983 to this case, but he summarily dismissed the possibility of using that legislation on the grounds that the stigma associated with that Act meant that patients would be less prejudiced by compulsory treatment outside that Act. Do you agree, especially in view of the fact that the 1983 Act contains statutory safeguards (discussed in Chapter 8) to protect those compulsorily treated under it? Does Lord Donaldson's attitude in itself reinforce the stigmatisation of mental illness? (See P. Fennell, "Informal Compulsion" [1992] *Journal of Social Welfare and Family Law* 311; Masson, *op. cit.* in note 2; Brazier and Bridge, *op. cit.* in note 5 at p.96.)

4. Should legislation be required to authorise coercive action by the state, such as the action taken in this case? (See A. Grubb, "Treatment Decisions: Keeping it in the Family" in A. Grubb (ed.), *Choices and Decisions in Health Care*, Chichester: John Wiley, 1993 at p.71.)

5. In this case do you agree with:

   (a) the outcome?
   (b) the reasoning?

6. John Harris argues that it is nonsensical to posit that a child could competently consent to treatment but not be competent to refuse it (J. Harris, "Consent and End of Life Decisions" (2003) 29 *Journal of Medical Ethics* 10) whereas Caroline Bridge contends that the "consequences of refusal are likely to be potentially dangerous and more significant than simply giving consent" (C. Bridge, "Religious Beliefs and Teenage Refusal of Medical Treatment" (1999) 62 M.L.R. 585; see also N. Lowe and S. Juss, "Medical Treatment—Pragmatism and the Search for Principle" (1993) 56 M.L.R. 865.) Which view do you prefer and why?

In the following case, even though the young woman was not suffering from any recognisable mental disorder, the court held that circumstances had impacted on her ability to decide on her treatment.

Re M (child: refusal of medical treatment) [1999] 2 F.C.R. 577

M was a 15-year-old girl who had suffered heart failure. Within a few weeks her condition had deteriorated to the point where doctors concluded that a heart transplant was necessary to save her life. M refused her consent to the proposed transplant, so the medics sought authorisation from the court to proceed.

JOHNSON J.
"M will remember her discussions with Mr Winter [the Official Solicitor's agent in the case] but the outcome of those conversations was communicated to me in the early hours of Saturday morning. I need not repeat here the whole of what I was told but, quoting from Mr Winter's notes, the important things were these:

'First knew I needed a transplant on Wednesday. I understand what a heart transplant means, procedure explained . . . checkups . . . tablets for the rest of your life. I feel depressed about that. I am only fifteen and don't want to take tablets for the rest of my life . . . It's all happened quickly . . . if I don't have the operation I will die. I really don't want a transplant—I am not happy with it—I don't want to die. It's hard to take it all in. I feel selfish. If I had the transplant I wouldn't be happy. If I were to die my family would be sad. If I had children and they were old enough my age, I would go with whatever is best—what they want I would not let them die. Death is final I know I can't change my mind. I don't want to die, but I would rather die than have the transplant and have someone else's heart, I would rather die with fifteen years of my own heart. If I had someone else's heart, I would be different from anybody else—being dead would not make me different from anyone else. I would feel different with someone else's heart, that's a good enough reason not to have a heart transplant, even if it saved my life. I don't want to write the Judge a letter.'

Mr Winter read his notes to M who agreed with what he had written.

My decision

The Official Solicitor telephoned me and recounted what M had said to Mr Winter. She would not consent to the operation because she did not want to have someone else's heart and also because she did not want to take medication for the rest of her life. Equally she did not wish to die. Mr Winter and the Official Solicitor then gave me their own opinions in the matter. Their view was that M is an intelligent 15-year-old girl whose wishes should carry considerable weight. Nevertheless their view was that M felt overwhelmed by her circumstances and the decision she was being asked to make. A few weeks before M had been a healthy active girl, who loved netball and swimming, but now she is very ill and close to death. Events have overtaken her so swiftly that she has not been able to come to terms with her situation. Whilst emphasising to me what M had said, the Official Solicitor submitted to me that what was best for M required that I should authorise the giving of treatment according to the consultant's clinical judgment, including a heart transplant.

If the operation is successful, then M will live with the consequence of my decision, in a very striking sense. There are risks attached to the operation itself and there are risks continuing thereafter, both in terms of rejection in the medical sense and rejection by M of the continuing medical treatment. There is the risk too that she will carry with her for the rest of her life resentment about what has been done to her. Whatever that risk may be, and it is impossible to assess, it has to be matched against not simply the risk but the certainty of death. Whilst I was very conscious of the great gravity of the decision I was making in overriding M's wish, it seemed to me that seeking to achieve what was best for her required me on balance to give the authority that was asked."

NOTES:

1. Note that there was no consideration in this case of whether M was *Gillick* competent, and the judge noted that a refusal by M "is important but not decisive". We are told that M's mother had parental responsibility and was prepared to consent. Johnson J. noted that her consent would have sufficed.
2. It was subsequently reported that (unusually) a donor heart of the right size and blood group became available within days and, faced with this and the judge's ruling, M consented to the transplant (C. Dyer and S. Boseley, "A matter of life and death", *The Guardian* July 16, 1999).

QUESTION:

1. Mason and Laurie suggest that this case "must surely represent the outermost reaches of acceptable paternalistic practices". They also question whether "it is ethically correct to earmark a scarce and expensive resource for someone who does not want it" (J.K. Mason and G.T. Laurie, *Mason and McCall Smith's Law and Medical Ethics* (7th edn), Oxford: OUP, 2006 at p.373). Do you agree with either point? (See also A. Morris, "Treating Children Properly: Law, Ethics and Practice" (1999) 15 *Professional Negligence* 249.)

(b) Refusal of Treatment by Adolescents on the Basis of Belief

Cases where adolescents refuse treatment on the basis of religious belief present some of the most difficult cases, because the decision to refuse treatment is made by intelligent adolescents suffering from no degree of mental disorder or confusion, which arguably may differentiate them from the young people in Section (a) above. Moreover, in these cases the minors concerned tend to have the support of at least one parent.

Re E (A Minor) (Wardship: Medical Treatment) [1993] 1 F.L.R. 386

A was a young man aged fifteen-and-three-quarters, who suffered from leukaemia. He and his parents were devout Jehovah's Witnesses, and following his admission to hospital, all three refused their consent to conventional treatment for his condition, which required the administration of four drugs and of blood transfusions. Consent was given to a lesser form of drug therapy, which avoided the need for blood transfusions, but offered only a 40–50 per cent chance of full remission as compared to an 80–90 per cent chance where conventional treatment, including blood transfusions, was undertaken. Having successfully applied for A to be made a ward of court, the hospital authority sought the leave of the High Court to treat A conventionally once it became apparent that in a matter of hours his haemoglobin and blood platelet levels would fall to dangerous levels, posing the risk of death from a heart attack or stroke. His parents contended that his decision should be respected, as he was so close to the age of 16, when his consent to treatment would be required under s.8 of the Family Law Reform Act 1969. However, since he was still three months short of his sixteenth birthday, the judge rejected this submission and instead considered whether he was "*Gillick* competent", so as to enable him to refuse treatment.

WARD J.

" . . . In deference to the submissions made to me by counsel I will deal with the issue as to whether or not the refusal by A is a refusal taken in circumstances such as would, so it is submitted, enable him to override the parental choice. I find that A is a boy of sufficient intelligence to be able to take decisions about his own well-being, but I also find that there is a range of decisions of which some are outside his ability fully to grasp their implications. Impressed though I was by his obvious intelligence, by his calm discussion of the implications, by his assertion even that he would refuse well knowing that he may die as a result, in my judgment A does not have a full understanding of the whole implication of what the refusal of that treatment involves . . .

I am quite satisfied that A does not have any sufficient comprehension of the pain he has yet to suffer, of the fear that he will be undergoing, of the distress not only occasioned by that fear but also—and importantly—the distress he will inevitably suffer as he, a loving son, helplessly watches his parents' and his family's distress. They are a close family, and they are a brave family, but I find that he has no realisation of the full implications which lie before him as to the process of dying . . .

If, therefore, this case depended upon my finding of whether or not A is of sufficient understanding and intelligence and maturity to give full and informed consent, I find he is not. Both, therefore, because s.8 does not apply and because, as I find, his veto is not a binding one, he not being in the position to take the decision . . .

In my judgment, whether or not he is of sufficient understanding to have given consent or to withhold consent is not the issue for me. In considering what his welfare dictates, I have to have regard to his wishes. What he wishes is an important factor for me to take into account and, having regard to the closeness to his attaining 16, a very important matter which weighs very heavily in the scales I have to hold in balance.

He is of an age and understanding at least to appreciate the consequence if not the process of his decision, and by reason of the convictions of his religion, which I find to be deeply held and genuine, he says 'no' to a medical intervention which may save his life. What weight do I place upon this refusal? I approach this case telling myself that the freedom of choice in adults is a fundamental human right. He is close to the time when he may be able to take those decisions. I should therefore be very slow to interfere. I have also to ask myself to what extent is that assertion of decision, 'I will not have a blood transfusion', the product of his full but his free informed thought? Without wishing to introduce into the case notions of undue influence, I find that the influence of the teachings of the Jehovah's Witnesses is strong and powerful. The very fact that this family can contemplate the death of one of its members is the most eloquent testimony of the power of that faith. He is a boy who seeks and needs the love and respect of his parents whom, he would wish to honour as the Bible exhorts him to honour them. I am far from satisfied that at the age of 15 his will is fully free. He may assert it, but his volition has been conditioned by the very powerful expressions of faith to which all members of the creed adhere. When making this decision, which is a decision of life or death, I have to take account of the fact that teenagers often express views with vehemence and conviction—all the vehemence and conviction of youth! Those of us who have passed beyond callow youth can all remember the convictions we have loudly proclaimed which now we find somewhat embarrassing. I respect this boy's profession of faith, but I cannot discount at least the possibility that he may in later years suffer some diminution in his convictions. There is no settled certainty about matters of this kind . . .

When, therefore, I have to balance the wishes of father and son against the need for the chance to live a precious life, then I have to conclude that their decision is inimical to his well-being . . .

My jurisdiction is a protective one . . . In my judgment, A has by the stand he has taken thus far already been and become a martyr for his faith. One has to admire—indeed one is almost baffled by—the courage of the conviction that he expresses. He is, he says, prepared to die for his faith. That makes him a martyr by itself. But I regret that I find it essential for his well-being to protect him from himself and his parents, and so I override his and his parents' decision. In this judgment—which has been truly anxious—I have endeavoured to pay every respect and give great weight to the religious principles which underlie the family's decision and also to the fundamental human right to decide things for oneself. That notwithstanding, the welfare of A, when viewed objectively, compels me to only one conclusion, and that is that the hospital should be at liberty to treat him with the administration of those further drugs and consequently with the administration of blood and blood products."

NOTES:

1. When he was 18 E exercised his right to refuse medical treatment and died.
2. As Brazier and Bridge point out, E may well have had more understanding of death and less potential for regret than the average adult, given that his adamant refusal was based on sincere religious belief (M. Brazier and C. Bridge, "Coercion or Caring: Analysing Adolescent Autonomy" (1996) 16 *Legal Studies* 84).

QUESTIONS:

1. In your opinion, did Ward J. underestimate E's level of competence? Do you think that a court would ever deem a young person under the age of 16 competent to make a decision to refuse treatment where that decision is likely to result in the patient's death?
2. Given the strength of E's religious background, was he really in a position, even at 18, to exercise free choice?

Re S (A Minor) (Medical Treatment) [1994] 2 F.L.R. 1065

S, a 15-year-old girl, had suffered from a life-threatening form of thalassaemia from birth. Her condition had required her to endure daily injections and monthly blood transfusions since birth. As she had become irregular in administering her daily injections of an iron-excreting drug, she had failed to grow normally, with the result that she suffered abuse from her peers. When S was 10, her mother converted to the Jehovah's Witness faith. She began to take S to religious meetings and began to influence her to stop her medical treatment. S subsequently failed to attend for her monthly blood transfusions and the local authority social services department requested the High Court to exercise its inherent jurisdiction and override S's refusal to consent to future transfusions.

JOHNSON J.

" . . . Dr S [a consultant psychiatrist] says that at one level S knows the basic facts of her medical condition, but she also seemed to genuinely believe a mistake might have been made in the diagnosis. S said:

> 'They may have got it wrong all these years, and when I stop treatment they'll find it's something else and will treat it. I might not have thalassaemia. Who knows?'

Dr S found her surprisingly confused over many details. For example, she was very vague about the need for Desferal (an iron chelating agent) and said that if anyone had explained everything to her earlier she would have kept to the treatment more closely.

As to her death, she did not know how that would occur. She hoped she would die in her sleep but, she said, 'You never know, there could be a miracle and God might save me'. As to why God was against her having blood, she seemed uncertain, referring to the risk of HIV, and so on. Strikingly, she spoke to Dr S of 'being free now, free from all these treatments'. Dr S said it was as though she had drawn a line and was going to stick to it . . .

Doctor S's conclusion was that S does not fully understand the implication of her decision. She doesn't know how death will occur; she certainly, in the view of Dr S, does not believe that a failure to have further transfusions will certainly result in death.

S is very fed up and negative and despondent about her illness, says Dr S. Like Dr J, she finds these feelings are always at their height in adolescence. In her oral evidence, Dr S said that she did not believe that S understood the implications of the decision:

> 'There were a lot of things that concerned me, the patness of her replies, some of her phrases. She and her mother were using exactly similar phraseology. S was not able to explain her thought except that, "it was said in the Bible". She had no understanding of the manner in which she might die.'

The most worrying thing for Dr S was that S seemed to have latched onto the idea that other Jehovah's Witnesses had thalassaemia and survived without transfusion. She said:

> 'I actually believe that she doesn't believe that she will die. Much of what she said is what I hear from other children who are chronically ill and who are fed up with their treatment. In age terms, this is the peak of such problems.'

Cross-examined on S's behalf, Dr S said that she did not consider that she had been tutored to give her answers. She was certainly very determined but she did not agree that S was expressing her own mind. Her feeling about being fed up with treatment makes her susceptible to influence.

I turn then to the manner in which the discretion of the court should be exercised. I start unhesitatingly from the position that S's wish should be given effect unless the balance is strongly to the contrary effect. S's right to determine what happens to her body should not be overridden lightly. If it is to be overridden it may be necessary for force to be used, and I proceed on the basis that it will be. That is startling and to me, as to Dr J, extremely distasteful . . .

As Mr Daniel emphasised, whatever the decision of the court today, in 2 years' time S will be able to make up her own mind in the matter. He told me that the young man, the subject of Ward J.'s and the Court of Appeal's intervention in *Re E* had done precisely that and had now died. Against the background of the misery, for that is what she thinks it is, of this continuing treatment which she has sustained now for over 15 years, one may sensibly ask what is the point of forcing this young woman to have further treatment for what may be just $2\frac{1}{2}$ years.

In contrast to many other cases which have come before the court, this is not a one-off transfusion of blood that is envisaged, it is a treatment that will be required regularly every month . . .

As to the consequences of rejection, death is in my judgment inevitable and would be difficult and painful. The therapy is one that S has had for 15 years and it would surely seem a pity to stop it now. There is the possibility that, if it is forced upon her, her mind may change as Dr J and Dr S say children's minds do change in this situation, but of course those are not children who have the faith of Jehovah's Witnesses. Moreover, there is the possibility that within the next few years gene therapy will become available that will provide a complete cure for S's thalassaemia, so that blood transfusion will no longer be necessary.

As to her competence to make these decisions, because she is disillusioned with the treatment—one might say, fed up with it—she is susceptible to influence from outside. I do not believe that the mother or any Jehovah's Witnesses have overborne the wish of S in the matter, but I do believe that she has been influenced by them in the sense that she has come to share their faith. She does not understand the full implications of what will happen. It does not seem to me that her capacity is commensurate with the gravity of the decision which she has made. It seems to me that an understanding that she will die is not enough. For her decision to carry weight she should have a greater understanding of the manner of the death and pain and the distress . . .

Is S then '*Gillick*-competent' as to this? In approaching the case beforehand and having the advantage of reading some of the papers over the weekend, I had thought that this was a case of a child who was '*Gillick*-competent'. She is, after all, 15 years old. But having seen her and heard about her I have no doubt at all but that she is not '*Gillick*-competent' . . .

Whilst as she gave evidence I was so very strongly impressed by her integrity and her commitment, I believe they were the integrity and commitment of a child and not of somebody who was competent to make the decision that she tells me she has made. She hopes still for a miracle. My conclusion is, therefore, that she is not '*Gillick*-competent' . . .

I am quite sure how I should exercise the discretion of the court. It is that I should override the expressed wish of S and give authority for Dr J if necessary, to force this treatment upon her . . . "

Notes:

1. Note that S's decision not to undergo further treatment may have been influenced by other factors in addition to her religion, particularly her low quality of life and the invasive nature of her treatment (see M. Brazier and C. Bridge, "Analysing Adolescent Autonomy: Coercion or Caring" (1996) 16 *Legal Studies* 84, at p.106).

2. As Grubb points out, one psychiatric witness doubted whether S was "seriously immature" for her age and, since she was 15 and a half years old, the finding of incompetence means that it is difficult to conceive of situations where a minor would be deemed legally competent to refuse such treatment (see A. Grubb, "Treatment without Consent: Child" (1995) 3 *Medical Law Review* 84).

Question:

1. Was Johnson J. right to conclude that S lacked the capacity to make an autonomous choice to discontinue blood transfusions? Did her lack of insight into her condition compromise her ability to make an autonomous choice? At age 18 will she be able to make such a choice?

Re L (Medical Treatment: Gillick Competency) [1998] 2 F.L.R. 810

L—a 14-year-old girl—was, like her mother and stepfather, a committed Jehovah's Witness. She suffered from epilepsy and had fallen into a bath of very hot water sustaining very severe burns, creating a life-threatening situation. Her proposed treatment would require at least three operations which necessitated blood transfusions. Although she knew that the treatment was essential to save her life, the consultant responsible for L's care deemed it inappropriate to explain to her the manner of her death from gangrene which was described as "horrible". The hospital authority sought leave to administer the transfusions without L's consent.

SIR STEPHEN BROWN P

" . . . Dr Cameron, a well-respected consultant child psychiatrist, has given evidence on behalf of the Official Solicitor who represents the girl at this hearing. Dr Cameron has not seen the girl because of her situation and the fact that it would be quite wrong, in his view, to subject her to perhaps an hour-long interview in order to make some assessment of his own, but he has seen all the papers in the case and has had a brief discussion about her condition with Mr Milling. He makes the point that the girl's view as to having no blood transfusion is based on a very sincerely, strongly held religious belief which does not in fact lend itself in her mind to discussion. It is one that has been formed by her in the context of her own family experience and the Jehovah's Witnesses' meetings where they all support this view. He makes the point that there is a distinction between a view of this kind and the constructive formulation of an opinion which occurs with adult experience. That has not happened of course in the case of this young girl.

Dr Cameron would not—and I would not—question the sincerity of this girl's belief. But I do not think that it should be overlooked that she is still a child. She is 14, or just over 14. She has led what has been expressed to have been a sheltered life, not an unrealistically sheltered life, but nevertheless a sheltered life. Her family circle is a tight one, in one sense, although there are a number of members of the family. She is a member of the Jehovah's Witness congregation which forms a very large part of her life. I think the nursing sister told us that she had said that she had spent some 60 hours in the week before her accident dealing with matters connected with the church.

It is, therefore, a limited experience of life which she has—inevitably so—but that is in no sense a criticism of her or of her upbringing. It is indeed refreshing to hear of children being brought up with the sensible disciplines of a well-conducted family. But it does necessarily limit her understanding of matters which are as grave as her own present situation. It may be that because of her belief she is willing to say, and to mean it, 'I am willing to accept death rather than to have a blood transfusion', but it is quite clear in this case that she has not been able to be given all the details which it would be right and appropriate to have in mind when making such a decision.

I do not think that in this case this young girl is 'Gillick competent'. I base that upon all the evidence that I have heard. She is certainly not 'Gillick competent' in the context of all the necessary details which it would be appropriate for her to be able to form a view about.

I have, therefore, to consider her best interests. I have no hesitation in saying that in the light of the evidence of Mr Martin Milling, a very experienced consultant surgeon, it is not only in her best interests but it is absolutely vital that she should receive the careful, experienced surgical attention which he is able to offer. I have no doubt that she should receive the treatment which is offered and which is expressed to be vital. Accordingly, I propose to make an appropriate order which will permit that treatment to be given despite the fact that she does not consent. It is also my view, without any doubt at all, that it would be the appropriate order to make even if I were not justified in coming to the conclusion that she was not so-called 'Gillick competent'. This is an extreme case and her position is grave indeed. It is vital, as I have already said, that she should receive this treatment . . . "

NOTES:

1. Grubb notes that the President wrongly asked himself whether L *actually* understood what was involved in her decision rather than whether she was *capable* of understanding it. As he points out, actual understanding was impossible because the details of her death had been withheld from her (A. Grubb, "Refusal of Treatment (Child): Competence" (1999) 7 *Medical Law Review* 58, at pp.59–60.) He also notes the very high level of competence demanded of her to make a valid refusal.

2. The rigidity of L's views is attributed to her immaturity. But as Bridge points out "absolute faith . . . is itself a feature of any fundamentalist religious belief" so this argument would apply equally to adults who refused treatment on religious grounds (C. Bridge, "Religious Beliefs and Teenage Refusal of Medical Treatment" (1999) 62 M.L.R. 585 at p.588.)

3. This line of cases was recently followed by *Re P (Medical Treatment: Best Interests)* [2004] 2 F.L.R. 1117. Once again the High Court, albeit with some reluctance, declared that should the need to arise to use blood products to treat P, who suffered from hypermobility syndrome, it would be lawful to do so in his best interests. The decision was reached even though P was almost 17 and throughout his life had been a "staunch and committed" Jehovah's Witness. Johnson J. did add that this should only apply if there were no alterative to using blood products.

QUESTIONS:

1. Would it be better if the courts in these cases simply acknowledged that adolescent autonomy is circumscribed, rather than going through the sham of finding, often on dubious grounds, that adolescents are incompetent to refuse life-saving treatment? (See Grubb, *op. cit.* in note 1; Bridge, *op. cit.* in note 2).

2. Should L have been told how she would die? (For an ethical analysis of such dilemmas, see T. Vince and A. Petros, "Should Children's Autonomy Be Respected by Telling them of their Imminent Death?" (2006) 33 *Journal of Medical Ethics* 21.)

3. Writing of a comparable Canadian case, Margaret Somerville argues that "[i]n our-turn-of the millennium secular societies, a young person's maturity is often assessed by how autonomous, independent, self determined and individualistic that person is. On these criteria, a child from [such a religious family] . . . is unlikely to be found sufficiently mature to be held competent to consent to or refuse treatment" (M. Somerville, *The Ethical Canary: Science, Society and the Human Spirit,* Toronto: Penguin, 2000 at p.192). How applicable is her observation to the adolescents in this line of cases?

4. Is this line of cases ultimately one in which paternalism is justified? (See J. Bridgeman, "Because We Care? The Medical Treatment of Children" in S. Sheldon and M. Thomson (eds) *Feminist Perspectives on Health Care Law*, London: Cavendish, 1998.)

5. Limits to the Parental Power of Consent

Much of this chapter has been concerned with the issue of when it is legitimate for parents to consent to or refuse medical or bodily interventions by and on behalf of their children, whether they are approaching adulthood themselves or are clearly too young to consent. The case law we have considered to date has concerned decisions about treating or withdrawing treatment from seriously ill minors. However, conflicts about decisions over more routine forms of medical treatment or bodily interventions have also reached the courts, and posed difficult and controversial questions about the limits of parental powers. In *Hewer v Bryant* [1969] 3 All E.R. 578, Lord Denning stressed that parental rights only exist for the benefit of the child. As we have seen, his assertion was expressly approved by Lords Fraser and Scarman in the *Gillick* case. However, those cases failed to address the limits which law may impose on the kinds of medical treatment to which a parent may give consent. This issue was considered by Lord Templeman in the following case:

Re B (A Minor) (Wardship: Sterilisation) [1987] 2 All E.R. 206, [1988] 1 A.C. 199, [1987] 2 W.L.R. 1213

The facts of this case are discussed in Chapter 13 at p.928, but it concerned an application by a local authority for a 17-year-old girl to be made a ward of court and for leave to be given for her to undergo a sterilisation operation. The application was supported by the girl's mother but not by the Official Solicitor, who was acting as guardian *ad litem*. At first instance, the judge granted the application. The Official Solicitor appealed unsuccessfully to the Court of Appeal and then to the House of Lords:

LORD TEMPLEMAN

" . . . In my opinion sterilisation of a girl under 18 should only be carried out with the leave of a High Court judge. A doctor performing a sterilisation operation with the consent of the parents might still be liable in criminal, civil or professional proceedings. A court exercising the wardship jurisdiction emanating from the Crown is the only authority which is empowered to authorise such a drastic step as sterilisation after a full and informed investigation. The girl will be represented by the Official Solicitor or some other appropriate guardian; the parents will be made parties if they wish to appear and where appropriate the local authority will also appear. Expert evidence will be adduced setting out the reasons for the application, the history, conditions, circumstances and foreseeable future of the girl, the risks and consequences of pregnancy, the risks and consequences of sterilisation, the practicability of alternative precautions against pregnancy and any other relevant information. The judge may order additional evidence to be obtained. In my opinion, a decision should only be made by a High Court judge. In the Family Division a judge is selected for his or her experience, ability and compassion. No one has suggested a more satisfactory tribunal or a more satisfactory method of reaching a decision which vitally concerns an individual but also involves principles of law, ethics and medical practice. Applications for sterilisation will be rare. Sometimes the judge will conclude that a sufficiently overwhelming case has not been established to justify interference with the fundamental right of a girl to bear a child; this was the case in *Re D (a minor) (wardship: sterilisation)* [1976] 1 All E.R. 326. But in the present case the judge was satisfied that it would be cruel to expose the girl to an unacceptable risk of pregnancy which could only be obviated by sterilisation in order to prevent child bearing and childbirth in circumstances of uncomprehending fear and pain and risk of physical injury. In such a case the judge was under a duty and had the courage to authorise sterilisation."

NOTES:

1. Note the similarity in the fundamental issues addressed in this case and *Gillick*, in that both are concerned with the extent to which individual autonomy can be overridden in the context of the reproductive autonomy of young women. Yet *Gillick* is not referred to by their Lordships. (See R. Lee and D. Morgan, "A Lesser Sacrifice? Sterilisation and Mentally Handicapped Women" in R. Lee and D. Morgan (eds), *Birthrights: Law and Ethics at the Beginnings of Life*, London: Routledge, 1989 at p.134.)
2. Where sterilisation is a necessary incident of other, necessary treatment, it is not necessary to obtain the court's sanction. In *Re E* at p.463 above, for example, it was said that parents might give a valid consent to a hysterectomy operation on their daughter without first obtaining a declaration from the court.
3. Lord Templeman's opinion has been approved in *Re HG* [1993] 1 F.L.R. 587.

QUESTION:

1. Which, if any, other medical procedures should also require judicial sanction in the case of a young person? Is the answer to this question dependent on being able to forge a distinction between therapeutic and non-therapeutic procedures? (See Chapter 6 at p.384 and Chapter 13 at p.932) Are there matters of policy at stake which might circumscribe the remit of parental competence?

Though expressed *obiter*, Lord Templeman's opinion has since received judicial approval in the following case:

In Re P (a Minor) (1981) 80 L.G.R. 301

P (Shirley) was a 15-year-old girl in the care of the local authority under the Children and Young Persons Act 1969. She had earlier given birth to a baby boy and she and her son were placed in a mother and baby unit with educational facilities. During school hours her son was cared for in the nursery and outside school hours she cared for him. In August 1980 she again became pregnant and, as with her first pregnancy, her parents refused their consent to abortion, although on this occasion Shirley herself was anxious to have a termination.

The local authority made her a ward of court and asked the court to make an order directing that her pregnancy be terminated. Her father suggested instead that she should carry her pregnancy to term and that he and his wife would bring up her first child.

BUTLER-SLOSS J.

" . . . I would not like it to be thought that because she says she does not want the child her wishes should be given such paramount importance as to mean that for that reason only she should have an abortion. But where her wishes coincide with the facts that she is in danger of injury to her mental health; that she is undoubtedly—when I consider her interests, as I do, as the first and paramount consideration—unable to fulfil her own growing up as a child or her schooling as a consequence of this second pregnancy; where she is endangering the future of her current child; and where I take into account all the aspects of her actual and reasonably foreseeable environment, I have no doubt that this case comes within section 1(a) of the Abortion Act 1967. The continuance of the pregnancy would involve injury to the mental health of Shirley and her existing child who is the child of her family and that risk is undoubtedly much greater than the risk of the pregnancy being terminated. Indeed I am told by the consultants that the risks involved in terminating a pregnancy of under 12 weeks is minimal . . .

I must take into account in considering the welfare of Shirley—and her welfare is what is paramount in my mind because she is the ward of court—and through her the effect on her son of having this unwanted child, the important aspect of her parents. I was helpfully reminded of what had been said in the House of Lords in *J v C* [1970] A.C. 668 about the rights and obligations of parents. These parents are in certain difficulties in that they do not have the day to day care of Shirley since she is in care, and they are not able to offer to take over the day to day care of Shirley. In the circumstances, although I must give weight to their feelings as a factor in the case to be taken into consideration, and I must take into account their deeply and sincerely held religious objection, in considering the best interest of the minor as to whether she should have her pregnancy terminated I draw to some extent an analogy with Jehovah's Witnesses and blood transfusions; nevertheless, if I am satisfied, as I am, that there is a risk of injury to the mental health of this minor, the factors raised by the grandfather on behalf of himself and his wife—which I have taken into account—cannot weigh in the balance against the needs of this girl so as to prevent the termination which I have decided is necessary in her best interests.

Therefore, I propose to direct that there shall be a termination of this pregnancy this week . . . "

NOTES:

1. For the relevant provisions of the Abortion Act 1967 see Chapter 12.
2. This decision was followed in the case of *Re B (Wardship: Abortion)* [1991] 2 F.L.R. 426. In that case L—a 12-year-old girl—wished to terminate her pregnancy. She was supported in her wish by the putative father, who was 16, and her maternal grandparents who had brought her up. However, her mother, who had maintained close contact with L, opposed an application by the local authority to have L's pregnancy terminated, on the ground that she didn't believe in abortion. Notwithstanding the mother's objection, Hollis J. held that it was in L's best interests to have the termination, given her age and small build, the trauma of an unwanted pregnancy and the disruption to her education. As we saw at p.444 above, according to the *Axon* case, if minors are *Gillick-*

competent then parents have no right to be consulted about abortion decisions.

3. For the limits of parental power to consent to other controversial treatments such as research, sterilisations and organ transplants see Chapters 10, 13 and 15.

QUESTIONS:

1. Was it justifiable for the court, in this case, to over-rule the parents' religious and other objections on the basis of the child's best interests?

2. Do you think that the court would ever deem it in the best interests of a minor to be compelled to have an abortion in her best interests against her wishes? (See J. Herring, "Children's Abortion Rights" (1997) 5 *Medical Law Review* 257; C. Bridge, "Religious Beliefs and Teenage Refusal of Medical Treatment" (1999) 62 M.L.R. 585 at p.594.)

Re C (A Minor) (HIV Test) [2000] 2 W.L.R. 270, [1999] 2 F.L.R. 1004

The parents of a two-year-old child refused their consent to have her HIV tested, although the child's mother was HIV positive, had refused medication during pregnancy and had breastfed the child since birth. Medical evidence suggested there was a 20–25 per cent chance that the child was HIV positive. The parents believed in alternative medicine and disputed conventional medical opinion about the links between HIV and AIDS and appropriate treatment. The local authority had applied for a specific issue order under s.8 of the Children Act 1989, which, as we have seen, enables the court to determine a specific question concerning the exercise of parental responsibility.

BUTLER-SLOSS L.J.
" . . . In my view, the child is clearly at risk if there is ignorance of the child's medical condition. The degree of intrusion into the child of a medical test is slight. The degree of intrusion into the family of taking the child to the hospital for a medical test would for most people be comparatively slight. The parents have magnified this into a major issue because they do not accept any of the premises upon which the tests will be carried out. But the welfare of the child is paramount. The court has been asked to deal with the case. It cannot shirk its duty. The space sought by Mr Horowitz [counsel for the mother who had argued that law had to recognise a space for parental decision-making within which parents were entitled to reject current orthodoxy] . . . undoubtedly exists, but it exists subject to s 1(1) of the Children Act. It does not matter whether the parents are responsible or irresponsible. It matters whether the welfare of the child demands that such a course should be taken and, as Evans LJ was asking during this hearing in argument: can it be in the child's best interests for the parents to remain ignorant of their own child's state of health? You only have to ask that question for most people to say no. We are not talking about the rights of parents. We are talking about the rights of the child. Wilson J set out various Articles of the UN Convention on the Rights of the Child 1989. We do not in a sense need that. It is all encapsulated in s 1 of the Children Act, but it does give added strength to this most important of all points, that the parents' views, which are not the views of the majority, cannot stand against the right of the child to be properly cared for in every sense. This child has the right to have sensible and responsible people find out whether she is or is not HIV positive, either as a result of the birth to her mother, or as a result of the breast-feeding. There is a 25% chance, according to the doctors, that she is

HIV positive because of the birth. There is an increased danger because of breast-feeding. There is a one in three or one in four chance that she may be HIV positive. What seems to me to be crucial is that someone should find out so that one knows how she should be looked after. The idea that she should have aggressive treatment, because doctors who know about it feel, because they do not know if she is or is not HIV positive, that they must give her additional treatment, when it would not be necessary if she was not HIV positive, seems to me as sad as if they will not give her adequate treatment because the parents did not tell the doctor and the child was in fact seriously ill and was not given adequate treatment. Either way this child has her own rights. Those rights seem to me to be met at this stage by her being tested to see what her state of health is for the question of knowledge. That is as far as it goes. I therefore would refuse the application for permission to appeal.

NOTES:

1. Andrew Grubb questions whether in reality there is much space in which parental decisions regarding treatment of their children are final (A. Grubb, "Incompetent Patient (Child): HIV Testing and Best Interests" (2000) 8 *Medical Law Review* 120). Note that where parents do agree on HIV testing for their child, the approval of the High Court is no longer necessary (*President's Direction: HIV Testing of Children* [2003] 1 F.L.R. 1299).

2. The case of *Re MM* [2000] 1 F.L.R. 224 also concerned a difference between parents and doctors over which decision best promoted the child's interests. MM, aged 7, suffered from primary immunodeficiency, which had been treated in Russia with a programme of immunostimulant therapy, which remained his parents' treatment of choice. However, when he moved with his parents to England for three years, the unanimous medical advice was that he should instead receive replacement immunoglobin intravenously. Black J. accepted medical evidence that with the recommended treatment, although it would be necessary for MM to undergo the therapy for life, it would enable him to live close to a normal life, whereas without it the result was likely to be increased incidence of infections, leading to organ damage and failure and eventually death. The judge thus approved an order authorising the intravenous treatment, notwithstanding his acknowledgment that the parents were well informed about MM's disorder, had reservations about an early misdiagnosis and concerns about the safety of blood products when they returned to Russia.

QUESTIONS:

1. Grubb, *op. cit* (in note 1) questions whether much weight should be given to the parent's views in *Re C (HIV)*, contending they were sufficiently flawed to be deemed irrelevant. Do you agree?

2. By contrast, given the well-informed reasoning of the parents in *MM* and the practical difficulties they would face on their return to Russia, should

their views have been respected in *Re MM*? Compare this case with *Re T* at p.420 above. Black J. did not directly consider that case in his judgment, whereas Butler-Sloss L.J. in *Re C (HIV)* noted that *Re T* was "at the other end of any spectrum that one might be considering" from *Re C (HIV)*. Compare also the very different approach to "family autonomy" evident in the Irish case of *North Western Health Board v W(H)* [2001] I.E.S.C. 70. (see G.T. Laurie, "Better to Hesitate on the Threshold of Compulsion: PKU Testing and the Concept of Family Autonomy in Eire" (2002) 25 *Journal of Medical Ethics* 136).

3. As John Harris argues in relation to *Re C (HIV)*, any lack of clarity that remains after this decision is not about whether to or not to protect children against the palpably harmful decisions of their parents, but rather how far back (if at all) to extend this principle prior to birth. (J. Harris, "Test is best", *The Guardian*, September 25, 1999; see also A. Marsh "Testing Pregnant Women and Newborns for HIV: Legal and Ethical Responses to Public Health Efforts to Prevent Pediatric AIDS" (2001) 13 *Yale Journal of Law and Feminism* 199; this issue of "policing" pregnancy will be addressed in Chapter 13.) Do you agree?

4. In considering the conjoined twins case at pp.434–439 above, we noted that Michael Freeman questioned why parental objections grounded in religious views should be accorded respect (see M. Freeman, "Whose Life Is It Anyway?" [2001] *Medical Law Review* 259, at p.264). Should such views have any greater respect than those of the parents in these two cases? Why/why not?

Another situation in which parents might make controversial choices on behalf of their children is in requesting circumcision for their male infants, a procedure which is tolerated by professional guidelines in this country (see M. Fox and M. Thomson, "A Covenant with the Status Quo? Male Circumcision and the New BMA Guidance to Doctors" (2005) 31 *Journal of Medical Ethics* 463). The legality of the practice was addressed obliquely in the following case:

Re J (A Minor) (Prohibited steps Order: Circumcision [2000] 1 F.L.R. 571

This case concerned J, a five-year-old-boy—who, after his parents' separation, lived with his mother, a non-practising English Christian. His father was a non-practising Turkish Muslim, who wanted J to be circumcised so as to identify him with his father and confirm him as a Muslim. Having considered the factors relevant to J's upbringing, the Court of Appeal concluded that J should not be circumcised because he was not, and nor was he likely to be, brought up in the Muslim religion. Instead he had "a mixed heritage and an essentially secular lifestyle" and was unlikely to have such a degree of involvement with Muslims as to justify circumcising him for social reasons. In these circumstances, Wall J. held that the boy was unlikely to derive any of social or cultural benefits from circumcision which would outweigh the medical risks of the procedure—a view upheld by the Court of Appeal:

THORPE L.J.
[began by approving the following passages from Wall J.:]

"' . . . Circumcision is an effectively irreversible surgical intervention which has no medical basis in J's case. It is likely to be painful and carries with it small but definable physical and psychological risks. For it to be ordered there would accordingly have to be clear benefits to J which would demonstrate that circumcision was in his interests notwithstanding the risks. The principal benefits put forward are J's identification as a Muslim and the strengthening of his bond with his father. The strength of each is substantially weakened, in my judgment, by the facts of J's lifestyle and his likely upbringing. As I have already made clear, he is not going to be brought up as a Muslim child, and the strength of his bond with his father—viewed from his perspective rather than the father's—is unlikely to be weakened if he is not circumcised unless the father chooses to allow the absence of circumcision to work to weaken it . . .

J's mother, who not only shares parental responsibility for him with his father but cares for him on a day-to-day basis and is currently the most important person in his life, is opposed to his circumcision, and there is a rational basis for her opposition. It is a strong thing to impose a medically unnecessary surgical intervention on a residential parent who is opposed to it. In my judgment, this should only be done if the evidence shows that J's welfare requires him to be circumcised. For the reasons I have given, I do not think that the evidence overall shows that it is in J's interests to be circumcised . . . The judge correctly held that the father's right to manifest his religion had to be balanced against the welfare of the child and the rights of the mother. That holding has not been challenged in the course of this appeal . . . '"

[Thorpe L.J. then continued.]
I have summarised the judgment in this important case at length and have cited extensive passages since I accept the submission of Mr Harris QC that it is impregnable . . .

The only point of principle that this appeal decides is to indorse the judge's conclusion that s 2(7) of the 1989 Act does not enable a parent to arrange circumcision without the consent of the other. Section 2(7) provides:

'Where more than one person has parental responsibility for a child, each of them may act alone and without the other (or others) in meeting that responsibility; but nothing in this Part shall be taken to effect the operation of any enactment which requires the consent of more than one person in a matter affecting the child.'

Mr Nicholls, for the Official Solicitor, submitted and the judge accepted that the operation of circumcision is of considerable consequence and irreversible. It must, therefore, join the exceptional categories where disagreement between holders of parental responsibility must be submitted to the court for determination. He has renewed that submission in this court. No one has opposed it and I would uphold it . . . "

NOTES:

1. Schiemann L.J. and Butler-Sloss L.J. ageed. The decision was followed in *Re S (Children) (Specific Issue: Religion: Circumcision)* [2005] 1 F.L.R. 236.
2. Similar ethico-legal issues are raised by the issue of intersex surgery which, in the past, was routinely performed on children soon after birth. Responsible medical practice is increasingly understood to require that surgery be postponed until children are mature enough to decide for themselves. (See P.L. Chau and J. Herring, "Defining, Assigning and Designing Sex" (2002) 16 *International Journal of Law, Policy and the Family* 327; M. Fox and M. Thomson, "Cutting It: Surgical Interventions and the Sexing of Children" (2006) 13 *Cardozo Journal of Law and*

Gender 101.) Note the difference in English law's response to female circumcision, to which even a competent adult cannot consent (see Chapter 6 at pp.356–357).

3. *Re C (Welfare of Child: immunisation)* [2003] 2 F.L.R. 1095 was another example of parental disagreement over a child's best interests. In two similar cases the mothers, who were the principal carers of the children, wished not to immunise their children (aged 4 and 10) against any of the common childhood illnesses. The children's fathers who had parental responsibility, disagreed, and having evaluated the medical evidence and found it overwhelmingly in favour of vaccination, Sumner J. ordered each mother to take her child for immunisation in accordance with a schedule of appointments attached to the order. The Court of Appeal dismissed the appeal by both mothers and upheld the specific issue orders. It held that, like male circumcision, neither parent had the right to make the decision alone. In the event of disagreement immunisation should be carried out only where a court decided that it was in the best interests of the child. Thorpe L.J. also noted that the case of *Re T* (see p.420 above) was "unique in our jurisprudence and . . . explained by the trial judge's erroneous focus on the reasonableness of the mother's rejection of medical opinion".

QUESTIONS:

1. Is the non-consensual removal of healthy genital tissue for non-medical reasons ever ethically justifiable? Should it be categorised as a legitimate parental choice where both parents agree? (See M. Fox and M. Thomson, "Short Changed? The Law and Ethics of Male Circumcision" (2005) 13 *International Journal of Children's Rights* 157.)

2. Would it be justifiable for cosmetic surgery to be performed on children if both parents agree? Is it ethical to carry out such surgery to "correct" the characteristic facial appearance of children with Down's syndrome? (See R.B. Jones, "Parental Consent to Cosmetic Facial Surgery in Down's syndrome" (2000) 26 *Journal of Medical Ethics* 101.) What about an operation to correct "bat ears"? (See F.M. Hodges *et al.*, "Prophylactic intervention in Children: Balancing Human Rights with Public Health" (2002) 28 *Journal of Medical Ethics* 10.) Or weight-loss surgery? Would it be ethical for parents to consent to the administration of growth hormone therapy, (a) to make a small child "normal" and (b) to make a "normal" child taller? (See M. Veweij and F. Kortmann, "Moral Assessment of Growth Hormone Therapy for Children with Idiopathic Short Stature" (1997) 23 *Journal of Medical Ethics* 305.

SELECT BIBLIOGRAPHY

M. Brazier and C. Bridge, "Coercion or Caring: Analysing Adolescent Authority" (1996) 16 *Legal Studies* 84.

C. Bridge, "Parental Religious Benefits and the Medical Treatment of Children" [1994] *Butterworth's Family Law Journal* 131.

J. Bridgeman, "Caring for Children with Severe Disabilities: Boundaries and Relational Rights" (2005) 13 *International Journal of Children's Rights* 99.

J. Bridgeman, "Old Enough to Know Best?" (1993) 13 *Legal Studies* 69.

J. Bridgeman, *Parental Responsibility, Young Children and Healthcare Law*, Cambridge: CUP, forthcoming 2007.

J. Bridgeman and D. Monk (eds), *Feminist Perspectives on Child Law*, London: Cavendish, 2000.

British Medical Association, *Consent, Rights and Choices in Health Care for Children and Young People*, London: BMJ Books, 2001.

G. Douglas, "The Retreat from *Gillick*" (1992) 55 M.L.R. 569.

J. Eekelaar, "The Emergence of Children's Rights" (1986) 6 O.J.L.S. 161.

M. Freeman (ed.) *Children's Health and Children's Rights* Leiden/Boston: Martinus Nijhoff, 2006.

A. Grubb, "Treatment Decisions: Keeping it in the Family" in A. Grubb (ed.), *Choices and Decisions in Health Care*, Chichester: John Wiley, 1993.

I. Kennedy, "The Doctor, the Pill and the 15-year-old Girl" in M. Lockwood (ed.), *Moral Dilemmas in Modern Medicine*, Oxford: Oxford University Press, 1985.

R. Lavery, "Routine Medical Treatment of Children" [1990] *Journal of Social Welfare Law* 375.

S. Lee, "Towards a Jurisprudence of Consent" in J. Eekelaar and S. Ball (eds), *Oxford Essays in Jurisprudence* (3rd series), Oxford: OUP, 1987.

C. Lyon, "What's Happened to the Child's Right to Refuse?" (1994) 6 *Journal of Child Law* 84.

R. Miller, *Children, Ethics and Modern Medicine*, Bloomington: Indiana University Press, 2003.

J. Montgomery, "Consent to Health Care for Children" (1993) 5 *Journal of Child Law* 117.

J. Murphy, "Circumscribing the Autonomy of '*Gillick* Competent' Children" (1992) 43 *Northern Ireland Legal Quarterly* 60.

J. Munby, "Consent to Treatment: Children and the Incompetent Patient" in A. Grubb (ed.), *Principles of Medical Law*, Oxford: OUP, 2004.

K. O'Donovan, "The Child as Legal Object" in K. O'Donovan, *Family Law Matters*, London: Pluto, 1993.

L.F. Ross, *Children, Families and Health Care*, Oxford: Clarendon Press, 1998.

R. Weir, *Selective Non-Treatment of Handicapped New Borns*, New York: OUP, 1988.

8

MENTAL HEALTH

1. INTRODUCTION

As we saw in Chapter 6, above, the general rule for treatment of an adult is that he must consent to the treatment and that such consent cannot be overridden. Other than the special rules relating to people who are not able to consent to treatment and the regime in relation to children, the most obvious exception to this rule is where treatment is carried out under the Mental Health Act 1983. For a person to be compulsorily admitted, it is not necessary that he be incompetent. Many, but not all, detained patients are competent. The Act allows for the treatment of a competent detained patient even if he wishes not to have the treatment. The main focus of this chapter is on treatment, but it is essential to consider the process of admission to hospital and its implications. These matters are considered by examining the law relating to what may be called "civil admission". The same treatment provisions exist in relation to patients detained as a result of contact with the criminal justice system, but they fall outwith the scope of this chapter.

(a) Reform

There is a need for reform of the Mental Health Act. This has two primary drivers: (a) the need to make it ECHR compliant where it is clearly currently not so; and (b) a principled approach to endeavour to achieve change to deliver a better piece of mental health legislation. In doing this and fully achieving both objectives, the preferred route is a completely new Mental Health Act. However, the process of moving towards that objective has been so difficult and has so clearly failed to gain the commitment and approval of, among other stakeholders, the professionals (whose engagement is vital to its effective implementation) that the Government, in March 2006, announced that it was no longer seeking a major reform, but was going for a more limited process of change that will involve the introduction of a piece of amending legislation. An advantage of this approach is that it will enable the new legislation to be implemented at the same time as the Mental Capacity Act 2005 comes into force, i.e. April 2007.

479

The process of full reform was commenced by the appointment of an expert committee to review the 1983 legislation and to make proposals for change. It is known as the Richardson Report, after the Chair (see *Report of the Expert Committee: Review of the Mental Health Act 1983* (1999)). While the Government initially proposed legislation that was widely divergent from its proposals (draft Mental Health Bill 2002 and see J. Peay, "Reform of the Mental Health Act 1983: Squandering an Opportunity?" (2000) 3 *Journal of Mental Health Law* 5), the 2004 Bill was much closer to the Richardson Report (see draft Mental Health Bill 2004). Even so, the Pre-Legislative Scrutiny Committee of both Houses of Parliament on that Bill raised very considerable concerns (House of Lords and House of Commons Joint Committee on the Draft Mental Health Bill, *Draft Mental Health Bill* Session 2004–05 HL Paper 79-I; HC 95-I) which, in part, led the Government to its current position. There are some interesting lessons to be drawn from the reform process and so selected aspects of it will be referred to in this chapter. The present position is that a Bill to reform the Mental Health Act 1983 will be introduced so as to make key changes to the 1983 Act.

The current position on reform is as stated in a Ministerial Statement of March 23, 2006 and in briefing sheets from the Department of Health of May 2, 2006.

Written Ministerial Statement on the Government's policy on mental health legislation by Minister of State, Department of Health (Ms Rosie Winterton) March 23, 2006

I should like to set out the Government's plans for a Mental Health Bill.

Mental health legislation is about the circumstances in which people with a mental disorder can be treated without their consent, in order to protect them and/or others from harm; and the processes that have to be followed if someone is to be treated without consent. The majority of people with a mental disorder will not require treatment under mental health legislation. At any point in time, one in six of the population has a common mental health problem. At 31 March 2004, there were about 14,000 patients who were being detained and treated in hospital for a mental disorder.

Through sustained investment and ongoing service reform, the mental health system is progressively achieving success in many areas. However, it is important that the present mental health legislation is amended to keep pace with changes in service delivery, to provide safeguards for patients and to prevent harm to individual patients and to the wider public.

We have spent the last 7 years consulting on, discussing and redrafting the Mental Health Bill. The draft Bill achieves many of our intentions but we have been reviewing its length and complexity. We have listened to the Joint Committee and our stakeholders, and have looked again at the arguments about amending the Mental Health Act 1983.

As a result, we will introduce a shorter, streamlined Bill that amends the Act. It will reflect the impact of service modernisation and will provide legislation that is easier to understand and implement. It will also help deliver our other objectives: to promote patient safeguards and to protect patients and the public from harm.

The Bill to amend the 1983 Act will:

- introduce supervised treatment in the community for suitable patients following an initial period of detention and treatment in hospital. This will help ensure that patients comply with treatment and enable action to be taken to prevent relapse and readmission to hospital. The introduction of treatment in the community reflects modern service provision enabling patients to be treated according to their individual needs and circumstances.

- expand the skill base of professionals who are responsible for the treatment of patients treated without their consent.
- improve patient safeguards by taking order-making powers with regard to the Mental Health Review Tribunal. We are currently considering across government the precise terms of the changes, and will continue to consult with stakeholders.
- reflect a widespread consensus and the views of the Joint Committee and will introduce a new, simplified single definition of mental disorder.
- keep, as recommended by the Joint Committee, the exclusion for drug and alcohol dependency, and preserve the effect of the Act as it relates to people with learning disabilities.
- replace the 'treatability' test with a test that appropriate treatment must be available. Unlike the treatability test, the availability of appropriate treatment will be a requirement for all groups of patients, regardless of their particular diagnosis. This is important to ensure that patients are not brought under compulsory powers unless appropriate treatment is available.
- amend the current Act to remedy an ECHR incompatibility in relation to the Nearest Relative. At the same time, we will bring the Act into line with the Civil Partnership Act 2004 in relation to the Nearest Relative provisions.

The Bill will be used as the vehicle for introducing the Bournewood safeguards, through amending the Mental Capacity Act 2005. These safeguards are for people who lack capacity and are deprived of their liberty but do not receive mental health legislation safeguards.

We will address safeguards for children treated on the basis of parental consent through the Children Act 1989. Children detained under the Mental Health Act will continue to receive the same safeguards as adults. We will also look at ways that we can continue to pursue other patient safeguards, such as advocacy, through other means.

We shall publish very soon a report on the outcome of the public consultation on Bournewood and the key features of our Bournewood proposals.

The Mental Health Bill: Plans to amend the Mental Health Act 1983—Briefing sheets on key policy areas where changes are proposed May 2, 2006

As part of its comprehensive strategy to reform and modernise mental health care, the Government plans to update the Mental Health Act 1983. The amending Bill will ensure that legislation reflects the modernisation of services and the move towards more treatment in the community. It will improve safeguards and increase the safety of individual patients, and protect the wider public from harm.

This series of briefing sheets covers key policy areas where changes to the Act are proposed (further updates will be posted on the website as they become available).

The key policy areas where changes to the Act are proposed are as follows:

- **Supervised community treatment**: which aims to ensure that patients who have been discharged from compulsory treatment in hospital continue to comply with treatment. It will be used in suitable cases to help prevent the relapse of patients and so will help to improve their safety and the safety of others.
- **Professional roles**: expanding the skill base of professionals who are responsible for the treatment of patients without their consent.
- **Nearest relative**: make it possible for some patients to appoint a different "nearest relative" to represent them.
- **Definition of mental disorder**: introduce a new, simplified definition of mental disorder throughout the Act.

- **Criteria for detention**: introduce a requirement that someone cannot be detained for treatment unless appropriate treatment is available and remove the "treatability" test.
- **Mental Health Review Tribunal (MHRT)**: improve patient safeguards by taking an order-making power which will allow us to vary the current time limit for automatic referral by hospital managers to the MHRT.

(b) Principles for Mental Health Legislation

The two classic justifications for the compulsory detention of people with mental ill health are by reference to a *parens patriae* power in the State to ensure that people are treated for illnesses when necessary and/or the police power of the State to control people causing harm to others. The *parens patriae* justification operates on the basis that the State has the right, as the parent of its citizens, to take action for the benefit of citizens, even though the citizens may not perceive a need for help or indeed even wish to reject it. The major obstacle to the acceptability of such an approach was identified by John Stuart Mill in his *Essay on Liberty* (1859) where he argued that interference in the freedoms of others could only be justified where the action was designed to "prevent harm to others". The best interests of the citizen, he argued, would not be sufficient justification, though they would indicate the obligation to inform, advise or even remonstrate with the citizen. Nevertheless, the *parens patriae* justification was part of the basis of the Percy Commission's proposals for reform of mental health law, which formed the basis of the Mental Health Act 1959 and, thus also, of the Mental Health Act 1983.

The Report of the Royal Commission on Mental Illness and Deficiency 1954–57 (Cmd. 169)

In our view, individual people who need care because of mental disorder should be able to receive it as far as possible with no more restriction of liberty or legal formality than is applied to people who need care because of other types of illness. But mental disorder has special features which require special measures. Mental disorder makes any patients incapable of protecting themselves or their interests, so that if they are neglected or exploited it may be necessary to have authority to insist on providing them with proper care. In many cases, it affects the patient's judgment so that he does not realize he is ill, and the illness can only be treated against the patient's wishes at that time. In many cases too it affects the patient's behaviour in such a way that it is necessary in the interests of other people or of society to insist on removing him for treatment even if he is unwilling.

Barnes, Bowl and Fisher criticised this justification for compulsory hospitalisation on the basis that: (1) the fact that people do not know they are ill and may not seek help may appear to be attractive, but it begs the question of what degree of deviation from health is sufficient to justify compulsory powers; and (2) the fact that society has a right to protect itself is accepted, but its application in this context begs the question of exactly what behaviour patterns will justify compulsory powers (M. Barnes, R. Bowl and M. Fisher, *Sectioned: Social Services and the 1983 Mental Health Act*, London: Routledge, 1990). The latter concern is also reflected in the debate about mental illness (see below). If deviant behaviour is a sufficient grounding for the use of compulsory power, there are real risks: first, any deviance may be sufficient to warrant action; secondly, identification of deviant behaviour may be subjective and not objective, and, more particularly, identifying the "norm" is culturally, racially and gender-based, thus allowing for, if not actively encouraging, discrimination in the use of compulsory powers.

The alternative to a *parens patriae* justification, which is also present in the extract from the Percy Commission, is the police power. This justification argues that, where individuals present a danger (or perhaps harm) to others, the State is entitled to take action by interfering with that individual's freedoms, thereby protecting others from the danger or harm. This clearly is a justification for action taken through the criminal law, but it is also argued to be a justification for compulsory admission to hospital. The Mental Health Act 1983 uses both justifications in establishing the criteria for admission to hospital, as is clearly demonstrated by reading s. 2(1)(b) and s. 3(2)(c) (below).

While the Government has changed significantly its approach to reform of the 1983 Act, there is considerable value in considering some of the views of the Expert Committee, at least as potential benchmarks against which the current and any future law should be measured.

Report of the Expert Committee: Review of the Mental Health Act 1983 (1999)

Underlying principles

2.1 The desire to encourage the treatment of mental ill health according to principles similar to those which govern the treatment of physical ill health is fundamental to our entire approach. This desire to promote non-discrimination on grounds of mental health has led inevitably to an emphasis on patient autonomy. In the context of physical health a patient with capacity is free to choose whether or not to accept treatment: his or her autonomy is respected.

2.2 In our Draft Proposals we indicated our views on non-discrimination and patient autonomy, which we defined as meaning 'the freedom to decide for oneself, the ability to make choices which others will respect'. While we received overwhelming support for the principle of patient autonomy many respondents pointed to both the contradiction inherent in the elevation of non-discrimination in a statute which then permits the compulsion of individuals essentially on the grounds of mental disorder, and to the failure of our Draft Proposals to maintain a consistent approach to patient autonomy throughout. We recognise the strength of both of these comments and therefore think it appropriate to set out the basis of our approach in more detail and the nature of the dilemmas as we see them.

2.3 We are convinced that whatever the precise scope of a mental health act it must primarily be seen as a health measure and must be consistent with the professional ethics of the health services. This is not to deny the importance of public protection but to place it within the appropriate context within which it can best be promoted. The importance of respecting and enhancing patient autonomy is now gaining increased recognition within the health services generally... and we are satisfied that it must acquire similar recognition within mental health services specifically.

2.4 Respect for patient autonomy implies respect for the treatment choices of those who have the capacity necessary to make them. Patient autonomy therefore brings with it an inevitable emphasis on capacity. In the context of mental health this becomes crucially relevant. Many people with a mental disorder will retain the capacity to make treatment decisions but others will not, at points in the course of their disorder they will lose that capacity either temporarily or for a more prolonged period. In order to ensure that people who lack the necessary capacity can none the less receive the care and treatment they require, the law must provide a framework to authorise the application of care and treatment in the absence of their consent, even in the face of their active objection. If the law did not do so it would be preventing their access to treatment.

2.5 Thus it is clear that one major objective of a mental health act must be to provide such a framework. To do so is congruent with the principles of both non-discrimination and patient autonomy. Indeed not to do so could be said to be discriminatory. That much is widely, if not universally, accepted. The difficulties arise in the case of patients with mental disorder who retain the capacity to make treatment choices and refuse the treatment proposed by clinicians. In the context of physical ill health such capable refusals would prevail, whatever the consequences for the patient. Thus to be faithful to the principle of non-discrimination and consistent in the application of patient autonomy a legislative scheme would have to permit intervention in the absence of consent only in the care of those who lacked capacity: a patient's capable refusal of treatment would have to be allowed to prevail.

2.6 . . . For some [respondents] the issue was clear: a mental health act should authorise treatment in the absence of consent only for those who lack capacity. The refusal to accept treatment by a person with capacity must be respected in the context of mental ill health just as it is in the context of physical ill health, whatever the consequences for the individual. If a person with a mental disorder who refused treatment was thought to pose a serious risk to others then he or she should be dealt with through the criminal justice system, not through a health provision.

2.7 Those who maintained such a pure approach were in a small minority. There was a much larger body of opinion which was prepared to accept the overriding of a capable refusal in health provision on grounds of public safety in certain circumstances. The reasons given were in part pragmatic and in part driven by principle. Essentially most of those who commented accepted that the safety of the public must be allowed to outweigh individual autonomy where the risk is sufficiently great and, if the risk is related to the presence of a mental disorder for which a health intervention of likely benefit to the individual is available, then it is appropriate that such intervention should be authorised as part of a health provision. Mental disorder unlike most physical health problems may occasionally have wider consequences for unconnected members of the public affected by the individual's behaviour, acts and omissions. The Committee supports this reasoning and in what follows we seek to describe a framework which adequately reflects it.

2.8 The issue of harm to self, however, presents a much more intractable dilemma and one on which no consensus has emerged . . . . A strict adherence to non-discrimination and patient autonomy would imply that a person's capable refusal must be respected whatever the consequences for him or herself. For many this is an unpalatable conclusion. Equally, however, few if any would wish to return to unchallenged paternalism. The overwhelming support achieved by the principle of patient autonomy indicates that the enforced treatment of the capable and objecting patient simply in the interests of his or her own health as defined by professionals is no longer acceptable.

2.9 The reasons for rejecting the full implications of patient autonomy, in the cases of self harm, while at the same time rejecting unrefined paternalism were again a mixture of principle and pragmatism. They include a belief that the consequences of untreated mental disorder may impact more directly and significantly on carers and relatives than do the consequences of untreated physical disorder, and a disinclination to allow someone with a mental disorder whether or not they formally retain capacity, to deteriorate beyond a certain point. There is also the practical concern that a failure to allow intervention to protect the patient from serious harm despite his or her capable refusal will lead in practice to the adaptation of a very broad interpretation of incapacity.

2.10 Those who would wish to give precedence to autonomy in the case of harm to self argue that, unlike the case of harm to others, there is no countervailing interest at stake which outweighs the principle of respect for autonomy. They also suggest that in the case of most forms of mental disorder the person who is vulnerable to serious harm if untreated is unlikely to retain capacity on any proper understanding of the term and would therefore be treated as lacking capacity. Further they point to clinical experience which suggests that for many disorders of personality, rather than mental illness, treatment under compulsion is likely to be counterproductive.

2.11 . . . We believe [these arguments] reflect a difference in fundamental philosophy which can only be resolved by according preference to one approach over the other. We have set out the alternative views as best we can and invited politicians to make the moral choice between them . . . .

Principles of Non-Discrimination

2.14 . . . [W]e regard the principle of non-discrimination as central to the provision of treatment and care to those suffering from mental disorder and by non-discrimination . . . we are referring to non-discrimination on grounds of mental health.

2.15 . . . Thus we recommend the recognition of the following principle:

- **that wherever possible the principles governing mental health care should be the same as those which govern physical health.**

2.16 However, we accept that it would not be appropriate to express the principle within the act itself . . . .

Express Principles—Patient Autonomy

2.20 The Committee considers that any new legislation must be expressly concerned with the recognition and enhancement of patient autonomy . . . Patient autonomy should only be disregarded in well defined circumstances set out by law.

Other Express Principles

2.21 . . . The principles which we wish to see included are as follows:

i. **Informal care**
Wherever possible care, treatment and support should be provided without recourse to compulsion.

ii. **Least restrictive alternative**
Service users should be provided with any necessary care, treatment and support both in the least invasive manner and in the least restrictive manner and environment compatible with the delivery of safe and effective care, taking account of the safety of other patients, carers and staff.

iii. **Consensual care**
Programmes of care, treatment and support should as far as possible reflect the preferences of the service user, even where intervention in the absence of consent is expressly permitted by law.

iv. **Participation**
Service users should be fully involved, to the extent permitted by their individual capacity, in all aspects of their assessment, care, treatment and support.

v. **Reciprocity**
Where society imposes an obligation on an individual to comply with a programme of treatment and care it should impose a parallel obligation on the health and social care authorities to provide appropriate services, including ongoing care following discharge form compulsion.

vi. **Respect for diversity**
Service users should receive care, treatment and support in a manner that accords respect for their individual qualities, abilities and diverse backgrounds, and properly takes into account their age, gender, sexual orientation, ethnic group and social, cultural and religious background.

vii. **Equality**
All powers under the act, particularly those relating to access to services, assessments and the provision of services shall be exercised without any direct or indirect discrimination on the grounds of physical disability, age, gender, sexual orientation, race, colour, language, religion, or national, ethnic or social origin.

viii. **Carers**
Those who provide care to service users on an informal basis should receive respect for their role and experience and have their views and needs taken into account.

ix. **Effective communication**
Service users are entitled to the benefit of the effective sharing of information, consistent with the obligations of confidentiality and the law, amongst those responsible for their care and treatment.

x. **Provision of information**
Service users should be provided with all the information necessary to enable them to participate fully in the sense of envisaged in [the participation principle] . . .

[The Committee was also in favour of the principle of evidence based medicine for effective treatment.]

ENTITLEMENTS

Consequences of the Principle of Reciprocity

3.5 The possibilities [are] as follows:

i. specific reference in the national service frameworks to the need to achieve the same quality of service irrespective of the user's legal status;
ii. specific reference within the duties of the Commission for Care Standards;
iii. inclusion within the requirements of clinical governance;
iv. clear guidance in the Code of Practice;
v. the introduction of a duty on the Secretary of State to monitor the quality of care provided as between those placed under compulsion and those in receipt of care informally.

3.6 [Following the responses received, we] therefore recommend the above for serious consideration.

Rights which Flow from Compulsion

3.7 . . . [We] recommend the introduction of a number of [further and] specific rights [which] should include:

i. the right to information about treatment and care;
ii. at the earliest possible opportunity the right to advocacy . . . ;
iii. the right of access to medical records . . . ;
iv. the right to receive care and treatment in accordance with the care plan during any period of compulsion;
v. the right to ongoing care after any period of compulsion;
vi. in the case of those detained in hospital, the right to safe containment with respect for human dignity;

vii. the right to information about and assistance with drawing up an advance agreement.

NOTES:

1. A number of people have indeed argued for legislation that (1) gives priority to capacity; (2) would apply mental capacity law where someone is incapable; and (3) would allow detention for a mental disorder causing harm to others and treatment for that mental disorder (alone) that causes the harm to others. See, for example, M. Gunn and T. Holland, "Some Thoughts on the Proposed Mental Health Act" (2002) 8 *Journal of Mental Health Law* 360. For an article that, originally, teased out the issues for relying on capacity, see D. Price, "Civil Commitment of the Mentally Ill: Compelling Arguments for Reform" (1994) 2 *Medical Law Review* 321.

2. The critical balance is, as Fennell comments in "Inscribing Paternalism in the Law: Consent to Treatment and Mental Disorder" (1990) 17 *Journal of Law and Society* 29, between autonomy and paternalism. He notes that there are two important organising concepts: legalism (which emphasises "the need to put limits on the power of mental health professionals and the rights of patients to respect their autonomously expressed wishes") and medicalism (stressing "the need to ensure that the safeguards for the individual rights of patients are not so cumbersome as to impede medical interventions aimed at serving those same patients' best interests"). Fennell states that "there is now widespread acknowledgement of the folly of rigid insistence upon the ascendancy of patient autonomy over paternalism where the result would be to harm the patient."

3. It is not essential that a person be not competent prior to admitting him to hospital or providing him with treatment in hospital. Indeed, many people admitted to hospital are capable of making decisions about entering hospital and accepting or refusing treatment. There is a trend for at least some psychiatrists to take it into account capacity in exercising their discretion whether to pursue compulsory detention in hospital.

4. The Mental Health Bill 2004, cl. 9(4) revealed the moral choice made by the Government as to whether compulsory powers can be used where there is self-harm. There were a number of conditions that would have had to be fulfilled as the basis for compulsory admission to hospital.

> cl. 9(4) The third condition is that it is necessary—
> (a) for the protection of the patient from—
> 1. suicide or serious self-harm, or
> 2. serious neglect by him of his health or safety, or
> (b) for the protection of other persons,
> that medical treatment be provided to the patient.

QUESTIONS:

1. Is the rationale adopted by the Percy Commission an adequate basis for the compulsory hospitalisation of people? Is the *parens patriae* justification

sufficient on its own? If so, would you expect that it be demanded that the condition be curable or would it be sufficient that the person be offered some prospect of their condition being alleviated?

2. Would a more appropriate basis for interference be the police power of the state?

3. If neither the *parens patriae* power nor the police power is sufficient justification for the use of compulsory powers, does this leave distressed and ill citizens to fend for themselves when help could easily be provided; if so, is that morally unacceptable? Do the answers to these questions assume that the individual is capable of exercising his rights?

4. Is compulsory admission acceptable only when it is predicated on some form of incompetence, so that to exercise compulsory powers on the competent, mentally ill person should not be permitted?

5. The Mental Health Act 1983, as will be seen below, does not demand that a prospective patient be a "danger" to others nor does it demand that the condition be curable (though some alleviation or prevention of deterioration may be necessary). Does this mean that compulsory admission may be justified on relatively flimsy grounds?

6. If there were to be more reliance on the concept of capacity, are reliability and validity sufficiently secure to carry such a weight of responsibility (see Chapter 5 on Capacity in considering this question)?

(c) The Significance of Safeguards

Despite the impact of the anti-psychiatry debate (for an introduction, see B. M. Hoggett, *Mental Health Law* (4th edn, London: Sweet & Maxwell, 1996, pp.27–29 and 46–49), a system of compulsory hospitalisation in some circumstances for people with mental illness is likely to continue to exist. Since the restrictions on freedom of liberty are severe, it is essential that the means by which compulsory admission is imposed are, and are seen to be, fair and based upon clear evidence. Sir Thomas Bingham M.R. in *Re SC* [1996] 1 All E.R. 532 said:

"Powers therefore exist to ensure that those who suffer from mental illness may, in appropriate circumstances, be involuntarily admitted to mental hospitals and detained. But, and it is a very important but, the circumstances in which the mentally ill may be detained are very carefully prescribed by statute. Action may only be taken if there is clear evidence that the medical condition of a patient justifies such action, and there are detailed rules prescribing the classes of person who may apply to a hospital to admit and detain a mentally disordered person. The legislation recognises that action may be necessary at short notice and also recognises that it will be impracticable for a hospital to investigate the background facts to ensure that all the requirements of the Act are satisfied if they appear to be so. Thus we find in the statute a panoply of powers combined with detailed safeguards for the protection of the patient. The underlying issue in the present appeal is whether those powers were properly exercised and whether the appellant was lawfully detained. One reminds oneself that the liberty of the subject is at stake in a case of this kind, and that liberty may be violated only to the extent permitted by law and not otherwise."

The European Convention on Human Rights accepts the necessity of a system of compulsory hospitalisation, subject to necessary safeguards. Article 5 provides:

Article 5

1. Everyone has the right to liberty and security of person. No one shall be deprived of his liberty save in the following cases and in accordance with a procedure prescribed by law:

. . .

(e) the lawful detention . . . of persons of unsound mind . . .

4. Everyone who is deprived of his liberty by arrest or detention shall be entitled to take proceedings by which the lawfulness of his detention shall be decided speedily by a court and his release ordered if the detention is not lawful.

NOTES:

1. The case law of the European Court of Human Rights has established that there are three minimum conditions which have to be satisfied for a State's law to comply with the requirements in Article 5. First, the prospective patient must be reliably shown by objective medical expertise to be of unsound mind; secondly, the patient's mental disorder must be of a kind or degree warranting compulsory confinement; and thirdly, the unsoundness of mind must continue throughout the period of detention. (See *Winterwerp v Netherlands* (1979), *Ashingdane v UK* (1985), *Johnson v UK* (1997), *H.M. v Switzerland* (2002), *Reid v UK (2003), and H.L. v UK* (2004), and R. Clayton and H. Tomlinson, *The Law of Human Rights* (Oxford: OUP, 2000, with updates) and M. G. Wachenfeld, *The Human Rights of the Mentally Ill in Europe* (Denmark: Danish Center for Human Rights, 1992).)

2. In general, the scheme of the Mental Health Act appears to be compliant. This is partly because the European Convention does not require treatability for application of the law and it does not engage with the philosophical debate about harm to self and harm to others. Partly, this compliance is because the 1983 Act was drawn up intending to comply with the then understanding of the requirements of the Convention. However, MIND, the National Association for Mental Health, some years ago took the view that there are many areas in which mental health law fails to comply with these obligations (see MIND and National Council of Civil Liberties, *People with Mental Illness and Learning Disabilities* (1993)). It is becoming clear that this is the position as more cases raising issues under the ECHR go through the English courts after the commencement of the Human Rights Act 1998.

   The impact of the ECHR continues to be significant. Declarations of incompatibility (under the Human Rights Act 1998, s. 4) of the Mental Health Act with the convention have been made in the following cases:

   - *R. (on the application of H) v Mental Health Review Tribunal* [2002] Q.B. 1 on the basis that the burden of proof in MHRT proceedings should not be on the patient, but on the detaining authority and this led to the Remedial Order which has amended the Mental Health Act to secure compliance (Mental Health Act 1983 (Remedial) Order 2001, SI 2001/3712);

- *R. (on the application of M) v Secretary of State for Health* [2003] EWHC Admin 1094 on the basis that the inability to replace an abusive relative as the nearest relative is a breach of Article 8 (following the decision *JT v United Kingdom* (1997); see also *R. (on the application of E) v Bristol City Council* [2005] EWHC Admin 74);
- *R. (on the application of D) v Home Secretary* [2003] 1 W.L.R. 1315 because an MHRT has no power to discharge a person on a discretionary life sentence who has been transferred to hospital from prison, where the normal tariff on their life sentence has passed.

One further particularly significant decision is *R. (on the application of Wilkinson) v Broadmoor Hospital* [2001] EWCA Civ 1545 in which it was held that, where a patient challenges the forcible administration of medical treatment, the court, in order for there to be compliance with Article 6, must be able to consider the merits of the medical decision and whether human rights were infringed, thus the traditional limits of judicial review cannot apply (see P. Bartlett and R. Sandland, *Mental Health Law: Policy and Practice* (2nd edn), Oxford: OUP, 2003 at pp.362–363). This case was the first of a series of cases that includes *R. (on the application of B) v Dr Haddock* [2005] EWHC 521 which summarises the current position at pp.538–541 below.

3. Paul Bowen has identified that "there has been a great deal of activity in the Courts" (P. Bowen, "Is this a Revolution? The Impact of the Human Rights Act on Mental Health Law" [2004] *Journal of Mental Health Law* 27, at p.29). While not engaging in a complete survey of all areas, Bowen identifies five areas where there has been considerable court activity: detention and discharge; compulsory treatment; seclusion; other conditions of detention; and protection of confidential information. He concludes his survey with the following predictions for the future, at p.33:

"The law is in a state of flux, and it is difficult to predict where it will end. However, it is likely that more is yet to be said by the Courts (both here and in Strasbourg) on the following issues:

- Powers and procedures of the Mental Health Review Tribunal. I expect challenges to the standard of proof in Tribunal proceedings; the current civil standard may be too low; the use of hearsay evidence will be more tightly regulated; the qualifications of those giving evidence in support of a patient's continuing detention will be more anxiously scrutinized.
- Whether Article 5 and/or 8 requires the tribunal to have power to transfer patients to lower security, or grant leave of absence, as a necessary precursor to discharge.
- Whether decisions of the Tribunal to discharge are binding on subsequent clinicians (including those in the community) in the absence of compelling reasons.
- Whether positive obligations may be derived from Article 6(1) upon public authorities to provide both in-patient and after-care treatment which will enable patients to be discharged.

- Bournewood: whether compliant incapacitated patients are to be given greater safeguards against arbitrary and mistaken detention or treatment.
- Whether the right of autonomy entitles a competent patient to refuse treatment other than in circumstances where he is a threat to others."

QUESTIONS:

1. Do you accept that there must be a form of compulsory admission?
2. If so, is an element of professional discretion necessary? Can professional discretion be controlled by the procedure for admission, ensuring that a multi-professional approach is adopted?
3. Would you involve lawyers and/or courts more in the decision-making process?

Reconsider these questions throughout the chapter and assess how close the Mental Health Act comes to your ideal approach.

The criteria and procedures for compulsory admission must be sufficient to avoid improper usage, so that only those people for whom compulsory hospitalisation is necessary are indeed admitted. The 1983 Act introduced many changes to the original provisions of the 1959 Act in a clear endeavour to meet the demands of civil libertarians (see, for example, L.O. Gostin, *A Human Condition*, (London: MIND, 1975). Thus, for example, the need for compulsory hospitalisation being the least restrictive alternative received statutory recognition in s.3(2); provisions were introduced to regulate treatment (Part IV); an independent watchdog body was created (the Mental Health Act Commission); and a multidisciplinary approach was used whenever possible (see, for example, the obligation on a responsible medical officer to consult others on renewal of detention and the involvement of two other professionals in advising the second opinion approved doctor in assessing the commencement or continuity of certain treatments).

A consequence of hospitalisation being the least restrictive alternative is that many people with mental disorder in need of some form of treatment and care will either not be detained in hospital, but will be informal patients or living in the community. The greatest need then is that the necessary support facilities are provided (see Bartlett and Sandland, *op. cit.* in note 2 at Chapter 9). The importance of improved service provision was recognised by the Government when considering reform of the Mental Health Act, indeed reform is to be seen in the context of the overall provision of mental health services (see, for example, *Government Response to the Report of the Joint Committee on the draft Mental Health Bill 2004* (2005) Cm. 6624, at pp.1–3 and the Written Ministerial Statement 2006, p.480, above).

Where a person is compulsorily hospitalised, there is an argument that that person must have, as a consequence, a right to treatment. This also flows from the Richardson principle of reciprocity (see above, p.485). No such legal right currently exists (but see the obligation to provide after-care under s.117 and after-care under supervision under s.25A; see below, p.555). Further, it is not a requirement of compliance with Article 5(1)(e), of the ECHR; see *Winterwerp v Netherlands* (1979) and *Reid v UK* (2003). Indeed, it is not the case that the condition of a person has to be treatable in the sense of it being curable (see p.515 below).

Finally, it is clear that resources for mental health services are inadequate. Bed occupancy rates have frequently been reported as being over 100 per cent, thus resulting in some patients having to be out of hospital on leave so as to allow a bed to be made available to a more pressing case. One consequence of this is the high number of prisoners who have mental health problems. This is a major dilemma for those working in the mental health services.

QUESTION:

1. If a person is compulsorily admitted to hospital, would you agree that there should be an obligation to provide treatment to the patient? If so, should the patient be able to challenge the treatment with which he is provided? Keep this question in mind when examining the Act.

2. ADMISSION TO HOSPITAL

Admission to hospital may be compulsory, voluntary or informal. Section 131(1) of the Mental Health Act 1983 permits admission without any formal procedures. A person who has attained the age of 16 and is competent may also be admitted informally (s.131(2)). Quite what s.131 permits was litigated up to the House of Lords in the following case.

R v Bournewood Community and Mental Health NHS Trust, Ex p. L
(Secretary of State for Health and others intervening) [1998] 3 All E.R. 289

The case concerned a 48-year-old man, Mr L, who was "profoundly mentally retarded". He was incapable of consenting to medical treatment. He was frequently agitated, had no sense of danger and a history of self-harming behaviour. For some 30 years, from the age of 13, he had been a resident at Bournewood Hospital. Since 1994, he had been discharged and was living in the community with paid carers, the Enderbys, who regarded him as one of the family. On July 22, 1997, at Cranstock Day Centre, he became particularly agitated, hitting himself on the head with his fists and banging his head against the wall. As the Enderbys could not be contacted, the day centre contacted a local doctor, who administered a sedative, and the social worker, who got Mr L taken to accident and emergency at Bournewood Hospital. Because of the sedative, he became calmer, but, after becoming agitated again, a psychiatrist assessed him as needing in-patient treatment. Mr L made no attempt to leave and was transferred to the behavioural unit under Dr M, the consultant. She decided that it was not necessary to detain him because he appeared to be fully compliant and did not resist admission. He was therefore admitted informally. The issue raised for the courts was whether Mr L had been unlawfully detained in hospital.

The Court of Appeal took a different view from that of Owen J. at first instance. They held that Mr L had in fact been detained. They said: "In our judgment a person is detained in law if those who have control over the premises in which he is have the intention that he shall not be permitted to leave those premises and have the ability to prevent him from leaving. We have concluded that this was and is the position of L."

Since he was detained, but not under the Act, Mr L won his appeal. The trust appealed to the House of Lords.

LORD GOFF OF CHIEVELY

"The impact of the Court of Appeal's judgment

There can be no doubt that the decision of the Court of Appeal has caused grave concern among those involved in the care and treatment of mentally disordered persons. As a result, three parties applied for, and were granted, leave to intervene in the appeal before this House. They were the Secretary of State for Health, the Mental Health Act Commission (the commission) and the Registered Nursing Homes Association (the RNHA) . . . .

. . . I am able to summarise the position which has arisen following the Court of Appeal's judgment, as follows. First and foremost, the effect of the judgment is that large numbers of mental patients who would formerly not have to be compulsorily detained under the 1983 Act will now have to be so detained. Inquiries by the commission suggest that 'there will be an additional 22,000 detained patients resident on any one day as a consequence of the Court of Appeal judgment plus an additional 48,000 admissions per year under the Act' . . . . This estimate should be set against the background that the average number of detained patients resident on any one day in England and Wales is approximately 13,000 . . . The commission considered it to be very likely that the majority of patients to whom the Court of Appeal judgment would be patients in need of long term care and further considered that if the judgment is held to apply to patients receiving medical treatment for mental disorder in mental nursing homes not registered to receive detained patients, the above estimates were likely to be very much higher. It is obvious that there would in the result be a substantial impact on the available resources . . . , not only for the mental health services and professionals who have to implement the 1983 Act, but also for mental health review tribunals and for the commission itself . . . Deep concern about the effect of the judgment was expressed, in particular, by the President of the Royal Society of Psychiatrists, and the chairman of the Faculty for Psychiatry and Old Age of that society and also by the executive director of the Alzheimer's Disease Society . . .

The commission also stated that the Court of Appeal's judgment had given rise to a number of legal uncertainties. Two particular questions . . . arose with regard to mental nursing homes, viz, whether such homes were required to be registered to receive patients detained under the 1983 Act before receiving patients like Mr L, and whether homes not so registered are now obliged to register or to discharge such patients from their care . . .

On the other hand . . . , if patients such as Mr L had to be compulsorily detained under the 1983 Act in order to be admitted to hospital, they would reap the benefit of the safeguards written into the Act for the protection of patients compulsorily detained . . . [T]he lack of statutory safeguards for patients informally admitted to hospital has been a matter of concern for the commission . . . However, under s121(4) of the 1983 Act there is, vested in the Secretary of State, the power 'to direct the commission to keep under review the care and treatment, or any aspect of the care and treatment, in hospitals and mental nursing homes of patients who are not liable to be detained under this Act.' During the course of the hearing, the Appellate Committee was assured by counsel for the Secretary of State that he has had the matter under consideration, but that hitherto he has not thought it right to exercise his power in this respect. In this connection, it is plain that he has to have regard to the resource implications of extension of the statutory safeguards to the very much larger number of patients who are informally admitted . . . .

Section 131(1) of the 1983 Act

Central to the argument advanced by [counsel, Mr Pleming] was the submission that . . . in-patients in hospital fall into two categories. (1) Those patients who are compulsorily, and formally, admitted into hospital, against their will or regardless of their will, who are detained or liable to be detained in hospital. This category may be called 'compulsory patient' . . . . (2) Those patients who enter hospital as in-patients for treatment either (a) who, having the capacity to consent, do consent ('voluntary patients') or (b) who, though lacking capacity to consent, do not object ('informal patients'). Both are admitted under s 131(1) without the formalities and procedures for admission necessary for detention under the Act. Strictly, therefore, both groups could be described as informal patients, but it is convenient to confine that description to those who are not voluntary patients.

[S] 131(1) of the 1983 Act is in identical terms to s 5(1) of the Mental Health Act 1959. Furthermore the 1959 Act was enacted following the *Report of the Royal Commission on the Law Relating to Mental Illness and Mental Deficiency* (Cmnd 169 (1954–1957)) (the Percy Commission), which recommended that compulsory detention should only be employed in cases where it was necessary to do so. The Percy Commission's views, and recommendation, on this point are to be found in paras 289, 290 and 291 of their report, which read as follows:

> '289. We consider compulsion and detention quite unnecessary for a large number, probably the great majority, of the patients at present cared for in mental deficiency hospitals, most of whom are childlike and prepared to accept whatever arrangements are made for them. There is no more need to have power to detain these patients in hospital than in their own homes or any other place which they have no wish to leave. We strongly recommend that the principle of treatment without certification should be extended to them. Such a step should help to alter the whole atmosphere of this branch of the mental health services. Many parents of severely sub-normal children at present feel that they lose all their rights as parents when their child is admitted to hospital and automatically becomes subject to compulsory detention there. We have no doubt that the element of coercion also increases the resentment of some feeble-minded psycho-paths, and of their parents, when they are placed under "statutory supervision" or admitted to mental deficiency hospitals after leaving school, and that this makes it even more difficult than it been be to persuade them to regard these services in the same way as other social services and other types of hospital treatment, as services which are provided for their own benefit . . .
>
> 290. Admission to hospital without using compulsory powers should also be possible for considerably more mentally ill patients than are at present admitted as voluntary patients . . . .
>
> 291. We therefore recommend that the law and its administration should be altered, in relation to all forms of mental disorder, by abandoning the assumption that compulsory powers must be used unless the patient can express a positive desire for treatment, and replacing this by the offer of care, without deprivation of liberty, to all who need it and are not unwilling to receive it. All hospitals providing psychiatric treatment should be free to admit patients for any length of time without any legal formality and without power to detain . . . .'

. . . Following the enactment of the 1959 Act, s 5(1) was duly implemented in the manner foreshadowed by the Percy Commission, a practice which . . . has been continued under s 131(1) of the 1983 Act, which is in identical terms. It is little wonder therefore that the judgment of the Court of Appeal . . . , which restricts s 131(1) to voluntary patients, should have caused the grave concern which has been expressed in the evidence . . . .

In the light of the statutory history, Mr Gordon, for Mr L, recognised that s 5(1) of the 1959 Act must have the meaning for which Mr Pleming contended; but he boldly suggested that s 131(1) of the 1983 Act should be given a different meaning and be restricted to voluntary patients ... [I]n my opinion, [his argument] is wholly untenable, bearing in mind not only that s 131(1) of the 1983 Act is in identical terms to 5(1) of the 1959 Act, but that I have been able to discover no trace, either in the 1982 Act or in the White Paper of November 1981 which preceded it ..., of any intention to depart from, or modify, the recommendations of the Percy Commission upon which s 5(1) was founded, or to amend s 5(1) itself ...

For these reasons, I am unable, with all respect, to accept the opinion of the Court of Appeal on the crucial question of the meaning of s 131(1) ...

Treatment and care of informal patients

... It was plainly the statutory intention that [informal] patients would be cared for, and receive such treatment for their condition as might be prescribed for them in their best interests. Moreover, the doctors in charge would, of course, owe a duty of care to such a patient in their care. Such treatment and care can, in my opinion, be justified on the basis of the common law doctrine of necessity, as to which see the decision of your Lordships' House in *F v West Berkshire Health Authority (Mental Health Act Commission intervening)* [1990] 2 AC 1 ...

Was the respondent unlawfully detained?

... In the course of their judgment, the Court of Appeal stated:

' ... a person is detained in law if those who have control over the premises in which he is have the intention that she shall not be permitted to leave those premises and have the ability to prevent him from leaving.'

I observe however that no mention here is made of the requirement that, for the tort of false imprisonment to be committed, there must *in fact* be a complete deprivation of, or restraint upon, the plaintiff's liberty. On this the law is clear. As Atkin LJ said in *Meering v Graham-White Aviation Co Ltd* (1920 122 LT 44 at 54, 'any restraint within defined bounds which is a restraint in fact may be an imprisonment'. Furthermore, it is well settled that the deprivation of liberty must be actual, rather than potential ...

In the light of [the evidence], the following conclusions may be drawn. The first is that ... Mr L ... had not been finally discharged. It followed that the appellant trust remained responsible for his treatment, and that it was in discharge of that responsibility that the steps ... were taken. The second is that when, on 22 July, Mr L became agitated and acted violently, an emergency in any event arose which called for intervention, as a matter of necessity, in his best interests and, at least in the initial stage, to avoid danger to others. Plainly it was most appropriate that the appellant trust, and Dr M in particular, should intervene in these circumstances; certainly Mr and Mrs E, as Mr L's carers, could not assert any superior position. Third, I have no doubt that all the steps in fact taken ... were in fact taken in the best interests of Mr L and, in so far as they might otherwise have constituted an invasion of his civil rights, were justified on the basis of the common law doctrine of necessity.

I wish to add that the latter statement is as true of any restriction upon his freedom of movement as then occurred, as it is of any touching of his person. There were times during the episode when it might be said that Mr L was 'detained' in the sense that, in the absence of justification, the tort of false imprisonment would have been committed. I have particularly in mind the journey by ambulance from the Day Centre to the Accident and Emergency Unit. But that journey was plainly justified by necessity, as must frequently be so in the case of removal to hospital by ambulance of unfortunate people who have been taken ill or suffered injury and as a result are incapacitated from expressing consent. I wish further to add that I cannot see that Dr M's statements to the effect that she would if necessary have taken steps compulsorily to detain Mr L under the 1983 Act have any impact on the above conclusions. Those concerned with the treatment and care of mentally disordered persons must always have this possibility in mind although, like Dr M, they will know that this power is only to be exercised in the last resort and they may hope, as in the present case, that it would prove to be unnecessary to exercise it. Such power, if exercised in accordance with the statute, is of course lawful. In the present case all the steps in fact taken by Dr M were, in my opinion, lawful because justified under the common law doctrine of necessity and this conclusion is unaffected by her realisation that she might have to invoke the statutory power of detention.

Finally, the readmission of Mr L to hospital as an informal patient under s 131(1) of the 1983 Act could not, in my opinion, constitute the tort of false imprisonment. His readmission, as such, did not constitute a deprivation of his liberty. As Dr M stated . . . , he was not kept in a locked ward after he was admitted and the fact that she . . . had it in her mind that she might thereafter take steps to detain him compulsorily under the Act, did not give rise to his detention in fact at an earlier date. Furthermore his treatment while in hospital was plainly justified on the basis of the common law doctrine of necessity. It follows that none of these actions constituted any wrong against Mr L.

For these reasons, I would allow the appeal.

Two subsidiary points

There are however two subsidiary points which I wish to mention . . . .

The second point relates to the function of the common law doctrine of necessity in justifying actions which might otherwise be tortious, and so has the effect of providing a defence to actions in tort. The importance of this was . . . first revealed in the judgments in *F* v *West Berkshire Health Authority* . . . . [O]ur attention was drawn [by counsel to] three earlier cases in which the doctrine was invoked . . . , all of which provide authority for the proposition that the common law permitted the detention of those who were a danger, to themselves or others, in so far as this was shown to be necessary . . . . The concept of necessity . . . is a concept of great importance. It is perhaps surprising, however, that the significant role it has to play in the law of torts has come to be recognise at so late a stage in the development of our law."

Lords Lloyd, Nolan and Hope agreed with Lord Goff.

Lord Steyn took a different view as to whether Mr L was detained, but reluctantly accepted that s.131(1) permitted the detention on compliant, incapacitated patients. These two aspects of his opinion are worthy of consideration.

LORD STEYN

"Detention

. . . In my view, this case falls on the wrong side of any reasonable line that can be drawn between what is or what is not imprisonment or detention. The critical facts are as follows. (1) When, on 22 July 1997 at the Day Centre, L became agitated and started injuring himself, he was sedated and then physically supported and taken to the hospital. (2) Health care professionals exercised effective power over him. If L had physically resisted, the psychiatrist would immediately have taken steps to ensure his compulsory admission. (3) In hospital, staff regularly sedated him. That ensured that he remained tractable. This contrasts with the position when he was with the carers; they seldom resorted to medication and then only in minimal doses. (4) The psychiatrist vetoed visits by the carers to L. She did so, as she explained to the carers, in order to ensure that L did not try to leave with them. The psychiatrist told the carers that L would be released only when she, and other health care professionals, deemed it appropriate. (5) While L was not in a locked ward, nurses closely monitored his reactions. Nurses were instructed to keep him under continuous observation and did so.

Counsel for the trust and the Secretary of State argued that L was in truth always free not to go to the hospital and subsequently to leave the hospital. This argument stretches credulity to breaking point. The truth is that for entirely bona fide reasons, conceived in the best interests of L, any possible resistance by him was overcome by sedation, by taking him to hospital and by close supervision of him in hospital and, if L had shown any sign of wanting to leave, he would have been firmly discouraged by staff and, if necessary, physically prevented from doing so. The suggestion that L was free to go is a fairy tale.

At one stage counsel for the trust suggested that L was not detained because he lacked the necessary will, or more precisely the capacity to grant or refuse consent. That argument was misconceived. After all, an unconscious or drugged person can be detained: see *Meering v Graham-white Aviation Co Ltd* (1920) 122 LT 44 at 53–54 per Atkin LJ, dictum approved in *Murray v Ministry of Defence* [1988] 2 All ER 521 . . . . In my view L was detained because the health care professionals intentionally assumed control over him to such a degree as to amount to complete deprivation of his liberty . . .

The effect of the decision of the House of Lords

The general effect of the decision of the House is to leave compliant incapacitated patients without the safeguards enshrined in the 1983 Act. This is an unfortunate result. The Mental Health Act Commission has expressed concern about such informal patients in successive reports. And in a helpful written submission the commission has again voiced those concerns and explained in detail the beneficial effects of the ruling of the Court of Appeal. The common law principle of necessity is a useful concept, but it contains none of the safeguards of the 1983 Act. It places effective and unqualified control in the hands of the hospital psychiatrist and other health care professionals. It is, of course, true that such professionals owe a duty of care to patients and that they will almost invariably act in what they consider to be the best interests of the patient. But neither habeas corpus nor judicial review are sufficient safeguards against misjudgments and professional lapses in cases of compliant incapacitated patients. Given that such patients are diagnostically indistinguishable from compulsory patients, there is no reason to withhold the specific and effective protections of the 1983 Act from a large class of vulnerable mentally incapacitated individuals. Their moral right to be treated with dignity requires nothing less. The only comfort is that counsel for the Secretary of State has assured the House that reform of the law is under active consideration."

NOTES:

1. Bartlett and Sandland (*Mental Health Law: Policy and Practice* (2nd edn), Oxford: OUP, 2003) present a serious critique of this decision on the basis that there was incomplete consideration of the Percy Report at pp. 135–136:

   "The House of Lords viewed [para. 291] as being essentially determinative of the case before it. That must be read as a considerable overstatement, for 14 paragraphs after paragraph 291, the Percy Commission considered the situation of such an acquiescing patient when a family member requested their discharge from the facility. In the event that the family member was the nearest relative, the Commission stated that 'there can be no question of a barring certificate, even on grounds of danger to the patient or to others, in relation to patients admitted informally, whom the hospital has no authority to detain' (para. 305(ii)) . . . . It is unfortunate that this paragraph was not cited to the House of Lords, for it makes reliance on the Percy Report considerably more problematic in L's case."

2. Once in hospital, the person so present would be treated under the doctrine of necessity as established in *Re F* [1990] 2 A.C. 1 and developed in subsequent cases (see Chapter 5 on Capacity).

QUESTIONS:

1. Do you agree with the analysis about whether L was detained of (i) Lord Goff and the majority or (ii) Lord Steyn?
2. Do you agree with the unanimous interpretation of s.131(1)?
3. Is the precursor of s.131(1), that is s.5(1) of the 1959 Act, predicated on an outdated view of appropriate approaches to people who are incapable (see the extracts from the Percy Commission report in Lord Goff's speech).
4. What protections for compliant incapacitated patients and for the staff caring for them are there? What qualities must a person have to exercise them? Does not a compliant incapacitated patient not, by definition, have them?

Subsequently, this matter was taken to the European Court of Human Rights, which has reached a conclusion that significantly differs from that of the House of Lords.

H.L. v United Kingdom (2004) Application no. 45508/99

"I. Alleged violation of Article 5(1) of the Convention

. . .

A. Was the applicant "deprived of his liberty" from 22 July to 29 October 1997?

89. It is not disputed that in order to determine whether there has been a deprivation of liberty [the phrase in Article 5(1)(e)], the starting-point must be the specific situation of the individual concerned and account must be taken of a whole range of factors arising in a particular case such as the type, duration, effects and manner of implementation of the measure in question. The distinction between deprivation of, and restriction upon, liberty is merely one of degree or intensity and not one of nature of substance . . . .

90. . . . The majority of the House of Lords specifically distinguished actual restraint of a person (which would amount to false imprisonment) and restraint which was conditional upon his seeking leave (which would not amount to false imprisonment). The Court does not consider such a distinction to be of central importance under the Convention. Nor, for the same reason, can the Court accept as determinative the fact relied upon by the Government that the regime applied to the applicant (as a compliant incapacitated patient) did not materially differ from that applied to a person who had the capacity to consent to hospital treatment, neither objecting to their admission to hospital. The Court recalls that the right to liberty is too important in a democratic society for a person to lose the benefit of Convention protraction for the single reason that he may have given himself up to be taken into detention . . . , especially when it is not disputed that that person is legally incapable of consenting to, or disagreeing with, the proposed action.

91. . . . the Court considers the key factor in the present case to be that the health care professionals treating and managing the applicant exercised complete and effective control over his care and movements from the moment he presented acute behaviour problems on 22 July 1997 to the date he was compulsorily detained on 29 October 1997 . . . .

Accordingly, the concrete situation was that the applicant was under continuous supervision and control and was not free to leave. Any suggestion to the contrary was, in the Court's view, fairly described by Lord Steyn as 'stretching credulity to breaking point' and as a 'fairy tale'.

92. The Court would therefore agree with the applicant that it is not determinative whether the ward was 'locked' or 'lockable' . . . .

93. [The Court distinguished *H.M. v Switzerland* as] each case has to be decided on its own particular "range of factors and, while there may be similarities between the present and the *H.M.* case, there are also distinguishing features. In particular, it was not established that *H.M* was legally incapable of expressing a view in her position, she had often stated that she was willing to enter the nursing home and, within weeks of being there, she had agreed to stay. This combined with a regime entirely different to that applied to the present applicant . . . allows a conclusion that the facts of the *H.M.* case were not of a 'degree' or 'intensity' sufficiently serious to justify the conclusion that she was detained . . . .

94. The Court therefore concludes that the applicant was 'deprived of his liberty' within the meaning of Article 5(1) . . . .

B. Was that detention 'in accordance with a procedure prescribed by law' and 'lawful' within the meaning of Article 5(1)(e)?

1. Was the applicant of unsound mind?

101. . . . the Court finds that the applicant has been reliably shown to have been suffering from a mental disorder of a kind or degree warranting compulsory confinement which persisted during his detention between 22 July and 5 December 1997.

2. Lawfulness and protection against arbitrary detention

. . .

(c) The relevant principles

114. The Court recalls that the lawfulness of detention depends on conformity with the procedural and with the substantive aspects of domestic law, the 'lawful' term overlapping to a certain extent with the general requirement in Article 5(1) to observe a 'procedure prescribed by law' . . . . It is also recalled that, given the importance of personal liberty, the relevant national law must meet the standard of 'lawfulness' set by the Convention which requires that all law be sufficiently precise to allow the citizen—if need be, with appropriate advice—to foresee, to a degree that is reasonable in the circumstances, the consequences which a given action might entail . . . .

115. It is further recalled that it must be established that the detention was in conformity with the essential objective of Article 5(1) . . . which is to prevent individuals being deprived of their liberty in an arbitrary fashion . . . . This objective, and the broader condition that detention be 'in accordance with a procedure prescribed by law' and 'fair and proper procedures' . . . .

(d) The court's assessment

116. The Court considers it clear that the domestic legal basis for the applicant's detention . . . was the common law doctrine of necessity . . . .

120. . . . the Court finds striking the lack of any fixed procedural rules by which the admission and detention of compliant incapacitated persons is conducted. The contrast between this dearth of regulation and the extensive network of safeguards applicable to psychiatric committals covered by the 1983 Act . . . is, in the Court's view, significant. In particular and most obviously, the Court notes the lack of any formalised admission procedures which indicate who can propose admission, for what reasons and on the basis of what kind of medical and other assessments and conclusions. There is no requirement to fix the exact purpose of admission (for example, for assessment or for treatment and, consistently, no limits in terms of time, treatment or care attach to that admission). Nor is there any specific provision requiring a continuing clinical assessment of the persistence of

a disorder warranting detention. The nomination of a representative of a patient who could make certain objections and applications on his or her behalf is a procedural protection accorded to those committed involuntarily under the 1983 Act and which would be of equal importance for patients who are legally incapacitated and have, as in the present case, extremely limited communication abilities.

121. As a result of the lack of procedural regulation and limits, the Court observes that the hospital's health care professionals assumed full control of the liberty and treatment of a vulnerable incapacitated individual solely on the basis of their own clinical assessments completed as and when they considered fit . . . . While the Court does not question the good faith of those professionals or that they acted in what they considered to be the applicant's best interests, the very purpose of procedural safeguards is to protect individuals against 'any misjudgments and professional lapses' . . . .

122. The Court notes, on the one hand, the concerns about the lack of regulation in this area . . . . On the other hand, it has also noted the Government's understandable concern . . . to avoid the full, formal and inflexible impact of the 1983 Act.

123. The Government's submission that detention could not be arbitrary . . . because of the possibility of a later review of its lawfulness disregards the distinctive and cumulative protections offered by paragraphs 1 and 4 of Article 5: the former strictly regulates the circumstances in which one's liberty can be taken away whereas the latter requires a review of its legality thereafter.

124. The Court therefore finds that this absence of procedural safeguards fails to protect against arbitrary deprivations of liberty on grounds of necessity and, consequently, to comply with the essential purpose of Article 5(1) . . . . On this basis, the Court finds that there has been a violation of Article 5(1) of the Convention.

II. Alleged violation of Article 5(4) of the Convention

. . .

B. The court's assessment

1. General principles

135. Article 5(4) provides the right to an individual deprived of his liberty to have the lawfulness of that detention reviewed by a court in the light, not only of domestic law requirements, but also of the test of the Convention, the general principles embodied therein and the aim of the restrictions permitted by paragraph 1: the scheme of Article 5 implies that the notion of 'lawfulness' should have the same significance in paragraphs 1(e) and 4 in relation to the same deprivation of liberty. This does not guarantee a right of review of such scope as to empower the court on all aspects of the case or to substitute its own discretion for that of the decision-making authority. The review should, however, be wide enough to bear on those conditions which are essential for the lawful detention of a person, in this case, on the ground of unsoundness of mind . . . .

2. Application to the present case

. . .

139. The Court considered that . . . even with the application of the 'super-Wednesbury' principles on judicial review, the bar of unreasonableness would at the time of the applicant's domestic proceedings have been placed so high as effectively to exclude any adequate examination of the merits of the clinical views as to the persistence of mental illness justifying detention. This is indeed confirmed buy the decision of the Court of Appeal in . . . *R (Wilkinson) v Broadmoor Hospital* . . . .

140. For these reasons, the Court finds that the requirements of Article 5(4) were not satisfied . . . by judicial review and habeas corpus proceedings . . . .

142. In such circumstances, the Court concludes that it has not been demonstrated that the applicant had available to him a procedure which satisfied the requirements of Article 5(4) of the Convention. There has been therefore a violation of this provision."

NOTES:

1. It is now for the Government to decide how to respond. One option is to make amendments to the Mental Health Act 1983 and to provide a procedural system for incapacitated, compliant patients. The other option would be to either rely upon the structure of the Mental Capacity Act as providing sufficient substantive and procedural protections or, as there are Article 5 issues at play, to introduce amendments to the Mental Capacity Act to deal with this particular issue. The Pre-Legislative Scrutiny Committee recommended (in recommendation 29) that the Government should "bring forward a comprehensive and universal set of proposals to deal with hospitalisation and treatment of patients affected by the Bournewood judgment, either as amendments to [the Mental Capacity Act 2005] (as it appears to be intending now), or, failing that, by introducing. Proposals in the Mental Health Bill, as soon as possible." In response, all the Government could say was that it "is committed to bringing forward proposals for new safeguards for those incapacitated patients who need to be treated in their best interests in a way that involves deprivation of liberty" (*Government response to the report of the Joint Committee on the draft Mental Health Bill 2004* (2005) Cm. 6624, p.17).
2. The Government's statement of intention appears in a Department of Health briefing note of May 2, 2006:

   "**Clarifying when detention under the Act should be used rather than the Mental Capacity Act or the proposed new 'Bournewood' procedure in respect of patients who lack capacity.** The Mental Capacity Act cannot be used to deprive anyone of their liberty. The new Bournewood procedure the Government plans to introduce will fill the gap for people who need to be detained in their own interests. Where there is potentially a choice between Bournewood and the Mental Health Act, the Government's intention is that the Mental Health Act will be used where people object to being detained or treated. That will put these people in broadly the same position as people who have capacity but refuse to consent to treatment."

QUESTIONS:

1. If the solution to the violations of the Convention is to look to the Mental Capacity Act, should that not suggest that this piece of legislation should take priority so that any Mental Health Bill only deals with other cases (such as the ability to detain and treatment people with a mental disorder who present a danger to others (and, perhaps, harm to self)?
2. What procedural protections do you think are necessary to ensure that any process is ECHR compliant?
3. Are the procedural protections in the Mental Capacity Act likely to be sufficient? In essence, the key question is whether challenges to decisions on behalf of incapable adults under the Mental Capacity Act are likely to occur in sufficient cases (accepting that 100 per cent success rate cannot be achieved) for there to be compliance. Considering this issue demands cross reference to Chapter 5 on Capacity.

3. Compulsory Admission to Hospital

Hospitals and mental nursing homes (the latter being privately run institutions, including private hospitals, which are specifically registered for such purposes under the Care Standards Act 2000) may compulsorily admit patients under the Mental Health Act 1983. Section 145(1) defines hospital as meaning:

(a) any health service hospital within the meaning of the National Health Service Act 1977; and
(b) any accommodation provided by a local authority and used as a hospital or on behalf of the Secretary of State under that Act . . .

NOTE:

1. In 2003–04, over 200,000 people would have been admitted to hospital informally, voluntarily and compulsory. Of these admissions, only 26,235 were compulsory admissions. Admissions under s.2 totalled 14,110 and those under s.3 totalled 8,887. The number of detentions were 45,600. At March 31, 2004, there were 14,000 detained patients (see Department of Health, *Inpatients Formally Detained in Hospitals under the Mental Health Act 1983 and Other Legislation*, 2004).

QUESTION:

1. From the definition of hospital in s.145(1), do you think that a hospital has to be a large institution or could a small building housing only a few patients be a hospital? If the latter, would it have to be staffed by nurses?

(a) The Main Admission Sections

Mental Health Act 1983, ss.2(2–4), 3(2–3)

2.—(2) An application for admission for assessment may be made in respect of a patient on the grounds that—

(a) he is suffering from mental disorder of a nature or degree which warrants the detention of the patient in a hospital for assessment (or for assessment followed by medical treatment) for at least a limited period; and
(b) he ought to be so detained in the interests of his own health or safety or with a view to the protection of other persons.

(3) An application for admission for assessment shall be founded on the written recommendations in the prescribed form of two registered medical practitioners, including in each case a statement that in the opinion of the practitioner the conditions set out in subsection (2) above are complied with.

(4) Subject to the provisions of section 29(4) below, a patient admitted to hospital in pursuance of an application for admission for assessment may be detained for a period not exceeding 28 days beginning with the day on which he is admitted, but shall not be detained after the expiration of that period unless before it has expired he has become

liable to be detained by virtue of a subsequent application, order or direction under the following provisions of this Act.

3.—(2) An application for admission for treatment may be made in respect of a patient on the grounds that—

(a) he is suffering from mental illness, severe mental impairment, psychopathic disorder or mental impairment and his mental disorder is of a nature or degree which makes it appropriate for him to receive medical treatment in a hospital; and

(b) in the case of psychopathic disorder or mental impairment, such treatment is likely to alleviate or prevent a deterioration of his condition; and

(c) it is necessary for the health or safety of the patient or for the protection of other persons that he should receive such treatment and it cannot be provided unless he is detained under this section.

(3) An application for admission for treatment shall be founded on the written recommendations in the prescribed form of two registered medical practitioners, including in each case a statement that in the opinion of the practitioner the conditions set out in subsection (2) above are complied with; and each such recommendation shall include:

(a) such particulars as may be prescribed of the grounds for that opinion so far as it relates to the conditions set out in paragraphs (a) and (b) of that subsection; and

(b) a statement of the reasons for that opinion so far as it relates to the conditions set out in paragraph (c) of that subsection, specifying whether other methods of dealing with the patient are available and, if so, why they are not appropriate.

Section 3 may be renewed at the end of the first six months and thereafter at annual intervals, provided section 20 is satisfied. It demands that the responsible medical officer examine the patient within two months of the end of the detention period and, after consulting two people professionally concerned with the patient's medical treatment, make a report to the hospital managers if satisfied that:

(4) . . .

(a) the patient is suffering from mental illness, severe mental impairment, psychopathic disorder or mental impairment, and his mental disorder is of a nature or degree which makes it appropriate form him to receive medical treatment in a hospital; and

(b) such treatment is likely to alleviate or prevent a deterioration of his condition; and

(c) it is necessary for the health or safety of the patient or for the protection of others that he should receive such treatment and that it cannot be provided unless he continues to be detained;

but, in the case of mental illness or severe mental impairment, it shall be an alternative to the condition specified in paragraph (b) above that the patient, if discharged, is unlikely to be able to care for himself, to obtain the care which he needs or to guard himself against serious exploitation.

QUESTIONS:

1. What are the substantive requirements to be satisfied so that a person may be admitted to hospital under the two admission sections?

2. In what circumstances may s.3 be renewed, and how do the requirements differ from those for the original admission? Does a patient have to present

a danger to others in order for the conditions to be satisfied? Does a patient's condition have to be treatable or curable for the conditions to be satisfied?

3. What procedural requirements must be satisfied under these two sections?

(b) Mental Disorder

From ss.2 and 3, it is apparent that there are two broad categories of mental disorder to consider. First, a person may be admitted under s.2 if he or she is suffering from *mental disorder*, which means "mental illness, arrested or incomplete development of mind, psychopathic disorder and any other disorder or disability of mind" (s.1(2)).

Secondly, a person may be admitted under s.3 (and that admission be renewed under s.20) if he or she is suffering from one of four specific forms of mental disorder, that is mental illness, severe mental impairment, mental impairment and psychopathic disorder.

"Severe mental impairment" means a state of arrested or incomplete development of mind which includes severe impairment of intelligence and social functioning and is associated with abnormally aggressive or seriously irresponsible conduct on the part of the person concerned.

"Mental impairment" means a state of arrested or incomplete development of mind (not amounting to severe mental impairment) which includes significant impairment of intelligence and social functioning and is associated with abnormally aggressive or seriously irresponsible conduct on the part of the person concerned.

"Psychopathic disorder" means a persistent disorder or disability of mind (whether or not including significant impairment of intelligence) which results in abnormally aggressive or seriously irresponsible conduct on the part of the person concerned.

"Mental illness" is a central diagnosis and definition. This diagnosis will be that ascribed to at least 90 per cent of patients admitted to or resident in mental hospitals. On March 31, 2004, 10,697 of the 14,000 people detained were diagnosed as suffering from mental illness.

"Mental illness" is, however, a rather elusive concept because it bears no agreed definition. As Hoggett points out, the approach to the identification of mental illness can be made reliable by the adoption of standard criteria, but this does not answer the question of validity where there is a lack of agreement between three schools of thought which she identified: (1) the belief that all mental illnesses have an organic cause, though not all have yet been discovered; (2) the psychotherapeutic approaches that are "aimed at the patient's individual psyche or at its interaction with family or societal pressures"; (3) the behavioural school which concentrates upon the identification of deviant behaviour. There are obvious dangers with all these schools, not only the problem that there is not necessarily any common ground upon which they might all agree, but also the fact that the organic school fails to allow that the patient's perceptions and rationality have a role to play; and finally labelling through these methods allows for the imposition of treatment on "socially inconvenient people". The lack of agreement means that the ascription of the label "mental illness" relies heavily upon the professional judgment and understanding of a psychiatrist, which may be highly subjective and vary from one psychiatrist to another in a way which would not be acceptable with other doctors. However, it can be replied that this anti-psychiatry approach fails to recognise that some people are really ill and need care and treatment. (B.M. Hoggett, *Mental Health Law* (4th edn), London: Sweet & Maxwell, 1996, at pp.27–34); see also P. Bartlett and R. Sandland, *Mental Health Law: Policy and Practice* (2nd edn, Oxford, OUP, 2003), at pp.56–70 and M. Cavadino, *Mental Health Law in Context: Doctor's Orders*, Aldershot: Gover, 1989, especially Chapters 4 and 5).

The reliability of the identification of mental illness can be achieved by all professionals using the various symptom descriptions provided by one of two manuals developed for statistical purposes: the *Diagnostic and Statistical Manual* of the American Psychiatric Association or the *International Classification of Diseases and Disorders* of the World Health Organization. Reliability, however, may not avoid the identification of some people as being mentally ill, for example, on inappropriate cultural or racial grounds.

Some of these issues faced the Court of Appeal in the following case:

St George's Healthcare NHS Trust v S [1998] 3 All E.R. 673

JUDGE L.J.
" . . . The Act cannot be deployed to achieve the detention of an individual against her will merely because her thinking process is unusual, even apparently bizarre and irrational, and contrary to the views of the overwhelming majority of the community at large. The prohibited reasoning is readily identified and easily understood. Here is an intelligent woman. She knows perfectly well that if she persists with this course against medical advice she is likely to cause serious harm, and possibly death, to her baby and to herself. No normal mother-to-be could possibly think like that. Although this mother would not dream of taking any positive steps to cause injury to herself or her baby, her refusal is likely to lead to such a result. Her bizarre thinking represents a danger to their safety and health. It therefore follows that she *must* be mentally disordered and detained in hospital in her own interests and those of her baby. The short answer is that she may be perfectly rational and quite outside the ambit of the Act, and will remain so notwithstanding her eccentric thought process.

Even when used by well-intentioned individuals for what they believe to be genuine and powerful reasons, perhaps shared by a large section of the community, unless the individual case falls within the prescribed conditions, the Act cannot be used to justify detention for mental disorder . . . ."

QUESTIONS:

1. Does the lack of a clearly agreed definition of mental illness mean that the compulsory hospitalisation of people should not be possible? Alternatively does it mean that, while mental illness is generally recognised as existing, great care must be taken in ensuring that compulsory hospitalisation is carried out only when necessary and with sufficient precautions being taken to avoid its usage on discriminatory or other unacceptable grounds? If the latter, assess whether the Mental Health Act provides sufficient

protections for the person who is to be admitted to hospital as a detained patient. Note that the *Mental Health Act Code of Practice* (1999), para. 1.1 establishes certain "Guiding Principles":

"The detailed guidance on the Code needs to be read in the light of the following broad principles, that people to whom the Act applies . . . should:
  – receive recognition of their basic human rights under the . . . ECHR;
  – be given the respect for their qualities, abilities and diverse backgrounds as individuals and be assured that account will be taken of their age, gender, sexual orientation, social, ethnic, cultural and religious background, but that general assumptions will not be made on the basis of any one of these characteristics;
  – have their needs taken fully into account, though it is recognised that, within available resources, it may not always be practicable to meet them in full;
  – be given any necessary treatment or care in the least controlled and segregated facilities compatible with ensuring their own health or safety or the safety of other people;
  – be treated an cared for in such a way as to promote to the greatest [practicable] degree their self determination and personal responsibility, consistent with their own needs and wishes;
  – be discharged from detention or other powers provided by the Act as soon as it is clear that their application is no longer justified."

2. Does the law provide sufficient clarity on the meaning of mental illness? Note that this is the one condition for which the Mental Health Act provides no definition. The question may be addressed by considering the following case.

W v L (Mental Health Patient) [1974] Q.B. 711, [1973] 3 W.L.R. 859, (1973) 117 S.J. 757

The central issue in the case was whether a woman should be replaced as the nearest relative of a prospective patient on the basis that she had acted unreasonably in objecting to the making of an application. In the course of considering this matter, the court had to consider whether her husband might be suffering from mental illness. He was a young man aged 23. He had carried out a number of bizarre acts over roughly a two-year period. A series of acts occurred before he had any treatment: threatening his wife with a knife at her throat; putting a cat in a gas oven (it was rescued by his wife); forcing a cat to inhale ammonia and cutting its throat with a broken cup, eventually burying the body; hanging a Labrador puppy from the garage beams; strangling a terrier pup with a wire noose. After one week's stay voluntarily in a hospital, the husband discharged himself, after which he stopped taking his medication and threatened to push his pregnant wife downstairs.

LAWTON L.J.:
" . . . For the purpose of seeing what was the intention of the Act, the court has looked at the Report of the Royal Commission on the Law Relating to Mental Illness and Mental Deficiency [(1957) Cmnd. 169]. The Royal Commission seem to have overlooked that their recommendations would not result in a definition of 'mental disorder' [Lawton L.J. must have meant 'mental illness']. The facts of this case show how difficult the fitting of particular instances into the statutory classification can be. Lord Denning M.R. and Orr

L.J. have pointed out that there is no definition of 'mental illness'. The words are ordinary words of the English language. They have no particular medical significance. They have no particular legal significance. How should the court construe them? The answer in my judgment is to be found in the advice which Lord Reid recently gave in *Cozens v. Brutus* [1973] A.C. 854, 861, namely, that ordinary words of the English language should be construed in the way that ordinary sensible people would construe them. That being, in my judgment, the right test, then I ask myself, what would the ordinary sensible person have said about the patient's condition in this case if he had been informed of his behaviour to the dogs, the cat and his wife? In my judgment such a person would have said: 'Well, the fellow is obviously mentally ill'. If that be right, then, although the case may fall within the definition of 'psychopathic disorder' in [section 1(2)], it also falls within the classification of 'mental illness'; and there is the added medical fact that when the EEG was taken there were indications of a clinical character showing some abnormality of the brain. It is that application of the sensible person's assessment of the condition, plus the medical indication, which in my judgment brought the case within the classification of mental illness and justified the finding of the county court judge.

NOTE:

1. It is important to read the last sentence of the extract from the judgment of Lawton L.J. very carefully as it indicates the central importance of there being a "medical indication" before the application of the ordinary words of the English language test applies. This means that there is not complete reliance upon medical evidence. Brenda Hoggett has described this as the "man must be mad test" (see B. Hoggett, *Mental Health Law* (4th edn), London: Sweet & Maxwell, 1996 at p.32).

2. The meaning of "severe mental impairment" has been considered in *Re F (Mental Health Act: Guardianship* [2000] 1 F.L.R. 192 where the concern was to endeavour to ensure that T, an 18-year-old daughter, did not return to live with her abusive father. One option considered was guardianship (see below) and thus it was necessary to establish whether she had "severe mental impairment". Clearly, as she had a learning disability from an early age, there was a state of arrested or incomplete development of mind and it was clear that this had produced both severe impairment of intelligence and of social functioning. The question was whether her preparedness to put herself in a position where abuse could continue, that is her failure to take action to protect herself could be regarded as seriously irresponsible conduct on her part. The Court of Appeal held it could not. Thorpe L.J. said:

   "The urge to return [home] is almost universal . . . The deficiencies of the home are more apparent to other adults than to the young who have known no other. Furthermore, any measure of irresponsibility must depend upon an evaluation of the consequences of return . . . Clearly each case must depend on its particular facts and we would not wish to be taken as offering any general guideline."

   This approach means that the Act cannot be an effective part of action against abuse. See further R. Sandland, "Mental Health Act Guardianship and the Protection of Children" (2000) 4 *Journal of Mental Health Law* 186.

3. "Psychopathic disorder" has no medical usage, where the concept now adopted is that of personality disorder. The critical question in relation to this question is its treatability (see below). For further consideration of the definitions, see R.M. Jones, *Mental Health Act Manual* (9th edn), London: Sweet & Maxwell, 2004, at paras 1–021—1–026.

4. Whether the diagnosis is to be the generic "mental disorder" or one of the four specific forms of mental disorder, some things are stated not to fall within these terms, since s.1(3) provides:

> "Nothing in subsection (2) above shall be construed as implying that a person may be dealt with under this Act as suffering from mental disorder, or from any form of mental disorder described in this section, by reason only of promiscuity or other immoral conduct, sexual deviancy or dependence on alcohol or drugs."

What amounts to sexual deviancy was briefly considered in *R. v MHRT, Ex p. Clatworthy* [1985] 3 All E.R. 699:

> "It may be at once observed that the effect of subsection (3) is apparently to prevent there being a condition of psychopathic disorder when the abnormally aggressive or seriously irresponsible conduct consequent on the persistent disorder or disability of mind is conduct which is a manifestation of sexual deviancy. It may also be observed that it can be contended that sexual deviancy does not mean tendency to deviation but means indulgence in deviation. That contention would achieve support from its context, the context being promiscuity or other immoral conduct and dependence on alcohol or drugs."

One possible view of this decision is that it is only where a person acts on their thoughts that there is sexual deviancy and so no mental disorder. If there are only thoughts or tendencies then there is no sexual deviancy and the Act can be used, see Bartlett and Sandland, pp.53–55.

QUESTIONS:

1. How helpful is the approach in *W v L* as a guide to anyone about the critical concept of mental illness? Do you agree with Hoggett that this approach "simply adds fuel to the fire of those who accuse the mental hygiene laws of being a sophisticated machine for the suppression of unusual, eccentric or inconvenient behaviour . . . "?

2. Would it have been more helpful to have adopted the proposed definition of mental illness in the DHSS Consultative Document on the 1959 Act? That document states:

> "Mental illness means an illness having one or more of the following characteristics:
> (i) More than temporary impairment of intellectual functions shown by a failure of memory, orientation, comprehension and learning capacity;
> (ii) More than temporary alteration of mood of such degree as to give rise to the patient having a delusional appraisal of his situation, his past or his future, or that of others or to the lack of any appraisal;

(iii) Delusional beliefs, persecutory, jealous or grandiose;
(iv) Abnormal perceptions associated with delusional misinterpretation of events;
(v) Thinking so disordered as to prevent the patient making a reasonable appraisal of his situation or having reasonable communication with others."

During the course of the reform process, there was much discussion about how mental disorder should be defined. In the 2004 Bill, the Government preferred a very broad definition, placing more emphasis upon the other criteria for admission. It intends to adopt this approach through amendment to the 1983 Act as indicated in the following briefing note issued by the Department of Health on May 2, 2006.

The Mental Health Bill (Plans to amend the Mental Health Act 1983)

THE DEFINITION OF MENTAL DISORDER

The Government intends to change the way the Act defines mental disorder, so that the same, simplified definition applies throughout the Act. This will make the Act easier to use and help to ensure that nobody who needs to be subject to the Act is arbitrarily excluded. These amendments will complement the changes the Government intends to make to the criteria for detention.

What changes are the Government proposing to make?

Introducing a new simplified definition of mental disorder to make the Act easier to use. The Government intends to simplify the definition of mental disorder, so that it more straightforwardly covers all disorders and disabilities of the mind.

Abolishing the separate categories of mental disorder to further simplify the Act and to help ensure that nobody who needs compulsion is arbitrarily excluded on the basis of a legal classification. The use of four separate categories of mental disorder risks arbitrary and unnecessary distinctions, does not relate to the categories used by clinicians and encourages some patients and their lawyers to argue about legal classifications in the hope of securing inappropriate discharge. Decisions ought to be based on the needs of patients and the degree of risk posed by their disorder, not on their diagnostic label.

The removal of the categories will mean that certain sections of the Act will in future cover certain mental disorders not currently covered by any of the categories. That will include, for example, mental disorders arising out of injury or damage to the brain in adulthood. This may mean that some people who cannot now be brought under compulsion could be in the future—which is a good thing if, as a result, they get the treatment they need. The Government does not expect this to affect many people.

Preserving the effect of the Act as it applies to learning disability. The effect of abolishing the four categories will be that all the powers in the Act will in future apply to all types of mental disorder. However, for those parts of the Act currently limited to particular categories of disorder, there will be a new special provision about learning disability. It will mean that learning disability will only be treated as a mental disorder for those purposes if it is associated with abnormally aggressive or seriously irresponsible conduct on the part of the patient concerned.

This special provision will preserve the way the Act operates now in relation to learning disability. It will only apply to learning disability and not, for example, to autistic spectrum disorders (ASD), because the intention is to preserve the effect of the Act, not to change it. At present, ASD per se, is not covered by the definition of mental or severe mental impairment. The Government believes that the minority of people with ASD who might need compulsory treatment will be better served by not being subject to any limitation in the Act.

As now, no one will be subject to compulsion under the Act simply because they have a learning disability. The use of compulsion is based on needs and risk, not diagnosis.

Even though it is obviously a very different kind of disorder to mental illness, the Government does not believe it would be right to exclude learning disability from the Act entirely. Doing so would risk the minority of people with learning disabilities who need compulsory treatment not getting it, or leave clinicians feeling they have to apply an in inappropriate diagnostic label to enable them to give someone the treatment they need.

The changes will ensure that the Act can, as now, still be used for the very small minority of people with learning disabilities who may need and benefit from compulsion, whether or not they are also suffering form a mental illness or another mental disorder. In particular it will ensure they can still be diverted from prison to hospital should they be convicted of an offence.

Removing the exclusion for promiscuity and other immoral conduct because it is obsolete. Promiscuity and immoral conduct are not mental disorders so it is unnecessary to exclude them from the definition. For the same reason, there are no plans to introduce new exclusions for things like cultural, political and religious beliefs or anti-social behaviour. Such beliefs and behaviours are not mental disorders—although sometimes anti-social behaviour can be a symptom of an underlying mental disorder.

Removing the exclusion for sexual deviancy because it has sometimes resulted in patients who need compulsory treatment for mental disorder being excluded because their disorder manifests itself in sexual deviancy or offending. The absence of this exclusion will not mean that the Act can be used on the basis of a person's sexual orientation as there is now no question that homo- or bi-sexual orientation is a mental disorder any more than heterosexual orientation.

Retaining the exclusion for dependence on alcohol and drugs—probably in a reworded form to make clear that the Act is not (and never has been) to be used to force people who are suffering from no other mental disorder to accept treatment for substance dependence. The exclusion may, however, be re-worded to make it even clearer that people who are dependent on alcohol and drugs are not excluded from the scope of the Act if they also suffer from another mental disorder (even if that other disorder is related to their alcohol or drug use).

The exclusion will not extend to substance misuse because misuse by itself is not a mental disorder and so does not need to be excluded.

QUESTION:

1. Would you simplify the definition of mental disorder? Does that contain risks of over-inclusivity and greater use of compulsory admission? How is that risk to be avoided?

(c) Other Criteria for Admission

While there are crucial differences between ss.2 and 3, the other criteria are considered together, with priority being given to a consideration of s.3. In *R. v Wilson, Ex p. Williamson, The Independent*, April 19, 1995, the judge confirmed that admission:

" . . . under section 2 is to be of short duration and for a limited purpose, assessment of the patient's condition with a view to ascertaining whether it is a case which would respond to treatment, and whether an order under section 3 would be appropriate . . . Although there is nothing to suggest that section 2 is a once and for all procedure, there is nothing in the Act which justifies successive or back to back applications under this section of the kind which occurred here. The powers under section 2 can only be used for the limited purpose for which they were intended, and cannot be utilised for the purpose of further detaining a patient for the purposes of assessment beyond the 28 day period, or used as a stop-gap procedure."

As to the interrelationship between and guidance on the preference to use s.2 or s.3, see the *Code of Practice*, Chapter 5 and Jones, *Mental Health Act Manual*, *op. cit.* in note 3 at para.1–033.

(i) The Need for Treatment in Hospital

Does the Act require that treatment must be provided in hospital in order for a section to be imposed? There is no explicit community treatment order (see below). In considering this matter, consider the problem presented by the person for whom treatment, usually medication, is successful, but who is not compliant. So when he is not in hospital and required to take that medication, he stops and so gets unwell until such point as hospitalisation becomes necessary and then, when stabilised, he is discharged and leaves hospital, only for the cycle to commence again. One solution is to recognise that sections can be used earlier than has often been thought to be the case so that the patient whose condition is known to be deteriorating does not have to be left in relapse because his medical history will reveal that the requirements of the Act are satisfied in that case (see Jones, *op. cit.* in note 3 at para.1–045). In a different attempt to solve the problem, "long leash treatment" was once used. A patient would be admitted to hospital under section 3 with the intention of granting leave of absence on the following day. There was never any intention that the person should spend any time in hospital for treatment, other than the initial overnight period. When on leave of absence, a treatment regime could continue under Part IV of the Act, since that Part applies to patients on leave of absence (granted under s.17). The section would be renewed, under s.20, as and when necessary, and the patient would be recalled to hospital every six months (now the maximum period for leave of absence is one year) so that the leave of absence could be renewed. It was argued that this satisfied the Act because the patient's condition and treatment needs demanded that he or she be on a section. However, the challenge to the use of this treatment was based upon the argument that the patient did not need treatment *in hospital* and so no section could be imposed nor renewed. These arguments were considered by the High Court.

R. v Hallstrom, Ex p. W; R. v Gardner, Ex p. L [1986] Q.B. 1090, [1985] 3 W.L.R. 1090, (1985) 129 S.J. 892

In this case W had been admitted to hospital under s.3 and granted leave of absence the following day, and L was a patient already in hospital who had been given leave of absence, and his s.3 was renewed under s.20 on being recalled to hospital over night.

McCULLOUGH J.

" . . . Section 3 is concerned with admission to hospital and detention there. A person 'admitted' to hospital becomes an in-patient. This is the sense in which the word is ordinarily used . . . Detention follows admission. As, on admission, the patient becomes an in-patient, it must follow that his detention is *as an in-patient*, at any rate initially . . . The ordinary meaning of the words used in the Act of 1983 as a whole is to this effect. Section 3 and section 20 are about detention *in* a hospital. Section 3(2)(a) refers to treatment *in* a hospital. Section 17 deals with leave of absence *from* a hospital and recall (or return) *to* a hospital.

The admission is 'for treatment'. Mr. Thorold submits that the treatment contemplated is treatment as an in-patient. But for the existence of section 17 this would certainly be so, since the treatment could only be given while the patient was detained, i.e. detained as an in-patient.

The argument [from counsel for the doctors] was that the mental disorder would have to require treatment in a hospital but not necessarily as an in-patient and that what was important was the use of the compulsory nature of the section rather than the hospital-isation.

Alternatively . . . if the meaning of section 3 is ambiguous, the construction for which [counsel] contends should be adopted because it enables doctors in such a situation to do what is, in accordance with good modern psychiatric practice, in the best interests of patients like W. i.e. treat them in the community, but compel them to accept the medication which their condition requires, but which, because of their illness, they do not think they need and therefore refuse.

There is, however, no canon of construction which presumes that Parliament intended that people should, against their will, be subjected to treatment which others, however professionally competent, perceive, however sincerely and however correctly, to be in their best interests. What there is is a canon of construction that Parliament is presumed not to enact legislation which interferes with the liberty of the subject without making it clear that this was its intention.

It goes without saying that, unless clear statutory authority to the contrary exists, no one is to be detained in hospital or to undergo medical treatment or even to submit himself to a medical examination without his consent. This is as true of a mentally disordered person as anyone else."

The judge recognised that there are various checks and controls within the legislation, such as: the various ways in which an authority to detain a patient may be discharged; the need for two doctors to give a reasoned opinion that the conditions of s.3 are met; the nearest relative's right to prevent a social worker from making an application for admission under s.3; the fact that a social worker who does so apply must first consult the nearest relative; and the fact that if the application is made by the nearest relative, a social worker must, as soon as practicable, interview the patient and report to the hospital managers on his social circumstances. But he concluded:

"In my judgment, these provisions do not help to construe the sections with which this case is concerned. Each of these checks and controls is as compatible with [each argument].

In my judgment, the key to the construction of section 3 lies in the phrase 'admission for treatment.' It stretches the concept of 'admission for treatment' too far to say that it covers admission for only so long as it is necessary to enable leave of absence to be granted, after which the necessary treatment will begin. 'Admission for treatment' under section 3 is intended for those whose condition is believed to require a period of treatment as an in-patient. It may be that such patients will also be thought to require a period of out-patient treatment thereafter, but the concept of 'admission for treatment' has no applicability to those whom it is intended to admit and detain for a purely nominal period, during which no necessary treatment will be given.

The phrase 'his mental disorder . . . makes it appropriate for him to receive medical treatment in a hospital' in section 3(2)(a) also leads to the conclusion that the section is concerned with those whose mental condition requires in-patient treatment. Treatment in a hospital does not mean treatment *at* a hospital . . . When it is remembered that the section authorises compulsory detention in a hospital it is at once clear why a distinction should be made between those whom it is appropriate to treat *in* a hospital, i.e. as in-patients, and those whom it is appropriate to treat otherwise, whether at the out-patient department of the hospital or at home or elsewhere.

It is true that the word 'appropriate' rather than 'necessary' is used in section 3(2)(a). This merely recognises the possibility that some forms of treatment required by a patient's mental disorder, although more appropriately given as an in-patient, might, as a matter of possibility be given elsewhere . . .

During the argument attention was focused on the word 'detained' in the phrase 'such treatment . . . cannot be provided unless he is detained under this section' in section 3(2)(c) . . . [This phrase should be read as meaning] 'such treatment cannot be given unless he is then under detention' [and so] it is impossible without violation to the meaning of words to embrace those then liable to be detained but not then detained. [This interpretation] is consistent with the meaning of 'admission for treatment' and of 'treatment in a hospital' and with the intention of the section as a whole."

After referring to assistance in his approach from ss.13 and 2 and by comparison with the corresponding provision in the Mental Health Act 1959, s.26 and drawing upon the differences which must have been deliberate, the judge continued:

"Even a night's detention is an infringement of personal liberty. Had Parliament intended to grant the power to overbear the refusal to consent of patients such as W, who could be maintained in the community provided they were given appropriate treatment, it would have so provided by a clear provision which involved no unnecessary detention. The differences between the Acts of 1959 and 1983 in relation to consent to treatment, to which I have already referred, underline the unlikelihood that Parliament intended in the later Act to provide for cases like W's in the indirect way contended for by counsel for the doctors.

For those various reasons, I conclude that section 3 only covers those whose mental condition is believed to require a period of in-patient treatment . . . "

By similar process of argument, the judge arrived at the analogous position with regard to s.20, and stated:

"The similarity of language between it and section 20 suggests that it too is concerned with those who are believed to require in-patient treatment. This tends to confirm that Parliament did not intend that the provisions for renewal would embrace those liable to be detained but not in fact detained . . . "

NOTE:

1. Since the treatment must be intended to take place in a hospital, it is possible that it means that the treatment to be offered must, in some way,

be efficacious, and that this is a requirement separate from the treatability requirement.

This decision has proved not to be the end of the matter.

R. (on the application of DR) v Merseycare NHS Trust [2002] All E.R. (D) 28

The detention of a person with schizophrenia under s.3 had been renewed under s.20. The treatment plan for the patient involved her attending occupational therapy at the hospital once a week and a review at the hospital once a week, but otherwise she was living in the community on leave of absence, except that a community psychiatric nurse called at her home once a fortnight to administer her drugs. The patient challenged the renewal of her detention by the hospital managers under s.20(4). The decision went against the patient.

WILSON J.
"It was held by the Court of Appeal in *B v Barking Havering and Brentwood Community Healthcare NHS Trust* [1999] 1 FLR 106, overruling on this point the decision of McCullough J. in *R v Hallstrom ex p. W, R v Gardner ex p. L* [1986] 1 QB 1090, that the words at the end of [s.20(4)(c)], namely 'unless he continues to be detained', mean 'unless he continues to be liable to be detained' and not 'unless he continues actually to be detained'; and that accordingly the conditions for renewal can be satisfied even in relation to a patient who is no longer actually detained but has been granted leave of absence under s. 17 of the Act . . . .
    In my view this case is centrally an enquiry into the words 'medical treatment in a hospital' set out in [s. 20(4)(a)] and repeated, by reference, in [s. 20(4)(b) and (c)]. The claimant clearly suffers from mental illness so the enquiry at (a) was whether it was of a nature or degree which made it appropriate for her to receive 'medical treatment in a hospital'. The enquiry at (b) . . . was whether 'such' treatment could not be provided unless she continued to be liable to be detained and unless it was necessary for the health or safety of herself or (for example) her daughter. To crystallise the point further: was it open to the doctor and the managers to conclude that his treatment plan for the claimant was for 'medical treatment in a hospital'? . . . There was no need for McCullough J., in the two plain cases of *Hallstrom* and *Gardner,* where there was no plan for any treatment in hospital, whether in-patient or out-patient, to hold that the hest embraced only in-patient treatment. His remarks, though entitled to very great respect, are obiter; and his distinction between treatment at hospital and treatment in hospital is too subtle for me. When I eat at a restaurant, I eat in a restaurant. In the *Barking* case, where the limited proposed treatment in hospital happened to be of an in-patient character, it was natural that that word might again be deployed. But that does not make it become the test, any more than the reference of Thorpe L.J. to a 'home base' renders that concept the test. The significance of the *Barking* case is that the renewal was lawful notwithstanding that only part of the plan was for treatment in hospital. It sufficed if that part of the plan was, to borrow another phrase from the judgment of Thorpe L.J., an essential ingredient. In my view it would be an impermissible—indeed an illogical—gloss upon the Act to make lawfulness depend upon a plan to put the patient at times into a hospital bed. There is no magic in a bed; indeed the facility for treatment at night, when the patient is in bed, must be much less than for treatment during the day.
    The question therefore in my judgment is whether a significant component of the plan for the claimant was for treatment in hospital. It is worth noting that, by s. 145(1) of the Act, the words 'medical treatment' include rehabilitation under medical supervision. There is no doubt, therefore, that the proposed leave of absence for the claimant is properly regarded as part of her treatment plan. As para. 20.1 of the Code of Practice states, 'leave of absence can be an important part of a patient's treatment plan'. Its purpose was to

preserve the claimant's links with the community, to reduce the stress caused by hospital surroundings which she found particularly uncongenial; and to build a platform of trust between her and the clinicians upon which dialogue might be constructed and insight on her part into her illness engendered. Equally, however, the requirement to attend hospital on Fridays between 9.00 am and 5.00 pm and on Monday mornings was also in my judgment a significant component of the plan. The role of occupational therapy as part of the treatment of mental illness needs no explanation. But the attendance at hospital on Monday mornings seems to me to be likely to have been even more important. Such was to be the occasion for the attempted dialogue; for monitoring; for assessment and for review. In the *Barking* case both Lord Woolf and Thorpe L.J. stressed the importance of the arrangements for weekly monitoring and assessment in the hospital.

I therefore hold that a significant component of the plan for the claimant was treatment in hospital and that the conditions for renewal set by s. 20(4) were satisfied."

NOTE:

1. Two other cases are important to take into account, since they underpin the view in *DR* that, provided there is treatment being provided in or at a hospital, the requirements in ss.3 and 20 are met: see *R v BHB Community Healthcare NHS Trust, Ex p. B* [1999] 1 F.L.R. 106 and *R (on the application of CS) v MHRT* [2004] EWHC 2958.

QUESTIONS:

1. Is the distinction between "treatment at hospital" and "treatment in hospital" as opaquely subtle as Wilson J. suggests?
2. Is there a credible distinction between "hospital" and "community"? Bear in mind the size of hospitals nowadays (and indeed the fact that a hospital can be a very small unit).
3. Has the Act's interpretation been stretched so far that it now provides, in effect, a community treatment order (and see further below)?

(ii) The Treatability Requirement

The requirement in s.3(2)(b) (see also s.20) is often referred to as the "treatability test", although strictly speaking it is not necessary that the patient is likely to be cured. It is a particular problem in relation to patients with psychopathic disorder, but the cases could equally apply to other patients.

R. v Cannons Park MHRT, Ex p. A [1994] 2 All E.R. 659

ROCH L.J.
" . . . I would suggest the following principles. First, if a tribunal were to be satisfied that the patient's detention in hospital was simply an attempt to coerce the patient into participating in group therapy, then the tribunal would be under a duty to direct discharge. Second, treatment in hospital will satisfy the treatability test although it is unlikely to alleviate the patient's condition, provided that it is likely to prevent a deterioration. Third, treatment in hospital will satisfy the treatability test although it will not immediately alleviate or prevent deterioration in the patient's condition, providing that alleviation or

stabilisation is likely in due course. Fourth, the treatability test can still be met although initially there may be some deterioration in the patient's condition, due for example to the patient's initial anger at being detained. Fifth, it must be remembered that medical treatment in hospital covers nursing and also includes care, habilitation and rehabilitation under medical supervision. Sixth, the treatability test is satisfied if nursing care etc. are likely to lead to an alleviation of the patient's condition in that the patient is likely to gain an insight into his problem or cease to be unco-operative in his attitude towards treatment which would potentially have a lasting benefit.

Subsequent developments are summarised by Jones, at paras 1–050 and 1–051:

"In the Scottish case of *R* v *Secretary of State for Scotland* 1998 S.C. 49 2 Div, the court identified a seventh principle namely 'that the patient's condition includes the symptoms or manifestations of it and behaviour caused by it, so that, if there was treatment likely to alleviate or prevent the deterioration of such symptoms, manifestations or behaviour, that would suffice to demonstrate treatability.' This case was appealed to the House of Lords (*Reid v Secretary of State for Scotland* [1999] 1 All E.R. 481) where it was held that the term 'medical treatment' was 'wide enough to include treatment which alleviates or prevents a deterioration of the symptoms of the disorder, not the disorder itself which gives rise to them' (*per* Lord Hope at 497) and that the treatability test could be satisfied in circumstances where 'the anger management of the [patient] in the structured setting of the State Hospital in a supervised environment resulted in his being less physically aggressive' (*per* Lord Hutton at 515). Lord Hope also said that the definition of 'medical treatment' included 'all manner of treatment the purpose of which may extend from cure to containment' (at 495) and concluded that the benefits to the patient behaviour of being in a 'structured setting' and a 'supervised environment' fell within the definition (at 531). *Canons Park* and *Reid* were considered by Elias J in *R. (on the application of Wheldon) v Rampton Hospital Authority* [2001] EWHC Admin 134. His Lordship said at para. 14 that it 'is plain from both these authorities that the concept [of treatability] is a very wide one, and that the responsible medical officer making the assessment can look to the future and consider whether the treatment is likely, in the future, to achieve beneficial results.' If the doctor has reason to believe that further and different treatment from that given to the patient in the past might alleviate the patient's condition or prevent a deterioration of it, the test will be satisfied. This is the case even though the benefits to the patient may be 'very limited' (paras 33, 34). It is not sufficient for the doctor to hope that the treatment might have a beneficial effect; he must believe this to be the case (para. 35)." (R.M. Jones, *Mental Health Act Manual* (9th edn), London: Sweet & Maxwell, 2004.)

For further consideration of issues in relation to psychopathy (or personality disorder), see Jones at paras 1–024 and 1–025; P. Bartlett and R. Sandland, *Mental Health Law: Policy and Practice* (2nd edn), Oxford: OUP, 2003, at pp.48–51, and B.M. Hoggett, *Mental Health Law* (4th edn), London: Sweet & Maxwell 1998 at pp.37–47).

QUESTION:

1. If the environment in a given hospital is merely incarcerative or in another hospital merely a form of asylum and no therapeutic work is done by any staff would the treatability requirement be satisfied?

(iii) The Least Restrictive Alternative

The latter part of s.3(2)(c) is a statutory expression of the least restrictive alternative. This is an internationally recognised principle demanding that detention should be used only when absolutely necessary and then imposing as little restriction on the freedom of the individual as possible.

QUESTION:

1. Does the Mental Health Act force approved social workers (ASWs) and doctors to consider whether sectioning is really necessary and what alternative facilities are available?

(iv) The Nature or Degree of the Mental Disorder

The first part of s.3(2)(c) does not demand that the prospective patient be dangerous. This criterion is satisfied if detention is for the prospective patient's health *or* safety *or* for the protection of others. (See the *Code of Practice*, paras 2.9 and 2.10.) Further, in *R. v Mental Health Review Tribunal for the South Thames Region, Ex p. Smith* [1999] C.O.D. 148, Popplewell J. held, in the words of Jones, *Mental Health Act Manual op. cit.* at para.1–049, that:

"(1) although the wording of this phrase is disjunctive, in very many cases the nature and degree of the patient's mental disorder will be inevitably bound up so that it matters not whether the issue is dealt with under nature or degree;

(2) the word 'nature' refers to the particular mental disorder from which the patient suffers, its chronicity, its prognosis, and the patient's previous response to receiving treatment for the disorder; and

(3) the word 'degree' refers to the current manifestation of the patient's disorder."

QUESTIONS:

1. What will satisfy the requirement that the patient's "health or safety" be affected? Is it necessary that the person's mental health be at risk? When is a person's safety sufficiently at risk to merit hospital detention?
2. Is it right that it is possible for a person to be admitted compulsorily to hospital when he or she is not a danger to another, indeed presents no risk to others at all?

(v) Reform

The Government has indicated, in a briefing note issued by the Department of Health on May 2, 2006, the changes that it intends to make to the criteria for admission.

The Mental Health Bill (Plans to amend the Mental Health Act 1983)

THE CRITERIA FOR DETENTION

The criteria in the Act must ensure that detention can be used only when properly justified. Where it is justified, there should be no arbitrary restrictions, so that the small minority of people with mental disorders who need compulsory treatment can get it.

The Government intends to make changes to the criteria to ensure that these objectives are met without changing the basic structure of criteria in the current Act.

These changes will benefit both patients and the wider public and will complement the simplifications the Government intends to make to the definition of mental disorder.

What improvements are the Government proposing to make?

Introducing a new, appropriate treatment test which will apply to all the longer-term powers of detention. This will ensure that detention under these powers cannot be used or continued unless medical treatment which is appropriate to the patient's mental disorder and all other circumstances of their case is available.

Decision makers will have to consider not only the clinical factors, but also, for example, whether treatment will be culturally appropriate, how far from the patient's home the proposed service is and what effect it will have on the patient's contact with family and friends.

The appropriate treatment must actually be available to the patient. It will not be enough for the treatment to exist "in theory", if it cannot actually be offered or accessed.

The appropriate treatment test will strengthen the criteria for detention by ensuring that:

- for the first time practitioners will be required by law to make a holistic assessment of whether appropriate treatment is available before detaining someone;
- clinicians have to decide what is clinically appropriate in the same way as for any other patient.

The other criteria already require that there must be a clinical purpose to detention. The appropriate treatment test will further strengthen this requirement. The Government remains firmly committed to mental health legislation only being used to detain people to enable them to get the specialist mental healthcare they need.

Retaining the current definition of medical treatment, with one small modification to ensure consistency with the way the Government proposed to modernise the Act in respect of certain key professional functions.

The definition of medical treatment in section 145(1) of the Act says that it: "includes nursing, and also includes care, habilitation and rehabilitation under medical supervision".

The Government proposes to open up the role of the responsible medical officer to suitably qualified and experienced practitioners from other professional disciplines. The definition of medical treatment will be amended to ensure that care, habilitation and rehabilitation supervised by such practitioners is covered.

Medical treatment has always had a deliberately wide meaning in the Act to recognise the diversity of services that people need. It need not be treatment which can be forced on patients against their will. Many treatments, particularly psychological therapies, require the patient's active participation, but the use of the Act may be instrumental in encouraging and sustaining such participation. Those treatments will therefore remain within the definition of medical treatment. To exclude them would be inconsistent with the reality of mental health care and might inadvertently encourage the use of medication even where there are more appropriate alternatives available.

Applying the new criterion to all groups of patients equally, to avoid arbitrary distinctions. The Government believes that the use of detention should be determined by the needs of patients and the risk posed by their disorder, not by their particular diagnostic label.

Because of the changes the Government intends to make to the way the Act defines mental disorder, the longer term powers of detention will in future apply to all forms of mental disorder, not just specific categories like mental illness, mental impairment and psychopathic disorder. The appropriate treatment test will therefore apply to all patients equally, regardless of the type of their disorder.

There will be a special provision to preserve the current effect of the Act in relation to learning disability.

Abolishing the so-called 'treatability test', which the Government believes does not serve the interests of patients of the wider public. The test is often misunderstood and has contributed to a culture where some patients in great need are labelled 'untreatable' and therefore denied the services that they need.

Because it singles out particular groups of patients, the test has lead to a false presumption that some — particularly those with severe personality disorders — are untreatable. This means that detention is sometimes not used when it ought to be, even though people with severe personality disorders can be — and are — treated compulsorily under the Act.

More generally, the test has not helped the development of much needed services for such people. As a result some people do not get the treatment they need, whether or not compulsion is being considered, which puts them and sometimes the other people at risk. It can also mean they end up in prison or with another criminal justice disposal even though they need treatment.

The test is too narrowly focused only on the likely outcome of treatment. That combined with the tendency to misunderstand what it really means, leads to the Mental Health Review Tribunal sometimes being asked to discharge dangerous patients categorised as having psychopathic disorder on the basis that they are not benefiting from the treatment they are receiving, even when treatment is both available and necessary.

Occasionally, this has resulted in such patients having to be discharged even though they still need treatment, which is not good for them or for the wider public.

Also, the treatability test primarily applies only to the minority of patients classified as having psychopathic disorder or mental impairment. At the point of initial decisions about detention, it does not apply to the large majority of patients who are classified as suffering from mental illness. (As noted above, these categories will be abolished).

The Government believes that the appropriate treatment test will be better because it calls for an holistic assessment of whether appropriate treatment is available, not focused only on the likely outcome of treatment

The Government's aim is to ensure that people get the services they need. Removing treatability and the categories of disorder will take away some unnecessary obstacles to practitioners' ability to used the Act where it is warranted by the needs of the patient and the degree of risk. The Government does not think that this will lead to any significant increase in people detained. It could have the opposite effect if it helps encourage better and earlier interventions for people with personality disorder.

Making equivalent changes to the criteria for renewal of detention and discharge by the Mental Health Review Tribunal (MHRT) in sections 20 and 72 respectively, so that they too incorporate the appropriate treatment test where relevant. This will ensure that detention can only continue so long as appropriate medical treatment remains available for the patient.

There will also be a further consequential change. Section 20 requires that patients suffering from mental illness or severe mental impairment must either meet the treatability test or else "the patient, if discharged, is unlikely to be able to care for himself, to obtain the care which he needs or to guard himself against serious exploitation". This same test is one of the factors that the MHRT considers when asked to review detention under section 3. With the introduction of the appropriate treatment test, this "grave incapacity" test is no longer needed in either provision . . . .

Otherwise retaining the basic structure of the criteria in the Act to avoid unnecessary changes and to allow practitioners to continue to work within a largely familiar legislative structure. This means that:

- practitioners will continue to have discretion about whether to apply for detention (and guardianship) for civil patients and whether to renew detention (and guardianship) even where the criteria are met;
- MHRTs will continue to have the same discretion they have now to discharge patients even where the criteria for mandatory discharge are not met;
- the criteria for detention for assessment under section 2 (for up to 28 days) will not change. Because section 2 is about assessment which may or may not be accompanied by treatment, it would not make sense to apply the appropriate treatment test to this section or to patients remanded to hospital for report under section 35;
- guardianship under s7 and guardianship orders under s37 will be retained, and neither the initial criteria under those sections, nor the criteria for renewal or discharge by the MHRT will change—except that they will now apply to all types of mental disorder;
- nearest relatives will continue to have the same rights as now to discharge civil patients. This can only be blocked in the case of detention if a clinician certifies that the patient is likely to act in a manner dangerous to themselves or others;
- the test of whether treatment is necessary for the health and safety of the patient or for the protection of others will not change.

The needs of the patient and the degree of risk must determine whether detention should be used, not the capacity or decision-making ability of the patient. The Government is not proposing to include in the criteria a test of whether a patient's judgement is impaired. Some people whose mental disorder puts them at very great risk to themselves or others are able to make unimpaired decisions about treatment. An impaired decision-making criterion would result in some patients going untreated or some clinicians feeling compelled to assess people as having impaired decision-making to enable them to be treated.

QUESTIONS:

1. Is it right to introduce the appropriate treatment test? Is it required by the ECHR?
2. What do you think will be the impact of moving from the "treatability" test to the "appropriate treatment" test? Will it expand or contract the potential range of people who can be compulsorily admitted to hospital?

(d) Procedural Issues

Under the Mental Health Act 1983, since the power of compulsory admission is exercised without recourse to a court receiving evidence, the procedural issues are intended to establish sufficient safeguards to ensure that the power is used when, and only when, the statutory criteria are satisfied and that the discretion whether to apply for the admission of a patient is exercised appropriately. This is achieved by identifying the people involved and setting procedural as well as substantive criteria.

(i) Applications for Admission to Hospital

An application for someone's admission to hospital is not made by a doctor, but is made by either an approved social worker (ASW) or the prospective patient's nearest relative (s.11). An ASW is an experienced social worker appointed to undertake this formal statutory work. While employed by the social services department, an ASW is expected to exercise independent judgment to provide a non-medical view and to be aware of alternative facilities to compulsory admission to hospital. The details of the role of an ASW in admissions are to be found in ss.11 and 13 and in the *Code of Practice* at paras 2.11–2.17.

Anyone could be a nearest relative. The Act provides, in s.26, a means of identifying both whether a person is a relative and whether they are the nearest relative. This is by no means always an easy task. Where an ASW applies for admission for assessment, he or she must inform the nearest relative (s.11(2)), and where an ASW applies for admission for treatment, he or she must consult the nearest relative who has the right of objection (s.11(3)). Laws J., in *R. v South West Hospital Managers, Ex p. M* [1993] Q.B. 683, made clear that the consultation must take place with the person the ASW genuinely believes, on the facts known, to be the nearest relative, but that such consultation may take place through another person when direct consultation is difficult. What is important is that the consultation be "full and effective". The nearest relative may be replaced as such by the county court on the application under s.29 of, among others, an ASW where the power of objection has been exercised unreasonably, as was the issue in *W v L*, considered above. Where the nearest relative applies for admission of a person to hospital, the ASW will be asked to make a social circumstances report under s.14 when and if the patient is admitted hospital. The *Code of Practice*, at paragraph 2.35, recommends that ordinarily the ASW ought to be the applicant.

Whoever applies, they must have personally seen the patient within the previous 14 days (s.11(5)). This is an obligation which cannot be fulfilled through an intermediary according to Laws J. in *R. v South West Hospital Managers, Ex p. M* [1993] Q.B. 683.

Paragraph 2.6 of the *Code of Practice* offers guidance on the exercise of the discretion whether to use compulsory power. It suggests that factors to be taken into account include:

"the guiding principles in Chapter 1; the patient's wishes and views of his own needs; the patient's social and family circumstances; the nature of the illness/ behaviour disorder and its course; what may be known about the patient by [others], assessing in particular how reliable this information is; other forms of care or treatment [available]; the needs of the patient's family or others with whom he or she lives; the need for others to be protected from the patient; the burden on those close to the patient of a decision not to admit under the Act . . . "

The Government proposes in its briefing note on professionals roles of May 2, 2006, that the ASW function (which will remain the same) "will be opened up to a wider role of trained and qualified mental health professionals, such as nurses and occupational therapists" and will be known as the approved mental health professional. They will be expected to bring "an alternative perspective to the medical view and to act independently".

The Government proposes in its briefing note on nearest relatives of May 2, 2006 to introduce significant changes which will meet ECHR requirements but without changing the powers of the nearest relative:

- patients will be able to apply to the county court to displace their nearest relative;
- new bases for replacing the nearest relative will be introduced;
- the county court will be able to make its order for an indefinite period;
- civil partners will be included in the list of relatives.

(ii) Doctors' Recommendations

Two doctors must make medical recommendations supporting the application. The Act seeks to secure their independence from one another in s.12. The *Code of Practice* at para.2.23 makes clear that the doctors are expected to undertake a "direct personal examination of the patient's mental state" and they must consider all the relevant medical information and take into account the guiding principles. On the basis of an examination the doctor must diagnose the patient with reference to the statutory concepts, decide whether the statutory criteria are satisfied, assess whether the person should be compulsorily admitted, and discover whether a hospital bed would be available (see the *Code of Practice*, para. 2.22).

(iii) Arrival at Hospital

Once the patient arrives at the hospital, a decision must be taken whether to admit him. No hospital is obliged to accept a patient. The usual scenario is that the admission will have been sorted out prior to the patient's arrival, but this is not always the case and, whether arranged before hand or not, a means of making or confirming decisions should be available at the actual time of admission.

Mental Health Act, s.6(1–3)

6.—(1) An application for the admission of a patient to a hospital under this Part of this Act, duly completed in accordance with the provisions of this Part of this Act, shall be sufficient authority for the applicant, or any person authorised by the applicant, to take the patient and convey him to the hospital at any time within the following period, that is to say

(a) in the case of an application other than an emergency application, the period of 14 days beginning with the date on which the patient was last examined by a registered medical practitioner before giving a medical recommendation for the purposes of the application;

(b) [for the case of emergency applications].

(2) Where a patient is admitted within the said period . . . the application shall be sufficient authority for the managers to detain the patient in hospital in accordance with the provisions of this Act.

(3) Any application for the admission of a patient under this Part of this Act which appears to be duly made and to be founded on the necessary medical recommendations may be acted upon without further proof of the signature or qualification of the person by whom the application or any such medical recommendation is made or given or of any matter of fact or opinion stated in it.

NOTES:

1. Section 6(3) does not require a detailed examination of the issues behind the forms at the time of admission. Further, some errors in the forms may be amended within 14 days of the admission under s.15. Errors which may not be rectified include "a defect which arises because a necessary event in the procedural chain . . . has simply not take place at all" according to Laws J. in *R. v South West Hospital Managers, Ex p. M.* [1993] Q.B. 683, nor can this section enable "a fundamentally defective application to be retrospectively validated" according to Sir Thomas Bingham M.R. in *Re SC* [1996] 2 All E.R. 532. So, for example, where personal interviews by ASWs and medical examinations do not take place, s.15 is of no avail to the hospital detaining the patient. See K. Keywood "Rectification of Incorrect Documentation under the Mental Health Act 1983" (1996) 7 *Journal of Forensic Psychiatry* 79.

2. Whether the hospital must institute any checks of the documentation was considered by Laws J. in *R. v South Western Hospital Managers, Ex p. M* [1994] 1 All E.R. 161. His Lordship said:

> "Section 6(1) and (2) confer authority to convey or detain the patient in hospital where the application is 'duly completed in accordance with the provisions of this Part of this Act'. In my judgment that is an objective requirement and means that the application must not only state that the relevant provisions (which include the requirements of s. 11(4)) have been fulfilled, but also that it be the case that they have actually been fulfilled . . .
>
> In my judgment, where an application on its face sets out all the facts which, if true, constitute compliance with the relevant provisions of Part II of the Act (again, including section 11(4)) it is an application which 'appears to be duly made' within section 6(3). If any of the facts thus stated are not true, then although the application appears to be duly made, it is not duly completed for the purposes of section 6(1) and 6(2). Here, Miss Stiller's application did state all the facts which, if true, constituted compliance with the relevant statutory provisions. Accordingly it was an application which appeared to be duly made. It follows that, although the managers were not authorised to detain the patient by section 6(2) standing alone, they were entitled to act upon the application, and thus to detain the patient, by virtue of section 6(3).
>
> Accordingly, the applicants detention is not unlawful."

That passage was considered by the Court of Appeal in *Re SC* [1996] 2 All E.R. 532, where Sir Thomas Bingham M.R. said:

> "Speaking for myself, I would accept almost everything in that passage as correct with the exception of the last sentence. The judge goes straight from a finding that

the hospital managers were entitled to act upon an apparently valid application to the conclusion that the applicant's detention was therefore not unlawful. That is, in my judgment, a *non sequitur*. It is perfectly possible that the hospital managers were entitled to act on an apparently valid application, but that the detention was in fact unlawful. If that were not so the implications would, in my judgment, be horrifying. It would mean that an application which appeared to be in order would render the detention of a citizen lawful even though it was shown or admitted that the approved social worker purporting to make the application was not an approved social worker, that the registered medical practitioners whose recommendations founded the application were not registered medical practitioners or had not signed the recommendations, and that the approved social worker had not consulted the patient's nearest relative or had consulted the patient's nearest relative and that relative had objected. In other words, it would mean that the detention was lawful even though every statutory safeguard built into the procedure was shown to have been ignored or violated.

Bearing in mind what is at stake, I find that conclusion wholly unacceptable. I am, for my part, satisfied that on present facts an application for *habeas corpus* is an appropriate, and possibly even *the* appropriate, course to pursue."

QUESTIONS:

1. Why do you think that a hospital is obliged to have an admission process making clear, exactly, when the patient became a detained patient?
2. Do you agree with the analysis of Laws J. or that of Sir Thomas Bingham? What, if any, implications follow from their alternative conclusions?

(iv) The Exercise of the Doctor's Discretion

As indicated above, the ASW and doctors must exercise their discretion, which must be based upon information and assessment. But they do not always know prospective patients nor have sufficient information to contemplate compulsory admission. If the prospective patient is at home, it can be particularly difficult to obtain sufficient information. Access may be provided to the house by someone with the power to do so, but, according to the Divisional Court, there is no right of entry for doctors to undertake an examination (*Townley v Rushworth* (1963) 62 L.G.R. 95). ASWs do have a power to enter and inspect premises under s.115, and this is supported by the offence of obstruction within s.129. But is any of this relevant to the function of the ASW in deciding whether or not to make an application?

Under s.135, an ASW has the power to seek a warrant from a magistrate for the police to enter the premises (by force if necessary) and remove certain people to a place of safety (such as a hospital, residential home, police station or other place where the occupier is willing to accept the patient), provided the necessary conditions are satisfied:

that there is reasonable cause to suspect that a person believed to be suffering from mental disorder:

(a) has been, or is being, ill-treated, neglected or kept otherwise than under proper control, in any place within the jurisdiction of the justice, or
(b) being unable to care for himself, is living alone in any such place . . .

(See P. Fennell, "The Beverley Lewis case: Was the Law to Blame?" (1989) 139 *New Law Journal* 1559.)

(v) Reform

One key strand in the now abortive Mental Health Bill 2004 was the introduction of an independent review of all detentions beyond 28 days through authorisation of continuing detentions by a mental health tribunal.

Improving Mental Health Law—Towards a new Mental Health Act (2004)

1.17 Where the clinical supervisor decides that the conditions continue to be met, assessment and treatment under the Act may only continue beyond 28 days if authorised by the Mental Health Tribunal . . . .

1.18 The patient or the nominated person [the equivalent of nearest relative, but compliant with Article 8] can request a Tribunal hearing during the initial assessment to see if the patient can be either discharged from treatment under formal powers or treated on a non-resident basis. The clinical supervisor may decide to bring forward an application for a Tribunal order so that both applications are dealt with at the same time. The Tribunal must appoint a medical practitioner from a specially appointed Expert Panel to examine the patient and provide a report on the application(s). The Tribunal may appoint other Panel members, e.g. a further specialist in learning disability. Expert Panel members can visit, interview and examine the patient and inspect any relevant records when preparing their report.

1.19 The Tribunal will consider whether all of the relevant conditions are met—if they are not it must discharge the patient. If it decides that all of the conditions are met, the Tribunal can decide to:

- Confirm the patient's liability to assessment, but may change the patient's residency status. This does not extend the original assessment procedure so the clinical supervisor must still decide whether to apply to the Tribunal within the original 28 day period;
- Make an order for a further 28 day period of assessment (which means there will need to be further consideration of the case by the Tribunal within 28 days of its decision) and may change the patient's residency status; or
- Make a treatment order that can be for up to six months and may change the patient's residency status.

2.20 On each occasion it considers a patient's case, the Tribunal will also approve the patient's care plan and where necessary may approve it with amendments agreed with the clinical supervisor.

2.21 Assessment or further assessment orders cannot be longer than 28 days and between them, assessment and further assessment cannot last more than 3 months. An assessment order cannot be given once a treatment order has been given.

2.22 A treatment order can be for up to six months in the first instance. If three treatment orders have been given, or where the total period a patient has been under treatment orders is 12 months, an order of up to 12 months can then be given.

2.23 The Tribunal must always be satisfied that all the relevant conditions are met before an order is made. If they are not met, it must discharge the patient from treatment under formal powers.

NOTES:

1. The Pre-Legislative Scrutiny Committee was particularly concerned about the resource implications for a tribunal sitting to hear all cases where

detention was to proceed beyond 28 days. The Government recognises the issue and has undertaken further work on the mechanics of the new tribunal.

2. It would appear that this change will not now be introduced as there is no reference to it in the written ministerial statement of March 2006 or the briefing notes of May 2006.

QUESTIONS:

1. Does the ECHR demand that there must be such a judicial phase at the outset of detention?
2. Why do you think the Government has decided not to pursue this change? Would you have made it?

(e) Admission for Assessment in Emergency

Section 4 provides for the possibility of an admission for assessment in an emergency. The criteria for admission are the same as for admission under s.2 (s.4(2) and (3)), except that there must be a statement on the application that "it is of urgent necessity for the patient to be admitted and detained under s.2 above, and that compliance with the provisions of this Part of this Act relating to applications under that section would involve undesirable delay" (s.4(2)). Only one medical recommendation is needed (s.4(3)). If the patient is admitted, the section ceases to have effect after 72 hours unless a second medical recommendation is forthcoming to turn it into a s.2 admission (s.4(4)). In order to make an application, the patient must have been personally seen within the previous 24 hours (ss.11(5) and 4(5)).

(f) Admission of Patients Already in Hospital

Section 5 provides for the possibility of detaining a patient who is already in hospital but is not detained under a section of the Mental Health Act 1983. In considering the position of a patient informally or voluntarily resident in hospital, it is important to bear s.5 in mind, since it significantly affects the reality of the assertion that an informal or voluntary patient is free to leave.

There are two means whereby a patient in hospital informally (which is the meaning of in-patient in s.5(6)) may be prevented from leaving: one is that holding power may be used by a doctor, the other, by a nurse. In 2003–04 in NHS facilities the doctor's power was used on 8,894 occasions and the nurse's power on 1,779 occasions.

(i) The Doctor's Holding Power

The holding power of doctors is covered in s.5(1) of the Act:

5.—(1) An application for admission of a patient to a hospital may be made under this Part of this Act notwithstanding that the patient is already an in-patient at that hospital or, in the case of an application for admission for treatment that the patient is for the time being liable to be detained in the hospital in pursuance of an application for admission for assessment; and where an application is so made the patient shall be treated for the purposes of this Part of the Act as if he had been admitted to the hospital at the time when that application was received by the managers.

Where the holding power is exercised by a report furnished or sent to the hospital managers, the patient may be detained in the hospital for 72 hours from the time the report is so furnished (s.5(2)).

QUESTIONS:

1. Must the in-patient be receiving treatment for a mental disorder? Compare the wording of s.5(4) below to assist you in considering this matter. If not, which doctor may institute this holding power?
2. What are the criteria for imposing this holding power? Are they clear and specific? If not, should they be?

The doctor in charge of the patient's medical treatment will not be on duty in the hospital at all times, so s.5(3) provides for the power to "nominate one (but not more than one) other" doctor on the hospital staff to exercise the power in his absence.

(ii) The Nurse's Holding Power

The holding power of nurses is covered in s.5(4–5):

5.—(4) If, in the case of a patient who is receiving treatment for mental disorder as an in-patient in a hospital, it appears to a nurse of the prescribed class:

(a) that the patient is suffering from mental disorder to such a degree that it is necessary for his health or safety or for the protection of others for him to be immediately restrained from leaving the hospital; and
(b) that it is not practicable to secure the immediate attendance of a practitioner for the purpose of furnishing a report under subsection (2) above,

the nurse may record that fact in writing; and in that event the patient may be detained in the hospital for a period of six hours from the time when that fact is so recorded or until the earlier arrival at the place where the patient is detained of a practitioner having power to furnish a report under that sub-section.

(5) A record made under subsection (4) above shall be delivered by the nurse (or by a person authorised by the nurse in that behalf) to the managers of the hospital as soon as possible after it is made; and where a record is made under that subsection the period mentioned in subsection (2) above shall begin at the time when it is made.

NOTE:

1. "Prescribed nurse" means, in old terminology, a nurse with a Registered Mental Nurse or Registered Nurse of the Mentally Handicapped qualification and does not refer to seniority or any other such criteria.

QUESTIONS:

1. Would you expect s.5(4) to be interpreted so that the form must be furnished to the managers before a patient can be stopped from leaving?
2. Might s.5 operate on the mind of a person contemplating entering hospital as an in-patient to enter voluntarily or compulsorily?
3. Should other professionals have a holding power?

4. IN HOSPITAL

Certain consequences flow from being a patient detained in a hospital. Of these, the most important, for present purposes, are the rules relating to treatment, but there are also other implications to be considered. A patient comes under the care of a doctor who, for the purposes of the Mental Health Act is the responsible medical officer. The Government proposes (in its briefing note of May 2, 2006) that this role should be replaced by that of a clinical supervisor which "will be opened up to mental health professionals with the appropriate training and competencies. They may include psychiatrists, psychologists, nurses, social workers and occupational therapists."

(a) Detention

The Mental Health Act 1983 permits the detention of a person in hospital. He can only be discharged if the procedures laid down in the Act are followed, and can only leave the hospital temporarily if granted leave of absence (s.17). If a patient is absent without leave, the Act provides for his return to hospital in s.18. The patient can be taken into custody and returned up until six months after going absent without leave (s.18(4) of the 1983 Act, as amended). Special provisions apply where the section would have terminated (but the termination is suspended under s.21) during the period of absence without leave and vary depending on whether the patient is returned within 28 days (s.21A) or six months (s.21B).

(b) Leave of Absence

Section 17(1) provides that a patient may be granted "leave to be absent from the hospital subject to such conditions (if any) as [the responsible medical officer] considers necessary in the interests of the patient or for the protection of other persons." Leave of absence may be granted "either indefinitely or on specified occasions or for any specified period; and where leave is so granted for a specified period, that period may be extended by further leave granted in the absence of the patient." The patient may be recalled from leave and the leave be revoked at any time if "it appears to the [RMO] that it is necessary to do so in the interests of the patient's health or safety or for the protection of others" (s.17(4)). Leave of absence can last until the s.3 comes up for renewal, in which case the patient must either be recalled to hospital or discharged (ss.17(5) and 20).

Great care has to be taken in the granting of leave of absence (as in discharge) because of the potential dangers presented by some, but by no means all, patients. The *Code of Practice* recommends, in para.20.6, that the "granting of leave and the conditions attached to it should be recorded in the patient's notes and copies given to the patient, any appropriate relatives or friends and any professionals in the community who need to know." Leave of absence is of real significance to a patient. It enables him to retain or obtain skills which will be necessary once he is discharged or allows him to retain contact with the "outside world". There are no limits imposed by the statute as to the purposes for which leave of absence may be granted. Further, when a patient is on leave of absence, he is liable to be detained and so the treatment regime provided for in Part IV of the Act applies. Reflecting back on the cases considered above, that is *R. v Hallstrom and Another, Ex p. W; R. v Gardner and Another, Ex p. L* [1986] 1 Q.B. 1090 and *R. (on the application of DR) v Merseycare NHS Trust* [1999] 1 F.L.R. 106, the use of s.17 with no requirement for any treatment in hospital must be impermissible, but granting leave of absence between the periods when the person is having treatment in the hospital, e.g. as an out-patient, is permissible. Thus, some forms of treatment in the community are permitted under the Act, because the patient may be admitted under s.3, that may be renewed under s.20, and the patient may be granted regular leaves of absence, where the patient is primarily living in the community but is attending the hospital for treatment. What is not permitted is where the patient has no contact with the hospital, whether as an in-patient or an out-patient.

QUESTIONS:

1. Would you agree that, since the person is a detained patient, any absence from the hospital or its grounds must be authorised by a leave of absence? If so, every shopping trip, for example, must be covered by a leave of absence. Would you agree, then, that it is good practice to allow RMOs to provide fairly open-ended leave of absence for some patients who, it is known, will be able to take regular journeys outside the hospital and for which the requirement to provide a fresh leave of absence on every occasion would be impracticable? If you disagree, can the power to grant leave of absence be delegated to overcome the problem that the RMO may not be available (on holiday, at the cinema, etc.)?

(c) Discipline and Control of Patient Activity

There is nothing in the Act which indicates what can be done with patients on a day-to-day basis, unless it falls within the definition of "treatment" — see below. There may, however, be some bodily interference which is necessary within the hospital, not as part of the therapeutic regime, but to ensure that the institution operates relatively efficiently, including the exercise of discipline and control. This appears to have been approved by the House of Lords as a necessary implication of compulsory admission:

Pountney v Griffiths [1976] A.C. 314

LORD EDMUND-DAVIES

" . . . [sectioning] 'warrants the detention of the patient in a hospital for medical treatment', and that necessarily involves the exercise of control and discipline. Suitable arrangements for visits to patients by family and friends are an obvious part of a patient's treatment. Such visits inevitably involve the ushering of him back to his quarters when the permitted visiting time is ended. The respondent was accordingly acting in pursuance of the 1959 Act when the incident complained of occurred and, before civil or criminal proceedings for assault could properly be brought against him, the leave of the High Court should have been sought and obtained."

Some patients may present management problems to staff since they may "disturb others around them, or their behaviour may present a risk to themselves or others around them or those charged with their care" (*Code of Practice*, para.19.1). In these cases, the *Code of Practice* encourages staff to consider the problems contributing to the behaviour and the possible causes of that behaviour (paras 19.2 and 19.3) and take general preventive measures (para. 19.5). Restraint may, though, be justified or excused as it is the use of reasonable force in the defence of self or others, as in Chapter 19 of the *Code of Practice*. Restraint includes physical restraint (paras 19.6–19.14), medication (para.19.15) and seclusion (the "supervised confinement of a patient alone in a room which may be locked for the protection of others from significant harm": para.19.16; on seclusion generally, see paras 19.16–19.23). The basis for these actions is *not*, it is suggested, that they are treatment under Part IV of the Act or common law, despite the view of Sullivan J. in *R (on the application of Munjaz) v Ashworth Hospital Authority* [2002] EWHC Admin 1521, at para.73 that it was "medical treatment" within s.145(1) of the Act. Indeed, it appears to be the view of the majority of the House of Lords in the protracted *Munjaz* litigation that seclusion is not justified as being treatment, see *R (on the application of Munjaz) v Mersey Care NHS Trust* [2005] UKHL 58.

But the implications of the use of a section go further. Of course, it permits the detention of a person in hospital, that is the patient is not free to leave and may be detained in a secure environment. It is implicit that certain controls over that individual's life must, therefore, follow. For example, there will be necessary rules relating to such matters as meal times, use of television, etc. that have to operate simply because of the numbers of people living in a given environment. Further, there will be security issues, so that it can be anticipated that ward doors will be locked at night, just as doors at home are locked at night. With detention, therefore, go significant infringements on the liberty of the individual. The extent of such infringements have been challenged in a series of recent cases that draw attention to the issue and to the relevance of Article 8 of the ECHR, such that some infringements on privacy will be a necessary corollary, under Article 8(2), of the permitted infringement on liberty, but such infringements must be necessary to achieve that purpose and must be in accordance with the law. In *R. (on the application of Munjaz) v Ashworth Hospital Authority* [2005] UKHL 58, it was accepted that a detained patient may be secluded and the *Code of Practice* on seclusion should, unless there is good reason to adopt a different general policy or

good individual reasons on the facts of the instant case, be followed. Further, in
R. v Broadmoor Hospital Authority, Ex p. S, H, D, the right randomly to search
a patient has been accepted.

QUESTIONS:

1. One element of the justification for the interference in many of the recent
   cases was that they were all patients in a high security hospital. Is it
   possible, therefore, that these rulings only apply to patients detained in
   such hospitals on the basis that they need a particular level of security or
   will the fact of detention under the Act be sufficient for some interferences
   in liberty, such as searching (at least, for example, for weapons for offence
   and drugs)?
2. Where there are rules relating to the running of the hospital or to the
   expected behaviour of the patients, should it be a requirement that these
   rules are clear, transparent and available, in understandable fashion, to the
   patients? See further G. Richardson, *Law, Process and Custody: Prisoners
   and Patients*, London: Weidenfield and Nicholson, 1993.

(d) Treatment

The 1959 Act contained no provisions clarifying the treatment position of
detained patients: Part IV of the 1983 Act does just that. If the justification for
compulsory admission is either *parens patriae* or police powers, it would appear
to follow that there is an obligation to provide treatment. This is reflected in the
Richardson principle of reciprocity.

   Not all compulsory sections involve the patient being admitted for treatment
(whether with assessment or not). Thus the treatment sections do not apply to
patients in hospital under ss.5(2) and (4), 135 and 136. In addition, since s.4 is an
emergency section, there is no good reason for applying the treatment provisions.
It is easy to change it to a s.2, which is a treatment section. These objectives are
achieved by s.56. For all these patients, the consent to treatment position is that
under the common law. It is important to note that s.56 also applies the
provisions of s.57 to informal patients, which is one of the very few provisions to
apply to such patients (and which explains why the patient in *R. v Mental Health
Act Commission, ex p. X*, below, concerns an out-patient).

   The phrase used in s.56(1)(a) is that a patient must be "liable to be detained"
under one of the sections which permits treatment (i.e. ss.2 and 3 for our purposes).

QUESTIONS:

1. Do you believe that there is an obligation to provide treatment under Part
   IV of the 1983 Act? If so, does it follow that it must be possible to provide
   that treatment compulsorily, even though this turns the common law on its
   head, in particular the assumption that a compulsorily detained patient is
   not capable of making her or his own treatment decisions? If the rationale

for admission is the police power, does it follow that only treatment for mental disorders causing danger to others should be permitted?

2. Using your knowledge gained so far, does a patient have to be detained in hospital to fall within this phrase? Refer back to the cases at pp.511–515.

The Mental Health Act separates treatment for mental disorder into three categories, covered by ss.57, 58 (and treatments covered by these sections in an emergency under s.62) and 63. Note that treatment may include a plan of treatment (s.59). Note also that a patient may withdraw consent, if it had been provided, at any time (s.60).

(i) Psychosurgery and the Surgical Implantation of Hormones to Reduce Male Sexual Drive

These treatments are covered by s.57(1–3) of the Act, as follows:

57.—(1) This section applies to the following forms of medical treatment for mental disorder

(a) any surgical operation for destroying brain tissue or for destroying the functioning of the brain tissue; and

(b) such other forms of treatment as may be specified for the purposes of this section by regulations made by the Secretary of State.

(2) Subject to section 62 below, a patient shall not be given any form of treatment to which this section applies unless he has consented to it and

(a) a registered medical practitioner appointed for the purposes of this Part of this Act by the Secretary of State (not being the responsible medical officer) and two other persons appointed for the purposes of this paragraph by the Secretary of State (not being registered medical practitioners) have certified in writing that the patient is capable of understanding the nature, purpose and likely effects of the treatment in question and has consented to it; and

(b) the registered medical practitioner referred to in paragraph (a) above has certified in writing that, having regard to the likelihood of the treatment alleviating or preventing a deterioration of the patient's condition, the treatment should be given.

(3) Before giving a certificate under subsection (2)(b) above the registered medical practitioner concerned shall consult two other persons who have been professionally concerned with the patient's medical treatment, and of those persons one shall be a nurse and the other shall be neither a nurse nor a registered medical practitioner.

NOTES:

1. Section 57(1)(a) is concerned with psychosurgery. (For further consideration, see L. Gostin, "Psychosurgery: a Hazardous and Unestablished Treatment? A Case for the Importation of American Legal Safeguards to Great Britain" (1982) *Journal of Social Welfare Law* 83.) It is carried out very rarely.

2. Section 57(1)(b) is concerned with a treatment which is carried out even more rarely than psychosurgery, and that is the surgical implantation of

hormones to reduce male sexual drive (Mental Health (Hospital, Guardianship and Consent to Treatment) Regulations 1983, SI 1983/893, reg. 16(1)(a)). It is interesting to note that this appears to be a treatment for sexual deviancy, placed in provisions relating to controlling consent to treatment for mental disorder. However, sexual deviancy is not a form of mental disorder and therefore it is doubtful whether it should be in the Act at all. In *R. v Mental Health Act Commission, Ex p. X* (1988) 9 B.M.L.R. 77, it was decided that this provision did not cover the administration of Goserelin, a drug the primary purpose of which was the treatment of prostate cancer, but which had the side effect of reducing testosterone to castrate levels. Three Mental Health Act Commissioners had taken the view that the administration of the drug was covered by s.57. Stuart-Smith J. stated that: (a) it was not a hormone. The fact that it was a synthetic substance did not matter. It was a synthetic analogue, having the opposite effect of a hormone by obstructing the messages sent. (b) It was not surgically implanted. It was administered in a polymer cylinder which degraded so as to release the substance gradually and was inserted subcutaneously via an injection, which did not comply with what would be regarded in common parlance as surgical implantation.

QUESTION:

1. If the administration of Goserelin does not fall within s.58, does it fall within any other provision of Part IV? If so, what consequences flow for what might be termed chemical castration? (You may wish to consider this question further after examining s.63 below. See P. Fennell, "Sexual Suppressants and the Mental Health Act" [1988] *Criminal Law Review* 660.)

(ii) Medication and Electro-convulsive Therapy

The provisions are as follows:

58.—(1) This section applies to the following forms of medical treatment for mental disorder—

(a) such forms of treatment as may be specified for the purposes of this section by regulations made by the Secretary of State;
(b) the administration of medicine to a patient by any means (not being a form of treatment specified under paragraph (a) above or section 57 above) at any time during a period for which he is liable to be detained as a patient to whom this Part of the Act applies if three months or more have elapsed since the first occasion in that period when medicine was administered to him by any means for his mental disorder. . . .

(3) Subject to section 62 below, a patient shall not be given any form of treatment to which this section applies unless—

(a) he has consented to that treatment and either the responsible medical officer or a registered medical practitioner appointed for the purposes of this Part of this Act by the Secretary of State has certified in writing that the patient is capable of understanding its nature, purpose and likely effects and has consented to it; or

(b) a registered medical practitioner appointed as aforesaid (not being the responsible medical officer) has certified in writing that the patient is not capable of understanding the nature, purpose and likely effects of that treatment or has not consented to it but that, having regard to the likelihood of its alleviating or preventing a deterioration of his condition, the treatment should be given.

(4) Before giving a certificate under subsection (3)(b) above the registered medical practitioner concerned shall consult two other persons who have been professionally concerned with the patient's medical treatment, and of those persons one shall be a nurse and the other shall be neither a nurse nor a registered medical practitioner.

Medication

The three-month rule, with regard to the continuation of medication (s.58(1)(b)), is often misunderstood and the *Code of Practice* attempts to clarify matters by providing that (in para.16.12) the "period starts on the occasion when medication for mental disorder was first administered by any means during any period of continuing detention" and that the "medication does not necessarily have to be administered continuously throughout the three month period". This period allows (para.16.11) "time for the doctor to create a treatment programme suitable for the patient's need. Even though the Act allows treatment to be given without consent during the first three months the rmo should ensure that the patient's valid consent is sought before any medication is administered. The patient's consent or refusal should be recorded in the case notes. If such consent is not forthcoming or is withdrawn during this period, the rmo must consider whether to proceed in the absence of consent, to give alternative treatment or no further treatment."

Electro-convulsive therapy

Electro-convulsive therapy was added by regulations (Mental Health (Hospital, Guardianship and Consent to Treatment) Regulations 1983, SI 1983/893, reg. 16(2)). Some people object to the use of ECT. On the other hand, the indicators for its use have been carefully researched by psychiatrists, and the observations of its effect have been carefully identified, even if it is not quite clear how it works. It would appear that the active agent is the fit induced by ECT rather than the electricity itself. Many would regard it as a "quick fix" treatment when other forms of treatment, though taking more time, would be as efficacious. In J. Cookson *et al.*, *The Use of Drugs in Psychiatry*, there is a summary of guidance on the use of ECT. The purposes for which ECT may be used include severe depressive illness, mania and catatonic stupor. Combined with a phenothiazine, a drug, it can assist in the short-term treatment of schizophrenia. The treatment is safe provided a muscle relaxant is given and it is avoided, if possible, for people with aneurysms, recent cerebral haemorrhage or raised intracranial pressure. Brief confusion, restlessness, headache and nausea are common following ECT. A cup of tea, a lie-down and an aspirin may help these after-effects disappear. Assessment for therapeutic benefit should be made the next day, after each treatment. Amnesia for events immediately before ECT (anterograde) and patchy memory losses of memory after ECT (retrograde amnesia), most often for less important matters, are common. Memory difficulties usually subside in two or three weeks but may persist longer. Depressive illness does appear to be associated with memory impairment and distinguishing between this and an ECT effect may be impossible. In 2003, NICE published guidelines for the use of ECT (NICE, *Guidelines on the Use of Electroconvulsive Therapy*, 2003). As the Mental Health Act Commission states in its 11th Biennial Report, *In Place of Fear?* (2006), at paras 4.68–4.70:

these sought to restrict the use of ECT to situations where all other alternatives had been exhausted and/or where the illness to be treated was life-threatening, and advised against "maintenance" ECT treatment . . . . Clinicians using ECT have subsequently published research questioning assumptions made by NICE over the likely effect of ECT on quality of life or function. In June 2005 a statement from the RCPsych Consensus Group was published as the first chapter of the College's revised ECT Handbook. This notes that, whilst health professional must take NICE guidelines into account, the latter cannot override the individual responsibility of doctors to make decisions appropriate to the circumstances of an individual patient. It envisages some circumstances when it might be considered in a patient's best interests to receive ECT treatment for depressive illness that is neither life-threatening nor severe, nor proven resistant to other treatments, or as a maintenance therapy . . . . In such circumstances, the Consensus Group recommends that clinical decisions to depart from NICE guidelines should:

- Have a fully documented assessment of the potential risks and benefits of treatment to which valid consent has been obtained;
- Exercise particular circumspection in the use of ECT outside of NICE guidelines where patients have never had the treatment before, and in all cases ensure that discussions with patients about potential side-effects, such as retrograde amnesia for personal memories, are undertaken and recorded;
- Obtain a second medical opinion; and
- Use unilateral electrode placement and, where possible, avoid supra-threshold electrical doses for at least initial treatment in a prescription.

We note that the RCPsych's Consensus Group assumes that departures from NICE guidelines will involve only consenting patients, and does not contemplate patients receiving ECT treatment outside of NICE guidelines under the powers of the Mental Health Act or, if incapacitated but informally admitted to hospital, under the common law . . . . [But] we do not feel able to prejudge that, in the case of a detained patient, a SOAD would necessarily decline to authorise [treatment outside NICE guidelines for a patient who refuses consent].

QUESTIONS:

1. When can ECT be given or drugs continued beyond the first three months?
2. What does the requirement with regard to consent in s.58(2)(a) mean? What is the procedural difference between s.57 and s.58 as regards validating the consent of the patient?

Consider the following view on the identical provision in s.57. Note the different procedures for identifying that the substantive issues are satisfied and read the following extract in that light.

R. v Mental Health Act Commission, Ex p. X (1988) 9 B.M.L.R. 77

STUART-SMITH J.

"... A number of points should be made. First, all three commissioners have to be satisfied before they can certify. [This does not apply to section 58] Secondly, the subsection is concerned both with capacity and consent, and the commissioners have to be satisfied on both heads. Thirdly, the words are 'capable of understanding' and not 'understands'. Thus the question is capacity and not actual understanding. Fourthly, it is capacity to understand the likely effects of the treatment and not possible side effects, however remote...

No doubt the consent has to be an informed consent in that he knows the nature and likely effect of the treatment. There can be no doubt that the applicant knew this. So too in this case, where the treatment was not routinely used for control of sexual urges and was not sold for this purpose, it was important that the applicant should realise that the use on him was a novel one and the full implications with use on young men had not been studied, since trials had only been involved with animals and older men. Again it is perfectly clear that the applicant knew this.

[The judge then dealt with the issue that the Commissioners first assessed X to be capable and then, three months later that his condition had so deteriorated that he had no longer the capacity to understand.] While I accept that there may be cases where a patient's mental condition has so gravely deteriorated over three months that his capacity to understand may have changed, I do not find the bald assertion that it had done so in this case persuasive... I cannot accept that a patient must understand the precise physiological process involved before he can be said to be capable of understanding the nature and likely effects of the treatment or can consent to it. In fact it is clear from his affidavit that the applicant had a remarkably good understanding of the physiological process involved. But I cannot accept that it is a necessary prerequisite.

The second ground, that he denied the possibility of any medium or long term side effects, is in contrast with his understanding in August. I think it is clear from the applicant's own affidavit that he was adopting a somewhat cavalier and less cooperative attitude to the questioning on November 17 as compared with that on August 18. This is regrettable but not difficult to understand, since he knew that the commissioners had already decided that he was capable of understanding and had consented to the treatment he was anxious to have."

The judge concluded that, if the treatment had fallen within s.57, he would have decided that:

"the decision to refuse a certificate under section 57(2) would have to be quashed on the grounds that the commissioners took into account matters which they should not have taken into account, applied the wrong test and reached a decision that was unreasonable in the *Wednesbury* sense."

While the main critique was addressed to the question of capacity, the judge also considered whether the treatment was likely to alleviate or prevent a deterioration of the patient's condition and noted:

"In his report Professor Bluglass [a psychiatrist] has drawn attention to the problems involved in finding two people with whom the medically qualified commissioner must consult before he can certify under section 57(2)(b), when the patient is a voluntary outpatient. Both must have been professionally concerned with the patient's treatment, one must be a nurse, and the other neither a nurse nor a doctor... [P]sychologists, speech therapists, social workers and probation officers might come into the latter category. But it is obvious that many, if not most, voluntary outpatients will not have been involved with people in these disciplines. Moreover, there may even be difficulty in finding a nurse who is involved in his treatment. Quite apart from these practical difficulties . . . it is not entirely clear why it is appropriate for non-medically qualified people to be consulted on the desirability of medical treatment, having regard to the likelihood of it alleviating the patient's condition or preventing its deterioration . . . I am far from saying that in every case the medical commissioner must discuss every reservation that he may have with the responsible medical officer, but most, if not all, [the matters indicated by the medical commissioner] are criticisms of Dr Silverman's approach and treatment . . . [T]he medical commissioner does not have to have regard only to the likelihood of the treatment in alleviating the patient's condition or preventing its deterioration . . . [T]here are two matters that he must have regard to. The commissioner must first consider whether the proposed treatment is likely to alleviate the condition or prevent its deterioration. If he concludes that it is not so likely, then he must refuse a certificate. If he concludes that it is likely to do so, then no doubt he may balance the benefit against what he conceives to be the disadvantages . . . I am satisfied that whether it be put on the ground of unfairness or the failure to take relevant matters into consideration, or taking irrelevant matters into consideration, the refusal to certify under section 57(2)(b) could not stand in the event that I am wrong on the question of jurisdiction."

NOTES:

1. Every time the patient's detention is renewed, there must be a report on treatment provided under s.57(2)(b) only (s.61). It is, however, only good practice to review the position where the patient is consenting, as provided in the *Code of Practice* (paras 16.35). The Mental Health Act Commission in its 11th Biennial Report, *In Place of Fear?* (2006) states, at para. 4.59:

   "In our Tenth Biennial Report we noted that visiting Commissioners had identified that RMOs had failed to submit a s. 61 report in a quarter of the 636 cases where Forms 39 had been issued and detention renewed. Because the MHAC does not receive notifications of individual detentions or renewals, we are unable effectively to police this aspect of services' duties towards their patients and towards us an organisation, but this could be corrected with arrangements for a future monitoring body or the Tribunal under the next Act."

2. The Mental Health Act Commission in its 11th Biennial Report, *op. cit.* in note 1, reports on second opinion activity in paras 4.64–4.67:

   "Whilst the numbers of Second Opinions overall continue to rise, the numbers of referrals for ECT treatment may be showing a slight decline, perhaps as a consequence of NICE guidelines which imply that ECT is a treatment of last resort. In our last report we suggested that a declining proportion of ECT referrals could skew the gender-balance of Second Opinion referrals, given that more men than women are referred for medication, and more women than men for ECT. In this reporting period male patients have accounted for 59% of referrals, an increase of 4% from the last reporting period.
   Perhaps more significantly, the biennially-grouped data . . . shows a steep and continuing rise in the number of Second Opinions for medication. The reasons for this may only be surmised, but the statistics *could* reflect:
   • Changing general clinical profiles of detained patients (e.g., an increasingly 'unwell' population who are less likely to be able or willing to consent to treatment); and/or
   • A growing appreciation and care on the part of clinicians to consider whether apparent consent from a patient has a genuine basis, rather than

being based upon inadequate understanding, capacity or freedom of choice; and/or

- An increasing desire on the part of clinicians to offset their accountability and liability in prescribing medication to detained patients in view of a perceived increase in litigation in this area . . . .

[In the period 2003–2005 where there were 16,931 Second Opinion requests received for medication and 3,811 for ECT], at least 478 patients' proposed treatment was significantly altered as a result of a Second Opinion . . . , and nearly 2,000 treatment plans were slightly changed . . . . We also have suggested that the value of the SOAD system's oversight of treatment plans cannot be measured simply by changes made, given that RMOs draw up treatment plans knowing that they will be subject to this system of scrutiny. It is important that the best elements of the SOAD system are preserved under the proposed legislative framework . . . ."

3. The SOAD should give reasons for his decision which should be available to the patient and which the courts may permit to be challenged (*R (on the application of Wooder) v Feggeter and Mental Health Act Commission* [2002] EWCA Civ 554).
4. Subsequent to the implementation of the Human Rights Act, there have been challenges to the procedures under the Mental Health Act 1983 and these are best summarised by reading the following extract.

R. (on the application of B) v Dr Haddock and others [2005] EWHC 921

"9. Since any form of treatment which is administered without a previous consent is capable of breaking at least Article 8 (respect for private life) and particular treatment may even breach Article 3 of the European Convention on Human Rights, the courts have had to consider claims by patients such as the claimant. There are two important decisions of the Court of Appeal. The first is *R (Wilkinson) v Broadmoor Special Hospital & Others* [2002] 1 W.L.R. 419. The claimant in that case contended that, in order to comply with his right to a fair trial under Article 6 of the European Convention on Human Rights, it was necessary that the doctors concerned, that is to say the RMO and the SOAD together with his own medical expert, should attend court to give evidence and be cross examined so that the court could reach its own view whether the treatment infringed the patient's human rights. The court upheld that contention.

10. Considerable reliance was placed by the court on the possibility of bringing a claim under s.7 of the Human Rights Act or in tort (subject to the protection provided for the doctors by s.139 of the 1983 Act, which requires proof of bad faith or lack of reasonable care and the leave of the High Court to bring proceedings). This coupled with the need to consider and to deal with possible breaches of human rights made it essential for there to be a full merits review and for the court to form its own view having so far as possible investigated and resolved the medical issues. In paragraph 26 Simon Brown LJ said this:—

'It seems to me that the court must inevitably now reach its own view both as to whether this claimant is indeed incapable of consenting (or refusing consent) to the treatment programme planned for him by the first defendant as his RMO and, depending upon the court's conclusion on that issue, as to whether the proposed forcible administration of such treatment (a) would threaten the claimant's life and so be impermissible under Article 2, (b) would be degrading and so impermissible under Article 3, and (c) would not be justifiable as both necessary and proportionate under Article 8(2) given the extent to which it would invade the claimant's right to privacy. (I cannot see that Article 14 adds anything to the debate)'.

He expressed the hope that cases such as this would be rare indeed. In paragraphs 30 and 31, he said this:—

'30. If in truth this claimant has the capacity to refuse consent to the treatment proposed here, it is difficult to suppose that he should nevertheless be forcibly subjected to it. True, Dr Horne appears to regard it as his only hope of eventual return to their community. That said, however, its impact on the claimant's rights above all to autonomy and bodily inviolability is immense and its prospective benefits (not least given his extreme opposition) appear decidedly speculative. Even, moreover, if the claimant is incompetent, the court will need to be satisfied, in the language of the European Court of Human Rights in *Herczegfalvy's* case 15 E.H.R.R. 437, 484 paras 82–83, "that the medical necessity has been convincingly shown to exist . . . according to the psychiatric principles generally accepted at the time".

31. Accordingly, were there to be a fresh decision to subject this claimant to forcible treatment which is then challenged, I would order the attendance of all three specialists for cross-examination at the review hearing. I recognise, of course, that this would substantially complicate and lengthen the course of proceedings. I recognise too the great inconvenience it would occasion the defendants and the potentially inhibiting effect it could have in future on the choice of treatment for unco-operative mental patients. I would, however, express the confident hope that challenges of this nature, so far from becoming commonplace, will be rare indeed and will arise only in the most exceptional circumstances. Dr Grounds, and others like him will surely hesitate long before being prepared to join issue both with those who have the express statutory responsibility for treating the patient (RMOs) and also, in section 58 cases like the present, those specifically appointed to safeguard the patient's interests (SOADs). SOADs, I should note, are experienced and entirely independent specialists drawn from a panel appointed by the Mental Health Act Commission ("MHAC") which was directed by the Secretary of State to discharge on his behalf that function under Part IV of the Act. Courts, after all, are likely to pay very particular regard to the views held by those specifically charged with the patient's care and well-being. I do not go so far as to say that a *Bolam/Bolitho* approach will be taken to their evidence—i.e. that the treatment which they propose will be sanctioned by the court provided only that a respected body of medical opinion would approve it. Certainly, however, courts will not be astute to overrule a treatment plan decided upon by the RMO and certified by a SOAD following consultation with two other persons'.

11. It was also made clear in Wilkinson that the SOAD must form his own independent view on the need for the treatment, bearing in mind the tests cited by Simon Brown LJ as set out by the ECHR in *Herczegfalvy* v *Austria* (1992) 15 E.H.R.R. 437 at 484 in Paragraphs 82 and 83. It is interesting to note that in Paragraph 83 the ECtHR said:—

'In this case it is above all the length of time during which the handcuffs and security bed were used which appears worrying. However, the evidence before the court is not sufficient to disprove the governments' argument that, according to the psychiatric principles generally accepted at the time, medical necessity justified the treatment in issue'.

The treatment had resulted in loss of teeth, broken ribs and bruises.

12. In *R(N)* v *M & Others* [2003] 1 W.L.R. 562 the Court of Appeal considered the issue again and to some extent qualified what had been said in Wilkinson. It made the point that the only question was whether the treatment had been convincingly shown to be medically necessary. If so, there would be no breach of Article 3, even if the high threshold were otherwise crossed, nor of Article 8 since the interference with the right to respect for private life would be proportionate and would be justified within the terms of Article 8.2. The court also made the point that the treatment could not be in the patient's best interests unless a responsible body of medical opinion agreed with it, but it did not follow that the treatment could not be in the patient's best interests or medically necessary merely because

there was a responsible body of medical opinion to the effect that the treatment was not in the patient's best interests and not medically necessary.

13. Mr Pezzani argued that the *Herczegfalvy* test had to be applied sequentially both to the determination whether the claimant suffered from a mental disorder and whether depot medication was a medical necessity. In paragraph 20 of *N*, albeit, as was said not having heard argument directed to the point, the court said:—

'Suppose that there is a good chance (but it has not been convincingly shown) that the patient is suffering from a treatable mental illness which, if he was suffering from it, would unquestionably be alleviated by the proposed treatment. On the compartmentalised approach as we understand it, the Herczegfalvy test would not be made out. That is surprising, and we would suggest, not a sensible outcome, at any rate in the case of a patient who does not have the capacity to consent to treatment". It seems to me that there is indeed a single question. That is consistent with the ECHR's approach in *Herczegfalvy*. It must be obvious that that test will not be met unless the RMO and the SOAD are convinced that the treatment will alleviate the patient's condition and so they must, after considering all the evidence, be at least persuaded that the patient is indeed suffering from a mental disorder for which the treatment is needed. It is, I think, important to bear in mind that precise diagnosis of mental disorders is not always possible and psychiatrists are often unable to be certain from what form of disorder the patient is suffering. But they may properly be convinced that a particular form of treatment will alleviate a condition from which they have good reason to believe the patient is suffering. It is clear that the more drastic the treatment, the more the doctor must be satisfied of the need for it and in this respect there is no difference in principle between physical and mental disorders.'

14. The Court indicated that it should not often be necessary to adduce oral evidence with cross-examination. In paragraph 38 this was said:—

'We suggest that it should not often be necessary to adduce oral evidence with cross-examination where there are disputed issues of fact and opinion in cases where the need for forcible medical treatment of a patient is being challenged on human rights grounds. Nor do we consider that the decision in *R (Wilkinson)* v *Broadmoor Special Hospital Authority* [2002] 1 W.L.R. 419 should be regarded as charter for routine applications to the court for oral evidence in human rights cases generally. Much will depend on the nature of the right that has allegedly been breached, and the nature of the alleged breach. Furthermore, although in some cases (such as the present) the nature of the challenge may be such that the court cannot decide the ultimate question without determining for itself the disputed facts, it should not be overlooked that the court's role is essentially one of review: see per Lord Steyn in *R (Daly)* v *Secretary of State for the Home Department* [2001] 2 AC 532, 547, para 27'.

15. I am bound to say that without the Court of Appeal decisions, particularly that of Wilkinson, I would have doubted that it was appropriate for the court to reach its own conclusion after, if necessary, hearing evidence. Parliament has required a second independent medical opinion in order to protect the patient's rights. S.139 of the 1983 Act limits in what in my opinion is a clearly proportionate fashion the ability of a patient to bring civil proceedings in connection with his treatment. Article 6 does not necessarily require in all cases that the independent and impartial tribunal (here, the court) must consider the whole matter afresh and reach its own conclusion having heard or considered all the evidence. The Court must naturally consider all the evidence put before it but it is difficult to follow why that should extend beyond consideration of written material. Furthermore, having regard to the fact that the issue is a medical one and that there are safeguards in the requirement of confirmation by an independent expert who must seek advice from at least a nurse and a non-medical person, it is difficult to see why the court should go beyond its normal review obligations, albeit, since human rights are involved, to the high level required. However, I recognise that I am bound by and must apply the

approach set down in Wilkinson. I note the last sentence of paragraph 39 in N's case. I confess that I do not find it easy to follow how an obligation to determine for myself the disputed facts, namely whether the claimant has capacity and whether the treatment is convincingly shown to be needed, fits in with a limitation to review.

16. A SOAD is required to give reasons for his decision. This was made clear by the Court of Appeal in *R (Wooder)* v *Feggetter* [2002] EWCA Civ 554. Brooke LJ said at paragraph 25:—

'With the coming into force of the Human Rights Act 1998 the time has come, in my judgment, for this court to declare that fairness requires that a decision by a SOAD which sanctions the violation of the autonomy of a competent adult patient should be accompanied by reasons. The fact that the critical decision is made by a doctor in the exercise of his clinical judgment and not by a tribunal following a more formal process, cannot, in my judgment, be allowed to diminish the significance of the doctor's decision'.

In my view, this principle applies equally to an incompetent as to a competent patient. The third defendant has in this case given full and detailed reasons for reaching his conclusion that he should issue a certificate enabling the treatment in its modified form to be administered."

QUESTIONS:

1. If the patient does not or cannot consent, can the treatment within s.58 still be given? If so, what are the requirements to be satisfied?
2. If the patient does not or cannot consent, what is the role of the Second Opinion Approved Doctor (known as a SOAD)?
3. Who is the nurse which the SOAD must consult? Should it be a qualified nurse, or can it be a nursing assistant? Must it be a nurse of a specific grade, e.g. the nurse in charge of the ward on which the patient is currently resident? The Act offers no definition of "nurse", although the Mental Health Act Commission prefers that the nurse, where possible, should be someone with an appropriate qualification, i.e. RMN or RNMH.
4. Who do you think is likely to be the other person consulted, and what might be their role?

In something like 80–90 per cent of cases the other person will be a social worker. However, there have been problems in finding suitable consultees. The *Code of Practice* states, at para. 16.32, that "Any person whom the SOAD proposes to consult must consider whether he or she is sufficiently concerned professionally with the patient's care to fulfil the function. If not, or if the person feels that someone else is better placed to fulfil the function, he or she should make this known to the patient's rmo and the SOAD in good time." The *Code* states that the matters upon which the consultee "should consider commenting upon are: the proposed treatment and the patient's ability to consent to it; other treatment options; the way in which the decision to treat was arrived at; the facts of the case, progress, attitude of relatives, etc; the implications of imposing treatment upon a non-consenting patient and the reasons for the patient's refusal of treatment; any other matter relating to the patient's care on which the consultee wishes to comment" (para.16.34).

(iii) Treatment in an Emergency

The need to contact the MHAC as required above and so satisfy the statutory criteria may delay necessary treatment. The need to follow the above procedures can be avoided if, in accordance with s.62, the treatment is:

62.—(1)(a) . . . immediately necessary to save the patient's life; or

(b) . . . (not being irreversible) . . . immediately necessary to prevent a serious deterioration of his condition; or

(c) . . . (not being irreversible or hazardous) . . . immediately necessary to alleviate serious suffering by the patient; or

(d) . . . (not being irreversible or hazardous) . . . immediately necessary and represent the minimum interference necessary to prevent the patient from behaving violently or being a danger to himself or others.

NOTES:

1. Section 62 has been alarmingly used for non-detained patients or patients under short-term holding powers even though it clearly does not apply. In *Treatment without Consent*, Fennell discovered that, in a sample of 1,009 statutory second opinions, "there were 114 cases where patients had been given emergency ECT under section 62 to save life or prevent a serious deterioration in health" (P. Fennell, *Treatment without Consent*, London: Routledge, 1996, at p.190).
2. Section 62(3) states that "treatment is irreversible if it has *unfavourable* physical or psychological consequences and hazardous if it entails *significant* physical hazard." (Emphasis added.)
3. When the treatment proposed is carried out under s.57 or 58, there is a recording system and referral to the Mental Health Act Commission for treatment under s.62. However, there is no form which needs to be filled in (but it is good practice to do so; see the *Code of Practice*, at paras 16.40 and 16.41).

QUESTIONS:

1. When is treatment "immediately necessary'? Note the timeframe to which this refers must be affected by the speed with which the Commission can respond.
2. When is treatment irreversible or hazardous?
3. Would you propose any further protections for a patient provided treatment under s.62?
4. Is s.62 likely to be used very often? (See P. Fennell, "Statutory Authority to Treat, Relatives and Treatment Proxies" (1994) 2 *Medical Law Review* 30 and Fennell, *op. cit.* in note 1, Chapters 12 and 13.)

(iv) Other Treatment

Section 63 of the Act covers other treatment:

> 63. The consent of a patient shall not be required for any medical treatment given to him for the mental disorder from which he is suffering, not being treatment falling within section 57 or 58 above, if the treatment is given by or under the direction of the responsible medical officer.

QUESTIONS:

1. If the drug Goserelin under consideration in *R. v Mental Health Act Commission, Ex p. X* (see p.536, above) was not a treatment falling within s.57, did it fall within either s.58 or s.63? Is it a treatment for mental disorder, bearing in mind that s.1(3) rules out sexual deviancy from being a form of mental disorder? If the drug is for a form of mental disorder, is it possible that it could be given without the consent of the patient?
2. Would you accept that the following are typical forms of treatment within s.63: drugs for the first three months, behaviour modification and milieu therapy?
3. How extensive is s.63? The forced feeding of someone with anorexia nervosa is a matter which has come to the courts' attention. Assess, in the following case, whether the person did satisfy the admission criteria and whether the treatment proposed really was for the mental disorder (if there was one).

B. v Croydon Health Authority [1995] 1 All E.R. 683

A woman, Miss B., was admitted to hospital under s.3 suffering from psychopathic disorder ("borderline personality disorder coupled with post traumatic stress disorder") and the treatment which she was to receive was psychotherapeutic psychoanalysis (the "core treatment"). In addition, she stopped eating as an "urge to punish herself". Although she had begun eating again at the time of the case, both Miss B and the health authority wished to know whether feeding her by nasogastric tube would have been lawful.

HOFFMANN L.J.
" . . . I first consider s. 63 . . .

[The question is] whether tube feeding would have been treatment for the mental disorder from which Ms B. was suffering. My initial reaction was that it could not be. Ms B. suffers from a psychopathic disorder which, according to the evidence, is incapable of treatment except by psychoanalytical psychotherapy. How can giving her food be treatment for that disorder?

Mr Gordon says that it cannot. It may be a prerequisite to a treatment for mental disorder or it may be treatment for a consequence of the mental disorder, but it is not treatment of the disorder itself . . .

This is a powerful submission. But I have come to the conclusion that it is too atomistic. It requires every individual element of the treatment being given to the patient to be directed to his mental condition. But in my view this test applies only to the treatment as a whole. Section 145(1) gives a wide definition to the term 'medical treatment'. It includes 'nursing . . . care, habilation and rehabilitation under medical supervision'. So a range of acts ancillary to the core treatment fall within the definition. I accept that by virtue of section 3(2)(b) a patient with a psychopathic disorder cannot be detained unless the proposed treatment, taken as a whole, is 'likely to alleviate or prevent a deterioration of his condition'. In my view, contrary to the submission of Mr Francis, 'condition' in this paragraph means the mental disorder on grounds of which the application for his admission and detention has been made. It follows that if there was no proposed treatment for Ms B.'s psychopathic disorder, s.63 could not have been invoked to justify feeding her by nasogastric tube. Indeed, it would not be lawful to detain her at all.

It does not however follow that every act which forms part of that treatment within the wide definition in section 145(1) must in itself be likely to alleviate or prevent a deterioration of that disorder. *Nursing and care concurrent with the core treatment or as a necessary prerequisite to such treatment or to prevent the patient from causing harm to himself or to alleviate the consequences of the disorder are, in my view, all capable of being ancillary to a treatment calculated to alleviate or prevent a deterioration of the psychopathic disorder.* [Emphasis added.] It would seem to me strange if a hospital could, without the patient's consent, give him treatment directed to alleviating a psychopathic disorder showing itself in suicidal tendencies, but not without such consent be able to treat the consequences of a suicide attempt. In my judgment the term 'medical treatment . . . for the mental disorder' in section 63 includes such ancillary acts.

I therefore agree with Ewbank J. in *Re KB (adult) (mental patient: medical treatment)* (1994) 19 B.M.L.R. 144 at 146 when he said of the tube-feeding of an anorexic: ' . . . relieving symptoms is just as much a part of treatment as relieving the underlying cause.' To similar effect is the judgment of Stuart-White J., quoted by Sir Stephen Brown P in *Riverside Mental Health NHS Trust* v. *Fox* [1994] 1 FLR 614 at 619. *Re C. (adult: refusal of medical treatment)* [1994] 1 All E.R. 819, in which a schizophrenic was held entitled to refuse treatment for gangrene, is distinguishable. The gangrene was entirely unconnected with the mental disorder.

Mr Gordon said that if the meaning of 'medical treatment for . . . mental disorder' was wide enough to include ancillary forms of treatment, section 63 would involve a breach of the Convention for the Protection of Human Rights and Fundamental Freedoms (the European Human Rights Convention (Rome, November 4, 1950; TS 71 (1953); Cmd 8969). He referred us to *Herczegfalvy* v. *Austria* (1992) 18 BMLR 48 at 68 in which the court said that a measure constituting an interference with private life and therefore *prima facie* contrary to article 8(1) (like involuntary tube feeding) can only be justified under article 8(2) if, among the other requirements of that article, its terms are sufficiently precise to enable the individual 'to foresee its consequences for him'. This requirement is necessary to prevent such measures from being a source of arbitrary official power, contrary to the rule of law. In my judgment section 63 amply satisfies this test. There is no conceptual vagueness about the notion of treating the symptoms or consequences of a mental disorder, although naturally there will be borderline cases. But there is no question of an exercise of arbitrary power.

I therefore think that the judge was right and would dismiss the appeal."

This decision has obviously wide potential consequences, as is evidenced by the following case:

Tameside and Glossop Acute Services Trust v CH (A Patient) [1996] 1 F.C.R. 753

CH, the defendant was 41 and in her 38th week of pregnancy. She had two children, aged 18 and 14 respectively. She suffered from schizophrenia and had been admitted to hospital under s.3 of the Mental Health Act 1983. In January

1995 there was evidence that the foetus had inter-uterine growth retardation. A consultant obstetrician and gynaecologist gave evidence that unless labour was induced, the foetus would die and there was the possibility that the patient would require a caesarian section. Both these steps would require the patient's agreement. While at that stage the patient agreed, the consultant was worried that she might change her mind. Evidence was also given by the psychiatrist who had initially seen the patient on her admission. He stated that she was a paranoid schizophrenic who was incapable of making a balanced rational decision about her treatment. He was of the view that she failed the three-part test for competency, in *Re C* (see p.308). He noted that during her pregnancy she had resisted persons going near her and she had shown an adverse reaction to tranquillisers. He was of the view that it was in her optimum interest to bear a healthy child.

Wall J. examined the interpretation of s.63 of the Mental Health Act 1983. He considered three questions as raised by Mr Francis, counsel for the patient. 1. Does the patient lack the capacity to consent or to refuse medical treatment in relation to the management of her pregnancy? 2. Is the proposed treatment necessary to save her life or prevent a deterioration in her physical or mental health? 3. Is the treatment in her best interests? His conclusions are set out below.

WALL J.
"As to the first of the questions posed by Mr. Francis, the evidence is overwhelming that the defendant lacks the capacity to consent to, or to refuse medical treatment in relation to the management of her pregnancy. Mr Francis accepts this on her behalf. I agree with Dr M.'s evidence that she fails all three of the tests laid down in *Re C* [1994] 2 FCR 151. In particular, she is suffering from the delusion that the doctors wish to harm her baby and is incapable of understanding the advice which she is given.

As to the second question, I accept the evidence of Dr M. that if the defendant is delivered of a still-born child this is likely to have a profound deleterious effect on the defendant's mental health in both the short and the long-term. I will not repeat the evidence that I have already summarised.

As to the third question it is in my view plainly in the defendant's interests to give birth to a live baby . . . "

Wall J. quoted s.63, above and noted the definition of "medical treatment" in s.145, above. He then referred to the decision in *B v Croydon HA* and continued . . .

" . . . Is the question of inducing the defendant's labour and/or causing her to be delivered of her child by Caesarian section 'entirely unconnected' with her mental disorder? At first blush it might appear difficult to say that performance of a Caesarian section is medical treatment for the defendant's mental disorder.

I am, however, satisfied that on the facts of this case so to hold would be 'too atomistic a view' to use Hoffmann L.J.'s phrase in the passage from *B v. Croydon HA* . . .

There are several strands in the evidence, which, in my judgment, bring the proposed treatment within s.63 of the Act. Firstly, there is the proposition that an ancillary reason for the induction and, if necessary, the birth by Caesarian section is to prevent a deterioration in the defendant's mental state. Secondly, there is the clear evidence of Dr M. that in order for the treatment of the schizophrenia to be effective, it is necessary for her to give birth to a live baby. Thirdly, the overall structure of her treatment requires her to receive strong anti-psychotic medication. The administration of that treatment has been necessarily interrupted by her pregnancy and cannot be resumed until her child is born. It is not, therefore, I think stretching language unduly to say that achievement of a successful outcome of her pregnancy is a necessary part of the overall treatment of her mental disorder. In *Re C. (An Adult: Refusal of Treatment)* [1994] 2 FCR 151 treatment of C's gangrene was not likely to effect his mental condition: the manner in which the delivery of the defendant's child is treated is likely to have a direct effect on her mental state.

I am therefore satisfied that the treatment of the defendant's pregnancy proposed by Dr G. is within the broad interpretation of s63 of the Mental Health Act approved by the Court of Appeal in *B* v. *Croydon HA*: it follows that since the defendant's consent is not required, Dr G is entitled, should he deem it clinically necessary, to use restraint to the extent to which it may be reasonably required in order to achieve the delivery by the defendant of healthy baby.

In these circumstances it becomes unnecessary for me to consider whether or not I could make a declaration authorising the use of reasonable force outwith the provisions of s.63. Mr. Lloyd for the trust, was prepared on the facts of this case to accept a declaration under s.63. He made it quite clear, however, that he did not accept that my power to make such a declaration was limited to a case which fell within s.63 and wished to reserve for another occasion the argument that the court has the power at common law to authorise the use of reasonable force as a necessary incident of treatment. I make it clear that I express no opinion on whether or not the power for which Mr. Lloyd contends exists, which must await argument in another case . . . "

Note:

1. It seems that the declaration authorising the caesarian section, if necessary, was based on the decision in *F v West Berkshire Health Authority* [1989] 2 All E.R. 545, although Wall J. seems to have been prepared to grant the declaration on the basis of s.63. Section 63 is clearly the basis for that part of the declaration authorising the use of restraint.

2. The House of Lords in *R (on the application of B) v Ashworth Hospital Authority* [2005] UKHL 20 has confirmed that treatment can be provided for any mental disorder, whether it is the mental disorder for which the patient was detained or not.

Questions:

1. Is anorexia nervosa a form of mental disorder?

2. Do you think that the *Croydon* case extends s.63 too far? Could it not be argued that almost any form of treatment falls within the criteria established in the case? If so, how does Hoffmann J. manage to distinguish the scenario in *Re C*? Is it convincing? How can you be sure that the case falls within or outwith s.63?

3. Do you agree with Wall J. that restraint to enable a Caesarian section is a treatment for the mental disorder from which CH was suffering? Or do you think that the interpretation of s.63 extends the law too far? (See also Chapter 13 below).

4. If the decision in these two cases is correct, where will the dividing line between physical treatment (not covered) and treatment for mental disorder (covered) be drawn? In considering this question, consider

whether termination of pregnancy could fall within s.63 (note the conditions for lawful termination under the Abortion Act 1967 as amended— see Chapter 12) and whether the removal of a brain tumour might fall within the section.

(v) Reform

There is no reference to change of the treatment provisions in either the Written Ministerial Statement of March 2006 or the briefing notes of May 2006. The most significant change was the introduction of the requirement to have intended care plans approved by a mental health tribunal before detention beyond the first 28 days was approved. As this tribunal stage is not being introduced, the care plan approval stage cannot be introduced either. Other changes, though apparently significant, were probably not that significant. Further, rather too much was left to secondary legislation and so maintaining the position in the 1983 Act may be preferable.

QUESTION:

1. Do you agree with the argument that maintaining the position in the 1983 Act is preferable?

(e) Information

Clearly, a detained patient will be in a better position if he or she has information about the effect of the Mental Health Act. Section 132 requires the managers of the hospital to provide such information "as soon as practicable after the commencement of the patient's detention". The information must be provided "both orally and in writing" (s.132(3)). Such information is also to be provided to the nearest relative, unless the patient objects (s.132(4)).

(f) Correspondence

Correspondence is not to be interfered with, unless such interference is permitted within s.134. Unless the person is detained in a special hospital when security factors are important, the restriction is that mail from the patient can only be stopped when it is addressed to someone who has requested that it should be withheld.

(g) Mental Health Act Commission

The Mental Health Act Commission has the broad remit to "keep under review the exercise of the powers and the discharge of the duties conferred or imposed by this Act so far as relating to the detention of patients or to patients liable to be detained under this Act" (s.120(1)). To that end it makes arrangements to visit all hospitals in which patients are detained and to meet with detained patients who make such a request. It has a complaints investigation jurisdiction (see s.120(1)(b)) when a complaint has been dealt with internally and the complainant wishes to pursue the matter further, has oversight of the correspondence limitations, and has specific roles within the consent to treatment provisions as mentioned earlier. It is a body which has a significant impact in providing an avenue for patients, and staff, to raise matters of concern about the operation of the legislation, other than the discharge of a patient, which is the remit of the Mental Health Review Tribunal. To gain an idea of the value of the role of the Mental Health Act Commission, see its 11th Biennial Report, covering the period 2003–2005, *In Place of Fear?* (2006).

Under the Mental Health Bill 2004, the Commission was to disappear, with its inspectorate functions being merged with those of the Healthcare Commission. *Improving Mental Health Law—Towards a New Mental Health Act* (2004) stated that "this will ensure that a single organisation can address issues about all aspects of the patient's care and treatment e.g. legal issues, clinical quality, safety, cleanliness, food standards, in a way that is more effective and efficient". It is unclear what the future holds, but if there were to be no change, the Pre-Legislative Scrutiny Committee would approve.

5. Discharge

The main focus of this chapter is on admission to hospital (and how to challenge it) and treatment in hospital, but there must be at least brief consideration of the question of discharge. Issues relating to leave of absence and challenging the initial admission have already been considered. A person may be discharged from section by the section simply ending. The patient may not need to leave hospital (indeed, some patients will not wish to do so). A patient may be discharged at any time in accordance with section 23, which gives certain people the power of discharge.

23.—(2) An order for discharge may be made in respect of a patient:

(a) where the patient is liable to be detained in a hospital in pursuance of an application for admission for assessment or for treatment by the responsible medical officer, by the managers or by the nearest relative of the patient . . .

(3) Where the patient is liable to be detained in a mental nursing home in pursuance of an application for admission for assessment or treatment, an order for discharge may, without prejudice to subsection (2) above, be made by the Secretary of State and, if the patient is maintained under a contract with a National Health Service trust, Health Authority, . . . or special health authority, by that trust or authority.

NOTES:

1. The powers of discharge granted to a trust or authority are exercisable by a committee of three members (s.23(4) and (5)).

2. Where a nearest relative wishes to discharge the patient, he or she must provide 72 hours' notice in writing of the decision to exercise the power (s.25). Within that time the discharge may be prevented if the RMO furnishes a report to the hospital managers stating that "the patient, if discharged, would be likely to act in a manner dangerous to other persons or himself". The nearest relative must be informed that a danger report has been issued (s.25(2)). The nearest relative has a right to apply to a mental health review tribunal seeking an order for discharge (s.66(1)(g)).

6. MENTAL HEALTH REVIEW TRIBUNALS

Mental health review tribunals were established under the 1959 Act to provide an independent body entitled to review the detention of a patient in hospital. Coincidentally, their existence and jurisdiction also satisfies, broadly speaking, the requirements of Article 5, particularly Article 5(4), of the European Convention on Human Rights. Patients may seek their discharge by making an application to the tribunal office. The patient must make the application, which need not be made in any formal manner; mere indication of a desire to be discharged by the tribunal is sufficient. A patient (and, on occasion, others) has a right to apply to an MHRT if he or she falls within the provisions of s.66.

66.—(1) Where—

(a) a patient is admitted to a hospital in pursuance of an application for assessment; or

(b) a patient is admitted to a hospital in pursuance of an application for treatment; or . . .

(d) a report is furnished under section 16 above in respect of a patient; or

(e) a patient is transferred from guardianship to a hospital in pursuance of regulations made under section 19 above; or

(f) a report is furnished under section 20 above in respect of a patient and the patient is not discharged; or

(g) a report is furnished under section 25 above in respect of a patient who is detained in pursuance of an application for admission for treatment; or . . .

(h) an order is made under section 29 above in respect of a patient who is or subsequently becomes liable to be detained or subject to guardianship under Part II of this Act,

an application may be made to a Mental Health Review Tribunal within the relevant period:

(i) by the patient (except in the cases mentioned in paragraphs (g) and (h) above) or, in the cases mentioned in paragraphs (d), (ga), (gb) and (gc) above, by his nearest relative if he has been (or was entitled to be) informed under this Act of the report or acceptance, and

(ii) in the cases mentioned in paragraphs (g) and (h) above, by his nearest relative.

(2) In subsection (1) above "the relevant period" means—

(a) in the case mentioned in paragraph (a) of that subsection, 14 days beginning with the day on which the patient is admitted as so mentioned;

(b) in the case mentioned in paragraph (b) of that subsection, six months beginning
     with the day on which the patient is admitted as so mentioned . . .
(d) in the cases mentioned in paragraphs (d), (g) and (gb) of that subsection, 28 days
     beginning with the day on which the applicant is informed that the report has been
     furnished;
(e) in the case mentioned in paragraph (e) of that subsection, six months beginning
     with the day on which the patient is transferred;
(f) in the case mentioned in paragraph (f) of that subsection, the period for which
     authority for the patient's detention or guardianship is renewed by virtue of the
     report;
(g) in the case mentioned in paragraph (h) of that subsection, 12 months beginning
     with the date of the order, and in any subsequent period of 12 months during which
     the order continues in force.

NOTES:

1. The Act does not necessarily expect that a patient initiate the procedure,
   since in some circumstances there will be an automatic referral of the
   patient's case to an MHRT. Section 68 provides that a case will be
   automatically referred where the patient has been detained for six months
   under a new s.3 and has not applied to an MHRT; where a patient has been
   detained under a s.3 for three years and has not applied to an MHRT
   within that time; and where a patient has been transferred from guardianship to a s.3 and has not applied within six months of the transfer.

2. The existence of the automatic power of referral in s.68 was sufficient to
   mean that there was no breach of the ECHR where the patient was not
   capable of making an application themselves, as decided by the House of
   Lords in *R. (on the application of MH) v Secretary of State for Health*
   [2005] UKHL 60. While it is possible for cases to get to the MHRT
   through this procedure, there is no guarantee that cases that ought to be
   referred will be so referred. While the power may be sufficient to meet the
   Article 6 requirement for access to the court, it might only be significant if
   incapable patients have sufficient assistance in launching applications. The
   proposals for Mental Health Act Advocacy within the Mental Health Bill
   2004 will, if implemented properly (with sufficient resources and powers),
   make a major difference.

3. Patients before MHRTs may be represented and that representation may
   be paid for under the Advice by Way of Representation scheme for which
   there are no eligibility limits, so that all detained patients qualify.
   Representation may be from solicitor members of the Law Society's
   Mental Health Panel, but need not be.

QUESTIONS:

1. How frequently may a patient detained under s.3 apply?
2. What explanation can there be to allow a patient detained under s.2 only
   to apply to an MHRT within the first 14 days of the section?

An MHRT has certain specific statutory powers which are set out in s.72 of the
Mental Health Act 1983.

72.—(1) Where application is made to a Mental Health Review Tribunal by or in respect of a patient who is liable to be detained under this Act, the tribunal may in any case direct that the patient be discharged, and:

(a)   the tribunal shall direct the discharge of a patient liable to be detained under section 2 above if they are satisfied:
   (i)   that he is not then suffering form mental disorder or from mental disorder of a nature or degree which warrants his detention in a hospital for assessment (or for assessment followed by medical treatment) for at least a limited period; or
   (ii)   that his detention as aforesaid is not justified in the interests of his own health or safety or with a view to the protection of other persons;
(b)   the tribunal shall direct the discharge of a patient liable to be detained otherwise than under section 2 above if they are satisfied:
   (i)   that he is not then suffering from mental illness, psychopathic disorder, severe mental impairment or mental impairment or from any of those forms of disorder of a nature or degree which makes it appropriate for him to be liable to be detained in a hospital for medical treatment; or
   (ii)   that it is not necessary for the health or safety of the patient or for the protection of other persons that he should receive such treatment; or
   (iii)   in the case of an application by virtue of paragraph (g) of section 66(1) above, that the patient, if released would not be likely to act in a manner dangerous to other persons or to himself.

(2) In determining whether to direct the discharge of a patient detained otherwise than under section 2 above on a case not falling within paragraph (b) of subsection (1) above, the tribunal shall have regard:

(a)   to the likelihood of medical treatment alleviating or preventing a deterioration of the patient's condition; and
(b)   in the case of a patient suffering from mental illness of severe mental impairment, to the likelihood of the patient, if discharged, being able to care for himself, to obtain the care he needs or to guard himself against serious exploitation.

(3) A tribunal may under subsection (1) above direct the discharge of a patient on a future date specified in the direction; and where a tribunal do not direct the discharge of a patient under that subsection the tribunal may:

(a)   with a view to facilitating his discharge on a future date, recommend that he be granted leave of absence or transferred to another hospital or into guardianship; and
(b)   further consider his case in the event of any such recommendation not being complied with.

(3A) Where, in the case of an application to a tribunal by or in respect of a patient who is liable to be detained in pursuance of an application for admission for treatment or by virtue of an order or direction for his admission or removal to hospital under Part III of this Act, the tribunal do not direct the discharge of the patient under subsection (1) above, the tribunal may:

(a)   recommend that the responsible medical officer consider whether to make a supervision application in respect of the patient; and
(b)   further consider his case in the event of no such application being made . . .

(6) Subsections (1) to (5) above apply in relation to references to a Mental Health Review Tribunal as they apply in relation to applications made to such a tribunal by or in respect of a patient.

NOTES:

1. An MHRT may defer discharge under s.72(3) for the purpose of ensuring that, for example, community support is provided to the patient. The discharge takes effect on the date stated by the MHRT even if the conditions are not fulfilled.
2. An MHRT has the power to recommend the use of after-care under supervision (see below).
3. The MHRT is required to give reasons for the decision (Mental Health Review Tribunal Rules, SI 1982/942, r. 23(2)). It enables the patient and/or his legal adviser to be able to ascertain the reasons sufficiently so as to assess whether it is appropriate to challenge the decision. There is no right of appeal against the decision of a tribunal.
4. It is important to recall (see p.489 above) that the burden of proof lies upon the detaining institution. It is also the case that the standard of proof is that of the ordinary civil balance of probabilities: *R. (on the application of AN) v MHRT* [2005] EWHC Civ 1605.
5. There appears to be little change in immediate prospect for tribunals (see the Written Ministerial Statement, March 2006).

QUESTIONS:

1. Section 72 indicates that a tribunal may discharge in any circumstances, but only has to discharge in the circumstances specifically stated in s.72(1) or (2), depending upon the section under which the patient is detained. In fact, it is only in these latter circumstances that the tribunal exercises the discharge power. Should the tribunal be prepared to exercise its power of discharge more generally? Would the general discretion allow the tribunal to take into account the legality of the original admission? Interestingly, the Pre-Legislative Scrutiny Committee was of the view that this power ought to be retained, though the Government disagreed.
2. Do you agree with Ackner L.J. in *R v. Hallstrom, ex p. W* [1985] 3 All E.R. 775 that a tribunal, in particular because of the use of the phrase "not then" in s.72(1)(a)(i) and (b)(i), has no power to consider the original admission only whether, at the time seen by it, it has the power to consider whether the patient should continue to be detained? It is on the assumption that this view is correct that the ability to challenge the original admission by either judicial review or writ of *habeas corpus* is of particular significance.

7. COMMUNITY CARE AND TREATMENT

Most of the Mental Health Act 1983 is concerned with admission to, treatment and care in, and discharge from hospital. However, the vast majority of people with a mental disorder spend little, if any, time in a hospital, even as an informal patient. It is also government policy to provide for care in the community. As regards mental health care, there is not only the general provision relating to community care (as to which, see P. Bartlett and R. Sandland, *Mental Health Law: Policy and Practice* (2nd edn), Oxford: OUP, 2003, pp.500–553), but also a specific obligation in the 1983 Act.

117.—(1) This section applies to persons who are detained under section 3 above, or admitted to a hospital in pursuance of a hospital order made under section 37 above, or transferred to a hospital in pursuance of a transfer direction under section 47 or 48 above, and then cease to be detained and (whether or not immediately after so ceasing) leave hospital.

(2) It shall be the duty of the Health Authority and of the local social services authority to provide, in co-operation with relevant voluntary agencies, after-care services for any person to whom this section applies until such time as the Health Authority and the local social services authority are satisfied that the person concerned is no longer in need of such services, but they shall not be so satisfied in the case of a patient who is subject to after-care under supervision at any time while he remains so subject.

In the context of the present work, it is more important to consider the treatment position of a person in the community. The only directly relevant powers to consider are those of guardianship and after-care under supervision, although the National Assistance Acts 1948 and 1951 provide for a power (exercisable also in an emergency) for the removal of certain categories of people, who are unable to cope or are living in insanitary conditions, to other accommodation.

(a) Guardianship

If the criteria of s.7 (see below) are satisfied, an application may be made to the social services department for the reception of the person in question into the guardianship of either the social services department or of a private guardian. The procedure for making an application is similar to that for an admission to hospital for treatment. An application can be made by either an ASW or the nearest relative (s.11(1). If an ASW makes an application, the nearest relative has right to object (subject to replacement as such by the county court under s.29) and, in any case, must be consulted (s.11(4)). There must be two medical recommendations (ss.7(3) and 12). The applications must then be "forwarded to the local social services authority named in the application as guardian, or, as the case may be, to the local social services authority for the area in which the person so named resides" (s.11(2)). Applications must be forwarded within 14 days of the last medical examination (s.11(2)). The guardian will be either the social services department or a private guardian, that is "any other person (including the applicant himself)" (s.7(5)). If the guardian is not the social services, the application is "of no effect unless it is accepted . . . by the local social services authority for the area in which [the prospective guardian] resides" (s.7(5)). A private guardian must be willing to act, as impliedly must the authority.

7.—(1) A patient who has attained the age of 16 years may be received into guardianship, for the person allowed by the following provisions of this Act, in pursuance of an application (in this Act referred to as "a guardianship application") made in accordance with this section.

(2) A guardianship application may be made in respect of a patient on the grounds that:

(a) he is suffering from mental disorder, being mental illness, severe mental impairment, psychopathic disorder or mental impairment and his mental disorder is of a nature or degree which warrants his reception into guardianship under this section; and
(b) it is necessary in the interests of the welfare of the patient or for the protection of other persons that the patient should be so received.

Once received into guardianship, the guardian has the limited powers in s.8, known as the essential powers. The powers were dramatically reduced from those of a father of a child under the age of 14 because, it was thought, the extent of the powers was a major explanation for the lack of usage of the power since 1959.

8.—(1) Where a guardianship application [has been duly made and accepted by the social services department, it shall] confer on the . . . guardian, to the exclusion of any other person:

(a) the power to require the patient to reside at a place specified by the authority or person named as guardian;
(b) the power to require the patient to attend at places and times so specified for the purpose of medical treatment, occupation, education or training;
(c) the power to require access to the patient to be given, at any place where the patient is residing, to any registered medical practitioner, approved social worker or other person so specified.

Guardianship ends either because it is not renewed (for renewal, see section 20(6) & (7)) or because the patient is discharged by the RMO, the social services department or the nearest relative (section 23(2)(b)) or a Mental Health Review Tribunal orders discharge under section 72(4) (patients have the right of application at the end of the first six months and thereafter once during each period of renewal, see section 66(1)(c) & (f) & (2)(c) & (f)).

NOTE:

1. In fact, guardianship is rarely used. (See M. Fisher, "Guardianship under the Mental Health Legislation: a Review" (1988) *Journal of Social Welfare Law* 316.) It has been said (M.J. Gunn, "Mental Health Act Guardianship: Where Now?" (1986) *Journal of Social Welfare Law* 144) that guardianship is rarely used for the following reasons: (1) Some people are excluded by the choice of definitions, in particular many people with mental handicap or learning disabilities for whom it might have been extremely useful. Consider, therefore, the definitions of severe mental impairment and mental impairment, which exclude most people with learning disabilities because of the end phrase that the impairment "is associated with abnormally aggressive or seriously irresponsible conduct on the part of the person concerned"; (2) The powers are not the essential powers, as they had been expected to be. In particular, the guardian does not have the power to consent to treatment. In the Mental Health Act 1959, a guardian had the powers of a father of a child under the age of 14; (3) Institutional

inertia and myth; that is social services believed that it was valueless, therefore it is valueless.

QUESTIONS:

1. Do you agree with the view of McCullough J. in *R. v Hallstrom, Ex p. W* [1986] 1 Q.B. 1090 that s.8 provides no power for the guardian to consent to treatment? Note that the comparable provision in the 1959 Act provides the guardian with the powers which a father would have over a child under the age of 14.
2. Might guardianship be of some value in assisting people who are elderly and confused or people with learning disabilities to live in the community?

(b) After-care under Supervision

To improve matters in the community, after-care under supervision was introduced by the Mental Health (Patients in the Community) Act 1995. It creates ss.25A–25H of the Mental Health Act 1983. It involves an application being made for a patient to be placed under supervision to secure that he or she receives the after-care services provided under s.117. The patient must be detained under s.3 and be at least 16 years old (s.25A(1)). The further criteria for making a supervision application are contained in the following provision.

25A.—(4) A supervision application may be made in respect of a patient only on the grounds that—

(a) the patient is suffering from mental disorder, being mental illness, severe mental impairment, psychopathic disorder or mental impairment;
(b) that there would be a substantial risk of serious harm to the health or safety of the patient or the safety of other persons, or of the patient being seriously exploited, if he were not to receive the after-care services to be provided for him under section 117 below after he leaves hospital; and
(c) his being subject to after-care under supervision is likely to help to secure that he or she receives the after-care services to be so provided.

An application is made by the patient's RMO (s.25A(5)) after (a) consulting and taking into account the views of the patient, one or more persons professionally concerned with the patient's medical treatment in hospital, one or more persons who will be professionally concerned with the provision of the after-care services, and any person who the RMO believes will play a substantial part in the patient's care after leaving hospital but will not be professionally concerned (i.e. a carer) (s.25B(1) and (2); (b) considering the after-care services to be provided; and (c) any requirements which may be imposed on the patient by the responsible after-care bodies (see below) (s.25B(1) and (3)). The application, which must make clear that the criteria are satisfied, among other things (s.25B(4)), must be accompanied by a written medical recommendation from the doctor who will be professionally concerned with the patient after discharge and a written recommendation from an ASW (s.25B(5)). It must also be accompanied by a statement from the doctor who is to be the community RMO that he or she is to be in charge of the medical treatment provided under s.117, a statement in writing from the person who is to be the patient's supervisor, details of the after-care services and details of any requirements to be imposed (s.25B(8)). The RMO must inform the patient, the consultees and the nearest relative, unless the patient objects, of the making of an application, the after-care services to be provided, any requirements to be imposed, and the names of the community RMO and supervisor (s.25B(9) and (10). For other details relating to the application, see s.25C.

The application is addressed to the health authority with the s.117 duty to the patient (s.25A(6)). Before accepting it, the authority must consult the relevant social services department (s.25A(7)). If the authority accepts the application, it must inform the patient, the people consulted by the RMO and, except where the patient objects, the nearest relative (s.25A(8)).

The responsible after-care bodies (that is those bodies with the duty to provide after-care under s.117) may impose any of the requirements on a patient subject to after-care under supervision (s.25D(1)). The requirements referred to are contained in the following provision:

25D.—(3) . . .

(a) that the patient reside at a specified place;
(b) that the patient attend at specified places and times for the purpose of medical treatment, occupation, education or training; and
(c) that access to the patient be given, at any place where the patient is residing, to the supervisor, any [doctor] or any approved social worker or to any other person authorised by the supervisor.

(4) A patient subject to after-care under supervision may be taken and conveyed by, or by any person authorised by, the supervisor to any place where the patient is required to reside or attend for the purpose of medical treatment, occupation, education or training.

The after-care services and any imposed requirements are to be kept under review and if necessary modified by the responsible after-care bodies (after a consultation process) where the patient refuses or neglects to receive any or all of the after-care services or to comply with any of the imposed requirements (s.25E(1)–(3), (5) and (6)). The amendments can include contemplating terminating the supervision or informing an ASW with a view to the patient being admitted to hospital (s.25E(4)). The patient and others are to be informed of any modifications (s.25E(7)).

After-care under supervision begins on leaving the hospital and ends six months later (s.25G(1)), but it may be renewed for six months and thereafter annually (s.25G(2)). The process for renewal is similar to that for renewal of admission for treatment in demanding a report from the community RMO after a full consultation exercise (s.25G(3)–(10). The conditions which must be satisfied for renewal are set out in s.25G.

25G.—(4) . . .

(a) the patient is suffering from mental disorder, being mental illness, severe mental impairment, psychopathic disorder or mental impairment;

(b) that there would be a substantial risk of serious harm to the health or safety of the patient or the safety of other persons, or of the patient being seriously exploited, if he were not to receive the after-care services to be provided for him under section 117 below after he leaves hospital; and

(c) his being subject to after-care under supervision is likely to help to secure that he or she receives the after-care services to be so provided.

After-care under supervision may be ended by the community RMO, after a consultation exercise, at any time (s.25H(1)–(3)). It is also ended if the patient is admitted to hospital for treatment or for assessment under s.2 (but not s.4) (s.25H(4)). Further, the patient has a right of application to a mental health review tribunal when a supervision application is accepted (the patient must apply within the first six months), when it is renewed (a patient has a right of application in every period of renewal) and if the patient's mental disorder is reclassified under s.25F (the patient must apply within 28 days of the report) (s.66(1), as amended). The nearest relative may also apply. The tribunal has the following power.

72.—(4A) . . . the tribunal may in any case direct that the patient shall cease to be so subject (or not become so subject) and shall so direct if they are satisfied:

(a) in a case where the patient has not yet left hospital, that the conditions set out in section 25A(4) above are not complied with; or

(b) in any other case, that the conditions set out in section 25G(4) above are not complied with.

QUESTION:

1. Do the powers of guardianship and after-care under supervision provide sufficient compulsory powers in the community? In considering this question take account of the following issues.

NOTES:

1. A community treatment order (CTO) involves creating a power whereby those admitted to it may be provided with treatment for their mental disorder whether or not they consent to it. No one in the recent debates appeared to be supporting such a power, although in some minds it would seem that the effect of other proposals might be to produce such a power, either explicitly or implicitly by the control and influence it would exercise over those within its remit.

2. A community supervision order (CSO) is what the Royal College of Psychiatrists turned to in 1993 after the rejection of the earlier proposal for a CTO. The purpose of a CSO is to "allow the compulsory supervision in the community of a patient previously compulsorily detained in hospital to prevent deterioration of his/her condition." To achieve this end, the potential supervisees would be people who have been detained under s.3 or s.37 of the Mental Health Act and "who have a history of frequent relapse

and deterioration of their condition with subsequent compulsory admission as a consequence of failure or refusal to comply with treatment in the community." The supervisee would have to agree to accept treatment and to receive supervision. The application for the order would come from the individual's responsible medical officer and one other doctor, and a report by an ASW would be obtained in support of the application. The application would then be presented to the hospital managers. The order would last initially for six months and could then be renewed annually by the responsible medical officer recommending so to the hospital managers. The sanction which would, it is presumed, ensure that the supervisee complies with the order is recall to hospital. Recall would be possible where "the patient refuses to accept supervision in the community [and as] a consequence of the patient's refusal, deterioration of his condition will not be prevented". Further, the patient "must be suffering from mental illness of a nature or degree such that it is necessary to recall him/her to hospital for treatment to prevent further deterioration of his/her condition". On recall, the supervisee would be regarded as a patient detained under s.3, and her/his case would be referred to a mental health review tribunal within 14 days.

3. Would it be permissible to have a community power which grants others powers of coercion? A community treatment order has been a serious proposal for consideration, and one criticism was the graphic objection to Community Psychiatric Nurses having forcibly to inject patients on their own kitchen tables. At its heart there is a very serious objection here. Can treatment be provided in the community without an individual's consent without seriously breaching privacy and resulting in degrading treatment? Can the treatment be provided without consent but with appropriate safeguards? Where the patient is competent and refusing, there must come a point, if it is not with all treatments, that compulsory treatment should only take place in the privacy of a hospital with all the attendant health care safeguards and where abuses are more easily safeguarded against than in the community.

4. Why do people not follow a treatment/medication regime and so why might a power be necessary? The central issue is the value of medication in curing and/or controlling mental illness. Its value is accepted by many, but even so there are doubts as to its efficacy and predictability. As was frequently pointed out in evidence to the House of Commons Health Select Committee (*Community Supervision Orders* (1993)), some people break down despite taking their medication and some people do not break down despite not taking their medication contrary to professional advice. Psychotropic medication may have severe side effects, some of which may be very long lasting. If an individual does not understand the drug or its effects or feels that information is being withheld, he or she is less likely to be willing to participate in a treatment regime involving the administration of medicine. There has been some success with depot clinics, where people are encouraged to attend for the administration of their medication via long-term methods and whereby they present themselves to a supportive,

information-providing environment. The provision of greater information to patients might well result in greater treatment compliance. Not providing information is counter-productive. Further, it is entirely possible that the mere existence of power makes an individual less interested in engaging with the programme proposed. There is some evidence that the more client-centred direction of the care programme approach, involving negotiation with the patient, is often effective with those people who have not traditionally engaged well with the ordinary services. Granting powers may not help.

5. The evidence available is unclear as to how many people might be subject to an order. Evidence before the Health Select Committee presented estimates which varied from 1,200 to 4,000. Of course, all estimates can only be guesses because saying that you will use a power and actually using it may be two very different things. Exactly what the power would allow and its procedure may affect people's preparedness to be involved, and there was some confusion between prevalence and incidence, i.e. between how many people at any given time might be subject to an order and how many new orders might be imposed. The state of confusion is perhaps not surprising and is not, in itself, a major reason not to introduce a new power.

6. Is it likely to work if anyone could agree to after-care under supervision (or a CSO) just to get out of hospital? It has been cogently suggested that any patient would agree to accept treatment and receive supervision if it meant getting out of hospital. So the essential prerequisite for the new power might well be fallacious.

7. Problems relate to whether a person may get off community-based orders. In hospital cases, a calculated risk may be taken on discharging the individual. It seems quite clear that the risk is likely to be exercised conservatively. This is certainly the outcome of the research into tribunal decision-making by Peay (J. Peay, *Tribunals on Trial*, Oxford: Clarendon Press, 1989). If the individual is living in the community, there is nowhere for him to go but stay where he or she already is. If one of the reasons for the imposition of the order is the "revolving door" syndrome, release becomes almost impossible since the history of the patient is bound to count against him. This is the group likely to be placed under such an order. The failure to impose an overall time limit upon a supervised discharge arrangement compounds the problems for the patient, even if the rationale for it may be compelling. There are, however, powers to terminate after-care under supervision.

8. The Mental Health Bill 2004 did not propose a compulsory treatment in the community order. Any compulsory treatment would have had to have been provided in a hospital. What it did was to allow the question of residency (in hospital or not) to be separated from the question of application of a section to a patient. The 2006 proposal is the introduce supervised community treatment, as explained in the following briefing note issued by the Department of Health on May 2, 2006, which also will not introduce compulsory treatment in the community.

The Mental Health Bill (Plans to amend the Mental Health Act 1983)

SUPERVISED COMMUNITY TREATMENT (SCT)

The Government wants to introduce Supervised Community Treatment (SCT) for patients following a period of detention in hospital. It will mean a small proportion of patients with mental disorder can live in the community under the powers of the Mental Health Act, to ensure they continue with the medical treatment that they need.

Tackling the problem of patients disengaging from services

SCT will address the specific problem where patients—who leave hospital—do not continue with their treatment, their health deteriorates and they require detention again—the so-called "revolving door".

Providing a positive alternative to detention in hospital

Increasingly, treatments for mental disorder can safely be given in the community. For patients who do not need to be detained in hospital, SCT will provide a positive alternative and an opportunity to minimise the disruption to their lives. This will help to reduce the risk of social exclusion that can result from detention under the Act.

How it will work

Not all patients who are detained under the Act will be suitable for SCT. It will benefit primarily those with a chronic mental disorder that has stabilised following treatment in hospital. Only people who would be a risk to their own health or safety or that of others if they did not continue to receive their treatment when discharged from hospital can be considered for SCT.

Decisions as to whether a patient should be subject to SCT will be based on a clinical judgement of the person's condition and circumstances. They will have to meet criteria set out in the Bill which are similar to those for admission for treatment under Section 3 of the Act. The Code of Practice will offer guidance on best practice.

Anyone going on to SCT will have been assessed and treated in hospital first. They must be under Section 3 of the Act or detained under a Part III power without restrictions. A patient's clinical supervisor will decide if, and when, SCT is appropriate. The clinical supervisor must obtain a second opinion from the Approved Mental Health Professional (AMHP) before a patient can be placed on SCT. An appropriate package of treatment and free support services will be put into place by the NHS and local authority social services before a patient leaves hospital on SCT.

There may be requirements on patients in the community to ensure that they stay in contact with mental health services and practitioners can monitor them for signs of deteriorating health, and if necessary decide that they must be recalled to hospital. The clinical supervisor must agree these requirements with the AMHP.

There will be clear criteria as to the circumstances in which people may be recalled to hospital for compulsory treatment. The clinical supervisor must obtain a second opinion from an AMHP in order to redetain a patient. Hospital managers must refer a patient's case to the tribunal if the patient is detained in hospital again for more than 72 hours.

Compulsory treatment

Patients who refuse to consent will not be treated against their will in the community, but may be recalled to hospital for treatment where clinically necessary.

Renewal of SCT and discharge from SCT

Renewal of SCT occurs along the same timeframe as renewal of detention under section 3—that is, after six months from the time a patient leaves hospital, at one year and then at yearly intervals. Renewal is via report to the Hospital managers.

Safeguards for patients

Patients on SCT will receive the same safeguards as patients detained in hospital including Nearest Relative rights. All patients on SCT will also have their treatment (if it involves giving medicines) reviewed and certified by a Second Opinion Doctor (SOAD) after three months.

People on SCT will have their case regularly reviewed in the same way as detained patients, and will be discharged when they no longer meet the criteria.

Access to a Mental Health Review Tribunal

Patients on SCT will have the same access to a tribunal as patients who are detained under section 3. The tribunal will be able to discharge patients from SCT in the same way as it can discharge them from detention in hospital.

NOTE:

1. It is clear that many, though not all, of the Pre-Legislative Scrutiny concerns about the 2004 proposals have been incorporated. So, the power is only available after someone has been in hospital and stabilised there, it will be limited to a clearly defined group of patients and it does not permit compulsory treatment in the community.

QUESTIONS:

1. Does this approach make an improvement on guardianship under the Mental Health Act without falling into the traps identified in relation to community treatment orders?
2. Does supervised community treatment offer much of an improvement over the position under the 1983 Act, where treatment can be provided when someone is on leave of absence and the s.3 can be maintained provided there is some treatment in or at a hospital?

SELECT BIBLIOGRAPHY

E. Baker and J. Crichton, "Ex parte: Psychopathy, Treatability and the Law" (1995) 6 *Journal of Forensic Psychiatry* 101.

P. Bartlett, "English Mental Health Reform: Lessons from Ontario?" (2001) 5 *Journal of Mental Health Law* 27.

P. Bartlett, "The Test of Compulsion in Mental Health Law: Capacity, Therapeutic Benefit and Dangerousness as Possible Criteria" (2003) 11 *Medical Law Review* 326.

P. Bartlett and R. Sandland, *Mental Health Law: Policy and Practice* (2nd edn), Oxford: OUP, 2003.

P. Bean, *Compulsory Admission to Mental Hospitals*, Chichester: Wiley & Sons, 1983.

J. Bellhouse, A. Holland, I.C.H. Clare, M. Gunn and P. Watson, "Capacity-based Mental Health Legislation and its Impact on Clinical Practice: (1) Admission to Hospital" (2003) 9 *Journal of Mental Health Law* 9.

J. Bellhouse, A. Holland, I.C.H. Clare, M. Gunn and P. Watson, "Capacity-based Mental Health Legislation and its Impact on Clinical Practice: (2) Treatment in Hospital" (2003) 9 *Journal of Mental Health Law* 24.

W. Bingley, "The Mental Health Act Commission: an Audit" (1991) 2 *Journal of Forensic Psychiatry* 135.

M. Cavadino, "Commissions and Codes: a Case Study in Law and Public Administration'" [1993] *Public Law* 333.

M. Cavadino, *Mental Health Law in Context: Doctor's Orders*, Aldershot: Gower 1988.

J. Crichton, "The *Bournewood* judgment and Mental Incapacity" (1998) 9 *Journal of Forensic Psychiatry* 513.

L. Davidson, "Human Rights versus Public Protection: English Mental Health Law in Crisis?" (2002) 25 *International Journal of Law and Psychiatry* 491.

J. Dawson, "Necessitous Detention and the Informal Patient" (1999) 115 *Law Quarterly Review* 40.

N. Eastman and J. Peay, *Law without Enforcement: Integrating Mental Health and Justice*, London: Hart Publishing, 1999.

A. Eldergill, "Is Anyone Safe? Civil Compulsion under the Draft Mental Health Bill" (2002) 8 *Journal of Mental Health Law* 331.

A. Eldergill, *Mental Health Review Tribunals: Law and Practice*, London: Sweet & Maxwell, 1998.

Expert Committee Report, *Review of the Mental Health Act 1983*, London: Department of Health, 1999 (Chair: G. Richardson).

P. Fennell, "Balancing Care and Control: Guardianship, Community Treatment Orders and Patient Safeguards" (1992) 15 *International Journal of Law and Psychiatry* 1.

P. Fennell, "Detention and Control of Informal Mentally Disordered Patients" (1984) *Journal of Social Welfare Law* 345.

P. Fennell, "Inscribing Paternalism in the Law: Consent to Treatment and Mental Disorder" (1990) 17 *Journal of Law and Society* 29.

P. Fennell, "Reforming the Mental Health Act 1983: 'Joined Up Compulsion'" (2001) 5 *Journal of Mental Health Law* 5.

P. Fennell, "Sexual Suppressants and the Mental Health Act" [1988] *Criminal Law Review* 660.

P. Fennell, "The Beverley Lewis Case: Was the Law to Blame?" (1989) 139 *New Law Journal* 559.

P. Fennell, *Treatment without Consent*, London: Routledge, 1996.

M. Fisher, "Guardianship under the Mental Health Legislation: a Review" [1988] *Journal of Social Welfare Law* 316.

Nicola Glover-Thomas, *Reconstructing Mental Health Law and Policy*, London: Butterworths, 2002.

L. Gostin, *Mental Health Services: Law and Practice* (looseleaf), London: Shaw & Sons.

L. Gostin, "Psychosurgery: a Hazardous and Unestablished Treatment?" [1982] *Journal of Social Welfare Law* 83.

L. Gostin and P. Fennell, *Mental Health: Tribunal Procedure* (2nd edn), London: Longman, 1992.

M.J. Gunn, "Judicial Review of Hospital Admissions and Treatment in the Community under the Mental Health Act 1983" (1986) *Journal of Social Welfare Law* 290.

M.J. Gunn, "Mental Health Act Guardianship: Where Now?'" (1986) *Journal of Social Welfare Law* 144.

M. Gunn, "Reforms of the Mental Health Act 1983: the Relevance of Capacity to Make Decisions" (2000) 3 *Journal of Mental Health Law* 39.

M. Gunn and T. Holland, "Some Thoughts on the Proposed Mental Health Act" (2002) 8 *Journal of Mental Health Law* 360.

R. Hargreaves, "'A Mere Transporter'—the Legal Role of the Approved Social Worker" (2000) 4 *Journal of Mental Health Law* 135.

D. Hewitt, "Something Less than Ready Access to the Courts: Section 139 & Local Authorities" (2000) 3 *Journal of Mental Health Law* 73.

B.M. Hoggett, *Mental Health Law* (4th edn), London: Sweet & Maxwell, 1996.

R.M. Jones, *Mental Health Act Manual* (8th edn), London: Sweet & Maxwell, 2003.

J.M. Laing, "Rights vs Risk? Reform of the Mental Health Act 1983" (2000) 8 *Medical Law Review* 210.

Mental Health Act Commission, *Biennial Reports*.

MIND and National Council on Civil Liberties, *People with Mental Illness and Learning Disabilities*, London: NCCL, 1993.

J. Peay, *Decisions and Dilemmas: Working with Mental Health Law*, Oxford: Hart Publishing, 2003.

J. Peay, "Reform of the Mental Health Act 1983: Squandering an Opportunity?" (2000) 3 *Journal of Mental Health Law* 5.

J. Peay, *Tribunals on Trial*, Oxford: Clarendon Press, 1989.

D.P.T. Price, "Civil Commitment of the Mentally Ill: Compelling Arguments for Reform" (1994) 2 *Medical Law Review* 321.

H. Prins, "Psychopathic Disorder—Concept or Chimera" (2002) 8 *Journal of Mental Health Law* 243.

G. Richardson, "Autonomy, Guardianship and Mental Disorder: one problem, two solutions" (2002) 65 *Modern Law Review* 702.

G. Richardson, *Law, Process and Custody: Prisoners and Patients*, London: Weidenfield and Nicholson, 1993.

R. Robinson, "ECT and the Human Rights Act 1998" (2003) 9 *Journal of Mental Health Law* 66.

R. Sandland, "Mental Health Act Guardianship and the Protection of Children" (2000) 4 *Journal of Mental Health Law* 186.

P. Walton, "Reforming the Mental Health Act 1983: an ASW perspective" (2000) 22 *Journal of Social Welfare and Family Law* 401

A. Zigmond and A.J. Holland, "Unethical Mental Health Law: History Repeats Itself" (2000) 3 *Journal of Mental Health Law* 49.

9

HEALTH CARE, PRIVACY AND CONFIDENTIALITY

1. INTRODUCTION

The requirement to protect patient confidentiality has long been included in the ethical codes of health care professionals. It has been argued that confidentiality is necessary to ensure that patients are willing to come forward to receive treatment. It is also claimed that confidentiality is part of the patient's right to control access to his own personal information, his right to informational privacy. Gostin defines health information privacy as being "An individual's claim to control the circumstances in which personal health information is collected, used, stored and transmitted". He goes on to define confidentiality as being "A form of health information privacy that focuses upon maintaining trust between two individuals engaged in an intimate relationship, characteristically a physician–patient relationship" (see further L.O. Gostin, *Public Health Law: Power, Duty and Restraint* Los Angeles: University of California Press, 2000 at p.128; see also G. Laurie, *Genetic Privacy* Cambridge: CUP, 2002).

Article 8 of the European Convention of Human Rights provides that:

"1. Everyone has the right to respect for his private and family life his home and correspondence.

2. There shall be no interference by a public authority with the exercise of this right except such as is in accordance with the law and is necessary in a democratic society in the interests of national security, public safety or the economic well being of the country, for the prevention of disorder or crime, for the protection of health or morals, or for the protection of the rights and freedoms of others."

Article 8 has been interpreted by the European Court of Human Rights as affording protection to individual privacy (*Malone v UK* Applications No. 8691/79) (1984) and this has also been extended to cover personal health information e.g. *MS v Sweden* (1997) 45 B.M.L.R. 133 and *Z v Finland* (1997) 25 E.H.R.R. 371). In English law there is no overarching protection given to privacy (*Wainwright v Home Office* [2003] 4 All E.R. 969), but nonetheless as we shall see considerations of Article 8 of the ECHR in relation to informational privacy underpin domestic law protection of the confidentiality of health care information (see *Campbell v MGN* below at p.573).

Today the obligation of a health care professional to maintain patient confidentiality frequently extends beyond his or her ethical codes. The terms and conditions of service of the NHS employee require her to keep patient information confidential. Unauthorised disclosure of confidential information may lead to an action under the equitable remedy of breach of confidence. In addition, certain specific statutory provisions safeguards confidentiality. Alternatively, breach of confidence may lead to the patient bringing a complaint under the NHS complaints procedure.

Protecting patient confidentiality may give rise to some very difficult moral and legal dilemmas. The provision of health care is more complex than it has ever been. The patient who enters hospital is cared for by many different health care practitioners, all with access to his records. The rise in the availability of personal genetic information has led to new challenges. Personal information obtained from DNA sequencing can reveal information not only about an individual but also information relevant to family members. Genetic information may also reveal a pre-disposition to illness in the future which may have implications for insurance and employment. The confidentiality of such information is both crucial and problematic (See further e.g. G. Laurie *Genetic Privacy* Cambridge: CUP, 2000; Human Genetics Commission *Inside Information* London: HGC 2004). In law the protection given to patient information is not absolute. In some situations the health professional may be required to break confidentiality by statute or at common law. In addition there is a grey area relating to information which, while generally protected by the obligation of confidentiality, may be disclosed in certain situations if, for example, it is in the public interest to do so.

While the patient has some means of redress where information is disclosed without his consent, until very recently the patient frequently faced considerable problems in obtaining access to his health care records. The position has gradually changed through the introduction of rights of access to computer records — initially in the Data Protection Act 1984, with statutory rights of access to manual files being granted in the Access to Health Records Act 1990. Today the majority of the principles governing this area are to be found in the Data Protection Act 1998. Nevertheless, these rights of access are not absolute. They can be restricted if, for example, disclosure is not in the patient's best interests because it would cause him significant physical or mental harm.

There is currently no comprehensive specific statutory protection accorded to personal health care information. While, as we noted above, particular statutes operate in certain areas to provide protection to confidential health information, such as the Human Fertilisation and Embryology Act 1990, their scope is limited. In 1981, in its report on *Breach of Confidence*, the Law Commission recommended that the equitable remedy of breach of confidence should be placed on a statutory footing (Law Commission Report No. 110, *Breach of Confidence*, Cmnd. 8388, 1981). At the time of writing, however, there appears no prospect of specific legislation being enacted providing comprehensive regulation of personal health information.

This chapter begins, in Section 2, with a consideration of the scope of confidentiality as highlighted in health care professions' ethical codes. Section 3 examines the obligation of confidentiality as it arises in the employment context. In Section 4 deals with the legal obligation of confidentiality at common law and discusses remedies for breach of confidence. Section 5 provides an examination of protection to patient confidentiality accorded by statute, while in Section 6 those situations in which statute requires that confidence be broken are explored. Section 7 considers disclosure of information and legal proceedings. Section 8 discusses patients' access to records.

2. The Obligation of Confidentiality and Professional Ethical Codes

All health professions include in their professional codes a requirement to preserve the confidentiality of health information. Below we provide some examples.

General Medical Council: Confidentiality, Protecting and Providing Information London: GMC (2004)

Principles

1. Patients have a right to expect that information about them will be held in confidence by their doctors. Confidentiality is central to trust between doctors and patients. Without assurances about confidentiality, patients may be reluctant to give doctors the information they need in order to provide good care. If you are asked to provide information about patients you must:

- inform patients about the disclosure, or check that they have already received information about it;
- anonymise data where unidentifiable data will serve the purpose;
- be satisfied that patients know about disclosures necessary to provide their care, or for local clinical audit of that care, that they can object to these disclosures but have not done so;
- seek patients' express consent to disclosure of information, where identifiable data is needed for any purpose other than the provision of care or for clinical audit—save in the exceptional circumstances described in this booklet;
- keep disclosures to the minimum necessary; and
- keep up to date with and observe the requirements of statute and common law, including data protection legislation.
-

2. You must always be prepared to justify your decisions in accordance with this guidance . . .

Protecting information

4. When you are responsible for personal information about patients you must make sure that it is effectively protected against improper disclosure at all times.

5. Many improper disclosures are unintentional. You should not discuss patients where you can be overheard or leave patients' records, either on paper or on screen, where they can be seen by other patients, unauthorised health care staff or the public. You should take all reasonable steps to ensure that your consultations with patients are private.

NOTES:

1. The courts have referred to the GMC guidelines when considering the scope of breach of confidence (see below *X v Y* at p.598, *W v Edgell* at p.607).
2. Breach of confidence may lead to disciplinary proceedings (see further Chapter 4 above).
3. For further discussion regarding HIV/AIDS see below at p.619.

A corresponding duty to maintain patient confidentiality is imposed upon members of the nursing profession.

Nursing and Midwifery Council: code of professional conduct; standards for performance, and ethics (2004)

5 As a registered nurse, midwife or specialist community public health nurse, you must protect confidential information.

5.1 You must treat information about patients and clients as confidential and use it only for the purposes for which it was given. As it is impractical to obtain consent every time you need to share information with others, you should ensure that patients and clients understand that some information may be made available to other members of the team involved in the delivery of care. You must guard against breaches of confidentiality by protecting information from improper disclosure at all times.

5.2 You should seek patients' and clients' wishes regarding the sharing of information with their family and others. When a patient or client is considered incapable of giving permission, you should consult relevant colleagues.

5.3 If you are required to disclose information outside the team that will have personal consequences for patients or clients, you must obtain their consent. If the patient or client withholds consent, or if consent cannot be obtained for whatever reason, disclosures may be made only where:

- they can be justified in the public interest (usually where disclosure is essential to protect the patient or client or someone else from the risk of significant harm)
- they are required by law or by order of a court.

5.4 Where there is an issue of child protection, you must act at all times in accordance with national and local policies.

NOTE:

1. Much of the debate in relation to the nurse's obligation of confidentiality in recent years has arisen in the context of the debate concerning "whistleblowing". (See below at pp.568–571.)

3. CONFIDENTIALITY IN THE CONTRACT OF EMPLOYMENT

As noted above, health care professionals employed by the NHS are required by their contract of employment to maintain confidentiality. In some situations this may conflict with other obligations contained in the health care professional's ethical code of conduct. This problem is graphically illustrated by the case of the "whistleblower" Grahame Pink. Pink was employed as a night duty charge nurse on a ward for acutely ill patients. Having observed what he believed was an unacceptable reduction in standards of patient care, and having, in his opinion, received no satisfactory response to his expressed concerns he decided to "go public". He gave an interview to a local paper, which was subsequently reprinted in *The Guardian*. He was accused of breaching patient confidentiality. Relatives of the patients claimed they could recognise their relatives from the descriptions in the paper. Pink was eventually dismissed. He challenged his dismissal at an industrial tribunal He claimed that his disclosure was justified under Article 10 of the UKCC code (now known as the NMC Code) because he was under a duty to bring to the attention of the appropriate authorities information which showed that standards of patient care had fallen. There is no special protection provided in employment law for a "whistleblowing employee". While an employee may assert before an industrial tribunal that his conduct was in the public interest, that does not by itself give rise to a claim for unfair dismissal. Mr Pink's case was settled out of court. Even if Mr Pink had won after a full hearing, any decision of such a tribunal would not set a precedent for subsequent cases. (See J.V. McHale, "Whistleblowing in the NHS" (1992) 5 *Journal of Social Welfare Law* 363). Reinstatement is also very unlikely.

The response of the Department of Health to the Pink case was to publish the *Guidance for Staff on Relations With the Public and Media* (DOH 1993). The guidance stated that health authorities should establish both formal and informal complaints systems for staff. They require that the complaints should be made internally, either through the existing management structure or to a complaints officer who would be the person appointed to receive patient complaints under the Hospital Complaints Act 1985. (See Chapter 4 above.) The guidance was the subject of considerable criticism (see J.V. McHale "Two Initiatives for Reform" in G. Hunt (ed.), *Whistleblowing in the Health Services*, London: Edward Arnold, 1994). There is no provision for external appeal. While the guidance notes that staff may consult external bodies such as the Mental Health Act Commission or the Health Service Commissioner, it emphasises the obligation of confidentiality and the fact that a member of staff who "goes public" risks disciplinary proceedings. There is no attempt to address the role of the nurse as advocate for her patient, nor the conflict which may face a health professional between his or her ethical code and contract of employment.

In 1992 Derek Fatchett M.P. published a NHS Freedom of Speech Bill which attempted to introduce a general ethical code for all health care employees—a "Charter of Values". Clause 8 provided that there should be:

"a duty and a right to report to any competent person any instruction, policy or practice which they would believe would result in inadequate or unsafe conditions which are likely to either harm the health and safety or well being of patients/clients or colleagues or be contrary to law or be to the detriment of the health service and public confidence in its operation."

The Bill also recommended that staff complaint procedures should be established, but it went beyond the Government proposals by providing for an external right of appeal. However, it left open what form the appellate body should take. The Bill failed to obtain parliamentary time. An attempt was made in 1995 to introduce a Whistleblower Protection Bill, which applied generally to whistleblowers rather than exclusively within the NHS. The Bill was drafted by Maurice

Frankel of the Freedom of Information campaign. In 1995 a charity—Public Concern at Work, was established with funding from the Joseph Rowntree foundation, to provide support for whistleblowers, including those within the health care professions.

In the years that followed the controversy over whistleblowing continued. Particularly notable was the case of Stephen Boisin, an anaesthetist, who blew the whistle over the cardiac paediatric unit at Bristol Royal Infirmary (see further Chapters 1 and 4 above and R. Klein "Competence, Professional Self-Regulation and the Public Interest "(1998) 316 British Medical Journal 1740). The unwillingness to blow the whistle as was illustrated in the inquiry into Rodney Ledward (see further *An Inquiry into Quality and Practice within the National Health Service arising from the actions of Rodney Ledward"*, London: Department of Health, 2000 at p.16).

Today this area is regulated by the Public Interest Disclosure Act 1998 (see generally J. Gobert and M. Punch, "Whistleblowers, the Public Interest and the Public Interest Disclosure Act 1998" (2000) 63 *Modern Law Review* 25: L. Vickers, "Whistling in the Wind? The Public Interest Disclosure Act 1998" (2000) 20 *Legal Studies* 428). This provides safeguards for workers who make what is known as a "protected disclosure" under the Act (Employment Rights Act 1996, s.43B). Those disclosures which are protected are those which relate to actual or apprehended breaches of law and dangers to health, safety and the environment.

The Act extends to cover "workers" who are both employees and also those consultants who provide services outside a professional–client relationship (Employment Rights Act 1996, s.43K) and this specifically includes those persons providing medical, dental, ophthalmic and pharmaceutical services under NHS provision. The legislation provides that a worker must have a "reasonable belief" that this is a protected disclosure (Employment Rights Act 1996, s.43(B)(1)). In addition, it is provided that a disclosure will be protected where it is in good faith, made to the employer or to a person other than the employer if it concerns that person or if it concerns something for which that person has legal responsibility. Furthermore it is provided that workers may disclose to bodies which are included in a list issued under regulations made under the Act by the Secretary of State. Interestingly, the GMC nor the Nursing and Midwifery Council are included as "prescribed bodies" under the legislation (a point noted by J. Burrows in "Telling Tales and Saving Lives: Whistleblowing—the Role of Professional Colleagues" (2001) 9 *Medical Law Review* 100 at p.114).

In addition the Public Interest Disclosure Act 1998 makes provision for a secondary category of disclosures and it is within this category which those disclosures which were made to the media are most likely to fall. The Act in s.43G also provides protection where disclosure has been made in good faith, the worker reasonably believes that the information disclosed and any information contained in it are substantially true, the disclosure is not made for any personal gain and that in all the circumstances of the case it is reasonable for him to make the disclosure. In addition the criteria in s.43G(2) must be complied with. These are that the worker reasonably believes that the employer will subject him to a detriment if he makes the disclosure to his employer in accordance with section 43F, that he reasonably believes the evidence will be lost or destroyed if he makes a disclosure to the employer or where there is no person who is prescribed under s.43F to whom the worker could disclose in relation to this particular failure. Factors to be taken into account when determining reasonableness of disclosure include the identity of the person, how serious is the failure and whether this is on going or is likely to re occur in the future and whether the disclosure itself has been made in breach of an obligation of confidentiality which is owed to the employer or another person.

A specific provision s.43H concerns disclosures which are of an exceptionally serious nature. It protects disclosures where they are made in good faith, where the worker reasonably believes that the information disclosed and any allegations contained in it are substantially true. In addition the disclosure must not be made for personal gain and it must be reasonable for the worker to make the disclosure in all the circumstances of the case. It is provided that in determining what constitutes "reasonableness" under this section, regard shall be had to the identity of the person to whom the disclosure is made (Employment Rights Act 1996, s.42H(2)).

The legislation provides that if a worker is dismissed for making what is a protected disclosure this will fall within the category of unfair dismissal (Employment Rights Act 1996, s.103). Further protection extends where the employee is victimised on the grounds that a protected disclosure was made (Employment Rights Act 1996, s.47B). Victimisation in this context will arise where an employer subjects the employee to a detriment (Employment Rights Act 1996, s.48(2)). Although the legislation can be seen as a safeguard and there is no upper limit on the award of compensation under the Act, nonetheless there are in such cases very limited prospects for the reinstatement of the employee.

Interestingly, the Public Interest Disclosure Act 1998 targets the so-called "gagging clauses" which caused controversy in the NHS. Section 43J of the Employment Rights Act 1998 now provides that such clauses cannot stop a worker from making what is a protected disclosure. Specific NHS guidance "Whistleblowing in the NHS", HSC 1999/198, now provides that NHS trusts and health authorities are to have policies in place to ensure compliance with the legislation.

QUESTION:

1. To what extent should a health care professional have a "political speech" right to disclose confidential information regarding poor NHS care standards in the public interest? (See further L. Vickers, "Holding the Chancellor to Account: Political Speech and Medical Staff" (2003) 25(2) *Journal of Social Welfare and Family Law* 151).

4. NON-STATUTORY PROTECTION IN LAW FOR CONFIDENTIAL INFORMATION: BREACH OF CONFIDENCE

(a) Basis for the Action

English law provides protection for confidential information through the equitable remedy of breach of confidence. The basis in law for restraint of disclosure of confidential information is usually that of the equitable remedy of breach of confidence. The grounds on which an action for breach of confidence may be brought are were stated in *A.-G. v. Guardian Newspapers (No. 2)* [1988] 3 All E.R. 545 at 658, [1990] 1 A.C. 109:

LORD GOFF

" . . . a duty of confidence arises where confidential information comes to the knowledge of a person (the confidant) in circumstances where he has notice, or is held to have agreed, that the information is confidential with the effect that it would be just in all the circumstances that he should be precluded from disclosing the information to others. I have used the word 'notice' advisedly in order to avoid the . . . question of the extent to which actual notice is necessary, though I of course understand knowledge to include circumstances in which the confidant has deliberately closed his eyes to the obvious. The existence of this broad general principle reflects the fact that there is such a public interest in the maintenance of confidentiality that the law will provide remedies for this protection.

I realise that, in the vast majority of cases, in particular those concerned with trade secrets, the duty of confidence will arise from a transaction or relationship between the parties, often a contract, in which event the duty may arise by reason of an express or implied term of that contract. It is in such cases as these the expression 'confider' and 'confidant' are perhaps most aptly employed. But it is well settled that a duty of confidence may exist in equity independently of such cases . . . "

NOTES:

1. Today it is generally recognised that the doctor–patient relationship is one of the category of relationships protected by the equitable remedy of breach of confidence. It appears virtually certain that the courts would extend this protection to other health care relationships such as, for example, nurse–patient.

2. Alternative grounds for legal proceedings do exist. Actions may be brought in contract and in negligence. Negligence was held in a New Zealand case to be the basis on which an obligation of confidentiality arose (*Furniss v Fitchett* [1958] N.Z.L.R. 396). There is no clear authority on this point in England and Wales in the medical context, although the potential for such an action can be seen by analogy to an action for negligent breach of disclosure of a police informers identity in *Swinnery v. Chief Constable of the Northumbria Police, The Times*, May 25, 1999. Here the principle of such an action was recognised although on its facts the case failed. (See further A. Laing and A. Grubb, "Confidentiality and Data Protection" in A. Grubb (ed.), *Principles of Medical Law* (2nd edn), Oxford: OUP, 2003, paras 9.98–9.98.) The action in contract, as we shall see below in the context of the child patient, may prove to be practically of some considerable importance.

3. The obligation of confidence is owed to the patient but it may also be the case that an obligation of confidentiality may also be owed to the hospital in relation to the patient's medical records; see further *Ashworth HA v Mirror Group Newspapers Ltd* [2001] 1 All E.R. 991, CA; [2002] UKHL 29, HL. See also *Merseycare NHS Trust v Ackroyd* [2003] EWCA Civ 663.

4. Difficulties may also arise in the context of the prisoner patient. While doctors are responsible for maintaining confidentiality, there has in the

past been erosion of confidentiality, particularly in relation to prisoners diagnosed as HIV positive. These prisoners were kept segregated from other prisoners under what are known as Viral Infectivity restrictions, thus effectively eliminating much of the confidentiality of their condition, (see J. McHale and A. Young, "Policy, Rights and the HIV Positive Prisoner" in S. McVeigh and S. Wheelar (eds), *Law, Health and Medical Regulation*, Aldershot: Dartmouth, 1993).

5. Where the obligation of confidentiality arises other than from contract, does a patient have to establish that some detriment has been suffered? There was disagreement on this point in the House of Lords in *A-G v Guardian Newspapers*. In the later case of *X v Y* [1988] 2 All E.R. 648 (see below at p.598) Rose J. seemed to recognise that this was not a requirement before an injunction was obtained.

(b) The Relationship between Confidentiality and Privacy

The relationship between confidentiality and privacy was explored further in the House of Lords in *Campbell v MGN* in 2004.

Campbell v MGN Ltd [2004] 2 A.C. 457, HL

The case concerned the model Naomi Campbell who brought an action for damages regarding the publication of an article in the *Daily Mirror* which stated that she had been receiving treatment for drug addiction. Campbell claimed that although there was justification in publication of information which corrected statements which she had made in public about her drug addiction that were false, publication of an article which detailed information regarding her treatment for drug addiction and contained an additional photograph constituted an invasion of privacy. The case was not a health professional–patient breach of confidence case, but it does have important implications for the relationship between confidentiality and privacy.

LORD HOPE OF CRAIGHEAD

"81 Paradoxically, for someone in Miss Campbell's position, there are few areas of the life of an individual that are more in need of protection on the grounds of privacy than the combating of addiction to drugs or to alcohol. It is hard to break the habit which has led to the addiction. It is all too easy to give up the struggle if efforts to do so are exposed to public scrutiny. The struggle, after all, is an intensely personal one. It involves a high degree of commitment and of self-criticism. The sense of shame that comes with it is one of the most powerful of all the tools that are used to break the habit. But shame increases the individual's vulnerability as the barriers that the habit has engendered are broken down. The smallest hint that the process is being watched by the public may be enough to persuade the individual to delay or curtail the treatment. At the least it is likely to cause distress, even to those who in other circumstances like to court publicity and regard publicity as a benefit.

82 The question in this case is whether the publicity which the respondents gave to Miss Campbell's drug addiction and to the therapy which she was receiving for it in an article which was published in the 'Mirror' newspaper on 1 February 2001 is actionable on the ground of breach of confidence. Miss Campbell cannot complain about the fact that publicity was given in this article to the fact that she was a drug addict. This was a matter of legitimate public comment, as she had not only lied about her addiction but had sought to benefit from this by comparing herself with others in the fashion business who were

addicted. As the Court of Appeal observed [2003] QB 633, 658, para 43, where a public figure chooses to make untrue pronouncements abut his or her private life, the press will normally be entitled to put the record straight.

83 Miss Campbell's case is that information about the details of the treatment which she was receiving for the addiction falls to be treated differently. This is because it was not the subject of any falsehood that was in need of correction and because it was information which any reasonable person who came into possession of it would realise was obtained in confidence. The argument was put succinctly in the particulars of her claim, where it was stated:

> 'Information about whether a person is receiving medical or similar treatment for addiction, and in particular details relating to such treatment or the person's reaction to it, is obviously confidential. The confidentiality is the stronger where, as here, disclosure would tend to disrupt the treatment and/or its benefits for the person concerned and others sharing in, or giving, or wishing to take or participate in, the treatment. The very name "Narcotics Anonymous" underlines the importance of privacy in the context of treatment as do the defendants' own words — "To the rest of the group she is simply Naomi, the addict." '

84 The respondents' answer is based on the proposition that the information that was published about her treatment was peripheral and not sufficiently significant to amount to a breach of the duty of confidence that was owed to her. They also maintain that the right balance was struck between Miss Campbell's right to respect for her private life under article 8(1) of the European Convention for the Protection of Human Rights and Fundamental Freedoms (1953) (Cmd 8969) and the right to freedom of expression that is enshrined in article 10(1) of the Convention.

85 The questions that I have just described seem to me to be essentially questions of fact and degree and not to raise any new issues of principle. As Lord Woolf CJ said in *A v B plc* [2003] QB 195, 207, paras 11(ix) and (x), the need for the existence of a confidential relationship should not give rise to problems as to the law because a duty of confidence will arise whenever the party subject to the duty is in a situation where he knows or ought to know that the other person can reasonably expect his privacy to be protected. The difficulty will be as to the relevant facts, bearing in mind that, if there is an intrusion in a situation where a person can reasonably expect his privacy to be respected, that intrusion will be capable of giving rise to liability unless the intrusion can be justified: see also the exposition in *Attorney General v Guardian Newspapers Ltd (No 2)* [1990] 1 AC 109, 282 by Lord Goff of Chieveley, where he set out the three limiting principles to the broad general principle that a duty of confidence arises when confidential information comes to the knowledge of a person where he has notice that the information is confidential. The third limiting principle is particularly relevant in this case. This is the principle which may require a court to carry out a balancing operation, weighing the public interest in maintaining confidence against a countervailing public interest favouring disclosure.

86 The language has changed following the coming into operation of the Human Rights Act 1998 and the incorporation into domestic law of article 8 and article 10 of the Convention. We now talk about the right to respect for private life and the countervailing right to freedom of expression. The jurisprudence of the European Court offers important guidance as to how these competing rights ought to be approached and analysed. I doubt whether the result is that the centre of gravity, as my noble and learned friend, Lord Hoffmann, says, has shifted. It seems to me that the balancing exercise to which that guidance is directed is essentially the same exercise, although it is plainly now more carefully focussed and more penetrating. As Lord Woolf CJ said in *A v B plc* [2003] QB 195, 202, para 4, new breadth and strength is given to the action for breach of confidence by these articles.

87 Where a case has gone to trial it would normally be right to attach a great deal of weight to the views which the judge has formed about the facts and where he thought the balance should be struck after reading and hearing the evidence. The fact that the Court

of Appeal felt able to differ from the conclusions which Morland J reached on these issues brings me to the first point on which I wish to comment.

Was the information confidential?

88 The information contained in the article consisted of the following five elements: (1) the fact that Miss Campbell was a drug addict; (2) the fact that she was receiving treatment for her addiction; (3) the fact that the treatment which she was receiving was provided by Narcotics Anonymous; (4) details of the treatment—for how long, how frequently and at what times of day she had been receiving it, the nature of it and extent of her commitment to the process; and (5) a visual portrayal by means of photographs of her when she was leaving the place where treatment had been taking place.

89 The trial judge drew the line between the first two and the last three elements. Mr Caldecott for Miss Campbell said that he was content with this distinction. So the fact that she was a drug addict was open to public comment in view of her denials, although he maintained that this would normally be treated as a medical condition that was entitled to protection. He accepted that the fact that she was receiving treatment for the condition was not in itself intrusive in this context. Moreover disclosure of this fact in itself could not harm her therapy. But he said that the line was crossed as soon as details of the nature and frequency of the treatment were given, especially when these details were accompanied by a covertly taken photograph which showed her leaving one of the places where she had been undertaking it. This was an area of privacy where she was entitled to be protected by an obligation of confidence.

90 Court of Appeal recognised at the start of their discussion of this point that some categories of information are well recognised as confidential: [2003] QB 633, 659, para 47. They noted that these include details of a medical condition or its treatment. But they were not prepared to accept that information that Miss Campbell was receiving therapy from Narcotics Anonymous was to be equated with disclosure of clinical details of the treatment of a medical condition: para 48. This was contrary to the view which Morland J appears to have taken when he said, at para 40, that it mattered not whether therapy was obtained by means of professional medical input or by alternative means such as group counselling or by organised meetings between sufferers. The Court of Appeal were also of the view that the publication of this information was not, in its context, sufficiently significant to shock the conscience and thus to amount to a breach of the duty of confidence which was owed to her. They accepted the respondents' argument that disclosure of these details was peripheral. They had regard too to the fact that some of the additional information that was given in the article was inaccurate.

91 I do not think that the Court of Appeal were right to reject the analogy which the judge drew between information that Miss Campbell was receiving therapy from Narcotics Anonymous and information about details of a medical condition or its treatment. Mr Brown for the respondents said that it was not his case that there was an essential difference or, as he put it, a bright line distinction between therapy and medical treatment. He maintained that the Court of Appeal were simply drawing attention to a difference of degree. But it seems to me that there is more in this passage in the Court of Appeal's judgment and its criticism of the judge's analogy than a difference of degree. The implication of the Court of Appeal's criticism of the judge's reasoning is that the details of non-medical therapy are less deserving of protection than the details of a medical condition or its treatment. That seems to be why, as they put it, in para 48, the two 'are not to be equated.'

92 The underlying question in all cases where it is alleged that there has been a breach of the duty of confidence is whether the information that was disclosed was private and not public. There must be some interest of a private nature that the claimant wishes to protect: *A v B plc* [2003] QB 195, 206, para 11(vii). In some cases, as the Court of Appeal said in that case, the answer to the question whether the information is public or private will be obvious. Where it is not, the broad test is whether disclosure of the information about the

individual ('A') would give substantial offence to A, assuming that A was placed in similar circumstances and was a person of ordinary sensibilities.

93 The trial judge applied the test which was suggested by Gleeson CJ in *Australian Broadcasting Corpn v Lenah Game Meats Pty Ltd* (2001) 208 CLR 199. In that case the respondent sought an interlocutory injunction against the broadcasting of a film about its operations at a bush tail possum processing facility. It showed the stunning and killing of possums. Gleeson CJ said, at p 204, paras 34–35, that information about the respondent's slaughtering methods was not confidential in its nature and that, while the activities filmed were carried out on private property, they were not shown, or alleged, to be private in any other sense. He observed, at p 226, para 42, that there was a large area in between what was necessarily public and what was necessarily private:

'An activity is not private simply because it is not done in public. It does not suffice to make an act private that, because it occurs on private property, it has such measure of protection from the public gaze as the characteristics of the property, the nature of the activity, the locality, and the disposition of the property owner combine to afford. Certain kinds of information about a person, such as information relating to health, personal relationships, or finances, may be easy to identify as private; as may certain kinds of activity, which a reasonable person, applying contemporary standards of morals and behaviour, would understand to be meant to be unobserved. The requirement that disclosure or observation of information or conduct would be highly offensive to a reasonable person of ordinary sensibilities is in many circumstances a useful practical test of what is private.'

Applying to the facts of the case the test which he had described in the last sentence of this paragraph, he said in para 43 that the problem for the respondent was that the activities secretly observed and filmed were not relevantly private.

94 The test which Gleeson CJ has identified is useful in cases where there is room for doubt, especially where the information relates to an activity or course of conduct such as the slaughtering methods that were in issue in that case. But it is important not to lose sight of the remarks which preceded it. The test is not needed where the information can easily be identified as private. It is also important to bear in mind its source, and the guidance which the source offers as to whether the information is public or private. It is taken from the definition of the privacy tort in the United States, where the right of privacy is invaded if the matter which is publicised is of a kind that (a) would be highly offensive to a reasonable person, and (b) is not of legitimate concern to the public: American Law Institute, Restatement of the Law, Torts, 2d (1977), section 625D. The reference to a person of ordinary sensibilities is, as Gleeson CJ acknowledged in his footnote on p 226, a quotation from William L Prosser, 'Privacy' (1960) 48 *California Law Review* 383. As Dean Prosser put it, at pp 396–397, the matter made public must be one which would be offensive and objectionable to a reasonable man of ordinary sensibilities, who must expect some reporting of his daily activities. The law of privacy is not intended for the protection of the unduly sensitive.

95 I think that the judge was right to regard the details of Miss Campbell's attendance at Narcotics Anonymous as private information which imported a duty of confidence. He said that information relating to Miss Campbell's therapy for drug addiction giving details that it was by regular attendance at Narcotics Anonymous meetings was easily identifiable as private. With reference to the guidance that the Court of Appeal gave in *A v B plc* [2003] QB 195, 206, para 11(vii), he said that it was obvious that there existed a private interest in this fact that was worthy of protection. The Court of Appeal, on the other hand, seem to have regarded the receipt of therapy from Narcotics Anonymous as less worthy of protection in comparison with treatment for the condition administered by medical practitioners. I would not make that distinction. Views may differ as to what is the best treatment for an addiction. But it is well known that persons who are addicted to the taking of illegal drugs or to alcohol can benefit from meetings at which they discuss and face up to their addiction. The private nature of these meetings encourages addicts to

attend them in the belief that they can do so anonymously. The assurance of privacy is an essential part of the exercise. The therapy is at risk of being damaged if the duty of confidence which the participants owe to each other is breached by making details of the therapy, such as where, when and how often it is being undertaken, public. I would hold that these details are obviously private.

96 If the information is obviously private, the situation will be one where the person to whom it relates can reasonably expect his privacy to be respected. So there is normally no need to go on and ask whether it would be highly offensive for it to be published. The trial judge nevertheless asked himself, as a check, whether the information that was disclosed about Miss Campbell's attendance at these meetings satisfied Gleeson CJ's test of confidentiality. His conclusion, echoing the words of Gleeson CJ, was that disclosure that her therapy for drug addiction was by regular attendance at meetings of Narcotics Anonymous would be highly offensive to a reasonable person of ordinary sensibilities. The Court of Appeal disagreed with this assessment. In para 53 they said that, given that it was legitimate for the respondents to publish the fact that Miss Campbell was a drug addict and that she was receiving treatment, it was not particularly significant to add the fact that the treatment consisted of attendance at meetings of Narcotics Anonymous. In para 54 they said that they did not consider that a reasonable person of ordinary sensibilities, on reading that Miss Campbell was a drug addict, would have found it highly offensive, or even offensive. They acknowledged that the reader might have found it offensive that what were obviously covert photographs had been taken of her, but that this of itself was not relied upon as a ground for legal complaint. Having drawn these conclusions they held, in para 58, that the publication of the information of which Miss Campbell complains was not, in its context, sufficiently significant to amount to a breach of duty of confidence owed to her.

97 This part of the Court of Appeal's examination of the issue appears to have been influenced by the fact that they did not regard disclosure of the fact that Miss Campbell was receiving therapy from Narcotics Anonymous capable of being equated with treatment of a clinical nature. If one starts from the position that a course of therapy which takes this form is of a lower order, it is relatively easy to conclude that a reasonable person of ordinary sensibilities would not regard the publication of the further details of her therapy as particularly significant. But I think that it is unrealistic to look through the eyes of a reasonable person of ordinary sensibilities at the degree of confidentiality that is to be attached to a therapy for drug addiction without relating this objective test to the particular circumstances.

98 Where the person is suffering from a condition that is in need of treatment one has to try, in order to assess whether the disclosure would be objectionable, to put oneself into the shoes of a reasonable person who is in need of that treatment. Otherwise the exercise is divorced from its context. The fact that no objection could be taken to disclosure of the first two elements in the article does not mean that they must be left out of account in a consideration as to whether disclosure of the other elements was objectionable. The article must be read as a whole along with the photographs to give a proper perspective to each element. The context was that of a drug addict who was receiving treatment. It is her sensibilities that needed to be taken into account. Critical to this exercise was an assessment of whether disclosure of the details would be liable to disrupt her treatment. It does not require much imagination to appreciate the sense of unease that disclosure of these details would be liable to engender, especially when they were accompanied by a covertly taken photograph. The message that it conveyed was that somebody, somewhere, was following her, was well aware of what was going on and was prepared to disclose the facts to the media. I would expect a drug addict who was trying to benefit from meetings to discuss her problem anonymously with other addicts to find this distressing and highly offensive.

99 The approach which the Court of Appeal took to this issue seems to me, with great respect, to be quite unreal. I do not think that they had a sound basis for differing from the conclusion reached by the trial judge as to whether the information was private. They were also in error, in my opinion, when they were asking themselves whether the disclosure

would have offended the reasonable man of ordinary susceptibilities. The mind that they examined was the mind of the reader: para 54. This is wrong. It greatly reduces the level of protection that is afforded to the right of privacy. The mind that has to be examined is that, not of the reader in general, but of the person who is affected by the publicity. The question is what a reasonable person of ordinary sensibilities would feel if she was placed in the same position as the claimant and faced with the same publicity.

100 In *P v D* [2000] 2 NZLR 591 the claimant was a public figure who was told that publicity was about to be given to that fact that he had been treated at a psychiatric hospital. In my opinion the objective test was correctly described and applied by Nicholson J, at p 601, para 39, when he said:

'The factor that the matter must be one which would be highly offensive and objectionable to a reasonable person of ordinary sensibilities prescribes an objective test. But this is on the basis of what a reasonable person of ordinary sensibilities would feel if they were in the same position, that is, in the context of the particular circumstances. I accept that P has the stated feelings and consider that a reasonable person of ordinary sensibilities would in the circumstances also find publication of information that they had been a patient in a psychiatric hospital highly offensive and objectionable.'

That this is the correct approach is confirmed by the Restatement, p 387, which states at the end of its comment on clause (a) of section 652D: 'It is only when the publicity given to him is such that a reasonable person would feel justified in feeling seriously aggrieved by it, that the cause of action arises.'

101 These errors have an important bearing on the question whether the Court of Appeal were right to differ from the decision of the trial judge on the question where the balance lay between the private interest of Miss Campbell and the public interest in the publication of these details.

102 In view of the conclusion that I have reached on this issue it is not necessary for me to say anything about the weight that the Court of Appeal attached to the inaccuracies, except to observe that there is a vital difference between inaccuracies that deprive the information of its intrusive quality and inaccuracies that do not. The inaccuracies that were relied on here fall into the later category. The length of time that Miss Campbell had been attending meetings was understated, while the frequency of her attendance at meetings was exaggerated. And the caption to the photograph in the first article stated that she was arriving at the meeting, when the fact was that she was leaving it. These were errors of a minor nature only, which did not affect the overall significance of the details that were published. I would hold that they did not detract from the private nature of what was being published.

. . .

125 Despite the weight that must be given to the right to freedom of expression that the press needs if it is to play its role effectively, I would hold that there was here an infringement of Miss Campbell's right to privacy that cannot be justified. In my opinion publication of the third, fourth and fifth elements in the article (see para 88) was an invasion of that right for which she is entitled to damages. I would allow the appeal and restore the orders that were made by the trial judge."

NOTES:

1. Lord Carswell and Baroness Hale agreed with Lord Hope. Lord Hoffmann agreed with Lord Nicholls' dissenting judgment.
2. In his dissenting judgment Lord Nicholls rejected the approach of breach of confidence rather instead taking a privacy approach. In contrast the judgments of the majority are rooted in confidentiality. Three tests are discernable from their Lordships' judgments. First, the "reasonable expectation" test, secondly, the test as to whether it is "highly offensive to a

reasonable person of ordinary sensibilities test" and thirdly, the "obviously private" test.

3. It has been commented that the implication of this case is that it removes the need to necessarily show a confidential relationship when in formulating an action for breach of confidence (see further S. Pattinson, *Health Care Law*, London: Thomson, 2006 at p.178). Thus private information may be seen as confidential information.

QUESTION:

1. Will the application of human rights analysis make a substantial difference to determining breach of confidence cases in relation to health care in the future? See Lord Hope above and also note *Z v Finland* (1998) 25 E.H.R.R. 371 and *MS v Sweden* (1999) 28 E.H.R.R. 313 and see further Pattinson, *op. cit.* in note 3 at pp.178–179.

(c) Confidentiality and Anonymised Information

While English law is concerned to safeguard the confidentiality of personal information, what is the position if the information while disclosed is anonymised? Does that mean that disclosure of the personal information in question would not give rise to any breach of confidence? This is the issue which arose in the following case.

R v Department of Health, Ex p. Source Informatics [2001] Q.B. 424, 438–439, CA

The case concerned disclosure of anonymised data concerning G.P.s' prescribing habits to a firm who wanted the information to sell to pharmaceutical companies. The issue was as to whether such disclosure would constitute a breach of confidentiality.

SIMON BROWN L.J.
"31 To my mind the one clear and consistent theme emerging from all these authorities is this: the confidant is placed under a duty of good faith to the confider and the touchstone by which to judge the scope of his duty and whether or not it has been fulfilled or breached is his own conscience, no more and no less. One asks, therefore, on the facts of this case: would a reasonable pharmacist's conscience be troubled by the proposed use to be made of patients' prescriptions? Would he think that by entering Source's scheme he was breaking his customers' confidence, making unconscientious use of the information they provide?

32 In contending for the answer 'Yes', Mr Sales urges in particular these considerations. The patient's sole purpose in handing over the prescription is so that the pharmacist may dispense the drugs prescribed. That, therefore, is the only use of it that is authorised. By anonymising the information the pharmacist does not cease to be under a duty of confidence with regard to it. Indeed the very act of anonymisation involves 'manipulation' of the information and is itself objectionable. The only reason the pharmacist has something to sell is because the patient has handed over his prescription. Even when it is anonymised, it is still not in the public domain. To sell any part of it is to misuse it.

33 For my part I find these arguments not merely unconvincing but wholly unreal. True it is that even when stripped of anything capable of identifying the patient, the information which the pharmacist proposes to sell to Source is still not in 'the public domain'. But whether or not that matters must surely depend upon the interest at stake. I referred earlier to the different classes of information identified by Dr Gurry as traditionally having attracted the law's protection. If, of course, government information is involved, then whether or not the information has entered the public domain may well prove decisive—as in the *Spycatcher* case [1990] 1 AC 109 itself. If trade secrets (which clearly include intellectual property rights) are involved, then the position may be different—consider the final passage quoted above from Dr Gurry and the springboard principle. What then of a case like the present which involves personal confidences? What interest, one must ask, is the law here concerned to protect?

34 In my judgment the answer is plain. The concern of the law here is to protect the confider's personal privacy. That and that alone is the right at issue in this case. The patient has no proprietorial claim to the prescription form or to the information it contains. Of course he can bestow or withhold his custom as he pleases—the pharmacist, note, has no such right: he is by law bound to dispense to whoever presents a prescription. But that gives the patient no property in the information and no right to control its use provided only and always that his privacy is not put at risk. I referred earlier to Mr Sales's plea for respect for 'the patient's autonomy'. At first blush the submission is a beguiling one. My difficulty with it, however, is in understanding how the patient's autonomy is compromised by Source's scheme. If, as I conclude, his only legitimate interest is in the protection of his privacy and, if that is safeguarded, I fail to see how his will could be thought thwarted or his personal integrity undermined. By the same token that, in a case concerning government information, 'once it has entered . . . the public domain . . . the principle of confidentiality can have no application to it' (*per* Lord Goff in the *Spycatcher* case [1990] 1 AC 109, 282), so too in a case involving personal confidences I would hold by analogy that the confidence is not breached where the confider's identity is protected.

35 This appeal concerns, as all agree, the application of a broad principle of equity. I propose its resolution on a similarly broad basis. I would not distinguish between Source's first and second arguments and nor would I regard the case as turning on the question of detriment. Rather I would stand back from the many detailed arguments addressed to us and hold simply that pharmacists' consciences ought not reasonably to be troubled by co-operation with Source's proposed scheme. The patient's privacy will have been safeguarded, not invaded. The pharmacist's duty of confidence will not have been breached."

NOTES:

1. Aldous L.J. and Schiemann L.J. agreed with Simon Brown L.J.
2. The fact that health care information is anonymised may not on the other hand necessarily preclude the imposition of an obligation of confidentiality see further *H (a health worker) v Associated Newspapers Ltd* [2002] EWCA Civ 195 discussed below and J. Laing (2003) 11 *Medical Law Review* 124.
3. The decision in *Source Informatics* has been subject to considerable criticism. It can be argued that anonymisation by itself may safeguard identity but can infringe an individual's rights to decision-making autonomy to control use of their personal information. (See generally for commentary on this case D. Beylved and E. Histed, "Betrayal of Confidence in the Court of Appeal" (2000) *Medical Law International* 277). Patterson has argued that such a narrow approach is no longer sustainable

following the House of Lords' ruling in *Campbell* (S. Pattinson *Health Care Law*, London: Thomson, 2006 at p.202.
4. In *Source Informatics* the claim that the patient owns his own information was rejected. See further on this issue p.645 below.

QUESTION:

1. Do you agree that the fact that information is anonymised mean that individual privacy is necessarily protected?

(d) Who Can Bring an Action for Breach of Confidence?

Usually an action for breach of confidence may be brought by the person to whom the confidence is owed (*Fraser v Evans* [1969] 1 All E.R. 8). This may be a patient where he or she is competent to do so, but it may equally be another person or body, for example, a health authority (see *X v Y* [1988] 2 All E.R. 648 below.)

(i) Children

The leading case on the question of children and consent to treatment is that of *Gillick*. The facts of this case are set out in Chapter 7. Here we consider the question of confidentiality and the child patient.

Gillick v West Norfolk and Wisbech Area Health Authority [1985] 3 All E.R. 402

LORD FRASER:
" . . . Once the rule of the parents' absolute authority over minor children is abandoned, the solution to the problem in this appeal can no longer be found by referring to rigid parental rights at any particular age. The solution depends on a judgment of what is best for the welfare of the particular child. Nobody doubts, certainly I do not doubt, that in the overwhelming majority of cases the best judges of a child's welfare are his or her parents. Nor do I doubt that any important medical treatment of a child under 16 would normally only be carried out with the parents' approval. That is why it would and should be 'most unusual' for a doctor to advise a child without the knowledge and consent of the parents on contraceptive matters. But, as I have already pointed out, Mrs Gillick has to go further if she is to obtain the first declaration that she seeks. She has to justify the absolute right of veto in a parent. But there may be circumstances in which a doctor is a better judge of the medical advice and treatment which will conduce to a girl's welfare than her parents. It is notorious that children of both sexes are often reluctant to confide in their parents about sexual matters, and the DHSS guidance under consideration shows that to abandon the principle of confidentiality for contraceptive advice to girls under 16 might cause some of them not to seek professional advice at all, with the consequence of exposing them to 'the immediate risks of pregnancy and of sexually-transmitted diseases'. No doubt the risk could be avoided if the patient were to abstain from sexual intercourse, and one of the doctor's responsibilities will be to decide whether a particular patient can reasonably be expected to act on advice to abstain. We were told that in a significant number of cases such abstinence could not reasonably be expected. An example is *Re P (A Minor)* (1981) 80 LGR 301, in which Butler-Sloss J. ordered that a girl aged 15 who had been pregnant

for the second time and who was in the care of a local authority should be fitted with a contraceptive appliance because, as the judge is reported to have said (at 312):

'I assume that it is impossible for this local authority to monitor her sexual activities, and, therefore, contraception appears to be the only alternative.'

There may well be other cases where the doctor feels that because the girl is under the influence of her sexual partner or for some other reason there is no realistic prospect of her abstaining from intercourse. If that is right it points strongly to the desirability of the doctor being entitled in some cases, in the girl's best interest, to give her contraceptive advice and treatment if necessary without the consent or even the knowledge of her parents. The only practicable course is, in my opinion, to entrust the doctor with a discretion to act in accordance with his view of what is best in the interests of the girl who is his patient. He should, of course, always seek to persuade her to tell her parents that she is seeking contraceptive advice, and the nature of the advice that she receives. At least he should seek to persuade her to agree to the doctor's informing the parents. But there may well be cases, and I think there will be some cases, where the girl refuses either to tell the parents herself or to permit the doctor to do so and in such cases the doctor will, in my opinion, be justified in proceeding without the parents' consent or even knowledge provided he is satisfied on the following matters: (1) that the girl (although under 16 years of age) will understand his advice (2) that he cannot persuade her to inform her parents or to allow him to inform the parents that she is seeking contraceptive advice (3) that she is very likely to begin or to continue having sexual intercourse with or without contraceptive treatment (4) that unless she receives contraceptive advice or treatment her physical or mental health or both are likely to suffer (5) that her best interests require him to give her contraceptive advice, treatment or both without the parental consent.

That result ought not to be regarded as a licence for doctors to disregard the wishes of parents on this matter whenever they find it convenient to do so. Any doctor who behaves in such a way would, in my opinion, be failing to discharge his professional responsibilities, and I would expect him to be disciplined by his own professional body accordingly. The medical profession have in modern times come to be entrusted with very wide discretionary powers going beyond the strict limits of clinical judgment and, in my opinion, there is nothing strange about entrusting them with this further responsibility which they alone are in a position to discharge satisfactorily.

No authority has been cited which prevents an infant from seeking medical or any other advice or which forbids a doctor to advise an infant who has not been tendered by the parent as a patient. No authority compels a doctor to disclose to a parent, otherwise than in the course of litigation, any information obtained as a result of a conversation between the doctor and the infant. On the other hand, in my opinion, confidentiality owed to an infant is not breached by disclosure to a parent responsible for that infant if the doctor considers that such disclosure is necessary in the interests of the infant. A doctor who gave a pledge to a girl under 16 that he would not disclose the fact or content of a conversation would no doubt honour that pledge, but the doctor ought to hesitate before committing himself. A doctor who gave an unconditional pledge of confidentiality to a girl under 16 would, for example, be in a difficult position if the girl then disclosed information which made the doctor suspect that she was being introduced to sexual intercourse by a man who was also introducing her to drugs.

Although a doctor is entitled to give confidential advice to an infant, the law will, in my opinion, uphold the right of a parent to make a decision which the infant is not competent to make. The decision to authorise and accept medical examination and treatment for contraception is a decision which a girl under 16 is not competent to make. In my opinion a doctor may not lawfully provide a girl under 16 with contraceptive facilities without the approval of the parent responsible for the girl save pursuant to a court order, or in the case of emergency or in exceptional cases where the parent has abandoned or forfeited by abuse the right to be consulted. Parental rights cannot be insisted on by a parent who is not responsible for the custody and upbringing of an infant or where the parent has abandoned or abused parental rights. And a doctor is not obliged to give effect to parental rights in an emergency.

A girl under 16 is usually living with a parent and is usually attending school. It is sufficient for the doctor to obtain the consent of the parent or guardian with whom the girl is living. It seems to me to be contrary to law and offensive to professional standards that a doctor should provide contraceptive facilities against the known or presumed wishes of such a parent and that the doctor should conspire with the girl to keep the parent in ignorance of the fact that the girl intends to participate in frequent, regular or casual sexual intercourse in the belief that the only bar to sexual intercourse is the risk of pregnancy and in complacent reliance on the doctor's contraceptive facilities to obviate that risk.

But parental rights may have been abandoned. If the doctor discovers, for example, that the girl is not living with a parent but has been allowed to live in an environment in which the danger of sexual intercourse is pressing, the doctor may lawfully provide facilities for contraception until the parent has been alerted to the danger and has been afforded the opportunity to reassert parental rights and to protect the girl by means other than contraception. The court will uphold the doctor's actions if the doctor reasonably believes that parental rights have, for the time being at any rate, been abandoned.

Parental rights may have been abused. The dangers of sexual intercourse may emanate from the girl's home. The doctor would be entitled to provide the girl with contraceptive facilities but would then be bound to consider whether the local welfare authorities should be alerted to the possibility that the girl is in need of care and protection. Again, the doctor may be satisfied that the parent is a brute and that the girl has been driven to seek solace outside the family. The doctor might decide that it was necessary to provide contraceptive facilities for the girl without informing the parent but the doctor would be bound to consider the possible consequences if the parent, known to be brutal, discovered the truth.

The doctor may also be faced with circumstances which could properly be described as a medical emergency. The doctor may decide that the girl is unable to control her sexual appetite or is acting under an influence which cannot be counteracted immediately. The doctor would be entitled to provide contraceptive facilities as a temporary measure but would, in my opinion, be bound to inform the parent. A subsequent decision to continue contraceptive treatment would be open to the doctor and the parent acting jointly in default of agreement between them, the welfare authority or the court could be asked to intervene.

There may be other exceptional circumstances and emergencies which would impel the doctor to provide contraceptive facilities without the prior consent of the parent but in most cases the doctor would be bound to inform the parent as soon as possible in order that the parent might have the opportunity of exercising parental rights in such manner as to deter or prevent the girl from indulging in sexual intercourse."

NOTES:

1. Whether a child patient can restrain disclosure of information on the basis of breach of confidence has been a disputed issue. If a child is under 16, then he or she has no statutory right to consent to treatment (see Chapter 7). However, after *Gillick*, it is recognised that a child under 16 may be competent to consent but that this is dependant upon an assessment of the child's maturity. It appears that such an analysis would be applicable to the disclosure of personal health information. Where a child is of sufficient maturity, he or she can determine the basis on which information could be disclosed. However, the position of the immature minor is less clear. Some have suggested that where a child is not *Gillick*-competent, then questions regarding disclosure of information and consent to treatment are to be left

to the child's parents (see A. Grubb and D. Pearl, "Medicine, Health, Family and the Law" (1986) *Family Law* 101). In contrast, Montgomery has argued that a child who approaches her doctor without telling her parents rightly expects that any disclosure which is made will be treated as confidential, then the "very action evidences the maturity required before the law will recognise this expectation" (see J. Montgomery, "Confidentiality and the Immature Minor" (1987) *Family Law* 101).

2. An alternative basis for the obligation of confidence is that of contract. There are certain difficulties in establishing an obligation on the basis of contract in the context of the child patient. If treatment is being given privately rather than within the NHS, then is the contract enforceable by the child? There is some authority to suggest that this may be the case if it can be shown that the contract was manifestly to the minor's advantage (*Clements v London & North Western Railway Co* [1894] 2 Q.B. 482 and see Montgomery *op. cit.* in note 1). In the case of the NHS patient there is no direct contract between patient and practitioner. The existence of a contractual obligation in such a situation has been disputed, although one argument advanced is that an independent contract arises between patient and doctor regarding a promise to maintain confidentiality (see Montgomery and Grubb and Pearl, both *op. cit.* in note 1).

3. Even if an obligation of confidence does arise, then as we shall see this obligation is not absolute in nature. In law the obligation of confidentiality may be outweighed by the public interest in disclosure. In what situations may information regarding the child patient be disclosed to others and in particular his family? Essentially, this is a question of where the public interest lies. A number of commentators have noted that sanctioning disclosure may not only have the effect of discouraging the particular patient from seeking treatment but will also affect other patients. (See generally I. Kennedy, "The Doctor, the Pill and the Fifteen Year Old Girl" in I. Kennedy (ed.), *Treat Me Right*, Oxford: OUP, 1989 and Montgomery, *op. cit.* in note 1).

4. The courts have subsequently confirmed that there is an obligation of confidentiality owed to a child. For example in *Venables v News Group Newspapers Limited* ([2001] Fam. 430, 469), "children, like adults, are entitled to confidentiality in respect of certain areas or information ... medical records are the obvious example" and see also *Re C (A Minor) (Wardship: Medical Treatment) (No. 2)* [1990] Fam. 39. However, these cases do not make clear the precise basis on which the obligation of confidence itself actually arose. See also the discussion in J. Loughrey, "Medical Information, Confidentiality and a Child's Right to Privacy" (2003) 23 *Legal Studies* 510.

QUESTION:

1. Should a doctor preserve the confidentiality of a 14-year-old boy who has contracted a sexually transmitted disease?

The issue of disclosure to parents of medical information regarding children was again considered by the courts in January 2006 in the following case:

R (on the application of Axon) v Secretary of State [2006] EWCA 37 (Admin), [2006] All E.R. (D) 148

In 2004 the Department of Health produced guidance called "Best Practice Guidance for Doctors and Other Health Professionals on the Provision of Advice and Treatment to Young People under Sixteen on Contraception, Sexual and Reproductive Health" (the 2004 Guidance). This provided that health professionals could provide such advice and treatment on sexual matters for persons under 16 years of age without parental knowledge or consent of their parents, subject to conditions. The guidance was rooted in the judgments of the majority of the House of Lords in *Gillick*. Mrs Axon, a mother of teenage daughters, applied for judicial review, challenging this and arguing that the doctor was not under any duty to maintain confidentiality unless disclosure could harm the child's physical or mental health. This case is also further discussed in Chapter 7 above in relation to the broader aspects of the issues raised.

SILBER L.J.
"(iii) What did Gillick decide about the need for parental notification on sexual matters?
85. The starting point to resolving this issue must be to consider the basis on which the majority of the Appellate Committee in *Gillick* reached their decision, which of course, only related to contraception in order to ascertain if their reasoning in that case throws any light on the duty of confidentiality owed by a medical professional in respect of proposed abortion advice and treatment.
86. I will not repeat the pertinent points in the reasoning of the majority in *Gillick* which I have set out in paragraph 13 above and which indicate when and how a doctor can give advice and treatment to a young person without parental consent or knowledge The speeches of Lord Fraser, Lord Scarman and Lord Bridge do not indicate or suggest that their conclusions depended in any way upon the nature of the treatment proposed because the approach in their speeches was and is of general application to all forms of medical advice and treatment. Indeed the approach of the majority was to consider in *general* terms the reasons why parental knowledge or consent might be required for medical advice and treatment and then again in general terms when that parental knowledge or consent would no longer be required . . .
(iv) . . .
In the light of the very important issues which have to be resolved before a young person can agree to an abortion, can Lord Fraser's Guidelines be adapted so as to permit a medical professional to give advice and treatment on a possible abortion without parental knowledge or consent?
88. As I have explained in paragraph 83 above, Mr Havers attaches importance to the very complex issues that have to be resolved before any woman can decide whether she should have an abortion. The issue that now has to be resolved is whether these issues are so important and so difficult that a medical professional is under no obligation to keep confidential advice and treatment which she proposed to give in respect of abortion unless to do so would or might prejudice the young person's physical or mental health . . .

[Silber J. looked at the guidelines issued in *Gillick* and continued:]

90. There is no reason why this approach cannot be adapted so that a girl could only be considered to have understood advice if she understands properly 'what is involved'. This

would constitute a high threshold and many young girls would be unable to satisfy the medical professional that they fully understood all the implications of the options open to them. These requirements would be underpinned by two matters of which the first is that the sanction for medical professionals was as explained by Lord Fraser that a doctor who did not adhere to his guidelines could 'expect . . . to be disciplined by his own professional body'. The second matter is that the medical professional is required to take into account all aspects of the young person's health in deciding if what he is proposing satisfies the test of showing that unless the girl receives the proposed abortion advice, her physical or mental health or both are likely to suffer. In summary, there is no reason why Lord Fraser's Guidelines and Lord Scarman's criteria should not be adapted and applied to advice and treatment for abortion even though abortions raise, as I have explained, more serious and more complex issues than contraception. I conclude that they should be adapted and I set out in paragraph 154 below how they should now read.

91. I am fortified in coming to this conclusion by the fact, as I have set out in paragraphs 67 to 69 above, that young people would be deterred from taking advice on sexual matters such as abortion without the assurance of confidentiality. In addition, as I have explained in paragraph 10 above, Lord Fraser pointed out at page 174 D that his guidelines were not 'a licence for doctors to disregard the wishes of parents on this matter whenever they find it convenient to do so'. I should add that as I will explain in Section XII below, the claimant cannot establish that her Article 8 rights are being infringed when she is not notified about proposed advice and treatment on abortion. For all these reasons, I do not consider that there should be any different rule on waiving confidentiality when abortion advice or treatment is discussed than when contraceptive advice or other treatment is under consideration. Hence I am bound to reject Mr Havers' submission.

XI. The provision of actual advice and treatment on sexual matters issue

92. Mr Havers contends that the claimant is entitled to a declaration that a medical professional is not entitled to provide actual advice and treatment on contraception, sexually transmitted infections and abortion without parental knowledge unless to do so would or might prejudice the young person's physical or mental health so that it is in the young person's best interest not to do so. Mr Sales and Miss Lieven submit that this claim is an attempt to reverse the decision in *Gillick* and should be rejected. I have already dealt with many aspects of these issues in sections IX and X above

93. Starting with the claim in respect of contraception, I agree with the submission of Mr Sales and Miss Lieven that the decision in *Gillick* is determinative as, in the words of Lord Fraser at page 166G, one of the strands of the argument in *Gillick* was 'whether giving [contraceptive] advice and treatment to a girl under 16 without her parents' consent infringes the parent's rights'. As I have explained, the majority of the Appellate Committee answered that question in the negative in relation to contraception, which was the only matter under consideration in that case. As I will explain, I have considered whether article 8 of the ECHR would mean that *Gillick* would now be decided differently but for the reasons set out in section XIII below, I have concluded that *Gillick* remains good law. I am bound by that decision in *Gillick* with the result that Mr Havers' submissions in respect of advice and treatment for contraception fail.

94. Turning to the claim in respect of advising on and providing treatment for abortion and sexually transmissible diseases, *Gillick* provides a very helpful starting point because, as I explained in paragraph 13 above, the majority decision is based on an analysis of the parental right to determine whether or not their minor child below the age of 16 will have medical treatment, which according to Lord Scarman at page 188H–189A: 'terminates if and when the child achieves a sufficient understanding and intelligence to enable him or her to fully understand what is proposed'. Lord Fraser also regarded the parent's authority as being a 'dwindling right' (page 172H) and 'that once the rule of the parents' absolute authority over minority children is abandoned, the solution to the problem in the appeal can no longer be found by referring to rigid parental rights at any particular age. The solution depends on what is best for the welfare of the particular child' (page 173D).

95. This reasoning is inconsistent with the relief sought by Mr Havers because his case depends on some form of parental authority, which continues until the sixteenth birthday of their offspring. Although, as I have explained, an abortion is a form of major invasive treatment with serious consequences, there is nothing in the speeches of the majority in *Gillick*, which suggests that parental authority has any place in decision-making for a young person, who in the words of Lord Scarman, which I have quoted in the last paragraph 'achieves a sufficient understanding and intelligence to enable him or her to fully understand what is proposed'. In fact as I have sought to explain in section XI above, Lord Fraser's Guidelines can be and should be adapted to deal with advising and providing treatment for all sexual matters. The approach of the medical professional to a young person who seeks advice and treatment on sexual issues without notifying his or her parents or permitting them to be notified should be in accordance with Lord Fraser's Guidelines as adapted for abortions and sexually transmitted illnesses . . .

. . .

(ii) *Does the failure of the 'Confidentiality' section in the 2004 Guidance to refer to the need to notify parents mean that parents are not notified unless they become involved because of local agreed Child Protection Protocols?*

108. Mr Havers contends that the section entitled 'Confidentiality' in the 2004 Guidance does not refer to any notification or involvement of the parents of the young person concerned unless they happen to be notified or become involved through the application of locally agreed child protection protocols. This submission focuses on just one section of the 2004 Guidance rather than on the whole document and which in Lord Scarman's words which I quoted in paragraph 99 above is 'how it would be understood by a doctor' or a medical professional if the 2004 Guidance is addressed to them. Such a person would also have correctly and inevitably attached importance to the section in the 2004 Guidance, which deals with 'Good practice in providing contraception and sexual health to young people under 16' which, as I have sought to explain, specifically refers to the fact that 'it is considered good practice' to follow Lord Fraser's guidelines, which themselves refer at page 174D to the doctor being unable to 'persuade [the girl] to inform her parents or allow [the doctor] to inform the parents that she is seeking contraceptive advice'.

109. This section of the 2004 Guidance also makes it clear that where an abortion is under consideration, the girl patient should if possible be persuaded 'to involve a parent'. Both these provisions show that this complaint of the claimant is unjustified especially as I have already explained in Sections IX, X and XI of this judgment above that the medical professional remains under a duty to respect the confidentiality of information from a young person and not to notify his or her parents . . .

(iv) Does the 2004 Guidance mean that the parents of a young person are excluded from involvement in important decision making about the life and welfare of the young person?

116. Mr Havers complains that the 2004 Guidance means that the parents of a young person are excluded from involvement in the making of important decisions about the life and welfare of the young person but this submission fails to appreciate that in *Gillick*, the majority of the House of Lords explained that the doctor could provide advice and treatment to a young person even if his or her parents did not consent provided that certain conditions were satisfied. I have already set out in paragraphs 11 and 12 what Lord Fraser and Lord Scarman considered appropriate conditions. It is quite true that the pre-Gillick Guidance stresses that it was 'most unusual to provide advice about contraception without parental consent' while the 2004 Guidance does not use this wording. As I have explained in paragraphs 103 to 107 above, the criticism concerning the absence of the words 'most exceptional' in the 2004 Guidance does not in any way invalidate this document.

117. Furthermore, I am unable to accept any of Mr Havers' complaints about the 2004 Guidance whether considered individually or cumulatively because, in my view, the 2004

Guidance is not unlawful unless the article 8 rights of the parents mean that the 2004 Guidance is unlawful and that is the issue to which I must now turn.

[Silber went on to consider whether failure to inform the parents would constitute a violation of their human rights under Article 8 of the ECHR.]

127. I am unable to accept Mr Havers' contention that by permitting a medical professional to withhold information relating to advice or treatment of a young person on sexual matters, the article 8 rights of the parents of the young person were thereby infringed. In considering this issue, it must always be remembered first, that in *Z v Finland* (supra) the European Court emphasized the significance and compelling nature of the patient's article 8(1) right to confidentiality of health information as I explained in paragraph 63 above. A similar approach was adopted in *MS v Sweden* [1999] 28 EHRR 313 in which it is said at page 337 in paragraph 41 that 'respecting the confidentiality of health data is a vital principle in the legal systems of all contracting parties to the Convention'. Although these cases deal with the position of an adult, there is no good reason why they could not apply to protect the confidentiality of health information concerning a young person, especially because, as I have explained in paragraphs 40 and 41 above, that a duty of confidentiality is owed to a young person by medical professionals.

128. Second, it is noteworthy that in *Kjeldsen and Others v Denmark* (1976) 1 EHRR 711, the Strasbourg Court rejected complaints by a group of parents some of whose children were under 11 years of age under, inter alia, article 8, that their children had received sex education at school without their consent. Although the Article 8 point might not have been fully argued in that case, if the parents in that case had no right to control what information their children should receive on these matters, it is not easy to see how and why they could have a sufficient interest under article 8 to override a young person's article 8 rights to seek to maintain confidentiality in relation to his or her private medical information on sexual matters.

129. In order to decide whether parents have what Mr Havers describes as 'the right to parental authority over a child' having regard to their having parental duties, the age and maturity of the young person is of critical importance. Lord Lester QC and Mr David Pannick QC state convincingly and correctly in my view that 'as a child matures, the burden of showing ongoing family life by reference to substantive links or factors grows' (*Human Rights Law and Practice*—2nd Edition (2004) paragraph 4.8.48). This conclusion presupposes correctly that any right to family life on the part of a parent dwindles as their child gets older and is able to understand the consequence of different choices and then to make decisions relating to them.

130. As a matter of principle, it is difficult to see why a parent should still retain an article 8 right to parental authority relating to a medical decision where the young person concerned understands the advice provided by the medical professional and its implications. Indeed, any right under article 8 of a parent to be notified of advice or treatment of a sexual matter as part of the right claimed by Mr Havers must depend on a number of factors, such as the age and understanding of their offspring. The parent would not be able to claim such an article 8 right to be notified if their son or daughter was, say, 18 years of age and had sought medical advice on sexual matters because in that case the young person was able to consent without parental knowledge or consent for the reasons set out in paragraph 1 above. The reason why the parent could not claim such a right is that their right to participate in decision-making as part of the right claimed by Mr Havers would only exist while the child was so immature that his parent had the right of control as was made clear in *Gillick*. As Lord Fraser explained in *Gillick*, 'the parental rights to control a child do not exist for the benefit of the parent. They exist for the benefit of the child and they are justified only in so far as they enable the parent to perform his duties towards the child and towards other children in the family' (page 170D). Lord Fraser and Lord Scarman in *Gillick* at pages 172H and 186D both adopted the statement of Lord Denning MR in *Hewer v Bryant* [1970] 1 QB 357, 369 that the parent's right as against a child is 'a dwindling right'. As Lord Scarman explained, a parental right yields to the young

person's right to make his own decisions when the young person reaches a sufficient understanding and intelligence to be capable of making up his or her own mind in relation to a matter requiring decision (page 186D) and this autonomy of a young person must undermine any article 8 rights of a parent to family life. In my view, any article 8 right of the kind advocated by Mr Havers must be seen in that light so that once the child is sufficiently mature in this way, the parent only retains such rights to family life and to be notified about medical treatment if but only if the young person so wishes.

131. Indeed whether there is family life and hence a right to family life in a particular family is a question of fact. The European Commission on Human Rights has explained that the existence of family ties depends upon 'the real existence in practice of close family ties' (*K v United Kingdom* (1986) 50 DR 199, 207). It is not clear why the parent should have an article 8 right to family life, where first the offspring is almost 16 years of age and docs not wish it, second where the parent no longer has a right to control the child for the reasons set out in the last paragraph and third where the young person in Lord Scarman's words at page 188 'has sufficient understanding of what is involved to give a consent valid in law'.

132. There is nothing in the Strasbourg jurisprudence, which persuades me that any parental right or power of control under article 8 is wider than in domestic law, which is that the right of parents in the words of Lord Scarman 'exists primarily to enable the parent to discharge his duty of maintenance, protection and education until he reaches such an age as to be able to look after himself and make his own decisions' (*Gillick* page 185E). The parental right to family life does not continue after that time and so parents do not have article 8 rights to be notified of any advice of a medical professional after the young person is able to look after himself or herself and make his or her own decisions. This leads to the next question which is whether the 2004 Guidance interferes with those rights.

133. As I explained in Section XII above, there is nothing in the 2004 Guidance, which enables or permits a medical professional to give advice or treatment on a sexual matter unless the medical professional is satisfied that in the words of the 2004 Guidance on 'Duty of Care' that the young person 'understands the advice provided and its implications'. Furthermore in the section of the 2004 Guidance which deals with 'good practice', it is stated that it is good practice for medical professionals 'to follow . . . the Fraser Guidelines [which required that the young person understands the health professional's advice]'.

134. There is the additional safeguard mentioned after both the provisions which is that the treatment and advice must be in the young person's best interests. In those circumstances, I conclude that there is nothing in the 2004 Guidelines, which interferes with any of a parent's article 8 rights.

135. Nevertheless, if I am wrong and that the 2004 Guidance interferes with a parent's article 8(1) rights, I must still consider whether the Secretary of State can invoke the provisions of article 8(2).

(v) The Secretary of State's Case on Article 8(2) that the 2004 Guidance will not be regarded as an interference with a parent's article 8 right

136. Mr Sales, with Miss Lieven's support, contends that even if the claimant's article 8 rights are infringed, I should conclude that the 2004 Guidance falls within article 8(2) with the result that any article 8 rights of the claimant would not have been interfered with because in the wording of article 8(2), the 2004 Guidance was 'in accordance with the law' and 'necessary in a democratic society . . . for the protection of health . . . or for the protection of the rights . . . of others' as well as being proportionate. Mr Havers disagrees and so I will have to consider each of these three requirements in turn.

(vi) " . . . in accordance with the law . . . ."

137. As I have explained my conclusion is that the 2004 Guidelines comply with the law of England and Wales in an area of the law which after *Gillick* must be regarded as clear

and sufficiently certain so 'that it be accessible to the persons concerned and formulated with sufficient precision to enable [the citizens] if need be, with appropriate advice to foresee to a degree that is reasonable in the circumstances the consequences which a given action may entail' (*MS v Sweden* (1997) 28 EHRR 313, 321 at paragraph 48). This requirement is satisfied after the decision in *Gillick*.

(vii) . . . **"necessary in a democratic society . . . for the protection of health . . . or for the protection of the rights . . . of others"**

138. Mr Havers submits correctly that the burden of proof of this exception is on the Secretary of State and he then contends that the expert evidence does not support the Secretary of State's case. It is true that the Secretary of State cannot in my view point to any statistical evidence which unequivocally supports his case that the abandonment of the principle of confidentiality would inevitably lead to increases in sexually transmitted illness and other matters. Nevertheless as I have explained, there is clear evidence that an assurance to young people of medical confidentiality increases the use of contraceptive and abortion services by those under the age of 16 and Mr Havers does not dispute this . . .

141. There are in my view four different ways in which the Secretary of State can establish that if, contrary to my conclusion in paragraph 134 above, there had been infringement of a parent's article 8(1) rights, such interference could be justified as being 'necessary in a democratic society for the protection of health . . . or the rights of others'. It is necessary to bear in mind that the word 'necessary' in article 8(2) is not synonymous with the word 'indispensable' but the treatment would be justified 'if the interference complained of [which in this case was the proposed advice or treatment] corresponded to a pressing social need, whether it was proportionate to the legitimate aim pursued, whether the reasons given by the national authority to justify it are relevant and sufficient' (*Sunday Times v UK* (1979) 2 EHRR 245 at 255, 275 and 277–278). This approach is logical because inherent in the interpretation of the Convention is its aim to strike a 'fair balance between the demands of the general interest of the community and the requirements of the protection of the individual's fundamental rights' (see *Sporrong and Lonroth v Sweden* (1992) 5 EHRR 35, 52). Any restriction on a guaranteed freedom, such as that set out in article 8(1) of the Convention, must be proportionate to the legitimate aim pursued (*Handyside v United Kingdom* (1976) 1 EHRR 737) and I will consider the requirements of proportionality as a separate issue in paragraphs 150 and 151 below.

142. First, as I have explained, there is clear evidence that confidentiality increases the use of contraceptive and abortion services for those under the age of sixteen and that conclusion corresponds with common sense. The use of contraceptives will also reduce the risk of the need subsequently for treatment for sexually transmitted diseases and for abortion. By the same token, in the case of sexually transmissible diseases, it is much more likely that a young person, who does not want his or her parents to know of his or her sexual activities, would go and obtain advice from a medical professional or if that young person knew that his or her parents would not be notified of the advice or of the young person's condition by a medical professional. In other words, many young people, who need help on sexual matters from medical professionals, would be or might be deterred from obtaining such advice and treatment if their parents would have to be notified and this conclusion justifies the approach in the 2004 Guidance.

143. A second and overlapping factor is the disturbing consequences of the young people being deterred from obtaining advice and treatment on sexual matters. The young person, who had or suspected that he had a sexually transmissible disease, might be deterred from obtaining advice or from being treated thereby causing the risk of a consequential deterioration not only of the health of that young person, his present and past partners as well as the risk of infection of his or her present and future partners. By the same token, the girl who was intent on sexual intercourse and who did not obtain professional medical advice on contraception because she knew that her parents would be notified might become pregnant and become a candidate for an abortion or she might also run the risk of picking up a sexually transmissible illness. There is also the risk that if the

pregnant girl knew that a medical professional would have to notify her parents, she might be deterred from obtaining advice or having an abortion and that she might instead use an unqualified abortionist with the inevitable risks to her health. All these are real dangers which would justify any interference with any article 8(1) rights of a parent.

144. A third reason why I do not consider that the 2004 Guidance interferes with any article 8 rights of a parent is that it is established that a child's article 8 rights overrides similar rights of a parent. In *Hendricks v Netherlands* (1992) EHRR 223, the Commission explained at paragraph 23 that:

'The Commission has consistently held that, in assessing the question of whether or not the refusal of the right of access to the non-custodial parent was in conformity with article 8 of the convention, the interests of the child pre-dominate.'

145. Similarly in *Yousef v Netherlands* (2003) 36 EHRR 345, it was said at paragraph 73 that:

'The court reiterates that in judicial decisions where the rights under article 8 of the parents and those of the child are at stake, the child's rights must be the paramount consideration'.

146. Clayton and Tomlinson explain that under ECHR Jurisprudence:

'the right of the child to respect for his private life or to exercise freedom or thought conscience and religion in a manner which is at variance with the new directives of his parent, has been receiving increased attention so that the weight given to parental authority may be reduced' (*The Law of Human Rights*, Volume 1 paragraph 13-116).

147. A final reason is that in this particular area relating as it does to social policy, the Judiciary should show a substantial deference to the Executive on these issues.

[Silber L.J. referred to Lord Bridge in *Gillick* and then stated:]

148. Indeed any judgment on the matters set out in the 2004 Guidance is one in respect of which the courts would and should give to the Executive a discretionary area of judgment. In *R v DPP ex parte Kebilene* [2000] 2 AC 326, at 380, 381, Lord Hope of Craighead said that:

'In some circumstances it will be appropriate for the court to recognize that there is an area of judgment within which the Judiciary will defer, on democratic grounds, to the considered opinion of the elected body or person whose act or decision is said to be incompatible with the Convention . . . It will be either for such an area of judgment to be recognized where the Convention requires a balance to be struck, much less so where the right is stated in terms which are unqualified. It will be easier for it to be recognized where the issues involve questions of social or economic policy, much less where the rights are of high constitutional importance of a kind where the courts are well placed to assess the importance of them'.

149. Applying Lord Hope's approach means that the Secretary of State is entitled to a substantial degree of deference when the 2004 Guidance is considered for two reasons, of which the first is that the issues raised on this application and in the 2004 Guidance relate to what Lord Hope describes as 'questions of social policy'. The second reason is that this case concerns article 8, which is a qualified right in the light of the provisions of article 8 (2)."

NOTE:

1. In *Axon* Silber J. confirms the application of *Gillick* in relation to patient confidentiality in relation to abortion as well as contraception and notes that this is applicable in the context of human rights jurisprudence.

QUESTION:

1. To what extent can the *Axon* case be reconciled with *Re R* (for general discussion of this case see Chapter 7 above). In this case the Court of Appeal indicated that a child's parents may be able to authorise treatment of a competent minor in the face of the minor's refusal. How can parents overrule their child's refusal of treatment unless they had been informed of the refusal and surrounding circumstances in the first place? Does this mean that in any situation in which a refusal takes place confidence may be broken? (See further A. Grubb, "Treatment Decisions: Keeping it in the Family" in A. Grubb (ed.), *Choices and Decisions in Health Care*, Chichester: John Wiley, 1994, at p.64.)

(ii) Adults Lacking Mental Capacity

Following the House of Lords decision in *Re F (Mental Patient Sterilisation)* [1990] 2 A.C. 1, it remained uncertain as to whether and to what extent an obligation of confidentiality arose in the context of an adult who lacked capacity. This issue was considered further in the following case.

R. (on the application of S) v Plymouth City Council [2002] EWCA Civ 388

S was a 26-year-old adult who lacked mental capacity. His mother wanted access to his medical records in her capacity as nearest relative under the Mental Health Act 1983 but was refused access because the local authority took the view that disclosure would constitute breach of confidence.

HALE L.J.
"41 But should the mother and her lawyers also have access to the information sought by her experts? The case put by Mr Murray Hunt on her behalf relied on the right of access to a court, and the right of access to legal advice in order to exercise that right, contained in article 6 of the European Convention on Human Rights and the jurisprudence of the European Court of Human Rights, in particular *Golder v United Kingdom* (1975) 1 EHRR 524. The mother has already been told that, if she exercises her right to discharge C, an application will be made to displace her. The two are part of the same process and it is unrealistic to regard them separately. In effect, the mother is placed in a position where she is likely to have to justify her decision before a court. Proper access to the court therefore requires that she have proper access to legal advice before she sets that process in motion. Proper access to legal advice requires that she have access to the information which will be relevant to the court's decision.
42 Two arguments are put against this on behalf of the authority. First, the proceedings before the county court are not 'the determination of her civil rights and obligations' for the purpose of article 6(1). Her status as nearest relative is given her by statute and not by virtue of her actual relationship with the patient. Her role as nearest relative is a public law

role of participating in the procedures for the imposition of compulsory powers under the 1983 Act. Second, there is not yet, and may never be, any question of court proceedings. They will only arise if and when she decides to discharge C from guardianship, and even then it will depend upon the professional judgments available to her and to the local authority at the time.

43 As to the first, it is plain that the common law also recognises a right of access to a court and access to legal advice for the purpose of exercising that right: see e.g. *Raymond v Honey* [1983] 1 AC 1, *R v Secretary of State for the Home Department, Ex p Leech* [1994] QB 198 and *R (Daly) v Secretary of State for the Home Department* [2001] 2 AC 532. The common law will protect the exercise of those rights irrespective of whether or not they would be classed as civil rights for the purpose of article 6: see *R v Secretary of State for the Home Department, Ex p Saleem* [2001] 1 WLR 443. In any event, article 6 does not prescribe or presume any particular content for civil rights, which is a matter for domestic law. Although the identity of the nearest relative is prescribed by statute, the object of the statute is to identify the person with the closest family relationship to the patient. The powers are given to the nearest relative partly for the protection of the patient and partly for the protection of the family which may otherwise face intolerable burdens in looking after him. Disputes between the state and the family about family relationships have long been regarded as falling within the ambit of article 6 as well as article 8: see, e.g., *W v United Kingdom* (1987) 10 EHRR 29.

44 Furthermore, the dispute between the mother and the local authority about where C was to live might well (and if Dr Morris had not recommended guardianship could only) have been resolved by way of a claim for a declaration in the Family Division as to what was in C's best interests: see, e.g., *In re S (Hospital Patient: Court's Jurisdiction* [1995] Fam 26. That would undoubtedly have fallen within article 6. It is artificial to draw a distinction here.

45 In the same way, it is artificial to draw a distinction between access to legal advice upon discharge and access to legal advice upon a displacement application. The two go hand in hand. In reality, the nearest relative cannot exercise her power of discharge without regard to the very real risk of displacement proceedings if she does so against the wishes of the local authority. She needs advice on them both together. The curious structure of these provisions means that she cannot lose her dispute with the local authority about whether or not to discharge C without also losing her status as his nearest relative and the statute gives her no power to seek reinstatement. It is also very much in C's interests for her to have that advice at the earlier stage. If she is advised not to discharge him, then the litigation may be avoided altogether. If she is advised to do so, then there must at least be a case which is worth putting before a court.

46 These considerations would arise at common law irrespective of the Human Rights Act 1998. The 1998 Act, however, introduces a further dimension in article 8. Both the mother and C have a right to respect for their family life. Not only is the mother C's closest relative in fact as well as in law, they lived together all his life until shortly before he was placed under guardianship. They still have a family relationship which requires respect. It is, of course, true that replacing the mother as nearest relative will not change their actual relationship. But the right to respect for family life goes deeper than that: the state is not permitted to interfere with that right unless this is (1) in accordance with the law, (2) in pursuit of a legitimate aim and (3) proportionate to that aim. The protection of the health and welfare of a young man who is unable to make decisions for himself must be a legitimate aim for this purpose. But, irrespective of article 6, the parent also has a right under article 8 to be involved in the decision-making process: see *W v United Kingdom* (1977) 10 EHRR 29, *McMichael v United Kingdom* (1995) 20 EHRR 205, and most recently, *TP and KM v United Kingdom* [2001] 2 FCR 289, 311, para 72:

'The court further recalls that whilst article 8 of the Convention contains no explicit procedural requirements, the decision-making process involved in measures of inter-ference must be fair and such as to afford due respect to the interests safeguarded by article 8.'

In that case, the failure of the local authority to disclose (or seek the court's guidance about disclosing) the video of a child psychiatrist's interview with the child, so as to give the mother a proper opportunity of challenging the evidence upon which their suspicions of child abuse were based, meant that she was not adequately involved in the decision-making process about the care of her daughter.

47 Article 8 also confers a right to respect for private life. Adults such as C have that right as much as anyone else. Indeed, many would think them more at risk, and therefore more worthy of respect by the authorities if, because of their mental disabilities, they are unable to protect it for themselves. But both his and his mother's right to respect for their family life under article 8, and the mother's right to a fair trial under article 6, would legitimate aims of interference with C's right to respect for his private life, provided as always that the interference was proportionate.

48 Hence both the common law and the Convention require that a balance be struck between the various interests involved. These are the confidentiality of the information sought; the proper administration of justice; the mother's right of access to legal advice to enable her to decide whether or not to exercise a right which is likely to lead to legal proceedings against her if she does so; the rights of both C and his mother to respect for their family life and adequate involvement in decision-making processes about it; C's right to respect for his private life; and the protection of C's health and welfare. In some cases there might also be an interest in the protection of other people, but that has not been seriously suggested here.

49 C's interest in protecting the confidentiality of personal information about himself must not be underestimated. It is all too easy for professionals and parents to regard children and incapacitated adults as having no independent interests of their own: as objects rather than subjects. But we are not concerned here with the publication of information to the whole wide world. There is a clear distinction between disclosure to the media with a view to publication to all and sundry and disclosure in confidence to those with a proper interest in having the information in question. We are concerned here only with the latter. The issue is only whether the circle should be widened from those professionals with whom this information has already been shared (possibly without much conscious thought being given to the balance of interests involved) to include the person who is probably closest to him in fact as well as in law and who has a statutory role in his future and to those professionally advising her. C also has an interest in having his own wishes and feelings respected. It would be different in this case if he had the capacity to give or withhold consent to the disclosure: any objection from him would have to be weighed in the balance against the other interests, although as *W v Egdell* [1990] Ch 359 shows, it would not be decisive. C also has an interest in being protected from a risk of harm to his health or welfare which would stem from disclosure; but it is important not to confuse a possible risk of harm to his health or welfare from being discharged from guardianship with a possible risk of harm from disclosing the information sought. As *In re D (Minors) (Adoption Reports: Confidentiality)* [1996] AC 593 shows, he also has an interest in decisions about his future being properly informed.

50 That balance would not lead in every case to the disclosure of all the information a relative might possibly want, still less to a fishing exercise amongst the local authority's files. But in most cases it would lead to the disclosure of the basic statutory guardianship documentation. In this case it must also lead to the particular disclosure sought. There is no suggestion that C has any objection to his mother and her advisers being properly informed about his health and welfare. There is no suggestion of any risk to his health and welfare arising from this. The mother and her advisers have sought access to the information which her own psychiatric and social work experts need in order properly to advise her. That limits both the context and the content of disclosure in a way which strikes a proper balance between the competing interests.

51 For those reasons I would allow this appeal. I would grant the relief sought in relation to the disclosure of the information required by the experts instructed by the mother to those experts and to the mother and her legal advisers."

NOTES:

1. This case is notable in that it is the first case to confirm that there is an obligation of confidentiality owed in relation to an adult who lacks mental capacity.
2. The issue of an obligation of confidentiality in relation to mental health issues was considered by the Government in relation to its proposals for the reform of the Mental Health Act 1983. See further Chapter 8 above.

(iii) Deceased Patients

General Medical Council: Confidentiality, Protecting and Providing Information London: GMC (2004)

Disclosure after a patient's death

30. You still have an obligation to keep personal information confidential after a patient dies. The extent to which confidential information may be disclosed after a patient's death will depend on the circumstances. If the patient had asked for information to remain confidential, his or her views should be respected. Where you are unaware of any directions from the patient, you should consider requests for information taking into account:

- whether the disclosure of information may cause distress to, or be of benefit to, the patient's partner or family;
- whether disclosure of information about the patient will in effect disclose information about the patient's family or other people;
- whether the information is already public knowledge or can be anonymised;
- the purpose of the disclosure.

If you decide to disclose confidential information you must be prepared to explain and justify your decision.

NOTES:

1. The GMC professional ethical code requires a doctor to keep patient information confidential, even after the patient's death. Winston Churchill's physician, Lord Moran, was subject to considerable criticism after he published the book *Churchill—A Struggle for Survival* following the prime minister's death. (See S. Lock and J. Loudan, "A Question of Confidence" (1984) 288 B.M.J. 123.)
2. To what extent can keeping patient information confidential after death be seen as required by European Convention of Human Rights obligations? This issue arose in connection with the publication of a book by a physician to the late President Mitterand of France after his death in January 1996. The book *Le Grand Secret* told of Mitterand's treatment for cancer—information which had been withheld from the French public (see further A. Dorozynski, "Mitterand Book Provokes Storm in France" (1996) 312 B.M.J. 201 and also J.K. Mason and G. Laurie, *Mason and McCall Smith's Law and Medical Ethics* (7th edn), Oxford, 2005 at pp.292–293. The French courts issued an injunction to stop further

publication, but this was challenged before the European Court of Human Rights. The ECHR held that while legal protection against breach of confidentiality was consistent with human rights jurisprudence, France was in violation of Article 10 as the ban placed on the book was disproportionate to the aim and no longer complied with a "pressing social need". (*Plon (Société) v France* Application No 58148/2000 May 18, 2004).

3. It is unclear whether a breach of confidence action could be brought to stop further publication of a patient's information after his death. It has been suggested that the courts may follow the approach taken in the tort of defamation, where an action cannot be brought after the person allegedly defamed has died because they have no interests in their reputation left to protect.

(e) Grounds for Disclosure

(i) Consent

General Medical Council: Confidentiality, Protecting and Providing Information London: GMC (2004)

Sharing information in the health care team or with others providing care

10. Most people understand and accept that information must be shared within the health care team in order to provide their care. You should make sure that patients are aware that personal information about them will be shared within the health care team, unless they object, and of the reasons for this. It is particularly important to check that patients understand what will be disclosed if you need to share identifiable information with anyone employed by another organisation or agency who is contributing to their care. You must respect the wishes of any patient who objects to particular information being shared with others providing care, except where this would put others at risk of death or serious harm.

11. You must make sure that anyone to whom you disclose personal information understands that it is given to them in confidence, which they must respect. All staff members receiving personal information in order to provide or support care are bound by a legal duty of confidence, whether or not they have contractual or professional obligations to protect confidentiality.

12. Circumstances may arise where a patient cannot be informed about the sharing of information, for example because of a medical emergency. In these cases you must pass relevant information promptly to those providing the patient's care.

Circumstances where patients may give implied consent to disclosure

Disclosing information for clinical audit

13. Clinical audit is essential to the provision of good care. All doctors in clinical practice have a duty to participate in clinical audit1. Where an audit is to be undertaken by the team which provided care, or those working to support them, such as clinical audit staff, you may disclose identifiable information, provided you are satisfied that patients:

- have been informed that their data may be disclosed for clinical audit, and their right to object to the disclosure; and
- have not objected.

14. If a patient does object you should explain why information is needed and how this may benefit their care. If it is not possible to provide safe care without disclosing information for audit, you should explain this to the patient and the options open to them.

15. Where clinical audit is to be undertaken by another organisation, information should be anonymised wherever that is practicable. In any case where it is not practicable to anonymise data, or anonymised data will not fulfil the requirements of the audit, express consent must be obtained before identifiable data is disclosed.

Disclosures where express consent must be sought

16. Express consent is usually needed before the disclosure of identifiable information for purposes such as research, epidemiology, financial audit or administration. When seeking express consent to disclosure you must make sure that patients are given enough information on which to base their decision, the reasons for the disclosure and the likely consequences of the disclosure. You should also explain how much information will be disclosed and to whom it will be given. If the patient withholds consent, or consent cannot be obtained, disclosures may be made only where they are required by law or can be justified in the public interest. Where the purpose is covered by a regulation made under s60 of the Health and Social Care Act 2001, disclosures may also be made without patients' consent. You should make a record of the patient's decision, and whether and why you have disclosed information.

17. Where doctors have contractual obligations to third parties, such as companies or organisations, they must obtain patients' consent before undertaking any examination or writing a report for that organisation. Before seeking consent they must explain the purpose of the examination or report and the scope of the disclosure. Doctors should offer to show patients the report, or give them copies, whether or not this is required by law.

NOTES:

1. No action for breach of confidence will arise if the patient has consented to the disclosure. Consent must be given freely. Difficulties may arise in relation to patients in teaching hospitals, who may feel under considerable pressure to consent. (See J.K. Mason and G. Laurie *Mason and McCall Smith Law and Medical Ethics* (7th edn), Oxford, OUP: 2005 at p.258).

2. Consent includes both express and implied consent. Determining the scope/reality of implied consent may be very difficult. While a patient who enters hospital may impliedly consent to information being passed to other health care professionals where it is necessary for his treatment, he may be unaware of the extent to which his information will be passed on within the health care team. (See M. Siegler, "Medical Confidentiality—a Decrepit Concept" (1982) 302 *New England Journal of Medicine* 1518.) This further illustrates the problematic nature of the GMC Code, which sanctions disclosure within the health care team.

3. Certain disclosures for the purposes of management practice are widely recognised in the health service. An example is information collected for the purposes of medical audit. All doctors working in the NHS are required to participate in medical audit, which is the analysis of quality of health care, including diagnosis and treatment. It remains questionable whether such disclosures can be justified on the basis of implied consent by patients, and it is submitted that if it is sought to disclose information on such a ground a better approach would be to attempt to justify it on the

basis of public interest. One further solution is to ensure that information disclosed is anomymised; see *Source Informatics* above at p.579.
4. Section 60 of the Health and Social Care Act 2001 is considered below at p.627.

(ii) The public interest

The law of breach of confidence allows information to be disclosed where it is in the public interest to do so. No single definition of what amounts to the public interest exists. But in certain cases the courts have provided guidance as to what will be deemed to be disclosure in the public interest. It was said by Wood V.C. in *Gartside v Outram* ((1857) 26 L.J. Ch. (NS) 113, 114) "there is no confidence as to the disclosure of iniquity". Iniquity goes beyond, for example, the disclosure of information relating to a crime. In *Beloff v Pressdram* [1973] 1 All E.R. 241, at p.260, Ungoed Thomas J. held that disclosure of information relating to "matters medically dangerous to the public" is justified. Nevertheless, while the public interest may justify disclosure, that does not necessarily mean that all members of the public need to know the information in question. In *Initial Services v Putterill* [1967] 3 All E.R. 145, Lord Denning held that disclosure would only be permitted if it was made to someone who had a proper interest in receiving the information. In *Lion Laboratories v Evans* [1984] 2 All E.R. 47, Lord Wilberforce stated that there was a difference between something which was of interest to the public and which was in the public interest to know. This is a matter to be determined on a case-by-case basis.

Freedom of expression and the public interest

X v Y [1988] 2 All E.R. 648

A national newspaper published details regarding two general practitioners (G.P.s) who had developed AIDS. The health authority brought proceedings to stop further publication of the health information of the G.P.s.

ROSE J.
" . . . Under the National Health Service (Venereal Disease) Regulations 1974 the plaintiffs and their servants have a statutory duty to take all necessary steps to secure that any information capable of identifying patients examined or treated for AIDS shall not be disclosed except to a medical practitioner, or a person under his direction, in connection with and for the purposes of treatment or prevention of the spread of the disease. Confidentiality is of paramount importance to such patients, including doctors. The plaintiffs take care to ensure it. Their servants are contractually bound to respect it. If it is breached, or if the patients have grounds for believing that it may be or has been breached they will be reluctant to come forward for and to continue treatment and, in particular counselling. If the actual or apprehended breach is to the press that reluctance is likely to be very great. If treatment is not provided or continued the individual will be deprived of its benefit and the public are likely to suffer from an increase in the rate of spread of the disease. The preservation of confidentiality is therefore in the public interest.
　. . . [I]s publication of this confidential information [in relation to the two G.P.'s with AIDS] justified in the public interest?
　Counsel for the second defendants accepted (as was indeed the evidence of every witness in the case) that public debate does not require the use of confidential information and he

also accepted that in any publication the doctors should not be identified. But he submitted, as did counsel for the first defendant, that the public's right to know is not limited to theoretical debate; they submitted that the public is entitled to be told, at the very least, that two general practitioners with AIDS have practised in the United Kingdom. This form of proposed publication, first suggested in the final speech of counsel for the second defendants is the fifth or sixth version suggested by the defendants. Earlier versions, progressively diminishing the degree of identification, were put forward in paragraph 18 of the first defendant's defence and paragraph 12 of the second defendant's defence (which conflict as to whether the editor's intention was or was not to name the doctors), a letter from the second defendants' solicitors dated October 7, 1987 and the second defendants' amended defence (adopted by the first defendant). Not until October 7, did the second defendants purport to abandon their expressed intention to name both the doctors and the hospital where they were treated and even then (in the letter) they wished to identify the alleged specialities of both the doctors.

I accept the submission of counsel for the second defendants that the last version would not lead to identification; none of the evidence suggests that it would. With regard to the version in paragraph 10 of the amended defence (repeated in paragraph 19 of the amended counterclaim) there is a conflict of evidence between the physician who saw no danger of identification or breach of confidence attributable to the hospital and Sir Donald Acheson and Professor Adler who thought it presented a risk of identification. Essentially the question is one for me rather than for medical opinion. But I suspect that Professor Adler may be right in saying that this version narrows down the issue too much and would lead to further media investigation and, ultimately, tracing of the doctors; and that suspicion, in the absence of any evidence from the first defendant, the second defendants' editor or any other journalist, is a healthy one. But for the purpose of considering whether there should be an injunction I am prepared to assume, without finding, that the version in paragraph 10 of the amended defence would not lead to identification or attributable breach of confidence.

Counsel for the second defendants next submitted that, if the identities are not revealed, an injunction should not be granted even though the information has the necessary quality of confidentiality. There must (as is common ground) be a substantial, not trivial, violation of the plaintiffs' rights to justify the equitable relief. He accepted that what the plaintiffs' unfaithful servant did was not trivial but said that publication in the form suggested in paragraph 10 of the amended defence would be. Accordingly, he submitted that there was no discernible detriment to the plaintiffs and detriment is essential; he relied on the reference to detriment in *Seager v Copydex Ltd* [1967] 2 All E.R. 415 at 417, 418, by Lord Denning M.R. and Salmon L.J. and suggested that, when in *Coco v A. N. Clarke (Engineers) Ltd* [1969] RPC 41 at 48 Megarry V.-C contemplates cases where the plaintiff may not suffer, that judgment has to be viewed in the light of the Court of Appeal judgments in *Seager v Copydex Ltd*.

Counsel for the plaintiffs submitted that detriment is not a separate question but part of the balancing exercise. Furthermore, he said there is detriment, first, in the breach of contract, second, in the special arrangements which had to be made in order to continue treatment of one of the doctors (as described by the physician), third, in the pursuit of one of the doctors as appears from the first defendant's notes of conversation and unpublished draft article and in the information that the other doctor was 'very suicidal' and, fourth, in the apparent breach of the plaintiff's duties of medical confidentiality and under the National Health Service (Venereal Disease) Regulations 1974.

In my judgment detriment in the use of the information is not a necessary precondition to injunctive relief. Although in *Seager v Copydex Ltd* the Court of Appeal held, by reference to the facts of the case, that the confidential information could not be used as a springboard for activities detrimental to the plaintiff, I do not understand any member of the court to have been saying that detrimental use is always necessary. I respectfully agree with Megarry V.-C that an injunction may be appropriate for breach of confidence where the plaintiff may not suffer from the use of the information and that is borne out by more recent observations in the Court of Appeal and House of Lords, to which I will refer later (in particular in *Lion Laboratories v Evans* [1984] 2 All E.R. 417, *Schering Chemicals v Falkman Ltd* [1981] 2 All E.R. 321, and *British Steel v Granada Television Ltd* [1981] 1 All E.R. 417), which contain no reference to the necessity for detriment in use and, indeed, point away from any such principle. In the present case, detriment occurred to the plaintiffs because patients' records were leaked to the press in breach of contract and breach of confidence, with the consequences, even without publication, to the plaintiffs and the patients listed by counsel for the plaintiffs. If use were made of that information in such a way as to demonstrate to the public (by identifying the hospital) the source of the leak, the plaintiffs would suffer further detriment. But use of the information (as the defendants now seek) in a way which identifies neither the hospital nor the patients does not mean that the plaintiffs have suffered no detriment. Significant damage, about which the plaintiffs are entitled to complain, has already been done. This is also the answer to the additional submission of counsel for the first defendant that, though there was a breach of confidence in obtaining the information there is, on the evidence, none in publishing it, if the doctors are not identified. In my judgment it is, in the present case, the initial disclosure and its immediate consequences, not subsequent publication, which found the plaintiffs' claim in breach of contract and breach of confidence.

The remaining, crucial, issue on the first question is public interest: does this require injunctive relief? . . . On the one hand, there are the public interests in having a free press and an informed public debate; on the other, it is in the public interest that actual or potential AIDS sufferers should be able to resort to hospitals without fear of this being revealed, that those owing duties of confidence in their employment should be loyal and should not disclose confidential matters and that, prima facie, no one should be allowed to use information extracted in breach of confidence from hospital records even if disclosure of the particular information may not give rise to immediately apparent harm.

It is to be noted that in the present case the plaintiffs' cause of action lies not just (as in most of the authorities) in breach of confidence but also in procurement of breach of contract. The onus of proving justification once the tort of interference with contractual rights is established (as is not here disputed) is on the defendants (see *South West Wales Miners' Federation v Glamorgan Coal Co. Ltd* [1904–7] All E.R. Rep. 211 at 214, 217, 219.

I keep in the forefront of my mind the very important public interest in freedom of the press. And I accept that there is some public interest in knowing that which the defendants seek to publish (in whichever version). But in my judgment those public interests are substantially outweighed when measured against the public interests in relation to loyalty and confidentiality both generally and with particular reference to AIDS patients' hospital records. There has been no misconduct by the plaintiffs. The records of hospital patients, particularly those suffering from this appalling condition should, in my judgment, be as confidential as the courts can properly keep them in order that the plaintiffs may 'be free from suspicion that they are harbouring disloyal employees'. The plaintiffs have 'suffered a grievous wrong in which the defendants became involved . . . with active participation'. The deprivation of the public of the information sought to be published will be of minimal significance if the injunction is granted; for, without it, all the evidence before me shows that a wide-ranging public debate about AIDS generally and about its effect on doctors is taking place among doctors of widely differing views, within and without the BMA, in medical journals and in many newspapers, including the *Observer*, the *Sunday Times* and the *Daily Express*. Indeed, the sterility of the defendants' argument is demonstrated by the edition of the second defendant's own newspaper dated on March 22, 1987. It is there expressly stated, purportedly quoting a Mr Milligan, that three general practitioners two of whom are practising (impliedly in Britain) have AIDS. Paraphrasing Templeman L.J. in the *Schering* case, the facts, in the most limited version now sought to be published, have already been made available and will again be made available if they are known otherwise than through the medium of the informer. The risk of identification is only one factor in assessing whether to permit the use of confidential information. In my judgment to allow publication in the recently suggested restricted form, would be to enable both defendants to procure breaches of confidence and then to make their own selection for publication. This would make a mockery of the law's protection of confidentiality when no justifying public interest has been shown. These are the considerations which guide me, whether my task is properly described as a balancing exercise, or an exercise in judicial judgment, or both. No one has suggested that damages would be an adequate remedy in this case."

NOTE:

1. This case was the first breach of confidence case concerning disclosure of confidential medical information in recent times. (See J.V. McHale "Doctors with AIDS—Dilemmas of Confidentiality" (1988) 4 *Professional Negligence* 76.)

QUESTION:

1. Would/should the decision of Rose J. to prevent further publication have been different had the doctors been surgeons as opposed to G.P.s?

The issue of disclosure of information concerning a health care professional who was HIV positive arose subsequently in the following case.

H (a health worker) v Associated Newspapers Ltd [2002] EWCA Civ 195

H, an NHS professional, was HIV positive. He stopped work when diagnosed. At that time Department of Health guidelines provided that where patients had undergone procedures in relation to which there was a risk of infection, they should be notified that they had been treated by a worker who was HIV positive and they should be offered counselling. The health authority (N) wanted to undertake a "look-back" study. H was asked to give the health authority details of both his NHS and his private patients. He alleged that the first look-back study was unlawful on the basis of clinical confidentiality. In addition he also asked if the N could be stopped from using information which he had previously supplied. The *Mail on Sunday* newspaper was informed of the case and wanted to publish details which would have identified both H and the N in question.

LORD PHILLIPS M.R.

"H's interest

27. The consequences to H if his identity were to be disclosed would be likely to be distressing on a personal level. More than this, there is an obvious public interest in preserving the confidentiality of victims of the AIDS epidemic and, in particular, of healthcare workers who report the fact that they are HIV positive. Where a lookback exercise follows, it may prove impossible to preserve the identification of the worker but, if healthcare workers are not to be discouraged from reporting that they are HIV positive, it is essential that all possible steps are taken to preserve the confidentiality of such reports. This is a point that is emphasised in the Guidelines.

28. H has another interest to which it is necessary to have regard when performing the balancing exercise. His patients have a right of confidentiality in relation to their medical

records. In *A Health Authority v X* [2001] Lloyd's Rep. Med. 349 at 351 Munby J. said of the duty of the doctor in that case:

> 'Dr X's ultimate obligation is to comply with whatever order the court may make. But prior to that point being reached his duty, like that of any other professional or other person who owes a duty of confidentiality to his patient or client, is to assert that confidentiality in answer to any claim by a third party for disclosure and to put before the court every argument that can properly be put against disclosure.'

In the Court of Appeal Thorpe LJ was inclined to endorse this statement—see transcript 21 December 2001 at paragraph 25. We would, however, express the reservation that a doctor's primary duty is to the welfare of his clients and that there will sometimes be circumstances in which it is in their interests to disclose their records.

29. H brought his first action in part to protect his patients' rights to confidentiality. He was not prepared to disclose records of his patients which would result in his patients being informed that he was HIV positive unless this was demonstrated to be in his patients' interests. The issue in the first action is whether H's patients' rights to confidentiality, and with them H's own right to keep confidential the fact that he is HIV positive, should give way to the requirements of a lookback exercise. If disclosure of N's identity is likely to set off a chain of events which will lead inexorably to a lookback exercise, pre-empting the result of the action, this is further justification for the order in the first action that N should remain anonymous.

N's standing in the dispute

32. We accept that N has a legitimate interest in striving to protect the information that they have obtained in confidence that one of their healthcare workers is HIV positive. In addition to this, however, DPH adverted to the consequences that would follow publication of the fact that one of N's healthcare workers was HIV positive in circumstances where N could not reassure the vast majority of patients who had had no contact with H. Widespread alarm would be caused to patients within the health area. Many help lines would have to be set up to deal with enquiries. Because N would not be able to reassure those who were not H's patients, they would have to offer HIV testing to anyone who sought it.

33. Before us DPH's evidence was supported by evidence adduced by Department of Health ('DH'). In her written submissions, which fairly summarised the Department's evidence, Miss Mulcahy said:

> 'The likelihood and degree of public anxiety should not be under-estimated. Communication of risk is a complex exercise. There is undoubtedly still stigma and ignorance surrounding the issue of HIV/AIDS, which can generate unjustified public alarm and the manner of communication in this sensitive area must be handled carefully. Even if patients are informed in the course of a typical patient notification exercise, some individuals may worry about the risk of contracting a potentially fatal illness to the extent that they may claim to have suffered diagnosable psychiatric illness. There is a higher risk of public alarm and of inaccurate public perception of risk if communication of the risk is through sensationalised news stories in the national media rather than directly through the health authority concerned as part of a responsibly conducted look back exercise. This is well illustrated by the case of *A & B v Tameside & Glossop Health Authority* [1997] 8 Med LR 91, CA in which an action was brought on behalf of patients who allegedly suffered psychiatric illness because they had been informed of the fact that they had previously been treated by an HIV-positive health care worker by a

letter instead of face to face from a GP or experienced health worker. The Judge at first instance found that publication of the issue in the national media (following a leak) at a time when helplines were not available may well have intensified the impact on patients of the notification letters received a couple of days later.

. . .

Resources: In order to maintain public confidence as far as possible, it seems likely that the Health Authority will have to be prepared to offer HIV testing and counselling to the entirety of the patient group treated by any clinical specialty in its Area within the last 10 years if a patient is concerned and does not wish to wait for the forthcoming decision on, and the implementation of, any lookback exercise. If so, it has the potential to be the largest and most costly exercise in the HIV notification field yet undertaken. If no lookback or a more limited lookback ultimately goes ahead, NHS resources will have been wasted. Even if a full lookback goes ahead, if patients who were not treated by the health care worker concerned have been offered HIV testing, it will have been a considerably more expensive exercise than would normally be the case.'

34. We had some doubt as to the extent to which these problems, however likely and serious, were matters that N could legitimately raise as a reason for restricting press freedom. We asked Mr Havers whether it was his case that N had a free standing interest that would have entitled them to seek an injunction, even if H's claim to confidentiality had not been in play. What if the story that ANL was proposing to publish was that one of N's healthcare workers had died of AIDS?

35. Mr Havers referred us to Article 10(2) of the Convention, which qualifies the freedoms of expression in this way:

'The exercise of these freedoms, since it carries with it duties and responsibilities, may be subject to such formalities, conditions, restrictions or penalties as are prescribed by law and are necessary in a democratic society, in the interests of national security, territorial integrity or public safety, for the prevention of disorder or crime, for the protection of health or morals, for the protection of the reputation or rights of others, for preventing the disclosure of information received in confidence, or for maintaining the authority and impartiality of the judiciary.'

36. We asked Mr Havers to identify the manner in which interference with freedom of expression to accommodate interests which were essentially administrative was, in this country, 'prescribed by law'. Mr Havers did not find it easy to answer this question. He submitted that, as a party to the first action, N had a right to be heard. This was never in doubt, but the right to be heard does not bear on the interests that can legitimately be advanced in the exercise of that right.

37. Ultimately Mr Havers submitted that, if he had to demonstrate a right to relief that was independent of H, he would rely on the decision of this Court in *Broadmoor Special Hospital v Robinson* [2000] QB 775. In that case, the majority—Lord Woolf MR and Waller L.J.—held that the Court had the following jurisdiction:

'if a public body is given a statutory responsibility which it is required to perform in the public interest, then, in the absence of an implication to the contrary in the statute, it has standing to apply to the court for an injunction to prevent interference with its performance of its public responsibilities and the court should grant such an application when, "it appears to the court to be just and convenient to do so" ' (see p.795)

38. The decision in *Robinson* represents a significant step down a path which our law appears to be treading towards using the injunction to restrain behaviour which, while

open to objection, does not represent a breach of duty owed under public or private law . . .

40. This trend is to be distinguished from the development of the law of privacy, under the stimulus of the Human Rights Act, under which the possibility of a new civil law right is being recognised as one that can be legitimately protected by the grant of an injunction—see *Douglas v Hello! Ltd* [2001] QB 967; *A v B and C* [2001] 1 WLR 2341. In *Venables v News Group Newspapers Ltd* [2001] 2 WLR 1038 the President, sitting in the Family Division, extended the law of confidence to justify the grant of an injunction in wide terms designed to ensure that the identity of the Bulger killers, now released into the community as young men, remains confidential. The remarkable and novel feature of the injunction granted in that case was that it was expressly stated to be against the whole world.

41. In *Venables* the President was at pains to reject the submission that the Court had jurisdiction to grant an injunction to prevent an interference with one of the fundamental human rights, where no breach of a duty owed under our private law was made out. We would view with concern any attempt to invoke the power of the Court to grant an injunction restraining freedom of expression merely on the ground that release of the information would give rise to administrative problems and a drain on resources. Such consequences are the price which has to be paid, from time to time, for freedom of expression in a democratic society. N's more cogent claim to be heard arises on behalf of the patients in N's health area for whose medical welfare N is responsible.

42. Gross J concluded (paragraph 29) 'the true focus of public interest lies with N not with H'. He weighed in the balance 'N's independent interest in preserving its anonymity'. He concluded that the balance still tilted in favour of freedom of expression. We consider that a somewhat different approach to the balancing exercise is called for.

43. The first action was commenced in order to obtain the decision of the Court as to whether a lookback exercise should take place, which would involve the disclosure of confidential medical records held by H and, in all probability, the confidential information that H was HIV positive. It has not been suggested that this action should not have been started, nor that the issues that it raises should not be determined by the Court. In these circumstances, we consider that the Court could properly make an Order in the proceedings restraining the publication of information made available in the course of or as a result of the conduct of the proceedings which, if disclosed, would pre-empt the decision of the Court on the issues before it. The power to make such an Order is inherent in the Judge's power to control the proceedings in such a manner as is necessary to achieve the due administration of justice and is implicitly recognised by the provisions of CPR 39.2. Third parties with knowledge of such an Order will be in contempt if they disclose information which the Court had ordered should not be disclosed. Justification for the restriction of freedom of expression inherent in such an Order is to be found in Article 10.2 of the Convention, for the Order is a necessary incident of ' the protection of health, the protection of the rights of others and the prevention of the disclosure of information received in confidence'.

44. Treating the Order of Scott-Baker J. as if made in the first action, we consider that it should only be maintained insofar as necessary to prevent the pre-emption of the determination of the issues before the Court in that action. The same is true of Master Leslie's Order permitting N's identity to be concealed. The immediate consequences to N if N's identity is disclosed are of importance insofar as they may lead to the pre-emption of the determination of the issues in the action. Putting this consideration on one side, it is plain that disclosure of N's identity is likely to cause alarm to patients within N's area, with consequent administrative and resource implications for N. Mr Wilson has not submitted that these considerations should be ignored. They weigh against disclosure of N's identity. How much weight they should carry is a question on which the views of individual members of the Court have differed. Ultimately, that question has not proved critical.

45. We turn, then, to consider what consequences would be likely to flow from disclosure of N's identity.

Deductive identification of H's identity

46. H contends that if N's identity is disclosed, this will lead to the identification of H because of the information that is already in the public domain by reason of the publication in the *Mail on Sunday* on 18 November 2001. H contends that if, to this information, there is added N's identity, it will be possible to deduce who H is.

47. Gross J. was not persuaded that this risk justified preserving N's anonymity. He held, in effect, that the casual reader of the November article would not have subjected it to the kind of scrutiny that would lead to deduction of information about A. If an investigative journalist were to put two and two together, the injunction would still restrain any publication of material that would lead to the deduction of H's speciality or of when he was diagnosed as HIV positive.

48. We are less sanguine than Gross J. about the risk of deductive disclosure of H's identity. The November article is in the public domain. The information in that article, coupled with the identification of N, could well lead anyone who had personal knowledge that H had retired through ill-health to deduce that the article was written about H. A prime, and not unreasonable, concern of H may well be that those whom he knows personally should not become aware of the nature of his illness.

49. We have, however, quite different concerns as to the manner in which disclosure of N's identity might lead to the identification of H. When addressing the concerns on the part of N at the public anxiety and alarm that would follow the naming of N the Judge concluded that these concerns were answered by the Guidelines. He said at paragraph 52:

> 'As it appears to me, paragraphs 11.41 and 11.45 of the guidelines make provision for and are readily applicable to the very situation which will arise as and when N's identity becomes known. It may well be that in responding to any publicity and in giving its version of events N will draw heavily on those paragraphs. In a nutshell, publication of N's identity does not take the matter out of the guidelines and into uncharted territory; instead the guidelines have contemplated and make provision for this eventuality.'

50. It is necessary to say a word about the Guidelines and to consider whether the Judge was correct to conclude that they would apply to the situation that would arise when N was named. The Guidelines were published in December 1998. Under the Guidelines the policy was that all patients who had undergone any exposure prone procedure performed by an infected health care worker should, as far as practicable, be notified of this (para. 8.2) and offered HIV testing. 'Exposure prone procedures' ('EPPs') are those where there is a risk that injury to the health care worker could result in his or her blood contaminating a patient's open tissues.

51. On being notified that a healthcare worker was HIV positive, a Health Authority had to carry out a period of evaluation before embarking on a lookback exercise. In the course of this evaluation, the exposed patient population had to be identified. The paragraphs of the Guidelines to which Gross J. referred made provision for the action that should be taken in the event of media interest. They gave the following advice:

> '11.41 In the event of media interest or other external enquiries during the period of evaluation prior to a patient notification exercise, the DPH should acknowledge that a case is being investigated. If necessary the media should be told that when the evaluation is complete anyone who is considered to have been at risk will be notified individually, counselled and offered HIV testing. At the same time an assurance should be given that the overall risk is considered very low.
> . . .
> 11.45 If, however, a proactive public announcement is judged necessary, it will normally be made through a press release. This should be as informative as possible whilst avoiding the inclusion of information which could lead to deductive disclosure of the health care worker's identity. The health care worker should not be named [see Section 10]. It should:

- refer to "a health care worker" unless more explicit information about the worker's profession has already entered the public domain;
- include details of arrangements which are being or have been made to contact patients;
- reassure that all patients who may have been exposed to risk will be or have been contacted individually, and offered HIV testing as appropriate.'

52. These Guidelines were designed for a situation where evaluation was already in progress. It does not seem to us that they can realistically be applied to cover the facts of the present case. At present there is no DH guidance in place as to the criteria to be applied in the evaluation exercise. The only advice is to do nothing until the new guidance is available. It was initially expected that this would be in mid-February. We are now told by Miss Mulcahy that it will not be until mid-March. We cannot be confident that this guidance will be in place before N's identity is disclosed.

53. If ANL are permitted to disclose N's identity, there is no doubt that they will make the most of this. They will be entitled to do so. The stance of the *Mail on Sunday* is that H's patients are entitled to know that they have been treated by someone who is HIV positive. The manner in which they break the news of N's identity is likely to lead to many of those who have received medical treatment of one kind or another in N's area ringing up N to find out whether they are potentially at risk.

54. N's original stance was that, when faced with such enquiries they would not be in a position to reassure those who had not had treatment from H that they were not at risk. They would simply have to say that it was not yet possible to say whether they were at risk, but that if they were the risk would be very slight and they would be informed of it in due course. Those who wanted reassurance would have to be offered HIV tests, which would involve the invasive procedures of taking blood and saliva samples. The overall cost of the operation might amount to £2 million.

55. We found this scenario disturbing and unrealistic. If N's identity were released tomorrow, N would be in a position to reassure the vast majority of those patients who telephoned in alarm that they were not at risk. Each patient could be asked what treatment had given rise to concern and, where the treatment was from someone other than H, they could be told that they had no cause for concern. To allow patients to submit to HIV testing as an alternative to this swift and simple reassurance would, so it seemed to us, be absurd. Any patient exposed to such a procedure would have justifiable cause for complaint.

56. The alternative would, however, almost inevitably involve the disclosure of H's identity. Those who phoned in would no doubt include some of H's patients. They would have to be told that they might be at risk, and thus H's identity would be likely to emerge. It seemed to us that this would be the lesser of two evils. The Guidelines recognise that the anonymity of the healthcare worker may have to be sacrificed in the interests of the patients. If N's identity were disclosed in the circumstances of the present case, the logical consequence would be a process of patient reassurance that would be likely to result in H's identification.

57. When we put these considerations to Mr Havers, he took instructions and informed us that, if N's identity were disclosed, N would indeed seek to be relieved of the obligation to do nothing that might reveal H's identity. N would do so in order to be free to reassure those who were not H's patients. We consider that the Court would be bound to accede to such an application. The disclosure of N's identity would thus set in train a course of events which would be likely to result in the disclosure of H's identity. H's patients would have to be offered HIV testing and counselling. The very state of affairs that H had sought, by the first action, to prevent would be brought about.

58. For these reasons, we have concluded that, in order to avoid the pre-emption of the determination of the issues raised in the first action, the Order that both H and N should only be identified by initials was appropriate, and that Gross J's modification of the Orders to permit the identification of N must be set aside.

Identification of H's speciality

59. We turn to the question of whether the embargo on disclosing H's speciality should remain in force. The Guidelines recognise that different specialisations give rise to different degrees of risk. H argued that even this information would be likely to lead to his identification. We do not agree. There must be a risk that some who know the details of H's retirement may suspect, and it can be no more than a suspicion, that he is the healthcare worker in this action. Provided, however, that the other restraints in Gross J's Order remain in force, which we consider that they should, we do not consider that this risk justifies continuing the restraint on disclosing H's speciality. As we indicated early in our judgment, this restraint is inhibiting debate on what is a matter of public interest. We have concluded that this restraint is not justified.

Disclosure to N of the medical records of H's patients

62. A significant period has elapsed since H was identified as HIV positive. This has been due in part to the hiatus caused by the withdrawal of the old Guidelines without replacement with new guidance. The hearing of the first action has been put back pending publication of the new guidance. Should it be determined, as it well may, that a lookback exercise should be carried out in relation to some of H's patients, it is important that there should be no further delay to the process of evaluation that is likely to be involved. H has indicated that, if the Court declares it necessary, he will hand over to N the records of his patients over the last ten years. We consider, for the reasons that we have given, that he should make available such records as are reasonably required for the purpose of evaluation. The records should be made available to N on terms that they do not disclose them, or take any action on the basis of them, without either the permission of H or the permission of the Court."

QUESTIONS:

1. In view of the very small risk of transmission by medical practitioners to patients, should disclosure be sanctioned at all?
2. How far should considerations of press freedom be taken into account in determining what protection should be given to patient confidentiality?
3. Should the fact that the doctor's identity was not disclosed be a relevant consideration in determining whether or not the article was in breach of confidence?
4. Can information be disclosed in the face of an explicit prohibition by the patient?

Public interest and risk disclosure

W v Egdell [1990] 1 All E.R. 835, [1990] Ch. 359, [1990] 2 W.L.R. 471

W was detained in hospital under a restriction order authorised by ss.60 and 65 of the Mental Health Act 1959, after being convicted of the manslaughter of five people. He applied to a mental health review tribunal for discharge from the hospital (Mental Health Act 1983, s.41). A psychiatrist, Dr Egdell, was commissioned to examine W and to compile a report on him. The report was unfavourable. Dr Egdell suggested that W had an abnormal personality which could be of a psychopathic nature and expressed his concern at W's interest in what W called fireworks, by which he meant such things as tubes of piping packed with explosive chemicals. On receipt of the report, W's solicitors decided to withdraw his application to the tribunal. Dr Egdell asked W's solicitors for a copy of his report to be put in W's hospital file. They refused. Dr Edgell then decided to disclose the contents of the report to W's responsible medical officer. Subsequently the report was disclosed to the Home Office. The Home Secretary is periodically required to refer cases of patients such as W to a mental health review tribunal (Mental Health Act 1983, s.67). After his own application to the tribunal had been withdrawn, W's case came up for review under this automatic procedure. W's solicitors obtained an injunction to restrain Dr Egdell from disclosing the contents of the report at the hearing. Unknown to them, however, the disclosure had already occurred. At the hearing the Home Secretary put forward the information obtained by Dr Egdell, alleging breach of confidence.

SIR STEPHEN BROWN
" . . . In the course of his judgment Scott J said ([1989] 1 All E.R. 1089 at 1101–1102:

'The basis of W's case is that his interview with Dr Egdell on July 23, 1987 and the report written by Dr Egdell on the basis of that interview is, or ought to have been, protected from disclosure by the duty of confidence resting on Dr Egdell as W's doctor. It is claimed that Dr Egdell was in breach of his duty of confidence in telling Dr Hunter about the report, in sending a copy of the report to Dr Hunter and in urging the despatch of a copy to the Home Office . . . It is convenient for me first to ask myself what duty of confidence a court of equity ought to regard as imposed on Dr Egdell by the circumstances in which he obtained information from and about W and prepared his report. It is in my judgment plain, and the contrary has not been suggested, that the circumstances did impose on Dr Egdell a duty of confidence. If, for instance Dr Egdell had sold the contents of his report to a newspaper, I do not think any court of equity would hesitate for a moment before concluding that his conduct had been a breach of his duty of confidence. The question in the present case is not whether Dr Egdell was under a duty of confidence he plainly was. The question is as to the breadth of that duty. Did the duty extend so as to bar disclosure of the report to the medical director of the hospital? Did it bar disclosure to the Home Office? In the *Spycatcher* case [*A.-G. v. Guardian Newspaper Ltd (No.2)*] [1988] 3 All E.R. 545 at 658–659, in the House of Lords Lord Goff, after accepting "the broad general principle . . . that a duty of confidence arises when confidential information comes to the knowledge of a person (the confidant) in circumstances where he has notice, or is held to have agreed, that the information is confidential, with the effect that it would be just in all the circumstances that he should be precluded from disclosing the information to others", formulated three limiting principles. He said: "The third limiting principle is of far greater importance. It is that, although the basis of the law's protection of confidence is that there is a public interest that confidences should be preserved and protected by the law, nevertheless that public interest may be outweighed by some other countervailing public interest which favours disclosure. This limitation may apply, as the learned judge pointed out, to all types of confidential information. It is this limiting principle which may require a court to carry out a balancing operation, weighing the public interest in maintaining confidence against a countervailing public interest favouring disclosure." In *X v. Y* [1988] 2 All E.R. 648 at 653, a case which concerned doctors who were believed to be continuing to practise despite having contracted AIDS, Rose J. said: "In the long run, preservation of confidentiality is the only way of securing public health otherwise doctors will be discredited as a source of education, for future individual patients will not come forward if doctors are going to squeal on them". Consequently, confidentiality is vital to secure public as well as private health, for unless those infected come forward they cannot be counselled and self-treatment does not provide the best care . . . "The question in a particular case whether a duty of confidentiality extends to bar particular disclosures that the confidant has made or wants to make requires the court to balance the interest to be served by non-disclosure against the interest served by disclosure. Rose J. struck that balance. It came down, he held, in favour of non-disclosure. In the *Spycatcher* case that balance too was struck. In that case the balance did not come down in favour of non-disclosure. I must endeavour to strike the balance in the present case.'

Counsel for W agreed that the judge was required to carry out a balancing exercise. He said that it is a question of degree.

As a starting point Scott J. turned to 'Advice on Standards of Professional Conduct and of Medical Ethics' contained in the General Medical Council's 'Blue Book' on professional conduct and discipline. The judge said ([1989] 1 All E.R. 1089 at 1103):

'These rules do not provide a definitive answer to the question raised in the present case as to the breadth of the duty of confidence owed by Dr Egdell. They seem to me valuable, however, in showing the approach of the General Medical Council to the breadth of the doctor/patient duty of confidence.'

These rules do not themselves have statutory authority. Nevertheless, the General Medical Council in exercising its disciplinary jurisdiction does so in pursuance of the provisions of the Medical Act 1983. Under the heading 'Professional Confidence', rr.79 to 82 provide as follows:

'79. The following guidance is given on the principles which should govern the confidentiality of information relating to patients.
    80. It is a doctor's duty, except in the cases mentioned below, strictly to observe the rule of professional secrecy by refraining from disclosing voluntarily to any third party information about a patient which he has learnt directly or indirectly in his professional capacity as a registered medical practitioner. The death of the patient does not absolve the doctor from this obligation.
    81. The circumstances where exceptions to the rule may be permitted are as follows:
    (a) If the patient or his legal adviser gives written and valid consent, information to which the consent refers may be disclosed.
    (b) Confidential information may be shared with other registered medical practitioners who participate in or assume responsibility for clinical management of the patient. To the extent that the doctor deems it necessary for the performance of their particular duties, confidential information may also be shared with other persons (nurses and other health care professionals) who are assisting and collaborating with the doctor in his professional relationship with the patient. It is the doctor's responsibility to ensure that such individuals appreciate that the information is being imparted in strict professional confidence.
    (c) If in particular circumstances the doctor believes it undesirable on medical grounds to seek the patient's consent, information regarding the patient's health may sometimes be given in confidence to a close relative or person in a similar relationship to the patient. However, this guidance is qualified in paragraphs 83–85 below.
    (d) If in the doctor's opinion disclosure of information to a third party other than a relative would be in the best interests of the patient, it is the doctor's duty to make every reasonable effort to persuade the patient to allow the information to be given. If the patient still refuses then only in exceptional cases should the doctor feel entitled to disregard his refusal.
    (e) Information may be disclosed to the appropriate authority in order to satisfy a specific statutory requirement, such as notification of an infectious disease.
    (f) If the doctor is directed to disclose information by a judge or other presiding officer of a court before whom he is appearing to give evidence, information may at that stage be disclosed. Similarly, a doctor may disclose information when he

has been summoned by authority of a court in Scotland, or under the powers of a Procurator -Fiscal in Scotland to investigate sudden, suspicious or unexplained deaths, and appears to give evidence before a Procurator-Fiscal. Information may also be disclosed to a coroner or his nominated representative to the extent necessary to enable the coroner to determine whether an inquest should be held. But where litigation is in prospect, unless the patient has consented to disclosure or a formal court order has been made for disclosure, information should not be disclosed merely in response to demands from other persons such as another party's solicitor or an official of the court.

(g) Rarely, disclosure may be justified on the ground that it is in the public interest which, in certain circumstances such as, for example, investigation by the police of a grave or very serious crime, might override the doctor's duty to maintain his patient's confidence.

(h) Information may also be disclosed if necessary for the purpose of a medical research project which has been approved by a recognised ethical committee.

82. Whatever the circumstances, a doctor must always be prepared to justify his action if he has disclosed confidential information. If a doctor is in doubt whether any of the exceptions mentioned above would justify him in disclosing information in a particular situation he will be wise to seek advice from a medical defence society or professional association.'

The judge said that paragraph (b) and (g) of regulation 81 seemed to him to be particularly relevant. He then rehearsed the circumstances of the disclosure by Dr Egdell of his report and asked the question ([1989] 1 All E.R. 1089 at 1104):

'Did these circumstances impose on Dr Egdell a duty not to disclose his opinions and his report to Dr Hunter, the medical director at the hospital? In my judgment they did not. Dr Egdell was expressing opinions which were relevant to the nature of the treatment and care to be accorded to W at the hospital. Dr Egdell was, in effect, recommending a change from the approach to treatment and care that Dr Ghosh was following. He was expressing reservations about Dr Ghosh's diagnosis. The case seems to me to fall squarely within paragraph (b) of 81. But I would base my conclusion on broader considerations than that. I decline to overlook the background to Dr Egdell's examina-tion of W. True it is that Dr Egdell was engaged by W. He was the doctor of W's choice. None the less, in my opinion, the duty he owed to W was not his only duty. W was not an ordinary member of the public. He was, consequent on the killings he had perpetrated, held in a secure hospital subject to a regime whereby decisions concerning his future were to be taken by public authorities, the Home Secretary or the tribunal. W's own interests would not be the only nor the main criterion in the taking of those decisions. The safety of the public would be the main criterion. In my view, a doctor called on, as Dr Egdell was, to examine a patient such as W owes a duty not only to his patient but also a duty to the public. His duty to the public would require him, in my opinion, to place before the proper authorities the result of his examination if, in his opinion, the public interest so required. This would be so, in my opinion, whether or not the patient instructed him not to do so.'

The judge then referred to the submission of counsel for W that the dominant public interest in the case was the public interest in patients being able to make full and frank disclosure to their doctors, and in particular to their psychiatrist, without fear that the doctor would disclose the information to others. The judge said ([1989] 1 All E.R. 1089 at 1104–1105):

'I accept the general importance in the public interest that this should be so. It justifies the General Medical Council's r.80 . . . In truth, as it seems to me, the interest to be served by the duty of confidence for which counsel for W contends is the private interest of W and not any broader public interest. If I set the private interest of W in the balance against the public interest served by disclosure of the report to Dr Hunter and the Home

Office, I find the weight of the public interest prevails . . . In my judgment, therefore, the circumstances of this case did not impose on Dr Egdell an obligation of conscience, an equitable obligation, to refrain from disclosing his report to Dr Hunter, or to refrain from encouraging its disclosure to the Home Office.'

In this court counsel for W acknowledges that, in addition to the duty of confidence admittedly owed by Dr Edgell to W, it was necessary for the judge to consider the public interest in the disclosure by Dr Egdell of his report to the authorities. There are two competing public interest considerations. However, he submits that the dominant public interest was the duty of confidence owed by Dr Edgell to W. The burden of proving that duty was overridden by public interest considerations in disclosing his opinion to the public authorities rested fairly and squarely on Dr Edgell. He contended that, where the public interest relied on to justify a breach of confidence is alleged to be the real reduction or elimination of a risk to public safety it must be shown (a) that such a risk is real, immediate and serious, (b) that it will be substantially reduced by disclosure, (c) that the disclosure is no greater than is reasonably necessary to minimise the risk and (d) that the consequent damage to the public interest protected by the duty of confidentiality is outweighed by the public interest in minimising such a risk. He relied on the decision of Rose J. in *X v. Y* [1988] 2 All E.R. 648. He also acted a passage from the judgment of Boreham J. in *Hunter v. Mann* [1974] 2 All E.R. 414 at 417–418.

> 'The second proposition is this: that in common with other professional men, for instance a priest and there are of course others, the doctor is under a duty not to disclose, without the consent of his patient, information which he, the doctor, has gained in his professional capacity, save, says counsel for the appellant, in very exceptional circumstances. He quoted the example of the murderer still manic, who would be a menace to society. But, says counsel, save in exceptional circumstances, the general rule applies. He adds that the law will enforce that duty.'

He referred to the American case of *Tarasoff v. Regents of the University of California* (1976) 17 Cal 3d 358 as an example of extreme circumstances and submitted that only in the most extreme circumstances could a doctor be relieved from observing the strict duty of confidence imposed on him by reason of his relationship with his patient. In this instance, said counsel for W, there was no immediate prospect of W being released or of being detained other than under secure conditions and furthermore any change in his circumstances would be conditional on further expert analysis and recommendation.

The two interests which had to be balanced in this case were both public interests. The judge was wrong to refer to W's 'private' interest. The judge was also in error, said counsel for W, in saying: The case seems to me to fall squarely within paragraph (b) of regulation 81' (of the General Medical Council's rules). Dr Egdell did not have any clinical responsibility for W and accordingly that particular rule could not be relied on by Dr Egdell in the present circumstances.

With reference to 'legal privilege', counsel for W submitted that in the context of this case it was highly relevant that the report was commissioned by solicitors acting for W in the matter of his application to the tribunal. He argued that, if legal privilege did not strictly apply to the report of Dr Egdell as distinct from his instructions, nevertheless the context in which it was prepared added strength to the duty of confidence. He used the phrase 'accumulative effect'.

Counsel for Dr Egdell argued that Dr Egdell is acknowledged to be a responsible and experienced consultant psychiatrist having particular knowledge of the procedures relating to the management and treatment of restricted patients detained in secure conditions under the provisions of the Mental Health Act 1983. His evidence on matters of fact was not challenged. It must be accepted that he was genuinely seriously concerned by the revelation of what seemed to him to be entirely new facts relating to W's long standing interest in guns and explosives. It is not challenged, he said, that he acted in good faith in disclosing his report to Dr Hunter and in urging its disclosure to the Home Secretary. He plainly believed that he was acting in the public interest.

The balance of public interest clearly lay in the restricted disclosure of vital information to the director of the hospital and to the Secretary of State who had the onerous duty of safeguarding public safety.

In this case the number and nature of the killings by W must inevitably give rise to the gravest concern for the safety of the public. The authorities responsible for W's treatment and management must be entitled to the fullest relevant information concerning his condition. It is clear that Dr Egdell did have highly relevant information about W's condition which reflected on his dangerousness. In my judgment the position came within the terms of r.81(g) of the General Medical Council's rules. Furthermore, Dr Egdell amply justified his action within the terms of r.82. The suppression of the material contained in his report would have deprived both the hospital and the Secretary of State of vital information, directly relevant to questions of public safety. Although it may be said that Dr Egdell's action in disclosing his report to Dr Hunter fell within the letter of r.81(b), the judge in fact based his conclusion on what he termed 'broader considerations', that is to say the safety of the public. I agree with him.

In so far as the judge referred to the 'private interest' of W, I do not consider that the passage in his judgment (see [1989] 1 All E.R. 1089 at 1105) accurately stated the position. There are two competing public interests and it is clear that by his reference to *X v. Y* [1988] 2 All E.R. 648 the judge was fully seised of this point. Of course W has a private interest, but the duty of confidence owed to him is based on the broader ground of public interest described by Rose J. in *X v. Y* . . . "

BINGHAM L.J.

" . . . The philosophy underlying the statutory regime which the judge described is in my view clear. A man who commits crimes, however serious, when subject to severe mental illness is not to be treated as if he were of sound mind. He requires treatment in hospital, not punishment in prison. So an order may be made committing him to hospital. He may, however, represent a great and continuing danger to the public. So his confinement in hospital may be ordered to continue until the Home Secretary, as guardian of the public safety, adjudges it safe to release him or relax the conditions of his confinement. But a decision by the Home Secretary adverse to the patient is not conclusive. The patient may have recourse to an independent tribunal which, if certain conditions are satisfied, must order his discharge either conditionally or absolutely and which may make non-binding recommendations. Lest an inactive patient be forgotten, his case must be reviewed by the tribunal at three-yearly intervals. These provisions represent a careful balance between the legitimate desire of the patient to regain his freedom and the legitimate desire of the public to be protected against violence. The heavy responsibility of deciding how the balance should be struck in any given case at any given time rests in the first instance on the Home Secretary and in the second instance on the tribunal. It is only by making a careful and informed assessment of the individual case that the potentially conflicting claims of humanity to the patient and protection of the public may be fairly and responsibly reconciled.

It has never been doubted that the circumstances here were such as to impose on Dr Egdell a duty of confidence owed to W. He could not lawfully sell the contents of his report to a newspaper, as the judge held. Nor could he, without a breach of the law as well as professional etiquette, discuss the case in a learned article or in his memoirs or in gossiping with friends, unless he took appropriate steps to conceal the identity of W. It is not in issue here that a duty of confidence existed.

The breadth of such a duty in any case is, however, dependent on circumstances. Where a prison doctor examines a remand prisoner to determine his fitness to plead or a proposer for life insurance is examined by a doctor nominated by the insurance company or a personal injury plaintiff attends on the defendant's medical adviser or a prospective bidder instructs accountants to investigate (with its consent) the books of a target company, the professional man's duty of confidence towards the subject of his examination plainly does not bar disclosure of his findings to the party at whose instance he was appointed to make his examination. Here, however, Dr Egdell was engaged by W, not by the tribunal or the hospital authorities. He assumed at first that his report would be communicated to the tribunal and thus become known to the authorities but he must, I think, have appreciated that W and his legal advisers could decide not to adduce his report in evidence before the tribunal.

The decided cases very clearly establish (1) that the law recognises an important public interest in maintaining professional duties of confidence but (2) that the law treats such duties not as absolute but as liable to be overridden where there is held to be a stronger public interest in disclosure. Thus the public interest in the administration of justice may require a clergyman, a banker, a medical man, a journalist or an accountant to breach his professional duty of confidence (*A.-G. v. Mulholland* [1963] 1 All E.R. 767 at 771, *Chantrey Martin & Co. v. Martin* [1953] 2 All E.R. 691). In *Parry Jones v. Law Society* [1968] 1 All E.R. 177, a solicitor's duty of confidence towards his clients was held to be overridden by his duty to comply with the law of the land, which required him to produce documents for inspection under the Solicitors' Accounts Rules. A doctor's duty of confidence to his patient may be overridden by clear statutory language (as in *Hunter v. Mann* [1974] 2 All E.R. 414). A banker owes his customer an undoubted duty of confidence, but he may become subject to a duty to the public to disclose, as where danger to the state or public duty supersede the duty of agent to principal (*Tournier v. National Provincial and Union Bank of England* [1923] All E.R. Rep 550 at 554, 561). An employee may justify breach of a duty of confidence towards his employer otherwise binding on him when there is a public interest in the subject matter of his disclosure (*Initial Services Ltd v. Putterill* [1967] 3 All E.R. 145, *Lion Laboratories v. Evans* [1984] 2 All E.R. 417). These qualifications of the duty of confidence arise not because that duty is not accorded legal recognition but for the reason clearly given by Lord Goff in his speech in (*A.-G. v. Guardian Newspapers Ltd (No. 2)* [1988] 3 All E.R. 545 at 659, the *Spycatcher* case), quoted by Scott J. [1989] 1 All E.R. 1089 at 1102:

'The third limiting principle is of far greater importance. It is that, although the basis of the law's protection of confidence is that there is a public interest that confidences should be preserved and protected by the law, nevertheless that public interest may be outweighed by some other countervailing public interest which favours disclosure. This limitation may apply, as the judge pointed out, to all types of confidential information. Is this limiting principle which may require a court to carry out a balancing operation, weighing the public interest in maintaining confidence against a countervailing public interest favouring disclosure?'

These principles were not in issue between the parties to this appeal. Counsel for W accepted that W's right to confidence was qualified and not absolute. But it is important to insist on the public interest in preserving W's right to confidence because the judge in his judgment concluded that while W had a strong private interest in barring disclosure of Dr Egdell's report he could not rest his case on any broader public interest (see [1989] 1 All E.R. 1089 at 1104–1105). Here, as I think, the judge fell into error. W of course had a strong personal interest in regaining his freedom and no doubt regarded Dr Egdell's report as an obstacle to that end. So he had a personal interest in restricting the report's circulation. But these private considerations should not be allowed to obscure the public interest in maintaining professional confidences. The fact that Dr Egdell as an independent psychiatrist examined and reported on W as a restricted mental patient under section 76 of the Mental Health Act 1983 does not deprive W of his ordinary right to confidence, underpinned, as such rights are, by the public interest. But it does mean that the balancing operation of which Lord Goff spoke falls to be carried out in circumstances of unusual difficulty and importance.

We were referred, as the judge was, to the current advice given by the General Medical Council to the medical profession pursuant to section 35 of the Medical Act 1983. Rule 80 provides:

'It is a doctor's duty, except in the cases mentioned below, strictly to observe the rule of professional secrecy by refraining from disclosing voluntarily to any third party information about a patient which he has learnt directly or indirectly in his professional capacity as a registered medical practitioner . . . '

I do not doubt that this accurately states the general rule as the law now stands, and the contrary was not suggested. A disclosure compelled by statute or court order is not voluntary. Rule 81 of the General Medical Council advice lists the exceptions. Our attention was drawn to paragraphs (b) and (d):

'(b) Confidential information may be shared with other registered medical practitioners who participate in or assume responsibility for clinical management of the patient. To the extent that the doctor deems it necessary for the performance of their particular duties, confidential information may also be shared with other persons (nurses and other health care professionals) who are assisting and collaborating with the doctor in his professional relationship with the patient. It is the doctor's responsibility to ensure that such individuals appreciate that the information is being imparted in strict professional confidence . . .

(d) If in the doctor's opinion disclosure of information to a third party other than a relative would be in the best interests of the patient, it is the doctor's duty to make every reasonable effort to persuade the patient to allow the information to be given. If the patient still refuses then only in exceptional cases should the doctor feel entitled to disregard his refusal.'

The judge regarded rule 81(b) as accurately stating the law and held that Dr Egdell's disclosure in the present case fell squarely within it. I have some reservations about this conclusion. It is true that the disclosure here may be said to fall within the letter of the first sentence of paragraph (b). But I think the paragraph is directed towards the familiar situation in which consultants or other specialised experts report to the doctor with clinical responsibility for treating or advising the patient, and the second sentence shows that the doctor whose duty is in question is regarded as having a continuing professional relationship with the patient. I rather doubt if the draftsman of paragraph (b) had in mind a consultant psychiatrist consulted on a single occasion—

'For the purpose of advising whether an application to a Mental Health Review Tribunal should be made by or in respect of a patient who is liable to be detained or subject to guardianship under Part II of this Act or of furnishing information as to the condition of a patient for the purposes of such an application . . . ' (See section 76(1) of the Mental Health Act 1983).

Nor do I think that Dr Egdell, in making disclosure, was primarily motivated by the ordinary concern of any doctor that a patient should receive the most efficacious treatment. Had that been his primary object, I think he would, consistently with the spirit of paragraph (d), have tried to reason with W to obtain his consent to disclosure in W's own interest. I need not, however, reach a final view. The judge preferred to rest his conclusion on a broader ground, which was in effect the exception set out in rule 81(g) of the General Medical Council advice, and I think that if the disclosure cannot be justified under that exception it would be unsafe to justify it under any other.

Rule 81(g) provides:

Rarely, disclosure may be justified on the ground that it is in the public interest which, in certain circumstances such as, for example, investigation by the police of a grave or very serious crime, might override the doctor's duty to maintain his patient's confidence.

It was this exception which, as I understand, the judge upheld and applied when he held, in what is perhaps the crucial passage in this judgment ([1989] 1 All E.R. 1089 at 1104):

'In my view, a doctor called on, as Dr Egdell was, to examine a patient such as W owes a duty not only to his patient but also a duty to the public. His duty to the public would require him, in my opinion, to place before the proper authorities the result of his examination if, in his opinion, the public interest so required. This would be so, in my opinion, whether or not the patient instructed him not to do so.'

Counsel for W criticised this passage as wrongly leaving the question whether disclosure was justified or not to the subjective decision of the doctor. He made the same criticism of a passage where Scott J. said ([1989] 1 All E.R. 1089 at 1105):

'If a patient in the position of W commissions an independent psychiatrist's report, the duty of confidence that undoubtedly lies on the doctor who makes the report does not, in my judgment, bar the doctor from disclosing the report to the hospital that is charged with the care of the patient if the doctor judges the report to be relevant to the care and treatment of the patient, nor from disclosing the report to the Home Secretary if the doctor judges the report to be relevant to the exercise of the Home Secretary's discretionary powers in relation to that patient.'

In my opinion these criticisms are just. Where, as here, the relationship between doctor and patient is contractual, the question is whether the doctor's disclosure is or is not a breach of contract. The answer to that question must turn not on what the doctor thinks but on what the court rules. But it does not follow that the doctor's conclusion is irrelevant. In making its ruling the court will give such weight to the considered judgment of a professional man as seems in all the circumstances to be appropriate.

The parties were agreed, as I think rightly, that the crucial question in the present case was how, on the special facts of the case, the balance should be struck between the public interest in maintaining professional confidences and the public interest in protecting the public against possible violence. Counsel for W submitted that on the facts here the public interest in maintaining confidences was shown to be clearly preponderant. In support of that submission he drew our attention to a number of features of the case, of which the most weighty were perhaps these.

(1) Section 76 of the Mental Health Act 1983 shows a clear parliamentary intention that a restricted patient should be free to seek advice and evidence for the specified purposes from a medical source outside the prison and secure hospital system. Section 129 ensures that the independent doctor may make a full examination and see all relevant documents. The examination may be in private, so that the authorities do not learn what passes between doctor and patient.

(2) The proper functioning of section 76 requires that a patient should feel free to bare his soul and open his mind without reserve to the independent doctor he has retained. This he will not do if a doctor is free, on forming an adverse opinion, to communicate it to those empowered to prevent the patient's release from hospital.

(3) Although the present situation is not one in which W can assert legal professional privilege, and although tribunal proceedings are not strictly adversarial, the considerations which have given rise to legal professional privilege underpin the public interest in preserving confidence in a situation such as the present. A party to a forthcoming application to a tribunal should be free to unburden himself to an adviser he has retained without fearing that any material damaging to his application will find its way without his consent into the hands of a party with interests adverse to his.

(4) Preservation of confidence would be conducive to the public safety: patients would be candid, so that problems such as those highlighted by Dr Egdell would become known, and steps could be taken to explore and if necessary treat the problems without disclosing the report.

(5) It is contrary to the public interest that patients such as W should enjoy rights less extensive than those enjoyed by other members of the public, a result of his

judgment which the judge expressly accepted (see [1989] 1 All E.R. 1089 at 1105).

Of these considerations, I accept (1) as a powerful consideration in W's favour. A restricted patient who believes himself unnecessarily confined has, of all members of society, perhaps the greatest need for a professional adviser who is truly independent and reliably discreet (2) also I, in some measure, accept, subject to the comment that if the patient is unforthcoming the doctor is bound to be guarded in his opinion. If the patient wishes to enlist the doctor's wholehearted support for his application, he has little choice but to be (or at least convince an expert interviewer that he is being) frank. I see great force in (3). Only the most compelling circumstances could justify a doctor in acting in a way which would injure the immediate interests of his patient, as the patient perceived them, without obtaining his consent. Point (4), if I correctly understand it, did not impress me. Counsel's submissions appeared to suggest that the problems highlighted by Dr Egdell could be explored and if necessary treated without the hospital authorities being told what the problems were thought to be. I do not think this would be very satisfactory. As to (5), I agree that restricted patients should not enjoy rights of confidence less valuable than those enjoyed by other patients save in so far as any breach of confidence can be justified under the stringent terms of r.81(g) . . .

When Dr Egdell made his decision to disclose, one tribunal had already recommended W's transfer to a regional secure unit and the hospital authorities had urged that course. The Home Office had resisted transfer in a qualified manner but on a basis of inadequate information. It appeared to be only a matter of time, and probably not a very long time, before W was transferred. The regional secure unit was to act as a staging post on W's journey back into the community. While W would no doubt be further tested, such tests would not be focused on the source of Dr Egdell's concern, which he quite rightly considered to have received inadequate attention up to then. Dr Egdell had to act when he did or not at all.

There is one consideration which in my judgment, as in that of the judge, weighs the balance of public interest decisively in favour of disclosure. It may be shortly put. Where a man has committed multiple killings under the disability of serious mental illness, decisions which may lead directly or indirectly to his release from hospital should not be made unless a responsible authority is properly able to make an informed judgment that the risk of repetition is so small as to be acceptable. A consultant psychiatrist who becomes aware, even in the course of a confidential relationship, of information which leads him, in the exercise of what the court considers a sound professional judgment, to fear that such decisions may be made on the basis of inadequate information and with a real risk of consequent danger to the public is entitled to take such steps as are reasonable in all the circumstances to communicate the grounds of his concern to the responsible authorities. I have no doubt that the judge's decision in favour of Dr Egdell was right on the facts of this case.

Counsel for W argued that even if Dr Egdell was entitled to make some disclosure he should have disclosed only the crucial paragraph of his report and his opinion. I do not agree. An opinion, even from an eminent source, cannot be evaluated unless its factual premise is known, and a detailed 10-page report cannot be reliably assessed by perusing a brief extract.

No reference was made in argument before us (or, so far as I know, before the judge) to the European Convention on Human Rights (Convention for the Protection of Human Rights and Fundamental Freedoms (Rome, November 4, 1950; TS 71 (1953) Cmd. 8969)), but I believe this decision to be in accordance with it. I would accept that art. 8(1) of the convention may protect an individual against the disclosure of information protected by the duty of professional secrecy. But art. 8(2) envisages that circumstances may arise in which a public authority may legitimately interfere with the exercise of that right in accordance with the law and where necessary in a democratic society in the interests of public safety or the prevention of crime. Here there was no interference by a public authority. Dr Egdell did, as I conclude, act in accordance with the law. And his conduct was in my judgment necessary in the interests of public safety and the prevention of crime."

NOTES:

1. This case differs from many doctor–patient encounters in that it involved a commissioned report by a specially appointed expert. The judgments in the Court of Appeal on the issue of disclosure can be usefully contrasted. Sir Stephen Brown followed the judgment of Scott J. at first instance. Bingham J., however, was more cautious. He stressed the obligation of confidentiality owed to a patient under a restriction order and that while, on the facts of this case, disclosure was warranted, he indicated that such disclosure should not be made lightly. He emphasised the need to show that there was a "real risk" to the public. All the judges took note of what were then the current GMC guidelines regarding disclosure of confidential information. As has been commented, these professional guidelines, which have never undergone the test of wider public debate effectively, became the legally enforced standard (see R. Lee "Deathly Silence" in R. Lee and D. Morgan, *Death Rites: Law and Ethics at the End of Life*, London: Routledge, 1994).

2. *W v Egdell* was considered in the later case of *R. v Crozier* (1990) *The Guardian*, May 8. In this case the defendant had pleaded guilty to attempted murder. The case had been adjourned for medical reports. Dr M was instructed to examine C (the defendant). The report did not reach defence counsel at the time of the hearing. The defendant was sentenced to nine years in prison. Dr M turned up late at the hearing by mistake. He approached the prosecution counsel and told him that in his opinion the defendant was suffering from a psychopathic disorder under the Mental Health Act 1983 and that another doctor who had originally been of the view that the defendant was not suffering from that mental disorder had changed his mind. The prosecution applied for and obtained variation of sentence. The judge quashed the original sentence and made an order under s.37 of the Mental Health Act 1983 and a restriction order under s.41. The defendant brought an appeal on the basis that disclosure was in breach of confidence. The defendant's appeal was rejected. The Court of Appeal said that Dr M had been in very much the same position as had Dr Egdell. Both doctors had believed that they were acting in the public interest.

3. In *W v Egdell* at first instance it was argued that the report compiled by Dr Edgell was subject to legal professional privilege and thus immune from disclosure. This argument was rejected by Scott J., the judge at first instance. This point was not the subject of consideration by the Court of Appeal in that case. (For discussion of legal professional privilege see below.)

4. It appears that to establish public interest in disclosure it is not necessary to prove that there is danger to the public as a whole and that it will be sufficient to establish that there is a risk of harm to one specified

individual, (see M. Jones, "Medical Confidentiality and the Public Interest" (1990) 6 *Professional Negligence* 16).

5. In *Egdell* the court placed considerable emphasis upon the fact that it was in the public interest for information to be disclosed. However, it has been suggested that some patients, such as those who are HIV positive, have a considerable private interest in maintaining confidentiality. It has been argued that in the case of *Egdell* W had a strong private interest in personal liberty. (See R. Lee, "Deadly Silence" in R. Lee and D. Morgan (eds), *Death Rites: Law and Ethics at the End of Life*, London: Routledge, 1994).

6. In the US, courts have been prepared to find practitioners who did not disclose confidential information revealed to them by their patients to third parties, who subsequently suffered harm, liable in negligence. The leading case *Tarasoff v Regents of the University of California* 551 p. 2d 334 131 Cal. R. 14 (1976) was cited in *Egdell*. It has been claimed that this case has had a considerable impact on the behaviour of psychiatrists in the United States, including greater willingness to breach confidentiality. The imposition of such a duty appears unlikely in this country. The English courts have been generally unwilling to impose duties on third parties (*Smith v Littlewood* [1987] All E.R. 710; *Palmer v Tees HA* [1999] Lloyd's Rep. Med. 351, CA).

7. The scope of public interest disclosure in the health care context is still uncertain. Genetic screening and testing have given rise to a number of dilemmas. Increasingly, tests are available to enable a person to determine the probability that they will develop one or more genetic diseases. There may be instances in which it is sought to inform a third party where he may himself have inherited that condition and be either at risk of developing it or being a carrier. In most instances disclosure could be undertaken with consent. If disclosure is made without the patient's consent, then a court would have to determine whether public interest justified disclosure. This may seem straightforward were a cure were to be available. Nevertheless, difficult issues could arise: for example, would disclosure to a woman, known to be contemplating pregnancy, of the fact that she is at risk of being a carrier of the lung disorder cystic fibrosis be in the public interest? The "harm" that she would be averting would be that of pregnancy (*cf.* discussion of "wrongful life" actions in Chapter 13 below). (See Nuffield Council on Bioethics report, *Genetic Screening*, 1993 and P. Boddington, "Confidentiality and Genetic Counselling" in A. Clarke (ed.), *Genetic Counselling: Practice and Principles*, London: Routledge, 1994.) Disclosure to relatives in such circumstances may be deemed to be in the public interest. (See generally K. O'Donovan and R. Gilbar "The Loved Ones: Families Intimates and Patient Autonomy" (2003) 23 Legal Studies 353.)

8. In some situations the courts have held that disclosure is in the public interest where this is for the purpose of disclosure obtained by police in the course of an investigation to a professional regulatory body as in *Woolgar v Chief Constable of Sussex Police* [1999] 3 All E.R. 604, CA. Here a police investigation of a matron and a registered nurse consequent upon a

death of a patient in a nursing home did not lead to a prosecution. The police passed the case to the UKCC, at that time the nursing regulatory body. Woolgar, however, objected to this disclosure. However, the Court of Appeal upheld the disclosure as justifiable to a regulatory body concerned with public health and safety issues where they thought that this was reasonably necessary in relation to the conduct of an investigation. (See commentary by P. Fennell (1999) 7 *Medical Law Review* 346.)

QUESTIONS:

1. What is the duty owed to the patient by his examining psychiatrist? In what ways does this duty differ from that owed to the patient by other medical practitioners?
2. What did Scott J. mean when he said that there was a duty upon Dr Egdell to disclose? What would have been the consequences for Dr Egdell had he failed to disclose?
3. An important factor influencing the decision in *Egdell* was the harm which W might cause. In what situations may a health care professional break confidence on the grounds that harm may be caused to another? Consider the following situations:

   (a) a doctor discovers that his patient, who is epileptic, is working as a lorry driver (See Legal Correspondant, "Doctors, Drivers and Confidentiality" (1974) 904 British Medical Journal 399);
   (b) a patient tells the doctor that he has been shoplifting.

A major point of discussion regarding the scope of disclosure on the basis of public interest grounds relates to persons who are HIV positive. The General Medical Council have issued guidance in relation to the issue of serious communicable disease.

General Medical Council Serious Communicable Diseases (October 1997)

CONFIDENTIALITY

Informing other health care professionals

18. If you diagnose a patient as having a serious communicable disease, you should explain to the patient:

(a) The nature of the disease and its medical, social and occupational implications, as appropriate.
(b) Ways of protecting others from infection.
(c) The importance to effective care of giving the professionals who will be providing care information which they need to know about the patient's disease or condition. In particular you must make sure that patient understands that general practitioners cannot provide adequate clinical management and care without knowledge of their patients' conditions.

19. If patients still refuse to allow other health care workers to be informed, you must respect the patients' wishes except where you judge that failure to disclose the information

would put a health care worker or other patient at serious risk of death or serious harm. Such situations may arise, for example, when dealing with violent patients with severe mentally illness or disability.

If you are in doubt about whether disclosure is appropriate, you should seek advice from an experienced colleague. You should inform patients before disclosing information. Such occasions are likely to arise rarely and you must be prepared to justify a decision to disclose information against a patient's wishes.

Disclosures to others

20. You must disclose information about serious communicable diseases in accordance with the law. For example, the appropriate authority must be informed where a notifiable disease is diagnosed. Where a communicable disease contributed to the cause of death, this must be recorded on the death certificate. You should also pass information about serious communicable diseases to the relevant authorities for the purpose of communicable disease control and surveillance.

21. As the GMC booklet *Confidentiality* makes clear, a patient's death does not of itself release a doctor from the obligation to maintain confidentiality. But in some circumstances disclosures can be justified because they protect other people from serious harm or because they are required by law.

Giving information to close contacts

22. You may disclose information about a patient, whether living or dead, in order to protect a person from risk of death or serious harm. For example, you may disclose information to a known sexual contact of a patient with HIV where you have reason to think that the patient has not informed that person, and cannot be persuaded to do so. In such circumstances you should tell the patient before you make the disclosure, and you must be prepared to justify a decision to disclose information.

23. You must not disclose information to others, for example relatives, who have not been, and are not, at risk of infection.

NOTE:

1. Imagine the situation where a patient of a G.P. refuses to tell his sexual partner that he is HIV positive. In such a situation both the GMC and a number of commentators would support disclosure to the sexual partner. (See, for example, A. Grubb and D. Pearl, *AIDS and DNA Profiling*, Bristol: Jordan, 1990; *cf.* R. Lee, "Deathly Silence" in R. Lee and D. Morgan (eds), *Death Rites: Law and Ethics at the End of Life*, London: Routledge, 1994. For furthur debate on the moral obligation to warn of HIV positive status, see J. Harris and C. Errin, "Is There an Ethics of Heterosexual AIDS?" in L. Sherr, *AIDS and the Heterosexual Population*, London: Harwood, 1993; R. Bennett, L. Frith and H. Draper "Ignorance is Bliss: HIV and Moral Duties and Legal Duties to Forewarn" (2000) 26 *Journal of Medical Ethics* 9.) Moreover there is today the issue that transmission of HIV to a sexual partner without informing them of the risks is a criminal offence. See further *R. v Dicca* [2004] 3 All E.R. 593 and discussion in Chapter 6 above.

QUESTIONS:

1. What amounts to a "serious risk" which would justify disclosure to third parties? See further J.K. Mason, "The Legal Aspects and Implications of Risk Assessment" (2000) 8 *Medical Law Review* 69.

2. Would a health care professional be justified in breaking confidentiality under her professional ethical code and under the public interest exception to breach of confidence where a HIV carrier is known to be having unprotected sexual intercourse with numerous partners? This situation occurred in Birmingham in 1992 (see M. Brazier "At Large with a Lethal Weapon", *The Guardian*, June 24, 1992).

(f) Conflicts of Disclosure where Doctors Have Dual Responsibilities

General Medical Council: Confidentiality, Protecting and Providing Information London: GMC (2004)

17. Where doctors have contractual obligations to third parties, such as companies or organisations, they must obtain patients' consent before undertaking any examination or writing a report for that organisation. Before seeking consent they must explain the purpose of the examination or report and the scope of the disclosure. Doctors should offer to show patients the report, or give them copies, whether or not this is required by law.

Further information is given under the "Frequently asked questions" section of this document

Q13 I am employed by a company to provide medical reports on people applying for life insurance. If they attend the consultation, can I assume they agree to the report being sent?

There are many circumstances in which doctors are asked to provide information to third parties, such as insurers or employers, either following an examination of a patient or from existing records. Although the circumstances vary in which doctors with 'dual obligations' may be asked to disclose information, the following principles of good practice generally apply. You should:

(a) Be satisfied that the patient has been told, at the earliest opportunity, about the purpose of the examination and/or disclosure, the extent of the information to be disclosed and the fact that relevant information cannot be concealed or withheld. You might wish to show the form to the patient before you complete it to ensure the patient understands the scope of the information requested.
(b) Obtain, or have seen, written consent to the disclosure from the patient or a person properly authorised to act on the patient's behalf. You may, however, accept written assurances from an officer of a government department that the patient's written consent has been given.
(c) Disclose only information relevant to the request for disclosure: accordingly, you should not usually disclose the whole record. The full record may be relevant to some benefits paid by government departments.
(d) Include only factual information you can substantiate, presented in an unbiased manner.
(e) The Access to Medical Reports Act 1988 entitles patients to see reports written about them before they are disclosed, in some circumstances. In all circumstances you should check whether patients wish to see their report, unless patients have clearly and specifically stated that they do not wish to do so

NOTE:

1. Particular difficulties may arise if advice is sought from an occupational health doctor. An employer will have a vested interest in discovering

information regarding the health of his or her employees. But at the same time the doctor owes an obligation of confidentiality to the patient. If the occupational health doctor intends to pass on information, then, as far as possible, this fact must be made clear to the employee and consent obtained. If information is to be disclosed without consent this must be justifiable in the public interest as indicated above in the GMC guidelines. (See generally D. Kloss, *Occupational Health Law* (3rd edn), Oxford: Blackwell, 2000).

5. Remedies for Breach of Confidence

A number of remedies may be available:

(a) Injunction

An injunction may be sought to prevent further publication. There has been some debate as to whether a court would be prepared to order an interlocutory injunction to prevent publication prior to the hearing (F. Gurry, *Breach of Confidence*, Oxford: OUP, 1986).

(b) Damages

Where the doctor–patient relationship is governed by a contract, then the patient who brings an action for breach of confidence may seek damages for psychiatric harm and physical injury. In *W v Egdell* there was a contractual relationship. Dr Egdell had been commissioned to prepare the report for W's solicitors. In that case Scott J. expressed his doubt as to whether damages for nervous shock and personal injury could be awarded. To recognise such an action would be to go against the authority of *Addis v Gramaphone Co* [1909] A.C. 488, which held that damages in contract could not be awarded for injured feelings. However, more recently in *Archer v Williams* [2003] EWCA 1670, a small damages award was made in a contractual breach of confidence action.

If there is no contract between doctor and patient, as is the case in relation to most NHS patients, then the scope of the award of damages for breach of confidence remains uncertain, although in some instances in recent years damages claims for breach of confidence, though nominal, have been upheld, as in *Campbell v MGN*, see above at p.573 and see also *Cornelius v de Taranto* [2001] 68 B.M.L.R. 62.

The Law Commission recommended reform of this area in their report *Breach of Confidence* ((1981) Report No. 110 Cmnd. 8388, para.4.75). It suggested that the breach of confidence action be placed on a statutory footing and that damages for mental distress should be recoverable. (See D. Capper, "Damages for Breach of the Equitable Duty of Confidence" (1994) 14 *Legal Studies* 313.) At present although damages to injured feelings are unlikely to be recovered, it appears that damage for any economic loss will be recoverable.

6. CONFIDENTIALITY REQUIREMENTS IMPOSED BY STATUTE

There is no general statutory protection for medical information. However certain statutory provisions require particular types of health information to be kept confidential. It is unsurprising that the statutory protection which does exist relates to areas of health care practice widely considered to be of a particularly sensitive nature, such as infertility treatment or treatment for venereal disease. By contrast, in certain other areas of health care practice, where confidentiality is regarded as being of paramount importance, such as psychiatry and psychotherapy there is no special statutory protection.

(a) Venereal Disease

National Health Service Venereal Disease Regulations (SI 1974/29)

Every strategic health authority, NHS trust, NHS Foundation Trust and primary care trust shall take all necessary steps to secure that any information capable of identifying any individual obtained by officers of the authority with respect to persons examined or treated for any sexually transmitted disease shall not be disclosed except:

(a) for the purpose of communicating that information to a medical practitioner or to a person employed under the direction of a medical practitioner in connection with the treatment of persons suffering from such disease or the prevention of the spread thereof, and
(b) for the purpose of such treatment or prevention.

NOTE:

1. For discussion of notifiable diseases and public health issues see Chapter 1 above.

(b) Infertility Treatment

Human Fertilisation and Embryology Act 1990 (as amended), s.33(1–7), (9)(a)

33.—(1) No person who is or has been a member of the Authority shall disclose any information mentioned in subsection (2) below which he holds or has held as such a member or employee.
(2) The information referred to in subsection (1) above is—

(a) any information contained or required to be contained in the register in pursuance of section 31 of this Act, and
(b) any other information obtained by any member or employee of the Authority on terms or in circumstances requiring it to be held in confidence.

(3) Subsection (1) above does not apply to any disclosure of information mentioned in subsection (2)(a) above made—

(a) to a person who is a member or employee of the Authority,
(b) to a person to whom a licence applies for the purpose of his functions as such,
(c) so that no individual to whom the information relates can be identified,
(d) in pursuance of an order of the court under section 34 or 35 of this Act or
(e) to the Registrar General in pursuance of a request under section 32 of this Act, or
(f) in accordance with section 31 of this Act.

(4) Subsection (1) above does not apply to any disclosure of information mentioned in subsection (2)(b) above—

(a) made to a person as a member or employee of the Authority,
(b) made with the consent of the person or persons whose confidence would otherwise be protected, or
(c) which has been lawfully made available to the public before the disclosure is made.

(5) No person who is or has been a person to whom a licence applies and no person to whom directions have been given shall disclose any information falling within section 31(2) of this Act which he holds or has held as such a person.

(6) Subsection (5) above does not apply to any disclosure of information made—

(a) to a person as member or employee of the Authority,
(b) to a person to whom a licence applies for the purposes of his functions as such,
(c) so far as it identified a person who, but for sections 27 to 29 of this Act, would or might be a parent of a person who instituted proceedings under section 1A of the Congenital Disabilities (Civil Liability) Act 1976, but only for the purpose of defending such proceedings, or instituting connected proceedings for compensation against that parent,
(d) so that no individual to whom the information relates can be identified,
(e) in pursuance of directions given by virtue of section 24(5) or (6) of this Act
(f) necessarily—
    (i) for any purpose preliminary to proceedings, or
    (ii) for the purposes of, or in connection with, any proceedings,
(g) for the purpose of establishing, in any proceedings relating to an application for an order under subsection (1) of section 30 of this Act, whether the condition specified in paragraph (a) or (b) of that subsection is met,
(h) under section 3 of the Access to Health Records Act 1990 (right of access to health records) [or]

(6A) Paragraph (f) of subsection (6) above, so far as relating to disclosure for the purposes of, or in connection with, any proceedings, does not apply—

(a) to disclosure of information enabling a person to be identified as a person whose gametes were used, in accordance with consent given under paragraph 5 of Schedule 3 to this Act, for the purposes of treatment services in consequence of which an identifiable individual was, or may have been, born, or
(b) to disclosure, in circumstances in which subsection (1) of section 34 of this Act applies, of information relevant to the determination of the question mentioned in that subsection.

(6B) In the case of information relating to the provision of treatment services for any identifiable individual—

(a) where one individual is identifiable, subsection (5) above does not apply to disclosure with the consent of that individual;

(b) where both a woman and a man are treated together with her are identifiable, subsection (5) above does not apply —

(i) to disclosure with the consent of them both, or

(ii) if disclosure is made for the purpose of disclosing information about the provision of treatment services for one of them, to disclosure with the consent of that individual.

(6C) For the purposes of subsection (6B) above, consent must be to disclosure to a specific person, except where disclosure is to a person who needs to know —

(a) in connection with the provision of treatment services, or any other description of medical, surgical or obstetric services, for the individual giving the consent,

(b) in connection with the carrying out of an audit of clinical practice, or

(c) in connection with the auditing of accounts.

(6D) For the purposes of subsection (6B) above, consent to disclosure given at the request of another shall be disregarded unless, before it is given, the person requesting it takes reasonable steps to explain to the individual from whom it was requested the implications of compliance with the request.

(6E) In the case of information which relates to the provision of treatment services for any identifiable individual, subsection (5) above does not apply to disclosure in an emergency, that is to say, to disclosure made —

(a) by a person who is satisfied that it is necessary to make the disclosure to avert an imminent danger to the health of any individual with whose consent the information could be disclosed under subsection (6B) above, and

(b) in circumstances where it is not reasonably practicable to obtain that individual's consent,

(6F) In the case of information which shows that any identifiable individual was, or may have been, born in consequence of treatment services, subsection (5) above does not apply to any disclosure which is necessarily incidental to disclosure under subsections (6B) or (6E) above.

(6G) Regulations may provide for additional exceptions from subsection (5) above, but no exception may be made under this subsection —

(a) for disclosure of a kind mentioned in paragraph (a) or (b) of subsection (6A) above, or

(b) for disclosure, in circumstances in which section 32 of this Act applies, of information having the tendency mentioned in subsection (2) of that section.

(7) This section does not apply to the disclosure to any individual of information which —

(a) falls within section 31(2) of this Act by virtue of paragraph (a) or (b) of that subsection, and

(b) relates only to that individual or, in the case of an individual treated together with another, only to that individual and that other . . .

(9) In subsection (6)(f) above, references to proceedings include any formal procedure . . . for dealing with a complaint.)

NOTES:

1. Section 33 of the 1990 Act was amended by the Human Fertilisation and Embryology (Disclosure of Information) Act 1992. This Act was passed after protests from the medical profession that the original s.33 imposed undue restrictions upon disclosure. The Act protects information concerning treatment and storage of gametes and embryos of identifiable persons held in the register of information required to be established under the Act as well as any other information obtained in confidence. Unauthorised disclosure is expressly made a criminal offence.

2. Section 33 allows disclosure to be made in relation to "any proceedings". During the second reading debate upon the 1992 Act in the House of Lords the Lord Chancellor indicated that "proceedings" were not limited to legal proceedings but also included GMC and UKCC (this would presumably now apply to NMC Proceedings) disciplinary procedures (HL Debates 1378, June 11, 1992). However, disclosure for these purposes does not include information relating to the donor of gametes. This may cause difficulties if such information is important for a doctor to establish his defence in civil proceedings.

3. Information may also be disclosed with the patient's consent. Section 33 states that a patient may consent to disclosure being made by the doctor to a specified person. This is in contrast to the original section which required the disclosure to be made personally by the patient. Consent may also be given to disclosure of information to a class of persons where this is necessary for medical treatment, clinical audit or accounts audit. Reasonable steps must be taken to explain to the patient the implications of giving consent.

4. Disclosure of information may take place in an emergency if the person disclosing the information is satisfied that the disclosure is necessary to avert imminent danger to the patient's health and at the time it is not reasonably practicable to gain the patient's consent.

QUESTION:

1. What constitutes information which can be disclosed to other practitioners on the basis that it is information that they "need to know"?

The Department of Health are now consulting on the confidentiality provisions consequent upon their review of the HFEA (see further Chapter 11 below).

Department of Health: Review of the Human Fertilisation and Embryology Act 1990: a Public Consultation, London: DOH, 2005

Confidentiality requirements

6.42 Both the Medical Research Council report referred to above and the Science and Technology Committee drew attention to the strict confidentiality requirements of the HFE

Act, as adversely affecting the conduct of research. The Science and Technology Committee concluded that the confidentiality provisions "are unnecessarily onerous and inconsistent with the widespread use of assisted reproductive technologies". Underlying this conclusion is the assumption that as the use of assisted reproduction technologies has become more common, so any perceived stigma associated with infertility and its treatment has diminished, and therefore the confidentiality provisions of the Act should be revised to be more in line with other areas of medical practice.

6.43 There is a wider concern that the confidentiality provisions of the HFE Act do not only adversely affect the capacity to undertake research, but also hamper activities such as clinical audit and other aspects of patient care. For instance, the fact that a patient has undergone a particular type of fertility treatment may be relevant to antenatal screening. There are currently restrictions that apply even where the patient has given consent to the release of information. In relation to information held by the clinic, a patient can currently only consent to disclosure to a specific person.

6.44 The Government proposes that the confidentiality provisions of the HFE Act should be revised so that information about assisted reproduction treatment is treated in the same way as other medical information and subject to the same safeguards. Do you agree? However, the Committee notes (in paragraph 262) that there is evidence that confidentiality remains extremely important for people from some ethnic groups who may object to certain forms of fertility treatment.

QUESTION:

1. Is there today a case for arguing that the confidentiality provisions in the 1990 Act are outdated as this is no longer an area with any need for specific protection due to considerations of particular sensitivity of personal information?

7. STATUTORY EXCEPTIONS

Health and Social Care Act 2001, s.60

Control of patient information

60.—(1) The Secretary of State may by regulations make such provision for and in connection with requiring or regulating the processing of prescribed patient information for medical purposes as he considers necessary or expedient—

(a) in the interests of improving patient care, or
(b) in the public interest.

This subsection and subsection (2) have effect subject to subsections (3) to (6).
  (2) Regulations under subsection (1) may, in particular, make provision—

(a) for requiring prescribed communications of any nature which contain patient information to be disclosed by health service bodies in prescribed circumstances—
  (i) to the person to whom the information relates,
  (ii) (where it relates to more than one person) to the person to whom it principally relates, or
  (iii) to a prescribed person on behalf of any such person as is mentioned in subparagraph (i) or (ii), in such manner as may be prescribed;

(b) for requiring or authorising the disclosure or other processing of prescribed patient information to or by persons of any prescribed description subject to compliance with any prescribed conditions (including conditions requiring prescribed undertakings to be obtained from such persons as to the processing of such information);

(c) for securing that, where prescribed patient information is processed by a person in accordance with the regulations, anything done by him in so processing the information shall be taken to be lawfully done despite any obligation of confidence owed by him in respect of it;

(d) for creating offences punishable on summary conviction by a fine not exceeding level 5 on the standard scale or such other level as is prescribed or for creating other procedures for enforcing any provisions of the regulations.

(3) Regulations under subsection (3) may not make provision requiring the processing of confidential patient information for any purpose if it would be reasonably practicable to achieve that purpose otherwise than pursuant to such regulations, having regard to the cost of and the technology available for achieving that purpose.

(4) Where regulations under subsection (3) make provision requiring the processing of prescribed confidential patient information, then the Secretary of State—

(a) shall, at any time within the period of one month beginning on each anniversary of the making of such regulations, consider whether any such provision could be included in regulations made at that time without contravening subsection (5), and

(b) if he determines that any such provision could not be so included, shall make further regulations varying or revoking the regulations made under subsection (3) to such extent as he considers necessary in order for the regulations to comply with that subsection.

(5) Regulations under subsection (3) may not make provision for requiring the processing of confidential patient information solely or principally for the purpose of determining the care and treatment to be given to particular individuals.

(6) Without prejudice to the operation of provisions made under subsection (4)(c), regulations under this section may not make provision for or in connection with the processing of prescribed patient information in a manner inconsistent with any provision made by or under the Data Protection Act 1998 (c. 29).

(7) Before making any regulations under this section the Secretary of State shall, to such extent as he considers appropriate in the light of the requirements of section 61, consult such bodies appearing to him to represent the interests of those likely to be affected by the regulations as he considers appropriate.

(8) In this section "patient information" means—

(a) information (however recorded) which relates to the physical or mental health or condition of an individual, to the diagnosis of his condition or to his care or treatment, and

(b) information (however recorded) which is to any extent derived, directly or indirectly, from such information, whether the identity of the individual in question is ascertainable from the information or not.

(9) For the purposes of this section, patient information is "confidential patient information" where—

(a) the identity of the individual in question is ascertainable—
    (i) from that information, or
    (ii) from that information and other information which is in the possession of, or is likely to come into the possession of, the person processing that information, and

(b) that information was obtained or generated by a person who, in the circumstances, owed an obligation of confidence to that individual.

(10) In this section—
"the health service" has the same meaning as in the 1977 Act;
"health service body" means any body (including a government department) or person engaged in the provision of the health service that is prescribed, or of a description prescribed, for the purposes of this definition;
"medical purposes" means the purposes of any of the following—

(a) preventative medicine, medical diagnosis, medical research, the provision of care and treatment and the management of health and social care services, and
(b) informing individuals about their physical or mental health or condition, the diagnosis of their condition or their care or treatment;

"prescribed" means specified in, or determined in accordance with, regulations made by the Secretary of State under this section;
"processing", in relation to information, means the use, disclosure or obtaining of the information or the doing of such other things in relation to it as may be prescribed for the purposes of this definition.

NOTE:

1. The Patient Information Advisory Group established under s.61 of the Act is required to advise the Secretary of State regarding the production of regulations under s.60.

Health Service (Control of Patient Information) Regulations 2002, SI 2002/1438

1.—(1) These Regulations may be cited as the Health Service (Control of Patient Information) Regulations 2002 and shall come into force on 1st June 2002.
(2) In these Regulations—
"the Act" means the Health and Social Care Act 2001,
"public authority" has the same meaning as in section 3(1) of the Freedom of Information Act 2000;
"public health laboratory service" means the microbiological service provided by the Public Health Laboratory Service Board under section 5(2)(c) and (4) of the National Health Service Act 1977;
"research ethics committee" means a local research ethics committee established or recognised by a health authority within its area or a multi-centre research ethics committee which is recognised by Secretary of State in respect of research carried out within five or more health authority areas or any other research ethics committee recognised by the Secretary of State.
(3) Any notice given under these Regulations shall be—

(a) in writing; or
(b) transmitted by electronic means in a legible form which is capable of being used for subsequent reference.

Medical purposes related to the diagnosis or treatment of neoplasia

2.—(1) Subject to paragraphs (2) to (4) and regulation 7, confidential patient information relating to patients referred for the diagnosis or treatment of neoplasia may be processed for medical purposes which comprise or include—

(a) the surveillance and analysis of health and disease;
(b) the monitoring and audit of health and health related care provision and outcomes where such provision has been made;
(c) the planning and administration of the provision made for health and health related care;
(d) medical research approved by research ethics committees;
(e) the provision of information about individuals who have suffered from a particular disease or condition where—
    (i) that information supports an analysis of the risk of developing that disease or condition; and
    (ii) it is required for the counseling and support of a person who is concerned about the risk of developing that disease or condition.

(2) For the purposes of this regulation, "processing" includes (in addition to the use, disclosure or obtaining of information) any operations, or set of operations, which are undertaken in order to establish or maintain databases for the purposes set out in paragraph (1), including—

(a) the recording and holding of information;
(b) the retrieval, alignment and combination of information;
(c) the organisation, adaptation or alteration of information;
(d) the blocking, erasure and destruction of information.

(3) The processing of confidential patient information for the purposes specified in paragraph (1) may be undertaken by persons who (either individually or as members of a class) are—

(a) approved by the Secretary of State, and
(b) authorized by the person who lawfully holds the information.

(4) Where the Secretary of State considers that it is necessary in the public interest that confidential patient information is processed for a purpose specified in paragraph (1), he may give notice to any person who is approved and authorized under paragraph (3) to require that person to process that information for that purpose and any such notice may require that the information is processed forthwith or within such period as is specified in the notice.

(5) A person who processes confidential patient information under this regulation shall inform the Patient Information Advisory Group of that processing and shall make available to the Secretary of State such information as he may require to assist him in the investigation and audit of that processing and in his annual consideration of the provisions of these Regulations which is required by section 60(4) of the Act.

Communicable disease and other risks to public health

3.—(1) Subject to paragraphs (2) and (3) and regulation 7, confidential patient information may be processed with a view to—

(a) diagnosing communicable diseases and other risks to public health;
(b) recognising trends in such diseases and risks;
(c) controlling and preventing the spread of such diseases and risks;
(d) monitoring and managing—

   (i) outbreaks of communicable disease;
  (ii) incidents of exposure to communicable disease;
 (iii) the delivery, efficacy and safety of immunisation programmes;
 (iv) adverse reactions to vaccines and medicines;
  (v) risks of infection acquired from food or the environment (including water supplies);
 (vi) the giving of information to persons about the diagnosis of communicable disease and risks of acquiring such disease.

(2) For the purposes of this regulation, "processing" includes any operations, or set of operations set out in regulation 2(2) which are undertaken for the purposes set out in paragraph (1).

(3) The processing of confidential patient information for the purposes specified in paragraph (1) may be undertaken by—

(a) persons employed or engaged for the purposes of the health service;
(b) other persons employed or engaged by a Government Department or other public authority in communicable disease surveillance.

(4) Where the Secretary of State considers that it is necessary to process patient information for a purpose specified in paragraph (1), he may give notice to any body or person specified in paragraph (2) to require that person or body to process that information for that purpose and any such notice may require that the information is processed forthwith or within such period as is specified in the notice.

(5) Where confidential information is processed under this regulation, the bodies and persons specified in paragraph (2) shall make available to the Secretary of State such information as he may require to assist him in the investigation and audit of that processing and in his annual consideration of the provisions of these Regulations which is required by section 60(4) of the Act.

Modifying the obligation of confidence

4. Anything done by a person that is necessary for the purpose of processing confidential patient information in accordance with these Regulations shall be taken to be lawfully done despite any obligation of confidence owed by that person in respect of it.

General

5. Subject to regulation 7, confidential patient information may be processed for medical purposes in the circumstances set out in the Schedule to these Regulations provided that the processing has been approved—

(a) in the case of medical research, by both the Secretary of State and a research ethics committee, and
(b) in any other case, by the Secretary of State.

Registration

6.—(1) Where an approval granted by the Secretary of State under regulation 5 permits the transfer of confidential patient information between persons who may determine the purposes for which, and the manner in which, the information may be processed, he shall record in a register the name and address of each of those persons together with the particulars specified in paragraph (2).

(2) The following particulars are specified for inclusion in each entry in the register—

(a) a description of the confidential patient information to which the approval relates;

(b) the medical purposes for which the information may be processed;
(c) the provisions in the Schedule to these Regulations under which the information may be processed; and
(d) such other particulars as the Secretary of State may consider appropriate to enter in the register.

(3) The Secretary of State shall retain the particulars of each entry in the register for so long as confidential patient information may be processed under an approval and for not less than 12 months after the termination of an approval.

(4) The Secretary of State shall, in such manner and to the extent to which he considers it appropriate, publish entries in the register.

Restrictions and exclusions

7.—(1) Where a person is in possession of confidential patient information under these Regulations, he shall not process that information more than is necessary to achieve the purposes for which he is permitted to process that information under these Regulations and, in particular, he shall—

(a) so far as it is practical to do so, remove from the information any particulars which identify the person to whom it relates which are not required for the purposes for which it is, or is to be, processed;
(b) not allow any person access to that information other than a person who, by virtue of his contract of employment or otherwise, is involved in processing the information for one or more of those purposes and is aware of the purpose or purposes for which the information may be processed;
(c) ensure that appropriate technical and organisational measures are taken to prevent unauthorised processing of that information;
(d) review at intervals not exceeding 12 months the need to process confidential patient information and the extent to which it is practicable to reduce the confidential patient information which is being processed;
(e) on request by any person or body, make available information on the steps taken to comply with these Regulations.

(2) No person shall process confidential patient information under these Regulations unless he is a health professional or a person who in the circumstances owes a duty of confidentiality which is equivalent to that which would arise if that person were a health professional.

(3) For the purposes of paragraph (2) "health professional" has the same meaning as in section 69(1) of the Data Protection Act 1998.

NOTE:

1. Section 60 and the subsequent regulations have proved extremely controversial. It is suggested that the impact of the provision is to fundamentally undermine the equitable remedy of breach of confidence. See generally regarding this provision P. Case, "Confidence Matters: the Rise and Fall of Informational Autonomy in Medical Law" (2003) 11 *Medical Law Review* 208. In contrast others have argued that s.60 impedes research through the time delays involved. See further L. Turnberg, "Common Sense and Common Consent in Communicable Disease Surveillance" (2002) 30 *Journal of Medical Ethics* 104.

8. INVESTIGATION OF CRIME

In certain situations statutes expressly require that patient confidentiality should be broken, for example, where information is required for the purposes of the investigation of crime or where disclosure is required on public health grounds. Medical records can be sought by the police when undertaking a criminal investigation. Such disclosure is regulated by the Police and Criminal Evidence Act 1984. This Act was amended during its passage to take account of the concerns expressed by the BMA that the reform of police powers rendered patient information unjustifiably vulnerable to access. Those seeking access to such records must now obtain a warrant from a circuit judge satisfying the provisions of ss.9–11 and Schedule 1.

Police and Criminal Evidence Act 1984, ss.9(1), 11(1–2), 12

Special provisions as to access

9.—(1) A constable may obtain access to excluded material . . . for the purposes of a criminal investigation by making an application under Schedule 1 below and in accordance with that Schedule . . . [this schedule makes reference to the need to apply to a circuit judge].

11.—(1) Subject to the following provisions of this section, in this Act, "excluded material" means—

(a)   personal records which a person has acquired or created in the course of any trade or business, profession or other occupation or for the purposes of any paid or unpaid office or which he holds in confidence;

(b)   human tissue or tissue fluid which had been taken for the purposes of diagnosis or medical treatment and which a person holds in confidence.

(2) A person holds material other than journalistic material in confidence for the purposes of this section if he holds it subject—

(a)   to an express or implied undertaking to hold it in confidence or

(b)   to a restriction on disclosure or any obligation of secrecy contained in any enactment including any enactment contained in an Act passed after this Act.

12.—In this Part of the Act "personal records" means documentary or other records concerning an individual (whether living or dead) who can be identified from them, and relating—

(a)   to his physical or mental health

(b)   to spiritual counselling or assistance given to him; or

(c)   to counselling or assistance given or to be given to him for the purposes of his personal welfare, by any voluntary organisation or individual who—
   (i) by reason of his office or occupation has responsibilites for his personal welfare; or
   (ii) by reason of an order of the court has responsibilities for his supervision.

NOTES:

1. In *R v Cardiff Crown Court, Ex p. Kellam* (1994) 16 B.M.L.R. 762 the court held that both clinical and administrative records were capable of being classed as excluded material within s.11.

2. The requirement to obtain a search warrant from a circuit judge appears to have acted as a restraint. Judges have been prepared to deny unmeritorious applications. For example, in 1988 a circuit judge rejected an application for disclosure of more than 1,000 names of men who shared the same blood group as blood stains found at the scene of a brutal murder. (See P. Schutte, "Medical Confidentiality and Crime" (1992) *Journal of the Medical Defence Union* 68.)

3. Despite the fact that a special warrant is necessary for excluded material and special procedure material, once the police officer is lawfully present on premises (for example, having obtained a warrant from a magistrate under s.9 of the 1984 Act), he or she may seize anything on the premises which is evidence of the offence which she is investigating or of another offence, under s.19 of the Police and Criminal Evidence Act 1984.

Other statutes requiring information to be notified includes the Abortion Act 1967 (see Abortion Regulations 1991, SI 1991/499), Public Health (Control of Disease) Act 1984 and Public Health (Infectious Disease) Regulations 1988; and, in connection with the investigation of crime, s.115 of the Crime and Disorder Act 1998 and ss.19 and 20 Terrorism Act 2000.

9. DISCLOSURE AND JUDICIAL PROCEEDINGS

Hunter v Mann [1974] 2 All E.R. 414, [1974] Q.B. 767, [1974] 2 W.L.R. 742

A car, taken without the owner's consent, was involved in an accident. After the accident both the driver and passenger left the scene and could not be traced. Later that day a doctor treated a man and a woman for injuries. The woman said that they had been involved in a car accident. The police later approached the doctor and asked for the names of those who had been treated. Section 168(3) of the Road Traffic Act 1972 provided that:

"Where the driver of a vehicle is alleged to be guilty of an offence to which this section applies.

. . .

(b) any other person shall be required as aforesaid give any information which is in his power to give and which may lead to the identification of the driver.

BOREHAM J.

" . . . The contentions of counsel for the appellant are directed towards a construction of section 168. His first contention is this. He says that the appellant does not fall within the limits of the expression in subsection (2)(b) 'any other person'. He says, and this is the basis of his submission on this aspect of the case, that it would not be right in the circumstances to give an unrestricted meaning to those words so as to include everyone except the driver or the keeper of the vehicle. He says that it would be wrong to give those words so unrestricted a meaning as to cause a doctor, or, as I understand it, any other professional man who stands in relation to his clients or patients in a position similar to a doctor, to act in breach of the duty of confidentiality on which a doctor's patient is entitled to rely.

He puts forward in support of that contention three propositions. He says first of all, and in effect this is a concession, that there is no absolute privilege in judicial proceedings for a doctor in respect of the disclosure of confidential information which was obtained by him in the course of his professional relationship with his patient. For my part at any rate I need no authority for that proposition; I accept it. The second proposition is this: that in common with other professional men, for instance a priest and there are of course others, the doctor is under a duty not to disclose, without the consent of his patient, information which he, the doctor, has gained in his professional capacity, save, says counsel for the appellant, in very exceptional circumstances. He quoted the example of the murderer still manic, who would be a menace to society. But, says counsel, save in such exceptional circumstances, the general rule applies. He adds that the law will enforce that duty.

I would accept that proposition if before the word 'disclosing' there were to be added the adverb 'voluntarily', as in the British Medical Association's handbook. I accept too counsel's cited authority for the proposition that the duty not to disclose information is enforceable at the behest of the patient in an action of contract or for breach of duty. But for my part at any rate I do not consider that that proposition covers the position where the doctor is compelled by law to disclose. In my judgment counsel for the appellant's second proposition relates only to voluntary disclosure. The third proposition is that protection is given to professional confidences to the extent that those who are bound by them are not ordinarily required to breach them and will only be compelled to do so by the order of a judge. Again counsel for the appellant has quoted authorities. I hope it will not indicate any lack of respect for him or for the authorities that he quoted if I do not cite them at this stage.

I would prefer to put the proposition in another way. I accept that the doctor, in accordance with the first proposition, has no right to refuse to disclose confidential information in the course of judicial or quasi-judicial proceedings; but I also accept that the judge in certain circumstances, and in the exercise of his, the judge's, judicial discretion, may refuse to compel him to do so. Further than this, in my judgment, the authorities which have been cited to us do not go. Moreover each one of those authorities was concerned with legal proceedings. In the present case it is important to bear in mind the distinction between privilege which is to be claimed in legal proceedings and a contractual duty not to disclose; that distinction is marked by a passage in the judgment of Diplock L.J. in *Parry-Jones v. the Law Society* [1968] 1 All E.R. 171 at 180,

'So far as the plaintiff's point as to privilege is concerned, privilege is irrelevant when one is not concerned with judicial or quasi-judicial proceedings because, strictly speaking, privilege refers to a right to withhold from a court, or a tribunal exercising judicial functions, material which would otherwise be admissible in evidence. What we are concerned with here is the contractual duty of confidence, generally implied though sometimes expressed, between a solicitor and client. Such a duty exists not only between solicitor and client, but, for example, between banker and customer, doctor and patient, and accountant and client. Such a duty of confidence is subject to, and overridden by, the duty of any party to that contract to comply with the law of the land. If it is the duty of such a party to a contract, whether at common law or under statute, to disclose in defined circumstances confidential information, then he must do so, and any express contract to the contrary would be illegal and void.'

With those words in mind I proceed to the conclusion drawn by counsel for the appellant from his contentions. He says that when one comes to construe the statute one should approach it thus; that Parliament must not be taken to have overridden or to have attempted to override the duty of confidence to which reference has been made, except by clear language or necessary implication. He says, and this is the burden of his whole contention, that 'any other person' in section 168 must be read in a restricted way so that that duty is not breached . . .

It seems to me that my first duty is to look at the section and give the words their ordinary natural meaning, and in the absence of equivocation or ambiguity to give effect to such meaning, unless of course there is something in the context of the section or of the Act itself which suggests that a special or restricted meaning should be given.

For my part I cannot find any ground for saying that a restricted meaning should be given. I find the words clear and unequivocal. I accept, as counsel for the appellant has suggested, that one should assume that Parliament has passed this Act, and this section in particular, with the existing law in mind. Accepting that, then it seems to me that Parliament must have been conscious of the use of very wide words here and, if it had been intended to create exceptions, it would have been easy enough to do so. It has not been done. Moreover I ask myself the question: if there is to be a restriction how far is it to go? Where is it to stop? I find it impossible to provide an answer to that question. In these circumstances I am driven to the conclusion that a doctor acting within his professional capacity, and carrying out his professional duties and responsibilities, is within the words 'any other person' in section 168(2)(b).

The next limb of counsel for the appellant's argument was directed to the words 'in his power' in the expression 'information which it is in his power to give'. He contends that power must include a legal right, that there is no legal right or power to disclose so far as a doctor is concerned and, therefore, that he is not caught by those words.

I am not going to attempt to define 'power'. It seems to me a word of fairly common understanding and reading it in its ordinary way I have no difficulty in coming to the conclusion that a doctor in the circumstances in which the appellant found himself had the power. It may be that but for the section in the Act he would not have exercised that power because of his duty to his patient, but that seems to me to beg the question, for that would have been in accordance with his duty not to make voluntary disclosure. Once it is decided that the appellant is a person to whom the statutory duty imposed by section 168 applies, then I have no doubt that he had the power. I think it would be no injustice to counsel for the appellant to say that this was the least strenuously argued of his points and I find it a point without substance.

In my view it is important when one is considering this section to have in mind that on many occasions serious accidents are caused by people who take away, without consent, other people's motor cars and who have no hesitation in leaving the scene as quickly as they possibly can so as to avoid detection. I therefore find it a comfort to think that the section gives the police a wide power for the purpose of detecting people who may cause damage to others.

May I say, before leaving this case, that I appreciate the concern of a responsible medical practitioner who feels that he is faced with a conflict of duty. That the appellant in this case was conscious of a conflict and realised his duty both to society and to his patient is clear from the finding of the justices, but he may find comfort, although the decision goes against him, from the following. First that he has only to disclose information which may lead to identification and not other confidential matters; secondly that the result, in my judgment, is entirely consistent with the rules that the British Medical Association have laid down . . . "

LORD WIDGERY C.J.

" . . . I agree also. With all deference to counsel for the appellant's argument, I felt that he was claiming a degree of medical confidence wider than that which his authorities would support. I would compliment the authors of the British Medical Association handbook to which reference has already been made, for a brief and, I think, effective statement of the position. I repeat it:

'A doctor should refrain from disclosing voluntarily to a third party information which he has learnt professionally or indirectly in his professional relationship with a patient, subject to exceptions, including the following . . .
   (2) the information is required by law.'

I would add one other point, namely, that if a doctor, giving evidence in court, is asked a question which he finds embarassing because it involves him talking about things which he would normally regard as confidential, he can seek the protection of the judge and ask the judge if it is necessary for him to answer. The judge, by virtue of the overriding discretion to control his court which all English judges have, can, if he thinks fit, tell the doctor that he need not answer the question. Whether or not the judge would take that line, of course, depends largely on the importance of the potential answer to the issues being tried."

NOTES:

1. The English courts have consistently rejected suggestions that a privilege be introduced allowing doctors to refuse to disclose confidential health information (*Duchess of Kingston's case* (1776) 20 State Trials 355, discussed in A.H. Ferguson, "The Lasting Legacy of a Bigamous Duchess: the Benchmark Precedent for Medical Confidentiality" (2006) 19(1) *Social History of Medicine* 37 and J.V. McHale, *Medical Confidentiality and Legal Privilege*, London: Routledge, 1993). It also appears that the remedy of breach of confidence may not be used to restrain the disclosure of confidential information in a court of law (see P. Matthews, "Legal Privilege and Breach of Confidence" (1980) 1 *Legal Studies* 77).
2. Medical information may, however, be withheld from disclosure prior to or during a trial if protected by legal professional privilege or public interest immunity. Legal professional privilege protects information passed between lawyer and client, see further *Three Rivers DC v Governor and Company of the Bank of England (No.5)* [2004] UKHL 48. Public interest immunity is the term used to describe exclusion of evidence on public policy grounds. In *Morrow and Others v DPP* (1993) 14 B.M.L.R. 54, abortion protestors were prosecuted under the Public Order Act 1986. They claimed in their defence that they had honestly believed that illegal abortions were to be undertaken at the centre where they were protesting. They applied for production by the British Pregnancy Advisory Service of information relating to all the abortions which were to be undertaken that day at that clinic. This application was rejected. The judge held that there was a strong public interest in maintaining confidentiality, illustrated by specific provisions contained in the Abortion Act 1967 and Abortion Regulations 1968. Disclosure of the documents was not essential to the defence—there was no need to show that the abortions which were to be undertaken were illegal, only that the defendant thought that they were. (For the operation of public interest immunity in relation to civil proceedings, see below and see C. Tapper (edn), Cross on Evidence, (8th edn), London: Butterworths, 1995, Chapter XII.)

10. DATA PROTECTION AND ACCESS TO HEALTH RECORDS

For many years the medical profession resisted calls for patients to be given rights of access to their medical records. It was argued that to allow the patient unrestricted access to his or her records might lead to harm because he might misunderstand their contents. In addition, if a doctor knew that the patient had a right of access, this could result in the doctor being less candid in the information which is included in the record. However, others opposed these views. They argued that access could be regarded as part of recognising patient autonomy. Some health professionals also believed that disclosure could assist in patients decision-making.

In the past the Department of Health was of the view that records were the property of the health authority, with general practice records being owned by the Family Health Service Authority. The current position is uncertain in the light of the NHS reorganisation which took place in 1996 (see Chapter 1 above). While the patient does not appear to have rights of ownership, he does have various rights of control over access to records, through the action of breach of confidence and through statutory rights of access to the contents of his own records.

The catalyst to change in the policy of access to patient records was the Data Protection Act 1984. This Act which gave rights of access to information held on computer. A number of statutes following this legislation widened the rights of access to health care records, culminating in the Access to Health Records Act 1990. Today the main legislation as noted above is that of the Data Protection Act 1998. This implemented the UK Data Protection Directive (EU Directive 95/46) (see further for the impact of the Directive the special Privacy edition of the *European Journal of Health Law* (2002) 9(3) *European Journal of Health Law*. The Data Protection Act 1998 governs data which is contained in both computer and manual files, while the Access to Health Records Act 1990 remains of relevance in relation to deceased patients. However, none of these statutory rights are absolute in nature. A standard limitation is that access may be withheld where disclosure of the information may be harmful to the physical/mental health of the patient or would involve revealing details concerning the health of others. (See M. Gilhooley and S.M. McGhee, "Medical Records: Practicalities and Principles of Patient Possession" (1991) 17 *Journal of Medical Ethics* 138.)

(a) Data Protection Act 1998

In contrast to the Data Protection Act 1984, the 1998 Act concerns both computerised and manual records. Manual records are those which are part of a relevant filing system, defined as information which is structured by reference to individuals (s.1(1)). Information is also regulated where it is part of an "accessible record". Individuals whose data is held are known as the "data subject". Data subjects have rights of access to their records from those who hold the records, who are known as "data controllers". The legislation is subject to enforcement by the Information Commissioner established under Pt V of the 1996 Act (formerly known as the Data Protection Comissioner). There are particular concerns to ensure the confidentiality of information held on computer and this led to a review of the area in the form of the Caldicott Review (*Report on the Review of Patient Identifiable Information*, 1997) and to the establishment of local "gate-keepers" of information known as Caldicott guardians (HSC 1999/012).

(i) The scope of the Data Protection Act 1998

Processing

1.—(1) In this Act unless the context otherwise requires—
"data" means information which—

(a) is being processed by means of equipment operating automatically in response to instructions given for that purpose,

(b) is recorded with the intention that it should be processed by means of such equipment,

(c) is recorded as part of a relevant filing system or with the intention that it should form part of a relevant filing system, or

(d) does not fall within paragraph (a), (b) or (c) but forms part of an accessible record as defined by section 68;

(e) is recorded information held by a public authority and does not fall within any of paragraphs (a) to (d);

"data controller" means, subject to subsection (4), a person who (either alone or jointly or in common with other persons) determines the purposes for which and the manner in which any personal data are, or are to be, processed;
"data processor", in relation to personal data, means any person (other than an employee of the data controller) who processes the data on behalf of the data controller;
'data subject" means an individual who is the subject of personal data;
'personal data" means data which relate to a living individual who can be identified—

(a) from those data, or

(b) from those data and other information which is in the possession of, or is likely to come into the possession of, the data controller,

and includes any expression of opinion about the individual and any indication of the intentions of the data controller or any other person in respect of the individual;
...
"processing" in relation to information or data means obtaining, recording or holding the information or data or carrying out any operation or set of operations on the information of the data, including—

(a) organisation, adaptation or alteration of the information or data,

(b) retrieval, consultation or use of the information or data

(c) disclosure of the information or data by transmission, dissemination or otherwise making available, or

(d) Alignment, combination, blocking, erasure or destruction of the information or data;

"relevant filing system" means any set of information relating to individuals to the extent that, although the information is not processed by means of equipment operating automatically in response to instructions given for that purpose, the set is structured, either by reference to individuals or by reference to criteria relating to individuals, in such a way that specific information relating to a particular individual is readily accessible.

NOTES:

1. Section 1(1) provides that the data must relate to living persons. Thus access to health records of the deceased are not regulated by the Data Protection Act 1998. Instead, personal representatives (s.3(1)(f) or those persons making application in relation to the estate of a deceased person (s.5(4)) will have to make an application under the Access to Health Records Act 1990.

2. In the context of health care, "data controllers" may be individual NHS professionals or NHS bodies.

3. Data "processing" is exceedingly broad and will include any procedure involving the person's health record—for a definition of health record see below.

4. A further issue is the extent to which the definition of "data subject" may also include other family members. This is a particularly difficult issue in relation to access to information where there is a genetic component. See further the European Commission's Article 29 Data Protection Working Group and the discussion in J.K. Mason and G. Laurie *Mason and McCall Smith's Law and Medical Ethics* (7th edn), Oxford: OUP, 2005, pp.275–276. See also *Durant v Financial Services Authority* [2003] EWCA Civ 1746, where it was suggested that personal data was information which affected the privacy of the data subject.

Sensitive personal data

2. In this Act "sensitive personal data" means personal data consisting of information as to—

(a) the racial or ethnic origin of the data subject,
(b) his political opinions,
(c) his religious beliefs or other beliefs of a similar nature,
(d) whether he is a member of a trade union (within the meaning of the Trade Union and Labour Relations (Consolidation) Act 1992),
(e) his physical or mental health or condition,
(f) his sexual life,
(g) the commission or alleged commission by him of any offence, or
(h) any proceedings for any offence committed or alleged to have been committed by him, the disposal of such proceedings or the sentence of any court in such proceedings.

The legislation further explicitly defines what constitutes "health records":

Health Records

68(2)
. . .
any record which

(a) consists of information relating to the physical or mental health or condition of an individual, and
(b) has been made by or on behalf of a health professional in connection with the care of that individual.

Health Professional

69.—(1) In this Act "health professional" means any of the following—

(a) a registered medical practitioner,
(b) a registered dentist as defined by section 53(1) of the Dentists Act 1984,
(c) a registered optician as defined by section 36(1) of the Opticians Act 1989,
(d) a registered pharmaceutical chemist as defined by section 24(1) of the Pharmacy Act 1954 or a registered person as defined by Article 2(2) of the Pharmacy (Northern Ireland) Order 1976,

(e)   a registered nurse, midwife or health visitor,
(f)   a registered osteopath as defined by section 41 of the Osteopaths Act 1993,
(g)   a registered chiropractor as defined by section 43 of the Chiropractors Act 1994,
(h)   any person who is registered as a member of a profession to which the Health Professions Order 2001 for the time being extends,
(i)   a clinical psychologist, child psychotherapist or speech therapist, and
(j)   a scientist employed by such a body as head of a department.

(ii) The Criteria Governing Data Processing

The Data Protection Act 1998 sets out a series of criteria concerning data processing which are to be found in the Schedules to the Act.

Data protection principles

Data processing is subject to the Data Protection principles.

Schedule 1—the Data Protection Principles

1. Personal data shall be processed fairly and lawfully and, in particular, shall not be processed unless—

(a)   at least one of the conditions in Schedule 2 is met, and
(b)   in the case of sensitive personal data, at least one of the conditions in Schedule 3 is also met.

2. Personal data shall be obtained only for one or more specified and lawful purposes, and shall not be further processed in any manner incompatible with that purpose or those purposes.
3. Personal data shall be adequate, relevant and not excessive in relation to the purpose or purposes for which they are processed.
4. Personal data shall be accurate and, where necessary, kept up to date.
5. Personal data processed for any purpose or purposes shall not be kept for longer than is necessary for that purpose or those purposes.
6. Personal data shall be processed in accordance with the rights of data subjects under this Act.
7. Appropriate technical and organisational measures shall be taken against unauthorised or unlawful processing of personal data and against accidental loss or destruction of, or damage to, personal data.
8. Personal data shall not be transferred to a country or territory outside the European Economic Area unless that country or territory ensures an adequate level of protection for the rights and freedoms of data subjects in relation to the processing of personal data.

NOTES:

1. If information is disclosed in breach of confidence, this will not constitute "lawful" processing.
2. Disclosure of information without the consent of the data controller constitutes a criminal offence under s.55 of the Data Protection Act 1998.

Conditions for data processing

Schedule 2 — Conditions relevant for purposes of the first principle processing of any personal data

1. The data subject has given his consent to the processing.
2. The processing is necessary —

(a) for the performance of a contract to which the data subject is a party, or
(b) for the taking of steps at the request of the data subject with a view to entering into a contract.

3. The processing is necessary for compliance with any legal obligation to which the data controller is subject, other than an obligation imposed by contract.
4. The processing is necessary in order to protect the vital interests of the data subject.
5. The processing is necessary —

(a) for the administration of justice . . .
(b) for the exercise of any functions conferred on any person by or under any enactment,
(c) for the exercise of any functions of the Crown, a Minister of the Crown or a government department, or
(d) for the exercise of any other functions of a public nature exercised in the public interest by any person.

6. — (1) The processing is necessary for the purposes of legitimate interests pursued by the data controller or by the third party or parties to whom the data are disclosed, except where the processing is unwarranted in any particular case by reason of prejudice to the rights and freedoms or legitimate interests of the data subject.

(2) The Secretary of State may by order specify particular circumstances in which this condition is, or is not, to be taken to be satisfied.

NOTE:

1. It has been suggested that it may be sufficient for this section for information to be provided in general terms, such as notices being put up in a surgery or hospital See, for example, A. Grubb and J. Laing, "Confidentiality and Data Protection" in A. Grubb (ed.), *Principles of Medical Law*, Oxford: OUP, 2003 at pp.614–615. However the willingness to assume consent here has been criticised by Pattinson who asks: "Is the failure to opt out a sufficient indication taking into account the vulnerable and distracted position of many of those in hospitals or GP's surgeries awaiting medical assistance? Overeagerness to infer or impute consent will render the patient's consent no more than a legal fiction". (See further S. Pattinson, *Medical Law and Ethics*, London: Sweet & Maxwell, 2006, at p.186). He does, however, go on to note that the breadth of the schedule will nonetheless allow processing despite this in a wide range of other situations.

Schedule 3 — Conditions relevant for purposes of the first principle: processing of sensitive personal data

1. The data subject has given his explicit consent to the processing of the personal data.

2.—(1) The processing is necessary for the purposes of exercising or performing any right or obligation which is conferred or imposed by law on the data controller in connection with employment.

(2) The Secretary of State may by order—

(a) exclude the application of sub-paragraph (1) in such cases as may be specified, or

(b) provide that, in such cases as may be specified, the condition in sub-paragraph (1) is not to be regarded as satisfied unless such further conditions as may be specified in the order are also satisfied.

3. The processing is necessary—

(a) in order to protect the vital interests of the data subject or another person, in a case where—
(i) consent cannot be given by or on behalf of the data subject, or
(ii) the data controller cannot reasonably be expected to obtain the consent of the data subject, or

(b) in order to protect the vital interests of another person, in a case where consent by or on behalf of the data subject has been unreasonably withheld.

4. The processing—

(a) is carried out in the course of its legitimate activities by any body or association which—
(i) is not established or conducted for profit, and
(ii) exists for political, philosophical, religious or trade-union purposes,

(b) is carried out with appropriate safeguards for the rights and freedoms of data subjects,

(c) relates only to individuals who either are members of the body or association or have regular contact with it in connection with its purposes, and

(d) does not involve disclosure of the personal data to a third party without the consent of the data subject.

5. The information contained in the personal data has been made public as a result of steps deliberately taken by the data subject.

6. The processing—

(a) is necessary for the purpose of, or in connection with, any legal proceedings (including prospective legal proceedings),

(b) is necessary for the purpose of obtaining legal advice, or

(c) is otherwise necessary for the purposes of establishing, exercising or defending legal rights.

7.—(1) The processing is necessary—

(a) for the administration of justice,

(b) for the exercise of any functions conferred on any person by or under an enactment, or

(c) for the exercise of any functions of the Crown, a Minister of the Crown or a government department.

(2) The Secretary of State may by order—

(a) exclude the application of sub-paragraph (1) in such cases as may be specified, or

(b) provide that, in such cases as may be specified, the condition in sub-paragraph (1) is not to be regarded as satisfied unless such further conditions as may be specified in the order are also satisfied.

8.—(1) The processing is necessary for medical purposes and is undertaken by—

(a) a health professional, or
(b) a person who in the circumstances owes a duty of confidentiality which is equivalent to that which would arise if that person were a health professional.

(2) In this paragraph "medical purposes" includes the purposes of preventative medicine, medical diagnosis, medical research, the provision of care and treatment and the management of healthcare services.

9.—(1) The processing—

(a) is of sensitive personal data consisting of information as to racial or ethnic origin,
(b) is necessary for the purpose of identifying or keeping under review the existence or absence of equality of opportunity or treatment between persons of different racial or ethnic origins, with a view to enabling such equality to be promoted or maintained, and
(c) is carried out with appropriate safeguards for the rights and freedoms of data subjects.

(2) The Secretary of State may by order specify circumstances in which processing falling within sub-paragraph (1)(a) and (b) is, or is not, to be taken for the purposes of sub-paragraph (1)(c) to be carried out with appropriate safeguards for the rights and freedoms of data subjects.

10. The personal data are processed in circumstances specified in an order made by the Secretary of State for the purposes of this paragraph.

Exceptions allowing data processing without further consent

The Act sanctions certain processing where this is without consent subject to certain specific statutory provisions. Here we note two exceptions which are particularly relevant in the context of health care information.

Research, history and statistics

33.—(1) In this section—
"research purposes" includes statistical or historical purposes;
"the relevant conditions", in relation to any processing of personal data, means the conditions—

(a) that the data are not processed to support measures or decisions with respect to particular individuals, and
(b) that the data are not processed in such a way that substantial damage or substantial distress is, or is likely to be, caused to any data subject.

(2) For the purposes of the second data protection principle, the further processing of personal data only for research purposes in compliance with the relevant conditions is not to be regarded as incompatible with the purposes for which they were obtained.

(3) Personal data which are processed only for research purposes in compliance with the relevant conditions may, notwithstanding the fifth data protection principle, be kept indefinitely.

(4) Personal data which are processed only for research purposes are exempt from section 7 if—

(a) they are processed in compliance with the relevant conditions, and
(b) the results of the research or any resulting statistics are not made available in a form which identifies data subjects or any of them.

(5) For the purposes of subsections (2) to (4) personal data are not to be treated as processed otherwise than for research purposes merely because the data are disclosed—

(a) to any person, for research purposes only,
(b) to the data subject or a person acting on his behalf,
(c) at the request, or with the consent, of the data subject or a person acting on his behalf, or
(d) in circumstances in which the person making the disclosure has reasonable grounds for believing that the disclosure falls within paragraph (a), (b) or (c).

NOTE:

1. The effect of this provision is to facilitate transmission of data for research purposes. Again it must be undertaken in connection with the law concerning breach of confidence discussed above.

Exceptions where information is required by law or in conjunction with legal proceedings

35.—(1) Personal data are exempt from the non-disclosure provisions where the disclosure is required by or under any enactment, by any rule of law or by the order of a court.
(2) Personal data are exempt from the non-disclosure provisions where the disclosure is necessary—

(a) for the purpose of, or in connection with, any legal proceedings (including prospective legal proceedings), or
(b) for the purpose of obtaining legal advice,

or is otherwise necessary for the purposes of establishing, exercising or defending legal rights.

NOTE:

1. This is in line with the exceptions to the principle of health care confidentiality noted above.

Anonymisation and data protection

One further issue is the extent to which anonymisation means that data may be transferred without the need for explicit consent from the data subject.

R v Department of Health Ex p. Source Informatics (discussed above at p.579)

SIMON BROWNE L.J.
"36 I turn to deal altogether more briefly with the remaining issues debated before us. First, there is Council Directive (95/46/EC) on the protection of individuals with regard to

the processing of personal data and on the free movement of such data, which fell to be implemented by 24 October 1998 and which the United Kingdom will finally implement on 1 March 2000 when the relevant provisions of the Data Protection Act 1998 come into force. Although all this postdates the Department of Health's policy guidance and, indeed, attracted no consideration in the court below, we cannot, I fear, entirely ignore it. Council Directive (95/46/EC) was first raised in these proceedings by Lord Lester on behalf of the General Medical Council ('GMC'), another intervening party. His argument (much over-simplified) is that, even if Source's proposal would involve a breach of confidence under domestic law, it does not offend Council Directive (95/46/EC) and so should be held compatible also with domestic law, the latter being read down if necessary for the purpose. By a linked submission, he further argues that the policy guidance (and/or any ruling by the court in support of it) would violate article 10 of the Convention for the Protection of Human Rights and Fundamental Freedoms (1953)(Cmd 8969), there being on the facts no countervailing interest in privacy to protect under article 8, and that domestic common law and, indeed, the scope of the Council Directive (95/46/EC) itself (see the reference to the Human Rights Convention in recital 1) should accordingly be determined as he contends so as to avoid such violation.

37 These arguments encouraged Mr Sales to advance mirror submissions on behalf of the Department of Health, namely that even if Source's proposal would not offend the common law (as I would hold) it should nevertheless be recognised to fall foul of Council Directive (95/46/EC) (and eventually the 1998 Act) so that domestic law ought accordingly to be read up for the purpose.

38 Let me put aside further complications such as whether or not Source are entitled to invoke the transitional provisions in article 32(2) of Council Directive (95/46/EC), and whether or not the Directive is directly effective pending its implementation, and turn to those of its articles upon which Mr Sales principally relies.

39 Article 2 (the definitions article) by paragraph (a) defines 'personal data' as meaning 'any information relating to an identified or identifiable natural person ("data subject")' and by paragraph (b) defines 'processing of personal data ("processing")' as meaning: 'any operation or set of operations which is performed upon personal data, whether or not by automatic means, such as collection, recording, organisation, storage, adaptation or alteration, retrieval, consultation, use, disclosure by transmission, dissemination or otherwise making available, alignment or combination, blocking, erasure or destruction . . . '

40 Article 8.1 requires that: 'Member states shall prohibit . . . the processing of data concerning health . . . '

41 Article 8.2(a) disapplies article 8.1 where: 'the data subject has given his explicit consent to the processing of those data . . . ' (a provision to which I shall briefly return later in this judgment).

42 Article 8.3, disapplies article 8.1:

'where processing of the data is required for the purposes of preventive medicine, medical diagnosis, the provision of care or treatment or the management of health-care services, and where those data are processed by a health professional [which includes, all parties agree, a pharmacist] . . . '

43 Mr Sales's argument put at its simplest is that the proposed anonymisation of the information contained in a prescription form will—under the very wide definition of "processing" set out in article 2(b)—constitute the processing of data concerning the patient's health, and that this is impermissible under article 8.1, such processing not being required for any of the stipulated purposes allowed for by article 8.3.

44 Lord Lester's best answer to this submission (and he is joined in it by Source) is that Council Directive (95/46/EC) can have no more application to the operation of anonymising data than to the use or disclosure of anonymous data (which, of course, by definition is not 'personal data' and to which, therefore, it is conceded that the Directive has no

application). He points to the several recitals emphasising the right to privacy as the principal concern underlying this Directive, and he places great reliance on recital (26):

'Whereas the principles of protection must apply to any information concerning an identified or identifiable person; whereas, to determine whether a person is identifiable, account should be taken of all the means likely reasonably to be used either by the controller or by any other person to identify the said person; whereas the principles of protection shall not apply to data rendered anonymous in such a way that the data subject is no longer identifiable; whereas codes of conduct within the meaning of article 27 may be a useful instrument for providing guidance as to the ways in which data may be rendered anonymous and retained in a form in which identification of the data subject is no longer possible . . . '

45 Although this is clearly not the appropriate occasion to attempt a definitive ruling on the scope of Council Directive (95/46/EC)—and still less of the impending legislation—I have to say that commonsense and justice alike would appear to favour the GMC's contention. By the same token that the anonymisation of data is, in my judgment, unobjectionable here under domestic law, so too, I confidently suppose, would it be regarded by other member states. Of course the processing of health data requires special protection and no doubt the 'erasure or destruction' of such data is included in the definition of processing for good reason: on occasion it could impair the patient's own health requirements. It by no means follows, however, that the process envisaged here should be held to fall within the definition: on the contrary, recital (26) strongly suggests that it does not."

NOTE:

1. The assumption is presently that use of anonymised data is legitimised in accordance with the Data Protection Act 1998, although this matter has yet to be conclusively resolved by the courts.

(iii) Rights of Access to Health Records under the Data Protection Act 1998

As with the Data Protection Act 1984 and the Access to Health Records Act 1990 data subjects have explicit rights of access to their data.

Right of access to personal data

7.—(1) Subject to the following provisions of this section and to sections 8, 9 and 9A, an individual is entitled—

(a) to be informed by any data controller whether personal data of which that individual is the data subject are being processed by or on behalf of that data controller,

(b) if that is the case, to be given by the data controller a description of—
   (i) the personal data of which that individual is the data subject,
   (ii) the purposes for which they are being or are to be processed, and
   (iii) the recipients or classes of recipients to whom they are or may be disclosed,

(c) to have communicated to him in an intelligible form—
   (i) the information constituting any personal data of which that individual is the data subject, and
   (ii) any information available to the data controller as to the source of those data, and

(d) where the processing by automatic means of personal data of which that individual is the data subject for the purpose of evaluating matters relating to him such as, for example, his performance at work, his credit worthiness, his reliability or his conduct, has constituted or is likely to constitute the sole basis for any decision significantly affecting him, to be informed by the data controller of the logic involved in that decision-taking.

(2) A data controller is not obliged to supply any information under subsection (1) unless he has received—

(a) a request in writing, and
(b) except in prescribed cases, such fee (not exceeding the prescribed maximum) as he may require.

(3) Where a data controller—

(a) reasonably requires further information in order to satisfy himself as to the identity of the person making a request under this section and to locate the information which that person seeks, and
(b) has informed him of that requirement,

the data controller is not obliged to comply with the request unless he is supplied with that further information.

(4) Where a data controller cannot comply with the request without disclosing information relating to another individual who can be identified from that information, he is not obliged to comply with the request unless—

(a) the other individual has consented to the disclosure of the information to the person making the request, or
(b) it is reasonable in all the circumstances to comply with the request without the consent of the other individual.

(5) In subsection (4) the reference to information relating to another individual includes a reference to information identifying that individual as the source of the information sought by the request; and that subsection is not to be construed as excusing a data controller from communicating so much of the information sought by the request as can be communicated without disclosing the identity of the other individual concerned, whether by the omission of names or other identifying particulars or otherwise.

(6) In determining for the purposes of subsection (4)(b) whether it is reasonable in all the circumstances to comply with the request without the consent of the other individual concerned, regard shall be had, in particular, to—

(a) any duty of confidentiality owed to the other individual,
(b) any steps taken by the data controller with a view to seeking the consent of the other individual,
(c) whether the other individual is capable of giving consent, and
(d) any express refusal of consent by the other individual.

(7) An individual making a request under this section may, in such cases as may be prescribed, specify that his request is limited to personal data of any prescribed description.

(8) Subject to subsection (4), a data controller shall comply with a request under this section promptly and in any event before the end of the prescribed period beginning with the relevant day.

(9) If a court is satisfied on the application of any person who has made a request under the foregoing provisions of this section that the data controller in question has failed to comply with the request in contravention of those provisions, the court may order him to comply with the request.

(10) In this section—

'prescribed" means prescribed by the [Secretary of State] by regulations;
'the prescribed maximum" means such amount as may be prescribed;
'the prescribed period" means forty days or such other period as may be prescribed;
"the relevant day", in relation to a request under this section, means the day on which the data controller receives the request or, if later, the first day on which the data controller has both the required fee and the information referred to in subsection (3).

(11) Different amounts or periods may be prescribed under this section in relation to different cases.

NOTES:

1. In contrast to the Access to Health Records Act 1990, the Data Protection Act 1998 does not specifically address either the issue of adults lacking mental capacity or children; see further A. Grubb and J. Laing, "Confidentiality and Data Protection" in A. Grubb (ed.), *Principles of Medical Law*, Oxford: OUP, 2003 at pp.620–630.
2. Note that there are exceptions in relation to information which is held for research purposes under s.33(4)of the Act, where data is not processed to support measures or decisions which relate to particular individuals, where processing is not done in such a way as to cause "substantial damage" or "substantial distress" to the patient and the research results do not identify any patient.
3. Specific exemptions to disclosure also exist in relation to information concerning fertility treatment (see further Data Protection (Miscellanous Subject Access Exemptions) Order 2000, SI 2000/419 and s.38 of the Data Protection Act 1998).

Regulations made under the legislation provide some further limitations on access rights to health information.

Data Protection Subject Access (Modification) (Health) Order 2000, SI 2000/413

2. In this Order—
"the Act" means the Data Protection Act 1998;
"the appropriate health professional" means—

(a) the health professional who is currently or was most recently responsible for the clinical care of the data subject in connection with the matters to which the information which is the subject of the request relates; or
(b) where there is more than one such health professional, the health professional who is the most suitable to advise on the matters to which the information which is the subject of the request relates; or
(c) where—
    (i) there is no health professional available falling within paragraph (a) or (b), or
    (ii) the data controller is the Secretary of State and data to which this Order applies are processed in connection with the exercise of the functions conferred on him by or under the Child Support Act 1991 and the Child Support Act 1995 or his functions in relation to social security or war pensions,
a health professional who has the necessary experience and qualifications to advise on the matters to which the information which is the subject of the request relates;

"care" includes examination, investigation, diagnosis and treatment;
"request" means a request made under section 7;
"section 7" means section 7 of the Act; and
"war pension" has the same meaning as in section 25 of the Social Security Act 1989 (establishment and functions of war pensions committees).

Personal data to which Order applies

3.—(1) Subject to paragraph (2), this Order applies to personal data consisting of information as to the physical or mental health or condition of the data subject.

(2) This Order does not apply to any data which are exempted from section 7 by an order made under section 38(1) of the Act.

Exemption from the subject information provisions

4.—(1) Personal data falling within paragraph (2) and to which this Order applies are exempt from the subject information provisions.

(2) This paragraph applies to personal data processed by a court and consisting of information supplied in a report or other evidence given to the court by a local authority, Health and Social Services Board, Health and Social Services Trust, probation officer or other person in the course of any proceedings to which the Family Proceedings Courts (Children Act 1989) Rules 1991, the Magistrates' Courts (Children and Young Persons) Rules 1992, the Magistrates' Courts (Criminal Justice (Children)) Rules (Northern Ireland) 1999, the Act of Sederunt (Child Care and Maintenance Rules) 1997 or the Children's Hearings (Scotland) Rules 1996 apply where, in accordance with a provision of any of those Rules, the information may be withheld by the court in whole or in part from the data subject.

Exemptions from section 7

5.—(1) Personal data to which this Order applies are exempt from section 7 in any case to the extent to which the application of that section would be likely to cause serious harm to the physical or mental health or condition of the data subject or any other person.

(2) Subject to article 7(1), a data controller who is not a health professional shall not withhold information constituting data to which this Order applies on the ground that the exemption in paragraph (1) applies with respect to the information unless the data controller has first consulted the person who appears to the data controller to be the appropriate health professional on the question whether or not the exemption in paragraph (1) applies with respect to the information.

(3) Where any person falling within paragraph (4) is enabled by or under any enactment or rule of law to make a request on behalf of a data subject and has made such a request, personal data to which this Order applies are exempt from section 7 in any case to the extent to which the application of that section would disclose information—

    (a) provided by the data subject in the expectation that it would not be disclosed to the person making the request;

    (b) obtained as a result of any examination or investigation to which the data subject consented in the expectation that the information would not be so disclosed; or

    (c) which the data subject has expressly indicated should not be so disclosed,

provided that sub-paragraphs (a) and (b) shall not prevent disclosure where the data subject has expressly indicated that he no longer has the expectation referred to therein.

(4) A person falls within this paragraph if—

    (a) except in relation to Scotland, the data subject is a child, and that person has parental responsibility for that data subject;

(b) in relation to Scotland, the data subject is a person under the age of sixteen, and that person has parental responsibilities for that data subject; or

(c) the data subject is incapable of managing his own affairs and that person has been appointed by a court to manage those affairs.

Modification of section 7 relating to data controllers who are not health professionals

6.—(1) Subject to paragraph (2) and article 7(3), section 7 of the Act is modified so that a data controller who is not a health professional shall not communicate information constituting data to which this Order applies in response to a request unless the data controller has first consulted the person who appears to the data controller to be the appropriate health professional on the question whether or not the exemption in article 5(1) applies with respect to the information.

(2) Paragraph (1) shall not apply to the extent that the request relates to information which the data controller is satisfied has previously been seen by the data subject or is already within the knowledge of the data subject.

Additional provision relating to data controllers who are not health professionals

7.—(1) Subject to paragraph (2), article 5(2) shall not apply in relation to any request where the data controller has consulted the appropriate health professional prior to receiving the request and obtained in writing from that appropriate health professional an opinion that the exemption in article 5(1) applies with respect to all of the information which is the subject of the request.

(2) Paragraph (1) does not apply where the opinion either—

(a) was obtained before the period beginning six months before the relevant day (as defined by section 7(10) of the Act) and ending on that relevant day, or

(b) was obtained within that period and it is reasonable in all the circumstances to re-consult the appropriate health professional.

(3) Article 6(1) shall not apply in relation to any request where the data controller has consulted the appropriate health professional prior to receiving the request and obtained in writing from that appropriate health professional an opinion that the exemption in article 5(1) does not apply with respect to all of the information which is the subject of the request.

Further modifications of section 7

8. In relation to data to which this Order applies—

(a) section 7(4) of the Act shall have effect as if there were inserted after paragraph (b) of that subsection

"or,

(c) the information is contained in a health record and the other individual is a health professional who has compiled or contributed to the health record or has been involved in the care of the data subject in his capacity as a health professional".

(b) section 7(9) shall have effect as if—

(i) there was substituted—

"(9) If a court is satisfied on the application of—

(a) any person who has made a request under the foregoing provisions of this section, or

(b) any other person to whom serious harm to his physical or mental health or condition would be likely to be caused by compliance with any such request in contravention of those provisions, that the data controller in question is about to comply with or has failed to comply with the request in contravention of those provisions, the court may order him not to comply or, as the case may be, to comply with the request."; and

(ii) the reference therein to a contravention of the foregoing provisions of that section included a reference to a contravention of the provisions contained in this Order.

(iv) Remedies

A number of remedies are explicitly recognised under the Data Protection Act 1998.

Right to require end of data processing likely to cause damage/distress

10.—(1) Subject to subsection (2), an individual is entitled at any time by notice in writing to a data controller to require the data controller at the end of such period as is reasonable in the circumstances to cease, or not to begin, processing, or processing for a specified purpose or in a specified manner, any personal data in respect of which he is the data subject, on the ground that, for specified reasons—

(a) the processing of those data or their processing for that purpose or in that manner is causing or is likely to cause substantial damage or substantial distress to him or to another, and

(b) that damage or distress is or would be unwarranted.

(2) Subsection (1) does not apply—

(a) in a case where any of the conditions in paragraphs 1 to 4 of Schedule 2 is met, or

(b) in such other cases as may be prescribed by the Secretary of State by order.

(3) The data controller must within twenty-one days of receiving a notice under subsection (1) ("the data subject notice") give the individual who gave it a written notice—

(a) stating that he has complied or intends to comply with the data subject notice, or

(b) stating his reasons for regarding the data subject notice as to any extent unjustified and the extent (if any) to which he has complied or intends to comply with it.

(4) If a court is satisfied, on the application of any person who has given a notice under subsection (1) which appears to the court to be justified (or to be justified to any extent), that the data controller in question has failed to comply with the notice, the court may order him to take such steps for complying with the notice (or for complying with it to that extent) as the court thinks fit.

(5) The failure by a data subject to exercise the right conferred by subsection (1) or section 11(1) does not affect any other right conferred on him by this Part.

NOTE:

1. This provision may be of use in a situation in which while there is no breach of confidence there has been misuse of the information (see further A. Grubb, *Kennedy and Grubb Medical Law* (3rd edn), London: Butterworths, 2001).

Action for damages where the data controller has contravened the legislation

13.—(1) An individual who suffers damage by reason of any contravention by a data controller of any of the requirements of this Act is entitled to compensation from the data controller for that damage.

(2) An individual who suffers distress by reason of any contravention by a data controller of any of the requirements of this Act is entitled to compensation from the data controller for that distress if—

(a) the individual also suffers damage by reason of the contravention, or
(b) the contravention relates to the processing of personal data for the special purposes.

(3) In proceedings brought against a person by virtue of this section it is a defence to prove that he had taken such care as in all the circumstances was reasonably required to comply with the requirement concerned.

NOTE:

1. It has been suggested that this provision is unlikely to provide any substantial change to the common law position given the fact that the onus is upon the claimant to prove damage and also there is a defence where the data controller took reasonable care (see further A. Grubb, *Kennedy and Grubb Medical Law* (3rd edn), 2000 at p.1045).

Right to rectification

14.—(1) If a court is satisfied on the application of a data subject that personal data of which the applicant is the subject are inaccurate, the court may order the data controller to rectify, block, erase or destroy those data and any other personal data in respect of which he is the data controller and which contain an expression of opinion which appears to the court to be based on the inaccurate data.

(2) Subsection (1) applies whether or not the data accurately record information received or obtained by the data controller from the data subject or a third party but where the data accurately record such information, then—

(a) if the requirements mentioned in paragraph 7 of Part II of Schedule 1 have been complied with, the court may, instead of making an order under subsection (1), make an order requiring the data to be supplemented by such statement of the true facts relating to the matters dealt with by the data as the court may approve, and
(b) if all or any of those requirements have not been complied with, the court may, instead of making an order under that subsection, make such order as it thinks fit for securing compliance with those requirements with or without a further order requiring the data to be supplemented by such a statement as is mentioned in paragraph (a).

(3) Where the court—

(a) makes an order under subsection (1), or
(b) is satisfied on the application of a data subject that personal data of which he was the data subject and which have been rectified, blocked, erased or destroyed were inaccurate, it may, where it considers it reasonably practicable, order the data

controller to notify third parties to whom the data have been disclosed of the rectification, blocking, erasure or destruction.

(4) If a court is satisfied on the application of a data subject—

(a) that he has suffered damage by reason of any contravention by a data controller of any of the requirements of this Act in respect of any personal data, in circumstances entitling him to compensation under section 13, and
(b) that there is a substantial risk of further contravention in respect of those data in such circumstances, the court may order the rectification, blocking, erasure or destruction of any of those data.

(5) Where the court makes an order under subsection (4) it may, where it considers it reasonably practicable, order the data controller to notify third parties to whom the data have been disclosed of the rectification, blocking, erasure or destruction.

(6) In determining whether it is reasonably practicable to require such notification as is mentioned in subsection (3) or (5) the court shall have regard, in particular, to the number of persons who would have to be notified.

(b) Access to Medical Reports Act 1988

This Act allows individuals a statutory right of access to medical records compiled for employment/insurance purposes.

Access to Medical Reports Act 1988, ss.2(1), 3(1–2), 4(1–4), 5(1–2), 6(1–3), 7(1–4)

2.—(1) In this Act—

"the applicant" means the person referred to in section 3(1) below;
"care" includes examination, investigation or diagnosis for the purposes of, or in connection with, any form of medical treatment;
"employment purposes", in the case of any individual, means the purposes in relation to the individual of any person by whom he is or has been, or is seeking to be, employed (whether under a contract of service or otherwise);
"health professional" has the same meaning as in the Data Protection (Subject Access Modification) (Health) Order 1987;
"insurance purposes", in the case of any individual, means the purposes in relation to the individual of any person carrying on an insurance business with whom the individual has entered into, or is seeking to enter into, a contract of insurance, and "insurance business" and "contract of insurance" have the same meaning as in the Insurance Companies Act 1982;
"medical practitioner" means a person registered under the Medical Act 1983;
"medical report", in the case of an individual, means a report relating to the physical or mental health of the individual prepared by a medical practitioner who is or has been responsible for the clinical care of the individual.

3.—(1) A person shall not apply to a medical practitioner for a medical report relating to any individual to be supplied to him for employment or insurance purposes unless—

(a) that person ("the applicant") has notified the individual that he proposes to make the application; and
(b) the individual has notified the applicant that he consents to the making of the application.

(2) Any notification given under subsection (1)(a) above must inform the individual of his right to withhold his consent to the making of the following rights under this Act, namely—

(a) the rights arising under sections 4(1) to (3) and 6(2) below with respect to access to the report before or after it is supplied,

(b) the right to withhold consent under subsection (1) of section 5 below, and

(c) the right to request the amendment of the report under subsection (2) of that section, as well as of the effect of section 7 below.

4.—(1) An individual who gives his consent under section 3 above to the making of an application shall be entitled, when giving his consent, to state that he wishes to have access to the report to be supplied in response to the application before it is so supplied; and, if he does so, the applicant shall—

(a) notify the medical practitioner of that fact at the time when the application is made, and

(b) at the same time notify the individual of the making of the application;

and each such notification shall contain a statement of the effect of subsection (2) below.

(2) Where a medical practitioner is notified by the applicant under subsection (1) above that the individual in question wishes to have access to the report before it is supplied, the practitioner shall not supply the report unless—

(a) he has given the individual access to it and any requirements of section 5 below have been complied with, or

(b) the period of 21 days beginning with the date of the making of the application has elapsed without his having received any communication from the individual concerning arrangements for the individual to have access to it.

(3) Where a medical practitioner—

(a) receives an application for a medical report to be supplied for employment or insurance purposes without being notified by the applicant as mentioned in subsection (1) above, but

(b) before supplying the report receives a notification from the individual that he wishes to have access to the report before it is supplied, the practitioner shall not supply the report unless:

(i) he has given the individual access to it and any requirements of section 5 below have been complied with, or

(ii) the period of 21 days beginning with the date of that notification has elapsed without his having received (either with that notification or otherwise) any communication from the individual concerning arrangements for the individual to have access to it.

(4) References in this section and section 5 below to giving an individual access to a medical report are references to—

(a) making the report or a copy of it available for his inspection; or

(b) supplying him with a copy of it;

and where a copy is supplied at the request, or otherwise with the consent, of the individual the practitioner may charge a reasonable fee to cover the costs of supplying it.

5.—(1) Where an individual has been given access to a report under section 4 above the report shall not be supplied in response to the application in question unless the individual has notified the medical practitioner that he consents to its being so supplied.

(2) The individual shall be entitled, before giving his consent under subsection (1) above, to request the medical practitioner to amend any part of the report which the individual considers to be incorrect or misleading; and, if the individual does so, the practitioner—

(a) if he is to any extent prepared to accede to the individual's request, shall amend the report accordingly;
(b) if he is to any extent not prepared to accede to it but the individual requests him to attach to the report a statement of the individual's views in respect of any part of the report which he is declining to amend, shall attach such a statement to the report.

(3) Any request made by an individual under subsection (2) above shall be made in writing.

6.—(1) A copy of any medical report which a medical practitioner has supplied for employment or insurance purposes shall be retained by him for at least six months from the date on which it was supplied.

(2) A medical practitioner shall, if so requested by an individual, give the individual access to any medical report relating to him which the practitioner has supplied for employment or insurance purposes in the previous six months.

(3) The reference in subsection (2) above to giving an individual access to a medical report is a reference to—

(a) making a copy of the report available for his inspection; or
(b) supplying him with a copy of it;

and where a copy is supplied at the request, or otherwise with the consent, of the individual the practitioner may charge a reasonable fee to cover the costs of supplying it.

7.—(1) A medical practitioner shall not be obliged to give an individual access, in accordance with the provisions of section 4(4) or 6(3) above, to any part of a medical report whose disclosure would in the opinion of the practitioner be likely to cause serious harm to the physical or mental health of the individual or others or would indicate the intentions of the practitioner in respect of the individual.

(2) A medical practitioner shall not be obliged to give an individual access, in accordance with those provisions, to any part of a medical report whose disclosure would be likely to reveal information about another person, or to reveal the identity of another person who has supplied information to the practitioner about the individual, unless—

(a) that person has consented; or
(b) that person is a health professional who has been involved in the care of the individual and the information relates to or has been provided by the professional in that capacity.

(3) Where it appears to a medical practitioner that subsection (1) or (2) above is applicable to any part (but not the whole) of a medical report—

(a) he shall notify the individual of that fact; and
(b) references in the preceding sections of this Act to the individual being given access to the report shall be construed as references to his being given access to the remainder of it; and other references to the report in sections 4(4), 5(2) and 6(3) above shall similarly be construed as references to the remainder of the report.

(4) Where it appears to a medical practitioner that subsection (1) or (2) above is applicable to the whole of a medical report—

(a) he shall notify the individual of that fact; but
(b) he shall not supply the report unless he is notified by the individual that the individual consents to its being supplied;

and accordingly, if he is so notified by the individual, the restrictions imposed by section 4(2) and (3) above on the supply of the report shall not have effect in relation to it.

NOTES:

1. A doctor may withhold information if it may cause serious harm to a person's physical or mental health and it would reveal a practitioner's intentions towards his patient.
2. A person may be ordered by a court to comply with the Act (s.8).
3. A medical practitioner is not obliged to inform the patient of the fact that the contents of any report compiled might be serious or damaging to the patient (see HC, Vol. 127, cols 660–661).
4. There has been considerable debate as to whether information that an individual has taken a HIV test should be withheld from his insurers. Evidence emerged that a positive answer to the question on an insurance form "have you ever had a HIV test" may lead to denial of insurance, although by taking the test itself an individual was not indicating that he had tested positive. The insurance industry have now indicated that such questions should be withdrawn. (See P. Roth and W. Gryk, "Aids and Insurance" in R. Haigh and D. Harris (eds), *AIDS and the Law*, London: Routledge, 1995, at p.96.) Should a medical practitioner be entitled to refuse to disclose such information on a medical report?
5. A further debate has arisen as to whether an individual is entitled to withhold from his medical report any information concerning a genetic screening test which he may have undertaken (see Nuffield Council on Bioethics Report *Genetic Screening*, 1993, Chapter 7). This is particularly problematic because even though an individual may have tested positive, that does not necessarily mean that he will actually develop that condition; it may mean simply that he has an increased chance of developing a particular illness. This problem is likely to become acute in the future as testing becomes increasingly common. (See further on this issue J. Harris, *Wonderwoman and Superman*, Oxford: OUP, 1992, Chapter 10 and Human Genetics Commission, *The Use of Genetic Information in Insurance: Interim Recommendations of the Human Genetics Commission*, London: HCG, 2001). The UK Government have agreed a moratorium on the use of test results with the Association of British Insurers which has currently been agreed up to November 1, 2011 (Department of Health and Association of British Insurers, *Concordat and Moratorium on Genetics and Insurance*, London: DOH, 2005).

QUESTIONS:

1. Are reports which are compiled solely for the purposes of insurance within the provisions of the Act?
2. The Act refers to doctors who have the "clinical care" of the patient? Does this include occupational health physicians? (See J. Montgomery, "Access to Medical Reports Act 1988" (1989) *Journal of Social Welfare Law* 129 at p.130.)

(c) Disclosure of Medical Records as a Preliminary to Legal Proceedings

Supreme Court Act 1981, s.34(1–4)

34.—(1) This section applies to any proceedings in the High Court in which a claim is made in respect of personal injuries to a person, or in respect of a person's death.

(2) On the application, in accordance with rules of court, of a party to any proceedings to which this section applies, the High Court shall, in such circumstances as may be specified in the rules, have power to order a person who is not a party to the proceedings and who appears to the court to be likely to have in his possession, custody or power any documents which are relevant to an issues arising out of the said claim—

(a) to disclose whether those documents are in his possession, custody or power;
(b) to produce such of those documents as are in his possession, custody or power to the applicant or, on such conditions as may be specified in the order:
    (i) to the applicant's legal advisers; or
    (ii) to the applicant's legal advisers and any medical or other professional adviser of the applicant; or
    (iii) if the applicant has no legal adviser, to any medical or other professional adviser of the applicant.

(3) On the application, in accordance with rules of court, of a party to any proceedings to which this section applies, the High Court shall, in such circumstances as may be specified in the rules, have power to make an order providing for any one or more of the following matters, that is to say—

(a) the inspection, photographing, preservation, custody and detention of property which is not the property of, or in the possession of, any party to the proceedings but which is the subject-matter of the proceedings or as to which any question arises in the proceedings;
(b) the taking of samples of any such property as is mentioned in paragraph (a) and the carrying out of any experiment on or which any such property.

(4) The preceding provisions of this section are without prejudice to the exercise by the High Court of any power to make orders which is exercisable apart from those provisions.

Provisions supplementary to sections 33 and 34

35.—(1) The High Court shall not make an order under section 33 or 34 if it considers that compliance with the order, if made, would be likely to be injurious to the public interest.

(5) In Sections 32A, 33 and 34 and this section:
"property" includes any land, chattel or other corporeal property of any description;
"personal injuries" includes any disease and any impairment of a person's physical or mental condition

Notes:

1. Despite the provisions of the Data Protection Act 1998 there may be circumstances in which it is sought to use s.31. Some health records are not compiled as part of "clinical care" and thus would fall outside the 1990 Act. Furthermore, while information may be withheld under the 1990 Act on the basis that disclosure may cause serious physical or mental harm to

the patient, there are no such limitations upon disclosure under the 1981 Act. (See generally M. Jones, *Medical Negligence* (3rd edn), London: Sweet & Maxwell, 2003.)

2. As a general rule, full disclosure of experts' reports prior to trial will be ordered. In *Naylor v Preston AHA* [1987] 2 All E.R. 353 criticism was made of the approach taken in the *Wilsher* case in which it was stated that the earlier case was "fought in the dark" (see Chapter 3 above). The courts have indicated that disclosure should not be delayed in medical negligence cases (*Hall v Wandsworth HA* (1985) 129 S.J. 181). This area was considerably impacted by the Woolf reforms of the civil justice process— see discussion in Chapter 3 above.

3. In both civil and criminal proceedings, access to documents may be refused if the documents are covered by legal professional privilege or by public interest immunity. In *Lee v South West Thames R.H.A.* [1985] 2 All E.R. 385 an infant suffered brain damage due to treatment in one of two hospitals, the first under the control of Hillingdon AHA and the second under the control of North East Thames AHA. Disclosure of reports compiled by the ambulance crew of South West Thames RHA for the purpose of Hillingdon obtaining legal advice was refused. The court held that they were covered by legal professional privilege. This was on the basis that a defendant should be able to obtain evidence without having to disclose the findings of the other party. In *W v Egdell*, at first instance, Scott J. held that the report which Dr Egdell had compiled was not covered by legal professional privilege. He said that a distinction could be drawn between the situation in which instructions were given to experts for the making of a report, which were covered by legal professional privilege, and the ultimate opinion given by the expert which was not. Dr Egdell's report was not privileged. Whether such a distinction is justifiable is questionable. This matter was not discussed fully in the Court of Appeal, although Sir Stephen Brown appeared to agree with the approach taken by Scott J. on this issue. (See J.V. McHale, "Confidentiality—An Absolute Obligation?" (1989) 52 *Modern Law Review* 715.)

4. Discovery will also be refused if the documents are covered by public interest immunity. In deciding whether to disclose information on the basis of public interest immunity, the court will balance the public interest in preserving the confidentiality of the information against the public interest in ensuring that there is a fair hearing at the subsequent proceedings. In *Re HIV Haemophiliac Litigation* [1990] N.L.J.R. 1349, a large number of haemophiliacs had received blood infected with HIV. They sought to bring an action against the Department of Health on the grounds that the Department was negligent in failing to ensure that there was enough blood available for donation in the United Kingdom, and as a result having to obtain blood for donation from the US. The Government refused disclosure of certain documents. These documents concerned briefings for ministers as to whether a policy for self-sufficiency in blood products should be established and what resources would be required for such a policy, planning decisions relating to the Blood Products Laboratory and

the decision whether and how to organise the National Blood Transfusion Service. The Court of Appeal held that discovery of the documents was necessary in order for the plaintiffs to make a thorough presentation of their case. (This litigation is further discussed in Chapter 1 above.) See also *AB v Glasgow and West of Scotland Blood Transfusion Service* (1989) 15 B.M.L.R. 91.

(d) Access to Health Records at Common Law

A patient seeking access to records compiled before 1991 when the Access to Health Records Act came into force has no automatic right of access. His only chance of obtaining the records, aside from undertaking litigation, is either to persuade his doctor to make a voluntary disclosure of the information or to attempt to claim that he has a right of access at common law.

R. v Mid Glamorgan Family Health Services Authority, Ex p. Martin [1995] 1 All E.R. 356

M was diagnosed as being a catatonic schizophrenic suffering from depression, psychopathy and intellectual immaturity. He received psychotherapy. M fell in love with the consultant psychiatrist treating him. As a result of this, she was withdrawn from treating him. M sought details of his records and of the decision to withdraw the psychiatrist. He was subsequently detained under the Mental Health Act 1959. He sought judicial review of the decision by Mid Glamorgan Family Health Services Authority to make consideration of disclosure of the records conditional upon an assurance from the applicant that no potential litigation was contemplated by him in respect of his treatment by South Glamorgan Health Authority. He also sought judicial review of the decision of South Glamorgan Health Authority on November 2, 1990 to refuse such disclosure to him.

At first instance the application was rejected by Popplewell J. He rejected the claim that there was a right of access and laid emphasis on the fact that legislation had been explicitly enacted for the purposes of granting access. He drew a distinction between treatment information, which the patient was entitled to receive in order to reach his decision regarding treatment and information which constituted a doctor's assessment of the patients condition to which the patient had no right of access. He said also that Article 8 of the European Convention of Human Rights was not applicable in this situation. Moreover Article 8 itself does not give unlimited access to medical records. Popplewell J. said that if he was wrong and there was a right of access at common law that still did not mean that Martin would be able to gain access since such rights were not absolute. Mr Martin appealed to the Court of Appeal.

NOURSE L.J.
"Popplewell J. said that the claim was a public law claim and did not depend on private rights. Although both these propositions are correct, a public body, as the owner of medical records, can be in a position no different from that of a private doctor, whose

relationship is governed by contract. In other words, a public body, in fulfilment of its duty to administer its property in accordance with its public purposes, is bound to deal with medical records in the same way as a private doctor. In that regard the observations of Lord Templeman in *Sidaway v Bethlem Royal Hospital Governors* [1985] 1 All E.R. 643 at 665–666 are pertinent:

'I do not subscribe to the theory that the patient is entitled to know everything nor to the theory that the doctor is entitled to decide everything. The relationship between doctor and patient is contractual in origin, the doctor performing services in consideration for fees payable by the patient. The doctor, obedient to the highest standards set by the medical profession, impliedly contracts to act at all times in the best interests of the patient. No doctor in his senses would impliedly contract at the same time to give to the patient all the information available to the doctor as a result of the doctor's training and experience and as a result of the doctor's diagnosis of the patient. An obligation to give a patient all the information available to the doctor would often be inconsistent with the doctor's contractual obligation to have regard to the patient's best interests. Some information might confuse, other information might alarm a particular patient Whenever the occasion arises for the doctor to tell the patient the result of the doctor's diagnosis, the possible methods of treatment and the advantages and disadvantages of the recommended treatment, the doctor must decide in the light of his training and experience and in the light of his knowledge of the patient what should be said and how it should be said.'

These observations provide a sensible basis for holding that a doctor, likewise a health authority, as the owner of a patient's medical records, may deny the patient access to them if it is in his best interests to do so, for example if their disclosure would be detrimental to his health. In the light of the offer made in the respondents' solicitor's letter of March 24, 1993, that is a complete answer to the appellant's application. I agree with Popplewell J. that the respondents have offered all that is necessary to comply with their duty to the appellant. The judge was entitled, in the exercise of his discretion, to refuse the appellant the relief that he sought and I would affirm his decision on that ground. Although the respondents have not taken this point, it might also, as a matter of discretion, have been affirmed on the ground that the appellant did nothing effective to pursue his rights against either of the respondents between 1981 and 1990.

It is inherent in the views above expressed that I do not accept that a health authority, any more than a private doctor, has an absolute right to deal with medical records in any way that it chooses. As Lord Templeman makes clear, the doctor's general duty, likewise the health authority's, is to act at all times in the best interests of the patient. Those interests would usually require that a patient's medical records should not be disclosed to third parties; conversely, that they should usually, for example, be handed on by one doctor to the next or made available to the patient's legal advisers if they are reasonably required for the purposes of legal proceedings in which he is involved. The respondents' position seems to be that no practical difficulty could arise in such circumstances, but that they would act voluntarily and not because they were under a legal duty to do so. If it ever became necessary for the legal position to be tested, it is inconceivable that this extreme position would be vindicated.

On all the other points taken by the appellant I agree with Popplewell J. I would dismiss this appeal."

EVANS L.J.
" . . . Like Nourse L.J., I do not consider that the fact that these are public law proceedings alters the nature of the central issue which is the extent of the appellant's common law rights and of the respondent's correlative duties to provide access. Like him, also, I consider that the essential issue is whether they are entitled to deny access on the ground that their disclosure would be harmful to him.

The statutory right under the 1990 Act is qualified in this way. Section 5(1) reads:

'5(1) Access shall not be given . . . to any part of a health record—
(a)   which, in the opinion of the holder of the record, would disclose—
(i) information likely to cause serious harm to the physical or mental health of the
patient or of any other individual . . . '

Mr Allen submits that this restriction forms no part of the common law. He relied upon
the fundamental right of self-determination which is expressed in art 8(1) of the
Convention For the Protection of Human Rights and Fundamental Freedom (Rome,
November 4, 1950 TS 71 (1953); Cmnd. 8969) as follows: 'Everyone has the right to
respect for his private and family life, his home and his correspondence. . . . ', and which
is recognised, as he submits, by common law decisions including *Sidaway v Bethlem Royal
Hospital Governors* [1985] 1 All E.R. 643, regarding the patient's right to know sufficient
of the relevant facts to enable him to make his own decision about medical treatment, and
Re T (adult: refusal of medical treatment) [1992] 4 All E.R. 649 regarding the rights of a
Jehovah's Witness to refuse medical treatment. The decision in *Re C (adult: refusal of
medical treatment)* [1994] 1 All E.R. 819, demonstrates, he submits that the right of self-
determination now outweighs the public interest in the sanctity of life. Therefore, the
applicant is entitled to decide for himself whether or not to incur whatever risk of damage
to his mental or physical health might accompany the disclosure of the records to him.

Mr Allen's reliance upon Art. 8 of the Convention, and on the decision of the European
Court of Human Rights in *Gaskin v U.K.* (1990) 12 E.H.R.R. 36, does not involve any
contention that the Convention forms part of English law or that its provisions are directly
enforceable here. Rather, he adopts the approach described in Sir John Laws' lecture to the
Administrative Law Bar Association: 'Is the High Court the Guardian of Fundamental
Constitutional Rights?' [1993] *Public Law* 59. The fact that the convention does not form
part of English law does not mean that its provisions cannot be referred to and relied upon
as persuasive authority as to what the common law is, or should be. Article 8 therefore
reflects the right of self-determination which now, he submits, forms part of the common
law.

For my part, I am prepared unreservedly to adopt this approach but I hope that it is not
unduly insular, or even parochial, to remind oneself at the outset that the object of the
inquiry is to establish the relevant rules of the common law. That inquiry in the present
case reduces itself to the question whether the common law right of access, if there is one,
is qualified in the same way as the statutory right now enacted is qualified by section
5(1)(a).

In my judgment, there is no good reason for doubting either that a right of access does
exist or that it is qualified to that extent at least. The record is made for two purposes
which are relevant here: first, to provide part of the medical history of the patient, for the
benefit of the same doctor or his successors in the future; and secondly, to provide a record
of diagnosis and treatment in case of future inquiry or dispute. Those purposes would be
frustrated if there was no duty to disclose the records to medical advisers or to the patient
himself, or his legal advisers, if they were required in connection with a later claim. Nor
can the duty to disclose for medical purposes be limited, in my judgment, to future medical
advisers. There could well be a case where the patient called for them in order to be able
to give them to a future doctor as yet unidentified, e.g. in case of accident whilst travelling
abroad.

But the present case is not one where the records are required for medical purposes, or
in connection with any dispute or projected litigation. Both are expressly disavowed. The
applicant wishes to have a greater knowledge of his 'childhood, development and history'
(see *Gaskin v U.K.* (1989) 12 E.H.R.R. 36) and he seeks disclosure for this reason
alone.

The respondents' solicitors' letter of March 24, 1993 offers to produce the records to a
medical adviser who can assess their likely effect upon the mental or physical health of the
applicant. It is more than 20 years since he was a patient of any doctor whose records they
hold, and so they cannot assess this for themselves. The assessment can only be carried out
by a medical adviser with knowledge of his present-day condition. To release the records

to the applicant himself, when there are grounds for supposing that they might cause harm to his physical or mental health, would be to risk causing or aggravating the kind of injury which previously they undertook to prevent or cure. These are valid reasons, in my judgment, for holding that any common law right of access is limited to this extent."

SIR ROGER PARKER:

" . . . I agree that this appeal must be dismissed for the reasons given in the judgment of Nourse L.J. I add only the following observations:

(1) I regard as untenable the proposition that, at common law, a doctor or health authority has an absolute property in medical records of a patient, if this means, which it appears to do, that either could make what use of them he or it chose. Information given to a doctor by a patient or a third party is given in confidence and the absolute property rights are therefore necessarily qualified by the obligations arising out of that situation.

(2) I regard as equally untenable the proposition that by reason of a 'right of self determination' a patient has an unfettered right of access to his medical records at all times and in all circumstances, indeed it is accepted for the applicant that this cannot be so.

(3) In my view the circumstances in which a patient or former patient is entitled to demand access to his medical history as set out in the records will be infinitely various, and it is neither desirable nor possible for this or any court to attempt to set out the scope of the duty to afford access or, its obverse, the scope of the patient's rights to demand access. Each case must depend on its own facts.

(4) There can, I think, be no doubt, for example, that a doctor should, if requested by the patient, or perhaps by a patient's doctor for the time being, afford access to such doctor but not necessarily to the entire contents of the records. There may, however, be circumstances when direct access to the records or some part of them should be given to the patient himself. If, for example, he is about to emigrate and his condition is such that he might need treatment before he can nominate a successor doctor, it would, it seems to me, be probable that the doctor with the records would be obliged either to give access to the records or to provide his departing patient with a letter giving the information necessary to enable a doctor, faced with his collapse, for example, on board ship, to treat him properly."

NOTES:

1. The Court of Appeal appeared to accept that there is a right of access to health care records, although this right is not absolute in nature. There has, been some speculation as to the source of such a right. One possibility is that it may be grounded in the doctor's duty of care in negligence. This has, however, been questioned. Grubb, for example, has argued that non-disclosure may be fully consistent with professional practice under *Bolam*. Secondly, there would be difficulties in some situations of establishing that non-disclosure constituted harm to the patient (see A. Grubb, "Access to Medical Records" (1994) 2 *Medical Law Review* 353).

2. At first instance, before Popplewell J., it was argued that the doctor owed an obligation of disclosure as part of her general fiduciary duty to her patient. This issue had arisen in the Canadian case of *McInerney v MacDonald* (1992) 93 D.L.R. (4th edn) 415 S.C.C. In that case the Canadian Supreme Court held that a right of access was derived from the doctor's fiduciary duty, because the doctor had a duty to act in the utmost good faith. A patient may not be able to establish that a doctor had acted in such a manner unless he was allowed access to information relating to his treatment. Popplewell J. rejected the existence of a fiduciary duty. In

reaching his decision he noted the rejection of a fiduciary duty in *Sidaway v Bethlem Royal Hospital Governors* [1984] 1 All E.R. 1018 (see Chapter 6 above) and stated that the opinion reached by the doctor was the doctor's property and could be distinguished from the information which she had been provided by the patient.

3. This case was subject to subsequent critical scrutiny in *Breen v Williams* in the High Court of Australia in 1996 (1996) 70 A.L.J.R. 772 and I. Kennedy (1997) 5 *Medical Law Review* 115. Here it was held that there was no obligation to provide access in the absence of a contractual term or where it would be negligent to fail to provide access in a particular situation.

QUESTIONS:

1. To what extent does the approach taken by Evans L.J. as to the basis on which information may be withheld differ from that adopted by Nourse L.J.?
2. What does Sir Roger Parker mean when he says that property rights in medical records are qualified?
3. Do you agree with the use made by Evans L.J. of Article 8 of the ECHR?
4. If the duty to disclose is derived from negligence, then will the patient be able to suceed in a claim for damages based upon failure to disclose?

SELECT BIBLIOGRAPHY

M. Beupré "Confidentiality, HIV/AIDS and Prison Health Care Services" [1994] 2 *Medical Law Reviews* 149.

P. Case, "Confidence Matters: the Rise and Fall of Informational Autonomy in Medical Law" (2003) 11(2) *Medical Law Review* 208.

R. Chadwick, M. Levitt, and D. Shickle (eds), *The Right to Know and the Right not to Know*, Ashgate, 1997.

J. Davis, "Patients' Rights of Access to their Health Records" [1996] 2 *Medical Law International* 189.

Department of Health Confidentiality; Code of Practice; London: DOH (2003).

H. Emson, "Confidentiality: a Modified Value" (1988), 14 *Journal of Medical Ethics* 87.

F. Gurry, *Breach of Confidence*, Oxford: Clarendon, 1985.

Human Genetics Commission Inside Information, London: HGC (2004).

G. Hunt (ed.), *Whistleblowing in the Health Services*, London: Edward Arnold, 1994.

M. Jones, "Medical Confidentiality and the Public Interest" (1990) 6 *Professional Negligence* 16.

I. Kennedy, "The Doctor, the Pill and the Fifteen Year Old Girl" in I. Kennedy (ed.), *Treat Me Right*, Oxford: OUP 1989.

M.H. Kottow, "Medical Confidentiality: an Absolute and Intransigent Obligation" (1986) 12 *Journal of Medical Ethics* 117.

G. Laurie, *Genetic Privacy*, Cambridge: CUP, 2002.

R. Lee, "Deathly Silence" in R. Lee and D. Morgan (eds), *Death Rites: Law and Ethics at the End of Life*, London: Routledge, 1994.

H. Lesser and Z. Pickup, "Law, Ethics and Confidentiality" (1990) 17 *Journal of Law and Society* 17.

J.V. McHale, *Medical Confidentiality and Legal Privilege*, London: Routledge, 1993.

J. Montgomery, "Confidentiality and the Immature Minor" [1987] *Family Law* 101.

10

CLINICAL RESEARCH

1. INTRODUCTION

Following the atrocities perpetrated by the Nazi regime, scientists have been pressurised to be accountable for the conduct of clinical research. International ethical declarations were drawn up in the form of the Nuremburg Code in 1949 and the Declaration of Helsinki in 1964. The Declaration of Helsinki is now in its sixth edition (World Medical Association, "Declaration of Helsinki Ethical Principles for Medical Research Involving Human Subjects", 6th edition, adopted October 2000) and has been followed by a series of major international and European statements on ethical clinical research practice (see further A. Plomer, *The Law and Ethics of Medical Research: International Bioethics and Human Rights*, London: Cavendish Publishing 2005). Guidance, for example, has been published with reference to some of the ethical challenges of conducting biomedical research particularly in developing countries (see, for example, the Council for International Organisations of Medical Sciences, *International Ethical Guidelines for Biomedical Research Concerning Human Subjects*, 2002). As we shall see in this chapter, despite the guidelines, the ethical controversy regarding research continues. This was illustrated, most notably, by the notorious Tuskegee experiment in the US on black males to determine the progression of syphilis, even though there had been an accepted treatment for many years (see further J. Jones, *Bad Blood: the Tuskegee Syphilis Experiment*, New York: Free Press, 1981). In 2001 Ellen Roche, a 24-year-old technician, died after acting as a volunteer in a non-therapeutic asthma study at Johns Hopkins University in the US. The review undertaken after her death was exceedingly critical of the project, inadequate consent procedures and failures regarding the reporting of adverse events. The statement of the external review committee looking into the incident commented that "many people at Hopkins believe that oversight and regulatory processes are a barrier to research and are to be reduced to the minimum". ("Death of Research Volunteer at Johns Hopkins Hospital", *Bulletin of Medical Ethics*, September 2001.) In 2006 an investigation undertaken by Professor Sir Ian Kennedy condemned the conduct of chemical experiments upon servicemen at Porton Down before the Second World War and during the Cold War, experiments in some instances undertaken on servicemen who thought they had volunteered for experiments concerning the common cold. ("Porton Down nerve gas trials breached standards of ethics", *The Times*, July 15, 2006.) Recent controversy surrounded the conduct of a trial at Northwick Park Hospital in London where healthy volunteers suffered a sudden violent reaction during a trial involving anti-inflamatory drugs (see "BBC News, "Six taken ill After drug trial", March 6, 2006 *http://news.bbc.co.uk/1/hi/england/london/4807042.stm*).

While much of the discourse concerns the protection of research subjects, some regard participation in scientific research as a moral obligation to society (see J. Harris, "Scientific Research is a Moral duty" (2005) 31 *Journal of Medical Ethics* 242; and in the context of genetic databases O. O'Neil, R. Chadwick and K. Berg, "Solidarity and Equity: New Ethical Frameworks for Genetic Databases" (2001) 2 *Nature Reviews Genetics* 318), even to the extent that those who refuse to participate in research should be refused access to treatment (see A. Caplan, "Is There an Obligation to Participate in Biomedical Research?" in S.F. Spicker, I. Alon, A. de Vries and H. Tristram Englehardt (eds), *The Use of Human Beings in Research*, Dordrecht: Kluwer 1988). In England and Wales, a movement towards the regulation of clinical research developed in the 1960s. In 1968 the then Minister of Health, in response to a report issued by the Royal College of Physicians, sent a letter to health authorities requesting that they establish research ethics committees. These were non-statutory bodies composed of members drawn predominantly from the health professions who sat part time to consider proposals for clinical trials. It was not, however, until 1984 that the first extensive guidance was provided to researchers, in the form of a document issued by the Royal College of Physicians. General guidelines to research ethics committees were issued by the Department of Health in 1991 (Department of Health, *Local Research Ethics Committees*, 2001—the "Red Book"). These were replaced in 2001 with the introduction of the Research Governance Framework and the Governance Arrangements for Research Ethics Committees (GAFREC). (For a critical commentary of these guidelines, see E. Cave and S. Holm, "New governance arrangements for research ethics committees: is facilitating research achieved at the cost of participant interest" (2002) 28 *Journal of Medical Ethics* 318). While the GAFREC guidelines are still in force, a revised Research Governance Framework was produced in 2005 ("Research Governance Framework for Health and Social Care", London: DOH, 2005). It should be noted that these are still non-statutory guidelines, although it is likely that reference would be made to them in any judicial proceedings. There is little explicit guidance provided to researchers on human subjects in the form of statutes and decided cases. This is perhaps ironic, since research upon animals is subject to a detailed statutory regulatory procedure under the Animals (Scientific Procedures) Act 1986. However, the European Union has recently had a considerable impact upon the regulation of the clinical trials process in the UK in relation to trials upon medicinal products through the implementation of the Clinical Trials Directive (Directive 2001/20).

In Section 3 we consider the mechanisms currently available for the scrutiny of clinical trials. In Section 4 we examine the basis on which subjects are recruited into clinical trials and the information which they should be given before they participate. In Section 5 the separate and distinct rule regarding participation in trials concerning medicinal products are discussed. Section 6 considers confidentiality issues. Section 7 examines the question of fraudulent research and Section 8 approval issues (including challenges to committee decisions and the liability of committee members). Section 9 considers compensation for research subjects. In Section 10 we consider one area of research which has been regarded as giving rise to particularly difficult dilemmas, that of embryo research. Finally, in Section 11 we consider the issue of animal research.

2. REGULATING RESEARCH: NATIONAL OVERSIGHT

Originally, regulation of clinical research was a matter entrusted solely to a local level of scrutiny. This position has altered as a result of two developments. First, research activity has been affected by the establishment of national regulatory organisations which have as part of their concern the question of research; these orgainisations include the Xenotransplantation Interim Regulatory Authority and the Gene Therapy Advisory Committee, which are considered below. Secondly, the UK has introduced national oversight of clinical trials consequent upon the Clinical Trials Directive (discussed below at p.703). The Medicines for Human Use Clinical Trials Regulations have now established a new UK Ethics Committee Authority.

The Medicines for Human Use (Clinical Trials) Regulations 2004 (SI 2004/1031)

United Kingdom Ethics Committees Authority

5.—(1) The body responsible for establishing, recognising and monitoring ethics committees in the United Kingdom in accordance with these Regulations is the United Kingdom Ethics Committees Authority, which is a body consisting of—

(a) the Secretary of State for Health;
(b) the National Assembly for Wales;
(c) the Scottish Ministers; and
(d) the Department for Health, Social Services and Public Safety for Northern Ireland.

(2) The functions of the Authority—

(a) may, by agreement between them, be performed by any one of the Secretary of State for Health, the National Assembly for Wales, the Scottish Ministers and the Department for Health, Social Services and Public Safety for Northern Ireland acting alone, or any two or more of them acting jointly; and
(b) may be performed by any one of the Secretary of State for Health, the National Assembly for Wales, the Scottish Ministers and the Department for Health, Social Services and Public Safety for Northern Ireland acting alone solely in relation to a part of the United Kingdom with respect to which the Secretary of State, the Assembly, the Ministers or the Department, as the case may be, have responsibilities.

(3) In accordance with the preceding provisions of this regulation, in these Regulations "the United Kingdom Ethics Committees Authority" ("the Authority") means any one or

more of the Secretary of State for Health, the National Assembly for Wales, the Scottish Ministers and the Department for Health, Social Services and Public Safety for Northern Ireland, and, in the case of anything falling to be done by the Authority, means any one or more of them acting as mentioned in paragraph (2).

Establishment of ethics committees

6.—(1) The Authority may establish ethics committees to act—

(a) for the entire United Kingdom or for such areas of the United Kingdom; and
(b) in relation to such descriptions or classes of clinical trials,

as the Authority consider appropriate.
(2) The Authority may—

(a) vary the area for which any committee they have established acts or, as the case may be, the descriptions or classes of clinical trials in relation to which such a committee acts; and
(b) abolish any such committee.

NOTES:

1. While these Regulations only apply to trials concerning medicinal products, in practice, nationally there has been an attempt to align law and practice consistent with these provisions.
2. In addition co-ordination of operation and training of research ethics committees is undertaken by the Central Office for Research Ethics Committees (COREC) which now operates as part of the National Patient Safety Agency (*http://www.npsa.nhs.uk*).

3. APPROVAL OF A CLINICAL TRIAL: THE RESEARCH ETHICS COMMITTEE

Before a clinical trial is undertaken, it is standard practice for the trial to be referred to a research ethics committee for its approval. Failure to obtain such approval may mean that the researcher is subsequently unable to secure publication of his findings in an academic journal. In the case of drug trials, these now have to be given approval by a research ethics committee consequent upon the Medicines for Human Use (Clinical Trials) Regulations 2004. Here we consider the general guidance concerning approval of clinical trials and below we consider specific issues consequent upon the Directive at p.703.

(a) The Remit of a Research Ethics Committee

Governance Arrangements for Research Ethics Committees (London: DOH, 2001)

3.1 Ethical advice from the appropriate NHS REC is required for any research proposal involving:

a. patients and users of the NHS. This includes all potential research participants recruited by virtue of the patient or user's past or present treatment by, or use of, the NHS. It includes NHS patients treated under contracts with private sector institutions

b. individuals identified as potential research participants because of their status as relatives or carers of patients and users of the NHS, as defined above

c. access to data, organs or other bodily material of past and present NHS patients

d. fetal material and IVF involving NHS patients

e. the recently dead in NHS premises

f. the use of, or potential access to, NHS premises or facilities

g. NHS staff—recruited as research participants by virtue of their professional role.

3.2 If requested to do so, an NHS REC may also provide an opinion on the ethics of similar research studies not involving the categories listed above in section 3.1, carried out for example, by private sector companies, the Medical Research Council (or other public sector organisations), charities or universities.

3.3 The appropriate REC in each case is one recognised for this purpose by the Health Authority within the area of which the research is planned to take place.

3.4 This will normally be one established by the Health Authority itself within its geographical area—currently called a Local Research Ethics Committee (LREC).

3.5 For the purposes of ethical review of the research proposal, a research "site" is defined as the geographical area covered by one Health Authority, whether the research is based in institution(s) or in the community. Even when the research may physically take place at several locations within that geographical boundary, a favourable ethical opinion on the research protocol is required from only one NHS REC within that Health Authority boundary.

3.6 Where the research is planned to take place at more than one "site" as defined above, different arrangements apply.

3.7 For research involving gene therapy, application should be made to the Gene Therapy Advisory Committee (GTAC).

3.8 For clinical research that involves xenotransplantation, application should be made to the United Kingdom Xenotransplantation Interim Regulatory Authority (UKXIRA).

3.9 Certain types of research specified under the Human Fertilisation and Embryology Act, 1990, may not proceed without a licence from the Human Fertilisation and Embryology Authority, from whom further information may be obtained. Research Ethics Committee approval is also required.

3.10 Specific arrangements are in place for ethical review of research on prisoners.

3.11 Research on clients of Social Services (i.e. participants recruited by virtue of their past or present status as clients of Social Services), including those cared for under contracts with private sector care providers, should have the favourable opinion of a Research Ethics Committee which meets the same general standards as NHS RECs in respect of composition, review process and general operating procedures.

NOTES:

1. As the above terms of reference indicate, research ethics committees scrutinise diverse issues, ranging from patient questionnaires to major surgical trials. Although there is no requirement for trials undertaken outside the NHS (except where these concern medicinal products) to receive research ethics committee approval, some private organisations have established their own ethics committees.

2. Research into the operation of research ethics committees discovered that many committees review a large number of projects with a maximum per

annum of 351 per committee (see C. Gilbert Foster, "The Annual Reports of Research Ethics Committees" (1995) 21 *Journal of Medical Ethics* 214). There is considerable variation in ethical review across the country, illustrated by a review of protocols regarding multi-centred trials (see further on this below at pp.675) and also in relation to the review of protocols by full committee as opposed to by chair's action (see further P. Glasziou and I. Chalmers, "Ethics Review Roulette: What Can We Learn?" (2004) 328 B.M.J. 121). There are concerns that the procedural impact of ethics committee review can delay research activity (see further D.J. Togerson and J.C. Dumville, "Research Governance also Delays Research" (2004) 328 B.M.J. 710).

3. While research ethics committees scrutinise clinical trials, they do not take decisions to include individual patients in trials. In this respect research ethics committees differ from bodies such as institutional ethics committees prevalent in the United States which do play a major role in the authorisation of treatment.

4. The research committee is expected to provide an annual report to the body which established it, setting out its operation over the past year.

5. The GAFREC document refers to the Gene Therapy Advisory Committee. One challenge for medical researchers is to determine whether it is possible to eradicate genetic illness through the use of what is known as "gene therapy". There are two types of gene therapy. First, somatic gene therapy. This involves gene therapy being undertaken on one particular patient. Secondly, germ-line gene therapy which would involve changing the gene line. Such therapy has implications for future generations. The ethics of research into gene therapy were considered by a government committee, the Clothier Committee, which reported in 1992, (Clothier Committee, *Report of the Committee on the Ethics of Gene Therapy*, Cmnd. 1788, 1992). It recommended the establishment of an expert advisory body to oversee the operation of gene therapy. It was opposed to the development of germ-line gene therapy but supported further research into somatic gene therapy. The Clothier Committee's rejection of germ-line therapy is reflective of the wide concern that has been expressed as to the implications of such a technique, with a fear that it could be a slippery slope leading to the wish to eliminate factors which are seen as "undesirable" (see J.K. Mason and G. Laurie, *Law and Medical Ethics* (7th edn), London: Butterworths, 2006, at p.248 and W. French Anderson, "Human Gene Therapy: Scientific and Ethical Considerations" in R. Chadwick (ed.), *Ethics, Reproductionism and Genetic Control*, London: Routledge, 1987). The Government accepted the Committee's recommendations and in 1993 established a new non-statutory body, the Gene Therapy Advisory Committee (*http://www.advisorybodies.doh.gov.uk/genetics/gtac/.*). This has now become the statutory body under the Medicines for Human Use (Clinical Trials) Regulations 2004 for the approval of clinical trials involving gene therapy products. (See further W.M. Kong, "The Regulation of Gene Therapy Research in Competent Adult Patients: Today and Tomorrow; The Implications of EU Directive 2001/20/EC" (2004) 12

Medical Law Review 164). The Gene Therapy Advisory Committee is obliged to give an ethical opinion on gene therapy products. The Committee will not consider applications for germ-line gene therapy as it is of the view that this has not developed to the stage where it could be considered for treatment.

6. The role of the Xenotransplantation Interim Regulatory Authority, a body established to review animal-human transplants is considered further in Chapter 15 below at p.1170. The operation of the Human Fertilisation and Embryology Authority in relation to embryo research is explored later in this chapter at p.721.

7. The ambit of NHS research ethics committees extends to cover social care issues in addition to health matters.

8. Prisoners may be regarded as a vulnerable group of research subjects. Because of their position they are at risk of being coerced into participation in a trial. For the purposes of medical treatment, prisoners are regarded as any other competent adult (*Freeman v Home Office* [1984] 1 All E.R. 1036). It is presumed that they can also give consent to therapeutic medical research. As far as non-therapeutic research is concerned, it is suggested that were a prisoner to bring an action in battery, claiming that he had not given valid consent, much would depend upon whether his consent was given freely.

(b) Membership of the Committee

Governance Arrangements for Research Ethics Committees (London: DOH, 2001)

6 COMPOSITION OF AN REC

6.1 An REC should have sufficient members to guarantee the presence of a quorum *(see 6.11)* at each meeting. The maximum should be 18 members. This should allow for a sufficiently broad range of experience and expertise, so that the scientific, clinical and methodological aspects of a research proposal can be reconciled with the welfare of research participants, and with broader ethical implications.

6.2 Overall the REC should have a balanced age and gender distribution. Members should be drawn from both sexes and from a wide range of age groups. Every effort should also be made to recruit members from black and ethnic minority backgrounds, as well as people with disabilities. This should apply to both expert and lay members

6.3 RECs should be constituted to contain a mixture of "expert" and "lay" members. At least three members must be independent of any organisation where research under ethical review is likely to take place.

Expert members

6.4 The "expert" members of the committee shall be chosen to ensure that the REC has the following expertise:

- relevant methodological and ethical expertise in:

  - clinical research

- non-clinical research
- qualitative or other research methods applicable to health services, social science and social care research.

- clinical practice including:

  - hospital and community staff (medical, nursing and other)
  - general practice
  - statistics relevant to research
  - pharmacy.

Lay members

6.5 At least one third of the membership shall be "lay" members who are independent of the NHS, either as employees or in a non-executive role, and whose primary personal or professional interest is not in a research area.

6.6 The "lay" membership can include non-medical clinical staff who have not practised their profession for a period of at least five years.

6.7 At least half of the "lay" members must be persons who are not, and never have been, either health or social care professionals, and who have never been involved in carrying out research involving human participants, their tissue or data.

Non-representative role

6.8 Despite being drawn from groups identified with particular interests or responsibilities in connection with health and social care issues, REC members are not in any way the representatives of those groups. They are appointed in their own right, to participate in the work of the REC as equal individuals of sound judgement, relevant experience and adequate training in ethical review.

NHS Staff as members

6.9 NHS organisations should provide encouragement to their staff who wishes to serve as members of RECs. The time required for undertaking such service and the necessary training should be protected, and form a recognised part of the individual's job plan.

Specialist referees

6.10 The Chair and Administrator may seek the advice of specialist referees on any relevant aspects of a specific research proposal that lie beyond the expertise of the members. These referees may be specialists in ethical aspects, specific diseases or methodologies, or they may be representatives of communities, patients, or special interest groups. Such referees are not voting members of the committee, and should not be involved in the business of the committee other than that related to the specific research proposal in question. Terms of reference for independent referees should be established. Their advice should be recorded in the minutes.

Note:

1. One criticism made in the past regarding the operation of REC was in relation to the lack of experience of REC members. The GAFREC guidelines now provide that:

   "4.10 REC members have a need for initial and continuing education and training regarding research ethics, research methodology and research governance.

4.11 Appointing Authorities shall provide, within the annual budget for its REC(s), resources for such training, guidance on which will be issued by the Department of Health."

QUESTIONS:

1. What is the ideal membership composition of a research ethics committee? Does it accord with that stated in the guidelines?
2. Should the chair always be a lay member?

(c) Approval of Multi-centred Research

Governance Arrangements for Research Ethics Committees (London: DOH, 2001)

8 MULTI-CENTRE RESEARCH

8.1 For the purpose of ethical review of research, a research "site" is defined as the geographical area covered by a single Health Authority, and includes all the research institutions and localities within it.

8.2 For the present, multi-centre research will continue to be defined as research carried out within five or more "sites", i.e. the area covered by five or more Health Authority boundaries, irrespective of the number of LRECs within each Authority.

8.3 For research taking place in from two to four sites, application should be made to one LREC within each of the Health Authority boundaries. However, when a favourable opinion has been obtained from the first Health Authority's LREC, the second, third and fourth Health Authorities may, on the advice of their own LRECs, accept that opinion with further review by their own LREC only of the "locality issues".

8.4 If recruitment is planned in five (or more) sites, irrespective of whether existing LREC approval in up to four sites has been already given, application is then required to a Multi-centre Research Ethics Committee (MREC). A favourable opinion of an MREC then covers the whole of the United Kingdom.

8.5 If the MREC declines to give a favourable opinion on the application, any existing approval by LRECs still stands, but those LRECs shall be informed of the MREC's decision (and its reasons).

8.6 Once an MREC has declined approval, no further application using the same proposal may be made to any LREC.

Consideration of "locality" issues

8.7 The MREC (or "lead" LREC—see 8.3 above) undertakes the review of the ethics of the research
protocol, including the content of the patient information sheet and consent form. No further ethical review of these items shall be undertaken by other RECs (except in the process of a "second review"described in 7.35 above).

8.8 The "locality issues" are limited to:

- the suitability of the local researcher
- the appropriateness of the local research environment and facilities
- specific issues relating to the local community, including the need for provision of information in languages other than English.

8.9 The LREC should satisfy itself that the "locality issues" have been adequately considered, and that it can approve them. In undertaking consideration of the "locality issues" the REC should work closely with the NHS host organisation, which also has a responsibility for research conduct and safety.

8.10 LRECs and local NHS trusts should set up administrative mechanisms to facilitate such joint working. The detailed assessment of the "locality issues" may be undertaken on behalf of the NHS either directly by an LREC itself (or its officers), or by the NHS host (if it is a Trust) with the prior agreement of the LREC. In the latter case the Trust shall inform the LREC of the outcome of the process. The LREC shall consider the advice of the Trust and, if accepted, shall record its approval in LREC minutes. For multi-centre research, the research may not proceed until the LREC has informed the approving MREC of its lack of objection with respect to the "locality issues".

8.11 The consideration of "locality issues" should occur in parallel with the consideration of ethical review of the research protocol by the MREC or "lead" LREC.

8.12 The decision on the "locality issues" should be made and communicated within 60 days of receipt of a valid application for this purpose.

Multi-centre research where there is no "local" researcher

8.13 For multi-centre research where there is no "local" researcher, and where this is confirmed by the MREC (or "lead" LREC—see 8.3 above) during its review of the research protocol, no specific consideration of "locality" issues by an LREC may be needed and the overall process of review may thus be expedited. Approval by the host NHS organisation is still required before the research may proceed.

NOTE:

1. The introduction of the MREC process followed years of critical comment regarding approval of clinical trials protocols across various regions. Originally the conduct of the trial would require approval by the research ethics committee in each area in which it is proposed to conduct the trial. This could result in the trial receiving approval in some areas of the country but not in others. For example, a study in 1995 noted that, in a situation in which the same proposal was submitted to 24 health authorities, in nine regions there was a wide range of variation in the manner in which the proposals were reviewed. Fourteen gave approval without modification; three rejected it and gave three different grounds for the rejection while six committees requested minor modifications. (See M. Redshaw, A. Harris and D. Baum, "Research Ethics, Committee Audit-Difference between Committee" (1996) 22 *Journal of Medical Ethics* 78.) However, research undertaken in the early years of the operation of MRECs indicated that problems still remained (see, for example, K.G.M.M. Alberti, "Multi-centre Research Ethics Committees: Has the Cure Been Worse than the Disease?" (2000) 320 B.M.J. 1157).

(d) Procedure for Reviewing Trials

The research ethics committees are given guidance as to the procedure for reviewing clinical trials protocol, currently in the form of the Governance Arrangements for Research Ethics Committee.

Governance Arrangements for Research Ethics Committees (London: DOH, 2001)

9 THE PROCESS OF ETHICAL REVIEW OF A RESEARCH PROTOCOL

9.1 All properly submitted and valid applications shall be reviewed in a timely fashion and according to an established review procedure described in the standard operating procedures. A valid application is one which has been submitted by an appropriate investigator, is complete, with all the necessary documents attached, and is signed and dated.

9.2 RECs shall meet regularly on scheduled dates that are announced in advance. Meetings should be planned in accordance with the needs of the workload, but RECs must meet the time standards for review.

9.3 REC members should be given enough time in advance of the meeting to review the relevant documents.

9.4 Meetings shall be minuted. There should be an approval procedure for the minutes.

9.5 The applicant (and if appropriate, the sponsor and/or other investigators) shall be invited to be available to elaborate on or clarify specific issues as required by the REC at its meeting. An REC should not cause unnecessary delay by deferring consideration of an application when the necessary further information it requires could have been obtained from the applicant at the first review meeting.

9.6 Independent expert referees may be invited by the Chairman to attend the meeting or to provide written comments, subject to applicable confidentiality agreements.

9.7 The primary task of an REC lies in the ethical review of research proposals and their supporting documents, with special attention given to the nature of any intervention and its safety for participants, to the informed consent process, documentation, and to the suitability and feasibility of the protocol.

9.8 The Research Governance Framework makes it clear that the sponsor is responsible for ensuring the quality of the science. Paragraphs 2.3.1 and 2.3.2 state that:

"● It is essential that existing sources of evidence, especially systematic reviews, are considered carefully prior to undertaking research. Research which duplicates other work unnecessarily or which is not of sufficient quality to contribute something useful to existing knowledge is in itself unethical.

● All proposals for health and social care research must be subjected to review by experts in the relevant fields able to offer independent advice on its quality. Arrangements for peer review must be commensurate with the scale of the research."

9.9 Thus, protocols submitted for ethical review should already have had prior critique by experts in the relevant research methodology, who should also comment on the originality of the research. It is not the task of an REC to undertake additional scientific review, nor is it constituted to do so, but it should satisfy itself that the review already undertaken is adequate for the nature of the proposal under consideration.

9.10 If the committee is of the opinion that the prior scientific review commensurate with the scale of the research is not adequate (including adequate statistical analysis), it should require the applicant to re-submit the application having obtained further expert review.

9.11 In addition to considering prior scientific review, RECs need to take into account the potential relevance of applicable laws and regulations. It is not the role of the REC to offer a legal opinion, but it may advise the applicant and the host NHS body whenever it is of the opinion that further expert legal advice might be helpful to them.

Requirements for a favourable opinion

9.12 Before giving a favourable opinion, the REC should be adequately reassured about the following issues, as applicable:

9.13 *Scientific design and conduct of the study*:

a. the appropriateness of the study design in relation to the objectives of the study, the statistical methodology (including sample size calculation where appropriate), and the potential for reaching sound conclusions with the smallest number of research participants
b. the justification of predictable risks and inconveniences weighed against the anticipated benefits for the research participants, other present and future patients, and the concerned communities
c. the justification for use of control arms in trials, (whether placebo or active comparator), and the randomisation process to be used
d. criteria for prematurely withdrawing research participants
e. criteria for suspending or terminating the research as a whole
f. the adequacy of provisions made for monitoring and auditing the conduct of the research, including the constitution of a data safety monitoring committee (DSMC)
g. the adequacy of the research site, including the supporting staff, available facilities, and emergency procedures. For multi-centre research, these locality issues will be considered separately from the ethical review of the research proposal itself
h. the manner in which the results of the research will be reported and published.

9.14 *Recruitment of research participants*

a. the characteristics of the population from which the research participants will be drawn (including gender, age, literacy, culture, economic statusand ethnicity) and the justification for any decisions made in this respect
b. the means by which initial contact and recruitment is to be conducted
c. the means by which full information is to be conveyed to potential research participants or their representatives
d. inclusion criteria for research participants
e. exclusion criteria for research participants.

9.15 *Care and protection of research participants*

a. the safety of any intervention to be used in the proposed research
b. the suitability of the investigator(s)'s qualifications and experience for ensuring good conduct of the proposed study
c. any plans to withdraw or withhold standard therapies or clinical management protocols for the purpose of the research, and the justification for such action
d. the health and social care to be provided to research participants during and after the course of the research
e. the adequacy of health and social supervision and psychosocial support for the research participants
f. steps to be taken if research participants voluntarily withdraw during the course of the research
g. the criteria for extended access to, the emergency use of, and/or the compassionate use of study products
h. he arrangements, if appropriate, for informing the research participant's general practitioner, including procedures for seeking the participant's consent to do so
i. a description of any plans to make the study product available to the research participants following the research
j. a description of any financial costs to research participants

k. the rewards and compensations (if any) for research participants (including money, services and/or gifts)

l. whether there is provision in proportion to the risk for compensation/treatment in the case of injury/disability/death of a research participant attributable to participation in the research; the insurance and indemnity arrangements

m. the nature and size of any grants, payments or other reward to be made to any researchers or research hosts

n. circumstances that might be lead to conflicts of interest that may affect the independent judgement of the researcher(s).

NOTES:

1. It may be the case that the conduct of a particular trial involves a difficult issue of public policy; for example, a trial involving the controlled distribution of drugs, such as heroin, to drug abusers. It is arguable that issues of this nature should not be left for local resolution but should be determined by a national forum. Controversy arose in relation to a video surveillance technique used in an attempt to detect whether child patients had been the victims of parental abuse, and particularly whether those who were harming the children were suffering from Munchausen's syndrome by proxy. The researchers said that they had referred the practice to a research ethics committee, but that they had asked the committee to treat it as an accepted technique and not as a matter of research. The issue was subsequently referred to a special ethics committee. It has been suggested that such surveillance is not a matter for the research ethics committee or for the hospital but for the police. Interestingly, when these researchers first undertook a similar study in London, the local police were involved. However, in Staffordshire, the police said that they would be unable to undertake such surveillance. Where a trial involves a difficult question of public policy, it is arguable that reference should be made to some form of national forum to examine the ethics and legality of the procedure. (See D. Evans, "The Investigation of Life-threatening Child Abuse and Munchausen's Syndrome by Proxy" (1995) 21 *Journal of Medical Ethics* 9; D.P. Southall and M.P. Samuels, "Some Ethical Issues Surrounding Covert Video Surveillance: a Response" (1995) 21 *Journal of Medical Ethics* 104; R. Gillon, "Editorial: 'Covert surveillance by doctor for life-threatening Munchausen's syndrome by proxy'" (1995) 21 *Journal of Medical Ethics* 131; and "Symposium on covert video surveillance" (1996) 22 *Journal of Medical Ethics* 16).

2. The research ethics committee will be particularly concerned to examine the potential risk levels of participation in the trial. It has been noted in the past that the perception of risk levels by scientists may differ considerably from the research subject's perception of risk.

3. Inducements may be offered to individual research subjects or to physicians to encourage participation in trials. Many trials would be impossible without the involvement of major pharmaceutical companies; nonetheless it is important to ensure that individuals participate freely in research and

that the judgment of the ethical acceptability of the trial is not impacted by the commercial advantages which may accrue through involvement, whether to the participant or indeed to a clinician who is involved (see further the Report of the Royal College of Physicians, *The Relationship between Physicians and the Pharmaceutical Industry*, London, 1986). Inducements may also lead to individuals being tempted to become involved in several trials simultaneously. For example, students may be tempted to enter a number of trials in order to alleviate financial pressures. Volunteers may put themselves at risk if drugs taken in different trials conflict. In addition, multiple participation may invalidate the success of a clinical trial. One possible way of dealing with the problem is for researchers to ask the subjects whether they are involved in another trial; it appears that some research ethics committees require that researchers include a question to that effect. The Royal College of Physicians' *Guidelines on Research with Healthy Volunteers* (London, 1986) suggests that medical students involved in clinical trials should inform the Dean of the Medical School. However this does not deal with the problem of students from other disciplines who may seek to enter such trials. It is suggested that failure to ask the research subject whether he was involved in any other clinical trial, and if so to give details, would constitute negligence. Nevertheless, such a claim may fail because causation is not established or the student may be found contributorily negligent in participation or to have assumed that risk under the principle of *volenti non fit injuria*. Of course cash-strapped students may not tell the truth. Perhaps one way in which this problem could be addressed would be through the use of a national register listing all those who are currently included in a clinical trial, say by reference to their NHS number. Admittedly, the costs of this proposal may prove a deterrent to its establishment and it would not totally overcome the difficulty of the dubious researcher, although it might represent an improvement on the present position.

4. GAFREC requires, in para.9.14, consideration to be given to the nature of the research participants. Over the years there has been a considerable debate as to whether some groups, such as women of child-bearing age, should be excluded from clinical research because of the differing physiological impact of research on men and women and also the impact on child-bearing capacity, and issues which may arise should a woman involved in a study become pregnant, with the prospect of harm for woman and foetus. The guidelines do not exclude such groups. Exclusion of women from research can be seen as discriminatory and indeed could have long-term adverse implications for the development of treatments which may benefit women. (See generally M. Fox, "Research Bodies: Feminist Perspectives on Clinical Research" in S. Sheldon and M. Thomson (eds), *Feminist Perspectives in Health Care Law*, London: Cavendish, 1998).

5. One notable development in the 2001 guidelines is that over recent years the language of research regulation has changed—now guidance makes reference to "research participants" as opposed to "research subjects".

(e) Reform of the Research Ethics Committee System

Over recent years the operation of research ethics committees has come under criticism. There is evidence of considerable variation in ethical review across the country, illustrated by a review of protocols regarding multi-centered trials and also in relation to the review of protocols by full committee as opposed to by chair's action (see further P. Glasziou and I. Chalmers, "Ethics Review Roulette: What Can We Learn?" (2004) 328 B.M.J. 121). There are considerable concerns that the procedural impact of ethics committee review can delay research activity (see further D.J. Togerson and J.C. Dumville, "Research Governance Also Delays Research" (2004) 328 B.M.J. 710). The criticism led to an Advisory Group being established to review the system. The group agreed that there was need for reform and suggested several steps to alter the existing system. They made the following recommendations.

Report of the Ad Hoc Advisory Group on the Operation of NHS Research Ethics Committees (London: DOH, 2005)

1. The remit of NHS RECs should not include surveys or other non research activity if they present no material ethical issues for human participants. COREC should develop guidelines to aid researchers and committees in deciding what is appropriate or inappropriate for submission to RECs.

2. RECs should not reach decisions based on scientific review. In the unusual situation of a REC having reservations about the quality of the science proposed, they should be able to refer to COREC for scientific guidance.

3. The recently introduced managed operating system has been well received. Its use of IT points the way to further efficiency and quality improvements. We believe that responsibility for site specific assessment should be transferred to NHS hosts as soon as acceptable mechanisms for quality assurance are in place.

4. The application form and application process call for improvement. The form should take more explicit account of differences between types of research and should also give more space and attention to ethical issues.

5. We strongly encourage NHS research hosts to adopt common national systems. Substantial improvement to local R&D procedures and their interaction with ethical review—including the ability to make multiple use of information supplied once—is required in order to reduce bureaucracy and timescales. This is the most pressing of all our recommendations.

6. We believe that a smaller number of RECs perhaps one for each Strategic Health Authority, with a limited number of exceptions would be more appropriate. Their operations would be more intense than at present, with a greater use of electronic communications. The time commitment required of members and support staff for training should be more formally recognised, as should the time taken in committee hearings and preparation. This implies paying REC members appropriately, either directly or through compensating their employers.

7. Research Ethics Committees must represent the public interest as well as patient perspectives on research. This means that membership needs to be drawn from a wider mix of society and that all members need to be supported by appropriate training. We believe that our recommendation that we move towards a system of fewer, paid RECs will support this objective.

8. The issue of excessive inconsistency amongst committees should be addressed by concentrating on the provision of appropriate training, and on capturing and sharing good practice where issues and arguments have been already explored. The newly introduced

system of quality assurance by peer review amongst committees and their members should assist this process and should be further developed.

9. We propose the creation of "Scientific Officers" in COREC to support the work of committees. They might undertake much of the preliminary assessment required, and review reports. Chairs, for whom it is a major burden, currently undertake this work.

NOTES:

1. The reform proposals of the Ad Hoc Group have been subject to considerable criticism. It has been suggested that the proposed separation between "scientific" and "ethical" issues is problematic. For example, Dawson has commented "such a view seems very odd. Surely a study's methodology can raise ethical issues? Is it not an ethical issue if the study will fail to answer the research questions set by the researcher. As anyone who has sat on a REC knows that these are rightly, serious concerns for many members of RECs. The review process will be poorer and perhaps even impossible if this discussion is now to be banned. The tidy separation between scientific and ethical review envisaged here is impossible. . . . " (See A.J. Dawson, "The Ad Hoc Advisory Group's Proposals for Research Ethics Committees: a Mixture of the Timid, the Revolutionary and the Bizarre" (2005) 31 *Journal of Medical Ethics* 435.)

2. The proposals for fewer paid ethics committees have also been subject to criticism. One issue is as to who will be prepared to undertake such a role. Will there be the necessary cohort of applicants one consequence will be the loss of many experienced research ethics committee members who wouldn't be in a position to sit on a committee on a full-time basis. In addition, this will in effect remove the "local" dimension from research ethics review. (See further discussion in Dawson *op. cit.* in note 1 and R. Aschroft, "Reforming Research Ethics Committees" (2005) 331 B.M.J. 587.)

3. It is also suggested that the Review did not adequately address a range of issues including when "student projects" become a research project (see further Aschroft, *op. cit.* in note 1).

4. Whether fewer committees will assist remains to be seen. In relation to the existing committees it appears that members are subject to a considerable workload. A recent article by a vice-chair of an REC who has been in post as a committee member for 20 years is illustrative. He notes that he averages eight hours a week on committee activities:

   "As well as assessing and then discussing the 10 new submissions at the monthly committee meeting I chair a weekly subcommittee that reviews about the same number of substantial amendments. There are inquiries to handle and occasional disputes to resolve, matters to discuss with our excellent administrative team, guidelines and operating procedures to review and advice to give to health care and governmental bodies." (See G. Masterton, "Two Decades on an Ethics Committee" (2006) 332 B.M.J. 615.)

5. This report was subject to a consultation exercise by the Department of Health, which closed in April 2006.

4. THE RESEARCH SUBJECT

(a) Obtaining Consent

As with medical treatment, the consent of the research subject should be obtained before he is included in a clinical trial. Failure to obtain any consent at all will render the researcher liable to an action in trespass (see *Chatterson v Gerson* [1981] 1 All E.R. 257 and Chapter 6). Even if some information is given, this may be inadequate, thus leading to proceedings in battery and negligence (see below pp.685). Consent in the context of the research process was the subject of some considerable controversy in the 1990s. The research governance guidelines on consent were revised in the light of a research study undertaken by Professor David Southall at the North Staffordshire Hospital NHS Trust. This study concerned the effects of continuous negative extra thoratic pressure rather than standard ventilation upon neonates who suffered respiratory failure. Following complaints made regarding the trial, an investigation was undertaken by Professor Rod Griffiths who was director of public health in the West Midlands. The consent procedure was subject to grave criticism. It was stated that "the apparent lack of adequate explanation of choice and consequent properly elicited and recorded consent and involvement in later decision making was unacceptable" (R. Griffiths, NHS Executive, West Midlands Regional Office, *Report of a Research Framework in North Staffordshire Hospital NHS Trust* 2001).

Governance Arrangements for Research Ethics Committees (London: DOH, 2001)

Applicants to research ethics committees are directed to examine the informed consent process.

9.17 *Informed consent process*

a. a full description of the process for obtaining informed consent, including the identification of those responsible for obtaining consent, the time-frame in which it will occur, and the process for ensuring consent has not been withdrawn
b. the adequacy, completeness and understandability of written and oral information to be given to the research participants, and, when appropriate, their legally acceptable representatives
c. clear justification for the intention to include in the research individuals who cannot consent, and a full account of the arrangements for obtaining consent or authorization for the participation of such individuals
d. assurances that research participants will receive information that becomes available during the course of the research relevant to their participation (including their rights, safety and well-being)
e. the provisions made for receiving and responding to queries and complaints from research participants or their representatives during the course of a research project.

QUESTIONS:

1. Can a patient ever give voluntary consent to entry into a clinical trial? (See H. Thornton, "Clinical Trials: a Brave New Partnership?" (1994) 20

Journal of Medical Ethics 19–22; M. Baum, "Clinical Trials: a Brave New Partnership: a response to Mrs Thornton" (1994) 20 *Journal of Medical Ethics* 23–25. Note also empirical work as to participant perceptions of information given to them by researchers consequent upon their entry into a clinical trial (P. Ferguson, "Patient's Perceptions of Information Provided in Clinical Trials (2002) 28 *Journal of Medical Ethics* 45.)

Further consideration of consent and the research process is given in the guidance issued to doctors by the General Medical Council.

General Medical Council: Research—the Role and Responsibility of Doctors (GMC 2001)

Consent

15. Seeking consent is fundamental to research involving people.

Valid consent

16. Participants' consent is legally valid and professionally acceptable only where participants are competent to give consent, have been properly informed, and have agreed without coercion.

Consent for research

17. Obtaining consent is a process involving open and helpful dialogue, and is essential in clarifying objectives and understanding between doctors and research participants.

18. Effective communication is the key to enabling participants to make informed decisions. When providing information you must do your best to find out about participants' individual needs and priorities. For example, participants' current understanding of their condition and treatment, beliefs, culture, occupation or other factors may have a bearing on the information they require. You must not make assumptions about participants' views, but discuss matters with them, and ask whether they have any concerns about the treatment or the risks involved in the research programme.

19. You must ensure that any individuals whom you invite to take part in research are given the information which they want or ought to know, and that is presented in terms and a form that they can understand. You must bear in mind that it may be difficult for participants to identify and assess the risks involved. Giving the information will usually include an initial discussion supported by a leaflet or sound recording, where possible taking into account any particular communication or language needs of the participants. You must give participants an opportunity to ask questions and to express any concerns they may have.

20. The information provided should include:

- what the research aims to achieve, an outline of the research method, and confirmation that a research ethics committee has approved the project;
- the legal rights and safeguards provided for participants;
- the reasons that the patient or volunteer has been asked to participate;
- if the project involves randomisation, the nature of the process and reasons for it, and the fact that in double-blind research trials neither the patient nor the treatment team will know whether the patient is receiving the treatment being tested or is in the control group;
- information about possible benefits and risks;
- an explanation of which parts of the treatment are experimental or not fully tested;

- advice that they can withdraw at any time and, where relevant, an assurance that this will not adversely affect their relationship with those providing care;
- an explanation of how personal information will be stored, transmitted and published;
- what information will be available to the participant about the outcome of the research, and how that information will be presented;
- arrangements for responding to adverse events;
- details of compensation available should participants suffer harm as a result of their participation in the research.

21. You must allow people sufficient time to reflect on the implications of participating in the study, and provide any further information they request, including a copy of the protocol approved by the research ethics committee. You must not put pressure on anyone to take part in the research. You should make a record of the discussion and the outcome.

22. When seeking consent it is also important to consider the needs of particular groups of people and situations that require special consideration, advice is given in paragraphs 43 to 58.

NOTES:

1. There are no decided cases or statutes regulating the quantity and content of information which should be disclosed to a subject in a clinical trial. At present it is uncertain whether the courts would follow the same approach in relation to therapeutic trials as they do in relation to medical treatment. (See Chapter 6 above.) It can be argued that in the context of a clinical trial the patient is entitled to a fuller explanation of the nature of the trial and of the risks than would be the case in relation to medical treatment. As far as negligence is concerned, as was noted in Chapter 6 (p.372 above), the obligation of disclosure of the risks of a particular treatment was set out by the House of Lords in *Sidaway v Bethlem Royal Hospital Governors* [1985] 3 All E.R. 643 and *Pearce v Bristol NHS Trust* [1999] P.I.Q.R. 53. It is perhaps questionable whether a court will require a different standard of disclosure in relation to therapeutic research as opposed to treatment. Nor would it necessarily be justified in doing so, particularly in view of the very fine line which exists between innovative treatment and research.

2. The position may be different in relation to non-therapeutic research. It is arguable that here the policy arguments weigh in favour of a broad duty of disclosure. The benefit of the trial is felt not directly by the individual participant but rather benefit the community as a whole. It is suggested that failure to disclose should give rise to liability in battery and in negligence. (see I. Kennedy, "The Law and Ethics of Informed Consent and Randomised Controlled Trials" in I. Kennedy (ed.), *Treat Me Right*, Oxford: OUP, 1989). A Canadian case frequently cited in support of the approach which should be taken to disclosure to volunteers in clinical trials is *Halushka v University of Saskatchewan* (1965) 53 D.L.R. (2d) 436. In this case Hall J. stated that: "The subject of medical experimentation is entitled to a full and frank disclosure of all the facts, probabilities and opinions which a reasonable man might be expected to consider before giving his consent". It has been suggested that such a rigorous standard

should be employed in relation to both patients and volunteers. (See, for example, M. Brazier, *Medicine, Patients and the Law,* (3rd edn), Harmondsworth: Penguin, 2002 at pp.418–419.)

3. Failure to obtain the consent of an individual before including him in a clinical trial may give rise, not only to an action in battery, but also to a criminal prosecution. In addition, even if consent has been given to inclusion in a clinical trial it is possible that a clinical procedure may be held to be a criminal offence. As we noted earlier (see Chapter 6 at p.355), there are certain types of harm to which the individual may not lawfully consent. If, for example, a trial involved a very high risk of death or serious injury, a criminal prosecution might be brought. The Law Commission considered the question of clinical trials and consent in their consultation paper (see *Consent in the Criminal Law,* Law Commission Consultation Paper No. 139, and London: HMSO, 1996, paras 8.38–8.52.) The report states that:

> 8.51 "We provisionally propose that
> (1) a person should not be guilty of an offence, notwithstanding that he or she causes injury to another, of whatever degree of seriousness, if such injury is caused during the course of properly approved medical research and with the consent of that other person; and
> (2) in this context the term 'properly approved medical research' should mean medical research approved by a local research ethics committee or other body charged with the supervision and approval of medical research falling within its jurisdiction."

QUESTIONS:

1. In view of the fact that the law does not allow an individual to consent to the infliction of certain types of harm, should a volunteer be able to consent to involvement in a clinical trial?
2. Is it likely that a responsible body of professional medical opinions would support full disclosure to patients of the risk of entry into a clinical trial?

(b) Randomised Clinical Trials

An important part of medical research is the randomised clinical trial. Randomisation is used as a technique to reduce the possibility that the patient's positive response to a new treatment is simply because of the psychological effect of being given a new drug. In a randomised clinical trial, one group of subjects is given the drug, while another group is given the placebo, or dummy treatment. A variant upon the randomised controlled trial is the double-blind trial in which the clinician is also unaware which drugs are being provided to the patient. Double-blind trials are undertaken to avoid the patient being influenced by the clinician's enthusiasm for a particular treatment. Such trials are used almost exclusively in relation to pharmaceutical research.

Royal College of Physicians, Research involving Patients (1990)

Ethical problems with controlled trials

7.98 Double-blind and placebo-controlled trials have sometimes been the source of anxiety on the part of the public or of prospective participants, usually because an element of deception seems to be involved, or because patients who are allocated to the control group (which might, for example, not receive a new treatment) may seem to be at an unfair advantage. Anxiety on both of these counts is quite proper if certain conditions fail to be met when the trial is proposed.

7.99 Where the administration of effective treatment is important for the future well being of the patient, it is ethical for a controlled trial to be undertaken only if, at the outset, the investigator does not know whether the trial treatment is more effective or less effective than the standard treatment with which it is to be compared (or than no treatment at all in the case of a placebo controlled study.) Obviously the fact that the study is initiated at all must mean that the investigator thinks that the question is worth asking. However, an investigator who holds the view that one treatment is known to be definitely superior to another is ethically unable to conduct a controlled study of this treatment and would also be unable to collaborate by inviting his patients to participate in such a trial arranged by another clinician. A different clinician who considered that there was no good evidence to indicate that either treatment was superior would be able to invite patients to participate in a controlled comparison of the new procedure with standard treatment. It is a matter of extending into the trial the same consideration for patient's interest which prevails in ordinary clinical practice.

Withholding effective treatment

7.100 Withholding effective treatment for a short time, whether or not it is substituted by a placebo, can sometimes be acceptable in order to validate a technique of measurement or confirm the sensitivity or discrimination of a therapeutic trial design. An investigator who proposes to do this should explicitly confirm his intention and the intended consent procedure to the Research Ethics Committee. Patient consent is necessary and the patient may agree that he need not know precisely when this will take place.

Use of placebos

7.101 The scientific justification for the use of placebo preparations is set out above. Their use is ethical if patients give consent in advance. Where consent is given there is no deception and the proper use of placebos constitutes a useful tool in evaluating treatment.

Giving consent for randomisation

7.102 Proper conduct of a randomised controlled trial requires the allocation of treatments to be conducted after the patient has given consent to participation in the study and has been enrolled. Otherwise, knowledge of which treatment would be allocated to a particular patient could influence recruitment to one or other treatment options and introduce a bias which could affect the outcome of the research.

7.103 Before making a choice about whether or not to participate, patients should be told of the alternative forms of treatment under study. It is sometimes difficult to ensure that patients understand that they are being invited to enrol in a study in which the treatment allocation will be determined by chance. If a patient expresses a strong preference for a particular treatment he is probably ineligible as a participant.

Randomisation of treatment without the consent of the patient

7.104 In some circumstances it may be proposed that a random allocation should be made but that the random basis on which the doctor recommends a particular treatment should not be declared to the patient.

7.105 We consider that in general, randomisation of treatment without the consent of the patient is unethical. Exceptional circumstances may exist in some research where there is an argument for not telling patients. But acceptance of this should be a deliberate decision as part of an ethical review.

Randomisation before seeking consent

7.106 Randomised allocation of treatment *before* seeking consent to participation in the study is sometimes proposed in order to make it easier for patients to understand what is being offered to them and to facilitate recruitment. This may occasionally be ethically acceptable provided that the patient is told about the other option in the trial. However, in general, we think it is to be discouraged on both scientific and ethical grounds because of the risk of over- persuasion when inviting subjects to accept the allocated treatment.

NOTES:

1. One danger in informing patients that they are being involved in a randomised trial is that a group of patients who are suffering from a terminal condition might sabotage the trial by deciding to pool the drugs in order that they obtain at least some available treatment. Difficulties arose in the United States where patients with AIDS involved in AZT randomised trials, pooled the drugs and thus frustrated the trial (see J. McHale and A. Young, "The Dilemmas of the HIV Positive Prisoner" (1992) 31 *Howard Journal of Criminal Justice* 89.)

2. The Helsinki Declaration provides in relation to this issue that:

   "29 The benefits, risks, burdens and effectiveness of a new method should be tested against those of the best current prophylactic, diagnostic and therapeutic methods. This does not exclude the use of placebos, or no treatment, in studies where no proven prophylactic diagnostic or therapeutic method exists."

   Helsinki Declaration (Clarification)

   "The World Medical Association is concerned that paragraph 19 of the revised declaration of Helsinki has led to diverse interpretations and possible confusion. It hereby affirms its position that extreme care must be taken in making use of a placebo trial and that in general this methodology should be used in the absence of existing proven therapy. However a placebo controlled trial may be ethically acceptable even if proven therapy is available under the following circumstances:
   – Where for compelling and scientifically sound methodological reasons its use is necessary to determine the efficacy or safety of a prophylactic, diagnostic or therapeutic method, or
   – Where a prophylactic, diagnostic or therapeutic method is being investigated for a minor condition and the patients who receive placebo will not be subject to any additional risk of serious or irreversible harm."

(c) Trials including Child Subjects

While much research can be undertaken using adult subjects, it is inevitable that there are situations in which the nature of the research dictates that child subjects must be used, for example, if it is proposed to undertake a trial into childhood diseases. In such cases the trials should be subjected to particularly careful scrutiny. Controversy over the consent processes for inclusion of children in clinical trials arose from the trial into the treatment of babies born prematurely with breathing difficulties at Staffordshire Hospital. The trial resulted in an investigation which was exceedingly critical of the conduct of the trial and of the consent procedures adopted (see R. Griffiths, *Report of a Review of the Research Framework in North Staffordshire Hospital NHS Trust*, London: NHSE, 2000). Whether a child has the right to decide himself to be included in a clinical trial is uncertain. The courts may be willing to apply the test set out in *Gillick v West Norfolk and Wisbech AHA* [1985] 3 All E.R. 402 (see Chapter 7 above). Where a child lacks sufficient maturity to give consent himself, then researchers would have to obtain consent from the person with the parental power of consent. It is perhaps questionable whether courts would compel a child to be involved in a therapeutic trial. There is a remote possibility that a court may be asked to rule on such an issue, if the therapy offered the only chance of recovery from a terminal condition. While the legal position regarding non-therapeutic trials is equally uncertain, it is suggested the court would be most unlikely to compel an unwilling child to be involved in such a trial, even where it could be shown that the trial only involved a minimal risk. Determining who has the power to decide who should be included in a clinical trial is only one issue; another equally important consideration is the basis on which clinical trials which involve child patients should be undertaken.

Royal College of Paediatrics and Child Health: Ethics Advisory Committee, Guidelines for the Ethical Conduct of Medical Research Concerning Children (2000) 82 Archives of Disease in Childhood 177

These guidelines are based on six principles:

(1) Research involving children is important for the benefit of all children and should be supported, encouraged and conducted in an ethical manner
(2) Children are not small adults; they have an additional, unique set of interests
(3) Research should only be done on children if comparable research on adults could not answer the same question
(4) A research procedure which is not intended directly to benefit the child subject is not necessarily either unethical or illegal
(5) All proposals involving medical research on children should be submitted to a research ethics committee
(6) Legally valid consent should be obtained from the child, parent or guardian as appropriate. When parental consent is obtained, the agreement of school age children who take part in research should also be requested by researchers . . .

The attempt to protect children absolutely from the potential harms of research denies any of them the potential benefits. We therefore support the premise that research that is of no intended benefit to the child subject is not necessarily unethical or illegal. Such research includes observing and measuring normal development, assessing diagnostic methods, the use of "healthy volunteers" and of placebos in controlled trials.

The importance of evaluating potential benefits, harms, and costs in research on human beings, and ways of doing so, have been discussed repeatedly. A summary of discussion points is included in these guidelines to illustrate how complex such evaluations can be. Our aim, rather than to provide answers, is to list questions for researchers and ethics committees to consider.

Assessment of potential benefit includes reviewing estimates of:

Magnitude

- How is the knowledge gained likely to be used?
- In research into treatment how severe is the problem which the research aims to alleviate?
- How common is the problem?

Probability

- How likely is the research to achieve its aims?

Beneficiaries

- Is the research intended to benefit the child subjects, and/or other children?

Resources

- Will potential benefits be limited because they are very expensive, or require unusually highly trained professionals?

Assessment of potential harm includes estimates of:

- How invasive or intrusive is the research? (psychosocial research should be assessed as carefully as physical research)

Magnitude

- How severe may the harms associated with research procedures be?

Probability

- How likely are the harms to occur?

Timing

- Might adverse effects be brief or long lasting, immediate or not evident until years later?

Equity

- Are a few children drawn into too many projects simply because they are available?

- Are researchers relying unduly on children who already have many problems?

Interim finding

- If evidence of harm in giving or withholding certain treatment emerges during the trial, how will possible conflict between the interests of the child subjects and of valid research be managed?

Assessment of potential harm also includes reviewing personal estimates

Children's responses are varied, often unpredictable, and alter as children develop, so that generalisations about risk tend to be controversial. A procedure that does not bother one child arouses severe distress in another. Researchers sometimes underestimate high risk of pain if the effects are brief, whereas the child or parents may consider the severe transient pain is not justified by the hoped for benefit. There is evidence that tolerance of pain increases with age and maturity when the child no longer perceives medical interventions as punitive.

Some potential harms may not be obvious without careful consideration of their consequences. For example, with research into serious genetic disorders that present in adult life, presymptomatic diagnosis in a child, while it may be beneficial, may also have very harmful effects, and may affect the child's opportunities and freedom of choice.

Risks may be estimated as minimal, low or high

Minimal (the least possible) risk describes procedures such as questioning, observing, and measuring children, provided that procedures are carried out in a sensitive way, and that consent has been given. Procedures with minimal risk include collecting a single urine sample (but not by aspiration), or using blood from a sample that has been taken as part of treatment.

Low risk describes procedures that cause brief pain or tenderness, and small bruises or scars. Many children fear needles and for them low rather than minimal risks are often incurred by injections and venepuncture.

High risk procedures such as lung or liver biopsy, arterial puncture, and cardiac catheterisation are not justified for research purposes alone. They should be carried out only when research is combined with diagnosis or treatment intended to benefit the child concerned.

We believe that research in which children are submitted to more than minimal risk with only slight, uncertain or no benefit to themselves deserves serious ethical consideration. The most common example of such research involves blood sampling. Where children are unable to give consent, by reason of insufficient maturity or understanding, their parents or guardians may consent to the taking of blood for non-therapeutic purposes, provided that they have been given and understand a full explanation of the reasons for blood sampling and have balanced its risk to their child. Many children fear needles, but with careful explanation of the reason for venepuncture and an understanding of the effectiveness of local anaesthetic cream, they often show altruism and allow a blood sample to be taken. We believe that this has to be the child's decision. We believe that it is completely inappropriate to insist on the taking of blood for non-therapeutic reasons if a child indicates either significant unwillingness before the start or significant stress during the procedure.

QUESTIONS:

1. Should inclusion of children in clinical trials be a matter for a research ethics committee or should a special national committee be established for the conduct of trials on child subjects?

2. Should children be allowed to participate in non-therapeutic trials? Is it unethical to include a child in a non-therapeutic trial where there is more than a minimal risk? Parents allow their children to participate in risky activities for pleasure—why not allow them to include a child in a trial on the basis of the public interest? (See R. Nicholson, "The Ethics of Research with Children" in M. Brazier and M. Lobjoit (eds), *Protecting the Vulnerable*, London: Routledge, 1991.)

3. Should a mature adolescent who is assessed as Gillick-competent be able to include herself in a high-risk trial despite her parents' objections? (See R. Nicholson, *Medical Research with Children*, Oxford: OUP, 1985.)

4. Should a child be deemed competent to refuse entry to a therapeutic clinical trial? Compare the position regarding refusal of treatment (see Chapter 7 above).

(d) Trials Involving Adults without Mental Capacity

(i) General Issues

While clinical trials will usually be undertaken with competent adult volunteers, there may be occasions in which research upon an adult lacking decision-making capacity is unavoidable because, for instance, the trial is into a particular disorder/mental disability. For many years the legality of inclusion of adults in such trials was the subject of some uncertainty. The decision of the House of Lords in *F v West Berkshire Area Health Authority* [1989] 3 All E.R. 545 makes it clear that no one can give consent on behalf of an adult lacking mental capacity (see Chapter 5 above at p.321.) Treatment may only be given if this is in the best interests of the patient, with in more recent cases the courts indicating that they have been prepare to take a more expansive approach to best interests—see, for example, *Re SL* [2000] 3 W.L.R. 1288 and Chapter 5 at p.326 above. It is unclear as to whether this test applies in relation to research. It appears likely that the court will follow a "best interests" test in deciding whether an incompetent patient should be included in a therapeutic research project. It should be noted that the courts have been prepared to sanction the conduct of experimental therapy upon an adult without capacity in *Sims v Sims and an NHS Trust* [2002] EWHC 2743, and see further J. Harrington, "Deciding Best Interests: Medical Progress, Clinical Judgement and the 'Good Family' " (2003) 2 *Web J of Current Legal Issues*. The Law Commission in its report, *Mental Incapacity* (Law Com. 231, HMSO: 1995) suggested that the decision whether or not to include a mentally incompetent person in a therapeutic trial was one which could be left to the broad general authority to act reasonably in the best interests of the incompetent person which they propose earlier in the report at para. 6.28 (see Chapter 5 and the Mental Capacity Act 2005 below at p.696. It should be noted that a patient with mental illness may have the capacity to consent to entry into a clinical trial. Nonetheless, care needs to be taken when it is proposed to include psychiatric patients in a clinical trial in view of the fact that such patients may be inherently emotionally vulnerable (see K.W.M. Fulford and K. Howse, "Ethics of

Research with Psychiatric Patients: Principles, Problems and the Primary Responsibilities of Researchers" (1993) 19 *Journal of Medical Ethics* 85).

QUESTION:

1. Does the *Bolam* test, albeit modified in *Re SL,* provide an appropriate basis to determine whether a mentally incompetent person may be included in a therapeutic research project or should this task be entrusted to a third-party decision-maker? (See Chapter 5 above.)

(ii) Non-therapeutic Research

At common law it appears that undertaking invasive non-therapeutic research upon the adult lacking mental capacity is prima facie unlawful. *F v West Berkshire Area Health Authority* [1989] 2 All E.R. 545 indicated that therapeutic procedures could be undertaken if they were in the best interests of the patient. Nevertheless, it appears that this does not extend to non-therapeutic procedures. That does not mean, however, that non-therapeutic medical research should never be undertaken upon such a person. This matter received extensive consideration by the Law Commission.

Law Commission, Mental Incapacity (Law Com. 231, 1995)

6.29 "Non-therapeutic" research, on the other hand, does not claim to offer any direct or immediate benefit to the participant. Such procedures may well be scientifically and ethically acceptable to those who are qualified to decide such matters. If, however, the participant lacks capacity to consent to his or her participation, and the procedure cannot be justified under the doctrine of necessity, then any person who touches or restrains that participant is committing an unlawful battery. The simple fact is that the researcher is making no claim to be acting in the best interests of that individual person and does not therefore come within the rules of law set out in *Re F.* It was made abundantly clear to us on consultation, however, that non-therapeutic research projects of this nature are regularly taking place. We were told of a research project into the organic manifestations of Alzheimer's disease which involves the administration of radioactive isotopes to sufferers, followed by extensive testing of blood and bodily functions. Another project was said to involve the examination of written patients' records, although they are unable to consent to this examination. In some cases relatives are asked to "consent" to what is proposed, and do so. It appears that some funding bodies and Ethics Committees stipulate for consent by a relative where the research participant cannot consent. As a matter of law, such "consent" is meaningless. It appears that the question of the legality of non-therapeutic research procedures is regularly misunderstood or ignored by those who design, fund and approve the projects.

6.30 A number of our respondents expressed concern about non-invasive research based on observations, photography or videoing of participants (sometimes covertly). We accept that questions of dignity and privacy arise in such situations where the project is not designed to benefit the research participant.

6.31 We suggested in our consultation paper that the balance of expert opinion favours the participation of people unable to consent in even non-therapeutic research projects, subject to strict criteria. The majority of our consulters argued that there is an ethical case for such participation. This case turns on the desirability of eradicating painful and distressing disabilities, where progress can be achieved without harming research subjects. The wide range of guidance and expert commentary on this matter shows a striking degree of consensus over the factors which make non-therapeutic research ethical, and we remarked a similar consensus in the responses submitted to us on consultation. In summary, the consensus appears to be that non-therapeutic research involving participants who cannot consent is justifiable where (1) the research relates to the condition from which the participant suffers, (2) the same knowledge cannot be gained from research limited to those capable of consenting, and (3) the procedures involve minimal risk and invasiveness. The recommendations which follow are intended to resolve the unacceptable anomaly that projects of this type, assessed by those with appropriate scientific and ethical expertise as being important and meritorious, in fact involve actionable unlawful conduct by the researchers. At the same time, our recommendations will place necessary protections for the participant without capacity on a statutory footing.

We recommend that research which is unlikely to benefit a participant, or whose benefit is likely to be long delayed, should be lawful in relation to a person without capacity to consent if (1) the research is into an incapacitating condition with which the participant is or may be affected and (2) certain statutory procedures are complied with (Draft Bill, clause 11(1))

A Mental Incapacity Research Committee

6.33 The Department of Health has instructed District Health Authorities to set up Local Research Ethics Committees (LRECs) "to advise NHS bodies on the ethical acceptability of research proposals involving human subjects". LRECs have no legal standing, a decision by a LREC does not make a researcher's actions lawful, and statute cannot enable a non-statutory body to achieve such an end. In the consultation paper we suggested that a judicial body should have power to make a declaration that proposed research involving persons without capacity would be lawful. Courts and adversarial process, however, are not well adapted to cases where there are no opposing parties to present evidence. Ordinary judges will have no relevant scientific expertise. Instead, therefore, we recommend that a new statutory committee should be established. This will supplement the "extra-legal" checks and balances which already exist, avoiding duplication of valuable time and effort.

We recommend that there should be a statutory committee to be known as the Mental Incapacity Research Committee (Draft Bill, clause 11(2).

6.34 A non-therapeutic research procedure should only be lawful in relation to a person who is without capacity to consent if the Mental Incapacity Research Committee approves the research. Although most research which would otherwise be unlawful will be "medical" in the broadest sense, we do not suggest that the remit of the committee should be expressly limited to medical research. The criteria to be applied by the committee should be set out in statute. They all refer to the one particular issue of participants without capacity. Wider scientific questions will still be investigated by the relevant funding bodies. If NHS patients are involved, then the ethical advice of the LREC will be required before the Department of Health guidance will be satisfied.

We recommend that the committee may approve the proposed research if satisfied:

(1) That it is desirable to provide knowledge of the causes or treatment of, or of the care of people affected by, the incapacitating condition with which any participant is or may be affected,

(2) that the object of the research cannot be effectively achieved without the participation of persons who are or may be without capacity to consent and

(3) that the research will not expose a participant to more than negligible risk, will not be unduly invasive or restrictive of a participant and will not unduly interfere with a participant's freedom of action or privacy (Draft Bill, clause 11(3)).

The draft bill makes provision for the composition and procedures of the committee. . . .

Protection for the individual participant

6.36 It is not realistic or practicable for the individual participation of a person without capacity in a particular project to be referred to the special statutory committee for approval. The committee's role is to approve the research protocol, and we anticipate this involving documentary submissions in most cases. There is, however, a need for a separate and individualised independent check to confirm whether any particular proposed participant should indeed be brought into the project. Our recommendations therefore involve a two-stage process. By way of example, researchers obtain the committee's approval to a project which envisages tests on those with advanced Alzheimer's disease. The researchers should not then be under the impression that this approval means they may involve in their project all the residents of a particular nursing home who have been diagnosed as suffering from Alzheimer's disease without the need for any further permission. They must approach each of these proposed participants as an individual. They must ask whether this particular person does indeed have the capacity to consent to what is proposed. It may be that an explanation in simpler or more appropriate terms would be quite comprehensible to the person, especially if given by a person familiar to him or her. If, however, it appears that the proposed participant is without capacity to consent to what is proposed then an independent check is required, and we describe the nature of this check below.

6.37 In most cases the appropriate person to carry out an independent check will be a registered medical practitioner who is not involved in the research project. This need not be an independent doctor appointed to consider such matters by the Secretary of State (as recommended in relation to "second opinion category" treatments). The important point is simply that this doctor should not be involved with the proposed research. The doctor who knows the person best, by virtue of having responsibility for his or her general medical care, will often be the best candidate. An attorney with express authorisation from a donor should be able to consent on the donor's behalf. Similarly, a court-appointed manager may have express authority to give such consent. In some cases the court itself may have made it clear whether the person concerned may participate in non-therapeutic research. In none of these situations need the "second opinion" doctor be involved. There will also be some rare cases where the research protocol does not contemplate any direct contact between researcher and participant. These might involve covert observation or photographing, or the inspection of written records. In such cases, the broad ethical issues still have to be weighed by the committee but there is no purpose in anyone else looking at individual circumstances. The committee should therefore have the power to designate a project as one which does not involve direct contact with participants, with no second stage check then required.

We recommend that, in addition to the approval of the Mental Incapacity Research Committee, non-therapeutic research in relation to a person without capacity should require either:

(1) court approval,
(2) the consent of an attorney or manager,
(3) a certificate from a doctor not involved in the research that the participation of the person is appropriate, or
(4) the designation of the research not involving direct contact. (Draft Bill, clause 11(1)(c) and (4).

6.38 Where the court, an attorney, a manager or an independent doctor is considering the question of a particular individual participating in a project then regard should be had to the factors in the best interest's checklist.

6.39 In accordance with the recommendations we have made elsewhere in this report, this should be a clear prohibition against anything being done to a research participant if he or she objects to what is being done. Equally, in the event that a person has made an effective advance refusal to participate in a non-therapeutic research project then no approval of the committee or third party's confirmation would have any effect.

NOTES:

1. The Law Commission recommends that trials undertaken upon an adult lacking capacity should be subject to approval by one of four decision-makers. The Commission does not, however, stipulate in which contexts which decision-maker should operate. In addition it recommends that such clinical trials should not expose the participant to more than a "minimal risk". One of the possible approaches is to refer the decision to a judicial decision-maker. But is judicial authorisation really required if, as the Law Commission suggests, the trial should never involve more than minimal risk? Furthermore, if judicial authorisation became the norm, regular referral of all intended research subjects to the courts would be expensive and time consuming.
2. The Government rejected the proposal of the Law Commission for a specialised committee to deal with these issues in their document *Making Decisions* in 1999 and did not take forward these recommendations in the Mental Capacity Act 2005.

QUESTIONS:

1. What are the advantages and disadvantages of establishing a national research committee to approve the conduct of trials upon those with mental incapacity?
2. Why should observational research be an exception to the "special consent" procedure proposed by the Law Commission?

(iii) Mental Capacity Act 2005

The Government finally introduced some statutory clarification of the conduct of research involving adults without capacity in the Mental Capacity Act 2005 (for further consideration of this legislation see Chapter 5 above).

Mental Capacity Act 2005

Research

30.—(1) Intrusive research carried out on, or in relation to, a person who lacks capacity to consent to it is unlawful unless it is carried out—

(a) as part of a research project which is for the time being approved by the appropriate body for the purposes of this Act in accordance with section 31, and

(b) in accordance with sections 32 and 33.

(2) Research is intrusive if it is of a kind that would be unlawful if it was carried out—

(a) on or in relation to a person who had capacity to consent to it, but
(b) without his consent.

(3) A clinical trial which is subject to the provisions of clinical trials regulations is not to be treated as research for the purposes of this section.

(4) "Appropriate body", in relation to a research project, means the person, committee or other body specified in regulations made by the Secretary of State as the appropriate body in relation to a project of the kind in question.

(5) "Clinical trials regulations" means—

(a) the Medicines for Human Use (Clinical Trials) Regulations 2004 (S.I. 2004/1031) and any other regulations replacing those regulations or amending them, and
(b) any other regulations relating to clinical trials and designated by the Secretary of State as clinical trials regulations for the purposes of this section.

Requirements for approval

31.—(1) The appropriate body may not approve a research project for the purposes of this Act unless satisfied that the following requirements will be met in relation to research carried out as part of the project on, or in relation to, a person who lacks capacity to consent to taking part in the project ("P").

(2) The research must be connected with—

(a) an impairing condition affecting P, or
(b) its treatment.

(3) "Impairing condition" means a condition which is (or may be) attributable to, or which causes or contributes to (or may cause or contribute to), the impairment of, or disturbance in the functioning of, the mind or brain.

(4) There must be reasonable grounds for believing that research of comparable effectiveness cannot be carried out if the project has to be confined to, or relate only to, persons who have capacity to consent to taking part in it.

(5) The research must—

(a) have the potential to benefit P without imposing on P a burden that is disproportionate to the potential benefit to P, or
(b) be intended to provide knowledge of the causes or treatment of, or of the care of persons affected by, the same or a similar condition.

(6) If the research falls within paragraph (b) of subsection (4) but not within paragraph (a), there must be reasonable grounds for believing—

(a) that the risk to P from taking part in the project is likely to be negligible, and
(b) that anything done to, or in relation to, P will not—
    (i) interfere with P's freedom of action or privacy in a significant way, or
    (ii) be unduly invasive or restrictive.

(7) There must be reasonable arrangements in place for ensuring that the requirements of sections 32 and 33 will be met.

Consulting carers etc

32.—(1) This section applies if a person ("R")—

(a) is conducting an approved research project, and

(b) wishes to carry out research, as part of the project, on or in relation to a person ("P") who lacks capacity to consent to taking part in the project.

(2) R must take reasonable steps to identify a person who—

(a) otherwise than in a professional capacity or for remuneration, is engaged in caring for P or is interested in P's welfare, and
(b) is prepared to be consulted by R under this section.

(3) If R is unable to identify such a person he must, in accordance with guidance issued by the Secretary of State, nominate a person who—

(a) is prepared to be consulted by R under this section, but
(b) has no connection with the project.

(4) R must provide the person identified under subsection (2), or nominated under subsection (3), with information about the project and ask him—

(a) for advice as to whether P should take part in the project, and
(b) what, in his opinion, P's wishes and feelings about taking part in the project would be likely to be if P had capacity in relation to the matter.

(5) If, at any time, the person consulted advises R that in his opinion P's wishes and feelings would be likely to lead him to decline to take part in the project (or to wish to withdraw from it) if he had capacity in relation to the matter, R must ensure—

(a) if P is not already taking part in the project, that he does not take part in it;
(b) if P is taking part in the project, that he is withdrawn from it.

(6) But subsection (5)(b) does not require treatment that P has been receiving as part of the project to be discontinued if R has reasonable grounds for believing that there would be a significant risk to P's health if it were discontinued.

(7) The fact that a person is the donee of a lasting power of attorney given by P, or is P's deputy, does not prevent him from being the person consulted under this section.

(8) Subsection (9) applies if treatment is being, or is about to be, provided for P as a matter of urgency and R considers that, having regard to the nature of the research and of the particular circumstances of the case—

(a) it is also necessary to take action for the purposes of the research as a matter of urgency, but
(b) it is not reasonably practicable to consult under the previous provisions of this section.

(9) R may take the action if—

(a) he has the agreement of a registered medical practitioner who is not concerned in P's treatment or care, or
(b) where it is not reasonably practicable in the time available to obtain that agreement, he acts in accordance with a procedure approved by the appropriate body at the time when the research project was approved under section 31.

(10) But R may not continue to act in reliance on subsection (9) if he has reasonable grounds for believing that it is no longer necessary to take the action as a matter of urgency.

Additional safeguards

33.—(1) This section applies in relation to a person who is taking part in an approved research project even though he lacks capacity to consent to taking part.

(2) Nothing may be done to, or in relation to, him in the course of the research—

(a) to which he appears to object (whether by showing signs of resistance or otherwise) except where what is being done is intended to protect him from harm or to reduce or prevent pain or discomfort, or
(b) which would be contrary to—
  (i) an advance decision of his which has effect, or
  (ii) any other form of statement made by him and not subsequently withdrawn, of which R is aware.

(3) The interests of the person must be assumed to outweigh those of science and society.

(4) If he indicates (in any way) that he wishes to be withdrawn from the project he must be withdrawn without delay.

(5) P must be withdrawn from the project, without delay, if at any time the person conducting the research has reasonable grounds for believing that one or more of the requirements set out in section 31(2) to (7) is no longer met in relation to research being carried out on, or in relation to, P.

(6) But neither subsection (4) nor subsection (5) requires treatment that P has been receiving as part of the project to be discontinued if R has reasonable grounds for believing that there would be a significant risk to P's health if it were discontinued.

NOTES:

1. The original Draft Mental Capacity Bill 2003 did not make reference to research. The Joint Select Committee recommended that it should be included to ensure that the ethical requirements underpinning research concerning persons with mental capacity were properly safeguarded. Research was included when the final version of the Bill was introduced in summer 2004.
2. Section 30(3) expressly excludes those clinical trials which are regulated under the provisions of the Clinical Trials Regulations—see p.703.
3. In contrast to the Clinical Trials Regulations, there is no requirement for consent to be given by a personal or professional legal representative.
4. Research must be approved by an "appropriate body". The Draft Mental Capacity Act 2005 (Appropriate Body) (England) Regulations 2006 provides:

   "2. For the purposes of sections 30, 31 and 32 of the Mental Capacity Act 2005, the appropriate body in relation to a research project is a committee [or other body]—

   (a) established to advise on, or on matters which include, the ethics of research investigations of the kind conducted, or intended to be conducted, as part of the project, including the ethics of intrusive research in relation to people who lack capacity to consent to it; and
   (b) recognised for those purposes by or on behalf of the Secretary of State or the National Assembly for Wales."

The Consultation Document issued at the same time as the drafts regulations in summer 2006 provides that:

   "16. During the passage of the Act the Government signalled a wish to retain flexibility in certain research related aspects of the legislation in order to cater for future eventualities such as the independent review of NHS Research Ethics Committees and any future evolution of the social care ethics system. The draft Regulations do not therefore provide a definitive list of ethics committees; but instead suggest the criterion that appropriate bodies have expertise including the ethics of research falling under the Act.

17. Certain ethics committees will receive training in application of the Act's principles and safeguards in readiness for implementation of the Act. This will ensure that new research projects involving those who lack the capacity to consent to participate can be reviewed by independent committees, consisting of lay and expert members, who are fully conversant with the legislation and its Code of Practice and have the competence to consider the ethics of the proposal."

5. In relation to non-therapeutic research, this may only go ahead where there is only "negligible risk".
6. The Act now makes reference to the need to consult carers in s.32. Carers do not have a power to consent, but they do have a right to consultation. It should also be noted that the requirement to consult carers is not absolute and may not for example, apply in an emergency situation.

In addition s.34 of the Mental Capacity Act also provides for regulations to deal with the situation in which a person had consented to inclusion in research before the Mental Capacity Act comes into force in 2007 but after giving that consent loses mental capacity. This issue is now dealt with in draft regulations issued for consultation in summer 2006.

Draft Mental Capacity (Loss of Capacity During Research Project) (England) Regulations 2006

Application

4. These Regulations apply where—

(a) a person ("P")—
   (i) has consented before [31 December 2007] to take part in a research project ("the project") begun before [1st April 2007] but
   (ii) before the conclusion of the project, loses capacity to consent to continue to take part in it, and
   (iii) research for the purposes of the project in relation to P would, apart from these Regulations, be unlawful by virtue of section 30 of the Act.

Research which may be carried out despite a participant's loss of capacity

5. Despite P's loss of capacity, research for the purposes of the project may be carried out using information or material relating to him if—

(a) the project satisfies the requirements set out in Schedule 1,
(b) all the information or material relating to P which is used in the research was obtained before P's loss of capacity, and
(c) the person conducting the project ("R") takes in relation to P such steps as are set out in Schedule 2.

Schedule 1 Regulation 3

Requirements which the project must satisfy

1. A protocol approved by an appropriate body and having effect in relation to the project makes provision for research to be carried out in relation to a person who has consented to take part in the project but loses capacity to consent to continue to take part in it.

2. The appropriate body must be satisfied that there are reasonable arrangements in place for ensuring that the requirements of Schedule 2 will be met.

Schedule 2 Regulation 3

Steps which the person conducting the project must take

1. R must take reasonable steps to identify a person who—

(a) otherwise than in a professional capacity or for remuneration, is engaged in caring for P or is interested in P's welfare, and
(b) is prepared to be consulted by R under this Schedule.

2. If R is unable to identify such a person he must, in accordance with guidance issued by the appropriate authority, nominate a person who—

(a) is prepared to be consulted by R under this Schedule, but
(b) has no connection with the project.

3. R must provide the person identified under paragraph 1, or nominated under paragraph 2, with information about the project and ask him—

(a) for advice as to whether research [of the kind proposed] should be carried out in relation to P, and
(b) what, in his opinion, P's wishes and feelings about such research being carried out would be likely to be if P had capacity in relation to the matter.

4. If, any time, the person consulted advises R that in his opinion P's wishes and feelings would be likely to lead him to wish to withdraw from the project if he had capacity in relation to the matter, R must ensure that P is withdrawn from it.

5. The fact that a person is the donee of a lasting power of attorney given by P, or is P's deputy, does not prevent him from being the person consulted under paragraphs 1 to 4.

6. R must ensure that nothing is done in relation to P in the course of the research which would be contrary to—

(a) an advance decision of his which has effect, or
(b) any other form of statement made by him and not subsequently withdrawn, of which R is aware.

7. The interests of P must be assumed to outweigh those of science and society.

8. If P indicates (in any way) that he wishes the research in relation to him to be discontinued, it must be discontinued without delay.

9. The research must be discontinued without delay if at any time R has reasonable grounds for believing that one or more of the requirements set out in Schedule 1 is no longer met in relation to research being carried out in relation to P.

10. R must conduct the research in accordance with the provision made in the protocol referred to in paragraph 1 of Schedule 1 for research to be carried out in relation to a

person who has consented to take part in the project but loses capacity to consent to take part in it.

NOTES:

1. Note that these regulations will apply both to human material and to information (see further, regarding the legal regulation of human material, Chapter 15 below, and regarding the use of information, Chapter 9 above). This is a rare situation in which the overlap which exists in practice between collection of material and information is reflected in the law. Generally the legal position on this has been to deal with the legal regulation of material and the legal regulation of information—even where obtained from that material, e.g. through DNA analysis—as totally separate.
2. The regulations will not apply to existing studies involving persons lacking capacity such as ongoing projects involving adults with dementia or learning difficulties. As a consequence these will require approval under s.30 of the Mental Capacity Act 2005.

QUESTION:

1. Compare the proposals in the Law Commission Report set out above with the final Mental Capacity Act 2005 and draft regulations. Do you agree with the Law Commission's proposal for a specialist Mental Capacity Research Ethics Committee?

(e) Follow-up by Research Ethics Committees

Governance Arrangements for Research Ethics Committees (London: DOH, 2001)

Following up and reports

7.23 Once the REC has given a favourable opinion, the researcher is required to notify the committee, in advance, of any proposed deviation from the original protocol. The committee may then wish to review its decision.

7.24 No deviation from, or changes to, the protocol shall be initiated by the researcher without the prior written approval of the REC, save where this is necessary to eliminate immediate hazards to research participants or when the change involves only logistical or administrative aspects of the research. In these cases, the changes may be implemented immediately, but the REC must be informed within seven days. The REC may then reconsider its opinion.

7.25 The research sponsor is responsible for ensuring that arrangements are in place to review significant developments as the research proceeds (particularly those which put the safety of individuals at risk) and to approve any modifications to the design of the research protocol. These modifications must be submitted to the REC and a favourable opinion obtained before implementation (except when there are immediate hazards to research participants, when the process laid out in 7.24 above shall apply).

7.26 The REC should indicate at the time of approval any progress reports it requires from time to time from the applicant. It shall request a final report to be delivered within three months of completion.

7.27 The REC shall require, as a minimum, an annual report from the researcher, and shall reconsider its opinion at that stage. Where the REC considers the degree of risk demands it, more frequent reports and subsequent interim review shall be required.

7.28 Where the research is terminated prematurely, a report shall be required within 15 days, indicating the reasons for early termination.

7.29 RECs may also ask to receive reports of inspections by other authorities.

7.30 Reports to the committee should also be required if there are any other unusual or unexpected results which raise questions about the safety of the research.

7.31 Reports on success (or difficulties) in recruiting participants provide the REC with useful feedback on perceptions of the acceptability of the project among potential research participants. RECs may wish to request such reports where they anticipate potential difficulties.

7.32 On the basis of any such reports, the REC may wish to review its decision. Failure to produce such required reports without a reason acceptable to the REC may result in suspension of the REC's favourable opinion, in which case the research must cease.

7.33 Other than by means of these required progress reports, the REC has no responsibility for pro-active monitoring of research, the accountability for which lies with the host NHS institution, but the REC may wish to be reassured of the process for such monitoring in certain specific cases.

7.34 A member of an REC who becomes aware of a possible breach of good practice in research should report this initially to the Chair and Administrator of the REC, who shall inform the appointing Authority. The Authority's officers shall be accountable for taking appropriate action.

Second ethical review when an REC declines to give a favourable opinion

7.35 Exceptionally, a further review of the protocol may be undertaken by a second REC.

NOTE:

1. These provisions in the Governance Arrangements are in contrast to the position under the 1991 guidelines. The 1991 guidelines were criticised because they did not provide for sufficient scrutiny—see further J. Neuberger, *Ethics and Health Care: the Role of Research Ethics Committees in the UK*, London: King's Fund Institute (1992). There is now provision for a degree of follow-up. One issue which remains, however, is the extent to which research ethics committees can be realistically expected to undertake such follow-up given their composition with members serving on an occasional basis (see also the discussion of the reform of the research ethics committee structure at pp.681 above).

5. TRIALS CONCERNING MEDICINAL PRODUCTS

The conduct of one particular type of clinical trial, that concerning medicinal products, has been considerably affected by EU Clinical Trials Directive (Directive 2001/20 of the European Parliament and of the Council of 4 April 2001 on the approximation of the laws, regulations and administrative provisions of the Member States relating to the implementation of good clinical practice in the conduct of clinical trials on medicinal products for human use) and the subsequent passage of the Medicines for Human Use (Clinical Trials) Regulations 2004 which places the conduct of such trials on a statutory basis in English law. (See further A.J. Baeyens, "Implementation of the Clinical Trials Directive: Pitfalls and Benefits" (2002) 9 *European Journal of Health Law* 31; T.K. Hervey and J.V. McHale, *Health Law and the European Union*, Cambridge: CUP, 2004, Chapter 7.) The aim of the Directive is to facilitate consistency in drug trial approval processes across the European Union, which has obvious benefits for the pharmaceutical industry as well as being advantageous in facilitating transparency in review of such trials across Europe. Implementation of the Directive has not however been without controversy and the UK research community expressed considerable objections to the new statutory regulatory framework which was to be imposed (see further R. Watson, "EU Legislation Threatens Clinical Trials" (2003) 326 B.M.J. 1348; R. Watson, "Research Bodies Lobby EU Governments over Trials Legislation" (2003) B.M.J. 1136; R. Watson, "Scientists Beg EU to Repeal New Rules for Clinical Trials" (2004) 328 B.M.J. 187). Nonetheless, the Medicines for Use (Clinical Trials) Regulations now align English law with the Directive.

Research Ethics Committees will thus have to operate in accordance with the regulations in the context of drug trials whilst making reference to other common law principles in relation to the approval of other research projects. Interestingly, COREC recently issued standard operating procedures, which provide that it will be Department of Health policy to apply the Clinical Trials Regulations approach more generally. It remains to be seen whether this causes some problems in practice, given the differing legal principles, for example in relation to consent, which exist as we shall see below under the regulations and at common law (COREC *Standard Operating Procedures for Research Ethics Committees* (2004), version 2, October 2004). Article 22 of the Directive required publication of the laws, regulations and administrative provisions necessary to comply with the Directive by May 1, 2003 and to come into effect by May 1, 2004. The impact of the Directive has been considerable. First, it has led the Government to introduce a statutory instrument incorporating the Directive into English law, the Medicines for Human Use (Clinical Trials) Regulations 2004. The Government has attempted to align the approach taken in the Directive with other areas of the clinical research process. This has caused particular controversy in that those conducting trials are now expected to have a "sponsor" to act as a back-stop. This provision came under heavy criticism because it was argued that it had an adverse effect on the trial process.

The Directive builds upon the original guidelines on good Clinical Practice. Article 1(2) provides that Good Clinical Practice is a set of internationally recognised ethical and scientific quality requirements which must be observed for designing, conducting, recording and reporting clinical trials that involve the participation of human subjects. Compliance with this good practice provides assurance that the rights, safety and well-being of trial subjects are protected, and that the results of the clinical trials are credible.

The Medicines for Human Use (Clinical Trials) Regulations 2004 (SI 2004/1031), Sch.1, Pt 2

PART 2
CONDITIONS AND PRINCIPLES WHICH APPLY TO ALL CLINICAL TRIALS

Principles based on International Conference on Harmonisation GCP Guideline

1. Clinical trials shall be conducted in accordance with the ethical principles that have their origin in the Declaration of Helsinki, and that are consistent with good clinical practice and the requirements of these Regulations.
2. Before the trial is initiated, foreseeable risks and inconveniences have been weighed against the anticipated benefit for the individual trial subject and other present and future patients. A trial should be initiated and continued only if the anticipated benefits justify the risks.
3. The rights, safety, and well-being of the trial subjects are the most important considerations and shall prevail over interests of science and society.
4. The available non-clinical and clinical information on an investigational medicinal product shall be adequate to support the clinical trial.
5. Clinical trials shall be scientifically sound, and described in a clear, detailed protocol.
6. A trial shall be conducted in compliance with the protocol that has a favourable opinion from an ethics committee.
7. The medical care given to, and medical decisions made on behalf of, subjects shall always be the responsibility of an appropriately qualified doctor or, when appropriate, of a qualified dentist.
8. Each individual involved in conducting a trial shall be qualified by education, training, and experience to perform his or her respective task(s).
9. Subject to the other provisions of this Schedule relating to consent, freely given informed consent shall be obtained from every subject prior to clinical trial participation.
10. All clinical trial information shall be recorded, handled, and stored in a way that allows its accurate reporting, interpretation and verification.
11. The confidentiality of records that could identify subjects shall be protected, respecting the privacy and confidentiality rules in accordance with the requirements of the Data Protection Act 1998 and the law relating to confidentiality.
12. Investigational medicinal products used in the trial shall be—

(a) manufactured or imported, and handled and stored, in accordance with the principles and guidelines of good manufacturing practice, and
(b) used in accordance with the approved protocol.

13. Systems with procedures that assure the quality of every aspect of the trial shall be implemented.

Conditions based on Article 3 of the Directive

14. A trial shall be initiated only if an ethics committee and the licensing authority comes to the conclusion that the anticipated therapeutic and public health benefits justify the risks and may be continued only if compliance with this requirement is permanently monitored.
15. The rights of each subject to physical and mental integrity, to privacy and to the protection of the data concerning him in accordance with the Data Protection Act 1998 are safeguarded.
16. Provision has been made for insurance or indemnity to cover the liability of the investigator and sponsor which may arise in relation to the clinical trial.

NOTE:

1. Some further guidance as to what constitutes "good clinical practice" in relation to such trials is set out in Directive 2005/28. This Directive provides for the approval of such trials by ethics committees, for consent procedures—which extend to adults with capacity, adults lacking mental capacity and children—and for monitoring of the safety of such trials.

The Medicines for Human Use (Clinical Trials) Regulations 2004 (SI 2004/1031)

12.—(1) No person shall—

(a) start a clinical trial or cause a clinical trial to be started; or
(b) conduct a clinical trial,

unless the conditions specified in paragraph (3) are satisfied.
(2) No person shall—

(a) recruit an individual to be a subject in a trial;
(b) issue an advertisement for the purpose of recruiting individuals to be subjects in a trial,

unless the condition specified in paragraph (3)(a) has been satisfied.
(3) The conditions referred to in paragraphs (1) and (2) are—

(a) an ethics committee . . . or an appeal panel appointed under Schedule 4 has given a favourable opinion in relation to the clinical trial; and
(b) the clinical trial has been authorised by the licensing authority.

(4) For the purposes of these Regulations, a clinical trial has been authorised by the licensing authority—

(a) in the case of a trial to which regulation 18 relates—
    (i) the trial is to be treated as authorised by virtue of regulation 18, or
    (ii) the authority has accepted the request for authorisation in accordance with the procedure specified in Schedule 5; or
(b) in the case of a clinical trial to which regulation 19 or 20 applies—
    (i) the authority has given a notice of authorisation in accordance with those regulations, or
    (ii) the authority has accepted the request for authorisation in accordance with the procedure specified in Schedule 5.

NOTES:

1. These regulations are the first situation in which research ethics approval was legally mandatory before a clinical trial could be undertaken in this country. Prior to this, reference to research ethics committees was simply discretionary.
2. As a consequence of the Clinical Trials Directive and reg.14(6) of the Medicines for Human Use (Clinical Trials) Regulations, clinical trials involving medicinal products must be approved by a research ethics committee. The UK has now placed those ethics committees which are concerned with the approval of clinical trials concerning medicinal prod-

ucts on a statutory basis. The Medicines for Human Use (Clinical Trials) Regulations provide in para.6 for the establishment of ethics committees. In addition the regulations enable the recognition of existing ethics committees for this purpose (para.7). Research ethics committees which scrutinised such trials must in turn be approved by the new UK Ethics Committee Authority established under the regulations (para.5).

3. In addition a trial concerning a medicinal product will require authorisation from the licensing body, which is the Medicines and Healthcare Products Regulatory Agency (Medicines for Human Use (Clinical Trials) Regulations, reg.11), and to undertake a trial without having obtained such an authorisation is a criminal offence.

4. Where applications concern gene therapy, they are to be made to the Gene Therapy Advisory Committee (reg.14(3)).

5. The trial can be suspended or prohibited a trial if there are doubts as to its scientific validity (Article 12 of the Directive).

6. Inspectors may inspect the sites where clinical trials may be conducted, sites where the product is investigated, laboratories used for analysis and sponsors' premises.

7. The Clinical Trials Directive also requires in Article 11 for the creation of a European database which will include information regarding the authorisation and conduct of clinical trials on medicinal products.

8. Article 16 of the Directive sets out procedures for notification of information concerning serious adverse events, including deaths consequent upon the trial and for the keeping of records concerning adverse events.

9. Article 17 of the Directive makes provision for notification of information concerning suspected serious unexpected adverse reactions that are fatal or life-threatening to be recorded and reported to the Member State's, ethics committee and sponsor.

10. Provision is made in Article 18 for the Commission to provide detailed guidance regarding production of adverse reaction reports.

(a) Scrutiny by the Research Ethics Committee of Trials Concerning Medicinal Products

Following the Directive, the regulations set out the general issues which an ethics committee should consider before approving a trial protocol.

The Medicines for Human Use (Clinical Trials) Regulations 2004 (SI 2004/1031)

Ethics committee opinion

15.—(1) Subject to paragraphs (3) and (4), an ethics committee shall within the specified period following receipt of a valid application, give an opinion in relation to the clinical trial to which the application relates.

(2) Where following receipt of a valid application it appears to the committee that further information is required in order to give an opinion on a trial, the committee may, within the specified period and before giving its opinion, send a notice in writing to the applicant requesting that he furnishes the committee with that information.

(3) Where the committee sends a request in accordance with paragraph (2), the specified period shall be suspended pending receipt of the information requested.

(4) If the clinical trial involves a medicinal product for xenogenic cell therapy, the time limits referred to in paragraphs (1) to (3) shall not apply and the ethics committee may give an opinion in relation to that trial or send a notice under paragraph (2) at any time after receipt of the valid application.

(5) In preparing its opinion, the committee shall consider, in particular, the following matters—

(a) the relevance of the clinical trial and its design;
(b) whether the evaluation of the anticipated benefits and risks as required under paragraph 2 of Part 2 of Schedule 1 is satisfactory and whether the conclusions are justified;
(c) the protocol;
(d) the suitability of the investigator and supporting staff;
(e) the investigator's brochure;
(f) the quality of the facilities for the trial;
(g) the adequacy and completeness of the written information to be given, and the procedure to be followed, for the purpose of obtaining informed consent to the subjects' participation in the trial;
(h) if the subjects are to include persons incapable of giving informed consent, whether the research is justified having regard to the conditions and principles specified in Part 5 of Schedule 1;
(i) provision for indemnity or compensation in the event of injury or death attributable to the clinical trial;
(j) any insurance or indemnity to cover the liability of the investigator or sponsor;
(k) the amounts, and, where appropriate, the arrangements, for rewarding or compensating investigators and subjects;
(l) the terms of any agreement between the sponsor and the owner or occupier of the trial site which are relevant to the arrangements referred to in sub-paragraph (k); and
(m) the arrangements for the recruitment of subjects.

(6) If—

(a) any subject of the clinical trial is to be a minor; and
(b) the committee does not have a member with professional expertise in paediatric care,

it shall, before giving its opinion, obtain advice on the clinical, ethical and psychosocial problems in the field of paediatric care which may arise in relation to that trial.

(7) If—

(a) any subject to the clinical trial is to be an adult incapable by reason of physical and mental incapacity to give informed consent to participation in the trial; and
(b) the committee does not have a member with professional expertise in the treatment of—
   (i) the disease to which the trial relates, and
   (ii) the patient population suffering that disease,

it shall, before giving its opinion, obtain advice on the clinical, ethical and pyschosocial problems in the field of that disease and patient population which may arise in relation to that trial.

(8) The ethics committee shall consider, and give an opinion on, any other issue relating to the clinical trial, if—

(a) the committee has been asked by the applicant to consider the issue;

(b) it is, in the committee's opinion, relevant to the other matters considered by the committee in accordance with this regulation.

NOTES:

1. The Clinical Trials Directive does not define "informed consent". This is left as a matter for national law. Paragraph 3(1) of Pt 1 of Sch.1 to the Medicines for Human Use (Clinical Trials) Regulations defines it as being:

> "a person gives informed consent to take part in a clinical trial only if his decision:
> (a) is given freely after that person is informed of the nature, significance, implications and risks of the trial and
> (b) either:
>   (i) is evidenced in writing, dated and signed or otherwise marked by that person so as to indicate his consent or
>   (ii) if the person is unable to sign or to mark a document so as to indicate his consent, is given orally in the presence of at least one witness and recorded in writing."

2. The regulations provide that the Committee should consider the provision for insurance and indemnity by the researcher and sponsor. This is a new requirement. The "sponsor" is in effect the backstop/guarantor for the project should something go wrong.

3. There are time limits contained in the regulations, and para.10 provides that

> "the specified period" means—
> (a) in the case of a clinical trial involving a medicinal product for gene therapy or somatic cell therapy or a medicinal product containing a genetically modified organism—
>   (i) where a specialist group or committee is consulted, 180 days, or
>   (ii) where there is no such consultation, 90 days; or
> (b) in any other case, 60 days;

(i) Consent and Research Involving Children: Who should consent be obtained from in the case of the child research participant in a drug trial?

The Medicines for Human Use (Clinical Trials) Regulations 2004 set out further guidance regarding the consent process in the case of children.

Medicines for Human Use (Clinical Trials) Regulations 2004 (SI 2004/1031), Sch.1, Pt 4

PART 4
CONDITIONS AND PRINCIPLES WHICH APPLY IN RELATION TO A MINOR

Conditions

1. A person with parental responsibility for the minor or, if by reason of the emergency nature of the treatment provided as part of the trial no such person can be contacted prior

to the proposed inclusion of the subject in the trial, a legal representative for the minor has had an interview with the investigator, or another member of the investigating team, in which he has been given the opportunity to understand the objectives, risks and inconveniences of the trial and the conditions under which it is to be conducted.

2. That person or legal representative has been provided with a contact point where he may obtain further information about the trial.

3. That person or legal representative has been informed of the right to withdraw the minor from the trial at any time.

4. That person or legal representative has given his informed consent to the minor taking part in the trial.

5. That person with parental responsibility or the legal representative may, without the minor being subject to any resulting detriment, withdraw the minor from the trial at any time by revoking his informed consent.

6. The minor has received information according to his capacity of understanding, from staff with experience with minors, regarding the trial, its risks and its benefits.

7. The explicit wish of a minor who is capable of forming an opinion and assessing the information referred to in the previous paragraph to refuse participation in, or to be withdrawn from, the clinical trial at any time is considered by the investigator.

8. No incentives or financial inducements are given—

(a) to the minor; or
(b) to a person with parental responsibility for that minor or, as the case may be, the minor's legal representative,

except provision for compensation in the event of injury or loss.

9. The clinical trial relates directly to a clinical condition from which the minor suffers or is of such a nature that it can only be carried out on minors.

10. Some direct benefit for the group of patients involved in the clinical trial is to be obtained from that trial.

11. The clinical trial is necessary to validate data obtained—

(a) in other clinical trials involving persons able to give informed consent, or
(b) by other research methods.

12. The corresponding scientific guidelines of the European Medicines Agency are followed.

Principles

13. Informed consent given by a person with parental responsibility or a legal representative to a minor taking part in a clinical trial shall represent the minor's presumed will.

14. The clinical trial has been designed to minimise pain, discomfort, fear and any other foreseeable risk in relation to the disease and the minor's stage of development.

15. The risk threshold and the degree of distress have to be specially defined and constantly monitored.

16. The interests of the patient always prevail over those of science and society.

Further guidance has been issued as to how to ascertain from whom informed consent should be obtained.

COREC Informed Consent in CTMPS (2005)

MINORS

13. The following guidance applies to England, Wales, Scotland and Northern Ireland without distinction.

Definition of a minor

14. Under the Regulations a minor is a person under the age of 16 years.

Hierarchy of consent

15. The Regulations prescribe a hierarchy for determining who should be approached to give informed consent on behalf of a minor prior to their inclusion in the trial. The provisions for informed consent by a legal representative only apply in the case of emergency treatment where no person with parental responsibility can be contacted prior to the proposed inclusion of the minor.

Table 1: Hierarchy of informed consent for a minor

	Person who may give consent	Definition	Commentary
1.	Parent	A parent or person with parental responsibility.	Should always be approached if available.
2.	Personal legal representative	A person not connected with the conduct of the trial who is: (a) suitable to act as the legal representative by virtue of their relationship with the minor, *and* (b) available and willing to do so.	May be approached if no person with parental responsibility can be contacted prior to the proposed inclusion of the minor, by reason of the emergency nature of the treatment provided as part of the trial.
3.	Professional legal representative	A person nominated by the relevant health care provider (e.g. an acute NHS Trust) . . . who is not connected with the conduct of the trial.	May be approached if no person suitable to act as a personal legal representative is available. Informed consent must be given before the minor is entered into the trial.

NOTE:

1. This builds upon the common law position (see Chapter 8 above) but goes beyond it in recognising provision for an external third-party-decision maker in relation to research.

(ii) Adults Lacking Mental Capacity

The regulations following the Directive also make specific reference to adults lacking mental capacity.

Medicines for Human Use (Clinical Trials) Regulations 2004, Sch.1, Pt 5

PART 5
CONDITIONS AND PRINCIPLES WHICH APPLY IN RELATION TO AN INCAPACITATED ADULT

Conditions

1. The subject's legal representative has had an interview with the investigator, or another member of the investigating team, in which he has been given the opportunity to understand the objectives, risks and inconveniences of the trial and the conditions under which it is to be conducted.

2. The legal representative has been provided with a contact point where he may obtain further information about the trial.

3. The legal representative has been informed of the right to withdraw the subject from the trial at any time.

4. The legal representative has given his informed consent to the subject taking part in the trial.

5. The legal representative may, without the subject being subject to any resulting detriment, withdraw the subject from the trial at any time by revoking his informed consent.

6. The subject has received information according to his capacity of understanding regarding the trial, its risks and its benefits.

7. The explicit wish of a subject who is capable of forming an opinion and assessing the information referred to in the previous paragraph to refuse participation in, or to be withdrawn from, the clinical trial at any time is considered by the investigator.

8. No incentives or financial inducements are given to the subject or their legal representative, except provision for compensation in the event of injury or loss.

9. There are grounds for expecting that administering the medicinal product to be tested in the trial will produce a benefit to the subject outweighing the risks or produce no risk at all.

10. The clinical trial is essential to validate data obtained—

(a)   in other clinical trials involving persons able to give informed consent, or
(b)   by other research methods.

11. The clinical trial relates directly to a life-threatening or debilitating clinical condition from which the subject suffers.

Principles

12. Informed consent given by a legal representative to an incapacitated adult in a clinical trial shall represent that adult's presumed will.

13. The clinical trial has been designed to minimise pain, discomfort, fear and any other foreseeable risk in relation to the disease and the cognitive abilities of the patient.

14. The risk threshold and the degree of distress have to be specially defined and constantly monitored.

15. The interests of the patient always prevail over those of science and society.

NOTES:

1.   The Directive's requirement that consent must be obtained from the legal representative introduces for the first time a proxy decision-maker in relation to the involvement of the adult without capacity in the clinical research process. It can be contrasted with the position both at common

law which does not provide for a third party to make health-related decisions on behalf of an adult lacking capacity and under the Mental Capacity Act 2005 which allows an individual to appoint an individual to exercise a power of attorney.

2. The definition of a legal representative is left to the individual Member State. Further guidance as to who should be approached to give consent in relation to an adult lacking mental capacity is given under the Medicines for Human Use (Clinical Trials) Regulations 2004.

3. The provisions in relation to the Directive now also need to be seen in the light of the Mental Capacity Act 2005, discussed above at p.696.

As with the child, further guidance is given as to who consent should be obtained from the 2005 COREC document.

Who should consent be obtained from in relation to a trial involving adults lacking mental capacity ?

COREC Informed consent in CTMP (2005)

Definition

17. The term used in the Regulations is *"an adult unable by virtue of physical or mental incapacity to give informed consent"*.

Hierarchy of consent

18. Table 2 sets out the hierarchy prescribed in the Regulations for determining what type of legal representative should be approached to give informed consent on behalf of an incapable adult prior to inclusion of the subject in the trial. The provisions in England, Wales and Northern Ireland differ from those in Scotland.

Table 2: Hierarchy of informed consent for an incapable adult

---

England, Wales and Northern Ireland

---

1. Personal legal representative

A person not connected with the conduct
of the trial who is:
(a) suitable to act as the legal
    representative by virtue of their
    relationship with the adult, *and*
(b) available and willing to do so.

---

2. Professional legal representative

A person not connected with the conduct
of the trial who is:
(a) the doctor primarily responsible for the
    adult's medical treatment, or
(b) a person nominated by the relevant
    health care provider (e.g. an acute NHS
    Trust or Health Board).
A professional legal representative may be
approached if no suitable personal legal
representative is available.

NOTE:

1. Some concerns have been expressed as to how the role of the professional
   legal representative will operate. In particular one concern is that it may be
   possible to "block book" consent by one professional legal representative
   in relation to a number of patients for example in a nursing home. (See
   further J. McHale, "Clinical Research" in A. Grubb (ed.), *Principles of
   Medical Law*, Oxford: OUP, 2004 at pp.884–888.)

6. CONFIDENTIALITY AND PRIVACY OF RESEARCH PARTICIPANTS' INFORMATION

As with other personal information, the use of information for research purposes
is subject to general common law principles of confidentiality and privacy and
also to the Data Protection Act 1998, discussed in Chapter 9 above.

General Medical Council: Research The Roles and Responsibilities of Doctors
(London: GMC (2002))

Confidentiality

30. Patients and people who volunteer to participate in research are entitled to expect
that doctors will respect their privacy and autonomy. Where data is needed for research,
epidemiology or public health surveillance you should:

- Seek consent to the disclosure of any information wherever that is practicable;
- Anonymise data where unidentifiable data will serve the purpose;
- Keep disclosures to the minimum necessary;
- Keep up to date with, and abide by, the requirements of statute and common law,
  including the Data Protection Act 1998 and orders made under the Health and Social
  Care Act 2001.

Use of existing records in research

Obtaining consent

31. Records made for one purpose, for example the provision of care, should not usually
be disclosed for another purpose without the patient's consent. If you are asked to disclose,

or seek access to, records containing personal information for research, you must be satisfied that express consent has been sought from the participant, wherever that is practicable.

32. Where it is not practicable for the person who holds the records either to obtain express consent to disclosure, or to anonymise records, data may be disclosed for research, provided participants have been given information about access to their records, and about their right to object. Any objection must be respected. Usually such disclosures will be made to allow a person outside the research team to anonymise the records, or to identify participants who may be invited to participate in a study. Such disclosures must be kept to the minimum necessary for the purpose. In all such cases you must be satisfied that participants have been told, or have had access to written material informing them:

- that their records may be disclosed to persons outside the team which provided their care.
- of the purpose and extent of the disclosure, for example, to produce anonymised data for use in research, epidemiology or surveillance.
- that the person given access to records will be subject to a duty of confidentiality.
- that they have a right to object to such a process, and that their objection will be respected, except where the disclosure is essential to protect the patient, or someone else, from risk of death or serious harm.

33. Where you control personal information or records about patients or volunteers, you must not allow anyone access, unless the person has been properly trained and authorised by the health authority, NHS trust or comparable body and is subject to a duty of confidentiality in their employment or because of their registration with a statutory regulatory body.

Where consent cannot be obtained

34. Where it is not practicable to contact participants to seek their consent to the anonymisation of data or use of identifiable data in research, this fact should be drawn to the attention of a research ethics committee so that it can consider whether the likely benefits of the research outweigh the loss of confidentiality to the patient. Disclosures may otherwise be improper, even if the recipients of the information are registered medical practitioners. The decision of a research ethics committee would be taken into account by a court if a claim for breach of confidentiality were made, but the court's judgement would be based on its own assessment of whether the public interest was served.

Projects which are not approved by research ethics committees

35. Some epidemiology, health surveillance and monitoring is, for good reason, undertaken without research ethics committee approval. Data can be used in these cases where there is a statutory requirement to do so, for example where the data relates to a known or suspected "notifiable" disease, or where there is a relevant order under the Health and Social Care Act 2001.

36. Where there is no statutory duty to disclose information, disclosures must be made in accordance with the principles set out in paragraph 30 above. Where it is not practicable to seek consent, nor to anonymise data, information may be disclosed or accessed where the disclosure is justified in the public interest.

Disclosures in the public interest

37. Personal information may be disclosed in the public interest, without the individual's consent, where the benefits to an individual or to society of the disclosure outweigh the public and the individual's interest in keeping the information confidential. In all cases where you consider disclosing information without consent from the individual, you must weigh the possible harm (both to the individual, and the overall trust between doctors and

participants) against the benefits which are likely to arise from the release of information.

38. Before considering whether disclosure of personal information would be justified, you must be satisfied that:

a. the participants are not competent to give consent; or,
b. it is not practicable to seek consent, for example because:
   • the records are of such age and/or number that reasonable efforts to trace patients are unlikely to be successful;
   • the patient has been or may be violent;
   • action must be taken quickly (for example in the detection or control of outbreaks of some communicable diseases) and there is insufficient time to contact participants; or
c. participants have been asked, but have withheld consent.

39. In considering whether the public interest in the research outweighs the privacy interests of the individual and society, you will need to consider the nature of the information to be disclosed, how long identifiable data will be preserved, how many people may have access to the data, as well as the potential benefits of the research project. A participant's wishes about the use of data can be overridden only in exceptional circumstances and you must be prepared to explain and justify such a decision.

40. Other circumstances in which disclosures may be made without consent are discussed below.

Records made during research

41. Records made during research should be kept securely and disclosed to people outside the research team only in accordance with the guidance in our booklet *Confidentiality: Protecting and Providing Information*.

NOTES:

1. This guidance is consistent with the decision in *R v Department of Health Ex p. Source Informatics* [2000] 1 All E.R. 786, which was discussed in Chapter 9 above at p.579 which sanctions the use of anonymised material.

2. Reference is made in the guidelines to the fact that use of some information for research purposes may be sanctioned under s.60 of the Health and Social Care Act 2001 and consequent regulations (see Chapter 10 above at p.627 and W. Lowrance, *Learning from Experience: Privacy and the Secondary Use of Data in Medical Research*, London: Nuffield Trust, 2002).

3. A further problematic question is the extent to which, where information is generated by a study, the individual who has provided that information is entitled to any feedback. The Council of Europe draft additional protocol to the Convention on Human Rights and Biomedicine in relation to Biomedical Research provides that:

   "Article 27
   If research gives rise to information of relevance to the current or future health or quality of life of research participant this information must be offered to them. That shall be done within a framework of healthcare or counselling. In

communication of such information due care must be taken in order to protect confidentiality and to respect the wish of the participant to receive such information."

This can be seen in terms of respect for human rights, in particular Article 8 of the ECHR—respect for privacy of home and family life. However, practical difficulties can arise: individuals may simply not want to know the information, nor might they wish that information to be included in their medical records. There is also the concern that information being fed back may relate to risks rather than to certainties (see, for example, a discussion of this issue in the context of genetic information: M.P.M. Richards, "Issues of Consent and Feedback in a Genetic Epidemiological Study of Women with Breast Cancer" (2003) 29 *Journal of Medical Ethics* 93). On the other hand, concerns have been voiced that failure to feed back information regarding certain clinical conditions may mean that the researcher is at risk of consequent litigation (see further C. Johnson and J. Kaye, "Does UK Biobank Have a Legal Obligation to Feedback Information to its Participants?"(2004) 12 *Medical Law Review* 239).

4. A further issue relates to the need to align the legal principles concerning use of human material for research purposes alongside those concerning confidentiality. This is clearly illustrated in relation to long-term genetic databases such as those where storage of samples is alongside the collection of personal information through links to medical records. A notable example of one such database in this country is the UK Biobank project which aims to collate the genetic information of 500,000 people between 40 and 69 over a period of 20 years. (See further J.V. McHale, "Regulating Genetic Databases: Some Legal and Ethical Issues" (2004) 11(1) *Medical Law Review* 70).

7. REGULATING FRAUDULENT RESEARCHERS

Considerable pressures are placed upon those who are involved in clinical research to show results for the money spent. There are also pressures upon the researcher to publish numerous papers for career advancement. The temptation to falsify results is thus considerable. This may impact upon patient care if drugs/ techniques are deemed "safe" from trials which are themselves inherently flawed. At present, misconduct by a researcher may lead to his or her being struck off the register by the General Medical Council (C. Dyer, "GP Struck Off for Fraud in Drug Trials" (1996) 312 BMJ 798 and S. Lock, F. Wells and M. Farthing (eds), *Fraud and Misconduct in Medical Research* (3rd edn), London: BMJ, 2001. The Royal College of Physicians have stated that two measures are required to ensure ethical research practice. First, there should be adherence to good practice in research. Secondly, there should be some form of mechanism for investigating allegations into fraud. (See *Fraud and Misconduct in Medical Research*, Royal College of Physicians, London: 1991, Chapter 6.) They suggest measures such as limiting the number of papers research applicants can cite when applying for jobs. They also propose that consideration should be given to the American approach, namely that research grants are conditional upon an institution having a mechanisam in place to deal with scientific misconduct.

In 1995 a meeting was held, convened by the Royal College of Physicians and attended by representatives from the Royal Society, General Medical Council and Medical Research Council to consider the establishment of a central body, though this was not taken further. There there have also been calls in both the *British Medical Journal* and the *Lancet* for this issue to be examined by the government (see R. Smith, "Time to Face up to Research Misconduct" (1996) 312 B.M.J. 789 and editorial, "dealing with deception" [1996] *Lancet* 843).

This has now led to the Committee on Publication Ethics being established in 1997 which has produced best practice guidelines on publication ethics ((1997) 315 B.M.J. 201). Nonetheless internationally controversy continues as illustrated by the resignation of a stem cell research expert over research fraud allegations in 2005 (see further S. Knight, "Stem cell research pioneer resigns over fraud", *The Times*, December 23, 2005). Finally in 2006 a panel was established in the UK to deal with research misconduct, the UK Panel for Health and Biomedical Research Integrity initially, on a three-year basis. It will begin by developing a code of practice for the NHS, universities and industry (see A. Cole, "UK Launches Panel to Deal with Research Misconduct" (2006) 332 B.M.J. 871.) The panel will be chaired by Professor Sir Ian Kennedy and will also provide information and support for whistleblowers.

8. Scrutinising the Approval of Clinical Trials

(a) Challenging the Decision of a Local Research Ethics Committee to Approve a Clinical Trial

A research ethics committee, as a public body, is liable to scrutiny of its action through judicial review. The decision of such a committee may be overturned on the basis that it had failed to act within the powers given to it by the Department of Health, failed to take into account relevant considerations when making the decision such as approving a protocol which is in contravention of existing law or if a committee failed to observe procedural proprieties when examining applications (see S. Baker, D. Beyleveld, S. Wallace and J. Wright, "Research Ethics Committees and the Law" in D. Beyleveld, D. Townend and J. Wright (eds), *Research Ethics Committees, Data Protection and Medical Research* (Aldershot: Ashgate, 2005). In both instances where judicial review actions have been brought against an ethics committee of an IVF unit, the actions were unsuccessful: *R v St Mary's Hospital Manchester Ex p. Harriot* [1988] 1 F.L.R. 51 and *R v Sheffield H.A. Ex p. Seale* (see Chapter 11 at p.809.) Nevertheless the potential for an action against a research ethics committee remains.

(b) Liability of Members of a Research Ethics Committee to a Research
Subject Injured in a Clinical Trial

Governance Arrangements for Research Ethics Committees (London: DOH,
2001)

Legal Liability

4.14 The appointing Authority will take full responsibility for all the actions of a
member in the course of their performance of his or her duties as a member of the REC
other than those involving bad faith, wilful default or gross negligence. A member should,
however, notify the appointing Authority if any action or claim is threatened or made, and
in such an event be ready to assist the Authority as required.

NOTES:

1. The introduction of indemnity for members of NHS research ethics
   committees followed concern regarding the accountability of the members
   of the NHS committee were an action to be brought against them by
   injured research subjects. (See M. Brazier, "Liability of Ethics Committees
   and their Members" (1990) 6 *Professional Negligence* 186.)
2. While such a negligence action is theoretically possible, it is likely that
   considerable practical difficulties would face a research subject bringing a
   negligence action against individual committee members. In the first place,
   the courts have indicated that they are unwilling to impose negligence
   liability upon regulatory bodies, (see *Yeu Keu-yen v Att.-Gen. of Hong
   Kong* [1988] A.C. 175). Moreover, even if they were prepared to entertain
   such a claim, the case might well founder on the issue of causation. It
   would be difficult to establish that it was the negligence of the committee
   member which caused the ultimate injury that the research subject suffered.

9. COMPENSATION FOR RESEARCH SUBJECTS WHO SUFFER HARM THROUGH PARTICIPATION IN A CLINICAL TRIAL

The present position regarding compensation for subjects injured in a clinical trial
is outlined in the Department of Health guidance. If a research subject is injured
due to defective drugs or surgical appliances, a strict liability action may be
brought under the Consumer Protection Act 1987 (for a general discussion of this
Act see Chapter 3). The NHS does not provide specific undertakings to
compensate those injured through involvement in clinical trials. However if the
research is undertaken by a commercial company, then undertakings for compensation may be given to the subject who is involved in the research. The
Association of British Pharmaceutical Industry guidelines provide for contractually binding undertakings to be made in volunteer trials. (See J.M. Barton
et al., "The Compensation of Patients Injured in Clinical Trials" (1995) 21
Journal of Medical Ethics 166.) While it does not advocate such guarantees in
therapeutic trials it suggests that the researcher should provide committees with

assurances that if injury occurs compensation will be given. Such compensation does not cover injury incurred where the physician continues to administer the drug even though the trial is itself at an end. In some cases limits have been imposed at the maximum amount claimed along with a requirement that claims be brought within three years of the trial. The Medical Research Council has indicated that it will make *ex gratia* payments in appropriate circumstances to volunteers injured in clinical trials which it sponsors but there is no absolute right to compensation.

The eclectic state of compensation arrangements needs to be considered alongside the difficulties which may face a research subject in bringing a tort action. This poses the question whether there should be any special provision for compensation for those involved in clinical research. The matter was considered by the Pearson Commission in its wide ranging study of personal injury matters in 1978.

Royal Commission on Civil Liability and Compensation for Personal Injury (Cmnd. 7054, 1978)

Volunteers for medical research

1339 People may volunteer to take part in research or clinical trials of new forms of treatment or new drugs. Strict precautions are imposed, including the screening of experiments by medical ethics committees. Nevertheless the Medical Research Council stated in their evidence to us; despite the exercise of the highest degree of care and skill by the medical investigator concerned, death or personal injury which was quite unforeseen and indeed quite unforeseeable might be suffered by a person who volunteers to participate in such an investigation. For example, a volunteer taking part in a recent trial of live attenuated influenza vaccine developed a neurological lesion shortly after the administration of the vaccine—the first known neurological sequela to any attenuated influenza virus despite the fact that many hundreds of thousands of such innoculations had been given during the previous ten years: a causal connection between the administration of the vaccine and the neurological lesion could neither be proved or disproved. In such a situation, the Medical Research Council would seek authority to make an *ex gratia* payment from public funds to the volunteer or to his dependants and such a payment has been approved for the volunteer who developed the lesion in question.

Patients undergoing clinical trials

1340 Patients as well as healthy volunteers may be asked if they will agree to accept a new form of treatment in the interests of research. If a patient is given such treatment and through it suffers injury or a worsening of his condition which would not have been expected with conventional treatment, he is in the same position as a healthy person volunteering to take part in research.

1341 We think that it is wrong that a person who exposes himself to some medical risk in the interests of the community should have to rely on *ex gratia* compensation in the event of injury. We *recommend* that any volunteer for medical research or clinical trials who suffers severe damage as a result should have a cause of action, on the basis of strict liability, against the authority to whom he has consented to make himself available.

QUESTION:

1. Should the government be obliged to provide compensation for persons injured in government-sponsored non-therapeutic clinical trials? (See R.

Gillon, "No-fault Compensation for Victims of Non-therapeutic Research—Should Government Continue to Be Exempt?" (1992) 18 *Journal of Medical Ethics* 59.)

10. EMBRYO RESEARCH

(a) General

Experimentation on embryos has been the subject of much controversy. It has been claimed that embryo research is justified by scientific advantages such as the development of new contraceptive techniques, more effective IVF procedures and an improved understanding of miscarriages. Some take the view that the conduct of embryo research does not give rise to any particular ethical difficulties, arguing that the embryo is a clump of cells with no special status and that it does not require special protection. (For discussion of the status of the embryo foetus see Chapter 12.) Nevertheless, embryo research has provoked considerable opposition. Some are of the view that research is unjustifiable because the embryo is a human being or a potential human being. Others perceive embryo research as sinister and are concerned as to the "slippery slope" which leads to an unjustifiable manipulation of the human race. (See Chapter 2 above.) Some feminist critics who oppose new reproductive techniques also oppose embryo research, regarding it as a manifestation of the exploitation of procreative activity. (See generally J. Harris and A. Dyson (eds), *Experiments on Embryos*, London: Routledge, 1991.)

The Warnock Committee which reported in 1984 considered the question of embryo research.

Report of the Committee of Enquiry into Human Fertilisation and Embryology (Warnock Committee Report), Cmnd. 9314, 1984)

Arguments against the use of human embryos

11.11 It is obvious that the central objection to the use of human embryos as research subjects is a fundamental objection based on moral principles. Put simply, the main argument is that the use of human embryos for research is morally wrong because of the very fact that they are human and much of the evidence submitted to us strongly submits this. The human embryo is seen as having the same status as a child or an adult by virtue of its potential for human life. The right to life is held to be the fundamental human right and the taking of human life on this view is always abhorrent. To take the life of the innocent is an especial moral outrage. The first consequence of this line of argument is that since an embryo used as a research subject would have no prospect of fulfilling its potential for life, such research should not be permitted.

11.12 Everyone agrees that it is completely unacceptable to make use of a child or an adult as the subject of a research procedure which may cause harm or death. For people who hold the views outlined in 11.11 research on embryos would fall under the same principle. They proceed to argue that since it is unethical to carry out any research harmful or otherwise on humans without first obtaining their informed consent, it must be equally unacceptable to carry out research on a human embryo, which by its very nature, cannot give consent.

11.13 In addition to the arguments outlined above, and well represented in the evidence, many people feel an instinctive opposition to research which they see as tampering with the creation of human life. There is widely felt concern at the possibility of unscruplous scientists meddling with the process of reproduction in order to create hybrids, or to indulge theories of selective breeding or eugenic selection.

11.14 Those who are firmly opposed to research on human embryos recognise that a ban on their use may reduce the volume not only of pure research but also research in potentially beneficial areas, such as the detection and prevention of inherited disorders, or the alleviation of infertility and that in some areas a ban would halt research completely. However, they argue that the moral principle outweighs any such possible benefits.

Arguments for the use of human embryos

11.15 The evidence showed that the views of those who support the use of embryos as research subjects cover a wide range. At one end is the proposition that it is only to *human persons* that respect must be accorded. A human embryo cannot be thought of as a person, or even as a potential person. It is simply a collection of cells which, unless it implants in a human uterine environment, has no potential for development. There is no reason therefore to accord these cells a protected status. If useful results can be obtained from research on embryos then such research should be permitted. We found that the more generally held position, however, is that though the human embryo is entitled to some added measure of respect beyond that accorded to other animal subjects that respect cannot be absolute and may be weighed against the benefits arising from research. Although many research studies in embryology and developmental biology can be carried out on animal subjects and it is possible in such cases to extrapolate these results and findings to man, in certain situations there is no substitute for the use of human embryos. This particularly applies to the study of disorders only occuring in humans, such as Downs syndrome, or research into the processes of human fertilisation or perhaps into the specific effect of drugs or toxic substances on human tissue.

The Warnock Committee went on to recommend that the human embryo should be given some special status in law.

11.19 The statutory body which we propose should issue licences for research will have as one of its main functions the regulation of research. First, it will have to be assured that no other research material is available for the particular project in mind, and second, it will have to limit the length of time for which an embryo can be kept alive *in vitro*. While as we have seen, the timing of the different stages of development is critical once the process has begun, there is no particular part of the developmental process that is more important than another: all are part of a continuous process, and unless each stage takes place normally at the correct time and in the correct sequence further development will cease. Thus biologically there is no one single identifiable stage in the development of the embryo beyond which the *in vitro* embryo should not be kept alive. However, we agreed that this was an area in which some precise decision must be taken in order to allay public anxiety.

11.20 The evidence showed a wide range of opinion on this question. One argument put forward may be termed the strictly utilitarian view. This suggests that the ethics of experiments on embryos must be determined by the balance of benefits over harm or pleasure over pain. Therefore, as long as the embryo is incapable of feeling pain, it is argued that its treatment does not weigh in the balance. According to this argument the time limit for some *in vitro* development and for research on embryos could be set at either when the first beginnings of the central nervous system can be identified or when functional activity first occurs. If the former is chosen then this would imply a limit of twenty two to twenty three days after fertilisation, when the neural tube begins to close. As to the latter, the present state of knowledge the onset of central nervous system functional activity could not be used to identify accurately the limits to research, because the timing is not known: however, it is generally thought to be considerably later in pregnancy. With either limit, proponents suggest subtracting a few days in order that there would be no possibility of the embryo feeling pain.

11.21 The Royal College of Obstretricians and Gynaceologists suggested that embryos should not be allowed to develop *in vitro* beyond a limit of seventeen days, as this is the point at which early neural development begins. The British Medical Association favoured a limit of fourteen days and a number of groups, including the Medical Research Council and the Royal College of Physicians suggested that the time limit should be at the end of the implantation stage. Again, some groups submitting evidence suggested that no embryo which had gone the beginning of the implantation stage should be used for research.

11.22 As we have seen, the objection to using human embryos in research is that each one is a potential human being. One reference point in the development of the human individual is the development of the human individuation in the performance of the primitive streak. Most authorities put this at fifteen days after fertilisation. This marks the beginning of individual development of the embryo. Taking such a time limit is consonant with the views of those who favour the end of the implantation stage as a limit. We have therefore regarded an earlier date than this as a desirable end-point for research. *We accordingly recommend that no live human embryo derived from in vitro fertilisation whether frozen or unfrozen, may be kept alive, if not transferred to a woman, beyond fourteen days after fertilisation. This fourteen day period does not include any time during which the embryo may have been frozen. We further recommend that it shall be a criminal offence to handle or to use as a research subject any live human embryo derived from in vitro fertilisation beyond that limit. We recommend that no embryo which has been used for research should be transferred to a woman.*

NOTES:

1. The Warnock Report noted the fact that the embryo has no specific legal status (see Chapter 12 below).
2. The Committee disagreed over whether embryos should be specially produced for research—see paras 11.25–11.30. Four members of the Committee, while supporting research in general, were opposed to the creation of embryos specifically for use in research. (See J. Harris, *The Value of Life*, London: Routledge, 1985, p.129 onwards, and also Chapter 11 below.)

The Warnock Committee recommended that embryo research should continue but subject to regulation. This recommendation was accepted by the Government. In the period prior to legislation, a voluntary regulatory regime was instituted in relation to new reproductive technologies (see Chapter 11 below). The Human Fertilisation and Embryology Act 1990 sets out the statutory framework within which treatment for infertility and embryo research are to be undertaken. The 1990 Act requires those proposing to undertake embryo research to obtain a licence from the Human Fertilisation and Embryology Authority, the regulatory body established under the statute. The grounds on which licences may be granted are set out below. (See generally on the passage of the 1990 Act D. Morgan and R. Lee, *Human Fertilisation and Embryology: Regulating the Reproductive Revolution*, London: Blackstone, 2001, Chapter 3.)

Human Fertilisation and Embryology Act 1990

Schedule 2, s.3(1–9)

3.—(1) A licence under this paragraph may authorise any of the following—

(a) bringing about the creation of embryos in vitro, and
(b) keeping or using embryos for the purposes of research specified in the licence.

(2) A licence under this paragraph cannot authorise any activity unless it appears to the Authority to be necessary or desirable for the purpose of—

(a) promoting advances in the treatment of infertility
(b) increasing the knowledge of congenital disease
(c) increasing knowledge about the cause of miscarriages,
(d) developing more effective means of contraception, or
(e) developing methods for detecting the prescence of gene or chromosome abnormalities in embryos before implantation, or for such other purposes as may be specified in regulations.

(3) Purposes may only be so specified with a view to the authorisation of projects of research which increase knowledge about the creation and development of embryos or about disease, or enable such knowledge to be applied.

(4) A licence under this paragraph cannot authorise altering the genetic structure of any cell while it forms part of an embryo, except in such circumstances (if any) as may be specified in or determined in pursuance of regulations.

(5) A licence under this paragraph may authorise mixing sperm with the egg of a hamster, or other animal specified in directions, for the purposes of developing more effective techniques for determining the fertility or normality of sperm, but only where anything which forms is destroyed when the research is completed, and in any event, not later than the two cell stage.

(6) No licence under this paragraph shall be granted unless the Authority is satisfied that any proposed use of embryos is necessary for the purposes of research.

(7) Subject to the provisions of this Act, a licence under this paragraph may be granted subject to such conditions as may be specified in the licence.

(8) A licence under this paragraph may authorise the performance of any of the activities referred to in sub paragraph (1) or (5) above in such a manner as may be so specified.

(9) A licence under this paragraph shall be granted for such period not exceeding three years as may be specified in the licence.

Section 15(1–4)

15.—(1) The following shall be conditions of every licence under paragraph 3 of schedule 2 to this Act.

(2) The records maintained in pursuance of the licence shall include such information as the Authority may specify in directions about such matters as the Authority shall so specify.

(3) No information shall be removed from any records maintained in pursuance of the licence before the expiry of such period as may be specified in directions for records of the class in question.

(4) No embryo appropriated for the purposes of any project of research shall be kept or used otherwise than for the purposes of such a project.

NOTES:

1. During the debates upon the 1990 Act M.P.s considered whether embryo research should be limited to spare embryos produced during infertility

treatment and whether a ban should be placed upon specially created embryos. This proposal was, however, rejected.

2. The 1990 Act only authorises use of an embryo up until the appearance of the "primitive streak" (s.3(1)). Save where the embryo has been frozen, this period runs from when the gametes are mixed. At the appearence of the primitive streak, it is possible to determine whether the embryo will develop into twins. However, some regard this limit as arbitrary. Other notable stages in the development of the foetus, which have been suggested as indicative of its development as a person, do not occur until much later, for example, it is not until at around 12 weeks that electrical activity can be detected in the brain of the foetus.

3. Human eggs can be mixed with hamster sperm but only up to the 2 cell stage. The value of this test is to assess male fertility levels. While there is a ban upon placing human embryos in an animal, it appears to be possible to license mixing human gametes inside an animal uterus. (See D. Morgan and R. Lee, *Human Fertilisation and Embryology: Regulating the Reproductive Revolution*, London: Blackstone, 2001 at p.82.)

4. The Human Fertilisation and Embryology Authority regulates the conduct of research. Research proposals are submitted for approval to academic referees (HFEA Code of Practice, 6th edn, 2003, para.10.10).

5. Each IVF centre should have access to a research ethics committee. Some units have established their own committees. Units within the NHS are expected to refer projects to the relevant MREC or LREC. No more than one-third of the members may be employed by or have a financial interest in the centre (Code of Practice, para.10.6).

6. The Code of Practice provides that research proposals should be referred to such a committee before a licence is obtained (Code of Practice, para.10.6).

7. As with abortion, embryo research is a subject on which certain persons hold strong ethical beliefs. The 1990 Act provides a right of conscientious objection in s.38 (see Chapter 11).

8. The 1990 Act also regulates experimental records (s.15).

QUESTIONS:

1. Is it justifiable to give statutory safeguards to embryos and animals while neglecting the human subject?

2. Does Sch.2, para.3 of the Human Fertilisation and Embryology Act 1990 give the Secretary of State unduly broad powers to make regulations?

(b) Cloning and Stem Cell Research

There has been a vast degree of controversy over one particular research technique involving embryos, that of cloning. The issue of cloning in general is considered in Chapter 11. Cloning came to the forefront of public attention with the cloning of Dolly the sheep and was the subject of much ethical debate (see for example, J. Harris, *Clones, Genes and Immortality*, OUP, Oxford, 1998, J.

Harris, "Goodbye Dolly? The Ethics of Human Cloning" (1997) 23 *Journal of Medical Ethics* 353, S.D. Pattison, "Reproductive Cloning: Can Cloning Harm the Clone?" [2002] 10 M*edical Law Review* 295). Here, we consider the legal responses to one aspect of cloning—in the context of stem cell research—for a discussion of reproductive cloning, see Chapter 11). Stem cells are the body's "master cells" and have an ability to be developed into any cell needed, e.g. for blood, bone or brain. Stem cells removed from embryos are a particularly rich source for research purposes. There it is noted that while there is a statutory prohibition upon cloning in s.3 of the Human Fertilisation and Embryology Act 1990 it is argued that this only covers certain types of cloning technique, namely the replacement of the nucleus of an embryo, but it does not explicitly refer to other techniques such as that used in relation to Dolly—the technique of cell nuclear replacement or replacing the nucleus of an egg and not an embryo. The ethics of cloning were considered in two major reports: the Human Fertilisation and Embryology Authority and Human Genetics Advisory Commission Report, *Cloning: Issues in Reproduction, Science and Medicine* and the Chief Medical Officers Expert Group Report, *Stem Cell Research: Medical Progress with Responsibility* (2000). Both reports supported stem cell cloning for therapeutic purposes, while at the same time being opposed to reproductive cloning. As a consequence, the Human Fertilisation and Embryology (Research Purposes) Regulations 2001 (SI 2001/188) were passed.

Human Fertilisation and Embryology (Research purposes) Regulations 2001 No 188

Further purposes for which research licences may be authorised

2.—(1) The Authority may issue a licence for research under paragraph 3 of Schedule 2 to the Act for any of the purposes specified in the following paragraph.
(2) A licence may be issued for the purposes of—

(a) increasing knowledge about the development of embryos;
(b) increasing knowledge about serious disease, or
(c) enabling any such knowledge to be applied in developing treatments for serious disease.

The HFEA indicated that it was to license stem cell research. However, the legality of the ability to undertake such research came under challenge in the following case:

R. (Quintavalle) v Secretary of State for Health [2003] 2 All E.R. 113

A pro-life campaigner sought to challenge the decision by the HFEA to license research which involved cell nuclear replacement. She argued that the legislation did not regulate stem cell cloning. The rationale for this was to push the Government into tightening the law in this area and ultimately restricting the development of cloning technology. At first instance, the claimant was successful, and Crane J. held that cell nuclear replacement was outside the legislation. In response, the Government swiftly passed the Human Reproductive Cloning Act

2001 to ban all reproductive cloning (see Chapter 11 at p.850).

The Human Reproductive Cloning Act 2001

(1) A person who places in a woman a human embryo which has been created otherwise than by fertilisation is guilty of an offence.

(2) A person who is guilty of the offence is liable on conviction on indictment to imprisonment for a term not exceeding 10 years or a fine or both.

(3) No proceedings for the offence may be instituted—

(a) in England and Wales, except with the consent of the Director of Public Prosecutions;

(b) in Northern Ireland, except with the consent of the Director of Public Prosecutions for Northern Ireland.

NOTE:

1. This Act bans reproductive cloning. However the consequence of the judgement at first instance was that research involving cell nuclear replacement was unregulated. This issue was subject to consideration by the Court of Appeal.

The first instance judgment was reversed by Lord Phillips M.R. on appeal. On appeal by Quintavelle to the House of Lords:

LORD BINGHAM OF CORNHILL

"1 My Lords, the issues in this appeal are whether live human embryos created by cell nuclear replacement (CNR) fall outside the regulatory scope of the Human Fertilisation and Embryology Act 1990 and whether licensing the creation of such embryos is prohibited by section 3(3)(d) of that Act . . .

2 This case is not concerned with embryos created in the ordinary way as a result of sexual intercourse. Nor is it directly concerned with the creation of live human embryos *in vitro* where the female egg is fertilised by the introduction of male sperm outside the body. CNR, a very recent scientific technique, involves neither of those things. In the Court of Appeal and in the House the parties were content to adopt the clear and succinct explanation given by the judge of what CNR means and involves [2001] 4 All ER 1013, 1016–1017:

'13. In the ovary the egg is a diploid germ (or reproductive) cell. It is described as "diploid" because its nucleus contains a full set of 46 chromosomes. By the process of meiotic division the nucleus divides into two parts. Only one of these, a pronucleus containing only 23 chromosomes (described as "haploid"), plays any further part in the process. Fertilisation begins when the male germ cell, the sperm, whose pronucleus contains 23 chromosomes, meets the haploid female germ cell and is a continuous process taking up to 24 hours. As part of the process the male and female pronuclei fuse to form one nucleus with a full complement of 46 chromosomes, a process known as syngamy. The one-cell structure that exists following syngamy is the zygote. After several hours the cell divides to create a two-cell zygote. At this stage it is generally referred to as an embryo. At about 15 days after fertilisation a heaping-up of cells occurs which is described as the "primitive streak".

14. Fertilisation may of course take place in the normal way or *in vitro*.

15. CNR is a process by which the nucleus, which is diploid, from one cell is transplanted into an unfertilised egg, from which . . . the nucleus has been removed. The [replacement] nucleus is derived from either an embryonic or a foetal or an adult cell.

The cell is then treated to encourage it to grow and divide, forming first a two-cell structure and then developing in a similar way to an ordinary embryo.

16. CNR is a form of cloning. Clones are organisms that are genetically identical to each other. When CNR is used, if the embryo develops into a live individual, that individual is genetically identical to the nucleus transplanted into the egg. There are other methods of cloning, for example, embryo splitting, which may occur naturally or be encouraged. Identical twins are the result of embryo splitting.

17. The famous Dolly the sheep was produced by CNR. Live young have since been produced by CNR in some other mammals. It has not yet been attempted in humans.

18. . . . CNR of the kind under consideration does not . . . involve fertilisation.'

The Act

3 The 1990 Act was passed

'to make provision in connection with human embryos and any subsequent development of such embryos; to prohibit certain practices in connection with embryos and gametes; to establish a Human Fertilisation and Embryology Authority',

and for other purposes. The sections at the heart of this appeal are sections 1 and 3 [see Chapter 11 at pp.755–756], which I should quote in full:

'*Principal terms used*

1(1) In this Act, except where otherwise stated–

(a) embryo means a live human embryo where fertilisation is complete, and
(b) references to an embryo include an egg in the process of fertilisation, and, for this purpose, fertilisation is not complete until the appearance of a two cell zygote. . . .

3(1) No person shall—

(a) bring about the creation of an embryo, or
(b) keep or use an embryo, except in pursuance of a licence. . . .

(3) A licence cannot authorise—
. . .
(d) replacing a nucleus of a cell of an embryo with a nucleus taken from a cell of any person, embryo or subsequent development of an embryo.

(4) For the purposes of subsection (3)(a) above, the primitive streak is to be taken to have appeared in an embryo not later than the end of the period of 14 days beginning with the day when the gametes are mixed, not counting any time during which the embryo is stored.'

4 The Act imposes three levels of control. The highest is that contained in the Act itself. As is apparent, for example from section 3(2) and (3), the Act prohibits certain activities absolutely, a prohibition fortified by a potential penalty of up to ten years' imprisonment (section 41(1)). The next level of control is provided by the Secretary of State, who is empowered to make regulations for certain purposes subject (so far as relevant here) to an affirmative resolution of both Houses of Parliament (section 45(1), (4)). Pursuant to section 3(3)(c) the Secretary of State may make regulations prohibiting the keeping or use of an embryo in specified circumstances. The third level of control is that exercised by the Authority. Section 3(1) prohibits the creation, keeping or use of an embryo except in pursuance of a licence, and the Act contains very detailed provisions governing the grant,

revocation and suspension of licences and the conditions to which they may be subject: see, among other references, sections 11 to 22 of and Schedule 2 to the Act. A power is also conferred on the Authority to give binding directions: sections 23 and 24.

5 The first argument of the Alliance is squarely based on the wording of section 1(1)(a) of the Act, fortified by that of subsection (1)(b). It hinges on the words 'where fertilisation is complete'. That makes clear, it is argued, that the live human embryos to which the Act applies are such embryos as are the product of fertilisation, for the obvious reason that if there is no fertilisation there can be no time when fertilisation is complete (and there is never an egg in the process of fertilisation). Therefore the Act does not apply to embryos created by CNR, unsurprisingly since in 1990 the creation of live human embryos was unknown to Parliament. The second argument of the Alliance is put as an alternative: if embryos created by CNR are, contrary to the first argument, embryos within the scope of the Act, then the CNR process is specifically prohibited by section 3(3)(d) and cannot be licensed.

The approach to interpretation

6 By the end of the hearing it appeared that the parties were divided less on the principles governing interpretation than on their application to the present case. Since, however, the Court of Appeal were said to have erred in their approach to construction, it is necessary to address this aspect, if relatively briefly.

7 Such is the skill of parliamentary draftsmen that most statutory enactments are expressed in language which is clear and unambiguous and gives rise to no serious controversy. But these are not the provisions which reach the courts, or at any rate the appellate courts. Where parties expend substantial resources arguing about the effect of a statutory provision it is usually because the provision is, or is said to be, capable of bearing two or more different meanings, or to be of doubtful application to the particular case which has now arisen, perhaps because the statutory language is said to be inapt to apply to it, sometimes because the situation which has arisen is one which the draftsman could not have foreseen and for which he has accordingly made no express provision.

8 The basic task of the court is to ascertain and give effect to the true meaning of what Parliament has said in the enactment to be construed. But that is not to say that attention should be confined and a literal interpretation given to the particular provisions which give rise to difficulty. Such an approach not only encourages immense prolixity in drafting, since the draftsman will feel obliged to provide expressly for every contingency which may possibly arise. It may also (under the banner of loyalty to the will of Parliament) lead to the frustration of that will, because undue concentration on the minutiae of the enactment may lead the court to neglect the purpose which Parliament intended to achieve when it enacted the statute. Every statute other than a pure consolidating statute is, after all, enacted to make some change, or address some problem, or remove some blemish, or effect some improvement in the national life. The court's task, within the permissible bounds of interpretation, is to give effect to Parliament's purpose. So the controversial provisions should be read in the context of the statute as a whole, and the statute as a whole should be read in the historical context of the situation which led to its enactment.

9 There is, I think, no inconsistency between the rule that statutory language retains the meaning it had when Parliament used it and the rule that a statute is always speaking. If Parliament, however long ago, passed an Act applicable to dogs, it could not properly be interpreted to apply to cats; but it could properly be held to apply to animals which were not regarded as dogs when the Act was passed but are so regarded now. The meaning of 'cruel and unusual punishments' has not changed over the years since 1689, but many punishments which were not then thought to fall within that category would now be held to do so. The courts have frequently had to grapple with the question whether a modern invention or activity falls within old statutory language: see Bennion, *Statutory Interpretation*, 4th ed (2002), Part XVIII, Section 288. A revealing example is found in *Grant v Southwestern and County Properties Ltd* [1975] Ch 185, where Walton J had to decide whether a tape recording fell within the expression 'document' in the Rules of the Supreme

Court. Pointing out, at p 190, that the furnishing of information had been treated as one of the main functions of a document, the judge concluded that the tape recording was a document.

10 Limited help is in my opinion to be derived from statements made in cases where there is said to be an omission in a statute attributable to the oversight or inadvertence of the draftsman: see *Jones v Wrotham Park Settled Estates* [1980] AC 74, 105 and *Inco Europe Ltd v First Choice Distribution* [2000] 1 WLR 586. This is not such a case. More pertinent is the guidance given by the late Lord Wilberforce in his dissenting opinion in *Royal College of Nursing of the United Kingdom v Department of Health and Social Security* [1981] AC 800. The case concerned the Abortion Act 1967 and the issue which divided the House was whether nurses could lawfully take part in a termination procedure not known when the Act was passed. Lord Wilberforce said, at p 822:

'In interpreting an Act of Parliament it is proper, and indeed necessary, to have regard to the state of affairs existing, and known by Parliament to be existing, at the time. It is a fair presumption that Parliament's policy or intention is directed to that state of affairs. Leaving aside cases of omission by inadvertence, this being not such a case, when a new state of affairs, or a fresh set of facts bearing on policy, comes into existence, the courts have to consider whether they fall within the parliamentary intention. They may be held to do so, if they fall within the same genus of facts as those to which the expressed policy has been formulated. They may also be held to do so if there can be detected a clear purpose in the legislation which can only be fulfilled if the extension is made. How liberally these principles may be applied must depend upon the nature of the enactment, and the strictness or otherwise of the words in which it has been expressed. The courts should be less willing to extend expressed meanings if it is clear that the Act in question was designed to be restrictive or circumscribed in its operation rather than liberal or permissive. They will be much less willing to do so where the subject matter is different in kind or dimension from that for which the legislation was passed. In any event there is one course which the courts cannot take, under the law of this country; they cannot fill gaps; they cannot by asking the question "What would Parliament have done in this current case—not being one in contemplation—if the facts had been before it?" attempt themselves to supply the answer, if the answer is not to be found in the terms of the Act itself.'

Both parties relied on this passage, which may now be treated as authoritative. Mr Gordon for the Alliance submitted that the Court of Appeal had fallen into error by asking the question which Lord Wilberforce said should not be asked, and by themselves supplying the answer.

[His Lordship considered the Warnock Committee report and its consideration of this area and continued:]

12 There is no doubting the sensitivity of the issues. There were those who considered the creation of embryos, and thus of life, *in vitro* to be either sacrilegious or ethically repugnant and wished to ban such activities altogether. There were others who considered that these new techniques, by offering means of enabling the infertile to have children and increasing knowledge of congenital disease, had the potential to improve the human condition, and this view also did not lack religious and moral arguments to support it. Nor can one doubt the difficulty of legislating against a background of fast-moving medical and scientific development. It is not often that Parliament has to frame legislation apt to apply to developments at the advanced cutting edge of science.

13 The solution recommended and embodied in the 1990 Act was not to ban all creation and subsequent use of live human embryos produced *in vitro* but instead, and subject to certain express prohibitions of which some have been noted above, to permit such creation and use subject to specified conditions, restrictions and time limits and subject to the regimes of control briefly described in paragraph 4 above. The merits of this solution are not a matter for the House in its judicial capacity. It is, however, plain that while Parliament outlawed certain grotesque possibilities (such as placing a live animal embryo

in a woman or a live human embryo in an animal), it otherwise opted for a strict regime of control. No activity within this field was left unregulated. There was to be no free for all.

Section 1(1)(a)

14 It is against this background that one comes to interpret section 1(1)(a). At first reading Mr Gordon's construction has an obvious attraction: the Act is dealing with live human embryos 'where fertilisation is complete', and the definition is a composite one including the last four words. But the Act is only directed to the creation of embryos *in vitro*, outside the human body (section 1(2)). Can Parliament have been intending to distinguish between live human embryos produced by fertilisation of a female egg and live human embryos produced without such fertilisation? The answer must certainly be negative, since Parliament was unaware that the latter alternative was physically possible. This suggests that the four words were not intended to form an integral part of the definition of embryo but were directed to the time at which it should be treated as such. This was the view taken by the judge (in paragraph 62 of his judgment) and by the Court of Appeal (paragraphs 29, 53, 58) and I agree with it. The somewhat marginal importance of the four words is in my opinion indicated by the fact that section 1(1)(b) appears to contradict them. The crucial point, strongly relied on by Mr Parker in his compelling argument, is that this was an Act passed for the protection of live human embryos created outside the human body. The essential thrust of section 1(1)(a) was directed to such embryos, not to the manner of their creation, which Parliament (entirely understandably on the then current state of scientific knowledge) took for granted.

15 Bearing in mind the constitutional imperative that the courts stick to their interpretative role and do not assume the mantle of legislators, however, I would not leave the matter there but would seek to apply the guidance of Lord Wilberforce quoted above in paragraph 10. (1) Does the creation of live human embryos by CNR fall within the same genus of facts as those to which the expressed policy of Parliament has been formulated? In my opinion, it plainly does. An embryo created by *in vitro* fertilisation and one created by CNR are very similar organisms. The difference between them as organisms is that the CNR embryo, if allowed to develop, will grow into a clone of the donor of the replacement nucleus which the embryo produced by fertilisation will not. But this is a difference which plainly points towards the need for regulation, not against it. (2) Is the operation of the 1990 Act to be regarded as liberal and permissive in its operation or restrictive and circumscribed? This is not an entirely simple question. The Act intended to permit certain activities but to circumscribe the freedom to pursue them which had previously been enjoyed. Loyalty to the evident purpose of the Act would require regulation of activities not distinguishable in any significant respect from those regulated by the Act, unless the wording or policy of the Act shows that they should be prohibited. (3) Is the embryo created by CNR different in kind or dimension from that for which the Act was passed? Plainly not: as already pointed out, the organisms in question are, as organisms, very similar. While it is impermissible to ask what Parliament would have done if the facts had been before it, there is one important question which may permissibly be asked: it is whether Parliament, faced with the taxing task of enacting a legislative solution to the difficult religious, moral and scientific issues mentioned above, could rationally have intended to leave live human embryos created by CNR outside the scope of regulation had it known of them as a scientific possibility. There is only one possible answer to this question and it is negative.

16 In support of his argument on construction Mr Gordon drew attention to three provisions of the Act which, he submitted, could not be applied to embryos created by CNR. The first of these was the starting point for the protection provided by the Act, specified in section 1(1) in relation to an embryo created by fertilisation but otherwise unprovided for. The second was the 14-day time limit provided in section 3(4), 'beginning with the day when the gametes are mixed', inapplicable in a case where gametes are not mixed. Third was the absence of any requirement of consent by the donor of the

replacement nucleus, in contrast with the stringent requirement of consent in other cases as provided by section 12(c) and Schedule 3. These are relevant points, and account must be taken of them when forming an overall judgment on the interpretation of section 1(1)(a). But once it is accepted that Parliament did not have embryos created by CNR specifically in mind when passing the Act, it almost inevitably follows that discrepancies will arise if the Act is applied to another member of the same genus. The real question is whether these discrepant features are of structural significance such that effect cannot be given to the intention of Parliament without observing them. Neither singly nor cumulatively do these three features have that effect. The appearance of a two cell zygote (section 1(1), which occurs however the embryo is created, provides a satisfactory starting point, there is a period before that occurs, but like Lord Phillips of Worth Matravers MR [2002] QB 628, 642, para 45 I do not think this is of practical significance. The 14-day time limit (section 3(4)) is alternative to appearance of the primitive streak (section 3(3)(a)), and it is open to the Secretary of State to prescribe a period shorter than 14 days (section 3(3)(c)). The Authority may impose a requirement of consent as a condition of any licence to create an embryo by CNR, and could be expected to do so. Given the clarity of Parliament's purpose, I do not regard these discrepancies as significant.

17 The criticisms made of the Court of Appeal's judgments are not, save in very minor respects, soundly based. I agree with the decision which that court reached on this interpretation question and substantially with the reasons given for it.

Section 3(3)(d)

18 It seems to me quite clear that CNR does not involve 'replacing a nucleus of a cell of an embryo' because there is no embryo until the nucleus of the recipient cell is replaced by the nucleus of the donor cell. I accordingly conclude that section 3(3)(d), which cannot have been drafted to prohibit CNR, does not, almost fortuitously, have that result. The target of section 3(3)(d) is in my opinion made plain by paragraph 12.14 of the Warnock Report, which need not be quoted but which was directed to a particular form of genetic manipulation, replacement of the nucleus of a fertilised human egg. The White Paper referred, at para 36, to 'techniques aimed at modifying the genetic constitution of an embryo', and proposed that legislation 'should clearly prohibit all such activities, but with a power for Parliament itself, by affirmative resolution, to make exceptions to these prohibitions if new developments made that appropriate'. Section 3(3)(d) was, I infer, enacted to give effect to this recommendation. If, as Mr Gordon contended, Parliament intended to ban all cloning by section 3(3)(d), it would have been possible so to provide; but it seems clear that Parliament did not intend to prohibit embryo-splitting, which creates clones, and to which the Warnock Report referred in paragraph 12.11. In my opinion, the subsection cannot be interpreted to prohibit CNR."

LORD STEYN

"The primary argument

26 Lord Phillips of Worth Matravers MR dealt with the primary argument in trenchant terms. He said [2002] QB 628, 641, para 38:

'To the question of whether it is necessary to bring embryos created by cell nuclear replacement within the regulatory regime created by the Act in order to give effect to the intention of Parliament, there can only be one answer. It is essential. There is no factor that takes embryos created by cell nuclear replacement outside the need, recognised by Parliament, to control the creation and use of human organisms. The consequence of Crane J's judgment is that anyone is free to create embryos by cell nuclear replacement and to experiment with these without limitation of time or any other restriction. There is no bar to placing a human embryo created in this way inside an animal. There is no bar to placing an animal embryo created in this way inside a woman. Until the

Government intervened with the Human Reproductive Cloning Act 2001 it was legal to use the process of cell nuclear replacement to produce and use an embryo to create a human clone. It is clear that these results are wholly at odds with the intention of Parliament when introducing the 1990 Act.'

I agree. I would summarise my reasons as follows. The long title of the 1990 Act makes clear, and it is in any event self-evident, that Parliament intended the protective regulatory system in connection with human embryos to be comprehensive. This protective purpose was plainly not intended to be tied to the particular way in which an embryo might be created. The overriding ethical case for protection was general. Not surprisingly there is not a hint of a rational explanation why an embryo produced otherwise than by fertilisation should not have the same status as an embryo created by fertilisation. It is a classic case where the new scientific development falls within what Lord Wilberforce called 'the same genus of facts' and in any event there is a clear legislative purpose which can only be fulfilled if an extensive interpretation is adopted. As Lord Bingham has demonstrated the makeweight arguments based on the difficulty of applying some regulatory provisions to the new development cannot possibly alter the clear legislative purpose. In the result I would either treat the restrictive wording of section 1(1)as merely illustrative of the legislative purpose or imply a phrase in section 1(1) so that it defines embryo as 'a live human embryo where [if it is produced by fertilisation] fertilisation is complete'. If it is necessary to choose I would adopt the former technique. It fits readily into section 1(1) since the words of 1(1)(b) plainly make otiose the words 'where fertilisation is complete' in section 1(1)(a). Treating the latter as merely illustrative requires no verbal manipulation.

27 For my part I am fully satisfied that cell nuclear replacement falls within the scope of the carefully balanced and crafted 1990 Act.

The alternative argument

28 The alternative argument was based on section 3(3)(d), which provides that a licence cannot authorise 'replacing a nucleus of a cell of an embryo with a nucleus taken from a cell of any person, embryo or subsequent development of an embryo'. The argument was that the development of cell nuclear replacement is prohibited under section 3(3)(d). Lord Phillips of Worth Matravers MR observed that he could see no basis for arguing that an unfertilised egg, prior to the insertion of the nucleus by the cell nuclear replacement process, is required to be treated under the Act as if it is an embryo: p 643, para 51. I agree.

Disposal

29 For the reasons given by Lord Bingham of Cornhill and Lord Hoffmann, as well as the reasons I have given, I would also dismiss the appeal."

NOTES:

1. Lord Scott agreed with Lords Bingham and Steyn.
2. The House of Lords followed the Court of Appeal and took a purposive approach. It has been questioned, however, whether it is correct to assume that Parliament was unaware of CNR when the legislation was enacted. It has been argued that "Its [CNR's] application to cloning may not have been thought to have scientific potential but as a procedure its technical aspects must have been within the contemplation of informed scientists at the time. They did not need to conceive of any futuristic (and yet to be discovered) technology to achieve it" (see A. Grubb, "UK Cloning (Cell-

Nuclear Replacment): the Scope of the Human Fertilisation and Embryology Act 1990" (2003) 11 *Medical Law Review* 135).

3. It has also been suggested that the Human Reproductive Cloning Act 2001 does not include all cloning technologies and does not prohibit expressly, for example, the insertion of a CNR embryo in an artificial uterus (see J. Herring, "Cloning in the House of Lords" (2003) 33 *Family Law* 663).

4. There have been attempts to regulate stem cell research across the EU and indeed to ban embryonic stem cell research during the passage of the EU Tissue Directive (see generally S. Halliday, "A Comparative Approach to the Regulation of Human Embryonic Stem Cells in Europe" (2004) 12 *Medical Law Review* 40 and T.K. Hervey and J.V. McHale, *Health Law and the European Union*, Cambridge: CUP, 2004, pp.274–280). Further controversy continues to rage internationally regarding stem cell cloning. In July 2006 President Bush used his presidential veto to stop a Bill approved by the US Congress which would have had the effect of lifting the ban on federal funding of stem cell research, despite considerable opposition from patient groups, high-profile campaigners such as the actor Michael J. Fox who suffers from Parkinson's disease and the scientific research community (see "Bush faces backlash for stem cell-veto", *The Times*, July 20, 2006).

5. An alternative to the use of embryonic stem cells is the use of stem cells from adults. This has the obvious advantage of avoiding controversy regarding the prospect of destruction of human life. When the House of Lords Select Committee considered the issue, evidence at that time indicated that the use of embryonic stem cells had far greater potential for research purposes than adult cells which were considered to have a more limited range (House of Lords *Stem Cell Research Committee*, (2002). However, there was some evidence to the Committee which suggested that adult stem cells may have much greater potential for use in the future. The Committee favoured going ahead with both embryonic and adult stem cell research and this was subsequently supported by the Government (see further *Government Response to the House of Lords Select Committee on Stem Cell Research*: London: DOH, 2002, Cm 561 and see further the discussion in R. Brownsword, "Stem Cells Superman and the Report of the Select Committee" (2002) 65 *Modern Law Review* 568).

QUESTIONS:

1. Should a decision such as the decision to license stem cell cloning be given to a regulator if there is no public consensus on the issue? (See further R. Brownsword, "Regulating Human Genetics: Dilemmas for a New Millennium" (2004) 12 *Medical Law Review* 14.)

2. Does the judgment of the House of Lords in *Quintavalle* illustrate that in cases of acute ethical controversy such as this, the issue should be left for Parliamentary determination as opposed to judicial deliberation?

Department of Health Review of the Human Fertilisation and Embryology Act 2005: A consultation document (London: DOH, 2005)

Research was considered in the government consultation document on the Human Fertilisation and Embryology Act 1990. The Government indicated that it "does not intend to re-open the fundamental issue of the permissibility of research involving embryos. However, the current review of the Act will cover the parameters of legitimate research—the activities which may lawfully be carried out—and the mechanisms through which they may be authorised and over-seen."

Cell Nuclear Replacement

9.21 The use of CNR on embryos for research was recently considered by the House of Commons Science and Technology Committee. In particular, the Committee considered the use of CNR for research into mitochondrial disorders which are known to cause more than fifty inherited metabolic diseases. As these problems occur in the outer part of a cell, rather than the nucleus, CNR could (in theory) be used to put an otherwise "healthy" nucleus into a cell which is free from mitochondrial disorders and therefore result in a "healthy" embryo. The law does not currently prohibit this type of research being undertaken on human eggs in order to create an egg free from mitochondrial disorders. The Committee concluded that there was no reason to distinguish in law between the use of CNR on eggs and on embryos for the purposes of research into mitochondrial diseases as the aim would be the same in both cases.

9.22 The Government believes that research undertaken on embryos using the cell nuclear replacement technique for the purpose of studying mitochondrial diseases should be permissible in law, subject to licensing.

9.23 Further, the Government invites views on removing the current prohibition on "replacing a nucleus of a cell of an embryo with a nucleus taken from the cell of any person, another embryo or a subsequent development of an embryo" for research purposes, subject to licensing.

Altering the genetic structure of an embryo

9.24 The HFE Act prohibits altering the genetic structure of any cell while it forms part of an embryo. This is currently an absolute ban with regard to assisted reproduction treatment, and section 5 considered what, if any, change should be made to this position.

9.25 However, with regard to research, the Act enables Parliament to pass regulations to permit this activity under licence from the HFEA. To date, no regulations under this section of the Act have been made.

9.26 This restriction overlaps with that discussed above insofar as replacing the nucleus of an embryo, or taking the nucleus of an embryo and placing it in another cell, is altering the embryo's genetic structure.

9.27 There could be several reasons for undertaking research involving altering the genetic structure of an embryo. It could, for example, aim to develop therapies to prevent the transmission of harmful gene variations to subsequent generations. If it could be done safely, such therapies might be a way of repairing gene defects before clinical manifestations and would also spare descendants the burden of serious diseases. The development of such therapies would, however, require extremely thorough research and testing.

9.28 The Government invites views on whether the law should permit altering the genetic structure of an embryo for research purposes, subject to licensing. . . .

Human–animal hybrids and chimeras

9.30 The Government has heard no compelling evidence that there is any reason to remove the prohibition on placing human embryos in animals (or vice-versa) and we have no intention of changing this position.

9.31 However, the Government is aware of arguments that there may be benefits in the research use of embryos created through the combination of human and animal material. At present the mixing of human and animal gametes is only allowed (under licence) for testing the fertility or normality of human sperm, and the result of the mixed gametes must be destroyed when the test is complete and definitely not later than the two cell stage. Other human–animal cell fusion products have been widely used in biosciences research for many years, for example in the development of treatments for some types of breast cancer.

9.32 Reasons for wanting to create hybrid or chimera embryos for research could include:

- to test the capacity of embryonic stem cells to differentiate into a range of bodily cell types, as part of research into the treatment of serious diseases.
- to derive human embryonic stem cells, thereby circumventing the shortage of good quality human eggs available for research.

9.33 The House of Commons Science and Technology Committee has recommended that new legislation should:

- define the nature of hybrids and chimeras
- make their creation legal for research purposes (provided they are destroyed in line with the 14 day rule)
- prohibit their implantation in a woman.

9.34 The Committee recognised that there are strongly held views both for and against this proposal, ranging from revulsion in some quarters to arguments that the creation and destruction of such creations pose fewer ethical problems than the creation and destruction of purely human embryos.

9.35 The Government invites views on whether the law should permit the creation of human–animal hybrid or chimera embryos for research purposes only (subject to the limit of 14 days culture in vitro, after which the embryos would have to be destroyed).

9.38 The Government invites views on whether the current list of legitimate purposes for licensed research involving embryos remains appropriate. . . .

Use of, and payments for, gametes in research

9.42 The HFE Act contains some restrictions on the use of gametes (sperm and egg) but does not generally seek to regulate their use in research. Use of gametes to create an embryo is a criminal offence without a licence from the HFEA, and the Act also prohibits the mixing of human and animal gametes and placing non-human gametes in a woman. Research use of gametes per se, not involving the creation of embryos or other prohibited activities, can therefore fall outside of the scope of regulation under the HFE Act.

9.43 The Government is, in particular, aware of concerns that the law does not prevent payments being made for the supply of gametes to be used in research (in circumstances where a licence is not required), and that this could lead to people being exploited or taking inappropriate risks.

9.44 Medical practitioners are, however, expected to follow the guidance published by the General Medical Council; Research: the Role and Responsibilities of Doctors, published in 2002. This makes clear that payments should not be offered at a level which could induce research participants to take risks that they otherwise would not take. Further, research must be conducted in accordance with the Department of Health's

Research Governance Framework, which includes referral to an independent research ethics committee.

9.45 The Government invites views on what, if any, additional regulatory requirements should apply to the procurement and use of gametes for purposes of research.

Creation of embryos for therapeutic purposes

9.46 Whereas research using embryos for the purpose of developing treatments for serious diseases is permissible under the HFE Act, the creation of embryos for the direct therapeutic benefit of a patient would be prevented by the wording of the Act in relation to licences. This is because the current wording of the Act sees the creation of an embryo for treatment purposes as being for the purpose of assisting a woman to carry children. This means that while an embryo could be created for a project of research involving experimental therapy on a patient, the same activity could not be undertaken under a treatment licence. Therefore, in effect, the therapy in question would be prevented once its effectiveness had been proved through research.

9.47 The Government invites comments on the desirability of allowing the creation of embryos for the treatment of serious diseases (as distinct from research into developing treatments for serious diseases which is already allowed).

NOTES:

1. The Government were of the view that there was no case for an extension of the 14-day time limit for research.
2. While recognising criticism that approval procedures in relation to research were bureaucratic, the Government stated that they wished to continue with the existing process which involved the HFEA as well as the research ethics committee process. They saw advantages here in terms of consistency and ensuring that approval processes were in accordance with the law of involving a national body (para.9.41).

11. ANIMAL RESEARCH

As was noted above, prior research on animals is generally a prerequisite of what is regarded as ethical clinical research. For instance Article 16(1) of the Council of Europe's Convention clearly presumes the necessity of animal research before experimental drugs or techniques are used on humans:

Article 16—Protection of persons undergoing research

Research on a person may only be undertaken if all the following conditions are met:

   i. there is no alternative of comparable effectiveness to research on humans;
   ii. the risks which may be incurred by that person are not disproportionate to the potential benefits of the research;
   iii. the research project has been approved by the competent body after independent examination of its scientific merit, including assessment of the importance of the aim of the research, and multidisciplinary review of its ethical acceptability;
   iv. the persons undergoing research have been informed of their rights and the safeguards prescribed by law for their protection;
   v. the necessary consent as provided for under Article 5 has been given expressly, specifically and is documented. Such consent may be freely withdrawn at any time.

Moreover, many of the biotechnological developments that are considered in this book, such as organ transplants, assisted conception and cloning, have only been made possible through the sacrifice of animal bodies. UK law does regulate the ways in which animals may be used in medical research under the Animals (Scientific Procedures) Act 1986. Indeed the provisions governing permissible research in the Human Fertilisation and Embryology Act 1990 (see p.721 above) are largely modelled on the 1986 Act which established the Animal Procedures Committee to license and oversee permissible research. (For more detail on this legislation see M. Fox, "Animal Rights and Wrongs: Medical Ethics and the Killing of Non-human Animals". In R. Lee and D. Morgan (eds), *Death Rites: Law and Ethics at the End of Life*, London: Routledge, 1994.)

Although the numbers of animals used in experiments have been steadily falling since the mid-1970s, the extensive use of genetically modified aninals in genetic and xeno technologies has led to an unprecedented increase in animal testing in the past ten years. Thus the years 1991–2001 witnessed a 1,017 per cent rise in the number of transgenic animals used in experiments (British Union for Abolition of Vivisection, *Designer Mice: BUAV Special Report into the Use of Mice in Genetic Experiments*, London, undated). In 2004 the number of animal procedures started was just over 2.85 million, a rise of about 63,000 (2.3 per cent) on 2003. Genetically modified animals were used in 914,000 regulated procedures representing 32 per cent of all procedures for 2004 (compared with 27 per cent in 2002 and 8 per cent in 1995) (Home Office, *Statistics of Scientific Procedures on Living Animals Great Britain 2004*, Norwich: HMSO, 2005). This illustrates the potential of new technologies to generate new ways of consuming animals. Such uses are often glossed over in discussions of the ethics of clinical research or using technologies (see the discussion of xenotransplantation in Chapter 15 at p.1170). Many commentators have attributed our reluctance to take animals status seriously to the fact that they (unlike human embryos for instance) are clearly classified as property in law. (For a critique of this legal construction of animals, see G. Francione, *Animals, Property and the Law*, Philadelphia: Temple University Press, 1995.)

Some of the ways in which animals are used in medical research and of the ethical issues posed by such research are canvassed in the following extract from an extensive recent report on the issue:

Nuffield Council on Bioethics, The Ethics of Research Involving Animals, 2005

1.8 Two questions are fundamental to the debate about research involving animals. First, does the scientific use of animals lead to valid, useful and relevant results in specific areas? Secondly, is it permissible for one species to cause pain, suffering and death to another to achieve aims that primarily benefit the former species? In order to consider these questions, we must explore a number of complex issues. These include a discussion of the arguments about the moral status of humans and animals, and ways of morally justifying specific kinds of treatment. The usefulness and relevance of the different kinds of research in which animals are involved need to be examined, as well as the degree of pain and suffering which they may experience in research.

1.9 It is unhelpful to consider these issues merely in the abstract. Rather, it is necessary to examine the types of research that give rise to particular concerns and we briefly consider four examples. First, knowledge about the genetics of animal traits enables researchers to "design" animals with specific features, using different methods of genetic modification (GM). Some people perceive such activities as an instance of increasing commodification of animals. Critics of the GM approach are also concerned about the large numbers of animals (mostly rodents) required to produce GM strains and the fact that the welfare implications of genetic modification are often unforeseeable . . .

1.10 The second example concerns the use of animals as models for human disease. In the case of hepatitis C, in the 1980s researchers infected chimpanzees in order to understand the pathology of the disease and to develop a vaccine . . . Researchers have also bred or created by other means animals that are affected by particular diseases so that they can study the processes involved, and develop possible interventions. These models include mice with diseases such as cystic fibrosis, rheumatoid arthritis (RA) or transmissible spongiform encephalopathies (TSEs) such as BSE (Bovine Spongiform Encephalopathy . . .). Many people object to the idea of producing animals that will exhibit the symptoms of a serious disease, whether by selective breeding, genetic modification or other means.

1.11 Thirdly, experiments on animals that, in evolutionary terms, are most closely related to humans, such as primates, have been particularly controversial. They are used in many areas of neurobiology because their brains share a great number of structural and functional features with human brains . . . While this similarity has scientific advantages, it poses some difficult ethical problems, because of an increased likelihood that primates experience pain and suffering in ways that are similar to humans.

1.12 Fourthly, the use of animals for toxicity testing in the development of pharmaceuticals and non-medical products such as agricultural and household chemicals has attracted criticism with regard to the degree of pain and suffering that is involved, and the numbers of animals killed. Some opponents of this type of animal use also consider that the scientific validity of such tests is doubtful.

. . .

3.59 The current regulatory framework in the UK requires that any research on vertebrate animals (and the common octopus) which may cause pain, suffering, distress or lasting harm must be licensed . . . A licence is not required where no harm will be caused or when the research involves only invertebrates (excluding the common octopus). Harmful experiments for the sake of mass entertainment (such as television entertainment) are prohibited by law, and research involving animals for the production of new cosmetic ingredients is also not permitted . . . Although not prohibited directly by law, licences for any research involving the great apes (gorillas, chimpanzees, pygmy chimpanzees and orang-utans) are not granted as a matter of current policy. In order for licences for specific research projects to be issued, the law requires that the likely benefits of the research, and the likely costs to the animals, are considered; that "the regulated procedures to be used are those which use the minimum number of animals, involve animals with the lowest degree of neurophysiological sensitivity, cause the least pain, suffering, distress or lasting harm, and are most likely to produce satisfactory results"; and that there are no available alternatives to achieving the goals of the experiment without using protected animals . . .

3.60 Pain and suffering of animals are treated with great seriousness in the current UK legislation. For example, licences may not be granted for research that is "likely to cause severe pain or distress that cannot be alleviated". Where possible, potentially harmful research must be conducted under anaesthetic or with the use of pain relieving medicines. By contrast, animal death, if brought about without pain or suffering, is regarded as a far less serious matter. Animals that are not used in regulated procedures but killed humanely to obtain tissue samples or because they are surplus to requirements are excluded from the controls of the A(SP)A.

. . .

10.44 The first part of this chapter summarised the findings of our description of the range of scientific uses of animals in research. Across and within each area the benefits take a wide range of forms. Research is undertaken to understand animal behaviour, and basic biological processes; to understand the mechanisms of diseases affecting humans and animals in order to develop effective preventative and therapeutic interventions, and to test the safety of compounds for humans, animals and the environment. Some of the research findings have immediate and directly applicable results, whereas others contribute primarily to the scientific body of knowledge.

10.45 The welfare implications for animals used in research are as varied as the benefits. In appropriately conducted purely observational research of animals in their natural habitat there are no negative effects at all. Whether or not animals used in laboratories experience pain, suffering or distress depends on a range of different aspects: of the animal's environment. In all kinds of laboratory-based research there are contingent factors, arising from the conditions of transport, breeding, housing, and handling. Then there may be effects associated with procedures connected directly to specific elements of the experimental design. For example, the taking of a blood sample is a typical procedure that is applied to many research animals. Animals that are used as disease models are likely to experience the symptoms typical for the disease. Whether or not animals experience pain, suffering and distress associated with experimental procedures is highly variable and depends on standards of handling and husbandry and whether or not the experiment permits the use of pain relieving medicines and anaesthetics.

10.46 The second part of this chapter addressed issues relating to transferability of results obtained from animal research to humans. Drawing on discussion in Chapters 5–9 we concluded that animal research has been, and can potentially be, scientifically valid, in that it is possible to extrapolate from animal models to humans (or other animals) in specific cases. Each type of research has to be judged on its own merits and must be subject to critical evaluation.

. . .

14.53 It is clear, then, that great moral disagreement exists both within and outside the Working Party. Nevertheless, as in other areas of ethically contentious issues, such as abortion or euthanasia, any society needs to settle on a single policy for practical purposes . . . [W]e are partially influenced by the concept of the "overlapping consensus", developed by the American philosopher John Rawls, who considered how to achieve fair agreements between reasonable moral agents on policies and procedures in societies that faced the "fact of pluralism". The concept relies on the possibility that each party to a consensus supports it for its own sake, or on its own merits, based on its individual moral or other normative framework

14.54 In trying to achieve an overlapping consensus it is necessary to produce a procedure or position that could be adopted from all reasonable perspectives. Could it be the case that the concept of the Three Rs [reduction, replacement and refinement of animal models], and the type of hybrid moral position (some absolute constraints, some balancing), which can be said to underlie the A(SP)A, could be accepted, at least in broad outlines, by all positions?

. . .

15.9 All research licensed in the UK under the A(SP)A [Animals (Scientific Procedures) Act 1986] has the potential to cause pain, suffering, distress or lasting harm to the animals used. Most animals are killed at the end of experiments. A world in which the important benefits of such research could be achieved without causing pain, suffering, distress, lasting harm or death to animals involved in research must be the ultimate goal . . .

15.11 While we trust that more progress in the moral debate can be made, we are aware that, for the near future, further moral argument alone cannot provide a universal answer as to whether or not research on animals is justified. But practical advances in scientific methods can reduce areas of conflict . . .

15.12 The Working Party therefore concludes that it is crucial that the Three Rs are, and continue to be, enshrined in UK regulation on research involving animals. The principle that animals may only be used for research if there is no other way of obtaining the results anticipated from an experiment is also fundamental. Furthermore, we observe that for moral justification of animal research it is insufficient to consider only those alternatives that are practicably available at the time of assessing a licence application. The question of why alternatives are not available, and what is required to make them available, must also be asked. The potential of the Three Rs is far from being exhausted. The Working Party therefore agrees that there is a moral imperative to develop as a priority scientifically rigorous and validated alternative methods for those areas in which Replacements do not currently exist. It is equally important to devise mechanisms that help in the practical implementation of available validated methods.

15.13 In applying the Three Rs it is crucial to consider not only the context of the experiments but also the many other factors that can affect animal welfare, including breeding, transportation, feeding, housing, and handling. The quality of these factors, and the ability of animals to satisfy their species-specific needs, can usually be improved.

15.14 We acknowledge that the UK has the most detailed legislative framework regarding animal research in the world. But proper attention to the welfare of animals involved in research and the accountability of scientists who conduct animal research cannot be achieved merely by having detailed regulations. Regulation can act as an emotional screen between the researcher and an animal, possibly encouraging researchers to believe that simply to conform to regulations is to act in a moral way. It is therefore crucial to promote best practice more actively and to improve the culture of care in establishments licensed to conduct experiments on animals.

15.15 When considering the replacement of specific types of research by alternative methods, it is important to take account of the international context in which research involving animals takes place. Many chemical and pharmaceutical compounds that have been developed are being marketed in countries or regions that have different regulatory frameworks for animal research and testing. Alternatives have been internationally accepted for safety testing. Nonetheless, many Replacements are not universally accepted, and the process of validation is lengthy. These processes need to be optimised and initiatives aimed at abandoning and replacing specific types of animal testing at national levels complemented by initiatives at the international level. This is not to say that initiatives in the UK can only be taken once there is consensus at an international level. In the past, the UK has been a leader in working towards change in international policies related to research involving animals. This leadership should be encouraged.

15.16 Scientific experiments involving animals are sometimes repeated by the same or other research groups. In considering whether the repetition of experiments should take place, it is important to distinguish between duplication and replication of experiments . . .

15.17 The Working Party acknowledges that academic competitiveness and commercial confidentiality can sometimes complicate the sharing of information. But at its best, science is an open process, and mechanisms that prevent the sharing of information need to be reviewed carefully in terms of their justification and implications for the use of animals in research.

NOTE:

1. Footnotes and subheadings have been omitted.

QUESTIONS:

1. Do you agree that the notion of an overlapping consensus can be developed on such a divisive issue as animal research, or are the Nuffield Working Party being overly optimistic in suggesting that something akin to the current regulatory position can attract widespread support?
2. Is it always more ethical to carry out research on animals than it is on humans? For instance, if a human being is incapacitated and unable to feel pain (for instance, because he or she is a persistent vegetative state) is it not more ethical to carry out research on him or her than on a sentient primate?

3. What, if any, types of animal research do you think law should rule out as morally impermissible?
4. In para.15.14 above the report makes the important point that conformity to law does not resolve the morality of all procedures carried out on animals.

SELECT BIBLIOGRAPHY

M. Baum, "The Ethics of Clinical Research" and S. Bottros, "Equipoise, Consent and the Ethics of Randomised Clinical Trials" in P. Byrne (ed.), *Ethics and Law in Health Care and Research*, Chichester: John Wiley, 1990.
D. Beyleveld, D. Townend and J. Wright (eds), *Research Ethics Committees, Data Protection and Medical Research*, Aldershot: Ashgate, 2005.
S. Bottros, "Abortion, Embryo Research and Foetal Transplantation: their Moral Interrelationship" in P. Byrne (ed.), *Medicine, Medical Ethics and the Value of Life*, Chichester: John Wiley, 1989.
M. Brazier, "Embryos 'Rights': Abortion and Research" in M. Freeman, *Medicine, Medical Ethics and Law*, London: Sweet & Maxwell, 1990.
C. Foster, *The Ethics of Medical Research on Humans*, Cambridge: CUP, 2001.
M. Fox, "Research Bodies: Feminist Perspectives on Clinical Research" in S. Sheldon and M. Thomson (eds), *Feminist Perspectives in Health Care Law*, London: Cavendish, 1998.
D. Giesen, "Civil Liability of Physicians for New Methods of Treatment and Experimentation Comparative Examination" (1995) 3 *Medical Law Review* 22.
J. Harris and A. Dyson (eds), *Experiments on Embryos*, London: Routledge, 1990.
I. Kennedy, "The Law and Ethics Informed Consent and Randomised Controlled Trials" in I. Kennedy, *Treat Me Right*, Oxford: OUP, 1988.
J.V. McHale "Clinical Research" in A. Grubb (ed.), *Principles of Medical Law* (2nd edn), Oxford: OUP, 2004.
J.V. McHale, "Guidelines for Medical Research, Some Ethical and Legal Problems" (1993) 1 *Medical Law Review* 160.
J.V. McHale and J. Miola, "Liability for and Insurability of Biomedical Research: Health Law Aspects in England" in J. Dute, M.G. Faure and H. Koziol (eds), *Liability for and Insurability of Biomedical Research with Human Subjects in a Comparative Perspective*, Vienna: Springer, 2004.
D. Morgan and R. Lee, *Human Fertilisation and Embryology: Regulating the Reproductive Revolution*, London: Blackstone, 2001.
A. Plomer, *The Law and Ethics of Medical Research*, London: Cavendish, 2005.
Freidman Ross, *Children in Medical Research: Access versus Protection*, Oxford: OUP, 2006.

M. Shea, "Embryonic Life and Human Life" (1985) *Journal of Medical Ethics* 205.

P. Singer *et al.*, *Embryo Experimentation: Ethical, Legal and Social Issues*, Cambridge: CUP, 1990.

PART IV

PART IV

This section of the book is concerned with reproductive choices, and the constraints, legal and otherwise, which limit those choices. Chapter 11 explores the issue of access to the growing menu of reproductive technologies, which individuals and couples may wish to use whether because of fertility problems, because they are gay or single or because they wish to avoid passing an inherited genetic disorder to a prospective child. By contrast, Chapter 12 focuses on the rights of the fertile woman to control her fertility through access to contraception and legal abortion. Although contraception and abortion my be viewed as private reproductive choices, requiring only that third parties (such as the state or health professionals) should not interfere with the right in question—an issue which we will return to in Chapter 13 when we consider involuntary sterilisation—it can be argued that there should also be a positive obligation on the state to provide abortion and contraceptive services as key aspects of a woman's right to health (see also Chapter 1). Similar claims have more recently been made about access to assisted conception. These have to some extent been recognised by the National Institute of Health and Clinical Excellence (NICE), which has recommended free IVF treatment for at least some infertile couples (see Chapter 11 at pp.812–814.) Chapter 13 shifts the focus to issues which arise once a pregnancy has been established, and the woman has chosen to carry her pregnancy to term. We explore whether the pregnant woman has the right to manage her pregnancy and the process of birth free from state or medical interference. In this context we examine the impact of medical technologies, such as ultrasound, amniocentesis and foetal surgery. On one level it is clear that such innovations increase the choices open to the pregnant woman, but it should be recognised that they may also serve to oblige her to undergo screening, tests or other medical procedures for the benefit of the foetus. They may even lead to pressure to terminate her pregnancy if such screening reveals that the foetus is disabled. Such technologies thus open up new possibilities for policing pregnancy. We go on to examine whether a child subsequently born alive has any cause of legal action if it is injured during pregnancy, or during assistant conception procedures, as a result of actions by third parties or the pregnant woman herself.

Taken as whole, these three chapters focus on the extent to which UK law promotes reproductive choice. Historically, it has shied away from explicit recognition of a right to reproduce, and in the first edition of this text we suggested that there was no clearly established right to reproduce. The only statement to contrary effect then dated from a High Court judgment by Heilbron J. in *Re D (a minor) (Wardship: surrogacy)* [1976] 1 All E.R. 326 (see Chapter 13 at p.927.) in which she stated that a woman's right to reproduce was a basic human right, which precluded in that case the sterilisation of an 11-year-old girl. However, subsequent appellate court rulings in a series of cases which endorsed sterilisation of incompetent women and girls cast doubt on even the negative conception of reproductive rights which Heilbron J. had endorsed.

Of course, one of the major changes in our legal culture since the first edition appeared in 1997 has been the enactment of the Human Rights Act 1998. While litigation asserting rights to reproduce or conversely staking a right to life on the part of the foetus (which many commentators anticipated), has not materialised, it is interesting that the cases which have been brought have asserted a positive right to reproduce on the part of prisoners who were denied access to assisted conception. The fact that these rights have been claimed in this very particular context, by prisoners who had committed serious crimes and been deprived of their liberty as a result, enabled the courts to avoid fully addressing the duties of the state to recognise and protect rights to reproduce (See the discussion of the Court of Appeal ruling in *R. v Secretary of State for the Home Department, Ex p. Mellor* [2001] 3 W.L.R. 533, which was subsequently endorsed by the European Court of Human Rights in *Dickson v the United Kingdom* (44362/2004) April 8, 2006, in Chapter 11 at pp.814–817.) It thus remains to be seen how valuable Articles 8 and 12 of the ECHR can be in protecting rights to reproduce, but what is clear is that any right to reproduce is not explicitly protected under the Human Rights Act. Thus, as Catherine MacKinnon and other feminist legal scholars have argued, it may be more productive for reproductive rights to be grounded in equality rather than notions of privacy or rights to found a family (see C. MacKinon, "Reflections on Sex Equality under Law" (1991) 100 *Yale Law Journal* 1309).

Nevertheless, it is arguable that, in less tangible ways, the 1998 legislation has impacted on our judicial culture. Certainly in sterilisation cases which have occurred since 1999 there has been a much greater willingness of the courts to call doctors to account and to justify proposals to sterilise incompetent citizens. In part this trend may be attributed to the retreat from the *Bolam* principle, which we have identified in Parts II and III of this text, but it may also speak to an increased rights consciousness on the part of the judiciary in the era of the Human Rights Act. Thus cases such as *Re S (Adult Patient: Sterilisation)* [2001] Fam. 15 (see Chapter 13 at p.941) may be contrasted with earlier rulings like *Re B* [1987] 2 All E.R. 206; [1988] A.C. 109 (at p.928), which failed to even pay lip service to the notion of human rights.

It remains true, however, that reproductive issues offer a good illustration of the limitations of rights discourse. In abortion debates and controversies which have surrounded the issue of whether a pregnant woman may be compelled to undergo a Caesarean delivery (see Chapter 13 at pp.954–961), legal discourse is often framed in adversarial terms, whereby the rights of the pregnant woman are pitted against those of the foetus. It is improbable that law or rights-based arguments can ever craft a satisfactory solution to dilemmas posed in this way. Furthermore, other challenges for human rights law would include the need to address the rights of men to reproduce—issues which are being asserted in the context of sterilisation (see Chapter 13 at pp.938–941), abortion (see Chapter 12 at pp.912–919) and surrogacy (see Chapter 11 at pp.791–799) as well as in the prisoner cases cited above. Other men (see Chapter 11 at pp.836–841) have also argued for the right not to be turned into a father against their will. Furthermore, as the children of the reproductive revolution have become more visible, their rights have also been asserted as evidence, particularly in the debates over a right to one's genetic heritage which are discussed in Chapter 11 at pp.830–835.

In the context of reproductive choice, then, law is constantly facing new challenges and the assertion of new rights by and on behalf of different groups. Furthermore, even when issues appear to have been resolved, it is always possible that judicial activism may unsettle the law. This is certainly true of the law on wrongful conception and birth. At the time of writing the first edition of this text, the Court of Appeal ruling in *Emeh v Chelsea and Kensington AHA* [1984] 3 All E.R. 1044 seemed to have confirmed the legal position that a woman who has an "unwanted" child as a result of a failed sterilisation can recover financial damages for the cost of bringing up that child. However, this ruling has subsequently been upset by the House of Lords decision in *McFarlane v Tayside Health Board* [2000] 2 A.C. 59, which has ruled out the payment of such damages—a holding which has caused subsequent appellate courts to struggle with attempts to carve out exceptions to this rule. The upshot is an area of law which has been thrown into considerable confusion (see Chapter 13).

At a more fundamental level, many issues of longer standing which underpin several of these debates—such as the how the foetus may be conceptualised in law—have never been satisfactorily resolved. Yet even in contexts like abortion, where some of the most intractable debates have taken place, discernible shifts have occurred in how matters are debated since the first edition of this book. Over the last decade it is notable that so-called "pro-life" activists have become increasingly litigious, bringing a number of judicial review cases on diverse issues, such as the legality of reproductive cloning (see Chapter 10 at pp.725–734 and Chapter 11 at pp.850–853) and decisions over alleged failures to prosecute in cases of unlawful abortion (see Chapter 12 at pp.886–887). However, such challenges tend now to be less concerned with opposition to abortion *per se*; and more with contesting particular aspects of abortion law where there may well be some popular support for their position. Thus, the abortion debate has recently focused on the ethico-legal challenges posed by late abortions, particularly when they are performed on the grounds of foetal handicap (see Chapter 12 at p.882).

Just as there seems to be widespread acceptance in this jurisdiction that lawful abortion will continue to be available, provided certain conditions are satisfied, so reproductive technologies have become a more accepted feature of health care provision. (For an excellent discussion of how reproductive techniques have been normalised, see C. Thomson, *Making Parents: the Ontological Choreography of Reproductive Technologies*, Cambridge, Massachusetts: MIT Press, 2005, Chapter 3.) This move towards popular acceptance of IVF and other forms of assisted conception has, however, been accompanied by technological developments, including new forms of cloning and new pre-implantation screening techniques, which highlight how outdated the 1990 Human Fertilisation and Embryology Act has already become. The need for legislative reforms has been addressed by the Science and Technology Committee, *Human Reproductive Technologies and the Law: Fifth Session 2004–5, Vols I and II* (HC 7-I, 7-II) and *Inquiry into Human Reproductive Technologies and the Law: Eight Special Report of Session 2004–5* (HC 491, London: The Stationary Office, 2005). Concerns over embryo mix-ups in clinics (see Chapter 11 at pp.824–828) have also prompted public concerns and all these factors have led to the Government's plans, announced in 2005, to conduct a major review of the Human Fertilisation and Embryology Act 1990. The law regulating reproductive technologies thus represents an area where we can predict substantial changes and in all probability an entirely new legal landscape when the time comes to write the third edition of this text.

11

REPRODUCTIVE CHOICE I: ASSISTED CONCEPTION

1. INTRODUCTION

This chapter focuses upon the reproductive choices available to those who are infertile or who decide not to have children via heterosexual intercourse. The alternative methods of reproduction discussed in this chapter have flourished in a social context where it is widely accepted that levels of infertility have risen to the point where approximately one in seven couples in the United Kingdom are alleged to be infertile or subfertile (HFEA, *The HFEA Guide to Infertility 2005/6*). While there is much debate about whether total levels of infertility have increased, it is clear that, whereas the problem used to be concentrated among older, poorer populations, it is now becoming highly visible among educated middle-class couples in their 30s. (It should also be noted, however, that recently more attention has been devoted to post-menopausal women asserting rights to reproduce in their 40s and 50s or even later—see pp.810–811 below.) The causes of such decreased fertility have been variously located. One factor seems to be changing patterns of sexual behaviour, which carry an increased incidence of sexually transmitted diseases, especially pelvic inflammatory disease and chlamydia. Decreasing fertility levels are also linked to certain contraceptive methods. The oral contraceptive pill, IUD and injectable and implantable forms of contraception, along with abortion, may carry some risk of decreased fertility (see Chapter 12 at pp.860–869). Changes in the social roles of women, which have entailed postponement of childbearing, have also played a role. More generally, fertility problems may be connected with a range of workplace hazards and environmental oestrogens. Allied with a decrease in the number of healthy babies available for adoption, all these factors have contributed to the high visibility of infertility. Although in the past there has been extensive debate about whether infertility is really an illness and how it can be defined (see S. Elliston and A. Britton, "Is Infertility an Illness?" (1994) 145 *New Law Journal Practitioner* 1552; J. Montgomery, "Rights, Restraints and Pragmatism: the Human Fertilisation and Embryology Act 1990" (1991) 54 M.L.R. 524; R.G. Lee and D. Morgan, *Human Fertilisation and Embryology: Regulating the Reproductive Revolution*, London: Blackstone, 2001, pp.43–47) the recommendation by the

National Institute for Health and Clinical Excellence (NICE) that at least some infertility treatment should be publicly funded (see pp.812–813 below) signals its acceptance as a routine part of health care law.

As infertility has become more high profile, medical technology has developed new techniques to assist conception over the past 30 years. There continues to be debate as to whether these methods offer an adequate solution to the problem of infertility. Critics argue that they are a technological fix which mask the real causes of infertility and suggest that conceptive technologies are a product of the same ideology which is to blame for causing or exacerbating fertility problems in the first place (see P. Spallone, *Beyond Conception: the New Politics of Reproduction*, London: Macmillan, 1989). Their criticisms are heightened by the fact that, notwithstanding the NICE recommendations, this menu of reproductive options is frequently only available to those with the resources to pay for them privately.

Furthermore, as single persons or gay and lesbian couples have increasingly sought to use reproductive technologies, the issue of who may access them has been rendered politically controversial. A further source of controversy stems from the fact that resort to the methods discussed in this chapter—use of donor gametes, surrogacy and *in vitro* fertilisation (IVF)—renders the whole process of reproduction more visible and technological and hence more open to medical control. Furthermore, in frequently separating out the processes of sex and reproduction, these conceptive techniques have called into question the extent to which traditional family structures can be regarded as "natural", and fundamentally questioned our notions of maternity, paternity and kinship. They have prompted a number of new variables to be considered by law. These include such issues as who can donate gametes and under what conditions; how and where fertilisation and gestation will take place; who will assume parental responsibility for the products of assisted reproduction and what is meant by the "family". In the future the possibility of human cloning has the potential to pose additional questions, although for now it remains firmly subject to legal prohibition.

Yet, notwithstanding the ethico-legal questions which reproductive technologies continue to raise, the extent to which many reproductive techniques have become normalised represents a crucial shift from the last edition of this text in 1997 (see C. Thomson, *Making Parents: the Ontological Choreography of Reproductive Technologies*, Cambridge, Massachusetts: MIT Press, 2005, Chapter 3). This shift, coupled with refinements and innovations in the technologies themselves, has prompted the Government in 2005 to announce a major review of the Human Fertilisation and Embryology Act 1990—the legislation which has shaped the legal landscape for regulating reproductive technologies in this country and proven influential elsewhere. This followed consideration of the law regulating assisted conception by the Science and Technology Committee, *Human Reproductive Technologies and the Law: Fifth Session 2004–5*, Vols I and II (HC 7-I, 7-II) and *Inquiry into Human Reproductive Technologies and the Law: Eight Special Report of Session 2004–5* (HC 491), London: The Stationary Office 2005. The documents contain a useful overview and critique of law and policy in this area. In that sense the issues we consider in this chapter are in a state of legal flux. We begin in Section 2 by considering the pivotal role of the Human Fertilisation and Embryology Authority (HFEA) in regulating the technologies. Section 3 explores the three main techniques of assisted conception—donation of gametes, IVF and surrogacy—and the extent to which they are regulated by law. Section 4 addresses the question of access to reproductive technologies, and how, as in the case of abortion, doctors have been installed as gate-keepers of these technologies, with Section 5 noting the right of health professionals to conscientiously object to involvement. In Section 6 we explore the funding of fertility services and in Section 7 the related issue of citizens' rights to reproduce. This is followed by an examination of the potential of assisted conception to create new forms of families and disrupt traditional understandings of motherhood and fatherhood, while also allowing choices to be made about genetic and other characteristics of potential children. Then we discuss the limitations of such choices and how law responds to the assertion of rights to information about genetic parentage, and disputes that arise over 'ownership' of stored gametes or embryos. We conclude with a consideration of particularly controversial options thrown up by bio-technology: pre-implantation genetic diagnosis, sex selection and reproductive cloning. In Section 11 we explore the way in which limiting reproductive choices has fuelled the phenomenon of procreative tourism and conclude by considering the legal implications if things go wrong with reproductive technologies.

2. The Human Fertilisation and Embryology Authority

The HFEA is the regulatory body established, in line with the Warnock recommendations, by the Human Fertilisation and Embryology Act 1990 to monitor and control embryo research and the provision of infertility services. It replaced the Voluntary (later Interim) Licensing Authority which had operated since the publication of the Warnock report. (For further detail see J. Gunning and V. English, *Human In Vitro Fertilisation: a Case Study in the Regulation of Medical Innovation*, Aldershot: Dartmouth, 1993.) The HFEA's principal duty is to regulate, by means of a licensing and monitoring system, any research or treatment which involves the creation, keeping and use of human embryos outside the body, or the storage or donation of human eggs and sperm. Its other duties include maintaining a register of information about all licensed treatment and children born as a result of such treatment. It also provides advice to the Secretary of State for Health on developments concerning infertility services and embryology, formulates a regularly updated Code of Practice, and produces information for consumers of reproductive technologies. The HFEA currently licenses 115 clinics to carry out all types of infertility treatment, and 85 to carry out IVF and DI (donor insemination) only (HFEA Response to the Toft Report, HFEA, 2004; see also *The HFEA Guide to Infertility and Directory of Clinics 2005/6*). (For more detail on the role and functions of the HFEA see Morgan and Lee, *Human Fertilisation and Embryology: Regulating the Reproductive Revolution*, London: Blackstone, 2001, Chapter 4; Science and Technology Committee, *Human Reproductive Technologies and the Law: Fifth Session 2004–5*, Vols I and II (HC 7-I, 7-II) and *Inquiry into Human Reproductive Technologies and the*

Law: Eight Special Report of Session 2004–5 (HC 491), London: The Stationary Office 2005.)

From April 2006 the HFEA is also designated as a "competent authority" for the purposes of implementing the requirements of the EU Tissue and Cells Directive (Directive 2004/23, Article 4) which introduces new legal requirements, which aim to harmonise standards of quality and safety for all establishments involved in the donation, processing and storage of human tissues and cells, including gametes and embryos (see further pp.763–768 below). The Directive will be incorporated into UK law by way of regulations that will amend the 1990 Act and increase the licensing and regulatory aspects of the HFEA's work. (The Department of Health is currently proposing to consult on the amending regulations in late-2006.)

(a) Constitution of HFEA

Human Fertilisation and Embryology Act 1990, s.5(1–3)

5.—(1) There shall be a body corporate called the Human Fertilisation and Embryology Authority.
 (2) The Authority shall consist of—

(a) a chairman and deputy chairman, and
(b) such number of other members as the Secretary of State appoints.

(3) Schedule 1 to this Act (which deals with membership of the Authority, etc) shall have effect.

Schedule 1

4.—(1) All the members of the Authority (including the chairman and deputy chairman who shall be appointed as such) shall be appointed by the Secretary of State.
 (2) In making the appointments the Secretary of State shall have regard to the desirability of ensuring that the proceedings of the Authority, and the discharge of its functions, are informed by the views of both men and women.
 (3) The following persons are disqualified from being appointed as chairman or deputy chairman of the Authority—

(a) any person who is, or has been, a medical practitioner registered under the Medical Act 1983 (whether fully, provisionally or with limited registration), or under any repealed enactment from which a provision of that Act is derived,
(b) any person who is, or has been, concerned with keeping or using gametes or embryos outside the body, and
(c) any person who is, or has been, directly connected with commissioning or funding any research involving such keeping or use, or has actively participated in any decision to do so.

(4) The Secretary of State shall secure that at least one-third but fewer than half of the other members of the Authority fall within sub-paragraph (3)(a), (b) or (c) above, and that at least one member falls within each of paragraphs (a) and (b).

NOTES:

 1. In the remainder of this chapter it will become apparent that the HFEA has been entrusted with considerable discretion to formulate policy and has

played an important role in stimulating public debate on developments in reproductive technology and influencing policy regarding regulation of these technologies. As we shall see, its decisions in recent years have also been increasingly subject to legal challenge. (For academic discussion of its role see M. Brazier, "Regulating the Reproductive Business" (1999) 7 *Medical Law Review* 166; R. Lee and D. Morgan, "Regulating Risk Society; Stigmata Cases, Scientific Citizenship and Biomedical Diplomacy" (2001) 23 *Sydney LR* 297; A. Dawson, "The Human Fertilisation and Embryology Authority: Evidence Based Policy Formation in a Contested Context" (2004) 12 *Health Care Analysis* 1–6.)

2. The Government is currently proposing to amalgamate the HFEA and the Human Tissue Authority (see Chapter 15 at p.1156) into a new Regulatory Authority for Tissues and Embryology (RATE), to come into being in 2008.

3. The HFEA is funded in the main by licence fees, supplemented by a Department of Health grant (HFEA Business Plan, 2005–6). It has been questioned whether it is acceptable that the HFEA is heavily dependent on licence fees for its funding, given its role in regulating and on occasion revoking licences. It is contended that this creates a potential conflict of interests, as some would argue that it is, effectively, funded by the reproductive industry (see S.D. Pattinson, *Medical Law and Ethics*, London: Sweet & Maxwell, 2006, p. 246; S. Fischel and C. Bennett, "Breeding debate", *The Guardian* August 30, 2003).

QUESTION:

1. Which, if any, special features of assisted conception justify the imposition of this degree of control over their use? (See E. Jackson, *Regulating Reproduction: Law, Technology and Autonomy*, Oxford: Hart, 2001, Chapter 5; J. Meikle, "Axe IVF watchdog, says fertility expert", *The Guardian*, December 11, 2004).

(b) The Legislative Framework of the Human Fertilisation and Embryology Act

The introductory sections of the 1990 Act lay down the basic legislative framework within which the HFEA currently works. This is couched in terms of certain express prohibitions (principally on any unlicensed research on or storage of human gametes and embryos, any research post 14 days, reproductive cloning and the creation of hybrids), coupled with a number of permissible purposes for which research may be carried out.

Human Fertilisation and Embryology Act 1990, ss.1–4

1.—(1) In this Act, except where otherwise stated—

(a) embryo means a live human embryo where fertilisation is complete, and

(b) references to an embryo include an egg in the process of fertilisation and, for this purpose, fertilisation is not complete until the appearance of a two cell zygote.

(2) This Act, so far as it governs bringing about the creation of an embryo, applies only to bringing about the creation of an embryo outside the human body; and in this Act—

(a) references to embryos the creation of which was brought about *in vitro* (in their application to those where fertilisation is complete) are to those where fertilisation began outside the human body whether or not it was completed there, and
(b) references to embryos taken from a woman do not include embryos whose creation was brought about *in vitro*.

(3) This Act, so far as it governs the keeping or use of an embryo, applies only to keeping or using an embryo outside the human body.

(4) References in this Act to gametes, eggs or sperm, except where otherwise stated, are to live human gametes, eggs or sperm but references below in this Act to gametes or eggs do not include eggs in the process of fertilisation.

2.—(1) In this Act—

"the Authority" means the Human Fertilisation and Embryology Authority established under section 5 of this Act, . . .

"licence" means a licence under Schedule 2 to this act and, . . .

"treatment services" means medical, surgical or obstetric services provided to the public or a section of the public for the purpose of assisting women to carry children.

(2) Reference in this Act to keeping, in relation to embryos or gametes, include keeping while preserved, whether preserved by cryopreservation or in any other way; and embryos or gametes so kept are referred to in this Act as "stored" (and "store" and "storage" are to be interpreted accordingly).

(3) For the purpose of this Act, a woman is not to be treated as carrying a child until the embryo has become implanted.

3.—(1) No person shall—

(a) bring about the creation of an embryo or
(b) keep or use an embryo, except in pursuance of a licence.

(2) No person shall place in a woman:

(a) a live embryo other than a human embryo, or
(b) any live gametes other than human gametes.

(3) A licence cannot authorise:

(a) keeping or using an embryo after the appearance of the primitive streak,
(b) placing an embryo in any animal,
(c) keeping or using an embryo in any circumstances in which regulations prohibit its keeping or use, or
(d) replacing a nucleus of a cell of an embryo with a nucleus taken from a cell of any person, embryo or subsequent development of an embryo.

(4) For the purpose of subsection (3)(a) above, the primitive streak is to be taken to have appeared in an embryo not later than the end of the period of 14 days beginning with the day when the gametes are mixed, not counting any time during which the embryo is stored.

3A.—No person shall, for the purposes of providing fertility services for any woman, use female germlines taken or derived from an embryo or a foetus or use embryos created by using such cells.

4.—(1) No person shall—

(a) store any gametes, or

(b) in the course of providing treatment services for any woman, use the sperm of any man unless the services are being provided for the woman and the man together or use the eggs of any other woman, or

(c) mix gametes with the live gametes of any animal,

except in pursuance of a licence.

(2) A licence cannot authorise storing or using gametes in any circumstances in which regulations prohibit their storage or use.

(3) No person shall place sperm and eggs in a woman in any circumstances specified in regulations except in pursuance of a licence.

(4) Regulations made by virtue of subsection (3) above may provide that, in relation to licences only to place sperm and eggs in a woman in such circumstances, sections 12 to 22 of this Act shall have effect with such modifications as may be specified in the regulations.

(5) Activities regulated by this section or section 3 of this Act are referred to in this Act as "activities governed by this Act".

Schedule 2

1.—(1) A licence under this paragraph may authorise any of the following in the course of providing treatment services—

(a) bringing about the creation of embryos *in vitro*,

(b) keeping embryos,

(c) using gametes,

(d) practices designed to secure that embryos are in a suitable condition to be placed in a woman or to determine whether embryos are suitable for that purpose,

(e) placing any embryo in a woman,

(f) mixing sperm with the eggs of a hamster, or other animal specified in directions, for the purpose of testing the fertility or normality of the sperm, but only where anything which forms is destroyed when the test is complete and, in any event, not later than the two cell stage, and

(g) such other practices as may be specified in, or determined in accordance with, regulations.

(2) Subject to the provisions of this Act, a licence under this paragraph may be granted subject to such conditions as may be specified in the licence and may authorise the performance of any of the activities referred to in sub-paragraph (1) above in such manner as may be so specified.

(3) A licence under this paragraph cannot authorise any activity unless it appears to the Authority to be necessary or desirable for the purpose of providing treatment services.

(4) A licence under this paragraph cannot authorise altering the genetic structure of any cell while it forms part of an embryo.

(5) A licence under this paragraph shall be granted for such period not exceeding five years as may be specified in the licence.

NOTES:

1. Sections 3 and 4 define actions which cannot be licensed, whereas Schedule 2 lists activities which may be the subject of licences. (For a comprehensive discussion of the licensing provisions, see M. Freeman, "Medically Assisted Reproduction" in A. Grubb (ed.), *Principles of Medical Law*, Oxford: OUP, 2004.)

2. Although the 1990 Act is broadly permissive, subsections 3(2) and (3) which rule out species mixing are designed to counter instinctive "yuk"

factor reactions and to dispel fears about the creation of a *Brave New World* scenario, with reproductive scientists out of control (see M. Thomson, *Reproducing Narrative: Gender, Reproduction and the Law*, Aldershot: Ashgate, 1998). Section 3A was inserted by s.156 of the Criminal Justice and Public Order Act 1994, in response to fears that the shortage of donated eggs for treatment of infertile women would lead to the use of eggs obtained from aborted female foetuses. The provision bans the use of foetal eggs, or embryos derived from foetal germlines (eggs), in fertility treatment (see Commentary by A. Grubb, [1995] 3 *Medical Law Review*, pp.203–204; A. Plomer and N. Martin Clement, "The Limits of Beneficence: Egg Donation under the Human Fertilisation and Embryology Act 1990" (1995) 15 *Legal Studies* 434). The fact that this provision was introduced as a late amendment to a criminal justice statute, which otherwise had nothing to do with infertility treatment, illustrates both the vagaries of the legislative process in this area, and how the activities of reproductive scientists are always circumscribed by criminal law.

QUESTIONS:

1. Carrying out any of the activities prohibited by the 1990 Act, or acting without a licence, are criminal offences with sanctions of up to 10 years' imprisonment (s.41). Although there appear to have been no prosecutions under the Act (see R.G. Lee and D. Morgan, *Human Fertilisation and Embryology: Regulating the Reproductive Revolution*: London, Blackstone, 2001, at p.150), are such heavy sentences, or indeed criminal prohibitions appropriate?

2. Alison Harveson Young has argued, in relation to a new Canadian law regulating reproductive technologies, which has introduced similar prohibitions to those operating under UK law, that criminal prohibitions in such legislation are problematic as "historically, the criminal law does not work well in the absence of significant consensus" (A.H. Young, "Let's Try Again . . . This Time with Feeling: Bill C-6 and New Reproductive Technologies" (2005) 38 *UBC Law Review* 123–45 at p.130.) Do you think that a societal consensus on prohibiting technologies like gamete mixing and reproductive cloning does exist?

3. TECHNIQUES FOR ALLEVIATING INFERTILITY

There are a variety of means by which the infertility of an individual, or a couple, can be overcome. Here, we explore the range of possibilities. In this section we consider those that are permitted by law, subject to conditions: the donation of human eggs and sperm, IVF and surrogacy. In the final section of this chapter we will consider the potential contribution of reproductive cloning, and whether law's ban on the practice is justifiable.

(a) Gamete Donation

The use of human sperm for the purposes of Assisted Insemination (AI) has a long history, having originated for use by humans in the 19th century. It has been a standard procedure for the last four decades and available on the NHS since 1968. AI can be used to overcome both female infertility problems (where the cervix or fallopian tubes pose barriers to normal insemination) and male infertility problems (by concentrating sperm before insemination). The process involves the collection of sperm outside the body and its introduction into the uterus for the purpose of inducing conception. Sperm is procured either from the partner of the woman who is to be inseminated (Assisted Insemination by Partner (AIP)), or from an donor who will not normally be legally related to the resulting offspring (Donor Insemination (DI), formerly referred to as Artificial Insemination by Donor or AID). In the former case, assisted insemination may be necessary because the partner's sperm count or its motility is abnormally low. A man's sperm count may be increased by laboratory manipulation of sperm density in a given sample. AIP may also be used where the male partner predicts damage to his testicles, e.g. because of workplace hazards or cancer treatment, and deposits semen in a "sperm bank". (For more detail on the technique, see R. Snowden and G. Mitchell, *The Artificial Family: a Consideration of Artificial Insemination by Donor*, London: Allen and Unwin, 1981.) Some commentators have argued that DI is not truly a therapy for male infertility; rather it is a way of enabling a woman whose male partner is unable to impregnate her to have a child. (See R. Hull, *Ethical Issues in the New Reproductive Technologies*, Belmont, California: Wadsworth, 1990 at p.54.) In most cases, unlike some of the reproductive technologies discussed below, assisted insemination is a fairly low tech procedure. It can be accomplished with nothing more sophisticated than a syringe, turkey baster or drinking straw. Under subs.4(1)(a) of the Human Fertilisation and Embryology Act 1990, DI is brought within the regulatory framework. However, subs.4(1)(b) of the Act (see above at p.757) effectively excludes AIP from the statutory scheme of regulation, since no donation of sperm is involved, and thus an individual performing AIP is not required to be licensed by the Act. Also in most AIP cases, fresh sperm will be used, whereas the 1990 Act only applies to gametes which have been placed in storage. However, the implementation of the EU Tissue and Cells Directive (see p.754 above) means that the HFEA's authority will extend to cover assisted insemination with a partner's sperm or the use of fresh sperm from a donor, as the Directive extends to the regulation of all gametes.

Largely due to its established history, assisted insemination is the most widely accepted of the alternative methods of reproduction, despite the fact that children born of donor insemination are often not told how they were conceived (see J. Dewar, "Fathers in Law? The Case of AID" in R. Lee and D. Morgan (eds), *Birthrights: Law and Ethics at the Beginning of Life*, London: Routledge, 1989.) However, when it was first introduced it created exactly the same moral panic about its threat to the family and society that are currently evoked by surrogacy and IVF. (See C. Smart, "'There is of course the distinction dictated by nature': Law and the Problem of Paternity" and N. Pfeffer, "Artificial Insemination,

In-vitro Fertilisation and the Stigma of Infertility" both in M. Stanworth (ed.), *Reproductive Technologies: Gender, Motherhood and Medicine*, Cambridge: Polity Press, 1987; M. Strathern, *After Nature: English Kinship in the Late Twentieth Century*, Cambridge: CUP, 1992, at pp.39–41.) The current widespread social acceptance of DI as a means of alleviating infertility in heterosexual couples is thus a good illustration of the process by which these techniques have been normalised. Since, in the past, DI was shrouded in secrecy, many of the ethical dilemmas it poses have only been debated fairly recently. The primary objection has been rooted in concern for the impact on the child produced as a result of DI, particularly where the sperm donor is genetically related to the male infertile partner. Historically, the main source of opposition to the practice comes from the Roman Catholic Church who have drawn analogies with adultery (see Congregation for the Doctrine of the Faith, *Instruction on Respect for Human Life in its Origin and on the Dignity of Procreation*, reprinted at pp.21–39 in R. Hull, *op. cit.*; on changing attitudes to AI see J. Dewar, *op cit.*; although other concerns have been raised about eugenicist underpinnings of the practice, post the Second World War—see Strathern, *op. cit.*). Legally, the main issue has been whether DI should be regulated by the medical profession. The issue of regulation, and consequently of the availability of the technique, has in the past proven contentious where single and lesbian women have sought to inseminate themselves, thus creating legally "fatherless" children. (See K. Harrison, "Lesbian Mothers, Sperm Donors and Limited Fathers" in M. Fineman and I. Karpin, *Mothers-in-Law: Feminist Theory and the Legal Regulation of Motherhood*, New York: Columbia University Press, 1995.) However, the normalisation of these techniques may be seen in the numbers of births produced. Between 1991 and 1998 in the UK 18,000 children have been born (officially) of donated gametes (Department of Health, *Donor Information Consultation: Providing Information about Gamete or Embryo Donors*—a figure which is set to rise as egg freezing becomes more widely available. Optimism about success rates in egg freezing has been heightened by recent reports of high success rates using a new "anti-freeze" technique developed by the Kato Ladies' Clinic in Tokyo which resulted in a fertilisation (via intra-uterine insemination (ICSI) (see p.778, Note 1 below) rate of over 90 per cent (K. Horsey, "Scientists report on new egg freezing technique" *Bionews* June 19, 2006).

Warnock Committee: Report of the Committee of Inquiry into Human Fertilisation and Embryology (1984) Cmnd. 9314

4.16 We have concluded that AID [DI] should no longer be left in a legal vacuum but should be subject to certain conditions and safeguards, and receive the protection of the law. It is certain that, for some people, [DI] will always remain unacceptable. Nevertheless we cannot accept their objections as a reason for denying the opportunity for treatment to those infertile couples who do not share their beliefs. Moreover the practice of [DI] will continue to grow, with or without official sanction and its clandestine practice could be very harmful. It is therefore desirable that [DI] should be available as a treatment for the alleviation of infertility, in a form subject to all possible safeguards. We regard it as a legitimate form of treatment for those infertile couples for whom it might be appropriate. Therefore *we recommend that [DI] should be available on a properly organised basis and subject to . . . licensing arrangements . . . to those infertile couples for whom it might be appropriate. Consequently we recommend that the provision of [DI] services without a licence for the purpose should be an offence.*

Notes:

1. The Warnock proposals on DI were incorporated into the Human Fertilisation and Embryology Act 1990, thus medicalising sperm donation by bringing the practice within the regulatory scheme established by the Act, and subjecting it to the control of the HFEA.
2. As Jackson notes, the success of ICSI in overcoming fertility problems in men with low sperm counts has reduced the incidence of AIP (E. Jackson, *Regulating Reproduction*, Oxford: Hart, 2001, pp. 164–165). On the alleged over-application of ICSI, see C. Thompson, *Making Parents: the Ontological Choreography of Reproductive Technologies*, Cambridge, Massachusetts: MIT Press, 2005 at pp.124–125.

At the time the 1990 Act was enacted it was much less common for eggs to be successfully used in fertility treatment, and the issue of egg donation was addressed in much less detail by Warnock. (For discussion of the market in human eggs which currently exists in the United States, the demand for particular genetic traits and the high prices commanded, see D.L. Spar, *The Baby Business: How Money, Science and Politics Drive the Commerce of Conception*, Boston, Massachusetts: Harvard Business School Press, 2006, at pp.29–30.)

Egg donation differs in a number of ways from sperm donation. First, since eggs are naturally much less plentiful than sperm, egg donation will require the donor to take superovulatory drugs for several days from days 3 to 7 of her menstrual cycle. Recently new concerns have been voiced about the safety of these drugs (L. Carpenter, "He'd like to have your babies", *The Observer*, August 6, 2006). In August 1996 ethical controversy was generated by the case of Mandy Allwood who allegedly became pregnant with octuplets as a result of fertility treatment which was administered without her partner's knowledge. This heralded calls for better regulation of the process of administering fertility drugs. (See "Octuplet woman's boyfriend 'not told of drugs'", *The Times*, August 12, 1996.) Following drug treatment, one or more follicles containing eggs will generally develop. Eggs were formerly collected via a surgical technique known as laparoscopy, but the process is now done vaginally under ultra-sound guidance, which is considerably less invasive. Following removal, oocytes are first placed in a specially prepared culture and incubated to develop into mature eggs.

A third key difference between the process of egg and sperm donation is that, whereas freezing of sperm has long been relatively straightforward, thus permitting cyropreservation or "spermbanking", it is much harder to successfully freeze eggs, which contain a higher percentage of water than sperm and are deemed to be less robust. Thus, in the past any "spare" eggs have tended to be fertilised and the resulting embryo is frozen, which raises a number of ethico-legal issues which we will address at pp.768–776 below. (See F. Price, "The Donor, the Recipient and the Child—Human Egg Donation in U.K. Licensed Centres" (1995) 7 *Child and*

Family Law Quarterly 145. Generally, on issues of gender differences between eggs and sperm, see T. Murphy, "Gametes, Law and Modern Preoccupations" (2000) 7 *Health Care Analysis* 155–169; M. Thomson, "Regulating (for) Sperm Donor Identity' in *Endowed: Regulating the Sexed Male Body*, New York: Routledge, forthcoming, 2007).

Techniques for freezing and storing eggs have now improved considerably, and in the UK by 2006 four so-called "ice babies" had been born as a result of successful egg freezing followed by IVF, while it is estimated that 150 have been born world-wide (see V. Groskop, 'Babies on ice', *The Guardian*, March 4, 2006). It is, however, important to note that this remains an experimental technique and that success rates (measured in terms of average live births per treatment cycle) are likely to be lower than for IVF using fresh gametes (currently around 17 per cent) or using frozen embryos (around 12 per cent) (HFEA, *Storage and Use of Frozen Eggs*, undated.) Another alternative for those who wish to store eggs prior to cancer treatment is to have ovarian tissue removed, frozen and subsequently implanted (M. Henderson, "Saving fertility before cancer treatment is harder for women", *The Times*, March 7, 2006).

The opportunities opened up by egg freezing does enhance choice for those with ethical objections to freezing embryos, especially since donated eggs are in such short supply. However, it simultaneously generates concerns regarding commercialisation of gametes and the potential of such technologies to facilitate controversial "lifestyle" choices for those with sufficient wealth to access the technologies (I. Sample, "Clinics prepare for 'lifestyle' fertility treatment', *The Guardian*, January 6, 2006). Media reports have suggested that, particularly in the wake of the removal of donor anonymity and the subsequent fall in gamete donation (see pp.830–835 below), "reproductive tourism" has flourished, with British women travelling to other EU jurisdictions for donor gametes (G. Tremlett, "Spain becomes the destination of choice for fertility tourists from Britain", *The Guardian*, May 12, 2006; L. France, "passport, tickets, suncream, sperm . . . ", *The Observer* January 15, 2006). Particular concerns have been voiced about exploitation of low-income egg donors in eastern Europe and Cyprus, and the adequacy of gamete screening in some jurisdictions (A. Barnett and H. Smith, "Cruel cost of the human egg trade", *The Observer*, April 30, 2006; see pp.773–775 below on payment for gametes).

Added impetus has been given to these concerns by the exposure of research fraud and unethical egg procurement in a high-profile Korean laboratory (see "Summary of the final report on Professor Woo Suk Hwang's research allegations by Seoul National University Investigation Committee", *New York Times*, January 9, 2006). Arguably, different issues are raised if women decide to donate eggs for research purposes as opposed to treating other women. At its open meeting in Belfast on May 10, 2006, the HFEA announced the launch of a consultation programme on egg donation for research and the ethical issues to which it gives rise (HFEA press release, "Authority decision on eggs for research", May 10, 2006). What is clear is that very few human eggs are available for research purposes.

The medically sanctioned form of DI via clinics, coupled with the increasing use of donated or stored eggs, raises issues concerning storage of and property rights in human gametes. These issues are addressed only to a limited extent in the 1990 Act, which contains provisions on the storage of gametes and embryos and also on the degree to which donors can control the subsequent use of "their" sperm, eggs or embryos. Schedule 3, as authorised by ss.12–14, requires written consent to the use and storage of donated sperm or eggs and of embryos produced by them. The consent is effective as long as it is not withdrawn.

Human Fertilisation and Embryology Act 1990, s.14(1–5)

14.—(1) The following shall be conditions of every licence authorising the storage of gametes or embryos—

(a) that gametes of a person or an embryo taken from a woman shall be placed in storage only if received from that person or woman or acquired from a person to whom a licence applies and that an embryo the creation of which has been brought about *in vitro* otherwise than in pursuance of that licence shall be placed in storage only if acquired from a person to whom a licence applies,

(b) that gametes or embryos which are or have been stored shall not be supplied to a person otherwise than in the course of providing treatment services unless that person is a person to whom a licence applies,

(c) that no gametes or embryos shall be kept in storage for longer than the statutory storage period and, if stored at the end of the period, shall be allowed to perish, and

(d) that such information as the Authority may specify in directions as to the persons whose consent is required under Schedule 3 to this Act, the terms of their consent and the circumstances of the storage and as to such other matters as the Authority may specify in directions shall be included in the records maintained in pursuance of the licence.

(2) No information shall be removed from any record maintained in pursuance of such a licence before the expiry of such period as may be specified in directions for records of the class in question.

(3) The statutory storage period in respect of gametes is such period not exceeding ten years as the licence may specify.

(4) The statutory storage period in respect of embryos is such period not exceeding five years as the licence may specify [see, now, Note 2 at p.770].

(5) Regulations may provide that subsection (3) or (4) above shall have effect as if for ten years or, as the case may be, five years there were substituted—

(a) such shorter period, or

(b) in such circumstances as may be specified in the regulations, such longer period as may be specified in the regulations.

Schedule 3: Consent to use of Gametes or Embryos

1. A consent under this Schedule must be given in writing and, in this Schedule, "effective consent" means a consent under this Schedule which has not been withdrawn.

2.—(1) A consent to the use of any embryo must specify one or more of the following purposes—

(a) use in providing treatment services to the person giving consent, or that person and another specified person together,

(b) use in providing treatment services to persons not including the person giving consent, or

(c) use for the purposes of any project of research,

and may specify the conditions subject to which the embryo may be so used.

(2) A consent to the storage of any gametes or any embryo must—

(a)   specify the maximum period of storage (if less than the statutory storage period), and
(b)   state what is to be done with the gametes or embryo if the person who gives the consent dies or is unable because of incapacity to vary the terms of the consent or to revoke it,

and may specify conditions subject to which the embryos or gametes may remain in storage . . .

5.—(1) A person's gametes must not be used for the purposes of treatment services unless there is an effective consent by the person to their being so used and they are used in accordance with the terms of the consent.

(2) A person's gametes must not be received for use for those purposes unless there is an effective consent by that person to their being so used.

(3) This paragraph does not apply to the use of a person's gametes for the purposes of that person, or that person and another together, receiving treatment services . . .

6.—(1) A person's gametes must not be used to bring about the creation of any embryo *in vitro* unless there is an effective consent by that person to any embryo the creation of which may be brought about with the use of those gametes being used for one or more of the purposes mentioned in paragraph 2(1) above . . .

7.—(1) An embryo taken from a woman [e.g. by lavage etc] must not be used for any purpose unless there is an effective consent by her to the use of the embryo for that purpose and it is used in accordance with the consent . . . .

According to s.13 (6) of the Act:

(6) A woman shall not be provided with any treatment services involving—

(a)   the use of any gametes of any person, if that person's consent is required under paragraph 5 of schedule 3 to this Act for the use in question,
(b)   the use of any embryo the creation of which was brought about *in vitro*, or
(c)   the use of any embryo taken from a woman if the consent of the woman from whom it was taken is required under paragraph 7 of that Schedule for the use in question,

unless the woman being treated and, where she is being treated together with a man, the man have been given a suitable opportunity to receive proper counselling about the implications of taking the proposed steps, and have been provide with such relevant information as is proper.

QUESTIONS:

1.   Are these consent provisions unduly onerous?
2.   Do you think the law should continue to set statutory maximum storage periods for gametes (and embryos) and if so, how should they be determined. (See question 23 of the current Department of Health Review of the 1990 Act—see p.752 above.)

The centrality of consent to the legislative scheme is highlighted particularly by the cases of *Evans v UK* (see p.836 below) and *Leeds Teaching Hospital v A* (see p.824 below), as well as by the following high-profile case:

R v HFEA, Ex p. Blood [1997] 2 W.L.R. 807; [1997] 2 All E.R. 687

In 1997, when Stephen Blood was dying from meningitis and was unconscious, his wife Diane asked doctors to take sperm from him via electro-ejaculation. The sperm was subsequently stored in a licensed clinic. When Mrs Blood requested that she be inseminated with the sperm after her husband's death, the HFEA refused on the basis that according to s.4(1) and Sch.3 of the 1990 Act, his written consent was necessary before his gametes could be stored and used; whereas Mrs Blood was only able to argue that he had verbally indicated his desire for children with her. The HFEA also refused to exercise its discretion under s.24(4) to allow the export of gametes which would have enabled Mrs Blood to travel to Belgium to avail herself of services lawfully available in another EU Member State under Articles 59 and 60 (now 49 and 50) of the EC Treaty. On this latter point the Court of Appeal allowed Mrs Blood's appeal:

LORD WOOLF M.R.
"Mrs Blood . . . wants to use the [sperm] samples to have her husband's child. However, so far, she has been frustrated in this desire because of the decisions which have been made under the provisions of the Human Fertilisation and Embryology Act 1990 . . .

Sperm can be used fresh or after it has been preserved. Its life, if not preserved is extremely limited, a matter of a few hours. If it is preserved, then it is being stored for the purposes of the 1990 Act and, therefore, is subject to the requirements of a licence. This is made clear by the definition of keeping or preserving sperm contained in s 2(2). The Act, therefore, takes the preservation process as the beginning of storage . . .

Mr Blood's sperm should not, in fact, have been preserved and stored. Technically, therefore, an offence was committed by the licence holder as a result of the storage under s 41(2)(b) of the 1990 Act by the licensee. There is, however, no question of any prosecution being brought in the circumstances of this case . . . From now on, however, the position will be different as these proceedings will clarify the legal position. Because this judgment makes it clear that the sperm of Mr Blood has been preserved and stored when it should not have been, this case raises issues as to the lawfulness of the use and export of sperm which should never arise again . . .

The fact is that whether or not it was proper to do so, treatment was being provided to Mr Blood even though he was unconscious when the sperm was obtained. The next question is, therefore, as to whether the obtaining of the sperm amounted to treatment services, which were being provided for Mr and Mrs Blood together in the sense that s 4(1)(b) refers to the provision of services 'for the woman and man together' . . .

As already indicated, treatment of a patient who is unaware of what is happening is not in itself a contravention of the 1990 Act. The important question is whether this position is altered as a result of Mr Blood dying before the sperm was used for the treatment of Mrs Blood. It is the time of treatment which is critical under s 4(1)(b).

In answering this question, it is to be borne in mind that s 4(1)(b) creates a criminal offence. In addition, s 4(1)(b) can interfere with Mrs Blood's ability to have a child by her former husband. Both these considerations suggest that a narrow interpretation should be given to its provisions. Lord Lester prays in aid s 28(6) as indicating that the 1990 Act contemplates the use of a person's sperm after his death . . .

The 1990 Act clearly regards the situation where the donor of the gametes dies before their use as being one which requires special safeguards. Thus, under para 2(2)(b) of Sch 3, a consent must state what is to happen to gametes if the donor dies. There are also the different provisions in the Act as to paternity where the father dies contained in s 28(6). This, together with the obvious difficulty in regarding a person who is dead as being treated together with someone else, means it is really not possible to regard treatment as being together for the purposes of s 4(1)(b), once the man who has provided the sperm has died. And, in any event, the exception to the need for written consent in the case of gametes for 'treatment together' only applies where the sperm is used at once and so does not need to be preserved. The keeping of sperm requires written consent under s 4(1)(a) and the terms of the licence.

This means that in this case, because of the effect of the section, Mrs Blood is not entitled to rely on the exception to s 4(1)(b) or to para 5 of Sch 3. Accordingly, the authority and Sir Stephen Brown P are correct so far as treatment in the United Kingdom is concerned. The absence of the necessary written consent means that both the treatment of Mrs Blood and the storage of Mr Blood's sperm would be prohibited by the 1990 Act. The authority has no discretion to authorise treatment in the United Kingdom . . . Our decision means that, unless fresh sperm are being used, there will always be a need for a written consent which complies with the schedule. It seems, therefore, that in the future, those who are responsible for treating a man and woman together should take the precaution of having the necessary consent not only to storage but also to enable that treatment to continue if the man should have the misfortune to die before the sperm is used . . .

Parliament was acting well within its powers in passing the 1990 Act, with its requirement for informed written consent from the donor before gametes were stored. And the authority were rightly faithful to and acting consistently with the clear intention of Parliament in giving the 1991 directions imposing a general restriction on export [of gametes]. But arts 59 and 60 give Mrs Blood the right to seek a particular direction permitting export in her case, under ss 23 and 24 of the 1990 Act . . .

Parliament did not place any express restriction on the authority's discretion. Parliament by the 1990 Act had left issues of public policy as to export to be determined by the authority. It is the authority's decision that, therefore, has to be capable of being justified in relation to art 59. In coming to its decision, the authority was required to take into account that to refuse permission to export would impede the treatment of Mrs Blood in Belgium and to ask whether, in the circumstances, this was justified.

Parliament has delegated to the authority the responsibility for making decisions in this difficult and delicate area, and the court should be slow to interfere with its decisions. However, the reasons given by the authority [for refusing to exercise its discretion to export the sperm], while not deeply flawed, confirm that the authority did not take into account two important considerations. The first being the effect of art 59 of the Treaty. The second being that there should be, after this judgment has been given, no further cases where sperm is preserved without consent . . .

[I]t is reasonably clear that it was a concern of the authority that if they gave Mrs Blood consent to export, this would create an undesirable precedent which could result in the flouting of the 1990 Act. While as already indicated this can, in the appropriate case, be a legitimate reason for impeding the provision of services in another member state it is a consideration which can not have any application here. The fact that storage cannot lawfully take place without written consent, from a practical point of view means that there should be no fresh cases . . .

If the authority had taken into account that Mrs Blood was entitled to receive treatment in Belgium unless there is some good reason why she should not be allowed to receive that treatment, the authority may well have taken the view that as the 1990 Act did not prohibit this, they should given their consent. The authority could well conclude that as this is a problem which will not reoccur there is not any good reason for them not to give their consent. If treated in Belgium, Mrs Blood is proposing to use a clinic which in general terms adopts the same standards as this country. The one difference being that they do not insist upon the formal requirements as to written consent which are required in this country. The need for formal requirements is not obvious in this situation.

Apart from the effect of Community law, the authority's view of the law was correct. It is not possible to say even taking into account Community law that the authority are bound to come to a decision in Mrs Blood's favour. What can be said is that the legal position having received further clarification, the case for their doing so is much stronger than it was when they last considered the matter . . .

If the authority is to reconsider their decision it will have to direct itself correctly as to the law, that is the law including Community law. This will involve starting from the premise that to refuse to allow the export of the sperm is contrary to art 59 of the Treaty unless there are appropriate reasons to justify this. The onus is, therefore, on the authority to provide reasons which meet the standards set by Community law. In deciding whether it can be justified, the authority are entitled to take into account the public interest."

NOTES:

1. Diane Blood subsequently gave birth to two sons conceived with her husband's sperm at a Belgium clinic.
2. In the wake of the outcry occasioned by this case, the Department of Health commissioned Professor Sheila McLean to report on its ramifications. Although critical of the Court of Appeal's reasoning, the review endorsed the importance of written consent and concluded that the consent provisions in the Act are basically sound (S. McLean, *Review of the Common Law Provisions Relating to the Removal of Gametes and of the Consent Provisions in the Human Fertilisation and Embryology Act 1990*, London: HMSO, 1997).
3. As Derek Morgan and Bob Lee argue, the case demonstrates the significance of the stipulation in s.13(5) of the Act that the child should have a father. Because, symbolically at least, Diane Blood acts in the name of her dead husband, she ultimately succeeds in very aggressively asserting her right to single parenthood. (See D. Morgan and R.G. Lee, "'In the Name of the Father?' *Ex parte Blood*: Dealing with Novelty and Anomaly" (1997) 60 Modern Law Review 840–856; H. Biggs, "Madonna Minus Child, or—Wanted: Dead or Alive! The Right to Have a Dead Partner's Child" (1997) 5 *Feminist Legal Studies* 225–234.)
4. In the later case of *U v Centre for Reproductive Medicine* [2002] EWCA Civ 565 a widow wished to use sperm which her husband had stored before his sudden death. Although he had signed a consent form agreeing to the posthumous use of his sperm when he has originally gone for treatment with his wife, Mr U had subsequently amended his form to withdraw his consent to this procedure, following a consultation with a specialist nurse who had told him that the clinic opposed the posthumous use of gametes. Mrs U failed in her claim that the pressure exerted on him amounted to undue influence which vitiated the purported withdrawal of consent. (See Chapter 6 at pp.401–402; and for a critique of the decision see S. Pattinson, "Undue Influence in the Context of Medical Treatment" (2002) 5 *Medical Law International* 305–317.)

QUESTIONS:

1. Do you agree with Lord Woolf that, under EU law, Mrs Blood has the right to be treated in Belgium with her husband's sperm unless there are good public policy reasons existed for not allowing this to happen? Why did those reasons not exist in this case? (On the application of EU law in this

case, see T. Hervey, "Buy Baby: the European Union and Regulation of Human Reproduction" (1998) *Oxford Journal of Legal Studies* 207.)

2. Can a national legislature prevent individuals from travelling abroad to avail themselves of services in other jurisdictions? Does this undermine the rationale for restrictive legislation in the UK? (For further consideration of "reproductive tourism", see pp.853–854 below.)

3. If the case had involved a husband asking doctors to take his wife's eggs, do you think that the court would have ruled out the possibility of prosecution so readily as they did in this case? Do you accept Lord Woolf's view that the case doesn't create any precedent?

4. Do you agree with the analysis of Morgan and Lee (*op. cit.* in note 3) that this case marks the beginning of the process of unravelling the legislative scheme established by the 1990 Act? (See also J. Wallbank, "Reconstructing the HFEA 1990: Is Blood Really Thicker than Water?" (2004) *Child and Family Law Quarterly* 387.)

The HFEA Code of Practice offers additional guidance for licensed clinics on issues such as the screening procedures applicable to donated eggs and sperm, counselling and limits placed on numbers of donations. (At the time of writing, the Code of Practice is under review and a new Code of Practice is due to be published later in 2006.)

HFEA Code of Practice (6th edn) 2003 (http://www.hfea.gov.uk/ HFEAPublications/CodeofPractice)

4.8 Before accepting gametes for the treatment of others, treatment centres are expected to consider the suitability of the intending donor. All potential donors must be given suitable opportunities to receive counselling. Where this involves embryos the counselling is expected to be offered to both partners of the donating couple. The views of all treatment centre personnel involved with the prospective donor are expected to be taken into account. In particular, treatment centres are expected to consider:

(i) Personal or family history of heritable disorders and
(ii) Personal history of transmissible infection and
(iii) The level of potential fertility indicated by semen analysis (where appropriate) and
(iv) If the prospective donor has children, the implications for the prospective donor in respect of the donation for themselves and their existing families and any offspring born of their donation both in the short and longer term and
(v) If the prospective donor does not have children, the implications for themselves and any future family . . .

4.10 It is expected that all reasonable steps should be taken to prevent the transmission of serious genetic disorders. This will usually be served by taking a thorough history from the prospective donor.

4.11 It is expected that genetic testing should be limited to the determination of carrier status for inherited recessive disorders in which abnormal test results carry no significant direct health implications for the prospective donor.

4.12 Centres are expected to ensure that where prospective donors are genetically tested, they have the same level of support and counselling as recipients. They are expected to be informed of the test results and offered post test counselling as applicable . . .

4.18 It is essential that all recipients of gamete donations receive information explaining the limitations of testing procedures and the risks associated with treatment. If any concerns are raised appropriate counselling is expected to be made available.

. . .

4.22 Sperm should not be taken for the treatment of others from donors over the age of 45, unless there are exceptional reasons for doing so.

4.23 Eggs should not be taken for the treatment of others from donors over the age of 35, unless there are exceptional reasons for doing so.

4.24 Gametes should not be taken for the treatment of others from anyone under the age of 18.

. . .

6.7 Treatment centres are expected to allow individuals seeking treatment, considering donation or storage sufficient time to reflect upon their decisions before obtaining their written consent.

It is expected that a copy of the signed consent form will be provided for those who have given consent.

6.8 Individuals may specify additional conditions subject to which their gametes or embryos may be stored or used. Consent may be varied or withdrawn at any time providing that the gametes and embryos have not already been used in treatment services or research.

6.9 Gametes must not be taken from anyone who is incapable of giving a valid consent, or has not given a valid consent to examination and treatment and effective consent to the use or storage of those gametes.

. . .

6.39 . . . [I]f there is an intention to donate gametes for the treatment of others (including the creation of an embryo for that purpose), the written consent of the potential donor(s) must be obtained.

6.40 Treatment centres are not required to obtain the consent of the donor's partner before the donor may donate gametes. Where the donor is married or in a long-term relationship, treatment centres are expected to nonetheless encourage the donor to seek the partner's consent in writing to the use of the gametes for donation.

6.41 Where a woman withdraws her consent for egg donation after preparation has commenced, the treatment centre is expected to accept any financial loss which it sustains as a result of the withdrawal of either the woman providing or receiving the eggs.

. . .

7.16 Where a couple is undergoing infertility treatment and the possibility of donation arises, donor implications counselling is expected to be undertaken separately from treatment implications counselling (see 7.11). Where the possibility of donation arises later in treatment, it is expected that treatment will not proceed unless the couple or woman, if being treated singly, have been given a suitable opportunity and time to receive counselling.

7.17 As well as considering the requirements of paragraphs 7.1–7.24 of this Code of Practice, counsellors are expected to invite people considering donation of gametes and embryos to consider in particular:

(i) The reasons for wanting to provide donated gametes and

(ii) Their attitudes to resulting children and their willingness to forego future knowledge and responsibility in respect of such children and

(iii) The possibility of their own childlessness and

(iv) Their perception of the needs of children born as a result of their donation and

(v) Their perception of the needs of any existing or future children of their own and

(vi) Possibility, with embryo donation, of the existence of full genetic siblings to their own children, resulting from their donation and

(vii) Their attitudes to allowing embryos produced from their gametes to be used for research.

NOTES:

1. Currently the Code of Practice requires screening for cystic fibrosis, Tay-Sachs disease, thalassaemia, sickle cell anaemia, HIV and cytomegalovirus (CMV) antibodies (paras 4.13–16.)

2. Under the 1990 Act the maximum storage period for gametes was 10 years. (We deal with the issue of embryo storage below at pp.835–841.) Where the gametes were supplied by a person under the age of 45 for their own subsequent use and their fertility has since become or is likely to become impaired, the Human Fertilisation and Embryology (Statutory Storage Period) Regulations 1991 (SI 1991/1540) provides for those periods to be extended as follows:

   > 2. (1) In the circumstances specified in paragraph (2) below, section 14(3) of the Human Fertilisation and Embryology Act 1990 . . . shall have effect in respect of any gametes as if for ten years there were substituted the appropriate period specified in the Schedule to these Regulations.
   > (2) The circumstances referred to in paragraph (1) are that the gametes were provided by a person—
   >
   > (a) whose fertility since providing them has or is likely to become, in the written opinion of a registered medical practitioner, significantly impaired.
   > (b) who was aged under 45 on the date on which the gametes were provided, and
   > (c) who does not consent to the gametes being used for the purpose of providing treatment services to persons other than that person, or that person and another together, and never has so consented while the gametes were ones to which this regulation applied.

3. Note that the consent provisions in Sch.3 are unusually stringent in requiring all consent to be in writing, following adequate counselling. However, notwithstanding this, the difficulties to which the requirement can give rise are demonstrated by *In Re D (A Child Appearing by her Guardian ad Litem)* [2005] UKHL 33 (See p.823, Note 1 below).

4. The HFEA has recently conducted a major review of gamete and embryo donation in the UK (HFEA, *SEED Report: a Report of the Human Fertilisation and Embryology Authority's review of sperm, egg and embryo donation in the United Kingdom*, London, 2005; *http://www.hfea.gov.uk/ AboutHFEA/HFEAPolicy/SEEDReview)* (hereafter the SEED review) It recommended that rather than the HFEA setting standards in relation to screening for disease or conditions, that could be more appropriately done by expert groups from within the relevant braches of the medical profession, such as the British Andrology Society and British Fertility Society, who should in the future have responsibility for issuing revised guidance in this regard (para.1.6). The HFEA would continue to have a role in monitoring compliance with the guidance.

5. Under the current Code of Practice licensed clinics are directed, where possible, to match the physical characteristics of the donor with those of the fertile partner, or of the woman seeking treatment if she is single.

However, in practice the limited number of donors often makes this impossible. Given this, the SEED Review recommends (at para.2.7) that the HFEA should produce only non-prescriptive guidance on issues to be taken into account in selecting appropriate donors.

6. In relation to limitations on the number of donors, the Warnock Committee (at para.4.26) suggested that any single sperm donor should only be permitted to "father" up to 10 children as a result of donor insemination. While this recommendation was not incorporated in the 1990 Human Fertilisation and Embryology Act, it was subsequently inserted in the Code of Practice (see paras 8.30–32 of the 6th edition). The SEED Review proposes a change to the way of calculating limits on the number of donors from one based on the number of live births to one based on number of families, in order to avoid fears of persons who are genetically related unknowingly reproducing. It proposes that while "donors should continue to be able to set their own limits on the use of their gametes which must never be exceeded, gametes from an individual donor should not be used to produce children for more than 10 families in the UK" (para.3.9).

7. Another significant ethico-legal issue arising out of gamete donation is the issue of whether children born as a result of donated gametes should be allowed to trace the donors. This is considered at pp.830–835 below when we consider the impact of reproductive technologies on the family, and address there the issue of whether children have a right to know their genetic parentage.

QUESTIONS:

1. Do you agree with Warnock's conclusion that DI should only be legally permissible when conducted through a statutorily licensed organisation? Do safety considerations justify subjecting gamete donation to the jurisdiction of the HFEA? If so, should the HFEA continue to oversee the relevant guidance in this area, or can this be entrusted to professional bodies, as the SEED review proposes? (Note also here the impact of the EU Tissue and Cells Directive 2004.)

2. Do you agree that the number of donations from any one sperm donor should be limited? If so, on what basis?

3. Warnock regarded DI as a "legitimate form of treatment" for couples. Should this include lesbian couples? What about single women? Is it ethically wrong for the medical profession to assist in the creation of fatherless children (see further pp.821–824 below)?

4. Given the shortage of donor eggs, was it justifiable for Parliament to ban the retrieval of eggs from aborted female foetuses, in the Criminal Justice and Public Order Act 1994? That legislation referred to female germlines rather than eggs, because of doubt about whether the term "gametes" covered immature eggs. Are different issues raised if eggs could be extracted from cadavers? (See the discussion of research on foetal tissue in Chapter 15 at p.1124, Note 3). More recent reports have suggested that stem cell research (see Chapter 10 at pp.725–734 affords the potential of

creating artificial sperm and eggs from stem cells. What ethico-legal issues, if any, do you think the culturing of artificial gametes would raise? (See D. Adam "Faking babies", *The Guardian*, May 19, 2005; J. Meikle, "Sperm and eggs could be created from stem cells, says new study", *The Guardian*, June 20, 2006.)

5. Are children born of donated gametes and embryos, or via IVF or surrogacy likely to be harmed in physical or psychosocial ways by collaborative reproduction, which involves a mixture of genetic, gestational and social parental roles? (See further pp.828–835 below; and J.A. Laing and D.S. Oderberg, "Artificial Reproduction, the 'Welfare Principle', and the Common Good" (2005) 13 *Medical Law Review* 328.) In what ways might any such harms manifest themselves?

6. Is egg donation analogous to organ or tissue donation? (See F. Price, "The Donor, the Recipient and the Child—Human Egg Donations in U.K. Licensed Centres" (1995) 7 *Child and Family Law Quarterly* 145.)

7. Are there valid ethical objections to permitting any woman who wishes to delay child-bearing to have her eggs frozen during her 20s when they are in peak condition, and re-implanted when she decides that she wishes to have a child?

8. In general, should a donor be screened for genetic disorders to determine whether she is an unwitting carrier of a genetic disease?

(i) Payment for Gametes

The question of payment for gametes has proven very controversial. Human gametes are widely available for sale over the internet, although obviously the purchase of sperm or eggs which do not come within the jurisdiction of the HFEA carries safety risks, as they will not be adequately screened and the rules concerning legal parentage under the 1990 Act would not apply. There has always been a shortage of donor eggs and it remains to be seen what impact the removal of sperm donor anonymity will have on sperm donation rates. Some commentators have advocated that remuneration should be allowed for those who permit their gametes to be used. Similar arguments about commodification are raised in the context of surrogacy (see pp.796–797 below) and as a way of overcoming shortages of organs and tissue for use in transplantation and research (see Chapter 15).

Section 12(e) of the Human Fertilisation and Embryology Act provides that "no money or other benefit may be given in respect of any supply of gametes or embryos unless authorised by [HFEA] directions".

Under a direction issued in 1991 (as amended in 1998), donors currently may be paid up to £15, plus "reasonable expenses" or benefits in kind—a position inserted in the 2003 Code of Practice (paras 4.2–3 and 4.26 of the HFEA Code of Practice, 2003).

This position, however, potentially contravenes the EU Tissues and Cells Directive 2004:

Article 12:

Member States shall endeavour to ensure voluntary and unpaid donations of cells and tissues.

Donors may receive compensation, which is strictly limited to making good the expenses and inconveniences related to the donation. In that case, Member States define the conditions under which compensation may be granted.

The current position on payment to gamete donors was reviewed in a major HFEA report which has significant implications for the next edition of the Code of Practice:

HFEA, SEED Report: a Report of the Human Fertilisation & Embryology Authority's review of sperm, egg and donation in the United Kingdom, London, 2005

5.1 Discussion of compensation payments to gamete donors has been ongoing since the HFEA first commenced its powers in 1991. The HFEA has always advocated the principle of non-payment although, recognising the persistent difficulty in recruiting donors, it has not so far imposed this on clinics. Instead, donors have been permitted to receive £15 in respect of each donation, as well as reimbursement of expenses. However, the regulatory environment within which gamete and embryo donation takes place is changing [with the adoption of the EU Tissues and Cells Directive [above] . . .

5.3 Despite the limitations of the Directive, some respondents to the consultation argued that donors should be free to sell their gametes on an unregulated market. Others said that compensation should be given in recognition of the disruption and physical inconvenience associated with gamete donation or even for the small health risk borne by egg donors.

5.4 Whilst some argued that donors were entitled to these payments, the assumption that additional monetary compensation would have an effect on the number of donors was widely challenged in the evidence we collected. Many respondents to the consultation, notably donors, said that compensation was largely unimportant and may even deter truly altruistic donors. Many felt that greater advertising and public awareness of the need for donors would have a greater effect on the number coming forward . . . .

5.5 In the course of the review we sought additional evidence from the authorities involved in blood, tissue and organ donation in the UK. This confirmed that payment for personal inconvenience (as distinct from expense and loss of earning) is not offered in return for blood, tissue or organ donation. There are a number of practical, as well as ethical, reasons for this, many of which may be applicable to gamete donation. Those reasons included the concern that additional payment might encourage donors to disregard risk to their health or to withhold medical information, or that it might attract donors whose motives, when disclosed, could be difficult for offspring to come to terms. Considerations like these moved some consultation respondents to say that donors should not be compensated at all, because any compensation was indistinguishable from payment for gametes, or because, as donors, they felt that bearing these costs was part of the donation.

5.6 Most respondents felt that donors should not be "out of pocket" as a result of donation and that there are costs, principally loss of earnings for which donors are entitled to be compensated. This is consistent with current practice in tissue and organ donation. It was generally acknowledged, however, that the value of such "hidden costs" might be difficult to establish for a number of reasons (such as donors being unwilling to disclose the reason for their absence to employers).

5.7 Among those supporting compensation for loss of earnings there were different opinions about whether there should be a maximum limit or even whether, for practical reasons, it would be desirable to offer a standardised level of compensation. At the stakeholder meeting, for example, a consensus emerged that a "flat rate" for donors should be considered as long as this was thought to be consistent with the requirements of the Directive. Sums suggested were £15 per donation for sperm donors and £300–500 per cycle for non patient egg donors.

5.8 Another argument put in favour of a standardised level of compensation was highly variable costs could end up being passed on to recipients, resulting in variations in charges for treatment with gametes from different donors. Others argued that if donors' variable costs were not always met and some maximum or standard rate was imposed, this might lead to some donors either losing out financially or declining to donate and to clinics focusing their recruitment efforts on "cheaper" donors.

Following the SEED Review, new directions on payment for gametes were published under s.12(e). These came into force on April 1, 2006 and revoke Directions D.1998/1.

Directions Ref D.2006/1

2. Individual donors of gametes may be given money or other benefits for the supply of their gametes, subject to the conditions of these Directions.

3. In money or money's worth, a donor may be reimbursed reasonable expenses which he or she has incurred, within the UK, in connection with the donation.

4. Donors may be compensated for loss of earnings (but not for other costs or inconveniences) up to a daily maximum of £55.19 but with an overall limit of £250 (or the equivalent in local currency) for each course of sperm donation or each cycle of egg donation.

5. There is no restriction on the value of other benefits which may be given to the donor, but the only benefits which may be offered for this purpose are treatment services. These services should be provided to the donor in the course of the donation cycle unless there is a medical reason why they cannot be provided at that time.

6. No establishment may accept as a donor any individual who is known by that establishment to have received or to be about to receive, or who is reasonably suspected by that establishment to have received or to be about to receive:

(a) money or money's worth in excess of reasonable expenses incurred in connection with the donation or compensation for loss of earnings permitted by these Directions;
   or
(b) other benefits of a kind not permitted to be given under these Directions, received through the means of and/or with the assistance of any agency or other intermediary.

NOTES:

1. "Other benefits" is defined as "services and benefits which cannot be measured in money". This could include treatment in exchange for egg donation (see p.775 below).

2. Kath O'Donnell suggests that many of the ethico-legal problems thrown up by commodification of gametes arise from the failure of Warnock and the 1990 legislation to address the legal status of gametes, which as a result is incoherent. She argues that the "legislation seems to compromise by stringent informed consent provisions, but this simply reaffirms the ambiguous status of gametes: they have the characteristics of a 'hybrid' or tightly limited form of property, despite official insistence that it is not property at all." (K. O'Donnell, "Legal Conceptions: Regulating Gametes and Gamete Donation" (2000) 8 *Health Care Analysis*, 137 at p.144. (See further the discussion of the *Blood* case at p.765 above.)

QUESTIONS:

1. Should gamete donors be paid for their services? If so, should they receive payment over and above reasonable expenses? If so, what level of payment is appropriate? If sperm donors should be paid, what would be appropriate payment for egg donation? Do you agree with the figures suggested in the SEED Review? (Compare this with the issue of payment for body parts in Chapter 15, or for surrogacy below.)

2. If spare eggs are produced as a result of administering fertility drugs, and are not donated or sold, how should they be disposed of?

3. The Canadian Assisted Human Reproduction Act 2004 makes it a criminal offence to buy, sell or trade in human eggs, sperm or embryos. Should the United Kingdom Government follow suit?

4. What criminal offence, if any, is committed, or what property rights violated, when "surplus" embryos are destroyed? (See A. Capron, "Alternative Birth Technologies: Legal Challenges" (1987) 20 *University of California at Davis Law Review* 679.)

(ii) Egg Sharing

In recognition of the obstacles to obtaining an adequate supply of donated eggs, the HFEA does permit a practice known as "egg sharing" whereby a woman undergoing IVF treatment, from whom "surplus" eggs have been procured, may agree to donate those eggs to another patient, in return for some free treatment. In recognition of the potential for conflicts of interest between egg provider and recipient, the HFEA has issued guidance on egg sharing which is designed to comply with Direction 2006/1 above on payment for gamete donation, and which will ultimately be incorporated in the 7th edition of the Code of Practice.

HFEA Practice Guidance Note: Egg Sharing (2006)

Information

3. Before the egg sharing cycle begins egg providers and recipients should be provided with separate written information which should include:

(i) a description of the criteria used for the selection of women providing and receiving eggs in egg sharing arrangements
(ii) a description of how the centre proposes to determine the allocation of eggs between provider and recipient(s)
(iii) a description of the screening that a woman providing eggs in an egg sharing arrangement will undergo
(iv) a description of the terms of the agreement to be entered into
(v) a description of the law relating to consent, in particular the rights of a woman providing eggs to vary or withdraw her consent and the implications of her doing so
(vi) a description of available alternative treatment options

Consent

4. The egg provider's consent should be recorded in such a way as to allow different conditions to be placed on the use of eggs and the use and storage of embryos created for

the egg provider's own treatment, on the one hand, from conditions placed on the use of eggs and the use and storage of embryos created for the treatment of the recipient(s), on the other hand.

5. Centres should emphasise to both the egg provider and recipient(s) that the egg provider may withdraw or vary her consent up to the time that an egg, or embryo created using her eggs, is transferred to a woman, used in a project of research or allowed to perish. The possible consequences of this should be made clear to both the egg provider and the recipient(s) before the egg sharing cycle begins and should be set out in the written patient information included with the egg sharing agreement.

Counselling

6. Independent counsellors should be aware of the medical procedures and the legal and social issues relevant to egg sharing arrangements.

7. Centres should encourage couples who intend to participate in an egg sharing arrangement to undergo implications counselling. Counselling should cover:

  (i) the implications of receiving information about the outcome of the treatment of the person(s) with whom the eggs are shared
 (ii) the implications of either the egg sharer or recipient(s), both the egg sharer and recipient(s), or neither the egg sharer nor recipient(s) having a live birth as a result of the treatment, in particular:
  (a) where both the provider and recipient(s) have a live birth, the implications of half-siblings who may not know each other being born and growing up as contemporaries
  (b) where a recipient has a live birth and the egg provider does not, the implications of a recipient having a live child whilst the egg provider might remain childless . . .

Egg sharing agreements

9. Licensed treatment centres offering an egg sharing arrangement should draw up separate agreements with the egg provider and with the egg recipient(s).

The centre's agreements with an egg provider and with those receiving eggs from that provider should be consistent with each other. Centres should abide by the terms of egg sharing agreements they have made.

10. Where benefits are offered to an egg provider those benefits should be given in connection with the cycle in which eggs are supplied for the treatment of a recipient unless there is a clinical reason to defer them. Where such a reason exists the egg provider may elect to donate all the eggs collected in the initial cycle and to take advantage of the benefits in a subsequent cycle.

11. Eggs collected from an egg provider in a single cycle should not be shared among more than two other recipients.

QUESTION:

1. Is it justifiable to offer treatment, such as sterilisation or IVF treatment cycles, at significantly reduced costs to women in return for a donation of eggs? Is this really distinguishable from paying women to donate eggs? Given estimates that 90 per cent of UK clinics have a donor egg shortage (H. Echlin, "How much would you pay for this?", *The Guardian*, July 25, 2005), which strategy to increase the supply of eggs (i.e. payment or egg sharing) would you support and why?

(b) In Vitro Fertilisation (IVF)

(i) Definitions and Attitudes

Compared to DI, IVF is a recent development in the treatment of infertility, dating from the birth of the first "test tube" baby—Louise Brown—in 1978. It is a unique form of reproductive technique in that fertilisation occurs outside the body. It thus brings the formerly invisible processes of fertilisation and early embryonic development into view, greatly extending the potential for medico-legal control of the reproductive process. IVF involves a three-stage process. First, multiple ovulation is induced in the woman by hormonal treatment and ovarian stimulation, in the same way as for egg donation (see p.775 above). Secondly, the ova are incubated with the sperm in a petri dish. A capacitating chemical may be used to endow sperm with the ability to pierce the egg's cellular wall. Thirdly, when the resulting zygote has developed to the 4–8 cell stage, it is transferred to the woman's uterine cavity in the hope that it will implant. At this stage the hormonal preparation of the woman and timing of the transfer are crucial in securing a successful implantation. If it is successful, pregnancy should be detectable 10–14 days later. As will be apparent, this treatment is extremely invasive and may have a significant impact on the health of the woman undergoing it. (See J. Raymond, *Women as Wombs: Reproductive technologies and the Battle over Women's Freedom*, New York: HarperCollins, 1994 at pp.9–14.)

Warnock Committee: Report of the Committee of Inquiry into Human Fertilisation and Embryology (1984) Cmnd. 9314, 1984 (footnotes omitted)

5.1 IVF is very much a new development. Of those women who are infertile a small proportion can produce healthy eggs but, although they have a normal uterus, have damaged or diseased fallopian tubes which prevent the egg passing from the ovary to the uterus. A certain proportion of these women can be helped by tubal surgery. Until IVF became a reality, the possibility of achieving a pregnancy for women with tubal problems was not great. IVF may be appropriate perhaps for 5 per cent of infertile couples. Recently claims have been made for IVF as a treatment for other forms of infertility including its use in the treatment of oligospermia and unexplained infertility . . .

5.5 Despite the technical difficulties of IVF, at the time we write, there have been some hundreds of such births throughout the world. These births continue to exercise considerable fascination. At the same time, this public interest creates, in itself, difficulties, adding to the pressure on doctors practising in this field who are not only trying to provide a new treatment for their patients, but are also constantly working in the public eye . . .

5.10 We have reached the conclusion that IVF is an acceptable means of treating infertility and *we therefore recommend that the service of IVF should continue to be available subject to the same type of licensing and inspection as we have recommended with regard to the regulation of [DI]* . . . For the protection and reassurance of the public this recommendation must apply equally to IVF within the NHS and in the private medical sector. At the present time IVF is available on a limited scale within the NHS and *we recommend that IVF should continue to be available within the NHS.* One member of the Inquiry would not like to see any expansion of NHS IVF services until the results obtained in using this technique are more satisfactory. IVF requires a concentration of skilled medical and scientific expertise, and it is appropriate for only a small proportion of infertile couples. Therefore we would not argue that it should be available at all district general hospitals, or even at all university teaching hospitals. However in order to minimise travelling and other inconvenience to patients, we believe that ultimately NHS centres should be distributed throughout the United Kingdom. We recognise that there will be those who will press for at least one in every region.

5.11 We are conscious that such specialised units with their distinctive organisational features, would have considerable cost implications. We are also mindful that IVF is only one of a range of treatments for infertility and . . . [that] there is scope for improvement in the provision of infertility services generally. We would not want to see IVF with its present relatively low success rate, cream off all the resources available for the treatment of infertility just because it has the glamour of novelty. Details of the financing of the service are outside our terms of reference, but these factors make it desirable that the early development of the service within the NHS be carefully monitored. *We recommend that one of the first tasks of the working group, whose establishment we recommend . . . should be to consider how best an IVF service can be organised within the NHS.*

NOTES:

1. There are a number of variations on the basic IVF procedure. In gamete intrafallopian transfer (GIFT), eggs harvested from a woman and sperm from her partner or a donor are injected into the woman's fallopian tube to enable fertilisation to occur *in vivo*. In some cases it appears to have a higher success rate than IVF, but it is not appropriate where a woman's fallopian tubes are damaged. As with IVF, ovarian hyperstimulation is a problem as is a higher risk of multiple pregnancy, since it is not open to the same degree of monitoring as IVF. ZIFT is a variation of GIFT in which the fertilised egg/zygote is transferred into the fallopian tube at the pronuclear stage when it is one day old. IUI (intra-uterine insemination) involves the insertion of sperm into the uterus of the woman. ICSI (intra cytoplasmic sperm injection) is a technique in which a sperm is injected into an egg using a fine glass needle. The technique was pioneered in Belgium in 1992, and is used in cases of low sperm count or low sperm motility or where there are high levels of antibodies in the semen. It has prompted health and safety concerns in relation to children born as a result of ICSI, as it has been linked to genetic and developmental defects, with some studies suggesting a rate of chromosomal abnormalities of the order of 3 per cent, whereas in the general population the rate is around 0.6 per cent (HFEA leaflet, ICSI, undated; for more information on the techniques see HFEA, *The HFEA Guide to Infertility 2005/6*). One important effect of ICSI has been how its increasing use has made men more visible as IVF patients, whereas in the past, as Thomson has noted, women were "over-implicated" as patients in this field (C. Thompson, *Making Parents: the Ontological Choreography of Reproductive Technologies*, Cambridge, Massachusetts: MIT Press, 2005 at p.121).

2. It would appear that GIFT and IUI fall outside the regulatory scheme of the 1990 Act, as s.1(3) states that the Act "applies only to keeping or using an embryo outside the human body". However, the difficulty of determining precisely when fertilisation takes place means that there is a possibility with GIFT that fertilisation could occur outside the body, thus bringing it within the regulatory scheme of the Act. (See G. Douglas, *Law, Fertility*

and Reproduction London: Sweet & Maxwell, 1991 at pp.117–118, and D. Morgan, "Assisted Conception and Clinical Practice: Whose Freedom Is It?" (1990) 140 New L.J. 600.) In any event, these procedures are now to be subject to regulation under the EU Tissues and Cells Directive 2004, although at the time of writing in mid-2006 the Department of Health estimate that it will not be fully implemented until autumn 2007 (Department of Health, *EU Directive on Tissues and Cells 2004/23/EC: Update on Implementation*, October 2005.)

(ii) IVF—A Proven Success?

A contested issue is the success rate of IVF. Even proponents of the technologies have to admit that success rates for IVF are low, and that they vary tremendously from one clinic to another. Moreover, according to the European Society for Human Reproduction and Embryology, UK clinics have one of the lowest success rates in Europe, recording a success rate of 28.6 per cent pregnancy rates (compared to 40.5 per cent in Belgium) (L. Rogers, "British fertility clinics at foot of IVF league", *Sunday Times*, March 26, 2006). Of course such indices of success depend crucially on how many cycles of IVF are offered and whether success is measured in terms of pregnancy or actually having a healthy baby at the end of the procedure. As rates of miscarriage are high (around 28 per cent), the most satisfactory measure of success is the "live birth" rate. For UK clinics this averages about 22 per cent (HFEA, *Response to the Toft Report*, 2004; HFEA, *The HFFEA Guide to Infertility 2005/6.*) Critics have suggested that the huge demand for IVF is surprising, since it is stressful, expensive if carried out privately, necessitates bodily invasion, has a number of side-effects ranging from dizziness to ovarian hyperstimulation and cysts and the possible long-term effects, e.g. ovarian cancer, and its success rates are low. (See J. Raymond, *Women as Wombs: Reproductive Technologies and the Battle over Women's Freedom*, San Francisco: HarperCollins, 1993, Chapter 1.) More recently the Medical Research Council has expressed concerns about the safety of these technologies. A Working Group found that "little research has been done to show whether [innovations in ART (assisted reproductive tecnology)] are superior to conventional procedures, and in particular what the long-term health implications might be for the mother or the resulting child" (MRC, *Assisted Reproduction: a Safe, Sound Future*, 2004, p.2). It recommended that existing provisions for monitoring by the HFEA were inadequate to allay safety concerns and that "A new approach should be adopted which encourages the use of high-quality clinical trials or other appropriate methodologies to evaluate ARTs" (MRC, *op. cit.* at p. 12; see also "Controversial conceptions" (letters, *The Guardian*, May 9, 2006; "IVF Risk of Pregnancy Complication", *BioEdge* May 30, 2006). As we noted above, such concerns may be especially acute in relation to particular technologies, such as ICSI.

QUESTIONS:

1. To what extent should societal resources be devoted to developing techniques for the alleviation of infertility? Is such expense justified when

the "solutions" work only for a relatively small percentage of those seeking treatment?

2. In the light of factors like the low success rate, expense and risks of IVF treatment, what factors do you think account for its popularity? Given these factors do you think that there is a problem in ensuring that consent to IVF treatment is truly voluntary? (See Chapter 6, pp.397–402 and B.J. Berg, "Listening to the Voices of the Infertile" in J.C. Callaghan (edn), *Reproduction, Ethics and the Law: Feminist Perspectives*, Bloomington and Indianapolis: Indiana University Press, 1995.)

3. Is the safety of IVF procedures sufficiently well established to qualify as proven medical treatment, or are some procedures, at least, better regarded as research, as suggested by the MRC at note 3 above? (See further Chapter 10.)

A further problem with IVF, fuelled by concern about success rates, has been the issue of multiple order births. Since a clinic's success rate can be enhanced if they replace more embryos per cycle, a potential conflict is introduced between the interests of the woman and clinic, as pressure to achieve high success rates may lead clinics to downplay the adverse consequences which multiple pregnancy may have for the health of the pregnant woman. Under the 2001 HFEA Code of Practice (paras 8.20–22), clinics are limited to implanting two embryos in any one treatment cycle unless the woman is over 40 (in which case three embryos may be implanted) in order to reduce the problems of selective reduction (see Chapter 12 at p.883) and the issues (including financial costs to the NHS) associated with multiple births. The high incidence of multiple births in successful IVF cases (around 23 per cent) has increased pressure to bring UK practice into line with some other European jurisdictions, where single embryo transfer is the norm. (See J. Meikle, "'One embryo' rule to cut multiple births in IVF", *The Guardian*, July 29, 2005; S. Hall. "Single embryos for older women could cut risk of multiple pregnancy", *The Guardian*, June 1, 2006.)

Notwithstanding this trend, some doctors have vociferously contested the HFEA's policy on embryo replacement, arguing that older women in particular are disadvantaged by a policy which limits the number of embryos that can be implanted. In one case a 46-year-old woman wanted five embryos which had been created to be implanted in a single cycle and sought a judicial review of the HFEA's (then) policy of only permitting three embryos to be transferred. The appellant was supported by her doctor, but the Court of Appeal upheld Ouseley J.'s view at first instance that the appellant had succeeded in showing only that two views were possible and not that the HFEA's decision was irrational.

R. (on the application of the Assisted Reproduction and Gynaecology Centre) and Another v HFEA [2003] 1 F.C.R. 266, CA

WALL J.
"[The HFEA] thought that future treatment for Mrs H was likely to fail but that, if she did succeed in becoming pregnant, there would be a higher risk of multiple pregnancy if five

embryos had been transplanted rather than three. The authority therefore considered that the possible marginal improvement in the chances of pregnancy were outweighed by the albeit small risk of multiple pregnancy . . .

Disagreements between doctors and scientific bodies in this pioneering field are inevitable . . . The authority is the body which is empowered by parliament to regulate. Like any public authority it is open to challenge by way of judicial review, if it exceeds or abuses the powers and responsibilities given to it by parliament; but where, as is manifest here from an examination of the facts, it considers requests for advice carefully and thoroughly, and produces opinions which are plainly rational, the court, in our judgment, has no part to play in the debate, and certainly no power to intervene to strike down any such decision. The fact that the appellants may disagree with the Authority's advice is neither here nor there."

NOTES:

1. Although this policy has continued to attract criticism from medical specialists (see I. Sample, "IVF embryo limit failing older women, warns specialist", *The Guardian*, October 18, 2005), the HFEA have announced a review of the current policy and are considering tightening existing restrictions so that only single embryo transfer should be permitted per cycle (see HFEA press release, "Fertility regulator looks to reduce the risks of IVF treatment", July 28, 2005). The HFEA have announced that a public consultation on this issue will take place in 2007.

2. In the earlier case of *Thompson v Sheffield Fertility Clinic* [2001] (unreported, accessible via Westlaw), a couple undergoing IVF treatment successfully sued for damages after the woman gave birth to triplets. Four embryos were created and three were transferred (in line with the Code of Practice in existence at the time), despite Mrs Thompson's express stipulation in her treatment plan that she wished only two embryos to be implanted, owing to her moral objections to abortion/foetal reduction. The award of damages was settled out of court.

QUESTION:

1. Would it be better to leave decisions about the numbers of embryos to be transferred to the discretion of the woman's doctor, taking account of the particular circumstances of her case?

(c) Surrogacy

(i) Definitions and Attitudes

Of all the alternative methods of conception, it is surrogacy which has provoked the most intense passion and the greatest public hostility, probably due to its very visible splitting of motherhood into genetic, gestational and social components (see M. Strathern, "Still Giving Nature a Helping Hand? Surrogacy: a Debate about Technology and Society" in R. Cook and S.D. Sclater with F. Kaganas (eds) *Surrogate Motherhood: International Perspectives*, Oxford: Hart, 2003, 281–298). The impact of surrogacy arrangements on definitions of motherhood and fatherhood is considered at p.828 below.

A surrogate pregnancy may be established through a variety of methods. "Partial surrogacy", which remains the most common form of arrangement, is where the carrying woman (the gestational or surrogate mother) is fertilised with the commissioning man's sperm either as a result of sexual intercourse or assisted insemination. Thus, she not only carries and gives birth to the baby, she also has a genetic link to it. "Full surrogacy" is where the commissioning couple provide both sperm and ovum so that the child is genetically entirely theirs, although carried by another woman. It necessarily involves the use of *in vitro* fertilisation (see section (b) above). Surrogacy can help alleviate infertility, where a woman suffers from severe pelvic disease, has no uterus, experiences repeated miscarriages, or where pregnancy is medically undesirable for other reasons. It is generally constructed as an option of last resort, and since it is relatively rare, may be regarded as on the fringes of infertility treatment.

The Warnock Committee neatly summarised the arguments for and against surrogacy.

Warnock Committee: Report of the Committee of Inquiry into Human Fertilisation and Embryology (1984) Cmnd. 9314

8.10 The objections turn essentially on the view that to introduce a third party into the process of procreation which should be confined to the loving partnership between two people, is an attack on the value of the marital relationship . . . Further, the intrusion is worse than in the case of [donor insemination], since the contribution of the carrying mother is greater, more intimate and personal, than the contribution of a semen donor. It is also argued that it is inconsistent with human dignity that a woman should use her uterus for financial profit and treat it as an incubator for someone's else's child. The objection is not diminished, indeed it is strengthened, where the woman entered an agreement to conceive a child, with the sole purpose of handing the child over to the commissioning couple after birth.

8.11 Again, it is argued that the relationship between mother and child is itself distorted by surrogacy . . . It is also potentially damaging to the child, whose bonds with the carrying mother, regardless of genetic connections, are held to be strong, and whose welfare must be considered to be of paramount importance. Further it is felt that a surrogacy agreement is degrading to the child who is to be the outcome of it, since, for all practical purposes, the child will have been bought for money.

8.12 It is also argued that since there are some risks attached to pregnancy, no woman ought to be asked to undertake pregnancy for another, in order to earn money. Nor, it is argued should a woman be forced by legal sanctions to part with a child, to which she has recently given birth, against her will.

8.13 If infertility is a condition which should, where possible, be remedied, it is argued that surrogacy must not be ruled out, since it offers to some couples their only chance of having a child genetically related to one or both of them. In particular, it may well be the only way that the husband of an infertile woman can have a child. Moreover, the bearing of a child for another can be seen, not as an undertaking that trivialises or commercialises pregnancy, but, on the contrary, as a deliberate and thoughtful act of generosity on the part of one woman to another. If there are risks attached to pregnancy, then the generosity is all the greater.

8.14 There is no reason, it is argued, to suppose that carrying mothers will enter into agreements lightly, and they have a perfect right to enter into such agreements if they so wish, just as they have a right to use their own bodies in other ways, according to their own decision . . .

8.15 As for intrusion into the marriage relationship, it is argued that those who feel strongly about this need not seek such treatment, but they should not seek to prevent others from having access to it.

8.16 On the question of bonding, it is argued that as very little is actually known about the extent to which bonding occurs when the child is *in utero*, no great claims should be made in this respect. In any case the breaking of such bonds, even if less than ideal, is not held to be an overriding argument against placing a child for adoption, where the mother wants this.

Having outlined the pros and cons of surrogacy the Warnock Committee reached the following conclusion:

8.17. . . . [W]e are all agreed that a surrogacy for convenience alone, that is, where a woman is physically capable of bearing a child but does not wish to undergo pregnancy, is totally ethically unacceptable. Even in compelling medical circumstances the danger of exploitation of one human being by another appears to the majority of us far to outweigh the potential benefits, in almost every case. That people should treat others as a means to their own ends, however desirable the consequences, must always be liable to moral objection. Such treatment of one person by another becomes positively exploitative when financial interests are involved. It is therefore with the commercial exploitation of surrogacy that we have been primarily, but by no means exclusively, concerned.

8.18. . . . *We recommend that legislation be introduced to render criminal the creation or the operation in the United Kingdom of agencies whose purposes include the recruitment of women for surrogate pregnancy or making arrangements for individuals or couples who wish to utilise the services of a carrying mother; such legislation should be wide enough to include both profit and non-profit making organisations. We further recommend that the legislation be sufficiently wide to render criminally liable the actions of professionals and others who knowingly assist in the establishment of a surrogate pregnancy.*

8.19 We do not envisage that this legislation would render private persons entering into surrogacy arrangements liable to criminal prosecution, as we are anxious to avoid children being born to mothers subject to the taint of criminality. We nonetheless recognise that there will continue to be privately arranged surrogacy agreements. While we consider that most, if not all, surrogacy arrangements would be legally unenforceable in any of their terms, we feel that the position should be put beyond any possible doubt in law. We recommend that it be provided by statute that all surrogacy agreements are illegal contracts and therefore unenforceable in the courts.

NOTE:

1. Commentators are virtually unanimous that the Warnock Committee's recommendations on surrogacy represent the weakest stage of the report, since the conclusions appear to have been based on public opposition to the practice rather than any considered philosophical position. (See M. Freeman, "Is surrogacy exploitative?" in S. McLean (ed.), *Legal Issues in Human Reproduction*, Aldershot: Gower, 1989; S. Lee, "Re-reading Warnock" in P. Byrne (ed.), *Rights and Wrongs in Medicine*, London: King Edward's Hospital Fund, 1986; M. Lockwood, "The Warnock Report: a Philosophical Appraisal" in M. Lockwood (ed.), *Modern Dilemmas in Modern Medicine*, Oxford: Oxford University Press, 1985; S. Roberts, "Warnock and Surrogate Motherhood: Sentiment or Argument" in Byrne *op. cit.* For a considered philosophical argument against surrogacy, see R. Hursthouse, *Beginning Lives*, Oxford: Blackwell, 1987.)

QUESTIONS:

1. Do you agree with the Warnock Committee's conclusions on this issue? Compare and contrast the Warnock proposals on surrogacy with those on *in vitro* fertilisation (discussed at p.777 above) and embryo research (see Chapter 10 at pp.721–734).

2. Do you think that the case against surrogacy is really grounded in arguments which oppose *commercial* surrogacy rather than the practice *per se*? Can commercial and altruistic surrogacy be distinguished? (Compare S. McLean, "Mother and Others: the Case for Surrogacy" in E. Sutherland and A. McCall Smith (eds), *Family Rights: Family Law and Medical Advance*, Edinburgh: Edinburgh University Press, 1990 with U. Narayan, "The Gift of a Child: Commercial Surrogacy, Gift Surrogacy and Motherhood" in P. Boling (ed.), *Expecting Trouble: Surrogacy, Foetal Abuse and New Reproductive Technologies*, Boulder, Colorado: Westview Press, 1995; see also E. Blyth and C. Potter, "Paying for it: Surrogacy, Market Forces and Assisted Conception" in R. Cook and S.D. Sclater with F. Kaganas (eds), *Surrogate Motherhood: International Perspectives*, Oxford: Hart, 2003, 227–242)

3. Do you agree with Freeman that, whereas Warnock strongly endorses the principles of autonomy and self-determination on issues like DI, IVF and egg and embryo donation, on the issue of surrogacy the report reverts to the paternalism and moralism which it had elsewhere eschewed, citing public opinion as justification? (See M. Freeman, "Is Surrogacy Exploitative?" in S. McLean (ed.), *Legal Issues in Human Reproduction*, Aldershot: Dartmouth, 1989.) If you agree that Warnock was overly paternalistic on this issue, who do you think was the object of such paternalism? Was its paternalism directed at the woman who wants a child, the carrying mother, the child, or the family unit?

4. Is the "work" involved in pregnancy and birth analogous to other forms of human labour which are the subject of contracts of employment? (See E. Anderson, "Is Women's Labor a Commodity?" (1990) 19 *Philosophy and Public Affairs* 71; M.L. Shanley, "Surrogate Mothering and Women's Freedom: a Critique of Contracts for Human Reproduction" in Boling, *op. cit.* in note 2). Can surrogacy be regarded as particularly exploitative? (See A. Wertheimer, "Two Questions about Surrogacy and Exploitation" (1992) 21 *Philosophy and Public Affairs* 211; L. Purdy, *Reproducing Persons: Issues in Feminist Bioethics*, Ithaca: Cornell University Press, 1996, Chapter 11.)

(ii) Judicial Attitudes towards Surrogacy

Although surrogacy is commonly discussed as part of a package of "reproductive technologies" it can, of course, like DI, be performed very simply without professional intervention. However, as with DI, its use has been shrouded in secrecy, making it difficult to establish the extent to which it has been practised. (See D. Morgan, "Surrogacy: an Introductory Essay" in R. Lee and D. Morgan (eds), *Birth Rights: Law and Ethics at the Beginnings of Life*, London: Routledge, 1989.) This difficulty in establishing accurate figures was also noted by the Brazier Review (see p.797 below) which estimated that there are between 100 and 180 surrogacy arrangements made each year in the UK (see M. Brazier, A. Campbell and S. Golombok, *Surrogacy: a Review for Health Ministers of Current Arrangements for Payment and Regulation*, London: The Stationary Office, 1998, para.6.22).

The first surrogacy case to be litigated in the UK was heard in 1978 (albeit reported in 1984), at a time when reproductive techniques were becoming a subject of public controversy, following the birth of Louise Brown, the first "test tube" baby. Compare judicial attitudes to surrogacy in the following two cases:

A v C [1985] F.L.R. 445, [1984] Fam. Law 241

This case concerned an unmarried couple in which the woman, who had children from a previous relationship, was unable to have any further children. Her partner, A, had a very strong desire to raise his own biological child. He found a woman, C, who was prepared to be inseminated with his sperm and agreed to hand the baby over at birth for adoption by him and his partner in return for a payment of £3,000. However, after the birth she decided to keep the child and forgo the money. A commenced wardship proceedings seeking custody of the child. In court proceedings, Conwyn J. held that the child should remain a ward of court until majority or further order. C was given care and control of the child, the father was granted access, and a supervisory order was made in favour of the local authority. In the Court of Appeal strong disapproval of surrogacy was evident.

ORMROD L.J.

" . . . It is unnecessary to make any more comment on the irresponsibility shown by all three of the adults in this case, which is perhaps only rivalled by the irresponsibility of the person who performed the insemination on the mother . . . We are dealing here with two people who have never had any sort of relationship together at all, not even a relationship amounting to one single isolated act of intercourse taking place casually on some occasion and never to be repeated. Here we have nothing but the clinical fact that the father has contributed the necessary male sperm to the conception of this child. That is the sum total of his contribution to this child . . .

There is always a close physical bond between mother and child which tends to get closer from the time of birth onwards for some considerable time and then, perhaps, to slacken off a little as the child gets older. The bond between father and child operates in the opposite direction. At first it is very slight indeed, but gradually, as association between father and child increases and lengthens in time, the bond becomes more and more real and lasts, sometimes, longer — not always. In this case we have a situation where there is no bond between the father and the child except the mere biological one. There has never been any association, except of the most exiguous character, between the father and the mother. There has never been anything between them except a sordid commercial bargain. The father has only had the intermittent contact provided by access to a very young child over the past year. He has been very assiduous in maintaining that access, bringing with him his present wife, whose role in this case, as I have said before, fills me with sympathy. What her position can be in that house during periods of access, I find very hard to imagine. Her emotions must be very mixed and I feel sorry for her.

But what is the future? The mother is 21. She is almost certain, given the chance and a little peace from litigation or the strain of access, to marry and set up a family of which this child will be part. By far the best thing that can happen to this child is that he should become a member of a family just like other children. This will give him as normal a life as possible . . .

So what is the good of keeping this wholly artificial, painful tie going? My answer is: No good will be done whatever . . .

I can see absolutely no advantage to this child in continuing to be in contact with the father, except possibly a financial advantage to which I attach no significance whatever, in this case."

NOTES:

1. Stamp and Cumming-Bruce L.JJ. delivered concurring judgments. Cumming-Bruce L.J. added that the fact that a child was conceived through "artificial" means, as compared to natural methods of conception, could have no effect on the duty of a court to seek to afford the child a life that would best promote the child's welfare.

2. By contrast, in the next UK surrogacy case, *Re C (A Minor) (Wardship: Surrogacy)* [1985] F.L.R. 846 Latey J. held that the best interests of the child necessitated that she be handed over to the commissioning couple, who had contacted a North American agency which secured a British woman to bear Mr A's child in return for payment. A nurse performed the insemination with Mr A's sperm, and the commissioning couple never met the surrogate. The couple came to England for the birth and the surrogate mother voluntarily left the baby in hospital in the care of nurses while its future was determined. The local authority which had made the child a ward of court carried out inquiries into the suitability of the prospective parents and concluded by fully endorsing the application that the baby be given into the care of Mr and Mrs A. The judge commented:

   "Mr A is the baby's father and he wants her, as does his wife. The baby's mother does not want her. Mr and Mrs A are a couple in their 30s. They are devoted to each other. They are both professional people, highly qualified. They have a very nice home in the country and another in a town. Materially they can give the baby a very good upbringing. But, far more importantly, they are both excellently equipped to meet the baby's emotional needs. They are most warm, caring, sensible people, as well as highly intelligent."

The surrogate mother in this case, Kim Cotton, went on to co-found COTS (Childlessness Overcome Through Surrogacy), an agency which facilitates surrogacy arrangements (see p.790 below).

QUESTIONS:

1. It seems that Ormrod L.J.'s attitude to infertility in 1978 was simply that the infertile person or couple should learn to accept it. Do you think that many judges would adopt such an attitude today? Do judicial views on such contested issues reflect, or help to shape, public opinion?

2. Do you agree with the manner in which Ormrod L.J. dismissed the claims of the commissioning male partner, effectively reducing his status to that of

a sperm donor? In what ways, if any, can a man who commissions a surrogate pregnancy be distinguished from a sperm donor, given that his biological involvement is the same in both cases?

3. What assumptions about the welfare of children and family structures does Ormrod L.J. make in his judgment? Do you agree with them?
4. What factors explain the shift in judicial opinion which *Re C* seems to represent? Is the different outcome solely due to the fact that there was no dispute in this case? (See L. Foxcroft, "Surrogacy—Warnock and After" (1997) 2 *Medical Law International* 337.)

(iii) The Legislative Approach

In 1985 the United Kingdom became the first country to legislate on surrogacy, acting remarkably quickly in this instance on the Warnock proposals to ban commercial surrogacy. However the Act did not go so far as to endorse Warnock's suggestion that the actions of any third party who facilitated the arrangement should be banned regardless of whether they received money. (See S. Sloman, "Surrogacy Arrangements Act 1985" (1985) 135 New L.J. 978.)

Surrogacy Arrangements Act 1985, ss.1(1–1A) and 2(1–4)

1.—(1) The following provisions shall have effect for the interpretation of this Act.
(2) "Surrogate mother" means a woman who carries a child in pursuance of an arrangement—

(a) made before she began to carry the child, and
(b) made with a view to any child carried in pursuance of it being handed over to, and parental responsibility being met (so far as practicable) by, another person or other persons.

(3) An arrangement is a surrogacy arrangement if, were a woman to whom the arrangement relates to carry a child in pursuance of it, she would be a surrogate mother.
(4) In determining whether an arrangement is made with such a view as is mentioned in subsection (2) above regard may be had to the circumstances as a whole (and, in particular, where there is a promise or understanding that any payment will or may be made to the woman or for her benefit in respect of the carrying of any child in pursuance of the arrangement, to that promise or understanding).
(5) An arrangement may be regarded as made with such a view though subject to conditions relating to handing over of any child.
(6) A woman who carries a child is to be treated for the purposes of subsection (2)(a) above as beginning to carry it at the time of the insemination or of the placing in her of an embryo, of an egg in the process of fertilisation or of sperm and eggs, as the case may be, that results in her carrying the child.
(7) "Body of persons" means a body of persons corporate or unincorporated.
(8) "Payment" means payment in money or money's worth.
(9) This Act applies to arrangements whether or not they are lawful.
1A.—No surrogacy arrangement is enforceable by or against any of the persons making it.
2.—(1) No person shall on a commercial basis do any of the following acts in the United Kingdom, that is—

(a) initiate or take part in any negotiations with a view to the making of a surrogacy arrangement;
(b) offer or agree to negotiate the making of a surrogacy arrangement, or
(c) compile any information with a view to its use in making, or negotiating the making of, surrogacy arrangements;

and no person shall in the United Kingdom knowingly cause another to do any of those acts on a commercial basis.

(2) A person who contravenes subsection (1) above is guilty of an offence; but it is not a contravention of that subsection—

(a) for a woman, with a view to becoming a surrogate mother herself, to do any act mentioned in that subsection or to cause such an act to be done, or
(b) for any person, with a view to a surrogate mother carrying a child for him, to do such an act or to cause such an act to be done.

(3) For the purposes of this section, a person does an act on a commercial basis (subject to subsection (4) below) if—

(a) any payment is at any time received by himself or another in respect of it, or
(b) he does it with a view to any payment being received by himself or another in respect of making, or negotiating or facilitating the making of, any surrogacy arrangement.

In this subsection "payment" does not include payment to or for the benefit of a surrogate mother or prospective surrogate mother.

(4) In proceedings against a person for an offence under subsection (1) above, he is not to be treated as doing an act on a commercial basis by reason of any payment received by another in respect of the act if it is proved that—

(a) in a case where payment was received before he did the act, he did not do the act knowing or having reasonable cause to suspect that any payment had been received in respect of the act; and
(b) in any other case, he did not do the act with a view to any payment being received in respect of it.

NOTES:

1. Section 1A above was inserted by s.36(1) of the Human Fertilisation and Embryology Act 1990. This amendment provides legislative endorsement for the position adopted in *A v C* (above). Section 36(2) extends the meaning of a surrogacy arrangement to cover the placing in the woman of sperm and eggs, or of an egg in the process of fertilisation as well as embryo transfer.
2. Section 3 of the 1985 Act prohibits advertisements in relation to surrogacy arrangements.
3. The 1985 Act proscribes only the actions of commercial agencies or individuals seeking to profit from surrogacy. Thus, the commissioning couple and the surrogate mother do not commit any offence, even if she is paid. However, they may be guilty of an offence under ss.95–96 of the

Adoption and Children Act 2002 which makes it a criminal offence to give or receive payment (aside from expenses) in relation to the adoption of a child, unless such payment is authorised by a court.

4. In *Re: An Adoption Application* [1987] 2 All E.R. 826, the third case concerning surrogacy to come before the British courts and the first to be considered after the passage of the 1985 Act, the High Court indicated a willingness to assist a couple who wished to adopt a surrogate baby born as a result of intercourse between the surrogate and the husband. Even though the couple had paid £10,000 to the surrogate mother, thus appearing *prima facie* to have breached the prohibition on payment in the Adoption Act 1976 (the legislation then in force), Latey J. held that the payment was for expenses rather than to procure the gestational mother's consent to adoption. Moreover, he added that even if he was wrong on that point, the court could authorise such payments retrospectively, in the interests of the child. This case thus represented another step in the progressive liberalisation of judicial attitudes towards surrogacy arrangements. A similar approach has been adopted in subsequent cases. In these, the courts have been prepared to sanction retrospectively breaches of adoption law, where the child's interests are deemed to lie with the commissioning parents. In *Re MW (Adoption) (Surrogacy)* [1995] 2 F.L.R. 759, the court retrospectively authorised payments to the surrogate mother even though it acknowledged such payments to be unlawful (see G. Douglas, "Commentary on *Re MW*" [1995] Fam. Law 666). As we shall see (at p.828 below,) in many cases of surrogacy the commissioning couple will be eligible to apply for a parental order, thus bypassing the adoption process. In such cases the courts have also been prepared to retrospectively authorise unlawful payments. Thus, in *Re C (Application by Mr and Mrs X under s.30 of the Human Fertilisation and Embryology Act 1990)* [2002] 1 F.L.R. 909 the court sanctioned the payment of £12,000 to a surrogate, which included £2,000 for loss of earnings, even though it subsequently emerged that she was also claiming income support. Freeman suggests that even had the commissioning couple known that she was claiming benefits, the welfare of the child would nevertheless have dictated that the court ratify the payment. (See M. Freeman, "Medically Assisted Reproduction" in A. Grubb (ed.), *Principles of Medical Law* (2nd edn), Oxford: OUP, 2004, p.734.) See also *Re Q* [1996] 1 F.L.R. 369. Note, however, that the case of *Briody v St Helens & Knowsley Health Authority* [2002] 2 W.L.R. 394 (see p.792 below) demonstrates judicial unwillingness to authorise such payments in advance. In the High Court, Ebsworth J. noted: "[i]t is one thing for a court retrospectively to sanction breaches of statute in the paramount interests of an existing child, it is quite another to award damages to enable such an unenforceable and unlawful contract to be entered into".

5. Legislative policy towards surrogacy also appeared to be softening with the enactment of s.30 of the 1990 Human Fertilisation and Embryology Act, which came into force in 1995, and appears to run counter to the policy of discouraging surrogacy in the 1985 Act (see p.828 below).

6. Other case law provides further evidence of the judiciary's increasing willingness to facilitate surrogacy arrangements. Even though s.30 of the 1990 Human Fertilisation and Embryology Act (which provides for the grant of a court order that the commissioning couple should be regarded in law as the parents of the child, discussed further below at p.828) was not then in force, in *Re W (minors) (surrogacy)* [1991] 1 F.L.R. 385, Scott Baker J. was prepared to treat twins born as a result of a "total" surrogacy arrangement as the children of the commissioning couple. In his view the paramount issue was how to facilitate any steps which would ensure that the child would bond with the genetic parents. Again such reasoning underpins later cases like *Re C.*

7. The choice of statutory judicial language is significant. Notice how the gestational mother is labelled the surrogate (substitute) mother although she is what most people would have regarded as the "natural" mother. What are the political and legal consequences of using such language?

8. There have been no prosecutions under the 1985 Act, and it is estimated that in the UK over 500 babies have been born to surrogate mothers. The voluntary organisation COTS (see p.786 above) was formed to bring together potential surrogates and infertile couples. Under the Act it cannot charge for its services, and as a consequence lacks resources to fully screen surrogates or commissioning couples. A Bill aimed at strengthening this legislation, sponsored by the Earl of Halsbury, failed (Surrogacy Arrangements (Amendment) Bill 1986) and as we shall below, the Brazier Review has advocated its repeal. In 2004 another voluntary organisation— Surrogacy UK—was established. It is more ambitious in its claims to screen and counsel commissioning couples and potential surrogates. (Though see R. Cook, "Safety in the Multitude of Counsellors: Do We Need Counselling in Surrogacy?" and "Emotional Aspects of Surrogacy: a Case for Effective Counselling and Support", both in R. Cook and S.D. Sclater with F. Kaganas (eds), *Surrogate Motherhood: International Perspectives*, Oxford: Hart, 2003, pp.179–208)

QUESTIONS:

1. Why do you think that the UK Government was so quick to act on surrogacy, whereas it procrastinated for a further six years on the issue of embryo research? Also, why do you think it failed to accept fully the recommendations of the Warnock Committee on surrogacy, whereas ultimately Warnock's proposals on embryo research were enacted (see Chapter 10 at pp.721–723)?

2. Would you agree with Freeman that the Act represents "an ill-considered and largely irrelevant panic measure"? (See M. Freeman, "Is Surrogacy Exploitative?" in S. McLean (ed.), *Legal Issues in Human Reproduction*, Aldershot: Dartmouth, 1989, at p.165.) Does it demonstrate the dangers of legislating too early before some sort of social, moral and public consensus has built up? Is such a consensus likely to accrue on an issue like surrogacy?

3. Is the strategy of applying criminal penalties only to those involved in facilitating surrogacy for commercial ends morally and rationally defensible? (Compare M. Gibson, "Contract Motherhood: Social Practice in Social Context" in C. Feinman (ed.), *Criminalization of a Woman's Body*, New York: The Haworth Press, 1992 with U. Narayan, "The 'Gift' of a Child: Commercial Surrogacy, Gift Surrogacy and Motherhood" in P. Rolling (ed.), *Expecting Trouble: Surrogacy, Foetal Abuse and New Reproductive Technologies*, Boulder, Colorado: Westview Press, 1995.)

4. Would it have been a better policy to stop short of banning commercial arrangements altogether and have regulated them instead? If so, in what ways would you have sought to regulate the practice? (See further p.797 below.)

5. Does the legislative failure to enforce surrogacy contracts violate the commissioning parties' "right to procreate"? (Compare J. Robertson, "Embryos, Families and Procreative Liberty: the Legal Structure of the New Reproduction" (1986) 59 *Southern California Law Review* 942 with M. Lyndon Shanley, " 'Surrogate Mothering' and Women's Freedom: a Critique of Contracts for Human Reproduction" in Rolling, *op. cit.* in note 3)

Although the 1985 Act made the position of commercial agencies clear, it failed to provide any ethical guidance for doctors who might be approached to facilitate the establishment of a surrogate pregnancy. In 1990 the British Medical Association published the report of a Working Party on Surrogacy it had established in response to a resolution passed at its Annual Representative Meeting calling for the production of ethical guidelines in relation to surrogacy. The report was extremely hostile to the practice of surrogacy and discouraged medical professionals from facilitating it (see BMA, *Surrogacy: Ethical Considerations*, Report of the Working Party on Human Infertility Services, 1990). However, in recognition of the increased prevalence and acceptability of surrogacy, the BMA later issued revised guidance, which evidenced a more tolerant attitude:

Changing Conceptions of Motherhood: the Practice of Surrogacy in Britain, London: BMA, 1996

Guidelines for Health Professionals

1. Surrogacy is an acceptable option of last resort in cases where it is impossible or highly undesirable for medical reasons for the intended mother to carry a child herself. In all cases the interests of the potential child must be paramount and the risks to the surrogate mother must be kept to a minimum.

2. Health professionals consulted about a surrogacy arrangement should inform themselves about the legal position before offering advice. In particular, health professionals should be aware of the non-enforceability of surrogacy arrangements and the legal position with regard to parentage of the child . . .

5. Practitioners approached by people considering self-insemination should encourage those concerned to consider the issues and implications very carefully and should ensure

that they are aware of how to obtain accurate information about the medical, psycho-logical, emotional and legal issues involved with the surrogacy.

6. Before agreeing to provide licensed treatment services aimed at establishing a surrogate pregnancy, for example through *in vitro* fertilisation or donor insemination, the health care team must take all reasonable steps to ensure that the medical, emotional and legal issues have been carefully considered and must, in all cases, take account of the welfare of the child who may be born as a result of the treatment. Such treatment services may only be provided in clinics licensed by the Human Fertilisation & Embryology Authority (HFEA) and in compliance with the HFEA's Code of Practice. Before proceeding with treatment, health professionals should also satisfy themselves that the intended parents have tried all other reasonable treatment options . . .

8. Health professionals providing treatment services or advice about surrogacy, should actively encourage those considering this option to seek counselling and testing for infectious diseases.

9. Health professionals providing advice or treatment services should also emphasise the importance of discussing with all parties, in advance, the decisions which may need to be made before, during and after the pregnancy. These include decisions about the number of embryos to be replaced in surrogacy using IVF, the level of prenatal testing, the preferred method of delivery and decisions about care in the immediate postpartum period. Ideally these decisions should be reached by mutual agreement but in all cases of dispute, the surrogate mother, in conjunction with the health professionals, should make the final decision . . .

12. The surrogate mother should usually have successfully borne at least one child prior to the surrogacy arrangement and preferably will have completed her own family and have a partner, family or friends to provide support throughout and after the pregnancy. In some cases, particular attention may be necessary where family support is to be given to the surrogate mother and the intended mother from the same family.

13. In view of the potential risks to the surrogate mother's health, the intended parents should be advised of the importance of ensuring that proper insurance cover has been arranged for the surrogate mother . . .

18. Health professionals with a conscientious objection to surrogacy are not obliged to participate in the arrangement but have an ethical duty to refer that patient to another practitioner who would be prepare to consider offering help and advice.

NOTE:

1. Notwithstanding this limited professional endorsement of surrogacy, it should be noted that in the medical negligence case of *Briody v St Helens & Knowsley Health Authority* [2002] 2 W.L.R. 394 the damages which the claimant sought in order to fund a surrogacy arrangement were denied. She argued that following a wrongful hysterectomy, surrogacy represented her only chance of a genetically related child. Interestingly, at first instance, while it was accepted by all the medical experts that the claimant's chances of conception via surrogacy were extremely remote, Sir Robert Winston, normally a staunch advocate of assisted conception, testified that the procedure was no longer performed at his Hammersmith clinic. He added that, "the majority of gynaecologists regard surrogacy as a rather ques-tionable procedure" and that "the pendulum of opinion is swinging further and further away from surrogacy" (*Briody v St. Helens & Knowsley Health Authority* [2000] 2 F.C.R. 13 at p.20 Hale L.J.'s judgment in the Court of Appeal contains a useful account of UK law on

surrogacy [2002] 2 W.L.R. 394. She concluded that relevant provisions in the HFEA Code of Practice:

> "do not indicate that surrogacy as such is contrary to public policy. They tend to indicate that the issue is a difficult one, upon which opinions are divided, so that it would be wise to tread with caution. This is borne out in the official publications which have considered the matter. If there is a trend, it is towards acceptance and regulation as a last resort rather than towards prohibition."

In the circumstances of this case she held that it would not be reasonable to expect a surrogacy arrangement organised by COTS to be funded, in part because the chances of success were low because of the woman's age (47). The case was distinguished from those in which damages had been awarded to cover IVF treatment. Hale L.J. also endorsed the view of the Court of Appeal in the *ex parte Mellor* case (see p.814) that the ECHR could not found any positive claim to be provided with a child.

QUESTIONS:

1. What factors do you think account for the change of attitude towards surrogacy on the part of the BMA? Do you agree with Hale L.J. that it is nevertheless wise to proceed with caution in endorsing surrogacy? (For an analysis of how this case fits into shifting judicial attitudes on the practice, see D. Morgan, "The Bleak House of Surrogacy: *Briody v. St Helens and Knowsley Health Authority*" (2001) 9 *Feminist Legal Studies* 57.)
2. Is it right that the final say in relation to the matters identified in guideline 9 is left to the surrogate mother in conjunction with the health professionals? What if they disagree?

(iv) Disputes between the Commissioning Couple and the Surrogate Mother

One of the risks of surrogacy highlighted by the BMA Working Party in 1990 was that of disputes between the parties. We have already seen that in *A v C* the Court of Appeal was not prepared to enforce a surrogacy arrangement when a dispute arose between the surrogate mother and the commissioning couple. A similar issue was raised in the following case.

Re P (Minors) (Wardship: Surrogacy) [1987] 2 F.L.R. 421

Mrs P offered her services as a surrogate mother to Mr and Mrs B who were seeking a woman to bear his biological child, as Mrs B was unable to carry a child to term. Mr and Mrs B contracted to pay Mrs P sums of money by instalment throughout the pregnancy, which was brought about by assisted insemination with Mr P's sperm. It was agreed that, following the birth of twins, Mrs P should take them home for a couple of months and hand them over to the commissioning couple for adoption on an agreed date. Mrs P had doubts throughout the pregnancy about her willingness to hand over the children, which crystallised after bringing the twins home. She expressed such doubts in a letter to Mr B but wrote that despite her unwillingness she still intended to give up the children. Both parties then approached the local authority, which applied to make the children wards of court.

SIR JOHN ARNOLD P.

" . . . In this, as in any other wardship dispute, the welfare of the children, or child, concerned is the first and paramount consideration which the court must, by statute, take into account and that is what I do.

These children have been, up to their present age of approximately 5 months, with, quite consistently, their mother and in those circumstances there must necessarily have been some bonding of those children with their mother and that is undoubtedly coupled with the fact that she is their mother, a matter which weighs predominantly in the balance in favour of leaving the children with their mother, but there are other factors which weigh in the opposite balance and which, as is said by Mr B through his counsel, outweigh the advantages of leaving the children with their mother and it is that balancing exercise which the court is required to perform . . .

What then are the factors which the court should take into account? I have already mentioned on the side of Mrs P the matters which weigh heavily in the balance are the fact of her maternity, that she bore the children and carried them for the term of their gestation and that ever since she has conferred upon them the maternal care which they have enjoyed and has done so successfully . . .

I start, therefore, from the position that these babies have bonded with their mother in a state of domestic care by her of a satisfactory nature and I now turn to the factors which are said to outweigh those advantages, so as to guide the court upon the proper exercise of the balancing function to the conclusion that the children ought to be taken away from Mrs P, and passed over, under suitable arrangements, to Mr and Mrs B. They are principally as follows. It is said, and said quite correctly, that the shape of the B family is the better shape of a family in which these children might be brought up, because it contains a father as well as a mother and that is undoubtedly true. Next, it is said that the material circumstances of the B family are such that they exhibit a far larger degree of affluence than can be demonstrated by Mrs P. That, also, is undoubtedly true. Then it is said that the intellectual quality of the environment of the B's home and the stimulus which would be afforded to these babies, if they were to grow up in that home, would be greater than the corresponding features in the home of Mrs P. That is not a matter which has been extensively investigated, but I suspect that that is probably true. Certainly, the combined effect of the lack of affluence on the part of Mrs P and some lack of resilience to the disadvantages which that implies has been testified in the correspondence to the extent that I find Mrs P saying that shortage of resources leads to her sitting at home with little E and overeating, because she has no ability from a financial point of view to undertake anything more resourceful than that. Then it is said that the religious comfort and support which the B's derive from their Church is greater than anything of that sort available to Mrs P. How far that is true, I simply do not know . . .

Then it is said, and there is something in this, that the problems which might arise from the circumstance that these children who are, of course, congenitally derived from the semen of Mr B and bear traces of Mr B's Asiatic origin would be more easily understood and discussed and reconciled in the household of Mr and Mrs B, a household with an Asiatic ethnic background than they would be if they arose in relation to these children while they were situated in the home of Mrs P, which is in an English village and which has no non-English connections . . . The situation in which Mrs P lives is not, as it seems to me, likely to breed that sort of intolerance. She lives in a smallish country community, large in terms of a village but small in terms of a town, where there is very little penetration by any immigrant citizens, which does not seem to me to be a community in which racial discrimination is very likely, but it is a factor which contingently at least may have some importance . . .

[B]ut I do not think, having given my very best effort to the evaluation of the case dispassionately on both sides, that they ought to be taken to outweigh the advantages to these children of preserving the link with the mother to whom they are bonded and who has, as is amply testified, exercised over them a satisfactory level of maternal care, and accordingly it is, I think, the duty of the court to award the care and control of these babies to their mother... "

NOTE:

1. The stance taken by the British judges in *A v C* and *Re P* may be contrasted with the approach adopted in many North American cases. Feminist scholars in the United States have argued that the reasoning in US cases has generally been detrimental to the "surrogate" mother, as it has focused on the material advantages of the commissioning couple, under the guise of promoting the best interests of the child. (See, for example, M.A. Field, *Surrogate Motherhood* (2nd edn), Cambridge, Massachusetts: Harvard University Press, 1994; R. Rao, "Surrogacy Law in the United States: the Outcome of Ambivalence" in R. Cook and S.D. Sclater with F. Kaganas (eds), *Surrogate Motherhood: International Perspectives*, Oxford: Hart, 2003, 23–34.) Other interesting comparisons may be made with Israeli law, under which the gestational mother has no right to withdraw from the arrangements unless there has been a pertinent change in the circumstance. (See P. Laufer-Ukeles, "Gestation: Work for Hire or the Essence of Motherhood? A Comparative Legal Analysis" (2002) 9 *Duke Journal of Gender, Law & Policy* p.91.)

QUESTIONS:

1. Of the factors outlined above by the President, which weighed heaviest upon the court? Do you agree with its assessment?
2. Are surrogacy cases really analogous to adoption cases? Note that in both scenarios, since new adoption legislation came into effect in 2004, the welfare of the child is the paramount consideration for the court (Children and Adoption Act 2002, s.1(2); Children Act 1989, s.1). Do you think that in cases of disputed surrogacy arrangements, the "best interests" of the child should always dictate the outcome?
3. Is the "best interests" test a meaningful test where a child is unaware of its genetic origins? Would it be better to have a presumption that the gestational mother is the best person to look after the child? Do you think this was the criterion which the President was actually using in this case? (On the best interests test generally, see Chapter 7.)
4. Is the President right in suggesting that the courts have no business dealing with the morality of surrogacy contracts? Can law and morality be so easily separated? (See Chapter 2 at pp.92–97.)
5. Can any conclusions about the motives of surrogate mothers be drawn from the British cases which have been litigated, or are they, by definition, unusual cases? (See K. Cotton and D. Winn, *Baby Cotton: For Love or*

Money, London: Dorling Kindersley, 1985.) In your view, is the "surrogate" mother capable of freely consenting to such a contract? (See S. Wilkinson, *Bodies for Sale: Ethics and Exploitation in the Human Body Trade*, London: Routledge, 2003, Chapter 8.)

6. Given that the surrogacy arrangement in English law cannot be regarded as a contract for the sale of a commodity, is it more appropriately viewed as a gift? (See J. Dolgin, "Status and Contract in Surrogate Motherhood", (1990) 38 *Buffalo Law Review* 515.) How do you think the parties to the contract would view it?

7. In April 1996 it was revealed that the NHS had funded a surrogate pregnancy for the first time, and was considering funding other cases. The first case cost Yorkshire Health Authority £5,000. ("Surrogate grandmother wants twins", *The Guardian*, April 15, 1996.) Is expenditure on surrogacy arrangements a justifiable use of NHS resources? (Note also the *Briody* decision—p.792 above.)

(v) The Terms of the Surrogacy Arrangement

Theoretically there are no limits to the types of clause which may be inserted into surrogacy contracts. This raises the question of what terms can justifiably be inserted into a surrogacy contract. For instance, the commissioning couple could seek to prohibit the surrogate mother from smoking or drinking during her pregnancy, or indeed to compel her to take certain forms of exercise or undergo medical tests in the interests of the foetus. The insertion of such clauses also raises the issue of what should happen in the event of breach of contractual conditions. Would breach entitle the commissioning couple to refuse payment or reject the baby? Could they compel the surrogate mother to abort the pregnancy? (See the case of *W and W v H* at p.800 below.) The issue is becoming more vexed as ultra sound, amniocentesis and other forms of screening throughout pregnancy are becoming more common (see Chapter 13), and as reproductive technologies are increasingly expected to deliver the perfect or "designer" baby (see p.850 below). Although all pregnancies are increasingly subject to medical scrutiny and legal regulation, the ability of the commissioning couple to dictate terms raises the question of the potentially exploitative nature of surrogacy. It is unlikely that women in well-paid occupations would agree to become surrogate mothers, which suggests that it may be a form of commercial exploitation of women to expect them to undertake surrogacy arrangements for other women. (See M. Radin, "Market-Inalienability" (1987) 100 *Harvard Law Review* 1849.) On the other hand, this suggestion may deny the agency and choice of the woman concerned. (See C. Shalev, *Birth Power*, New Haven: Yale University Press, 1989.) Since many feminists would argue that male/female sexual relationships are inherently unequal economic bargains, perhaps relations which are explicit in surrogacy arrangements are simply pervasive in women's condition. (See M. Freeman, "Is Surrogacy Exploitative?" in S. McLean (ed.), *Legal Issues in Human Reproduction*, Aldershot: Gower, 1989; U. Narayan, "The Gift of a Child: Commercial Surrogacy, Gift Surrogacy and Motherhood" in P. Boling (ed.), *Expecting Trouble: Surrogacy, Fetal Abuse and New Reproductive Technologies*,

Boulder, Colorado: Westview Press, 1995; S. Wilkinson, *op. cit.* in question 5.) It would, however, be easier to avoid the charge of exploitation if there was some sort of statutory regulation of the contents of surrogacy arrangements. For instance, it could be provided that the gestational mother be allowed the same sort of revocation period available to a woman who offers her baby for adoption. A further issue is whether there is anything to prevent the insertion of a clause permitting the commissioning couple to reject the child, for example, if it is born disabled. So far, all the British cases have involved disputes where both parties want the child. An even more distressing case would be where neither party to the couple wanted the child, as has happened in the US—see, for instance, *Buzzanca v Buzzanca* 72 Cal. Rptr. 2d 280 (Cal.App. 4 Dist. 1998).

(vi) Reforming the Law on Surrogacy

In 1997 calls for reforms to the hastily enacted 1986 Surrogacy Arrangements Act intensified owing to the media outcry over one high-profile case. A Dutch couple entered into a surrogacy arrangement with an English woman, which was facilitated by COTS. The surrogate subsequently changed her mind amid media outrage over reports that she had threatened to have an abortion. Concerns about the ability of ill-resourced voluntary groups to adequately regulate the procedure prompted the establishment by the Department of Health of an independent review chaired by Professor Margaret Brazier. The Review Group was given fairly limited terms of reference, *viz.* to consider whether payments, including expenses to surrogate mothers, should continue to be allowed; and if so, on what basis; to examine whether a case existed for the regulation of surrogacy arrangements through a recognised body; and to advise on any consequent changes needed to existing regulation. Thus, questions as to the whether surrogacy contracts should be legally enforceable and whether commercial surrogacy should be allowed were excluded from their remit.

Even assuming the current unenforceability of surrogacy contracts and the prohibition of commercial surrogacy the Review Group concluded that both the Surrogacy Arrangements Act 1985 and s.30 of the Human Fertilisation and Embryology Act 1990 (see p.828 below) should be repealed and replaced by a new Surrogacy Act. Having sought to ascertain the practice in relation to compensation, the Review proposed that only "actual expenses" arising from the surrogacy should be allowed:

M. Brazier, A. Campbell and S. Golombok, *Surrogacy: a review for Health Ministers of Current Arrangements for Payment and Regulation*, London: The Stationary Office, 1998

5.4 We have received accounts from COTS and elsewhere suggesting that payments of £15,000 or more are being made by commissioning couples to surrogate mothers, with a number of payments being in the range of £10,000–£15,000.

5.5 Although systematic records of families with a child born as a result of a surrogacy arrangement have not been kept, it has been possible to obtain some information about the practice of surrogacy from Guardians *ad litem* [reference omitted].

5.6 In the 34 cases of surrogacy in which Guardians were involved, payments made to the surrogate were found to range from nothing to £12,000 (see table at Annex C). In 22%

of cases where the sum paid was known, the payment was between £0–£999 (with 16% receiving £100 or less); in 47% of cases it was between £1000–£4999; in 28% of cases it was between £5000–£9999; and in 3% of cases payment was more than £10,000. Payments were usually made in instalments throughout the pregnancy rather than in a lump sum.

5.11 . . . [I]t is a fundamental belief in our society that children should not be viewed as commodities to be bought or sold. This principle is also enshrined in the law on adoption. Although a theoretical distinction can be made between payment for the purchase of a child and payment for a potentially risky, time-consuming and uncomfortable service, in practice it is difficult to separate the two, and it remains the case that payment other than for genuine expenses constitutes a financial benefit for the surrogate mother.

5.12 The policy of the Human Fertilisation and Embryology Authority is to withdraw payments for egg and sperm donors on the grounds that it is not appropriate for people to donate their genetic material to create new life for financial reasons. Allowing a woman to gain financially from hosting a pregnancy for someone else, whether or not her genetic material has been used, would be at odds with the spirit of gamete donation as a gift, freely and voluntarily given.

5.13 Parallels have also been drawn between surrogacy and blood or live organ donation. In the UK, bodily parts may be donated only as a gift for which no payments are allowed. We believe that surrogacy should be informed by the same values.

5.24 We recommend that payments to surrogate mothers should cover only genuine expenses associated with the pregnancy. Any additional payments should be prohibited in order to prevent surrogacy arrangements being entered into for financial reasons. Details of expenses should be established before any attempt is made to create a surrogacy pregnancy, and a mechanism should be put in place to ensure that documentary evidence of expenses incurred in association with the surrogacy arrangement is produced by the surrogate mother.

5.25 We recommend that allowable expenses should be:

Maternity clothing
Counselling fees
Healthy food
Legal fees
Domestic help
Life and disability insurance
Travel to and from hospital/clinic
Medical expenses
Telephone and postal expenses
Ovulation and pregnancy tests
Overnight accommodation
Insemination and IVF costs
Child care to attend hospital/clinic
Medicines and vitamins

5.26 If the surrogate mother is employed when she enters into the surrogacy arrangement and has to take time off work in connection with the pregnancy or birth, her actual loss of earnings should be reimbursed. The time taken off work should be in accordance with medical advice and statutory guidelines. We would expect actual loss of earnings to be minimal, and to represent no more than the difference between the surrogate mother's usual earnings and state benefits. Documentary proof of actual loss of earnings should be provided. No compensation should be allowed for loss of potential earnings.

Having reached this conclusion, the Review Group then considered various options for regulation. It first rejected the option of extending the regulatory role of the HFEA to encompass surrogacy:

6.13 . . . we have rejected this option for a number of reasons. Although infertility is clearly a reason for seeking surrogacy, we do not believe that surrogacy arrangements are correctly perceived as merely another treatment for infertile people. The involvement of the surrogate mother requires a consideration of other factors, much more akin to the dilemmas of adoption than those of infertility, both from the point of view of her welfare and of the child's welfare. We do not believe, therefore, that fertility clinics are necessarily the correct setting for negotiating surrogacy arrangements, though we accept that they have an important part to play, especially in IVF surrogacy.
. . .

A second option of establishing a new statutory body with the express aim of regulating surrogacy was also dismissed, before the Review Group set out its preferred regulatory strategy:

6.23 In this third option all agencies involved in surrogacy arrangements would be required to be registered by the UK Health Departments and to operate in accordance with a statutory Code of Practice, but no new Authority would be set up. As a first step the Department of Health, in consultation with the other UK Health Departments, would draw up a Code of Practice after discussion with relevant bodies and individuals. We believe that this option has the merit of simplicity and that the Health Departments already have relevant experience of registration procedures of this kind [reference omitted].

6.24 Clearly some additional resources would be required, but this would be much less than that entailed in creating and supporting a new authority. As an interim measure (prior to the necessary legislation) the Departments would draw up and promulgate a voluntary code and invite relevant bodies to seek voluntary registration. The Code would also be drawn to the attention of professional bodies and of the HFEA, so that they could consider incorporating relevant aspects of it into the guidance they issue to practitioners and clinics.

6.25 Although the Code will of necessity be modified and refined during the consultation process and with experience of its use during the interim period, we consider that it must contain the following broad provisions [reference omitted]:

– a statement of allowable expenses, as defined in paragraph 5.25–5.26 above;
– a description of the range of information which must be made available to all parties prior to any agreement being reached, including clear guidance on the legal aspects and a guarantee of access to independent legal advice (at no expense to the surrogate);
– procedures for the minimisation of physical risk to the surrogate and the child (e.g. safe insemination methods);
– criteria for minimum counselling and follow-up procedures to be made available to all parties;
– criteria for the selection of both commissioning couples and surrogates; and
– a model memorandum of understanding between the parties.

6.26 In addition to the Code, the Health Departments would also need to give consideration to establishing requirements for full record keeping; reporting of specified statistics; and clear guidelines on how research will be facilitated into the outcomes of the arrangements, with a description of appropriate procedures for independent ethical appraisal of all proposed research projects.
. . .

NOTES:

1. Under this scheme any breach of the prohibition on payments would disqualify the commissioning couple from seeking a parental order, rather than attracting criminal sanctions.

2. To date no action has been taken to implement the Brazier proposals. They have been subject to academic critique. For instance, Stephen Wilkinson takes issue with some of the underlying assumptions in the Brazier review, such as its treatment of surrogacy as analogous to baby selling, its estimation of the impact of surrogacy on child welfare, and its view of commercial surrogacy as exploitative. He argues that the proposals, if enacted, would constitute an unwarranted interference with procreative choices (see S. Wilkinson, *Bodies for Sale: Ethics and Exploitation in the Human Body Trade*, London: Routledge, 2003, Chapter 8; see also E. Jackson, *Regulating Reproduction*, Oxford: Hart, 2001, 284–292; *cf.* M. Brazier, "Can You Buy Children?" (1999) 11 *Child and Family Law Quarterly* 345). Michael Freeman is especially critical of the recommendation that, although her body and services are central to the surrogacy arrangement, the surrogate herself is not entitled to remuneration. He also warns of the danger of driving the practice underground or overseas (see M. Freeman, "Does Surrogacy Have a Future after Brazier?" (1999) 7 *Medical Law Review* 1). This view was echoed in the media by Kim Cotton who announced her resignation as the chair person of COTS partially in response to the Review—see Wilkinson, *op. cit.* at p.138. For a defence of the form of regulation envisaged by the Review team (by one of its authors), see A.V. Campbell, "Surrogacy, Rights and Duties: a Partial Commentary" (2000) 8 *Health Care Analysis* 35, and H. McLahlan and J.K. Swales, "Surrogate Motherhood, Rights and Duties: a Reply to Campbell" (2001) 9 *Health Care Analysis* 101.

3. Emily Jackson has proposed instead that the law should be reformed so as to more accurately reflect the intention of the parties. She advocates that, provided certain preconditions are satisfied, including the absence of any undue influence, a surrogacy contract should be regarded as a legally enforceable contract for services. In the case of a surrogate who changes her mind, she would be liable to pay damages to the commissioning couple (see Jackson, *op. cit.* in note 2 at pp.308–316).

4. As Freeman (*op. cit.* in note 2) highlights, a problem for any national regulatory scheme is the possibility that those who wish to avail themselves of services will travel to other less regulated jurisdictions (see also D. Morgan, "Enigma Variations: Surrogacy, Rights and Procreative Tourism" in R. Cook and S.D. Sclater with F. Kaganas (eds), *Surrogate Motherhood: International Perspectives*, Oxford: Hart, 2003, pp.75–92.) The legal problems to which such reproductive tourism can give rise are well illustrated by the case of *W and W v H (Child Abduction: surrogacy) No. 2* [2002] 2 F.L.R. 252. Helen Beasley—a surrogate mother from England—entered into a contract with a commissioning couple in California to bear a child created with an egg from an anonymous donor and the sperm of the

commissioning male partner. When it emerged that the surrogate was carrying twins this prompted a legal dispute over various issues, including Beasley's refusal to agree to a selective reduction of the pregnancy (see Chapter 12 at p.883, Note 11). Beasley refused to return to California as agreed for the birth of the twins, whereupon the commissioning couple brought abduction proceedings under the Hague Convention on International Child Abduction which had been given effect in English law by the Child Abduction and Custody Act 1985. While the abduction proceedings failed, on the grounds that the children were not habitually resident either in England or the US (see judgment of Hedley J. at [2002] 1 F.L.R. 1008), at a second hearing the judge ordered the removal of the twins to California as the appropriate jurisdiction for determination of the merits of the case. In California, in contrast to the UK, surrogacy contracts are enforceable. Freeman questions whether the same decision would have been reached had the surrogate mother had a genetic link to the child (see M. Freeman, "Medically Assisted Reproduction" in A. Grubb (ed.), *Principles of Medical Law* (2nd edn), Oxford: OUP, 2004, at p.738). Hedley J.'s passing comment in the first hearing that the cost of the case "in terms of human unhappiness let alone its future implications for these children, may serve to caution against an imbalance between our scientific and ethical capacities" is further evidence that the tide of judicial opinion may be turning against surrogacy once again. In relation to reproductive tourism, recent reports suggest that India may be the destination of choice for those seeking to establish surrogacy arrangements (R. Ramesh, "British couples desperate for children travel to India in search of surrogates", *The Guardian*, March 20, 2006).

5. Robin MacKenzie argues that a private ordering of family arrangements, based on a pre-conceptual agreement which presumes that the arrangement is enforceable, is more appropriate than heavy-handed state regulation. She argues that this facilitates reproductive autonomy by allowing individuals "to design a kin network as they see fit". (See R. MacKenzie, "Beyond Genetic and Gestational Dualities: Surrogacy Agreements, Legal Parenthood and Choice in Family Formation" in K. Horsey and H. Biggs (eds), *Human Fertilisation and Embryology: Reproducing Regulation* (London: UCL Press, 2006 at p.253).

6. Contemporaneously with the Brazier Review, a number of (mainly critical) surrogacy stories surfaced in the media (see Wilkinson, *op. cit.* in note 2 for discussion). For more recent examples see S. Jones, "Visa for twins born to their grandmother", *The Guardian*, July 27, 2004; M. Wainwright, "Surrogate mother jailed for internet fraud", *The Guardian*, May 22, 2004; "Woman slams agencies as her daughter dies after surrogate birth", *The Observer*, January 30, 2005. The outcome of recently litigated cases are not in the public domain owing to reporting restrictions.

7. Recent technological advances in transplant surgery hold the promise of bypassing the need for surrogacy in the case of women who are born without wombs or have hysterectomies. The first human womb transplant was carried out in 2002 in Saudi Arabia, although it had to be removed

after 99 days owing to blood clotting (S. Boseley, "Surgeons hail world's first womb transplant", *The Guardian*, March 7, 2002). Experiments in Sweden the following year which resulted in allegedly healthy mice being born from transplanted wombs led to predictions that the technology could be transferred to humans in the near future (I. Sample, "Womb transplant babies 'within three years' " *The Guardian*, July 2, 2003).

QUESTIONS:

1. Do you think the Brazier Review and recent judicial dicta signal a return to the sort of hostility which surrogacy used to attract and which is evident in the Warnock Report? Note Derek Morgan's point that "surrogacy has undergone a metamorphosis, or more accurately, several forms of metamorphosis; from (i) the sexual to the medical; (ii) the private and invisible to the public and intermittently visible; (iii) the altruistic to the commercial and back again; and (iv) the contested and controversial to the accepted and clinically mediated; and (v) back again" (D. Morgan, "The Bleak House of Surrogacy: *Briody v St Helens and Knowsley Health Authority*" (2001) 9 *Feminist Legal Studies* 57 at p.65).
2. Do you agree that if attempts were made to tighten up the regulation of expenses then the practice would be driven underground (or abroad)?
3. Are you convinced by Brazier's view that regulation of surrogacy requires a different kind of expertise from that offered by the HFEA? (See J.K. Mason and G.T. Laurie, *Mason and McCall Smith's Law and Medical Ethics* (7th edn), Oxford: OUP, 2005, p.118.) If so, what do you make of the current proposals to amalgamate the HFEA and the Human Tissue Authority (see above at p.755)?

4. ACCESS TO REPRODUCTIVE TECHNOLOGIES

(a) The Welfare of the Child

The question of access to reproductive technologies has proven one of the most contentious aspects of IVF provision, raising questions of justice, human rights and resource allocation (see Chapters 1 and 2). Two major practical obstacles to accessing the technologies exist: first, the issue of resources to pay for treatment which arises with hi-tech procedures like IVF, and secondly the shortage of donor gametes, especially eggs. These factors, coupled with the high demand for these procedures, have meant that although the legislation itself has little to say about who is eligible for treatment, in practice, for those unable to fund treatment privately, clinics are able to impose stringent eligibility criteria. Significantly, the test of child welfare has been used to limit access to IVF treatment. In this area of the law, as in general with laws concerning children (see Chapter 7), the policy has been to stress the best interests of the potential child. Thus, those who seek to access treatment services will be screened by clinics to assess their suitability as parents. Access is effectively governed by the individual policies of each clinic, operating under the guidance of Ethics Committees. They are also put into practice by individual consultants. The question of access was canvassed in the following reports:

Warnock Committee, Report of the Committee of Inquiry into Human Fertilisation and Embryology (1984) Cmnd. 9314

2.9 . . . the various techniques for assisted reproduction offer not only a remedy for infertility, but also offer the fertile single woman or lesbian couple the chance of parenthood without the direct involvement of a male partner. To judge from the evidence, many believe that the interests of the child dictate that it should be born into a home where there is a loving, stable, heterosexual relationship and that, therefore, the *deliberate* creation of a child for a woman who is not a partner in such a relationship is morally wrong. On the other side some expressed the view that a single woman or lesbian couple have a right under the European Convention to have children even though those children may have no legal father. It is further argued that it is already accepted that a single person, whether man or woman, can in certain circumstances provide a suitable environment for a child, since the existence of single adoptive parents is specifically provided for in the Children Act 1975 . . .

2.11 We have considered these arguments, but nevertheless, we believe that as a general rule it is better for children to be born into a two-parent family, with both father and mother, although we recognise that it is impossible to predict with any certainty how lasting such a relationship will be.

2.12 We have considered very carefully whether there are circumstances where it is inappropriate for treatment which is solely for the alleviation of infertility to be provided. In general we hold that everyone should be entitled to seek expert advice and appropriate investigation. This will usually involve referral to a consultant. However, at the present time services for the treatment of infertility are in short supply, both for initial referral and investigation and for the more specialized treatments considered in this report. In this situation of scarcity some individuals will have a more compelling case for treatment than others.

NOTE:

1. A more liberal approach is adopted in *Fertility and the Family: the Glover Report on Reproductive Technologies to the European Commission*, London: Fourth Estate, 1989.

QUESTIONS:

1. Should the provision of fertility services be available only to those who are proven to be infertile? Would such a position unacceptably discriminate against fertile lesbians and single women? (See K. Dawson and P. Singer, "Should Fertile People Have Access to *in vitro* Fertilisation?" (1990) 300 *British Medical Journal* 167; S. Golombok and J. Rust, "The Warnock Report and Single Women: What about the Children? (1986) 12 *Journal of Medical Ethics* 182.)

2. The Warnock Committee referred to "the feminist position" on single motherhood. Is there an identifiable (and unitary) "feminist position" on single motherhood? How adequately did Warnock address feminist issues (see Chapter 2)?

The following action for judicial review of the decision-making process was brought by a candidate who was not selected for IVF treatment. It arose out of the criteria then used at St Mary's hospital in Manchester.

R. v Ethical Committee of St Mary's Hospital (Manchester), Ex p. Harriott, [1988] 1 F.L.R. 512, [1988] Fam. Law 165

Mrs H was experiencing difficulty in becoming pregnant and had applied to her local authority's social services department to adopt or foster a child. Her application was turned down, because of her criminal record (which included soliciting for prostitution) and her allegedly poor understanding of the role of a foster-parent. She subsequently applied for IVF under the National Health Service and once again her application was refused. She unsuccessfully sought judicial review of the decision to refuse her treatment:

SCHIEMANN J.
" . . . In the spirit of [the Warnock] report, a local committee exists at St Mary's Hospital, Manchester. Its constitution and functions were decided in June 1985, although it evolved from separate committees of those individuals providing IVF and [DI] . . . services at the hospital . . . It is clear that the committee, with its wide range of expertise, is intended as an advisory rather than a decision-making body . . .

The Notice of Application . . . seeks amongst other things to quash an alleged decision of the committee . . . to remove the applicant from the hospital's IVF programme. The applicant also seeks relief against the managers of the regional IVF unit . . .

Mr Blom Cooper [counsel for the applicant] does not suggest that the general policy pursued by the regional IVF unit, namely, that 'couples accepted on to the waiting list must, in the ordinary course of events, satisfy the general criteria established by adoption societies in assessing suitability for adoptions' is in any way illegal. He submits, however, that once the committee had been asked for advice on whether a treatment should be given to a particular individual, the committee was obliged itself to investigate the matter and give advice following such investigation. He points out that the membership of the committee was such that it was well placed to give advice and perhaps better placed than an obstetrician and a gynaecologist.

I do not accept Mr Blom Cooper's submission. In my judgment, the committee's function was to provide a forum for discussion amongst professionals. It is essentially an informal body. If the committee in a particular case refuses to give advice or does not have a majority view as to what advice should be given, then I do not consider that the courts can compel it to give advice or to embark upon a particular investigation.

Mr Bell, for the committee, submitted that judicial review does not lie to review any advice given by the committee. As at present advised, I would be doubtful about accepting that submission in its full breadth. If the committee had advised, for instance, that the IVF unit should in principle refuse all such treatment to anyone who was a jew or coloured, then I think the courts might well grant a declaration that such a policy was illegal . . . But I do not need to consider that situation in this case. Here the complaint is that the committee's advice was that the consultant must make up her own mind as to whether the treatment should be given. That advice was, in my judgment, unobjectionable.

Mr Blom Cooper's second complaint about the committee is a procedural one. He submits that the committee should have given the applicant an opportunity to put evidence and submissions before the committee. I also reject that submission. If I am right in holding that the committee was entitled not to give advice and that it was set up to provide a forum for professionals to talk things over and to provide general guidelines, then I think the court should be slow, if indeed it has the power, to force such a committee to receive representations before it decides not to give advice . . .

I turn now to consider the position of the consultant. The complaint against her is entirely a procedural one. Mr Blom Cooper submits that when a consultant is making a decision removing a woman from the IVF list and is taking that decision on social grounds, either exclusively or mainly where those social grounds involve issues of contested fact, then the doctor has a duty to act fairly.

Mr Bell submits that the doctor/patient relationship is outside the purview of administrative law. I am prepared for the purposes of this judgment to assume that Mr Blom Cooper's submission is correct in law. But even on that assumption, I am not prepared to grant his client any relief. I can see arguable grounds for criticism of Dr Buck's decision in December 1984 not to treat the applicant. That decision was made without first giving her an opportunity to try to establish that the case was an extraordinary one in some way and that, therefore, the applicant should be accepted for treatment notwithstanding that she did not satisfy the general criteria established by adoption societies in assessing suitability for adoptions. I can see further arguable grounds for criticism of Dr Buck's decision not to inform the applicant of the true reason for refusal until September 1985. She was misled and is understandably furious that time went by in what now appears to have been shadow-boxing. However, it must be remembered that decisions by doctors as to whether to give or refuse treatment are not ones which, once made, render the doctor powerless to change her view in the light of new arguments and new facts. I consider that the applicant has since that time had opportunities to put more information in front of Dr Buck and the Health Authority. She has used those opportunities. I have no reason to suppose that they have acted unfairly in the matter or shut their ears to her representations in the sense of being unwilling to entertain them. It is not, and could not be, suggested that no reasonable consultant could have come to the decision to refuse treatment to the applicant.

In those circumstances, I see no reason to grant the applicant the relief she seeks against the consultant, namely, an order requiring the consultant to consider her case after giving her a further opportunity to make representations. In consequence, I do not need to decide the question whether or not in principle judicial review will lie in respect of such a decision."

NOTE:

1. This case demonstrates that issues of resource allocation must always be addressed on a number of levels (see Chapter 1). At the macro level, decisions are taken regarding whether particular services should be provided at all. It is only when the decision is made to provide a service that micro allocation questions arise as to whether particular patients should be given treatment. Thus, but for the fact that Manchester was one of the first areas in the United Kingdom that had fully funded IVF services on the NHS, this question might never have arisen.

QUESTIONS:

1. Is it meaningful to talk of the welfare of an unborn child, or is the welfare test too artificial to be workable in this context? (See p.806 below; and E. Jackson, "Conception and the Irrelevance of the Welfare Principle" (2002) 65 *Modern Law Review* 176; "Re-thinking the Pre-conception Welfare Principle" in K. Horsey and H. Biggs (eds), *Human Reproduction and Embryology: Reproducing Regulation*, London: UCL Press, 2006.) In what ways, if any, is the welfare of a child threatened by the fact that his mother has convictions for prostitution? Does the judgment imply that workers in the sex industry should not be allowed to become parents?

2. Is the model of adoption an appropriate one to use in assessing the suitability of persons seeking infertility services? (See G. Douglas, *Law, Fertility and Reproduction*, London: Sweet & Maxwell, 1991, Chapter 6.) What distinguishes a family created via adoption and one created via assisted conception? (See R. MacKenzie, "Beyond Genetic and Gestational Dualities: Surrogacy Agreements, Legal Parenthood and Choice in Family Formation" in Horsey and Biggs, *op. cit.* in note 1).

3. As a result of the decision in *Ex p. Harriott*, it would seem that an IVF clinic which denies treatment to an ex prostitute is acting reasonably; but one which denies treatment to members of ethnic minorities is introducing unlawful and irrelevant considerations. Would a reasonable IVF clinic debar a white couple from having a black or mixed race child?

4. Should decisions about who will receive infertility treatment services be left in the hands of medical practitioners? Given that the Warnock Committee accepted that such judgments were not purely medical, was it justifiable to leave responsibility to doctors? (See S. Millns, "Making 'Social Judgments that Go Beyond the Purely Medical': The Reproductive Revolution and Access to Fertility Treatment Services" in J. Bridgeman and S. Millns (eds), *Law and Body Politics*, Aldershot: Dartmouth, 1995; I. Kennedy, "What is a Medical Decision" in *Treat Me Right: Essays in Medical Law and Ethics*, Oxford: Oxford University Press, 1988.)

5. Does the *Ex p. Harriott* decision offer any solace to parties aggrieved by the decision to deny them treatment? (See D. Longley, *Public Law and Health Service Accountability*, Buckingham: Open University Press, 1993.)

6. Although the case was decided before the 1990 Act came into force, do you think there would be any significant difference in how the case would be decided now? Should there have been provision in the Act for a review mechanism, so that aggrieved parties could appeal against a decision to deny them treatment? (See Chapter 1 on the issue of the right to treatment.)

Perhaps surprisingly, very little mention was made in the 1990 Act of eligibility for treatment or the best interests of the resultant child.

Human Fertilisation and Embryology Act 1990, s.13(5)

13.—(5) A woman shall not be provided with treatment services unless account has been taken of the welfare of any child who may be born as a result of the treatment (including the need of that child for a father), and of any child who may be affected by the birth.

NOTE:

1. The most striking aspect of the provision is that the only express guidance to clinics is the reference to the child's need for a father. Freeman points out that this is incoherent and bizarre in a statue which creates legally fatherless children. (See M. Freeman, "Medically Assisted Reproduction"

in A. Grubb (ed.), *Principles of Medical Law*, Oxford: OUP, 2004 at p.677; E. Jackson, "Conception and the Irrelevance of the Welfare Principle" (2002) 65 *Modern Law Review* 176.) Indeed, the former chair of the HFEA, Suzi Leather, has criticised this provision in a media interview as "anachronistic" (J. Laurance, "Fathers no longer required: Fertility chief signals an IVF Revolution", *The Independent*, January 21, 2004). For an analysis of the Parliamentary debates on this provision, see S. Sheldon, "Fragmenting Fatherhood: the Regulation of Reproductive Technologies" (2005) 68 M.L.R. 523, at pp.532–537.) This aspect of the welfare calculation is now under consideration in the Government's review of the 1990 Act, and looks likely to be deleted.

QUESTIONS:

1. Does s.13(5) provide adequate guidance about how to assess the best interests of the child? Is there a need for such guidance, or is this provision really a covert way of discriminating against certain parents? (See M. Brazier, "Liberty, Responsibility, Maternity" (1999) 52 *Current Legal Problems* 359; M. Thomson, "Legislating for the Monstrous: Access to Reproductive Services and the Monstrous Feminine" (1997) 6 *Social and Legal Studies* 401; S. McLean, "Women, Rights and Reproduction" in *Legal Issues in Human Reproduction*, Aldershot: Dartmouth, 1990.)
2. Is the need of a child for a father so significant that it should be the only factor specifically referred to in the legislation with regard to child welfare? Is this requirement in accordance with human rights? (See pp.814–817 below.)
3. If you think that it is justified to include a provision on child welfare, is it appropriate to leave fuller guidance to be fleshed out in the Code of Practice?

The current provisions in the HFEA Code of Practice were inserted in 2005 after the HFEA had reviewed the advice following a consultation (HFEA, *Welfare of the Child: Tomorrow's Children: Report of the Policy Review of Welfare of the Child Assessments in Licensed Assisted Conception Clinics*, 2005).

HFEA, Code of Practice, 6th edition, 2003, Part 3

3.1 There is a general presumption in favour of providing treatment for patients who seek it. However, in accordance with the requirements of the Act to take account of the welfare of any child who may be born as a result of treatment, treatment centres should assess the risk of harm to the welfare of such a child or any existing children in the family. Where it is judged that the child is likely to experience serious harm, treatment should not be provided.

3.2 Treatment centres are expected to take into account the welfare of any child who may be born as a result of treatment and of any other child who may be affected by the birth before providing any treatment service, as defined in section 2 of the Human Fertilisation and Embryology (HFE) Act . . .

3.7 Those seeking treatment are entitled to a fair assessment. Treatment centres are expected to conduct the assessment with skill and care, and have regard to the wishes of all those involved.

3.8 In order to take into account the welfare of the child, treatment centres are expected to consider factors which are likely to cause serious physical, psychological or medical harm, either to the child to be born or to any existing child of the family. These factors should include:

   (i) Any aspect of the patient's past or current circumstances which means that either the child to be born or any existing child of the family is likely to experience serious physical or psychological harm or neglect. Such aspects might include:
     (a) previous convictions relating to harming children;
     (b) child protection measures taken regarding existing children; or
     (c) serious violence or discord within the family environment.
  (ii) Any aspect of the patient's past or current circumstances which is likely to lead to an inability to care for the child to be born throughout its childhood or which are already seriously impairing the care of any existing child of the family. Such aspects might include:
     (a) mental or physical conditions; or
     (b) drug or alcohol abuse.
 (iii) Any aspect of the patient's medical history which means that the child to be born is likely to suffer from a serious medical condition.
 (iv) Any other aspects of the patient's circumstances which treatment centres consider to be likely to cause serious harm to the child to be born or any existing child of the family.

3.9 Where the child will have no legal father, the treatment centre is expected to assess the prospective mother's ability to meet the child's/children's needs and the ability of other persons within the family or social circle willing to share responsibility for those needs.

3.10 Where the child will not be raised by the carrying mother, treatment centres are expected to take into account the possibility of a breakdown in the surrogacy arrangement and whether this is likely to cause serious harm to the child to be born or any existing children in the surrogate's family.

   . . .

3.17 In deciding whether to refuse treatment, treatment centres are expected to take into account views from all staff who have been involved with the care of the patient(s). The patient(s) are expected to be given the opportunity to respond to adverse information and objections before a final decision is made . . .

3.19 Where treatment is refused, treatment centres are expected to:

   (i) Explain the reasons for such refusal to the woman and, where appropriate, her partner, together with any circumstances which may cause the centre to reconsider its decision; and
  (ii) Explain any remaining options; and
 (iii) Explain opportunities for obtaining appropriate counselling.

NOTE:

   1. The most significant amendment to pre-existing guidance is that the burden of proof shifts to a presumption in favour of treating potential parents. Rather than requiring subjective assessment of matters such as "the commitment to raise children", the focus is now placed squarely on those factors which indicate risk of serious harm to children, such as mental and physical impairment of the potential parents which would affect their responsibility to care for a child or evidence of past drug or alcohol abuse on their part. Significantly, the need of a child for a father has been completely downplayed. A further change is that the earlier

requirement to routinely contact G.P.s has been removed in favour of assessments being carried out by clinicians at licensed clinics.

QUESTIONS:

1. How adequate is the new guidance in relation to child welfare? Should any other factors have been explicitly referred to in Part 3 of the Code of Practice? Should such guidance be enshrined in the legislation itself?
2. Is it right in principle for those administering IVF programmes to screen parents as to their suitability? What is the difference between screening them in order to assess their suitability to benefit medically from the procedures, and screening them to assess their suitability as parents *per se*? Which is the more important? Who is qualified to assess the potential suitability of parents? (G. Douglas, "Assisted Reproduction and the Welfare of the Child" (1993) *Current Legal Problems* 53.)
3. Do you agree with Harris's argument that it is absurd to attempt to deny single persons the right to assisted conception when single women clearly cannot be forced to use contraception or to abort after pregnancy has occurred? (See J. Harris, *Wonderwoman and Superman*, Oxford: Oxford University Press, 1992, at pp.73–78; M.J. Campion, *Who's Fit to be a Parent?* London: Routledge, 1995.)

(b) The Woman's Age

Perhaps surprisingly, since the passage of the Act there has only been one further challenge to denial of treatment in the courts:

R. v Sheffield Health Authority, Ex p. Seale, 1994, unreported

Having experienced difficulty in conceiving, Mrs Seale, who was aged 36, applied to Sheffield Area Health Authority for IVF treatment. The authority rejected her application. In a letter, the authority explained that, due to competing health priorities, only £200,000 could be allocated to fertility services, and consequently some form of rationing was necessary.

AULD J.
" . . . Mr Straker [for the applicant] challenges the decision made in this case . . . under three heads. The first is illegality. As I understand his submission, it is that as the Secretary of State has given no directions or imposed no limitations on the provision of *in vitro* fertilisation, and it is not for the district health authority, once it has committed itself to providing such a service, to restrict that provision if in the case of any patient there is a chance, a reasonable probability, a possibility—I do not quite know where the line is to be drawn—of the treatment being effective . . . I reject as unarguable any submission based on illegality here. In my view it is clear that if the Secretary of State has not limited or given directions as to the way in which such a service once undertaken should be provided, the authority providing it is entitled to form a view as to those circumstances and when they justify provision and when they do not.

The second argument of Mr Straker is that the decision here is irrational, that is, absurd . . . He says it is irrational because it is not founded on any sustainable, clinical approach. The basis of that argument appears to be that there is more than one view of the appropriate 'cut-off' age for such treatment. In short, he submits, and refers me to the views of other doctors, that 35 years old is too low an age. It is possible to achieve success certainly up to the age of 42. I cannot, nor could the Court when deciding the matter as a substantive issue, if it came to that, form a view as to the rightness or wrongness of competing medical views on the effective cut-off date for the utility of such treatment. The decision letter does not say that the treatment cannot be effective after the age of 35, but merely that it is 'generally less effective in women aged over 35 years'. If that is so, can Mr Straker challenge the decision as irrational on the basis that it is absurd to apply the age of 35 years as a blanket cut-off point, taking no account of individual circumstances? His submission is that every case should be considered individually. Clinically speaking, there is no doubt good sense in such a submission. And a clinical decision on a case by case basis is clearly desirable and, in cases of critical illness, a necessary approach. However, it is reasonable, or it is at least not *Wednesbury* unreasonable, of an authority to look at the matter in the context of the financial resources available to it to provide this and the many other services for which it is responsible under the National Health Service legislation. I cannot say that it is absurd for this Authority, acting on advice that the efficacy of this treatment decreases with age and that it is generally less effective after the age of 35, to take that as an appropriate criterion when balancing the need for such a provision against its ability to provide it and all the other services imposed upon it under the legislation.

The third matter upon which Mr Straker relied as part of his argument based on irrationality was a reference to a particular condition from which this applicant suffers for which pregnancy is said to be a cure. However, that matter does not appear to have loomed large, or at all, in the circumstances giving rise to the decision of 22 April. Nor does it appear to have been particularly prominent as a reason for special treatment in this case in the correspondence that followed that decision. Under the heading of 'Irrationality' Mr Straker relies upon the fact that privately paying patients can secure such treatment until the age of 42. It seems to me that that argument does not meet the central problem here of an authority coping with a finite budget and a myriad of services which it is bound to provide under it. I am, therefore, of the view that there is no arguable case that this decision was irrational, applying the high test that that word imports under the *Wednesbury* decision."

NOTES:

1. In 1996 Mrs Seale gave birth to a baby boy as a result of IVF treatment paid for privately by an anonymous business person (*The Independent*, June 21, 1996).

2. Nothing in the 1990 Act imposes an age limit on recipients of IVF treatment. However, age is a factor which ethics committees may take into account in reviewing applications for treatment. Many clinics do include age limits in their own guidelines, and, as noted above, the latest HFEA Code of Practice highlights the importance of parental age when assessing the best interests of any potential children. Freeman suggests that a future challenge to an inflexible age policy may succeed, and is certainly more open to challenge than other criteria commonly inserted by NHS clinics, such as evidence of stability in relationships and the requirement that a woman is close to her ideal body weight (see M. Freeman, "Medically Assisted Reproduction" in A. Grubb (ed.), *Principles of Medical Law* (2nd edn), Oxford: OUP, 2004, pp.682–683.)

3. The pregnancies of post-menopausal women who have been treated abroad have attracted intense scrutiny and criticisms of the lack of

restrictions which allow fertility clinics in other countries to treat women in their 60s. (See, for instance, "The world's oldest mother?" (BBC News Online, January 17, 2005) reporting that a Romanian woman of 66 had given birth to a baby girl by Caesarean section after nine years of fertility treatment; S. Boseley, "The child psychiatrist who is at ease with becoming a mother at 63" (*The Guardian*, May 5, 2006) concerning a 63-year-old English woman who has been treated by the controversial Italian fertility specialist Severino Antinori in Russia. (See also M. Frith, "Antinori: a miracle worker or just an amoral egotist?", *The Independent*, May 15, 2006; J. Glover, "Nazi eugenics, Virginia Woolf and the morality of designer babies", *The Guardian*, May 6, 2006.) It should be noted that many British clinics do impose age limits and it was thought that 50 was a common cut-off point. However, in the wake of these high-profile cases, it has recently emerged that approximately 100 women aged 50 or over are treated at UK clinics each year ("Dozens of babies being born to mothers over 50", *The Telegraph*, May 8, 2006).

QUESTIONS:

1. Should the Human Fertilisation and Embryology Act 1990 have set an upper age limit beyond which access to IVF services would have been barred? On what grounds would you support or oppose the inclusion of such a provision? If you support such a measure, what should the upper age limit be? Should it apply equally to fathers? (F. Fisher and A. Sommerville, "To Everything There is a Season? Are there Medical Grounds for Refusing Fertility Treatment to Older Women?" in J. Harris and S. Holm (eds), *The Future of Human Reproduction: Choice and Regulation*, Oxford: OUP, 1998.) Should your grandmother be permitted to have IVF treatment provided she is physically fit and has access to donor eggs?

2. If a couple have been diagnosed to be HIV+ should they be allowed access to IVF treatment? Does it make a difference if only the male partner is HIV+? (See J.R. Smith *et al.*, "Infertility Management in HIV Positive Cases: a Dilemma" (1991) 302 *British Medical Journal* 1447; L. Delaney and K. Doyle, "The Childless HIV Couple" [1995] *New L.J.* 1517; K. Stephen, "Infertility Treatment and the HIV Positive Woman" in A. Morris and S. Nott (eds), *Well Women: the Gendered Nature of Healthcare Provision*, Aldershot: Dartmouth, 2002.) In May 1996 Hammersmith hospital's IVF unit decided to give IVF treatment to an HIV+ woman in her 30s. The woman was a former heroin addict who had had the virus for 10 years. For five years she had been in what was described as a "completely supportive" relationship, but was unable to conceive naturally because of damaged Fallopian tubes. It was estimated that there was a 10–15 per cent chance of the baby being infected by the virus, although a Caesarian section delivery, and administration to the woman of anti-viral drugs during pregnancy would probably reduce the risk to about 7 per cent. ("Fertility treatment for HIV woman sparks controversy", *The Guardian*,

May 13, 1996.) Do you think that this decision can be squared with the decision of St Mary's Hospital in Manchester not to treat Mrs Harriott?

5. Conscientious Objection

Not only are health care professionals entrusted with huge power to decide who may access fertility services, but those who object on moral grounds to being involved in the provision of reproductive treatment services or IVF are provided, under the Act, with a basis on which to object to such participation.

Human Fertilisation and Embryology Act 1990, s.38

38.—(1) No person who has a conscientious objection to participating in any activity governed by this Act shall be under any duty however arising, to do so.

(2) In any legal proceedings the burden of proof of conscientious objection shall rest on the person claiming to rely on it.

Note:

1. As we shall see, a similar statutory right of conscientious objection applies in the case of abortion (see Chapter 12 and M.R. Wiclair, "Conscientious Objection in Medicine" (2000) 14 *Bioethics* 205–227).

Question:

1. Michael Thomson has suggested that such clauses are significant in constructing the provision of fertility treatment, like abortion as morally dubious (M. Thomson, *Reproducing Narrative*, Aldershot: Ashgate, 1998.) Do you agree?

6. Allocation of Resources and Treating Infertility

The provision of IVF services on the NHS has raised in acute form the issue of how scarce resources can be rationed. The huge variation which exists from one NHS region to another, both in funding policies and in eligibility for treatment criteria, has fuelled political debate. Policies have ranged from fairly generous funding in some regions to a refusal to fund *any* IVF services in others. For instance, according to a survey by the National Association of Health Authorities in 1996, 11 authorities, including Hertfordshire and Northamptonshire refused to purchase IVF treatment. ("Health ration decisions must be made public", *The Independent*, June 21, 1996; A. Plomer *et al.*, "Rationing Policies on Access to IVF in the NHS" (1999) 7 *Reproductive Health Matters* 60.) Concerns about the existence of this postcode lottery, coupled with political pressure for more rational funding decisions prompted the National Institute for Health and Clinical Excellence (NICE) to issue the following guidance on infertility:

CG11 Fertility: NICE Guideline (February 2004)

Couples in which the woman is aged 23–39 years at the time of treatment and who have an identified cause for their fertility problems (such as azoospermia or bilateral tubal occlusion) or who have infertility of at least 3 years' duration should be offered up to three stimulated cycles of in vitro fertilisation treatment.

However, the subsequent announcement by the then Secretary of State for Health, John Reid, committed the Government only to fund a single treatment cycle of IVF for women under 40 from April 2005. Moreover, no time scale was given for full implementation of the NICE recommendation (G. Hinsliff, "Infertile couples to get just 'one shot' at IVF treatment", *The Observer*, February 22, 2004; J. Meikle, "Reid acts to end IVF post code lottery", *The Guardian*, February 25, 2004.) Critics argue that the low success rate for one cycle of treatment means that this policy fails to take infertility seriously, especially as the UK is usually located towards the bottom of European league tables for access to reproductive treatment (D. Derbyshire, "Britain the worst place in western Europe for IVF access", *Daily Telegraph*, July 3, 2003).

Furthermore, a recent investigation by the *Independent on Sunday* newspaper found that in fact only 40 per cent of NHS trusts fulfilled their obligation to offer free IVF treatment (M.Woolf and S. Carrell, "IVF: How a generation of women is being denied the chance to give birth", *Independent on Sunday*, April 9, 2006; see also N. Fleming, "Fertility treatment 'to be only for the rich'" *Daily Telegraph*, March 29, 2006). In August 2006, Northamptonshire NHS announced it was temporarily suspending funding for all IVF treatment as part of a financial recovery plan.

NOTES:

1. Note that this guidance limits treatment provision to infertile couples. Moreover, even the ability to pay does not guarantee access to IVF treatment in certain clinics. In 2005 it was reported that the Wessex Fertility Clinic in Southampton was refusing to treat women who were 42 or over, notwithstanding their ability to pay, in order to "keep the waiting list manageable" (R. Nikkhah, "You're too old to be mothers at 42, says fertility clinic", *Daily Telegraph*, March 27, 2005.)
2. High fees at UK clinics, coupled with shortages of donor gametes (see pp.834–835 below) and long waiting lists have sparked a surge in reproductive tourism ("Slovenia beckons with cut-price IVF", *Daily Telegraph*, July 3, 2004; N. Fleming, "Couples warned of dangers in fertility tourism" *Daily Telegraph*, April 28, 2006; N. Fleming, "Where Britons go, and what they pay", *Daily Telegraph*, May 17, 2006).

QUESTIONS:

1. Given that estimates suggest that full implementation of the NICE recommendation would cost £100 million annually in England and Wales (S. Boseley, "Huge NHS bill for infertility rights", *The Guardian*, August 26, 2003; C. Hall, "Free IVF service could cost NHS £100m a year", *Daily*

Telegraph August 26, 2003), is this a defensible use of scarce health care resources, especially given the low success rates of the treatment? (See p.779 above; E. Jackson, *Regulating Reproduction*, Oxford: Hart, 2001, pp.197–202.)

2. Is it fair to limit access to publicly funded treatment to those under 40 and who are demonstrably infertile? (See J.R. McMillan, "NICE, the draft fertility guideline and dodging the big question" (2003) 29 *Journal of Medical Ethics* 313–314.)

7. Rights to Reproduce

With the enactment of the Human Rights Act 1998, it might have been expected that a number of challenges would have been brought on denial of access. To date, however, such claims have been asserted only in the context of prisoners who were refused access to assisted conception (*R. v Secretary of State for the Home Department Ex p. Mellor* [2001] EWCA Civ 472; [2001] W.L.R. 533). The first case was brought by Mellor, a life prisoner who had been convicted of murder. He argued that since his wife, whom he had married in prison, would be 31 when he was released, she might have difficulty in conceiving and that they should be able to avail themselves of assisted insemination (AI). The Secretary of State decided that no exceptional circumstances existed in this case, and Mellor's application for judicial review of the decision was refused. Mellor contended that this breached Articles 8 (right to respect for private and family life) and 12 (right to marry and found a family) of the European Convention on Human Rights. The Court of Appeal dismissed the claim, holding that the denial of AI was proportionate to the aim of maintaining a penal system, and that the Secretary of State's decision was not irrational.

LORD PHILLIPS M.R.
"[44] . . . The fact that there is no jurisprudence bearing directly on the issue suggests that it has not to date been considered that fundamental human rights include the right of a prisoner to inseminate his wife by artificial means. I have concluded that they do not . . .

[60] . . . Mr Pannick [counsel for the applicant] accepted that if his submissions on behalf of the appellant were to succeed, he had to demonstrate that this policy was irrational. That is because it is not possible to demonstrate that any exceptional circumstances apply in the case of the appellant and his wife. Mr Pannick submitted that the reasons given by Mr Sanderson for the Secretary of State's policy were indeed irrational.

[61] . . . [Mr Sanderson] sets out three reasons for the policy that restricts the provision of facilities for artificial insemination to exceptional circumstances. I propose to start by considering those reasons.

[62] (a) It is an explicit consequence of imprisonment that prisoners should not have the opportunity to beget children whilst serving their sentences, until they come to a stage where they are allowed to take leave on temporary licence. Mr Pannick criticised the use of the adjective 'explicit'. I agree that this word does not seem appropriate. I suspect that Mr Sanderson meant that deprivation of the right to beget children is part and parcel of the deprivation of liberty that imprisonment is intended to effect. Such a statement does no more than restate the policy. It indicates that it is deliberate policy that the deprivation of liberty should ordinarily deprive the prisoner of the opportunity to beget children.

[63] (b) Serious and justified public concern would be likely if prisoners continued to have the opportunity to conceive children while serving sentences. Mr Pannick criticised

this reason also. He argued that public concern was not an appropriate touchstone for penal policy...

[65] ... Penal sanctions are imposed, in part, to exact retribution for wrongdoing. If there were no system of penal sanctions, members of the public would be likely to take the law into their own hands. In my judgment it is legitimate to have regard to public perception when considering the characteristics of a penal system...

[67] (c) The disadvantage of single parent families. Here again Mr Pannick submitted that this was not a material consideration when formulating penal policy. He argued that there were many circumstances in which children came to be brought up in single parent families and there could be no justification for the state to attempt to prevent this in the case of prisoners. Again, I do not agree. By imprisoning the husband the state creates the situation where, if the wife is to have a child, that child will, until the husband's release, be brought up in a single parent family. I consider it legitimate, and indeed desirable, that the state should consider the implications of children being brought up in those circumstances when deciding whether or not to have a general policy of facilitating the artificial insemination of the wives of prisoners or of wives who are themselves prisoners.

[68] For those reasons Mr Pannick has failed to make out his case that the Secretary of State's policy only to facilitate artificial insemination in exceptional circumstances is irrational. Mr Pannick accepted that there were in this case no exceptional circumstances, and he was right to do so... I would simply observe that it seems to me rational that the normal starting point should be a need to demonstrate that, if facilities for artificial insemination are not provided, the founding of a family may not merely be delayed, but prevented altogether.

[69] For these reasons I have concluded that the refusal to permit the appellant the facilities to provide semen for the artificial insemination of his wife was neither in breach of the Convention, unlawful nor irrational. It follows that I would dismiss the appeal.

The *Mellor* decision was subsequently confirmed, although only by the narrowest majority, by the European Court of Human Rights in the following case:

Dickson v the United Kingdom (44362/2004) April 8, 2006

The applicants, Kirk and Lorraine Dickson, had formed a relationship and subsequently married in prison. Mr Dickson had been sentenced to life imprisonment for murder with a tariff of 15 years. After Mrs Dickson's release the couple requested AI facilities to enable them to have a child together (Mrs Dickson already had three children from earlier relationships), arguing that it would not otherwise be possible, given Mr Dickson's earliest release date and Mrs Dickson's age. The Secretary of State refused their application. In September 2004 the Court of Appeal rejected their application for judicial review on the grounds that the Secretary of State's refusal to grant the treatment requested was irrational. The applicants took their case to Strasbourg arguing, once again, that the refusal of access to AI facilities breached their Article 8 and 12 rights:

JUDGMENT OF THE COURT
"31. The requirements of the notion of 'respect' for private and family life in Article 8 are not clear-cut, especially as far as the positive obligations inherent in that concept are concerned, and vary considerably from case to case having regard, notably, to the diversity of situations obtaining in Contracting States and the choices which must be made in terms of the State's priorities and resources. These considerations are particularly relevant in the present case. The issues raised by the case touch on an area where there is little common ground amongst the member States of the Council of Europe. The present applicants did

not suggest that there was any European consensus in favour of granting artificial insemination facilities to prisoners and indeed were unable to point to any other Contracting State which affords prisoners access to such facilities. Nor can the Court discern in this regard any 'evolving convergence as to the standards to be achieved' (*Christine Goodwin* v the United Kingdom [GC], no. 28957/95, §74, ECHR 2002 VI) . . . Accordingly, this is an area in which the Contracting States enjoy a wide margin of appreciation in determining the steps to be taken to ensure compliance with the Convention with due regard to the needs and resources of the community and of individuals . . .

33. The Court notes that, as a matter of general policy, requests by prisoners in the United Kingdom for artificial insemination are only granted by the authorities in exceptional circumstances. In reaching a decision as to whether such circumstances exist in any individual case, particular attention is given by the authorities to a number of general considerations which are set out in the Secretary of State's letter of 28 May 2003. As explained by the respondent Government, and as reflected in the judgments of the Court of Appeal in the . . . *Mellor* case and in the present case, two principal aims underlie the policy: the maintenance of public confidence in the penal system and the welfare of any child conceived as a result of artificial insemination and, therefore, the general interests of society as a whole.

34. . . . in developing and applying the policy, the authorities retained certain criteria which concerned the interests of any child to be conceived. The very object of a request for artificial insemination is the conception of a child and the State has positive obligations to ensure the effective protection and the moral and material welfare of children.

35. As to the policy itself, the Court attaches particular importance to the fact that . . . it did not operate to impose a blanket restriction on a prisoner's access to artificial insemination facilities, without any consideration of individual circumstances. On the contrary, as was explained in the letter of the Secretary of State, requests for artificial insemination were carefully considered on individual merit and according to the various criteria set out in the letter. Having examined these criteria, the Court does not find them to be arbitrary or not reasonably related to the underlying aims of the policy. Nor, on the material before the Court, can it be suggested that the examination of an individual case in the light of the considerations set out in the letter is merely theoretical or illusory: the unchallenged evidence before the Court of Appeal was that the Secretary of State had already allowed access to insemination facilities in certain cases, while two applications were struck out by the former Commission when artificial insemination facilities were granted to the applicants (*P.G. v. the United Kingdom*, no. 10822/84, Commission decision of 7 May 1987; and *G. and R.S. v. the United Kingdom*, no. 17142/90, Commission decision of 10 July 1991, both unpublished) . . .

38. . . . the Court notes that careful consideration was given by the Secretary of State to the individual circumstances of the present applicants, including the unlikelihood of conception after the date of the first applicant's release from prison, before concluding that these factors were outweighed by the other factors to which reference was made—in particular, the nature and gravity of the first applicant's crime and the welfare of any child who might be conceived, in the light of the prolonged absence of the father for an important part of its childhood years and the apparent lack of sufficient material provision and immediate support network in place for the mother and child. The Court further notes that the decision of the Secretary of State was examined by the High Court and the Court of Appeal which found not only that the policy was rational and lawful but that, in applying the policy in the circumstances of the present case, the decision of the Secretary of State to refuse the facilities was neither unreasonable nor disproportionate.

39. In these circumstances and having regard to the wide margin of appreciation afforded to the national authorities, the Court finds that it has not been shown that the decision to refuse facilities for artificial insemination in the present case was arbitrary or unreasonable or that it failed to strike a fair balance between the competing interests. Accordingly, there is in the present case no appearance of a failure to respect the applicants' rights to private and family life."

NOTES:

1. The majority held, on the basis of previous ECHR jurisprudence, that an interference with family life which is justified under para.8(2) cannot constitute a violation of Article 12. Judge Bonello delivered a concurring opinion, while three judges dissented. In his dissenting opinion Judge Borrego noted:

   "I find the British authorities' approach, endorsed in the present judgment, paternalist. The same reasoning would militate against the conception of a child where one parent is suffering from a fatal illness and has very little chance of surviving later than its birth. The judgment is therefore hostile to the conception of a baby unless, among other conditions, the stability of the couple is guaranteed and so on."

   Given the narrow four to three majority, it is likely that the applicant will appeal to the grand Chamber of the ECHR.
2. As Emily Jackson points out, a noteworthy feature of Judge Bonello's concurring opinion is that he appears to treat the interests of a child yet to be conceived as worthy of protection under Article 8(2) (E. Jackson, "Prisoners, their Wives and the Right to Reproduce", *Bionews*, 356, April 24, 2006).

QUESTION:

1. In other cases not involving prisoners, do you think that Articles 8 and 12 of the ECHR could be interpreted as affording a positive right to provision of infertility services by the state? (See G. Douglas, *Law, Fertility and Reproduction*, London: Sweet & Maxwell, 1991, Chapter 2.) Are resources more likely to be devoted to infertility services if they are conceptualised as health care matters, rather than being conceptualised as rights to privacy or to found a family?

8. THE IMPACT OF REPRODUCTIVE TECHNOLOGIES ON "THE FAMILY"

Many commentators have argued that the most profound effect of reproductive technologies may well be their potential to further disrupt traditional notions of the family (see C. Smart and B. Neale, *Family Fragments*, Cambridge: Polity, 1999). The ability to separate and recombine the various factors of reproduction necessary to produce a child seriously undermines the conventional nuclear family unit. Furthermore, due to the pace of technological development, there has been little opportunity to assess the impact upon children born as a result of the "reproductive revolution" (see P. Singer and D. Wells, *The Reproduction Revolution: New Ways of Making Babies*, Oxford: Oxford University Press, 1984.) However, as we shall see, law has often been concerned to contain the disruption to accepted family forms that reproductive technologies could unleash. (See, for instance, E. Sutherland, " 'Man Not Included'—Single Women, Female Couples and Procreative Freedom in the UK" (2003) 15 *Child and Family Law Quarterly* 155.) Nevertheless, given this disruptive potential (see D. Morgan, "Technology and the Political Economy of Reproduction" in M. Freeman (ed.), *Medicine, Ethics and the Law,* London: Stevens, 1988; and "Frameworks of Analysis for Feminism's Accounts of Reproductive Technology" in S. Sheldon and M. Thomson (eds), *Feminist Perspectives on Healthcare Law,* London: Cavendish, 1998), it is convenient to consider together the provisions in the legislation defining the status and responsibilities of mothers and fathers, and the status of children born as a result of assisted conception. Significantly, when disputes have arisen over frozen embryos that have been placed in storage, the discourse of family law in often invoked, although, as we shall see, with limited success. Recently, the importance of genetics in defining parents has been highlighted, and discourses of genetics have also played a key role in instituting the concept of a child's right to know his or her genetic heritage. Having considered disputes over embryo ownership and rights to genetic knowledge, we will then turn to consider the still more fundamental ways in which reproductive technologies may be used to create children with particular characteristics or "designer babies", focusing on the issue of pre-implantation genetic diagnosis and its use for sex selection or in order to create "saviour siblings".

(a) Mothers

The much publicised cases on surrogacy and "test-tube babies" in the 1970s and 1980s focused attention on the fact that procreative roles can now be divided up into various components. We can no longer rely on the presumption that the mother is the woman who gave birth to the child. (See D. Morgan, "Surrogacy: an Introductory Essay" in R. Lee and D. Morgan (eds), *Birthrights: Law and Ethics at the Beginnings of Life,* London: Routledge, 1989.) The genetic mother is the woman who provides the ova, the gestational mother is the woman who bears and gives birth to the child, and the social mother is the woman who assumes parental responsibility for the child after birth. As we saw above, in relation to the early surrogacy cases, the courts were faced with the difficult issue of adjudicating on the competing claims of gestational mothers and those of genetic fathers and their partners. The issue of which "mother" is to be regarded in law as the mother of the child has now been settled by the 1990 Act.

Human Fertilisation and Embryology Act 1990, s.27(1)–(3)

27.—(1) The woman who is carrying or has carried a child as a result of the placing in her of an embryo or sperm and eggs, and no other woman, is to be treated as the mother of the child.

(2) Subsection (1) above does not apply to any child to the extent that the child is treated by virtue of adoption as not being the child of any person other than the adopter or adopters.

(3) Subsection (1) above applies whether the woman was in the United Kingdom or elsewhere at the time of the placing in her the embryo or the sperm and eggs.

NOTE:

1. The potential for yet more fragmentation in the concept of motherhood was highlighted by the HFEA's decision to license researchers at Newcastle University to create embryos in which sperm was fused with an egg and the resulting embryo transplanted into an egg donated by another woman, in order to leave defective mitochondria behind and prevent mitochondrial diseases being passed on to offspring. The resultant embryo would thus have genetic material from two women (I. Sample, "Human embryo from two mothers gets go-ahead", *The Guardian*, September 2005).

QUESTIONS:

1. What policy arguments do you think were instrumental in the decision to define the gestational mother as the legal mother of the child she carries? Do you agree with those policy arguments? (See R. Tong, "Feminist Perspectives and Gestational Motherhood: the Search for a Unified Legal Focus" and P. Smith, "The Metamorphosis of Motherhood", both in J.C. Callaghan (ed.), *Reproduction, Ethics and the Law: Feminist Perspectives*, Bloomington and Indianapolis: Indiana University Press, 1995.)
2. Julie Wallbank has offered compelling reasons to question the desirability of the legal insistence on a single mother, which underpins UK policy and legislation (J. Wallbank, "Too Many Mothers? Surrogacy, Kinship and the Welfare of the Child" (2002) 10 *Medical Law Review* 271). Do you agree with the legal approach that the concept of a single mother is important to a child's welfare?

(b) Fathers

The issue of paternity has always been more contested than maternity, as a man could never be absolutely sure of his status as father. This, combined with the fact that inheritance of property and privilege was dependent upon descent through the male line, ensured that, unlike motherhood, the issue of establishing fatherhood has always posed problems for the legal system. The lack of certainty regarding legal fatherhood accounted for the introduction of a common law presumption that children of a marriage were the legitimate children of the husband. Thus, it is marriage, rather than any blood tie, which confers automatic paternity on men. The advent of conception in a petri dish has given, of course, men a firmer guarantee that they are the genetic fathers of their future children. (See C. Smart, " 'There is of course the distinction dictated by nature': Law and the Problem of Paternity" in M. Stanworth (ed.), *Reproductive Technologies: Gender, Motherhood and Medicine*, Cambridge: Polity Press, 1987.)

Human Fertilisation and Embryology Act 1990, s.28(1)–(9)

28.—(1) This section applies in the case of a child who is being or has been carried by a woman as the result of the placing in her of an embryo or of sperm and eggs or her artificial insemination.

(2) If—

(a)   at the time of the placing in her of the embryo or the sperm and eggs or of her insemination, the woman was a party to a marriage, and
(b)   the creation of the embryo carried by her was not brought about with the sperm of the other party to the marriage,

then, subject to subsection (5) below, the other party to the marriage shall be treated as the father of the child unless it is shown that he did not consent to the placing in her of the embryo or the sperm and eggs or to her insemination (as the case may be).

(3) If no man is treated, by virtue of subsection (2) above, as the father of the child but—

(a)   the embryo or the sperm and eggs were placed in the woman, or she was artificially inseminated, in the course of treatment services provided for her and a man together by a person to whom a licence applies, and
(b)   the creation of the embryo carried by her was not brought about with the sperm of that man,

then, subject to subsection (5) below, that man shall be treated as the father of the child.

(4) Where a person is to be treated as the father of the child by virtue of subsection (2) or (3) above, no other person is to be treated as the father of the child.

(5) Subsections (2) and (3) above do not apply—

(a)   in relation to England and Wales and Northern Ireland, to any child who, by virtue of the rules of common law, is treated as the legitimate child of the parties to a marriage,
(b)   in relation to Scotland, to any child who, by virtue of any enactment or other rule of law, is treated as the child of the parties to a marriage, or
(c)   to any child to the extent that the child is treated by virtue of adoption as not being the child of any person other than the adopter or adopters.

(6) Where—

(a)   the sperm of a man who had given such consent as is required by paragraph 5 of Schedule 3 to this Act was used for a purpose for which such consent was required, or
(b)   the sperm of a man, or any embryo the creation of which was brought about with his sperm, was used after his death,

he is not to be treated as the father of the child.

(7) The references in subsection (2) above to the parties to a marriage at the time there referred to—

(a)   are to the parties to a marriage subsisting at that time, unless a judicial separation was then in force, but
(b)   include the parties to a void marriage if either or both of them reasonably believed at that time that the marriage was valid; and for the purpose of this subsection it shall be presumed, unless the contrary is shown, that one of them reasonably believed at the time that the marriage was valid.

(8) This section applies whether the woman was in the United Kingdom or elsewhere at the time of the placing in her of the embryo or the sperm and eggs or her artificial insemination.

(9) In subsection (7)(a) above, "judicial separation" includes a legal separation obtained in a country outside the British Islands and recognised in the United Kingdom.

Notes:

1. Subsection 28(2) effectively re-enacts and expands s.27 of the Family Law Reform Act 1987, which provided that a child born to a married couple as a result of DI should be treated as a legitimate child of the marriage, *unless* the husband proves that he did not consent to his wife being inseminated. The burden of proof is an onerous one since acquiescence in, or ignorance of, his wife's insemination will result in him being treated as the father of the child.

2. Subsection 28(5)(a) states that the common law presumption of paternity attaching to the man to whom the woman is married at the time of the birth, takes precedence over either of the statutory presumptions contained in subss.28(2) or (3). Accordingly, the first step for any man denying the paternity of a child born to his wife by virtue of treatment services is to rebut the common law presumption of paternity. This may now be done by recourse to DNA testing (which may raise difficult issues in relation to consent if he wishes the child to be tested). The fact that he can rebut the *common law* presumption of paternity merely allows the statutory presumption in subs.28(2) to operate. Thus, the husband who denies paternity must also show that he did not consent to his wife receiving treatment.

3. Subsection 28(3) provides that where an unmarried heterosexual couple seek treatment together, the male partner will be regarded in law as the child's father, with the same limited legal rights as any other unmarried father. Thus he can agree with the mother to share parental responsibility or seek a court order to that effect under the Children Act 1989, s.4. Furthermore subs.29(1) provides that he is to be treated in law as the father of the child for all purposes, except transmission of titles of honour.

4. According to s.29 of the Act, ss.27 and 28 apply for all legal purposes except succession to dignities or transmission of titles of honour. Brazier notes how this provision ensures the primacy of certain aristocratic blood lines (see M. Brazier, "Reproductive Rights: Feminism or Patriarchy" in J. Harris and S. Holm (eds), *The Future of Human Reproduction*, Oxford: Clarendon Press, 1998). Since s.29 allows women who have received treatment services to be treated as the mother for all practical purposes, the combined effect of ss.27 and 29 is to endorse egg and embryo donation, at least for heterosexual couples.

5. Subsection 28(6) creates a new legal class of child: the "fatherless child". Subsection 28(6)(a) operates to protect men who act as sperm donors. Provided DI is performed in a licensed clinic, all legal links between the sperm donor and any resulting child are severed. Thus if a woman presents for treatment by herself, or if she is married and her husband has not consented, any resulting child is legally fatherless.

The issue of how s.28 is to be interpreted has recently been addressed by the courts. The following decision, variously referred to as *Re R* or *Re D* reached the

House of Lords, but we extract here the leading judgment of the Court of Appeal by Hale L.J., which was upheld by the Law Lords.

Re R (a child) [2003] EWCA Civ 182, [2003] 2 All E.R. 131, [2003] 2 W.L.R. 1485

Ms D and Mr B sought infertility treatment together and Ms D signed a consent form for IVF treatment involving egg removal, donor insemination and embryo replacement. Mr B countersigned the consent form acknowledging that they were being treated together and that he would become the legal father of any resulting child, pursuant to s.28(3). After unsuccessful treatment the couple separated, and Ms D began a relationship with a new partner. She became pregnant as a result of further treatment, carried out without informing the clinic that the couple had separated and without Mr B's knowledge. However, after the birth of the child he applied for parental responsibility and contact orders under the Children Act 1989. The Official Solicitor was appointed to act for the child. Both parties agreed that the respondent was the child's legal father. The judge ordered indirect contact and adjourned the application for parental responsibility generally. Mr B was refused permission to appeal against that decision, but the court expressed concern that jurisdiction had been assumed on the basis of a concession made without proper exploration of the facts leading to the birth of the child where the application of s.28(3) was "not beyond reasonable argument". The respondent sought to clarify the situation by reinstating his parental responsibility application and asking for consideration of his status under s.28(3) as a preliminary issue. Hedley J. granted the respondent a declaration of paternity which Ms D appealed successfully.

HALE L.J.
"[1] This is a mother's appeal from the order of Hedley J made on 27 March 2002 in the Family Division of the High Court, when he granted the respondent's application for a declaration of paternity pursuant to s 28(3) of the Human Fertilisation and Embryology Act 1990. That subsection provides that a man who is neither the genetic father of a child nor married to the mother is nevertheless to be treated in law as the father in certain circumstances . . .

[8] It was argued for the mother that the application of s 28(3) was a question of fact. These embryos were not placed in her 'in the course of treatment services provided for her and a man together' if at the time when those embryos were so placed they had separated and he took no part in the treatment which she then received. The treatment given to them together ended when the treatment cycle involving the first attempt at implantation ended . . .

[20] In our judgment, the argument of the mother and the child's guardian is correct. We start from the proposition, advanced by Mr Jackson for the child's guardian, that s 28(3) is an unusual provision, conferring the relationship of parent and child on people who are related neither by blood nor by marriage. Conferring such relationships is a serious matter, involving as it does not only the relationship between father and child but also between the whole of the father's family and the child. The rule should only apply to those cases which clearly fall within the footprint of the statutory language.

[21] The wording of s 28 makes it clear that the time at which legal paternity is created is the time when the embryo or the sperm and eggs which subsequently result in the birth of the child are placed in the woman. Section 28(2) expressly refers to the mother being married at that time. Section 28(3) expressly refers back to s 28(2) for the purpose of

ensuring that the mother's husband is excluded from paternity. This suggests that they both refer to the same time. Section 28(3) also focuses on the act of placing the embryo or sperm and eggs in the mother, further suggesting that the question whether this is done 'in the course of treatment services provided for her and a man together' should be answered at that time and no other.

[22] The natural and ordinary meaning of the expression 'in the course of' is 'during' or 'at a time when'. The subsection cannot require that the man is also given medical treatment, because in a case such as this he is provided with no treatment whatsoever . . . Gametes and embryos can be stored for up to ten years or even longer in some circumstances. There must be a point in time when the question has to be judged. The simple answer is that the embryo must be placed in the mother at a time when treatment services are being provided for the woman and the man together . . .

[27] While it is clearly in a child's interests to have a legal father if possible, the Act not only contemplates but expressly provides for two situations in which the child will have no legal father. One is where anonymous sperm donation results in the birth of a child in circumstances where s 28(2) or (3) do not apply, for example to a single woman or a woman in a lesbian relationship. The other, perhaps more surprising, is where the sperm of a man, or any embryo the creation of which was brought about by his sperm, was used after his death: see s 28(6). That is why the Code expressly refers to the extra factors to be considered where the child will have no legal father. It is not self-evident that a child in the situation of this child will benefit from the presence of the respondent in her life: if she would, then the court has ample power to recognise it through sensible contact arrangements without making the child a member of his family.

[28] There is no 'family life' between the child and the respondent which is entitled to respect under art 8(1) of the European Convention for the Protection of Human Rights and Fundamental Freedoms 1950 (as set out in Sch 1 to the Human Rights Act 1998). Family life does not inevitably flow from genetic fatherhood, although it often will. It may flow from looking after a child to whom one is not related by blood, but the length and intensity of that relationship will be particularly relevant. Where there is neither a genetic link nor a personal relationship of a family nature, there is no family life to respect: this case is stronger than that of the sperm donor who enabled a lesbian couple to have a child for whom he babysat for a while: see *JRM v Netherlands* App no 16944/90 (8 February 1993, unreported)."

NOTES:

1. D's appeal to the House of Lords against this ruling on paternity was dismissed—see *Re D (A Child Appearing by her Guardian ad Litem* [2005] UKHL 33, [2005] 2 F.C.R. 223, thus confirming that the child in this case was legally fatherless. (See also *Re Q (Parental Order)* [1996] 1 F.L.R. 369, at p.830 below.)

2. Sally Sheldon notes that the decision demonstrates the weight which courts attach to genetic factors. Effectively B is allowed to claim limited parental rights, not because of a genetic connection *per se*, but because of the role he has to play in explaining his daughter's genetic origins—thus further fragmenting fatherhood. She goes on to point out that at no level do courts seem concerned by the mother's argument that introducing B to the child's life is liable to be disruptive. Instead, it is she who is constructed as morally dubious in misrepresenting to the clinic her relationship status. As Sheldon speculates, this may be understandable given the Act's hostility to single motherhood (S. Sheldon, "Reproductive Technologies and the Legal Determination of Fatherhood" (2005) 13 *Feminist Legal Studies* 347;

"Fragmenting Fatherhood: the Regulation of Reproductive Technologies" (2005) 68 *Modern Law Review* 523–53, at pp.543–544.)

3. As Hale L.J. notes in her judgment, another type of legally fatherless child was created by subs.28(6)(b), which provided that where a woman was inseminated with frozen sperm or implanted with an embryo created from such sperm after her partner's death, he was not to be treated post-humously as the father. The Warnock Committee had recommended the insertion of such a provision to ensure that estates could be administered with some degree of finality. (For a trenchant critique of the provision, see C. Smart, *Law, Crime and Sexuality: Essays on Feminism*, London: Sage, 1995, pp.226–227.) As a result of campaigning by Diane Blood (see p.765) this position was amended by the Human Fertilisation and Embryology (Deceased Fathers) Act 2003 which provides that a deceased father may be recorded as the father on the birth certificate of a child born as a result of assisted conception provided that he had given specific written consent. However, deceased men will not be recognised as fathers for inheritance purposes.

A further dispute over legal fatherhood and the question of consent arose in the following case:

Leeds Teaching Hospital NHS Trust v A and Others [2003] EWHC 259, [2003] 1 F.L.R. 1091

Mr and Mrs A, a white couple, underwent treatment together at a licensed clinic run by the claimant NHS trust. Mr and Mrs B—a black couple—were also undergoing treatment at the clinic. Following ICSI treatment, Mrs A gave birth to twins of mixed race. It subsequently emerged that during the procedure Mr B's sperm had been injected into the eggs of Mrs A. Although it was agreed that Mr and Mrs A would raise the twins, both Mr A and Mr B sought declarations of paternity.

DAME ELIZABETH BUTLER-SLOSS P:
"[1] . . . In order to establish the legal parentage of the twins, it is necessary to consider whether certain provisions of the 1990 Act, principally ss 28 and 29 and Sch 3, apply to the facts of this case. If s 28(2) or (3) applies, Mr A will be treated for all purposes as the father. If this case does not come within the provisions of s 28(2) or (3), Mr B, as the biological father, will be the legal father . . .

[7] At common law, Mr B has the status of an unmarried father. He would not have parental responsibility by virtue of s 2(2)(b) of the Children Act 1989. The main argument in this case concerns the effect of the 1990 Act on the common law and the 1989 Act . . .

[20] The two most important principles to be found in the 1990 Act are the welfare of any children born by treatment under the provisions (see for instance s 13(5)), and the requirements of consent . . .

[26] Miss Hamilton [counsel for the As] submitted that on strict statutory interpretation Mr and Mrs A came within sub-s (2). It was not necessary in the case of a married couple for the husband to give 'effective' or written consent. There was a rebuttable presumption that he had consented. Miss Hamilton argued that Mr A gave a broad consent to the placing of an embryo sufficient to treat him as the father unless it could be shown that Mr A had not consented. He did not raise the issue nor seek to set aside the presumption.

[27] The insurmountable problem, in my view, to that approach, is the question—to what did he consent? The whole procedure is governed by written consent forms which are filled in and signed by both intended parents after careful discussion and counselling in the clinic. Mr A gave his written consent in the standard form which is at Annex C of the Code of Practice. He consented to the 'course of treatment outlined above', as interpreted in s 2(1). The 'course of treatment' to which he consented was that outlined in Mrs A's consent form. As I set out above, Mrs A consented to her eggs being used and mixed with her husband's sperm. She did not consent to her eggs being mixed with named or anonymous donated sperm. She consented to the placing of not more than two resulting embryos in her uterus.

[28] Mr A certainly gave his consent to the placing in his wife of 'an embryo'. The embryo actually placed in Mrs A was a fundamentally different embryo from one that might have been created by the use of Mr A's sperm. Mr A has indicated that he does not wish to seek to withdraw his consent and wishes to take advantage of the irrebuttable presumption set out in s 28(2) and become the legal father. It is not, however, a matter of endorsement by the husband of his consent. The question whether the husband consented is a matter of fact which may be ascertained independently of the views of those involved in the process. On the clear evidence provided in the consent forms Mr A plainly did not consent to the sperm of a named or anonymous donor being mixed with his wife's eggs. This was clearly an embryo created without the consent of Mr and Mrs A.

[29] Miss Hamilton and Mr Francis, on behalf of the NHS Trust, argued that the use of Mr B's sperm for the eggs of Mrs A was by way of a mistake which did not vitiate the meaning of sub-s (2). Mr Eadie argued that such a mistake was fatal. I was asked to look at a number of cases where mistakes were held not to be fundamental and a number of other cases where they were. In my judgment, this line of cases does not assist me, since the mixing of the sperm of Mr B with the eggs of Mrs A was not within the contemplation of either family and was entirely contrary to the written consents given by Mr A. This mistake went to the root of the whole process and has had irreparable consequences ... I am satisfied that, on the proper interpretation of s 28(2) in the absence of any consideration of the human rights legislation and its jurisprudence, Mr A did not consent to the placing in his wife of the embryo which was actually placed. Accordingly, s 28(2) does not apply.

[30] Miss Hamilton argued that the literal wording of sub-s (3) covered the present circumstances. In a situation where no man is treated as the father by virtue of sub-s (2), if sub-s (3)(a) applied to married men as well as unmarried men and the court was satisfied that Mr and Mrs A were treated together by a person to whom a licence applies, then on a strict statutory interpretation, sub-s (3) would apply. She submitted that Wilson J was in error in *U v W* in holding that sub-s (3) applied only to a man who was not married to the woman (see [1998] 1 FCR 526 at 536, [1998] Fam 29 at 37). Treatment together was a course of conduct and it would be wrong in the context of treatment not to look at the whole enterprise. She urged a robust interpretation of 'treatment together', in keeping with the approach taken in other decisions of the Court of Appeal and the High Court to which I shall turn below. She recognised that the strict interpretation that she submitted did not sit comfortably with the Code of Practice which clearly presumed a distinction between married men within s 28(2) and unmarried men within s 28(3). A literal interpretation would, however, cover the situation and meet the welfare requirements of the children who saw Mr A as their father. She suggested that, if the facts of this case took it outside s 28, then this part of the Act was incompatible with the 1998 Act. She suggested that it would be possible for the court to be human rights compliant if her interpretation of sub-s (3) was adopted.

[31] I have found s 28(3) more difficult to interpret than s 28(2). The first question is whether it was intended to apply to husbands or whether it was designed solely to deal with efforts to have children by those who were not married to each other. Subsection (3) requires in the case of the placing of an embryo in the woman that it was 'in the course of treatment provided for her and a man together by a person to whom a licence applies and the creation of the embryo was not brought about with the sperm of that man'. Subsection

(2), although limited to husbands, appears to be broader than sub-s (3). The husband is to be treated as the father, unless it is shown that he did not consent, that he 'opted out'. In sub-s (3) the boot is on the other foot. The acceptance of fatherhood has to be shown. The man has to show commitment and that commitment has to be demonstrated by his active involvement. In other words, he must 'opt in'. Further in sub-s (2), in contrast to sub-s (3), it does not have to be shown that the husband played an active part in the course of treatment provided for his wife and him together by a person to whom a licence applies . . . I agree with Mr Garnham's final submission and that s 28(3) was not intended to include husbands . . .

[33] Since the hearing, I have seen the judgments of the Court of Appeal in *Re R (a child)* [2003] EWCA Civ 182, [2003] 1 FCR 481 [above], which dealt with s 28(3). I am reassured in my conclusions that s 28(3) was not intended to apply to husbands by the judgment of Hale LJ . . .

A fundamental error resulting in the use of the sperm of another in place of the use of sperm of the man taking part in the treatment must vitiate the whole concept of 'treatment together' for the purposes of the 1990 Act. I am therefore satisfied, even if s 28(3) could be construed as applying to married couples as well as unmarried couples, that Mr and Mrs A were not being treated together within the meaning of the subsection. Accordingly, s 28(3) cannot cover the present facts . . .

[39] I have heard submissions on arts 6, 8, 12 and 14 of the European Convention. In my judgment the articles of the Convention other than art 8 are not infringed and it is not necessary for me to explore them further. Clearly, however, art 8 is engaged and I shall therefore look in turn at the positions of Mrs B, Mr B, Mrs A and Mr A, and the twins . . .

[58] I am entirely satisfied that the issue of potential incompatibility of the 1990 Act with the human rights legislation does not arise in respect of any of the parties to these proceedings. As I have set out above, the rights of Mr and Mrs B are not infringed. In relation to the rights of Mr and Mrs A, it would be possible, if I was compelled to do so by my duty to ensure the compatibility of domestic legislation with the 1998 Act, so to construe s 28(3) as to squeeze into it the present situation and thereby avoid a situation of incompatibility. But more to the point, there are alternative routes through domestic family legislation which can give to Mr and Mrs A adequate protection and relief from the unhappy situation in which they find themselves. The twins require love, security and protection within their existing family, all of which can be ensured by domestic legislation and they do not require, nor would it be to their advantage, for there to be any consideration of incompatibility.

NOTES:

1. Once again this case demonstrates the centrality of consent to the legislative framework. Because Mr A was found not to have consented to the placing in his wife of these particular embryos, he could not be deemed to be the father by virtue of s.28(2) and because he did not consent to the use of another man's sperm, Mr and Mrs A could not be regarded as having had "treatment together" under s.28(3). In this respect it echoes the *Blood* decision—see p.765 above.

2. As Sheldon points out, although the court decided that the fundamental mistake involved vitiated Mr A's consent, it could equally plausibly have found in favour of Mr A, given the clear desire to protect the sanctity of the nuclear family evidenced in parliamentary debates preceding the 1990 Act. Instead, she argues that the judgment can be located within a more recent shift "towards recognising a fragmentation of fatherhood, with a number of different parental figures potentially important for different reasons" (S.

Sheldon, "Fragmenting Fatherhood: the Regulation of Reproductive Technologies" (2005) 68 *Modern Law Review* 523–553 at p.544).

3. A further issue which has arisen before the courts is the extent to which a man who is deemed by law to be a father under s.28 is protected once the marriage breaks up. In the case of *Re CH (Contact: Parentage)* [1996] 1 F.L.R. 569, the parties had been married for eight years. The husband had a daughter from a previous marriage and had been sterilised subsequent to her birth. It proved impossible to have the vasectomy reversed when he and his second wife decided that they wanted children. Eventually they decided to have a child by donor insemination. The husband gave his written consent to the procedure, was present at the birth of the child in April 1993, and was registered as the father at the time of birth. The parties separated in March 1994 as a result of the husband's drunkenness and violence. Having remarried, the wife sought to deny contact to her former husband on the basis that he was not the biological father and consequently there was no presumption in his favour that contact should take place.

   However, Callman J. held that the mother's wish to sever the legal ties between her child and her ex-husband on the grounds that he was not the biological father was contrary both to the express wishes of Parliament in the 1990 Act and to principles of justice. He stated that without the father's consent to and participation in treatment there would have been no child, and that he could see no reason why the father should be denied contact given that he had displayed no violence to the child. Like *Re R/Re D* (above) the case is interesting for its dissection of the concept of fatherhood into three components—social fatherhood (the mother's new husband); legal fatherhood (her ex-husband); and biological fatherhood (the sperm donor).

4. In the wake of the *Leeds* case the Chief Medical Officer commissioned an inquiry, which found that there had been a catalogue of mistakes at two clinics in Leeds, including the accidental destruction of embryos as well as the sperm mix-up (B. Toft, *Independent Review of the Circumstances Surrounding Four Adverse Events that Occurred in the Reproductive Medicine Units at Leeds Teaching Hospitals NHS Trust, West Yorkshire*, London, Department of Health, 2004.) In its response to the report, the HFEA indicated that most of the measures recommended in the report to tighten up regulation were by then in place (HFEA, *The HFEA Response to Professor Brian Toft's Report*, June 2004).

5. Clearly the "mistake" in this case only came to light because of the different races of the parents. Mason and Laurie suggest the case is atypical (K. Mason and G. Laurie, *Mason & McCall Smith's Law and Medical Ethics* (7th edn), Oxford: OUP, 2006 at p.90). However, Ford and Morgan note that a similar case occurred in Manhattan in 1999 when a woman gave birth to twins one of whom was white and one black (M. Ford and D. Morgan, "Misconceived Conceptions" (2004) 30 *Journal of Medical Ethics* 478–479); while media reports in the wake of the Leeds case pointed to another sperm mix-up in a Dutch clinic in 1993. It was also reported

that the HFEA acknowledged the detection of a small number of errors in clinics each year, but claimed that these were usually picked up prior to implantation. Such reports do, however, flag up concerns about how adequately licensed clinics are monitored in practice (D. Derbyshire, "Mix-up may have happened before, admits watchdog", *Daily Telegraph* May 20, 2006).

QUESTIONS:

1. Do you agree with the judge's reasoning as to why human rights based arguments are not applicable in this case? Was this the decision which best furthered the interests of the child, in your view?
2. Do you agree with the legal definitions of parents in the 1990 Act? Does s.28 place the burden of proof in the right place?
3. Do you agree with Ford and Morgan (*op. cit.* in note 5 at p.49) that the Leeds decision "appears to swim against the tide of legal and cultural change, which has in recent years, been moving towards an acknowledgement that 'what really matters' about family is not genetic relationship, but bonds of care between people who may or may not be biologically related"?

(c) Children of the Reproductive Revolution

In this section we address two issues pertaining to children born through assisted conception. The first concerns their status within the family, the second their right to knowledge about their genetic heritage. Until 1987 a sperm donor was regarded in law as the father of any ensuing child. In 1987 the status of children born as a result of DI was clarified by the Family Law Reform Act which removed the taint of illegitimacy. As noted above, s.27 of that Act provided that where the woman's husband had not refused consent to her insemination, any child born to her was to be treated also as the child of her husband. Section 30 of the 1990 Act extends the approach of s.27 of the Family Law Reform Act 1987 to children born via surrogacy involving egg or embryo donation.

Human Fertilisation and Embryology Act 1990, s.30(1–7)

30.—(1) The court may make an order providing for a child to be treated in law as the child of the parties to a marriage (referred to in this section as "the husband" and "the wife") if—

(a) the child has been carried by a woman other than the wife as the result of the placing in her of an embryo or sperm and eggs or her artificial insemination,
(b) the gametes of the husband or the wife, or both, were used to bring about the creation of the embryo, and
(c) the conditions in subsections (2) to (7) below are satisfied.

(2) The husband and the wife must apply for the order within six months of the birth of the child or, in the case of a child born before the coming into force of this Act, within six months of the coming into force.

(3) At the time of the application and of the making of the order —

(a) the child's home must be with the husband and the wife, and
(b) the husband or the wife, or both of them, must be domiciled in a part of the United Kingdom or in the Channel Islands or the Isle of Man.

(4) At the time of the making of the order both the husband and the wife must have attained the age of eighteen.

(5) The court must be satisfied that both the father of the child (including a person who is the father by virtue of section 28 of this Act), where he is not the husband, and the woman who carried the child have freely, and with full understanding of what is involved, agreed unconditionally to the making of the order.

(6) Subsection (5) above does not require the agreement of a person who cannot be found or is incapable of giving agreement and the agreement of the woman who carried the child is ineffective for the purposes of that subsection if given by her less than six weeks after the child's birth.

(7) The court must be satisfied that no money or other benefit (other than for expenses reasonably incurred) has been given or received by the husband or the wife for or in consideration of —

(a) the making of the order,
(b) any agreement required by subsection (5) above,
(c) the handing over of the child to the husband and the wife, or
(d) the making of any arrangements with a view to the making of the order,

unless authorised by the court.

NOTES:

1. The effect of s.30, which came into force in 1995, is that where a married couple have commissioned a woman (the "surrogate mother") to carry a child, the couple may apply for a court order (a "parental order") that they shall be regarded as the child's parents under this section provided one or both of them have donated gametes. The section was added as a late amendment arising out of the case of *Re W (minors) (surrogacy)* [1991] 1 F.L.R. 385, discussed at p.790 above). This provision will only be of use in uncontested cases, where both the surrogate mother and her partner consent to the handing over of the child. The effect of a "parental order" under this section is that the child will be regarded in law as the child of the commissioning married couple. It thus effectively reverses the provisions of ss.27–29 above, which would deem the surrogate to be the mother and her partner to be the father. The procedure is considerably less cumbersome than procedures under the adoption legislation, which would produce the same end result.

2. The Parental Orders (Human Fertilisation and Embryology) Regulations 1994 (SI 1994/2767) amend and apply certain provisions in the Adoption legislation to parental order cases under s.30. The regulations specify that hearings should be in private and that the paramount consideration is "the need to safeguard and promote the welfare of the child throughout his

childhood". The effect of a parental order under s.30 is to extinguish any "parental responsibility" on the part of the surrogate mother and her partner. The Registrar General is required to maintain a distinct "Parental Order Register" to record the effects of parental orders made by the court. A person who is the subject of a parental order will be allowed to obtain details of their birth once they have reached the age of 18. (See A. Grubb, Commentary (1995) 3 *Medical Law Review* 204.)

3. In the case of *Re Q* (Parental Order) [1996] 1 F.L.R. 369, the question arose as to who was to be treated as a father for the purpose of giving consent to the making of a parental order under s.30. The facts of the case were that an unmarried woman had acted as a surrogate mother for a married couple, and she carried a child created from the egg of the wife of the commissioning couple fertilised by sperm from a licensed donor. Johnson J. held that as the surrogate mother was not married, she had no husband who could be treated as the father under subs.28(2); and that as the husband of the commissioning couple had not presented himself for "treatment services" with the surrogate mother he could not be deemed to be the father under subs.28(3). The sperm donor was excluded because he had donated via a licensed clinic. Thus the child was legally fatherless (see p.821, Note 5 above) and only the surrogate mother's consent was needed before a parental order could be made.

QUESTIONS:

1. Is s.30 out of line with the general legislative policy of discouraging surrogacy? If so, what explains this provision? (See R.G. Lee and D. Morgan, *Human Fertilisation and Embryology: Regulating the Reproductive Revolution* London: Blackstone Press, 2001, at pp.219–221; B.E. Blythe, "Section 30 — the Acceptable Face of Surrogacy?" [1993] *Journal of Social Welfare and Family Law* 248.)

2. Why does s.30 only operate in favour of *married* couples? Is it inconsistent with s.28 which allows an unmarried man to be treated as a father where his partner receives treatment? Note that it is likely that this anomaly will be removed as a result of the current review of the 1990 Act.

The issue of whether children born via assisted reproduction have a right to know about their genetic origins and method of conception has proven troublesome. Some commentators have asserted that children born as a result of DI (and by implication as a result of egg or embryo donation) should be able to trace their conceptual origins. Such a contention is rooted in the convention that individuals have a desire to know their family history, which is now validated by the medical benefits of such knowledge; and that by analogy with adoption, children conceived through DI should be granted the same rights to counselling and information concerning ethnic origin and genetic health which are available to adopted children. The Warnock Committee addressed this issue briefly:

Warnock Committee: *Report of the Committee of Inquiry into Human Fertilisation and Embryology* (1984) Cmnd. 9314

4.21 As a matter of principle we do not wish to encourage the possibility of prospective parents seeking donors with specific characteristics by the use of whose semen they hope to give birth to a particular type of child. We do not therefore want detailed descriptions of donors to be used as a basis for choice, but we believe that the couple should be given sufficient relevant information for their reassurance. This should include some basic facts about the donor such as his ethnic group and his genetic health. A small minority of the Inquiry, while supporting the principle set out above, and without compromising the principle of anonymity, consider that a gradual move towards making more detailed descriptions of the donor available to prospective parents, if requested, could be beneficial to the practice of AID, provided this was accompanied by appropriate counselling. *We recommend that on reaching the age of eighteen the child should have access to the basic information about the donor's ethnic origin and genetic health and that legislation should be enacted to provide the right of access to this* ...

Warnock's recommendation was partially adopted in the 1990 Act.

Human Fertilisation and Embryology Act 1990, s.31(1–4)

31.—(1) The Authority shall keep a register which shall contain any information obtained by the Authority which falls within subsection (2) below.

(2) Information falls within this subsection if it relates to—

(a)   the provision of treatment services for any identifiable individual, or
(b)   the keeping or use of the gametes of any identifiable individual or of an embryo taken from any identifiable woman,

or if it shows that any identifiable individual was, or may have been, born in consequence of treatment services.

(3) A person who has attained the age of eighteen ("the applicant") may by notice to the Authority require the Authority to comply with a request under subsection (4) below, and the Authority shall do so if—

(a)   the information contained in the register shows that the applicant was, or may have been, born in consequence of treatment services, and
(b)   the applicant has been given a suitable opportunity to receive proper counselling about the implications of compliance with the request.

(4) The applicant may request the Authority to give the applicant notice stating whether or not the information contained in the register shows that a person other than a parent of the applicant would or might, but for sections 27 to 29 of this Act, be a parent of the applicant and, if it does show that—

(a)   giving the applicant so much of that information as relates to the person concerned as the Authority is required by regulations to give (but no other information), or
(b)   stating whether or not that information shows that, but for sections 27 to 29 of this Act, the applicant, and a person specified in the request as a person who the applicant proposes to marry, would or might be related ...

NOTES:

1. Commentators have suggested that the real motivation for the policy of sperm donor anonymity was to protect the nuclear family. As Thomson

states, "the [Warnock] Report has a strong tone of bringing this practice of [DI] within a regulatory framework and legally securing the family unit": (M. Thomson, "Regulating (for) sperm donor identity" in *Endowed: Regulating the Male Sexed Body* New York: Routledge, forthcoming, 2007; see also E. Haimes, "Recreating the Family? Policy Considerations Relating to the 'New' Reproductive technologies" in M. McNeil *et al.* (eds), *The New Reproductive Technologies*, Basingstoke: Macmillan, 1990, p.169; Kath O'Donnell, "Legal Conceptions: Regulating Gametes and Gamete Donation" (2000) 8 *Health Care Analysis* 137.)

2. No regulations were issued under s.31 specifying what information may be divulged to a child conceived using donated materials until 2004 (see below). Note, however, that the Act does not stipulate that donors must be anonymous—thus relatives or friends can donate to one another. Donors can also specify that gametes may be used only by named friends or relatives.

3. Section 33 of the 1990 Act imposes limits on disclosure of registered information under s.31 and of other information obtained in confidence by the HFEA. (For discussion of this provision see Chapter 9.)

4. Note that under s.30 of the 1990 Act a person who is the subject of a "parental order" was allowed details of their birth at 18 years of age, thus granting them the same rights as adopted children under the Adoption Act 2002, but until 2005 they were the only children born as a result of assisted conception granted this right.

Reform of the law to abolish donor anonymity was given impetus by the following case, which was supported by Liberty:

Rose v Secretary of State for Health and Human Fertilisation and Embryology Authority [2002] EWHC 1593 (Admin), [2003] 2 F.L.R. 962

The claimants in this case—Joanna Rose, an adult born before the 1990 legislation was enacted, and EM, a child represented by her mother as litigation friend—had been born as a result of donor insemination. Both requested that the Secretary of State make available non-identifying information and either a contact register or, where possible, identifying information, in respect of the anonymous donors. The Secretary of State's response was that there was to be a consultation exercise and that the issue would be considered by ministers following completion of the consultation exercise. The claimants sought judicial review of that decision, arguing that their rights under Articles 8 and 14 of the European Convention on Human Rights were engaged, and that in order to discharge its duties under those articles, the State had a positive obligation to ensure that certain vital non-identifying information about donors was collected and made available to children born as a result of DI, including all the information routinely recorded in adoption cases. The court acknowledged that Article 8 was engaged but held, given the caveats in Article 8(2), that this did not necessarily establish that UK law had breached Article 8.

SCOTT BAKER J.

[17] It is necessary at the outset to say that Ms Carss-Frisk QC, who has appeared for the claimants, has made it clear that for the purposes of this litigation it is not sought to achieve compulsory disclosure of the identity of donors. This seems to me to be an entirely realistic position for her to take. The donors donated the sperm voluntarily for the purposes of relieving the affliction of infertility and on the clear understanding, if not promise, that their identity would remain undisclosed forever. Any failure now to honour that long-standing understanding, quite apart from being manifestly unfair to the donors, would drive a coach and horses through the [DI] system . . .

[20] The only question for the court at the present juncture is whether Art 8 is engaged at all. If it is, it will be necessary at any adjourned hearing to go on and consider the balancing exercise under Art 8(2) and whether Art 8 has been breached . . .

[40] What the claimants in reality want is as much information as possible, including, if appropriate, the identity of the donor. Realistically, they realise that because of the circumstances of confidentiality in which donations of semen are made, they are most unlikely to be able to force disclosure of the donor's identity . . .

[45] What therefore are the principles to be drawn from the authorities that are relevant to this case? They seem to me to be these:

- Private and family life is a flexible and elastic concept incapable of precise definition.
- Respect for private and family life can involve positive obligations on the State as well as protecting the individual against arbitrary interference by a public authority.
- Respect for private and family life requires that everyone should be able to establish details of their identity as individual human beings. This includes their origins and the opportunity to understand them. It also embraces their physical and social identity and psychological integrity.
- Respect for private and family life comprises to a certain degree the right to establish and develop relationships with other human beings.
- The fact that there is no existing relationship beyond an unidentified biological connection does not prevent Art 8 from biting.

[46] These principles lead me to the following conclusions. Article 8 is engaged both with regard to identifying and non-identifying information, albeit in this case the identity of the donors is not directly sought. What is wanted is non-identifying information and a voluntary contact register. I do emphasise, lest there be any doubt about it, that the fact that Art 8 is engaged is far from saying that there is a breach of it. That question, which may fall to be decided on a further occasion, involves consideration of other matters and may depend on any future action taken by the Secretary of State.

[47] It is to my mind entirely understandable that [DI] children should wish to know about their origins and in particular to learn what they can about their biological father or, in the case of egg donation, their biological mother. The extent to which this matters will vary from individual to individual. In some instances, as in the case of the claimant Ms Rose, the information will be of massive importance. I do not find this at all surprising bearing in mind the lessons that have been learnt from adoption. A human being is a human being whatever the circumstances of his conception and [a DI] child is entitled to establish a picture of his identity as much as anyone else. We live in a much more open society than even 20 years ago. Secrecy nowadays has to be justified where previously it did not. The distinction between identifying and non-identifying information is not relevant at the engagement stage of Art 8, but it is likely to become very relevant when one comes to the important balancing exercise of the other considerations in Art 8(2).

[48] Respect for private and family life has been interpreted by the European Court to incorporate the concept of personal identity (see Gaskin). Everyone should be able to establish details of his identity as a human being (*Johnston v Ireland* (1986) 9 EHRR 303, para 55). That, to my mind, plainly includes the right to obtain information about a biological parent who will inevitably have contributed to the identity of his child. There is

in my judgment no great leap in construing Art 8 in this way. It seems to me to fall naturally into line with the existing jurisprudence of the European Court . . .

[52] The question is whether if the claimants' arguments succeed they would be capable of justifying a declaration of incompatibility under s 4 of the 1998 Act . . .

[54] There are two reasons why, in my judgment it is premature to rule on this issue now. First, it is unclear in what precise circumstances the issue might arise and secondly, the law is not presently clear and it is possible that it will be clarified by higher courts before the final conclusion of this case.

NOTES:

1. Following the consultation exercise mentioned in *Rose*, the HFEA (Disclosure of Information) Regulations 2004, SI 2004/1511 were passed under ss.31(4)(a) and 45(1)–(3) of the 1990 Act. They prescribe the information which the Authority will provide in response to a request from a person who has attained the age of 18 and who was, or may have been, born in consequence of treatment services provided under the 1990 Act. A person conceived via treatment provided under the Act is now entitled to access non-identifying information (covered by reg.2(2)). Regulation 2(3) removes anonymity for donations made after April 2005 and entitles children born as result of donated gametes to receive identifying information once they have reached 18.

2. Obviously the right to access information under the 2004 regulations will depend upon parents being truthful about the means of conception. In this regard it is noteworthy that one European study found that only 8 per cent of children born via DI had been told about their genetic origins (S. Golombok *et al.*, "The European Study of Assisted Reproduction Families: the Transition to Adolescence" (2002) 17 *Human Reproduction* 830). It seems that such reluctance may be attributed to the contradiction of the sperm donor as disruptive even as he facilitates conception. (On the double-edged nature of the practice of DI, which is constructed as potentially destabilising, as well as rehabilitating, see M. Thomson, "Regulating (for) sperm donor identity" in *Endowed: Regulating the Male Sexed Body*, New York: Routledge, forthcoming, 2007.)

3. Sheldon points out that debates regarding donor anonymity are frequently premised on a binary between social and genetic fathers and revolve around the question of who is the "real" father (or mother), but notes that the "disclosure of information sought in *Rose* is presented as necessary not to provide a genetic father who can replace the social father, but rather to give a further source of information about one's own genetic identity" (S. Sheldon, "Fragmenting Fatherhood: the Regulation of Reproductive Technologies" (2005) 68 *Modern Law Review* 523, at p.548).

4. It is difficult to predict what the effect of donor anonymity will be on the number of donations and the kinds of people who donate (see Thomson, *op. cit.* in note 2). However, recent media reports have suggested that the removal of donor anonymity has led to a drastic decline in sperm donations and caused UK patients to resort to unregulated internet sperm banks or reproductive tourism in order to avail themselves of treatment

with donated gametes ("Where have all the donors gone?", *Daily Tele-graph*, May 1, 2006). A government scheme recently established to recruit sperm donors has attracted criticism for being wasteful and inefficient (C. McDonald-Gibson, "Every sperm donor recruited costs public £6,250, say critics", *Daily Telegraph*, May 20, 2006). Increased use of unregulated internet sites has raised the prospect, canvassed in the Review of the HFEA Act, that the Government may seek to legislate to ban the selling of sperm via fertility websites.

QUESTIONS:

1. Should all children be able to trace their genetic origins? Should parents have a duty to tell their children if they were born as a result of gamete donation? (Compare J. Wallbank, "The Role of Rights and Utility in Instituting a Child's Right to Know her Genetic History" (2004) 13 *Social and Legal Studies* 245 with K. O'Donovan, "'What shall we tell the children?' Reflections on Children's Perspectives and the Reproductive Revolution" in R. Lee and D. Morgan (eds), *Birthrights: Law and Ethics at the Beginnings of Life*, London: Routledge, 1989.)

2. To what extent should the interests of gamete donors be taken into account? (See F. Price, "The Donor, the Recipient and the Child—Human Egg Donation in U.K. Licensed Centres" (1995) 7 *Child and Family Law Quarterly* 145.) How should those be weighed against the interests of the children who may be born? (See S. Maclean and M. Maclean, "Keeping Secrets in Assisted Reproduction—the Tension between Donor Anonymity and the Need of the Child for Information" (1996) 8 *Child and Family Law Quarterly* 243.) Does the current law get the balance right?

3. Are children born of donated gametes and embryos, or of surrogates, or as a result of IVF likely to be harmed in physical or psychosocial ways by collaborative reproduction, which involves a mixture of genetic, gestational and social parental roles? In what ways might such harms manifest themselves?

4. Is it ultimately secrecy, rather than anonymity, that is damaging to children born from donated gametes? Should there be a duty on parents, or the State, to inform children that they were born as a result of assisted conception? (See T. Callus, "Tempered Hope? A Qualified Right to Know One's Genetic Origin: *Odievre v. France*" (2004) 67 *Modern Law Review* 658–669.)

9. DONATION AND STORAGE OF EMBRYOS

The preceding section has highlighted some ethico-legal issues that can arise when children are born as result of reproductive technologies. Earlier we addressed some of the issues involved in donating and storing gametes for fertility treatment. Even more intractable questions arise with the issue of storage and donation of frozen embryos. Here we are confronted with the vexed question of the moral and legal status of the human embryo that also arises in the context of abortion (see Chapter 12) and embryo research (see Chapter 10). We saw above at pp.763 that s.14 of the Act established maximum storage period for gametes for embryos. Initially, because of safety concerns, the statutory storage period for embryos was five years, but in May 1996, the Government introduced regulations to extend this to 10 years (the Human Fertilisation and Embryology (Statutory Storage Period for Embryos) Regulations, SI 1996/375). In exceptional cases the 10-year period may also be extended—for instance in the case of a woman about to undergo cancer treatment who may wish to keep open the possibility of having more than one child in the future (R.G. Lee and D. Morgan, *Human Fertilisation and Embryology: Regulating the Reproductive Revolution* 2001, London: Blackstone Press, at p.122.) For those who had stored embryos during the first five years of the Act's operation, the regulations provided that they had to communicate their consent to the five-year extension by August 2, 1996. The failure of many persons to communicate the requisite consent to clinics by the deadline resulted in the destruction of over 3,300 frozen embryos. In a striking example of the problems to which stored embryos can give rise, the anti-abortion group LIFE called upon the Official Solicitor to intervene to stop the destruction. He rejected such appeals on the ground that his jurisdiction extends only to legal persons and that embryos are not recognised by English law as persons. (See Chapter 12 at pp.902–919; "Clinics start destruction of embryos", *The Guardian*, August 2, 1996; M. Fox, "Pre-persons, Commodities or Cyborgs: the Legal Construction and Representation of the Embryo" (2000) 8 *Health Care Analysis* 171–188.)

The fact that embryos are not persons, coupled with the centrality of the notion of consent to the legislative framework proved to be the decisive factors in the following case:

Case of Evans v The United Kingdom (Application 6339/2005)

This case originated as one of two UK cases where a relationship had broken up after the couple had stored embryos and the woman wished the embryos to be implanted while the man refused his consent on the basis that he did not want to be a father (*Natalie Evans v Amicus Healthcare Ltd and Others; Lorraine Hadley v Midland Fertility Services Ltd and Others* [2003] EWHC 2161, [2004] 1 F.L.R. 67 (Fam); *Natalie Evans v Amicus Healthcare Ltd and Others* [2004] EWCA (Civ) 72, [2004] 2 F.L.R. 766, CA). In 2001 Natalie Evans was informed by her doctors that both of her ovaries would have to be removed because of cancer. She and her partner Howard Johnston agreed that she would have eggs harvested and fertilised with his sperm. Upon removal of her ovaries she was unable to conceive spontaneously although she could carry a pregnancy to term. Use of the stored embryos thus afforded her only opportunity to have a child genetically related to her. However, after the breakdown of the couple's relationship in 2002, Mr Johnston wrote to the clinic requesting that the embryos be destroyed. Ms Evans brought a joint action with another woman in the High Court requesting permission to use their stored embryos. Their claims were rejected by Wall J. in the High Court. He held that since the HFEA's Form for Consent to Storage and Use of Eggs and Embryos stipulated the right of partners to withdraw consent to storage or use, it was open to the male partner to do so. Moreover, despite assurances he had allegedly made to Ms Evans when the embryos were stored, Mr Johnston was not estopped from revoking his consent. Wall J. also rejected arguments under the Human Rights Act, which are discussed in more detail below. The Court of Appeal rejected Ms Evans' appeal against the judgment and the House of Lords refused leave to appeal, which led her to take her case to the European Court of Human Rights.

JUDGMENT OF THE COURT
"56. The Court observes at the outset that, like the Court of Appeal, it accepts the facts as found by the High Court, which had the benefit of hearing the witnesses in person . . . In particular, it accepts that J acted in good faith in embarking on the IVF treatment with the applicant, but that he did so only on the basis that their relationship would continue.

57. It is not disputed between the parties that Article 8 is applicable and that the case concerns the applicant's right to respect for her private life . . .

59. The Court does not . . . find it to be of central importance whether the case is examined in the context of the State's positive or negative obligations. The boundaries between the two types of obligation under Article 8 do not always lend themselves to precise definition and the applicable principles are similar. In both contexts, regard must be had to the fair balance that has to be struck between the competing interests of the individual and of the community as a whole, and in both cases the State enjoys a certain margin of appreciation . . . The breadth of this margin will vary in accordance with the nature of the issues and the importance of the interests at stake . . .

60. The applicant argues that while the State may have a broad margin in deciding whether or not to intervene in the area of IVF treatment, once it does so, the relative importance of the competing interests entails that the State's margin in deciding where to strike the balance is extremely limited or non-existent.

61. The Court observes that there is no international consensus with regard to the regulation of IVF treatment or to the use of embryos created by such treatment. As appears from the comparative material summarised above . . . while certain States have adopted specific legislation in this area, others have either not legislated, or have only partially legislated, relying instead on general legal principles and professional ethical guidelines. Again, there is no consensus as to the point at which consent to the use of genetic material provided as part of IVF treatment may be withdrawn by one of the parties; in certain States, it appears that consent may be withdrawn only up to the point of fertilisation, whereas in other States such withdrawal may occur at any time prior to the implantation of the embryo in the woman; in still other States the point at which consent may be withdrawn is left to the courts to determine on the basis of contract or according to the balance of interests of the two parties.

62. Since the use of IVF treatment gives rise to sensitive moral and ethical issues against a background of fast-moving medical and scientific developments, and since the questions raised by the case touch on areas where there is no clear common ground amongst the Member States, the Court considers that the margin of appreciation to be afforded to the respondent State must be a wide one. In this regard, the Court is unable to accept the distinction drawn by the applicant between the intervention of the State in the field of IVF treatment, on the one hand, and its regulation of such treatment, on the other. The two questions are inseparably linked and the State's wide margin must in principle extend both to its decision to intervene in the area and, once having intervened, to the detailed rules it lays down in order to achieve a balance between the competing public and private interests.

63. The Court next observes that the legislation at issue in the present case was the culmination of an exceptionally detailed examination of the social, ethical and legal implications of developments in the field of human fertilisation and embryology. The United Kingdom was particularly quick to respond to the scientific advances in this

field . . . Central to the [Warnock] Committee's recommendations and to the policy of the legislation was the primacy of the continuing consent to IVF treatment by both parties to the treatment . . . It is true that, as noted by Arden LJ, neither the Warnock Report nor the Green Paper discussed what was to happen if the parties became estranged during treatment. However, the White Paper emphasised that donors of genetic material would have the right under the proposed legislation to vary or withdraw their consent at any time before the embryos were used and, as the Court of Appeal found in the present case, the policy of the Act was to ensure continuing consent from the commencement of treatment to the point of implantation in the woman . . .

64. Thus, Schedule 3 to the 1990 Act places a legal obligation on any clinic carrying out IVF treatment to explain to a person embarking on such treatment that either gamete provider has the freedom to terminate the process at any time prior to implantation. To ensure further that this position is known and understood, each donor must by law sign a form setting out the necessary consents . . . In the present case, while the pressing nature of the applicant's medical condition required that she and J reach a decision about the fertilisation of her eggs without as much time for reflection and advice as might ordinarily be desired, it is undisputed that it was explained to them both that either was free to withdraw consent at any time before any resulting embryo was implanted in the applicant's uterus.

65. The Court recalls that on several previous occasions it has found that it was not contrary to the requirements of Article 8 of the Convention for a State to adopt legislation governing important aspects of private life which did not allow for the weighing of competing interests in the circumstances of each individual case . . . As the Court of Appeal observed, to have made the withdrawal of the male donor's consent relevant but not conclusive, or to have granted a power to the clinic, to the court or to another independent authority to override the need for a donor's consent, would not only have given rise to acute problems of evaluation of the weight to be attached to the respective rights of the parties concerned, particularly where their personal circumstances had changed in the period since the outset of the IVF treatment, but would have created "new and even more intractable difficulties of arbitrariness and inconsistency" . . .

66. The Court is not persuaded by the applicant's argument that the situation of the male and female parties to IVF treatment cannot be equated and that a fair balance could in general be preserved only by holding the male donor to his consent. While there is clearly a difference of degree between the involvement of the two parties in the process of IVF treatment, the Court does not accept that the Article 8 rights of the male donor would necessarily be less worthy of protection than those of the female; nor does it regard it as self-evident that the balance of interests would always tip decisively in favour of the female party. In his judgment in the present case, Wall J noted that the provisions of Schedule 3 to the Act applied equally to all patients undergoing IVF treatment, regardless of their sex, and observed that it would not be difficult to imagine an infertile man facing a dilemma similar to that which confronted the present applicant . . .

67. The Court, like the national courts, has great sympathy for the plight of the applicant who, if implantation does not take place, will be deprived of the ability to give birth to her own child. However, like the national courts, the Court does not find that the absence of a power to override a genetic parent's withdrawal of consent, even in the exceptional circumstances of the present case, is such as to upset the fair balance required by Article 8. As noted by Arden LJ . . . the personal circumstances of the parties are different from what they were at the outset of the treatment and, even in the present case, it would be difficult for a court to judge whether the effect on the applicant of J's withdrawal of consent would be greater than the impact the invalidation of that withdrawal of consent would have on J . . . The Court accepts that a different balance might have been struck by Parliament, by, for instance, making the consent of the male donor irrevocable or by drawing the "bright-line" at the point of creation of the embryo. It notes in this regard that this latter solution has been adopted in a number of Member States of the Council of Europe . . . However, the central question in terms of Article 8 of

the Convention is not whether a different solution might have been found by the legislature which would arguably have struck a fairer balance, but whether, in striking the balance at the point at which it did, Parliament exceeded the margin of appreciation afforded to it under that Article. In determining this question, the Court attaches some importance to the fact that, while, as noted above, there is no international consensus as to the point at which consent to the use of genetic material may be withdrawn, the United Kingdom is by no means alone among the Member States in granting to both parties to IVF treatment the right to withdraw consent to the use or storage of their genetic material at any stage up to the moment of implantation of the resulting embryo. The Court further notes a similar emphasis on the primacy of consent reflected in the relevant international instruments concerned with medical interventions . . .

69. For the above reasons, the Court finds that, in adopting in the 1990 Act a clear and principled rule, which was explained to the parties to IVF treatment and clearly set out in the forms they both signed, whereby the consent of either party might be withdrawn at any stage up to the point of implantation of an embryo, the United Kingdom did not exceed the margin of appreciation afforded to it or upset the fair balance required under Article 8 of the Convention.

There has not therefore been a violation of Article 8 of the Convention."

NOTES:

1. In addition to finding by five votes to two that there had been no breach of Article 8, the court held unanimously that there had been no breach of Article 2 because an embryo lacks independent rights or interests, nor of Article 14. Ms Evans had also argued that she was discriminated against on the basis of her infertility, since fertile women and their embryos enjoy the protection of ECHR rights from the point of conception (see Chapter 12 at pp.902–912). However, this point was also rejected unanimously.

2. The two dissenting judges on the Article 8 point (Judges Traja and Miljovic) held that the majority had been overly concerned with considerations of public policy and the margin of appreciation open to Member States and as a result had neglected the individual rights at stake. They noted that:

    "The dilemma between the applicant's right to have a child and J's right not to become a father cannot be resolved, in our view, on the basis of such a rigid scheme and the blanket enforcement by the law of one party's withdrawal of consent. The dilemma should instead be resolved through careful analysis of the circumstances of the particular case, to avoid the unjust preservation of one person's right by negating the rights of the other."

3. Of course, had Ms Evans elected to store eggs rather than embryos the case would never have arisen and, as we saw (p.761–762 above), this is now a feasible option in such cases.

4. Sheldon has questioned the adequacy of consent in this case, noting that the "lack of space for confidential, private discussions between each party and clinic staff on the one hand, and between the two parties themselves, on the other, makes for rather less than the quality of consent which might be thought desirable" (S. Sheldon, "Case Commentary: *Evans v Amicus*

Healthcare, Hadley v Midland Fertility Services—Revealing cracks in the 'twin pillars'?" (2004) 16 *Child and Family Law Quarterly* 437–452 at p.447). She argues that cracks are emerging in the "twin pillars" which underpin the legislation (the concepts of consent and the welfare of the child requirement), thus lending weight to calls for reform of the 1990 Act.

5. Because an embryo created *in vitro* may only lawfully be kept in storage with the consent of both partners, it seems that if one partner dies the other has no *right* to insist on treatment. Morgan and Lee argue that the effect of reading together ss.14(1)(b) and 4(1)(b) renders it a matter for the exercise of clinical judgment and discretion if the clinic decides to honour the wishes of the deceased partner, as expressed in the written consent s/he was required to give. (See D. Morgan and R. Lee, *Blackstone's Guide to the Human Fertilisation and Embryology Act 1990*, London: Blackstone Press, 1991; see also A. Grubb, "The Legal Status of the Frozen Embryo" in *Challenges in Medical Care*, Chichester: John Wiley 1992.)

6. In the situation where a couple stores embryos with a view to implanting them in a surrogate mother, the HFEA will not entertain applications for an extension to the statutory storage period. A British couple, in an application reminiscent of the *Blood* case (see p.762 above), recently sought permission from the HFEA to export their embryos to a Belgian clinic in order to avoid their destruction and store them until a suitable surrogate can be found ("IVF clinic breaks law to help couple searching for a surrogate mother", *The Independent*, May 11, 2006). The HFEA, in these circumstances, agreed to permit continued storage.

QUESTIONS:

1. Should there be a duty to transfer all embryos to a uterus? If so, whose uterus? Does it make a difference to the moral and/or legal status of the embryo whether or not it is one which is intended to be transferred to a uterus or one which is essentially a "spare" embryo—a by-product of the IVF process? Does its potential to come into existence as a person make a difference? (See J. Harris, *The Value of Life*, London: Routledge and Kegan Paul, 1985, Chapter 6.)

2. If spare eggs are produced as a result of administering fertility drugs, and are not donated or sold, how should they be disposed of? What criminal offence is committed, or what property rights violated, in destroying surplus gametes or embryos? (See A. Capron, "Alternative Birth Technologies: Legal Challenges" (1987) 20 *University of California at Davis Law Review* 679.)

3. What do *you* think should happen to spare embryos or gametes where one of the partners dies or the couple separate? Given how women and men are differently situated in cases like *Evans*, is it possible to achieve a just outcome in the cases?

10. Reproductive Choices: the Limits of Permissible Choice—PGD and the Ethics of Tissue Typing and Sex Selection

A key role of the 1990 Act has been to police the choices that reproductive technologies open up for individuals. As we shall see, this involves the drawing of lines between choices defined as permissible and those regarded as illegitimate. One of the most controversial topics has been regulation of pre-implantation diagnosis (PGD) which has become increasingly common as IVF has become more widespread (see Chapter 2 at pp.133–136). This procedure allows a cell biopsy to be performed on embryos at the 6–10 cell stage, prior to implantation. This causes no harm to the embryo, but allows it in to be screened for features like disease or sex. It offers IVF parents the choice of selecting against embryos which are not of the desired sex or which carry certain genetic disorders. This ability to choose certain features of embryos to be implanted has led critics of the procedure to accuse health professionals of creating "designer babies".

As the practice of PGD largely developed after the enactment of the 1990 legislation, with the first successful use occurring in 1990, it is not explicitly addressed in the legislation. However since the procedure involves interference with an *in vitro* embryo it can only be lawfully carried out with a licence. Since the early 1990s, PGD for genetic disorders has been licensed by the HFEA. (For discussion of the ethical challenges which the practice poses, see S. Holm, "Ethical Issues in Preimplantation Diagnosis" in J. Harris and S. Holm (eds), *The Future of Human Reproduction*, Oxford: Clarendon Press, 1998); HGC, *Choosing the Future: Genetics and Reproductive Decision Making*, HGC, London, 2004; on the law see S. Pattinson, *Influencing Traits before Birth*, Aldershot: Ashgate, 2002.) In most cases the procedure will be sought by parents who have already given birth to a child affected by a genetic disorder, or who know they are carriers, and wish to avoid passing the disorder on to any future child. It currently allows the identification of approximately 200 inherited disorders, including cystic fibrosis and Huntington's disease. However the growing list of screenable diseases and variety of uses to which PGD may be put has posed regulatory problems, which are not clearly addressed in the 1990 Act. The following two case studies demonstrate the difficulties the HFEA has faced in drawing the boundaries of permissible PGD:

(a) The Selection of Saviour Siblings

One variation of PGD involves not only screening embryos to ensure that they are free of disease but then using Human Leukocyte Antigen (HLA) tissue typing to ascertain if the embryo could be a tissue match for an existing person. In 2001 the HFEA agreed to license tissue-typing procedures on a case-by-case basis, and eight centres have been licensed by the HFEA to date. The following case concerned a challenge to the HFEA's decision to authorise tissue typing:

R. (on the application of Quintavelle) v HFEA [2003] 3 All E.R. 257, [2005] 2 All E.R. 555

Mr and Mrs Hashmi had a three-year-old son, Zain, who was suffering from B-thalassaemia, a potentially fatal blood disorder, which required him to undergo regular blood transfusions. The parents wised to use PGD and tissue typing in order to conceive a child who would be free of this hereditary disease and who would also be a tissue march for Zain. They then intended to authorise the use of stem cells from the umbilical cord of the resulting child in order to benefit Zain. The HFEA granted permission for the procedure to take place, with the then Chair, Ruth Deech, explaining:

> "We have considered the ethical, medical and technical implications of the treatment very carefully indeed. Where PGD is already being undertaken we can see how the use of tissue typing to save the live of a sibling could be justified. We would see this happening only in very rare circumstances and under strict controls."

Simultaneously the HFEA issued guidance to govern its decision-making in future cases, which included the following criteria:

> "(b) the embryos conceived in the course of this treatment should themselves be at risk from the condition by which the existing child is afflicted . . .
>   (d) the intention should be to take only cord blood for the purposes of the treatment, and not other tissues or organs."

(HFEA press release, "HFEA to allow tissue typing in conjunction with pre-implantation genetic diagnosis", December 13, 2001, cited in S. Sheldon and S. Wilkinson, "Hashmi and Whitaker: an Unjustifiable and Misguided Distinction?" (2004) 12 *Medical Law Review* 137–163.)

Josephine Quintavalle, on behalf of the pro-life pressure group Comment on Reproductive Ethics (CORE), sought judicial review of the HFEA decision to license tissue typing. CORE relied on the arguments that HLA testing was not a procedure "designed to assist women to carry children", and did not constitute "treatment services" for the purposes of Sch.2, so that it could not be licensed under the Act. The Court of Appeal ([2004] QB 168), overturning the decision of Maurice Kay J., held that this was within HFEA powers, as PGD constituted "treatment for the purpose of assisting women to bear children" in that it imparted knowledge that the child would not be born with a genetic disease which might otherwise have deterred the woman from having children. CORE appealed to the House of Lords:

LORD HOFFMAN
    "24 Subject to these prohibitions [in ss. 3 & 4 of the 1990 Act], the licensing power of the authority is defined in broad terms. Paragraph 1(1) of Schedule 2 enables it to authorise a variety of activities (with the possibility of others being added by regulation) provided only that they are done "in the course of" providing IVF services to the public and appear to the authority "necessary or desirable" for the purpose of providing those services. Thus,

if the concept of suitability in sub-paragraph (d) of 1(1) is broad enough to include suitability for the purposes of the particular mother, it seems to me clear enough that the activity of determining the genetic characteristics of the embryo by way of PGD or HLA typing would be "in the course of" providing the mother with IVF services and that the authority would be entitled to take the view that it was necessary or desirable for the purpose of providing such services.

25 The chief argument of Lord Brennan [for Quintavalle] against interpreting suitability in this sense was that, once one allowed the mother's choice to be a legitimate ground for selection, one could not stop short of allowing it to be based upon such frivolous reasons as eye or hair colour as well as more sinister eugenic practices. It was, he said, inconceivable that Parliament could have contemplated the possibility of this happening.

26 Let it be accepted that a broad interpretation of the concept of suitability would include activities highly unlikely to be acceptable to majority public opinion. It could nevertheless be more sensible for Parliament to confine itself to a few prohibitions which could be clearly defined but otherwise to leave the authority to decide what should be acceptable. The fact that these decisions might raise difficult ethical questions is no objection. The membership of the authority and the proposals of the Warnock committee and the White Paper make it clear that it was intended to grapple with such issues.

27 In this case . . . Maurice Kay J thought that suitable meant no more than suitable to produce a viable foetus but Lord Brennan, understandably unwilling to argue that Parliament might have outlawed PGD, said that it meant suitable to produce a healthy foetus, free of genetic defects. But this definition is itself not free from difficulty. What amounts to a genetic defect? Marie Stopes, an enthusiastic believer in eugenics, cut off relations with her son because she considered that the woman he chose to marry suffered from a genetic defect: she was short-sighted and had to wear spectacles. Surely it would be more sensible to concentrate on whether choice on such grounds was ethically acceptable rather than to argue over whether it counted as a genetic defect. The great advantage which Parliament would have seen in using broad concepts to define the remit of the authority is that it would avoid sterile arguments over questions of definition and focus attention upon the ethical issues.

28 Even in cases in which one could clearly say that the ground for selection was not a genetic defect, a total prohibition might exclude cases which many people would think ethically acceptable. Mr Pannick [for the HFEA] drew attention to the facts of *Leeds Teaching Hospitals NHS Trust v. A* [see p.824 above] In the course of providing IVF treatment to a husband and wife, the hospital mixed up the sperm provided by the husband with that of another man. As a result, a woman gave birth to twins, the father of whom was a stranger. But they suffered from no genetic defects and Mr Pannick points out that if the muddle had been suspected before implantation of the embryo, Lord Brennan's construction of suitability would have prevented any tests to check the embryo's DNA. Likewise, many people might agree with the authority that the tests proposed to be conducted in the present case would be ethically acceptable. It often seemed that an unstated assumption in Lord Brennan's argument was that the authority was likely to authorise anything that it was not positively prohibited from authorising or that it could not be trusted to make proper ethical distinctions. But these assumptions are in my opinion illegitimate. The authority was specifically created to make ethical distinctions and, if Parliament should consider it to be failing in that task, it has in reserve its regulatory powers under section 3(3)(c).

29 Perhaps the most telling indication that Parliament did not intend to confine the authority's powers to unsuitability on grounds of genetic defects is, as Mance LJ pointed out [2004] QB 168, 209, para 143, the absence of any reference in the Act to selection on grounds of sex. It could be said that the Act made no reference to HLA typing because neither the Warnock committee nor Parliament in 1990 foresaw it as a possibility. But there was intense discussion, both in the report and in Parliament, about selection for sex on social grounds. If ever there was a dog which did not bark in the night, this was it. It is hard to imagine that the reason why the Act said nothing on the subject was because

Parliament thought it was clearly prohibited by the use of the word 'suitable' or because it wanted to leave the question over for later primary legislation. In my opinion the only reasonable inference is that Parliament intended to leave the matter to the authority to decide. And once one says that the concept of suitability can include gender selection on social grounds, it is impossible to say that selection on the grounds of any other characteristics which the mother might desire was positively excluded from the discretion of the authority, however unlikely it might be that the authority would actually allow selection on that ground.

30 Lord Brennan referred to the well known remarks of Lord Wilberforce in *Royal College of Nursing v. DHSS* [See Chapter 12 at pp.888].

33 But, like all guidance on construction, Lord Wilberforce's remarks are more appropriate to some cases than others. This is not a case in which one starts with the presumption that Parliament's intention was directed to the state of affairs existing at the time of the Act. It obviously intended to regulate research and treatment which were not possible at the time. Nor is it a case, like the first *Quintavelle* case [see Chapter 10 at p.727], in which the statutory language needs to be extended beyond the 'expressed meaning'. The word 'suitable' is an empty vessel which is filled with meaning by context and background. Nor is it helpful in this case to ask whether some new state of affairs falls within 'the same genus' as those to which the expressed policy has been formulated. That would beg the question because the dispute is precisely over what the genus is. If 'suitability' has the meaning for which the authority contends, then plainly PGD and HLA typing fall within it. If not, then not. Finally, Lord Wilberforce's recommendation of caution in the construction of statutes concerning controversial subjects 'involving moral and social judgments on which opinions strongly differ' would be very much to the point if everything which the Act did not forbid was permitted. It has much less force when the question is whether or not the authority has power to authorise it.

34 Lord Brennan and Mr Pannick each relied upon different statements made by ministers in Parliament during the debates on the Bill which became the 1990 Act. As is almost invariably the case when such statements are tendered under the rule in *Pepper v. Hart* [1993] AC 593, I found neither of any assistance.

35 I would therefore accept Mr Pannick's argument and hold that both PGD and HLA typing could lawfully be authorised by the authority as activities to determine the suitability of the embryo for implantation within the meaning of paragraph 1(1)(d).

36 Lord Brennan made some criticism of the way in which the authority had from time to time stated its policy and relaxed some of the conditions upon which licences were granted. For example, the authority originally gave a licence for HLA typing only if the cell biopsy was also required for PGD, because it considered that the risk to the embryo from removal of a cell did not warrant it being done for HLA typing alone. More recently, after further study of the effects of a cell biopsy, it has decided that the risk is low enough to justify a licence for HLA typing alone. That seems to me exactly in accordance with the duty of the authority to keep the state of the art under constant review.

37 Another point on which the authority has shifted its position is the use of bone marrow rather than umbilical cord blood as a source of stem cells. Bone marrow may in some cases be more suitable but involves a far more intrusive operation upon the donor child than taking cord blood. The policy formulated by the authority in 2001 (under which the licence which authorised the treatment of Mrs Hashmi was granted) required a condition that 'the intention' should be only to take cord blood. After a review in 2004, the authority decided to delete this condition. It was in practice unenforceable because once the embryo had been implanted and the child conceived, the case passed out of the jurisdiction of the authority. On 21 July 2004 the authority endorsed with amendment the following recommendation of its Ethics and Legal Committee:

'It was acknowledged that the authority did not have any power to impose a condition that would prohibit any future attempt to obtain bone marrow. However the committee noted that obtaining bone marrow for the treatment of siblings from children from the age of one year was a relatively routine treatment strategy where no other matched donor was available. The committee also noted that under common law the test for the type of medical procedures that may be performed on a child is very much higher when such treatment is non-therapeutic. Although parents usually give consent to a child's medical treatment, the courts always have the power to overrule their consent where the procedure would not be in the child's best interests.'

38 These reasons appear to be valid. I have no doubt that medical practitioners take very seriously the law that any operation upon a child for which there is no clinical reason relating to the child itself must be justified as being for other reasons in the child's best interests. If the question appears to be doubtful, a ruling from the court may be obtained. The authority is in my opinion entitled to assume that a child conceived pursuant to its licence will, after birth, receive the full protection of the law.

39 In my opinion, however, it is unnecessary to express any view about Lord Brennan's criticisms of the way the authority has exercised its jurisdiction. There has never been any suggestion that the authority acted unreasonably in granting a licence. The case has always been that it had no power to do so. In my opinion it did, and I would therefore dismiss the appeal."

NOTES:

1. At first instance the Authority had also argued that tissue typing on a biopsied cell did not constitute "use" of an embryo and therefore did not need to be licensed. When Kay J. ruled against the Authority on this point, it effectively abandoned this argument on appeal.

2. Roger Brownsword has suggested that some parallels may be drawn between the "saviour sibling" situation and the arguments underpinning the conjoined twins case—*Re A*—which we considered in Chapter 7. In his view both can be read as cases of "instrumentalism" where the donor of tissue or the twin whose life is terminated are treated as a means only (R. Brownsword, "Reproductive Opportunities and Regulatory Challenges" (2004) 67 *Modern Law Review* 304–21 at p.315).

3. Following the HFEA's decision to grant the licence, 14 embryos were produced via IVF, but as was the case with their second child conceived through sexual intercourse, none were a tissue match for Zain. After the decision, the Hashmis were reported to be continuing their attempts to conceive a sibling who would be a tissue match (See S. Sheldon and S. Wilkinson, "Hashmi and Whitaker: an Unjustifiable and Misguided Distinction?" (2004) 12 *Medical Law Review* 137, at p.140.)

4. Shortly after granting the licence in the *Hashmi* case, the HFEA refused a licence for similar treatment requested by the Whittaker family, on the grounds that the disease from which their three-year-old son Charlie suffered—Diamond-Blackfan anaemia—was not hereditary. It therefore did not satisfy one of the HFEA's conditions for granting a licence at that time, viz. "that the embryos conceived in the course of this treatment should themselves be at risk from the condition by which the existing child is afflicted . . . ". Consequently the Authority decided that PGD should not be licensed in this case since it would be carried out solely in order to benefit Charlie, and not to ensure that the embryos themselves were free of genetic disorders. Subsequently the Whittakers travelled to Chicago where

the procedures was carried out and produced a successful tissue match (see R. Dobson, "'Saviour Sibling' is Born after Embryo Selection in the United States" (2003) 326 B.M.J. 1416).

5. In the wake of academic critique (see Sheldon and Wilkinson, *op. cit.* in note 3) and new research demonstrating a lack of evidence that embryo biopsy poses a risk to future children, the HFEA, as predicted by Brownsword (*op. cit.* in note 3 at pp.317–318) amended its policy on tissue typing (HFEA press release, "HFEA agrees to extend policy on tissue typing", July 21, 2004.) The new guidance (HFEA, *Revised Pre-implantation Testing Guidance*, August 4, 2004 CH(04)(05)—see p.848 below) no longer requires the genetic disorder to be inherited but stipulates the PGD should be a last resort.

6. The difficulties in drawing regulatory boundaries in this area were evident in a HFEA public consultation on whether licensing for PGD should be extended to a group of inherited cancer conditions. The consultation was designed to solicit public views on whether these conditions would count as a "serious genetic condition", given that they are potentially treatable, are late onset diseases which do not develop until adulthood, and that they create a susceptibility to the cancer rather than a certainty of getting it. Perhaps predictably, given the controversial nature of PGD, there was no consensus in the responses (HFEA, *Choices and Boundaries Report: a Summary of Responses to the HFEA Public Discussion*, 2006). Subsequently, the Authority accepted a recommendation from its ethics and law committee to allow licences to be granted to test embryos for these conditions. This will permit licensed researchers to test embryos for the BRAC 1 and BRAC 2 genes linked to breast and ovarian cancer and for HNPCC gene mutations which confer a high risk of colon cancer. ("Watchdog approves embryo selection to help prevent cancer, *The Guardian*, May 11, 2006; A. Thornhill, "Designer Babies or Designer News?" *BioNews*, May 15, 2006.) However, notwithstanding this extension of the list of screenable diseases, parents are still being driven abroad for screening for conditions which have not been licensed in the UK—as in the case of the Baum family who travelled to Belgium for screening to avoid having another child afflicted with the inherited genetic condition tuberous sclerosis ("We had to go abroad to get our baby screened", *Daily Telegraph*, May 15, 2006). Generally, see R. Scott, "Choosing between Possible Lives: Legal and Ethical Issues in Preimplantation Genetic Diagnosis" (2006) 26 *Oxford Journal of Legal Studies* 153.

7. Even greater ethical controversy is likely to be generated by requests to select embryos for implantation *because* they carry certain disorders, such as deafness. However, legally such requests would almost certainly be ruled out by application of the welfare of the child test. (See E. Jackson, *Medical Law: Text, Cases and Materials*, Oxford: OUP, 2006 at pp.842–844.)

8. A recent refinement of the technique by licensed researchers at Guy's and St Thomas' Hospital in London, known as pre-implantation genetic haplotyping (PGH), has the potential to greatly expand the use of PGD by allowing the identification of many other rarer heritable genetic condi-

tions, such as Prader-Willi syndrome and Angelman syndrome. It will also allow testing of specific male embryos for sex-linked disorders, such as Duchene muscular dystrophy and haemophilia, meaning that potential parents can avail themselves of more discriminating tests that would allow them to select healthy male embryos for implantation as well as female ones. Critics of such testing have argued that the potential to eliminate such inherited diseases can adversely impact on our attitudes to disability. (See M. Henderson, "Embryo screening set to take giant step in battling hereditary disease", *The Times*, June 19, 2006.)

QUESTIONS:

1. Do you agree with the broad, purposive construction of the phrase "treatment services" endorsed by the Court of Appeal and House of Lords in the *Hashmi* case? (See Sheldon and Wilkinson, *op. cit.* in note 3 at p.145 for the argument that this interpretation best accords with protecting the notion of reproductive autonomy.) Were the appellate level judges right to be so reluctant to interfere with the policy decisions of the HFEA? (See Commentary, "In vitro fertilisation, 'Treatment Services' and Embryo 'Suitability'" [2003] *Medical Law Review* 241–246, at pp.245–246.)

2. Brownsword has contended that the Court of Appeal decision in this case failed to adequately address the key question raised by CORE, which is whether HLA testing involves a different kind of technology or brings in a fresh dimension. He suggests the Court glossed over "the possibility that there is a significant difference between a standard PGD test designed to confirm that an embryo is healthy (and thus suitable for implantation) and a test of the kind authorised for the Hashmis where the purpose is to confirm that an embryo has a profile that will render it suitable to serve as a donor for an already born child." He adds that "if there is a genuine question about whether (and, if so, where) the new technology falls within the spirit and intent of the regulatory scheme, then the courts do us no favour by stretching the regulatory framework in such a way that the issues are not freely debated" (R. Brownsword, "Reproductive Opportunities and Regulatory Challenges" (2004) 67 *Modern Law Review* at p.304). Is this critique applicable to the House of Lords' view as well?

3. Do you think that the deliberate creation of "saviour siblings" is ethically defensible? (Compare S.M. Wolf, J.P. Kahn and J.E. Wagner, "Using Pre-implantation Genetic Diagnosis to Create a Stem Cell Donor: Issues, Guidelines and Limits" (2003) 13 *Journal of Law, Medicine and Ethics* 327 with S. Sheldon and S. Wilkinson, "Should Selecting Saviour Siblings be Banned?" (2004) 30 *Journal of Medical Ethics* 533.)

4. Should PGD be publicly funded by the NHS? (See S.K. Templeton, "NHS pays for first 'designer baby'", *Sunday Times*, March 21, 2004.) If so on what grounds? (See V. Chico, "Savour Siblings: Trauma and the Law" (2006) 14 *Medical Law Review* 180–218.)

Guidance on the practice of PGD is contained in the current Code of Practice:

HFEA, Code of Practice, 6th edn 2003 (as amended by HFEA, Revised Pre-implantation Testing Guidance, August 4, 2004 CH(04)(05))

14.6 Centres may only carry out preimplantation tests for those genetic conditions,chromosomes or traits (or combinations of these),and using those specific tests (or combinations of tests), listed in the preimplantation testing Annex to their licence or approved by a licence committee in any particular case.

14.7 Centres must submit an application to the HFEA for each new condition for which they wish to test and for each new test that they wish to use . . .

14.20 The decision to use PGD is expected to be made in consideration of the unique circumstances of those seeking treatment, rather than the fact that they carry a particular genetic condition.

14.21 Indications for the use of PGD are expected to be consistent with current practice in the use of (post-implantation) prenatal diagnosis (PND).

14.22 It is expected that PGD will be available where there is a significant risk of a serious genetic condition being present in the embryo. The perception of the level of risk by those seeking treatment is an important factor in the decision making process. The seriousness of the condition is expected to be a matter for discussion between the people seeking treatment and the clinical team.

14.23 In any particular situation the following factors are expected to be considered when deciding the appropriateness of PGD:

   (i) the view of the people seeking treatment of the condition;
  (ii) their previous reproductive experience;
 (iii) the likely degree of suffering associated with the condition;
  (iv) the availability of effective therapy, now and in the future;
   (v) the speed of degeneration in progressive disorders;
  (vi) the extent of any intellectual impairment;
 (vii) the extent of social support available; and
(viii) the family circumstances of the people seeking treatment . . .

14.27/1 Where preimplantation tissue typing is to be used in conjunction with preimplantation genetic diagnosis for heritable genetic disease, the requirements applicable to a PGD service (set out in paragraphs 14.12–14.23 [of the Code of Practice]) are expected to be followed.

14.27/2 Applications to carry our preimplantation tissue typing are expected to be made to the Authority on a case-by-case basis. It is expected that applications will be accompanied by a statement from the consultant responsible for the care of the affected child. The application is expected to demonstrate that all possible alternative treatments have been investigated, including searches of bone marrow registries and cord blood banks, and to explain the reasons why preimplantation tissue typing is the preferred option. The authority may require the application to be supported by an additional expert report on the suitability of using cord blood or bone marrow for the particular disease in question.

NOTE:

1. For a defence of the current regulatory position on PGD and tissue typing see N. R. Ram, "Britain's New Pre-implantation Tissue-Typing Policy: an Ethical Defence" (2006) 32 *Journal of Medical Ethics* 278–282.

(b) Sex Selection

In Lord Hoffmann's opinion in *Hashmi* above he noted that Parliament had made no express provision regarding sex selection when it passed the 1990 Act.

Nothing in the legislation prohibits sex selection which does not involve manipulation of an embryo, for instance techniques based on sperm sorting and selection. In the case of PGD, we have seen above that the technique may be used to select only female embryos when there is a danger of passing on a sex-linked disorder which manifests itself in boy children, such as Duchenne muscular dystrophy or haemophilia. However, many commentators endorse the position adopted by the Council of Europe's Convention on Human Rights and Biomedicine (1997) that sex selection for non-medical reasons is ethically unacceptable:

Article 14 (Non selection of sex)

The use of techniques of medically assisted procreation shall not be allowed for the purpose of choosing a future child's sex, except where serious hereditary sex-related disease is to be avoided.

A similar prohibition underpins the current HFEA Code of Practice:

HFEA, Code of Practice, 6th edn, 2003

14.10 Centres may not use any information derived from tests on an embryo, or any material removed from it or from the gametes that produced it, to select embryos of a particular sex for social reasons.

With the growing efficacy of sex selection techniques, and concerns about drawing regulatory boundaries in this area, the Secretary of State for Health asked the HFEA to hold a second public consultation exercise on sex selection in 2002 (having initially consulted in 1993). Following responses to HFEA, *Sex Selection: Choice and Responsibility in Human Reproduction*, 2002, the HFEA proposed that in view of public hostility, sex selection should not be licensed for "social" reasons:

HFEA, Sex Selection: Options for Regulation. A Report on the HFEA's 2002–03 Review on Sex Selection Including a Discussion of Legislative and Regulatory Options, 2003

147. In reaching a decision we have been particularly influenced by the considerations set out above relating to the possible effects of sex selection for non-medical reasons on the welfare of children born as a result, and by the quantitative strength of views from the representative sample polled by MORI and the force of opinions expressed by respondents to our consultation. These show that there is very widespread hostility to the use of sex selection for non-medical reasons. By itself this finding is not decisive; the fact that a proposed policy is widely held to be unacceptable does not show that it is wrong. But there would need to be substantial demonstrable benefits of such a policy if the state were to challenge the public consensus on this issue. In our view the likely benefits of permitting sex-selection for non-medical reasons in the UK are at best debateable and certainly not great enough to sustain a policy to which the great majority of the public are strongly opposed. Accordingly we advise that treatment services provided for the purpose of selecting the sex of children, by whatever means this is to be achieved, should be restricted under licence to cases in which there is a clear and overriding medical justification.

QUESTIONS:

1. Is evidence of widespread public revulsion towards a practice a good reason to ban it or refuse to license it? What weight should such moral intuitions (sometimes labelled the "yuk" factor) have in framing law and policy? (See Chapter 2 at pp.92–97.)

2. What arguments do you think can be made in favour of sex selection for non-medical reasons? Consider the case of the Mastersons. Mrs Masterson was 42 and she and her husband already had five children when their only daughter, then aged three, was killed in a tragic bonfire accident. They sought permission from the HFEA to use IVF and embryo selection in order to ensure they conceived another girl. Although a clinic in Nottingham was reportedly willing to carry out the procedure, the HFEA refused a licence. The then Chair of the Authority, Ruth Deech, justified the decision on the basis that the case would create a dangerous precedent. The Mastersons ultimately spend £30,000 undertaking IVF treatment with sex-screened embryos abroad. All the attempts failed (see R. Shabi, "Baby chase", *The Guardian*, June 26, 2004). How valid is the "slippery slope" argument invoked in this instance? Are there any other strong reasons for ruling out sex selection in this case?

3. Is sex selection sexist? (See H. Bequaert Holmes, "Choosing Children's Sex: Challenges to Feminist Ethics" in J.C. Callaghan (ed.), *Reproduction, Ethics and the Law: Feminist Perspectives*, Bloomington and Indianapolis: Indiana University Press, 1995.)

4. Aside from sex, should parents ever be given the right to select other offspring characteristics, such as race? Can you think of other characteristics that parents might want to select? (See R. Chadwick, "The Perfect Baby: Introduction" in R. Chadwick (ed.), *Ethics, Reproduction and Genetic Control*, London: Routledge, 1989.) Does it make a difference whether parents wish to select "normal" characteristics, such as choosing an embryo which is not affected by achondroplaia (which leads to retarded growth), or that they wish to choose an embryo which is better than the norm, such as a child who is taller or more intelligent than average? (Not that such genes exist, as size and intelligence are also contingent on socio-environmental factors.) What, if any, ethical arguments justify the medical profession or the government stepping in to limit procreative choices? When do the interests of resulting offspring or society justify regulation of reproductive decisions made by freely consenting persons in the private sector? (See J. Harris, *Wonderwoman and Superman*, Oxford: Oxford University Press, 1992, Chapter 7.)

(c) Reproductive Cloning

Another potential reproductive option, albeit one which has been firmly ruled out by the UK and other governments, is human reproductive cloning (see Chapter 2 at pp.131–133). We saw in Chapter 10 at pp.725–734 that UK law and policy has drawn a sharp distinction between therapeutic cloning, which is permitted by licence under the 1990 Act, and reproductive cloning which has been deemed unlawful in the UK by the House of Lords interpretation of the 1990 Act in *R v Secretary of State for Health, Ex p. Quintavalle* [2003] 2 W.L.R. 692 and the Human Reproductive Cloning Act of 2001. The upshot of both the Act and the House of Lords decision is that the HFEA does not have any power to issue a licence for human reproductive cloning. Moreover as Andrew Grubb notes:

"The 1990 Act covers embryos produced by fertilisation; the 2001 Act covers all others, i.e. those produced otherwise than by fertilisation. As a consequence there are no loopholes. Whatever technique is used—whether CNR [cell nuclear replacement, the method used to create Dolly] or some yet to be developed one—the 2001 Act will apply." (A. Grubb, "The Human Reproductive Cloning Act 2001" [2002] *Medical Law Review* 327 at p.328.)

The government response was predictable in the wake of the outcry which greeted the announcement of the birth of Dolly the sheep in 1997. On the supranational level, it prompted the addition of a protocol on cloning to the Convention on Human Rights and Biomedicine:

Council of Europe, Additional Protocol to the Convention for the Protection of Human Rights and the Dignity of the Human Being with regard to the Application of Biology and Medicine, On the Prohibition of Cloning Human Beings (Strasbourg, 1997)

Noting scientific developments in the field of mammal cloning, particularly through embryo splitting and nuclear transfer;
   Mindful of the progress that some cloning techniques themselves may bring to scientific knowledge and its medical application;
   Considering that the cloning of human beings may become a technical possibility;
   Having noted that embryo splitting may occur naturally and sometimes result in the birth of genetically identical twins;
   Considering however that the instrumentalisation of human beings through the deliberate creation of genetically identical human beings is contrary to human dignity and thus constitutes a misuse of biology and medicine;
   Considering also the serious difficulties of a medical, psychological and social nature that such a deliberate biomedical practice might imply for all the individuals involved;
   Considering the purpose of the Convention on Human Rights and Biomedicine, in particular the principle mentioned in Article 1 aiming to protect the dignity and identity of all human beings,

Have agreed as follows:

Article 1

Any intervention seeking to create a human being genetically identical to another human being, whether living or dead, is prohibited.
   For the purpose of this article, the term human being "genetically identical" to another human being means a human being sharing with another the same nuclear gene set.

In the UK the then Secretary of State for Health, Frank Dobson, responded to concerns about the use of the Dolly technique in humans by stating that:

"We regard the deliberate cloning of human beings as ethically unacceptable. Under UK law, cloning of individual humans cannot take place whatever the origin of the material and whatever technique is used" (June 1997).

However, as we saw in Chapter 10, the HFEA along with the Human Genetics Commission (then called the Human Genetics Advisory Commission) did issue a report into human cloning. It concluded that a valid distinction could be drawn between "reproductive" and "therapeutic" cloning. Whereas the latter was regarded as permissible, the strength of public opposition to reproductive cloning was deemed sufficient to rule it out as a reproductive option for individuals who wished to have a genetically linked child, or couples who wished for a child with a genetic link to at least one parent. Although it was of the opinion that the 1990 Act was adequate to prohibit reproductive cloning (a view subsequently confirmed by the House of Lords in the *Quintavalle* case), the Report did conclude that the Government may nevertheless wish to consider passing legislation with the express purpose of clarifying this, as subsequently happened with the 2001 Act (extracted in Chapter 10 at p.727).

HFEA and HGAC, Cloning Issues in Reproduction, Science and Medicine (December 1998)

4.3 The response to the consultation was conclusive. There was very little support for reproductive cloning, though there were a few who saw benefit in certain circumstances, mainly in connection with infertility treatment. 80% of the respondents thought it was an ethically unacceptable procedure . . .

4.8 In relation to using reproductive cloning as a means to relieve infertility it is also necessary to consider the wider question of public policy. Decisions about what may be done involve not only the couple themselves and their medical advisors but also society as a whole. For any type of infertility treatment to function satisfactorily there has to be a degree of social acceptability of the measures being taken. It is quite clear that human reproductive cloning is unacceptable to a substantial majority of the population. A total ban on it use for any purpose is the obvious and straightforward way of recognising this. The results of the consultation fully support Government policy in this respect.

NOTE:

1. In response to the Report, Tessa Jowell, Minister for Public Health, commented that:

> "The government reaffirms its policy that human reproductive cloning is ethically unacceptable and cannot take place in this country. However, we recognise that regulations to allow therapeutic research should be very carefully considered".

Susan Squier has located such responses as part of a series of attempts by law to resettle the boundaries, such as gender, species, individual identity and age, which cloning potentially disrupts. It does so by separating out good and bad forms of cloning and reproduction in order to subject them to medico-legal management (see S. Squier, "Negotiating Boundaries" in E.A. Kaplan and S.M. Squier (eds), *Playing Dolly: Technocultural Formations, Fantasies and Fictions of Assisted Reproduction*, New York: Rutgers

UP, 1999 at p.112.) In this it resembles legal attempts to contain the potential of other reproductive technologies to disrupt the family, which we saw play out in Section 9 above. Similar negative responses to reproductive cloning were evident in the United States and throughout Europe and in the United States (see S. Pattinson, "Reproductive Cloning: Can Cloning Harm the Clone?" (2002) 10 *Medical Law Review* 295-307; J.F. Daar, "The Prospect of Human Cloning: Improving Nature or Dooming the Species?" (2003) 33 *Seton Hall Law Review* 511–572).

QUESTIONS:

1. Is the distinction between therapeutic and reproductive cloning valid?
2. How persuasive are the arguments against permitting reproductive cloning? (See E. Jackson, *Regulating Reproduction*, Oxford: Hart, 2001, Chapter 5; Pattinson, *op. cit.* in note 1; J. Harris, *On Cloning*, Oxford: Oxford University Press, 2004; L. Macintosh, *Illegal Beings: Human Clones and the Law*, Cambridge: CUP, 2005; D. Gurnham, "The Mysteries of Human Dignity and the Brave New World of Human Cloning" (2005) 14 *Social and Legal Studies 197.*)
3. Is public revulsion at a practice a good reason to legally ban it? (See N. Biller-Andorno, "It's cloning again" (2005) 31 *Journal of Medical Ethics* 63; discussing the difficulties in reaching any consensus on reproductive cloning in the formulation of United Nations policy; and Daar *op. cit.* in note 1 for scepticism about the ability of any prohibition to keep pace with advances in human cloning.)

11. PROCREATIVE TOURISM

A recurring theme in this chapter has been that, in cases where reproductive options are ruled out by UK law, then individuals with sufficient resources will travel abroad to avail themselves of those services. Indeed, as we saw in the case of Diane Blood (at pp.765 above), European Union law affords UK residents the right to travel to access reproductive services lawfully available in other EU Member States. We have seen cases where people have travelled to Europe and further afield to avail of PGD, IVF free of age restrictions, surrogacy and sex selection. The HFEA have expressed concerns about the inherent risks that may be entailed by inadequate regulation elsewhere, such as the absence of screening or counselling facilities. (See S. Leather, "Enhancing Life, Extending Life", speech to the World Forum on Science & Civilization, Oxford, 2006.) In addition to the possible health repercussions, the legal consequences of the global market in reproductive services do need to be borne in mind by individuals. These legal ramifications are demonstrated in the following case:

U v W (Attorney-General Intervening) [1997] 3 W.L.R. 739

A couple sought fertility treatment together at a clinic run by Dr Antinori in Italy. They were advised to use donor sperm due to the poor quality of the male partner's sperm and twins were born. When the relationship subsequently ended, the woman sought child support and her ex-partner contended that the children were not his and denied parental responsibility. Although finding that the couple were treated together in Rome, the judge held that s.28(3) of the Human Fertilisation and Embryology Act (dealing with the legal paternity of unmarried fathers—see pp.820 above) only applied where treatment was carried out in a HFEA licensed clinic.

WILSON J.

"One of Parliament's major purposes in passing the Human Fertilisation and Embryology Act 1990 was to set up a system of tight control within the United Kingdom of 'treatment services,' defined in section 2(1) of the Act of 1990 as 'medical, surgical or obstetric services provided to the public or a section of the public for the purpose of assisting women to carry children.' No doubt the profound ethical issues as to the nature and extent of permissible medical intervention in the reproductive process were considered to compel such control . . .

The applicant contends that the requirement in section 28(3) of the Human Fertilisation and Embryology Act 1990 that the treatment services should be provided by a person to whom a licence applies constitutes a restriction on the freedom of those who are nationals of, and established within, other member states, such as Dr. A., to provide services for United Kingdom nationals such as the applicant and the respondent . . .

[S]ection 28(3) would substantially incline most such couples to seek treatment under licence in the United Kingdom rather than in another member state. I consider that most such men would want to be the legal father of any resultant child; that most such women, concerned (I would suggest) less with the financial responsibility of the man for the child following any breakdown of their relationship than with the creation of a fully integrated family life, would want him to be the legal father; and that, in reaching those conclusions, both of them would in particular consider that it was in the child's interests that the man, rather than an anonymous donor, should be his father. . . .

Section 28(3) is a unique and, to many, a surprising provision. In no other area of English law can the male unmarried partner acquire parenthood along with the mother even though he is not the genetic father . . .

Paragraph 6.13 [of the HFEA Code of Practice then in existence] provides:

'Treatment with donated material should not proceed unless the woman and, where appropriate, her partner have been given a suitable opportunity to receive counselling about it.'

Where a couple seek treatment outside the United Kingdom, it would be unrealistic to expect any analogous exposition to the man of the consequences for him of such treatment under English law. Take, for example, the facts of this case. It is true that the respondent signed the declaration in which he agreed to undertake both to acknowledge paternity and not to disclaim it in the future. But there was no prior discussion about its effect; its ramifications in English law never crossed his mind; and he never considered that his signature upon it or his general conduct in Rome might create an obligation upon him to maintain any child born as a result of donated sperm.

NOTES:

1. See also the case of *W and W v. H (Child Abduction: Surrogacy) No. 2* [2002] 2 F.L.R. 252.
2. To some extent concerns about procreative tourism should be reduced by supranational initiatives such as the EU Tissue Directive (see p.754 above) which should go some way towards harmonising reproductive laws within the EU.

12. LIABILITY FOR DISABILITY

If a child born as a result of IVF or DI suffers from a disability at birth which is attributable to negligence on the part of the licensed clinic the parents will have a right to sue the clinic. In such a situation the trauma that the parents will suffer is clearly foreseeable. However, there may be difficulties in establishing who was the negligent party. If the treatment is undertaken on the NHS, the health authority or NHS trust will owe a direct duty to the parents (see Chapter 3). If the treatment is undertaken privately patients should ensure that the clinic is under a contractual duty to underwrite the whole course of treatment (see M. Brazier, *Medicine, Patients and the Law* (3rd cdn), London: Penguin, 2003, p.306.) As far as actions by the child are concerned, s.44 of the 1990 Human Fertilisation and Embryology Act 1990 amends the Congenital Disabilities (Civil Liability) Act 1976 to allow for an action resulting from negligence in the course of providing infertility treatment (see Chapter 13 at pp.962–967). Victoria Chico raises the possibility that a child born as a result of PGD and tissue typing who turned out to be disabled may bring a claim under this Act. She discusses in more depth the chances of parents succeeding in a "wrongful birth" (see Chapter 13 at pp.961–988) action, where the selected embryo turns out to not to be a tissue match (V. Chico, "Saviour Siblings: Trauma and Tort Law" (2006) 14 *Medical Law Review* 180–218).

One issue which has not been resolved by the 1990 Act is whether gametes or embryos could ever amount to a "product" for the purposes of the Consumer Protection Act 1987. (This legislation is discussed in Chapter 3 at pp.203–209.) Lee and Morgan point out that, although subs.6(3) of the Consumer Protection Act specifically incorporates claims for congenital disability, this was probably intended to cover only claims based on pharmaceutical products. Given judicial hostility to "wrongful life" claims (see Chapter 13 at pp.967–971), they suggest that courts are unlikely to countenance claims under the 1987 Act, alleging that gametes or embryos were defective. They add that "the whole tone of the 1987 Act seems inappropriate for this body of law." (See R.G. Lee and D. Morgan, *Human Fertilisation and Embryology Act: Regulating the Reproductive Revolution*, London: Blackstone Press, 2001 at pp.261–262.) However, it should be noted that in 2001 it was held in *A and Others v The National Blood Authority and Others* [2001] 3 All E.R. that human products, such as blood, may be deemed products. Moreover, in the context of assisted conception, Stern has argued that, by applying the Consumer Protection Act, courts may award compensation in cases where donated gametes cause injury, provided it was possible to detect the risk that injury would be so caused (See K. Stern, "Strict Liability and the Supply of Donated Gametes" (1994) 2 *Medical Law Review* 261.)

She suggests that a screening process may enable some assessment of safety. Where gametes are taken from a donor who has been screened and found to be healthy, the gametes can be deemed to be safe as the risk has been screened out. However, liability would be imposed in a situation in which gametes were used from unhealthy donors who should have been screened out. Stern argues that, because the courts are required to assess the risk of disease, taking into account public policy considerations, they would probably find some risk of disease transmission to be acceptable (Stern, *op. cit.*).

QUESTION:

1. Is it appropriate to seek to apply the language of property, contract and consumer law in this context? Can you think of any alternative discourse that could be adopted? (For a suggestion that the concept of the cyborg, which serves to destabilise notions of property and personhood, may be usefully deployed here, see M. Fox, "Pre-persons, Commodities or Cyborgs: the Legal Construction and Representation of the Embryo" (2000) 8 *Health Care Analysis* 171–188 and H.V. McLachlan, "Persons and their Bodies: How We Should Think about Human Embryos" (2002) 10 *Health Care Analysis* 155–164.)

SELECT BIBLIOGRAPHY

R. Arditti *et al.* (eds), *Test-tube Women: What Future for Motherhood?*, London: Pandora Press, 1989.

P. Boling (ed.), *Expecting Trouble: Surrogacy, Foetal Abuse and New Reproductive Technologies*, Boulder, Colorado: Westview Press, 1995.

J.C. Callaghan (ed.), *Reproduction, Ethics and the Law: Feminist Perspectives*, Bloomington and Indianapolis: Indiana University Press, 1995.

R. Cook and S.D. Sclater with F. Kaganas (eds), *Surrogate Motherhood: International Perspectives*, Oxford: Hart, 2003.

G. Corea, *The Mother Machine: Reproductive Technologies from Artificial Insemination to Artificial Wombs*, London: The Women's Press, 1988.

D. Cuisine, *New Reproductive Techniques*, Aldershot: Gower, 1989.

G. Douglas, *Law, Fertility and Human Reproduction*, London: Sweet & Maxwell, 1991.

M. Fox and J. McHale (eds), *Regulating Human Body Parts and Property: Special Issue* (2000) 8 (2) *Health Care Analysis* 83–201.

J. Harris, *On Cloning*, Oxford: Oxford University Press, 2004.

J. Harris and S. Holm (eds), *The Future of Human Reproduction: Choice and Regulation*, Oxford: OUP, 1998.

K. Horsey and H. Biggs (eds), *Human Fertilisation and Embryology: Reproducing Regulation*, London: UCL Press, 2006.

E. Jackson, "Conception and the Irrelevance of the Welfare Principle" (2002) 65 M.L.R. 176.

E. Jackson, *Regulating Reproduction*, Oxford: Hart, 2001.

R.G. Lee and D. Morgan (eds), *Birthrights: Law and Ethics at the Beginning of Life*, London: Routledge, 1989.

R.G. Lee and D. Morgan, *Human Fertilisation and Embryology: Regulating the Reproductive Revolution*, London: Blackstone Press, 2001.

K.L. Macintosh, *Illegal Beings: Human Clones and the Law*, Cambridge: Cambridge University Press, 2005.

J. Maienschein, *Whose View of Life? Embryos, Cloning and Stem Cells*, Cambridge, Massachusetts: Harvard University Press, 2003.

J.K. Mason, *Medico-legal Aspects of Reproduction and Parenthood* (2nd edn), London: Butterworths, 1998.

S. McLean (ed.), *Law Reform and Human Reproduction*, Aldershot: Dartmouth, 1992.

S. McLean (ed.), *Legal Issues in Human Reproduction*, Aldershot: Gower, 1989.

M.C. Nussbaum and C.R. Sunstein, *Clones and Clones: Facts and Fantasies About Human Cloning*, New York: Norton, 1998.

L. Purdy, *Reproducing Persons: Issues in Feminist Bioethics*, Ithaca and London: Cornell University Press, 1996.

J. Robertson, "Embryos, Families and Procreative Liberty: The Legal Structure of the New Reproduction" (1986) 59 *Southern California Law Review* 942.

R. Scott, "Choosing between Possible Lives: Legal and Ethical Issues in Pre-implantation Genetic Diagnosis" (2006) 26 *Oxford Journal of Legal Studies* 153.

S. Sheldon, "Fragmenting Fatherhood: the Regulation of Reproductive Technologies" (2005) 68 *Modern Law Review* 523–553.

P. Spallone, *Beyond Conception: the New Politics of Reproduction*, London: Macmillan, 1989.

M. Stanworth, *Reproductive Technologies: Gender, Motherhood and Medicine*, Cambridge: Polity Press, 1987.

B. Steinbock (ed.), *Legal and Ethical Issues in Human Reproduction*, Aldershot: Ashgate, 2002.

C. Thompson, *Making Parents: the Ontological Choreography of Reproductive Technologies*, Cambridge, Massachusetts: MIT Press, 2005.

M. Warnock, *Making Babies*, Oxford: OUP, 2002.

12

REPRODUCTIVE CHOICE II: CONTRACEPTION AND ABORTION

1. INTRODUCTION

As we saw in the preceding chapter, a host of legal, ethical and socio-political issues are raised when individuals or couples seek to assert a positive right to reproduce. However, over the past three decades, as many forms of assisted reproduction have been normalised, the involvement of health professionals in such procedures has become routine. Equally, if not more, complex issues, of somewhat longer standing, are raised by the assertion of a right *not* to reproduce by women claiming rights to bodily autonomy, privacy and equality. Each of these rights has been asserted by women in the context of family planning decisions. Although contraceptive choices have proven controversial, it is abortion which arguably remains the most contentious issue in health care law. The intractable nature of the abortion debate is reflected in the strategy adopted by legislators around the world, which is to avoid, if at all possible, having to legislate on such a divisive social issue on which there are no votes to be won (see M. Fox and T. Murphy, "Irish Abortion: Seeking Refuge in Jurisprudence of Doubt and Delegation" (1992) *Journal of Law and Society*; L. Hessini, "Global Progress in Abortion Advocacy and Policy: an Assessment of the Decade since ICPD" (2005) 13 *Reproductive Health Matters* 88–100). This is certainly true in the United Kingdom where the main legislation—the 1967 Abortion Act—resulted from a private member's bill introduced by the Liberal M.P. David Steele. It was thus preceded by none of the consideration and consultation, however flawed, which characterised the enactment of the 1990 Human Fertilisation and Embryology Act. As a result, the drafting of the abortion legislation has been the subject of judicial and academic criticism (see pp.878–886 below). The refusal of the British Government squarely to confront the abortion issue is further evidenced by its failure to extend the 1967 legislation to Northern Ireland and the reluctance of both main political parties to reform the 1967 law (despite numerous attempts by private members' bills to amend or repeal it) until forced to do so when abortion became linked with the issues addressed by the Human Fertilisation and Embryology Act 1990. (For discussion of proposed amendments to the law between 1967 and 1990 see J. Keown, *Abortion, Doctors and the Law*, Cambridge: CUP, 1988).

In this chapter, as throughout the book, we focus on UK law, but in order to draw comparisons with two other jurisdictions where abortion has proven particularly contentious, you may want to check the following excellent web sites which focus on legal strategies–Center for Reproductive Rights (US) (*www.repro ductiverights.org/st_legislatiiveacticity.html* and Irish Family Planning Association (*www.ifpa.ie*). In Section 2 we consider the law on contraception. We start our consideration of abortion in Section 3 with a discussion of the moral and legal status of the foetus and the ethics of abortion. Given the divergence of views on abortion, as with most contested issues, legislators adopted what is essentially a pragmatic compromise. In Section 4 we consider in detail the law on abortion, which in the United Kingdom is subject to medical control. We examine the criminal prohibitions on procuring a miscarriage, the grounds on which abortion may be lawfully carried out, and legal regulation of where and how abortions may be performed. We then address in Section 5 the interests of other parties affected by the decision whether or not to abort. We conclude in Section 6 with a discussion of conscientious objection and its impact on the choice to terminate.

2. CONTRACEPTION

In Great Britain in recent years the provision of contraceptive advice and treatment has generally not been legally contentious. However, controversy has arisen regarding the overlap between certain forms of contraception and abortion (see pp.891–898 below); in the context of providing confidential contraceptive advice and treatment to minors (see Chapter 7) and to those incapable of consenting by reason of mental disability or severe learning difficulties (see Chapter 13 at pp.926–947); and feminist commentators have criticised the lack of safe and effective contraceptive options. While there has never been a general ban in English law on the use of contraceptive devices, in the past the availability of contraception has been indirectly regulated under obscenity legislation and through the scrutiny of the divorce court. (See G. Douglas, *Law, Fertility and Reproduction*, London: Sweet & Maxwell, 1991, at pp.42–46; K. McK. Norrie, *Family Planning Practice and the Law*, Aldershot: Dartmouth, 1991, at pp.7–15, and for an account of opposition to birth control in the 19th century, see M. Thomson, "Women, Medicine and Abortion in the Nineteenth Century" (1995) 3 *Feminist Legal Studies* 159). The subject continues to be contentious in Northern Ireland (see, Medico Legal Enquiry Group, *The Brook Clinic in Northern Ireland—An Agenda for Debate*, Belfast, 1992). Elsewhere in the United Kingdom the major issue has concerned access to adequate contraceptive advice and treatment, especially since a crucial factor in the take-up of contraceptive advice and services is the manner in which treatment is provided. Contraception has been available on NHS prescription since the passage of the NHS (Family Planning) Act 1967. In 1974 the NHS assumed responsibility for the provision of family planning clinics, which generally offer a much broader range of advice and services than G.P.s are able to offer. The current legislation places the Secretary of State for Health under a statutory duty to arrange:

" . . . to such extent as he considers necessary to meet all reasonable requirements in England and Wales, for the giving of advice on contraception, the treatment of such persons and the supply of contraceptive substances and appliances." (National Health Service Act 1977, s.5(1)(b))

However, although contraceptive advice and treatment should form an important element of primary care provision, and government policy consistently emphasises the importance of ensuring the development and effective provision of family planning services in order to maximise uptake, in recent years many clinics have been closed (see F. Godlee, "Regions co-ordinate family planning services" [1992] *British Medical Journal* 304, 401). Following concerns expressed by the Family Planning Service in relation to the closure of family planning clinics, DHSS guidance issued in 1989 urged health authorities to take account of the following factors:

- the need to give choice to encourage full uptake of services;
- the need for separate, more informal arrangements for young people;
- the wider health role of family planning services, such as the provision of cervical cytology screening facilities (NHSME, HC (89)24, LAC89(11), H.N. (FP)(89)17, Department of Health, 1989).

The provision of contraceptive services by G.P.s has grown substantially over the last 30 years, reflecting both increased contraceptive availability within general practice and reduced availability of family planning clinic services. Unfortunately, detailed information about contraceptive services is currently only available for NHS family planning clinics and Brook Advisory Centres. Available statistics show that in 2002–03 there were about 2.6 million attendances at family planning clinics by about 1.2 million women and 93,000 men (see Government Statistical Service, *NHS Contraceptive Services, England: 2002–03*, September 2003). While the range of contraceptive services available within general practice varies considerably, such surgeries rarely provide a full range of contraceptive methods. In particular, G.P.s are usually unable to provide free condoms for financial reasons. Moreover, they will have less expertise in fitting contraceptive devices than staff in family planning clinics. Available research suggests that there is a demand for provision of less "medicalised" contraceptive services, although it is unlikely that this demand will be met (see Contraceptive Education Service, *Contraceptive Choices: Supporting Effective Use of Methods*, London: Family Planning Association, 1996). Even among clinic attenders, however, the most common form of contraceptive is the oral contraceptive pill—see p.864 below.

Constraints on contraceptive choices are not limited to control of the service by medical professionals. Although the apparent proliferation of contraceptive drugs and devices seems to have increased choice in the field of family planning, Douglas warns that:

"the provision of effective contraception may have been a mixed blessing for women. While it may have freed them from the fear of an unplanned pregnancy, this has been at the cost of having to face new potential health risks, and of surrendering effective control over the decision of when and how to use contraception to the medical profession, thanks to the way the judiciary and legislature have dealt with contraceptive issues" (G. Douglas, Law, *Fertility and Reproduction*, London: Sweet & Maxwell, 1991, at p.41).

Moreover, notwithstanding a high-profile campaign by the Government to reduce teenage pregnancies in the wake of revelations that the UK had the highest teenage pregnancy rate in Western Europe (see Social Exclusion Unit, *Teenage Pregnancies*, London: HMSO, 1999, Cm. 4342), pregnancies among those under 14 have continued to rise ("£150m plan has failed to cut teenage pregnancies", *Daily Telegraph*, February 24, 2006).

Available contraceptive methods can be divided into two broad categories: surgical and non-surgical. Surgical sterilisation offers the most permanent form of contraception. Female sterilisation may be accomplished by clipping the fallopian tubes which carry the eggs from the ovaries to the uterus. More radically, hysterectomy involves the complete removal of the womb and may be used in the case of women suffering from heavy periods, although doctors have been criticised for performing the operation too readily. Male sterilisation or vasectomy is effected by cutting and tying back the *vas deferens*—the tube which leads through the testes epidemus to the urethra and enables the sperm to pass through. As we noted in Chapter 6 at pp.352–358, individuals do not have absolute freedom to consent to any surgical operation. The legality of sterilisation was formerly contested on public policy grounds. In *Bravery v Bravery* [1954] 3 All E.R. 59, a woman sought to divorce her husband on the grounds of his cruelty in having undergone a vasectomy contrary to her wishes. In his dissenting judgment Lord Denning suggested that sterilisation for non-therapeutic reasons was "plainly injurious to the public interest". By contrast, the majority judges took the view that there was no legal obligation to obtain spousal consent for a sterilisation operation, although they did consider that it was good medical practice to obtain a partner's consent. While clauses requiring the consent of a spouse or partner are no longer used on the relevant form, the BMA suggests that it remains good practice to obtain the consent of both parties. It is, however, unlikely that the courts would be prepared to accord the partner a legal right to be consulted, particularly since a sexual partner has no right in law to be consulted regarding abortion (see pp.912–919 below).

As we shall see in Chapter 13 (at pp.971–988), the fact that courts have been prepared to compensate for failed sterilisations, and in some circumstances to sanction the sterilisation of allegedly mentally disabled women in their best interests (see Chapter 13 at pp.926–947) has removed any taint of illegality attaching to the procedure.

Non-surgical contraceptive techniques include barrier methods such as the male condom, the female condom (Femidom) and the diaphragm or cap, which is inserted in the vagina so as to cover the cervix prior to intercourse. Barrier methods have an important role to play in preventing sexually transmissible diseases and have thus featured heavily in health promotional materials. Such methods have no medical side effects, although they may not be as effective as other methods, and also require a high degree of motivation on the part of those using them. Non-barrier methods include the intrauterine device. This is available in two forms. The more traditional form consists of a copper ring placed in the uterus which releases a copper irritant, thus rendering the uterus inhospitable to fertilised eggs. It has been linked to pelvic inflammatory disease and other infections. A more recent type, the Mirena IUD, is a levonorgestral intrauterine system which releases a dose of progestogens every 24 hours. The most common form of non-barrier contraceptive is the oral contraceptive pill. While highly effective if properly used, it does carry the risk of side effects, as we will see below. The combined oral contraceptive pill, in particular, can cause side effects ranging from headaches, nausea, breast tenderness, acne or weight gain through poor menstrual cycle control to more serious side effects such as thrombosis, breast cancer and infertility. Longer-lasting contraceptives which give protection for up to five years have also been developed. These include contraceptive patches, Depo Provera—an injectable contraceptive—and Norplant, which involved the insertion (and subsequent surgical removal) of capsules or rods, containing the progestin levonorgestrel, into the arm. These long-term methods have proven contentious due to their increased risk of side effects and the delayed return of fertility after use. The constant controversy which dogged Norplant in the UK, including the establishment in 1995 of an action group to sue the manufacturers for complications that occurred when implants were removed (see J. Burne, "Protection Racket", *Sunday Telegraph*, June 23, 1996), ultimately prompted the decision by its UK distributors, Hoescht Marion Roussel, to discontinue its distribution here in October 1999.

Thus, although a variety of contraceptive methods exist, choice is limited by either their safety or effectiveness or both. According to figures for those attending NHS or Brook family planning clinics, 42 per cent of attenders chose oral contraceptive pills. The male condom was the the method of choice for 34 per cent attenders; IUDs accounted for 7 per cent, injectable methods for 8 per cent, and female sterilisation 0.1 per cent (see Government Statistical Service, *NHS Contraceptive Services, England: 2002–3*, September 2003). It has been suggested that these "methods of fertility regulation from which most couples choose represent a choice among unpleasant alternatives" (R. Snowden, *Consumer Choices in Family Planning*, London, Family Planning Association, 1985). This unsatisfactory position underlines the need for care in prescribing, the necessity of adequate disclosure of risks and counselling as to alternatives. To this end, the Contraceptive Education Service has emphasised the importance of communication between doctor and patient, stressing the need for the doctor to listen to the client and to "provide information, verbally and in writing, about the method, how effective it is and about any concerns that the client may have about its use" (see Contraceptive Education Service, *Contraceptive Choices: Supporting Effective Use of Methods*, London: Family Planning Association, 1996 at p.19.) A significant proportion of the women surveyed by the Contraceptive Education Service would have liked more information about their contraceptive options. The report also stressed the significance of health promotion strategies in this context, finding that by the time a woman approaches a health professional for contraceptive treatment, she has usually already reached a decision on the method she intends to use, based for the most part on negative perceptions of those she has chosen not to use. This finding highlights the importance of health promotion information in ensuring that women's contraceptive choices are also informed by the positive characteristics of methods which they could choose. The report stressed that positive information about the advantages of different contraceptive methods must be made available to women before they take active steps to choose or change a contraceptive method. It concluded that:

"[p]oorly informed or misinformed contraceptive choices are associated with reduced user satisfaction, lower user effectiveness and discontinuation of method use while still at risk of unintended pregnancy. By the consistent and co-ordinated provision of information which is standardised, accurate, appropriately targeted, and impartially presented, all members of the health care team can promote and support informed contraceptive choices, and improve user satisfaction and user effectiveness" (Contraception Education Service, *op. cit.* at p.34).

G.P.s are especially likely to prescribe the oral contraceptive pill, exemplifying Foster's argument that doctors are predisposed to recommend methods of contraception which are simple to prescribe and leave them in control. Moreover, she suggests that pharmaceutical companies have a vested interest in persuading doctors to prescribe their products. (See P. Foster, "Contraception and Abortion" in *Women and the Health Care Industry: An Unhealthy Relationship?*, Buckingham: Open University Press, 1995.) The prescription of long-lasting contraceptives, such as the Mirena IUD (which may require a general anaesthetic for insertion and removal) may also be influenced by doctors' perception of certain woman as feckless and unable to manage their own contraceptive regimes. In such cases the consent of the woman is questionable. (See L. Arthur, "The Norplant Prescription: Birth Control, Women Control or Crime Control?" (1992) 40 U.C.L.A. LR 1; J. Hoyal and M. Dutton, "The Right to Reproduce— Sterilisation and the Mirena IUD" [1996] *Family Law* 376; E. Jackson, *Regulating Reproduction*, Oxford: Hart, 2001, pp.49–53.)

QUESTIONS:

1. Is the provision of contraceptive treatment of such importance that it should be the only medical product supplied free to all users, without any form of means testing or financial contribution? If it is so crucial, would it make economic sense for doctors, as well as family planning clinics, to provide free condoms? Should oral contraceptives be available without prescription?
2. Conversely, should the provision of contraceptives be limited to specialist family planning clinics, especially given the numerous demands on the time of G.P.s, the fact that adequate advice and counselling is essential to the

effective use of contraception, and that doctors are not actually obliged to provide contraceptive services?

3. Why do you think that research on contraceptive drugs and devices has focused almost exclusively on women? Despite numerous reports that a so-called "male pill" is in development, the marketing of contraceptive patches for men still seems some way off (see I. Hollingshead, "Whatever happened to . . . the male pill", *The Guardian*, December 17, 2005).

In the past, as we saw in Chapter 6 (at pp.384–387), English courts have considered the issue of information disclosure in cases involving relatively new contraceptives and non-therapeutic sterilisation, and taken the view that the provision of such information was a clinical matter wholly within the doctor's discretion. However, given the significance of social and personal factors, as well as medical ones, in contraceptive decision-making, the better view is surely that there is a particular need for full disclosure of risks and benefits, as well as advice and counselling on alternatives, in this context. Thus the status of *Gold v Haringey* and *Blyth v Bloomsbury Health Authority*, discussed in Chapter 6 at pp.384–387), as precedents must now be regarded as extremely dubious. As Margaret Brazier notes, "I would argue that in the light of *Bolitho v. City & Hackney Health Authority* and *Pearce v. United Bristol Health NHS Trust*, women must be advised of any risk that the Pill poses to them that a sensible woman would consider material to a reasonable decision about the sort of contraceptive to use." (M. Brazier, *Medicine, Patients and the Law*, (3rd edn), London: Penguin, 2003, p. 265.)

The side effects of contraceptive products have led to litigation. The most notorious example was the Dalkon Shield IUD which was heavily marketed in the United States in the early 1970s before it was withdrawn, having caused at least 20 deaths in the US alone and injured and rendered infertile tens of thousands of women worldwide, in addition to failing to prevent pregnancy. (See K.M. Hicks, *Surviving the Dalkon Shield: WOMEN v The Pharmaceutical Industry*, New York: Teachers' College Press, 1994; P. Foster, *Women and the Health Care Industry: an Unhealthy Relationship?* Buckingham: Open University Press, 1995 at p.19). Other types of IUD have also caused side effects (see P. Ferguson, *Drug Injuries and the Pursuit of Compensation*, London: Sweet & Maxwell, 1996, at pp.6–8). It has been argued that more recent IUDs which do not suffer from the design flaws of the Dalkon Shield have a valuable role to play in increasing women's reproductive choices (see D. Hubacher, "The Checkered History and Bright Future of Intrauterine Contraception in the United States" (2002) 34 *Perspectives on Sexual and Reproductive Health*).

As with any other drugs or medical products a person who suffers side effects may seek legal redress (see Chapter 3). A private patient may be able to sue for breach of contract under s.13 of the Supply of Goods and Services Act 1982. Where contraceptives are obtained on the NHS, the patient's remedy will be in negligence, for instance if she suffered a perforated uterus because a doctor fell below the expected standard in inserting an IUD. The major hurdle that complainants face in such cases is the difficulty of proving causation. The difficulty in overcoming this obstacle prompted the Legal Aid Board to withdraw funding in the Norplant litigation noted above (see E. Jackson, *Regulating Reproduction*, Oxford: Hart, 2001 at p.40) and accounts for the failure of the claimant in the following case:

Vadera v Shaw 45 (1999) B.M.L.R. 162

The claimant—a 22-year-old woman—was prescribed Logynon, one of the third generation of low oestrogen oral contraceptive pills, having sought contraceptive advice from her G.P. The G.P., Dr Shaw, gave what the judge described as "her usual low-key warning about side effects". Just over a month after she started taking the pill, the complainant suffered a serious brain stem stroke as a result of thrombosis in the basilar artery, and was rendered almost completely disabled. She was conscious, had some understanding, vision and hearing, but could barely communicate, as she was suffering the condition known as "locked-in syndrome". The claimant's case was based on negligence in the prescribing of Logynon, owing to concerns about an initial high blood pressure reading on the day she was prescribed the pill (which the complainant's family argued was indicative of hypertension) and disputed evidence over whether she had communicated to Dr Shaw that she suffered from headaches before and after taking the pill. The negligence case was dismissed by Alliott J. One of the issues raised on appeal was whether the judge could properly find that the stroke suffered by the plaintiff was not caused in whole or in part by her taking of the oral contraceptive. The Court of Appeal signalled its reluctance to interfere with the findings of fact by the judge, who had had the opportunity to hear witnesses. It concluded that he had been entitled to find that the plaintiff was not suffering from hypertension on October 11 when Dr Shaw first tested her blood pressure, since a single recording of high blood pressure was not sufficient to establish hypertension, and that notwithstanding her family's testimony, there was no medical evidence of migraines. In the leading judgment Henry L.J. then turned to the general issue regarding causation:

HENRY L.J.
" . . . . We now know (and knew in 1986) that the risk of thrombosis associated with oral contraception (though always a low risk) is related to the oestrogen content of the Pill. The belief that the oral contraceptive increased the risk of a stroke (and, it is suggested, the warnings in the literature addressed to users) were based on the early pills which contained a high dose of oestrogen (50 micrograms or more). Logynon was a third generation pill, which contained, over the cycle, 16 tablets containing 30 micrograms of oestrogen and five tablets containing 40 micrograms. This case concerns the risks of those third generation pills with a lower oestrogen content . . . .

The judge properly approached the issue of causation on the basis of his findings of fact: that is, that Miss Vadera had not been suffering from hypertension on 11 October 1986 (or, it would seem, subsequently); and that there had been no history of (relevant) headaches. He was concerned, therefore, only with the general question of whether without those special factors the plaintiff was none the less able to prove that the Logynon had caused her stroke. As we have already indicated, that inquiry was, for the purposes of this appeal, academic, since the plaintiff accepts that it was not negligent to prescribe Logynon unless she was suffering from hypertension, migraine or both. However, Mr

Coonan QC for the defendant took us carefully through the evidence on causation on which the judge had based his conclusion. He was right to do that, because, as will be apparent, proper consideration of the cases where a patient suffers a stroke when taking Logynon at the same time as she is suffering from hypertension and migraine can only be undertaken on the basis of a clear understanding of the effect and operation of Logynon on a normal patient. That evidence included a substantial number of epidemiological studies, as well as the evidence of persons who had studied the relationship between taking the Pill and the incidence of stroke: . . . On the basis of that evidence, the judge concluded that it could not be established, applying the discipline of statistics to the available figures, that the association between a person taking Logynon and that person suffering a stroke was more than a relationship of chance. It followed (bearing in mind that the burden of proof on this issue rested with the plaintiff) that it could not be established on a balance of probabilities that this plaintiff suffered her stroke by reason of the taking of the Logynon.

We did not understand Mr Croxon QC . . . to challenge those statistical conclusions . . . Rather, he suggested that such studies might be misused in an inquiry into legal causation, which he reminded us is a jury question based on common sense. He had, indeed, so submitted to the judge in the course of the trial, but the judge made it plain that he was unable to ignore the statistical evidence and, as it were, simply draw his own conclusion. The judge was right to take that view. From the plaintiff's point of view, there was in fact no evidence that Logynon had caused Miss Vadera's stroke. Dr Lidegaard was called in an attempt to remedy that difficulty. The judge concluded, and in our respectful view was right on the evidence to conclude, that the studies carried out and referred to by Dr Lidegaard did not establish a statistically significant connection between Logynon and strokes. Such evidence cannot be ignored by a judge. It is as common sense a conclusion as one could wish to say that if the connection between A and B cannot be shown with confidence to be other than a coincidence, then it cannot be held on a balance of probabilities that A caused B. This is not to allow scientists or statisticians to usurp the judge's function, but rather to permit him to use their skills to discern a connection, or a lack of connection, between two phenomena.

Mr Croxon, however, argued further on another front . . . that doctors generally suspected a connection between Logynon and strokes. That, for instance, had been the reaction of the doctors at Charing Cross who, having unsuccessfully sought for some reason for this very unusual event in a young patient, had suggested in the discharge letter that the cause might be Logynon. It had also been the reaction of physicians called on behalf of the plaintiff. For instance, Dr Greenwood, consultant neurologist, having discussed the possible effect of migraine . . . said in his second report, apparently about the case generally and without relying on the presence of either migraine or hypertension, that 'It is difficult to avoid the conclusion that, on a balance of probabilities, the Logynon played some part in the causation of her stroke'.

However, when cross-examined, Dr Greenwood very fairly said that while, as a clinician, he would find it difficult to dissociate the Logynon from the stroke, to establish that connection with any certainty he would have to turn to the statisticians:

'[In answer to the question] "How can you say that on the balance of probabilities the pill contributed?" [I would say] I would ask the statistician, but as a clinician I could not dissociate oral contraceptives from the occlusion . . . All I am saying is that I would view it as my responsibility as a clinician to view them as associated unless I was told by the epidemiologist, for example, that that was not the case.'

On the basis of this answer, and other similar answers from other medical witnesses, it is impossible to contend that there is a medical view implicating Logynon that transcends or overrides the evidence on which the judge acted. The judge was right to make the findings that he did, on the comparatively limited question that, in view of his findings of fact, remained to him at the end of the case . . . "

NOTES:

1. Is the judge's conclusion that causation could not be proven on the balance of probabilities justified? As Mason and Laurie point out, "there is no doubt that compounds with a high oestrogen content will predispose to intravascular thrombosis" (J.K. Mason and G.T. Laurie, *Mason & McCall Smith's Law and Medical Ethics* (7th edn), 2005, p. 125). They note that the dearth of claims in relation to contraception are probably explained by the fact that adequate warning of risk has been given—see *Coker v Richmond, Twickenham and Roehampton Area Health Authority* [1996] 7 Med. L.R. 58. For criticism of *Vadera v Shaw*, see R. Goldberg, "The Contraceptive Pill, Negligence and Causation: Views on *Vadera v. Shaw*" (2000) 8 *Medical Law Review* 316.

2. Both private and NHS patients may also have a remedy against the manufacturer of defective products under the Consumer Protection Act 1987, as in the *XYZ v Schering* case below (and see further Chapter 3).

3. In *Vadera v Shaw* Henry L.J. is clear that judges cannot disregard statistical evidence in favour of common sense judgments on causation. Yet more difficult issues are raised when judges are called upon to adjudicate between competing expert views as in *XYZ and Others v Schering Health Care Ltd* [2002] EWHC 1420, where a mass of conflicting evidence was produced by numerous experts. This was a group litigation under the Consumer Protection Act 1987 (see further Chapter 3 at pp.203–209), alleging that third generation oral contraceptive pills manufactured by three pharmaceutical companies were defective under the provisions of the Consumer Protection Act 1987 and/or the Product Liability Directive 85/374 of July 25, 1985. The trial concerned the various cardio-vascular injuries, including deep vein thrombrosis (DVY) and strokes, which the seven lead applicants alleged had resulted from their use of these pills. The litigation followed a pill scare sparked by a letter which the UK Committee on the Safety of Medicine (CSM) wrote to all relevant prescribers stating that three unpublished studies into the safety of Combined Oral Contraceptive pills (COCs) in relation to venous-thromboembolism (VTE) had indicated "around a two-fold increase in the risk" of such conditions as against the preceding generation of COCs. (See, "What every woman knows", *The Guardian*, October 21, 1995.) The claimants' case was that a proper consideration of those studies supported their claim, whereas the defendants claimed that the warning from the CSM was misjudged and that it should never have been given. It was agreed that the action would fail unless the enhanced risk was twice that of the second generation of oral contraceptives. The experts called were asked specifically to testify on the risks of these third generation contraceptives. Significantly, they disagreed on issues of methodology and design as well as on the likely risks. The judgment of MacKay J. contains an exhaustive examination of very complex statistical evidence, which was hotly disputed by the various experts. Ultimately the judge expressed a clear preference for a particular

analysis which concluded that any enhanced risk was of the order of 1.7, rather than a doubling of the risk associated with these third generation pills over earlier oral contraceptives. The case is an excellent examples of the complexities of scientific risk analysis in such cases.

4. For a consideration of the liability history of various contraceptive devices and products, and of the impact of fears of litigation on the development of new forms of contraception, see S.A. Law, "Tort Liability and the Availability of Contraceptive Drugs and Devices in the US" (1997) 23 NYU Rev L & Soc Change 339.

5. Gillian Douglas has argued, writing before the 1995 pill scare, that doubts about the safety of female contraceptives and criticism of the cavalier attitude taken to women's concern about side effects are increasing. Furthermore, she contends that all women who wish to use contraceptives are effectively treated as guinea pigs, given the fact that information about long-term side effects of prolonged contraceptive use is still unavailable. (G. Douglas, *Law, Fertility and Reproduction*, London: Sweet & Maxwell, 1991, at pp.62–66).

6. Liability for failure of contraceptive measures is considered in the context of failed sterilisation in Chapter 13 at pp.971–988.

QUESTION:

1. Do you think that judges are well equipped to adjudicate on which of these complex studies is most valid? (See the special edition of the Royal Statistical Society magazine, *Significance*, March 2005, which addresses the problems faced in court because the disciplines of statistics and law have radically different ways of approaching the issue of decision-making under conditions of uncertainty.)

3. The Ethics of Abortion

(a) The Construction of the Ethical Debate

As we shall see below (at pp.891–898), until recently it seemed that there was no clear distinction between certain forms of contraception on the one hand and abortifacients on the other. However, notwithstanding some continuity between methods of contraception and abortion, abortion has provoked much greater controversy. In the last two decades, the debate on abortion has become increasingly polarised around the world. Although Britain has escaped the excesses witnessed elsewhere (particularly in the United States—see R. Dworkin, *Life's Dominion: an Argument about Abortion and Euthanasia*, London: Harper-Collins, 1993, Chapter 1), the abortion debate has nevertheless continued to be construed as a debate between two polarised camps, one claiming to be "pro life" and the other "pro choice". "Pro life" pressure groups, such as LIFE and SPUC (the Society for the Protection of the Unborn Child), maintain that the life of the human embryo/foetus is sacrosanct, and consequently that termination of pregnancy cannot be tolerated unless the life of the pregnant woman is at serious risk. For proponents of this position, life begins at conception when the sperm and ovum merge to create a (potential) human being with her or his own unique genetic pattern. (Though note the problems in defining the point of conception — see R.G. Lee and D. Morgan, *Human Fertilisation and Embryology: Regulating the Reproductive Revolution*, London: Blackstone Press, 2001 at pp.59–64). "Pro choice" advocates, on the other hand, see pregnancy as a uniquely female experience which must be controlled by the individual woman concerned. They view the life of the foetus as subordinate to the needs of the pregnant woman. For them the real issue at stake is the right of the pregnant woman to control her own body free from intrusion by third parties, including the state, which may seek to intervene on behalf of the foetus. However, although these competing moral and political positions seem logically irreconcilable, they encompass many different shades of opinion, which lead us to the conclusion that the abortion issue is best viewed as a spectrum encompassing a range of opinions. As McLean points out, it is likely that most people who reflect on the abortion issue are not necessarily or inevitably committed to the extreme positions (see S. McLean, "Abortion Law: Is Consensual Reform Possible?" (1990) 17 *Journal of Law and Society* 106 at p.107).

(b) The Moral Status of the Foetus

There is an extensive philosophical literature on the moral status of the foetus, which mainly focuses on the point at which personhood may be attributed to the foetus. Commentators variously argue for conception, implantation, the development of a nervous system or acquisition of humanness, viability, birth or when personhood is acquired. A detailed philosophical discussion of foetal status is beyond the scope of this text. (For an overview see BMA, *Abortion Time Limits: a Briefing Paper from the BMA*, Part 2, May 2005.) Nevertheless, the issue arises in various contexts — in relation to arguments about personhood in Chapter 2; the morality of embryo research and the use of foetal tissue in Chapter 10, and in terms of its impact on the management of pregnancy in Chapter 13. (For a full philosophical discussion of the issue see R. Hursthouse, *Beginning Lives*, Oxford: Basil Blackwell, 1987.) In recent years there has been increased recognition of the necessity of finding some common ground on the abortion issue. (See R. Colker, *Abortion and Dialogue: Pro Choice, Pro Life and American Law*, Bloomington: Indiana University Press, 1992.) In this regard various suggestions have been made to find ways out of the moral and political impasse. For example, Dworkin has suggested that each side may lack a clear grasp of what they are disagreeing about, and that common ground between the two groups and a basis for dialogue may be found in the fact that "[a]lmost everyone shares, explicitly or intuitively, the idea that human life has objective, intrinsic value that is quite independent of its personal value for anyone, and disagreement about the right interpretation of that shared idea is the actual nerve of the great debate about abortion" (Dworkin, *op. cit.* at p.67). He contends that in practice no one holds the belief that from conception a human life is of the same value as that of a child or adult. He argues that it follows that the foetus cannot have rights until it is born and thus that it is nonsensical to attempt to balance its rights against the rights of the pregnant woman. However, Dworkin does concede that the foetus has value, and argues that there is general agreement, albeit from different perspectives, on the intrinsic value of human life. Thus, he suggests that from the moment of conception a foetus embodies a form of human life which is sacred, although he maintains that this claim need not imply that a foetus has interests of its own. Roberston adopts a similar position. He argues for an intermediate position of special respect for prenatal life on the basis that it is "genetically unique, living, human tissue that, as pregnancy progresses, increases in capacity, and eventually becomes a newborn infant". He suggests that adopting this view of the embryo/foetus is symbolically significant of our membership in the human community, although that does not require that everyone must find the same symbolic meaning or that everyone must act according to the meaning that others find (see J. Robertson, *Children of Choice: Freedom and the New Reproductive Technologies*, Princeton, New Jersey: Princeton University Press, 1994, at pp.50–57). Many British commentators also share this "gradualist" view that the foetus grows in moral worth. (See G. Douglas, *Law, Fertility and Reproduction*, London: Sweet & Maxwell, 1991, Chapter 3; J. Glover, *Causing Death and Saving Lives*, Harmondsworth: Penguin, 1977, Chapter 9; J. Harris, *The Value of Life*, London: Routledge & Kegan Paul, 1985, Chapter 1; I. Kennedy, "The Moral Status of the Embryo" in I. Kennedy, *Treat Me Right*, Oxford: Oxford University Press, 1988.) Such a view was translated into law in the landmark United States Supreme Court case of *Roe v Wade* 410 U.S. 113 (1973), in which the United States Supreme Court decided that the constitutional right to privacy enshrined in the United States Constitution was broad enough to encompass a woman's right to terminate her pregnancy. The Supreme Court adopted a trimester framework for analysing pregnancy. It held that the pregnant woman's right to privacy must prevail in the first trimester, but suggested that by the third trimester the state's interest in protecting foetal life should prevail unless there was a risk to the life or health of the pregnant woman. Although the trimester framework was subsequently invalidated in *Planned Parenthood of S.E. Pennsylvania v Casey* (1992) 112 St. 2791, it did seem to accord with the intuitive views of many commentators that the foetus grows in moral worth throughout the pregnancy. The notion that the foetus has some sort of "intermediate" moral status, which is less than that of a person but more than a body part, and of its complex relationship to the pregnant woman has also been recognised in much feminist writing. (See C. MacKinnon, "Reflections on Sex Equality under Law" (1991) 100 *Yale Law Journal* 1281; B. Steinbock, *Life before Birth*, New York: Oxford University Press, 1992, Chapter 1.)

Such a position, commanding as it does a widespread consensus at least among legal and philosophical scholars, has led McLean to suggest that the issue of late abortions provides one example of common ground, since all parties to the debate can agree that late terminations should be avoided (see McLean, *op. cit.*). However, even on this issue debate has raged on matters such as the ethics of anaethetising foetuses in late abortions and the stage at which the foetus feels pain (see pp.882–886 below). There may be more space for progressive dialogue on the need to reduce the number of abortions through the provision of better sex education and improved access to contraception, although many "pro life" advocates are almost equally vehemently opposed to these developments.

A few other factors are worth noting about the abortion debate. First, it provides a good illustration of the political importance of terminology, since all the available language in which the issue may be debated—including the designation "pro choice" or "pro life"—are morally loaded. Thus, we recognise that speaking in terms of the "pregnant woman" and "foetus", as we have elected to do, rather than using the words "mother" and "unborn child" has the potential to skew the debate in particular ways. We have chosen this language to reflect the fact that law has traditionally accorded the foetus a different status from a human being, and in order to avoid the ideology of maternity that comes with adopting the term "mother". (See E. Fegan, "Fathers, Foetuses and Abortion Decision-making: the Reproduction of Maternal Ideology" (1996) 5 *Social and Legal Studies* 75). Secondly, the abortion debate exemplifies the problematic nature of rights-based arguments and their tendency to lead to a political and moral impasse, as in this situation where the pregnant woman's right to autonomy is pitted against the right to life of the foetus. Rights arguments also have a tendency to represent the debate in a way which is at odds with the experiences of the pregnant woman. (See C. Smart, *Feminism and the Power of Law*, Routledge: London, 1989 at pp.138–159; E. Kingdom, *What's Wrong with Rights: Problems for a Feminist Politics of Law*, Edinburgh: Edinburgh University Press, 1991, Chapter 3.) Thirdly, it is worth noting that many leading commentators on the abortion law issue are North American, and that "solutions" to complex social issues like abortion may not be easily transplanted to other jurisdictions. (See S. Gibson, "Continental Drift: The Question of Context in Feminist Jurisprudence" (1990) I *Law and Critique* 173.)

(c) The Relationship between Ethics and Law

In practice, legislators in Britain have largely sidestepped the ethical debate by opting for the pragmatic course of permitting abortion in a limited range of circumstances. Our legislators have thus failed to address the status of the foetus, or indeed the rights of any of the parties concerned (see below at pp.899–919). In part this is a result of the main statute's origin as a private member's bill, the form of which was dictated largely by the medical profession, which was concerned about the uncertainty of the common law regarding the circumstances in which abortion was permissible. (See T. Newburn, *Permission and Regulation: Law and Morals in Post-War Britain*, London: Routledge, 1989 at pp.136–157.) For the most part, the 1967 Abortion Act (which, like most legislation on contentious social issues, was the subject of a free vote in parliament) was a compromise premised largely on pragmatic arguments. Thus it was argued that unless law tolerates abortions performed by doctors, we would face the spectre of backstreet abortions, since prior to the passage of the 1967 legislation unlawful terminations were frequently carried out by medically untrained persons in unhygienic conditions and at extortionate rates. Other concerns focused on the girl who was raped, the woman who was carrying a foetus disabled by thalidomide or the older woman who accidentally becomes pregnant, having thought her family was complete. As Sally Sheldon has noted, in the parliamentary debates the woman seeking abortion is often figured as desperate (see S. Sheldon, "Who is the Mother to Make the Judgment? The Construction of Women in English Abortion Law" (1993) *Feminist Legal Studies* 3).

A further pragmatic argument in favour of abortion rests on the principle of "double effect", which operates to permit terminations where the intention of the physician is to save the life of the woman and the destruction of the foetus is an unintended side effect of the overall good end of preserving the life of the woman (see further Chapter 2 at pp.136–140; and T. Beauchamp and R. Childress, *Principles of Biomedical Ethics*, Oxford: OUP, 5th edn, 2001 at pp.128–132 on the applicability of the doctrine to the issue of abortion).

The lack of sustained discussion of the moral and legal status of the foetus has served to medicalise and consequently depoliticise the issue of abortion in the United Kingdom. (See S. Sheldon, "Subject Only to the Attitude of the Surgeon Concerned: the Judicial Protection of Medical Discretion" (1996) 5 *Social and Legal Studies* 95.) One consequence of the pragmatic stance adopted by English law is that the legal status of the foetus may be inconsistent. In Chapter 10 we saw that the law permits embryo experimentation only up to 14 days, yet as we shall see, provided the 1967 Act is satisfied, abortions may be performed up to 24 weeks, or in certain circumstances right up to birth. (See J. Harris, "Should We Experiment on Embryos?" in R. Lee and D. Morgan, *Birthrights: Law and Ethics at the Beginning of Life*, London: Routledge, 1989.) What is clear is that English law has not recognised the foetus as a person to whom rights may be attributed. Any rights which the foetus has are contingent on it being born alive (see pp.902–912 below). However, it has been argued that attempts to vindicate foetal rights in law by "pro life" individuals and groups, even though they have not been successful to date, have shifted the moral terrain in favour of "pro life" forces. (See S. Sheldon, "The Law of Abortion and the Politics of Medicalisation" in J. Bridgman and S. Millns (eds), *Law and Body Politics*, Aldershot: Dartmouth, 1995.) Indeed, even to focus on the debate about foetal status and personhood as means of deciding the debate may be misdirected. (See C. Wells and D. Morgan, "Whose Foetus Is It?" (1991) 81 *Journal of Law and Society* 431.) Such a focus may obscure both the role of the woman and "important connections between unwanted pregnancies and broader social factors. Moreover, it fosters a climate where it seems possible to deal with the problem of unwanted pregnancy merely by the provision of abortion without ever listening to women in order to explore the problems which lead to unwanted pregnancy itself" (S. Sheldon, "Subject only to the Attitude of the Surgeon Concerned: the Judicial Protection of Medical Discretion" (1996) 5 *Social and Legal Studies* 95). Furthermore, as we shall see in Chapter 13, the effect of technological interventions during pregnancy which have rendered the foetus *in utero* increasingly visible, has been to construct the foetus as a separate individual and "second patient" in medical and scientific discourse. (See R. Petchesky, "Foetal Images: the Power of Visual Culture in the Politics of Reproduction" in M. Stanworth (ed.), *Reproductive Technologies*, Cambridge: Polity Press, 1987; A. Young, "Decapitation or Feticide: the Fetal Laws of the Universal Subject" (1993) 4 *Women: a Cultural Review* 288; V.

Hartouni, *Cultural Conceptions: On Reproductive Technologies and the Remaking of Life*, Minneapolis: University of Minnesota Press, 1997; M. Fox, "Prepersons, Commodities or Cyborgs: the Legal Construction and Representation of the Embryo" (2000) 8 *Health Care Analysis* 171–188.)

QUESTION:

1. The abortion debate provides a good context in which to explore the relationship between law and morality addressed in Chapter 2. Thus, whatever your view of the morality of abortion and the moral status of the foetus, can you make a convincing case for your arguments to be translated into law? (See M. Brazier, "Embryo's 'Rights': Abortion and Research" in M.D.A. Freeman (ed.), *Medicine, Ethics and the Law*, London: Stevens, 1988.)
2. Do you think a different model of legislation might have been more appropriate than that chosen in Britain? For example, France permits abortion on demand up to 12 weeks and therapeutic abortion afterwards. What would be the pros and cons of this system compared to the current English legislation? (See M. Latham, *Regulating Reproduction*, Manchester: Manchester University Press, 2002.)

4. THE LAW OF ABORTION

Since the 19th century, the law of abortion has formed part of the criminal law. For a history of English abortion law, see J. Keown, *Abortion, Doctors and the Law*, 1988, and the discussion in the judgment of Munby J. in *R. (on the application of Smeaton) v SoS for Health*—see p.895 below) Under the current statutory framework, those who unlawfully terminate (or, in some circumstances, attempt to terminate) a pregnancy are liable to be convicted of serious criminal offences, as may those who procure the means of unlawfully terminating a pregnancy. These offences are now contained in the Offences Against the Person Act 1861 and centre on the notion of procuring a miscarriage.

(a) The Criminal Prohibition on Procuring a Miscarriage

Offences Against the Person Act 1861, ss.58–59

58. Every woman being with child, who, with intent to procure her own miscarriage, shall unlawfully administer to herself any poison or other noxious thing, or shall unlawfully use any instrument or other means whatsoever with the like intent and whosoever, with intent to procure the miscarriage of any woman whether she be or be not with child, shall unlawfully administer to her or cause to be taken by her any poison or other noxious thing, or shall unlawfully use any instrument or other means whatsoever with the like intent, shall be guilty of an offence, and being convicted thereof shall be liable . . . to be kept in penal servitude for life . . .

59. Whosoever shall unlawfully supply or procure any poison or other noxious thing, or any instrument or thing whatsoever, knowing that the same is intended to be unlawfully used or employed with intent to procure the miscarriage of any woman, whether she be or

not be with child, shall be guilty of an offence, and being convicted thereof shall be liable . . . to be kept in penal servitude for a term not exceeding five years.
(Note: words omitted were repealed by the Statute Law Revision Act 1892 and the Statute Law Revision (No. 2) Act 1893.)

NOTES:

1. The 1861 Act proscribes three kinds of conduct: the self-induction of miscarriage, things done by a third party to procure the miscarriage of a woman (whether or not she is in fact pregnant), and the supply or procurement of an abortifacient (*i.e.* an implement or drug designed to bring about a miscarriage).
2. A woman cannot be convicted of attempting to self-induce a miscarriage where she is not in fact pregnant: the act makes any offence by her conditional upon her "being with child".

QUESTION:

1. Is it necessary that the act of a person other than the woman should be successful in producing a miscarriage so long as the act in question was done with the intent to procure a miscarriage? (Reread s.59 carefully!)

In 1929 Parliament passed a second statute which continues to be relevant to the legal regulation of abortion, the Infant Life Preservation Act of 1929. This Act was introduced for two main reasons. The first was to fill a lacuna in the law. As we have seen, the 1861 Act affords protection to the foetus *in utero*. The law of homicide (see Chapter 14) protects a child once it has been born. However, no legal protection was afforded to the baby while it was in the process of being born. In 1928 a defendant charged with procuring a miscarriage had been acquitted on the grounds that the child was in the process of being born, and the legislation was introduced to close this loophole. The second reason for the passage of the 1929 Act was to protect a doctor who performed a craniotomy, an operation in which the impacted head of a foetus was crushed in order to save the mother's life. This operation was commonly practised before Caesarean sections became routine.

Infant Life (Preservation) Act 1929, s.1(1)–(2)

1.—(1) Subject as hereinafter in this subsection provided, any person who, with intent to destroy the life of a child capable of being born alive, by any wilful act causes a child to die before it has an existence independent of its mother, shall be guilty of felony, to wit, of child destruction, and shall be liable on conviction thereof on indictment to penal servitude for life.
Provided that no person shall be found guilty of an offence under this section unless it is proved that the act which caused the death of the child was not done in good faith for the purpose only of preserving the life of the mother.
(2) For the purposes of this Act, evidence that the woman had at any material time been pregnant for a period of twenty-eight weeks or more shall be *prima facie* proof that she was at that time pregnant with a child capable of being born alive.

NOTE:

1. The crucial threshold criterion for the operation of the 1929 Act is the attainment, by the foetus, of the capacity to be born alive. However this phrase is not clearly defined. Its meaning is a crucial issue since s.1(2) of the Act simply provided a (rebuttable) presumption that a child attains this capacity at 28 weeks' gestation. (For the position at present see pp.879–881 below.)

Just as the 1929 Act rendered craniotomies lawful, so s.58 of the 1861 Act, by using the word "unlawful", seemed to envisage some situations in which abortion would be lawful. This issue was addressed in the leading case prior to the passage of the 1967 legislation.

R v Bourne [1938] 3 All E.R. 615; [1939] 1 K.B. 687

The case concerned the prosecution of Mr Bourne, a gynaecologist who deliberately challenged the English law on abortion in order to clarify the scope of defences available to doctors who performed abortions. Having performed an abortion on a 14-year-old girl who had been subjected to gang rape by a group of soldiers and become pregnant as a result, he presented himself to the authorities and was charged with unlawfully procuring a miscarriage, contrary to s.58.

MACNAUGHTEN J.
" . . . The charge against Mr Bourne is the very grave charge under the Offences Against the Person, 1861, s.58, that he unlawfully procured the abortion of the girl . . . [J]udging by the cases that come before the court, it is a crime by no means uncommon. This is the second case at these July sessions at this court where a charge of an offence against that section has been preferred, and I mention that case only to show you how different the case now before you is from the type of case which usually comes before a criminal court. In that case, a woman without any medical skill or any medical qualifications did what is alleged against Mr Bourne here: she unlawfully used an instrument for the purpose of procuring the miscarriage of a pregnant girl. She did it for money . . . The case here is very different. A man of the highest skill, openly, in one of our great hospitals, performs the operation. Whether it was legal or illegal you will have to determine, but he performs the operation as an act of charity, without fee or reward, and unquestionably believing that he was doing the right thing, and that he ought, in the performance of his duty as a member of a profession devoted to the alleviation of human suffering, to do it . . .
 The question that you have got to determine is whether the Crown has proved to your satisfaction beyond reasonable doubt that the act which Mr Bourne admittedly did was not done in good faith for the purpose only of preserving the life of the girl . . . But is there a perfectly clear line of distinction between danger to life and danger to health? I should have thought not. I should have thought that impairment of health might reach a stage where it was a danger to life . . . If that is a view which commends itself to you, so that you cannot say that there is this division into two separate classes with a dividing line between them, then it may be that you will accept the view that Mr Oliver put forward when he invited you to give to the words 'for the purpose of preserving the life of the mother' a wide and liberal view of their meaning. I would prefer the word 'reasonable' to the words 'wide and liberal'. Take a reasonable view of the words 'for the preservation of the life of the mother'. I do not think that it is contended that those words mean merely for the

preservation of the life of the mother from instant death. There are cases, we were told—and indeed I expect you know cases from your own experiences—where it is reasonably certain that a woman will not be able to deliver the child with which she is pregnant. In such a case, where the doctor expects, basing his opinion upon the experience and knowledge of the profession, that the child cannot be delivered without the death of the mother, in those circumstances the doctor is entitled—and, indeed, it is his duty—to perform this operation with a view to saving the life of the mother, and in such a case it is obvious that the sooner the operation is performed the better. The law is not that the doctor has got to wait until the unfortunate woman is in peril of immediate death and then at the last moment to snatch her from the jaws of death. He is not only entitled, but it is his duty, to perform the operation with a view to saving her life . . .

[I]f the doctor is of opinion, on reasonable grounds and with adequate knowledge, that the probable consequence of the continuance of the pregnancy will be to make the woman a physical or mental wreck, the jury are quite entitled to take the view that a doctor, who, in those circumstances, and in that honest belief, operates, is operating for the purpose of preserving the life of the woman . . . "

NOTES:

1. As the jury acquitted Mr Bourne, this authority was never confirmed by an appellate court. The uncertainty of the parameters of the *Bourne* decision gave impetus to the movement to reform the law on abortion, especially given the uncertainty pertaining to abortions on grounds of foetal abnormality following this case.

2. It was confirmed in three unreported cases that the precedent of *Bourne* governs the law on abortion in Northern Ireland, where the Abortion Act 1967 has never applied. (See S. Lee, "An A to K to Z of Abortion Law in Northern Ireland: Abortion on Remand" in A. Furedi (ed.), *The Abortion Law in Northern Ireland: Human Rights and Reproductive Choice*, Belfast: Family Planning Association, 1995; T. McGleenan, "*Bourne* again? Abortion Law in Northern Ireland from *Re K to Re A*" (1994) 46 *Northern Ireland Legal Quarterly* 389.) As Lee notes, although in the past most abortions in Northern Ireland were performed on the ground of foetal disability, it is difficult to see how *Bourne* could be stretched to encompass terminations on this basis (see S. Lee, "Abortion Law in Northern Ireland: the Twilight Zone" in Furedi, *op. cit.* at p.21). More recently it would appear that concern about the legality of such terminations has stopped doctors from performing abortions on this ground (see A. Simpson, "Abortion Law in Northern Ireland" in E. Lee (ed.), *Abortion Law and Politics Today*, London: Macmillan, 1998.) In *Family Planning Association of Northern Ireland v Minister for Health, Social Services and Public Safety* [2004] NICA 39, the FPANI sought judicial review of the failure to issue guidance to women and doctors on the availability and provision of abortion services in Northern Ireland. The NI Court of Appeal held that the Department of Health, Social Services and Public Policy was in breach of its duty to provide guidance to health care practitioners about treating abortion-seeking women, although to date no such guidance has been forthcoming. (See B. Hewson, "The Law of Abortion in Northern Ireland" [2004] Public Law 234–245; see also pp.883 below for UK guidance.) Ruth Fletcher notes the focus in the

arguments put forward in this case on procedural arguments concerning fairness and clarity in law, as opposed to the human rights reasoning which could have been employed (see R. Fletcher, "Abortion Needs or Abortion Rights? Claiming State Responsibility for Reproductive Welfare" (2004) 13 *Feminist Legal Studies* 123–124).

QUESTIONS:

1. Was Macnaughten J.'s summing up to the jury unduly favourable to Mr Bourne? (See Chapter 3 at pp.157–167 for the argument that tests propounded by the courts have historically favoured the medical profession.)
2. Are medical qualifications really necessary to perform an abortion? (See *Royal College of Nursing v Department of Health and Social Security* [1981] 1 All E.R. 545 at p.888 below; R. Chalker and C. Dovner, *A Woman's Book of Choices*, Four Walls and Eight Windows, 1992.)
3. Is it justifiable to refuse to extend the Abortion Act to Northern Ireland, given that an estimated 2,000 Northern Irish women travel to Britain annually for abortion. (See E. Fegan, "Northern Ireland's Abortion Law: the Morality of Silence and the Censure of Agency" (2003) 11 *Feminist Legal Studies* 1–34.) According to the statistics for 2004, 8,764 abortions were performed in England and Wales on residents of other jurisdictions, principally from Northern Ireland (15 per cent) and the Republic of Ireland (71 per cent)—Government Statistical Services, *Abortion Statistics, England and Wales, 2004*, July 2005, para. 3.3.

(b) The Statutory Grounds for Lawful Termination

The circumstances in which a termination can lawfully be performed were significantly extended by the enactment of the Abortion Act 1967. This statute, as has already been observed, was intended in large part to eradicate the problem of "back street" abortions. It thus requires that, except in emergencies, a termination performed under the Act must be performed in an NHS (trust) hospital or other approved place. This was clearly designed to minimise the effects of a medical mishap during termination as well as to reduce the likelihood of infection.

The statutory pre-conditions for a lawful termination are contained in s.1 of the 1967 Act (as amended by s.37 of the Human Fertilisation and Embryology Act 1990).

Abortion Act 1967, ss.1(1–2), 5, 6

1.—(1) Subject to the provisions of this section, a person shall not be guilty of an offence under the law relating to abortion when a pregnancy is terminated by a registered medical practitioner if two registered medical practitioners are of the opinion, formed in good faith—

(a) that the pregnancy has not exceeded its twenty fourth week and that the continuance of the pregnancy would involve risk, greater than if the pregnancy were terminated, of injury to the physical or mental health of the pregnant woman or any existing children of her family; or

(b) that the termination is necessary to prevent grave permanent injury to the physical or mental health of the pregnant woman; or

(c) that the continuance of the pregnancy would involve risk to the life of the pregnant woman, greater than if the pregnancy were terminated; or

(d) that there is a substantial risk that if the child were born it would suffer from such physical or mental abnormalities as to be seriously handicapped.

(2) In determining whether the continuance of a pregnancy would involve such risk of injury to health as is mentioned in paragraph (a) or (b) of subsection (1) of this section, account may be taken of the pregnant woman's actual or reasonably foreseeable environment . . . [For the remaining provisions of this section see p.886 below.]

5.—(1) No offence under the Infant Life (Preservation) Act 1929 shall be committed by a registered medical practitioner who terminates a pregnancy in accordance with the provisions of this Act.

(2) For the purposes of the law relating to abortion, anything done with intent to procure a woman's miscarriage (or, in the case of a woman carrying more than one foetus, her miscarriage of any foetus) is unlawfully done unless authorised by section 1 of this Act and, in the case of a woman carrying more than one foetus, anything done with intent to procure her miscarriage of any foetus is authorised by that section if—

(a) the ground for termination of the pregnancy specified in subsection (1)(d) of that section applies in relation to any foetus and the thing is done for the purpose of procuring the miscarriage of that foetus, or

(b) any of the other grounds for termination of the pregnancy specified in that section applies.

6.—In this Act, the following expressions have meanings hereby assigned to them: "the law relating to abortion" means sections 58 and 59 of the Offences against the Person Act 1861, and any rule of law relating to the procurement of abortion; . . .

NOTES:

1. Perhaps the most significant omission in the 1967 Abortion Act prior to its amendment in 1990 was that it set no time limit as to when abortions could lawfully be performed. However, the 1967 Act did contain a provision that nothing in it affected the operation of the 1929 Infant Life (Preservation) Act. As we have seen, that statute provided that if a woman had been pregnant for 28 weeks that was prima facie evidence that the child was capable of being born alive. Thus, it was assumed that abortions under the 1967 Act were lawful if they were performed before the foetus was 28 weeks old. However, the 1967 Act did not preclude the possibility that a foetus could be deemed capable of being born alive at some earlier gestational age. This issue received judicial consideration in two cases decided before the 1990 amendments. In *C v S* [1987] 1 All E.R. 1230 (considered further at p.916 below) a single woman wished to terminate her pregnancy, which was dated at between 18 and 21 weeks. Two medical practitioners were satisfied that continuance of the pregnancy would involve a risk of injury to her physical or mental health greater than if the pregnancy was terminated. The putative father nevertheless sought to restrain the proposed termination on the basis that it would contravene the Infant Life (Preservation) Act 1929. Crucial to his case was the claim that a foetus of between 18 and 21 weeks is capable of being born alive (in

which case a termination could only lawfully be performed to preserve the life of the pregnant woman). The meaning of the phrase was therefore judicially considered both at first instance, and in the Court of Appeal. At both levels the judges stated that they need not provide an authoritative interpretation of what the phrase "capable of being born alive" meant, since they accepted that a foetus of 19–21 weeks gestation was not capable of being born alive.

The later case of *Rance and Another v Mid Downs Health Authority and Another* [1991] 1 All E.R. 801 concerned an action for negligence brought by a man and his wife who gave birth to a baby boy suffering from spina bifida. The gist of their action was that the defendant health authority's employees ought to have diagnosed the disability and to have offered the plaintiffs the possibility of having the pregnancy legally terminated. The defendant authority, however, contended that their failure to diagnose the foetal disability was immaterial since, as Mrs Rance was then about 26 weeks pregnant, a legal termination could not have been performed in any event. It followed, the health authority argued, that no action for failure to advise of the possibility of an abortion could possibly lie. Brooke J. held that a 26-week-old foetus was capable of being born alive, so that it would have been too late for a lawful abortion to be performed and consequently the claim for damages failed. For him the crucial issue was whether the child was capable of "breathing and living by reason of its breathing through its own lungs alone, without deriving any of its living or power to live by or through any connection with the mother". (See J. Murphy, "Grey Areas and Green Lights: Judicial Activism in the Regulation of Doctors" (1991) 42 *Northern Ireland Legal Quarterly* 260; R.G. Lee and D. Morgan, *Human Fertilisation and Embryology: Regulating the Reproductive Revolution*, London: Blackstone Press, 2001 at pp.242–246.) A recent BMA briefing paper suggests that the concept of meaningful life seems to require "as a minimum, a reasonable period of survival" (see BMA, *Abortion Time Limits: a Briefing Paper* May 2005, at p.16.)

Whereas the original 1967 Abortion Act had specifically preserved the effect of the Infant Life Preservation Act, that saving is removed by s.37(4) of the 1990 Act which inserts a new s.5(1) into the Abortion Act. Hence, since 1990 provided an abortion is carried out in accordance with s.1 no prosecution will lie, even if the foetus destroyed is "capable of being born alive".

The insertion of the 24-week time limit into s.1(1)(a) of the 1967 Act by the 1990 Human Fertilisation and Embryology Act purported to settle this issue. (See D. Morgan and R.G. Lee, *Blackstone's Guide to the Human Fertilisation and Embryology Act 1990* London: Blackstone Press, 1991 at p.49 for the complicated pattern of voting in the House of Commons on the time limits issue.) However, as we shall see, debates still rage about appropriate time limits.

2. After the 1990 amendments there is no time limit on the grounds in s.1(1)(b)–(d) which may all be invoked until the point of birth. One of the

few points of consensus in the abortion debate is that late abortions are best avoided although, as we discuss below, this is sometimes not possible and generally at post 24 weeks abortions are performed under s.1(1)(d). (See S. Sheldon and S. Wilkinson, "Termination of Pregnancy for Reason of Foetal Disability: Are There Grounds for a Special Exception in Law?" (2001) 9 *Medical Law Review* 85.)

3. The justification for abortion enshrined in s.1(1)(a) is sometimes referred to as the "social grounds" for abortion. This is because, in assessing the risk to the woman's health (or that of any existing children), or the threat to her life, account may be taken of her home environment, pursuant to s.2. In 2004, consistent with figures for previous years, 95 per cent of abortions were performed on this ground (Government Statistical Services, *Abortion Statistics, England and Wales, 2004*, July 2005, para. 4.2.2.)

Indeed statistics would appear to demonstrate that the risks of continuing with the pregnancy and birth are always greater than the risk of abortion within the first 12 weeks. Potentially, however, a consideration of the social grounds may lead to the conclusion that abortion is not the best option. For instance, in the case of a pregnant teenage girl from an ethnic minority or strict religious denomination, the social ground might well necessitate consideration of the fact that, if the girl undergoes a termination, she is likely to be shunned or ostracised within her community or by her family. The fact that there is external pressure on her may also affect the validity of her consent to the termination. (See further D. Pearl, "Legal Issues Arising out of Medical Provision for Ethnic Groups" in A. Grubb (ed.), *Justice and Health Care: Comparative Perspectives*, Chichester: John Wiley, 1995.)

4. Particular problems arise with respect to dating pregnancies for the purposes of s.1(1)(a). Doctors have traditionally dated pregnancies from the last menstrual period (see J. Murphy, "Cosmetics, Eugenics and Ambivalence: the Reform of the Abortion Act 1967" [1991] *Journal of Social Welfare and Family Law* 375). However, the National Institute for Clinical Excellence now recommends that gestational age should be calculated by measurement of the crown-rump length during the ultrasound scan which takes place between 10 and 13 weeks into the pregnancy (National Institute for Clinical Excellence, *Antenatal care. Routine care for the healthy pregnant woman. Clinical guideline 6*. London: NICE, October 2003, para 4.6). This should lead to more precision in the calculation of gestational age.

5. Subsection 1(1)(b) was a new ground for abortion inserted by the 1990 Act. It seems that "grave permanent injury" to the woman's physical or mental health must mean something less serious than either "a risk to her life greater than if the pregnancy was terminated" (the ground specified in subs.1(1)(c)), or "an immediate risk to her life" dealt with in subs.1(4). Morgan and Lee suggest that this puts into statutory form the reading given to the Infant Life (Preservation) Act 1929 in *Bourne* above; and would include conditions such as mild pre-eclampsia or uncontrolled diabetes in which the risk to the woman increases during pregnancy due to

hormonal changes. (See Lee and Morgan, *Human Fertilisation and Embryology, op. cit.* at p.249.)

6. The ground in s.1(1)(c)—that a termination is justified where the pregnant woman's life is at risk—overlaps with s.1(1)(b) and is relatively uncontroversial.

7. The meaning of the foetal abnormality ground in s.1(1)(d) is not settled under English law, thus leaving doctors to decide what constitutes "substantial risk" and "seriously handicapped". Some discussion of its possible import—that in certain circumstances it is better not to be born than to suffer disabilities—was supplied by Stephenson L.J. in *McKay v Essex AHA* [1982] 2 All E.R. 771 (see Chapter 13 at p.917). Morgan has noted that this provision has (until recently) attracted relatively little attention although it was always the most difficult ground to interpret— see D. Morgan, "Abortion: the Unexamined Ground" [1990] *Criminal Law Review* 687. Only approximately 1 per cent of abortions in 2004 were performed under s.1(1)(d); but more recently this provision has attracted critical scrutiny, largely as a result of the case of *Jepson v Chief Constable of West Mercia Police Constabulary* [2003] EWHC 3318. A curate was granted standing to seek judicial review of a police decision that a doctor who allegedly performed a termination on the basis that the foetus had a cleft palate should not be prosecuted. Jepson contended that such a termination would not satisfy s.1(1)(d) because the condition did not constitute a serious handicap. (See B. Hewson, "Abortion and Disability: Who Should Decide What Abortion Laws We Should Have?" 2003, available from *http://www.prochoiceforum.org.*) The case was ultimately dropped when the police decided there was insufficient evidence to prosecute. However, it could be argued that its likely impact will be to make doctors wary of certifying that certain medical conditions satisfy ground 1(1)(d).

8. As the *Jepson* case demonstrates, late abortion, specifically for foetal abnormality has become the new platform for anti-abortion campaigns. In practice many doctors refuse to authorise abortions beyond 16 weeks, and BPAS provides over 75 per cent of abortions which are performed between 20 and 24 weeks. As the BPAS have pointed out, this leaves them uniquely well placed to comment on women's reason for choosing late abortions. A diagnosis of foetal abnormality is a key factor and in some cases a definitive diagnosis is impossible until the latter part of the second trimester. (See BPAS briefing note on late abortion *http://www.prochoice forum.org.uk/ocrabortlaw9.asp*; BMA, "Abortion Time Limits: a Briefing Paper from the BMA, May 2005.)

9. Abortions on the basis of foetal abnormality have generated controversy, not only because of claims that they show a lack of respect for the lives of disabled people, but because these tend to be the most common late abortions. Given that many commentators view sentience, or the ability to feel pain, as a relevant ethical criterion, considerable controversy was generated by reports that foetuses can experience pain at an earlier point in gestation than had commonly been presumed. (See for instance V.

Glover and N. Fisk, "Fetal pain: implications for research and practice" (1999) 106 *British Journal of Obstetrics and Gynaecology* 881–886.) Following a review of available evidence, the Royal College of Obstetricians and Gynaecologists have ruled out the possibility of foetal awareness and thus pain before 26 weeks' gestation (see RCOG, *Fetal Awareness: Report of a Working Party*, London: RCOG Press, 1997.)

10. Some late abortions may be requested for reasons other than foetal abnormality, such as relationship break-up or failure to diagnose pregnancy. In 2004, 124 abortions were performed at post 24 weeks' gestation (0.1 per cent of the total). A media outcry followed reports in the *Sunday Telegraph*, October 10, 2004 that BPAS was referring British women to Spanish clinics for abortions. These were alleged to be unlawful, as they were being carried out post 24 weeks. Following a report by the Chief Medical Officer, it was established that the organisation had acted lawfully, since women were entitled to travel to other EU Member States for abortion, although recommendations were made in respect of the BPAS procedures for dealing with such requests (*An Investigation into the BPAS Response to Requests for Late Abortions*, Report by the Chief Medical Officer, September 2005).

    In 2004 the RCOG issued revised abortion guidance which recommended that heath authorities accept responsibility for the abortions needed by women resident in their districts. A key recommendation was that:

    "7. Service arrangements should be such that:

    - ideally, all women requesting abortion are offered an assessment appointment within 5 days of referral.
    - as a minimum standard, all women requesting abortion are offered an assessment appointment within 2 weeks of referral.
    - ideally, all women can undergo the abortion within 7 days of the decision to proceed being agreed.
    - as a minimum standard, all women can undergo the abortion within 2 weeks of the decision to proceed being agreed.
    - as a minimum standard, no woman need wait longer than 3 weeks from her initial referral to the time of her abortion.
    - women should be seen as soon as possible if they require termination for urgent medical reasons."

    (Royal College of Obstetricians and Gynaecologists (RCOG). *The Care of Women Requesting Induced Abortion*. Evidence-based Guideline No. 7. London: RCOG, 2004.)

    However, see p.900 below for evidence that regional variations in compliance with such guidelines persist.

11. The "selective reduction" of pregnancy—that is, termination of one or more foetuses in the case of multiple pregnancy—is legally permissable where the terms specified in s.5(2) are met. This provision was inserted by the Human Fertilisation and Embryology Act 1990, in recognition of the increase in multiple pregnancies which initially resulted from *in vitro* fertilisation. It permits the destruction of one or more foetuses in the interests of the one or more which will survive. (See J. Keown, "Selective

Reduction of Multiple Pregnancy" (1987) New L.J. 1165; D. Price, "Selective Reduction and Feticide: the Parameters of Abortion" [1988] *Criminal Law Review* 199.) In the early years of IVF treatment, it was estimated that approximately 100 selective terminations were performed every year on women who have undergone IVF treatment. In August 1996 a national debate on the ethics of selective termination erupted when it emerged that a 28-year-old woman who was 16 weeks pregnant with healthy twins had aborted one foetus on the ground that she could not cope with twins. It was initially suggested that she was a single mother in "socially straitened" circumstances, although it later became apparent that she was in fact a married professional woman. (See " 'No new issue' in abortion of twin", *The Guardian*, August 5, 1996.) Later in the same month the issue was aired again as a result of the high-profile media coverage of Mandy Allwood, who became pregnant with octuplets as a result of taking ovulatory drugs and rejected medical advice that some of the foetuses should be selectively reduced (see "Pregnancy that should be viewed as a catastrophe for all involved", *The Times*, August 12, 1996). Both cases raise important issues about the parameters of acceptable reproductive choices. (See S. Sheldon, "Multiple Pregnancy and Re(pro)ductive Choice: *R v. Queen Charlotte Hospital et al ex parte SPUC, ex parte Philys Bowman*" (1997) 5 *Feminist Legal Studies* 99–106.) Revised HFEA guidance on single embryo transfer should avoid the issue of multiple pregnancies, thus obviating the need for selective reductions (see Chapter 11).

QUESTIONS:

1. If the point of viability can change through time (and from one part of the world to another, depending on the level of medical technology available), can viability be regarded as a point of moral significance in the development of the foetus?

2. Do you think that the statutory provisions as to the circumstances in which abortion is lawful are more workable than the test in *Bourne*? If so, is this an argument for further statutory regulation of health care law as opposed to leaving such issues to be settled by the judiciary?

3. What, for the purposes of s.1, amounts to the absence of good faith on the part of the two registered medical practitioners who certify a termination? How would one prove the absence of good faith? (See *Paton v British Pregnancy Advisory Service and Another* [1978] 2 All E.R. 987 at p.914 below.)

4. Certain ethnic minority groups place great emphasis on the importance of having a male son, which means that a woman who seems able only to give birth to daughters might find herself pressurised (even ostracised) within her community to the extent that her mental or physical health begin to suffer. Would it be possible, in such circumstances, to provide abortion as a means of sex selection? Is subs.1(1)(a), read in the light of subs.2—wide enough to permit such terminations? (See D. Morgan, "Foetal Sex Identification, Abortion and the Law" (1988) 18 *Family Law* 355.)

Recently a special report in *The Observer* newspaper highlighted the widespread practice of abortion of female foetuses by British Asian women, and the practice of travelling to India for late abortions if they were denied in the Britain (D. McDougal, "Desperate British Asians fly to India to abort baby girls", *The Observer*, January 22, 2006; for other examples of procreative tourism see Chapter 11 at pp.853–854.)

5. Would the risk of harm to psychological health suffice for the purposes of subs.1(1)(b)?

6. Would subs.1(1)(b) (construed in accordance with subs.1(2)) entitle a doctor to take account of risks to mental health caused by the effects of child rearing if the pregnancy were not terminated?

7. Is it wrong in principle to allow terminations on the basis of foetal disability? Can aborting a very mature foetus be justified on this, or any other, ground where, if the foetus was born, it would probably survive? In the case of *R v Hamilton* (1983) *The Times* September 16, it was reported that a foetus which had been born alive was left to die, but the magistrates decided that there was no case to answer. During the passage of the 1990 Human Fertilisation and Embryology Act, Baroness Cox did attempt, unsuccessfully, to insert an amendment which would have required doctors to use all reasonable steps to ensure a live birth. Recent media reports have suggested that such a practice is not uncommon (see L. Rogers, "Fifty babies a year are alive after abortion", *The Sunday Times* November 27, 2005). However, RCOG guidance advises that for abortions post 21 weeks and six days, where there is the possibility of live birth, potassium chloride injections should be administered *in utero* to avoid the possibility of a live birth (see RCOG, "Further Issues Relating to Late Abortion, Fetal Viability and Registration of Births and Deaths", RCOG, April, 2001; (RCOG), *The Care of Women Requesting Induced Abortion. Evidence-based Guideline* No. 7, London: RCOG, 2004, para. 6.6).

For discussion of the interface between termination of pregnancy and induction of labour and the potential liability of doctors should an abortion result in live birth, see E. Wicks, M. Wyldes and M. Kilby, "Late Termination of Pregnancy for Fetal Abnormality: Medical and Legal Perspectives" (2004) 12 *Medical Law Review* 285–305, at pp.296–304; see also Chapter 14 at pp.1014–1016). The Nuffield Council on Bioethics is currently working on this issue, having established a working party, chaired by Margaret Brazier to consult on the ethics of prolonging life in foetuses and the newborn. Its terms of reference require it, *inter alia*, to examine "recent evidence on the capacity of foetuses and the newborn to experience pain and suffering" (Nuffield Council on Bioethics, *Consultation Paper: The Ethics of Prolonging Life in Fetuses and the Newborn* (2005). The public consultation closed in June 2005 and a report is expected to be published in late 2006.

8. What is the level of (a) risk and (b) disability necessary for a termination on the basis of subs.1(1)(d)? Do you agree with Joanna Jepson that a termination on the basis of a cleft palate would not suffice? (See E. Wicks,

et al, *op. cit.* in question 7). Is it relevant that the condition is often associated with other "abnormalities"? Who should decide the meaning of the subsection: doctors, the courts or the pregnant woman? (See D. Morgan, "Abortion: the Unexamined Ground" [1990] *Criminal Law Review* 687.) Should this ground for abortion be subject to a time limit? (See S. Sheldon and S. Wilkinson, "Termination of Pregnancy for Reason of Foetal Disability: Are There Grounds for a Special Exception in Law?" (2001) 9 *Medical Law Review* 85.)

9. Should there be a common time limit for all abortions, as Tom Shakespeare has argued, on the basis that otherwise law discriminates against the impaired foetus? (T. Shakespeare, "Choice and Rights: Eugenics, Genetics and Disability Equality" (1998) 13 *Disability and Society* 665.)

(c) Where and How May Lawful Abortions Be Performed?

One of the objectives of the 1967 Act was to eradicate "back street" abortions, performed by persons who frequently were not medically qualified, and carried out in unhygienic conditions. The Act therefore requires that, in addition to satisfying one of the grounds in s.1(1) that terminations must, save in emergencies, be carried out in a hospital or other regulated environment.

Abortion Act 1967, s.1(3), (3A), (4), s.2(1), (2), (4)

1.—(3) Except as provided by subsection (4) of this section, any treatment for the termination of pregnancy must be carried out in a hospital vested in the Secretary of State for the purposes of his functions under the National Health Service Act 1977 or the National Health Service (Scotland) Act 1978 or in a hospital vested in a National Health Service trust or in a place approved for the purposes of this section by the Secretary of State.

(3A) The power under subsection (3) of this section to approve a place includes power, in relation to treatment consisting primarily in the use of such medicines as may be specified in the approval and carried out in such manner as may be so specified, to approve a class of places.

(4) Subsection (3) of this section, and so much of subsection (1) as relates to the opinion of two registered medical practitioners, shall not apply to the termination of a pregnancy by a registered medical practitioner in a case where he is of the opinion, formed in good faith, that the termination is immediately necessary to save the life or to prevent grave permanent injury to the physical or mental health of the pregnant woman.

NOTE:

1. Section 3A was inserted by the Human Fertilisation and Embryology Act 1990 subs.37(3) in anticipation of the abortion pill and its administration by G.P.s—see p.892, below.

Before a termination will be lawful, proper certification that the terms of the 1967 Act have been met must take place in accordance with s.2 of the Act.

Abortion Act 1967, s.2(1–4)

2.—(1) The Minister of Health in respect of England and Wales, and the Secretary of State in respect of Scotland, shall by statutory instrument make regulations to provide:

(a) for requiring any such opinion as is referred to in section 1 of this Act to be certified by the practitioners or practitioner concerned in such form and at such time as may be prescribed by the regulations, and for requiring the preservation and disposal of certificates made for the purposes of the regulations;

(b) for requiring any registered medical practitioner who terminates a pregnancy to give notice of the termination and such other information relating to the termination as may be so prescribed;

(c) for prohibiting the disclosure, except to such persons or for such purposes as may be so prescribed, of notices given or information furnished pursuant to the regulations.

(2) The information furnished in pursuance of regulations made by virtue of paragraph (b) of subsection (1) of this section shall be notified solely to the Chief Medical Officer of the Department of Health, or of the Welsh Office, or of the Scottish Home and Health Department.

(3) Any person who wilfully contravenes or wilfully fails to comply with the requirements of regulations under subsection (1) of this section shall be liable on summary conviction to a fine not exceeding level 5 on the standard scale.

(4) Any statutory instrument made by virtue of this section shall be subject to annulment in pursuance of a resolution of either House of Parliament.

The requisite certification must be on one of two prescribed forms. The first relates to the ordinary case where two doctors' testimonies are required. The second covers those cases where a doctor treats a woman on her own in an emergency to save her life or prevent her suffering irreparable, grave ill health.

Since 1967 there has only been one successful prosecution of a doctor owing to failure to comply with the terms of the Act. The doctor in question performed an abortion without examining the woman or enquiring about her medical history (*R. v Smith* [1974] 1 All E.R. 376).

In 2003 it was reported that the GMC had found a doctor guilty of serious professional misconduct after he performed an abortion in Birmingham during which a woman's uterus was ripped open. Nevertheless he was permitted to continue working as a doctor subject to oversight and random audit. Following a tabloid newspaper campaign against the doctor concerned, which prompted 35 further complaints from women patients, a closed tribunal of the GMC heard 15 of the cases but, for a second time cleared him to continue practising among reports that some of the women's lawyers would refer the GMC decision to the Council for Healthcare Regulatory Excellence (Polly Curtis, "GMC lets doctor stay on register," *The Guardian*, January 14, 2006; see further Chapter 4, Professional Regulation).

One important question concerning the drafting of s.1 of the Abortion Act is how wide a construction ought to be placed on the phrase "when a pregnancy is terminated by a registered medical practitioner". In practice medically induced terminations are usually performed by nurses, since it is they who administer the hormone which induces labour (*i.e.* a series of uterine contractions which culminates in the birth of the child).

Royal College of Nursing v Department of Health and Social Security [1981] 1
All E.R. 545; [1981] A.C. 800

The Royal College of Nursing brought the proceedings out of which this case
arose, seeking to clarify the lawfulness of nursing involvement in terminations
obtained by medical induction. The College was unconvinced by the contents of
a Department of Health and Social Security circular which had stated that no
offence was committed by nurses who administer fluids to a pregnant woman
with the result that premature birth would be induced and that the foetus would
be born dead.

The College sought a declaration that the advice contained in the circular was
wrong and that the administration by a nurse of prostaglandin (or some other
such substance) was contrary to s.58 of the Offences Against the Person Act
1861.

LORD KEITH
" . . . My Lords, this appeal is concerned with the question whether s.1(1) of the Abortion
Act 1967 applies, so as to relieve the participants from criminal liability, to the procedures
normally followed in operating a modern technique for inducing abortion by medical
means.

The technique, which has been evolved and become common practice over the past ten
years for the purpose of terminating pregnancy during the third trimester, is considered in
medical circles to involve less risk to the patient than does surgical intervention . . . Its
main feature is the introduction via a catheter into the interspace between the amniotic sac
and the wall of the uterus of an abortifacient drug called prostaglandin. The purpose of
this is to induce uterine contractions which in most cases, but not in all, result in the
expulsion of the foetus after a period of between 18 and 30 hours. The process is assisted
by the introduction into the blood stream, via a cannula inserted in a vein, of another drug
called oxytocin. Responsibility for deciding on and putting the procedure into operation
rests with a registered medical practitioner who himself inserts the catheter and the
cannula. The attachment of the catheter and the cannula to a supply of prostaglandin and
of oxytocin respectively and the initiation and regulation of the flow of these drugs are
carried out by a nurse under the written instructions of the doctor, who is not normally
present at those stages. He or a colleague is, however, available on call throughout.

Section 1(1) of the 1967 Act can operate to relieve a person from guilt of an offence
under the law relating to abortion only 'when a pregnancy is terminated by a registered
medical practitioner'. Certain other conditions must also be satisfied, but no question
about these arises in the present case. The sole issue is whether the words I have quoted
cover the situation where abortion has been brought about as a result of the procedure
under consideration.

The argument for the Royal College of Nursing is, in essence, that the words of the
subsection do not apply because the pregnancy has not been terminated by any registered
medical practitioner but by the nurse who did the act or acts which directly resulted in the
administration to the pregnant woman of the abortifacient drugs.

In my opinion this argument involves placing an unduly restricted and unintended
meaning on the words 'when a pregnancy is terminated'. It seems to me that these words,
in their context, are not referring to the mere physical occurrence of termination. The side-
note to section 1 is 'Medical termination of pregnancy'. 'Termination of pregnancy' is an
expression commonly used, perhaps, rather more by medical people than by laymen, to
describe in neutral and unemotive terms the bringing about of an abortion. So used, it is
capable of covering the whole process designed to lead to that result, and in my view it
does so in the present context. Other provisions of the Act make it clear that termination

of pregnancy is envisaged as being a process of treatment. Section 1(3) provides that, subject to an exception for cases of emergency, 'treatment for the termination of pregnancy' must be carried out in a national health service hospital or a place for the time being approved by the minister. There are similar references to treatment for the termination of pregnancy in section 3, which governs the application of the Act to visiting forces. Then by section 4(1) it is provided that no person shall be under any duty 'to participate in any treatment authorised by this Act to which he has a conscientious objection'. This appears clearly to recognise that what is authorised by section 1(1) in relation to the termination of pregnancy is a process of treatment leading to that result. Section 5(2) is also of some importance. It provides:

'For the purposes of the law relating to abortion, anything done with intent to procure the miscarriage of a woman is unlawfully done unless authorised by section 1 of this Act.'

This indicates a contemplation that a wide range of acts done when a pregnancy is terminated under the given conditions are authorised by section 1, and leads to the inference that, since all that section 1 in terms authorises is the termination of pregnancy by a registered medical practitioner, all such acts must be embraced in the termination.

Given that the termination of pregnancy under contemplation in section 1(1) includes the whole process of treatment involved therein, it remains to consider whether, on the facts of this case, the termination can properly be regarded as being 'by a registered medical practitioner'. In my opinion this question is to be answered affirmatively. The doctor has responsibility for the whole process and is in charge of it throughout. It is he who decides that it is to be carried out. He personally performs essential parts of it which are such as to necessitate the application of his particular skill. The nurse's actions are done under his direct written instructions. In the circumstances I find it impossible to hold that the doctor's role is other than that of a principal, and I think he would be very surprised to hear that the nurse was the principal and he himself only an accessory. It is true that it is the nurse's action which leads directly to the introduction of abortifacient drugs into the system of the patient, but that action is done in a ministerial capacity and on the doctor's orders. Even if it were right to regard the nurse as a principal, it seems to me inevitable that the doctor should also be so regarded. If both the doctor and the nurse were principals, the provisions of the subsection would be still satisfied, because the pregnancy would have been terminated by the doctor notwithstanding that it had also been terminated by the nurse.

I therefore conclude that termination of pregnancy by means of the procedures under consideration is authorised by the terms of section 1(1). This conclusion is the more satisfactory as it appears to me to be fully in accordance with that part of the policy and purpose of the Act which was directed to securing that socially acceptable abortions should be carried out under the safest conditions attainable. One may also feel some relief that it is unnecessary to reach a decision involving the very large numbers of medical practitioners and others who have participated in the relevant procedures over several years past should now be revealed as guilty of criminal offences.

My Lords, for these reasons I would allow the appeal, and restore the declaration granted by Woolf J."

LORD WILBERFORCE (DISSENTING)
" . . . Section 1 of the 1967 Act created a new defence, available to any person who might be liable under the existing law. It is available (i) *'when a pregnancy is terminated by a registered medical practitioner'* (these are the words of the Act), (ii) when certain other conditions are satisfied, including the expressed opinion of two registered medical practitioners as to the risks (specified in paragraphs (a) and (b)) to mother, or child, or existing children, and the requirement that the treatment for the termination of pregnancy

must be carried out in a national health service hospital or other approved place. The present case turns on the meaning to be given to condition (i).

The issue relates to a non-surgical procedure of medical induction by the use of a drug called prostaglandin. This operates on the mother's muscles so as to cause contractions (similar to those arising in normal labour) which expel the foetus from the womb. It is used during the second trimester. The question has been raised by the Royal College of Nursing as to the participation of nurses in this treatment, particularly since nurses can be called on (subject to objections of conscience which are rarely invoked) to carry it out. They have felt, and express grave concern as to the legality of doing so and seek a declaration, that a circular issued by the Department of Health and Social Security, asserting the lawfulness of the nurses' participation, is wrong in law.

There is an agreed statement as to the nature of this treatment and the part in it played by the doctors and the nurses or midwives. Naturally this may vary somewhat from hospital to hospital, but, for the purpose of the present proceedings, the assumption has to be made of maximum nurse participation, *i.e.* that the nurse does everything which the doctor is not required to do. If that is not illegal, participation of a lesser degree must be permissible.

1. The first step is for a thin catheter to be inserted via the cervix into the womb so as to arrive at, or create, a space between the wall of the womb and the amniotic sac containing the fetus. This is necessarily done by a doctor. It may, sometimes, of itself bring on an abortion, in which case no problem arises: the pregnancy will have been terminated by the doctor. If it does not, all subsequent steps except no. 4 may be carried out by a nurse or midwife. The significant steps are as follows (I am indebted to Brightman L.J. for their presentation):

2. The catheter (*i.e.* the end emerging from the vagina) is attached, probably via another tube, to a pump or to a gravity feed apparatus. The function of the pump or apparatus is to propel or feed the prostaglandin through the catheter into the womb. The necessary prostaglandin infusion is provided and put into the apparatus.

*3. The pump is switched on, or the drip valve is turned, thus causing the prostaglandin to enter the womb.

4. The doctor inserts a cannula into a vein.

*5. An oxytocin drip feed is linked up with the cannula. The necessary oxytocin (a drug designed to help the contractions) is supplied for the feed.

6. The patient's vital signs are monitored; so is the rate of drip or flow.

*7. The flow rates of both infusions are, as necessary, adjusted.

*8. Fresh supplies of both infusions are added as necessary.

9. The treatment is discontinued after discharge of the fetus, or expiry of a fixed period (normally 30 hours) after which the operation is considered to have failed.

The only steps in this process which can be considered to have a direct effect leading to abortion (abortifacient steps) are those asterisked. They are all carried out by the nurse, or midwife. As the agreed statement records 'the causative factor in inducing . . . the termination of pregnancy is the effect of the administration of prostaglandin and/or oxytocin and not any mechanical effect from the insertion of the catheter or cannula'.

All the above steps 2 to 9 are carried out in accordance with the doctor's instructions, which should, as regards important matters, be in writing. The doctor will moreover be on call, but may in fact never be called.

    . . . I am of the opinion that the development of prostaglandin induction methods invites, and indeed merits, the attention of Parliament. It has justly given rise to perplexity in the nursing profession. I doubt whether this will be allayed when it is seen that a majority of the judges who have considered the problem share their views. On this appeal I agree with the judgments in the Court of Appeal that an extension of the 1967 Act so as to include all persons, including nurses, involved in the administration of prostaglandin is not something which ought to, or can, be effected by judicial decision. I would dismiss the appeal."

NOTES:

1. Lords Diplock and Roskill delivered speeches concurring with Lord Keith, while Lord Edmund-Davies delivered a dissenting judgment.
2. Elizabeth Kingdom has argued that the issue of competence to perform abortions is of crucial significance, and that had the Law Lords upheld the Court of Appeal's ruling it would have represented a setback to feminists' hopes that trained personnel other than medical practitioners might, in the future, lawfully terminate pregnancies (see E. Kingdom, *What's Wrong with Rights? Problems for Feminist Politics of Law*, Edinburgh: Edinburgh University Press, 1991 at pp.52–53.)
3. The outcome of the *RCN* case is indicative of the reluctance of courts to interfere with "good medical practice" (see S. Sheldon, "Subject Only to the Attitude of the Surgeon Concerned: the Judicial Protection of Medical Discretion" (1996) 5 *Social and Legal Studies* 95 at pp.102–103.)

QUESTIONS:

1. Do you prefer the reasoning employed by the majority, or the powerful dissent in the *RCN* case?
2. Does the outcome of the *RCN* case reinforce the hierarchal relationship between doctors and nurses? (See J. Montgomery, "Doctors' Handmaidens: the Legal Contribution" in S. McVeigh and S. Wheeler (eds), *Law, Health and Medical Regulation*, Aldershot: Dartmouth, 1992; "Professional Regulation: a Gendered Phenomenon?" in S. Sheldon and M. Thomson (eds), *Feminist Perspectives on Healthcare Law*, London: Cavendish, 1998.)
3. In recognition of the growing expertise and specialisation of nurses, in 2004 the Family Planning Association proposed that nurses should be trained and permitted to oversee abortions which involved simple surgery such as vacuum procedure or medical abortions induced by drugs (see below) (G. Hinscliff, "Nurses set to perform abortions", *The Guardian*, April 25, 2004). How would such a policy square with the decision in the *RCN* case? (See also the controversy in relation to nurses performing medical roles in Chapter 6 at p.365).

The *RCN* case was concerned with the legality of one method of performing abortion, and its outcome seemed to entrench medical control of abortion. This has been a feature of abortion provision in the United Kingdom and has led to calls from some feminist commentators for women to be given more control over abortion, which need not be a highly technical medical procedure.

The other main issue raised by the various techniques for performing abortion is whether some of the methods can be meaningfully distinguished from contraceptive techniques.

(i) Aspiration termination (surgical abortion)

In the early stages of pregnancy (during the first 12 weeks), until the advent of medical abortion—see below—most abortions were performed using this technique. The cervix is first dilated in proportion to the size of the uterus, which is then evacuated with a suction curette. Up to eight weeks the procedure can be done using only a local anaesthetic, but it is now thought preferable to use medical abortion for gestations below seven weeks.

(ii) Prostaglandin termination

After 12 weeks, aspiration termination is hazardous. Thus, after this point, abortions are induced through the administration of prostaglandins, either extra amniotically (introduced through a cervical catheter) or intra amniotically (introduced by amniocentesis).

(iii) Anti progestin terminations (medical/chemical abortion)

The most significant recent innovation in abortion techniques has been the development of anti-progestin abortions. The "abortion pill", commonly referred to as RU486 (and marketed under the names mifepristone and mifegyne), is an anti-progestin drug. It works by preventing progesterone (a reproductive hormone necessary to maintain a pregnancy) from entering the cells in the lining of the uterus, and thus stops the uterine wall from thickening. This means that it is not receptive to implantation by the fertilised ovum. Even if an ovum is implanted in the uterine wall, the lack of progesterone will cause it to be discharged in the menstrual flow. Thus the drug has a double action, both rendering the uterus inhospitable and dislodging any implantations that have not been prevented. It was discovered in the early 1970s, tested on human volunteers in Switzerland in 1982, and marketed in France in 1988 in the face of huge anti-abortion opposition which led to its temporary withdrawal (see M. Latham, *Regulating Reproduction*, Manchester: Manchester University Press, 2002, Chapter 5). It was licensed in the United Kingdom on July 3, 1991, having been approved for abortions up to a maximum of 63 days. The drug has been used on the NHS since September 1991 and was approved for use in the private sector by the Department of Health in December 1991.

RU486 is used in combination with a prostaglandin pessary administered 48 hours later, which induces uterine contractions. Within a few hours 90 per cent of women have completed their termination, and the remainder will usually do so within a few days. The success rate of the method is approximately 96 per cent. For those who fail to abort, a surgical abortion is required. Side effects may include bleeding, pain (which varies greatly in severity), nausea, vomiting and diarrhoea. About 1 per cent of women bleed severely enough to require a blood transfusion. (On side effects of RU486, see J. Raymond, "RU486: Progress or Peril?" in J. Callaghan (ed.), *Reproduction, Ethics and the Law: Feminist Perspectives*, Bloomington and Indianapolis: Indiana University Press, 1995.) The woman must return to the clinic within 12 days to check whether the abortion is complete and the severity of side effects. As we noted above at p.886, subs.37(3) of the Human Fertilisation and Embryology Act 1990 amended the Abortion Act by empowering the Secretary of State to authorise classes of places for the administration of such drugs. In July 2002 this form of abortion became available through family planning clinics.

The major advantage of RU486 over existing forms of abortion is that, in addition to obviating the need for surgery and anaesthetic, it can be administered as soon as the woman knows she is pregnant, whereas with a surgical abortion she has to wait until at least six weeks after her last menstrual period. It thus facilitates the performance of terminations at an early stage in pregnancy, which many people are prepared to concede is at least a lesser evil. (See S. McLean, "Abortion Law: Is Consensual Reform Possible?" (1990) 17 *Journal of Law and Society* 106.) Conversely, its disadvantage in comparison to surgical abortion is that it takes more time for the process of abortion to be completed.

In the United Kingdom, the introduction of RU486 attracted less debate and opposition than it did in France and the United States. The RCOG have recognised it as the most effective method of abortion at gestations of not less than seven weeks (RCOG, *The Care of Women Requesting Induced Abortion* 2004). However, in comparison with other jurisdictions, taken up rates of RU 486 have been low (S. Sheldon, *Beyond Control: Medical Power and Abortion Law*, London: Pluto Press, 1997). For instance, in the first two years of availability, only 2 per cent of NHS abortions were performed using this method, whereas in France, where the health minister described RU486 as the "moral property of women", it accounts for approximately one-third of abortions. Nevertheless there has been a continuous upward trend in use of this method and by 2004 medical abortions accounted for approximately 19 per cent of abortions performed in England and Wales (Government Statistical Service, *Abortion Statistics, England and Wales, 2004*, July 2005, para. 4.9.2). Since RU486 is only effective up to 12 weeks and is recommended before nine weeks, it is particularly important that delays are minimised.

Legally, anti-progestin abortions fall within the terms of the Abortion Act 1967 and are subject to the same regulations as surgical abortions. Thus, RU486 abortion must be approved by two doctors and administered on licensed premises, except for its availability through GP surgeries and family planning clinics. In relation to the ethics of abortion and contraception, it has been argued that RU486 offers the potential to irrevocably change the nature of the abortion debate, since the earlier abortion is performed, the less convincing may be the opposition of "pro-life" groups, as the line between post-coital contraception and abortion becomes blurred. It thus has the potential to undermine the entire "pro-life" campaign. (See L.A. Cole, "The End of the Abortion Debate" (1989) 138 *University of Pennsylvania Law Review* 217; M.J. Lees, "I Want a New Drug: RU486 and the Right to Choose" (1990) 63 *Southern California Law Review* 1113.)

NOTE:

1. Although many commentators have objected to the tight controls on its use, it is likely that RU486 would not have been made available at all but

for the fact that it is subject to such strict regulation, given the fear of manufacturers of being sued for side effects or harm (see Lees, *op. cit.*).

QUESTIONS

1. Since medical abortions are considerably cheaper to perform than surgical abortions, would the medical profession be justified in encouraging women to undergo this form of abortion in order to conserve resources?
2. Some commentators have argued that early abortion should be promoted as a form of contraception to be used as a back-up method where barrier methods fail. They suggest that this would be preferable to the negative effects on women's health of more "effective" forms of contraception. Do you agree? (See P. Foster, *Women and the Health Care Industry: an Unhealthy Relationship?*, Buckingham: Open University Press, at pp.24–26.)
3. In February 2006 it was reported that a pilot study involving 172 women had found that it would be safe for women to be prescribed mifepristone to take at home. Do you agree that this would be a desirable policy, in the light of anti-abortion arguments that it will simply make the procedure easer and result in more women having terminations? (P. Curtis, "Abortions at home are safe—pilot study", *The Guardian*, February 16, 2006.)

The issue of the blurring between contraception and abortifacient is a long-standing one. In 1981 pro-choice campaigners urged the Director of Public Prosecutions to prosecute a doctor for inserting a coil as an abortifacient, in the hope of obtaining a ruling that this was lawful. However the Government's Law Officers—the DPP and the Attorney General—took the view that a prosecution would be inappropriate and that "interceptive" methods of post-coital birth control need not comply with the terms of the Abortion Act. (See written answer by the Attorney-General, HC, Vol. 142 (May 1983), 238 at p.239). The correctness of this view was confirmed in the case of *R (on the application of Smeaton) v. SoS for Health* below.

R (on the application of Smeaton) v SoS for Health [2002] 2 F.L.R. 146

The background to this case was an internal report of the Royal Pharmaceutical Society (*Annual Report*, 1995, at p.6), which recommended that post-coital contraception should be made available over the counter to women over 16 years of age, a proposal which attracted the support of family planning experts and academics (see M. Latham, "Emergency Contraception: Why the Law Should Make it Available 'over the counter'" (1999) 149 *New Law Journal* 366–367. The policy was given legal effect in a statutory instrument, the Prescription Only Medicines Act (Human Use) Amendment (No 3) Order 2000, which came into effect on January 1, 2001. This reclassified a prescription-only drug called Levonelle, which acts as an emergency contraceptive if taken up to 72 hours after intercourse, and permitted it to be dispensed over the counter by pharmacists.

The claimant sought judicial review of the order, arguing that because Levonelle acted post-fertilisation, the supply of this drug breached the criminal prohibition on "procuring a miscarriage" unless it complied with the terms of the 1967 Abortion Act, *i.e.* that two registered medical practitioners had certified that a pregnant woman satisfied the grounds for lawful abortion contained in the Act.

MUNBY J.

"[340] [Mr Gordon, Counsel for SPUC] helpfully and correctly identifies the question upon which SPUC's claim turns as being whether one who causes the expulsion or destruction of an embryo prior to implantation procures a miscarriage within the meaning of ss 58 and 59 of the 1861 Act.

[341] SPUC's case that this question must be answered in the affirmative was summarised by Mr Gordon in the following propositions.

(i) The primary legal question is the meaning of the word 'miscarriage' in the 1861 Act. That has to be addressed having regard to the purpose of the 1861 Act and contemporary understanding of the meaning of the word.

(ii) The purpose of the 1861 Act was to protect the life of the unborn and also to protect the health of women by criminalising the procuring of miscarriage. The intention of the 1861 Act was to remove the previous temporal limitation on the scope of the offence and to provide that a miscarriage could occur at any time after life had started, or at least at any time after fertilisation.

(iii) When the 1861 Act was passed the word 'miscarriage' was understood to include the expulsion or destruction of the embryo prior to implantation . . . .

[343] There are, in my judgment, a number of separate reasons why SPUC is wrong and why, as I have concluded, (i) the word 'miscarriage' when used in ss 58 and 59 of the 1861 Act presupposes that the fertilised ovum has become implanted in the endometrium of the uterus; and (ii) accordingly there is nothing in ss 58 and 59 of the 1861 Act which in any way criminalises, makes unlawful, or otherwise prohibits or inhibits the prescription, supply, administration or use of the pill, the mini-pill or the morning-after pill (or, so far as the evidence before me bears on this aspect of the case, of IUDs).

[344] In *R v Dhingra* . . . Wright J expressed his conclusion in these words:

'I . . . adopt the narrower interpretation of this part of s 58, and hold that the word "miscarriage" in this context relates to the spontaneous expulsion of the products of pregnancy. I further hold, in accordance with the uncontroverted evidence that I have heard, that a pregnancy cannot come into existence until the fertilized ovum has become implanted in the womb . . . It follows from this—and I so hold—that the insertion of an intra-uterine contraceptive device before a pregnancy has become established, with the intention of preventing the successful implantation in the uterine wall of any fertilized ovum that may result from a prior act of sexual intercourse, does not amount to an offence under s 58 of the Offences Against the Person Act 1861.'

[345] I entirely agree.

[346] In my judgment the prescription, supply, administration or use of the morning-after pill does not—indeed cannot—involve the commission of any offence under either s 58 or s 59 of the 1861 Act. On the evidence I have heard—corresponding in all material respects, so far as I can see, with the evidence which Wright J heard—neither the 1861 Act nor the 1967 Act has anything whatever to do with the use of the pill, the mini-pill or the morning-after pill.

The meaning of the 1861 Act

[347] The first, and, on its own, determinative, reason for coming to this conclusion is simple and, in my judgment, unanswerable.

[348] SPUC's entire argument in effect requires one, as Mr Parker put it, to 'freeze the frame' in 1861 and to give the word 'miscarriage' the meaning it was then understood as having. In effect SPUC's case is put on the basis that Parliament intended a particular construction in 1861 and that nothing which has happened subsequently has altered or is capable of altering that construction.

[349] Now quite apart from the artificiality of freezing the frame in 1861, when the word had been consistently used in this context ever since the beginning of the century, and the impossibility in fact of ascertaining 'the' meaning of the word in 1861, SPUC's whole approach is, with respect to Mr Gordon, entirely inapt—in fact quite inconsistent with a proper application of the principles of updating construction.

[350] Applying the principles to be found, in particular, in *R v Ireland*, *Fitzpatrick's* case and *Oakley's* case, the correct approach can be set out in the form of four propositions: (i) the 1861 Act is an 'always speaking' Act; (ii) the word 'miscarriage' is an ordinary English word of flexible meaning which Parliament in 1861 chose to leave undefined; (iii) it should accordingly be interpreted as it would be currently understood; and (iv) it should be interpreted in the light of the best current scientific and medical knowledge that is available to the court.

[351] Now whatever Mr Gordon may say, there is in truth no substantial dispute as to the current meaning of the word 'miscarriage'. Pregnancy begins once the blastocyst has implanted in the endometrium. More particularly, miscarriage is the termination of such a post-implantation pregnancy. Current medical—and, indeed, I would add, current lay and popular—understanding of what is meant by 'miscarriage' plainly excludes results brought about by IUDs, the pill, the mini-pill and the morning-after pill. That, in my judgment, is clear in the light of Professor Drife's evidence and the various current medical dictionaries to which I have referred-just as it was clear to Wright J in the light of the very similar evidence he heard.

[352] At the end of the day—and despite the length of this judgment—the resolution of this case is as short and simple as that . . .

[357] Further support—though in the view I take of it further support is unnecessary—is afforded for this conclusion when the 1861 Act is considered in the context of the 1967 Act.

[358] Parliament when it originally enacted the 1967 Act did so, as s 6 shows, expressly by reference to ss 58 and 59 of the 1861 Act. Section 5(2) of the 1967 Act, read in conjunction with s 6, provides avowedly for the 1967 Act to define that which is (un)lawful for the purposes of the 1861 Act. The 1861 Act and the 1967 Act operate as a statutory code in relation to the procuring of abortions or miscarriages—the two words being used synonymously—the 1967 Act defining that which is lawful and the 1861 Act that which is criminal.

[359] Bearing in mind that IUDs had been in popular use since 1959 and the pill since 1961, and that the National Health Service (Family Planning) Act 1967 had been enacted only some four months previously, I find it quite inconceivable that Parliament when it enacted the 1967 Act intended to bring the use of IUDs and the pill within the limited confines of the 1967 Act . . . .

[386] On 10 May 1983, as I have already mentioned, the Attorney-General, Sir Michael Havers QC, gave a written answer in the House of Commons. I think I should set out the question and the answer:

'Dr Hampson asked the Attorney General how many complaints have been received, either by himself or by the Director of Public Prosecutions, which relate to the supply of what is commonly called the "morning after" pill; and whether he proposes to institute criminal proceedings in connection with any of the complaints. The Attorney General: One complaint has been made direct to my Department and three to the Director of Public Prosecutions. Each complaint alleges that the supply and administration of such post-coital medications contravenes sections 58 and 59 of the Offences against the Persons Act 1861 and that a woman using such medication may commit an offence under section 58 of the Act. Such pills are intended to be taken by women following unprotected intercourse to inhibit implantation in the womb of any fertilised ovum. The sole question for resolution therefore is whether the prevention of implantation constitutes the procuring of a miscarriage within the meaning of sections 58 or 59 of the Offences against the Persons Act 1861. The principles relating to interpretation of statutes require that the words of a statute be given the meaning which they bore at the time the statute was passed. Further, since the words were used in a general statute, they are prima facie presumed to be used in their popular, ordinary or natural sense. In this context it is important to bear in mind that a failure to implant is something which may occur in the manner described above or quite spontaneously. Indeed in a significant proportion of cases the fertilised ovum is lost either prior to implantation or at the next menstruation. It is clear that, used in its ordinary sense, the word "miscarriage" is not apt to describe a failure to implant—whether spontaneous or not. Likewise, the phrase "procure a miscarriage" cannot be construed to include the prevention of implantation. Whatever the state of medical knowledge in the 19th century, the ordinary use of the word "miscarriage" related to interference at a stage of pre-natal development later than implantation. In the light of the above I have come to the conclusion that this form of post-coital treatment does not constitute a criminal offence within either sections 58 or 59 of the Offences against the Persons Act 1861. No proceedings are to be instituted.'

It follows from what I have already said that I agree entirely with everything Sir Michael said.

[387] In the course of a debate in the House of Commons on 2 July 1998 the Minister of Public Health, Ms Tessa Jowell MP, said:

'Emergency contraception is precisely that: contraception to be used in an emergency, possibly when the regular form of contraception fails . . . However, it is intended to be used occasionally, and is not a form of long-term birth control. As the hon Lady said—I want to underline this—neither is it a form of abortion.'

[388] On 19 July 2000, as I have said, the matter was again referred to in the House of Commons by the Minister of Public Health, on this occasion Ms Yvette Cooper MP:

'Mr Gummer: To ask the Secretary of State for Health if he defines the morning-after pill as an abortifacient; and if he will make a statement.

Yvette Cooper: The accepted legal and medical view is that emergency contraception is not a method of abortion. Emergency contraception pills work before implantation and so before a pregnancy has been established. Emergency contraceptive pills will not cause an abortion if taken after implantation.

My right hon Friend the Attorney General, in answering a parliamentary question in 1983, stated that medical practitioners would not be prosecuted for illegal abortion if they sought to prevent implantation by the use of the "morning-after pill" or an inter-uterine device.'

[389] On 24 January 2001, in the course of debate on the 2000 order in the House of Commons Standing Committee on Delegated Legislation, the Minister of Public Health, Ms Cooper, said this: 'Levonorgestrel . . . works prior to implantation and prevents pregnancy. The accepted legal and medical view is that emergency contraception is not a method of abortion.'

[390] Again, I agree entirely with everything said by successive Ministers of Public Health."

NOTES:

1. The effect of the judgment is twofold. First, it clarifies the meaning of the phrase "to procure a miscarriage", thereby debunking Keown's argument

that a miscarriage could be effected prior to implantation (see J. Keown, " 'Miscarriage': a Medico-legal Analysis" [1984] *Criminal Law Review* 604). Secondly, it draws a clear demarcation between abortion and emergency contraception (see B. Hewson, "SPUC and the Morning After Pill Saga" [2002] 152 N.L.J. 1004–1005.)

2. Campaigners for women's reproductive autonomy have argued that notwithstanding the availability of emergency contraception over the counter, it has still not been accepted as part of a menu of contraceptive options and has been under-promoted (see G. Bedell, "Waking up to the morning after pill", *The Observer*, May 1, 2005).

3. In contrast to emergency contraception, methods which may work after implantation—like RU486—clearly must comply with the terms of the Abortion Act. The same is true of IUDs, especially if they are not fitted immediately after unprotected intercourse. In *R. v Price* [1968] 2 All E.R. 282 a prosecution was brought under s.58 of the 1861 Act against a doctor who had fitted a patient with an intra-uterine device when he believed her to be about 14 weeks pregnant. So doing caused the woman to suffer a miscarriage shortly afterwards. The Court of Appeal upheld his conviction under s.58 Offences Against the Person Act 1861, as it was clear in the circumstances that he did intend to procure a miscarriage. As Andrew Grubb points out, the key issue is thus whether the doctor has the requisite intent (A. Grubb, "Abortion" in A. Grubb (ed.), *Principles of Medical Law* (2nd edn), Oxford: OUP, 2004 at p.746). Consequently, in the later case of *R. v Dhingra* (1991) *Daily Telegraph*, January 25, where the insertion of the IUD took place 11 days after unprotected intercourse, a doctor was acquitted of the offence. Wright J. stated that, "It is highly unlikely that any ovum became implanted and only at completion of implantation does an embryo become a foetus." His view that miscarriage could only occur post-implantation was, as we have noted, approved in *Smeaton* above.

QUESTIONS:

1. What factors account for the policy of making emergency contraception available over the counter? Is such a policy justifiable? (See M. Latham, "Deregulation and Emergency Contraception: a Way Forward for Women's Health Care?" (2001) 9 *Feminist Legal Studies* 221–246.)

2. In July 2004 it was reported that 13 of Northern Ireland's hospital accident and emergency departments refused to prescribe emergency contraception to patients who requested it (see "Morning after pill 'scandal' ", July 20, 2004, *bbc.co.uk*). In hospitals emergency contraception would normally be distributed free. Would such a refusal amount to a breach of the hospital's duty of care to its patients?

(d) Emergency Abortions

Much feminist opposition to the medicalisation of abortion has questioned the need for *two* registered medical practitioners to certify that one or more of the specified grounds for abortion exist. As Douglas points out, this requirement adds to the delay in abortion being performed (G. Douglas, *Law, Fertility and Reproduction*, London: Sweet & Maxwell, 1991, at p.87). Section 1(4) of the Act (at p.886 above) provides a defence for the doctor who terminates a pregnancy without such second opinion only in an emergency situation where she considers the termination to be immediately necessary. This issue came before the courts in the unreported case of Reginald Dixon in 1995. Mr Dixon, a consultant gynaecologist and obstetrician, performed a hysterectomy on Barbara Whitten, a 35-year-old woman who suffered from a painful and chronic disease of the womb. Having tried for several years to become pregnant, she believed that the disease had left her unable to conceive and thus opted for a hysterectomy. During the operation Mr Dixon noticed that Mrs Whiten's uterus was enlarged, which could have been an indication of pregnancy. Rather than delaying the hysterectomy operation so that a scan could determine the cause of the swelling, he elected to go ahead with the operation. The following day he informed her that she had been pregnant and that he had, in accordance with "the usual practice", removed a healthy 11-week-old foetus. Dixon was charged under s.58 of the Offences Against the Person Act 1861 with unlawfully procuring a miscarriage. Although it was accepted that he had failed to obtain a second signature as required by the 1967 Act, he was acquitted of the offence on the grounds that he had acted within the terms of subs.1(4) of the Act, which permits a registered medical practitioner to carry out a termination in "emergency" situations without complying with certain formalities (see *The Guardian*, December 22, 1995). The case demonstrates how the crucial ethical issue of whether or not the pregnant woman had consented to abortion is deemed legally irrelevant under the Abortion Act. Its emphasis instead is on protecting the medical relationship from outside challenge. As Sheldon notes, the only other potential criminal action—a charge of battery—has never been sustained against a doctor acting in good faith (see S. Sheldon, "Subject Only to the Attitude of the Surgeon Concerned: the Judicial Protection of Medical Discretion" (1996) 5 *Social and Legal Studies* 95.)

QUESTIONS:

1. Should the test of whether the situation constitutes an emergency be judged subjectively according to what the doctor believed in good faith, or should the test be the objective one of whether the reasonable doctor would have judged it to be an emergency?
2. Do you agree with Sheldon (*op. cit.*) that, in the case law on abortion, medical paternalism is actively enforced and condoned by law?

5. CONFLICTING INTERESTS AT STAKE IN ABORTION DECISIONS

There are a number of parties affected by any decision to abort, and, as noted above, English law has failed to fully address the competing claims at stake in making abortion decisions, or the legal weight to be given to those competing interests. The parties most intimately affected by the decision to abort are as follows:

(a) The Pregnant Woman

Although the pregnant woman has been recognised in other jurisdictions as the person most directly affected by the abortion decision (see, for instance, *Planned Parenthood of SE Pennsylvania v Casey* (1992) 112 St 2791; *R v Morgantaler* [1988] 44 DLR (4th) 385), the Abortion Act 1967 does not accord the woman any legal right to decide that she will have an abortion, not even in the very early stages of pregnancy. (For a contrast with the legal position in France, see M. Latham, *Regulating Reproduction*, Manchester: Manchester University Press, 2002.) It is clear from the decision in *Re T (adult: refusal of medical treatment)* [1992] 4 All E.R. 649 (see Chapter 5 at p.310) that a competent adult woman has a right to refuse treatment, so that no third party would be able to compel an adult woman to undergo a termination against her will. As Slade L.J. noted in *Emeh v Kensington and Chelsea and Westminster AHA* [1985] QB 1012:

"Save in the most exceptional circumstances, I cannot think it right that the court should ever declare it unreasonable for a woman to decline to have an abortion in a case where there is no evidence that there were any medical or psychiatric grounds for terminating the particular pregnancy".

However, the woman has no right to demand an abortion. Rather, English law has accorded rights only to doctors, who have the right to decide whether a woman's situation falls within the terms of the 1967 Act. (See L. Clarke, "Abortion: a Rights Issue?" in R. Lee and D. Morgan, *Birthrights: Law and Ethics at the Beginnings of Life*, London: Routledge, 1989.) However, in *D v An NHS Trust* [2003] E.W.H.C. 2793 Coleridge J. held that an application to the court should always be made where there was any doubt about capacity or the assessment of best interests, especially where there was some disagreement between either health professionals or where the woman's family or the putative father were opposed to termination. (See Chapter 5, on assessing capacity.)

One impact of the discretion accorded to UK doctors by the 1967 Act is considerable regional variation in the provision of abortion. A survey conducted by the Family Planning Association in 2003 found the following variations in regional access to abortion: 79 per cent of women in North East Lincolnshire obtained an abortion before 10 weeks in 2001, compared to 26 per cent in Great Yarmouth; 96 per cent of abortions were NHS funded in Coventry, but only 50 per cent of those performed in Kingston and Richmond. The women reported that these delays caused unnecessary distress and ultimately led to late abortions (U. Kumar, P. Baraitser, S. Mortan and H. Massil, "Decision Making and Referral prior to Abortion: a Qualitative Study of Women's Experiences" (2004) 30 *Journal of Family Planning and Reproductive Health Care* 51–54).

QUESTIONS:

1. Should the decision whether to abort be entrusted to the woman alone, given the impact of pregnancy and becoming a mother on her life? Is the current abortion law out of line with the general trend in English law towards allowing patients more control and autonomy in health care decision-making? (See Chapter 6; and E. Jackson, *Regulating Reproduction*, Oxford: Hart, 2001, Chapter 3.)
2. What factors do you think explain regional variations in the numbers of abortions performed in the public sector?

(b) The Incompetent Pregnant Woman

Although the Act is explicit in requiring the approval of two medical practitioners, it is also implicit that a legal termination will not be performed against the wishes of the pregnant woman. This is unlikely to prove problematic unless the pregnant woman is over 18 years old and lacks capacity to consent to the termination. In such a case, the question arises whether her pregnancy can lawfully be terminated. The answer—according to *T v T* [1988] 1 All E.R. 613, which concerned a severely mentally disabled woman of 19 years—appears to be that an abortion is not unlawful provided it is (a) in the woman's best interests and (b) in accordance with good medical practice. This also seems in accordance with the Mental Capacity Act 2005 (see Chapter 5). The issue of performing abortions on a patient detained under the Mental Health Act 1983 arose in the case of *Re SS (an adult: medical treatment)* [2002] 1 F.L.R. 445. The case concerned a 34-year-old woman, S, who was 24 weeks pregnant and suffered from schizophrenia. S already had four children; the three oldest lived with her husband and the fourth had been given up for adoption. The putative father was not her husband but a man who was a Schedule 1 offender under the 1983 Act and also suffered from mental illness. An added complication was that the putative father was white whereas S and her husband were Indian, so the child, if born, would be of mixed race, and thus more difficult to place for adoption. S had previously expressed a desire for termination and applied to the court for two declarations: (i) that she lacked the capacity to make a decision about the termination of her pregnancy; and (ii) that it was, in the existing circumstances, in her best interests to undergo a termination of the pregnancy. Wall J. ultimately held that, notwithstanding the parents' difficulties and the obstacles to placing any child for adoption, "on a fine balance" the continuation of the pregnancy carried the lesser detriment to the applicant, and that, accordingly, a termination of pregnancy in these circumstances was not in her best interests. The judge was particularly influenced by the fact that termination of pregnancy at 21 weeks, which involves going into labour and effectively giving birth to the unviable foetus, was likely to be very stressful and upsetting for S, even if it was her preferred option. He pointed to the need for procedures to deal with termination of pregnancies in psychiatric hospitals, noting that such protocols should be designed to address the issue in good time so that, wherever practicable and in the interests of the patient, a termination could be carried out at the earliest opportunity. Furthermore, any such protocol should "ensure that the patient is referred at an early stage to independent legal advice". In the case of *Re SG (adult mental patient: abortion)* [1991] 2 F.L.R. 329, the application of the best interests test led to the conclusion that a termination was in the woman's best interests. Because the matter was governed by the Abortion Act, Sir Stephen Brown took the view that specific court approval for abortions was not necessary. (Compare the situation with regard to performing sterilisations—see Chapter 13 at pp.926–948.) On the legal definition of capacity to consent in the Mental Capacity Act 2005 see Chapter 5.

(c) The Foetus

Since virtually no one would dispute that the foetus is a form of human life, which deserves ethical consideration, the real question is whether the foetus should be accorded any legal rights independent of the pregnant woman who is carrying it. This issue was addressed in the following case:

Attorney-General's Reference (No. 3 of 1994) [1996] 2 All E.R. 10, CA; [1997] 3 All ER, HL

The defendant stabbed his partner, whom he knew to be 22–24 weeks pregnant with their child. Initially no injury to the foetus was detected and the woman appeared to make a good recovery. However, six weeks later she was admitted to hospital and gave birth to a grossly premature baby. It was then apparent that when she was stabbed, the knife had penetrated the uterus and injured the foetus. It lived for 120 days. Prior to the child's death the defendant had been charged with wounding his partner with intent to do her grievous bodily harm, to which he pleaded guilty. Following the child's death he was charged with murdering the child. The trial judge upheld a defence submission that the facts could not give rise to a homicide conviction, and therefore directed the jury to acquit. The Attorney-General referred the following questions to the Court of Appeal:

(i) whether, subject to proof of the requisite intent, the crimes of murder or manslaughter could be committed where unlawful injury was deliberately inflicted to a child *in utero* or to a mother carrying a child *in utero* where the child was subsequently born alive, existed independently of the mother and then died, the injuries *in utero* either having caused or made a substantial contribution to the death, and

(ii) whether the fact that the child's death was caused solely as a consequence of injury to the mother rather than as a consequence of direct injury to the foetus could remove any liability for murder or manslaughter in those circumstances.

The Court of Appeal decided that the defendant was guilty of murder under the doctrine of transferred intent:

LORD TAYLOR C.J.

" . . . We have concluded that there is no requirement that the person who dies needs to be a person in being at the time that the act causing death is perpetrated. That, we are satisfied, was the position at common law and to hold otherwise would produce anomalies of an unacceptable kind. For example, a defendant who poisoned the water of a pregnant woman intending her to drink it and be killed, would not be guilty of murder if the woman gave birth to a child and then made up a bottle for the baby using the poisoned water which killed the child. On the other hand, if at the time of the poison being added, the child had already been born, and the mother for whom it was intended used the poisoned water in precisely the same way with the same consequences, it would amount to murder . . .

It is . . . necessary to consider the concept of transferred malice in order to answer the questions posed in this reference. At its simplest the concept is that if a defendant intends to kill or cause really serious injury to A but instead kills B, he is guilty of the murder of B as if the object of his intentions had been B rather than A.

We can see no reason to hold that malice can only be transferred where the person to whom it is transferred was in existence at the time of the act causing death. It is perhaps pertinent to observe that a sufficient intention may be directed at no individual but rather there may be an indiscriminate intention which will suffice. Thus a defendant who introduces poison into baby food on a supermarket shelf with an intention to kill some wholly unidentified child is clearly guilty of murder if a child later dies from eating the poisoned food. It would be a remarkable state of affairs if such a person was only guilty of murder if the child had already been born at the date when the poison was introduced to the food. If in such cases of general malice there is no requirement that the child should already have been born, it is not easy to see why there should be a distinction drawn when malice is instead transferred from an intended victim to an unintended one . . . It is clear from *Mitchell's* case that it is unnecessary for the precise mechanism of death to be foreseen in manslaughter and we are satisfied that the same is true for murder. We do not think it is right or necessary to reintroduce any question of causation at the stage when mens rea falls to be considered. Provided that the jury are satisfied that the death was caused by the defendant's act, then we see no reason why the concept of transferred malice should not operate.

Obviously, if the mode of death is utterly remote, there may be circumstances in which this could be regarded as severing the chain of causation, but in the instant case we cannot see that it should matter whether the child dies after birth as a result of a stab wound suffered by the foetus before birth or as a result of premature birth induced by the stabbing.

Equally, we can see no justification for the proposed qualification that some degree of negligence towards the intended victim is required. Thus we can see no reason to conclude that the doctrine of transferred malice is excluded in a situation such as falls to be considered in the reference."

The House of Lords disagreed both on the issue of liability for murder and on the way in which the relationship between the pregnant woman and the foetus should be conceptualised:

LORD MUSTILL

" . . . The decision of the Court of Appeal founded on the proposition that the foetus is part of the mother, so that an intention to cause really serious bodily injury to the mother is equivalent to the same intent directed towards the foetus. This intent could be added to the actus reus, constituted (as I understand it) by the creation of such a change in the environment of the foetus through the injury to the mother that the baby would be born at a time when, as events proved, it would not survive. I must dissent from this proposition for I believe it to be wholly unfounded in fact. Obviously, nobody would assert that once M. had been delivered of S., the baby and her mother were in any sense "the same." Not only were they physically separate, but they were each unique human beings, though no doubt with many features of resemblance. The reason for the uniqueness of S. was that the development of her own special characteristics had been enabled and bounded by the collection of genes handed down not only by M. but also by the natural father. This collection was different from the genes which had enabled and bounded the development of M., for these had been handed down by her own mother and natural father. S. and her mother were closely related but, even apart from differing environmental influences, they were not, had not been, and in the future never would be "the same." There was, of course, an intimate bond between the foetus and the mother, created by the total dependence of the foetus on the protective physical environment furnished by the mother, and on the supply by the mother through the physical linkage between them of the nutrients, oxygen and other substances essential to foetal life and development. The emotional bond between the mother and her unborn child was also of a very special kind. But the relationship was one of bond, not of identity. The mother and the foetus were two distinct organisms living symbiotically, not a single organism with two aspects. The mother's leg was part of the mother; the foetus was not.

. . .

My Lords, the purpose of this inquiry has been to see whether the existing rules are based on principles sound enough to justify their extension to a case where the defendant acts without an intent to injure either the foetus or the child which it will become. In my opinion they are not. To give an affirmative answer requires a double 'transfer' of intent: first from the mother to the foetus and then from the foetus to the child as yet unborn. Then one would have to deploy the fiction (or at least the doctrine) which converts an intention to commit serious harm into the mens rea of murder. For me, this is too much. If one could find any logic in the rules I would follow it from one fiction to another, but whatever grounds there may once have been have long since disappeared. I am willing to follow old laws until they are overturned, but not to make a new law on a basis for which there is no principle.

. . .

Accordingly, I would differ from the thoughtful judgments delivered in Reg. v. Kwok Chak Ming [1963] H.K.L.R. 226 and Reg. v. Kwok Chak Ming (No. 2) [1963] H.K.L.R. 349, and hold that on the presumed facts the judge was right to direct an acquittal on the count of murder.

. . .

[On the manslaughter charge:]

All that it is needed, once causation is established, is an act creating a risk *to anyone*; and such a risk is obviously established in the case of any violent assault by the risk to the person of the victim herself (or himself). In a case such as the present, therefore, responsibility for manslaughter would automatically be established, once causation has been shown, simply by proving a violent attack even if (which cannot have been the case here) the attacker had no idea that the woman was pregnant. On a broader canvas, the proposition involves that manslaughter can be established against someone who does any wrongful act leading to death, in circumstances where it was foreseeable that it might hurt anyone at all; and that this is so even if the victim does not fall into any category of persons whom a reasonable person in the position of the defendant might have envisaged as being within the area of potential risk. This is strong doctrine, the more so since it might be said with some force that it recognises a concept of general malice (that those who do wrong must suffer the consequences of a resulting death, whether or not the death was intended or could have been foreseen) uncomfortably similar to the one rejected more than 150 years ago by the courts and commentators in the context of murder; and one which, it is proper to add, I have proposed in the first part of this speech, should be rejected once again in that context.

It is this feature which has caused me to hesitate long in joining the remainder of your Lordships to hold that a verdict of manslaughter can be available in circumstances as broad as this. I am, however, entirely convinced by the speech of Lord Hope that this is the present state of English law. To look for consistency between and within the very different crimes of murder and manslaughter is, I believe, hoping for too much. One can, however, look for a result which does substantial justice, and this is what I believe verdicts that B. was not guilty of murder and guilty of manslaughter would have achieved."

NOTES:

1. At all levels this case confirms existing precedent that the foetus is not to be regarded as a person for the purposes of the criminal law. (See *R. v Tait* [1989] 3 All E.R. 682.)
2. Grubb notes that the "unity of persons" doctrine espoused by the Court of Appeal in this case would have justified the artificial ventilation of a pregnant woman, who, owing to an accident, was in a state of coma and had no hope of recovery, for long enough to allow the foetus to be born by Caesarean section. (See A. Grubb, Commentary (1995) 3 *Medical Law Review* 302 at pp.308–309; see further Chapter 13 at p.954; K. de Gama, "Posthumous Pregnancies: Some Thoughts on Life and Death" in S. Sheldon and M. Thomson (eds), *Feminist Perspectives on Healthcare Law*, London: Cavendish, 1998.)

QUESTIONS:

1. Even though the foetus is not recognised as a legal person with rights, does the House of Lords effectively acknowledge foetal interests in this case? (See S. Fovargue and J. Miola, "Policing Pregnancy: Implications of the Attorney-General's Reference (No 3 of 1994)" [1988] 6 *Medical Law Review* 265.)
2. Do you agree with the Law Lords that manslaughter was the appropriate verdict in this case? (See M. Seneviratne, "Post-natal Injury and Trans-ferred Malice: The Invented Other" (1996) 59 *Modern Law Review* 884; J.K. Mason, "A Lord's Eye View of Fetal Status" (1999) 3 *Edinburgh Law Review* 246.)
3. Which is the better way of conceptualising the maternal/foetal relationship—Lord Taylor's view that the interests of the pregnant woman and the foetus are the same so that effectively there is only one legal person in existence, or Lord Mustill's view that they exist in an organic relation-ship? Is either model realistic, given the conflict that often characterises debates about abortion and reproductive rights? (See J. Mair, "Maternal/ Foetal Conflict: Defined or Defused?" in S. McLean (ed.), *Contemporary Issues in Law, Medicine and Ethics*, Aldershot: Dartmouth, 1996. For an argument that this "conflict" could be replaced by one rooted in notions of property, see Mary Ford, "A Property Model of Pregnancy" (2005) 1 *International Journal of Law in Context* 261–293. Note the parallels that may be drawn between the difficulties which law faces in dealing with conjoined bodies in the contexts of pregnancy and separating conjoined twins, an issue considered in Chapter 7 at pp.434–439. (See V. Munro, "Square Pegs in Round Holes: the Dilemma of Conjoined Twins and Individual Rights" (2001) 10 *Social and Legal Studies* 459–482.)

As we have seen above, and will note in the cases considering the interests of putative fathers below, the foetus has no status or rights in law. The decision of the European Commission in the *Paton* case (see p.912 below) did leave open the issue of whether there may be grounds to challenge a late abortion under Article 2 of the ECHR on the grounds that it offended the right to life. (See M. Fox, " 'A Woman's Right to Choose? A Feminist Critique" in J. Harris and S. Holm (eds), *The Future of Human Reproduction*, Oxford: OUP, 1998). This issue, however, seems to have been resolved in the following case which was heard by the European Court of Human Rights:

Vo v France (2005) 10 EHRR 12

Owing to a mix-up in the identity of two patients with similar names, Mrs Vo, who had presented herself at approximately 21 weeks' gestation for a routine medical examination was subjected to procedure to remove a contraceptive coil. During the procedure, the doctor negligently pierced the amniotic sac, necessitating a termination. Mrs Vo took her case to the European Court of Human Rights at Strasbourg complaining that the failure of the French courts to classify the taking of her unborn child's life as intentional homicide amounted to a violation of Article 2. By 14 votes to three, the court held that there had been no violation:

JUDGMENT OF THE COURT
"74. The applicant complained that she had been unable to secure the conviction of the doctor whose medical negligence had caused her to have to undergo a therapeutic abortion. It has not been disputed that she intended to carry her pregnancy to full term and that her child was in good health. Following the material events, the applicant and her partner lodged a criminal complaint, together with an application to join the proceedings as civil parties, alleging unintentional injury to the applicant and unintentional homicide of the child she was carrying. The courts held that the prosecution of the offence of unintentional injury to the applicant was statute-barred and, quashing the Court of Appeal's judgment on the second point, the Court of Cassation held that, regard being had to the principle that the criminal law was to be strictly construed, a foetus could not be the victim of unintentional homicide. The central question raised by the application is whether the absence of a criminal remedy within the French legal system to punish the unintentional destruction of a foetus constituted a failure on the part of the State to protect by law the right to life within the meaning of Article 2 of the Convention.

1. Existing case-law

75. Unlike Article 4 of the American Convention on Human Rights, which provides that the right to life must be protected 'in general, from the moment of conception', Article 2 of the Convention is silent as to the temporal limitations of the right to life and, in particular, does not define 'everyone' (*'toute personne'*) whose 'life' is protected by the Convention. The Court has yet to determine the issue of the 'beginning' of 'everyone's right to life' within the meaning of this provision and whether the unborn child has such a right.

To date it has been raised solely in connection with laws on abortion. Abortion does not constitute one of the exceptions expressly listed in paragraph 2 of Article 2 but the Commission has expressed the opinion that it is compatible with the first sentence of Article 2 § 1 in the interests of protecting the mother's life and health because 'if one assumes that this provision applies at the initial stage of the pregnancy, the abortion is covered by an implied limitation, protecting the life and health of the woman at that stage, of the "right to life" of the foetus' (see *X v. the United Kingdom*, Commission decision cited above, at p. 253).

76. Having initially refused to examine *in abstracto* the compatibility of abortion laws with Article 2 of the Convention (see *X v. Norway*, no. 867/60, Commission decision of 29 May 1961, Collection of Decisions 6, p. 34, and *X v. Austria*, no. 7045/75, Commission decision of 10 December 1976, DR 7, p. 87), the Commission acknowledged in the case of *Brüggemann and Scheuten v. the Federal Republic of Germany* that women complaining under Article 8 of the Convention about the Constitutional Court's decision restricting the availability of abortions had standing as victims. It stated on that occasion: ' . . . pregnancy cannot be said to pertain uniquely to the sphere of private life. Whenever a woman is pregnant her private life becomes closely connected with the developing foetus' (ibid., at p. 116, § 59). However, the Commission did not find it 'necessary to decide, in this context, whether the unborn child is to be considered as "life" in the sense of Article 2 of the Convention, or whether it could be regarded as an entity which under Article 8 § 2 could justify an interference "for the protection of others" ' (ibid., at p. 116, § 60). It expressed the opinion that there had been no violation of Article 8 of the Convention because 'not every regulation of the termination of unwanted pregnancies constitutes an interference with the right to respect for the private life of the mother' (ibid., at pp. 116–117, § 61), while emphasising: 'There is no evidence that it was the intention of the Parties to the Convention to bind themselves in favour of any particular solution' (ibid., at pp. 117–118, § 64).

77. In the *X v. the United Kingdom* decision [*Paton*—see below at p.912] the Commission considered an application by a man complaining that his wife had been allowed to have an abortion on health grounds. While it accepted that the potential father could be regarded as the 'victim' of a violation of the right to life, it considered that the term 'everyone' in several Articles of the Convention could not apply prenatally, but observed that 'such application in a rare case—e.g. under Article 6, paragraph 1—cannot be excluded' (see *X v. the United Kingdom*, cited above, at p. 259, § 7; for such an application in connection with access to a court, see *Reeve v. the United Kingdom*, no. 24844/94, Commission decision of 30 November 1994, DR 79-A, p. 146). The Commission added that the general usage of the term 'everyone' ('*toute personne*') and the context in which it was used in Article 2 of the Convention did not include the unborn. As to the term 'life' and, in particular, the beginning of life, the Commission noted a 'divergence of thinking on the question of where life begins' and added: 'While some believe that it starts already with conception, others tend to focus upon the moment of nidation, upon the point that the foetus becomes "viable", or upon live birth' (see *X v. the United Kingdom*).

The Commission went on to examine whether Article 2 was 'to be interpreted: as not covering the foetus at all; as recognising a "right to life" of the foetus with certain implied limitations; or as recognising an absolute "right to life" of the foetus'. Although it did not express an opinion on the first two options, it categorically ruled out the third interpretation, having regard to the need to protect the mother's life, which was indissociable from that of the unborn child: 'The "life" of the foetus is intimately connected with, and it cannot be regarded in isolation of, the life of the pregnant woman. If Article 2 were held to cover the foetus and its protection under this Article were, in the absence of any express limitation, seen as absolute, an abortion would have to be considered as prohibited even where the continuance of the pregnancy would involve a serious risk to the life of the pregnant woman. This would mean that the "unborn life" of the foetus would be regarded as being of a higher value than the life of the pregnant woman'. The Commission adopted that solution, noting that by 1950 practically all the Contracting Parties had 'permitted abortion when necessary to save the life of the mother' and that in the meantime the national law on termination of pregnancy had 'shown a tendency towards further liberalisation'.

78. In the case of *H. v. Norway*, concerning an abortion carried out on non-medical grounds against the father's wishes, the Commission added that Article 2 required the State

not only to refrain from taking a person's life intentionally but also to take appropriate steps to safeguard life. It considered that it did not have to decide 'whether the foetus may enjoy a certain protection under Article 2, first sentence', but did not exclude the possibility that 'in certain circumstances this may be the case notwithstanding that there is in the Contracting States a considerable divergence of views on whether or to what extent Article 2 protects the unborn life'. It further noted that in such a delicate area the Contracting States had to have a certain discretion, and concluded that the mother's decision, taken in accordance with Norwegian legislation, had not exceeded that discretion.

79. The Court has only rarely had occasion to consider the application of Article 2 to the foetus. In the case of *Open Door and Dublin Well Woman* the Irish Government relied on the protection of the life of the unborn child to justify their legislation prohibiting the provision of information concerning abortion facilities abroad. The only issue that was resolved was whether the restrictions on the freedom to receive and impart the information in question had been necessary in a democratic society, within the meaning of paragraph 2 of Article 10 of the Convention, to pursue the 'legitimate aim of the protection of morals of which the protection in Ireland of the right to life of the unborn is one aspect' (see *Open Door and Dublin Well Woman*), since the Court did not consider it relevant to determine 'whether a right to abortion is guaranteed under the Convention or whether the foetus is encompassed by the right to life as contained in Article 2'. Recently, in circumstances similar to those in the above-mentioned case of *H. v. Norway*, where a woman had decided to terminate her pregnancy against the father's wishes, the Court held that it was not required to determine 'whether the foetus may qualify for protection under the first sentence of Article 2 as interpreted [in the case-law relating to the positive obligation to protect life]', and continued: 'Even supposing that, in certain circumstances, the foetus might be considered to have rights protected by Article 2 of the Convention, . . . in the instant case . . . [the] pregnancy was terminated in conformity with section 5 of Law no. 194 of 1978'—a law which struck a fair balance between the woman's interests and the need to ensure protection of the foetus (see *Boso v. Italy* (dec.), no. 50490/99, ECHR 2002-VII).

80. It follows from this recapitulation of the case-law that in the circumstances examined to date by the Convention institutions—that is, in the various laws on abortion—the unborn child is not regarded as a 'person' directly protected by Article 2 of the Convention and that if the unborn do have a 'right' to 'life', it is implicitly limited by the mother's rights and interests. The Convention institutions have not, however, ruled out the possibility that in certain circumstances safeguards may be extended to the unborn child. That is what appears to have been contemplated by the Commission in considering that 'Article 8 § 1 cannot be interpreted as meaning that pregnancy and its termination are, as a principle, solely a matter of the private life of the mother' (see *Brüggeman and Scheuten*) and by the Court in the above-mentioned *Boso* decision. It is also clear from an examination of these cases that the issue has always been determined by weighing up various, and sometimes conflicting, rights or freedoms claimed by a woman, a mother or a father in relation to one another or *vis-à-vis* an unborn child.

2. Approach in the instant case

81. The special nature of the instant case raises a new issue. The Court is faced with a woman who intended to carry her pregnancy to term and whose unborn child was expected to be viable, at the very least in good health. Her pregnancy had to be terminated as a result of an error by a doctor and she therefore had to have a therapeutic abortion on account of negligence by a third party. The issue is consequently whether, apart from cases where the mother has requested an abortion, harming a foetus should be treated as a criminal offence in the light of Article 2 of the Convention, with a view to protecting the foetus under that Article. This requires a preliminary examination of whether it is advisable for the Court to intervene in the debate as to who is a person and when life begins, in so far as Article 2 provides that the law must protect 'everyone's right to life'.

82. As is apparent from the above recapitulation of the case-law, the interpretation of Article 2 in this connection has been informed by a clear desire to strike a balance, and the Convention institutions' position in relation to the legal, medical, philosophical, ethical or religious dimensions of defining the human being has taken into account the various approaches to the matter at national level. This has been reflected in the consideration given to the diversity of views on the point at which life begins, of legal cultures and of national standards of protection, and the State has been left with considerable discretion in the matter, as the opinion of the European Group on Ethics at Community level appositely puts it: 'the . . . Community authorities have to address these ethical questions taking into account the moral and philosophical differences, reflected by the extreme diversity of legal rules applicable to human embryo research . . . It is not only legally difficult to seek harmonisation of national laws at Community level, but because of lack of consensus, it would be inappropriate to impose one exclusive moral code' (see paragraph 40 above).

It follows that the issue of when the right to life begins comes within the margin of appreciation which the Court generally considers that States should enjoy in this sphere, notwithstanding an evolutive interpretation of the Convention, a 'living instrument which must be interpreted in the light of present-day conditions' (see *Tyrer v. the United Kingdom*, judgment of 25 April 1978, Series A no. 26, pp. 15-16, § 31, and subsequent case-law). The reasons for that conclusion are, firstly, that the issue of such protection has not been resolved within the majority of the Contracting States themselves, in France in particular, where it is the subject of debate (see paragraph 83 below) and, secondly, that there is no European consensus on the scientific and legal definition of the beginning of life (see paragraph 84 below).

83. The Court observes that the French Court of Cassation, in three successive judgments delivered in 1999, 2001 and 2002, considered that the rule that offences and punishment must be defined by law, which required criminal statutes to be construed strictly, excluded acts causing a fatal injury to a foetus from the scope of Article 221-6 of the Criminal Code, under which unintentional homicide of 'another' is an offence. However, if, as a result of unintentional negligence, the mother gives birth to a live child who dies shortly after being born, the person responsible may be convicted of the unintentional homicide of the child. The first-mentioned approach, which conflicts with that of several courts of appeal, was interpreted as an invitation to the legislature to fill a legal vacuum. That was also the position of the Criminal Court in the instant case: 'The court . . . cannot create law on an issue which [the legislature has] not yet succeeded in defining.' The French parliament attempted such a definition in proposing to create the offence of involuntary termination of pregnancy, but the Bill containing that proposal was lost, on account of the fears and uncertainties that the creation of the offence might arouse as to the determination of when life began, and the disadvantages of the proposal, which were thought to outweigh its advantages. The Court further notes that alongside the Court of Cassation's repeated rulings that Article 221–6 of the Criminal Code does not apply to foetuses, the French parliament is currently revising the 1994 bioethics laws, which added provisions to the Criminal Code on the protection of the human embryo and required re-examination in the light of scientific and technological progress. It is clear from this overview that in France, the nature and legal status of the embryo and/or the foetus are currently not defined and that the manner in which it is to be protected will be determined by very varied forces within French society.

84. At European level, the Court observes that there is no consensus on the nature and status of the embryo and/or foetus, although they are beginning to receive some protection in the light of scientific progress and the potential consequences of research into genetic engineering, medically assisted procreation or embryo experimentation. At best, it may be regarded as common ground between States that the embryo/foetus belongs to the human race. The potentiality of that being and its capacity to become a person—enjoying protection under the civil law, moreover, in many States, such as France, in the context of inheritance and gifts, and also in the United Kingdom—require protection in the name of human dignity, without making it a 'person' with the 'right to life' for the purposes of

Article 2. The Oviedo Convention on Human Rights and Biomedicine, indeed, is careful not to give a definition of the term 'everyone' and its explanatory report indicates that, in the absence of a unanimous agreement on the definition, the member States decided to allow domestic law to provide clarifications for the purposes of the application of that Convention. The same is true of the Additional Protocol on the Prohibition of Cloning Human Beings and the draft Additional Protocol on Biomedical Research, which do not define the concept of 'human being'. It is worth noting that the Court may be requested under Article 29 of the Oviedo Convention to give advisory opinions on the interpretation of that instrument.

85. Having regard to the foregoing, the Court is convinced that it is neither desirable, nor even possible as matters stand, to answer in the abstract the question whether the unborn child is a person for the purposes of Article 2 of the Convention (*'personne'* in the French text). As to the instant case, it considers it unnecessary to examine whether the abrupt end to the applicant's pregnancy falls within the scope of Article 2, seeing that, even assuming that that provision was applicable, there was no failure on the part of the respondent State to comply with the requirements relating to the preservation of life in the public-health sphere. With regard to that issue, the Court has considered whether the legal protection afforded the applicant by France in respect of the loss of the unborn child she was carrying satisfied the procedural requirements inherent in Article 2 of the Convention.

86. In that connection, it observes that the unborn child's lack of a clear legal status does not necessarily deprive it of all protection under French law. However, in the circumstances of the present case, the life of the foetus was intimately connected with that of the mother and could be protected through her, especially as there was no conflict between the rights of the mother and the father or of the unborn child and the parents, the loss of the foetus having been caused by the unintentional negligence of a third party.

. . .

94. In conclusion, the Court considers that in the circumstances of the case, an action for damages in the administrative courts could be regarded as an effective remedy that was available to the applicant. Such an action, which she failed to use, would have enabled her to prove the medical negligence she alleged and to obtain full redress for the damage resulting from the doctor's negligence, and there was therefore no need to institute criminal proceedings in the instant case.

95. The Court accordingly concludes that, even assuming that Article 2 was applicable in the instant case (see paragraph 85 above), there has been no violation of Article 2 of the Convention."

NOTES:

1. Three other judges—two dissenting and one concurring with the majority on the outcome of the case—concluded that a foetus could be covered by Article 2. For discussion of the implications of the case for foetal status, see J.K. Mason, "What's in a Name? The Vagaries of *Vo v. France*" (2005) 17 CFLQ 97; A. Plomer, "A Foetal Right to Life? The Case of *Vo v. France*" (2005) 5 *Human Rights Law Review* 311–338; T. Goldman, "*Vo v France* and Fetal Rights: the Decision Not to Decide" (2005) 15 *Harvard Human Rights Journal* 277–282.

2. Katherine O'Donovan has argued that the Court's judgment displays an unwillingness to grapple with the issue of foetal status and a reluctance to upset the consensus that, by using the "margin of appreciation" doctrine, it will not interfere with national legislation. She suggests that it would have been better to make Article 12 (the right to found a family) the basis of the application in this case as that would have focused attention on the

woman's freedom to procreate. (K. O'Donovan, "Taking a Neutral Stance on the Legal Protection of the Fetus" (2006) 14 *Medical Law Review* 115–123.)

3. There were reports that Joanna Jepson (see above at p.882) planned to challenge the compatibility of s.1(1)(d) of the Abortion Act with Article 2 of the ECHR. Do you think that any such action would be successful, given the decision in *Vo*? (For discussion of the applicable provisions of the ECHR, see M. Staunch, "Pregnancy and the Human Rights Act" in A. Garwood-Gowers *et al.* (eds), *Health Care Law: the Impact of the Human Rights Act 1998*, London: Cavendish, 2001.)

4. The issue of a woman's right to abortion is currently before the European Court of Human Rights in a case brought by a Polish woman which poses a direct challenge to the law in her country (Decision as to the admissibility of Application 5410/2003, *Tysiac v Poland* 2006). This may mean that the court is unable to avoid dealing with the conflicting rights of the woman and foetus. Since 1993, the Polish Family Planning (Protection of the Human Foetus and Conditions Permitting Pregnancy Termination) Act has permitted abortion only if the woman's health is at serious risk, if the foetus is irreparably damaged, or if the pregnancy was the result of rape or incest. The applicant suffered from severe myopia, and when she became pregnant for the third time in 2000, three opthalmologists concluded that continuing the pregnancy to term would pose a serious risk to her eyesight. Notwithstanding such expert opinion, her repeated requests for abortion were refused. After giving birth she suffered a retinal haemorrhage and is classified as disabled. Her challenge is based on the fact that Poland is in violation of the ECHR, since there is no legal framework for women to assert their right to abortion on medical grounds. Specifically the applicant is arguing that this failure to provide a legal framework, and to offer her therapeutic abortion when needed, violates her Article 8 right to respect for her private life and her physical and moral integrity. She also alleges violation of Article 3, which prohibits "inhuman and degrading treatment"; Article 13 as no effective remedy was provided with regard to the State's failure to respect her private life; and Article 14 on the basis she was discriminated against on grounds of sex and disability.

5. The implications of the *Tysiac* case may be significant for Irish women. In *S v Ireland* (application 26499/2002), an Irish woman, who was forced to travel to Britain for a termination when it emerged that the foetus she was carrying suffered a chromosonal abnormality, argued that the failure to provide abortion in such circumstances violated her right to life. However, the case was held inadmissible for failure to exhaust domestic remedies. More recently, a complaint has been lodged by a group of three Irish women, all of whom have recent experience of crisis pregnancies which required them to travel abroad for terminations (see Irish Family Planning Association press release, "European Court: legal initiative" August 8, 2005.) As we saw (above at pp.877–878), these cases could also have repercussions within the UK given the failure to clarify grounds for abortion in the North of Ireland.

(d) The Putative Father

As we have seen, under the terms of the Abortion Act it is ultimately a matter for the pregnant woman's doctor to determine whether she qualifies for an abortion under the criteria laid down in the 1967 Act. This raises the issue of whether any third party could veto the woman's decision to have an abortion if a doctor certifies that the terms of the 1967 Act are fulfilled. The third party most likely to be affected is the putative father of the child. In the past men have sought to intervene legally to prevent terminations, but always without success.

Paton v Trustees of the British Pregnancy Advisory Service and Another
[1978] 2 All E.R. 987; [1979] Q.B. 276; [1978] 3 W.L.R. 687

The second defendant (the plaintiff's wife) consulted two medical practitioners with a view to obtaining a termination under the provisions of the Abortion Act 1967. Following the consultation, the two doctors were of the opinion, formed in good faith, that the continuance of the pregnancy would constitute a sufficient threat to her physical and mental health to justify a termination under s.1 of the Act. Her husband sought an injunction to restrain the first defendants (the British Pregnancy Advisory Service) from proceeding with the operation.

In effect, since his allegation was that the abortion could not be undertaken without his consent, his claim was that he possessed a right to veto the termination. The case was heard by Sir George Baker P. sitting as an additional judge of the Queen's Bench Division. His Lordship first made plain the basis on which injunctive relief is available in English law.

SIR GEORGE BAKER P.
" . . . In considering the law the first and basic principle is that there must be a legal right enforceable at law or in equity before the applicant can obtain an injunction from the court to restrain an infringement of that right. That has long been the law . . . The law relating to injunctions has been considered recently in the House of Lords, in *Gouriet v. Union of Post Office Workers* [1977] 3 All E.R. 70. Many passages from their Lordships' speeches have been cited. I do not propose to go through them because it is now as clear as possible that there must be, first, a legal right in an individual to found an injunction and, second, that the enforcement of the criminal law is a matter for the authorities and for the Attorney-General . . .

[Sir George Baker then went on to consider whether the father of an unborn child possessed any right to veto a termination.]

The first question is whether this plaintiff has a right at all. The foetus cannot, in English law, in my view, have any right of its own at least until it is born and has a separate existence from the mother. That permeates the whole of the civil law of this country (I except the criminal law, which is now irrelevant), and is, indeed, the basis of the decisions in those countries where law is founded on the common law . . .

The husband's case must therefore depend on a right which he has himself. I would say a word about the illegitimate, usually called the putative, but I prefer myself to refer to the illegitimate, father. Although American decisions to which I have been referred concern illegitimate fathers, and statutory provisions about them, it seems to me that in this country the illegitimate father can have no rights whatsoever except those given to him by statute. That was clearly the common law.

One provision which makes an inroad into this is s.14 of the Guardianship of Minors Act 1971, and s.9(1) and some other sections of that Act applicable to illegitimate children, giving the illegitimate father or mother the right to apply for the custody of or access to an illegitimate child. But the equality of parental rights provision in s.1(1) of the Guardianship Act 1973 expressly does not apply in relation to a minor who is illegitimate: see s.1(7).

So this plaintiff must, in my opinion, bring his case, if he can, squarely within the framework of the fact that he is a husband. It is, of course, very common for spouses to seek injunctions for personal protection in the matrimonial courts during the pendency of or, indeed, after divorce actions, but the basic reason for the non-molestation injunction often granted in the family courts is to protect the other spouse or the living children, and to ensure that no undue pressure is put on one or other of the spouses during the pendency of the case and during the breaking-up of the marriage . . .

The law is that the court cannot and would not seek to enforce or restrain by injunction matrimonial obligations, if they be obligations such as sexual intercourse or contraception (a non-molestation injunction given during the pendency of divorce proceedings could, of course, cover attempted intercourse). No court would ever grant an injunction to stop sterilisation or vasectomy. Personal family relationships in marriage cannot be enforced by the order of a court. An injunction in such circumstances was described by Judge Marger in *Jones v Smith* (1973) 278 So 2d 339 (at 344) in the District Court of Appeal of Florida as 'ludicrous'.

I ask the question 'If an injunction were ordered, what could be the remedy?' And I do not think I need say any more than that no judge could even consider sending a husband or wife to prison for breaking such an order. That, of itself, seems to me to cover the application here; this husband cannot by law by injunction stop his wife having what is now accepted to be a lawful abortion within the terms of the Abortion Act 1967.

The case which was first put forward to me a week ago, and indeed is to be found in the writ, is that the wife had no proper legal grounds for seeking a termination of her pregnancy and that, not to mince words, she was being spiteful, vindictive and utterly unreasonable in seeking so to do. It now appears I need not go into the evidence in the affidavits because it is accepted and common ground that the provisions of the 1967 Act have been complied with, the necessary certificate has been given by two doctors and everything is lawfully set for the abortion.

The case put to me finally by counsel for the husband (to whom I am most indebted for having set out very clearly and logically what the law is) is that while he cannot say here that there is any suggestion of a criminal abortion nevertheless if doctors did not hold their views, or come to their conclusions, in good faith, which would be an issue triable by a jury (see *R v Smith (John)* [1974] 1 All E.R. 376), then this plaintiff might recover an injunction. That is not accepted by counsel for the first defendants. It is unnecessary for me to decide that academic question because it does not arise in this case. My own view is that it would be quite impossible for the courts in any event to supervise the operation of the 1967 Act. The great social responsibility is firmly placed by the law on the shoulders of the medical profession: *per* Scarman L.J., in *R v Smith (John)* [1974] 1 All E.R. 376 at 378.

I will look at the 1967 Act very briefly. Section 1 provides:

'(1) . . . a person shall not be guilty of an offence under the law relating to abortion when a pregnancy is terminated by a registered medical practitioner if two registered medical practitioners are of the opinion, formed in good faith, (a) that the continuance of the pregnancy would involve risk . . . of injury to the physical or mental health of the pregnant woman . . . [Then there are other provisions which I need not read].

(2) In determining whether the continuance of pregnancy would involve such risk of injury to health as is mentioned in paragraph (a) of subsection (1) of this section,

account may be taken of the pregnant woman's actual or reasonably foreseeable environment . . . '

That does not now arise in this case. The two doctors have given a certificate. It is not and cannot be suggested that that certificate was given in other than good faith and it seems to me that there is the end of the matter in English law. The 1967 Act gives no right to a father to be consulted in respect of the termination of a pregnancy. True, it gives no right to the mother either, but obviously the mother is going to be right at the heart of the matter consulting with the doctors if they are to arrive at a decision in good faith, unless, of course, she is mentally incapacitated or physically incapacitated (unable to make any decision or give any help) as, for example, in consequence of an accident. The husband, therefore, in my view, has no legal right enforceable at law or in equity to stop his wife having this abortion or to stop the doctors from carrying out the abortion . . .

This certificate is clear, and not only would it be a bold and brave judge (I think counsel for the husband used that expression) who would seek to interfere with the discretion of doctors acting under the 1967 Act, but I think he would really be a foolish judge who would try to do any such thing, unless possibly, there is clear bad faith and an obvious attempt to perpetrate a criminal offence. Even then, of course, the question is whether that is a matter which should be left to the Director of Public Prosecutions and the Attorney-General. I say no more for I have stated my view of the law of England . . . "

Notes:

1. The effect of the *Paton* decision has been to more fully entrench medical control over the abortion decision (see L. Clarke, "Abortion: a Right's Issue?" in R. Lee and D. Morgan (eds), *Birthrights: Law and Ethics at the Beginnings of Life*, London: Routledge, 1989; S. Sheldon, "Subject only to the Attitude of the Surgeon Concerned: the Judicial Protection of Medical Discretion" (1996) *Social and Legal Studies* 95.)
2. The holding in *Paton* that the foetus lacks legal standing has been affirmed in later appellate cases, including *Re MB* (see Chapter 13 at p.955).

When he was refused an injunction by the British courts, Paton took his case to the European Commission of Human Rights, arguing that the foetus had a right to life which he had standing to protect:

Paton v United Kingdom (1980) 3 EHRR 408

FROM THE OPINION OF THE EUROPEAN COMMISSION
"6. Article 2(1), first sentence, provides: 'Everyone's right to life shall be protected by law'.

7. The Commission first notes that the term 'everyone' ('toute personne') is not defined in the Convention. It appears in Article 1 and Section I, apart from Article 2(1), in Articles 5, 6, 8 to 11 and 13. In nearly all these instances the use of the word is such that it can apply only postnatally. None indicates clearly that it has any possible prenatal application, although such application in a rare case—e.g. under Article 6(1)—cannot be entirely excluded . . . .

23. The Commission considers that it is not in these circumstances called upon to decide whether Article 2 does not cover the foetus at all or whether it recognises a 'right to life' of the foetus with implied limitations. It finds that the authorisation, by the United Kingdom authorities, of the abortion complained of is compatible with Article 2(1), first sentence because, if one assumes that this provision applies at the initial stage of the

pregnancy, the abortion is covered by an implied limitation, protecting the life and health of the woman at that stage, of the 'right to life' of the foetus.

24. The Commission concludes that the applicant's complaint under Article 2 is inadmissible as being manifestly ill-founded within the meaning of Article 27(2)."

The Commission then considered Paton's argument that his right to "respect for his private and family life" guaranteed by Article 8 of the ECHR had been violated by British law.

"25. . . . . [T]he Commission has next had regard to Article 8 of the Convention which, in paragraph (1), guarantees to everyone the right to respect for his family life. The Commission here notes, apart from his principal complaint concerning the permission of the abortion, the applicant's ancillary submission that the 1967 Act denies the father of the foetus a right to be consulted, and to make applications, about the proposed abortion . . .

26. As regards the principal complaint concerning the permission of the abortion, the Commission recalls that the pregnancy of the applicant's wife was terminated in accordance with her wish and in order to avert the risk of injury to her physical or mental health. The Commission therefore finds that this decision, in so far as it interfered in itself with the applicant's right to respect for family life, was justified under paragraph (2) of Article 8 as being necessary for the protection of the rights of another person.

The Commission also considered briefly, the argument that the putative father has a right to be consulted, and equally briefly rejected it.

27. The Commission has next considered the applicant's ancillary complaint that the Abortion Act 1967 denies the father of the foetus a right to be consulted, and to make applications, about the proposed abortion. It observes that any interpretation of the husband's and potential father's right, under Article 8 of the Convention, to respect for his private and family life, as regards an abortion which his wife intends to have performed on her, must first of all take into account the right of the pregnant woman, being the person primarily concerned in the pregnancy and its continuation or termination, to respect for her private life. The pregnant woman's right to respect for her private life, as affected by the developing foetus, has been examined by the Commission in its Report in the *Bruggemann and Scheuten* case (1978) 10 D. & R. 100. In the present case the Commission, having regard to the right of the pregnant woman, does not find that the husband's and potential father's right to respect for his private and family life can be interpreted so widely as to embrace such procedural rights as claimed by the applicant, *i.e.* a right to be consulted, or a right to make applications, about an abortion which his wife intends to have performed on her."

NOTES:

1. As in the *Attorney-General's Reference* case (see p.902, above), the Commission stresses the inseparability of the interests of the woman and the foetus.
2. As we saw in the case of *Vo* (p.906 above) any ambiguity about whether a different decision would have been reached in the case of a more advanced pregnancy seems now to have been resolved in the negative.

QUESTION:

1. Do you think that a putative father would be more likely to succeed in preventing a termination if he based his argument on Article 12 of the European Convention which invests adults of marriageable age with "the right to marry and *found a family*"?

C v S [1987] 1 All E.R. 1230; [1988] 1 Q.B. 135; [1987] 2 W.L.R. 1108; [1987] 2 FLR 5

In this case, it was the woman's partner rather than her husband who applied for an injunction to prevent the proposed termination. (An account of the facts has already been given at p.879 above.)

HEILBRON J.
" . . . The first plaintiff, Mr C, a single man and a postgraduate student, is the father of the second plaintiff, who is named as 'a child en ventre sa mere' and sues by his father and next friend.

Mr C applies on his own behalf, and on behalf of the second plaintiff for orders restraining Miss S from having an abortion and the area health authority, the second defendants, from causing or permitting, by itself or its servants or agents, the abortion to be performed . . .

Counsel's case on behalf of Mr C is that he has the *locus standi* to bring these proceedings, based on his personal interest, which he does not put as high as a legal right, and because the proposed termination encompasses, he submits, a threatened crime concerning the life of his child.

If it were to be decided that there were no such threat, he concedes that he has no standing *qua* father, for he does not contend that as a father he has any special right. He concedes too that a husband has no special rights *qua* husband, and he accepts the correctness of the decision in *Paton v Trustees of BPAS* . . .

The question of the plaintiff's *locus standi* both as husband and father was also considered in *Paton's* case by Baker P., who decided that, since an unborn child had no rights of his own and since a father had no rights at common law over his illegitimate child, the plaintiff's right to apply for an injunction had to be made on the basis that he had the status of a husband and had rights of consultation and consent under the 1967 Act. But the judge pointed out that the Act gives the husband no such rights and, in his view, therefore, the husband had no legal right enforceable at law or in equity (a necessary basis for issuing the injunction) to stop his wife having the abortion or to stop the doctors from carrying it out.

Counsel for Mr C does not seek to argue for the contrary; but he submits that the instant case is distinguishable, because no suggestion was made in *Paton's* case, as here, that there is a potential criminal abortion and that, if it is carried out, the doctor would be contravening the provisions of s1 of the 1929 Act and would be guilty because he would be aborting a foetus of 18 weeks. Indeed, he further submitted that any doctor who since 1967 had aborted, or who proposed to abort, a foetus of that duration must be found guilty of the offence.

[Having decided that the weight of expert evidence indicated that a foetus of 18–21 weeks was not viable, Heilbron J. continued:]

I now, finally, come to consider the alleged criminality and to decide, as I am asked to do, whether or not I should grant the injunction which is sought . . .

Counsel for Mr C no longer claims *qua* father, but it is not unimportant to point out, as Baker P. did in *Paton v. Trustees of BPAS* [1978] 2 All E.R. 987 at 990 that, apart from a right to apply for custody of or access to an illegitimate child, the father has no other rights whatsoever, and the equality of parental rights provision in s1(1) of the Guardianship of Minors Act 1971 and s1(7) of the Guardianship Act 1973 expressly does not apply to an illegitimate child; parental rights are exclusively vested in the mother.

An injunction of the nature sought is rare. Indeed, a case of this sort is rare. *Paton's* case was, I understand, the first to be heard in this country. Such an injunction should not issue, in any event, on evidence which is conflicting, or uncertain, as here, and, in my opinion, for such an injunction to issue there must, most importantly, be strong evidence against the proposed defendant and virtual certainty that what is being complained of constitutes a defined criminal offence. Every case depends on its own facts and circumstances and none more so than this, for the graver the offence the more vital it is that, before an injunction issues to interfere with the operative procedures because of the risk to the health of Miss S, it is shown that an offence is virtually certain to be committed if no injunction issues. Moreover, the statute whose terms have to be interpreted in order to found this alleged offence is a penal one and the offence which it is said will be committed is one which attracts a penalty, as I have indicated, of life imprisonment. Such a statute must be strictly construed . . .

In my view, there is no sufficient basis for saying that there is a threatened crime and, if a case were brought, the judge would in my judgment be bound to stop the case, as I would. I have no hesitation in coming to the conclusion that counsel for Mr C has not made out his case for an injunction.

In view of of my conclusion, which disposes of the matter, I have not thought it necessary to add to this already long judgment by considering another hurdle that counsel might have encountered by reason of the decisions with regard to a private individual seeking to prevent the commission of an offence by way of an injunction, following the *Gouriet* line of cases (see *Gouriet v Union of Post Office Workers* [1977] 3 All E.R. 70).

The applications are dismissed."

NOTES:

1. Heilbron J.'s decision was upheld by the Court of Appeal, see [1987] 1 All E.R. 1241; and the Appellate Committee of the House of Lords refused leave to appeal.
2. In *C v S* the court conveniently "medicalised" the issue before it, thus side-stepping the difficult question of whether a putative father has the right to parenthood, since the pregnancy in *C v S* could lawfully be terminated (see C. Smart, Feminism and the Power of Law, London: Routledge, 1989, pp.17–19)

QUESTION:

1. If the pregnant woman was acting as a surrogate mother, and she had become pregnant by virtue of *in vitro* fertilisation using an embryo created with the commissioning couple's gametes, would (or should) the putative father have any greater say in any termination decision in this case? (For one possible solution see C. Farsides, "Body Ownership" in S. McVeigh and S. Wheeler (eds), *Law, Health and Medical Regulation*, Aldershot: Dartmouth, 1992).

In a later Scottish case an estranged husband who tried to restrain his wife from having an abortion under the 1967 Act attempted to argue that, since an action for damages lay at the instance of a child's guardian with regard to injuries inflicted in utero, it must be possible to prevent such harm from arising. However, the Scottish Court of Session reiterated the position that no such injuries were actionable before the child was born and had acquired personhood in law.

Kelly v Kelly [1997] 2 F.L.R. 828

"The question for this court is a question of law and not a question of policy. As Sir George Baker observed in Paton: 'My task is to apply the law free of emotion or predilection'

(278). None of the decisions to which we were referred appear to us to provide support for the view that a foetus has a legal persona, or is otherwise recognised as capable of being vested in personal rights for the protection of which the remedy of interdict may be invoked. Mr Sutherland submitted that none of the decisions in jurisdictions outside Scotland had answered the question—If it was legally wrong to damage the foetus, why was it not capable of being interdicted as a wrong? However, that question itself begs a further question, namely, given that a claim can be made by or on behalf of a child who has been born in respect of an injury caused by what was done before his or her birth, does it follow that injury to the foetus as such is actionable before the birth? In our opinion it does not and our answer to that question appears to be supported by the general approach which has been followed in Scotland and in other jurisdictions. Whether it is an actionable wrong to the unborn foetus for an abortion to be terminated depends essentially on whether Scots law confers on the foetus a right to continue to exist in the mother's womb. Our conclusion is that Scots law recognises no such right of the foetus. It follows that no person can invoke the power of the court to vindicate such a right.

While it is sufficient for us to reach a conclusion as to the law, there are a number of considerations which, while they form no part of the reasons for our conclusion, tend to support the maintaining of the law as it is. It is sufficient to refer to two of them.

First, to recognise the right of the foetus to continue in the womb would inevitably create a conflict with the policy of the Act to enable women to exercise their right to terminate the pregnancy in accordance with its terms. We note that the case of *Paton* was the subject of an application to the European Commission of Human Rights which declared that the application was inadmissible. In the report of their decision (*Paton v United Kingdom* (1980) 3 EHRR 408) the Commission rejected the proposition that Art 2 of the Convention recognised an absolute 'right to life' of the foetus. At para 19 they observed that this would involve a serious risk to the life of the pregnant woman: 'This would mean that the "unborn life" of the foetus would be regarded as being of a higher value than the life of the pregnant woman'. In *Re F (In Utero)* May LJ observed that to apply the principle that the interest of the child was to be predominant was bound to create conflict between the existing legal interests of the mother and those of the unborn child; that the enforcement of the wardship order against the mother would pose insuperable difficulties.

Secondly, if the foetus had the right to its own protection which could be vindicated on its behalf by interdict there would be no reason why it should be confined to cases of abortion. If such a right existed it could be used as the basis for a father taking legal action with a view to restraining the mother from some form of activity which was claimed to be harmful to the foetus—such as smoking, and certain sports and occupations. There is plainly room for conflicting views as to what would be adverse to the interests of the foetus.

In these circumstances we are of opinion that the legal proposition on which the pursuer's case for interdict is based is without foundation."

QUESTIONS:

1. Does the law relating to abortion unacceptably discriminate against men? Or, given the greater impact on women of pregnancy and childbirth, coupled with the gendered pattern of taking responsibility for contraception (see above), is it fair that decision-making rights are accorded only to the woman in this context? (See M. Fox, "Abortion Decision-making—Taking Men's Needs Seriously" and D. Nolan, "Abortion: Should Men Have a Say", both in E. Lee (ed.), *Abortion Law and Politics Today*, London: Macmillan, 1998; S. Sheldon, "Unwilling Fathers and Abortion: Terminating Men's Child Support Obligations?" (2003) 66 *Modern Law Review* 175–194.)

2. Do these cases demonstrate that medicalisation can be advantageous for women?

(e) The Parents of an Under-age Girl

A further interest which may need to be considered is whether the parents of a girl under the age of 16 have a right to veto her decision to have an abortion or to be consulted about it; or indeed to compel her to undergo a termination if they consider it to be in her best interests. As in the case of incompetent pregnant women, the courts will adopt the "patient's best interests approach", but they must be cautious to examine the girl's best interests from a suitably wide perspective, and not focus simply upon whether an abortion is desirable purely in medical terms. (This issue is discussed in Chapter 7.) In the recent case of *R (on the application of Axon) v SoS for Health*, the Administrative Court re-iterated the importance of protecting the rights of young people to confidential advice and treatment in relation to abortion, contraception and matters of sexual health (see Chapter 8 at p.585).

6. CONSCIENTIOUS OBJECTION

As we observed in the early part of this chapter, the liberalisation of abortion in England under the 1967 Act represented a compromise: it allowed for medically certified terminations but did not confer an absolute right on pregnant women to demand abortion. Furthermore, it conferred a right to abstain from participation upon those persons who hold a conscientious objection to abortion.

Abortion Act 1967, s.4(1)–(2)

4.—(1) Subject to subsection (2) of this section, no person shall be under any duty, whether by contract or by any statutory or other legal requirement, to participate in any treatment authorised by this Act to which he has a conscientious objection:
   Provided that in any legal proceedings the burden of proof of conscientious objection shall rest on the person claiming to rely on it.
   (2) Nothing in subsection (1) of this section shall affect any duty to participate in treatment which is necessary to save the life or to prevent grave permanent injury to the physical or mental health of a pregnant woman.

The main issue raised by subs.4(1) is the meaning of the words "participate in any treatment authorised by this Act"? Does this phrase only cover those who actually perform the termination or is it of broader compass?

Janaway v Salford Area Health Authority [1988] 3 All E.R. 1079; [1989] A.C. 537; [1988] 3 W.L.R. 1350; [1989] 1 F.L.R. 1

Mrs Janaway was a doctor's receptionist who refused to type a letter of referral for an abortion on the grounds of conscientious objection. She was dismissed from her position for her alleged breach of the health authority's disciplinary rules. According to the authority she was guilty of an "unjustified refusal of a lawful and reasonable instruction". She then sought, by way of judicial review, to obtain both a declaration that she was not (because of her conscientious objection) obliged to type the letter, and an order of certiorari to quash the authority's decision. She pursued her contention all the way to the House of Lords seeking to rely on s.4(1) of the 1967 Act.

LORD KEITH
" . . . The applicant claims the protection of s4(1). The issue in the case turns on the true construction of the words in that subsection 'participate in any treatment authorised by this Act'. For the applicant it is maintained that the words cover taking part in any arrangements preliminary to and intended to bring about medical or surgical measures aimed at terminating a pregnancy, including the typing of letters referring a patient to a consultant. The health authority argues that the meaning of the words is limited to taking part in the actual procedures undertaken at the hospital or other approved place with a view to the termination of a pregnancy.

The argument for the applicant proceeds on the lines that the acts attracting the protection afforded by s4(1) are intended to be coextensive with those which are authorised by s1(1) [*i.e.* actual terminations] and which in the absence of that provision would be criminal. The criminal law about accessories treats one who aids and abets, counsels or procures a criminal act as liable to the same extent as a principal actor. In the absence of s1(1) the applicant by typing a letter of referral would be counselling or procuring an abortion, or at least helping to do so, and subject to a possible defence on the principle of *R v. Bourne* [1938] 3 All E.R. 615, would be criminally liable. Therefore any requirement to type such a letter is relieved, in the face of a conscientious objection, by s4(1).

The majority of the Court of Appeal (Slade and Stocker L.JJ) accepted the main thrust of the applicant's argument, to the effect that ss1(1) and 4(1) are coextensive, but decided against her on the ground that her intention in typing a letter of referral would not be to assist in procuring an abortion but merely to carry out the obligations of her employment. In their view the typing of such a letter by the applicant would not be a criminal offence in the absence of s1(1).

Nolan J., however, and Balcombe L.J. in the Court of Appeal rejected the applicant's main argument. They accepted the argument for the health authority that on a proper construction the word 'participate' in s4(1) did not import the whole concept of principal and accessory residing in the criminal law, but in its ordinary and natural meaning referred to actually taking part in treatment administered in a hospital or other approved place in accordance with s1(3), for the purpose of terminating a pregnancy.

In my opinion Nolan J. and Balcombe L.J. were right to reach the conclusion they did. I agree entirely with their view about the natural meaning of the word 'participate' in this context. Although the word is commonly used to describe the activities of accessories in the criminal law field, it is not a term of art there. It is in any event not being used in a criminal context in s4(1). Ex hypothesi treatment for termination of a pregnancy under s1 is not criminal. I do not consider that Parliament can reasonably have intended by its use to import all the technicalities of the criminal law about principal and accessory, which can on occasion raise very nice questions about whether someone is guilty as an accessory. Such niceties would be very difficult of solution for an ordinary health authority. If Parliament had intended the result contended for by the applicant, it could have procured it very clearly and easily by referring to participation 'in anything authorised by this Act' instead of 'in any treatment [so] authorised'. It is to be observed that s4 appears to represent something of a compromise in relation to conscientious objection. One who believes all abortion to be morally wrong would conscientiously object even to such treatment as is mentioned in sub-s (2), yet the subsection would not allow the objection to receive effect."

Note:

1. The other Law Lords agreed with the judgment of Lord Keith.

The narrow construction of "participate in any treatment" supplied by Lord Keith gives rise to the following question. If a G.P. considers that one of the grounds in s.1(1) is satisfied, is she obliged to sign the requisite certificate (known as "the green form") herself, or is she entitled to rely upon s.4(1)? The question was acknowledged but not conclusively dealt with by Lord Keith, who observed:

> "The regulations do not appear to contemplate that the signing of the certificate would form part of treatment for the termination of pregnancy, since reg. 3(2) provides:
> 'Any certificate of an opinion referred to in section 1(1) of the Act shall be given before the commencement of the treatment for the termination of the pregnancy to which it relates.'
> It is unclear whether or not there are any circumstances under which a doctor might be under any legal duty to sign a green form, so as to place in difficulties one who had a conscientious objection to doing so. The fact that during the 20 years that the 1967 Act has been in force no problem seems to have surfaced in this connection may indicate that in practice none exists. So I do not think it appropriate to express any opinion on the matter."

Questions:

1. Where the risk of continuing the pregnancy is that the woman concerned would suffer psychological harm, is this a sufficient basis to trigger s.4(2)—which compels assistance in emergency cases—thus debarring a doctor from invoking the conscience clause?
2. Were Mrs Janaway's human rights adequately protected in the above case? Do you think it would be decided the same way now, given the enactment of the Human Rights Act 1998? Which of the European Convention rights might be engaged in such a case?

In *Janaway* Lord Keith might usefully have considered the question of whether, if the G.P. refuses to sign the certificate, he is obliged to refer the pregnant woman to either another G.P. or a consultant whom he knows has no moral objection to abortion. The matter is governed by the G.P.'s contractual duties which are set out in her terms of service. Although patients do not pay for the services provided by their G.P., it is nonetheless the case that her professional obligations are to be discharged in favour of such patients. For this reason, the duty (if any) to make referrals turns upon the construction of the relevant terms of service.

National Health Service (General Medical Services) Regulations 1992 (SI 1992/635), Sch.2

3.—Where a decision whether any, and if so what, action is to be taken under these terms of service requires the exercise of professional judgment, a doctor shall not, in reaching that decision, be expected to exercise a higher degree of skill, knowledge and care than—

. . .

(b) . . . that which general practitioners as a class may reasonably be expected to exercise.

12.—(1) Subject to paragraphs 3, 13 and 44, a doctor shall render to his patients all necessary and appropriate personal medical services of the type usually provided by general medical practitioners.

(2) The services which a doctor is required by sub-paragraph (1) to render shall include the following:

. . .

(d) arranging for the referral of patients, as appropriate, for the provision of any services under the [National Health Services] Act [1977].

Barr v Matthews [1999] 52 B.M.L.R. 217

The claimant—a 23-year-old woman—sought the the advice of her G.P. on her unwanted pregnancy. The G.P.—Dr Matthews—opposed abortion on the basis of her Christian beliefs. The G.P.'s medical notes were sketchy and the evidence of the parties conflicted, with the woman and her estranged partner claiming that they were told by the G.P. that because she was 16 weeks pregnant she did not fit the criteria under the Abortion Act. Ultimately, having seen a counsellor who did raise the possibility of abortion at a private clinic, the couple opted to continue with the pregnancy, and the child was born with cerebral palsy as a result of a disastrous antepartum haemorrhage. The claimant sought to sue Dr Matthews for negligence in the provision of advice on the viability of termination of pregnancy. Although the claim failed, as Alliott J. preferred the doctor's evidence to that of the couple, i.e. that their options were left open, he did add *obiter dicta*:

"[I]t is apparent that that the medical profession is very alive to ethical dilemmas posed to those of the defendant's persuasion. The practice arrangements spoken to by Dr Turner [a partner in Dr Barr's practice who testified] that she had made her position clear at interview and they had agreed that abortion requests would be referred to another [doctor] is a sensible way of avoiding those dilemmas, and I hope I will not be considered impertinent if I indicate my view that, once a termination of pregnancy is recognised as an option, the doctor invoking the conscientious objection clause should refer the plaintiff to a colleague at once."

QUESTIONS:

1. Do you agree with the legislative position that health professionals have a right to conscientiously object to participation in abortions?
2. Is the effect of Sch.2, para.3 of the regulations to make the doctor liable for failure to observe the terms of service only where he or she would be deemed negligent by courts under the test in *Bolitho*? (On the *Bolitho* standard, see further Chapter 3.)

SELECT BIBLIOGRAPHY

M. Boyle, *Re-thinking Abortion: Psychology, Gender, Power and the Law*, London: Routledge: 1997.

M. Brazier, "Embryos' 'Rights': Abortion and Research" in M.D.A. Freeman (ed.), *Medicine, Ethics and Law*, London: Stevens, 1988.

L. Clarke, "Abortion: a Rights Issue?" in R. Lee and D. Morgan (eds), *Birthrights: Law and Ethics at the Beginnings of Life*, London: Routledge, 1989.

R. Dworkin, *Life's Dominion: an Argument about Abortion and Euthanasia*, London: HarperCollins, 1993.

E. Fegan, "Subjects of Regulation/Resistance? Postmodern Feminism and Women's Agency in Abortion Decision-making" (1999) 7 *Feminist Legal Studies* 241.

P. Foster, "Contraception and Abortion" in *Women and the Health Care Industry: An Unhealthy Relationship*, Buckingham: OUP, 1995.

M. Fox, "A Woman's Right to Choose: a Feminist Critique" in J. Harris and S. Holm (eds), *The Future of Human Reproduction*, Oxford: OUP, 1998.

A. Grubb, "Abortion" in A. Grubb (ed.), *Principles of Medical Law* (2nd edn), Oxford: OUP, 2004.

A. Grubb, "The New Law of Abortion: Clarification or Ambiguity" [1991] *Criminal Law Review* 659.

E. Jackson, "Abortion, Autonomy and Prenatal Diagnosis" (2000) 9 *Social and Legal Studies* 467–494.

I. Kennedy, *Treat Me Right*, Oxford: OUP, 1991.

J. Keown, *Abortion, Doctors and the Law*, Cambridge: CUP, 1988.

E. Kingdom, "Body Politics and Rights" in J. Bridgeman and S. Millns (eds), *Law and Body Politics: Regulating the Female Body*, Aldershot: Dartmouth, 1995.

E. Lee (ed.), *Abortion Law and Politics Today*, London: Macmillan,1998.

E. Lee (ed.), *Abortion: Whose Right?*, London: Hodder and Stoughton, 2002.

E. Lee, "Tensions in the Regulation of Abortion in Britain" (2003) 30 *Journal of Law and Society* 532.

R.G. Lee and D. Morgan, *Human Fertilisation and Embryology: Regulating the Reproductive Revolution*, London: Blackstone, 2001.

C. Mackenzie, "Abortion and Embodiment" (1992) 70 *Australian Journal of Philosophy* 136–155 (reprinted in S. Sherwin and B. Parish (eds), *Women, Medicine, Ethics and the Law*, Aldershot: Ashgate, 2002).

C. Mackinnon, "Reflections on Sex Equality under Law" (1991) 100 *Yale Law Journal* 1281.

S. McLean, "Abortion Law: Is Consensual Reform Possible?" (1990) 17 *Journal of Law and Society* 106.

S. Sheldon, *Beyond Control: Medical Power and Abortion Law*, London: Pluto Press, 1997.

S. Sheldon, "Subject Only to the Attitude of the Surgeon Concerned: the Judicial Protection of Medical Discretion" (1996) 5 *Social and Legal Studies* 95.

S. Sheldon, "The Law of Abortion and the Politics of Medicalisation" in J. Bridgeman and S. Millns (eds), *Law and Body Politics: Regulating the Female Body*, Aldershot: Dartmouth, 1995.

P. Skegg, *Law, Ethics and Medicine*, Oxford: OUP, 1988.

M. Thomson, *Reproducing Narrative: Gender, Production and Law*, Aldershot: Ashgate, 1998.

M. Thomson, "Women, Medicine and Abortion in the Nineteenth Century" (1995) 3 *Feminist Legal Studies* 159.

13

REPRODUCTIVE CHOICE III

1. Introduction

Whereas the previous two chapters examined issues raised by attempts to control fertility and to challenge infertility, this chapter focuses on how the state or others may seek to control permanently the fertility of incompetent citizens, the ways in which law may aim to police pregnancy once a woman has decided to carry her pregnancy to term, and how law deals with cases where contraception or sterilisation fails. Each of these situations give rise to different sets of reproductive choices from those considered earlier. In many respects, this chapter is concerned with the fragility of reproductive choices, notwithstanding the technological advances we have explored. For instance, in the past it has been doubtful whether the discourse of reproductive choice was meaningful as regards mentally incompetent women (see R. Lee and D. Morgan, "A Lesser Sacrifice? Sterilisation and Mentally Handicapped Women" in R. Lee and D. Morgan (eds), *Birthrights: Law and Ethics at the Beginnings of Life*, London: Routledge, 1989 at pp.139–142; C. Heginbotham, "Sterilising People with Mental Handicaps" in S. McLean (ed.), *Legal Issues in Human Reproduction*, Aldershot Dartmouth, 1989). However, since the first edition of this book in 1997, there are indications that legal attitudes towards reproductive autonomy do seem to be changing, perhaps fostered by the changes wrought by the Human Rights Act 1998.

We saw in the context of assisted conception how technological developments may facilitate reproductive choices, and this is also true of pregnancy itself, where techniques such as ultrasound, amniocentesis and foetal surgery have increased information and choice. However, such developments have been double-edged for women's reproductive autonomy and have opened up pregnancy to surveillance and policing by health professionals and the law. For instance, awareness that adopting a particular lifestyle or indulging in certain behaviour, such as smoking, alcohol and drug consumption, brings the question of whether a woman owes obligations to her foetus during pregnancy into sharp focus. To what extent should a woman be able to manage her own pregnancy free of medical intervention? In the United States, where the issue has proved particularly controversial, there have been attempts to use criminal sanctions against women who place themselves and the foetus at risk of harm during pregnancy (see V. Toscano, "Misguided Retribution: Criminalization of Pregnant Women who Take Drugs" (2005) 14 *Social and Legal Studies* 359). By contrast, the UK judiciary have largely refused to intervene in regulating behaviour during pregnancy, so that legal regulation of pregnancy has centred on the process of childbirth itself.

As we saw in Chapter 11, the opportunities opened up by prenatal diagnosis have, in some quarters, heralded a search for "designer babies". While sex may be chosen and disabilities screened out, the potential for the process to go wrong also opens up new possibilities for litigation which raise difficult policy issues. Should a child who is born disabled be able to sue for damages? Should a woman be able to claim damages for the birth of a healthy child because medical negligence meant her sterilisation failed? It is little wonder that obstetrics and gynaecology have become an area of practice where health professionals are particularly liable to negligence suits (see Chapter 3).

In Section 2 of the chapter we discuss sterilisation of the incompetent patient. In Section 3 we explore the management of pregnancy, examining the available choices and the extent to which women are subject to pressures which may operate as constraints upon those choices. In the final section we consider the question of litigation consequent upon the failures of reproductive choices.

2. Authorising Sterilisation of the Incompetent Patient

(a) General Principles

Where it is proposed to sterilise a mentally incompetent person, whether child or adult, court approval must be sought unless the operation is performed purely for medical reasons. A number of such cases have come before the courts during the last three decades. The cases in this section involve both child and adult patients, but are dealt with together as they are governed by similar principles. As Emily Jackson has noted, "similarities in the treatment of mentally incapacitated women and girls are perhaps reinforced by the tendency to infantilise incompetent adult women" (E. Jackson, *Regulating Reproduction: Law, Technology and Autonomy*, Oxford: Hart, 2001 at p.57.)

The assessment of the best interests of the incompetent, which we considered in Chapter 5, are particularly sensitive in the sterilisation context, since such procedures invariably raise the spectre of eugenics. Advocates of eugenics argued that traits such as intellectual disability, epilepsy, criminality, alcoholism and pauperism were hereditary. In the early years of the 20th century, some schools of thought, both in England and abroad, advocated sterilisation of the mentally incompetent. Unsuccessful attempts were made to introduce legislation permitting sterilisation of the mentally unfit by Major Archibald Church in 1931. Stephen Trombley has argued that such concerns also persisted in later government campaigns against teenage pregnancy (Stephen Trombley, *The Right to Reproduce: a History of Coercive Sterilisation*, London: Weidenfeld & Nicolson, 1988; see also P. Fennell, *Treatment Without Consent*, London: Routledge, 1996, Chapter 6.) In examining the cases that follow you may wish to consider how far eugenic considerations have influenced judicial approaches.

(b) Sterilising the Mentally Incompetent Minor: the Early Case Law

Re D [1976] 1 All E.R. 326; [1976] Fam. 185

D was an 11-year-old girl who suffered from Sotos syndrome (which causes accelerated growth during infancy), epilepsy, a generalised clumsy appearance, behavioural problems and certain aggressive tendencies. She had reached puberty and, though she had not shown any marked interest in sex, her mother was concerned about the consequences should she become pregnant. She sought to have her daughter sterilised, an opinion supported by her doctor, but opposed by D's social worker.

HEILBRON J.

" . . . The type of operation proposed is one which involves the deprivation of a basic human right, namely the right of a woman to reproduce, and therefore it would, if performed on a woman for non-therapeutic reasons and without her consent, be a violation of such right . . .

It is of course beyond dispute that the welfare of this child is the paramount consideration, and the court must act in her best interests.

The question of the sterilisation of a minor is one aspect of a sensitive and delicate area of controversy into which I do not propose to enter. I am dealing here with the case of this particular young girl, but the evidence, including that which disclosed that Dr Gordon has recommended and Miss Duncan had performed two prior operations of this nature on handicapped children in Sheffield, indicates the possibility that further consideration may need to be given to this topic, consideration which would involve extensive consultation and debate elsewhere.

Dr Gordon's reason for wishing this operation to be performed was, of course, to prevent D ever having a child. He recognised, as did Mrs B, that there are other methods of achieving that objective, but his view was that D could not satisfactorily manage any form of contraception. Mrs B was concerned lest D might be seduced and become pregnant. She too was against all forms of contraception.

A good deal of evidence was directed to ascertaining whether Mrs B's fears were soundly based or not. The answer is in the nature of things somewhat speculative, but it was common ground that D had as yet shown no interest in the opposite sex, and that her opportunities for promiscuity, if she became so minded, were virtually non-existent, as her mother never leaves her side and she is never allowed out alone. Much of the evidence, which I found convincing, was to the effect that it was premature even to consider contraception, except possibly to allay the mother's fears.

Mrs B's genuine concern, however, cannot be disregarded. A body of evidence was produced, therefore, to indicate the advantages and disadvantages of various forms of contraception. I shall not, however, burden this judgment with any detailed examination of it, save to say that I do not accept on the evidence Dr Gordon's contention that this young girl, if and when the time arrived, would not be a suitable subject for one of the various methods described by the doctors. I think it is only necessary to refer to the fact that Miss Duncan herself stated in evidence that if Mrs B had been willing to accept one of the methods of contraception, she would have advised one before sterilisation, and I entirely accept Professor Huntingford's evidence that there were certainly two methods, either one of which could be safely and satisfactorily used. I think it was a pity that both Dr Gordon and Mrs B were so reluctant to accept this possibility, or even the alternative of abortion, if, unhappily, it ever proved necessary, rather than the proposed use of such an irrevocable procedure.

It was common ground that D had sufficient intellectual capacity to marry, in the future of course, and that many people of a like kind are capable of, and do so. Dr Gordon agreed that this being so, she and her future husband would then be the persons most concerned in any question of sterilisation, and such an operation might have a serious and material bearing on a future marriage and its consequences. The purpose of performing this operation is permanently to prevent the possibility of reproduction. The evidence of Professor Huntingford, consultant and professor of obstetrics and gynaecology at the University of London and at St Bartholomew's Hospital and the London Hospital Medical Colleges, was that in his view such an operation was normally only appropriate for a woman who consented to it, possibly at the conclusion of child-bearing, and then only after careful and anxious consideration by her and her husband of many factors and, what is most important, with full knowledge of all its implications.

Professor Huntingford, Dr Snodgrass and Dr Newton were all agreed that such an operation was not medically indicated in this case, and should not be performed. Dr Snodgrass said he was firmly of the view that it was wrong to perform this operation on an 11-year-old, on the pretext that it would benefit her in the future ... Dr Gordon, however, maintained that, provided the parent or parents consented, the decision was one made pursuant to the exercise of his clinical judgment, and that no interference could be tolerated in his clinical freedom. The other consultants did not agree. Their opinion was that a decision to sterilise a child was not entirely within a doctor's clinical judgment, save only when sterilisation was the treatment of choice for some disease, as, for instance, when in order to treat a child and to ensure her direct physical well-being, it might be necessary to perform a hysterectomy to remove a malignant uterus. Whilst the side effect of such an operation would be to sterilise, the operation would be performed solely for therapeutic purposes. I entirely accept their opinions. I cannot believe, and the evidence does not warrant the view, that a decision to carry out an operation of this nature performed for non-therapeutic purposes on a minor, can be held to be within the doctor's sole clinical judgment.

It is quite clear that once a child is a ward of court, no important step in the life of that child, can be taken without the consent of the court, and I cannot conceive of a more important step than that which was proposed in this case ... "

QUESTION:

1. Do you agree with Heilbron J. that the right to reproduce is a basic human right?

Re B [1987] 2 All E.R. 206; [1988] A.C. 109; [1987] 2 W.L.R. 1212

B was 17 years old, but was assessed as having a mental age of 5–6, and was epileptic. It was claimed that she did not understand and was unable to learn the causal connection between intercourse, pregnancy and the birth of children, but did have the sexual inclinations of a "normal" 17-year-old. Medical evidence suggested that oral contraceptives might interfere with her existing drug regime and would not necessarily prevent pregnancy. B's mother and the local authority, advised by the social worker, gynaecologist and physician, applied for sterilisation to be authorised.

LORD HAILSHAM OF ST MARYLEBONE L.C.
" ... There is no doubt that, in the exercise of its wardship jurisdiction, the first and paramount consideration is the well-being, welfare or interests (each expression occasionally used, but each, for this purpose, synonymous) of the human being concerned, that is the ward herself or himself. In this case I believe it to be the only consideration involved.

In particular there is no issue of public policy other than the application of the above principle which can conceivably be taken into account, least of all (since the opposite appears to have been considered in some quarters) any question of eugenics. The ward has never conceived and is not pregnant. No question therefore arises as to the morality or legality of an abortion.

The ward in the present case is of the mental age of five or six. She speaks only in sentences limited to one or two words. Although her condition is controlled by a drug, she is epileptic. She does not understand and cannot learn the causal connection between intercourse and pregnancy and the birth of children. She would be incapable of giving a valid consent to contracting a marriage. She would not understand, or be capable of easily supporting, the inconveniences and pains of pregnancy. As she menstruates irregularly, pregnancy would be difficult to detect or diagnose in time to terminate it easily. Were she to carry a child to full term she would not understand what was happening to her, she would be likely to panic, and would probably have to be delivered by Caesarean section, but, owing to her emotional state, and the fact that she has a high pain threshold she would be quite likely to pick at the operational wound and tear it open. In any event, she would be 'terrified, distressed and extremely violent' during normal labour. She has no maternal instincts and is not likely to develop any. She does not desire children, and, if she bore a child, would be unable to care for it.

In these circumstances her mother, and the local authority under whose care she is by virtue of a care order, advised by the social worker who knows her, a gynaecologist, and a paediatrician, consider it vital that she should not become pregnant, and in any case she would not be able to give informed consent to any act of sexual intercourse and would thus be a danger to others. Notwithstanding this, she has all the physical sexual drive and inclinations of a physically mature young woman of 17, which is what in fact she is. In addition, she has already shown that she is vulnerable to sexual approaches, she has already once been found in a compromising situation in a bathroom, and there is significant danger of pregnancy resulting from casual sexual intercourse. To incarcerate her or reduce such liberty as she is able to enjoy would be gravely detrimental to the amenity and quality of her life, and the only alternative to sterilisation seriously canvassed before the court is an oral contraceptive to be taken daily for the rest of her life whilst fertile, which has only a 40 per cent chance of establishing an acceptable regime, and has serious potential side effects. In addition, according to the evidence, it would not be possible in the light of her swings of mood and considerable physical strength to ensure the administration of the necessary daily dose. As her social worker put it, 'If she [the ward] is . . . in one of her moods . . . there is no way' she would try to give her a pill.

In these circumstances, Bush J. and the Court of Appeal both decided that the only viable option was sterilisation by occlusion of the Fallopian tubes (not hysterectomy). Apart from its probably irreversible nature, the detrimental effects are likely to be minimal. For my part, I do not myself see how either Bush J. or the Court of Appeal could sensibly have come to any other possible conclusion applying as they did as their first and paramount consideration the correct criterion of the welfare of the ward.

The ward becomes of age (18) on May 20 next. There seems some doubt whether some residual *parens patriae* jurisdiction remains in the High Court after majority (*cf.* Hoggett, *Mental Health Law* (2nd ed., 1984) p.203 and 8 *Halsbury's Laws* (4th ed.) para. 901, note 6). I do not take this into account. It is clearly to the interest of the ward that this matter be decided now and without further delay. We should be no wiser in 12 months' time than we are now and it would be doubtful then what legal courses would be open in the circumstances.

We were invited to consider the decision of Heilbron J. in *Re D* (a minor) (wardship: sterilisation) [at p.927 above] when the judge rightly referred to the irreversible nature of such an operation and the deprivation, which it involves, of a basic human right, namely the right of a woman to reproduce. But this right is only such when reproduction is the result of informed choice of which this ward is incapable. I have no doubt whatsoever that that case was correctly decided, but I venture to suggest that no one would be more astonished than that wise, experienced and learned judge herself if we were to apply these proper considerations to the extreme and quite different facts of the present case.

We were also properly referred to the Canadian case of *Re Eve* (1986) 31 DLR (4th) 1. But whilst I find La Forest J.'s history of the *parens patriae* jurisdiction of the Crown (at 14–21) extremely helpful, I find, with great respect, his conclusion (at 32) that the procedure of sterilisation 'should never be authorised *for non-therapeutic purposes*' (my emphasis) totally unconvincing and in startling contradiction to the welfare principle which should be the first and paramount consideration in wardship cases. Moreover, for the purposes of the present appeal I find the distinction he purports to draw between 'therapeutic' and 'non-therapeutic' purposes of this operation in relation to the facts of the present case above as totally meaningless, and, if meaningful, quite irrelevant to the correct application of the welfare principle. To talk of the 'basic right' to reproduce of an individual who is not capable of knowing the causal connection between intercourse and childbirth, the nature of pregnancy, what is involved in delivery, unable to form maternal instincts or to care for a child appears to me wholly to part company with reality . . . "

LORD BRIDGE OF HARWICH

" . . . The sad fact in the instant case is that the mental and physical handicaps under which the ward suffers effectively render her incapable of ever exercising that right or enjoying that privilege. It is clear beyond argument that for her pregnancy would be an unmitigated disaster. The only question is how she may best be protected against it. The evidence proves overwhelmingly that the right answer is by a simple operation for occlusion of the Fallopian tubes and that, quite apart from the question whether the court would have power to authorise such an operation after her eighteenth birthday, the operation should now be performed without further delay. I find it difficult to understand how anybody examining the facts humanely, compassionately and objectively could reach any other conclusion . . . "

LORD OLIVER OF AYLMERTON

" . . . My Lords, none of us is likely to forget that we live in a century which, as a matter of relatively recent history, has witnessed experiments carried out in the name of eugenics or for the purpose of population control, so that the very word 'sterilisation' has come to carry emotive overtones. It is important at the very outset, therefore, to emphasise as strongly as it is possible to do so, that this appeal has nothing whatever to do with eugenics. It is concerned with one primary consideration and one alone, namely the welfare and best interest of this young woman, an interest which is conditioned by the imperative necessity of ensuring, for her own safety and welfare, that she does not become pregnant . . . [I]t is, in my judgment, essential to appreciate, in considering the welfare of this young woman which it is the duty of the court to protect, the degree of her vulnerability, the urgency of the need to take protective measures and the impossibility of her ever being able at this age or any later age either to consent to any form of operative treatment or to exercise for herself the right of making any informed decision in matters which, in the case of a person less heavily handicapped, would rightly be thought to be matters purely of personal and subjective choice.

My Lords, the arguments advanced against the adoption of the expedient of a sterilisation operation are based almost entirely (and, indeed, understandably so) on its irreversible nature . . .

[The Court of Appeal] was faced, as your Lordships are faced, with the necessity of deciding here and now what is the right course in the best interests of the ward. The danger to which she is exposed and the speculative nature of the alternative proposed are such that, on any footing, the risk is not one which should properly be taken by the court . . . [T]he right to reproduce is of value only if accompanied by the ability to make a choice and in the instant case there is no question of the minor ever being able to make such a choice or indeed to appreciate the need to make one. All the evidence indicates that she will never desire a child and that reproduction would in fact be positively harmful to her. Something was sought to be made of the description of the operation for which authority was sought in *Re D* as 'non-therapeutic', using the word 'therapeutic' as connoting the treatment of some malfunction or disease. The description was, no doubt, apt enough in that case, but I do not, for my part, find the distinction between 'therapeutic' and 'non-therapeutic' measures helpful in the context of the instant case, for it seems to me entirely immaterial whether measures undertaken for the protection against future and foreseeable injury are properly described as 'therapeutic'. The primary and paramount question is only whether they are for the welfare and benefit of this particular young woman situate as she is situate in this case . . .

I desire to emphasise once again that this case is not about sterilisation for social purposes, it is not about eugenics it is not about the convenience of those whose task it is to care for the ward or the anxieties of her family and it involves no general principle of public policy. It is about what is in the best interests of this unfortunate young woman and how best she can be given the protection which is essential to her future well-being so that she may lead as full a life as her intellectual capacity allows. That is and must be the paramount consideration as was rightly appreciated by Bush J. and by the Court of Appeal. They came to what, in my judgment, was the only possible conclusion in the interests of the minor. I would accordingly dismiss the appeal."

NOTES:

1. Lords Brandon and Templeman agreed. Lord Templeman added that sterilisation of a minor should only be carried out with the leave of a High Court judge.

2. There was some urgency in *B* to perform the sterilisation before her 18th birthday as the legality of the performance of a sterilisation operation upon a mentally incompetent adult was unclear, since this case was decided before *F v West Berkshire Health Authority* (see below at p.933). After the House of Lords decision in that case, it is clear that a court may authorise a mentally incompetent adult to be sterilised where it is in her best interests. At least this ruling should afford more opportunity to monitor how a girl may develop and then, if necessary, sterilise when she is older.

3. An alternative to making a minor a ward of court is to apply for a specific issue order under s.8 of the Children Act 1989 as happened in the case of *Re HG (Specific Issue: Sterilisation)* [1993] 1 F.L.R. 587. The deputy judge in this case noted that the case was "sufficiently overwhelming" to justify sterilisation.

4. In these cases one needs to be particularly wary of accepting the stated facts at face value. As Lee and Morgan point out, what are treated as settled facts in *Re B* are actually highly selective and in reality constitute a series of assessments as to the girl's capabilities and prospects. (See R. Lee and D. Morgan, "A Lesser Sacrifice? Sterilisation and Mentally Handicapped Women" in R. Lee and D. Morgan (eds), *Birthrights: Law and Ethics at the Beginnings of Life*, London: Routledge, 1989 at pp.139–142.)

5. It has also been questioned whether decisions to sterilise are gender biased. It is notable that until recently the cases where sterilisation has been ordered have all concerned female patients (see M. Freeman, "For Her Own Good" (1987) 84 *L.S.Gaz.* 949). For a consideration of the different issues raised by proposed a sterilisation of a man, see *Re A* (at p.938 below).

6. The speeches in *Re B* emphasised B's mental age. Yet Christopher Heginbotham argues that mental age is not a static concept:

> "People with mental handicaps have complex personalities like everyone else. To talk of a mental age of two or three is meaningless. Although intellectually he/she may only function at that level, life skills may approximate to those of a child of five or six or eight or nine, and, socially, the person may be capable of adolescent or adult interaction." (C. Heginbotham, "Sterilising People with Mental Handicaps" in S. McLean (ed.), *Legal Issues in Human Reproduction*, Aldershot: Dartmouth, 1989; M. Freeman, "Sterilising the Mentally Handicapped" in M. Freeman (ed.), *Medicine, Ethics and Law*, London: Sweet & Maxwell, 1988.)

7. One difficulty identified in this case was B's incomprehension of the information provided to her. Kirsty Keywood has suggested that many of the problems in this case could have been overcome with better sex education. (See K. Keywood, "Sterilising the Woman with Learning Disabilities" in J. Bridgeman and S. Millns (eds), *Law and Body Politics*, Aldershot: Dartmouth, 1995.)

8. A further complication, glossed over in *Re B*, is that s.7 of the Sexual Offences Act 1956, which was then in force, provided that sexual intercourse with a "mental defective" was a criminal offence. (See now Sexual Offence Act 2003).

9. In reaching its decision, the House of Lords in *Re B* deemed sterilisations to be irreversible. However, in *Re P (A Minor) (Wardship: Sterilisation)* [1989] 1 F.L.R. 182 where it was proposed to sterilise a 17-year-old girl, Professor Robert Winston testified that sterilisation operations which involved clipping the fallopian tubes could be reversed by subsequent micro-surgical anastomosis, which carried a 95 per cent chance of reversal. In the earlier case of *Re M (A Minor) (Wardship: Sterilisation)* [1988] 2 F.L.R. 497 medical evidence had suggested that in 50 per cent to 75 per cent of cases micro-surgery allowed reversal of the procedure. However, as Brazier points out, average success rates for reversals may not accord with those quoted by leading experts (M. Brazier, "Down the Slippery Slope" (1990) 6 *Professional Negligence* 25; and note the dicta in the judgment of Cazalet J. in *A National Health Trust v C* (at p.946 below).

QUESTIONS:

1. Do you agree with the House of Lords' rejection of the approach taken in *Re Eve*? Is it correct to say that a distinction between therapeutic and non-therapeutic sterilisation is meaningless? (See Lee and Morgan, *op. cit.* in Note 4; G. Douglas, *Law, Fertility and Reproduction*, London: Sweet & Maxwell, 1991 at pp.56–71.) Is sterilisation of an incompetent person for contraceptive purposes ever justifiable? (See I. Kennedy, "Patients, Doctors and Human Rights" in I. Kennedy, *Treat Me Right*, Oxford: OUP, 1989.)

2. Was pregnancy really the worst misfortune that could befall B, as their Lordships' opinions seem to suggest? In the light of the speeches in *Re B*,

can a mentally incompetent person be said to have a "right to reproduce" (see Lee and Morgan, *op. cit.* in Note 4).

3. Notwithstanding the Law Lords' denials, do you think that that the case was covertly about eugenics? Note that in *Re M (A Minor) (Wardship: Sterilisation)* [1988] 2 F.L.R. 497 Bush J. took into account the fact the woman had a 50 per cent chance, should she become pregnant, of giving birth to a disabled child. (see M. Brazier, "Down the Slippery Slope" (1990) 6 *Professional Negligence* 25).

4. How likely is it that once a sterilisation has been carried out on an incompetent woman it will be reversed?

5. Were the judges in these cases unduly deferential to the opinion of medical experts? What about the human rights of the girls concerned? (See S. Lee, "Towards a Jurisprudence of Consent" in J. Bell and J. Eekelaar (eds) *Oxford Essays in Jurisprudence* (3rd series), Oxford: OUP 1987.)

(c) Sterilising Mentally Incompetent Adult Patients: the Early Case Law

In the following case the House of Lords considered the circumstances in which an incompetent adult could be sterilised:

Re F [1989] 2 All E.R. 545; [1990] 2 A.C. 1; [1989] 2 W.L.R. 938

F was a 36-year-old mentally disabled woman who lived as a voluntary in-patient in a mental hospital. She was stated to have a mental age of four or five, and the verbal ability of a two-year-old. Concern arose when she formed a close relationship of a sexual nature with a male patient. The opinion of the hospital medical staff was that she would be unable to cope with pregnancy. As was seen in Chapter 5, the House of Lords held that, in the case of the adult patient, they had no jurisdiction consent to treatment. Nevertheless, they held that treatment could be authorised on the basis of necessity where it was in the patient's best interests to do so.

LORD GRIFFITHS

" . . . My Lords, the argument in this appeal has ranged far and wide in search of a measure to protect those who cannot protect themselves from the insult of an unnecessary sterilisation. Every judge who has considered the problem has recognised that there should be some control mechanism imposed on those who have the care of infants or mentally incompetent women of child bearing age to prevent or at least inhibit them from sterilising the women without approval of the High Court. I am, I should make it clear, speaking now and hereafter of an operation for sterilisation which is proposed not for the treatment of diseased organs but an operation on a woman with healthy reproductive organs in order to avoid the risk of pregnancy. The reasons for the anxiety about sterilisation which it is proposed should be carried out for other than purely medical reasons, such as the removal of the ovaries to prevent the spread of cancer, are readily understandable and are shared throughout the common law world.

We have been taken through many authorities in the United States, Australia and Canada which stress the danger that sterilisation may be proposed in circumstances which are not truly in the best interests of the woman but for the convenience of those who are charged with her care. In the United States and Australia the solution has been to declare that, in the case of a woman who either because of infancy or mental incompetence cannot give her consent, the operation may not be performed without the consent of the court. In Canada the Supreme Court has taken an even more extreme stance and declared that sterilisation is unlawful unless performed for therapeutic reasons, which I understand to be as a life-saving measure or for the prevention of the spread of disease: see *Re Eve* (1986) 31 DLR (4th) 1. This extreme position was rejected by this House in *Re B (A Minor) (Wardship: Sterilisation)* [see p.928 above], which recognised that an operation might be in the best interests of a woman even though carried out in order to protect her from the trauma of a pregnancy which she could not understand and with which she could not cope. Nevertheless Lord Templeman stressed that such an operation should not be undertaken without the approval of a High Court judge of the Family Division. In this country *Re D (A Minor) (Wardship: Sterilisation)* [1976] 1 All E.R. 326, stands as a stark warning of the danger of leaving the decision to sterilise in the hands of those having the immediate care of the woman, even when they genuinely believe that they are acting in her best interests.

. . . I agree that an action for a declaration is available as a mechanism by which a proposed sterilisation may be investigated to ensure that it is in the woman's best interests.

But I cannot agree that it is satisfactory to leave this grave decision with all its social implications in the hands of those having the care of the patient with only the expectation that they will have the wisdom to obtain a declaration of lawfulness before the operation is performed. In my view the law ought to be that they must obtain the approval of the court before they sterilise a woman incapable of giving consent and that it is unlawful to sterilise without that consent. I believe that it is open to your Lordships to develop a common law rule to this effect. Although the general rule is that the individual is the master of his own fate the judges through the common law have, in the public interest, imposed certain constraints on the harm that people may consent to being inflicted on their own bodies . . .

The common law has, in the public interest, been developed to forbid the infliction of injury on those who are fully capable of consenting to it. The time has now come for a further development to forbid, again in the public interest, the sterilisation of a woman with healthy reproductive organs who, either through mental incompetence or youth, is incapable of giving her fully informed consent unless such an operation has been inquired into and sanctioned by the High Court. Such a common law rule would provide a more effective protection than the exercise of *parens patriae* jurisdiction which is dependent on some interested party coming forward to invoke the jurisdiction of the court. The *parens patriae* jurisdiction is in any event now only available in the case of minors through their being made wards of court. I would myself declare that on grounds of public interest an operation to sterilise a woman incapable of giving consent on grounds of either age or mental incapacity is unlawful if performed without the consent of the High Court. I fully recognise that in so doing I would be making new law. However, the need for such a development has been identified in a number of recent cases and in the absence of any parliamentary response to the problem it is my view that the judges can and should accept responsibility to recognise the need and to adapt the common law to meet it. If such a development did not meet with public approval it would always be open to Parliament to reverse it or to alter it by perhaps substituting for the opinion of the High Court judge the second opinion of another doctor as urged by counsel for the Mental Health Act Commission . . . "

LORD GOFF OF CHIEVELEY
"Upon what principle can medical treatment be justified when given without consent? We are searching for a principle upon which, in limited circumstances, recognition may be given to a need, in the interests of the patient, that treatment should be given to him in circumstances where he is (temporarily or permanently) disabled from consenting to it. It is this criterion of a need which points to the principle of necessity as providing justification.

That there exists in the common law a principle of necessity which may justify action which would otherwise be unlawful is not in doubt . . . We are concerned here with action taken to preserve the life, health or well-being of another who is unable to consent to it . . .

We can derive some guidance as to the nature of the principle of necessity from the cases on agency of necessity in mercantile law . . . from them can be derived the basic requirements, applicable in these cases of necessity, that, to fall within the principle, not only (1) must there be a necessity to act when it is not practicable to communicate with the assisted person, but also (2) the action taken must be such as a reasonable person would in all the circumstances take, acting in the best interests of the assisted person . . .

[I]n the case of a mentally disordered person, as in the case of a stroke victim, the permanent state of affairs calls for a wider range of care than may be requisite in an emergency which arises from accidental injury. When the state of affairs is permanent, or semi-permanent, action properly taken to preserve the life, health or well-being of the assisted person may well transcend such measures as surgical operation or substantial medical treatment and may extend to include such humdrum matters as routine medical or dental treatment, even simple care such as dressing and undressing and putting to bed . . . [W]here the state of affairs is permanent or semi-permanent, as may be so in the case of a mentally disordered person, there is no point in waiting to obtain the patient's consent. The need to care for him is obvious; and the doctor must then act in the best interests of his patient, just as if he had received his patient's consent so to do. Were this not so, much useful treatment and care could, in theory at least, be denied to the unfortunate. It follows that, on this point, I am unable to accept the view expressed by Neill L.J. in the Court of Appeal . . . that the treatment must be shown to have been necessary. Moreover, in such a case, as my noble and learned friend Lord Brandon of Oakbrook has pointed out, a doctor who has assumed responsibility for the care of a patient may not only be treated as having the patient's consent to act, but may also be under a duty so to act. I find myself to be respectfully in agreement with Lord Donaldson of Lymington M.R., when he said:

'I see nothing incongruous in doctors and others who have a caring responsibility being required, when acting in relation to an adult who is incompetent, to exercise a right of choice in exactly the same way as would the court or reasonable parents in relation to a child, making due allowance, of course, for the fact that the patient is not a child, and I am satisfied that that is what the law does in fact require.'

In these circumstances, it is natural to treat the deemed authority and the duty as interrelated. But I feel bound to express my opinion that, in principle, the lawfulness of the doctor's action is, at least in its origin, to be found in the principle of necessity. This can perhaps be seen most clearly in cases where there is no continuing relationship between doctor and patient. The 'doctor in the house' who volunteers to assist a lady in the audience who, overcome by the drama or by the heat in the theatre, has fainted away, is impelled to act by no greater duty than that imposed by his own Hippocratic oath. Furthermore, intervention can be justified in the case of a non-professional, as well as a professional, man or woman who has no pre-existing relationship with the assisted person—as in the case of a stranger who rushes to assist an injured man after an accident. In my opinion, it is the necessity itself which provides the justification for the intervention.

I have said that the doctor has to act in the best interests of the assisted person. In the case of routine treatment of mentally disordered persons, there should be little difficulty in applying this principle. In the case of more serious treatment, I recognise that its application may create problems for the medical profession; however, in making decisions about treatment, the doctor must act in accordance with a responsible and competent body of relevant professional opinion, on the principles set down in *Bolam v Friern Hospital Management Committee* [1957] 1 W.L.R. 582. No doubt, in practice, a decision may involve others besides the doctor. It must surely be good practice to consult relatives and others who are concerned with the care of the patient. Sometimes, of course, consultation with a specialist or specialists will be required; and in others, especially where the decision involves more than a purely medical opinion, an inter-disciplinary team will in practice participate in the decision. It is very difficult, and would be unwise, for a court to do more than to stress that, for those who are involved in these important and sometimes difficult decisions, the overriding consideration is that they should act in the best interests of the person who suffers from the misfortune of being prevented by incapacity from deciding for himself what should be done to his own body, in his own best interests.

... In the present case, your Lordships have to consider whether the foregoing principles apply in the case of a proposed operation of sterilisation on an adult woman of unsound mind, or whether sterilisation is (perhaps with one or two other cases) to be placed in a separate category to which special principles apply. Again, counsel for the Official Solicitor assisted your Lordships by deploying the argument that, in the absence of any *parens patriae* jurisdiction, sterilisation of an adult woman of unsound mind, who by reason of her mental incapacity is unable to consent, can never be lawful. He founded his submission on a right of reproductive autonomy or right to control one's own reproduction, which necessarily involves the right not to be sterilised involuntarily, on the fact that sterilisation involves irreversible interference with the patient's most important organs, on the fact that it involves interference with organs which are functioning normally, on the fact that sterilisation is a topic on which medical views are often not unanimous and on the undesirability, in the case of a mentally disordered patient, of imposing a 'rational' solution on an incompetent patient. Having considered these submissions with care, I am of the opinion that neither singly nor as a whole do they justify the conclusion for which counsel for the Official Solicitor contended. ...

Although the *parens patriae* jurisdiction in the case of adults of unsound mind is no longer vested in courts in this country, the approach adopted by the courts in the United States and in Australia provides, in my opinion, strong support for the view that, as a matter of practice, the operation of sterilisation should not be performed on an adult person who lacks the capacity to consent to it without first obtaining the opinion of the court that the operation is, in the circumstances, in the best interests of the person concerned, by seeking a declaration that the operation is lawful . . .

In my opinion, that guidance should be sought in order to obtain an independent, objective and authoritative view on the lawfulness of the procedure in the particular circumstances of the relevant case, after a hearing at which it can be ensured that there is independent representation on behalf of the person on whom it is proposed to perform the operation. This approach is consistent with the opinion expressed by Lord Templeman in *Re B (A Minor) (Wardship: Sterilisation)* . . .

I recognise that the requirement of a hearing before a court is regarded by some as capable of deterring certain medical practitioners from advocating the procedure of sterilisation but I trust and hope that it may come to be understood that court procedures of this kind, conducted sensitively and humanely by judges of the Family Division, so far as possible and where appropriate in the privacy of chambers, are not to be feared by responsible practitioners . . . "

NOTES:

1. Lords Bridge, Brandon and Jauncey concurred; Lord Griffiths also concurred that necessity was the basis for treatment in such cases.
2. The view taken by the House of Lords in *Re F* (disagreeing with the Court of Appeal on this point) that "best interests" was to be determined with reference to the standard set by a responsible body of medical practitioners was much criticised (see further Chapter 5 at pp.321–327; J. Shaw, "Regulating Sexuality: a Legislative Framework for Non-Consensual Sterilisation" in S. McVeigh and S. Wheeler (eds), *Law, Health and Medical Regulation*, Aldershot: Dartmouth, 1991; P. Fennell, *Treatment*

without Consent, London: Routledge 1996, Chapter 6; E. Jackson, *Regulating Reproduction*, Oxford: Hart, 2001, Chapter 1). Note how little attention is paid in the case to the determination of F's incapacity.

3. In *Re W (Mental Patient)* [1993] 1 F.L.R. 381, W was a 20-year-old woman with the mental age of a young child, who also suffered from severe learning disabilities, mild epilepsy and mobility problems related to dislocation of the hips which had resulted from a congenital disability. Sterilisation was sought on the grounds that pregnancy would aggravate her epilepsy. While she showed limited understanding of issues such as pregnancy and childbirth, it appeared that there was little immediate chance of her becoming pregnant because she was well supervised. Moreover, medical opinion on the question was divided. Nevertheless Hollis J. granted a declaration authorising sterilisation, noting that it would be undesirable for her to become pregnant and that contraception was unsuitable. He stated that he did not regard sterilisation as being to W's detriment.

4. In *Re E (A Minor) (Medical Treatment)* [1991] 2 F.L.R. 585 Sir Stephen Brown P. ruled that it was not necessary to seek the court's approval if the proposed sterilisation was to be performed on purely therapeutic grounds. In this case it was proposed to sterilise J, a 17-year-old mentally disabled girl, who suffered from severe menstrual problems. Because J was overweight, any attempt to treat the menstrual problems hormonally would have worsened the obesity factor. The judge ruled that the case was entirely different from *Re F* and that as she was a minor, parental consent to a therapeutic hysterectomy would suffice. This decision was followed in *Re GF* [1992] 1 F.L.R. 293, where the same judge held that a court declaration approving a sterilisation operation was unnecessary provided that two doctors agreed that the operation was necessary for therapeutic purposes, was in the patient's best interests, and that no practicable less intrusive treatment was available. It is unclear how these decisions can be reconciled with the view taken in *Re B* (at p.928 above) that there is no valid distinction between therapeutic and non-therapeutic sterilisation operations (see G. Douglas, *Law, Fertility and Reproduction*, London: Sweet & Maxwell, date at p.58). See also the comments of Thorpe L.J. in the Court of Appeal, in *Re S* at p.944 below.

5. *Re X (Adult Patient: Sterilisation)* [1998] 2 F.L.R. 1124 concerned a 31-year-old woman who was described as "severely mentally retarded". She attended an adult training centre, where she appeared to enjoy physical contact with men, and had a formed a particularly close relationship with one male user of the centre. Although it was accepted that she was incapable of looking after a child, she had stated that she would like to have a baby. She had been fitted with a contraceptive coil, but when it had to be replaced, X's parents, supported by the Official Solicitor, sought a declaration that sterilisation would be in X's best interests. Holman J. granted the declaration on the basis that there was a real risk that X would have a sexual relationship and become pregnant, and be traumatised by the physical processes of pregnancy and birth, coupled with the subsequent

inevitable removal of the baby. Sterilisation was therefore held to be in her best interests.

QUESTIONS:

1. It has been suggested in the context of these sterilisation decisions that "the courts' somewhat misplaced concern for the woman's vulnerability seems to be at the expense of recognising her sexual needs and desires". (See K. Keywood, "Sterilising the Woman with Learning Disabilities" in J. Bridgeman and S. Millns (eds), Law and Body Politics, Aldershot: Dartmouth, 1995.) Do you agree?
2. Would it have been preferable, rather than using the *Bolam* test, to apply the more stringent test proposed by Wood J. in *T v T* [1988] 1 All E.R. 613 at p.621 that sterilisation would only be permitted if there were "no two views" that the procedure was in the best interests of the incompetent patient? (See J.E.S. Fortin, "Sterilisation, the Mentally Ill and Consent to Treatment" (1988) 51 *Modern Law Review* 634; for another alternative, see Kennedy's reading of Scottish law in I. Kennedy, "Non-consensual Treatment: Incompetent Adult, Sterilisation" (1997) 5 *Medical Law Review* 325.)
3. Is a sterilisation performed for reasons of "menstrual management" properly regarded as therapeutic sterilisation? Note that in its 1995 Report on Mental Incapacity, the Law Commission took the view that sterilisation for these purposes should not require court approval but it should require certification by an independent medical practitioner (Law Commission, *Mental Incapacity*, Law Com. No. 231, London: HMSO 1995, paras 6.4–6.9).
4. It subsequently emerged that the man with whom F was sexually involved had formed relationships with other women in the hospital. Should this have affected the outcome of the case?

(d) A New Approach to Sterilisation Cases?

The different issues raised by an application to sterilise a man were addressed in the following case. While it may be that the difference in approach is attributable to the fact that it involved a man, it is also arguable that the courts have, since 2000, adopted an approach which is more respectful of the interests and rights of disabled people.

Re A (medical treatment: male sterilisation) [2000] 1 F.L.R. 549

A was a 28-year-old man with Down's syndrome. He lived with his 63-year-old mother who provided a high degree of supervision of his behaviour. However, acknowledging that her own ability to supervise A was fading, that he was moving into local authority care and that he was likely to be sexually active, his mother applied to the High Court for a declaration that it would be lawful and in his best interests to perform a vasectomy on A, notwithstanding his inability to consent. The Official Solicitor opposed the application and it was rejected by Sumner J. The mother appealed.

BUTLER-SLOSS L.J.
" . . . The starting point for consideration of the principles to be applied on an application for sterilisation of an adult who is unable to consent is the decision of the House of Lords in *Re F* . . .

[Noting that, in the light of subsequent cases, 'best interests' encompasses medical, emotional and all other welfare issues, she continued:]

Another question which arises from the decision in *Re F* is the relationship of best interests to the '*Bolam* test'. Doctors charged with the decisions about the future treatment of patients and whether such treatment would, in the cases of those lacking capacity to make their own decisions, be in their best interests, have to act at all times in accordance with a responsible and competent body of relevant professional opinion. That is the professional standard set for those who make such decisions. The doctor, acting to that required standard, has, in my view, a second duty, that is to say, he must act in the best interests of a mentally incapacitated patient. I do not consider that the two duties have been conflated into one requirement. To that extent I disagree with the passage in the Law Commission's *Report on Mental Incapacity* (Law Com No 231) (1995) p 43, para 3.26 and I prefer the alternative suggestion in footnote 40. In any event, in the case of an application for approval of a sterilisation operation, it is the judge, not the doctor, who makes the decision that it is in the best interests of the patient that the operation be performed . . .

The concerns of the mother of A and Dr Campbell [who supported the mother's application] can be seen as relating as much, if not more it seems to me, to the protection of vulnerable women from the unintended consequences of sexual intercourse with A and the undesirability in the public interest of allowing a pregnancy or a birth to occur, as they do to the best interests of A himself. Those are understandable concerns in the wider context of society but are not relevant in themselves to the issue before this court. Social reasons for carrying out of non-therapeutic invasive surgery is not part of the present state of the law. With the direct application of the European Convention on Human Rights to English domestic law imminent, the courts should be slow to take any step which might infringe the rights of those unable to speak for themselves. The facts of *Re D* (a minor) (wardship: sterilisation) [at p.927 above] demonstrate the dangers of well-meaning professionals of different disciplines confusing the welfare of the child with social considerations. I agree however with Thorpe LJ that the question whether third party interests should ever be considered in a case concerned with the best interests of a patient ought to be left open . . .

Since *Re F* there has been a number of first instance decisions. In *Re W (an adult: sterilization)* [1993] 2 FCR 187 Hollis J approved the operation to sterilise a 20-year-old mentally incapacitated woman with severe epilepsy. There was evidence accepted by the judge of the detrimental effect of pregnancy and the Official Solicitor did not actively oppose the application. In *Re LC (medical treatment: sterilisation)* (1993) [1997] 2 FLR 258, Thorpe J dismissed the application by a local authority in respect of a 21-year-old woman with an intellectual age of three and a half living in a specialist residential home. She had previously been indecently assaulted in a different home with less good standards of care. In her present home there was a high level of supervision and minimal risk for the future. The Official Solicitor and the key social worker opposed the application. In *Re X (adult patient: sterilisation)* [1999] 3 FCR 426 Holman J granted the declaration in respect of a 31-year-old woman who was severely mentally retarded. The application was supported by the Official Solicitor.

It is clear from the outline of the cases to which I have referred above that, whether the application was concerned with an adult or with a child, the decision of the court was made in the best interests of that person and that principle was applied to the individual facts of each case.

An application on behalf of a man for sterilisation is not the equivalent of an application in respect of a woman. It is not a matter of equality of the sexes but a balancing exercise on a case by case basis. There are obvious biological differences and sexual intercourse for a woman carries the risk of pregnancy which patently it does not for a man. Indeed there is no direct consequence for a man of sexual intercourse other than the possibility of sexually transmitted diseases. There may be psychological consequences for him in pregnancy or in the birth of his child. He may be required to take responsibility for the child after birth and may, in certain circumstances attract disapproval and criticism. In the case of a man who is mentally incapacitated, neither the fact of the birth of a child nor disapproval of his conduct is likely to impinge on him to a significant degree other than in exceptional circumstances. His freedom of movement might in certain instances be restricted and consequently his quality of life might be diminished. It is possible that there may be other disadvantages to the person concerned which might lead a court to decide to approve the operation. It may be necessary to evaluate the nature and degree of risk attached to approval of or refusal to approve the operation to sterilise. But the task in each case is to balance all the relevant factors and to decide what are the best interests of the person unable to make his own decision.

In the present appeal it is necessary to focus upon the best interests of A himself. It is clear from the evidence of his mother that, as long as she cares for him, he will continue to be subjected to the present regime of close supervision. The refusal to approve the operation will inevitably upset A's mother but her care of him will not be diminished nor will he be aware that she is upset. If sterilisation did take place, it would not save A from the possibility of exploitation nor help him cope with the emotional implications of any closer relationship that he might form. It is also clear from the evidence of those who care for him in the day centre that the level of supervision does not depend upon his fertility. His mother has raised her concerns with them over inappropriate behaviour with women attending the day centre. The supervisors stop inappropriate behaviour because it is conducted in a public place and, it would appear, will continue to do so whether or not he has the operation. From my understanding of the evidence, Dr Campbell's assessment of the present supervision of A is incorrect and that the operation will not free him to enjoy a more relaxed regime. When in due course he goes into local authority care, the degree of freedom might be affected by the fear that he might form a sexual relationship with another resident. It would however, in my view, be likely that the woman concerned would be the object of protection rather than A. If his quality of life were, however, to be diminished, that would be a reason to seek at that time a hearing before a High Court judge to grant a declaration that sterilisation would then be in A's best interests . . . "

NOTES:

1. Thorpe L.J. delivered a concurring judgement and Schiemann L.J. agreed with both judgments. Thorpe L.J. noted that, given the mother's laudable desire to plan for her son's future, another application on fresh evidence was not precluded by the decision. He also proposed that judges faced with determining best interests should draw up a check list of relevant considerations (see Chapter 5 at p.327).

2. According to *Practice Note (Official Solicitor: Declaratory Proceedings: Medical and Welfare Proceedings for Adults Who Lack Capacity)* [2001] 2 F.L.R. 158:

   Declarations should be sought where there are disputes as to the patient's capacity or their best interests. The courts have given guidance in relation to sterilisation in *B (A Minor) (Wardship: Sterilisation, Re* [1988] AC 199 and *F v. West Berkshire HA* [1990] 2 AC 1 [above] . . . Issues involving the medical treatment or welfare of children are to be dealt with under the the Children Act 1989 or the inherent jurisdiction. Applications for the Official Solicitor's involvement are to be on the basis that the applicant lacks capacity and treatment, or its discontinuation, is required. Evidence as to capacity and best interests is to be submitted with the application and the claimant should be the appropriate NHS trust with the patient as the defendant. Unless the matter is urgent, a directions hearing should be set for no later than eight weeks after the date of the issue of proceedings to allow the Official Solicitor to make inquiries. Directions hearings should set a timetable for the Official Solicitor's inquiries and for the establishment of a time for a final hearing. The Official Solicitor will conduct appropriate inquiries including meeting with the patient, reviewing medical and social work records and interviewing the patient's family, carers and other relevant parties.

QUESTIONS:

1. How far do you think that the decision in *Re A* can be attributed the following factors:

   (a) that A was a man?
   (b) the imminent introduction of the Human Rights Act?
   (c) the gradual incursions into the *Bolam* principle discussed in Chapters 3, 5 and 6?

   (See K. Keywood, " 'I'd Rather Keep Him Chaste'. Retelling the Story of Sterilisation, Learning Disability and (Non)Sexed Embodiment" (2001) 9 *Feminist Legal Studies* 185.)

2. In weighing up the competing rights of the incompetent individual, how much weight, if any, ought to be given to the rights of mentally incompetent individuals to sexual pleasure and autonomy? (See the US decision of *Re Grady* 85 J 235 426 A 2d 467 (1981); K. Keywood, "Disabling Sex: Some Legal Thinking about Sterilisation, Learning Disability and Embodiment" in A. Morris and S. Nott (eds), *Well Women: The Gendered Nature of Health Care Provision*, Aldershot: Dartmouth, 2002.)

3. Do you agree with Butler-Sloss L.J. that different issues arise when the application is to sterilise a man? (Note that Gillian Douglas had predicted the outcome in *Re A*, suggesting that a difficulty with sterilising a mentally incompetent man is that it cannot be regarded as in his best interests (see G. Douglas, *Law, Fertility and Reproduction*, London: Sweet & Maxwell, 1991, at p.89).

Re S (Adult Patient: Sterilisation) [2001] Fam 15

S was a 29-year-old woman with severe learning difficulties. She had hitherto lived with her mother, but in recognition of the fact that S would have ultimately to move into sheltered accommodation provided by the local authority, the mother sought a declaration that it would be lawful in her best interests for a hysterectomy to be performed. The Official Solicitor opposed the application, as medical experts testified that a Mirena coil should be tried before performing surgery. Wall J. granted the declaration on the grounds that both options were in S's best interests. The decision was overturned on appeal.

BUTLER-SLOSS P.

" . . . S follows a regular routine in her mother's home. She attends a day centre and a social club and enjoys physical activities including riding and swimming. She is not easy to care for. She has very limited speech and is prone to irritability and mood swings. There are two interrelated aspects of her care which have prompted the application by the mother. The first reason might be termed the social reason. As I have already said, S is an extremely attractive girl who is at present being cared for by her mother who keeps a close watch on her activities and supervises her. If she goes into a local authority home, there is a risk that she might move unsupervised in mixed circles and might either form a close emotional attachment or be the victim of a sexual assault with the possibility of a pregnancy. The evidence before the judge was that she would not be able to understand the concept of pregnancy and would be totally unable to cope with a child. The judge said that it was agreed that a pregnancy would be disastrous for her and the whole process would be frightening and traumatic. The second reason is therapeutic. The judge said . . . ' . . . S suffers from heavy menstrual bleeding, which she does not understand, which causes her distress and with which she has great difficulty coping.' It was common ground that S did not have the capacity to give an informed consent to treatment of any kind, in particular for the proposed hysterectomy. The two issues before the judge were therefore: (1) whether it was in the best interests of S to be sterilised in order to avoid the risk of pregnancy; and (2) whether it was in her best interests to undergo therapeutic treatment to eliminate her menstrual periods by way of laparoscopic subtotal hysterectomy, which would have the incidental effect of sterilisation . . . .

. . . On the first issue the judge came to the conclusion that it would be highly detrimental to S's welfare to become pregnant . . . . Mr Munby for the Official Solicitor, who appeals on behalf of S on the second issue, doubts whether the judge was right, on the facts, to find an identifiable risk of pregnancy. I share his doubt but it is not necessary to consider it since the appeal does not turn on the issue of sterilisation as such.

I turn therefore to the second issue and the facts about the proposed therapeutic treatment. A laparoscopic subtotal hysterectomy . . . was described as major invasive surgery but far less severe than a total hysterectomy and there would be less complications and blood loss and faster recovery . . . . The alternative treatment was to use a Mirena coil which, once inserted by general anaesthetic, would have the effect of significantly reducing the menstrual flow so that, after about three months, it would be minimal or stop altogether. The coil had a useful life, as a contraceptive device, of five years or so after which it would have to be replaced. It had the disadvantage that it might be dislodged and would then have to be reinserted . . . .

Mr Munby raised two main grounds of appeal. His first ground was that the decision of the judge was contrary to the expert medical evidence and did not have sufficient regard to the principle of *primum non nocere*. The second main ground asserted that the judge erred in law in his application of *Re F* [1990] 2 A.C. 1 [at p.933 above] and in his approach to the *Bolam* test . . . .

The first ground requires this court to look at the weight given by the judge to the evidence. This is an exercise not lightly undertaken by an appellate court . . . . The judge had clear advice, in particular from Dr K, an acknowledged expert in her field, as to the better course to follow. He did not accept that advice and it is necessary for this court to look at the strengths of that evidence, always bearing in mind the advantage uniquely given to the trial judge of seeing and hearing the witnesses. There was in fact no medical evidence that S was suffering from abnormal menstrual bleeding . . . . [Dr K said] ' . . . This is a normal woman and we would not dream of doing [a partial hysterectomy] for a normal woman just because of socially unacceptable periods.'

. . . [Dr K] used the word 'normal' in the physical sense and did not relate it to the cognitive ability of the patient. It appears that, most unusually, this experienced judge had misunderstood or misrecollected the answer Dr K gave . . . . The judge's failure to appreciate the point of that piece of evidence led him to give significantly less weight to the evidence of Dr K that it deserved.

The judge also failed to take sufficiently into account, in my view, the present state of medical research in this field . . . . Once the judge accepted the evidence of Dr K, he did not then explain why he formed the clear view that to try out the less intrusive method [the Mirena coil] and wait to see the outcome of medical advances would clearly not be the right course. The clear advice of Dr K was that inserting a Mirena coil was the best answer they had available at the moment for S's problems. She was wholly opposed to the more invasive surgery for the problems experienced by S until, at least, the Mirena coil had been attempted and failed . . . . This evidence was highly relevant to the choice of procedures available for S and the option of a reasonable two-step approach.

The evidence of Professor T . . . supported the evidence of Dr K. [The evidence of Dr E on the psychological impact of an operation on S] was the only psychiatric evidence and was not challenged. It also supported the evidence of Dr K.

. . . I agree, in principle, that the forensic medical evidence is given to assist the judge who must weigh the value of that evidence and make his own decision. I also agree . . . that 'best interests' is wider in concept than medical considerations. In *In re A (Medical Treatment: Male Sterilisation)* [above] I said: 'In my judgment best interests encompasses medical, emotional and all other welfare interests.'

It therefore falls to the judge to decide whether to accept or reject the expert medical opinion than an operation is, or is not, in the best interests of a patient. The context in which Lord Goff of Chievely, in *Re F*, warned of the need for special care and indicated the desirability of obtaining an independent, objective and authoritative view from the court was that of the protection of mentally incompetent women from over-zealous advocates of sterilisation: see *In re D (A Minor) (Wardship: Sterilisation)* [at p.927 above]. It does not necessarily support the contrary conclusion. It is relevant to remember that the focus of judicial decisions has been to rein in excessive medical enthusiasm. A judge, of course, has a discretion to go beyond undue medical caution in an appropriate case. In the present case the judge heard evidence from a witness whom he found to be impressive and whose evidence was supported by the other medical evidence. The weight of that unanimous evidence appears to me to be impressive and it supported the less invasive method as the preferred option, at least in the first instance. Was there any countervailing evidence of equal weight upon which the judge could rely to offset the medical evidence? [T]he understandable concerns of a caring mother and the problems of dealing with S during her menstrual periods do not, on the facts of this case, tilt the balance towards major irreversible surgery for therapeutic reasons when they are unsupported by any gynaeco-logical, psychological or other medical evidence . . . . There is a question of proportionality and in my judgment the remedy proposed by the judge is out of proportion at this stage to the problem to be solved. The patient has the right, if she cannot choose, not to have drastic surgery imposed upon her unless or until it has been demonstrated that it is in her best interests. The decision also offends against the doctrine of *primum non nocere*. In my judgment the first ground of appeal . . . is made out . . . .

The second ground of appeal . . . raises a question of law as to the correct approach of the court to the best interests of a patient without the mental capacity to consent to an operation and the relevance of the *Bolam* test to that judicial inquiry.

The starting point is the decision of the House of Lords in *Re F*. . . . Since *Re F* there has been a number of decisions in the High Court where an operation, which would have the effect of sterilisation, has been proposed to be performed upon a mentally incompetent female adult for therapeutic reasons, in connection with the menstrual cycle. *In re GF (Medical Treatment)* [1992] 1 F.L.R. 293 was such a case, where the application to sterilise a woman of 29 with a mental age of five was based on excessively heavy menstrual bleeding and the unanimous conclusion of the general practitioner and two consultant gynaecologists was that the only practicable method of treating her condition was by performing a hysterectomy. There was, in the circumstances of that case, no less intrusive means of treating the condition . . . .

There are no two lines of cases, relating to those unable through mental disability to make their own decisions, where declarations have been made by the High Court, the first for non-therapeutic reasons and the second for treatment of the patient. In each type of case the doctor, it seems to me, has two duties. I said in *In re A (Medical Treatment: Male Sterilisation)* [at p.938 above]:

> 'another question which arises from the decision in *Re F* is the relationship of best interests to the "*Bolam* test". Doctors charged with the decisions about the future treatment of patients and whether such treatment would, in the cases of those lacking capacity to make their own decisions, be in their best interests, have to act at all times in accordance with a responsible and competent body of relevant professional opinion. That is the professional standard set for those who make such decisions. The doctor, acting to that required standard has, in my view, a second duty, that is to say, he must act in the best interests of a mentally incapacitated adult. I do not consider that the two duties have been conflated into one requirement . . . .'

I would suggest that the starting point of any medical decision would be the principles enunciated in the *Bolam* test and that a doctor ought not to make any decision about a patient that does not fall within the broad spectrum of the *Bolam* test. The duty to act in accordance with responsible and competent professional opinion may give the doctor more than one option since there may well be more than once acceptable medical opinion. When the doctor moves on to consider the best interests of the patient he/she has to choose the best option, often from a range of options. As Mr Munby has pointed out, the best interests ought, logically, to give only one answer.

In these difficult cases where the medical profession seeks a declaration as to lawfulness of the proposed treatment, the judge, not the doctor, has the duty to decide whether such treatment *is* in the best interests of the patient. The judicial decision ought to produce the best answer not a range of alternative answers. There may, of course, be situations where the answer may not be obvious and alternatives may have to be tried. It is still at any one point the best option of that moment which should be chosen. I recognise that there is distinguished judicial dicta to the contrary in the speech of Lord Browne-Wilkinson in *Airedale NHS Trust v Bland* [1993] A.C. 789, 884 (see Chapter 14). The passage in his speech was not however followed by the other members of the House. Hale J in *In re S (Hospital Patient: Court's Jurisdiction)* [1995] Fam 26, 32 followed the same approach . . . . [B]ut I do not read *Re F . . .* as relieving the judge who is deciding the best interests of the patient from making a choice between the available options. I respectfully disagree with Lord Browne-Wilkinson and Hale J. I have had the opportunity to read Thorpe LJ's judgment in draft and I agree with his analysis. As I have set out earlier in this judgment, the principle of best interests as applied by the court extends beyond the considerations set out in the *Bolam* case. The judicial decision will incorporate broader ethical, social, moral and welfare considerations.

In my judgment the judge misapplied the *Bolam* test . . . . The question . . . for the judge was not was the proposed treatment within the range of acceptable opinion among competent and responsible practitioners, but was it in the best interests of S? The *Bolam* test was, in my view, irrelevant to the judicial decision, once the judge was satisfied that the range of options was within the range of acceptable opinion among competent and responsible practitioners. If it was not, I would hope a surgeon would not operate, even if a declaration *was* given by the court . . . . I would allow the appeal and set aside the declarations and invite the medical advisers to insert the Mirena coil as has been recommended."

THORPE L.J.
"I have had the advantage of reading in draft the judgment of Dame Elizabeth Butler-Sloss P., and am in complete agreement with all that she has said . . . .

The *Bolam* test was of course developed in order to enable courts to determine the boundaries of medical responsibility for treatment that has gone wrong . . . . So at first blush it would seem an unlikely import in determining the best interests of an adult too disabled to decide for him- or herself. True the decision relates to whether or not the adult should receive medical treatment but that is not treatment already delivered but treatment prospectively available and the medical opinion under judicial review is likely to be forensic rather than from a doctor as part of a treatment package. That said there can be no doubt that the speeches in *Re F* determined that the *Bolam* test is relevant to the judgment of the adult's best interests when a dispute arises as to the advisability of medical treatment. But subsequently there has been some divergence of judicial opinion as to the extent of the contribution that the *Bolam* test makes to the determination of best interests . . .

I would therefore accept Mr Munby's submission that in determining the welfare of the patient the *Bolam* test is applied only at the outset to ensure that the treatment proposed is recognised as proper by a responsible body of medical opinion skilled in delivering that particular treatment. That may be a necessary check in an exercise where it would be impossible to be over scrupulous. But I find it hard to imagine in practice a disputed trial before a judge of the Division in which a responsible party proposed for an incompetent patient a treatment that did not satisfy the *Bolam* test. As most of us know from experience a patient contemplating treatment for a physical condition or illness is often offered a range of alternatives with counter-balancing advantages and disadvantages. One of the most important services provided by a consultant is to explain the available alternatives to the patient, particularly concentrating on those features of advantage and disadvantage most relevant to his needs and circumstances. In a developing relationship of confidence the consultant then guides the patient to make the choice that best suits his circumstances and personality. It is precisely because the patient is prevented by disability from that exchange that the judge must in certain circumstances either exercise the choice between alternative available treatments or perhaps refuse any form of treatment. In deciding what is best for the disabled patient the judge must have regard to the patient's welfare as the paramount consideration. That embraces issues far wider than the medical. Indeed, it would be undesirable and probably impossible to set bounds to what is relevant to a welfare determination. In my opinion the *Bolam* case has no contribution to make to this second and determinative stage of the judicial decision.

Mr. Munby has quite rightly drawn attention to contrary dicta to be found in the speech of Lord Browne-Wilkinson in *Airedale NHS Trust v Bland* [1993] AC 789, 884 and the judgment of Hale J in *In re S (Hospital Patient: Court's Jurisdiction)* [1995] Fam 26, 32. However, I accept his submission that the passage in the speech of Lord Browne-Wilkinson did not have general support and that such an approach has little practical attraction. Disputes as to the treatments of competent adults are only referred to the court in extreme cases that often generate much emotional distress for the family concerned. One of the important functions of the judge is to instil into the situation certainty and finality, which the family may well have difficulty in adjusting to but which they can at least accept as the judgment of the appointed impartial authority. Equally it is the function of the judge to protect the medical professionals from the threat of criminal or civil proceedings as a consequence of the exercise of their best endeavours. It is simply not helpful for either the family or the doctors to be presented with a declaration that two or more possible treatments are lawful on the grounds that both or all satisfied the *Bolam* test. It is the judge's function to declare that treatment which is in the best interests of the patient and, as Mr. Munby submits, only one treatment can be best.

During the course of his submission Mr. Munby expressed the Official Solicitor's reservations concerning the test set by Sir Stephen Brown P in *In re GF (Medical Treatment)* [1992] 1 FLR 293, 294 when he said:

'I take the view that no application for leave to carry out [a sterilisation] operation need be made in cases where two medical practitioners are satisfied that the operation is: (1) necessary for therapeutic purposes, (2) in the best interests of the patient, and (3) that there is no practicable, less intrusive means of treating the condition'

First let it be said that the Official Solicitor did not then seemingly dispute that formulation and nine years later Mr. Munby did not suggest that the Official Solicitor had any evidence that Sir Stephen Brown P's definition had produced difficulties or miscarriages of justice.

The purpose of his ruling was to set a boundary to enable professionals to determine whether or not it was their responsibility to refer an issue concerning the treatment of an adult lacking capacity to the court for a ruling. In other words it seeks to define what is and what is not the business of the courts. Although this appeal does not raise that question directly we have heard argument on the point and I would wish to state this opinion. Sir Stephen Brown P's test was necessarily expressed in broad terms. Anything so stated offers a margin to whoever interprets and applies it. In my opinion any interpretation and application should incline towards the strict and avoid the liberal. The courts are not overburdened with applications in this field. Indeed they are rare. In view of the importance of the subject, if a particular case lies anywhere near the boundary line it should be referred to the court by way of application for a declaration of lawfulness."

Notes:

1. Mason and Laurie note that in the general context of an attack on the *Bolam* principle, *Re S* "provides a particularly strong barrier to any extension of its application" (J.K. Mason and G.T. Laurie, *Mason and McCall-Smith's Law and Medical Ethics* (7th edn), Oxford: OUP, 2006 at p.141).

2. *Re Z (Medical Treatment: Hysterectomy)* [2000] 1 F.L.R. 523 was factually similar to *Re S*. Again the issue was whether a hysterectomy or the insertion of a Mirena coil better promoted the woman's interests. Z was a 19-year-old woman with Down's syndrome who suffered menstrual problems. Z was incapable of managing her own hygiene and the evidence of her mother and sister was that her heavy and irregular periods caused her distress and embarrassment. She also had a boyfriend and was to move form home to live in residential unit. Bennett J. distinguished two relevant questions: (1) is it in Z's best interests for there to be a complete cessation of her periods? and (2) is it in her best interests for there to be complete protection from pregnancy? Although the medical evidence favoured the less invasive option, the judge noted that "In making my assessment the responsibility for that assessment falls on the court alone. Experts are what they are—experts. They must be listened to with respect, but their opinions must be weighed and judged by the court." He determined that, notwith-standing the risks of a hysterectomy, it was in Z's best interests to have the surgery, both to protect her from pregnancy and to improve the quality of her life by eliminating her periods.

3. In *A National Health Trust v. C* (2000, unreported, but available via LEXIS) Cazalet J. was faced with a split in the medical evidence. The parents of a 21-year-old woman with Down's syndrome wished her to be sterilised. She had been in their full-time care until she was 19, when she started a course at a residential mixed college which she attended during the week. The plan was for C to move to sheltered accommodation when she had completed college. She had a boyfriend and appeared to enjoy physical contact, and had been prescribed the oral contraceptive pill since she was found in a compromising situation with a boy when was 14. Two medical experts supported the family's view that C should be sterilised as it was likely that she would engage in a sexual relationship, had no understanding of the relationship between sex and childbirth and would be

very traumatised if she became pregnant and had a child removed from her. The medical expert called by the Official Solicitor agreed that C should not become pregnant; but was of the view that sterilisation was premature and that while she was being properly supervised at home and college she should continue to take the combined oral contractive pill. Having engaged in the balancing test recommended by Thorpe L.J. in *Re A* (see p.940 above), the judge concluded that the substantially safer protection against conception offered by sterilisation meant that the operation was in C's best interests. Surprisingly, there was no consideration of other contraceptive options like the Mirena coil or injectable contraceptives in this case. Two features of the judgment are worth noting. First, the judge, sensibly, stated that, notwithstanding evidence that the procedure was reversible he would proceed on the basis that it was irreversible (cf *Re P* and *Re M* at p.932 above.) Secondly, Cazalet J. indicated that it might be valid to take into account the interests of her carers, as there would be less strain and worry for her family if she was sterilised. In turn he added that this might result in them allowing C more autonomy. He did note, however, that he attached "limited importance" to this point.

4. It is clear from the cases we have surveyed above that assessments of best interests in this context are decided on a case-by-case basis, which is in line with the flexibility of this test in other health care contexts; see for instance its application to the situation of disabled neonates considered in Chapter 7.

QUESTIONS:

1. Notwithstanding the readiness of judges to question the need for sterilisations in the more recent cases, and the fact that the procedure was not authorised in the cases of *Re LC, Re A* and *Re S*, do judges nevertheless remain unduly deferential to health professionals in reaching decisions on this issue? (See K. Keywood, "Disabling Sex: Some Legal Thinking about Sterilisation, Learning Disability and Embodiment" in A. Morris and S. Nott (eds), *Well Women: the Gendered Nature of Health Care Provision*, Aldershot: Dartmouth, 2002.)

2. Emily Jackson has contended that the following conditions must be satisfied before a court will authorise sterilisation:

   "(1) The patient must be incompetent;
   (2) The patient must be fertile;
   (3) There must be a real likelihood of sexual contact;
   (4) Pregnancy must pose an unacceptable risk to the patient's well-being;
   (5) It must be impossible for the patient to use a less invasive contraceptive method."

   (E. Jackson, *Regulating Reproduction*, Oxford: Hart, 2001 at page 63.)

   Do you agree with these criteria? Were they satisfied in the above cases? Would you add any further conditions before a sterilisation should be deemed lawful?

3. MANAGEMENT OF PREGNANCY

The development of a range of biomedical technologies has resulted in increased levels of medical intervention in the management of pregnancy (see A. Oakely, *The Captured Womb,* Oxford: Blackwell, 1984; J. Murphy-Lawless, *Reading Birth and Death: A History of Obstetric Thinking,* Cork: Cork University Press, 1998). At the pre-conception stage, we explored in Chapter 11 the growing potential of pre-natal genetic diagnosis and screening in order to select only healthy embryos for implantation. As Robin MacKenzie notes:

"Women are faced with hard choices here. Quite apart from the social and economic difficulties involved in raising children who suffer from genetic disorders, the diagnostic tools with which these disorders may be predicted or cured are far from certain."

(R. MacKenzie, "From Sanctity to Screening: Genetic Disabilities, Risk and Rhetorical Strategies in Wrongful Birth and Wrongful Conception Cases" (1999) 7 *Feminist Legal Studies* 175 at p.176. See also R. Rapp, "Refusing Prenatal Diagnosis: the Uneven Meanings of Bioscience in a Multicultural World" in R. David-Floyd and J. Dumit (eds), *Cyborg Babies: From Techno-Sex to Techno-Tots,* NewYork: Routledge, 1998.)

Pregnancy itself has become increasingly subject to medical and techno-logical management to the point where, as Emily Jackson observes, it become pathologised and "[o]bstetric practice is . . . concerned with the management of risks in *all* pregnancies, rather than with interventions in exceptional cases" (E. Jackson, *Regulating Reproduction,* Oxford: Hart, 2001 at pp.120–121). During pregnancy a woman may be offered tests to determine whether the foetus she is carrying is suffering from, or will later develop, a disability, such as rubella or Down's syndrome. Such tests have certainly increased women's choices, whether that might be to terminate a pregnancy or to be given the information which will enable her to plan for the birth of a disabled child. It appears likely that in the future it will be possible to undertake tests for the propensity to develop a whole range of genetic conditions. Indeed, failure to offer ante-natal tests may lead to a subsequent negligence action. However, as MacKenzie notes, given their potential for misdiagnosis, procedures such as ultra sound entail considerable anxiety for the pregnant woman as well as leading to the termination of foetuses that may have been healthy or suffering only a mild degree of disability. Additionally screening procedures during pregnancy are not risk free. For instance, amniocentesis (which involves taking amniotic fluid from the sac surrounding the foetus by means of a needle) and chorionic villus sampling (which involves the removal of a small sample of placental tissue) are used to detect Down's syndrome but carry an increased risk of miscarriage. Although ultrasound—a technique undertaken at around 16–20 weeks of pregnancy which enables detection of a malformation of the foetus—has been constructed as a benign visualisation technique, it has been linked to changes in body cells and low birth weight (see P. Foster, *Women and the Health Care Industry*, Buckingham: Open UP, 1995, at p.34; Jackson, *op. cit.* at p.121.) It has also been argued that ultrasound has played an important role in the foetal rights movement, by marginalising the pregnant woman while simultaneously subjecting her to increased surveillance (see L.M. Mitchell and E. Georges, "Baby's First Picture: the Cyborg Fetus of Ultrasound Imaging" in David-Floyd and Dumit, *op. cit.*). Other procedures, which have become an integral part of medicalised births, such as the replacement of the stethoscope by electronic fetal monitoring, have undoubtedly contributed to a rise in induced births and Caesarean deliveries as well as hampering a woman's freedom to give birth in positions which she finds comfortable (see E. Cartwright, "Electronic Fetal Monitoring and Biomedically Constructed Birth" in David-Floyd and Dumit (eds) *op. cit.*). More generally it has been argued that women become bystanders rather than participants in the process of birth as it is increasingly technologised (see R. Davis-Floyd, "The Technocratic Body: American Childbirth as Cultural Expression" (1994) 38 *Social Science and Medicine* 1125; S. Mentor, "Witches, Nurses, Midwives and Cyborgs: IVF, ART and Complex Agency in the World of Technobirth" in David-Floyd and Dumit (eds), *op. cit.*), However, as they become a routine part of medicalised birth, such technologies are increasingly hard to resist or refuse, thus calling into question how meaningful the choices they offer are.

QUESTION:

1. Should there ever be a legal obligation on a pregnant woman to avail herself of tests during pregnancy to reveal genetic defects in the foetus? Is she under an *ethical* obligation to undergo such tests?

The management of pregnancy increasingly incorporates elements of health promotion, with women being encouraged to adopt healthy lifestyles (see Chapter 1). Since the early 1970s there have been campaigns which target pregnant women and emphasise the dangers of smoking (see Foster, *op. cit.* at page 131.) Studies have found links between smoking during pregnancy and low birth rates; while it has been contended that alcohol consumption by the pregnant mother may result in "foetal alcohol syndrome", which is linked to mental disorders and learning difficulties. It may be acceptable to strongly encourage pregnant women to adopt a particular lifestyle, although as Emily Jackson notes, health promotion campaigns have a tendency to label certain lifestyles as morally reprehensible as well as foolish, and in the case of pregnancy to downplay the impact of men's behaviour on the health of the next generation (E. Jackson, *Regulating Reproduction*, Oxford: Hart, 2001 at pp.155–159; see also C. Daniels, "Fathers, Mothers and Fetal Harm" in L.M. Morgan and M.W. Michaels (eds), *Fetal Subjects: Feminist Positions*, Philadelphia: Pennsylvania University Press, 1999.) It is still more questionable whether legal enforcement of moral obligations would ever be justified. The dangers of such compulsion were highlighted in the following case:

Re F (In Utero) [1988] 2 All E.R. 193; [1988] 2 W.L.R. 1288

This case concerned a pregnant woman with a history of mental disturbance and drug abuse. A child to whom she had given birth in 1977 had been placed in care and then with foster parents after the mother embarked on a nomadic existence around Europe. When she became pregnant again and disappeared from her flat, the local authority attempted to make the unborn child a ward of court. This involved, first, an order directed to the tipstaff who could involve the police to search for the mother; and secondly, an order requiring the mother to live at a particular place and attend a particular hospital; thirdly, orders relating to the care and control of the child once it was born. At first instance the judge rejected the application, but granted leave to appeal.

BALCOMBE L.J.

" . . . Of particular significance in the present case is that there is no recorded instance of the courts having assumed jurisdiction in wardship over an unborn child. Indeed, the whole trend of recent authority is to the contrary effect. In *Paton v. Trustees of BPAS* [1978] 2 All E.R. 987, [discussed in Chapter 12 at p.912] Baker P. said:

'The first question is whether this plaintiff has a right at all. The foetus cannot, in English law, in my view, have any right of its own at least until it is born and has a separate existence from the mother. That permeates the whole of the civil law of this country . . . To the like effect is the judgment of Heilbron J. in *C. v. S.*' [see Chapter 12 at p.916] . . .

However, these decisions only relate directly to the legal rights of the foetus: they are not decisive of the question before us, namely has the court power to protect a foetus by making it a ward of court?

The statutory provisions relating to wardship afford no assistance in answering this question as they are negative in character. Section 41 of the Supreme Court Act 1981 refers to a minor being made a ward of court and section 1(1) of the Family Law Reform Act 1969 provides that minority ends on the attainment of the age of 18; neither Act contains anything to indicate whether it is possible for a person to be a minor before birth . . .

Counsel also sought to rely on Art 2(1) of the European Convention for the Protection of Human Rights and Fundamental Freedoms: 'Everyone's right to life shall be protected by law.' However, in *Paton v. U.K.* [see Chapter 12 at p.914] . . . the European Commission of Human Rights ruled that on its true construction art. 2 is apt only to apply to persons already born and cannot apply to a foetus (at 413 (para. 8)). They continued (at 415 (para. 19)):

'The "life" of the foetus is intimately connected with, and cannot be regarded in isolation from, the life of the pregnant woman. If Article 2 were held to cover the foetus and its protection under this Article were, in the absence of any express limitation, seen as absolute, an abortion would have to be considered as prohibited even where the continuance of the pregnancy would involve a serious risk to the life of the pregnant woman. This would mean that the "unborn life" of the foetus would be regarded as being of a higher value than the life of the pregnant woman. The "right to life" of a person already born would thus be considered as subject not only to the express limitations mentioned in paragraph 8 above but also to a further, implied limitation'. . . .

In the end it seems to me that the question is one of first principles on which there is no direct authority.

Approaching the question as one of principle, in my judgment there is no jurisdiction to make an unborn child a ward of court. Since an unborn child has, *ex hypothesi*, no existence independent of its mother, the only purpose of extending the jurisdiction to include a foetus is to enable the mother's actions to be controlled. Indeed, that is the purpose of the present application. In the articles already cited Lowe gives examples of how this might operate in practice. [Lowe argues]

'It would mean, for example, that the mother would be unable to leave the jurisdiction without the court's consent. The court being charged to protect the foetus' welfare would surely have to order the mother to stop smoking, imbibing alcohol and indeed any activity which might be hazardous to the child. Taking it to the extreme were the court to be faced with saving the baby's life or the mother's it would surely have to protect the baby's.'

Another possibility is that the court might be asked to order that the baby be delivered by Caesarian section: in this connection see Fortin 'Legal Protection for the Unborn Child' (1988) 51 M.L.R. 54 at 81 and the United States cases cited . . .

If the law is to be extended in this manner, so as to impose control over the mother of an unborn child, where such control may be necessary for the benefit of that child, then under our system of parliamentary democracy it is for Parliament to decide whether such controls can be imposed and, if so, subject to what limitations or conditions . . . If Parliament were to think it appropriate that a pregnant woman should be subject to controls for the benefit of her unborn child, then doubtless it will stipulate the circumstances in which such controls may be applied and the safeguards appropriate for the mother's protection. In such a sensitive field, affecting as it does the liberty of the individual, it is not for the judiciary to extend the law."

NOTES:

1. Staughton L.J. and May L.J. agreed.
2. In *Re F* the court emphasised the fact that the foetus is not a legal person for the purposes of English civil or criminal law. This was subsequently confirmed by the Court of Appeal in *Attorney-General's Reference (No. 3 of 1994)* (see Chapter 12 at p.902) and in *Re MB* below at p.955).
3. Judicial unwillingness to impose constraints on the pregnant woman in this country can be contrasted with the approach in the United States. (See J. Robertson, *Children of Choice*, Princeton, New Jersey: University of Pennsylvania Press, 1995, Chapter 8; B. Steinbock, "Maternal–Foetal Conflict" in D.R. Brahamet, *et al.* (eds), *Ethics in Reproductive Medicine*, London: Springer-Verlag, 1992.) There women have been prosecuted for child abuse after taking drugs during pregnancy (see V. Toscano, "Misguided Retribution: Criminalization of Pregnant Women Who Take Drugs" (2005) 14 *Social and Legal Studies* 359; E. Pickworth, "Substance Abuse in Pregnancy and the Child Born Alive" (1998) 27 *Anglo-American Law Review* 472.)
4. Although, *Re F* rules out the possibility of courts imposing controls on a pregnant woman for the benefit of her foetus, her conduct during pregnancy may lead health and social services professionals to conclude that it is in the child's best interests for him to be taken away from the mother at birth — see *D (A Minor) v Berkshire County Council* [1987] 1 All E.R. 20, in which a child was born suffering from drug withdrawal

symptoms. The mother was a registered drug addict who had taken drugs for 10 years. She continued to take drugs during pregnancy, although she knew that this could harm the foetus. The child was kept in intensive care in hospital for several weeks immediately following the birth. A place of safety order, followed by care orders were obtained by Berkshire social services. At the time of the hearing the child had not been in the care or control of either the mother or father since birth. The House of Lords upheld the care order as valid in this extreme situation.

5. If a woman behaves recklessly during pregnancy, and the foetus dies as a result, this could result in a prosecution for manslaughter. A prosecution might also be attempted under the Infant Life Preservation Act 1929, which, as we saw in Chapter 12, makes it an offence to destroy the life of a child capable of being born alive. However, it has been noted that it would be exceedingly difficult to establish a wilful act causing the ultimate injury under that statute (P. Glazebrook, "What Care Must Be Taken of an Unborn Baby?" (1993) 52 *Cambridge Law Journal* 20 and I. Kennedy, "A Woman and her Unborn Child" in P. Byrne (ed.), *Ethics and Law in Health Care and Research*, Chichester, John Wiley: 1990). (For further discussion of the imposition of criminal liability where a foetus is injured by a third party during pregnancy, see Chapter 12, at p.902).

6. Judicial unwillingness to coerce lifestyle choices during pregnancy is linked with a general reluctance to use legal regulation to control such intimate choices. One of the limited respects in which such choices may be constrained is through the employment process and laws which regulate safe employment and exposure to industrial hazards. (See further M. Thompson, "Employing the Body: the Reproductive Body and the Employment Exclusion" (1996) 5 *Social Legal Studies* 243; E. Jackson, *Regulating Reproduction*, Oxford: Hart, 2001 at pp.152–155.)

QUESTIONS:

1. Would it ever be appropriate for the wardship jurisdiction to be used to resolve potential conflicts between a pregnant woman and a foetus? (See A. Bainham, *Parents, Children and the State*, London: Sweet & Maxwell, 1988, Chapter 6 and *cf.* G. Douglas, *Law, Fertility and Reproduction*, London: Sweet & Maxwell, 1991, at p.188.)

2. Should a woman's partner be held responsible for his conduct during the pregnancy and any injury that may result to the foetus? (See J. Robertson, *Children of Choice*, Princeton: Pennsylvania University Press, 1994, at p.191 and chapter 12 at pp.912–919.)

4. CHILDBIRTH

(a) The Choice of Where and How to Give Birth

A woman may wish to choose where to give birth and the manner in which she gives birth. In the 19th century, as a general rule, women who had the means gave birth at home, with only the poor going into hospital. Before the First World War, births in homes, hospitals or institutions established under the Poor Law only amounted to 1 per cent of the total number of births (see P. Foster, *Women and the Health Care Industry: an Unhealthy Relationship*, Buckingham: Open UP, 1995, at p.29.) During the last 30 years, women have been encouraged to give birth in hospital, so that currently fewer than 1% of births take place at home (E. Jackson, *Regulating Reproduction*, Oxford: Hart, 2001 at p.116). This has been accompanied by a greater medicalisation of childbirth, including increased reliance on technology, a high incidence of induced births (see RCOG, *Induction of Labour: Evidence-based Clinical Guideline 9*, London: RCOG Press, 2001) and a growth in the number of Caesarean sections. Such procedures are medically necessary in some cases, they may facilitate healthy births and in certain circumstances can enhance a woman's control over her body. However, the emphasis on hospital births was heavily criticised in official documents in the 1990s. A House of Commons Committee on Maternity Services in 1992 concluded that the policy of encouraging hospital births could not be justified on safety grounds (*The Winterton Report*, H. Committee 2nd Report HC Maternity Services, Vol. 1, 1992, para. 25), a view reiterated in the influential Report of the Expert Maternity Group, *Changing Childbirth (London: Department of Health*, 1993) which emphasised the importance of respecting women's choices. (See generally P. Foster, *Women and the Health Care Industry*, Buckingham: Open UP, 1995, at Chapter 3; M. Thomson, *Reproducing Narrative* 1998, Chapter 2). More recently, the Royal College of Midwives launched an initiative called the Campaign for Normal Birth (RCM, 2005). The initiative is "underpinned by the RCM's philosophy of pregnancy and birth as normal physiological processes, with a commitment to a positive reduction in medication". It seeks to contest defensive practices, arguing that institutions are introducing defensive practices in order "to reduce their exposure to litigation . . . [n]ot because the practice of normal birth is riskier (the evidence shows it to be safer) but because it is more difficult to defend." The campaign stresses that home births are safe, provided adequate emergency backup systems are in place, and questions over-reliance on electronic foetal heart monitoring, which has become established as best practice, but is often used unnecessarily. The campaign has been criticised, however, for downplaying the difficulties of "natural" birth (J. Revill, "Why mothers should be offered caesareans (Special Report)" *The Observer*, March 5, 2006; "Leading article: A mother's birthright", *The Independent*, May 19, 2006). Notwithstanding the RCM's attempt to promote home births, this may be undermined by local policies and legal requirements.

Nurses, Midwives and Health Visitors Act 1997

16.—(1) A person other than a registered midwife or a registered medical practitioner shall not attend a woman in childbirth.
(2) Subsection (1) does not apply—

(a) where the attention is given in a case of sudden or urgent necessity; or
(b) in the case of a person who, while undergoing training with a view to becoming a medical practitioner or to becoming a midwife, attends a woman in childbirth as

part of a course of practical instruction in midwifery recognised by the General Medical Council or one of the National Boards.

NOTES:

1. The requirement that a midwife be present may limit the choice of birth place. If a particular health authority does not favour home births, then it may not make NHS midwives available. Thus, a woman who chose a home birth would have to pay for a private midwife. Recent research by the Royal College of Midwives has highlighted a severe shortage of midwives, undermining government guidance about the importance of women in labour receiving "one-to-one treatment" (B. Marsh, "Half of all NHS hospital can't afford to replace midwives," *Daily Telegraph*, May 7, 2006).
2. The meaning of "attend" is left undefined in the legislation (See J. Finch, "Paternalism in Childbirth" (1982) 132 *New L.J.* 1012).

QUESTION:

1. Eeeklaar and Dingwall contend: "At the end of the day parents should not ultimately be free to dictate the terms under which their children are born" (J. Eeeklar and R. Dingwall, "Some Legal Issues in Obstetric Practice" [1984] *Journal of Social Welfare Law* 258). Do you agree?

(b) Controlling Childbirth: Enforced Caesareans

Particular controversy has surrounded Caesarean sections and the question of their risks and benefits. Evidence has suggested that women who have Caesarean sections have a higher maternal mortality rate, increase the risk of haemorrhage and post-natal depression and can experience impaired bonding with their infant. (See L. Miller, "Two Patients or One: Problems of Consent in Obstetrics" (1993) 1 *Medical Law International* 97.) The rising number of Caesarean deliveries is often cited as one manifestation of the "defensive medicine" practised by obstetricians and gynaecologists who operate in a very high-risk area of clinical practice. According to figures contained in NICE-funded guidance, in England and Wales Caesarean section rates have increased from 9 per cent of deliveries in 1980 to 21 per cent in 2001, meaning that approximately 120,000 Caesareans are performed annually in England and Wales (National Collaborating Centre for Women's and Children's Health, *Caesarean Section: Clinical Guidance* (London: RCOG Press, 2004). However, while defensive practice may account for some of the increased incidence of Caesareans, it has also been claimed that the increase is partially attributable to a greater desire on the part of women for elective Caesareans (see Education and Debate "Should doctors perform an elective caesarean section on request?" (1998) 317 *British Medical Journal* 462). In 2004 the NICE guidance, *op. cit.*, recommended that woman should be fully informed of the benefits and risks of Caesareans as compared to vaginal birth, specific to the woman and her pregnancy. It stressed that "[m]aternal request is not on its own an indication for CS and specific reasons for the request should be explored, discussed and recorded." The guidance has been criticised as being driven by the need to cut costs as much as reduce risks (see J. Revill, "Why mothers should be offered caesareans", *The Observer* March 5, 2006 and K. Luckhuirst *et al.*, "Caesarean births: the big debate" *The Observer*, March 12, 2004).

Subject to such advice, a pregnant woman will routinely agree a "birthing plan" with her midwife, which will stipulate her wishes in relation to matters such as pain relief and the extent of medical intervention. Difficulties may arise if departure from the birth plan appears to be appropriate. In some situations a woman's opinion concerning management of her pregnancy may differ from that of the health professional.

The courts have been confronted with this issue in a number of cases where women have refused medical advice that it is in the interests of both herself and her unborn child to have a Caesarean delivery. In the first of these cases, *Re S (Adult: Refusal of Treatment)* [1992] 4 All E.R. 671, Sir Stephen Brown P. granted a declaration authorising surgeons and staff of a hospital to carry out an emergency Caesarean operation upon a 30-year-old woman who was admitted to hospital with ruptured membranes and in spontaneous labour. When the court heard the application, the mother was six days overdue beyond the expected date of birth and was refusing medical intervention on the grounds that she and her husband were "born again Christians". The brief judgment was subjected to a trenchant critique by medical lawyers and was confidently expected to be a one-off decision. (See M. Thomson, "After Re S" (1994) 2 *Medical Law Review* 127; K. Stern, "Court Ordered Caesareans—Whose Interests?" (1993) 56 *Modern Law Review* 238; B. Hewson, "Mother Knows Best" (1992) *New Law Journal* 1538; K. De Gama, "A Brave New World? Rights Discourse and the Politics of Reproductive Autonomy" (1995) *Journal of Law and Society* 114, though *cf.* C. Wells, "On the Outside Looking In: Perspectives on Enforced Caesareans" in S. Sheldon and M. Thomson (eds), *Feminist Perspectives on Health Care Law*, London: Cavendish, 1998). However, it was followed in at least seven High Court cases subsequently, in many of which, unlike in *Re S* itself, the woman was found incompetent on very dubious grounds. Aurora Plomer notes of this line of case law that "the concern raised by [these cases] is that medical decisions which are really intended to benefit the unborn foetus could be rationalised with the court's approval as decisions intended to benefit the allegedly mentally incompetent or mentally disordered woman instead" (A. Plomer, "Judicially Enforced Caesareans and the Sanctity of Life" (1997) 26 *Anglo-American Law Review* 235 at p.235.)

Re MB

The leading case is now the Court of Appeal decision in *Re MB*, which was discussed in relation the common law test for capacity in Chapter 5. The case concerned a 23-year-old pregnant woman who suffered from a needle phobia and had steadfastly refused to allow blood samples to be taken since she was first seen at an ante-natal clinic when she was 33 weeks pregnant. At 40 weeks an ultrasound examination revealed that the foetus was in the breach position, and Ms MB was advised that although there was little risk to her from this complication, unless she consented to a Caesarean delivery, there was a 50 per cent risk of foetal death or brain damage. At that point she consented to the Caesarean but subsequently she refused to have blood samples taken, to have an anaesthetic by way of injection or to be fitted with an intravenous line or catheter. The possibility of anaesthesia by mask was canvassed, but once in the operating theatre MB refused to proceed. Hollis J. granted a declaration that it would be lawful for the consultant gynaecologist to operate on her, using reasonable force if necessary. Later that night the Court of Appeal dismissed the patient's appeal from that order, reserving its reasons. On the following morning the patient co-operated in the operation and was delivered of a healthy baby. As we saw in Chapter 5, the key ruling of the court was that, everyone, including a pregnant woman, is to be presumed competent unless and until that presumption is rebutted; and a competent woman who has the capacity to decide may, for religious reasons, other reasons, for rational or irrational reasons or for no reason at all, choose not to have medical intervention, even though the consequence may be the death or serious injury to the child she bears, or her own death. It broadly speaking confirmed the test for capacity laid down in *Re C* (see further Chapter 5).

Butler-Sloss L.J. delivered the judgment of the court:

BUTLER-SLOSS L.J.
" . . . A feature of some of the cases to which we have referred has been the favourable reaction of the patient who refused treatment to the subsequent medical intervention and the successful outcome. Having noted that, we are none the less sure that however desirable it may be for the mother to be delivered of a live and healthy baby, on this aspect of the appeal it is not a strictly relevant consideration. If therefore the competent mother refuses to have the medical intervention, the doctors may not lawfully do more than attempt to persuade her. If that persuasion is unsuccessful, there are no further steps towards medical intervention to be taken. We recognise that the effect of these conclusions is that there will be situations in which the child may die or may be seriously handicapped because the mother said no and the obstetrician was not able to take the necessary steps to avoid the death or handicap. The mother may indeed later regret the outcome, but the alternative would be an unwarranted invasion of the right of the woman to make the decision.

We have, helpfully, been provided by Mr Francis [counsel for MB] with the guidelines from the Royal College of Obstetricians and Gynaecologists entitled 'A Consideration of the Law and Ethics in Relation to Court-Authorised Obstetric Intervention' . . . The committee concluded that:

' . . . it is inappropriate, and unlikely to be helpful or necessary, to invoke judicial intervention to overrule an informed and competent woman's refusal of a proposed medical treatment, even though her refusal might place her life and that of her fetus at risk.'

In our judgment the advice of the committee accurately reflects the present state of the law. The only situation in which it is lawful for the doctors to intervene is if it is believed that the adult patient lacks the capacity to decide.

So we turn now to consider the best interests of Miss MB.

Mr Francis submitted that the judge did not find, and there was no evidence to find that it was in the mother's best interests to have the medical intervention. It is in my view implicit in his necessarily short judgment that the judge considered that it was in her best interests. Best interests are not limited to best medical interests . . .

In a number of first instance decisions the declarations have concluded that it would be lawful for reasonable force to be used in the course of such treatment. That declaration was granted by Hollis J in the present case and is criticised by Mr Francis. It would however follow, in our view, from the decision that a patient is not competent to refuse treatment, that such treatment may have to be given against her continued objection if it is in her best interests that the treatment be given despite those objections. The extent of force or compulsion which may become necessary can only be judged in each individual case and by the health professionals. It may become for them a balance between continuing treatment which is forcibly opposed and deciding not to continue with it. This is a difficult issue which may have to be considered in greater depth on another occasion. In our view the judge was justified in granting the declaration. All that was involved here was the prick of a needle to enable the first part of the anaesthesia to be given to the patient. In the events which happened, these problems did not arise. Miss MB, on hearing the decision of this court, then signed the consent form on the following morning and co-operated in the initial administration of the anaesthesia. No force was necessary . . .

In our judgment the court does not have the jurisdiction to take the interests of the foetus into account in a case such as the present appeal and the judicial exercise of balancing those interests does not arise. The nearest one might get to the view that the unborn child should in these circumstances be considered is to be found in the judgment of Lord Donaldson MR in *Re T* [1993] Fam 95, 102, [1992] 2 FLR 458, 460D [see Chapter 5]:

> 'An adult patient who, like Miss T, suffers from no mental incapacity has an absolute right to choose one rather than another of the treatments being offered. The only possible qualification is a case in which the choice may lead to the death of a viable foetus. That is not this case and, if and when it arises, the courts will be faced with a novel problem of considerable legal and ethical complexity.'

The situation postulated by him arose later in 1992 in *Re S* (above). The interest of the foetus prevailed. It is a decision the correctness of which we must now call in doubt. That is not to say that the ethical dilemma does not remain. None the less, as has so often been said, this is not a court of morals. In the light of earlier authority to which we now turn, the position in English law appears clear and contrary to the view expressed by Lord Donaldson and by the President . . .

On the present state of the English law, the submissions made by Mr Grace that we should consider and weigh in the balance the rights of the unborn child, are untenable. The only support in Lord Donaldson's observation in *Re T* (above) cannot stand, in our view, against the weight of earlier decisions, which are far more persuasive as to the present state of the law and which are applicable by analogy to the present appeal. The law is, in our judgment, clear that a competent woman who has the capacity to decide may, for religious reasons, other reasons, or for no reasons at all, choose not to have medical intervention, even though, as we have already stated, the consequence may be the death or serious handicap of the child she bears or her own death. She may refuse to consent to the anaesthesia injection in the full knowledge that her decision may significantly reduce the chance of her unborn child being born alive. The foetus up to the moment of birth does not have any separate interests capable of being taken into account when a court has to consider an application for a declaration in respect of a caesarian section operation. The court does not have the jurisdiction to declare that such medical intervention is lawful to protect the interests of the unborn child even at the point of birth.

We respectfully agree with Balcombe LJ in *Re F (In Utero)* [above at p.950] who also considered the possibility of the court being asked to order delivery of the baby by Caesarean section. He said:

> 'If Parliament were to think it appropriate that a pregnant woman should be subject to controls for the benefit of her unborn child, then doubtless it will stipulate the circumstances in which such controls may be applied and the safeguards appropriate for the mother's protection. In such a sensitive field, affecting as it does the liberty of the individual, it is not for the judiciary to extend the law.' "

NOTES:

1. Ian Kennedy argues that in this case it is important to look behind the judicial rhetoric and examine what the court actually does in the case, i.e. authorise the Caesarean section against the woman's wishes. He points out that, as in numerous other cases, "it is when a patient does not accede to a doctor's advice that the question of capacity arises". He argues that instead of making everything turn on capacity, "[w]hat the Court of Appeal should have done is to admit that paternalism remains the bottom line" in these cases (I. Kennedy, "Consent: Adult, Refusal of Consent, Capacity" (1997) 5 *Medical Law Review* 317; see also C. Wells, "On the Outside Looking In: Perspectives on Enforced Caesareans" in S. Sheldon and M. Thomson (eds), *Feminist Perspectives on Health Care Law*, London: Cavendish, 1998).

2. In response to criticisms of the procedural inadequacies of the earlier High Court decisions, Butler-Sloss L.J. concluded her judgment with some procedural guidance on practice to be followed when the medical profession feel it necessary to seek a declaration from the courts, the guidance was revised in the *St George's* case below. This guidance emphasises that cases should only come to court where there is concern over competence; that any such concern should be identified as early as possible; that the patient should have legal representation; and that the judge must be provided with all relevant information.

QUESTIONS:

1. Do you think that a woman has a moral obligation to submit to an unwanted Caesarean delivery if this is necessary to save the life of the foetus? If so, should this be a legally enforceable obligation? (See J. Eekelaar, "Does a Mother Have Legal Duties to her Unborn Child" in P. Byrne (ed.), *Medical Law and Ethics*, Oxford: King's Fund Press and OUP, 1988; W. Kluge, "When Caesarean Section Operations Imposed by a Court are Justified" (1988) 14 *Journal of Medical Ethics* 206; B. Bennett, "Pregnant Women and the Duty to Rescue: a Feminist Response to the Fetal Rights Debate" (1991) 9 *Law in Context* 70; R. Scott, "The Pregnant Woman and the Good Samaritan: Can a Pregnant Woman have a Duty to Undergo a Caesarean Section?" (2000) 20 *Oxford Journal of Legal Studies* 407–436.)

2. To what extent can the adversarial nature of the relationship constructed between the pregnant woman and her foetus in these cases be attributed to the medical model of pregnancy outlined above? (See Wells, *op. cit.* at pp.242–243).

3. Could the dispute between MB and the health professionals in this case have been avoided with better communication and management of her case? (See S. Fovargue, Case Note on *Re MB* (1998) 20 *Journal of Social Welfare and Family Law* 427.)

4. Notwithstanding the court's view of foetal status in law, do you think that foetal interests are still taken into account by judges in deciding whether a Caesarean is in the woman's best interests? (See Wells, *op. cit.* and S. Fovargue and J. Miola, "Policing Pregnancy: Implications of the Attorney-General's Reference (No 3 of 1994)" (1998) 6 *Medical Law Review* 265.)

The following is the only case in which a UK court has decided that the pregnant woman's autonomous refusal of medical treatment should have been respected:

St George's Healthcare NHS Trust v S, R v Collins [1998] 3 All E.R. 673

S, a 29-year-old veterinary nurse, was diagnosed with pre-eclampsia when she was seen at a general practice at 36 weeks pregnant, having received no ante-natal care prior to that point. She was advised by two doctors and a social worker of the risks her condition posed if untreated, *viz* that her baby would die and she too might die or become severely disabled. They recommended an early induced delivery. When S refused all intervention, an application was made under s. 2 of the Mental Health Act 1983 which provides for a patient to be detained in order for their condition to be assessed (see Chapter 8). After she had been hospitalised, a declaration was sought authorising treatment without her consent, and a Caesarean section was performed against her will. S subsequently experienced difficulties in accepting her baby girl, and at one point lost custody of her. S applied for judicial review and appealed against the declaration authorising the Caesarean section. In the Court of Appeal, the actions of the doctors and social worker were heavily criticised, especially for their failure to distinguish between S's need to be treated in relation to obstetrical complications and the issue of whether she was suffering from a mental disorder which justified her detention in hospital.

    Judge L.J. delivered the judgment of the Court:

JUDGE L.J.
" . . . In our judgment while pregnancy increases the personal responsibilities of a woman it does not diminish her entitlement to decide whether or not to undergo medical treatment. Although human, and protected by the law in a number of different ways set out in the judgment in *In re M.B.* [above], an unborn child is not a separate person from its mother. Its need for medical assistance does not prevail over her rights. She is entitled not to be forced to submit to an invasion of her body against her will, whether her own life or that of her unborn child depends on it. Her right is not reduced or diminished merely because her decision to exercise it may appear morally repugnant. The declaration in this case involved the removal of the baby from within the body of her mother under physical compulsion. Unless lawfully justified this constituted an infringement of the mother's autonomy. Of themselves the perceived needs of the foetus did not provide the necessary justification.
    The Mental Health Act 1983 cannot be deployed to achieve the detention of an individual against her will merely because her thinking process is unusual, even apparently bizarre and irrational, and contrary to the views of the overwhelming majority of the community at large. The prohibited reasoning is readily identified and easily understood. Here is an intelligent woman. She knows perfectly well that if she persists with this course against medical advice she is likely to cause serious harm, and possibly death, to her baby

and to herself. No normal mother-to-be could possibly think like that. Although this mother would not dream of taking any positive steps to cause injury to herself or her baby, her refusal is likely to lead to such a result. Her bizarre thinking represents a danger to their safety and health. It therefore follows that she must be mentally disordered and detained in hospital in her own interests and those of her baby. The short answer is that she may be perfectly rational and quite outside the ambit of the Act, and will remain so notwithstanding her eccentric thought process.

Even when used by well intentioned individuals for what they believe to be genuine and powerful reasons, perhaps shared by a large section of the community, unless the individual case falls within the prescribed conditions the Act cannot be used to justify detention for mental disorder...

So even assuming lawful admission and detention in accordance with the Act the patient is not deprived of all autonomy. Part IV of the Act provides a carefully structured scheme setting out the circumstances in which the patient's consent to treatment may be dispensed with. Section 63 of the Act may apply to the treatment of any condition which is integral to the mental disorder (*B. v. Croydon Health Authority* [1995] Fam. 133) provided the treatment is given by or under the direction of the responsible medical officer. The treatment administered to M.S. was not so ordered: she was neither offered nor did she refuse treatment for mental disorder. Her detention under the Act did not undermine or restrict her right to self-determination unless she was deprived 'either by long-term mental capacity or retarded development or by temporary factors such as unconsciousness or confusion or the effects of fatigue, shock, pain or drugs' of her capacity to decide for herself: In *re J.T. (Adult: Refusal of Medical Treatment)* [1998] 1 F.L.R. 48 . . .

In this case the judge made a declaratory order (i) on an ex parte application in proceedings which had not then been (and at the start of the hearing of this appeal still had not been) instituted by the issue of a summons, (ii) without M.S.'s knowledge or even any attempt to inform her or her solicitor of the application, (iii) without any evidence, oral or by affidavit, and (iv) without any provision for M.S. to apply to vary or discharge the order. The order declared that St. George's could subject M.S. to invasive surgery. It is inappropriate (for the reasons given by Lord Diplock) to describe such an order as void, or made without jurisdiction. But it is an order which M.S. is entitled to have set aside *ex debito justitiae*. That may involve some unfairness to the doctors and nurses at St. George's who were all conscientiously, and in very anxious circumstances, seeking to do the right thing. But the unfairness (indeed, injustice) to M.S. would be much greater if the order were not set aside.

It is unnecessary to re-emphasise our conclusions about M.S.'s autonomy. The Caesarean section performed on her (together with the accompanying medical procedures) amounted to trespass. The appeal against Hogg J.'s order will be allowed. While it may be available to defeat any claim based on aggravated or exemplary damages, in the extraordinary circumstances of this case the declaration provides no defence to the claim for damages for trespass against St. George's Hospital . . . "

NOTES:

1. For discussions of how conventional conceptions of autonomy are inadequate in these cases, thus necessitating new paradigms for addressing them, see J. Herring, "The Caesarean Section Cases and the Supremacy of Autonomy" in M. Freeman and A. Lewis (eds), *Law and Medicine: Current Legal Issues*, Vol. 3, Oxford: OUP, 2000; J. Herring, "Caesarean Sections and the Right of Autonomy" (1998) *Cambridge Law Journal* 438; H. Lim, "Caesareans and Cyborgs" (1999) 7 *Feminist Legal Studies* 133-73.

2. Note the emphasis in these cases on the risks of treatment refusal, but how these risks are not fully analysed in the decisions. As Wells points out

"pregnancy and childbirth have been subjected to increasing medicalisation, and obstetric fashions are highly volatile, and . . . challenges to the social control vision of pregnancy and birth have played a key role in achieving a retreat from some of the more interventionist orthodoxies, such as induction of labour. How are these risks to be weighed and by whom?" (C. Wells, "On the Outside Looking In: Perspectives on Enforced Caesareans" in S. Sheldon and M. Thomson (eds), *Feminist Perspectives on Health Care Law*, London: Cavendish, 1998 at p.249; see also J. Weaver, "Court-ordered Caesarean Sections" in A. Bainham *et al.* (eds), *Body Lore and Laws*, Oxford: Hart, 2002.)

3. In *Bolton Hospitals NHS Trust v O* [2003] 1 F.L.R. 824 Dame Butler-Sloss ruled that where a patient's actions were so irrational that they ceased to act as a competent person because of panic, then it was lawful to override a purported refusal. In this case the woman had had four previous Caesarean sections and experienced post-traumatic stress when she was taken to the operating theatre, which led her to withdraw her consent. Medical evidence suggested that a vaginal delivery had a 95 per cent chance of failure and that there was a high chance that O and her baby would die. The President held that she could not see the consequences of her actions because of her panic. Once again, the case demonstrates how the courts can act paternalistically by ruling that the woman is incompetent.

QUESTIONS:

1. Do you think that the Court of Appeal ruling in this case finally endorses the pregnant woman's autonomy, or does the case turn on its particular facts? (See R. Bailey-Harris, "Patient-Autonomy—A Turn in the Tide" in M. Freeman and A. Lewis (eds), *Law and Medicine: Current Legal Issues*, Vol. 3, Oxford: OUP, 2000; A. Morris, "Once upon a Time in a Hospital . . . the Cautionary Tale of *St George's Health Care NHS Trust v. S*" (1999) 7 *Feminist Legal Studies* 75.)
2. Rebecca Bailey-Harris suggests (*op. cit.* in Question 1 at p.127) that this "decision is concerned primarily with the power of the patient against the medical profession, rather than any conflict between mother and unborn child." Do you agree?

5. LIABILITY FOR INJURY IN CONNECTION WITH FAILED STERILISATION AND CHILDBIRTH

If a sterilisation operation proves unsuccessful or if the child is harmed or damaged during birth, an action may be brought seeking damages. These actions fall into two broad categories, actions brought on behalf of a child patient and those brought by the parents. (Actions concerning defective drugs are considered in Chapter 3 at pp.203–209, and damage caused by reproductive technologies in Chapter 11 at pp.855–856.)

At the outset it is important to note the conceptual difficulties that surround analysis of many of those actions. A number of different terms have been used to describe the actions brought. Dickens explains them as follows.

B. Dickens, "Wrongful Birth and Life, Wrongful Death before Birth and Wrongful Law" in S. McLean (ed.), Legal Issues in Human Reproduction, Aldershot: Dartmouth, 1989)

- "Wrongful pregnancy" is a claim that another's negligence resulted in a plaintiff's unplanned conception of a child, whether or not the pregnancy was carried to term.
- "Wrongful conception" is a narrower claim that negligent performance of a sterilisation procedure resulted in a conception which the purportedly sterilised plaintiff intended should not occur, but no child was born due to spontaneous or induced abortion.
- "Wrongful birth" is a claim that a health care provider violated a legal duty owed to a parent to give information or to perform a medical procedure with due care, resulting in the birth of a defective child.
- "Wrongful life" is a claim by, or on behalf of, a person born with predictable physical or mental handicaps that, but for the defendant's negligence, the person would not have been conceived or, having been conceived, would not have been born alive.

NOTE:

1. Note that these terms are not used consistently by commentators. (See A. Grubb (ed.), "Conceiving: a New Cause of Action" in M. Freeman (ed.), *Medicine, Ethics and Law,* London: Sweet and Maxwell, 1988; H. Teff, "The Action for Wrongful Life in England" (1985) 34 ICLQ 432; J.K. Mason, "Wrongful Pregnancy, Wrongful Birth and Wrongful Terminology" (2002) 6 *Edinburgh Law Review* 46; S. Pattinson, *Medical Law and Ethics,* London: Sweet & Maxwell, 2006 at pp.283–286.)

(a) Actions Brought on Behalf of the Child

(i) Where a Child is Born Dead

An action claiming that the birth of a still-born child is attributable to the defendant's negligence is not sustainable after the passage of the Congenital Disabilities (Civil Liability) Act 1976. This statute requires a child to be born alive (s.4(2)(a)). It was suggested by Dillon L.J. in *B v. Islington AHA* [1992] 3 All E.R. 832, that such an action may have been available at common law.

(ii) Actions under the Congenital Disabilities (Civil Liability) Act 1976

An action brought on behalf of a child claiming damages for negligent conduct resulting in handicap will today lead to proceedings under the Congenital Disabilities (Civil Liability) Act 1976.

In the 1960s the drug Thalidomide was marketed as a treatment for morning sickness in pregnancy. The drug was responsible for congenital and physical deformities in children. Although legal actions brought against the manufacturer, Distillers, resulted in settlements, the case highlighted the inadequacy of avenues for legal redress. As a result, the question of compensation for injuries caused to a child prior to birth was referred to the Law Commission. Following its report, the Congenital Disabilities (Civil Liability) Act was passed in 1976.

Congenital Disabilities (Civil Liability) Act 1976, s.1(1–7), s.1A(1–4), s.2, s.4(1–6)

1.—(1) If a child is born disabled as the result of such an occurrence before its birth as is mentioned in subsection (2) below, and a person (other than the child's own mother) is under this section answerable to the child in respect of the occurrence, the child's disabilites are to be regarded as damage resulting from the wrongful act of that person and actionable accordingly at the suit of the child.

(2) An occurrence to which this section applies is one which—

(a) affected either parent of the child in his or her ability to have a normal, healthy child; or
(b) affected the mother during her pregnancy, or affected her or the child in the course of its birth, so that the child is born with disabilities which would not otherwise have been present.

(3) Subject to the following subsections, a person (here referred to as "the defendant") is answerable to the child if he was liable in tort to the parent or would, if sued in due time, have been so; and it is no answer that there could not have been such liability because the parent suffered no actionable injury, if there was a breach of legal duty which, accompanied by injury, would have given rise to the liability.

(4) In the case of an occurrence preceding the time of conception, the defendant is not answerable to the child if at that time either or both of the parents knew the risk of their child being born disabled (that is to say, the particular risk created by the occurrence); but should it be the child's father who is the defendant, this subsection does not apply if he knew of the risk and the mother did not.

(5) The defendant is not answerable to the child, for anything he did or omitted to do when responsible in a professional capacity for treating or advising the parent, if he took reasonable care having due regard to then received profesional opinion applicable to the particular class of case; but this does not mean that he is answerable only because he departed from received opinion.

(6) Liability to the child under this section may be treated as having been excluded or limited by contract made with the parent affected, to the same extent and subject to the same restrictions as liability in the parent's own case; and a contract term which could have been set up by the defendant in an action by the parent, so as to exclude or limit his liability to him or her, operates in the defendant's favour to the same, but no greater, extent in an action under this section by the child.

(7) If in the child's action under this section it is shown that the parent affected shared the responsibility for the child being born disabled, the damages are to be reduced to such extent as the court thinks just and equitable having regard to the extent of the parent's responsibility.

1A.—(1) In any case where—

(a) a child carried by a woman as the result of the placing in her of an embryo or of sperm and eggs or her artificial insemination is born disabled,
(b) the disability results from an act or omission in the course of the selection, or the keeping or use outside the body, of the embryo carried by her or of the gametes used to bring about the creation of the embryo, and

(c) a person is under this section answerable to the child in respect of the act or omission,

the child's disabilities are to be regarded as damage resulting from the wrongful act of that person and actionable accordingly at the suit of the child.

(2) Subject to subsection (3) below and the applied provisions of section 1 of this Act, a person (here referred to as "the defendant") is answerable to the child if he was liable in tort to one or both of the parents (here referred to as "the parent or parents concerned") or would, if sued in due time, have been so; and it is no answer that there could not have been such liability because the parent or parents concerned suffered no actionable injury, if there was a breach of legal duty which, accompanied by injury, would have given rise to the liability.

(3) The defendant is not under this section answerable to the child if at the time the embryo, or the sperm and eggs, are placed in the woman or the time of her insemination (as the case may be) either or both of the parents knew the risk of their child being born disabled (that is to say, the particular risk created by the act or omission).

(4) Subsections (5) to (7) of section 1 of this Act apply for the purposes of this section as they apply for the purposes of that but as if references to the parent or the parent affected were references to the parent or parents concerned.

2.—A woman driving a motor vehicle when she knows (or ought reasonably to know) herself to be pregnant is to be regarded as being under the same duty to take care for the safety of her unborn child as the law imposes on her with respect to the safety of other people; and if in consequence of her breach of that duty her child is born with disabilities which would not otherwise have been present those disabilities are to be regarded as damage resulting from her wrongful act and actionable accordingly at the suit of the child . . .

4.—(1) References in this Act to a child being born disabled or with disabilities are to its being born with any deformity, disease or abnormality, including predisposition (whether or not susceptible of immediate prognosis) to physical or mental defect in the future.

(2) In this Act—

(a) "born" means born alive (the moment of a child's birth being when it first has a life separate from its mother), and "birth" has a corresponding meaning; and
(b) "motor vehicle" means a mechanically propelled vehicle intended or adapted for use on roads

[and references to embryos shall be construed in accordance with section 1 of the Human Fertilisation and Embryology Act 1990].

(3) Liability to a child under section 1 [1A] or 2 of this Act is to be regarded—

(a) as respects all its incidents and any matters arising or to arise out of it; and
(b) subject to any contrary context or intention, for the purpose of construing references in enactments and documents to personal or bodily injuries and cognate matters,

as liability for personal injuries sustained by the child immediately after its birth.

(4) No damages shall be recoverable under [any] of those sections in respect of any loss of expectation of life, nor shall any such loss be taken into account in the compensation payable in respect of a child under the Nuclear Installations Act 1965 as extended by section 3, unless (in either case) the child lives for at least 48 hours.

(4A) In any case where a child carried by a woman as the result of the placing in her of an embryo or of sperm and eggs or her artificial insemination is born disabled, any reference in section 1 of this Act to a parent includes a reference to a person who would be a parent but for sections 27 to 29 [of the Human Fertilisation and Embryology Act 1990.]

(5) This Act applies in respect of births after (but not before) its passing, and in respect of any such birth it replaces any law in force before its passing, whereby a person could be

liable to a child in respect of disabilities with which it might be born; but in section 1(3) of this Act the expression "liable in tort" does not include any reference to liability by virtue of this Act, or to liability by virtue of any such law.

(6) References to the Nuclear Installations Act 1965 are to that Act as amended; and for the purposes of section 28 of that Act (power by Order in Council to extend the Act to territories outside the United Kingdom) section 3 of this Act is to be treated as if it were a provision of that Act.

NOTES:

1. The Act allows recovery for pre-conception injuries. The Law Commission cited a defective contraceptive pill which was ineffective and also damaged the foetus as an example of the type of injury which would be covered. (See *Report on Injuries to Unborn Children*, Law Commission Report No. 60, Cmnd. 5709, 1974.) The statute also applies to injuries *in utero* (s.1(2)(b)) and during childbirth. The reference to "parents" suggests that liability is limited to first generation injuries.

2. For liability to accrue it must be shown that the defendant is liable in tort to the parents. It is not necessary to show that the parents had suffered an "actionable injury" (s.1(3)).

3. The Act rules out an action being brought against the mother for negligent conduct against the foetus *in utero*. The only exception is where a child is injured because of the negligent driving of the mother, as such costs are borne by insurers due to compulsory third-party insurance. The Law Commission recommended that claims should not be brought against the child's mother on the grounds that it could harm relationships within families and that it would raise problematic issues regarding conduct during pregnancy (Law Com. No. 60, Cmnd. 5709.)

4. A claim may only be brought in connection with a child who has been born alive (subs.4(2)). Objections were voiced by the Law Commission and in Parliament to the idea that a child who had only had a very brief existence could bring a claim for lost expectation of life. This needs to be understood in the context of a wider contemporary debate as to whether damages for lost expectation of life should be replaced by a claim by relatives for damages for bereavement. (See, for example, Ian Gow M.P., *Hansard*, Vol. 910, cols 730–740 (1976).). Section 4(4) precludes an action for damages for loss of expectation of life where the child had lived for up to 48 hours after birth.

5. Section 1A, which was inserted by the Human Fertilisation and Embryology Act 1990, gives a right of action to children born disabled where harm had been caused, for example, to the embryo in the course of infertility treatment. This would, it appears, cover both harm caused during storage of gametes and also during embryo selection. (See Chapter 11 at pp.855–856.) There are, however, some question marks as to the application of the section where an embryo has been obtained by lavage from one woman and implanted in another. In certain situations when bringing proceedings under s.1A, it may be necessary to trace the donor of gametes. Section 31 of the Human Fertilisation and Embryology Act 1990 provides

that an application may be made to the court for an order to require disclosure of persons who may be parents of the child.

6. Liability generally does not arise if the parents knew of the risk of harm to the child. But an exception exists in a situation in which the father did have such knowledge but the mother was unaware that her partner had been affected by the defendant's negligence.

7. There may be a problem in establishing liability if a child is injured due to delivery procedures, e.g. inexpert manipulation of forceps or monitoring equipment. In such a situation Dingwall and Eeklaar suggest that although there is a duty owed to the *child* it may be difficult to establish a duty to the *mother*. (see J. Eeklaar and R. Dingwall, "Some Legal Issues in Obstetric Practice" [1984] *Journal of Social Welfare Law* 258.)

8. Where a child has been damaged by administration of a defective drug during pregnancy, this may also give rise to an action under the Consumer Protection Act 1987. However, as we discussed in Chapter 3 at p.208, the "development risk defence" is a major obstacle to claims under this statute.

9. Damages awarded may be reduced if it can be shown that the parents were contributorily negligent in relation to the harm which occurred (s.1(7)). This reflects the recommendations of the Law Commission, which stated:

> "65. Our provisional conclusion as to a mother's liability to her own child led us, almost inevitably, to the opinion that a mother's contributory negligence ought not to effect any reduction in her child's damages. On consultation many have expressed the opinion that such a rule would be grossly unfair to tortfeasors and their insurers in a fault based tort system, and that the physical fact of identification between mother and foetus during pregnancy ought to mean that the mother's own negligence should reduce the damages payable by a tortfeasor. The medical treatment and medication of a pregnant woman depends so much on the cooperation and care for herself that the possibility of joint liability (perhaps with the mother herself most to blame) is one which cannot be ignored. In such circumstances we think it would be wrong if, perhaps for very slight carelessness in comparison with the mother's own negligence, a doctor, chemist or drug manufacturer had to compensate the child in full for his disability."

Thus, while the pregnant woman is under no explicit obligation to take care of herself during pregnancy it appears that some obligations are implicit.

QUESTIONS:

1. Section 4(2)(a) provides that an action accrues when a child has a life separate from that of its mother. When does this occur? (See C. Pace, "Civil Liability for Pre-natal Injuries" (1977) 40 *Modern Law Review* 141.)

2. If a woman refuses a Caesarean section despite medical advice and the child suffers brain damage during a prolonged labour, can an action be brought under the 1976 Act? (See J. Eeklaar and R. Dingwall, "Some Legal Issues in Obstetric Practice" [1984] *Journal of Social Welfare Law* 258.)

3. Is there a viable distinction between "disability" and "injury", thus allowing actions for the latter at common law while rejecting the former?

(See J. Murphy, "The Tortious Liability of Physicians for Injuries Sustained in Childbirth" (1995) 10(2) *Professional Negligence* 82.)

4. Do you agree with the policy of exempting the mother from liability for injuries? (See E. Sutherland, "Regulating Pregnancy: Should We and Can We?" in E. Sutherland & A. McCall Smith, *Family Rights,* 1990.) Why should fathers not have a similar exemption?

The position at common law was considered in the case of *B v Islington AHA,* a case in which the action accrued prior to the 1976 Act coming into force. We noted earlier (see Chapter 12 at pp.902–912) that a foetus is not a legal person. In *B* the court held that an action could be brought at common law claiming damages for injury which occurred *in utero.* In addition it appears that such an action would have been sustainable for a pre-conception injury, for example, where a woman's pelvis is harmed and this causes injury when a child is subsequently conceived and develops in the uterus. (See A. Whitfield, "Common Law Duties to Unborn Children" (1993) 1 *Medical Law Review* 28.) The harm was foreseeable and the cause of action arose at birth. As we shall see below, the courts have expressed the view that no residual common law action applies to claims arising after the 1976 Act.

(iii) Wrongful Life

A child who is born with disabilities as a result of negligence may seek to bring an action claiming that, but for the defendant's negligence, she would have never been born—a so called "wrongful life" action. However, courts in this jurisdiction and elsewhere have been very hostile to such cases.

McKay v Essex Area Health Authority [1982] 2 All E.R. 771; [1982] Q.B. 1160

Mary McKay was born in 1975. She had been infected in the womb with rubella (German measles). As a result she was born partially blind and deaf. It was claimed that one doctor had acted negligently in failing to treat rubella infection, when the mother told him she suspected it. Another doctor was alleged to have *either* negligently mislaid a blood sample which the mother had given or to have failed to interpret test results correctly. Mary McKay claimed that the doctor owed her a duty of care when she was *in utero,* which would have involved advising her mother as to the advisability of having an abortion, advice which the mother said she would have accepted.

STEPHENSON L.J.
" . . . I have come, at the end of two days' argument, to the same answer as I felt inclined to give the question before I heard argument, namely that plainly and obviously the claims disclose no reasonable cause of action. The general importance of that decision is much restricted by the Congenital Disabilities (Civil Liability) Act 1976, and in particular s.4(5) to which counsel for the doctor called our attention. That enactment has the effect explained by Ackner L.J. of depriving any child born after its passing on 22 July, 1976 of this cause of action . . . The importance of this cause of action to this child is somewhat

reduced by the existence of her other claim and the mother's claims, which, if successful, will give her some compensation in money or in care.

However, this is the first occasion on which the courts of this country or the Commonwealth have had to consider this cause of action, and I shall give my reasons for holding that it should be struck out.

If, as is conceded, any duty is owed to an unborn child, the authority's hospital laboratory and the doctor looking after the mother during her pregnancy undoubtedly owed the child a duty not to injure it, if she had been injured as a result of lack of reasonable care and skill on their part after birth, she could have sued them (as she is suing the doctor) for damages to compensate her for injury they have caused her in the womb. (*cf.* the thalidomide cases, where it was assumed that such an action might lie: e.g. *Distillers Co. (Biochemical) Ltd v. Thompson* [1971] 1 All E.R. 694.) But this child has not been injured by either defendant, but by the rubella which has infected the mother without fault on anybody's part. Her right not to be injured before birth by the carelessness of others has not been infringed by either defendant, any more than it would have been if she had been disabled by disease after birth. Neither defendant has broken any duty to take reasonable care not to injure her. The only right on which she can rely as having been infringed is a right not to be born deformed or disabled, which means, for a child deformed or disabled before birth by nature or disease, a right to be aborted or killed; or, if that last plain word is thought dangerously emotive, deprived of the opportunity to live after being delivered from the body of her mother. The only duty which either defendant can owe to the unborn child infected with disabling rubella is a duty to abort or kill her of that opportunity.

It is said that the duty does not go as far as that, but only as far as a duty to give the mother an opportunity to choose her abortion and death. That is true as far it goes . . . But the complaint of the child, as of the mother, against the health authority, as against the doctor, is that their negligence burdened her (and her mother) with her injuries. That is another way of saying that the defendants' breaches of their duties resulted not just in the child's being born but in her being born injured or, as the judge put it, with deformities. But, as the injuries or deformities were not the result of any act or omission of the defendants, the only result for which they were responsible was for her being born. For that they were responsible because if they had exercised due care the mother would have known that the child might be born injured or deformed, and the plaintiffs' pleaded case is that, if the mother had known that, that she would have been willing to undergo an abortion, which must mean she would have undergone one or she could not claim that the defendants were responsible for burdening her with an injured child. If she would not have undergone an abortion had she known the risk of the child being born injured, any negligence on the defendants' part could not give either plaintiff a cause of action in respect of the child being born injured.

I am accordingly of opinion that, though the judge was right in saying that the child's complaint is that she was born with deformities without which she would have suffered no damage and have no complaint, her claim against the defendants is a claim that they were negligent in allowing her, injured as she was in the womb, to be born at all, a claim for 'wrongful entry into life' or 'wrongful life'.

This analysis leads inexorably on to the question: how can there be a duty to take away life? How indeed can it be lawful? It is still the law that it is unlawful to take away the life of a born child or of any living person after birth. But the Abortion Act 1967 has given mothers a right to terminate the lives of their unborn children and made it lawful for doctors to help to abort them.

That statute (on which counsel for the plaintiffs relies) permits abortion in specified cases of risks to the mother's interests, but there is one provision relevant to the interests of the child. Section 1(1) provides:

'Subject to the provisions of this section, a person shall not be guilty of an offence under the law relating to abortion when a pregnancy is terminated by a registered medical practitioner if two registered medical practitioners are of the opinion, formed in good faith . . . (b) that there is a substantial risk that if the child were born it would suffer from such physical or mental abnormalities as to be seriously handicapped.'

That paragraph may have been passed in the interests of the mother, the family and the general public, but I would prefer to believe that its main purpose, if not its sole purpose, was to benefit the unborn child; and, if and in so far as that was the intention of the legislature, the legislature did not make a notable inroad on the sanctity of human life by recognising that it would be better for a child, born to suffer from such abnormalities as to be seriously handicapped, not to have been born at all. That inroad, however, seems to stop short of a child capable of being born alive, because the sanctity of the life of a viable fetus is preserved by the enactment of s.5(1) that 'Nothing in this Act shall affect the provisions of the Infant Life (Preservation) Act 1929 (protecting the life of the viable foetus).' [Though see now the amendments affected by the 1990 Human Fertilisation and Embryology Act which permit abortion until term in the case of foetal handicap.] . . .

There is no doubt that this child could legally have been deprived of life by the mother's undergoing an abortion with the doctor's advice and help so the law recognises a difference between the life of a fetus and the life of those who have been born. But, because a doctor can lawfully by statute do to a fetus what he cannot lawfully do to a person who has been born, it does not follow that he is under a legal obligation to a fetus to do it and terminate its life, or that the foetus has a legal right to die.

Like this court when it had to consider the interests of a child born with Down's syndrome in *Re B (A Minor) (Wardship Medical Treatment* [see Chapter 7], I would not answer until it is necessary to do so the question whether the life of a child could be so certainly 'awful' and 'intolerable' that it would be in its best interests to end it and it might be considered that it had a right to be put to death. But that is not this case. We have no exact information about the extent of this child's serious and highly delibitating congenital injuries; the judge was told that she is partly blind and deaf, but it is not and could not be suggested that the quality of her life is such that she is certainly better dead, or would herself wish that she had not been born or should now die.

I am therefore compelled to hold that neither defendant was under any duty to the child to give the child's mother an opportunity to terminate the child's life. That duty may be owed to the mother, but it cannot be owed to the child.

To impose such a duty towards the child would, in my opinion, make a further inroad on the sanctity of human life of a handicapped child as not only less valuable than the life of a normal child, but so much less valuable that it was not worth preserving, and it would even seem that a doctor would be obliged to pay damages to a child infected with rubella before birth who was in fact born with some mercifully trivial abnormality. These are the consequences of the necessary basic assumption that a child has a right to be born whole or not at all, not to be born unless it can be born perfect or 'normal', whatever that may mean.

Added to that objection must be the opening of the courts to claims by children born handicapped against their mothers for not having an abortion . . .

Finally, there is the nature of the injury and damage which the court is being asked to ascertain and evaluate.

The only duty of care which court of law can recognise and enforce are duties owned to those who can be compensated for loss by those who owe the duties, in most cases, including cases of personal injury, by money damages which will as far as possible put the injured party in the condition in which he or she was before being injured. The only way in which a child injured in the womb can be compensated in damages is by measuring what it has lost, which is the difference between the value of its life as whole and healthy normal child and the value of its life as an injured child. But to make those who have not injured the child pay for that difference is to treat them as if they injured the child, when all they have done is not taken steps to prevent its being born injured by another cause.

The only loss for which those who have not injured the child can be held liable to compensate the child is the difference between its condition as a result of their allowing it to be born alive and injured and its condition if its embryonic life had ended before its life in the world had begun. But how can a court of law evaluate that second condition and so measure the loss to the child? Even if a court were competent to decide between the conflicting views of theologians and philosophers and to assume an 'afterlife' or non-existence as the basis for the comparison, how can a judge put a value on the one or the other, compare either alternative with the injured child's life in this world and determine that the child has lost anything, without the means of knowing what, if anything, it has gained?

. . . To measure loss of expectation of death would require a value judgment where a crucial factor lies altogether outside the range of human knowledge and could only be achieved, if at all, by resorting to the personal beliefs of the judge who has the misfortune to attempt the task. If difficulty in assessing damages is a bad reason for refusing the task, impossibility of assessing them is a good one . . . If a court had to decide whether it were better to enter into life maimed than not to enter it at all, it would, I think, be bound to say it was better in all cases of mental and physical disability, except possibly those extreme cases already mentioned, of which perhaps the recent case of *Croke v Wiseman* [1981] 3 All E.R. 852 is an example, but certainly not excepting such a case as the present. However that may be, it is not for the courts to take such a decision by weighing life against death or to take cognisance of a claim like this child's. I would regard it on principle as disclosing no reasonable cause of action and would accordingly prefer the master's decision to the judge's . . .

The defendants must be assumed to have been careless. The child suffers from serious disabilities. If the defendant had not been careless, the child would not be suffering now because it would not be alive. Why should the defendants not pay the child for its suffering? The answer lies in the implications and the consequences of holding that they should. If public policy favoured the introduction of this novel cause of action, I would not let the strict application of logic or the absence of precedent defeat it. But as it would be, in my judgment, against public policy for the courts to entertain claims like those which are the subject of this appeal, I would for this reason and for other reasons which I have given, allow the appeal, set aside the judge's order and restore the master's order."

NOTES:

1. Ackner and Griffiths L.JJ. agreed. It is questionable whether a wrongful life action should be rejected on the basis that the damages are difficult to evaluate. Difficulty in assessing damages has not prevented the award of damages elsewhere in the law of tort. (See, for example, *Lim Po Chew v Camden Area Health Authority* [1989] A.C. 176.) It is worthy of note that when the action in *McKay* was brought, establishment of a wrongful birth action would have been more difficult than it subsequently became.

2. One argument advanced in *McKay* for the rejection of the claim was that it was wrong for a child plaintiff to be able to bring a tortious action against her mother. Such a policy is reflected in the Congenital Disabilities (Civil Liability) Act 1976 where generally a child cannot sue his or her mother (see p.965 above). However, Robert Lee argues that this consideration should not debar actions for "wrongful life": "whatever reasons for the mother's wish to bear a handicapped child, it seems improbable in the extreme that her failure to prevent birth will result from negligence". (See R. Lee, "To be or Not to Be: Is that the Question? The Claim of Wrongful Life" in R. Lee and D. Morgan (eds), *Birthrights: Law and Ethics at Beginning of Life*, London: Routledge, 1989).

3. Jane Fortin suggests that s.4(5) of the 1976 Act does not preclude a wrongful life action if the basis for the claim is that the health professional was negligent in failing to advise the woman of the quality of life which the child was likely to have in the light of the disabilities suffered (J. Fortin, "Is the Wrongful Life Action Really Dead?" (1987) *Journal of Social Welfare Law* 306).

4. The Law Commission based its rejection of wrongful life claims on fears that they could cause doctors to recommend abortions. This was questioned by Griffiths L.J. in *McKay*, who pointed out that no liability would arise as long as the doctor explained the risk in the continuation of pregnancy.

5. For responses to such claims in France and Germany see N. Priaulx, "Conceptualising Harm in the Case of the 'Unwanted' Child" (2002) 9 *European Journal of Health Law* 337, A. Morris and S. Saintier, "To Be or Not To Be: Is that the Question? Wrongful Life and Misconceptions" (2003) 11 *Medical Law Review* 167; and in North America see R. MacKenzie, "From Sanctity to Screening: Genetic Disabilities, Risk and Rhetorical Strategies in Wrongful Birth and Wrongful Conception Cases" (1999) 7 *Feminist Legal Studies* 175.

QUESTIONS:

1. Given the end of life cases considered in Chapter 14 and the disabled neonate rulings examined in Chapter 7, is it still possible for a judge to claim that life is worth preserving at all costs? (Note that Nicolette Priaulx has pointed out that while judges are reticent to enter into debates about harm in wrongful life cases, due to the impossibility of comparing existence with non-existence, in fact they do this in a range of cases considered in Chapters 7 and 14 when they determine whether it is in the best interests of a person to exist (Priaulx, *op. cit.* in Note 5).

2. Is it possible to reject a wrongful life action while accepting a "wrongful" birth action? (See discussion below at p.978.)

3. Robin MacKenzie has suggested that "wrongful life and wrongful birth case law is plagued by folk demons and moral panics" and that "formulating the duty in terms of imposing an obligation to on medical professionals to kill or abort" has raised all sorts of unsavoury spectres for the courts (MacKenzie, *op. cit.* in Note 5 at pp.178, 181.) Do you agree? How else could the duty be formulated? (See Lee, *op. cit.* in Note 2, Priaulx, *op. cit.* in Note 5).

(b) Actions Brought by Parents

(i) **Claims in Contract**

Sterilisation procedures are frequently undertaken privately. If the operation fails, a claim may be grounded in breach of contract, that the defendant breached either an express or an implied warranty to render the plaintiff permanently sterile. Alternatively, an action may be brought claiming negligent misrepresentation.

Eyre v Measday [1986] 1 All E.R. 488

The plaintiff was a 35-year-old woman who had three children. She and her husband did not want any more children. She was advised that continued use of the contraceptive pill was potentially harmful. Mr Measday, a well-known gynaecologist carried out the sterilisation operation privately under a budget scheme, which meant it was a low-cost private operation. Subsequently Mrs Eyre discovered that she was pregnant and she gave birth to a healthy boy. The plaintiff decided to let the pregnancy run full term and not to return to work until her child was about 10 years old. She brought an action claiming negligence and breach of contract. By the time the case reached the Court of Appeal the negligence claim had been abandoned.

SLADE L.J.
" . . . It is, I think, common ground that the relevant contract between the parties in the present case was embodied as to part in the oral conversations which took place between the plaintiff and her husband and the defendant at the defendant's consulting rooms, and as to the other part in the written form of consent signed by the plaintiff, which referred to the explanation of the operation which had been given in that conversation. It is also common ground, I think, that, in order to ascertain what was the nature and what were the terms of that contract, this court has to apply an objective rather than a subjective test . . .

I now turn to the first of the two principal issues which I have indicated. At the start of his argument for the plaintiff counsel indicated that his primary ground of appeal would be that the effect of the contract between the plaintiff and the defendant was one by which the defendant contracted to render the plaintiff absolutely sterile. Nevertheless, on the facts of this case, I, for my part, find this contention quite impossible to sustain. It seems to me quite clear from the evidence which we have as to the conversation which took place between the plaintiff and her husband and the defendant at the defendant's consulting rooms that he explained to them that the operation which he would propose to perform on the plaintiff was an operation by way of *laparoscopic sterilisation* and that was the method he intended to adopt and no other. Equally, that was the nature of the operation to which the plaintiff herself agreed, as is shown by the form of consent which she signed. The contract was, to my mind, plainly a contract by the defendant to perform that particular operation.

The matter may be tested in this way. Suppose that when the plaintiff had been under anaesthetic the defendant had formed the view that an even more effective way of sterilising her would be to perform a hysterectomy and had carried out that operation, the plaintiff would, of course, have had the strongest grounds for complaint. She could have said:

'I did not give you a general discretion to perform such operation as you saw fit for the purpose of sterilising me. I gave my consent to one particular form of operation. That was the operation I asked you to do and that was the operation you agreed to do.'

In the end, as I understood him, counsel for the plaintiff did not feel able to press his argument on the first issue very strongly. The nature of the contract was, in my view, indubitably one to perform a laparoscopic sterilisation.

That, however, is by no means the end of the matter. The question still arises: did the defendant give either an express warranty or an implied warranty to the effect that the result of the operation when performed would be to leave the plaintiff absolutely sterile? In response to our inquiry counsel for the plaintiff helpfully listed the two particular passages in the evidence on which he relied for the purpose of asserting that there was an express warranty. The first was a passage where, in the course of examination by her counsel, the plaintiff said:

'We went to the consulting rooms and we saw Mr Measday and we discussed sterilisation. He told us the method that he used for sterilising was the clip. He told us once I had had it done it was irreversible.'

Counsel for the plaintiff also relied on a passage in which the plaintiff was asked in chief:

'Q. Did he show you a clip?
A. He showed us a clip and he also showed us the diagram and told us where the the clips would go on the tubes. He said once I had the operation done there was no turning back, I could not have it reversed.'

Counsel for the plaintiff referred us to paragraph 2 of the defence in the action which read as follows:

'On the October 30, 1978 the Plaintiff consulted the Defendant about an operation of sterilisation. The Defendant examined her and agreed to carry out the operation and advised her that it must be regarded as a permanent procedure. He did not warn the Plaintiff of the slight risk of failure, nor did he guarantee success.'

There was thus a specific admission in the defence that the defendant advised the plaintiff that it must be 'regarded as a permanent procedure'.
In the light of these various representations or statements by the defendant, counsel for the plaintiff submitted that it was being expressly represented to the plaintiff that the effect of the operation would be to render her sterile absolutely and for ever. I, for my part, cannot accept that submission. There has been some discussion in the course of argument on the meaning of the phrase 'irreversible' and as to the relevance of the statement, undoubtedly made by the defendant to the plaintiff, that the proposed operation must be regarded as being irreversible. However, I take the reference to irreversibility as simply meaning that the operative procedure in question is incapable of being reversed, that what is about to be done cannot be undone. I do not think it can reasonably be construed as a representation that the operation is bound to achieve its acknowledged object, which is a different matter altogether. For my part, I cannot spell out any such express warranty as is asserted from the particular passages in the evidence and in the pleadings relied on by counsel for the plaintiff to support it, or from any other parts of the evidence.
In the alternative, however, counsel for the plaintiff relies on an implied warranty . . .
The test to be applied by the court in considering whether a term can or cannot properly be implied in a contract is that embodied in what is frequently called the doctrine of *The Moorcock* [1886–90] All E.R. Rep 530. It is conveniently set out in 9 Halsbury's Laws (4th edn) para. 355:

'A term can only be implied if it is necessary in the business sense to give efficacy to the contract that is if it is such a term that it can confidently be said that if at the time the contract was being negotiated someone had said to the parties, "What will happen in such a case", they would both have replied, "Of course, so and so will happen we did not trouble to say that it is too clear." ' . . .

Applying *The Moorcock* principles, I think there is no doubt that the plaintiff would have been entitled reasonably to assume that the defendant was warranting that the operation would be performed with reasonable care and skill. That, I think, would have been the inevitable inference to be drawn, from an objective standpoint, from the relevant discussion between the parties. The contract did, in my opinion, include an implied warranty of that nature. However, that inference on its own does not enable the plaintiff to succeed in the present case. She has to go further. She has to suggest, and it is suggested on her behalf, that the defendant, by necessary implication, committed himself to an unqualified guarantee as to the success of the particular operation proposed, in achieving its purpose of sterilising her, even though he were to exercise all due care and skill in performing it. The suggestion is that the guarantee went beyond due care and skill and extended to an unqualified warranty that the plaintiff would be absolutely sterile.

On the facts of the present case, I do not think that any intelligent lay bystander (let alone another medical man), on hearing the discussion which took place between the defendant and the other two parties, could have reasonably drawn the inference that the defendant was intending to give any warranty of this nature."

NOTE:

1. Purchase L.J. and Cummings Bruce L.J. agreed with Slade L.J.

Thake v Maurice [1986] 1 All E.R. 497; [1986] Q.B. 644

Mr and Mrs Thake already had four children when Mrs Thake became pregnant again. As the family were short of money and did not want more children, Mr Thake underwent a vasectomy. The defendant made it clear that they must regard the procedure as final. The defendant held both arms horizontally with clenched fists together, he pulled his arms apart to indicate the gap that is formed when the piece of the *vas deferens* is removed during the procedure. He bent his wrists backwards to show how the ends of the vas are tied back to face in the opposite direction. The defendant said that his usual warning about the possibility of reversal had been given, but the judge rejected this. The operation appeared to be a success; however three years later, Mrs Thake began to miss her periods. Initially she assumed it was the early onset of the menopause, but her doctor discovered that she was four months pregnant. The Thakes brought an action against the defendants both in contract and in negligence.

KERR L.J. (DISSENTING)
" . . . [I]t is plain on the evidence that Mr and Mrs Thake intended that Mr Thake should be rendered permanently sterile and believed that this is what the defendant had agreed to do. No submission on these lines was made below, and it would clearly have been rejected by the judge. The only issue is as to the objective interpretation of the offer made by the defendant once he had agreed to perform the operation.

On this issue I have reached the same conclusion as the judge. Having regard to everything that passed between the defendant and the plaintiffs at the meeting, coupled with the absence of any warning that Mr Thake might somehow again become fertile after two successful sperm tests, it seems to me that the plaintiffs could not reasonably have concluded anything other than that his agreement to perform the operation meant that, subject to successful sperm tests, he had undertaken to render Mr Thake permanently sterile. In my view this follows from an objective analysis of the undisputed evidence of what passed between the parties, and it was also what the plaintiffs understood and intended to be the effect of the contract with the defendant."

NEILL L.J.
" . . . The question for consideration is whether in the circumstances of the instant case the defendant further undertook that he would render Mr Thake permanently sterile by means

of this operation . . . It is not in dispute that the task of the court is to seek to determine objectively what conclusion a reasonable person would have reached having regard to (a) the words used by the defendant, (b) the demonstration which he gave and (c) the form which Mr and Mrs Thake were asked to sign.

Counsel for the plaintiffs placed particular reliance on the following matters: (1) that on more than one occasion the defendant explained to the plaintiffs that the effect of the operation was 'irreversible', subject to the remote possibility of later surgical intervention, and counsel pointed out that his explanation was reinforced by the statement in the form: 'I understand that the effect of the operation is irreversible'; (2) that the defendant agreed in evidence that the word 'irreversible' would have been understood by the plaintiff as meaning 'irreversible by God or man'; (3) that the demonstration which the defendant gave with his hands and arms and the sketch which he drew would have led the plaintiffs to believe that, because a piece of the *vas* was to be severed and the severed ends were to be turned back, there was no possibility whatever of the channels being reunited unless some further surgery took place; (4) that the defendant stated that two sperm tests were required to ensure that the operation was successful; this statement would have strengthened the impression given to his listeners that the operation when completed would render the patient sterile.

I recognise the force of the submissions put forward on behalf of the plaintiffs and I am very conscious of the fact that both the trial judge and Kerr L.J. have reached the conclusion that the case in contract has been established. For my part, however, I remain unpersuaded. It seems to me that it is essential to consider the events of 25 September, 1975 and the words which the defendant used against the background of a surgeon's consulting room. It is the common experience of mankind that the results of medical treatment are to some extent unpredictable and that any treatment may be affected by the special characteristics of the particular patient . . .

Both the plaintiffs and the defendant expected that sterility would be the result of the operation; the defendant appreciated that that was the plaintiff's expectation. This does not mean, however, that a reasonable person would have understood the defendant to be giving a binding promise that the operation would achieve its purpose or that the defendant was going further than he expected and believed that it would have the desired result. Furthermore, I do not consider that a reasonable person would have expected a responsible medical man to be intending to give a guarantee. Medicine, though a highly skilled profession, is not, and is not generally regarded as being, an exact science. The reasonable man would have expected the defendant to exercise all the proper skill and care of a surgeon in that speciality; he would not in my view have expected the defendant to give a guarantee of 100 per cent success.

Accordingly, though I am satisfied that a reasonable person would have left the consulting room thinking that Mr Thake would be sterilised by the vasectomy operation, such a person would not have left thinking that the defendant had given a *guarantee* that Mr Thake would be absolutely sterile."

NOTES:

1. Nourse L.J. agreed with Neill L.J.
2. In a case of failed sterilisation, there is a possibility of claiming under s.2(1) of the Misrepresentation Act 1967 for negligent misrepresentation. A duty arises at common law if there is a special relationship between the parties and the following conditions are satisfied. First, it must be reasonably foreseeable by the representor that the representee would rely upon the statement made to him. Secondly, there must be sufficient proximity between the parties. Thirdly, it must be just and reasonable for the law to impose such a duty. However, following the approach taken in *Eyre v Measday* the imposition of such a duty appears unlikely. Furthermore in

Gold v Haringey (see Chapter 6 at p.384) Lloyd L.J. stated that the fact that the plaintiff was told that the operation was irreversible did not mean that it was bound to succeed.

QUESTION:

1. Is it reasonable to assume that in all such cases the surgeon would not have guaranteed the success of the operation?

(c) Claims in Negligence

(i) Basis for the Action

Claims in negligence regarding pregnancy and childbirth relate to issues ranging from inadequate provision of information concerning clinical procedures to negligent conduct of such procedures.

Thake v Maurice [1986] 1 All E.R. 497; [1986] Q.B. 644

The facts of this case are as stated at p.974 above.

KERR L.J.
" . . . The evidence relevant to this issue can be summarised as follows. In the course of the defendants evidence he was taken through medical publications dealing with 'late recanalisation' and he agreed that he was aware that there was a slight risk that this might occur. The opening part of his cross-examination was then in the following terms:

'Q. Mr Maurice, I take it from your evidence (and please tell me whether this is right or wrong) that in 1975 you considered it necessary to give a warning about the risk of recanalisation.
A. Yes.
Q. Thank you. I would understand from that (and again would you tell me whether this is right or wrong) that if it was necessary to give a warning it had to be such a warning that it was going to be understood and sufficiently clear to be understood.
A. Yes.'

In addition to this evidence it must be remembered that the defendant agreed that, if he had failed to give any warning on these lines, then the plaintiffs would have been left with the mistaken impression that, subject only to confirmation by the two sperm tests, Mr Thake had been rendered permanently sterile, and, as discussed hereafter, that if Mrs Thake nevertheless became pregnant again, she might not realise that this had happened, having regard to her age, until it was too late for her to have the pregnancy terminated.
The submission made on behalf of the defendant was that this material was not sufficient to entitle the judge to conclude, as he did, that the defendant's failure to give his usual warning amounted to an inadvertent negligent omission on his part. The ground for this submission was that no independent expert evidence had been called on either side on the question whether the absence of any such warning in these circumstances would have been regarded as breach of professional duty, by applying the test laid down in *Bolam v Friern Hospital Management Committee* [1957] 2 All E.R. 118, as approved by the House of Lords in *Sidaway v Bethlem Royal Hospital Governors* [1985] 1 All E.R. 643. The judge rejected this and I entirely agree with his reasoning. There was no appeal against his refusal to allow a urologist to be called on behalf of the defendant after the completion of his

evidence, but it should be mentioned that it was explained to us, as I accept, that the failure to disclose his evidence in advance in the form of a written report, as had been ordered in relation to any expert that either side might wish to call, was merely due to inadvertence. In the event, therefore, no independent medical evidence was called by either party. But I cannot accept that in these circumstances the judge was not entitled to conclude that the defendant's failure to give his usual warning amounted to an inadvertent breach on his part of the duty of care which he owed to the plaintiffs. Unless and until rebutted, which they never were, the defendant's own evidence and the surrounding circumstances to which I have referred speak for themselves . . .

In the present case there was nothing to be placed in the balance against the need for the warning which the defendant himself recognised in his evidence. He was a general surgeon with high professional qualifications whose competence was not in question, and I think that the plaintiffs were entitled to rely on his evidence just as if it had been given by an independent expert with the same qualifications. Since there is nothing to be placed against it, I consider that the judge was entitled to conclude, as he did, that the plaintiffs had established an inadvertent breach of duty on the part of the defendant sufficient to amount to negligence both in contract and in tort."

NOTES:

1. As with other medical negligence cases, the level of information given must be in accordance with that proposed by a responsible body of professional practice but since *Bolitho* this will have to be a defensible practice (see Chapter 6 above).
2. In *Lybart v Warrington AHA* (1995) 25 B.M.L.R. 91, a woman was sterilised after having given birth to her third child by Casearean section. She was informed prior to sterilisation that the procedure was irreversible and she signed a NHS consent form. Subsequently she became pregnant. She brought an action in negligence claiming damages. Her claim succeeded. In the Court of Appeal it was held that she had not been given an adequate warning. The court stated that the gynaecologist had not taken reasonable steps to ensure that the information given had been understood. (See A. Grubb, "Failed Sterilisation: Duty to Provide Adequate Warning" (1995) 3 *Medical Law Review* 297.)
3. In *Goodwill v British Pregnancy Advisory Service* [1996] 2 All E.R. 161, the Court of Appeal stated that a duty was not owed to a pregnant woman who had commenced a sexual relationship with M three years after a vasectomy had been performed and who, having been told by M that he had undergone a vasectomy, did not take further contraceptive precautions.

(ii) Causation

An important aspect of a negligence action is to establish that the defendant's conduct caused the harm suffered. The plaintiffs must show either that had they known of the risks they would not have undergone the sterilisation operation or that the woman, once she became pregnant, would have chosen an abortion.

But if a woman discovers that she has an unwanted pregnancy, must she terminate? If she refuses the option of an abortion, will her refusal constitute a *novus actus interveniens*, breaking the chain of causation? One first instance judge ruled that a refusal to have an abortion when a sterilisation failed was unreasonable but this ruling was rejected by on appeal in *Emeh v Chelsea and Kensington Area Health Authority* [1984] 3 All E.R. 1044. The matter has been conclusively settled by the case of *McFarlane v Tayside Health Board* considered below. Lord Steyn stated:

> "Counsel for the health authority rightly did not argue that it is a factor against the claim that the parents should have resorted to abortion or adoption. I cannot conceive of any circumstances in which the autonomous decision of the parents not to resort to even a lawful abortion could be questioned. For similar reasons the parents' decision not to have the child adopted was plainly natural and commendable. It is difficult to envisage any circumstances in which it would be right to challenge such a decision of the parents. The starting point is the right of parents to make decisions on family planning and, if those plans fail, their right to care for an initially unwanted child. The law does and must respect these decisions of parents which are so closely tied to their basic freedoms and rights of personal autonomy."

On the relationship between abortion and wrongful birth, see R. Scott, "Prenatal Screening, Autonomy and Reasons: The Relationship between the Law of Abortion and Wrongful Birth" (2003) 11 *Medical Law Review* 265.

(iii) Award of Damages

In negligence actions based on the birth of an "unwanted" child, claims may be brought for both pecuniary and non-pecuniary loss. In the first case to address the issue, Jupp J. ruled in *Udale v Bloomsbury AHA* [1983] 2 All E.R. 522 that public policy militated against such damages on the grounds no child should discover that he had been "unwanted". The judge regarded the birth of a child as a "blessing". In subsequent cases, however, it was recognised that damages should be awarded in recognition of the costs of bringing up an unwanted child—see *Emeh v Chelsea and Kensington AHA op. cit. Thake v Maurice, op. cit.* and *Allen v Bloomsbury AHA* [1993] 1 All E.R. 65.

The matter thus appeared to have been settled until the ruling by the House of Lords in the following case, which has thrown it into confusion:

McFarlane v Tayside Health Board [2000] 2 A.C. 59

Mr McFarlane had a vasectomy carried out in a hospital run by Tayside Health Board, after which doctors assured him he was sterile and need no longer use contraception. His wife subsequently became pregnant and gave birth to their fifth child. Mrs McFarlane claimed damages for the pain and inconvenience of pregnancy and birth, and she and her husband claimed damages for the cost of rearing their healthy child, Catherine. Although the Health Board argued that conception, pregnancy and child birth were natural processes, the House of Lords by a four to one majority found that the mother was entitled to recover for the pain and inconvenience of pregnancy and for expenses directly arising from pregnancy. However, the Law Lords unanimously held that costs could not be recovered for the birth of a healthy child, although they differed in their reasoning on this point.

LORD STEYN

" . . . It may be helpful to state at the outset the nature and shape of the case before the House. First, a distinction must be made between two types of claims which can arise from the failure of a sterilisation procedure, resulting in the birth of a child. There is the action (if permitted) for 'wrongful life' brought by a disadvantaged or disabled child for damage to himself arising from the fact of his birth. The present case does not fall within this category. It is what in the literature is called an action for 'wrongful birth'. It is an action by parents of an unwanted child for damage resulting to them from the birth of the child. Secondly, the claim before the House is framed in delict. Counsel cited observations to the effect that it is immaterial whether such an action is brought in contract or in delict. The correctness of this assumption may depend on the nature of the term of the contract alleged to have been breached. Usually, since a contract of services is involved, it may be an obligation to take reasonable care. On the other hand, the term may be expressed more stringently and may amount to a warranty of an outcome. It is unnecessary in the present case to consider whether different considerations may arise in such cases. My views are confined to claims in delict . . .

It is possible to view the case simply from the perspective of corrective justice. It requires somebody who has harmed another without justification to indemnify the other. On this approach, the parents' claim for the cost of bringing up Catherine must succeed. But one may also approach the case from the vantage point of distributive justice. It requires a focus on the just distribution of burdens and losses among members of a society. If the matter is approached in this way, it may become relevant to ask of the commuters on the Underground the following question: Should the parents of an unwanted but healthy child be able to sue the doctor or hospital for compensation equivalent to the cost of bringing up the child for the years of his or her minority, ie until about 18 years? My Lords, I have not consulted my fellow travellers on the London Underground but I am firmly of the view that an overwhelming number of ordinary men and women would answer the question with an emphatic No. And the reason for such a response would be an inarticulate premise as to what is morally acceptable and what is not. Like Ognall J in *Jones v Berkshire Area Health Authority* (2 July 1986, unreported) they will have in mind that many couples cannot have children and others have the sorrow and burden of looking after a disabled child. The realisation that compensation for financial loss in respect of the upbringing of a child would necessarily have to discriminate between rich and poor would surely appear unseemly to them. It would also worry them that parents may be put in a position of arguing in court that the unwanted child, which they accepted and care for, is more trouble than it is worth. Instinctively, the traveller on the Underground would consider that the law of tort has no business to provide legal remedies consequent upon the birth of a healthy child, which all of us regard as a valuable and good thing.

My Lords, to explain decisions denying a remedy for the cost of bringing up an unwanted child by saying that there is no loss, no foreseeable loss, no causative link or no ground for reasonable restitution is to resort to unrealistic and formalistic propositions which mask the real reasons for the decisions. And judges ought to strive to give the real reasons for their decision. It is my firm conviction that where courts of law have denied a remedy for the cost of bringing up an unwanted child the real reasons have been grounds of distributive justice. That is, of course, a moral theory. It may be objected that the House must act like a court of law and not like a court of morals. That would only be partly right. The court must apply positive law. But judges' sense of the moral answer to a question, or the justice of the case, has been one of the great shaping forces of the common law. What may count in a situation of difficulty and uncertainty is not the subjective view of the judge but what he reasonably believes that the ordinary citizen would regard as right . . . ."

In my view it is legitimate in the present case to take into account considerations of distributive justice. That does not mean that I would decide the case on grounds of public policy. On the contrary, I would avoid those quick sands. Relying on principles of distributive justice I am persuaded that our tort law does not permit parents of a healthy unwanted child to claim the costs of bringing up the child from a health authority or a doctor. If it were necessary to do so, I would say that the claim does not satisfy the requirement of being fair, just and reasonable.

This conclusion is reinforced by an argument of coherence. There is no support in Scotland and England for a claim by a disadvantaged child for damage to him arising from his birth: see *McKay v Essex Area Health Authority* [see p.967 above] . . . "

LORD MILLETT (DISSENTING)
" . . . The contention that the birth of a normal, healthy baby 'is not a harm' is not an accurate formulation of the issue. In order to establish a cause of action in delict, the pursuers must allege and prove that they have suffered an invasion of their legal rights (*injuria*) and that they have sustained loss (*damnum*) as a result. In the present case the injuria occurred when (and if) the defenders failed to take reasonable care to ensure that the information they gave was correct. The *damnum* occurred when Mrs McFarlane conceived. This was an invasion of her bodily integrity and threatened further damage both physical and financial. Had Mrs McFarlane miscarried, or carried to full term only to be delivered of a still-born child, it is impossible to see on what basis she could have been denied a cause of action, though the claim would have been relatively modest. The same would apply if Mr and Mrs McFarlane had adhered to their determination not to have another child and had proceeded to restore the status quo ante by an abortion. Damages would be recoverable for the pain and distress involved as well as for any expenses incurred. The issue, therefore, is not whether Catherine's birth was a legal harm or injury, that is to say, whether the pursuers have a completed cause of action, but whether the particular heads of damage claimed, and in particular the costs of maintaining Catherine throughout her childhood, are recoverable in law.

The admission of a novel head of damages is not solely a question of principle. Limitations on the scope of legal liability arise from legal policy, which is to say 'our more or less inadequately expressed ideas of what justice demands' (see Prosser and Keeton Law of Torts (5th edn, 1984) p 264). This is the case whether the question concerns the admission of a new head of damages or the admission of a duty of care in a new situation. Legal policy in this sense is not the same as public policy, even though moral considerations may play a part in both. The court is engaged in a search for justice, and this demands that the dispute be resolved in a way which is fair and reasonable and accords with ordinary notions of what is fit and proper. It is also concerned to maintain the coherence of the law and the avoidance of inappropriate distinctions if injustice is to be avoided in other cases . . .

Nevertheless I am persuaded that the costs of bringing Catherine up are not recoverable. I accept the thrust of both the main arguments in favour of dismissing such a claim. In my opinion the law must take the birth of a normal, healthy baby to be a blessing, not a detriment. In truth it is a mixed blessing. It brings joy and sorrow, blessing and responsibility. The advantages and the disadvantages are inseparable. Individuals may choose to regard the balance as unfavourable and take steps to forego the pleasures as well as the responsibilities of parenthood. They are entitled to decide for themselves where their own interests lie. But society itself must regard the balance as beneficial. It would be repugnant to its own sense of values to do otherwise. It is morally offensive to regard a normal, healthy baby as more trouble and expense than it is worth.

This does not answer the question whether the benefits should be taken into account and the claim dismissed or left out of account and full recovery allowed. But the answer is to be found in the fact that the advantages and disadvantages of parenthood are inextricably bound together. This is part of the human condition. Nature herself does not permit parents to enjoy the advantages and dispense with the disadvantages. In other contexts the law adopts the same principle. It insists that he who takes the benefit must take the burden.

In the mundane transactions of commercial life, the common law does not allow a man to keep goods delivered to him and refuse to pay for them on the ground that he did not order them. It would be far more subversive of the mores of society for parents to enjoy the advantages of parenthood while transferring to others the responsibilities which it entails.

Unlike your Lordships, I consider that the same reasoning leads to the rejection of Mrs McFarlane's claim in respect of the pain and distress of pregnancy and delivery. The only difference between the two heads of damage claimed is temporal. Normal pregnancy and delivery were as much an inescapable precondition of Catherine's birth as the expense of maintaining her afterwards was its inevitable consequence. They are the price of parenthood. The fact that it is paid by the mother alone does not alter this.

It does not, however, follow that Mr and Mrs McFarlane should be sent away empty-handed. The rejection of their claim to measure their loss by the consequences of Catherine's conception and birth does not lead to the conclusion that they have suffered none. They have suffered both injury and loss. They have lost the freedom to limit the size of their family. They have been denied an important aspect of their personal autonomy. Their decision to have no more children is one the law should respect and protect. They are entitled to general damages to reflect the true nature of the wrong done to them. This should be a conventional sum which should be left to the trial judge to assess, but which I would not expect to exceed £ 5,000 in a straightforward case like the present.

In addition, Mr and Mrs McFarlane may have a claim for special damages. A baby may come trailing clouds of glory, but it brings nothing else into the world. Today he requires an astonishing amount of equipment, not merely the layette but pushchair, car seat, carry cot, high chair and so on. The expense of acquiring these is considerable, but in my opinion it is not recoverable. It falls into the same category as the costs of maintaining the baby. But most parents keep such items, bought for their first child, to await the arrival of further children. If Mr and Mrs McFarlane disposed of them in the belief that they would have no more children, the cost of replacing them should be recoverable as a direct and foreseeable consequence of the information they were given being wrong."

NOTES:

1. Lord Millett not only dissents on the issue of allowing the mother to recover for the harms of pregnancy, but he also differs from Lords Slynn, Hope and Clyde who had held that damages for raising a child were a form of pure economic loss and not recoverable on this basis. Lord Millett notes that the distinction between pure and consequential economic loss is "technical and artificial".

2. The ruling has attracted huge criticism. In additional to academic critique (see L.C.H. Hoyano, "Misconceptions about Wrongful Conception" (2002) 65 *Modern Law Review* 883; A. Maclean, "*McFarlane v Tayside Health Board*: a Wrongful Conception in the House of Lords" (2000) 3 *Web Journal of Current Legal Issues* 1; J.K. Mason, "Unwanted Pregnancy: a Case of Retroversion" (2000) 4 *Edinburgh Law Review* 191; N. Priaulx, "Joy to the World! A (Healthy) Child Is Born: Reconceptualizing 'Harm' in Wrongful conception" (2004) 13 *Social and Legal Studies* 5, *cf.* T. Weir, "The Unwanted Child" (2002) 6 *Edinburgh Law Review* 244). Lady Justice Hale (as she then was) has written that "left to myself, I would not regard the upbringing of a child as pure economic loss, but loss which is consequential upon invasion of bodily integrity and loss of personal autonomy involved in unwanted pregnancy" (Hale, D.B.E., "The Value of Life and the Cost of Living—Damages for Wrongful Birth", The Staple

Inn, Reading (2001) *British Actuarial Journal* 755. Moreover, in the Australian case *Cattanach v Melchior* (2003) 199 A.L.R. 131, Kirby J. castigated the decision as a departure "from the ordinary principles governing the recovery of damages for the tort of negligence".

QUESTIONS:

1. Priaulx (*op. cit.* in Note 2 at p.6) argues that central to the case is a tension regarding the meaning of harm, "Is unsolicited parenthood 'part of the normal vicissitudes of life' . . . or a '*harmful*' event that should be the subject of litigation, sounding in damages?" Do you think the birth of an unplanned child should be counted as harm, and if so on what basis? Is this a completely new "wrong" that the courts are being asked to recognise?
2. Can the courts avoid making moral judgments in a case of this sort? Can they avoid arguments rooted in public policy? Is there a difference between "legal policy" and "public policy"?
3. Does this ruling demonstrate that the "sanctity of life" principle still has a role to play in English law? (See J. Mee, "Wrongful Conception: the Emergence of a Full Recovery Rule" (1992) 70 *Washington University Law Quarterly* 887; Priaulx, *op. cit.*, in Note 2 at p.12.)
4. To what extent do you think scarce resources in the NHS are taken into account by judges deciding these cases? Is this a legitimate consideration? (See Weir, *op. cit.* in Note 2 *cf.* R. Lee, "To Be or not to Be: Is that the Question? The Claim of Wrongful Life" in R. Lee and D. Morgan (eds), *Birthrights: Law and Ethics at the Beginning of Life*, London: Routledge, 1987; N. Priaulx, "Conceptualising Harm in the Case of the 'Unwanted' Child" (2002) 9 *European Journal of Health Law* 337 at p.355.)

The subsequent history of claims of wrongful conception and birth cases in English law reveals a concern on the part of judges to limit the impact of the *MacFarlane* ruling.

Parkinson v St James and Seacroft University Hospital NHS Trust [2002] Q.B. 266, [2001] 3 W.L.R. 376

This was a wrongful conception case in which, following a negligently performed sterilisation, P gave birth to her fifth child who was disabled. The stress of an additional pregnancy, coupled with the issue of whether or not to abort, and the prospect caring for a disabled child led to the breakdown of P's marriage. The Court of Appeal upheld the ruling of Longmore J. that P was entitled to damages to cover the costs of providing for the child's special needs and care attributable to his disability, but that this did not extend to basic costs of his maintenance.

BROOKE L.J.
" . . . 49 . . . In *Fassoulas [v Ramey* (1984) 450 So 2d 822,] the Supreme Court of Florida followed the reasoning later to be adopted by the House of Lords in relation to the cost of rearing a healthy, normal child. It added, however, at p 824, para 4:

'We agree with the district court below that an exception exists in the case of special upbringing expenses associated with a deformed child . . . Special medical and educational expenses, beyond normal rearing costs, are often staggering and quite debilitating to a family's financial and social health; "indeed, the financial and emotional drain associated with raising such a child is often overwhelming to the affected parents" . . . There is no valid policy argument against parents being recompensed for these costs of extraordinary care in raising a deformed child to majority. We hold these special upbringing costs associated with a deformed child to be recoverable.'

50 Unless we are bound by authority to the contrary, I find this argument persuasive. On this side of the Atlantic I would apply the battery of tests which the House of Lords has taught us to use, and arrive at the same answer. My route would be as follows: (i) for the reasons given by Waller LJ in *Emeh v Kensington and Chelsea and Westminster Area Health Authority* [1985] QB 1012, the birth of a child with congenital abnormalities was a foreseeable consequence of the surgeon's careless failure to clip a fallopian tube effectively; (ii) there was a very limited group of people who might be affected by this negligence, viz Mrs Parkinson and her husband (and, in theory, any other man with whom she had sexual intercourse before she realised that she had not been effectively sterilised); (iii) there is no difficulty in principle in accepting the proposition that the surgeon should be deemed to have assumed responsibility for the foreseeable and disastrous economic consequences of performing his services negligently; (iv) the purpose of the operation was to prevent Mrs Parkinson from conceiving any more children, including children with congenital abnormalities, and the surgeon's duty of care is strictly related to the proper fulfilment of that purpose; (v) parents in Mrs Parkinson's position were entitled to recover damages in these circumstances for 15 years between the decisions in *Emeh's* case and *McFarlane's* case [2000] 2 AC 59, so that this is not a radical step forward into the unknown; (vi) for the reasons set out in (i) and (ii) above, Lord Bridge of Harwich's tests of foreseeability and proximity are satisfied, and for the reasons given by the Supreme Court of Florida in *Fassoulas v Ramey* 450 So 2d 822 an award of compensation which is limited to the special upbringing costs associated with rearing a child with a serious disability would be fair, just and reasonable; (vii) if principles of distributive justice are called in aid, I believe that ordinary people would consider that it would be fair for the law to make an award in such a case, provided that it is limited to the extra expenses associated with the child's disability.

51 I can see nothing in any majority reasoning in McFarlane's case to deflect this court from adopting this course, which in my judgment both logic and justice demand . . .

52 What constitutes a significant disability for this purpose will have to be decided by judges, if necessary, on a case by case basis. The expression would certainly stretch to include disabilities of the mind (including severe behavioural disabilities) as well as physical disabilities. It would not include minor defects or inconveniences, such as are the lot of many children who do not suffer from significant disabilities. I have had the opportunity of reading in draft the judgment of Hale LJ, and I agree with what she says about this matter in paragraph 91 of her judgment.

53 In this judgment I am concerned only with the loss that arises when the child's significant disabilities flow foreseeably from his or her unwanted conception . . . "

HALE L.J.
" . . . 87 At the heart of it all [the reasoning in *McFarlane*] is the feeling that to compensate for the financial costs of bringing up a healthy child is a step too far. A child brings benefits as well as costs; it is impossible accurately to calculate those benefits so as to give a proper discount; the only sensible course is to assume that they balance one another out . . .

There are many who would challenge that assumption. They would argue that the true costs to the primary carer of bringing up a child are so enormous that they easily outstrip any benefits . . .

89 The notion of a child bringing benefit to the parents is itself deeply suspect, smacking of the commodification of the child, regarding the child as an asset to the parents . . . But if, as Lord Millett observed, society is bound to regard its new member as an asset, whatever the views and experience of the parents, an equally rational response might have been to attribute a conventional sum as the benefit to be assumed to be gained from the pleasure of a child's company, the pride in his achievements, the hope of reciprocation of family feelings, the passing on of one's genes. This is a solution sometimes adopted by the law when faced with a rationally necessary but impossible task. Lord Millett would have adopted it for the "true nature of the wrong done" to the pursuers, the denial of an important aspect of their personal autonomy.

90 The solution of deemed equilibrium also has its attractions and is in any event binding upon us. Indeed, it provides the answer to many of the questions arising in this case. The true analysis is that this is a limitation on the damages which would otherwise be recoverable on normal principles. There is therefore no reason or need to take that limitation any further than it was taken in McFarlane's case. This caters for the ordinary costs of the ordinary child. A disabled child needs extra care and extra expenditure. He is deemed, on this analysis, to bring as much pleasure and as many advantages as does a normal healthy child. Frankly, in many cases, of which this may be one, this is much less likely. The additional stresses and strains can have seriously adverse effects upon the whole family, and not infrequently lead, as here, to the break-up of the parents' relationship and detriment to the other children. But we all know of cases where the whole family has been enriched by the presence of a disabled member and would not have things any other way. This analysis treats a disabled child as having exactly the same worth as a non-disabled child. It affords him the same dignity and status. It simply acknowledges that he costs more . . .

92 Another question is when the disability must arise. Mr Stuart-Smith argued that there was no rational cut-off point, as any manner of accidents and illnesses might foreseeably affect a child throughout his childhood. But that is part of the ordinary experience of childhood, in which such risks are always present, and the balance of advantage and disadvantage is deemed to be equal. The two serious contenders are conception and birth. The argument for conception is that this is when the major damage was caused, from which all else flows. This was what the defendants undertook to prevent. But there are at least two powerful arguments for birth. The first is that, although conception is when the losses start, it is not when they end. The defendants also undertook to prevent pregnancy and childbirth. The normal principle is that all losses, past, present or future, foreseeably flowing from the tort are recoverable. The second is that it is only when the child is born that the deemed benefits begin. And it is those deemed benefits which deny the claim in respect of the normal child. In practice, also, while it may be comparatively straightforward to distinguish between ante- and post-natal causes of disability, it will be harder to distinguish between ante- and post-conception causes. Further, the additional risks to mother and child (for example because of the mother's age or number of previous pregnancies) may be among the reasons for the sterilisation. I conclude that any disability arising from genetic causes or foreseeable events during pregnancy (such as rubella, spina bifida, or oxygen deprivation during pregnancy or childbirth) up until the child is born alive, and which are not *novus actus interveniens*, will suffice to found a claim . . . "

NOTES:

1. Sir Martin Nourse agreed with both judgments.
2. The issue which Hale L.J. addressed at he end of her judgment arose shortly afterwards in the case of *Groom v Selby* [2001] EWCA Civ 1522. Here a doctor negligently failed to detect a pregnancy after G had undergone sterilisation. He thus denied her the opportunity to terminate the unwanted pregnancy. G's daughter was born prematurely and three

weeks later developed meningitis, due to an infection with samonella in the birth canal, which led to brain damage. The Court of Appeal ruled that the child's exposure to bacteria during birth was a foreseeable consequence of the defendant's failure to detect her pregnancy, and therefore damages relating to the upbringing of a disabled child could be recovered. Mason and Laurie have questioned whether the *McFarlane* rule should have been undermined "in such indefinite terms" (J.K. Mason and G.T. Laurie, *Mason & McCall-Smith's Law and Medical Ethics* (7th edn), Oxford: OUP, 2006 at p.182.)

QUESTION:

1. Andrew Grubb points out that, given that recoverability of damages depends on whether the child is disabled, it is vitally important to define the term. (A. Grubb, "Failed Sterilisation: Damages for the Birth of a Disabled Child" (2002) 10 *Medical Law Review* 78 at p.81.) Does the Court of Appeal define the concept sufficiently clearly? Is it a tenable distinction?

Rees v Darlington Memorial Hospital Trust

R suffered from retinus pigmentosa and had chosen to be sterilised because she feared that her eyesight would prevent her from caring for a child. It had already caused her to give up work. The operation was negligently performed and she gave birth to a son. R claimed that, following *Parkinson*, it would be " just, fair and reasonable" to award her the costs of bringing up a healthy child which were attributable to her disability. She failed at first instance but by a 2–1 majority the Court of Appeal allowed her appeal. On appeal to the House of Lords, their Lordships overturned the Court of Appeal ruling by a 4–3 majority. They held that the instant case could not be distinguished from *McFarlane,* as the child was healthy; thus there could be no recovery for any costs associated with the child's upbringing. Nevertheless, the majority held that the mother should be given a conventional award of £15,000, to reflect the wrong she had suffered:

LORD BINGHAM
" . . . 7 I am of the clear opinion, for reasons more fully given by my noble and learned friends, that it would be wholly contrary to the practice of the House to disturb its unanimous decision in *McFarlane* given as recently as four years ago, even if a differently constituted committee were to conclude that a different solution should have been adopted. It would reflect no credit on the administration of the law if a line of English authority were to be disapproved in 1999 and reinstated in 2003 with no reason for the change beyond a change in the balance of judicial opinion. I am not in any event persuaded that the arguments which the House rejected in 1999 should now be accepted, or that the policy considerations which (as I think) drove the decision have lost their potency. Subject to one gloss, therefore, which I regard as important, I would affirm and adhere to the decision in *McFarlane.*
8 My concern is this. Even accepting that an unwanted child cannot be regarded as a financial liability and nothing else and that any attempt to weigh the costs of bringing up a child against the intangible rewards of parenthood is unacceptably speculative, the fact remains that the parent of a child born following a negligently performed vasectomy or

sterilisation, or negligent advice on the effect of such a procedure, is the victim of a legal wrong. The members of the House who gave judgment in *McFarlane* recognised this by holding, in each case, that some award should be made to Mrs McFarlane (although Lord Millett based this on a ground which differed from that of the other members and he would have made a joint award to Mr and Mrs McFarlane). I can accept and support a rule of legal policy which precludes recovery of the full cost of bringing up a child in the situation postulated, but I question the fairness of a rule which denies the victim of a legal wrong any recompense at all beyond an award immediately related to the unwanted pregnancy and birth. The spectre of well-to-do parents plundering the National Health Service should not blind one to other realities: that of the single mother with young children, struggling to make ends meet and counting the days until her children are of an age to enable her to work more hours and so enable the family to live a less straitened existence; the mother whose burning ambition is to put domestic chores so far as possible behind her and embark on a new career or resume an old one. Examples can be multiplied. To speak of losing the freedom to limit the size of one's family is to mask the real loss suffered in a situation of this kind. This is that a parent, particularly (even today) the mother, has been denied, through the negligence of another, the opportunity to live her life in the way that she wished and planned. I do not think that an award immediately relating to the unwanted pregnancy and birth gives adequate recognition of or does justice to that loss. I would accordingly support the suggestion favoured by Lord Millett in *McFarlane*, at p 114, that in all cases such as these there be a conventional award to mark the injury and loss, although I would favour a greater figure than the £5,000 he suggested (I have in mind a conventional figure of £15,000) and I would add this to the award for the pregnancy and birth. This solution is in my opinion consistent with the ruling and rationale of *McFarlane*. The conventional award would not be, and would not be intended to be, compensatory. It would not be the product of calculation. But it would not be a nominal, let alone a derisory, award. It would afford some measure of recognition of the wrong done. And it would afford a more ample measure of justice than the pure *McFarlane* rule.

9 I would for my part apply this rule also, without differentiation, to cases in which either the child or the parent is (or claims to be) disabled. (1) While I have every sympathy with the Court of Appeal's view that Mrs Parkinson should be compensated, it is arguably anomalous that the defendant's liability should be related to a disability which the doctor's negligence did not cause and not to the birth which it did. (2) The rule favoured by the Court of Appeal majority in the present case inevitably gives rise to anomalies such as those highlighted by Waller LJ in paragraphs 53–54 of his dissenting judgment. (3) It is undesirable that parents, in order to recover compensation, should be encouraged to portray either their children or themselves as disabled. There is force in the points made by Kirby J in paragraphs 163–166 of his judgment in *Melchior*. (4) In a state such as ours, which seeks to make public provision for the consequences of disability, the quantification of additional costs attributable to disability, whether of the parent or the child, is a task of acute difficulty. This is highlighted by the inability of the claimant in this appeal to give any realistic indication of the additional costs she seeks to recover.

10 I would accordingly allow the appeal, set aside the orders of the Court of Appeal and of the deputy judge, and order that judgment be entered for the claimant for £15,000. I would invite the parties to make written submissions on costs within 14 days."

LORD STEYN (DISSENTING)

"28 I do not propose to undertake the gruesome task of discussing the judgments in *McFarlane* . . .

[I]if the appellants are to succeed on this count, either this House must reverse that decision or there must be sufficient grounds for distinguishing this case . . . In the general interest of certainty in the law we must be sure that there is some very good reason before we so act . . . I think that however wrong or anomalous the decision may be it must stand and apply to cases reasonably analogous unless or until it is altered by Parliament.

In *McFarlane* the House examined the applicable principles and relevant analogies in great depth. It is not argued that the House overlooked any arguments of substance. Rather counsel for the claimant invites the House to say that the Law Lords in *McFarlane* made the wrong choice. For my part it would be entirely wrong for the House, differently constituted today, to depart from *McFarlane* even if some Law Lords had been persuaded that they would have decided the case differently.

33 Having listened to the argument of counsel for the claimant that *McFarlane* was wrongly decided—an argument somewhat less detailed and rigorous than was before the House in *McFarlane*—I have to say I am satisfied that the House came to the correct conclusion four years ago . . .

34 Throughout the speeches in *McFarlane* runs the strong emphasis on the birth of a healthy and normal child. The opinions show that the House was fully alive to the different considerations which arise if the child is seriously disabled. But the case then before the House did not require a decision on such a case.

35 When the issue involving a disabled child came before the Court of Appeal in *Parkinon* the ruling was unanimous that such a case is not affected by *McFarlane*. While not wishing to endorse everything said in the detailed judgments of Brooke and Hale LJJ, I agree with the decision . . .

37 Unlike the position of the disabled child, it is not possible to regard the disabled mother of a healthy and normal child as unaffected by the principle in *McFarlane*. On the contrary, an award of damages in the present case is only possible if an exception is created.

. . . On the basis of distributive justice I believe that ordinary people would think that it was not fair that a disabled person should recover when mothers who may in effect become disabled by ill-health through having a healthy child would not. . . .

In jurisprudential and positive law terms this is a truly hard case. It is unrealistic to say that there is only one right answer. But a decision must be made, and that decision must represent the best available choice and hopefully a decision defensible as delivering justice. For reasons which are apparent from this opinion it is logically not straightforward to treat the present case as simply an extension of *Parkinson*. On the other hand, I consider (like Hale and Robert Walker LJJ) that the law should give special consideration to the serious disability of a mother who had wanted to avoid having a child by undergoing a sterilisation operation. I am persuaded that the injustice of denying to such a seriously disabled mother the limited remedy of the extra costs caused by her disability outweighs the considerations emphasised by Waller LJ.

VII. A conventional award

40 Lord Bingham has explained why he favours a conventional award of £15,000 in the present case. His opinion makes clear that to this extent he would depart from *McFarlane* in the case of a healthy and normal child. He has further observed that he would apply this rule, without differentiation, to cases in which either the child or the parent is (or claims to be) disabled. This involves overruling the majority of the Court of Appeal in the present case. It also involves overruling the Court of Appeal decision in *Parkinson* against which there was no appeal. The other opinions in the present case speak for themselves.

For my part it is a great disadvantage for the House to consider such a point without the benefit of the views of the Court of Appeal. And the disadvantage cannot be removed by calling the new rule a 'gloss'. It is a radical and most important development which should only be embarked on after rigorous examination of competing arguments.

46 Like Lord Hope I regard the idea of a conventional award in the present case as contrary to principle. It is a novel procedure for judges to create such a remedy. There are limits to permissible creativity for judges. In my view the majority have strayed into forbidden territory. It is also a backdoor evasion of the legal policy enunciated in *McFarlane*. If such a rule is to be created it must be done by Parliament. The fact is, however, that it would be a hugely controversial legislative measure."

NOTES:

1. Lord Nicholls and Lord Scott agreed with the award of conventional damages. Lord Nicholls comments that the award applied "not for the birth of the child, but for the denial of an important aspect of their personal autonomy, viz, the right to limit their family".
2. As Jackson points out, the criticism of the *Parkinson* ruling by the Law Lords renders its legal status uncertain (E. Jackson, *Medical Law: Text, Cases and Materials*, Oxford: OUP, 2006, at pp.681–682).

QUESTIONS:

1. Would it have been better if, instead of carving out another exception to *McFarlane*, the House of Lords had simply used it powers under the 1966 Practice Statement to depart from its own previous decision, in light of the sustained critique it has received? (See N. Priaulx, "That's One Heck of an 'Unruly Horse'! Riding Roughshod over Autonomy in Wrongful Conception" (2004) 12 *Feminist Legal Studies* 317.)
2. Do you agree with Priaulx (*op. cit.* in Question 1 at p.329) that "the current approach [of English law] suggests that negligence resulting in the birth of a child is a harmless and inevitable part of life, for which individuals, in particular women, must be prepared to bear the costs"?
3. Mason and Laurie argue that a fair solution to the dilemma these cases raise would be "to see the 'conventional award" as recognition of a new head of damages, that is, a breach of autonomy or interference with the right to plan one's life as one wishes" (J.K. Mason and G.T. Laurie, *Mason & McCall-Smith's Law and Medical Ethics*, Oxford: OUP, 2006 at p.184.) Do you agree?
4. Morris and Santier have claimed that wrongful birth actions are "unjust and demeaning" since they treat the child as "a legal parasite" and as a "burden to his parents" (A. Morris and S. Santier, "To Be or Not to Be: Is that the Question? Wrongful Life and Misconceptions" (2003) 11 *Medical Law Review* 167 at p.192). Is their argument equally applicable to the wrongful life claims considered at pp.967–971 above, given that, in reality, "the decision to sue for wrongful life ordinarily is not made by the plaintiff [child], but by the parents charged with [the] plaintiff's care and education" (see P. J. Kelley, "Wrongful Life, Wrongful Birth and Justice in Tort Law" [1979] *Washington University Law Quarterly* 919, at p.942)?
5. A different analysis is offered by Julian Savulescu, who argues that so-called "wrongful birth" cases "are not primarily about some "right not to be born". They are about the rights of couples and other people engaging in procreative activities to be given a reasonable range of options and good-quality information relevant to those options" (J. Savulescu, "Is There a 'Right not to Be Born'? Reproductive Decision Making, Options and the Right to Information" (2002) 28 *Journal of Medical Ethics* 65). Do you agree that such cases represent an important aspect of reproductive choice?

SELECT BIBLIOGRAPHY

R. Davis-Floyd and J. Dumit (eds), *Cyborg Babies: From Techno-Sex to Techno-Tots*, New York: Routledge, 1998.

B. Dickens, "Wrongful Birth and Life, Wrongful Death before Birth and Wrongful Law", S. McLean (ed.), *Legal Issues in Human Reproduction*, Aldershot: Dartmouth, 1989.

G. Douglas, *Law, Fertility and Reproduction*, London: Sweet & Maxwell, 1991.

V. Harpwood, *Legal Issues in Obstetrics*, Aldershot: Dartmouth, 1996.

E. Jackson, *Regulating Reproduction: Law, Technology and Autonomy*, Oxford, Hart, 2001, Chapters 1 and 4.

R. Lee, "To Be or not to Be: Is that the Question? The Claim of Wrongful Life" and R. Lee and D. Morgan, "A Lesser Sacrifice, Sterilisation and the Mentally Handicapped Woman", in R. Lee and D. Morgan (eds), *Birthrights: Law and Ethics at the Beginning of Life*, London: Routledge, 1987.

R. MacKenzie, "From Sanctity to Screening: Genetic Disabilities, Risk and Rhetorical Strategies in Wrongful Birth and Wrongful Conception Cases" (1999) 7 *Feminist Legal Studies* 175

J.K. Mason, *The Troubled Pregnancy*, Cambridge: CUP, 2007 (forthcoming).

S. Pattinson, "Wrongful Life Actions as a Means of Regulating Use of Genetic and Reproductive Technologies" (1999) 7 *Health Law Journal* 19.

N. Priaulx, "Conceptualising Harm in the Case of the 'Unwanted' Child" (2002) 9 *European Journal of Health Law* 337.

N. Priaulx, "Joy to the World! A (Healthy) Child Is Born: Reconceptualizing 'Harm' in Wrongful Conception" ((2004) 13 *Social and Legal Studies* 5.

N. Priaulx, "That's One Heck of an 'Unruly Horse'! Riding Roughshod over Autonomy in Wrongful Conception" (2004) 12 *Feminist Legal Studies* 317.

N. Priaulx, *The Harm Paradox: Tort Law and the Unwanted Child in an Era of Choice*, London: Routledge Cavendish, 2007 (forthcoming).

R. Scott, *Rights, Duties and the Body: Law and Ethics of the Maternal–Fetal Conflict*, Oxford: Hart, 2002.

H. Teff, "The Action for Wrongful Life in England" (1985) 34 ICLQ 432.

V. Toscano, "Misguided Retribution: Criminalization of Pregnant Women who Take Drugs" (2005) *Social and Legal Studies* 35.

C. Wells, " On the Outside Looking In: Perspectives on Enforced Caesareans" in S. Sheldon and M. Thomson (eds), *Feminist Perspectives on Healthcare Law*, London: Cavendish, 1998.

A. Whitfield, "Actions Arising from Birth" in A. Grubb (ed.), *Principles of Medical Law*, Oxford: OUP, 2004.

PART V

Medical technology has wrought many changes at the end of life. The very concept of death itself has altered over time, from the recognition of death as being cessation of the heart to the current position in which death is generally recognised by the medical profession as being brain stem death (irreversible degeneration of the brain stem). Today, life support systems through the provision of artificial ventilation and nutrition and hydration offer the potential for life to be sustained and considerably prolonged. However, such technologies bring with them costs. Almost invariably not all patients can be sustained in such a manner. Health professionals are left to choose when therapies should be given or withdrawn. In the past, many of these choices were left hidden but the position has changed and the issue is now the subject of heated public debate. We noted in Chapter 6 above that a competent patient has the right to consent or refuse consent to medical treatment even if death results. The law supports the autonomy of the patient to refuse treatment *(see, for example, Re B* [2002] 2 All E.R. 449) but at the same time there is no "right to die" as such recognised in law. English law rejects euthanasia and assisted suicide and this approach has been confirmed as consistent with the European Convention of Human Rights by both the House of Lords and the European Court of Human Rights (*R (on the application of Pretty) v DPP* [2002] 1 All E.R. 1, *Pretty v UK* and see Chapter 14 below at pp.1001–1014). Recent attempts to introduce legislation to change the law on this issue have been unsuccessful, although at the time of writing Lord Joffee's Assisted Dying Bill is still ongoing. There is also no automatic right "to live" in that patients cannot demand access to whatever medical resources they wish (see further Chapter 1 above at pp.51–68 and also *R (Burke) v GMC* [2005] EWCA 1003, Chapter 14 below at pp.1000–1071).

Difficulties arise if it is sought to withdraw treatment from a patient lacking mental capacity. This dilemma is particularly acute when the patient is being sustained through the provision of nutrition and hydration through artificial means. The medical profession have for many years expressed adherence to the principle set out in Arthur Hough's satirical piece "The Latest Decalogue": "thou shalt not kill but needst not strive officiously to keep alive". The courts have affirmed their support for the sanctity of life. Yet some commentators are of the view that in many situations there is a very fine line between the withdrawal of treatment resulting in death and taking active steps to bring a patient's life to an end (see Chapter 2). Over a number of years the courts have shown themselves willing to sanction courses of non-active treatment , initially in a series of cases concerning new-born infants with severe handicaps and subsequently in relation to adult patients in a persistent vegetative state, that is to say those lacking cognitive functions. In *Airedale NHS Trust v Bland* [1993] 1 All E.R. 821, the House of Lords authorised the withdrawal of artificial nutrition and hydration from Tony Bland who had been injured during the disaster at Hillsborough Football ground and left in a persistent vegetative state. The courts confirmed that such decisions were to be made on the basis of the individual's "best interests". Consistent with the decision in *F v West Berkshire Health Authority* [1989] 2 All

E.R. 545, which we examined in Chapter 5 above "best interests" is to be determined with reference to what a responsible body of professional practice would deem to be in a patient's best interests. The approach in *Bland* has been subsequently confirmed to be in line with the Human Rights Act 1998 (*NHS Trust A v M, NHS Trust B v H* [2000] 2 F.L.R. 348). Difficulties in decision-making regarding treatment withdrawal may also revolve around problems of diagnosis. More recently questions have been raised as to the conclusiveness of the diagnosis of patients in a persistent vegetative state. The courts are likely to be faced with decisions relating to whether treatment should be continued on the basis that the patient's quality of life is likely to be poor.

Decision-making in this area will be affected by the Mental Capacity Act 2005 when it comes into force in spring 2007. This provides for advance decisions—more commonly known as advance directives—to be placed upon a statutory basis. Individuals will be also able to appoint a person to have a lasting power of attorney to make treatment decisions on their behalf if they lack mental capacity (see Chapter 14 below at pp.1078–1082).

The individual may have the right to control treatment decisions with regard to his body during his lifetime, but how much autonomy does he have to determine use of material removed from his body during his lifetime or after his death? Such material may be of vital importance for clinical purposes for transplantation or for researchers attempting to develop new treatments for illness and greater understanding of the manner in which disease progresses in the body. Yet individuals may object to the use of their human material in such a way, perhaps because they have religious and cultural objections to certain procedures or indeed to certain types of clinical research. At one extreme it could be argued that a patient has no rights, claims or interests over his excised material. So, for example, it could be argued that in the context of removal of material from the dead that the dead have no continuing interests. Such an approach would allow an individual's organs (where clinically suitable) to be routinely salvaged and used for transplantation and other material be used for research purposes. At the other extreme it can be argued that the human material excised from the patient is the patient's property and to use that material without the consent of the patient constitutes unauthorised dealing in their property which should be actionable in the tort of conversion (see, for example, *Moore v University of California* 793 Pd 479 (Cal 1990) and Chapter 15 below at pp.1112–1121).

The law in this area has been subject to radical reform following major controversy concerning unauthorised retention of human material leading to inquries, including that at the Royal Liverpool Children's Hospital at Alder Hey (M. Redfern, *Report of the Inquiry into the Royal Liverpool Children's Hospital*, (Alder Hey), 2001 *http://www.rclinquiry.org.uk*. This led ultimately to the passage of the Human Tissue Act 2004, a wide-ranging piece of legislation governing the use of human material from cadaver and live subjects. This Act is considered at length in Chapter 15. It is predicated upon the principle of "appropriate consent", although as can be seen in that chapter the consent principle is not regarded as absolute in nature and the Act recognises a number of exceptions which may yet prove controversial.

This part of the book ends with a case study examining the propects of increasing the supply of organs for transplantation through the use of legislative reform. The shortage of organs for transplantation has led to a number of proposals to increase the supply, from legislative reform to the development of new scientific techniques such as the use of organs transplanted from animals. As with many such technologies, the efficacy of transplantation has been questioned not least in the light of the costs entailed. In addition, as we noted earlier in this book, treatment options may be influenced by personal ethical and religious beliefs and this is particularly the case in relation to organ transplantation where mutiliation of the body after death has met with some opposition.

14

END OF LIFE

1. Introduction

In 1993 the House of Lords was asked to make a declaration approving the withdrawal of artificial feeding from Tony Bland, a young man who was in a persistent vegetative state resulting from injuries sustained in the Hillsborough Football Stadium disaster. A year before, Dr Cox had stood trial for murder of an elderly female patient. The woman, who had pleaded with him to put her out of her misery, was suffering from rheumatoid arthritis, gastric ulcers and body sores and was in great pain. He eventually gave her a lethal dose of potassium chloride. In 2001 Dianne Pretty, a woman terminally ill with motor neurone disease, was refused a guarantee that if her husband assisted in ending her life he would not be prosecuted for assisted suicide. In the same year Ms B died following the court upholding her decision to have the ventilator which was sustaining her life switched off. These four cases illustrate some of the most difficult dilemmas in health care practice. Medical technology enables life to be prolonged, but at what point should such treatment cease? Is it ever justifiable to take steps to deliberately end a person's life on their request? English law has never sanctioned "mercy killing" and yet a patient may be given a high dosage of pain-killing drugs even if the incidental effect is that the patient's death is hastened. An individual patient may bring their own life to an end, suicide is not a crime, yet patient autonomy here does not extend to a competent patient being allowed assistance in dying.

This chapter examines English law as it regulates decisions at the end of life. In Section 2, the position in criminal law is considered. At present deliberate termination of the life of the patient is likely to result in a prosecution for murder. The courts have nevertheless recognised that it may in some situations be legitimate to withhold treatment or to take the decision not to recommence therapy. Judicial approaches to making such orders are considered in Section 3. The final section of the chapter concerns the proposals advanced for reform of the present position and new measures introduced in the Mental Capacity Act 2005 are considered. These include the recognition of active euthanasia, the reform of the grounds on which treatment may be withdrawn and the enactment of legislation governing living wills or recognition of proxy decision-makers for the mentally incompetent.

2. ENDING THE LIFE OF A PATIENT: CRIMINAL LAW

(a) Suicide

Until relatively recently English law did not recognise a right to suicide. For a person to take their own life was a criminal offence. This position was changed by s.1 of the Suicide Act 1961 which legalised suicide. Nevertheless, the 1961 Act provides that assistance in suicide is a criminal offence.

Suicide Act 1961, ss.1, 2(1)–(2)

1.—The rule of law whereby it is a crime for a person to commit suicide is hereby abrogated.

2.—(1) A person who aids, abets, counsels or procures the suicide of another, or an attempt by another to commit suicide, shall be liable on conviction on indictment to imprisonment for a term not exceeding fourteen years . . .

(2) If on the trial on an indictment for murder or manslaughter it is proved that the accused aided, abetted, counselled or procured the suicide of the person the jury may find him guilty of that offence.

NOTES:

1. Persons who have assisted in ending the life of a terminally ill relative have been prosecuted under this section. In the case of *R v Beecham* (1988) the defendant assisted the suicide of his daughter who was suffering from cancer, multiple sclerosis and persistent severe pain. The daughter had previously made two suicide attempts. The defendant was convicted of aiding and abetting suicide. The judge gave him a suspended prison sentence of 12 months (see D. Meyer, *The Human Body and the Law* (2nd edn), Edinburgh: Edinburgh University Press, 1990 at p.285).

2. In *Re Z* [2004] EWHC 2817, Z, who was suffering from an incurable condition, cerebella axtia, wished to end her life in Switzerland. Her husband told the local authority who had been involved in her care of the intention to travel abroad to end her life. The local authority sought to stop Z from travelling to Switzerland. Hedley J. rejected the claim. Here the obligation of the local authority extended to informing the criminal authorities, which had been done in the case, but did not extend beyond this. He was of the view that civil law proceedings were inappropriate in this case. He also stated that section 1 of the Suicide Act 1961 removed suicide as a punishable act and thus "our law does not penalise the decision of a competent person to take their own life. Moreover nor does the law prohibit them from doing so." (See further P. de Cruz, "The Terminally Ill Adult Seeking Assisted Suicide Abroad: The Extent of Duty Owed by a Local Authority" (1995), 13 *Medical Law Review* 257.)

(i) What Constitutes Aiding and Abetting Suicide?

Att.-Gen. v Able [1984] 1 All E.R. 277; [1984] Q.B. 795

The defendants were members of the Voluntary Euthanasia Society. They published a booklet entitled *A Guide to Self Deliverance* to be distributed to members of the society, subject to certain qualifications. The booklet was supplied on payment of a fee and only to members of the society who were 25 and over and who had been members for at least three months. The booklet set out five different ways in which suicide could be committed. There was evidence that in the 18 months after the booklet had been first distributed 15 suicide cases were linked to it. In a further 19 documents had been found which indicated that the deceased was a member, or had corresponded with, the society. The Attorney-General sought for a declaration that future supply of the booklet constituted an offence under s.2(1) of the 1961 Act.

WOOLF J.
" . . . The fact that the supply of the booklet could be an offence does not mean that any particular supply is an offence. It must be remembered that the society is an unincorporated body and there can be no question of the society committing an offence. Before an offence under s.2 can be proved, it must be shown that the individual concerned 'aided, abetted, counselled or procured' an attempt at suicide or a suicide and intended to do so by distributing the booklet. The intention of the individual will normally have to be inferred from facts surrounding the particular supply which he made. If, for example, before sending a copy of the booklet, a member of the society had written a letter, the contents of which were known to the person sending the booklet, which stated that the booklet was required because the member was intending to commit suicide, then, on those facts, I would conclude that an offence had been committed or at least an attempted offence contrary to s.2 of the 1961 Act. However, in the majority of cases, a member requesting the booklet will not make clear his intentions and the supply will be made without knowledge of whether the booklet is required for purposes of research, general information, or because suicide is contemplated. Is it, therefore, enough that in any particular case the person responsible for making the supply would appreciate that there is a real likelihood that the booklet is required by one of the substantial number of members of the society who will be contemplating suicide? It is as to this aspect of the case that there is the greatest difficulty and little assistance from the authorities.

Counsel on behalf of the respondents contends that before a person can be an accessory, there must be a consensus between the accessory and the principal, and there can be no consensus where the alleged accessory does not even know whether the principal is contemplating (in this case) suicide. As, however, is pointed out in Smith & Hogan *Criminal Law* (4th edn. 1978), while counselling implies consensus, procuring and aiding do not. The authors say (p.116):

'the law probably is that: (i) "Procuring" implies causation "but not consensus" (ii) "abetting" and "counselling" imply consensus but not causation and (iii) "aiding" requires actual assistance but neither consensus nor causation.'

As a matter of principle, it seems to me that as long as there is the necessary intent to assist those who are contemplating suicide to commit suicide if they decide to do so, it does not matter that the supplier does not know the state of mind of the actual recipient. The requirement for the necessary intent explains why in those cases where, in the ordinary course of business a person is responsible for distributing an article, appreciating that some individuals might use it for committing suicide, he is not guilty of an offence. In the ordinary way such a distributor would have no intention to assist the act of suicide. An intention to assist need not however, involve a desire that suicide should be committed or attempted.

In this connection, I must refer to *R v. Fretwell* (1862) 9 Cox C.C. 152. In that case the Court of Criminal Appeal decided that the mere provision of the means of committing a crime is not sufficient to make the provider guilty as an accessory. In giving the judgment of the court, Erle C.J. (said, at p.154):

'In the present case the prisoner was unwilling that the deceased should take the poison; it was at her instigation and under the threat of self-destruction that he procured it and supplied it to her; but was found that he did not administer it to her or cause her to take it. It would be consistent with the facts of the case that he hoped she would change her mind; and it might well be that the prisoner hoped and expected that she would not resort to it.'

While I accept that this reasoning does not accord with mine. I do not regard the case as requiring me to come to a different conclusion from that which I have indicated. That case is inconsistent with *National Coal Board v. Gamble* [1958] 3 All E.R. 203, and I regard it as confined to its own facts, for the reasons indicated in Smith & Hogan, *Criminal Law* (4th edn, 1978 pp.120, 121). Counsel for the respondents points out, and this I accept that in some cases the booklet, far from precipitating someone to commit suicide might have the effect of deterring someone from committing suicide when they might otherwise have done so. In such circumstances, he submits it would be quite nonsensical to regard the supply of the booklet as being an attempted offence contrary to s.2 of the 1961 Act. I agree, though I recognise that on one approach the result would be different. The reason why I agree with the submission is because, in such a case, the booklet has not provided any assistance with a view to a contemplated suicide. Such assistance is necessary to establish the actus reus for even the attempted offence.

There will also be cases where, although the recipient commits or attempts to commit suicide, the booklet has nothing to do with the suicide or the attempted suicide; for example, a long period of time may have elapsed between the sending of the booklet and the attempt. In such a case, again, I would agree with counsel for the respondents that there would not be a sufficient connection between the attempted suicide and the supply of the booklet to make the supplier responsible. This does not mean that it has to be shown that the suicide or attempted suicide would not have occurred but for the booklet. However, if 'procuring' alone is relied upon, this may be the case. As Lord Widgery C.J. stated in *Attorney-General's Reference (No. 1 of 1975)* [1975] 2 All E.R. 684 at 686–687:

'To procure means to produce by endeavour. You procure a thing by setting out to see that it happens and taking the appropriate steps to produce that happening. You cannot procure an offence unless there is a causal link between what you do and the commission of the offence.'

However, you do not need to procure to be an accessory and the same close causal connection is not required when what is being done is the provision of assistance.

I therefore conclude that to distribute the booklet can be an offence. But, before an offence can be established to have been committed, it must at least be proved: (a) that the alleged offender had the necessary intent, that is, he intended the booklet to be used by someone contemplating suicide and intended that person would be assisted by the booklet's contents, or otherwise encouraged to attempt to take or to take his own life; (b) that while he still had that intention he distributed the booklet to such a person who read it; and, (c) in addition, if an offence under s.2 is to be proved, that such a person was assisted or encouraged by so reading the booklet to attempt to take or to take his own life, otherwise the alleged offender cannot be guilty of more than an attempt.

If these facts can be proved, then it does not make any difference that the person would have tried to commit suicide anyway. Nor does it make any difference, as the respondents contend, that the information contained in the booklet is already in the public domain. The distinguishing feature between an innocent and guilty distribution is that in the former case the distributor will not have the necessary intent, while in the latter case he will.

However, in each case it will be for a jury to decide whether the necessary facts are proved. If they are, then normally the offence will be made out. Nevertheless, even if they are proved, I am not prepared to say it is not possible for there to be some exceptional circumstance which means that an offence is not established."

NOTES:

1. This action took the form of an action for a declaration by the Attorney-General to clarify the law in this area (see J. Bridgeman, "Declared Innocent" (1993) 1 *Medical Law Review* 117).
2. Assisting in suicide may also be charged as attempted murder. For example, see *R v Hough* (1984) 6 Cr.App.R.(S) 404 where the defendant pleaded guilty to attempted murder after she had assisted an elderly woman who was blind and deaf to commit suicide.

QUESTION:

1. What is meant by "almost certainly know that a significant number of those to whom the booklet would be sent would be contemplating suicide"? (See K.J.M. Smith, "Assisting in Suicide—The Attorney-General and the Voluntary Euthanasia Society" [1983] Crim.L.R. 579.)

(ii) Assisted Suicide and the Human Rights Act 1998

The statutory prohibition on assisted suicide came under challenge in the first major case concerning end of life decision-making to be litigated under the Human Rights Act 1998.

R (on the application of Pretty) v DPP [2001] UKHL 61; [2002] 1 All E.R. 1; [2002] 1 FCR 1

Mrs Dianne Pretty was 42 years old and suffered from a degenerative condition, motor neurone disease. She was confined to a wheelchair and was paralysed from the waist down. Unable to take her own life she asked the DPP for an assurance that if her husband assisted her to die he would not be prosecuted. The DPP refused to provide this assurance. She challenged the DPP's decision and also argued that s.2 (1) of the Suicide Act 1961 infringed the ECHR as incorporated in the Human Rights Act 1998. The action was rejected at first instance in the Divisional Court. On appeal to the House of Lords, three issues were raised, first, did the DPP have the power to undertake not to prosecute in advance of a proposed assistance in suicide? Secondly, if he did have that power, taking into account Articles 2, 3, 8, 9 and 14 of the ECHR, was he required not to prosecute? Thirdly, if not, was s.2(1) of the Suicide Act 1961 incompatible with Articles 2, 3, 8, 9 and 14 of the ECHR?

LORD BINGHAM

His Lordship began by considering Article 2 of the Convention, the right to life.

"On behalf of Mrs Pretty it is submitted that article 2 protects not life itself but the right to life. The purpose of the article is to protect individuals from third parties (the state and public authorities). But the article recognises that it is for the individual to choose whether or not to live and so protects the individual's right to self-determination in relation to issues of life and death. Thus a person may refuse life-saving or life- prolonging medical treatment, and may lawfully choose to commit suicide. The article acknowledges that right of the individual. While most people want to live, some want to die, and the article protects both rights. The right to die is not the antithesis of the right to life but the corollary of it, and the state has a positive obligation to protect both.

The Secretary of State has advanced a number of unanswerable objections to this argument which were rightly upheld by the Divisional Court. The starting point must be the language of the article. The thrust of this is to reflect the sanctity which, particularly in western eyes, attaches to life. The article protects the right to life and prevents the deliberate taking of life save in very narrowly defined circumstances. An article with that effect cannot be interpreted as conferring a right to die or to enlist the aid of another in bringing about one's own death. In his argument for Mrs Pretty, Mr Havers was at pains to limit his argument to assisted suicide, accepting that the right claimed could not extend to cover an intentional consensual killing (usually described in this context as 'voluntary euthanasia', but regarded in English law as murder). The right claimed would be sufficient to cover Mrs Pretty's case and counsel's unwillingness to go further is understandable. But there is in logic no justification for drawing a line at this point. If article 2 does confer a right to self-determination in relation to life and death, and if a person were so gravely disabled as to be unable to perform any act whatever to cause his or her own death, it would necessarily follow in logic that such a person would have a right to be killed at the hands of a third party without giving any help to the third party and the state would be in breach of the Convention if it were to interfere with the exercise of that right. No such right can possibly be derived from an article having the object already defined.

It is true that some of the guaranteed Convention rights have been interpreted as conferring rights not to do that which is the antithesis of what there is an express right to do. Article 11, for example, confers a right not to join an association (*Young, James and Webster v UK* (1981) 4 EHRR 38, article 9 embraces a right to freedom from any compulsion to express thoughts or change an opinion or divulge convictions (*Clayton & Tomlinson, The Law of Human Rights* (2000), p 974, para 14.49) and I would for my part be inclined to infer that article 12 confers a right not to marry (but see Clayton & Tomlinson, p 913, para 13.76). It cannot however be suggested (to take some obvious examples) that articles 3, 4, 5 and 6 confer an implied right to do or experience the opposite of that which the articles guarantee. Whatever the benefits which, in the view of many, attach to voluntary euthanasia, suicide, physician-assisted suicide and suicide assisted without the intervention of a physician, these are not benefits which derive protection from an article framed to protect the sanctity of life.

There is no Convention authority to support Mrs Pretty's argument. To the extent that there is any relevant authority it is adverse to her.

In *Osman v UK* (1998) 29 BHRC 293 the applicants complained of a failure by the United Kingdom to protect the right to life of the second applicant and his deceased father. At p 305 the court said:

'115. The court notes that the first sentence of article 2(1) enjoins the state not only to refrain from the intentional and unlawful taking of life, but also to take appropriate steps to safeguard the lives of those within its jurisdiction. It is common ground that the state's obligation in this respect extends beyond its primary duty to secure the right to life by putting in place effective criminal law provisions to deter the commission of offences against the person backed up by law-enforcement machinery for the prevention, suppression and sanctioning of breaches of such provisions. It is thus accepted by those appearing before the court that article 2 of the Convention may also imply in certain well-defined circumstances a positive obligation on the authorities to take preventive operational measures to protect an individual whose life is at risk from the criminal acts of another individual. The scope of this obligation is a matter of dispute between the parties.

116. For the court, and bearing in mind the difficulties involved in policing modern societies, the unpredictability of human conduct and the operational choices which must be made in terms of priorities and resources, such an obligation must be interpreted in a way which does not impose an impossible or disproportionate burden on the authorities. Accordingly, not every claimed risk to life can entail for the authorities a Convention requirement to take operational measures to prevent that risk from materialising. Another relevant consideration is the need to ensure that the police exercise their powers to control and prevent crime in a manner which fully respects the due process and other guarantees which legitimately place restraints on the scope of their action to investigate crime and bring offenders to justice, including the guarantees contained in articles 5 and 8 of the Convention.'

The context of that case was very different. Neither the second applicant nor his father had had any wish to die. But the court's approach to article 2 was entirely consistent with the interpretation I have put upon it . . .

In the Convention field the authority of domestic decisions is necessarily limited and, as already noted, Mrs Pretty bases her case on the Convention. But it is worthy of note that her argument is inconsistent with two principles deeply embedded in English law. The first is a distinction between the taking of one's own life by one's own act and the taking of life through the intervention or with the help of a third party. The former has been permissible since suicide ceased to be a crime in 1961. The latter has continued to be proscribed. The distinction was very clearly expressed by Hoffmann LJ in *Airedale NHS Trust v Bland* (1993) AC 789 at, 831:

'No one in this case is suggesting that Anthony Bland should be given a lethal injection. But there is concern about ceasing to supply food as against, for example, ceasing to treat an infection with antibiotics. Is there any real distinction? In order to come to terms with our intuitive feelings about whether there is a distinction, I must start by considering why most of us would be appalled if he was given a lethal injection. It is, I think, connected with our view that the sanctity of life entails its inviolability by an outsider. Subject to exceptions like self-defence, human life is inviolate even if the person in question has consented to its violation. That is why although suicide is not a crime, assisting someone to commit suicide is. It follows that, even if we think Anthony Bland would have consented, we would not be entitled to end his life by a lethal injection.'

The second distinction is between the cessation of life-saving or life-prolonging treatment on the one hand and the taking of action lacking medical, therapeutic or palliative justification but intended solely to terminate life on the other . . . It was very succinctly expressed in the Court of Appeal in *Re J (a minor) wardship medical treatment* [1990] 3 All ER 930, (1991) Fam 33, in which Lord Donaldson of Lymington MR said, at p 46:

'What doctors and the court have to decide is whether, in the best interests of the child patient, a particular decision as to medical treatment should be taken which *as a side effect* will render death more or less likely. This is not a matter of semantics. It is fundamental. At the other end of the age spectrum, the use of drugs to reduce pain will often be fully justified, notwithstanding that this will hasten the moment of death. What can never be justified is the use of drugs or surgical procedures with the primary purpose of doing so.' (see [1990] 3 All ER 930 at 938, [1991] Fam 33 at 46).

Similar observations were made by Balcombe LJ, at p 51, and Taylor LJ, at p 53. While these distinctions are in no way binding on the European Court of Human Rights there is nothing to suggest that they are inconsistent with the jurisprudence which has grown up around the Convention. It is not enough for Mrs Pretty to show that the United Kingdom would not be acting inconsistently with the Convention if it were to permit assisted suicide; she must go further and establish that the United Kingdom is in breach of the Convention by failing to permit it or would be in breach of the Convention if it did not permit it. Such a contention is in my opinion untenable, as the Divisional Court rightly held.

Article 3 of the Convention

Article 3 of the Convention provides:

Prohibition of torture

'No one shall be subjected to torture or to inhuman or degrading treatment or punishment.'

This is one of the articles from which a member state may not derogate even in time of war or other public emergency threatening the life of the nation: see article 15. I shall for convenience use the expression 'proscribed treatment' to mean 'inhuman or degrading treatment' as that expression is used in the Convention.

In brief summary the argument for Mrs Pretty proceeded by these steps. (1) Member states have an absolute and unqualified obligation not to inflict the proscribed treatment and also to take positive action to prevent the subjection of individuals to such treatment (*A v UK* (1998) 27 EHRR 611: *Z v UK* [2001] 2 FCR 264 at 265). (2) Suffering attributable to the progression of a disease may amount to such treatment if the state can prevent or ameliorate such suffering and does not do so: *D v UK* (1997) 2 BHRC 273 at 283 (para 47),(3) In denying Mrs Pretty the opportunity to bring her suffering to an end the United Kingdom (by the Director) will subject her to the proscribed treatment. The state can spare Mrs Pretty the suffering which she will otherwise endure since, if the Director undertakes not to give his consent to prosecution, Mr Pretty will assist his wife to commit suicide and so she will be spared much suffering. (4) Since, as the Divisional Court held, it is open to the United Kingdom under the Convention to refrain from prohibiting assisted suicide, the Director can give the undertaking sought without breaking the United Kingdom's obligations under the Convention. (5) If the Director may not give the undertaking, s1(2) of the 1961 Act is incompatible with the Convention.

For the Secretary of State it was submitted that in the present case article 3 of the Convention is not engaged at all but that if any of the rights protected by that article are engaged they do not include a right to die. In support of the first of these submissions it was argued that there is in the present case no breach of the prohibition in the article. The negative prohibition in the article is absolute and unqualified but the positive obligations which flow from it are not absolute: (see *Osman v UK* (1998) 5 BHRC 293, *Rees v UK* (1986) 9 EHRR 56). While states may be obliged to protect the life and health of a person in custody (as in the case of *Keenan v UK*), and to ensure that individuals are not subjected to proscribed treatment at the hands of private individuals other than state agents . . . , and the state may not take direct action in relation to an individual which would inevitably involve the inflicting of proscribed treatment upon him (in *D v UK* (1997) 24 EHRR 423), none of these obligations can be invoked by Mrs Pretty in the present case. In support of the second submission it was argued that, far from suggesting that the state is under a duty to provide medical care to ease her condition and prolong her life, Mrs Pretty is arguing that the state is under a legal obligation to sanction a lawful means for terminating her life. There is nothing, either in the wording of the Convention or the Strasbourg jurisprudence, to suggest that any such duty exists by virtue of article 3. The decision how far the state should go in discharge of its positive obligation to protect individuals from proscribed treatment is one for member states, taking account of all relevant interests and considerations; such a decision, while not immune from review, must be accorded respect. The United Kingdom has reviewed these issues in depth and resolved to maintain the present position.

Article 3 enshrines one of the fundamental values of democratic societies and its prohibition of the proscribed treatment is absolute: *D v UK* (1997) 2 BHRC at 283. Article 3 is, as I think, complementary to article 2. As article 2 requires states to respect and safeguard the lives of individuals within their jurisdiction, so article 3 obliges them to respect the physical and human integrity of such individuals. There is in my opinion nothing in article 3 which bears on an individual's right to live or to choose not to live. That is not its sphere of application; indeed, as is clear from *X v Germany* above, a state may on occasion be justified in inflicting treatment which would otherwise be in breach of article 3 in order to serve the ends of article 2. Moreover, the absolute and unqualified prohibition on a member state inflicting the proscribed treatment requires that 'treatment' should not be given an unrestricted or extravagant meaning. It cannot, in my opinion, be plausibly suggested that the Director or any other agent of the United Kingdom is inflicting the proscribed treatment on Mrs Pretty, whose suffering derives from her cruel disease.

The authority most helpful to Mrs Pretty is *D v UK*, which concerned the removal to St Kitts of a man in the later stages of AIDS. The Convention challenge was to implementation of the removal decision having regard to the applicant's medical condition, the absence of facilities to provide adequate treatment, care or support in St Kitts and the disruption of a regime in the United Kingdom which had afforded him sophisticated treatment and medication in a compassionate environment. It was held that implementation of the decision to remove the applicant to St Kitts would amount in the circumstances to inhuman treatment by the United Kingdom in violation of article 3. In that case the state was proposing to take direct action against the applicant, the inevitable effect of which would be a severe increase in his suffering and a shortening of his life. The proposed deportation could fairly be regarded as 'treatment'. An analogy might be found in the present case if a public official had forbidden the provision to Mrs Pretty of pain-killing or palliative drugs. But here the proscribed treatment is said to be the Director's refusal of proleptic immunity from prosecution to Mr Pretty if he commits a crime. By no legitimate process of interpretation can that refusal be held to fall within the negative prohibition of article 3.

If it be assumed that article 3 is capable of being applied at all to a case such as the present, and also that on the facts there is no arguable breach of the negative prohibition in the article, the question arises whether the United Kingdom (by the Director) is in breach of its positive obligation to take action to prevent the subjection of individuals to proscribed treatment. In this context, the obligation of the state is not absolute and unqualified."

Lord Bingham considered *Osman v UK* and *Rees v UK* (1986) 9 EHRR 56 at pp.63–64 before continuing:

" . . . It stands to reason that while states may be absolutely forbidden to inflict the proscribed treatment on individuals within their jurisdictions, the steps appropriate or necessary to discharge a positive obligation will be more judgmental, more prone to variation from state to state, more dependent on the opinions and beliefs of the people and less susceptible to any universal injunction. For reasons more fully given . . . below, it could not in my view be said that the United Kingdom is under a positive obligation to ensure that a competent, terminally ill, person who wishes but is unable to take his or her own life should be entitled to seek the assistance of another without that other being exposed to the risk of prosecution.

Article 8 of the Convention

Counsel for Mrs Pretty submitted that this article conferred a right to self-determination: (see: *X v Netherlands* (1985) 8 EHRR 235. *Rodriguez v Attorney General of Canada* [1994] 2 LRC 136; *Re A (conjoined twins)* [2000] 4 All ER 961). This right embraces a right to choose when and how to die so that suffering and indignity can be avoided. S1(2) of the 1961 Act interferes with this right of self-determination: it is therefore for the United

Kingdom to show that the interference meets the Convention tests of legality, necessity, responsiveness to pressing social need and proportionality: (see *R v A* (No 2) [2001] UKHL 25; *R(Q) v Secretary of State for the Home Department* [2001] EWCA 1151 Civ). Where the interference is with an intimate part of an individual's private life, there must be particularly serious reasons to justify the interference. . . . The court must in this case rule whether it could be other than disproportionate for the Director to refuse to give the undertaking sought and, in the case of the Secretary of State, whether the interference with Mrs Pretty's right to self-determination is proportionate to whatever legitimate aim the prohibition on assisted suicide pursues. Counsel placed particular reliance on certain features of Mrs Pretty's case: her mental competence, the frightening prospect which faces her, her willingness to commit suicide if she were able, the imminence of death, the absence of harm to anyone else, the absence of far-reaching implications if her application were granted. Counsel suggested that the blanket prohibition in section 2(1), applied without taking account of particular cases, is wholly disproportionate, and the materials relied on do not justify it . . .

The Secretary of State questioned whether Mrs Pretty's rights under article 8 were engaged at all, and gave a negative answer. He submitted that the right to private life under article 8 relates to the manner in which a person conducts his life, not the manner in which he departs from it. Any attempt to base a right to die on article 8 founders on exactly the same objection as the attempt based on article 2, namely, that the alleged right would extinguish the very benefit on which it is supposedly based. Article 8 protects the physical, moral and psychological integrity of the individual, including rights over the individual's own body, but there is nothing to suggest that it confers a right to decide when or how to die. The Secretary of State also submitted that, if it were necessary to do so, section 2(1) of the 1961 Act and the current application of it could be fully justified on the merits. He referred to the margin of judgment accorded to member states, the consideration which has been given to these questions in the United Kingdom and the broad consensus among Convention countries. Attention was drawn to *Laskey v UK* (1997) 24 EHRR 39 in which the criminalisation of consensual acts of injury was held to be justified; it was suggested that the justification for criminalising acts of consensual killing or assisted suicide must be even stronger . . .

There is no Strasbourg jurisprudence to support the contention of Mrs Pretty. In *R v United Kingdom* 33 DR 270 the applicant had been convicted and sentenced to imprisonment for aiding and abetting suicide and conspiring to do so. He complained that his conviction and sentence under s1(2) of the 1961 Act constituted a violation of his right to respect for his private life under article 8 and also his right to free expression under article 10. In para 13 of its decision the Commission observed:

'The Commission does not consider that the activity for which the applicant was convicted, namely aiding and abetting suicide, can be described as falling into the sphere of his private life in the manner elaborated above. While it might be thought to touch directly on the private lives of those who sought to commit suicide, it does not follow that the applicant's rights to privacy are involved. On the contrary, the Commission is of the opinion that the acts of aiding, abetting, counselling or procuring suicide are excluded from the concept of privacy by virtue of their trespass on the public interest of protecting life, as reflected in the criminal provisions of the 1961 Act.'

This somewhat tentative expression of view is of some assistance to Mrs Pretty, but with reference to the claim under article 10 the Commission continued, in para 17 of its decision, at p 272:

'The Commission considers that, in the circumstances of the case, there has been an interference with the applicant's right to impart information. However, the Commission must take account of the state's legitimate interest in this area in taking measures to protect, against criminal behaviour, the life of its citizens particularly those who belong to especially vulnerable categories by reason of their age or infirmity. It recognises the right of the state under the Convention to guard against the inevitable criminal abuses that would occur, in the absence of legislation, against the aiding and abetting of suicide. The fact that in the present case the applicant and his associate appear to have been well intentioned does not, in the Commission's view, alter the justification for the general policy.'

That conclusion cannot be reconciled with the suggestion that the prohibition of assisted suicide is inconsistent with the Convention . . .

I would for my part accept the Secretary of State's submission that Mrs Pretty's rights under article 8 are not engaged at all. If, however, that conclusion is wrong, and the prohibition of assisted suicide in s2(1) of the 1961 Act infringes her Convention right under article 8, it is necessary to consider whether the infringement is shown by the Secretary of State to be justifiable under the terms of article 8(2). In considering that question I would adopt the test advocated by counsel for Mrs Pretty, which is clearly laid down in the authorities cited."

Lord Bingham noted that the issue as to whether assisted suicide should be decriminalised had been reviewed several times since 1961 and then continued:

"It would be by no means fatal to the legal validity of section 2(1) of the 1961 Act if the response of the United Kingdom to this problem of assisted suicide were shown to be unique, but it is shown to be in accordance with a very broad international consensus. Assisted suicide and consensual killing are unlawful in all Convention countries except the Netherlands, but even if the Dutch Termination of Life on Request and Assisted Suicide (Review Procedures) Act 2001 and the Dutch Criminal Code were operative in this country it would not relieve Mr Pretty of liability under article 294 of the Dutch Criminal Code if he were to assist Mrs Pretty to take her own life as he would wish to do.

On behalf of Mrs Pretty counsel disclaims any general attack on section 2(1) of the 1961 Act and seeks to restrict his claim to the particular facts of her case: that of a mentally competent adult who knows her own mind, is free from any pressure and has made a fully-informed and voluntary decision. Whatever the need, he submits, to afford legal protection to the vulnerable, there is no justification for a blanket refusal to countenance an act of humanity in the case of someone who, like Mrs Pretty, is not vulnerable at all. Beguiling as that submission is, Dr Johnson gave two answers of enduring validity to it. First, 'Laws are not made for particular cases but for men in general.' Second, 'To permit a law to be modified at discretion is to leave the community without law. It is to withdraw the direction of that public wisdom by which the deficiencies of private understanding are to be supplied' (*Boswell, Life of Johnson,* Oxford Standard Authors, 3rd ed (1970), pp 735, 496). It is for member states to assess the risk and likely incidence of abuse if the prohibition on assisted suicide were relaxed, as the Commission recognised in its decision in *R v United Kingdom* 33 DR 270 quoted above in paragraph 24. But the risk is one which cannot be lightly discounted. The Criminal Law Revision Committee recognised how fine was the line between counselling and procuring on the one hand and aiding and abetting on the other (report, p 61, para 135). The House of Lords Select Committee recognised the undesirability of anything which could appear to encourage suicide (report, p 49, para 239):

'We are also concerned that vulnerable people—the elderly, lonely, sick or distressed— would feel pressure, whether real or imagined, to request early death. We accept that, for the most part, requests resulting from such pressure or from remediable depressive illness would be identified as such by doctors and managed appropriately. Nevertheless we believe that the message which society sends to vulnerable and disadvantaged people should not, however obliquely, encourage them to seek death, but should assure them of our care and support in life.'

It is not hard to imagine that an elderly person, in the absence of any pressure, might opt for a premature end to life if that were available, not from a desire to die or a willingness to stop living, but from a desire to stop being a burden to others.

If section 2(1) infringes any Convention right of Mrs Pretty, and recognising the heavy burden which lies on a member state seeking to justify such an infringement, I conclude that the Secretary of State has shown ample grounds to justify the existing law and the current application of it. That is not to say that no other law or application would be consistent with the Convention; it is simply to say that the present legislative and practical regime do not offend the Convention.

Article 9 of the Convention

It is unnecessary to recite the terms of article 9 of the Convention, to which very little argument was addressed. It is an article which protects freedom of thought, conscience and religion and the manifestation of religion or belief in worship, teaching, practice or observance. One may accept that Mrs Pretty has a sincere belief in the virtue of assisted suicide. She is free to hold and express that belief. But her belief cannot found a requirement that her husband should be absolved from the consequences of conduct which, although it would be consistent with her belief, is proscribed by the criminal law. And if she were able to establish an infringement of her right, the justification shown by the state in relation to article 8 would still defeat it.

Article 14 of the Convention

Mrs Pretty claims that s2(1) of the 1961 Act discriminates against those who, like herself, cannot because of incapacity take their own lives without assistance. She relies on the judgment of the European Court of Human Rights in *Thlimmenos v Greece* (2000) 31 EHRR 411 BHRC where the court said:

'The court has so far considered that the right under article 14 not to be discriminated against in the enjoyment of the rights guaranteed under the Convention is violated when states treat differently persons in analogous situations without providing an objective and reasonable justification. However, the court considers that this is not the only facet of the prohibition of discrimination in article 14. The right not to be discriminated against in the enjoyment of the rights guaranteed under the Convention is also violated when states without an objective and reasonable justification fail to treat differently persons whose situations are significantly different.'

The European Court of Human Rights has repeatedly held that article 14 is not autonomous but has effect only in relation to Convention rights. As it was put in *Van Raalte v Netherlands* (1997) 24 EHRR 507, 516, para 33:

'As the court has consistently held, article 14 of the Convention complements the other substantive provisions of the Convention and the Protocols. It has no independent existence since it has effect solely in relation to "the enjoyment of the rights and freedoms" safeguarded by those provisions. Although the application of article 14 does not presuppose a breach of those provisions—and to this extent it is autonomous—there can be no room for its application unless the facts at issue fall within the ambit of one or more of the latter.'

If, as I have concluded, none of the articles on which Mrs Pretty relies gives her the right which she has claimed, it follows that article 14 would not avail her even if she could establish that the operation of it is discriminatory. A claim under this article must fail on this ground.

If, contrary to my opinion, Mrs Pretty's rights under one or other of the articles are engaged, it would be necessary to examine whether section 2(1) of the 1961 Act is discriminatory. She contends that the section is discriminatory because it prevents the disabled, but not the able-bodied, exercising their right to commit suicide. This argument is in my opinion based on a misconception. The law confers no right to commit suicide.

Suicide was always, as a crime, anomalous, since it was the only crime with which no defendant could ever be charged. The main effect of the criminalisation of suicide was to penalise those who attempted to take their own lives and failed, and secondary parties. Suicide itself (and with it attempted suicide) was decriminalised because recognition of the common law offence was not thought to act as a deterrent, because it cast an unwarranted stigma on innocent members of the suicide's family and because it led to the distasteful result that patients recovering in hospital from a failed suicide attempt were prosecuted, in effect, for their lack of success. But while the 1961 Act abrogated the rule of law whereby it was a crime for a person to commit (or attempt to commit) suicide, it conferred no right on anyone to do so. Had that been its object there would have been no justification for penalising by a potentially very long term of imprisonment one who aided, abetted, counselled or procured the exercise or attempted exercise by another of that right. The policy of the law remained firmly adverse to suicide, as section 2(1) makes clear.

The criminal law cannot in any event be criticised as objectionably discriminatory because it applies to all. Although in some instances criminal statutes recognise exceptions based on youth, the broad policy of the criminal law is to apply offence-creating provisions to all and to give weight to personal circumstances either at the stage of considering whether or not to prosecute or, in the event of conviction, when penalty is to be considered. The criminal law does not ordinarily distinguish between willing victims and others. Provisions criminalising drunkenness or misuse of drugs or theft do not exempt those addicted to alcohol or drugs, or the poor and hungry. 'Mercy killing', as it is often called, is in law killing. If the criminal law sought to proscribe the conduct of those who assisted the suicide of the vulnerable, but exonerated those who assisted the suicide of the non-vulnerable, it could not be administered fairly and in a way which would command respect.

I would dismiss this appeal."

Notes:

1. *Pretty* was the first case which had the potential for the English courts to consider the issue of euthanasia in relation to the Human Rights Act 1998. Keown suggests that "the outcome was as predictable as it was important" and comments that "For one thing the courts are as reluctant to interfere with prosecutorial discretion as they are to trespass on what they consider to be the province of a democratically elected legislature . . . For another this was not a case in which the applicant sought to establish that assisted suicide would be openly and carefully performed by a doctor as a last resort to put an end to otherwise unbearable suffering. As the Divisional Court put it 'We are being asked to allow a family member to help a loved one die, in circumstances in which we know nothing, in a way in which we know nothing and with no continuing scrutiny by an outside person' ". (See J. Keown, *Euthanasia, Ethics and Public Policy*, Cambridge: CUP, 2002, at p.289.)

2. The House of Lords in *Pretty* also considered the judgments of the Supreme Court of Canada in the earlier *Rodriguez v Attorney General of Canada* [1994] 2 L.R.C. 136. This case had comparable facts to that of *Pretty*, involving an attempt by a woman with a degenerative condition to obtain assistance in ending her life and challenging an analogous provision of the Canadian Criminal Code, s.241b, under the Canadian Charter of Rights and Freedoms. Here a majority of five to four upheld the Criminal Code (see further the notable dissent in that case by MacLachlin J. and A.

Grubb, "Assisting Suicide: *Sue Rodriguez v Attorney General of Canada*" 1991 (*Medical Law Review* 119).

3. The rejection of the argument that Article 8 was inapplicable has been criticised by some commentators. Mason, McCall Smith and Laurie comment that "the concept of autonomy as it is generally understood, includes decisions about dying. Dying is a part of life, even if death is not, and it is difficult to imagine how at least some decisions about the nature of one's death could be seen to have nothing to do with the exercise of self-determination". (See J.K. Mason, and G. Laurie, *Mason and McCall Smith's Law and Medical Ethics* (7th edn), Oxford: OUP, 2006 at p.622.

4. The Article 14 claim was rejected because it is only applicable in conjunction with another right under the Convention, although it is not necessary to show that the related right has been breached, simply that it is engaged.

5. In rejecting the Article 14 claim, Lord Steyn noted the vulnerability of the majority of those individuals who are terminally ill. This approach has been questioned by Freeman who commented, "Do we know the majority are not vulnerable? We know Mrs Pretty was not. And is there not a non sequitur in the argument. If we 'protect' those who do not need or want protection do we not discriminate against them?" (See M. Freeman, "Denying Death its Dominion: Thoughts on the Dianne Pretty case" (2002) 10(3) Med L.R. 245).

6. It has been suggested that the availability of palliative care is a consideration in determining whether individuals decide to seek assistance in dying (see p.1076 below). Only limited information in relation to available palliative care was provided to the court in *Pretty*. Lord Hope, for example, noted that the information provided as to what may be offered by palliative care put into doubt Mrs Pretty's claim that refusal of treatment here was inhuman or degrading contrary to Article 3. Lord Steyn also made reference to the lack of agreement as to what palliative care was available to Mrs Pretty.

7. Mrs Pretty also lost on the claim that the DPP should have exercised his discretion under s.2(4)of the Suicide Act 1961 not to prosecute her husband. As with the lower courts, the House of Lords refused to intervene and provide a guarantee against prosecution before a criminal action had taken place. Tur comments that there is an argument to suggest that s.2(4) is a legislative qualification on s.2(1) and that *Pretty* provides a "formidable candidate" for inclusion in the category of cases where the DPP exercises his discretion not to prosecute (see further R. Tur, "Legislative Technique and Human Rights: the Sad Case of Assisted Suicide" (2003) *Criminal Law Review* 3).

QUESTIONS:

1. To what extent does the *Pretty* decision illustrate that the English courts are an ineffective forum to determine fundamental human rights issues in the area of health care?

2. The House of Lords in *Pretty* were concerned as to the prospect of abuse should assisted dying be allowed in such a situation. To what extent are these concerns justifiable? See further the discussion of euthanasia at p.1072 below in the light of the Netherlands experience.

Mrs Pretty then took her case to the European Court of Human Rights in Strasbourg. The ECHR accepted the reasoning of the House of Lords in respect of the majority of the provisions which were pleaded but they differed in respect of their interpretation of Article 8.

Pretty v UK (2002) 35 EHRR 1

JUDGMENT OF THE EUROPEAN COURT OF HUMAN RIGHTS

"1. Applicability of Article 8(1) of the Convention

As the Court has had previous occasion to remark, the concept of 'private life' is a broad term not susceptible to exhaustive definition. It covers the physical and psychological integrity of a person. It can sometimes embrace aspects of an individual's physical and social identity. Elements such as, for example, gender identification, name and sexual orientation and sexual life fall within the personal sphere protected by Article 8.

Article 8 also protects a right to personal development, and the right to establish and develop relationships with other human beings and the outside world. Though no previous case has established as such any right to self-determination as being contained in Article 8 of the Convention, the Court considers that the notion of personal autonomy is an important principle underlying the interpretation of its guarantees.

The Government has argued that the right to private life cannot encapsulate a right to die with assistance, such being a negation of the protection that the Convention was intended to provide. The Court would observe that the ability to conduct one's life in a manner of one's own choosing may also include the opportunity to pursue activities perceived to be of a physically or morally harmful or dangerous nature for the individual concerned. The extent to which a State can use compulsory powers or the criminal law to protect people from the consequences of their chosen lifestyle has long been a topic of moral and jurisprudential discussion, the fact that the interference is often viewed as trespassing on the private and personal sphere adding to the vigour of the debate. However, even where the conduct poses a danger to health, or arguably, where it is of a life-threatening nature, the case-law of the Convention institutions has regarded the State's imposition of compulsory or criminal measures as impinging on the private life of the applicant within the scope of Article 8(1) and requiring justification in terms of the second paragraph.

While it might be pointed out that death was not the intended consequence of the applicants' conduct in the above situations, the Court does not consider that this can be a decisive factor. In the sphere of medical treatment, the refusal to accept a particular treatment might, inevitably, lead to a fatal outcome, yet the imposition of medical treatment, without the consent of a mentally competent adult patient, would interfere with a person's physical integrity in a manner capable of engaging the rights protected under Article 8(1) of the Convention. As recognised in domestic case law, a person may claim to exercise a choice to die by declining to consent to treatment which might have the effect of prolonging his life.

In the present case, though medical treatment is not an issue, the applicant is suffering from the devastating effects of a degenerative disease which will cause her condition to deteriorate further and increase her physical and mental suffering. She wishes to mitigate that suffering by exercising a choice to end her life with the assistance of her husband. As stated by Lord Hope, the way she chose to pass the closing moments of her life is part of the act of living, and she has a right to ask that this too must be respected.

The very essence of the Convention is respect for human dignity and human freedom. Without in any way negating the principle of sanctity of life protected under the Convention, the Court considers that it is under Article 8 that notions of the quality of life take on significance. In an era of growing medical sophistication combined with longer life expectancies, many people are concerned that they should not be forced to linger on in old age or in states of advanced physical or mental decrepitude which conflict with strongly held ideas of self and personal identity.

In the case of *Rodriguez v. Attorney General of Canada*, ([1994] 2 L.R.C. 136) which concerned a not dissimilar situation to the present, the majority opinion of the Supreme Court considered that the prohibition on the appellant in that case from receiving assistance in suicide contributed to her distress and prevented her from managing her death. This deprived her of autonomy and required justification under principles of fundamental justice. Although the Canadian court was considering a provision of the Canadian Charter framed in different terms from those of Article 8 of the Convention, comparable concerns arose regarding the principle of personal autonomy in the sense of the right to make choices about one's own body.

The applicant in this case is prevented by law from exercising her choice to avoid what she considers will be an undignified and distressing end to her life. The Court is not prepared to exclude that this constitutes an interference with her right to respect for private life as guaranteed under Article 8(1) of the Convention. It considers below whether this interference conforms with the requirements of the second paragraph of Article 8.

2. Compliance with Article 8(2) of the Convention

An interference with the exercise of an Article 8 right will not be compatible with Article 8(2) unless it is 'in accordance with the law', has an aim or aims that is or are legitimate under that paragraph and is 'necessary in a democratic society' for the aforesaid aim or aims.

The only issue arising from the arguments of the parties is the necessity of any interference, it being common ground that the restriction on assisted suicide in this case was imposed by law and in pursuit of the legitimate aim of safeguarding life and thereby protecting the rights of others.

According to the Court's established case law, the notion of necessity implies that the interference corresponds to a pressing social need and, in particular, that it is proportionate to the legitimate aim pursued; in determining whether an interference is 'necessary in a democratic society', the Court will take into account that a margin of appreciation is left to the national authorities, whose decision remains subject to review by the Court for conformity with the requirements of the Convention. The margin of appreciation to be accorded to the competent national authorities will vary in accordance with the nature of the issues and the importance of the interests at stake.

The Court recalls that the margin of appreciation has been found to be narrow as regards interferences in the intimate area of an individual's sexual life. Though the applicant has argued that there must therefore be particularly compelling reasons for the interference in her case, the Court does not find that the matter under consideration in this case can be regarded as of the same nature, or as attracting the same reasoning.

The parties' arguments have focused on the proportionality of the interference as disclosed in the applicant's case. The applicant attacked in particular the blanket nature of the ban on assisted suicide as failing to take into account her situation as a mentally competent adult who knows her own mind, who is free from pressure and who has made a fully informed and voluntary decision, and therefore cannot be regarded as vulnerable and requiring protection. This inflexibility means, in her submission, that she will be compelled to endure the consequences of her incurable and distressing illness, at a very high personal cost.

The Court would note that although the Government argued that the applicant, as a person who is both contemplating suicide and severely disabled, must be regarded as vulnerable, this assertion is not supported by the evidence before the domestic courts or by the judgments of the House of Lords which, while emphasising that the law in the United Kingdom was there to protect the vulnerable, did not find that the applicant was in that category.

Nonetheless, the Court finds, in agreement with the House of Lords and the majority of the Canadian Supreme Court in the *Rodriguez* case, that States are entitled to regulate through the operation of the general criminal law activities which are detrimental to the life and safety of other individuals . . . The more serious the harm involved the more heavily will weigh in the balance considerations of public health and safety against the countervailing principle of personal autonomy. The law in issue in this case, of the 1961 Act, was designed to safeguard life by protecting the weak and vulnerable and especially those who are not in a condition to take informed decisions against acts intended to end life or to assist in ending life. Doubtless the condition of terminally ill individuals will vary. But many will be vulnerable and it is the vulnerability of the class which provides the rationale for the law in question. It is primarily for States to assess the risk and the likely incidence of abuse if the general prohibition on assisted suicides were relaxed or if exceptions were to be created. Clear risks of abuse do exist, notwithstanding arguments as to the possibility of safeguards and protective procedures.

The applicant's counsel attempted to persuade the Court that a finding in this case would not create a general precedent or any risk to others. It is true that it is not this Court's role under Article 34 of the Convention to issue opinions in the abstract but to apply the Convention to the concrete facts of the individual case. However, judgments issued in individual cases establish precedents albeit to a greater or lesser extent and a decision in this case could not, either in theory or practice, be framed in such a way as to prevent application in later cases.

The Court does not consider therefore that the blanket nature of the ban on assisted suicide is disproportionate. The Government has stated that flexibility is provided for in individual cases by the fact that consent is needed from the DPP to bring a prosecution and by the fact that a maximum sentence is provided, allowing lesser penalties to be imposed as appropriate. The Select Committee report indicated that between 1981 and 1992 in 22 cases in which 'mercy killing' was an issue, there was only one conviction for murder, with a sentence for life imprisonment, while lesser offences were substituted in the others and most resulted in probation or suspended sentences . . . It does not appear to be arbitrary to the Court for the law to reflect the importance of the right to life, by prohibiting assisted suicide while providing for a system of enforcement and adjudication which allows due regard to be given in each particular case to the public interest in bringing a prosecution, as well as to the fair and proper requirements of retribution and deterrence.

Nor in the circumstances is there anything disproportionate in the refusal of the DPP to give an advance undertaking that no prosecution would be brought against the applicant's husband. Strong arguments based on the rule of law could be raised against any claim by the executive to exempt individuals or classes of individuals from the operation of the law. In any event, the seriousness of the act for which immunity was claimed was such that the decision of the DPP to refuse the undertaking sought in the present case cannot be said to be arbitrary or unreasonable.

The Court concludes that the interference in this case may be justified as 'necessary in a democratic society' for the protection of the rights of others and, accordingly, that there has been no violation of Article 8 of the Convention.

V. Alleged violation of Article 14 of the Convention

B. The Court's assessment

The Court has found above that the applicant's rights under Article 8 of the Convention were engaged . . . It must therefore consider the applicant's complaints that she has been discriminated against in the enjoyment of the rights guaranteed under that provision in that domestic law permits able-bodied persons to commit suicide yet prevents an incapacitated person from receiving assistance in committing suicide.

For the purposes of Article 14 a difference in treatment between persons in analogous or relevantly similar positions is discriminatory if it has no objective and reasonable justification, that is if it does not pursue a legitimate aim or if there is not a reasonable relationship of proportionality between the means employed and the aim sought to be realised. Moreover, the Contracting States enjoy a margin of appreciation in assessing whether and to what extent differences in otherwise similar situations justify a different treatment. (*Camp v Bourini v Netherlands* (2002) ECHR 59. Discrimination may also arise where States without an objective and reasonable justification fail to treat differently persons whose situations are significantly different (*Thimmenos v Greece* (2000) 9 BHRC 12 at 22).

Even if the principle derived from the case is applied to the applicant's situation however, there is, in the Court's view, objective and reasonable justification for not distinguishing in law between those who are and those who are not physically capable of committing suicide. Under Article 8 of the Convention, the Court has found that there are sound reasons for not introducing into the law exceptions to cater for those who are deemed not to be vulnerable. Similar cogent reasons exist under Article 14 for not seeking to distinguish between those who are able and those who are unable to commit suicide unaided. The borderline between the two categories will often be a very fine one and to seek to build into the law an exemption for those judged to be incapable of committing suicide would seriously undermine the protection of life which the 1961 Act was intended to safeguard and greatly increase the risk of abuse.

Consequently, there has been no violation of Article 14 in the present case."

NOTES:

1. This ECHR decision was the first case in which the ECHR had to determine an issue in which the UK House of Lords had delivered a decision based upon the provisions of the Human Rights Act 1998. As with the issue of abortion, the ECHR is here giving a considerable margin of appreciation to individual Member States in determining what is a controversial ethical issue (see Chapter 12 above at p.906).
2. In *Pretty*, the ECHR recognises the inconsistency with the fact that an individual who is able to do so may refuse treatment (see further the discussion of *Ms B* below at p.1058).
3. Mrs Pretty died of natural causes in a hospice on May 11, 2002 after the ECHR had delivered its ruling.

(b) Murder/Manslaughter

(i) Basic Principles

Deliberate termination of the life of the terminally ill patient will constitute murder or manslaughter. One of the most celebrated cases was that of *R v Arthur* in 1981. In *R v Arthur* (*The Times*, November 6, 1981) a baby, John Pearson, was born with Down's syndrome but apparently no other complications. Dr Arthur was a paediatrician caring for the child. He wrote in the notes "Parents do not wish it to survive, nursing care only". Dr Arthur also prescribed a strong pain-killing drug, DF118, which was a drug not normally given to infants. Some 69 hours later the baby died. Dr Arthur was charged initially with murder but this was later reduced to a charge of attempted murder. He was eventually acquitted. The judge asked the jury to consider whether Dr Arthur's actions amounted to a holding operation:

"setting a condition where the child could if it contradicted pneumonia die peacefully? Or was it a positive act on behalf of Dr Arthur which was likely to kill the child and represented an attempt accompanied by an intent on his part that it should as a result of the treatment that he prescribed die."

The concept used of a "holding operation" has been the subject of much criticism. It is argued that administration of the drug DF118 was a positive act causing death. The issues discussed in *Arthur* have now been largely superseded by the approach taken by the House of Lords in *Bland*. (See M. J. Gunn and J.C. Smith, "Arthur's Case and the Right to Life of a Down's Syndrome Child" [1985] Crim.L.R. 705. See also comments by D. Poole, D. Brahams and reply by Gunn and Smith [1986] Crim.L.R. 383. For discussion of *Bland* see below at pages 1021–1037). The case of *R v Arthur* can usefully be contrasted with the contemporaneous decision in *Re B* (see Chapter 7 above).

There have been a number of prosecutions of doctors who have deliberately ended the life of a terminally ill adult patient. In *R v Carr, Sunday Times*, November 1986, Dr Carr was charged with murder. He had injected a massive dose of phenobarbitone into a patient with inoperable lung cancer. He was acquitted of the charge, but Mars Jones J. emphasised that the patient was entitled to every hour that God had given him, however seriously ill he might be. In *R v Lodwig, The Times*, March 16, 1990 the doctor was on an 80-hour shift for the last 18 hours of which he had been continuously on duty. The relatives of a patient terminally ill with cancer of the pancreas who was writhing in pain begged the doctor to put him out of his misery. The doctor eventually said that there was something that he could do but that it might put the patient "over the top". He gave the patient a dose of an anaesthetic to kill the pain. Five minutes later the patient died peacefully. The doctor was charged with murder, but this charge was dropped when the main prosecution witness admitted it was possible that the man might have died from natural causes as opposed to a potassium overdose. In *R v Cox* (*The Times*, September 22, 1992; (1992) 12 B.M.L.R. 38) a doctor was convicted of attempted murder. His patient, a 70-year-old woman, was terminally ill with rheumatoid arthritis and this was complicated by gastric ulcers, gangrene and body sores. He gave her a dose of potassium chloride after repeated doses of heroin had failed to ease her agony. The doctor was given a sentence of one year's imprisonment, suspended for 12 months. The General Medical Council admonished him. They noted that his actions had been taken in good faith. (See C. Dyer, "Rheumatologist Convicted of Attempted Murder" (1993) 305 British Medical Journal 731). It is possible that if the death appears to be a "mercy killing" by a relative, then the prosecution may decide to accept a plea of manslaughter rather than prosecute for murder. There is, however, no specific defence of mercy killing in English law, something which was confirmed by the House of Lords in *Airedale NHS Trust v Bland* (see below p.1021). It is interesting to note that the prosecutions of both Dr Arthur and of Dr Cox resulted from a nurse alerting the authorities to what had transpired—the whole issue of whistleblowing is considered in Chapter 8 above. In 1997 Dr David Moor was charged and subsequently acquitted of the murder of retired ambulanceman George Liddell. Mr Liddell was 85 years old and terminally ill. It was alleged that he had been killed through the administration of a large dose of diamorphine. Dr Moor had commented in a television interview that he had helped patients to die but that he "would be very surprised if he had to defend himself in court". The relatives of Mr Liddell gave evidence in support of Dr Moor. "News: GP on trial for murder (1999) 318 British Medical Journal 1095: "News: British GP cleared of murder charge" (1999) 318 British Medical Journal 953.

(ii) Administration of Pain-killing Drugs

Deliberate termination of life through administration of a drug may lead to a prosecution under s.23 of the Offences Against the Person Act 1861 which makes it an offence to "unlawfully administer to or cause to be administered to or taken by any other person any poison or other destructive or noxious thing, so as to thereby endanger the life of such a person . . . ". This section carries a penalty of up to 10 years' imprisonment. However, while a doctor may not deliberately end the life of his or her patient, it has been suggested that he or she may administer pain killing drugs, even at a high dosage which may result in the patient's death.

R v. Bodkin Adams (1957)

Dr Bodkin Adams, who had treated many elderly patients and had been rewarded by many in their wills, was tried for murder. He had been treating an 81-year-old lady who had suffered from a stroke. She was prescribed heroin and morphia by Dr Adams and subsequently died. She had left Dr Adams a chest of silver and a Rolls Royce in her will. Dr Adams was acquitted.

H. Palmer, "Adam's Trial for Murder" [1957] Crim.L.R. 365

Devlin J., summing up to the jury, said that murder was an act or series of acts, done by the prisoner, which were intended to kill, and did in fact kill. It did not matter whether Mrs Morell's death was inevitable and that her days were numbered. If her life were cut short by weeks or months it was just as much murder as if it was cut short by years. There had been a good deal of discussion as to the circumstances in which doctors might be justified in administering drugs which could shorten life. Cases of severe pain were suggested and also cases of helpless misery. The law knew of no special defence in this category, but that did not mean that a doctor who was aiding the sick and dying had to calculate in minutes or even hours, perhaps not in days or weeks, the effect on a patient's life of the medicines which he would administer. If the first purpose of medicine, the restoration of health, could no longer be achieved, there was still much for the doctor to do, and he was entitled to do all that was proper and necessary to relieve pain and suffering even if the measures he took might incidentally shorten life by hours or perhaps even longer. The doctor who decided whether or not to administer the drug could not do his job if he were thinking in terms of hours or months of life. The defence in the present case was that the treatment given by Dr Adams was designed to promote comfort, and if it was the right and proper treatment, the fact that it shortened life did not convict him of murder.

NOTES:

1. A detailed account of the trial is provided in a book written by the trial judge Lord Patrick Devlin, *Easing the Passing*, Oxford: Bodley Head (1985).

2. It has been suggested that this case introduces the doctrine of double effect into English law. (See M. Brazier, *Medicine, Patients and the Law*, Harmondsworth: Penguin, 2003 (3rd edn) page 441; (see also discussion in Chapter 2 above.)

3. The question of the administration of pain-killing drugs was also addressed in *Bland* (see below at p.1021). However the existence of the double-effect doctrine in health care decision making may be questioned in the light of the decision of the House of Lords in *R v Woolin* [1999] A.C. 82. There it was stated that "intention" should be assessed in considering whether death was a "reasonably foreseeable consequence" of the action. An action was regarded as intentional if the actor was " virtually certain it would occur". It was considered in *Re A (children) (conjoined twins: surgical separation)* [2001] Fam. 147 but left open. Ward L.J. noted the difficulty with *Woolin* while suggesting that the doctrine may be applicable in the case of the administration of pain-killers to deal with extreme pain. The implications of the *Woolin* decision are still uncertain. Pattinson suggests that there are in effect three options. First, that double-effect still applies but only in relation to medical treatment; secondly, that it provides juries with a discretion to hold that the doctrine of double-effect is applicable or rather to infer intention and thirdly, that the doctrine of double-effect is no longer applicable (see the discussion in S. Pattinson, *Medical Law and Ethics*, London, Sweet & Maxwell, 2006 at pp.487–489). It has been criticised on the basis that if it has overruled *Bodkin Adams*, then doctors who administer pain-killing drugs would have to do so on the basis of necessity. Keown has argued that this would be unacceptable as it would mean that doctors involved in palliative care would be subject to culpability in the criminal law and have to rely on the doctrine of necessity (see further J. Keown, *Euthanasia, Ethics and Public Policy: an argument against Legalisation*, Cambridge: CUP, 2002 at pp.28–29).

QUESTION:

1. Is the use of the "doctrine of double effect" in this context justifiable? (See Chapter 2 above)? Would a better approach be to acknowledge that the morally right action in these circumstances is the action which hastens death?

(iii) Infanticide

If a mother kills a newly born handicapped child who is gravely suffering then, as with any so-called "mercy killing", she is liable to be prosecuted for murder. But in some instances a prosecution may be brought for the alternative offence of infanticide. This offence can be seen to reflect medical evidence that a high proportion of women following pregnancy suffer from depression and thus, in this situation, a charge other than murder would be appropriate.

Infanticide Act 1938, s.1(1)

1.—(1) Where a woman, by any wilful act or omission causes the death of her child, being a child under the age of twelve months, but at the time of the act or omission the balance of her mind was disturbed by reason of her not having fully recovered from giving birth to the child or by the reason of the effect of lactation consequent upon the birth of the child, then, notwithstanding that the circumstances were such that but for this Act the offence would have amounted to murder, she shall be guilty of felony, to wit of infanticide, and may, for such offence, be dealt with and punished as if she had been guilty of the manslaughter of the child.

NOTES:

1. This offence was introduced at a time when there was no partial defence of diminished responsibility to murder. The Criminal Law Revision Committee advocated the retention of the offence of infanticide because it avoided the necessity of charging the mother with murder (Criminal Law Revision Committee, *Offences Against the Person*, Working Paper No. 26). These recommendations were followed by the Law Commission in its draft criminal code in 1988. Clause 64(1) of this provides that:

   "A woman who, but for this section, would be guilty of murder or manslaughter of her child is not guilty of murder or manslaughter but is guilty of infanticide, if her act is done where the child is under the age of twelve months and when the balance of her mind is disturbed by reason of the effect of giving birth or of circumstances consequent upon the birth." (Law Com. No. 177.)

2. The proposals of the Law Commission may be seen as reflecting the fact that the decision to charge a woman with infanticide is not necessarily primarily related to the fact that her mental capacity is unduly impaired. Instead it may be seen as a tacit recognition that the death has arisen in a situation in which the mother is unable to cope because the child is severely handicapped or because of straitened financial circumstances. (See further K. O'Donovan, "The Medicalisation of Infanticide" [1984] Crim. L.R. 259.)

(iv) Liability for Failure to Provide Care

While there is generally no obligation to act for the benefit of another in English law, in some situations the law imposes a positive duty. For example, such an obligation may be imposed by statute. As we saw above, liability under the Infanticide Act 1938 can be established by an omission. Furthermore s.1 of the Children and Young Persons Act 1933 provides that:

"(1) If any person who has attained the age of sixteen years and has the responsibility, charge, or care of any young person under that age, wilfully assaults, ill treats, neglects, abandons, or exposes him . . . in a manner likely to cause him unnecessary suffering or injury to health . . . that person shall be guilty of a misdemeanour."

Liability under the 1933 Act would extend to a parent who failed to seek medical assistance resulting in the death of the child. In *R v Senior* [1899] 1 Q.B. 283 the defendant was a member of a sect who had religious objections to the use of medical assistance and medicines. His child fell ill and medical aid was not sought. The child died of diarrhoea and pneumonia. Evidence was given to the effect that had medical help been given the child would probably have lived. Except for the non-provision of medical help, the child was treated well by its parents. It was held that the action of the parents constituted neglect under the Prevention of Cruelty to Children Act 1896, s.1 (the statutory predecessor of the 1933 Act). In addition, the fact that the defendant had caused or accelerated death, meant that he was rightly convicted of manslaughter. A successful prosecution for manslaughter as a result of non-compliance with the 1933 Act now appears to be unlikely. In *R v Lowe* [1973] Q.B. 702, the court indicated that neglect by itself will not necessarily mean that a prosecution for manslaughter will succeed. In that case Phillimore L.J. suggested that while, for example, striking a child in a manner likely to cause it harm would lead to a prosecution for manslaughter, a simple failure to act with the consequence that death results would not inevitably result in a manslaughter prosecution. In 1993 a child's parents were prosecuted and convicted of manslaughter consequent upon negligence in care of their child. The couple, who were vegans and believed in homeopathic remedies, discharged their diabetic daughter from hospital. They treated her with homeopathic remedies but the girl subsequently died (*The Independent*, October 29, 1993).

What constitutes "wilful neglect" within s.1 was considered in *R v Sheppard* [1981] A.C. 394.

R v Sheppard [1981] A.C. 394

A 16-month-old child died of hypothermia and malnutrition. The child had suffered from gastroenteritis but the parents who were poor and of low intelligence had not sought medical attention. The parents were convicted, the judge having directed the jury that to establish liability under the section it was necessary to show that a reasonable parent with knowledge of these facts would have appreciated that this was likely to cause the child unnecessary suffering or injury to health. In the House of Lords, the appeal was allowed.

LORD DIPLOCK

" . . . the verb 'neglect' cannot, in my view, of itself import into the criminal law the civil law concept of negligence. The *actus reus* in a case of wilful neglect is simply a failure for whatever reason, to provide the child whenever it in fact needs medical aid with the medical aid it needs. Such a failure as it seems to me could not properly be described as 'wilful' unless the parent either (1) had directed his mind to the question whether there was some risk (though it might fall far short of a probability) that the child's health might suffer unless he was examined by a doctor and provided with such curative treatment as the examination might reveal as necessary, and had made a conscious decision, for whatever reason, to refrain from arranging for such medical examination, or (2) had so refrained because he did not care whether the child might be in need of medical treatment or not.

The section speaks of an act or an omission that is 'likely' to cause unnecessary suffering or injury to health. This word is imprecise. It is capable of covering a whole range of possibilities from 'it's on the cards' to 'it's more probable than not'; but having regard to the ordinary parent's lack of skill in diagnosis and to the very serious consequences which may result from failure to provide a child with timely medical attention, it should, in my view be understood as excluding only what would fairly be described as highly unlikely . . ."

LORD KEITH

" . . . This appeal is concerned solely with a failure to provide adequate medical care. The word 'adequate' as applied to medical care may mean no more than 'ordinarily competent'. If it is related to anything, I think it is related to the prevention of unnecessary suffering an injury to health as mentioned in section 1(1) where the adjective 'unnecessary' qualifies both 'suffering' and 'injury to health'. There could be no question of a finding of neglect against a parent who provided ordinarily competent medical care, but whose child nevertheless suffered further injury to its health, for example paralysis in a case of poliomyelitis, because the injury to health would not in the circumstances be unnecessary, in the sense that it could have been prevented by the provision by the parent of adequate medical care. Failure to provide adequate medical care may be deliberate as when the child's need for it is perceived yet nothing is done, negligent, as where the need ought reasonably to have been perceived but was not, or entirely blameless as when the need is not perceived but ought to have been perceived by the ordinary reasonable parent. I would say that in all three cases the parent has neglected the child in the sense of the statute, since I am of the opinion that in a proper construction of section 1(2)(a) it is to be ascertained objectively and in the light of events whether the parent failed to provide ordinarily competent medical care which as a matter of fact the child needed in order to prevent unnecessary suffering or injury to its health."

NOTE:

1. Lord Edmund-Davies agreed with Lords Diplock and Keith. Lords Scarman and Fraser dissented.

In addition, if a person undertakes care of another, then abandonment of care may lead to liability at common law. In *R v Gibbins & Proctor* (1918) 13 Cr.App.R. 134, Gibbins, along with Proctor, the woman with whom he was living, were convicted of murdering Gibbins' child by withholding food. The child died of starvation. By living with the man and receiving money from him for food, the woman had also assumed a duty to care for the man's child. In this case the jury reached the conclusion that the defendants were liable for murder because there was evidence that the woman had deliberately witheld food. In *R v Stone* [1977] 2 All E.R. 341, Stone's sister, F came to live with Stone and his mistress. The sister suffered from anorexia nervosa. Her condition deteriorated. Stone (who was 67, of low intelligence, partly deaf and nearly blind) and his mistress took certain measures to care for F but these were largely ineffectual. F subsequently died and a manslaughter charge was brought against Stone and his mistress. The Court of Appeal held that the judge at first instance had been correct to direct the jury that the minimal attention given by Stone and his mistress was sufficient to give rise to a duty of care and that they had been grossly negligent in the performance of that duty. A doctor who takes on the duty to care for a sick child and neglects that child also risks prosecution at common law. For the scope of doctor's duties to their patients see Chapter 3, above.

3. Judicial Sanctioning of the Removal of Life Support Systems from an Incompetent Patient

While active termination of life is a criminal offence, and in certain situations criminal liability will also arise for failure to provide care, in some cases the courts have been prepared to authorise withdrawal of treatment. In order to ascertain whether cessation of treatment is lawful, it has become increasingly common for an application to be made to the court for a declaration approving a course of treatment. Indeed, in the case of withdrawal of treatment from an incompetent adult patient in a persistent vegetative state (PVS), such referral seems mandatory. The ethics of recognising withdrawal of treatment ("passive" euthanasia) while rejecting active euthanasia are a source of dispute. The medical profession recognise passive euthanasia as being acceptable while active euthanasia is not. However, it has been questioned as to whether it is possible for a satisfactory distinction to be drawn between the two (see Chapter 2 at p.136). One final point is that the cases largely concern removal of treatment, but in some situations extend to decisions not to recommence therapy should a particular incident occur. As was noted in Chapter 7 above, the first cases which came before the courts in relation to non-treatment concerned handicapped infants (see Chapter 7 at p.409).

The cases which concern non-treatment of the handicapped infant now need to be read in the light of the approach taken by the courts to applications for orders in relation to withdrawal of treatment from the incapacitated adult patient. Particular difficulties may arise in relation to adult patients in a persistent vegetative state, who have no prospect of recovery and who are supported through artificial nutrition and hydration. (For further discussion as to the meaning of persistent vegetative state, see Chapter 15 below.) The leading case on this issue of the House of Lords in *Airedale NHS Trust v Bland*.

(a) Withdrawal of Treatment from Adult Patients

Airedale NHS Trust v Bland [1993] 1 All E.R. 521; [1993] A.C. 879

Tony Bland was a spectator who was injured at the tragedy at Hillsborough football ground in April 1989. He suffered a severely crushed chest during the incident and this gave rise to hypoxic brain damage. He entered a persistent vegetative state. He remained in this state and showed no signs of recovery. He was fed through a naso-gastric tube. The hospital, the Airedale NHS Trust, which was caring for him, sought a declaration authorising the discontinuation of all life-sustaining treatment and medical support mechanisms. Sir Stephen Brown in granting the declaration said that it was in the patient's best interests that the feeding regime be withdrawn. He said that while Mr Bland's life would come to an end as a consequence, the true cause of death was the injuries suffered at Hillsborough. In the Court of Appeal the appeal of the Official Solicitor was dismissed. There was then an appeal to the House of Lords. The judgments in the House of Lords in *Bland* present a rich analysis of the problems in relating to withdrawal of treatment. Here the extracts are largely drawn from the judgment of Lord Goff which can be regarded as the leading judgment in the case.

LORD GOFF OF CHIEVELEY
" . . . The central issue in the present case has been aptly stated by Sir Thomas Bingham M.R. to be whether artificial feeding and antibiotic drugs may lawfully be withheld from an insensate patient with no hope of recovery when it is known that if that is done the patient will shortly thereafter die. . . .
     I start with the simple fact that, in law, Anthony is still alive. It is true that his condition is such that it can be described as a living death; but he is nevertheless still alive. This is because, as a result of developments in modern medical technology, doctors no longer associate death exclusively with breathing and heart beat, and it has come to be accepted that death occurs when the brain, and in particular the brain stem, has been destroyed (see Professor Ian Kennedy's Paper entitled 'Switching off Life Support Machines: The Legal Implications,' reprinted in *Treat Me Right, Essays in Medical Law and Ethics* (1988), esp. at 351–352, and the material there cited). There has been no dispute on this point in the present case, and it is unnecessary for me to consider it further. The evidence is that Anthony's brain stem is still alive and functioning and it follows that, in the present state of medical science, he is still alive and should be so regarded as a matter of law. It is on this basis that I turn to the applicable principles of law. Here the fundamental principle is the sanctity of human life—a principle long recognised not only in our own society but in most civilised societies across the world as is indeed evidenced by recognition both in Article 2 of the European Convention for the Protection of Fundamental Rights and Freedoms (1953) (Cmd 8969) and in Article 6 of the International Convenant for Civil and Political Rights 1966.
     But this principle, fundamental though it is, is not absolute. Indeed there are circumstances in which it is lawful to take another man's life, for example by a lawful act of self-defence, or (in the days when capital punishment was acceptable in our society) by lawful execution. We are not however concerned with cases such as these. We are concerned with circumstances in which it may be lawful to withhold from a patient medical treatment or care by means of which his life may be prolonged. But here too there is no absolute rule that the patient's life must be prolonged by such treatment or care, if available, regardless of the circumstances.
     First, it is established that the principle of self-determination requires that respect must be given to the wishes of the patient, so that if an adult patient of sound mind refuses, however unreasonably, to consent to treatment or care by which his life would or might be prolonged, the doctors responsible for his care must give effect to his wishes, even though they do not consider it to be in his best interests to do so (see *Schloendorf v. Society of New York Hospital* (1914) 211 N.Y. 125 at 129–30, *per* Cardozo J.; *S v. S; W. v. Official Solicitor* [1970] 3 All E.R. 107 at 111, *per* Lord Reid; and *Sidaway v. Board of Governors of Bethlem Royal Hospital and the Maudsley Hospital* [1985]1 All E.R. 643 at 649, *per* Lord Scarman). To this extent, the principle of the sanctity of human life must yield to the principle of self-determination (see *ante*, pages p.851, *per* Hoffmann L.J.), and, for present purposes perhaps more important, the doctor's duty to act in the best interests of his patient must likewise be qualified. On this basis, it has been held that a patient of sound mind may, if properly informed, require that life support should be discontinued: see *Nancy v. Hotel Dieu de Quebec* (1992) 86 DLR (4th) 385. Moreover the same principle applies where the patient's refusal to give his consent has been expressed at an earlier date, before he became unconscious or otherwise incapable of communicating it; though in such circumstances especial care may be necessary to ensure that the prior refusal of consent is still properly to be regarded as applicable in the circumstances which have subsequently

occurred: see, e.g., *Re T (Adult: refusal of medical treatment)* [1992] 4 All E.R. 649. I wish to add that, in cases of this kind, there is no question of the patient having committed suicide, nor therefore of the doctor having aided or abetted him in doing so. It is simply that the patient has, as he is entitled to do, declined to consent to treatment which might or would have the effect of prolonging his life, and the doctor has, in accordance with his duty, complied with his patient's wishes.

But in many cases not only may the patient be in no condition to be able to say whether or not he consents to the relevant treatment or care, but also he may have given no prior indication of his wishes with regard to it. In the case of a child who is a ward of court, the court itself will decide whether medical treatment should be provided in the child's best interests, taking into account medical opinion. But the court cannot give its consent on behalf of an adult patient who is incapable of himself deciding whether or not to consent to treatment. I am of the opinion that there is nevertheless no absolute obligation upon the doctor who has the patient in his care to prolong his life, regardless of the circumstances. Indeed, it would be most startling, and could lead to the most adverse and cruel effects upon the patient, if any such absolute rule were held to exist. It is scarcely consistent with the primacy given to the principle of self-determination in those cases in which the patient of sound mind has declined to give his consent that the law should provide no means of enabling treatment to be withheld in appropriate circumstances where the patient is in no condition to indicate, if that was his wish, that he did not consent to it. The point was put forcibly in the judgment of the Supreme Judicial Court of Massachusetts in *Superintendent of Belchertown State School v. Saikewicz* (1977) 373 Mass 728 at 747, as follows:

> 'To presume that the incompetent person must always be subjected to what many rational and intelligent persons may decline is to downgrade the status of the incompetent person by placing a lesser value on his intrinsic human worth and vitality.'

I must however stress, at this point, that the law draws a crucial distinction between cases in which a doctor decides not to provide, or to continue to provide, for his patient treatment or care which could or might prolong his life, and those in which he decides, for example by administering a lethal drug, actively to bring his patient's life to an end. As I have already indicated, the former may be lawful, either because the doctor is giving effect to his patient's wishes by withholding the treatment or care, or even in certain circumstances in which (on principles which I shall describe) the patient is incapacitated from stating whether or not he gives his consent. But it is not lawful for a doctor to administer a drug to his patient to bring about his death, even though that course is prompted by a humanitarian desire to end his suffering, however great that suffering may be: see *Reg v. Cox* (unreported, September 18, 1992, *per* Ogden J. in the Crown Court at Winchester). So to act is to cross the Rubicon which runs between on the one hand the care of the living patient and on the other hand euthanasia actively causing his death to avoid or to end his suffering. Euthanasia is not lawful at common law. It is of course well known that there are many responsible members of our society who believe that euthanasia should be made lawful; but that result could, I believe, only be achieved by legislation which expresses the democratic will that so fundamental a change should be made in our law, and can, if enacted, ensure that such legalised killing can only be carried out subject to appropriate supervision and control. It is true that the drawing of this distinction may lead to a charge of hypocrisy; because it can be asked why, if the doctor, by discontinuing treatment, is entitled in consequence to let his patient die, it should not be lawful to put him out of his misery straight away, in a more humane manner, by a lethal injection, rather than let him linger on in pain until he dies. But the law does not feel able to authorise euthanasia, even in circumstances such as these; for once euthanasia is recognised as lawful in these circumstances, it is difficult to see any logical basis for excluding it in others.

At the heart of this distinction lies a theoretical question. Why is it that the doctor who gives his patient a lethal injection which kills him commits an unlawful act and indeed is guilty of murder, whereas a doctor who, by discontinuing life support, allows his patient to die, may not act unlawfully and will not do so, if he commits no breach of duty to his patient? Professor Glanville Williams has suggested (see his *Textbook of Criminal Law* (2nd edn.), (1983), p.282) that the reason is that what the doctor does when he switches off a life support machine 'is in substance not an act but an omission to struggle,' and that 'the omission is not a breach of duty by the doctor, because he is not obliged to continue in a hopeless case.'

I agree that the doctor's conduct in discontinuing life support can properly be categorised as an omission. It is true that it may be difficult to describe what the doctor actually does as an omission, for example where he takes some positive step to bring the life support to an end. But discontinuation of life support is, for present purpose, no different from not initiating life support in the first place. In each case, the doctor is simply allowing his patient to die in the sense that he is desisting from taking a step which might, in certain circumstances, prevent his patient from dying as a result of his pre-existing condition; and as a matter of general principle an omission such as this will not be unlawful unless it constitutes a breach of duty to the patient I also agree that the doctor's conduct is to be differentiated from that of, for example, an interloper who maliciously switches off a life support machine because, although the interloper may perform exactly the same act as the doctor who discontinues life support, his doing so constitutes interference with the life-prolonging treatment then being administered by the doctor. Accordingly, whereas the doctor, in discontinuing life support, is simply allowing his patient to die of his pre-existing condition, the interloper is actively intervening to stop the doctor from prolonging the patient's life, and such conduct cannot possibly be categorised as an omission.

The distinction appears, therefore, to be useful in the present context in that it can be invoked to explain how discontinuance of life support can be differentiated from ending a patient's life by a lethal injection. But in the end the reason for that difference is that, whereas the law considers that discontinuance of life support may be consistent with the doctor's duty to care for his patient, it does not, for reasons of policy, consider that it forms any part of his duty to give his patient a lethal injection to put him out of his agony.

I return to the patient who, because for example he is of unsound mind or has been rendered unconscious by accident or by illness, is incapable of stating whether or not he consents to treatment or care. In such circumstances, it is now established that a doctor may lawfully treat such a patient if he acts in his best interests, and indeed that, if the patient is already in his care, he is under a duty so to treat him: see *F v. West Berkshire Health Authority* [1989] 2 All E.R. 545, in which the legal principles governing treatment in such circumstances were stated by this House. For my part I can see no reason why, as a matter of principle, a decision by a doctor whether or not to initiate, or to continue to provide, treatment or care which could or might have the effect of prolonging such a patient's life, should not be governed by the same fundamental principle. Of course, in the great majority of cases, the best interests of the patient are likely to require that treatment of this kind, if available, should be given to a patient but this may not always be so. To take a simple example given by Thomas J. in the High Court of New Zealand in *Auckland Area Health Board v. Att.-Gen.* [1993] 1 NZLR 235 at 253, to whose judgment in that case I wish to pay tribute, it cannot be right that a doctor, who has under his care a patient suffering painfully from terminal cancer, should be under an absolute obligation to perform upon him major surgery to abate another condition which, if unabated, would or might shorten his life still further. The doctor who is caring for such a patient cannot, in my opinion, be under an absolute obligation to prolong his life by any means available to him, regardless of the quality of the patient's life. Common humanity requires otherwise, as do medical ethics and good medical practice accepted in this country and overseas. As I see it, the doctor's decision whether or not to take any such step must (subject to his patient's ability to give or withhold his consent) be made in the best interests of the patient. It is this principle too which, in my opinion, underlies the established rule that a doctor may, when caring for a patient who is, for example, dying of cancer, lawfully administer painkilling drugs despite the fact that he knows that an incidental effect of that application will be to abbreviate the patient's life. Such a decision may properly be made as part of the care of the living patient, in his best interests; and, on this basis, the treatment will be lawful. Moreover, where the doctor's treatment of his patient is lawful, the patient's death will be regarded in law as exclusively caused by the injury or disease to which his condition is attributable.

It is of course the development of modern medical technology, and in particular the development of life support systems, which has rendered cases such as the present so much more relevant than in the past. Even so, where (for example) a patient is brought into hospital in such a condition that, without the benefit of a life support system, he will not continue to live, the decision has to be made whether or not to give him that benefit, if available. That decision can only be made in the best interests of the patient. No doubt, his best interests will ordinarily require that he should be placed on a life support system as soon as necessary, if only to make an accurate assessment of his condition and a prognosis for the future. But if he neither recovers sufficiently to be taken off it nor dies, the question will ultimately arise whether he should be kept on it indefinitely. As I see it, that question (assuming the continued availability of the system) can only be answered by reference to the best interests of the patient himself, having regard to established medical practice. Indeed, if the justification for treating a patient who lacks the capacity to consent lies in the fact that the treatment is provided in his best interests, it must follow that the treatment may, and indeed ultimately should, be discontinued where it is no longer in his best interests to provide it. The question which lies at the heart of the present case is, as I see it, whether on that principle the doctors responsible for the treatment and care of Anthony Bland can justifiably discontinue the process of artificial feeding upon which the prolongation of his life depends.

It is crucial for the understanding of this question that the question itself should be correctly formulated. The question is not whether the doctor should take a course which will kill his patient, or even take a course which has the effect of accelerating his death. The question is whether the doctor should or should not continue to provide his patient with medical treatment or care which, if continued, will prolong his patient's life. The question is sometimes put in striking or emotional terms, which can be misleading. For example, in the case of a life support system, it is sometimes asked: should a doctor be entitled to switch it off, or to pull the plug? And then it is asked: can it be in the best interests of the patient that a doctor should be able to switch the life support system off, when this will inevitably result in the patient's death? Such an approach has rightly been criticised as misleading, for example by Professor Ian Kennedy in his paper in *Treat Me Right, Essays in Medical Law and Ethics*, (1988) and by Thomas J. in *Auckland Health Board v. Att.-Gen.* [1993] NZLR 235 at 247. This is because the question is not whether it is in the best interests of the patient that he should die. The question is whether it is in the best interests of the patient that his life should be prolonged by the continuance of this form of medical treatment or care.

The correct formulation of the question is of particular importance in a case such as the present, where the patient is totally unconscious and where there is no hope whatsoever of any amelioration of his condition. In circumstances such as these, it may be difficult to say that it is in his best interests that the treatment should be ended. But if the question is asked, as in my opinion it should be, whether it is in his best interests that treatment which has the effect of artificially prolonging his life should be continued, that question can sensibly be answered to the effect that it is not in his best interests to do so.

Even so, a distinction may be drawn between (I) cases in which, having regard to all the circumstances (including, for example, the intrusive nature of the treatment, the hazards involved in it, and the very poor quality of the life which may be prolonged for the patient if the treatment is successful), it may be judged not to be in the best interests of the patient to initiate or continue life-prolonging treatment, and (II) cases such as the present in which, so far as the living patient is concerned, the treatment is of no benefit to him because he is totally unconscious and there is no prospect of any improvement in his condition. In both classes of case, the decision whether or not to withhold treatment must be made in the best interests of the patient. In the first class, however, the decision has to be made by weighing the relevant considerations. For example, in *Re J (A Minor) Wardship: Medical*

Treatment) [1990] 3 All E.R. 930 at 945, the approach to be adopted in that case was stated by Taylor L.J. as follows:

'I consider that the correct approach is for the court to judge the quality of life the child would have to endure if given the treatment and decide whether in all the circumstances such a life would be so afflicted as to be intolerable to that child.'

With this class of case, however, your Lordships are not directly concerned in the present case; and though I do not wish to be understood to be casting any doubt upon any of the reported cases on the subject, nevertheless I must record that argument was not directed specifically towards these cases, and for that reason I do not intend to express any opinion about the precise principles applicable in relation to them.

By contrast, in the latter class of case, of which the present case provides an example, there is in reality no weighing operation to be performed. Here the condition of the patient, who is totally unconscious and in whose condition there is no prospect of any improvement, is such that life-prolonging treatment is properly regarded as being, in medical terms, useless. As Sir Thomas Bingham M.R. pointed out, in the present case, medical treatment or care may be provided for a number of different purposes. It may be provided, for example, as an aid to diagnosis; for the treatment of physical or mental injury or illness; to alleviate pain or distress, or to make the patient's condition more tolerable. Such purpose may include prolonging the patient's life, for example, to enable him to survive during diagnosis and treatment. But for my part I cannot see that medical treatment is appropriate or requisite simply to prolong a patient's life, when such treatment has no therapeutic purpose of any kind, as where it is futile because the patient is unconscious and there is no prospect of any improvement in his condition. It is reasonable also that account should be taken of the invasiveness of the treatment and of the indignity to which, as the present case shows, a person has to be subjected if his life is prolonged by artificial means, which must cause considerable distress to his family—a distress which reflects not only their own feelings but their perception of the situation of their relative who is being kept alive. But in the end, in a case such as the present it is the futility of the treatment which justifies its termination. I do not consider that, in circumstances such as these, a doctor is required to initiate or to continue life-prolonging treatment or care in the best interests of his patient . . .

In *F v. West Berkshire Health Authority* [1989] 2 All E.R. 545 it was stated that, where a doctor provides treatment for a person who is incapacitated from saying whether or not he consents to it, the doctor must, when deciding on the form of treatment, act in accordance with a responsible and competent body of relevant professional opinion, on the principles set down in *Bolam v. Friern Hospital Management Committee* [1957] 2 All E.R. 118. In my opinion, this principle must equally be applicable to decisions to initiate, or to discontinue, life support, as it is to other forms of treatment. However, in a matter of such importance and sensitivity as discontinuance of life support, it is to be expected that guidance will be provided for the profession; and, on the evidence in the present case, such guidance is for a case such as the present to be found in a Discussion Paper on Treatment of Patients in Persistent Vegetative State, issued in September 1992 by the medical ethics committee of the British Medical Association. Anybody reading this substantial paper will discover for himself the great care with which this topic is being considered by the profession. Mr Francis, for the respondents, drew to the attention of the Appellate Committee four safeguards in particular which, in the committee's opinion, should be observed before discontinuing life support for such patients. They are: (1) every effort should be made at rehabilitation for at least six months after the injury; (2) the diagnosis of irreversible PVS should not be considered confirmed until at least 12 months after the injury, with the effect that any decision to withhold life-prolonging treatment will be delayed for that period; (3) the diagnosis should be agreed by two other independent doctors; and (4) generally, the wishes of the patient's immediate family will be given great weight.

In fact, the views expressed by the committee on the subject of consultation with the relatives of PVS patients are consistent with the opinion expressed by your Lordships' House in *F v. West Berkshire Health Authority* [1989] 2 All E.R. 545 that it is good practice for the doctor to consult relatives. Indeed the committee recognises that, in the case of PVS patients, the relatives themselves will require a high degree of support and attention. But the committee is firmly of the opinion that the relatives' views cannot be determinative of the treatment. Indeed, if that were not so, the relatives would be able to dictate to the doctors what is in the best interests of the patient, which cannot be right. Even so, a decision to withhold life-prolonging treatment, such as artificial feeding, must require close co-operation with those close to the patient; and it is recognised that, in practice, their views and the opinions of doctors will coincide in many cases.

Study of this document left me in no doubt that, if a doctor treating a PVS patient acts in accordance with the medical practice now being evolved by the Medical Ethics Committee of the BMA, he will be acting with the benefit of guidance from a responsible and competent body of relevant professional opinion, as required by the *Bolam* test. I also feel that those who are concerned that a matter of life and death, such as is involved in a decision to withhold life support in case of this kind, should be left to the doctors, would do well to study this paper. The truth is that, in the course of their work, doctors frequently have to make decisions which may affect the continued survival of their patients, and are in reality far more experienced in matters of this kind than are the judges. It is nevertheless the function of the judges to state the legal principles upon which the lawfulness of the actions of doctors depend; but in the end the decisions to be made in individual cases must rest with the doctors themselves. In these circumstances, what is required is a sensitive understanding by both the judges and the doctors of each other's respective functions, and in particular a determination by the judges not merely to understand the problems facing the medical profession in cases of this kind, but also to regard their professional standards with respect. Mutual understanding between the doctors and the judges is the best way to ensure the evolution of a sensitive and sensible legal framework for the treatment and care of patients, with a sound ethical base, in the interest of the patients themselves . . .

I wish however to refer at this stage to the approach adopted in most American courts, under which the court seeks, in a case in which the patient is incapacitated from expressing any view on the question whether life-prolonging treatment should be withheld in the relevant circumstances, to determine what decision the patient himself would have made had he been able to do so. This is called the substituted judgment test, and it generally involves a detailed inquiry into the patient's views and preferences: see, e.g. *Re Quinlan* (1976) 50 N.J. 10, and *Belchertown State School Superintendent v. Saikewicz* (1977) 373 Mass 728. In later cases concerned with PVS patients it has been held that, in the absence of clear and convincing evidence of the patient's wishes, the surrogate decision-maker has to implement as far as possible the decision which the incompetent patient would make if he was competent. However, accepting on this point the submission of Mr Lester, I do not consider that any such test forms part of English law in relation to incompetent adults, on whose behalf nobody has power to give consent to medical treatment. Certainly, in *F v. West Berkshire Health Authority* [1989] 3 All E.R. 545 your Lordships' House adopted a straightforward test based on the best interests of the patient; and I myself do not see why the same test should not be applied in the case of PVS patients, where the question is whether life-prolonging treatment should be withheld. This was also the opinion of Thomas J. in *Auckland Area Health Board v. A.G.* [1993] NZLR 235, unreported, August 13, 1992, a case concerned with the discontinuance of life support provided by ventilator to a patient suffering from the last stages of incurable Guillain-Barre syndrome. Of course, consistent with the best interests test, anything relevant to the application of the test may be taken into account; and if the personality of the patient is relevant to the application of the test (as it may be in cases where the various relevant factors have to be weighed), it may be taken into account, as was done in *Re J (A Minor) (Wardship: Medical Treatment)*[1990] 3 All E.R. 930. But, where the question is whether life support should be withheld from a PVS patient, it is difficult to see how the personality of the patient can be relevant, though it may be of comfort to his relatives if they believe, as in the present case, and indeed may well be so in many other cases, that the patient would not have wished his life to be artificially prolonged if he was totally unconscious and there was no hope of improvement in his condition.

I wish to add however that, like the courts below, I have derived assistance and support from decisions in a number of American jurisdictions to the effect that it is lawful to discontinue life-prolonging treatment in the case of PVS patients where there is no prospect of improvement in their condition. Furthermore, I wish to refer to the section in Working Paper No. 28 (1982) on *Euthanasia, Aiding Suicide and Cessation of Treatment* published by the Law Reform Commission of Canada concerned with cessation of treatment, to which I also wish to express my indebtedness. I believe the legal principles as I have stated them to be broadly consistent with the conclusions summarised at pages 65–66 of the Working Paper, which was substantially accepted in the Report of the Commission (1983), pages 32–35. Indeed, I entertain a strong sense that a community of view on the legal principles applicable in cases of discontinuing life support is in the course of development and acceptance throughout the common law world.

In setting out my understanding of the relevant principles, I have had very much in mind the submissions advanced by Mr Munby on behalf of the Official Solicitor, and I believe that I have answered, directly or indirectly, all his objections to the course now proposed. I do not, therefore, intend any disrespect to his argument if I do not answer each of his submissions *seriatim*. In summary, his two principal arguments were as follows. First, he submitted that the discontinuance of artificial feeding would constitute an act which would inevitably cause and be intended to cause, Anthony's death; and as such, it would be unlawful and indeed criminal. As will be plain from what I have already said, I cannot accept this proposition. In my opinion, for the reasons I have already given, there is no longer any duty upon the doctors to continue with this form of medical treatment or care in his case, and it follows that it cannot be unlawful to discontinue it. Second, he submitted that discontinuance of the artificial feeding of Anthony would be a breach of the doctor's duty to care for and feed him; and since it will (as it is intended to do) cause his death, it will necessarily be unlawful. I have considered this point earlier in this opinion, when I expressed my view that artificial feeding is, in a case such as the present, no different from life support by a ventilator, and as such can lawfully be discontinued when it no longer fulfils any therapeutic purpose. To me, the crucial point in which I found myself differing from Mr Munby was that I was unable to accept his treating the discontinuance of artificial feeding in the present case as equivalent to cutting a mountaineer's rope, or severing the air pipe of a deep sea diver. Once it is recognised, as I believe it must be, that the true question is not whether the doctor should take a course in which he will actively kill his patient, but rather whether he should continue to provide his patient with medical treatment or care which, if continued, will prolong his life, then, as I see it, the essential basis of Mr Munby's submissions disappear. I wish to add that I was unable to accept his suggestion that recent decisions show that the law is proceeding down a 'slippery slope', in the sense that the courts are becoming more and more ready to allow doctors to take steps which will result in the ending of life. On the contrary, as I have attempted to demonstrate, the courts are acting within a structure of legal principle, under which in particular they continue to draw a clear distinction between the bounds of lawful treatment of a living patient, and unlawful euthanasia.

I turn finally to the extent to which doctors should, as a matter of practice, seek the guidance of the court, by way of an application for declaratory relief, before withholding life-prolonging treatment from a PVS patient. The President considered that the opinion of the court should be sought in all cases similar to the present. In the Court of Appeal, Sir Thomas Bingham M.R. expressed his agreement with Sir Stephen Brown P. in the following words.

'This was in my respectful view a wise ruling, directed to the protection of patients, the protection of doctors, the reassurance of patients' families and the reassurance of the public. The practice proposed seems to me desirable. It may very well be that with the passage of time a body of experience and practice will build up which will obviate the need for application in every case, but for the time being I am satisfied that the practice Sir Stephen Brown P. described should be followed.'

Before the Appellate Committee, this view was supported both by Mr Munby, for the Official Solicitor, and by Mr Lester, as amicus curiae. For the respondents, Mr Francis suggested that an adequate safeguard would be provided if reference to the court was required in certain specific cases, i.e. (1) where there was known to be a medical disagreement as to the diagnosis or prognosis, and (2) problems had arisen with the patient's relatives—disagreement by the next of kin with the medical recommendation; actual or apparent conflict of interest between the next of kin and the patient; dispute between members of the patient's family; or absence of any next of kin to give their consent. There is, I consider, much to be said for the view that an application to the court will not be needed in every case, but only in particular circumstances, such as those suggested by Mr Francis. In this connection I was impressed not only by the care being taken by the medical ethics committee to provide guidance to the profession, but also by information given to the Appellate Committee about the substantial number of PVS patients in the country, and the very considerable cost of obtaining guidance from the court in cases such as the present. However, in my opinion this is a matter which would be better kept under review by the President of the Family Division than resolved now by your Lordships' House. I understand that a similar review is being undertaken in cases concerned with the sterilisation of adult women of unsound mind, with a consequent relaxation of the practice relating to applications to the court in such cases. For my part, I would therefore leave the matter as proposed by Sir Thomas Bingham M.R.; but I wish to express the hope that the President of the Family Division, who will no doubt be kept well informed about developments in this field, will soon feel able to relax the present requirement so as to limit applications for declarations to those cases in which there is a special need for the procedure to be invoked.

I wish to add one footnote. Since preparing this opinion, I have had the opportunity of reading in draft the speech of my noble and learned friend, Lord Browne-Wilkinson, in which he has expressed the view that a doctor, in reaching a decision whether or not to continue, in the best interests of his patient, to prolong his life by artificial means, may well be influenced by his own attitude to the sanctity of human life. The point does not arise for decision in the present case. I only wish to observe that it has implications not only in the case of a patient who, like Anthony Bland, is totally unconscious, but also one who may be suffering from great physical pain or (as in the case of one suffering from Guillain-Barre syndrome) extreme mental distress; and it would in theory fall to be tested if the patient's relatives, dismayed by the artificial prolongation of the agony of their loved one, were to seek to restrain by injunction a doctor who was persisting in prolonging his life. I cannot help feeling, however, that such a situation is more theoretical than real. I suspect that it is unlikely to arise in practice, if only because the solution could be found in a change of medical practitioner. It is not to be forgotten, moreover, that doctors who for conscientious reasons would feel unable to discontinue life support in such circumstances can presumably, like those who have a conscientious objection to abortion, abstain from involvement in such work. For present purposes, however, it is enough to state that the best interests test is broad and flexible in the sense that room must be allowed for the exercise of judgment by the doctor as to whether the relevant conditions exist which justify the discontinuance of life support."

LORD MUSTILL
"An alternative approach is to develop the reasoning of *F v. West Berkshire Health Authority* [1989] 2 All E.R. 545, by concentrating on the best interests, not of the community at large, but of Anthony Bland himself. Just as in *F v. West Berkshire Health Authority*, so the argument runs, the best interests of the patient demand a course of action which would normally be unlawful without the patient's consent. Just as in *F v. West Berkshire Health Authority* the patient is unable to decide for himself. In practice, to make no decision is to decide that the care and treatment shall continue. So that the decision shall

not thus be made by default it is necessary that someone other than Anthony Bland should consider whether in his own best interests his life should now be brought to an end, and if the answer is affirmative the proposed conduct can be put into effect without risk of criminal responsibility.

I cannot accept this argument which, if sound, would serve to legitimate a termination by much more direct means than are now contemplated. I can accept that a doctor in charge of a patient suffering the mental torture of Guillain-Barre syndrome, rational but trapped and mute in an unresponsive body, could well feel it imperative that a decision on whether to terminate life could wait no longer and that the only possible decision in the interests of the patient, even leaving out all the other interests involved, would be to end it here and now by a speedy and painless injection. Such a conclusion would attract much sympathy, but no doctrine of best interests could bring it within the law.

Quite apart from this the case of Anthony Bland seems to me quite different. He feels no pain and suffers no mental anguish. Stress was laid in argument on the damage to his personal dignity by the continuation of the present medical regime, and on the progressive erosion of the family's happy recollections by month after month of distressing and hopeless care. Considerations of this kind will no doubt carry great weight when Parliament comes to consider the whole question in the round. But it seems to me to be stretching the concept of personal rights, beyond breaking point to say that Anthony Bland has an interest in ending these sources of others distress. Unlike the conscious patient he does not know what is happening to his body, and cannot be affronted by it; he does not know of his family's continuing sorrow. By ending his life the doctors will not relieve him of a burden become intolerable, for others carry the burden and he has none. What other considerations could make it better for him to die now rather than later? None that we can measure, for of death we know nothing. The distressing truth which must not be shirked is that the proposed conduct is not in the best interests of Anthony Bland, for he has no best interests of any kind.

I. Best interests: the termination of treatment

After much expression of negative opinions I turn to an argument which in my judgement is logically defensible and consistent with the existing law. In essence it turns the previous argument on its head by directing the inquiry to the interests of the patient, not in the termination of life but in the continuation of his treatment. It runs as follows. (i) The cessation of nourishment and hydration is an omission not an act. (ii) Accordingly the cessation will not be a criminal act unless the doctors are under a present duty to continue the regime. (iii) At the time when Anthony Bland came into the care of the doctors decisions had to be made about his care which he was unable to make for himself. In accordance with *F v. West Berkshire Health Authority* [1989] 2 All E.R. 545 these decisions were to be made in his best interests. Since the possibility that he might recover still existed his best interests required that he should be supported in the hope that this would happen. These best interests justified the application of the necessary regime without his consent. (iv) All hope of recovery has now been abandoned. Thus, although the termination of his life is not in the best interests of Anthony Bland, his best interests in being kept alive have also disappeared, taking with them the justification for the non-consensual regime and the co-relative duty to keep it in being. (v) Since there is no longer a duty to provide nourishment and hydration a failure to do so cannot be a criminal offence.

My Lords, I must recognise at once that this chain of reasoning makes an unpromising start by transferring the morally and intellectually dubious distinction between acts and omissions into a context where the ethical foundations of the law are already open to question. The opportunity for anomaly and excessively fine distinctions, often depending more on the way in which the problem happens to be stated than on any real distinguishing features, has been exposed by many commentators, including in England the authors above-mentioned, together with Smith and Hogan *Criminal Law* (6th ed., 1988), p.51, H. Beynon 'Doctors as Murderers' [1982] Crim.L.R. 17 and M. J. Gunn and J. C. Smith

'*Arthur's* case and the right to life of a Down's Syndrome Child" [1985] *Crim.L.R.* 705. All this being granted we are still forced to take the law as we find it and try to make it work. Moreover, although in cases near the borderline the categorisation of conduct will be exceedingly hard, I believe that nearer the periphery there will be many instances which fall quite clearly into one category rather than the other. In my opinion the present is such a case, and in company with Compton J. in *Barber v. Superior Court of Los Angeles County* (1983) 147 Cal. App. 3d 1006 at 1017, amongst others I consider that the proposed conduct will fall into the category of omissions.

I therefore consider the argument to be soundly-based. Now that the time has come when Anthony Bland has no further interest in being kept alive, the necessity to do so, created by his inability to make a choice, has gone; and the justification for the invasive care and treatment, together with the duty to provide it have also gone. Absent a duty, the omission to perform what had previously been a duty will no longer be a breach of the criminal law.

In reaching this conclusion I have taken into account the fact that whereas for almost all concerned the adoption of the proposed course will be a merciful relief, this will not be so for the nursing staff, who will be called on to act in a way which must be contrary to all their instincts, training and traditions. They will encounter the ethical problems, not in a court or in a lecture room, but face to face. As the United Kingdom Council for Nursing, Midwifery and Health Visiting has emphasised, for the nurses involved the interval between the initiation of the proposed conduct and the death of Anthony Bland will be a very stressful period. Acknowledging this I hope that the nurses will accept, as I believe, that sadly it is for the best.

For these reasons I would uphold the declarations. Whilst there is no need to go further it is better to mention one further point. The reasoning which I propose is, I believe, broadly in line with that of your Lordships. But I venture to feel some reservations about the application of the principle of civil liability in negligence laid down in *Bolam v. Friern Hospital Management Committee* [1957] 2 All E.R. 118 to decisions on best interests in a field dominated by the criminal law. I accept without difficulty that this principle applies to the ascertainment of the medical raw material such as diagnosis, prognosis and appraisal of the patient's cognitive functions. Beyond this point, however, it may be said that the decision is ethical, not medical, and that there is no reason in logic why on such a decision the opinions of doctors should be decisive. If there had been a possibility that this question might make a difference to the outcome of the appeal I would have wished to consider it further, but since it does not I prefer for the moment to express no opinion upon it.

. . .

IV. The ethical question

After discussing the legal issues at length I will deal only briefly with the ethical question which must be for most lay people what the case is really about. With the general tenor, if not with the details, of what was said in the courts below I respectfully agree. But I prefer to advance on a narrower front. In law, if my conclusion is right, the way is clear for the doctors to proceed as they and the family think best. If the principle of *Bolam* applies that is the end of the matter, since nobody could doubt that a body of reasonable medical opinion would regard the proposed conduct as right. But even if *Bolam* is left aside, I still believe that the proposed conduct is ethically justified, since the continued treatment of Anthony Bland can no longer serve to maintain that combination of manifold character-istics which we call a personality. Some who have written on this subject maintain that this is too narrow a perspective, so I must make it clear that I do not assert that the human condition necessarily consists of nothing except a personality, or deny that it may also comprise a spiritual essence distinct from both body and personality. But of this we can know nothing, and in particular we cannot know whether it perishes with death or transcends it. Absent such knowledge we must measure up what we do know. So doing, I have no doubt that the best interests of Anthony Bland no longer demand the continuance of his present care and treatment. This is not at all to say that I would reach the same conclusion in less extreme cases, where the glimmerings of awareness may give the patient an interest which cannot be regarded as null. The issues, both legal and ethical, will then be altogether more difficult. As Mr Munby has pointed out, in this part of the law the court has moved a long way in a short time. Every step forward requires the greatest caution. Here however I am satisfied that what is proposed, and what all those who have considered the matter believe to be right, is in accordance with the law."

Anthony Bland died on March 3, 1993 of renal failure.

NOTES:

1. The decision of the House of Lords in *Bland* confirms the existence of the act/omission distinction in English law (see discussion in Chapter 2 above). The House of Lords stated that the removal of the tube was not to be classed as an action causing death, rather it could be categorised as an omission. As we saw above, the fact that conduct constitutes an omission does not mean that there is no liability in criminal law. Some omissions are culpable. In *Bland* the House of Lords held that withdrawal of treatment would not be a culpable omission if it was in the patient's best interests. The approach taken in *Re F (Mental Patient Sterilisation)* was followed and the "substituted judgment" test used in certain other jurisdictions was rejected. (See further Chapter 5 above.) The majority of the court in *Bland* (four out of five law lords) stated that what amounted to best interests was to be determined by reference to the *Bolam* test although Lord Mustill was not prepared to accept the *Bolam* approach.

2. In the past there has been much discussion as to the distinction between ordinary and extra-ordinary treatment. It was suggested that while failure to provide a basic level of care would be culpable in criminal law failure to continue more advanced types of medical treatment—"extraordinary treatment"—would not lead to liability. But whether such a clear-cut distinction can be drawn between the categories has been questioned, since advancing medical technology may make today's extraordinary measures commonplace within a short period of time. The House of Lords in *Bland* did not base their decision on such a distinction.

3. In *Bland* the application was made for the removal of artificial nutrition/hydration. Two members of the House of Lords (Lords Keith and Lowry) referred to this as medical treatment, Lord Goff stated that it was medical treatment or "part of the medical care of the patient". One difficult issue to be resolved in the future is whether "spoon feeding" would be classed as medical treatment. It could be argued that the distinction between spoon feeding and artificial nutrition/hydration is that the latter is invasive. Moreover the insertion of a feeding tube may lead to greater complications. (See generally J.M. Finnis, "Bland: Crossing the Rubicon" (1993) 109 L.Q.R. 329.)

4. One issue left open after the decision in *Bland* was as to whether artificial ventilation could be regarded as treatment and thus withdrawn. If the patient is conscious then he may be able to disengage mechanical support

himself by flicking a switch. (The situations in which a patient is competent while supported on a ventilator are limited, examples including a patient with motor neurone disease.) Examples in other jurisdictions exist of judicial approval being given to the withdrawal of treatment in such situations. (See, for example, *Nancy B. v Hotel-Dieu de Quebec* (1992) 86 DLR (4th) 385, (1992) 1 B.M.L.R. 95). It should be noted that withdrawal of ventilation may not result in death. A celebrated instance of such a case is the US case of Karen Quinlan, a case that led to a heated debate regarding the right to die in the United States. In *Quinlan's* case, although ventilator support was withdrawn, Quinlan herself lived on (*Re Quinlan* 355 A 2d 664 (N.J., 1976)). Subsequently the courts have authorised the withdrawal of ventilation from a competent but incapacitated patient—see *Re AK* [2001] 2 FLR 35 and *Re B* below.

5. Lord Browne-Wilkinson suggested that not only was withdrawal of treatment lawful but that in a situation in which continued treatment was not in the patient's best interests, it would be actually unlawful to continue with treatment:

> "What then is the extent of the right to treat Anthony Bland which can be deduced from *F v. West Berkshire Health Authority*? Both Lord Brandon of Oakbrook, and Lord Goff, make it clear that the right to administer invasive medical care is wholly dependent upon such care being in the best interests of the patient. Moreover, a doctor's decision whether invasive care is in the best interests of the patient falls to be assessed by reference to the test laid down in *Bolam v. Friern Hospital Management Committee* [1957] 2 All E.R. 118 *viz* is the decision in accordance with a practice accepted at the time by a responsible body of medical opinion ([1989] 2 All E.R. 545 at 559, 567 per Lord Brandon and Lord Goff). In my judgment it must follow from this that if there comes a stage where the responsible doctor comes to the reasonable conclusion (which accords with the views of a responsible body of medical opinion) that further continuance of an intrusive life support system is not in the best interests of the patient, he can no longer lawfully continue that life support system: to do so would constitute the crime of battery and the tort of trespass to the person. Therefore he cannot be in breach of any duty to maintain the patient's life. Therefore he is not guilty of murder by omission."

This statement by Lord Browne-Wilkinson has implications for any attempt to undertake a non-therapeutic procedure on an incompetent patient and is one reason why procedures for the harvesting of organs such as elective ventilation may be unlawful. (See Chapter 15 below). Furthermore were life to be prolonged at the relatives request where this was not in the patient's best interests, then it appears that this would be unlawful.

6. In *Bland* Lord Goff appeared to follow the approach in *Bodkin Adams* namely that the administration of pain-killing drugs is lawful even though the incidental effect may be to shorten a patient's life.

7. The proceedings in *Bland* took the form of a declaration. While this by itself does not preclude subsequent criminal proceedings, as Lord Goff noted, the fact that a declaration has been obtained will normally have the effect of inhibiting prosecution. In addition the Attorney-General could

enter a *nolle prosequi* to stop later proceedings. The court emphasised the exceptional nature of the case and the fact that cases concerning withdrawal of treatment from patients in PVS should be referred to the courts. (See J. Bridgeman, "Declared Innocent" (1995) 3 *Medical Law Review* 117.) Guidance now exists in the form of a practice note as to the procedure which should be adopted for reference of such cases to the courts (Practice Note (Official Solicitor: Declaratory Proceedings: Medical and Welfare Decisions for Adults Who Lack Capacity [2001] 2 FLR 158.)

8. After the *Bland* case a minister, the Revd Morrow, attempted to start criminal proceedings against Bland's doctor for murder and he laid an information before Bingley magistrates to that effect (*R v Bingley Magistrates Court, ex p. Morrow*, April 13, 1994, Q.B.D., and see A. Grubb, "Declaration: Effect on Subsequent Criminal Proceedings" (1995) 3 *Medical Law Review* 86.) They refused, and Mr Morrow brought an application for judicial review of the magistrates' decision. His application was rejected. The court agreed with the statement by Lord Goff in *Bland* that a civil declaration would normally preclude a subsequent criminal prosecution.

9. In the *Bland* case, the Law Lords suggested that there was a need for the issues raised in the case to receive further consideration by Parliament. Subsequently a House of Lords Select Committee on Euthanasia was established (HL Paper 21-2, London: HMSO, 1994). The conclusions of this Committee are considered more fully in the section on reform below. The Select Committee recommended that a definition of PVS be drawn up and a Code of Practice for the management of PVS patients be developed.

10. One potential problem is precisely how conclusive should the evidence be before treatment should be withdrawn and what should be done about the emergency situation. The issue of whether treatment should be withdrawn from a patient in a PVS state came before the courts in later cases. In *Frenchay Healthcare National Health Service Trust v S* [1994] 2 All E.R. 403; [1994] 1 W.L.R. 601; [1994] 1 F.L.R. 485, S took a drug overdose. As a consequence he suffered brain damage. He was treated in hospital where he was diagnosed as being in a persistent vegetative state. He was fed via a naso-gastric tube in his stomach. The tube became disconnected. The consultant surgeon treating him did not believe that the tube could be reconnected and thought that the only alternative was to insert another tube. The doctor took the view that continued treatment was not in the best interests of S. The hospital sought an order from the court that it would be lawful not to reinsert the tube. On appeal to the Court of Appeal, Sir Thomas Bingham took the view that in an emergency as here, not all the guidelines as set out in *Bland* could be complied with that case is not one of them. In *Frenchay* the issue of treatment was urgent because the tube had become dislodged. The judge also noted that the diagnosis was not as conclusive as in the *Bland* case. The case illustrates some of the difficulties which are likely to arise in the future because these applications

will frequently be made as emergency orders (see A. Palmer, "Withdrawal of Medical Treatment: the Emergency Case" [1995] *Family Law* 195). This may be seen as particularly problematic in view of concerns expressed as to practices in relation to the diagnosis of PVS. A study undertaken at the Royal Hospital for Neurodisability in Putney found that out of 40 patients referred to the hospital with a diagnosis of persistent vegetative state between 1992 and 1995 some 17 had been wrongly diagnosed (see K. Andrew, L. Murphy, R. Munday, and C. Littlewood, "Misdiagnosis of the Vegetative State: Retrospective Study in a Rehabilitation Unit" (1996) 313 British Medical Journal 13).

11. The withdrawal of treatment has also been authorised where the patient was being treated in the community in *Swindon & Marlborough NHS Trust v S* [1995] Med. Law Rev. 84.) S, a 48-year-old married woman in a PVS state, was being cared for primarily by her family at home, although there were also certain periods of care in hospital. She was receiving nutrition through a gastrostomy tube. The tube became blocked and an operation was required to insert a new tube. An application was made to the court for an order that further treatment should not be pursued. The court granted the order. Waite J. made the point that in a situation in which the patient was being cared for at home proceedings regarding the withdrawal of treatment should be brought either by the hospital caring for the patient or by the G.P. to avoid the burden of bringing such proceedings falling on the family. (See J. Stone, "Withholding of Life Sustaining Treatment" (1995) New Law Journal 354 and M. Hinchliffe, "Vegetative State Patients" (1996) 146 New Law Journal 1579 .

12. Following *Bland* one of the characteristics of later decisions has been that of judicial willingness to approve withdrawal of treatment in cases which fell outside the PVS guidelines. So, for example, in *Re D (Medical Treatment)* [1998] 1 FLR 411 the patient had suffered severe head injuries following a road accident. She returned from hospital to live with her parents who were caring for her. She had both mental and physical disabilities. While she chould communicate, as she realised her condition was not going to further improve she became depressed and indicated that she was very dissatisfied with her life. She suffered an injury to the brain in September 1995 and in March 1996 was diagnosed as being in PVS. She was given artificial nutrition and hydration. The tube became dislodged in March 1997. An application was made to the court to determine whether it was lawful not to reinsert the tube. The Official Solicitor opposed the declaration as medical evidence indicated she fell outside the guidelines which had been produced by the Royal Medical Colleges regarding the diagnosis of PVS. The judge did accept the view of those medical experts who held her to be in PVS and in addition took the approach that there was no evidence that she had any life whatsoever and that she was suffering a "living death" and that it was not in her best interests to be kept alive artificially. In the later case of *Re H* [1998] 2 F.L.R. 36, H was 43 years old and had suffered serious brain damage in a road accident. He was kept alive through artificial feeding and was not aware of his environment.

Some evidence was given to the effect that not all the guidelines regarding diagnosis of PVS were fulfilled, however Sir Stephen Brown made the order stating that "I am satisfied that it is in the best interests of this patient that the life-sustaining treatment should be brought to a conclusion".

13. A contrasting case is that of *W Healthcare Trust v H and Another* [2004] EWCA Civ 1324, where the patient was suffering from multiple sclerosis, a condition which she had had for some 30 years. She was conscious. She was tube-fed and was given round-the-clock nursing care. When her feeding tube became dislodged, her family did not want it reinserted; however, the health care professionals wanted feeding continued. At first instance the decision to continue feeding was upheld and this was approved in the Court of Appeal. Here there was no indication of any advance directive or decision by the patient. Furthermore it was clear that as the patient did have awareness she would have known that she was starving to death. Brooke L.J. stated that:

> " The Court cannot in effect sanction the death by starvation of a patient who is not in a PVS state other than with their clear and informed consent or where their condition is so intolerable as to be beyond doubt . . . "

14. In a further notable case concerning newly born children, *Re A (children): (conjoined twins)* [2001] Fam. 147, the Court of Appeal sanctioned the separation of conjoined twins in a situation in which the consequence of the operation was that of certain death for Mary, the weaker twin, although there was parental opposition to surgery. This case is discussed in full in Chapter 7 above. It should be noted that in the Court of Appeal any attempt to class the operation to separate the twins as an omission as opposed to an action was rejected. (See Chapter 7 above and generally the special edition of the *Medical Law Review* devoted to this case (2001) 9 *Medical Law Review* 3.)

15. The approach of the House of Lords in *Bland* has been followed in other jurisdictions including Scotland: *Laws Hospital NHS Trust v The Lord Advocate* (1996) S.L.T. 848, and Ireland: *In the Matter of a Ward of Court* [1995] 2 I.L.R.M. 401 (Ireland). See also discussion in A. Grubb, P. Walsh and N. Lamb, "Reporting on the Persistent Vegetative State in Europe" (1998) 6 *Medical Law Review* 161.

QUESTIONS:

1. Why did the court grant the declaration in *Bland*? What is the effect of such a declaration in criminal and in civil law?
2. Why is the conduct of a doctor who discontinues nutrition/hydration not murder? (See J.M. Finnis, "Bland: Crossing the Rubicon" (1993) 109 *Law Quarterly Review* 329.)
3. What is meant by the "sanctity of life" and did the House of Lords misunderstand this principle? (See J. Keown, "Restoring Moral and Intellectual Shape to the Law After Bland" (1997) 113 *Law Quarterly Review* 481.)

4. Should the appropriate test to apply in such cases be whether an accepted body of medical opinion would be of the view that treatment should be withheld?
5. Is it correct to say that in a case, such as that of Tony Bland, death can be in the patient's best interests? Examine Lord Mustill's judgment.
6. The weighing up of medical resources in reaching the decision was rejected by the House of Lords in the *Bland* case, but should medical resources be a factor taken into consideration?
7. Lord Goff suggests that doctors who have a conscientious objection could probably abstain from work in this area. However, there are only two specific statutory provisions which allow for conscientious objection in health care, neither of which relate to the end of life. Should the doctor or other health professional be allowed to opt out on an ad hoc basis? Examine Lord Mustill's judgment above at p.1031 in relation to the role of the nurse. What may be the effect of the Human Rights Act 1998 today and in particular Article 9, the right to freedom of conscience and belief (see Chapter 1 above).
8. What are the implications of the *Bland* case for cases involving the withdrawal of treatment from neonates? (See Lord Goff's judgment above at p.1025 and see discussion in Chapter 7 above.)
9. Lord Goff talks in terms of it not being appropriate to prolong care where treatment is "futile". But what constitutes "futility"? Is it "futile" to treat a 10-year-old suffering from leukaemia where there is a success rate of 1–4 per cent. (See C. Newdick, *Who Should We Treat?* (2nd edn) Oxford: OUP, 2005 at pp.103–107, Chapter 1 above.)
10. Should the question of withdrawal of a patient from artificial nutrition/ventilation be referred automatically to the court?

(b) Discontinuation of Treatment and the Human Rights Act 1998

The *Bland* decision pre-dated the Human Rights Act 1998 by several years. To what extent is *Bland* in accordance with the Human Rights Act itself? This was an issue which came for judicial consideration in the following case:

NHS Trust A v M; NHS Trust B v H [2001] 1 All E.R. 801

Mrs M was a 49-year-old married woman who had three adult children, She had suffered a cardio-respiratory arrest while she was under general anaesthetic and this resulted in hypoxic brain damage. She was diagnosed as being in a chronic vegetative state. At the time of the case she had been in that state for over three years. Mrs H was a 36-year-old divorced woman who lived with her 10-year-old son. She had a history of epilepsy and the side-effects of her medication led to episodes of pancreatitis. She collapsed on holiday with her fiancée in 1999 and was admitted to hospital in October 1999 on her return to England. She was discharged but readmitted and then collapsed in an asystolic cardiac arrest and suffered anoxic brain damage. She was diagnosed as being in PVS. At the time of the hearing she had been in that state for nine months. Butler Sloss L.J. commented that:

"On the evidence presented to me it would not be in the best interests of either patient to continue treatment and the case for granting the declarations in respect of each patient is very strong if it is lawful to withdraw the provision of artificial nutrition and hydration."

She continued:

BUTLER SLOSS L.J.

"**Article 2 (the right to life)**

Mr Emmerson for the Official Solicitor in his submissions posed three key questions. (1) Is a patient diagnosed as in a permanent vegetative state alive? (2) Does the withdrawal of artificial nutrition and hydration constitute an 'intentional deprivation of life' within the meaning of article 2.1? That question breaks down into two further questions. (a) Is the 'intention' of the withdrawal of treatment to bring about the patient's death or shorten his or her life? (b) Does an omission to provide life-sustaining treatment constitute 'an intentional deprivation'? (3) If the withdrawal does not constitute an intentional deprivation of life, are the circumstances such that article 2 must be taken to impose a positive obligation to provide life-sustaining treatment? I have found the questions very helpful in my approach to this case and therefore adopt them.

1 Is a patient diagnosed as in a permanent vegetative state alive?

The answer to question (1) is clearly 'Yes' from the description of permanent vegetative state in the report of the college. The brain stem of the patient remains intact. All the judges in *Bland's* case [1993] AC 789, supported by the medical experts, accepted that Anthony Bland was alive despite the diagnosis that he was suffering from persistent vegetative state, as it was then described. Article 2 therefore clearly protects Mrs M and Mrs H.

2(a) Is the 'intention' of the withdrawal of treatment to bring about the patient's death or shorten his or her life?

Turning to question 2(a) Mr Emmerson, and Mr Grace for the trusts, disagree in their submissions on the issue whether the intention to withdraw artificial nutrition and hydration is to bring about the patient's death or to shorten life. Mr Grace argued that it was not the intention of the trust to bring about death. Withdrawing treatment would not be ending the life of either patient by the act of another, nor by culpable omission if carried out within the guidelines laid down in *Bland's* case. The cause of death would be the disease or injury that created their condition. In my view the issue was decided by the House of Lords in *Bland's* case. Although, since the implementation of the European Convention on Human Rights, I am no longer bound by the decision in *Bland's* case [1993] AC 789, the speeches of Lord Browne-Wilkinson where he said, at p 881, 'the whole purpose of stopping artificial feeding is to bring about the death of Anthony Bland', and of Lord Lowry, at pp 876–877, are most persuasive. I do not consider there is any difference in principle in this context between intention and purpose.

2(b) Does an omission to provide a life-sustaining treatment constitute an intentional deprivation?

The question of discontinuing artificial nutrition and hydration to a patient in a permanent vegetative state has not yet arisen in the European Court of Human Rights, and guidance on the applicability of article 2 has to be gleaned from decisions of that court dealing with entirely different situations . . .

Article 2 clearly contains a *negative* obligation on the state, to refrain from taking life intentionally. Question 2(b) raises the issue of the extent of the negative obligation not intentionally to deprive a patient of life within the meaning of article 2.1. Robert Walker LJ in *Re A*, 589 said:

'The Convention is to be construed as an autonomous text, without regard to any special rules of English law, and the word "intentionally" in article 2(1) must be given its natural and ordinary meaning. In my judgment the word, construed in that way, applies only to cases where the purpose of the prohibited action is to cause death.'

In *Widmer v Switzerland* (1993) Application No 20527/92 (unreported), on a petition by a son that the hospital in which his father had died had engaged in 'passive euthanasia', the Commission held that the failure of the Swiss state to criminalise 'passive euthanasia' did not amount to a breach of the Convention since the state sufficiently punished attacks on life. In *Association X v United Kingdom* (1978) 14 D&R 31 the Commission held that where a small number of children had died as a result of a vaccination scheme whose sole purpose was to protect the health of society by eliminating infectious diseases, it could not be said that there had been an intentional deprivation of life within the meaning of article 2, or that the state had not taken adequate and appropriate steps to protect life.

It is clear from the judgment of Robert Walker LJ in *Re A* and the decisions of the Commission in the *Widmer* and *Association X* cases that there are limits to the extent of the negative obligation under article 2.1.

The medical profession cannot treat patients who are competent without their consent. To do so, without consent, would be unlawful. A competent adult would have the absolute right to refuse artificial nutrition and hydration even though such refusal would lead to his death. This position is clear from English common law. Lord Goff of Chieveley said in *Bland*: "I start with the fundamental principle, now long established, that every person's body is inviolate."

That fundamental principle of English law is also to be found in article 8 of the Convention. If a patient does not have the capacity to accept or refuse treatment it is the duty of the doctor, under the doctrine of necessity, to treat such a patient if it is in his best interests: . . . As the speeches of the House of Lords showed in *Airedale NHS Trust v Bland* [1993] AC 789, the duty of the doctor is to treat the patient as long as it is in his best interests to have that treatment. If, however, it is no longer in the patient's best interests to have that treatment, it is not the duty of the medical team to continue it. Lord Goff of Chieveley said in *Bland's* case, at p 867:

'if the justification for treating a patient who lacks the capacity to consent lies in the fact that the treatment is provided in his best interests, it must follow that the treatment may, and indeed ultimately should, be discontinued where it is no longer in his best interests to provide it.'

Lord Browne-Wilkinson went further. In his speech in *Bland's* case he said, at pp.884–885:

'Unless the doctor has reached the affirmative conclusion that it is in the patient's best interest to continue the invasive care, such care must cease . . . Only if the doctors responsible for [Anthony Bland's] care held the view that, though he is aware of nothing, there is some benefit to him in staying alive, would there be anything to indicate that it is for his benefit to continue the invasive medical care. In Anthony Bland's case, the doctors do not take that view. The discontinuance of life support would be in accordance with the proposals contained in the Discussion Paper on Treatment of Patients in Persistent Vegetative State issued in September 1992 by the Medical Ethics Committee of the British Medical Association. Therefore the requirement is satisfied. In these circumstances, it is perfectly reasonable for the responsible doctors to conclude that there is no affirmative benefit to Anthony Bland in continuing the invasive medical procedures necessary to sustain his life. Having so concluded, they are neither entitled nor under a duty to continue such medical care. Therefore they will not be guilty of murder if they discontinue such care.'

Although lack of entitlement to treat an incompetent patient if it is not in his best interests was not specifically referred to in the other speeches in *Bland's* case, such treatment would violate the patient's personal autonomy which he retains despite being incompetent. Lord Browne-Wilkinson's analysis is clearly correct both at common law and under article 8.

If a decision to cease medical treatment in the best interests of the patient is to be characterised as intentional deprivation of life, in view of the absolute nature of the prohibition on intentional killing, Mr Emmerson submitted that there would be a duty in every case to take steps to keep a terminally ill patient alive by all means possible, and to continue those steps indefinitely, until the patient's body could no longer sustain treatment, irrespective of the circumstances or the prognosis. I agree with Mr Emmerson that such an interpretation of article 2 cannot be correct.

Although the intention in withdrawing artificial nutrition and hydration in PVS cases is to hasten death, in my judgment the phrase 'deprivation of life' must import a deliberate act, as opposed to an omission, by someone acting on behalf of the state, which results in death. A responsible decision by a medical team not to provide treatment at the initial stage could not amount to intentional deprivation of life by the state. Such a decision based on clinical judgment is an omission to act. The death of the patient is the result of the illness or injury from which he suffered and that cannot be described as a deprivation. It may be relevant to look at the reasons for the clinical decision in the light of the positive obligation of the state to safeguard life, but, in my judgment, it cannot be regarded as falling within the negative obligation to refrain from taking life intentionally. I cannot see the difference between that situation and a decision to discontinue treatment which is no longer in the best interests of the patient and would therefore be a violation of his autonomy, even though that discontinuance will have the effect of shortening the life of the patient.

The analysis of these issues by the House of Lords in *Bland's* case [1993] AC 789 is entirely in accordance with the Convention case law on article 2 and is applicable to the distinction between negative and positive obligations. An omission to provide treatment by the medical team will, in my judgment, only be incompatible with article 2 where the circumstances are such as to impose a positive obligation on the state to take steps to prolong a patient's life. Mr Grace made clear the concern of the trusts that my judgment dealing with omission to provide treatment should not in future be applied to cases which might arise, in which treatment was given which had the effect of shortening life. I understand his concern. This judgment is dealing only with the situation where treatment is to be discontinued and is not concerned with nor relevant to acts by doctors or other members of the health service, such as the giving of palliative drugs to a terminally ill patient, which might have the effect of shortening his life.

Mr Grace advanced the argument that the quality of life of a patient was relevant to the protection under article 2. I agree, however, with Mr Emmerson that the quality of life may be relevant to the clinical assessment of whether it is in the patient's best interests for treatment to continue but does not form part of the question whether this is an intentional deprivation of life within the meaning of article 2.

3 If the withdrawal does not constitute an intentional deprivation of life, are the circumstances such that article 2 must be taken to impose a positive obligation to provide life-sustaining treatment?

However, article 2 also contains a *positive* obligation, to take adequate and appropriate steps to safeguard life: . . . In answer to question 3 that positive obligation upon a state to protect life is not absolute. In the case the European Commission explained, in *Osman v UK* (1998) 5 BHRC 293 at 321:

'The first sentence of article 2(1) also imposes a positive obligation on contracting states that the right to life be protected by law. In earlier cases, the Commission considered that this may include an obligation to take appropriate steps to safeguard life . . . While effective investigation procedures and enforcement of criminal law prohibitions in respect of events which have occurred provide an indispensable safeguard and the protective effect of deterrence, the Commission is of the opinion that for article 2 to be given practical force it must be interpreted also as requiring preventive steps to be taken to protect life from known and avoidable dangers. However, the extent of this obligation will vary inevitably having regard to the source and degree of danger and the means available to combat it. Whether risk to life derives from disease, environmental factors or from the intentional activities of those acting outside the law, there will be a range of policy decisions, relating, inter alia, to the use of state resources, which it will be for contracting states to assess on the basis of their aims and priorities, subject to these being compatible with the values of democratic societies and the fundamental rights guaranteed in the Convention.'

The court held *Osman v UK* (1998) 5 BHRC 293 at 321, at p 306, para 116:

'For the court, and having regard to the nature of the right protected by article 2, a right fundamental in the scheme of the Convention, it is sufficient for an applicant to show that the authorities did not do all that could be reasonably expected of them to avoid a real and immediate risk to life of which they have or ought to have knowledge. This is a question which can only be answered in the light of all the circumstances of any particular case.'

The standard applied by the European Court of Human Rights bears a close resemblance to the standard adopted in the domestic law of negligence and approximates to the obligation recognised by the English courts in the best interests test: see *Airedale NHS Trust v Bland* [1993] AC 789. In a case where a responsible clinical decision is made to withhold treatment, on the grounds that it is not in the patient's best interests, and that clinical decision is made in accordance with a respectable body of medical opinion, the state's positive obligation under article 2 is, in my view, discharged. In *Widmer v Switzerland* (unreported) the Commission considered the claim that there was negligent failure on the part of the hospital to treat the applicant's father. The Commission rejected the petition and said that 'the idea that the right of any person to life is protected by law requires the state . . . to take all reasonable steps to protect life'.

It considered that Switzerland in its legislation had taken sufficient steps to carry out the duty imposed upon it by article 2. The court in *Widmer*, 305, para 116 said that the positive obligation under article 2 'must be interpreted in a way which does not impose an impossible or disproportionate burden on the authorities'.

Article 2 therefore imposes a positive obligation to give life-sustaining treatment in circumstances where, according to responsible medical opinion, such treatment is in the best interests of the patient but does not impose an absolute obligation to treat if such treatment would be futile. This approach is entirely in accord with the principles laid down in *Airedale NHS Trust v Bland* [1993] AC 789 where Lord Goff of Chieveley said, at p 869:

'for my part I cannot see that medical treatment is appropriate or requisite simply to prolong a patient's life, when such treatment has no therapeutic purpose of any kind, as where it is futile because the patient is unconscious and there is no prospect of any improvement in his condition.'

In our use of the declaratory jurisdiction of the High Court in PVS cases we impose in our domestic law a higher test than the standard set by the European Court of Human Rights, since the High Court reviews the medical conclusion on best interests and may not necessarily accept the medical opinion . . . .

[Dame Butler Sloss noted that withdrawal of PVS treatment has been regarded as legitimate in many countries across the world and then continued:]
The decision of the House of Lords forms an important part of international jurisprudence on this subject. The existing practice in the United Kingdom is accordingly compatible with the values of democratic societies.

Article 8

As I have already said article 8 protects the right to personal autonomy, otherwise described as the right to physical and bodily integrity. It protects a patient's right to self-determination and an intrusion into bodily integrity must be justified under article 8.2: see *X and Y v The Netherlands* (1985) 8 EHRR 235 and *Peters v The Netherlands* (1994) 77-A D&R 75. Mr Grace suggested that article 8 may be in conflict with article 2 and is to be balanced against article 2. I prefer, however, the submission of Mr Emmerson that, in seeking to determine the scope of the positive obligation in article 2, assistance can be derived from the provisions of article 8. Mr Grace asked me to take into account under article 8 the views and feelings of the families. They are, of course, important considerations for the hospitals treating these patients to take into account. It is not necessary for me in the present cases to come to a conclusion whether the wishes and feelings of the families form part of the patient's right to respect for family life under article 8 in situations where the patient is insensate. If they are relevant they cannot outweigh any positive obligation on the state to maintain the patient's life. I rather doubt that the families have rights under article 8 separate from the rights of the patient, but a decision on that issue also is not a necessary part of my overall decision.

Article 3

I am asked by Mr Grace to consider the implications of article 3 to the continuation of treatment which is futile. Mr Wood, on behalf of ALERT, wished me to consider article 3 on the basis that it was relevant to the withdrawal of artificial nutrition and hydration and would be breached during the short period leading up to the death of the two patients. I am satisfied that article 3 does not apply to either situation. Clearly the continuation of futile treatment or the withdrawal of such treatment cannot be described either as torture or as punishment. The issue is whether either is 'degrading treatment'. In *Ireland v United Kingdom* (1978) 2 EHRR 25, 80, para 167 the court said, in the context of interrogation tactics in Northern Ireland, that degrading treatment meant ill-treatment designed 'to arouse in their victims feelings of fear, anguish and inferiority capable of humiliating and debasing them and possibly breaking their physical or moral resistance'.

In *D v UK* (1997) 24 EHRR 423 a broader approach was adopted in respect of the proposed deportation of an AIDS patient from the United Kingdom to St Kitts. The court said, at p 447, para 49:

'the court must reserve to itself sufficient flexibility to address the application of that article in other contexts which might arise. It is not therefore prevented from scrutinising an applicant's claim under article 3 where the source of the risk of proscribed treatment in the receiving country stems from factors which cannot engage either directly or indirectly the responsibility of the public authorities of that country, or which, taken alone, do not in themselves infringe the standards of that article. To limit the application of article 3 in this manner would be to undermine the absolute character of its protection.'

The court held that to return him to St Kitts would amount to inhuman treatment.

Mr Grace submitted that article 3 can be invoked to ensure protection of a PVS patient's right to die with dignity and that it was degrading to enforce the continuation of life in those circumstances. He suggested that it was not necessary in order for article 3 to apply that the person within its protection had to be aware of the treatment complained of. The purpose of article 3 was to outlaw treatment which is inhuman or degrading and is objective as well as subjective. Mr Emmerson submitted that article 3 did not apply to an insensate patient and that for it to apply a person so treated had to be conscious of suffering. He further submitted that administration of medical treatment in good faith is unlikely to be a violation of article 3.

Two decisions of the European Court of Human Rights support Mr Emmerson's submission. In *T v UK* (1999) 7 BHRC 659 at 682–683 the court said:

'68. Ill-treatment must attain a minimum level of severity if it is to fall within the scope of article 3. The assessment of this minimum is, in the nature of things, relative; it depends on all the circumstances of the case, such as the nature and context of the treatment or punishment, the manner and method of its execution, its duration, its physical or mental effects and, in some instances, the sex, age and state of health of the victim . . .

'69. Treatment has been held by the court to be "inhuman" because, inter alia, it was premeditated, was applied for hours at a stretch and caused either actual bodily injury or intense physical and mental suffering, and also "degrading" because it was such as to arouse in its victims feelings of fear, anguish and inferiority capable of humiliating and debasing them. In order for a punishment or treatment associated with it to be "inhuman" or "degrading", the suffering or humiliation involved must in any event go beyond that inevitable element of suffering or humiliation connected with a given form of legitimate treatment or punishment. The question whether the purpose of the treatment was to humiliate or debase the victim is a further factor to be taken into account . . . but the absence of any such purpose cannot conclusively rule out a finding of violation of article 3.'

In *Herczegfolvy v Austria* (1992) 15 EHRR 437 at 484, para 82 the court said: 'as a general rule, a measure which is a therapeutic necessity cannot be regarded as inhuman or degrading. The court must nevertheless satisfy itself that the medical necessity has been convincingly shown to exist.' See also *X v Federal Republic of Germany* (1984) 7 EHRR 152 (forcible feeding of a prisoner on hunger strike not in violation of article 3).

On the assumption that article 3 requires to be considered, I am satisfied that the proposed withdrawal of treatment from these two patients has been thoroughly and anxiously considered by a number of experts in the field of PVS patients and is in accordance with the practice of a responsible body of medical opinion. The withdrawal is for a benign purpose in accordance with the best interests of the patients not to continue life-saving treatment; it is legitimate and appropriate that the residual treatment be continued until death. I am, moreover, satisfied that article 3 requires the victim to be aware of the inhuman and degrading treatment which he or she is experiencing or at least to be in a state of physical or mental suffering. An insensate patient suffering from permanent vegetative state has no feelings and no comprehension of the treatment accorded to him or her. Article 3 does not in my judgment apply to these two cases . . . "

NOTES:

1. In considering the interpretation of Article 2, Butler Sloss L.J. took a narrow approach to intention which is consistent with the approach taken in the Court of Appeal in *Re A* [2000] 4 All ER 961 (see Chapter 7 above at p.434).
2. Butler Sloss also took the approach that as long as a decision to withhold treatment satisfied the *Bolam* test, this was ECHR-compliant. Grubb has commented that the effect of this is that "we see the Convention as providing 'a floor' rather than a 'ceiling' for the protection of an

individual's human rights . . . The upshot is, however, that Article 2 will have little or no impact on the so-called treatment-limiting cases which have become so familiar to medical law. Decisions will still be made in the patient's best interests" (see A. Grubb, "Incompetent Patient (Adult): Bland and the Human Rights Act 1998' (2000) *Medical Law Review* 342).

3. The judgment has been criticised by Keown. In relation to Article 3 he asks "Why is it not inhuman or degrading for a doctor to subject an insensate patient to a lingering death from dehydration if the doctor does so to end a life he considers no longer worthwhile?" In addition he suggests that the judgment shows some confusion between autonomy and a right which, he argues, the adult without capacity possesses, the right to bodily integrity (see J. Keown, " Dehydration and Human Rights" (2001) *Cambridge Law Journal* 53).

4. In *R (Burke) v GMC* [2004] EWHC 1878, Mumby J also criticised the argument that Article 3 did not apply in the case of the patient who was unaware of the inhuman/degrading treatment or in a state of physical or mental suffering. He suggested that the implication of this finding was that "the Convention's emphasis on the protection of the vulnerable may be circumvented" (see further discussion of *Burke* below).

5. Despite the criticism, this judgment was followed in later cases, see *Re G* (2002) 65 B.M.L.R. 6, and *NHS Trust v I* [2003] E.H.C. 2243.

6. One notable feature of the post *Bland* cases has been the tendency for the courts to cross-refer those cases concerning adults and young children, even though the jurisdictional basis for review of such decisions is different. (see Chapter 7 above).

QUESTIONS:

1. Is it appropriate to deal with decisions to withdraw treatment from adults and children in the same way? (see further J.K. Mason and G. Laurie, *Mason and McCall Smith's Law and Medical Ethics* (Oxford: OUP, 2006) at pp.565–568.)

2. Is the best interests test the same in relation to adults lacking mental capacity and young children? (See Chapter 7 above.)

(c) Do Not Resuscitate Orders

Most of the cases which we have considered up until now concern the withdrawal of treatment once begun. But difficult issues also concern the commencement of therapy. The decision whether to treat at all is a medical decision and one made initially when the patient is brought in to hospital. This difficult assessment, known as "triage", is a rationing decision and is a matter of relatively low public visibility, which has not been the subject of judicial or legislative consideration. (See S. F. Spicker, "ICU Triage: the Ethics of Scarcity, the Ideal of Impartiality and the Inadvertent Endorsement of Evil" in R. Lee and D. Morgan (eds), *Death rites: Law and Ethics at the End of Life,* London: Routledge, 1994.) Another issue is not whether a particular therapy should be continued but whether therapy should be initiated at all. Once X is treated, then the issue may arise as to whether further "active" treatment should be continued. A patient may be made the subject of what is known as a "do not resuscitate order". These are directions given that, should a particular event occur, this patient should not be given one or more types of treatment. The directions are given by health practitioners. These directives were the subject of consideration in *Re R* [1996] 2 F.L.R. 99. R was a man of 23 with cerebral palsy, brain malformation and consequent learning difficulties. He was unable to walk or sit upright without help. While he was not in PVS he was in what was termed a low awareness state. He was totally dependent upon professional care and evidence was given to the effect that he was deteriorating neurologically and physically. The consultant stated that it was in R's best interests to let nature take its course when a "life-threatening crisis" took place. The parents agreed that if R suffered a cardiac arrest he should not be resuscitated. A doctor caring for R signed a "do not resuscitate" (DNR) direction. The staff of the day centre where R was being cared for challenged this order. They sought judicial review, claiming that the DNR policy was irrational and unlawful because it allowed treatment to be withheld on the basis of an assessment of a patient's quality of life. The NHS trust also went to court seeking a declaration to the effect that their actions were lawful. In the proceedings eventually heard before Sir Stephen Brown, the trust sought a declaration to the effect that it would be lawful to withhold cardio-pulmonary resuscitation of the patient and the administration of antibiotics in the event of the patient developing of potentially life-threatening infection which would otherwise call for the administration of antibiotics. This was upheld by Sir Stephen Brown P.

SIR STEPHEN BROWN P
" . . . In March 1993 the British Medical Association and the Royal College of Nursing published a joint statement entitled 'Cardio-Pulmonary Resuscitation: A Statement from the R.C.N. and the B.M.A.' A copy of the statement is to be found in the documents before the court. The introduction reads

'Cardio-Pulmonary Resuscitation (C.P.R.) can be attempted on any individual in whom cardiac or respiratory function ceases. Such events are inevitable as part of dying and thus C.P.R. can theoretically be used on every individual prior to death. It is therefore essential to identify patients for whom Cardio-pulmonary arrest respresents a terminal event in their illness and in whom C.P.R. is inappropriate.'

Under the heading 'Background' appears the following:

'Do not resuscitate (DNR) orders may be a potent source of misunderstanding and dissent amongst doctors, nurses and other involved in the care of patients. Many of the problems in this, difficult area would be avoided if communication and explanation of the decision were improved . . .
   These guidelines therefore should be viewed as a framework providing basic principles within which decisions regarding local policies on CPR may be formulated. Further assistance for doctors and nurses where individual problems arise, can be obtained from their respective professional organisations.

Guidelines

   1. It is appropriate to consider a do-not-resuscitate (D.N.R.) decision in the following circumstances:

(a) where the patient's condition indicates that effective cardio-pulmonary resuscitation (C.P.R.) is unlikely to be successful;

(b) where C.P.R. is not in accord with the recorded sustained wished of the patient who is mentally competent;

(c) where successful C.P.R. is likely to be followed by a lengthened quality of life which would not be acceptable to the patient.

2. Where a D.N.R. order has not been made and the express wishes of the patient are unknown, resuscitation should be initiated if cardiac or pulmonary arrest occurs. Anyone initiating C.P.R. in such circumstances, should be supported by their senior and medical nursing colleagues.

3. The overall responsibility for a D.N.R. decision rests with the consultant in charge of the patient's care. This should be be made after appropriate consultation and consideration of all aspects of the patients condition. The perspectives of other members of the medical and nursing team, the patient, and with due regard to patient confidentiality, the patient's relatives or close friends, may all be valuable in forming the consultants's decision.

. . .

5. Although responsibility for C.P.R. policy rests with the consultant, he or she should be prepared always to discuss the decision for an individual patient with other health professionals involved in the patient's care.'

Paragraph 9 states:

'when the basis for a D.N.R. Order is the absence of any likely medical benefit, discussion with the patient, or others close to the patient, should aim at securing an understanding and acceptance of the clinical decision which has been reached. If a D.N.R. decision is based on quality of life considerations, the views of the patient where these can be ascertained are particularly important. If the patient cannot express a view, the opinion of others close to the patient may be sought regarding the patient's best interests.'

In December 1993 the NHS Trust in question published its own version of the statement issued jointly by the BMA and the RCN. Its wording was slightly different and in particular in para. 2(c) used the phrase 'because of unacceptable quality of life'. That differed slightly from the wording of the joint BMA/RCN guidance which referred to 'the length of and quality of life which would not be acceptable to the patient'. However, the document issued by this NHS Trust made it clear in the first paragraph that 'the overall responsibility for such a D.N.R. decision rests with the consultant in charge of the patient's care. This should be made after appropriate consultation and consideration of all aspects of the patient's condition'.

. . . Dr Andrews points out that a 'do not resuscitate' policy is a well-recognised procedure in health care. He draws attention to the joint statement of the British Medical Association and the Royal College of Nurses to which I have already referred . . . He points out that (b) and (c) involve the views of the patient and therefore are not appropriate to this particular situation. It is (a) where the guideline deals with the effectiveness of CPR which is particularly relevant in the present case. Dr Andrews said that even in hospital settings, on average, only about 13 per cent of patients receiving CPR survive to discharge. In a residential home without medical staff present the chances of a successful resuscitation would be almost nil. There would also be a very real risk in the case of someone with deformities of the kind which the patient R has of his receiving injuries, such as broken ribs, from the procedure. Dr Andrews, gave it as his considered opinion that in the light of the extremely small potential for success and the distress which injuries would cause it would be wholly inappropriate to give this treatment to R. Accordingly, a 'do not resuscitate' policy in his view is appropriate based on the likely futility of attempts to resuscitate R successfully in a residential setting . . . "

The judge noted the unanimous view of the medical expert that to undertake resuscitation was inappropriate here and evidence to the effect that it could result in further brain damage and harm by excessive pressure being applied to an already fragile bone structure and continued:

"So far as the withholding of antibiotics is concerned Dr Andrews stated that this is a matter which can only properly be decided at the time when a potentially life threatening situation from infection arises. There should not be, as it were, a global 'Do Not Treat' policy. The plaintiff trust has indicated that it is content to accept that position. The decision as to the withholding of the administration of antibiotics in a potentially life threatening situation is a matter fully within the responsibility of the consultant having the responsibility for treating the patient. It is a matter which should be considered in conjunction with the general practitioner and, futhermore, in the case of R, with his parents. The Official Solicitor submits that it would be appropriate for the court at this stage to make a declaration that it would be lawful to withhold the administration of antibiotics in the event of the patient developing a potentially life-threatening infection which would otherwise call for the administration of antibiotics but only if immediately prior to withholding the same.

(a) The trust is so advised both by the general medical practitioner and by the consultant psychiatrist having the responsibility at the time of the patient's treatment and care and

(b) One or other or both of the parents first give their consent thereto.

Such a declaration would recognise the ultimate and effective responsibility of the consultant having responsibility at the time for the patient's treatment and care. A declaration in these terms would be a modification of the declaration which was initially sought in the originating summons

In this case there is no question of the Court being the phrase 'because of unacceptable quality of life'. That differed slightly from the wording of the joint BMA/RCN guidance which referred to 'the length and quality of life which would not be accepted to the patient'. However, the document issued by this NHS Trust made it clear in the first paragraph on page 2 that the overall responsibility for such a DNR decision rests with the consultant in charge of the patient's condition.

. . . The court is concerned with circumstances in which steps should be taken to prolong life. The facts are very different from those in the case of *Airedale NHS Trust v. Bland* [1993] A.C. 789. The principle of law to be applied in this case is that of the 'best interests of the Patient' as made clear by the Court of Appeal in *Re J* [1991] Fam. 33 . . . "

The judge referred to the facts in *Re J* and continued:

"In the course of his judgment Taylor L.J. said:

'The plight of baby J is appalling and the problem facing the court in the exercise of its wardship jurisdiction is of the greatest difficulty. When should the court rule against the giving of treatment aimed at prolonging life?' . . .

At 55F and 383M respectively Taylor L.J. said:

'I consider the correct approach is for the court to judge the quality of life the child would have to endure if given the treatment and decide whether in all circumstances such a life would be so afflicted as to be intolerable to that child.'

Although this present case concerns a handicapped adult and not a child who is a ward of court the overriding principle in my judgment is the same. The operative words in this passage from the judgment of Taylor L.J. to which I have referred are 'so afflicted as to be intolerable'. The extensive medical evidence in this case is unanimous in concluding that it would not be in the best interests of R to subject him to cardio-pulmonary resuscitation in the event of his suffering a cardiac arrest. The conclusions of the doctors are supported by R's parents. The Official Solicitor on behalf of R agrees that this is an appropriate course to be followed. He submits that in the context of the facts of this case it would be appropriate for the Court to make a declaration that it shall be lawful as being in the patient's best interests for the Trust and/or the responsible medical practitioners having the responsibility at the time for the patient's treatment and care to withhold cardio-pulmonary resuscitation of the patient. I agree that this declaration should be made.

The withholding in the future of the administration of antibiotics in the event of the patient developing a potentially life-threatening infection which would otherwise call for the administration of antibiotics is a decision which can only be taken at the time by the patient's responsible medical practitioners in the light of the prevailing circumstances. This requires a clinical judgment in the light of the prevailing circumstances. Mr Munby Q.C. on behalf of the Official Solicitor has referred to a passage in the speech of Lord Goff of Chieveley in the case of *Airedale NHS Trust v. Bland* [1993] A.C. 789. Lord Goff said:

'I turn finally to the extent to which doctors should, as a matter of practice, seek the guidance of the Court, by way of an application for declaratory relief, before withholding life prolonging treatment from a PVS patient. The President considered that the opinion of the Court should be sought in all cases similar to the present. In the Court of Appeal, Sir Thomas Bingham M.R. expressed his agreement with Sir Stephen Brown P. in the following words:

"This was in my respectful view a wise ruling, directed to the protection of patients, the protection of doctors, the reassurance of patients' families and the reassurance of the public. The practice proposed seems to me to be desirable. It may very well be that with the passage of time a body of experience and practice will build up which will obviate the need for application in every case, but for the time being I am satisfied that the practice which the President described should be followed."

Before the Appellate Committee, this view was supported both by Mr Munby for the Official Solicitor, and by Mr Lester, as amicus curiae. For the Respondents Mr Francis suggested that an adequate safeguard would be provided if reference to the Court was required in certain specific cases.'

Lord Goff then gave certain examples [and] . . . then said:

'For my part, I would therefore leave the matter as proposed by the Master of the Rolls; but I wish to express the hope that the President of the Family Division, who will no doubt be kept well informed about developments in this field, will soon feel able to relax the present requirement so as to limit applications for declarations to those cases in which there is a special need for the procedure to be invoked.'

Mr Munby, relying upon that passage in Lord Goff's speech, submits that in the light of the medical evidence and all the factual material in this case it would be appropriate for the Court to make a declaration in terms which would not require a future application to the Court. He suggests a declaration in the following terms:

'To withhold the administration of antibiotics in the event of the patient developing a potentially life threatening infection which would otherwise call for the administration of antibiotics but only if immediately prior to withholding the same

(a) the trust is so advised both by the general medical practitioner and by the consultant psychiatrist having the responsibility at the time for the patient's treatment and care and
(b) one or other or both of the parents first give their consent thereto.'

Counsel for the plaintiff trust agrees with that proposal. In my judgment it would reflect the reality of the situation. The decision to withhold antibiotics in a given situation falls fairly and squarely within the clinical responsibility of the consultant treating the patient. I am quite satisfied on the evidence in this case that the consultant and the general practitioner having the responsibility for R's treatment do have R's best interests in mind. They are fully supported by the parents. I am accordingly satisfied that it would be in the best interests of R to make a declaration in these terms . . . "

NOTES:

1. This case represents the first judicial consideration of "do not resuscitate orders". The use of such orders was considered by the House of Lords Select Committee on Euthanasia, who were opposed to the enactment of legislation on this subject (HL Paper 21-2, London: HMSO, 1994).
2. A number of reasons have been advanced as to why cardio-pulmonary resuscitation should be withheld from patients. CPR is costly; even if resuscitated, the patient may then suffer a relapse; and furthermore it is an invasive procedure. (See further J. Saunders, "Medical Futility: CPR" in R. Lee and D. Morgan (eds), *Death rites: Law and Ethics at the End of Life*, London: Routledge, 1994.)
3. In situations in which patient approval has been obtained for a DNR, it may be regarded as being a "living will" or "advance directive" (see further below at p.1080)
4. Despite the guidelines some later research in an audit of a hospital in North London suggested that only 9 per cent of consultants were involved in DNR decisions and there were no records in which any case had been discussed with the patient ((1999) 33 *Journal of the Royal College of Physicians* 348).

QUESTIONS:

1. Sir Stephen Brown rejected the use of the term "because of an unacceptable quality of life", but is such an assessment implicit in the order made? Consider the above cases concerning non-treatment of the newly born infant. To what extent is this case analogous and how far are the principles applied in those cases of assistance also applicable in a case of this type with regard to the issues of both resuscitation and administration of antibiotics?

(d) Conflicts between Family Members and Clinicians Regarding the
Continuation of Treatment

In *Bland* the family supported the decision to withdraw treatment, but what of the situation in which there is a disagreement? The extent to which the wishes of relatives should be taken into account in determining the treatment of PVS patients was considered in the later case of *Re G* [1995] 2 F.L.R. 528. Following a motorcycle accident in 1991, G had been in a persistent vegetative state. G's wife, along with the doctors treating him, supported the withdrawal of treatment. However, his mother wanted treatment continued. The matter was referred to the court. Sir Stephen Brown P. said that while relatives should be consulted, these views could not be conclusive and that in this case the opinion of the consultant orthopaedic surgeon that further treatment was not in the best interests of G should be followed. (See A. Grubb, "Incompetent Patient in PVS: Views of Relatives; Best Interests" (1995) 3 *Medical Law Review* 80.) Conflicts with family members may give rise to human rights considerations, an issue which is considered below.

R v Portsmouth Hospitals NHS Trust, Ex p. Glass [1999] Lloyd's Rep. Med. 367, [1999] 3 F.C.R. 145, [1999] 2 F.L.R. 905, [1999] Fam. Law 696, 50 B.M.L.R. 269

David Glass was a 12-year-old severely disabled boy. He was admitted to hospital in October 1998 after he had suffered from various infections following an operation. Clinical staff were of the view that the child was dying, and wished to administer diamorphine to alleviate his distress. His mother was opposed to such treatment, but a diamorphine infusion was commenced without her consent. Violent incidents between members of the child's family and two of his doctors followed, as a result of which both civil and criminal proceedings were commenced. In the melee Mrs Glass resuscitated her son. Subsequently a "do not resuscitate" order was placed in his notes without consulting his mother. David Glass survived and was subsequently discharged and treated by his general practitioner. The NHS trust wrote to the applicant saying that in view of their differences, it would be more sensible that if the child required further in-patient care, he should be treated at a different hospital. The applicant applied for judicial review, making complaints as to the trust's treatment of the child, and seeking various declarations concerning the lawfulness of the actions of an NHS trust in its treatment of or withdrawal of life-saving treatment from a child against the wishes of the child's parent. At first instance, the application was dismissed. This was on the basis that the case was not susceptible to judicial review. Secondly, it was not appropriate to grant relief since it would be very difficult to frame any declaration in meaningful terms in a hypothetical situation, so as not to unnecessarily restrict proper treatment by the doctors in an ongoing and developing matter. At first instance Scott Baker rejected the claim for judicial review.

SCOTT BAKER J.
"If there is serious disagreement, the best interests procedure can be involved at short notice and the court will resolve it on the basis of the facts as they are then. They will almost inevitably be different from the facts as they were in October 1998 . . . In any event it is unclear precisely what the facts were in October 1998 on the evidence that is before this court . . . Furthermore, if there is a crisis in the future, I am confident that if the matter is brought before the court the Official Solicitor will again provide assistance."

Moreover, he was unwilling to make an order on a hypothetical issue, although he stressed in conclusion:

"Nothing, I would finally say, should be read into this judgment to infer that it is my view that the [Portsmouth Hospital] in this case acted either lawfully or unlawfully."

The Court of Appeal (Lord Woolf, Butler Sloss L.J. and Robert Walker L.J.) refused the application.

LORD WOOLF M.R.

"There are questions of judgment involved. There can be no doubt that the best course is for a parent of a child to agree on the course which the doctors are proposing to take, having fully consulted the parent and for the parent to fully understand what is involved. That is the course which should always be adopted in a case of this nature. If that is not possible and there is a conflict, and if the conflict is of a grave nature, the matter must then be brought before the court so the court can decide what is in the best interests of the child concerned. Faced with a particular problem, the courts will answer that problem . . .

. . . This difficulty in this area is that there are conflicting principles involved. The principles of law are clearly established, but how you apply those principles to particular facts is often very difficult to anticipate. It is only when the court is faced with that task that it gives an answer which reflects the view of the court as to what is in the best interests of the child. In doing so it takes into account the natural concerns and the responsibilities of the parent. It also takes into account the views of the doctors, and considers what is the most desirable answer taking the best advice it can obtain from, among others, the Official Solicitor. That is the way, in my judgment, that the courts must react in this very sensitive and difficult area."

Mrs Glass complained to the GMC and alleged that the doctors had committed an assault by the administration of heroin without court authorisation and against her wishes but her complaint was not upheld by the GMC. In addition the Glass family complained to the Hampshire police but the DPP ultimately decided not to bring charges.

The Glass family took their case to the European Court of Human Rights.

Glass v UK [2004] 1 F.L.R. 1019

JUDGMENT OF THE COURT

"II. RELEVANT DOMESTIC LAW AND PRACTICE

45 Paragraph 24 of the General Medical Council's guidance *Seeking Patients' Consent: the Ethical Considerations* provides:

'Where a child under 16 years old is not competent to give or withhold the informed consent, a person with parental responsibility may authorise investigations or treatment which are in the child's best interests. This person may also refuse any intervention where they consider that refusal to be in the child's best interest, but you are not bound by such a refusal and may seek a ruling from the court. In an emergency, where you consider that it is in the child's best interest to proceed, you may treat the child, provided it is limited to that treatment which is reasonably required in an emergency'.

In *Re J (A Minor) (Wardship: Medical Treatment)*, [1991] 2 W.L.R. 140; [1990] 3 All E.R. 930, CA, Lord Donaldson M.R. stated:

'The doctors owe the child a duty to care for it in accordance with good medical practice recognised as appropriate by a competent body of professional opinion . . . This duty is however subject to the qualification that, if time permits, they must obtain the consent of the parents before undertaking serious invasive treatment.

The parents owe the child a duty to give or withhold consent in the best interests of the child and without regard to their own interests.

The court when exercising the *parens patriae* jurisdiction takes over the rights and duties of the parents, although this is not to say that the parents will be excluded from the decision-making process. Nevertheless in the end the responsibility for the decision whether to give or to withhold consent is that of the court alone.

No one can dictate the treatment to be given to the child—neither court, parents nor doctors. There are checks and balances. The doctors can recommend treatment A in preference to treatment B. They can also refuse to adopt treatment C on the grounds that it is medically contra-indicated or for some other reason is a treatment which they could not conscientiously administer. The court or parents for their part can refuse to consent to treatment A or B or both, but cannot insist on treatment C. The inevitable and desirable result is that choice of treatment is in some measure a joint decision of the doctors and the court or parents.'

In *National Health Service Trust v D*, [2000] 2 F.L.R. 677; [2000] 2 F.C.R. 577, it was held:

'The court's clear respect for the sanctity of human life must impose a strong obligation in favour of taking all steps capable of preserving life, save in exceptional circumstances'.

46 In that case, the court accepted the views of doctors treating a child that resuscitation of the child in the event of respiratory or cardiac arrest would be inappropriate.

47 According to the Government, English law recognises that it may be in the best interests of a child or of an adult to be treated with medication which relieves his symptoms but has the side-effect of hastening death.

According to Part 3B of the guidance drawn up by the British Medical Association on *Withholding and Withdrawing Medical Treatment: Guidance for Decision-Making*:

'... where there is reasonable uncertainty about the benefit of life-prolonging treatment, there should be a presumption in favour of initiating it, although there are circumstances in which active intervention (other than basic care) would not be appropriate since best interests is not synonymous with prolongation of life ... If the child's condition is incompatible with survival or where there is broad consensus that the condition is so severe that treatment would not provide a benefit in terms of being able to restore or maintain the patient's health, intervention may be unjustified. Similarly, where treatments would involve suffering or distress to the child, these and other burdens must be weighed against the anticipated benefit, even if life cannot be prolonged without treatment'.

Paragraph 15.1 of the 2001 British Medical Association Guidance on *Withholding and Withdrawing Life-prolonging Medical Treatment* states:

'Those with parental responsibility for a baby or young child are legally and morally entitled to give or withhold consent to treatment. Their decisions will usually be determinative unless they conflict seriously with the interpretation of those providing care about the child's best interests'.

Paragraph 15.2 states:

"The law has confirmed that best interests and the balance of benefits and burdens are essential components of decision making and that the views of parents are a part of this. However, parents cannot necessarily insist on enforcing decisions based solely on their own preferences where these conflict with good medical evidence".

48 At the time of the facts giving rise to the instant application, guidance had been published by the Royal College of Paediatrics and Child Health indicating the procedures that should normally be followed in the event that a parent dissents from the opinion of the health care team that treatment should be withheld from a child. The guidance states

that a second opinion should normally be offered and the parent should be allowed time to consult advisers of their choice. Paragraph 3.4.3 states:

'In most cases, with proper explanation and adequate time, parents can accept medical advice, but if the parents do not consent to withdrawal or withhold consent, a second opinion should be obtained and then the courts should be consulted. The Official Solicitor's Office can be telephoned for advice which will help clarify the need for court involvement'.

Guidance published by the Department of Health in 2001, entitled *Consent: Working with Children* deals explicitly with the situation where clinicians believe that treatment which the parents want is not appropriate. It states:

'One example would be where a child is very seriously ill, and clinicians believe that the suffering involved in further treatment would outweigh the possible benefits. Parents cannot require you to provide a particular treatment if you do not believe that it is clinically appropriate, but again the courts can be asked to rule if agreement cannot be reached. While a court would not require you to provide treatment against your clinical judgment, it could require you to transfer responsibility for the child's care to another clinician who does believe that the proposed treatment is appropriate" . . .

49 In the case of *Re A (Conjoined Twins: Surgical Separation)*, [2001] Fam. 147; [2001] 2 W.L.R. 480, CA, Ward L.J. stated:

'Since the parents are empowered at law, it seems to be that their decision must be respected and in my judgment the hospital would be no more entitled to disregard their refusal than they are to disregard an adult person's refusal. I derive this from *Re R (A Minor) (Wardship: Consent to Treatment)* [1992] Fam. 11, at p.22, where Lord Donaldson of Lymington M.R. said:
    "It is trite law that in general a doctor is not entitled to treat a patient without the consent of someone who is authorised to give that consent. If he does so, he will be liable in damages for trespass to the person and may be guilty of a criminal assault" '.

50 Under English law, there may be circumstances in which it is not practicable to seek a declaration from the courts, for example in an emergency situation where speedy decisions have to be taken concerning appropriate treatment. In *Re C (A Minor)*, 1998] 1 F.L.R. 384; [1998] Lloyd's Rep. Med. 1.
    Sir Stephen Brown affirmed that the decision of a doctor whether to treat a child:

'is dependent upon an exercise of his own professional judgment, subject only to the threshold requirement that save in exceptional cases usually of an emergency he has the consent of someone who has authority to give that consent'.
    . . .

52 In *Re T (Adult: Refusal of Treatment)*, [1994] 1 W.L.R. Fam. 95, Lord Donaldson stated:

'If in a potentially life threatening situation or one in which irreparable damage to the patient's health is to be anticipated, doctors or health authorities are faced with a refusal by an adult patient to accept essential treatment and they have real doubts as to the validity of that refusal, they should in the public interest, not to mention that of the patient, at once seek a declaration from the courts as to whether the proposed treatment would or would not be lawful. This step should not be left to the patient's family, who will probably not know of the facility and may be inhibited by questions of expense. Such cases will be rare, but when they do arise . . . the courts can and will provide immediate assistance'.

53 The Department of Health's Aide-Memoire on Consent provides:

'4. Giving and obtaining consent is usually a process, not a one-off event. Patients can change their minds and withdraw consent at any time. If there is any doubt, you should always check that the patient still consents to your caring for or treating them.

Can children consent for themselves?

5. Before examining, treating or caring for a child, you must also seek consent. Young people aged 16 and 17 are presumed to have the competence to give consent for themselves. Younger children who understand fully what is involved in the proposed procedure can also give consent (although their parents will ideally be involved). In other cases, someone with parental responsibility must give consent on the child's behalf, unless they cannot be reached in an emergency.

. . .

What information should be provided?

7. Parents need sufficient information before they can decide whether to give their consent: for example information about the benefits and risks of the proposed treatment, and alternative treatments. If the patient is not offered as much information as they reasonably need to make their decision, and in a form they can understand, their consent may not be valid'.

Non-resuscitation

54 Guidelines published in March 1993 by the British Medical Association and the Royal College of Nursing in conjunction with the Resuscitation Council provide in para.1:

'It is appropriate to consider a Do-Not-Resuscitate order (DNR) in the following circumstances:
  (a) Where the patient's condition indicates that effective Cardiopulmonary Resuscitation (CPR) is unlikely to be successful.
  (b) Where CPR is not in accord with the recorded, sustained wishes of the patient who is mentally competent.
  (c) Where successful CPR is likely to be followed by a length and quality of life which would not be acceptable to the patient'.

55 Paragraph 3 states:

'The overall responsibility for a DNR decision rests with the consultant in charge of the patient's care. This should be made after appropriate consultation and consideration of all aspects of the patient's condition. The perspectives of other members of the medical and nursing team, the patient and with due regard to patient confidentiality, the patient's relatives or close friends, may all be valuable in forming the consultant's decision'.

56 Paragraph 10 provides:

'Discussions of the advisability or otherwise of CPR will be highly sensitive and complex and should be undertaken by senior and experienced members of the medical team supported by senior nursing colleagues. A DNR order applies solely to CPR. It should be made clear that all other treatment and care which are appropriate for the patient are not precluded and should not be influenced by a DNR order'.

57 Current Departmental Guidance is set out in Resuscitation Policy. It states:

'Resuscitation decisions are amongst the most sensitive decisions that clinicians, patients and parents may have to make. Patients (and where appropriate their relatives and carers) have as much right to be involved in those decisions as they do other decisions about their care and treatment. As with all decision-making, doctors have a duty to act in accordance with an appropriate and responsible body of professional opinion'.

JUDGMENT

I. Alleged violation of Article 8 of the Convention

B. The Court's assessment

1. As to the existence of an interference with Article 8

70 The Court notes that the second applicant, as the mother of the first applicant—a severely handicapped child—acted as the latter's legal proxy. In that capacity, the second applicant had the authority to act on his behalf and to defend his interests, including in the area of medical treatment. The Government has observed that the second applicant had given doctors at St Mary's Hospital on the previous occasions on which he had been admitted authorisation to pursue particular courses of treatment. However, it is clear that, when confronted with the reality of the administration of diamorphine to the first applicant, the second applicant expressed her firm opposition to this form of treatment. These objections were overridden, including in the face of her continuing opposition. It considers that the decision to impose treatment on the first applicant in defiance of the second applicant's objections gave rise to an interference with the first applicant's right to respect for his private life, and in particular his right to physical integrity. [On the latter point, see, *mutatis mutandis*, *X and Y v Netherlands* (A/91): (1986) 8 E.H.R.R. 235, para.[22]; *Pretty v United Kingdom*: (2002) 35 E.H.R.R. 1, paras [61] and [63]; App. No. 24209/94, *YF v Turkey*, July 22, 2003, para.[33].] It is to be noted that the Government has also laid emphasis on its view that the doctors were confronted with an emergency (which is disputed by the applicants) and had to act quickly in the best interests of the first applicant. However, that argument does not detract from the fact of interference. It is, rather, an argument which goes to the necessity of the interference and has to be addressed in that context.

71 The Court would add that it has not been contested that the hospital was a public institution and that the acts and omissions of its medical staff were capable of engaging the responsibility of the Government under the Convention.

72 It would further observe that although the applicants have alleged that the impugned treatment also gave rise to an interference with the second applicant's right to respect for her family life, it considers that it is only required to examine the issues raised from the standpoint of the first applicant's right to respect for his personal integrity, having regard, of course, to the second applicant's role as his mother and legal proxy.

2. Compliance with Article 8(2)

73 An interference with the exercise of an Art.8 right will not be compatible with Art.8(2) unless it is 'in accordance with the law', has an aim or aims that is or are legitimate under that paragraph and is 'necessary in a democratic society' for the aforesaid aim or aims. [See the above-mentioned *Pretty* decision, para.[68].]

74 The Court observes that the applicants have questioned the adequacy of the domestic legal framework for resolving conflicts arising out of parental objection to medical treatment proposed in respect of a child. It is their contention that the current situation confers too much discretion on doctors in deciding when to seek the intervention of the courts when faced with the objection of a parent to treatment which might, as a secondary effect, hasten the death of the child. However, it considers that, in the circumstances of this case, it is not required to address that issue from the standpoint of whether or not the qualitative criteria which have to satisfied before an interference can be said to have been 'in accordance with the law' have been complied with. [As to those criteria, see, among many other authorities, *Herczegfalvy v Austria* (A/244): (1993) 15 E.H.R.R. 437, paras [88]–[91]. Nor does it consider it necessary to pronounce on the applicants' contention that the authorities failed to comply with the positive obligations inherent in an effective respect for the first applicant's right to personal integrity by failing to adopt measures designed to secure respect for his personal integrity. [See, for example, *X and Y v Netherlands*, cited above, para.[23]; more recently, *Odièvre v France*: (2004) 38 E.H.R.R. 43.]

The Court would, however, make two observations in this connection with reference to the facts of this case. First, the regulatory framework in the respondent state is firmly predicated on the duty to preserve the life of a patient, save in exceptional circumstances. Secondly, that same framework prioritises the requirement of parental consent and, save in emergency situations, requires doctors to seek the intervention of the courts in the event of parental objection. It would add that it does not consider that the regulatory framework in place in the United Kingdom is in any way inconsistent with the standards laid down in the Council of Europe's Bioethics and Human Rights Convention in the area of consent nor does it accept the view that the many sources from which the rules, regulations and standards are derived only contribute to unpredictability and an excess of discretion in this area at the level of application.

. . .

76 For the Court, the applicants' contention in reality amounts to an assertion that, in their case, the dispute between them and the hospital staff should have been referred to the courts and that the doctors treating the first applicant wrongly considered that they were faced with an emergency. However, the Government firmly maintains that the exigencies of the situation were such that diamorphine had to be administered to the first applicant as a matter of urgency in order to relieve his distress and that it would not have been practical in the circumstances to seek the approval of the court. However, for the Court, these are matters which fall to be dealt with under the 'necessity' requirement of Art.8(2), and not from the standpoint of the 'in accordance with the law' requirements.

77 As to the legitimacy of the aim pursued, the Court considers that the action taken by the hospital staff was intended, as a matter of clinical judgment, to serve the interests of the first applicant. It recalls in this connection that it rejected in its partial decision on admissibility of March 18, 2003 any suggestion under Art.2 of the Convention that it was the doctors' intention unilaterally to hasten the first applicant's death whether by administering diamorphine to him or by placing a DNR notice in his case notes.

78 Turning to the 'necessity' of the interference at issue, the Court considers that the situation which arose at St Mary's Hospital between October 19 and 21, 1998 cannot be isolated from the earlier discussions in late July and early September 1998 between members of the hospital staff and the second applicant about the first applicant's condition and how it should be treated in the event of an emergency. The doctors at the hospital were obviously concerned about the second applicant's reluctance to follow their advice, in particular their view that morphine might have to be administered to her son in order to relieve any distress which the first applicant might experience during a subsequent attack. It cannot be overlooked in this connection that Dr Walker recorded in his notes on September 8, 1998 that recourse to the courts might be needed in order to break the deadlock with the second applicant. Dr Hallet reached a similar conclusion following his meeting with the second applicant on September 9.

79 It has not been explained to the Court's satisfaction why the Trust did not at that stage seek the intervention of the High Court. The doctors during this phase all shared a gloomy prognosis of the first applicant's capacity to withstand further crises. They were left in no doubt that their proposed treatment would not meet with the agreement of the second applicant. Admittedly, the second applicant could have brought the matter before the High Court. However, in the circumstances it considers that the onus was on the Trust to take the initiative and to defuse the situation in anticipation of a further emergency.

80 The Court can accept that the doctors could not have predicted the level of confrontation and hostility which in fact arose following the first applicant's readmission to the hospital on October 18, 1998. However, in so far as the Government have maintained that the serious nature of the first applicant's condition involved the doctors in a race against time with the result that an application by the Trust to the High Court was an unrealistic option, it is nevertheless the case that the Trust's failure to make a High Court application at an earlier stage contributed to this situation.

81 That being said, the Court is not persuaded that an emergency High Court application could not have been made by the Trust when it became clear that the second applicant was firmly opposed to the administration of a diamorphine to the first applicant.

However, the doctors and officials used the limited time available to them in order to try to impose their views on the second applicant. It observes in this connection that the Trust was able to secure the presence of a police officer to oversee the negotiations with the second applicant but, surprisingly, did not give consideration to making a High Court application even though 'the best interests procedure can be involved at short notice'. [See the decision of Scott Baker J. in the High Court proceedings at para. [38] above.]

82 The Court would further observe that the facts do not bear out the Government's contention that the second applicant had consented to the administration of diamorphine to the first applicant in the light of the previous discussions which she had had with the doctors. Quite apart from the fact that those talks had focused on the administration of morphine to the first applicant, it cannot be stated with certainty that any consent given was free, express and informed. In any event, the second applicant clearly withdrew her consent, and the doctors and the Trust should have respected her change of mind and should not have engaged in rather insensitive attempts to overcome her opposition.

83 The Court considers that, having regard to the circumstances of the case, the decision of the authorities to override the second applicant's objection to the proposed treatment in the absence of authorisation by a court resulted in a breach of Art.8 of the Convention. In view of that conclusion, it does not consider it necessary to examine separately the applicants' complaint regarding the inclusion of the DNR notice in the first applicant's case notes without the consent and knowledge of the second applicant. It would however observe in line with its admissibility decision that the notice was only directed against the application of vigorous cardiac massage and intensive respiratory support, and did not exclude the use of other techniques, such as the provision of oxygen, to keep the first applicant alive.

Notes:

1. The ECHR ordered a payment of compensation of €10,000 in respect of non-pecuniary damages and €15,000 in respect of costs and expenses.

2. The case illustrates that NHS bodies will need to carefully review their procedures for referring cases for judicial determination. What is striking about the case, given the disagreement with the family, was that this did not occur. It is particularly striking given the arguments advanced that medical practice is becoming increasingly defensive in its nature—see Chapter 3 above.

3. Bridgeman has argued that the judgment "is to be welcomed for the clarity it brings to the role of parents, professionals and the court in relation to the medical treatment of dependent children—that decisions are made by parents, not healthcare professionals, and in the event of disagreement by the court". (See further J. Bridgeman, "Caring for Children with Severe Disabilities: Boundaried and Relational Rights" (2005) 13 *International Journal of Children's Rights* 99).

Question:

1. To what extent can the *Glass* case be seen as a revitalisation of parental authority with an increasing emphasis upon parental involvement in the decision-making process? (See further R. Huxtable and K. Forbes, "Glass v UK: Maternal Instinct v Medical Opinion" (2004) *Child and Fam Law Quarterly* 239).

(e) Judicial Sanctioning of Withdrawal of Life-saving Treatment from a Competent Patient

As we saw in Chapter 5, above competent patients have the right to refuse treatment even if it is the case that death will result (see *Re T (Adult: Refusal of Treatment)* [1992] 4 All E.R. 649 and *Re C (Adult refusal of medical treatment)* [1994] 1 All E.R. 849). But what if the patient is supported on life-support systems and to comply with their refusal this will mean that they will have to be withdrawn from these? This issue arose in the following case.

Re B [2002] 2 All ER 449

Ms B was a social worker by training who had been working as a head of department and principal officer for training and staff development (This case is also discussed in Chapter 5 above). She was admitted to hospital on August 26, 2001 when she suffered a haemorrhage of the spinal column in her neck. As a result she was paralysed and was supported on a ventilator. She requested that the ventilator be turned off. The clinicians treating her refused. Initially she was declared incompetent to refuse treatment by two psychiatrists. Subsequently she was found to be competent. However the hospital treating her did not want her removed from ventilation and suggested that she should attend an independent rehabilitation clinic. As was seen in Chapter 6 above, Butler-Sloss L.J. held that Ms B possessed decision-making capacity. She referred to the judgment of the House of Lords in *Bland* and continued:

BUTLER-SLOSS L.J.

"b. The sanctity of life

22. Society and the medical profession in particular are concerned with the equally fundamental principle of the sanctity of life. The interface between the two principles of autonomy and sanctity of life is of great concern to the treating clinicians in the present case. Lord Keith of Kinkel in *Airedale NHS Trust v Bland*, said at page 859

'. . . the principle of the sanctity of life, which it is the concern of the state, and the judiciary as one of the arms of the state, . . . is not an absolute one. It does not compel a medical practitioner on pain of criminal sanctions to treat a patient, who will die if he does not, contrary to the express wishes of the patient.'

Lord Goff of Chieveley said at page 864

'First, it is established that the principle of self-determination requires that respect must be given to the wishes of the patient, so that if an adult patient of sound mind refuses, however unreasonably, to consent to treatment or care by which his life would or might be prolonged, the doctors responsible for his care must give effect to his wishes, even though they do not consider it to be in his best interests to do so . . . To this extent, the principle of the sanctity of human life must yield to the principle of self-determination and for present purposes perhaps most important, the doctor's duty to act in the best interests of his patient must likewise be qualified. On this basis, it has been held that a patient of sound mind may, if properly informed, require that life support should be discontinued: see *Nancy B v Hôtel-Dieu de Québec* (1992) 86 DLR (4th) 385 . . . . I wish to add that, in cases of this kind, there is no question of the patient having committed suicide, nor therefore of the doctor having aided or abetted him in doing so. It is simply that the patient has, as he is entitled to do, declined to consent to treatment which might or would have the effect of prolonging his life, and the doctor has, in accordance with his duty, complied with his patient's wishes.'

. . .

24. Lord Mustill said at pages 891 and 1062

'Any invasion of the body of one person by another is potentially both a crime and a tort . . .

How is it that, consistently with the proposition just stated, a doctor can with immunity perform on a consenting patient an act which would be a very serious crime if done by someone else? The answer must be that bodily invasions in the course of proper medical treatment stand completely outside the criminal law. The reason why the consent of the patient is so important is not that it furnishes a defence in itself, but because it is usually essential to the propriety of medical treatment. Thus, if the consent is absent, and is not dispensed with in special circumstances by operation of law, the acts of the doctor lose their immunity . . .

Even if the patient is capable of making a decision whether to permit treatment and decides not to permit it his choice must be obeyed, if on any objective view it is contrary to his best interests. A doctor has no right to proceed in the face of objection, even if it is plain to all, including the patient, that adverse circumstances and even death will or may ensue.'

25. In the *Bland* case the issue concerned a patient in the permanent vegetative state. *In re T (Adult: Refusal of Treatment)* (see above) the issue was the state of competence of a pregnant young woman who had been injured in a car crash and was refusing a blood transfusion. Lord Donaldson of Lymington M.R. said at page 112

'This situation gives rise to a conflict between two interests, that of the patient and that of the society in which he lives. The patient's interest consists of his right to self-determination—his right to live his own life how he wishes, even if it will damage his health or lead to his premature death. Society's interest is in upholding the concept that all human life is sacred and that it should be preserved if at all possible. It is well established that in the ultimate the right of the individual is paramount.'

26. I note with interest that a situation similar to that of Ms B was considered by the Quebec Superior Court in *Nancy B v Hôtel-Dieu de Québec et al.* (1992) 86 DLR (4th) 385, in which a competent 25 year old woman with an incurable neurological disorder sought an injunction to enforce her refusal of artificial ventilation, without which she was incapable of breathing independently. The court in that case decided that the plaintiff was entitled to the injunction sought, and ordered that the treating doctor be permitted to stop ventilation if and when the plaintiff so instructed.

27. In the evidence of Dr I, to which I refer later in this judgment, he said that, in his view, the principles of autonomy and beneficence would appear to be in conflict in this case. In accordance with the principle set out so clearly by Lord Mustill and Lord Donaldson (above), the right of the competent patient to request cessation of treatment must prevail over the natural desire of the medical and nursing profession to try to keep her alive."

NOTES:

1. Following this judgment, ventilation was withdrawn and Ms B died.
2. *Re B* has been contrasted with the the *Pretty* case discussed above at p.1001. Some academic commentators regard the difference in approach

taken by the courts as wholly anomalous while others argue that the prohibition against intentional killing in law should remain. (See, for example, P. Singer, "Ms B and Dianne Pretty: a Commentary" (2002) *Journal of Medical Ethics* 234 and *cf.* J. Keown, "The Case of Miss B: Suicide's Slippery Slope?"(2002) *Journal of Medical Ethics* 238.)

3. *Re AK (adult: medical patient) (consent)* [2001] 2 F.L.R. 35 pre-dated the B decision. Here a patient with motor neurone disease was able to breathe with a ventilation. He had a limited ability to communicate due to the impact of the disease but he could communicate with movement of the eyelids. He communicated that he should be allowed to die two weeks after it became impossible to communicate. Next day he was asked again about his wishes when we was with his mother and another carer and he confirmed this. His wishes were confirmed by two consultants. The court held that his wish was genuine and a declaration was made that the NHS trust could withdraw treatment in accordance with the request of the patient provided that he did not indicate that his wishes had been changed.

(f) The "Right to Live"

While the majority of the cases which have been the source of debate within and without the courtroom have concerned the right to die, a recent case concerned the "right to live".

R (on the application of Oliver Leslie Burke) v GMC [2005] 3 W.L.R. 1132

Leslie Burke, a disability rights adviser, suffered from cerebellar ataxia, a progressively degenerative disorder which, as his condition worsened, would require treatment by artificial nutrition and hydration (ANH). The claimant would be likely to lose the ability to communicate his wishes but would retain full cognitive faculties right up to the end stage of his disease, at which point he would lapse into a coma, probably a few days before his death. He sought to challenge General Medical Council (GMC) guidance *Withholding and Withdrawing Life-prolonging Treatments: Good Practice in Decision-making* on the withdrawal of ANH by way of judicial review, contending that it was incompatible with his rights under Articles 2, 3, 6, 8 and 14 of the European Convention for the Protection of Human Rights and Fundamental Freedoms 1950 (as set out in Sch.1 to the Human Rights Act 1998) and sought certain declaratory relief. The guidance provided in particular as follows:

General Medical Council : Withdrawing or Withholding Life-Prolonging Treatment

81. Where patients have capacity to decide for themselves, they may consent to, or refuse, any proposed intervention of this kind. In cases where patients lack capacity to decide for themselves and their wishes cannot be determined, you should take account of the following considerations:

- Where there is a reasonable degree of uncertainty about the likely benefits or burdens for the patient of providing either artificial nutrition or hydration, it may be appropriate to provide these for a trial period with a pre-arranged review to allow a clearer assessment to be made.
- Where death is imminent, in judging the benefits, burdens or risks, it usually would not be appropriate to start either artificial hydration or nutrition, although artificial hydration provided by the less invasive measures may be appropriate where it is considered that this would be likely to provide symptom relief.
- Where death is imminent and artificial hydration and/or nutrition are already in use, it may be appropriate to withdraw them if it is considered that the burdens outweigh the possible benefits to the patient.
- Where death is not imminent, it usually will be appropriate to provide artificial nutrition or hydration. However, circumstances may arise where you judge that a patient's condition is so severe, and the prognosis so poor that providing artificial nutrition or hydration may cause suffering, or be too burdensome in relation to the possible benefits. In these circumstances, as well as consulting the health care team and those close to the patient, you must seek a second or expert opinion from a senior clinician (who might be from another discipline such as nursing) who has experience of the patient's condition and who is not already directly involved in the patient's care. This will ensure that, in a decision of such sensitivity, the patient's interests have been thoroughly considered, and will provide necessary reassurance to those close to the patient and to the wider public.
- It can be extremely difficult to estimate how long a patient will live, especially for patients with multiple underlying conditions. Expert help in this should be sought where you, or the health care team, are uncertain about a particular patient.

82. Where significant conflicts arise about whether artificial nutrition or hydration should be provided, either between you and other members of the health care team or between the team and those close to the patient, and the disagreement cannot be resolved after informal or independent review, you should seek legal advice on whether it is necessary to apply to the court for a ruling.

83. Where you are considering withdrawing artificial nutrition and hydration from a patient in a permanent vegetative state (PVS), or condition closely resembling PVS, the courts in England, Wales and Northern Ireland currently require that you approach them for a ruling. The courts in Scotland have not specified such a requirement, but you should seek legal advice on whether a court declaration may be necessary in an individual case."

At first instance Mumby J. made a series of wide-ranging declarations:

"(1) Any decision by the claimant while competent, or contained in a valid advance directive, that he requires to be provided with artificial nutrition and hydration is determinative that such provision is in the best interests of the claimant at least in circumstances where death is not imminent and the claimant is not comatose.

(2) Where the claimant has decided, or made a valid advance directive, that he wishes to be provided with artificial nutrition and hydration, any refusal by a hospital who has assumed the care of the claimant to arrange for the provision of such artificial nutrition and hydration at any time until the claimant's death is imminent and the claimant is comatose would be a breach of the claimant's rights under article 3 and article 8 of the European Convention on Human Rights.

(3) Where the claimant has decided, or made a valid advance directive, that he wishes to be provided with artificial nutrition and hydration and where a doctor has assumed the care of the claimant, the doctor must either continue to arrange for the provision of artificial nutrition and hydration or arrange for the care of the claimant to be transferred to a doctor who will make such arrangements, in the period until the claimant's death is imminent and the claimant is comatose.

(4) Para 81 of the guidance issued by the General Medical Council entitled *Withholding and Withdrawing Life-prolonging Treatments: Good Practice in Decision-making* is unlawful in that (a) it fails to recognise that the decision of a competent patient that artificial nutrition and hydration should be provided is determinative of the best interests of the patient, (b) it fails to acknowledge the heavy presumption in favour of life-prolonging treatment and that such treatment will be in the best interests of a patient unless the life of the patient, viewed from that patient's perspective, would be intolerable, and (c) provides that it is sufficient to withdraw artificial nutrition and hydration from a patient who is not dying because it may cause suffering or be too burdensome in relation to the possible benefits;

(5) Paras 13, 16, 32 and 42 of the guidance issued by the General Medical Council entitled *Withholding and Withdrawing Life-prolonging Treatments: Good Practice in Decision-making* are unlawful as they fail to recognise that the decision of a competent patient on whether artificial nutrition and hydration is determinative in principle of whether or not such treatment is in the patient's best interests.

(6) Paras 38 and 82 of the guidance issued by the General Medical Council entitled *Withholding and Withdrawing Life-prolonging Treatments: Good Practice in Decision-making* are unlawful as they fail to reflect the legal requirement that in certain circumstances artificial nutrition and hydration may not be withdrawn without prior judicial authorisation but provide that it is sufficient to consult a clinician with relevant experience or to take legal advice."

On appeal, the Court of Appeal was exceedingly critical of the wide-ranging approach taken to the examination of the issues by Mumby J. at first instance and allowed the appeal. Many of the findings made by Mumby were dismissed as unnecessary for the decision or were in error.

LORD PHILLIPS M.R.

"Concern at the possible withdrawal of ANH from Mr Burke while he is competent and expresses the wish to continue to receive ANH

26 The following parts of the declarations made by Munby J relate to this concern. (i) Mr Burke's decision that he requires ANH is determinative that this is in his best interests: declaration 1. (ii) Withdrawal of ANH contrary to Mr Burke's expressed wish would breach his rights under articles 3 and 8 of the Convention for the Protection of Human Rights and Fundamental Freedoms: declaration 2. (iii) Where Mr Burke expresses that he wishes to receive ANH a doctor who has assumed his care must either provide it or arrange for someone else to provide it: declaration 3. (iv) Paras 13, 16, 32 and 42 and 81 of the guidance are unlawful in that they fail to recognise that a decision of a patient that he wishes to receive ANH is in his best interests: declarations 4 and 5. We will deal with each of these in turn.

Best interests and autonomy

27 A theme running through Munby J's judgment is that, provided that there are no resource implications, doctors who have assumed the care of a patient must administer such treatment as is in the patient's best interests and that, where a patient has expressed an informed wish for a particular treatment, receipt of such treatment will be in the patient's best interests. This theme thus equates best interests with the wishes of the competent patient. Paras 88 to 115 of his judgment are devoted to developing this theme in terms which range over the position both where the patient is competent and where he is incompetent.

. . .

31 The proposition that the patient has a paramount right to refuse treatment is amply demonstrated by the authorities cited by Munby J [2005] QB 424, paras 54–56, under the

heading 'Autonomy and self-determination'. The corollary does not, however, follow, at least as a general proposition. Autonomy and the right of self-determination do not entitle the patient to insist on receiving a particular medical treatment regardless of the nature of the treatment. In so far as a doctor has a legal obligation to provide treatment this cannot be founded simply upon the fact that the patient demands it. The source of the duty lies elsewhere.

32 So far as ANH is concerned, there is no need to look far for the duty to provide this. Once a patient is accepted into a hospital, the medical staff come under a positive duty at common law to care for the patient. The authorities cited by Munby J, at paras 82–87, under the heading 'The duty to care' establish this proposition, if authority is needed. A fundamental aspect of this positive duty of care is a duty to take such steps as are reasonable to keep the patient alive. Where ANH is necessary to keep the patient alive, the duty of care will normally require the doctors to supply ANH. This duty will not, however, override the competent patient's wish not to receive ANH. Where the competent patient makes it plain that he or she wishes to be kept alive by ANH, this will not be the source of the duty to provide it. The patient's wish will merely underscore that duty.

33 In so far as the law has recognised that the duty to keep a patient alive by administering ANH or other life-prolonging treatment is not absolute, the exceptions have been restricted to the following situations: (1) where the competent patient refuses to receive ANH and (2) where the patient is not competent and it is not considered to be in the best interests of the patient to be artificially kept alive. It is with the second exception that the law has had most difficulty. The courts have accepted that where life involves an extreme degree of pain, discomfort or indignity to a patient, who is sentient but not competent and who has manifested no wish to be kept alive, these circumstances may absolve the doctors of the positive duty to keep the patient alive. Equally the courts have recognised that there may be no duty to keep alive a patient who is in a persistent vegetative state. In each of these examples the facts of the individual case may make it difficult to decide whether the duty to keep the patient alive persists.

34 No such difficulty arises, however, in the situation that has caused Mr Burke concern, that of the competent patient who, regardless of the pain, suffering or indignity of his condition, makes it plain that he wishes to be kept alive. No authority lends the slightest countenance to the suggestion that the duty on the doctors to take reasonable steps to keep the patient alive in such circumstances may not persist. Indeed, it seems to us that for a doctor deliberately to interrupt life-prolonging treatment in the face of a competent patient's expressed wish to be kept alive, with the intention of thereby terminating the patient's life, would leave the doctor with no answer to a charge of murder.

Would withdrawal of ANH contrary to the wishes of Mr Burke infringe articles 3 and 8 of the Convention?

35 Munby J's consideration of the effect of the Convention spans paras 117 to 214 — that is nearly half — of his judgment. His conclusion, as we understand it, was that article 2 of the Convention would not be infringed if the doctors ceased to provide ANH to Mr Burke contrary to his expressed wishes, but that article 3 would be infringed because the effect would be to subject Mr Burke to acute mental and physical suffering and article 8 would be engaged because Mr Burke's dignity and autonomy would have been flouted.

36 In this section of his judgment Munby J ranged widely over a mass of jurisprudence, giving consideration to the position of Mr Burke if ANH were withdrawn thereby causing him to die in a manner that involved acute mental and physical suffering. In doing so he considered the position of a patient who was both competent and incompetent. He identified three stages that Mr Burke might pass through: the first when he was competent and aware, the second when aware of his surroundings and predicament but unable to communicate, and the third after lapsing into a coma. He assumed that Mr Burke would, by the time he reached the second stage, have made an advance directive. He postulated

that to withdraw ANH in the first or second stage would infringe Mr Burke's article 3 and article 8 rights. As to the final stage, he said, at paras 175 and 176:

'175. Whether there will in fact be a breach either of article 3 or of article 8 if ANH is withdrawn from the claimant once he has entered into the third and final stage and has finally lapsed into a coma is not a matter capable of decision this far in advance of an event which, as I understand it, is unlikely to occur for many years yet. I decline therefore to express any conclusion on the point.

176. Much may turn upon the precise terms of the claimant's advance directive. More importantly, much will depend upon the claimant's condition once that stage is reached. It may be that by then—and on the evidence before me we are probably talking here only about the last few hours of life—ANH will be serving absolutely no purpose other than the very short prolongation of the life of a dying patient who has slipped into his final coma and who lacks all awareness of what is happening. In that event it might very well be said that the continuation of ANH would be bereft of any benefit at all to the claimant and that it would indeed be futile.'

37 As to this reasoning, we would comment that it is not clear to us that ANH will prolong Mr Burke's life at stage 2 or 3, nor that if he decides to make an advance directive, this will necessarily require that he be given ANH on the chance that this will gain him a few more hours or days of life, provided that its cessation will not be likely adversely to affect his comfort before he lapses into coma. We do not consider that there was any justification for embarking on speculation as to what the position might be when Mr Burke reaches the final stages of his life.

38 Turning to Mr Burke's concern that ANH may be withdrawn, contrary to his expressed wishes, so as to cause him to die of hunger and thirst while he is still competent, we have been unable to follow Munby J's reasoning and fear that he may have lost the wood for the trees. In particular, we have not been able to follow his reason for concluding that articles 3 and 8 of the Convention would be infringed, but not article 2. Munby J considered a body of authority that establishes that article 2 will not be violated when death follows withdrawal of treatment that has been rejected by the patient, in exercise of his right of self-determination, or because withdrawal of treatment was considered in the best interests of an incompetent patient for whom life offered intolerable suffering. He concluded [2005] QB 424, para 162:

'Article 2 does not entitle anyone to continue with life-prolonging treatment where to do so would expose the patient to "inhuman or degrading treatment" breaching article 3. On the other hand, a withdrawal of life-prolonging treatment which satisfies the exacting requirements of the common law, including a proper application of the intolerability test, and in a manner which is in all other respects compatible with the patient's rights under article 3 and article 8 will not, in my judgment, give rise to any breach of article 2.'

39 We endorse this conclusion. It does not, however, lead to the further conclusion that if a National Health doctor were deliberately to bring about the death of a competent patient by withdrawing life-prolonging treatment contrary to that patient's wishes, article 2 would not be infringed. It seems to us that such conduct would plainly violate article 2. Furthermore, if English law permitted such conduct, this would also violate this country's positive obligation to enforce article 2. As we have already indicated, we do not consider that English criminal law would countenance such conduct. However, the fact that articles 2, 3 and 8 of the Convention may be engaged does not, in our judgment, advance the argument or alter the common law . . .

The doctor with care of Mr Burke must either comply with his wish to be given ANH or arrange for another doctor to do so.

40 For the reasons that we have given we consider that the doctor with care of Mr Burke would himself be obliged, so long as the treatment was prolonging Mr Burke's life, to

provide ANH in accordance with his expressed wish. We do not believe that this has ever been open to doubt.

The lawfulness of the guidance

41 At this stage we are concerned with what should have been considered to be the only relevant question in relation to the guidance. Is it compatible with the duty of a doctor to administer ANH to a competent patient where this is necessary to keep the patient alive and the patient expresses a wish to be kept alive? . . .

Paragraph 81

46 This is the only paragraph to which the judge has taken exception that deals expressly with ANH. The first sentence requires the doctor to comply with the expressed wishes of a patient with capacity. No exception can be taken to this. The remainder deals with the approach to be taken where the patients lack capacity to decide for themselves and their wishes cannot be determined. We cannot see that this has any relevance to Mr Burke's predicament.

47 For these reasons, we do not consider that, in so far as the guidance relates to Mr Burke's predicament, there was any ground for declaring it unlawful.

Concerns about the wider implications of Munby J's judgment

48 We have identified the following topics explored by Munby J in his judgment in passages which have given rise to concern because of apparent implications which extend beyond the predicament of Mr Burke: (i) the right of a patient to select the treatment that he will receive; (ii) the circumstances in which life-prolonging treatment can be withdrawn from a patient who is incompetent; (iii) the duty to seek the approval of the court before withdrawing life-prolonging treatment.

The right of a patient to select the treatment that he will receive

49 Munby J identifies that the duty to care for a patient involves the duty to provide the treatment that is in the patient's best interests, referring to a statement by Lord Brandon of Oakbrook in *In re F (Mental Patient: Sterilisation)* [1990] 2 AC 1, 56, a passage dealing with the duty owed to an incompetent patient. Munby J then identifies that what is in the best interests of a patient depends upon the wishes of the patient, which may be influenced by matters which go beyond wanting to be cured, to continue to live or to avoid pain and suffering-all matters which the doctor might otherwise consider to be in the patient's best interest. He then postulates that it is the duty of the doctor to provide that treatment which complies with the wishes of the patient. At one point he states [2005] QB 424, at para 99:

'If the patient is competent (or, although incompetent, has made an advance directive which is both valid and relevant to the treatment in question) there is no difficulty in principle: the patient decides what is in his best interests and what treatment he should or should not have.'

50 The GMC is concerned that these passages suggest that a doctor is obliged, if the patient so requires, to provide treatment to a patient, or to procure another doctor to provide such treatment, even though the doctor believes that the treatment is not clinically indicated. No such general proposition should be deduced from Munby J's judgment, nor do we believe that he intended to advance any such general proposition. So far as the general position is concerned, we would endorse the following simple propositions advanced by the GMC. (i) The doctor, exercising his professional clinical judgment, decides what treatment options are clinically indicated (i e will provide overall clinical benefit) for his patient. (ii) He then offers those treatment options to the patient in the

course of which he explains to him/her the risks, benefits, side effects, etc involved in each of the treatment options. (iii) The patient then decides whether he wishes to accept any of those treatment options and, if so, which one. In the vast majority of cases he will, of course, decide which treatment option he considers to be in his best interests and, in doing so, he will or may take into account other, non-clinical, factors. However, he can, if he wishes, decide to accept (or refuse) the treatment option on the basis of reasons which are irrational or for no reasons at all. (iv) If he chooses one of the treatment options offered to him, the doctor will then proceed to provide it. (v) If, however, he refuses all of the treatment options offered to him and instead informs the doctor that he wants a form of treatment which the doctor has not offered him, the doctor will, no doubt, discuss that form of treatment with him (assuming that it is a form of treatment known to him) but if the doctor concludes that this treatment is not clinically indicated he is not required (i e he is under no legal obligation) to provide it to the patient although he should offer to arrange a second opinion.

51 The relationship between doctor and patient usually begins with diagnosis and advice. The doctor will describe the treatment that he recommends or, if there are a number of alternative treatments that he would be prepared to administer in the interests of the patient, the choices available, their implications and his recommended option. In such circumstances the right to refuse a proposed treatment gives the patient what appears to be a positive option to choose an alternative. In truth the right to choose is no more than a reflection of the fact that it is the doctor's duty to provide a treatment that he considers to be in the interests of the patient and that the patient is prepared to accept.

52 Munby J was not, however, concerned with the extent to which, in general, a patient has a right to insist on a particular treatment. He was concerned with the choice of whether or not to receive life-prolonging treatment and the right to decide 'how one chooses to pass the closing days and moments of one's life and how one manages one's death': para 62. The passages of general discussion in his judgment must be read in this context.

53 We have indicated that, where a competent patient indicates his or her wish to be kept alive by the provision of ANH any doctor who deliberately brings that patient's life to an end by discontinuing the supply of ANH will not merely be in breach of duty but guilty of murder. Where life depends upon the continued provision of ANH there can be no question of the supply of ANH not being clinically indicated unless a clinical decision has been taken that the life in question should come to an end. That is not a decision that can lawfully be taken in the case of a competent patient who expresses the wish to remain alive.

54 There is one situation where the provision of ANH will not be clinically indicated that is not relevant to Mr Burke's concern but which received a disproportionate amount of attention in this case. In the last stage of life the provision of ANH not only may not prolong life, but may even hasten death. Unchallenged evidence from Professor Higginson illustrated the latter proposition. At this stage, whether to administer ANH will be a clinical decision which is likely to turn on whether or not it has a palliative effect or is likely to produce adverse reactions. It is only in this situation that, assuming the patient remains competent, a patient's expressed wish that ANH be continued might conflict with the doctor's view that this is not clinically indicated.

55 As we understand Munby J's judgment, he considered that in this situation the patient's wish to receive ANH must be determinative. We do not agree. Clearly the doctor would need to have regard to any distress that might be caused as a result of overriding the expressed wish of the patient. Ultimately, however, a patient cannot demand that a doctor administer a treatment which the doctor considers is adverse to the patient's clinical needs. This said, we consider that the scenario that we have just described is extremely unlikely to arise in practice.

The position of the incompetent patient

56 A large part of Munby J's judgment and the submissions placed before us related to the position of the incompetent patient. Three situations were discussed: (i) the patient in

a PVS; (ii) the incompetent but sentient patient capable of being kept alive for an indefinite period by the provision of ANH; (iii) the patient in the final stages of life. We would reiterate that Mr Burke's legitimate concern at this stage of his life does not relate to any of these situations.

57 The situation of a patient in a PVS was only referred to in passing. It fell, however, within the compass of Mr Gordon's general submission that, if the patient has made an advance directive that he is to be kept alive, this must be complied with as a matter of law. The position of a patient in a PVS was addressed at length by the House of Lords in *Airedale NHS Trust v Bland* [1993] AC 789 and we do not consider it appropriate in this case to add to what was said by their Lordships, other than to make the following observation. While a number of their Lordships indicated that an advance directive that the patient should not be kept alive in a PVS should be respected, we do not read that decision as requiring such a patient to be kept alive simply because he has made an advance directive to that effect. Such a proposition would not be compatible with the provisions of the Mental Capacity Act 2005, which we consider accords with the position at common law. While section 26 of that Act requires compliance with a valid advance directive to refuse treatment, section 4 does no more than require this to be taken into consideration when considering what is in the best interests of a patient.

58 There are tragic cases where treatment can prolong life for an indeterminate period, but only at a cost of great suffering while life continues. Such a case was *In re J (A Minor) (Wardship: Medical Treatment)* [1991] Fam 33. There are other cases, and these are much more common, where a patient has lost competence in the final stages of life and where ANH may prolong these final stages, but at an adverse cost so far as comfort and dignity are concerned, sometimes resulting in the patient's last days being spent in a hospital ward rather than at home, with family around.

59 It is to these situations that so much of the debate in this case has been directed. Apprehensions have been expressed by some who have intervened that those in charge of patients may too readily withdraw, or fail to provide, ANH or other life prolonging treatment on the ground that the patient's life, if prolonged, will not be worth living. . . . "

The Master of the Rolls considered evidence advanced by the Disability Rights Alliance and then continued:

"61 These reports did not constitute admissible evidence, but underlined the importance of clear law and guidance in this area. After a lengthy analysis of jurisprudence under the heading 'Best interests and life-prolonging treatment' the judge set out a summary of his conclusions [2005] QB 424, para 116, which included the following:

'There is a very strong presumption in favour of taking all steps which will prolong life, and save in exceptional circumstances, or where the patient is dying, the best interests of the patient will normally require such steps to be taken. In case of doubt that doubt falls to be resolved in favour of the preservation of life. But the obligation is not absolute. Important as the sanctity of life is, it may have to take second place to human dignity. In the context of life-prolonging treatment the touchstone of best interests is intolerability. So if life-prolonging treatment is providing some benefit it should be provided unless the patient's life, if thus prolonged, would from the patient's point of view be intolerable.'

62 We do not think that any objection could have been taken to this summary had it not contained the final two sentences, which we have emphasised. The suggestion that the touchstone of 'best interests' is the 'intolerability' of continued life has, understandably, given rise to concern. The test of whether it is in the best interests of the patient to provide or continue ANH must depend on the particular circumstances. The two situations that we have considered above are very different. As to the approach to be adopted in the former,

this court dealt with that in *In re J* [1991] Fam 33 and we do not think that it is appropriate to review what the court there said in a context that is purely hypothetical.

63 As to the approach to best interests where a patient is close to death, it seems to us that the judge himself recognised that 'intolerability' was not the test of best interests. He said, at para 104: 'where the patient is dying, then the goal may properly be to ease suffering and, where appropriate, to "ease the passing" rather than to achieve a short prolongation of life . . . ' We agree. We do not think it possible to attempt to define what is in the best interests of a patient by a single test, applicable in all circumstances. We would add that the disturbing cases referred to in paras 57 and 58, if correctly reported, were cases where the doctors appear to have failed to observe the guidance. They are not illustrative of any illegality in the guidance. The guidance expressly warns against treating the life of a disabled patient as being of less value than the life of a patient without disability, and rightly does so."

The guidance

Lord Phillips made reference to para.81 and then continued:

"66 Declaration (4) goes on to declare that para 81 is unlawful because it does not make it clear that ANH can only be withdrawn from a patient who is not dying if his continued life would be intolerable. We do not consider that the terms of para 81 are unlawful. We do, however, feel that the wording of that part of the paragraph which deals with the position where death is not imminent could be better drafted. We believe that it is attempting to spell out the circumstances in which it may be lawful to withdraw ANH in a case such as *In re J* [1991] Fam 33. The statement that the provision of ANH "may cause suffering or be too burdensome in relation to the possible benefits" is not a clear or helpful description of the circumstances in which life is so burdensome that there is no duty to prolong it. This inadequacy of drafting does not, however, justify the judge's declaration.

Is there a legal requirement to obtain court authorisation before withdrawing ANH?

67 The judge's declaration (6) suggests that 'in certain circumstances' this question must be answered in the affirmative. What circumstances did the judge have in mind? The answer is given by para 214(g) of his judgment:

'Where it is proposed to withhold or withdraw ANH the prior authorisation of the court is required as a matter of law (and thus ANH cannot be withheld or withdrawn without prior judicial authorisation): (i) where there is any doubt or disagreement as to the capacity (competence) of the patient; or (ii) where there is a lack of unanimity amongst the attending medical professionals as to either (1) the patient's condition or prognosis or (2) the patient's best interests or (3) the likely outcome of ANH being either withheld or withdrawn or (4) otherwise as to whether or not ANH should be withheld or withdrawn; or (iii) where there is evidence that the patient when competent would have wanted ANH to continue in the relevant circumstances; or (iv) where there is evidence that the patient (even if a child or incompetent) resists or disputes the proposed withdrawal of ANH; or (v) where persons having a reasonable claim to have their views or evidence taken into account (such as parents or close relatives, partners, close friends, long-term carers) assert that withdrawal of ANH is contrary to the patient's wishes or not in the patient's best interests.'

68 We would observe that even if this paragraph accurately states the law, it does not follow that the guidance is illegal in that it directs the doctor concerned to seek legal advice rather than to seek the authority of the court to the withdrawal of ANH. On the contrary, even if the judge is correct about the legal duty, we consider that paras 38 and 82 of the guidance are proper and lawful. We note that the judge inaccurately summarises the effect of those paragraphs by saying that they direct the doctor to consult a clinician or take legal advice, when what in fact they direct is that the doctor should do both.

69 Declaration (6) has caused considerable concern. The Intensive Care Society informed us that each year approximately 50,000 patients are admitted to intensive care units and of these 30% die in the unit or on the wards before hospital discharge. Most of these die because treatment is withdrawn or limited, albeit in circumstances where the clinicians conclude that such treatment would be likely merely to prolong the process of dying. There is not always agreement on the part of all concerned as to the withdrawal of treatment. This is hardly surprising. Grief stricken relatives may not be able to accept that the patient is beyond saving. The ICS calculates that, if Munby J's criteria were applied, approximately ten applications a day would have to be made to the courts.

70 In the event, we do not consider that the judge is right to postulate that there is a legal duty to obtain court approval to the withdrawal of ANH in the circumstances that he identifies.

. . .

72 The judge's reasoning appears at paras 195–211. His starting point was the identification by the courts of a special category of cases where medical procedures required the sanction of the court, even if all concerned were agreed that the procedures were desirable. He observed, at para 195, that initially the requirement to obtain prior judicial sanction 'was not a matter of law but rather a matter of good practice'.

73 The judge then observed, at para 196, that more recently the courts had identified a further category of important decisions where the requirement for judicial intervention arose 'if there is disagreement between those involved'. He cited at length from the decision of Coleridge J in *D v An NHS Trust (Medical Treatment: Consent: Termination)* [2004] 1 FLR 1110. That was a case where the treatment under consideration was the termination of the pregnancy of an incompetent adult. Coleridge J identified a number of circumstances where, because the legitimacy of such treatment was open to doubt, it was 'necessary' to seek the authorisation of the court.

74 We do not read Coleridge J's judgment as purporting to transform the requirement to seek the approval of the court from a matter of good practice into a legal requirement. He did, however, observe, at para 31:

'The advent of the Human Rights Act 1998 has enhanced the responsibility of the court to positively protect the welfare of these patients, and in particular to protect the patient's right to respect for her private and family life under article 8(1) of the European Convention . . . '

75 Munby J emphasised this passage, before turning to consider the implications of decisions of the European Court of Human Rights first on admissibility and subsequently on the merits in *Glass v United Kingdom* [2004] 1 FLR 1019. He concluded [2005] QB 424, para 210, that the latter decision converted what had previously been only 'a matter of good practice' into 'a matter of legal requirement' by reason of the Human Rights Act 1998. He observed that this was 'a significant and potentially very important change'. If the judge was correct we would concur. Accordingly it is necessary to consider the Glass case with some care."

Lord Phillips examined the *Glass* decision considered above at p.1050 and continued:

"80 This was not a decision which made 'a significant and potentially very important change in English law'. The European court did no more than consider the implications of the doctors' conduct in the light of what the European court understood to be English law. The true position is that the court does not 'authorise' treatment that would otherwise be unlawful. The court makes a declaration as to whether or not proposed treatment, or the withdrawal of treatment, will be lawful. Good practice may require medical practitioners to seek such a declaration where the legality of proposed treatment is in doubt. This is not, however, something that they are required to do as a matter of law. For these reasons declaration (6) made by Munby J misstated the law."

Notes:

1. This case provides a good illustration of the extent to which end of life decision making is today governed by guidelines issued by the health professional bodies. One potential problem with such guidance is its low visibility for patients. While guidance may be published and/or made available on the internet, such guidelines are generally unlikely to be routinely drawn to the attention of patients in advance.

2. The decision is notable for the criticism of the Court of Appeal of the broad judgment by Mumby J. at first instance and in many respects can be seen as a return to judicial orthodoxy. For an analysis of the Mumby approach and a characterisation of him as a "new model judge", see further J. Montgomery "Law and the Demoralisation of Medicine" (2006) 26 *Legal Studies* 185 at pp.204–206.

3. The Court of Appeal agreed with Mumby J. that the ECHR was engaged and to fail to treat and to feed Burke after he had made a valid refusal would amount to a violation of Articles 3 and 8 of the ECHR.

4. The tensions between the first instance and Court of Appeal decisions illustrate the problems in attempting to rationalise respect for autonomy with the discretion inherent in clinical decision-making. Mumby J.'s judgment can be seen very much as pro-patient autonomy and also indicative that the Human Rights Act truly makes a difference to the decision-making process in this area. In contrast the Court of Appeal affirms judicial orthodoxy as illustrated in *Re J* above and the resource allocation cases considered in Chapter 1, namely that patients are unable to compel administration of treatment in a situation in which the clinician does not believe them to have a clinical need. Gurnham suggests that "It makes good practical sense for doctors to be given some legal lee-way when a patient demands resources which cannot justifiably be provided to the detriment of other needs" (see further D. Gurnham, "Losing the Wood for the Trees: Burke and the Court of Appeal" (2006) 14 *Medical Law Review* 253).

5. One of the criticisms made by the Court of Appeal of the judgment in *Burke* at first instance was that it had been unnecessary to deal with that issue as the issue had not yet arisen. They also rejected the approach by Mumby J. that the test to be employed here was as to whether life was intolerable.

6. McLean has suggested that the statement made by the Court of Appeal that "Where life depends upon the continued provision of AHN there can be no question of the supply of AHN not being clinically indicated unless a clinical decision has been taken that the life in question should come to an end" is unusual. She comments that "Generally courts go to great lengths to avoid characterising non-treatment decisions in this way by, however disingenuously, declaring that the court does not sanction the taking of a life; rather it simply pronounces on whether or not is is in a patient's best interests to have their life sustained. This distinction, which has always been suspect, did not commend itself to the Court of Appeal

whose honesty is to be commended, even if—taken to its logical conclusion—it would turn current law on its head" (see further S. McLean, "From Bland to Burke: The Law and Politics of Assisted Nutrition and Hydration" in S. McLean (ed.), *First Do No Harm: Law, Ethics and Healthcare*, Aldershot: Ashgate, 2006) at p.441).

7. The Court of Appeal further disagreed with Mumby J. as to the extent to which judicial approval was required after *Glass v UK* in relation to such cases. Mumby J. suggests that it is, whereas the Court of Appeal disagreed. Gurnham notes that this gives rise to an inconsistency between cases concerning patients in a permanent vegetative state and other end of life cases (discussed above) (see further D. Gurnham, "Losing the Wood for the Trees: Burke and the Court of Appeal" [2006] 14 *Medical Law Review* 253).

QUESTIONS:

1. To what extent, if at all does the *Burke* case mean that there is no "right to live" in English law?
2. Was Mr Burke making an impossible request, given that treatment decisions are fundamentally impacted by clinical judgment and resource allocation issues?
3. Were the Court of Appeal right to conclude that the *Glass* case has not had a "significant and very important change in English law"? See *Glass* discussed above at p.1050).

Mr Burke then took his case to the ECHR. As this book goes to press in August 2006, press reports have noted that the ECHR rejected his application on the basis that there was "no real and imminent threat" that artificial nutrition or hydration would be withdrawn. The ECHR also stated that it was satisfied that the presumption of English law was in favour of prolonging life wherever possible. They confirmed that the GMC guidance simply confirmed the law. Where a competent patient refused treatment, this refusal should be respected. In the case of an incompetent patient ANH should be continued for as long as this prolonged life, but there may be situations in which clinical judgment was reached that ANH hastened death. It confirmed the approach of the Court of Appeal that a judgment could not be made in relation to circumstances which had not finally been determined. Furthermore it took the approach that it was not for the High Court to authorise medical actions but simply to declare whether they were lawful.

However his solicitor commented that this was problematic as, if the issue could not be resolved when he was competent then Mr Burke would of course be unable to make an application himself once he lost decision-making capacity (BBC News, "Patient loses right to food-fight", Tuesday August 8, 2006; *http:/ /www.bbc.co.uk*: "Right to life case: Leslie Burke's appeal rejected by the ECHR", Media Information; Irwin Mitchell, August 8, 2008). Just after the judgment was delivered Mr Burke's brother died of the same genetic condition. Mr Burke has now indicated that he intends to make a living will setting out his wishes.

4. ENGLISH LAW REFORM

(a) Active Termination of Life

It has been argued that just as an individual who has the means and necessary physical strength can end his own life, so a person unable to end his own life should be able to request another to assist him in that process. (For strong support of active voluntary euthanasia see, L. Kennedy, "Euthanasia" in A. Grubb (ed.), *Choices and Decisions in Health Care*, Chichester: John Wiley 1993; G. Williams, "Euthanasia" (1973) 41 *Medico-Legal Journal* 4; see also the discussion in E. Jackson, "Whose Death Is It Anyway? Euthanasia and the Medical Profession" (2004) 57 *Current Legal Problems* 415.) "Euthanasia" is the term used to describe the deliberate ending of the life of a person suffering from a painful illness. Several different categories of euthanasia have been recognised— voluntary euthanasia: life terminated at the patient's request; non-voluntary euthanasia: termination of life of an incompetent patient; involuntary euthanasia: ending of life of the patient on paternalistic or other grounds disregarding any wishes expressed by the patient. The latter category is almost universally regarded as unacceptable, not least because it overrides the individual's autonomy and their right to life. The other two categories have been the source of considerable controversy. Two further distinctions should be noted: "active euthanasia" which, as the name suggests, is positive action terminating life; and "passive euthanasia" which concerns the shortening of life through an omission to act. English law, as we have already seen, rejects active euthanasia while accepting passive euthanasia. The issue of euthanasia received consideration by a House of Lords Select Committee established following the *Bland* case (HL Paper 21-2, London: HMSO, 1994). The Committee, who received an extensive quantity of evidence from leading experts, recommended that there should be no change in the law to allow active euthanasia. They were motivated in their decision by a concern to prohibit intentional killing, the slippery slope argument, the position of the elderly and others who may feel vulnerable and the availability of pallative care. (See further L. Gormally, "Walton, Davies, Boyd and the legalisation of euthanasia" in J. Keown (ed.), *Euthanasia Examined*, Cambridge: CUP, 1995).

One of the first instances of statutory recognition being given to the practice of euthanasia took place in Australia. The Rights of the Terminally Ill Act was passed in Northern Territory in 1995, providing that a person could request assistance to terminate life. A request had to be voluntary, the patient had to be of sound mind and over 18, and the patient has to be suffering from an illness that the medical practitioner believed will result in the patient's death. The assessment of the need for euthanasia also had to be confirmed by a second medical practitioner. The request was not to be effective where medically acceptable pallative care options existed. The legislation required there to be notification that the criteria under the statute had been complied with. This statute proved controversial and was eventually struck down (see also C.J. Ryan and M. Kaye, "Euthanasia in Australia—the Northern Territory Rights of the Terminally Ill Act 1995" (1996) *New England Journal of Medicine* 326). In Oregon, the Death with Dignity Act was passed in 1985. This gives patients with six months or less to live the right to ask their doctor for drugs to end their lives. It explicitly excludes lethal injection/mercy killing and active euthanasia. The number of patients who have taken advantage of the legislation has been small in number and it has been subject to a series of constitutional challenges.

In the Netherlands, while euthanasia itself was not recognised, there was a policy of non-prosecution of doctors who followed a series of guidelines and also reported an assisted death to a regional committee comprised of doctors, lawyers and ethicists. Recently legislation was passed giving legal effect to the existing position and legitimising assistance in dying; the legislation came into force in October 2001 (J. De Haan, "The New Dutch Law on Euthanasia" (2002) 10 *Medical Law Review* 57). The Termination of Life on Request and Assisted (Review Procedure) Act amends the Dutch Criminal Code. It is not a crime for a doctor to terminate the life of another on their request if the legislation is complied with. The doctor must satisfy the review committee that the patient has made a voluntary and well-considered request, that he is convinced that the patient was suffering unbearably and hopelessly, that he had informed the patient about his situation and the prospect for improvement; that he has reached the decision that the patient's condition is hopeless along with that of the patient; he has consulted one other independent doctor and he has terminated life with all due care and attention. In contrast to the previous legal situation, the new law applies to children. Those persons over 16 may take the decision themselves. Those between 12–15 can seek euthanasia but the doctor must only act with parental consent. The doctor who administers euthanasia is required to inform the regional pathologist and he must then report, without delay, to the regional review committee in his district. The task of the committee is to see whether the doctor has fulfilled the "due care" criteria. Now the review committee only has to send the case to the prosecutor where it believes that the criteria have not been satisfied. This was followed by similar legislation in Belgium in 2002, which applies to those who are conscious and who have an incurable illness. In contrast to the Netherlands, this legislation only applies to those persons over 18 and each euthanasia case has to be reported to a national committee. (M. Adams and H. Nys, "Comparative Reflections on the Belgium Euthanasia Act 2002" (2003) 11 *Medical Law Review* 353). There is also currently some consideration as to whether French law should also allow assisted dying (see further P. Lewis, "The Evolution of Assisted Dying in France: A Third Way" (2006) 14 *Medical Law Review* 44).

In recent years, in the absence of assisted dying legislation in the UK, there has been some evidence of euthanasia tourism, with UK citizens travelling to Switzerland to receive assistance in dying. In January 2003 Reginald Crew, a 74-year-old patient with advanced motor neurone disease, travelled with his wife and daughter to Zurich and ended his life by taking a drink laced with barbiturates (News in brief: "Briton ends his life at assisted suicide clinic" (2003) 326 British Medical Journal 180). In December 2004, a 65-year-old British woman with a degenerative brain disease, known only as Mrs Z, committed suicide in a Zurich clinic after a High Court judge refused to intervene to stop her husband taking her abroad ("News round-up: High Court upholds right of woman to travel abroad for suicide" (2004) British Medical Journal 1364). Here the law limits those situations in which euthanasia is a crime. Thus, in contrast to the jurisdictions already discussed in Switzerland, life may be ended without the involvement of a doctor (S. Hurst and A. Mauron, "Assisted suicide and euthanasia in Switzerland: allowing a role for non-physicians" (2003) 326 British Medical Journal 271; O. Guillod and A. Schmidt, "Assisted Suicide under Swiss Law" (2005) 12 *European Journal of Health Law* 23). Article 115 of the Swiss Penal Code provides that assisting suicide is only a crime if the motive is selfish. In *Re Z* [2004] EWHC 2817 an attempt to stop a woman who suffered from a degenerative brain condition to travel to Switzerland to end her life was unsuccessful. However, the judgment suggested that her husband may have committed an offence by helping her to travel abroad to end her own life (see p.998 above).

In 2004 a Bill, the Assisted Dying for the Terminally Ill Bill, was introduced into Parliament by Lord Joffe with the aim of legalising physician-assisted dying. This Bill fell on the dissolution of Parliament for the General Election in April 2005. However, the House of Lords Select Committee report on the Bill called for this matter to be debated early in the next parliament (Assisted Dying for the Terminally Ill Bill, HL, Vol.1: Report, 2005. They also proposed several amendments which were included in the redrafted Bill which was introduced into Parliament in November 2005. The amended Bill allows "assisted dying", which refers to euthanasia or assistance in suicide where a request was made by a competent, terminally ill patient. A doctor would have to assess that the patient was competent, had a terminal illness and was suffering unbearably. The patient would need to be informed of the doctor's diagnosis, the patient's prognosis and the process of being assisted to die and what alternatives were available including palliative care. If the patient still persisted in wanting to be assisted to die, then the doctor must be satisfied that this was a voluntary request and as a result as an informed decision. If these requirements were complied with then the patient should be referred to a consulting physician. This doctor would also have to confirm that the patient had complied with the same criteria as the assessing physician. In addition an offer of palliative care should be made available. Only when all those criteria were established could a patient make a written declaration which must be witnessed by two persons , one of whom must be a solicitor. This written declaration would then be valid for a six-month period. Again before assisting the patient to die a doctor must inform the patient of the right to revoke the declaration, ascertain that the declaration is still valid and again immediately before assisting the patient to die ask if they wish to revoke the declaration.

The Bill provided that the patient could revoke the declaration at any time. It also contained a right of conscientious objection for health care professionals to opt out of its provisions but provided that if a doctor did have such an objection, the patient should be referred to another doctor. In a situation in which the patient's competence was under question, then a referral should be made to a psychiatrist. In addition the Bill provided that the attending doctor should recommend to the patient that they inform their next of kin of their request for assistance in dying. Patients were also to be entitled to receive all necessary pain-relieving drugs. The Bill contained provision providing that doctors and members of the medical care team who act in good faith in assisting a patient to die will not be guilty of an offence where they act in what they reasonably believe to be the requirements of the Act. A further safeguard for the patient was the statement that doctors and members of the medical team could not participate in assistance in dying if they had grounds for believing that they would benefit financially from the patient's death. The Bill also provided for various criminal offences consequent upon contravention of terms of the legislation. Analagous with Belgium and the Netherlands, it also provided for the establishment of "monitoring commissions" comprising medical, legal and lay members around the country and for formal reporting requirements regarding compliance with the legislation. The Select Committee had proposed a number of amendments to the Bill, including a distinction being clearly drawn between euthanasia and assisted suicide. The Committee was also concerned that the words "terminal illness" were problematic, given the difficulty of conclusivity of medical diagnosis. Moreover, it found the subjectivity of the criteria of "unbearable suffering" potentially difficult and proposed that instead it should be necessary to show "unrelievable" or "intractable" suffering. In addition it suggested that the conscientious objection provision should include the requirement of reference of the patient to another doctor. The majority of these recommendations were not, however, included.

The Joffe Bill was by no means the first example of an attempt to introduce such legislation into English law. The Euthanasia Bill 1936 set out conditions for enthanasia for a patient who was over 21, suffering from an incurable and fatal illness, and able to sign a form in the presence of two witnesses asking to be put to death. The form and certificates were to be submitted to a euthanasia referee who was to have the task of interviewing the patient and other interested parties. The matter was then to go to a court which had the right to consider the case, review evidence and if they were satisfied then to issue a certificate authorising a doctor to perform euthanasia in the presence of an official witness. The Voluntary Euthanasia Bill 1969 authorised doctors to end the life of a patient who was over 21, who requested it and who was certified by two doctors as suffering from "serious physical illness or impairment reasonably thought in the patient's case to be incurable and expected to cause him severe distress or render him incapable of rational existence". The patient was to execute a declaration requesting euthanasia. A series of Incurable Patients Bills were introduced during the 1970s. One such Bill would have granted an incurable patient a right to receive whatever quantity of drugs he might need to get full relief from pain or physical distress and to be rendered unconscious if there was no treatment which could give him such relief.

An alternative and less complex proposal to that of the Joffe Bill is that suggested by Mason, McCall Smith and Laurie who suggest the inclusion of an amending subsection into the Suicide Act 1961 to the effect that "The provisions of s2(1) shall not apply to a registered medical practitioner who, given the existence of a competent directive, is providing assistance to a patient who is suffering from a progressive and irremediable condition and who is prevented, or will be prevented, by physical disability from ending his or her own life without assistance." See J.K. Mason and G. Laurie, *Law and Medical Ethics* (6th edn), Oxford: OUP, 2006 at p.647.

Those who oppose active euthanasia argue that it is not possible to either satisfactorily enact a euthanasia statute or provide legal defences to euthanasia which will provide sufficient safeguards against abuse. Some regard the introduction of voluntary euthanasia as one step down the slippery slope to involuntary euthanasia. Critics of euthanasia point to the experience in the Netherlands where it has been claimed the legislative safeguards do not provide satisfactory protection against abuses. (The dangers of the "slippery slope" are discussed in D. Lamb, *Down the Slippery Slope*, Croom Helm, 1988, Chapter 2, "It Started from Small Beginnings"; S. Smith, "Evidence for the Practical Slippery Slope in the Debate on Physician-Assisted Suicide and Euthanasia" (2006) 13 *Medical Law Review* 17, J. Keown, "Law and Practice of Euthanasia" (1992) 108 L.Q.R. 51; H. Jochemsem, "Euthanasia in Holland: an Ethical Critique of the New Law" (1994) 20 *Journal of Medical Ethics* 212. It has also been argued that the elderly may be particularly vulnerable to such legislation and it has been argued that this may be particularly the case in the context of elderly women who do not wish to be seen as a burden to their families (see further H. Biggs, " I don't want to be a burden! A Feminist Reflects on Women's Experiences of Death and Dying" in S. Sheldon and M. Thomson (eds), *Feminist Perspectives on Health Care Law*, London: Cavendish, 1998).

It has also been argued that active euthanasia is less of an issue today in view of the extensive development of palliative care along with the administration of pain-killing drugs. Alongside this has been the growth of the hospice movement. (See R.G. Twycross, "Where There is Hope, There is Life: a View from the Hospice" in J. Keown (ed.), *Euthanasia Examined*, Cambridge: CUP, 1995.) In 1967 Dame Cecily Saunders funded St Christopher's Hospice to care for dying patients and their families at home and on the wards, aimed also at teaching and research. Her initiative led subsequently to the development of a network of hospices across the country (see N. James, "From Vision to System" in R. Lee and D. Morgan (eds), *Death rites: Law and Ethics at the End of Life*, London: Routledge, 1994). Finally, some health care professional bodies such as the British Medical Association have argued that recognition of active euthanasia would result in the doctor acquiring a function which was at odds with his or her traditional role as healer.

(b) Defence to those Prosecuted for Active Cessation of Life of a Neonate

In the aftermath of *R v Arthur*, it was suggested that a doctor who terminated the life of a neonate should not be prosecuted for murder but rather for some alternative offence. Diana and Malcolm Brahams proposed a Limitation of Treatment Bill. No criminal offence would be committed where a doctor refused or stopped treatment of an infant under 28 days old, subject to two conditions being satisfied. First, the parents must give their written consent. Secondly, two doctors, both of at least seven years' standing and one of them being a paediatrician, must certify in writing that the infant suffered from a severe mental or physical handicap which was either irreversible or of such gravity that after receiving all available treatment the child would enjoy no worthwhile quality of life. In determining the issue of quality of life the doctors were to take into account various factors. These would include the degree of pain and suffering likely to be endured, the child's potential to communicate, the extent to which the parents were willing to care for the child and the effect that the child might have on the parent's physical and mental health. (See D. and M. Brahams, "*R. v. Arthur*" (1981) 78 L.S.Gaz. 1342.) Legislative reform has also been proposed by J.K. Mason and R.A. McCall Smith, *Law and Medical Ethics* (6th edn), Butterworths, 2002, p.502. They suggest that: "In the event of positive treatment being necessary for a neonate's survival, it will not be an offence to withhold such treatment if two doctors, one of whom is a consultant paediatrician, acting in good faith and with the consent of both parents if available, decide against treatment in the light of reasonably clear medical prognosis which indicates that the infant's further life would be intolerable by virtue of pain or suffering or because of severe cerebral incompetence."

QUESTIONS:

1. Is legislation necessary in order to safeguard the position of medical practitioners?
2. Do you think that the safeguards built into the legislative proposals outlined above are adequate?
3. Who should make decisions to cease treatment of neonates? What qualities are required in such a decision-maker? (See R. Weir, *Selective Non Treatment of the Handicapped Newborn*, Oxford: OUP, 1979, Chapter 9.)

(c) Statutory Recognition of Mercy Killing

Murder carries a mandatory life sentence. It can be argued that a person who kills another out of compassion for his or her suffering should not be classed in the same way as other murderers. One alternative approach to recognition of euthanasia would be the legislative recognition of mercy killing. This could take one of several forms. First, there could be a special offence of "mercy killing". Such an option was considered by the Criminal Law Revision Committee in their 14th Report *Offences Against the Person* (Cmnd.7844, p.53, section F). In their 12th report they had suggested that even if the mandatory life sentence was retained the judge should be given the option of not passing a custodial sentence. Subsequently in their Working Paper they suggested that:

"We suggested tentatively that there should be a new offence which would apply to a person who, from compassion, unlawfully kills another person who is or is believed by him to be:
(1) permanently subject to great bodily pain or suffering, or
(2) permanently helpless from bodily or mental incapacity, or
(3) subject to rapid and incurable bodily or mental degeneration.
We suggested that 2 years' imprisonment would be an appropriate maximum penalty."

This proposal was subject to considerable opposition. It was suggested that it could give rise to definitional difficulties. In addition it was suggested that it:

"would not prevent suffering but would cause suffering, since the weak and the handicapped would receive less effective protection from the law than the fit and well because the basis of the suggested new offence would rest upon the defendant's evaluation of the condition of the victim. That evaluation might be made in ignorance of what medicine would do for the sufferer."

In the light of the controversy it was decided to withdraw the proposal. However the approach of the Criminal Law Revision Committee has been criticised, not least because of its unwillingness to deal with an issue on the basis that that it controversial. It has been suggested that reliance on the plea of diminished responsibility in the case of mercy killers may be unsatisfactory because the courts have taken a more restrictive approach to the definition of diminished responsibility, requiring at least some evidence of mental imbalance (see R. Leng, "Mercy Killing and the CLRC" (1982) 132 New L.J. 76.)

An alternative approach is for mercy killing to operate as a defence to a prosecution for murder. A plea of mercy killing could reduce a charge of murder to manslaughter or alternatively operate as a total defence. The House of Lords Select Committee on Euthanasia considered this option (HL Paper 2-1, London: HMSO, 1994). Evidence was presented to the Committee to the effect that there was not a pressing case at that time for such a defence. Home Office statistics revealed that between 1982 and 1991 "mercy killing" was an issue in 22 cases of homicide; none of those cases concerned health professionals. Although in all cases a prosecution was begun for murder only one conviction and sentence of life imprisonment eventually resulted. In all other cases other sentences were substituted. The House of Lords Select Committee did suggest that the mandatory penalty of life imprisonment for murder should be abolished. (See M. Otlowski, "Active Voluntary Euthanasia" (1994) 2 *Medical Law Review* 161.) A final option would be that in a situation in which a judge determines that a mercy killing has taken place, he should have the power to reduce the sentence imposed. This would require a departure from the existing mandatory life sentence for murder. The Law Commission in their report "A New Homicide Act for England and Wales" did not make any special provision for the healthcare professional who acts as a "mercy killer", see Law Commission "A New Homicide Act for England and Wales", Law Commission Consultation Paper No.177, London: Law Commission (2005).

QUESTIONS:

1. What are the difficulties facing a legislative draftsman attempting to define a mercy killing offence?
2. Would a mercy killing offence place a patient in an unduly vulnerable position?

(d) Advance Directives

Advance directives (also known as living wills) are documents which allow a person to state the criteria on which they would wish treatment to be given should they become incapable of making their own decisions (see further J. Montgomery,

"Power over Death: the Final Sting" in R. Lee and D. Morgan (eds), *Death Rites: Law and Ethics at the End of Life*, London: Routledge, 1994). Use of advance directives has become increasingly common. Draft living wills have been drawn up by a number of organisations; a notable early illustration was that of the Terence Higgins Trust, a well-known charitable organisation which assists persons who are HIV positive or who have AIDS. We noted in Chapter 6 that patients have the right to refuse treatment where competent to do so, even if it means that death results. The courts have now confirmed that an advance refusal of treatment should be respected, (see *Re B*, discussed above at p.1058, and *Re T*, discussed in Chapter 5 above). Indeed, failure to respect a valid refusal of consent may give rise to an action in battery. Support was also given to advance directives by the Court of Appeal and the House of Lord in *Airedale NHS Trust v Bland* (see p.1021 above). In *Bland* the court indicated that it would be unlawful to ignore a valid refusal of treatment. That of course does not mean that a doctor would always be bound by an advance directive. He or she would have to consider the scope and applicability of the directive. The House of Lords Select Committee on Medical Ethics favoured advance directives but opposed legislation on the basis that doctors were recognising the ethical obligation to act in accordance with advance directives and that judicial support had been given to this. They proposed the development of a Code of Practice. (See D. Morgan had been given to this "Odysseus and the Binding Directive" (1994) 14 *Legal Studies* 411.) The applicability of an advance refusal was considered in *HE v Hospital NHS Trust* [2003] EWCA. Here there was a written advance refusal of blood by a Jehovah's Witness. The health care professionals wanted authorisation to administer a blood transfusion. Since the advance refusal had been drawn up the patient had become engaged to a Muslim and was intending to convert to that faith. Mumby J. held that the blood transfusion could go ahead. He went on to say that:

"A free man can no more sign away his life by executing an irrevocable advance directive refusing life-saving treatment than he can sign away his liberty by subjecting himself to slavery. Any condition in an advance directive purporting to make it irrevocable is contrary to public policy and void."

Advance directives were the subject of extensive consideration by the Law Commission in their *Mental Incapacity* report in 1995. The Law Commission proposed that there should be a rebuttable presumption that living wills should be valid if they were in writing, signed by the maker and witnessed. But the Law Commission did not accept that a person should be able to execute an advance directive refusing all types of care, including spoon feeding. To adopt such an approach would be to create a division between the approach taken in law to a competent patient who is refusing all treatment, including feeding, and the patient expressing his views through an advance directive. It has been suggested that such a restriction is justifiable because it protects the sensibilities of the medical staff and indeed that such an exception should be extended to the competent patient. (See A. Grubb, (1993) 1 *Medical Law Review* 84.) Recognition of the patient's right to refuse treatment should not, the Law Commission emphasised, mean that a person could require through the use of an advance directive that a doctor undertake an illegal positive action or an action contrary to the doctor's clinical judgment (para.5.6). The Law Commission recommended that there should be a new offence of concealing/destroying an advance directive (para.5.38). In addition they recommend that a Code of Practice for the use of advance directives should be drawn up. One of the problems was that the individual drawing up the living will may change their mind as to what may/may not be an acceptable approach to treatment. It was suggested that there should be a presumption that an advance directive should not apply in the case of treatment of a pregnant woman. (For discussion of treatment in face of opposition from a pregnant woman, see Chapter 13 above.) The Law Commission recommend that a treatment provider who has acted in the reasonable belief that an advance directive applies in that situation shall be exempt from liability in future legal proceedings (para.5.27.)

The Law Commission report proved highly controversial, particularly its recommendations in the area of end of life decision-making. This led initially to the Law Commission's recommendations on advance directives not being taken forward and nor did not form part of the draft Mental Incapacity Bill published in 2003 (For a discussion of the progress of the reforms, see Chapter 5 above and also J.V. McHale, "Mental Incapacity: Some Proposals for Legislative Reform" (1998) 24 *Journal of Medical Ethics* 322). However, subsequently, when the Mental Capacity Bill was published in June 2004, it did contain explicit reference to advance decisions refusing treatment as does the final Mental Capacity Act 2005.

Mental Capacity Act 2005 ss.24–25

ADVANCE DECISIONS TO REFUSE TREATMENT

Advance decisions to refuse treatment: general

24.—(1) "Advance decision" means a decision made by a person ("P"), after he has reached 18 and when he has capacity to do so, that if—

(a) at a later time and in such circumstances as he may specify, a specified treatment is proposed to be carried out or continued by a person providing health care for him, and

(b) at that time he lacks capacity to consent to the carrying out or continuation of the treatment, the specified treatment is not to be carried out or continued.

(2) For the purposes of subsection (1)(a), a decision may be regarded as specifying a treatment or circumstances even though expressed in layman's terms.

(3) P may withdraw or alter an advance decision at any time when he has capacity to do so.

(4) A withdrawal (including a partial withdrawal) need not be in writing.

(5) An alteration of an advance decision need not be in writing (unless section 25(5) applies in relation to the decision resulting from the alteration.

Validity and applicability of advance decisions

25.—(1) An advance decision does not affect the liability which a person may incur for carrying out or continuing a treatment in relation to P unless the decision is at the material time—

(a) valid, and
(b) applicable to the treatment.

(2) An advance decision is not valid if P—

(a) has withdrawn the decision at a time when he had capacity to do so,
(b) has, under a lasting power of attorney created after the advance decision was made, conferred authority on the donee (or, if more than one, any of them) to give or refuse consent to the treatment to which the advance decision relates, or
(c) has done anything else clearly inconsistent with the advance decision remaining his fixed decision.

(3) An advance decision is not applicable to the treatment in question if at the material time P has capacity to give or refuse consent to it.
(4) An advance decision is not applicable to the treatment in question if—

(a) that treatment is not the treatment specified in the advance decision,
(b) any circumstances specified in the advance decision are absent, or
(c) there are reasonable grounds for believing that circumstances exist which P did not anticipate at the time of the advance decision and which would have affected his decision had he anticipated them.

(5) An advance decision is not applicable to life-sustaining treatment unless—

(a) the decision is verified by a statement by P to the effect that it is to apply to that treatment even if life is at risk, and
(b) the decision and statement comply with subsection (6).

(6) A decision or statement complies with this subsection only if—

(a) it is in writing,
(b) it is signed by P or by another person in P's presence and by P's direction,
(c) the signature is made or acknowledged by P in the presence of a witness, and
(d) the witness signs it, or acknowledges his signature, in P's presence.

(7) The existence of any lasting power of attorney other than one of a description mentioned in subsection (2)(b) does not prevent the advance decision from being regarded as valid and applicable.

Effect of advance decisions

26.—(1) If P has made an advance decision which is—

(a) valid, and
(b) applicable to a treatment,

the decision has effect as if he had made it, and had had capacity to make it, at the time when the question arises whether the treatment should be carried out or continued.
(2) A person does not incur liability for carrying out or continuing the treatment unless, at the time, he is satisfied that an advance decision exists which is valid and applicable to the treatment.
(3) A person does not incur liability for the consequences of withholding or withdrawing a treatment from P if, at the time, he reasonably believes that an advance decision exists which is valid and applicable to the treatment.
(4) The court may make a declaration as to whether an advance decision—

(a) exists;
(b) is valid;
(c) is applicable to a treatment.

(5) Nothing in an apparent advance decision stops a person—

(a) providing life-sustaining treatment, or
(b) doing any act he reasonably believes to be necessary to prevent a serious deterioration in P's condition,

while a decision as respects any relevant issue is sought from the court.

NOTES:

1 In contrast to the Law Commission proposals, the Mental Capacity Act instead builds upon the common law position. It includes some formal criteria/guidelines relating to the refusal of treatment, such as the requirement that such advance decisions should be in writing.
2. The Act makes reference to treatment refusals. Consistent with the common law a patient cannot use the Act to compel medical practitioners to provide treatment.
3. The Mental Capacity Act applies only to those who are over 18. This is in line with the common law which enables competent minors under 18 to consent but not to refuse medical treatment. Nonetheless as we saw above at p.1058, this is by no means uncontroversial. It can be contrasted with the position in the Netherlands where those under 18 can currently seek assistance in dying.
4. The Act ensures that those who follow an advance directive will not be subject to legal liability, a real concern in the current position where the advance refusal is a matter for the common law and following in this respect the Law Commission recommendation.
5. The Mental Capacity Act does not exclude explicitly certain types of decision, such as the Law Commission's suggestion, noted above, for excluding pregnant women.

QUESTION:

1. Should an individual be able to make an advance refusal of treatment where there is a chance that if treatment were given, some health may be restored? (See C. Ryan, "Betting your Life: an Argument against Certain Advance Directives" (1996) 22 *Journal of Medical Ethics* 95 and S. Luttrell and A. Somerville, "Limiting Risks by Curtailing Rights: a Response to Dr Ryan" (1996) 22 *Journal of Medical Ethics* 100.)

(e) Power of Attorney

As was made clear by the House of Lords in *Re F (Mental Patient: Sterilisation)* [1989] 2 All E.R. 545, no one has the power to consent on behalf of an incompetent patient. Nevertheless, there may be situations in which an individual would wish another to have powers to make decisions about medical treatment. If a living will exists, it may be that some provisions may be unclear, and require interpretation. It is equally unlikely that a living will would be sufficiently comprehensive to cover all situations. Where a living will is unclear, a proxy decision-maker may be of considerable benefit. The Enduring Power of Attorney Act 1985 allows an individual to appoint a proxy to make decisions regarding financial matters once they became incapacitated, but such powers were not extended in relation to medical treatment. In its report, *Mental Incapacity* (Report No. 231, 1995), the Law Commission proposed that a scheme should be established allowing for the appointment of a proxy decision-maker by persons over 18 (see Part VII of the report). The Law Commission recommended that a proxy should be able to act only in the patient's "best interests" (see Chapter 5). They recommended that only persons over 18 should be able to appoint a power of attorney. The document containing the power of attorney should contain a statement by the donee that she understands that it is her duty to act in the best interests of the donor. This power should be registered by a registration authority appointed by the Lord Chancellor. The donor would have the right to revoke the power while he has capacity to do so. The Law Commission also suggested that the donee's powers should be capable of being modified by court order save where a contrary intention has been expressed by the donor. Consistent with its recommendations regarding living wills, it proposes limitations upon the power which a proxy would be able to exercise. Thus while a proxy may facilitate the process, there are still likely to be situations in which the wishes of the incompetent person will be unascertainable with the ultimate decision being thrown back onto medical discretion.

The Law Commission proposals have now been taken forward in the Mental Capacity Act 2005.

Mental Capacity Act 2005, ss.9–11, 13, 22, 23

POWERS OF THE COURT IN RELATION TO LASTING POWERS OF ATTORNEY

Lasting powers of attorney

9.—(1) A lasting power of attorney is a power of attorney under which the donor ("P") confers on the donee (or donees) authority to make decisions about all or any of the following—

   (a) P's personal welfare or specified matters concerning P's personal welfare, and
   (b) P's property and affairs or specified matters concerning P's property and affairs, and which includes authority to make such decisions in circumstances where P no longer has capacity.

(2) A lasting power of attorney is not created unless—

   (a) section 10 is complied with,
   (b) an instrument conferring authority of the kind mentioned in subsection (1) is made and registered in accordance with Schedule 1, and
   (c) at the time when P executes the instrument, P has reached 18 and has capacity to execute it.

(3) An instrument which—

(a) purports to create a lasting power of attorney, but
(b) does not comply with this section, section 10 or Schedule 1,

confers no authority.

(4) The authority conferred by a lasting power of attorney is subject to—

(a) the provisions of this Act and, in particular, section 1 (the principles), section 4 (best interests),
    and
(b) any conditions or restrictions specified in the instrument.

Appointment of donees

10.—(1) A donee of a lasting power of attorney must be—

(a) an individual who has reached 18, or
(b) if the power relates only to P's property and affairs, either such an individual or a trust corporation.

(2) An individual who is bankrupt may not be appointed as donee of a lasting power of attorney in relation to P's property and affairs.

(3) Subsections (4) to (7) apply in relation to an instrument under which two or more persons are to act as donees of a lasting power of attorney.

(4) The instrument may appoint them to act—

(a) jointly, or
(b) jointly and severally, or
(c) jointly in respect of some matters and jointly and severally in respect of others.

(5) To the extent to which it does not specify whether they are to act jointly or jointly and severally, the instrument is to be assumed to appoint them to act jointly.

(6) If they are to act jointly, a failure, as respects one of them, to comply with the requirements of subsection (1) or (2) or Part 1 or 2 of Schedule 1 prevents a lasting power of attorney from being created.

(7) If they are to act jointly and severally, a failure, as respects one of them, to comply with the requirements of subsection (1) or (2) or Part 1 or 2 of Schedule 1—

(a) prevents the appointment taking effect in his case, but
(b) does not prevent a lasting power of attorney from being created in the case of the other or others.

(8) An instrument used to create a lasting power of attorney—

(a) cannot give the donee (or, if more than one, any of them) power to appoint a substitute or successor, but
(b) may itself appoint a person to replace the donee (or, if more than one, any of them) on the occurrence of an event mentioned in section 13(6)(a) to (d) which has the effect of terminating the donee's appointment.

Lasting powers of attorney: restrictions

11.—(1) A lasting power of attorney does not authorise the donee (or, if more than one, any of them) to do an act that is intended to restrain P, unless three conditions are satisfied.

(2) The first condition is that P lacks, or the donee reasonably believes that P lacks, capacity in relation to the matter in question.

(3) The second is that the donee reasonably believes that it is necessary to do the act in order to prevent harm to P.

(4) The third is that the act is a proportionate response to—

(a) the likelihood of P's suffering harm, and
(b) the seriousness of that harm.

(5) For the purposes of this section, the donee restrains P if he—

(a) uses, or threatens to use, force to secure the doing of an act which P resists, or
(b) restricts P's liberty of movement, whether or not P resists, or if he authorises another person to do any of those things.

(6) But the donee does more than merely restrain P if he deprives P of his liberty within the meaning of Article 5(1) of the Human Rights Convention.

(7) Where a lasting power of attorney authorises the donee (or, if more than one, any of them) to make decisions about P's personal welfare, the authority—

(a) does not extend to making such decisions in circumstances other than those where P lacks, or the donee reasonably believes that P lacks, capacity,
(b) is subject to sections 24 to 26 (advance decisions to refuse treatment), and
(c) extends to giving or refusing consent to the carrying out or continuation of a treatment by a person providing health care for P.

(8) But subsection (6)(c)—

(a) does not authorise the giving or refusing of consent to the carrying out or continuation of life- sustaining treatment, unless the instrument contains express provision to that effect, and
(b) is subject to any conditions or restrictions in the instrument.
families or among friends or associates.

Revocation of lasting powers of attorney etc.

13.—(1) This section applies if—

(a) P has executed an instrument with a view to creating a lasting power of attorney, or
(b) a lasting power of attorney is registered as having been conferred by P, and in this section references to revoking the power include revoking the instrument.

(2) P may, at any time when he has capacity to do so, revoke the power.

Protection of donee and others if no power created or power revoked

14.—(1) Subsections (2) and (3) apply if—

(a) an instrument has been registered under Schedule 1 as a lasting power of attorney, but
(b) a lasting power of attorney was not created,

whether or not the registration has been cancelled at the time of the act or transaction in question.

(2) A donee who acts in purported exercise of the power does not incur any liability (to P or any other person) because of the non-existence of the power unless at the time of acting he—

(a) knows that a lasting power of attorney was not created, or
(b) is aware of circumstances which, if a lasting power of attorney had been created, would have terminated his authority to act as a donee.

(6) Where two or more donees are appointed under a lasting power of attorney, this section applies as if references to the donee were to all or any of them.

Powers of court in relation to validity of lasting powers of attorney

22.—(1) This section and section 23 apply if—

(a) a person ("P") has executed or purported to execute an instrument with a view to creating a lasting power of attorney, or
(b) an instrument has been registered as a lasting power of attorney conferred by P.

(2) The court may determine any question relating to—

(a) whether the requirements for the creation of a lasting power of attorney have been met;
(b) whether the power has been revoked or has otherwise come to an end.

(3) Subsection (4) applies if the court is satisfied—

(a) that fraud or undue pressure was used to induce P—
    (i) to execute an instrument for the purpose of creating a lasting power of attorney, or
    (ii) to create a lasting power of attorney, or
(b) that the donee (or, if more than one, any of them) of a lasting power of attorney—
    (i) has behaved, or is behaving, in a way that contravenes his authority or is not in P's best interests, or
    (ii) proposes to behave in a way that would contravene his authority or would not be in P's best interests.

(4) The court may—

(a) direct that an instrument purporting to create the lasting power of attorney is not to be registered, or
(b) if P lacks capacity to do so, revoke the instrument or the lasting power of attorney.

(5) If there is more than one donee, the court may under subsection (4)(b) revoke the instrument or the lasting power of attorney so far as it relates to any of them.
(6) "Donee" includes an intended donee.

Powers of court in relation to operation of lasting powers of attorney

23.—(1) The court may determine any question as to the meaning or effect of a lasting power of attorney.
(2) The court may—

(a) give directions with respect to decisions—
    (i) which the donee of a lasting power of attorney has authority to make, and
    (ii) which P lacks capacity to make;
(b) give any consent or authorisation to act which the donee would have to obtain from P if P had capacity to give it.

(3) The court may, if P lacks capacity to do so—

(a) give directions to the donee with respect to the rendering by him of reports or accounts and the production of records kept by him for that purpose;
(b) require the donee to supply information or produce documents or things in his possession as donee;
(c) give directions with respect to the remuneration or expenses of the donee;
(d) relieve the donee wholly or partly from any liability which he has or may have incurred on account of a breach of his duties as donee.

NOTES:

1. Schedule 1 to the Act sets out the required formalities in relation to the lasting power of attorney. These are subject to regulations to be enacted by the Secretary of State. The schedules do provide that the attorney must set out the donor's confirmation that he has read the "prescribed information" (to be determined under regulations) and intends the authority to apply when he no longer has capacity to make the decision, and for a statement by the donee that he has read the "prescribed information" and understands the duty imposed on the donee.
2. An application is to be made to the Public Guardian for registration of the power of attorney (Sch.1(4)). The donor may change their mind and object to registration where they have capacity to do so; provision is made for this under (Sch.1(13)).
3. The lasting power of attorney has the advantage that it provides for greater flexibility in decision-making than is afforded by advance decisions, in that it entrusts the decision to a particular person. Equally, however, such discretion may prove problematic, given the uncertainty for the person entrusted with the power of attorney to determine the issue.

SELECT BIBLIOGRAPHY

H. Biggs, *Euthanasia, Death with Dignity and the Law*, Oxford: Hart, 2001.

M. Brazier, *Medicine, Patients and the Law* (3rd edn) Harmondsworth: Penguin, 2003, Chapter 13.

A.G.M. Campbell, "The Right to be Allowed to Die" (1985) 11 *Journal of Medical Ethics* 136.

R. Dworkin, *Life's Dominion: an Argument about Abortion and Euthanasia*, London: HarperCollins, 1993.

M. Ford, "The Person Paradox and the Right to Die" (2005) 13 *Medical Law Review* 80.

J. Glover, *Causing Death and Saving Lives*, Oxford: OUP, 1987.

R. Goff, "A Matter of Life and Death" (1995) 3 *Medical Law Review* 1.

J. Harris, "The Right to Die Lives: There is No Personhood Paradox" [2005] 13 *Medical Law Review* 386.

H. Jochemsem, "Euthanasia in Holland: an Ethical Critique of the New Law" (1994) 20 *Journal of Medical Ethics* 212.

I. Kennedy, *Treat Me Right*, Oxford: OUP, 1991, Chapters 7, 8, 15 and 17.

J. Keown *Euthanasia, Ethics and Public Policy: an Argument against Legalisation*, Cambridge: CUP, 2002.

J. Keown (ed.), *Euthanasia Examined: Ethical, Clinical and Legal Perspectives*, Cambridge: CUP, 1995.

M. Khuse and P. Singer, *Should the Baby Live?*, Oxford: OUP, 1985.

R. Lee and D. Morgan (eds), *Death rites: Law and Ethics at the End of Life*, London: Routledge, 1994.

R. Magnusson, "Underground Euthanasia and the Harm Minimisation Debate" (2004) 42 *Journal of Law, Medicine and Ethics* 486.

J.K. Mason and G. Laurie, Mason & McCall Smith's, *Law and Medical Ethics* (7th edn), London: Butterworths, 2006, Chapters 16 and 17.

R.A. McCall Smith, "Euthanasia: the Strengths of the Middle Ground" (1999) 7 *Medical Law Review* 194.

S.A.M. McLean (ed.), *Death, Dying and the Law*, Aldershot: Dartmouth, 1996.

J. Montgomery, "Power over Death—The Final Sting" in R. Lee and D. Morgan (eds), *Death rites: Law and Ethics at the End of Life*, London: Routledge, 1994, Chapter 3.

D. Morgan, "Odysseus and the Binding Directive; only a Cautionary Tale" (1994) 14 *Legal Studies* 411.

M. Otlowski, "Active Voluntary Euthanasia: Options for Reform" (1994) 2 *Medical Law Review* 161.

M. Otlowski, *Voluntary Euthanasia and the Common Law*, Oxford: Clarendon Press, 1997.

S. Pattinson, *Medical Law and Ethics*, London: Sweet and Maxwell, 2005, Chapters 14 and 15.

J. Rachels, *The End of Life,* Oxford: OUP, 1985.

P. Singer, *Rethinking Life and Death: the Collapse of our Traditional Ethics,* Oxford: OUP, 1995.

P. Skegg, "The Edges of Life" [1988] *Otago Law Review* 517.

R.G. Twycross, "Euthanasia—a Physician's Viewpoint" (1982) 8 *Journal of Medical Ethics* 86.

15

DEATH AND LEGAL REGULATION OF THE USE OF LIVE AND CADAVER MATERIAL

1. INTRODUCTION

Medical technology, with its potential to redefine the boundaries of life, has forced radical reconsideration of what is meant by death. Traditionally, death was classified as cardiac death. But this definition became outdated as life could be prolonged through artificial ventilation. A new definition of death was formulated, the irreversible degeneration of the brain stem, although it was only after some time that brain stem death became generally accepted by the medical profession. Ascertaining the point at which death occurs may be of considerable practical importance, not least in relation to the law of succession, where it may be crucial for determining who succeeds under a will (see, for example, M. Brazier, *Medicine, Patients and the Law* (3rd edn), London: Penguin, 2002 at p.434). Today, brain stem death is recognised, both by the medical profession and by the courts, as the point of death. Nevertheless some have argued that the definition of death should be extended to encompass those persons in a state of cognitive death or upper brain death. Such reclassification would allow the person in a persistent vegetative state to be recognised as "dead". But, as we shall see below, such an extension is likely to meet considerable opposition.

Death is not simply a legal but is also a philosophical concept raising many issues, for example, issues of personhood (see D. Lamb, *Death, Brain Death and Ethics*, Beckenham: Croom Helm, 1985).

Scientific advances have meant that after the death of a person, parts of his body or tissue may be used by others. Transplantation of organs and tissue is common today. The range and sophistication of such transplants has dramatically increased over past decades from kidney, lung and heart to most recently, in France, the first face transplant (see D. Lamb, *Organ Transplants and Ethics*, London: Routledge, 1990; D. Price, *Legal and Ethical Aspects of Organ Transplantation*, Cambridge: CUP, 2000 at pp.1–20; and see also BBC News, November 30, 2005, "Woman has first face transplant", *http://news.bbc.co.uk/ 1/hi/health/ 4484728.stm*; *The Observer* "UK set for first face transplant", June 16, 2006). The conduct of transplantation surgery is inhibited by a considerable shortage in the availability of organs for transplantation. Some proposals advanced to increase the supply of organs are discussed.

Use of tissue, organs and other body products gives rise to the question, what rights has a person to control the use of such bodily products? To what extent, if at all, we possess any property rights over bodily products is an issue of increasing importance at a time when it is possible for certain bodily products to be used to produce substances of commercial value. Section 2 considers what constitutes "death" for the purposes of law and medical practice. Section 3 considers the legal regulation of the use of human material. This is a vast area and the aim of the chapter is to provide an overview of the main issues. We focus on many of the dilemmas concerned with organ transplantation. The discussion of the legal regulation of the use of human material begins by examining the common law position regarding consent to use human material from living subjects with particular reference to organ transplantation. Secondly, it considers the question of ownership of human material. Thirdly, it considers the statutory regulation of the use of human material under the Human Tissue Act 2004. Finally it examines as a case study the role of the law in increasing the supply of donor organs for transplantation.

2. Death

The definition of death has been the source of much academic commentary. (See further C. Pallis and D.H. Harley, *An ABC of Brain Stem Death* (2nd edn), London: BMJ, 1996.) A summary of the background to the current scientific exposition of death is provided by Lamb in the following extract:

D. Lamb, *Organ Transplants and Ethics*, London: Routledge, 1990 (references omitted)

Until the early 1960s and the advent of techniques for taking over the functions of the lungs and heart, the public had shown almost complete acceptance of medical practice concerning the diagnosis of death. This has not always been the case. Distrust of the profession's competence had been evident in scores in pamphlets and tracts written in the eighteenth and nineteenth centuries. In 1740 it had been suggested by Jacques Baeenigne Winslow that putrefaction was the only sure sign of death. Such a proposal reflected a total loss of public confidence in their doctors. Yet putrefaction has never been seriously advanced as a definition of death by either physicians or philosophers.

The prestige of physicians increased however, during the mid-nineteenth century as health care sought to become more scientific and professional, although distrust of the kind expressed in Edgar Allan Poe's novel, *The Tell-Tale Heart*, continued throughout the century. Nevertheless, the development of certain technological aids, such as the stethoscope, enabled a more accurate detection of heart beat and respiration, and was an important factor in the growth of public confidence in the ability to diagnose death. In the twentieth century scepticism has returned in some areas. It will be argued that this scepticism is without foundation, and that refinements in diagnostic criteria have reached the point where public acceptance is justified.

The earliest references in the neurological literature to states resembling brain death go back to the 1890s. In 1898 Sir Dyce Duckworth reported on four cases with structural brain lesions in which "the function of respiration had earlier ceased for some hours before that of the circulation." Then in 1902 Harvey Cushing described a patient whose spontaneous respiration ceased as a result of an intracranial tumour, but whose heart was kept beating for 23 hours with artificial respiration.

The concept of brain death really emerged in France in 1959. Early that year a group of French neurosurgeons described a condition which they termed "death of the central nervous system". The characteristics of that state were "persistent apnoeic coma, absent brain stem and tendon reflexes, and an electrically silent brain." These patients had no detectable electrophysiological activity in either the superficial or deeper parts of their brains. Whilst they looked like cadavers a regular pulse could be discerned as long as ventilation was maintained. Although the authors did not directly address the issue of whether this state was equivalent to death, they concluded that the persistence of this condition for 18 to 24 hours warranted disconnection from the ventilator. Later that year a more complete account of the condition was published by two Parisian neurologists, Mollaret and Goulon who called it coma daepassae (a state beyond coma). They were not prepared to equate coma dépassé with death and, unlike their predecessors, they did not advocate the withdrawal of ventilatory support. The patients had all sustained massive, irreversible structural brain damage. Patients in a state of *coma dépassé* were in a state of irreversible coma associated with an irreversible loss of the capacity to breathe. They had not only lost all capacity to respond to external stimuli, they could not even cope with their internal mileu: they were poikilothermic, had diabetes insipidus, and could not sustain their own blood pressure. The cardiac prognosis of the condition was at most a few days, but sometimes as little as a few hours.

Outside France the term *coma dépassé* never really caught on. The condition was of course encountered wherever resuscitation was sufficiently well organised and intensive care units adequately equipped, to prevent irreversible apnoea immediately resulting in the cessation of cardiac action. During this period there was no attempt to relate observations of this condition to any well founded concept of death. Neither of the two French groups discussed the meaning of death (which is probably why they suggested different courses of action for what is essentially the same condition). By the late 1960s an increasing rate of organ transplantation and greater successes in resuscitation provided a background to the need for greater philosophical clarity concerning what it meant to be dead. The lack of such clarity was reflected in the ambiguous and often confusing terminology used at the time. The term "irreversible coma" was sometimes employed to refer to a condition which was equivalent to "*coma dépassé*". The term "brain death" referred to the same state. Although the terminology was in a state of flux, the construct "brain death" achieved a degree of precision that allowed it to be used in a popular way. The term *coma dépassé* survived in France until May 24, 1988 when it was rejected in favour of "brain death" by the French Academy of Medicine, who commented that their decision "ends semantic ambiguity which leads to clinical ambiguity".

In 1968 the Ad Hoc Committee of the Harvard Medical School to Examine the Definition of Brain Death published its report and brain death (which was exactly what the French had described as coma dépassé) achieved world wide recognition (Ad Hoc Committee of the Harvard Medical School, 1968). The Harvard criteria for brain death were fourfold:

(1) absence of cerebral responsiveness;
(2) absence of induced or spontaneous movement;
(3) absence of spontaneous respiration;
(4) absence of brain stem and deep tendon reflexes.

An isolectric EEG was deemed to be of "great confirmatory value" but the performance of an EEG was not considered mandatory. The report specified two conditions which were capable of mimicking the state of brain death and which had to be excluded in each case: hypothermia and drug intoxication. Finally, the report recommended that tests be repeated over a period of 24 hours to document the persistence of the condition. Since then numerous patients throughout the world have been diagnosed as brain dead, maintained on ventilators and observed until their hearts stopped. No patient meeting the Harvard criteria has ever recovered despite the most heroic management.

In the years following the publication of the Harvard report it was gradually realised that the clinically testable component of brain death was the death of the brain stem (brain stem death). In 1971 the work of two neurosurgeons Mohandas and Chouc, in Minneapolis, had a profound influence on thinking and practice regarding the diagnosis of death on neurological grounds. From detailed observations of patients who has sustained massive intracranial damage they concluded that irreversible damage to the brain stem was the "point of no return in the dying process," and that a diagnosis of this state "could be based on clinical judgment". Their recommendations became known as the Minnesota criteria, which were significant in that they introduced aetilogical preconditions to the diagnosis of brain death. A valid diagnosis of a dead brainstem, they held, was context dependant in the sense that an essential precondition was knowledge of "irreparable intracranial lesions".

This point about context dependency has not been fully appreciated by critics of brainstem death in the popular media, who frequently assume that tests are conducted in ignorance of the causes of the coma. Later guidelines stress that the all-important characteristic of irreversibility can only be established with reference to crucial preconditions. Not only must there be a known primary diagnosis which accounts for the cause of the coma, there must also be evidence that all reversible causes of brainstem dysfunction (such as hypothermia and drug intoxication) have been excluded. This of course, may take time, which is why it is misleading to speak simply of tests for brain stem death.

(a) Diagnosing Death

The basis for the brain stem death test in England was set out in guidance published in 1976 by the Royal Medical Colleges (published as "The Diagnosis of Brain Death" (1976) *British Medical Journal* 1187) and this was subsequently consolidated and updated in the following statement.

Department of Health, *A Code of Practice for the Diagnosis of Brain Stem Death* (1996)

2. CONDITIONS UNDER WHICH THE DIAGNOSIS OF BRAIN STEM DEATH SHOULD BE CONSIDERED

2.1 There should be no doubt that the patient's condition is due to irremediable brain damage of known aetiology. It may be obvious within hours of a primary intracranial event such as a severe heard injury, or spontaneous intracranial haemorrhage that the condition is irremediable. However, when a patient has suffered primarily from cardiac arrest, hypoxia or severe circulatory insufficiency with an indefinite period of cerebral hypoxia, or is suspected of having cerebral air or fat embolism it may take longer to establish the diagnosis and to be confident of the prognosis. In some patients the primary pathology may be a matter of doubt and a confident diagnosis may only be reached by continuing clinical observation and investigation.

2.2 The patient is deeply unconscious.

2.2.1 There should be no evidence that this state is due to depressant drugs. Narcotics, hypnotics and tranquillisers may have prolonged action, particularly when hypothermia coexists or in the context of renal or hepatic failure. The benzodiazepines are markedly cumulative and persistent in their actions and are commonly used as anticonvulsants or to assist synchronisation with mechanical ventilators. It is therefore essential that the drug history should be carefully reviewed and any possibility of intoxication being the cause of, or contributing to, the patient's comatose state should preclude a diagnosis of brain stem death. It is important to recognise that, in some patients, hypoxia may have followed the ingestion of a drug but in this situation the criteria for brain stem death will not be applicable until such a time as the drug effects have been excluded as a continuing cause of the unresponsiveness.

2.2.2 Primary hypothermia as the cause of unconsciousness must have been excluded.

2.2.3 Potentially reversible circulatory, metabolic and endocrine disturbances must have been excluded as the cause of the continuation of unconsciousness. It is recognised that circulatory, metabolic and endocrine disturbances are a likely accompaniment of brain stem death (eg hypernatraemia, diabetes insipidus) but these are the effect rather than the cause of that condition and do not preclude the diagnosis of brain stem death.

2.3 The patient is being maintained on the ventilator because spontaneous respiration has been inadequate or ceased altogether. Relaxants (neuromuscular blocking agents) and other drugs must have been excluded as the cause of respiratory inadequacy or failure. Immobility, unresponsiveness, and lack of spontaneous respiration may be due to the use of neuromuscular blocking drugs and the persistence of their effects should be excluded by elicitation of deep tendon reflexes or by the demonstration of adequate neuromuscular conduction with a conventional nerve stimulator. Persistent effects of hypnotics or narcotics must be excluded as the cause of respiratory failure.

3. THE DIAGNOSIS OF BRAIN STEM DEATH

Fulfilment of the clinical criteria for the diagnosis of brain death specified by the Conference of Colleges during the period 1976–1981 is followed by cessation of the heart beat within a short period. This has been confirmed in all published series and has therefore been adequately validated. The following paragraphs recapitulate the criteria in the conference guidelines, with the addition of notes on how they may be elicited, based on intervening experience.

3.1 All brain stem reflexes are absent

3.1.1 The pupils are fixed and do not respond to sharp changes in the intensity of incident light.

3.1.2 There is no corneal reflect—care should be taken to avoid damage to the cornea.

3.1.3 The vestibulo-ocular reflexes are absent. No eye movements are seen during or following the slow infection of at least 50mls of ice cold water over one minute into each external auditory meatus in turn. Clear access to the tympanic membrane must be established by direct inspection and the head should be flexed at 30°. The performance of this manoeuvre may be prevented on one or other side by local injury or disease but this does not invalidate the diagnosis of brain stem death.

3.1.4 No motor responses within the cranial nerve distribution can be elicited by adequate stimulation of any somatic area. There is no limb response to supraorbital pressure.

3.1.5 There is no gag reflex or reflex response to bronchial stimulation by suction catheter placed down the trachea.

3.1.6 No respiratory movements occur when the patient is disconnected from the mechanical ventilator. During this test it is necessary for the arterial carbon dioxide to exceed the threshold for respiratory stimulation, that is, the $PaCO_2$ should reach 6.65kPa. This should be ensured by measurement of the blood gases. The patient may be moderately hypothermic, flaccid and with a depressed metabolic rate such that the arterial carbon dioxide tension rises slowly during apnoea. Hypoxia during disconnection should be prevented by delivering oxygen at 6 litres per minute through a catheter in the trachea. If the facility for administering 5% CO_2 in oxygen exists, this is the preferred method for performing this test. The patient should first be ventilated with 100% oxygen for 10 minutes, then with 5% CO_2 in oxygen for 5 minutes. The ventilator should then be disconnected for 10 minutes. During this period, oxygen should be delivered through a catheter as above. Those patients with pre-existing chronic respiratory disease who may be responsive only to supra-normal levels of carbon dioxide and who depend upon hypoxic drive are special cases who should be managed in consultation with an expert in respiratory disease.

3.2 Children

A report of a working party of the British Paediatric Association of 1991 supported by the Council of the Royal College of Physicians suggested that, in children over the age of 2 months, the brain stem death criteria should be the same as those in adults. Between 37 weeks of gestation and 2 months of age, it is rarely possible confidently to diagnose brain stem death and below 37 weeks of gestation, the criteria for brain stem death cannot be applied. A Working Party of the Conference of Colleges on Organ Transplantation in Neonates recommended that organs for transplantation may be removed from anencephalic infants when two doctors, who are not members of the transplant team, agree that spontaneous respiration has ceased. The conclusions of these reports are endorsed by the current Working Party.

3.3 Repetition of testing

The diagnosis of brain stem death should be made by at least two medical practitioners who have been registered for more than five years, are competent in this field and are not members of the transplant team, at least one of the doctors should be a consultant. Two sets of tests should always be performed, these may be carried out by the two practitioners separately or together. The tests are repeated to remove the risk of observer error. The timing of the interval between the tests is a matter for clinical judgement but the time should be adequate for the reassurance of all those directly concerned. The interval between the tests will depend upon the primary pathology, the clinical course of the disease and the progress of the patient. Although death is not pronounced until the second test has been completed the legal time of death is when the first test indicates brain stem death.

3.4 The beating heart in brain stem death

Even if ventilation is continued both adults and children will suffer cessation of heart beat within a few days, very occasionally a few weeks, of the diagnosis of brain stem death.

3.5 Endocrine, metabolic and circulatory abnormalities

Abnormalities, such as diabetes insipidus, hypo or hypernatraemia, hypothermia and disturbance of cardiac rhythm or blood pressure may occur in patients following anoxic, haemorrhagic or traumatic cerebral injury. These abnormalities may be consequences of brain stem failure and must be differentiated from abnormalities of endocrinological, biochemical or autonomic function contributing to failure of brain stem function.

3.6 Limb and trunk movements

Reflex movements of the limbs and torso may occur after brain stem death has been identified. The doctor should be able to explain clearly the significance of these movements to relatives, nurses and other staff who should be given sufficient information to enable them to understand that they are of spinal reflex origin and do not involve the brain at all.

3.7 Investigations

The safety of the clinical criteria for the diagnosis of brain stem death during the past 17 years provides justification for not including the results of neurophysiological or imaging investigations as part of those criteria. At present there is no evidence that imaging, electroencephalography or evoked potentials assist in the determination of brain stem death and, although such techniques will be kept under review, they should not presently form part of the diagnostic requirements.

3.8 Peripheral neurological syndromes of intensive care

There is a range of overlapping neuropathic, neuromuscular and myopathic syndromes which may occur in the context of intensive therapy and may cause problems in weaning a patient from a ventilator. This is not true apnoea (respiratory centre paralysis) and should not be taken as evidence for brain stem death.

3.9 The permanent vegetative state

Problems relating to the diagnosis and management of the permanent vegetative state must not be confused with those relating to brain stem death and the guidelines endorsed by the Conference of the Royal Colleges emphasise the important differences.

4. MANAGEMENT

It is essential that relatives, partners and carers be kept fully informed of the clinical condition of the patient and that explanation be given to them regarding the condition and prognosis. Relatives, partners and carers of the patient should be given explanation of the investigations being undertaken and of their interpretation throughout the process of the determination of brain stem death in a sympathetic, timely and appropriate fashion by those concerned with the management of the patient.

4.1 Maintenance of therapy

The maintenance of normal homeostasis by attempting to ensure adequate fluid intake, electrolyte balance, normal blood pressure, the monitoring of urine output by catheter collection and the use of other therapeutic agents, is part of the standard medical care of the patient where brain stem death has not been conclusively established and may be continued after brain stem death is confirmed to maintain the condition of organs to be donated.

4.2 Cessation of respiration

Sometimes a patient who is not receiving ventilatory assistance is thought to have irreversible brain damage but stops breathing before it has been possible to undertake testing. In cases of this kind brain stem death will not have been diagnosed and it will be possible to say with certainty that it will inevitably occur. In such cases the initiation of artificial ventilation as part of resuscitation is only justified if it is of potential benefit to the patient.

NOTES:

1. The Code of Practice was compiled by a Working Party of the Royal College of Physicians on behalf of the Academy of Medical Royal Colleges at the request of the Health Departments. In May 2005 a new draft code of practice, "A Code of Practice for the Diagnosis and Certification of Brain Stem Death", was drawn up by a Working Party of the Royal College of Anaethetists at the request of the Academy of Medical Royal Colleges and the English Department of Health (draft for consultation, May 14, 2006). This is subject to consultation at present.

2. What constitutes death must be seen in the context of cultural and religious traditions. (See further D. Lamb, *Death, Brain Death and Ethics*, Beckenhem: Croom Helm, 1985; S. Younger, R. Arnold and R. Schapiro, *The Definition of Death: Contemporary Controversies*, Baltimore: Johns Hopkins University Press, 1999.)

3. Despite the widespread acceptance of brain stem death among the medical profession, it has some critics (see M. Evans, "Against the Definition of Brain Stem Death" in R. Lee and D. Morgan (eds), *Death Rites*, London: Routledge, 1994). It has been suggested that considerable moral significance can be placed upon the fact that an individual is still breathing, both from intuition and traditional medical wisdom. It is perhaps worthy of note that while brain stem death is recognised in many countries, it does not command universal acceptance. For example, there has been a movement back towards recognition of cardiac death in Denmark. (See M. Evans, "Death in Denmark" (1990) 16 *Journal of Medical Ethics* 191 and D. Lamb, "Death in Denmark—A Reply" (1991) 17 *Journal of Medical Ethics* 100.)

4. The procedure used to detect brain stem death in the United Kingdom is not standard worldwide. In certain countries, it is also necessary to show that there is a negative electroencephalogram (EEG) test to ascertain blood flow in the brain, although it may be that such tests are redundant if the brain stem death test is accurately employed. (See J.K. Mason and G. Laurie, *Law and Medical Ethics* (7th edn), London: Butterworths, 2005 at pp.469–470, and see generally P. McCullagh, *Brain Death, Brain Absent, Brain Donors*, Chichester: John Wiley, 1993.)

(b) Deciding the Point of Death—the Law

(i) Defining Death—Common Law

While the medical profession had reached consensus as to the point of death, for a considerable period of time the legal definition of death was unclear. In *R v Malcherek and Steel* [1981] 2 All E.R. 422 the defendants were charged with murder. The defence claimed that the chain of causation was broken because after the assault the victims had been supported on a ventilator, and it was only when they were subsequently removed from the ventilator that brain stem death was diagnosed. Lord Lane stated that:

"Where the medical practitioner using generally acceptable methods, came to the conclusion that the patient was, for all practical purposes dead and that such vital functions as remained were being maintained solely by mechanical means and accordingly discontinued treatment, that did not break the chain of causation between the initial injury and death."

This statement appeared to amount to judicial acceptance of recognition of brain stem death as death. Nevertheless, the precise position remained uncertain for over a decade before finally being confirmed in *Re A*:

Re A [1992] 3 Med. L.R. 303

A was a young child just under two years of age. He was taken to hospital where he was found to have no heartbeat. He was suffering from non-accidental injuries, including blood on the brain. He was put on a ventilator. There were no signs of recovery. The court considered the question of whether the child had died and thus could be removed from the ventilator.

JOHNSON J.

" . . . The present criteria of death has been the subject of recommendations by both the Royal College of Surgeons and the Royal College of Physicians and a working party of the British Paedatric Association. Applying the criteria laid down by her profession the consultant concluded on January 20 that A was not brain stem dead. On the following day she again carried out the tests which are necessary to determine whether the necessary criteria are satisfied. The consultant described each test to me and she explained to me that each one was satisfied. The tests lasted overall about half an hour.

Describing the criteria and her observations of A and expressing myself in lay terms, her evidence was to the following effect. A's pupils were fixed and dilated. On movement of the head his eyes moved with his head. What is called a 'doll's eye response' was absent. On his eye being touched with a piece of cotton wool there was no response. On cold water being passed into his ear there was no reflex reaction neither was there reaction to pain being applied to his central nervous system. Finally, on his temporary removal from the ventilator to enable the carbon dioxide content of his body to increase there was no respiratory response. All in all the consultant was satisfied that A was brain stem dead . . .

On the same day the consultant had arranged for a colleague consultant paediatrician neurologist to carry out the same tests that she had, herself, carried out the previous day with a view to confirming or otherwise the validity of her professional conclusions. Under professional guidelines it was not necessary for her to seek a second opinion in that way, but she decided that in the particular circumstances of the case it would be a wise thing for her to do. Accordingly the tests were carried out again on Wednesday of last week, January 22, by this colleague who reached the same conclusion as had been reached by the first consultant.

Both doctors were at pains to exclude other possibilities for A's state, including the possibility of his suffering from extreme hypothermia or some abnormality of his biochemistry. Moreover, they tested for drug, lest his brain-stem functions should have been suppressed by the administration of some drug of which they had not been aware, although he had, in fact, been under the consultants supervision for three days in Guy's hospital and they would have been aware had drugs been administered to him. Nonetheless they carried out the necessary checks and satisfied themselves that no such drug was present.

Both doctors concluded that A was brain stem dead . . .

It is now Monday January 27. I have no hesitation at all in holding that A has been dead since Tuesday of last week January 21 . . . ".

NOTES:

1. This approach also received the support of the House of Lords in *Airedale NHS Trust v Bland* [1993] 1 All E.R. 821 (see Chapter 14 above at p.1021).
2. If a doctor fails to follow the accepted professional criteria for the diagnosis of brain stem death, this may result in a civil action or criminal

prosecution although in the absence of a statutory definition of death there is otherwise no specific sanction.

(ii) No Statutory Definition of Death

The existing definition of death is dependent upon the common law. The question of whether there should be a statutory definition of death was examined by the Criminal Law Revision Committee in 1980.

Criminal Law Revision Committee, *Fourteenth Report: Offences Against the Person*, Cmnd. 7844 (1980), HMSO

37. We have considered whether there should be a statutory definition of death. A memorandum issued by the honorary secretary of the Conference of Medical Royal Colleges and Faculties in the United Kingdom on January 15, 1979 refers to an earlier report of the Conference which expressed their unanimous opinion that "brain death" could be diagnosed with certainty. The memorandum states that the report published by the Conference has been widely accepted and says that the identification of brain death means that a patient is truly dead, whether or not the function of some organs. such as a heart beat, is still maintained by artificial means. Brain death is said to be when all the functions of the brain have permanently and irreversibly ceased. We are however extremely hesitant about embodying in a statute (which is not always susceptible of speedy amendment) an expression of present medical opinion and knowledge derived from a field of science which is continually progressing and inevitably altering its opinions in the light of new information. If a statutory definition of death were to be enacted there would, in our opinion, be a risk that further knowledge would cause it to lose the assent of the majority of the medical profession. In that event, far from assisting the medical profession, for example, in cases of organ transplants, the definition might be a hindrance to them. Moreover while there might be agreement that the statutory definition was defective there might be differences of view about the proper content of any new definition. An additional reason for not recommending a definition of death is that such a definition would have wide repercussions outside offences against the person and the criminal law. A legal definition of death would also have to be applicable in the civil law. It would be undesirable to have a statutory definition confined only to offences against the person, which is the extent of our present remit. For these reasons therefore we are not recommending the enactment of a statutory definition of death.

NOTE:

1. The new Human Tissue Act 2004 provides that the Human Tissue Authority is required to issue a Code of Practice giving a definition of death for the purposes of the legislation Human Tissue Act 2004, (s.26(2)(d) and see further the discussion of the Human Tissue Act from p.1121 below).

QUESTION:

1. Should the issue of brain stem death be subject to consideration in Parliament rather than left to judicial and clinical determination? (See P.D.G. Skegg, "The Case for a Statutory Definition of Death" (1976) *Journal of Medical Ethics* 190; while for a contrasting view see I. Kennedy, "Alive or Dead" (1969) 22 *Current Legal Problems* 102.)

(c) Extending the Definition of Death—Cognitive Death

While support has been given by courts and the medical profession to the concept of brain stem death, some have suggested that the definition of death could be extended still further to encompass cognitive death. This is death of upper hemispheres of the brain while the brain cells are still functioning. The status of cognitive death was considered in the *Bland* case.

Airedale NHS Trust v Bland [1993] 1 All E.R. 821; [1993] A.C. 789

For the facts of this case see p.1021, above.

LORD KEITH

" . . . Anthony Bland has for over three years been in the condition known as persistent vegetative state (PVS). It is unnecessary to go into all the details about the manifestations of this state which are already set out in the judgment of the courts below. It is sufficient to say that it arises from the destruction, through prolonged deprivation of oxygen, of the cerebral cortex, which has resolved into a watery mass. The cortex is that part of the brain which is the seat of cognitive function and sensory capacity. Anthony Bland cannot see, hear or feel anything. He cannot communicate in any way. The consciousness which is the essential feature of individual personality has departed for ever. On the other hand the brain stem, which controls the reflexive functions of the body, in particular heartbeat, breathing and digestion, continues to operate. In the eyes of the medical world and of the law a person is not clinically dead so long as the brain stem retains its function. In order to maintain Anthony Bland in his present condition, feeding and hydration are achieved artificially by means of a nasogastric tube and excretionary functions are regulated by a catheter and by enemas. The catheter from time to time gives rise to infections which have to be dealt with by appropriate medical treatment. The undisputed consensus of eminent medical opinion is that there is no prospect whatever that Anthony Bland will ever make any recovery from his present condition, but that there is every likelihood that he will maintain his present state of existence for many years to come, provided that the medical care which he is now receiving is continued."

NOTES:

1. Recognition of a cognitive definition of death would be in line with the approach taken by those commentators who define humans in terms of personhood and afford them rights accordingly (see Chapter 2 above). Destruction of the ability to reason could be seen as commensurate with the destruction of personhood. Nevertheless recognition of cognitive death would create considerable problems. As the judgments in *Bland* illustrate, one such problem concerns a patient who is in a persistent vegetative state. Should such a patient be recognised as dead? (See I. Kennedy and A. Grubb, "Withdrawal of Artificial Nutrition and Hydration: Incompetent Adult" (1993) 1 *Medical Law Review* 359.) Note the American case of *Re Quinlan*, 70 N.J. 10 353A 2d 647 (1976), regarding a patient in PVS who, after ventilation was withdrawn, continued to live for several years.
2. Recognition of cognitive death would also require clarification of the position of anencephalic infants. Anencephalic infants are born with some

or all of the upper hemispheres of the brain absent. They are capable of living for some days. Recognition of cognitive death would result in such infants being declared "dead" at birth. This would mean that, for example, their organs could be used immediately for the purposes of transplantation. Whether this approach should be adopted has been questioned. (See P. McCullagh, *Brain Dead, Brain Absent, Brain Donors*, Chichester: John Wiley, 1993, Chapters 4 and 5). There are also varying degrees of anencephaly combined with a risk of misdiagnosis (see A.D. Shewman, "Anencephaly: Selected Medical Aspects" (1988) 11 *Hastings Centre Report* and D. Lamb, *Organ Transplants and Ethics*, London: Routledge, 1990).

3. LEGAL REGULATION OF THE USE OF HUMAN MATERIAL

(a) Introduction

There was no statutory regulation of the medical use of cadaver tissue until the Anatomy Act 1832. This statute was passed following the prosecution for murder of the "body snatchers", of whom some of the most notorious were Burke and Hare who supplied corpses for payment to the medical schools of Edinburgh. (See generally R. Richardson "Fearful Symmetry: Corpses for Anatomy, Organs for Transplantation?" in S.J. Youngner, R.C. Fox and L.J. O'Connell, *Organ Transplantation: Meanings and Realities*, University of Wisconsin Press, 1996 and R. Richardson, *Death, Dissection and the Destitute*, University of Chicago Press, 2001). The 1832 Act allowed a person to make a declaration donating their body after their death for the purposes of medical science. The Corneal Grafting Act in 1952 allowed individuals to donate the use of their eyes for therapeutic purposes after their death. This was followed in 1961 by the Human Tissue Act which governed the use of material from cadavers. The legislation enabled people to choose to donate material before their death through a declaration in writing or orally in the prescence of two witnesses (s.1(1)) or enabled the person "lawfully in possession" of the body to authorise removal after their death where such enquiries had been made as were reasonably practicable of spouse and surviving relatives. Over time the legislation was the subject of criticism. One major difficulty identified with the Act was uncertainty surrounding the nature and extent of inquiries to be made. In addition the Act was widely regarded as was outdated in that, while enquiries were to be made of the spouse, it did not cover persons who were in long-term non-marital relationships (see further P.D.K. Skegg, "Human Tissue Act 1961" (1976) 16 *Medicine, Science and Law* 197 and G. Dworkin, "The Law Relating to Organ Transplantation in England" (1970) 30 *Modern Law Review* 353). A further difficulty was that the Act was silent as to the age at which a declaration under s.1(1) of the Act could be made. Consequently, the position regarding child donors was unclear. (See D. Lanham, "Transplants and the Human Tissue Act 1961" (1971) 11 *Medicine, Science and the Law* 16.)

The Human Tissue Act 1961 was subject to the powers of the coroner to require state-ordered post mortems (s.1(5)). However, the Government indicated that, wherever possible, the coroner should not inhibit transplantation (HC (77) August 28, 1975). The government guidance also suggested that the coroner should only reject a request for an organ to be removed in a situation in which the organ would be needed in evidence, where the organ might be the cause or partial cause of death, or where removal might inhibit further investigations. It was suggested that one method of facilitating transplantation would be to follow the Scottish system of allowing the coroner to be present when the transplantation operation was undertaken. The operation itself also constitutes the post mortem. (See J.K. Mason, "Organ Donation and Transplantation" in C. Dyer (ed.), *Doctors, Patients and the Law*, Oxford: Blackwell, 1992). In addition the Human Tissue Act 1961 also remained silent as to the legality of maintaining the corpse in a suitable condition to facilitate organ removal, for example, ventilating the corpse and keeping the heart operational—the "beating heart donor". (See further J.K. Mason and G. Laurie, *Law and Medical Ethics* (7th edn) London: Butterworths, 2005), at p.495.) Furthermore, the 1961 Act did not make provision for specific criminal offences for non-compliance.

The Human Tissue Act 1961 only regulated the use of cadaver tissue and for many years the use of human material from living persons, whether in the context of treatment or in relation to research, was governed by the common law. The common law position itself was fraught with uncertainties, not least the boundaries of consent to and legitimacy of transplantation procedures in relation to children and adults lacking mental capacity. However in 1989 the Human Organ Transplants Act was passed, following a scandal concerning trading in organs—see below at p.1150. This led to a ban on the commercial dealing in organs and established a regulatory structure concerning live organ transplantation. Because of concerns that unrelated donors were more likely to be subject to commercial pressures, the legislation introduced specific procedures concerning use of material from unrelated donors and established a new body, the Unrelated Live Transplants Regulatory Authority.

In the years which followed, transplantation technology developed apace. Today transplants are undertaken of many organs and tissues from hearts to corneas and bone marrow. Currently research is being undertaken into the use of substitutes for human organs in the form of artificial organs (and animal organs/tissue, which are known as xenographs (see p.1170 below)). However, these alternative forms have not reached a stage at which they will supplant the use of human tissue. The use of xenographs also poses some acute ethical dilemmas (see further at p.1170 below). There is a further question, namely whether transplantation technology should be increasing as fast as it is or whether medical resources should be expended in other ways (see Chapter 2 above).

The difficulty facing health professionals involved in transplant surgery at present is that there is a discrepancy between the number of organs available for transplantation and the number of organs required. This shortage of organs has led to considerable debate as to the means by which the supply can be improved. At p.1164 below we consider the legal implications of various proposals which

have been put forward for increasing the supply. Many ethical issues arise
regarding other transplantation procedures which we do not have the space to
consider here (see further, for example, D. Price, *Legal and Ethical Aspects of
Organ Transplantation*, Cambridge: CUP, 2000).

The law concerning the legal regulation of human material, other than that
covered already by the Human Fertilisation and Embryology Act 1990, has now
been subject to radical change through the Human Tissue Act 2004. The trigger
for legislation came not from concerns regarding the shortage of organs for
transplantation but rather from the huge public controversy which resulted from
the discovery that there were large stores of human material retained in hospitals
and medical schools around the country which had been obtained without
authorisation having been given for their retention. Particularly notable was the
retention of organs and body parts of babies and young children. This discovery
led to the establishment of the Alder Hey Inquiry chaired by Michael Redfern
QC, and a report was also issued as part of the on-going review into the events
at Bristol Royal Infirmary, conducted by Ian Kennedy (Report of the Inquiry into
the Royal Liverpool Children's Hospital (Alder Hey) (2001) *http://www.rclin
quiry.org.uk*; (Alder Hey report); Bristol Inquiry Interim Report Removal and
Retention of Human Material (2000) *http://www.bristol-inquiry.org.uk*, and see
further regarding the law and ethics of organ and tissue retention L. Skeane,
"Property Rights in Human Bodies, Body Parts and Tissue: Regulatory Contexts
and Proposals for New laws" (2002) *Legal Studies* 102). In Scotland a review was
undertaken by Professor Shelia McLean for the Scottish Executive (*Final Report
of the Independent Review on the Retention of Organs at Post Mortem*) 2002).
Further reports followed. The Retained Organs Commission established by the
Government in the aftermath of the Alder Hey report also undertook its own
investigations into organ retention (Retained Organs Commission, *Organ Retention at Central Manchester and Manchester Children's University Hospitals Trust*
July 2002 *http://www.nhs.uk/retainedorgans/index.htm*), and in 2003 Her Majesty's Inspector of Anatomy published a report revealing the extensive non-
consensual retention of brains in the Issacs report, *Investigation of the Events
which Followed the Death of Cyril Mark Issacs* (DOH, May 2003). See also in
Northern Ireland *Report of the Human Organ Inquiry* (2002). Organ retention
has also provoked controversy in other jurisdictions, e.g. G.D. Jones, *Speaking
for the Dead*, Aldershot: Ashgate, 2000, regarding the New Zealand position.).

The inquiry reports have highlighted the uncertainty as to the existing legal
position in this area and the assumption across the medical and scientific
community of the legitimacy of the retention and use of such materials for
education and research use without consent. In relation to the use of cadaver
material the reports also starkly illustrated differences in perception regarding the
use of material from the body after death, some believing that there is no ongoing
interest in the corpse after death, while others see treatment of the body after
death as imbued with a religious and cultural significance which relates to how
the body should be treated. (For a debate on the contrasting positions, see J.
Harris, "Law and Regulation of Retained Organs: the Ethical Issues" (2002) 22
Legal Studies 527; M. Brazier, "Retained Organs: Ethics and Humanity" (2002)
22 *Legal Studies* 550.) Such differing attitudes are reflected in the controversy

surrounding Dr Gunther von Hagens, who performed the first public autopsy for 170 years in November 2002, a procedure which was televised on Channel 4. ("Controversial autopsy goes ahead" *http://news.bbc.co.uk/1/hi/health/2493291* November 20, 2003). Von Hagens also put on an exhibition, "Bodyworlds", made up of "plastinated" corpses in London in 2002, which led to heated public debate (see discussion in D. Singh, "Scientist or Showman?" (2003) 326 B.M.J. 468). There remain also a range of differing perspectives regarding the use of material from living persons. Again there may be religious and cultural perspectives on the use of human material. In addition, as Liddell and Hall note, "Some feel that tissue communicates their identity or characteristics and as such is something to which they feel a special connection. Others feel that tissue obtained from them bears some form of personal stamp: that it is them, albeit in a transposed form." (See further K. Liddell and A. Hall, "The Future of Human Tissue" (2005) 13 *Medical Law Review* 170 at p.176.) In contrast, others would simply regard the material removed after surgery as being discarded or "waste" material—see the discussion of this below at p.1139.

Following the Alder Hey and Bristol inquiry reports and the media storm around the organ retention scandals, the Chief Medical Officer published a report which revealed the full extent of the retention of tissue and organs across the country (Chief Medical Officer, *Report of a Census of Organs and Tissue Retained by Pathology Services in England*, London: CMO, 2001). Subsequently the Government published the consultation document, *Human Bodies: Human Choices* in 2002 (see D. Price, "From Cosmos and Damien to Van Velzen: the Human Tissue Saga Continues" (2003) 11 *Medical Law Review* 1) and finally in 2003 introduced the Human Tissue Bill. This broad piece of legislation, which came into force in September 1, 2006, regulates the use of human material from both cadavar and live donors. The Act is considered in detail below at p.1121.

In this section first we consider the common law position concerning use of human material from the living. Secondly we consider the question of ownership of human material. Thirdly we consider the legal regulation of the use of human material under the Human Tissue Act 2004.

(b) Human Material from the Living—Common Law

One of the complexities of this area is that it is governed by common law as well as by statute, and consequently the Human Tissue Act 2004 operates alongside the common law principles. We therefore need to consider the legitimacy of the removal of human material at common law for research or treatment purposes. This needs to be seen alongside the discussion in Chapters 5 and 6 above in relation to consent to treatment. Removal of human material without consent will constitute potentially liability in the tort of battery and also liability in criminal law whether in relation to battery or one of the more serious offences under the Offences Against the Person Act 1861. Much of the discussion here is focused upon the legitimacy of the use of material for organ transplantation but the same principles are applicable in the context of use of material in relation to research.

(i) Human Material Removed from Live Subjects

Consent to removal of human material

THE COMPETENT ADULT

Law Commission, *Consent in the Criminal Law: a Consultation Paper*, Law Commission Consultation Paper No. 139 (1996)

Although the practice of taking kidneys and other tissue material from live donors has been an established therapeutic procedure for decades, the principles that make it lawful to remove organs from living donors have never been set out clearly in any English case. In 1969 Lord Justice Edmund-Davies said, extra-judicially, that he would be surprised if any liability, civil or criminal, attached to the surgeon who performed a transplant operation on a competent donor who freely consented to the operation, provided that it did not present an unreasonable risk to the donor's life or health. The existence of the risk to the donor has led to a distinction being drawn between the use of regenerative tissue (such as blood or bone marrow), non-regenerative tissue that is essential for life (such as the heart or the liver), and other non-regenerative tissue.

There are no special principles relating to the nature of the consent that must be obtained, although when the donor is closely related to the potential donee, the doctor in performing the operation needs to be conscious of the psychological pressure on the donor and to ensure that consent is indeed freely given. What is more difficult is to identify the principles on which English law sanctions these operations, since they do not confer any therapeutic benefit on the donors.

Professor Dworkin has suggested that legal justification might be derived from treating a volunteer donor as favourably as the courts have traditionally treated rescuers. Professor Skegg has argued that the shortage of organs available for transplantation means that the courts may be expected to accept that there is a just cause or good reason for transplant operations on living donors. Whatever the true legal analysis, there can be no doubt that, once a valid consent has been forthcoming, English law now treats as lawful operative procedures designed to remove regenerative tissue and also non-regenerative tissue that is not essential for life.

NOTES:

1. An individual is not able to consent to removal of an organ where death would be the inevitable consequence. In such a situation the surgeon would also be liable to be prosecuted for murder.
2. It has also been suggested that it would be unlawful to accept organs, such as an animal organ (see below at p.1176), where there is a high probability that such an organ will be rejected. (See J.K. Mason, "Organ Transplantation" in C. Dyer (ed.), *Doctors, Patients and the Law*, Oxford: Blackwell, 1992.) The legality of the performance of organ transplant procedures is considered more fully in relation to the discussion on consent to treatment in Chapter 5 above.

THE ADULT WITHOUT MENTAL CAPACITY

At common law it was unclear whether mentally incompetent adults may act as organ donors. While the House of Lords in *F v West Berkshire Health Authority* [1989] 2 All E.R. 454 made it clear that medical treatment may be undertaken where it is in the person's best interests (see Chapter 5) the person who is an organ donor is not being "treated" for an illness; rather, by donating an organ he is acting as a means to cure another. It is questionable whether the donation of an organ by a mentally incompetent person could ever be regarded as being in his best interests. In its report, *Mental Incapacity*, Law Commission Report No. 231, 1995, the Law Commission stated that:

"Para 65 . . . Respondents supported our suggestion that an operation to facilitate the donation of non-regenerative tissue or bone marrow by a person without capacity should automatically be referred to the court. The need for any such decision will not stem from any existing distressing condition of the person without capacity but from the illness of some other person. Organ donation will only rarely, if ever, be in the best interests of a person without capacity, since the procedures and their aftermath often carry considerable risk to the donor. There is however authority from another jurisdiction that where a transplant would ensure the survival of a close family member it may be in the best interests of the person without capacity to make such a donation.

We recommend that any treatment or procedure to facilitate the donation of non-regenerative tissue or bone marrow should require court authorisation (Draft Bill, clause 7(2)(b))."

NOTE:

1. The Law Commission referred here to the United States case of *Strunk v Strunk* (1969) 35 A.L.R. (3d) 683. In that case the court sanctioned the donation of a kidney from a 26-year-old mentally handicapped man to his brother who was dying of kidney disease. In making the order the court emphasised the strong emotional bond in existence between the two brothers.

The issue of donation of material from adults without capacity arose subsequently in the case of *Re Y*.

Re Y (Mental Patient: Bone Marrow Donation) (1996) F.L.R. 791

The case concerned a 25-year-old woman with impaired mental capacity. It was proposed that she should act as a bone marrow donor for her 36-year-old sister. It was likely that without the transplant the sister would develop acute myloid leukaemia within three months. Connell J. authorised the performance of a test on Y to ascertain her suitability and, if necessary, the bone marrow harvesting operation.

CONNELL J.

The test to be applied in a case such as this is to ask whether the evidence shows that it is in the best interests of the defendant for such procedures to take place. The fact that such a process would obviously benefit the plaintiff is not relevant unless, as a result of the defendant helping the plaintiff in that way, the best interests of the defendant are served . . .

This case is different from *In re F. (Mental Patient: Sterilisation)* because it involves the concept of donation of bone marrow by a donor who is incapable of giving consent where a significant benefit will flow to another person. There was no other person in *In re F.* who would have benefited directly as a result of the declaration sought, the benefits of sterilisation attaching solely to the mentally incapacitated subject of the application.

Nonetheless, I am satisfied that the root question remains the same, namely, whether the procedures here envisaged will benefit the defendant and accordingly benefits which may flow to the plaintiff are relevant only in so far as they have a positive effect upon the best interests of the defendant.

As indicated, the defendant's family are a very close, supportive family. They are convinced that the defendant would give her consent to the proposals if she were in a position to do so. There are some American authorities which suggest that a substitute judgment test should be applied, but in the light of the observations of Lord Goff of Chieveley, and Lord Mustill in *Airedale N.H.S. Trust v. Bland* [1993] A.C. 789, in particular at pp.871–872, 894–895, *such a test is not relev*ant to the issue in this jurisdiction . . .

So far as any benefits to the defendant are concerned, I have previously referred to the fact that this is a closely knit family. For the first 10 years of her life, the defendant lived at home where she was looked after by her mother, assisted by her father and her sisters."

The judge noted that there was some suggestion from psychiatric evidence that she might have some recollection of living in the family home. He continued:

"The information provided by those who now care for the defendant in the residential home make it apparent that the defendant benefits from the visits which she receives from her family and from her occasional involvement in family events, e.g. the wedding of one of her sisters, particularly because these visits maintain for her a link with the outside world which is helpful to her and which would otherwise be lost to her.

In addition, the Official Solicitor's representative observed affection between mother and daughter during a recent visit which demonstrated that her mother holds a special place in the defendant's world even if the defendant does not appreciate that this lady is in fact her mother.

If this application is not successful, the chances that the plaintiff will not survive are materially increased. She might be able to receive bone marrow from one of the two unrelated donors but the evidence shows that the recipient's chances of survival for 18 months following transplant from a sibling are at least 40 per cent. whereas those chances after donation from a stranger in the case of the plaintiff's illness are at best 30 per cent. The match from strangers is never quite as good as the match from a sibling.

Further, if the plaintiff survives the first six months post transplant then the prospects for survival semi-indefinitely are good. On the other hand, without any transplant her prospects of survival are very poor and are deteriorating fast. If the plaintiff dies, this is bound to have an adverse affect upon her mother who already suffers from significant ill-health. One lay witness took the gloomy view that this event would prove fatal to the mother, but in any event her ability to visit the defendant would be handicapped significantly, not only by a likely deterioration in her health, but also by the need which would then arise for her to look after her only grandchild, E.

In this situation, the defendant would clearly be harmed by the reduction in or loss of contact with her mother. Accordingly, it is to the benefit of the defendant that she should act as donor to her sister, because in this way her positive relationship with her mother is most likely to be prolonged. Further, if the transplant occurs, this is likely to improve the defendant's relationship with her mother who in her heart clearly wishes it to take place and also to improve her relationship with the plaintiff who will be eternally grateful to her.

The disadvantages to the defendant of the harvesting procedure are very small. Expert evidence from two anaesthetists has been placed before me. Both agree that, subject to examination of the defendant by an independent anaesthetist to ensure that she has no so far undetected personal aversion to anaesthetic and that there is nothing in her medication or her physical state which makes her an unsuitable subject for a general anaesthetic, the risks in her case of such a process are extremely low, i.e. less than one per 10,000 and are no greater than those faced by the average patient in hospital. It would be advisable for the responsibility for her clinical management to be shared by two consultant anaesthetists and I have been told that this would present no problem.

It is an advantage that the defendant has in fact experienced a general anaesthetic on many occasions in her life including for a hysterectomy, without any apparent adverse effects. She can be accompanied to the operating theatre by a relative who can be present during induction and recovery and any subsequent pain can readily be controlled by at most two doses of intramuscular morphine.

Of course, none of these problems would fall for consideration if the defendant did not act as donor for the plaintiff and it is relevant to ask the question, why subject the defendant to this process? To this the answer, in my judgment and in the judgment of the Official Solicitor, is because it is to her emotional, psychological and social benefit. This is the expert opinion of Dr. B., who is very experienced in these matters, and it is the conclusion to which I come on the evidence in this case.

I should perhaps emphasise that this is a rather unusual case and that the family of the plaintiff and the defendant are a particularly close family. It is doubtful that this case would act as a useful precedent in cases where the surgery involved is more intrusive than in this case, where the evidence shows that the bone marrow harvested is speedily regenerated and that a healthy individual can donate as much as two pints with no long term consequences at all. Thus, the bone marrow donated by the defendant will cause her no loss and she will suffer no real long term risk."

NOTES:

1. Cornell J. granted the declaration.

2. The judge made reference to Calvo J. in the US case of *Curran v Bosze* (1990) 566 N.E.2d 1319 where an application designed to permit bone marrow harvesting from twins for the benefit of their brother was considered. He stated that:

   "there must be an existing, close relationship between the donor and recipient. . . . Only where there is an existing relationship between a healthy child and his or her ill sister or brother may a psychological benefit to the child from donating bone marrow to a sibling realistically be found to exist. The evidence establishes that it is the existing sibling relationship, as well as the potential for a continuing sibling relationship, which forms the context in which it may be determined that it will be in the best interests of the child to undergo a bone marrow harvesting procedure for a sibling."

3. It should be noted that the judge in this case emphasised that the decision concerned bone marrow and suggested noted that the same approach may not be followed in a situation where the material was not regenerative, e.g. a solid organ such as the kidney.

4. Further consideration is now given to the legality of the use of material from adults lacking mental capacity under the Human Tissue Act 2004 (see below at p.1135.

QUESTIONS:

1. To what extent is it ever legitimate for adults lacking mental capacity to act as organ or tissue donors?
2. Is it possible to objectively establish a close family relationship in ascertaining "best interests"?

CHILDREN

Removal of human material from children for transplants or for research purposes raises a number of difficult legal and ethical issues. First, whether the child can actually consent at all to become the recipient of an organ. Transplantation is a major procedure. In the case of an older child it can be questioned whether such a child would be *Gillick*-competent to give consent herself. In most situations it is arguable that a child would be required to have a high degree of competence before being capable of giving consent to such a major surgical procedure. In practice it would appear that parental consent would, in effect, be required before the transplantation operation could be undertaken. Difficulties may arise in a situation in which a child's parents refuse to give consent to a transplantation operation being undertaken on the basis that the child had "suffered enough" and they do not believe it appropriate to take therapy further. It may be also the case that a transplant procedure is of a pioneering nature and the parents do not wish to take the risk of including their child in such a therapy. An example of such parental opposition which came before the courts in 1996 was the case of *Re T* (a minor) (wardship; medical treatment) [1997] 1 All ER 906. (See further discussion of this case in Chapter 7 above). Here parents refused consent to their child undergoing a liver transplant. This case is however highly exceptional in its nature and may in the future be seen as distinguishable upon its unusual facts. An analogy can be drawn here with clinical research and the performance of therapeutic research procedures: is it legitimate to subject children to a procedure where there may be a high degree of risk in the face of parental opposition? (See Chapter 10). Where a dispute arises between health care professionals and parents as to the efficacy of the transplantation procedure, this is a matter which should be referred to the court under one of the available orders (see Chapter 7 above).

The second issue relates to whether a child may lawfully act as an organ donor. Where a child is very young, this would again be a matter for parental consent. Can a parent authorise such a procedure? Parents may consent to clinical procedures on the basis that this clinical procedure is in the child's best interests. But can the donation of an organ be truly said to be in a child's best interests? Similar problematic issues arises here as in the context of the mentally incompetent adult. Such uncertainty surrounds the basis on which parents may legitimately consent to the inclusion of their children in non-therapeutic procedures in general (see Chapter 7). (It is worthy of note that some jurisdictions prohibit donation of organs by minors, e.g. Human Tissue and Transplant Act 1982, Western Australia, ss.12 and 13.)

What of a situation in which it is proposed to use an older child as an organ donor? Can such a child herself give consent at common law to such a procedure? This matter received some judicial discussion by the Court of Appeal in the case of *Re W* [1992] 4 All E.R. 627. This case was discussed in Chapter 7 above in connection with the refusal of treatment by a competent minor. Here we extract statements from the judgment of Lord Donaldson.

Re W (A Minor) (Medical Treatment: Court's Jurisdiction) [1992] 4 All E.R. 627, [1993] Fam. 64, [1992] 3 W.L.R. 758

The facts of the case are as stated at p.457, above. Lord Donaldson discussed the scope of the Family Law Reform Act 1969, s.8 of which provides that persons over 16 could give consent to "surgical, medical or dental treatment" as if they were of full age. The section provided that

"s8(2) In this section 'surgical, medical or dental treatment' includes any procedure undertaken for the purposes of diagnosis and this section applies to any procedure (including, in particular the administration of an anaesthetic) which is ancillary to any treatment as it applies to that treatment."

Lord Donaldson considered the report of the Latey Committee (Report of the Committee on the Age of Majority (1967) (Cmnd. 3342) which formed the basis for the 1969 Act and then continued:

LORD DONALDSON M.R.
"The section extends not only to treatment, but also to diagnostic procedures: see subsection (2). It does not, however, extend to the donation of organs or blood since, so far as the donor is concerned, these do not constitute either treatment or diagnosis. I cannot remember to what extent organ donation was common in 1967, but the Latey Committee expressly recommended that only 18-year-olds and older should be authorised by statute to consent to giving blood: see paragraphs 485–489. It seems that Parliament accepted this recommendation, although I doubt whether blood donation will create any problem as a '*Gillick* competent' minor of any age would be able to give consent under the common law.

Organ transplants are quite different and, as a matter of law, doctors would have to secure the consent of someone with the right to consent on behalf of a donor under the age of 18 or, if they relied upon the consent of the minor himself or herself, be satisfied that the minor was '*Gillick* competent' in the context of so serious a procedure which could not benefit the minor. This would be a highly improbable conclusion. But this is only to look at the question as a matter of law. Medical ethics also enter into the question. The doctor has a professional duty to act in the best interests of his patient and to advise accordingly. It is inconceivable that he should proceed in reliance solely upon the consent of an under-age patient, however '*Gillick* competent,' in the absence of supporting parental consent and equally inconceivable that he should proceed in the absence of the patient's consent. In any event he will need to seek the opinions of other doctors and may be well advised to apply to the court for guidance, as recommended by Lord Templeman in a different context in *Re B (A Minor) (Wardship: Sterilisation)* [1987] 2 All E.R. 206 at 214–215.

NOTES:

1. The Court of Appeal in *Re W* clearly states that the Family Law Reform 1969 Act does not cover donation of organs or blood and thus who is and who is not able to consent is a matter for the common law.

2. One difficulty relating to live organ donation, which may be particularly acute in the case of children, is ensuring that the donation is voluntary. The emotional pressure placed upon a child by relatives to donate to a sibling may be considerable. There may be a case for the introduction of some special procedure for independent supervision of child donors. Nevertheless, it appears that this matter may be of more theoretical than practical import because removal of organs from living child donors would be undertaken only in very rare cases. (See J.K. Mason, "Organ Transplantation" in C. Dyer (ed.), *Doctors, Patients and the Law,* Oxford: Blackwell, 1992). Donations of other body products from child patients are more common. Bone marrow donations involve tests, with the child being admitted to hospital for up to two nights and the administration of a general anaesthetic. There is also the risk of severe pain and discomfort consequent upon the transplantation. Sibling donations may lead to considerable pressure being placed upon the child donor. It has been argued that the donation of bone marrow by a child patient should be subject to regulation. Delaney has suggested that donation should be only authorised where these are in the best interests of the child determined by reference to a checklist of factors. In addition an independant forum should authorise each graft. (See L. Delaney, "Protecting Children from Forced Altruism: the Legal Approach" (1996) B.M.J. 240.) This view has been disputed by those who argue that it is a safe procedure (S. Month, "Preventing Children from Donating May not be in their Best Interests"; J. Savulescu, "Substantial Harm but Substantial Benefit"; P. Browett and S. Palmer, "Legal Barriers Might Have Catastrophic Effects" (1996) 312 B.M.J. 242). See further now the new procedures for approving transplantation from living donors in the Human Tissue Act 2004, discussed below at p.1143.

3. In *Re M* [1999] 2 F.L.R. 1097, a 15-year-old girl required a heart transplant, without which she was likely to die within the week. M refused consent and claimed that she did not want to follow the long-post operative course of therapy with a daily course of tablets for the rest of her life and that she would rather die than live on with the heart of another person inside her. Johnson J. in the Family Division held that M was in effect incompetent. He commented, "events have overtaken M so swiftly that she has not been able to come to terms with her situation". While there were consequent risks in the heart transplant operation itself being undertaken, as Johnson J. noted, these were overridden by what was otherwise the certainty that in this situation M would die.

COULD A PERSON EVER BE FORCED TO DONATE?

We noted earlier in relation to consent to treatment that in certain exceptional situations the courts have authorised treatment despite the patient's expressed objections (see, for example, *Re T* [1992] 4 All E.R. 649, *Re S* [1992] 4 All E.R. 671). But such cases are exceptional. In both these cases authorisation of treatment enabled the life of the patient to be prolonged and moreover it should be noted that the courts have subsequently firmly stated that autonomous patients have the right to make their own decisions in *Re MB* [1997] 2 F.C.R. 541. It would thus appear inconceivable that an individual would be compelled to undergo a transplant operation or to undergo a procedure to obtain material for research purposes.

THE ANENCEPHALIC INFANT

There has been considerable debate as to whether it is appropriate to harvest organs from anencephalic infants. Such infants are born with all or part of the upper hemispheres of the brain missing. They live usually for only some 24 hours, though in rare cases this has extended to weeks or months.

Working Party of the Medical Royal Colleges on Organ Transplantation in Neonates (1988)

Tests of brain stem functions are applied in adults because the absence of such function establishes that the brain is dead: they are clearly inapplicable when the forebrain is missing. Such infants clearly have a major neurological deficiency incompatible with life for longer than a few hours. A view which commended itself to the Working Party was that organs could be removed from an anencephalic infant when two doctors (who are not members of the transplant team) agreed that spontaneous respiration had ceased. In the adult the diagnosis of brain death plus apnoea is recognised as death. The Working Party felt by analogy that the absence of a forebrain in these infants plus apnoea would similarly be recognised as death.

NOTES:

1. Some believe that it is justifiable to harvest organs from anencephalic infants because they are not "persons" since they lack cognitive functions. However, such reasoning throws into question the status of those individuals who are in a persistent vegetative state. Could they too be made available as organ donor banks? Others are strongly critical of such an approach, questioning, for example, the adverse effect which the use of anencephalic infants would have upon the status of handicapped infants generally. (See A. Shewman and A. Capron *et al.*, "Use of Anencephalic Infants as Organ Sources: a Critique" (1989) 261 *Journal of the American Medical Association* 12; A. Davies, "The Status of Anencephalic Babies: Should their Bodies be Used as Donor Banks?" (1988) 14 *Journal of*

Medical Ethics 150). In the Supreme Court of Florida in the case of *Re TAC P* 609 So 2d 588 (Fla 1992) the request of parents that a kidney should be removed from an anencephalic infant although she had not been declared brain dead was rejected. The court stated that "We acknowledge the possibility that some infants lives might be saved by using organs from anencephalics who do not meet the traditional definition of 'death' we affirm today . But weighed against this is the utter lack of consensus, and the questions about the overall utility of such organ donations. The scales clearly tip in favour of not extending the common law in this instance."

2. It may be the case that the debate regarding the use of anencephalics becomes in the future one of simply historical interest. The increased use of screening during pregnancy and other medical developments have led to a steady fall in the number of anencephalic infants being born.

QUESTIONS:

1. Is treating the anencephalic infant as a donor currently lawful?
2. Should a specific statutory provision allow anencephalics to be used as organ donors?
3. In view of the limited availability of organs for transplantation, should patients in a persistent vegetative state whose relatives agree be used as organ donors? (Refer back to the discussion of PVS earlier and also to the decision in *Airedale NHS Trust v Bland*, discussed above at p.1021.)

(c) Organ and Tissue Ownership—Common Law

To what extent does an individual have any rights of ownership in their human material? The traditional approach is that human tissue and organs are not susceptible of ownership. *Dr Handyside's* case (1749) 3 East PC 652 is cited as authority for the proposition that there is no property in an unburied corpse, as is the case of *Williams v Williams* (1852) 20 Ch.D. 657 (see also *Dobson and Another v North Tyneside H.A.* [1997] 1 W.L.R. 596). While the strength of these authorities has been called into question, it appears to be the case that they are generally accepted as existing law, as confirmed in *R v Kelly* [1998] 3 All E.R. 741. (See generally P. Matthews, "Whose Body: People As Property" (1983) 36 *Current Legal Problems* 195). In contrast, human substances such as urine and hair may be stolen (*R. v Welsh* [1974] R.T.R. 478; *R v. Kelly*; and see G. Dworkin and I. Kennedy, "Human Tissue: Rights in the Body and its Parts" (1993) 1 *Medical Law Review* 291; A. Grubb, "I Me Mine; Bodies, Parts and Property" (1998) *Medical Law International* 247).

The catalyst for recent interest as to whether there is property in organs and tissue in this country was a US case, *Moore v University of California* 793 Pd 479 (Cal 1990) (see generally B. Dickens, "Living Tissue and Organ Donors and Property Law: More on Moore" (1992) *Journal of Contemporary Health Law and Policy* 73). Moore had part of his spleen removed as part of treatment for hairy cell leukaemia. Unknown to Moore, some of his cells were used in the development of a lucrative cell line. Whilst the Californian Supreme Court held that Moore had no or "at least only limited" property rights in the cells removed, they acknowledged that he should have been informed as to the use of the cells and that failure to do so was in contravention of the requirement of informed consent (see also *Greenberg et al v Miami Children's Hospital Research Institute Inc*, 264 F Supp 2D 1064 (SD Fla 2003) and J.K. Mason and G. Laurie, *Law and Medical Ethics* (5th edn), 2005 at pp.522–523). In English law there has been no comparable case to date. Consideration has been given to the question of tissue ownership by the Nuffield Council on Bioethics. Below is an extract from a report of the Council examining claims which a person, from whom tissue is removed, can assert in relation to that tissue.

Nuffield Council on Bioethics, *Human Tissue: Ethical and Legal Issues*, 1995

9.4 At common law the issue has not been tested in English law. It is instructive to enquire why the question of a claim over tissue once removed has not received legal attention. The answer seems simple. In the general run of things a person from whom tissue is removed has not the slightest interest in making any claim to it once it is removed. This is obviously the case as regards tissue removed as a consequence of treatment. It is equally true in the case of donation of tissue whether, for example, blood, bone marrow or an organ. The word donation clearly indicates that what is involved is a gift.

9.5 It is certainly true, of course, that an appendix or gallstone may be returned to a patient who may refer to it as her appendix or gallstone. But this says nothing about any legal claim that she may have to the appendix. In fact, in the case of the returned appendix, one view of the legal position may be as follows: the patient consents to the operation which involves the removal of her appendix: by her consent to the operation she abandons any claims to the appendix, on removal the appendix acquires the status of a *res* (a thing) and comes into the possession of the hospital authority prior to disposal; in response by a request of the patient that it can be returned the hospital gives the appendix to the patient as a gift; the appendix then becomes the property of the patient.

9.6 While what has been said about the lack of interest of the patient in the fate of tissue removed from him may be true, some have enquired whether a claim to tissue which has been removed can be advanced in certain circumstances. One such circumstance is the removal of foetal tissue subsequent to an abortion. Does a mother, it may be asked, have any claim to the tissue? The report of the Polkinghorne Committee did not claim to resolve the question. Instead it provided for a scheme whereby the woman has to give explicit and unconditional consent to the use of the foetal tissue before it may be used. The same scheme of consents, circumventing the need to resolve questions of property and ownership, was employed in the Human Fertilisation and Embryology Act.

9.7 But there are other circumstances in which the question posed in paragraph 9.6 may arise. In some circumstances, it could be argued, and has been by a number of commentators, that tissue once removed becomes the property of the person from whom it is removed. This is to say that consent to removal does not entail an intent to abandon. The tissue may well, in fact, be abandoned or donated, but these imply a prior coming into existence of a *res* and the exercise of rights over it. Indeed, such an analysis is logically essential, it is argued, even if the resulting property (i.e. a person's assertion of a property right over the new res) exists merely for the moment (a *scintilla temporis*). On this view the person from whom tissue is removed must have a property right in the tissue which expressly or by implication he could waive on the removal so that the property passes to another. The consequence is, of course, that if the property right were not waived, it would be retained. To return to the example in paragraph 9.5, the appendix would have become (and remained) the patient's property had she not by implication waived any right to it.

9.8 The case of *Venner v. State of Maryland* decided by the Court of Special Appeals in Maryland USA, may be of assistance. Powers J. held that, 'By the force of social custom . . .

when a person does nothing and says nothing to indicate an intent to assert his rights of ownership, possession and control over [bodily] material, the only rational inference is that he intends to abandon the material'. The emphasis of this approach is clear.

1. The legal presumption is in favour of abandonment
2. Abandonment may be prospective
3. Where, however, the circumstances are such that abandonment may not be presumed, it must follow that if no consent were given, or a consent expressed to be 'on terms' were given, property rights over the tissue would not necessarily pass but would be retained by the person from whom the property was removed.

9.9 It is fair to say that some support for this approach can be derived from various statutes already referred to. While we have seen (in paragraph 9.3) that no claim arises by reference to these statutes, the approach to tissue adopted by them may assist in understanding the current state of the common law. While the Human Tissue Act 1961 is of no assistance, both the Human Organ Transplants Act 1989 and the Human Fertilisation and Embryology Act 1990 appear to endorse a property approach. Indeed the latter, though relying upon a scheme of consents so as to avoid the need to decide the issue of property, contemplates that the control and disposal of gametes and embryos rests with the donor(s) and allows for the transfer of the reproductive material between those with a licence to deal with them. A final statutory provision section 25 of the National Health Service Act 1977 also seems implicitly to adopt a property approach. The section provides that:

where the Secretary of State has acquired:

(a) supplies of human blood . . . or
(b) any part of a human body . . .

he may arrange to make such supplies or that part available (on such terms, including terms as to charges as he thinks fit) to any person . . .

The statutory language is therefore, that of things, of property, of the reification of blood and body parts . . .
   . . .

9.11 . . . we have noticed the following as a possible legal approach to any claims made by the person from whom tissue is removed: either

1. consent to removal entails abandonment; or
2. on removal, property rights vest in the person from whom it is removed. It is presumed that these are abandoned, but they can be retained.

A further legal approach is to argue that tissue once removed becomes property, but at the time of its removal it is *res nullis*, i.e. that it belongs to no one until it is brought under domininion (the traditional legal example is the wild animal or plant). This would reflect the traditional view of 'no property in the body'. It would also mean that a person could not prospectively donate 'his' tissue once removed from the body. All he could do would be to consent to the removal. If this analysis were adopted, the tissue would be the property of the person who removed it or subsequently came into possession of it. The person from whom it was removed would not, however, have any property claim to it.

9.12 The current state of English law makes it unclear (at best) which of these approaches (or another) represents the law. Interest in the validity of property claims over removed tissue has, however, been rekindled because of the awareness of circumstances in which tissue has been removed and then developed in some way so as to serve as the basis for a commercial product. The *locus classicus* is the well known *Moore* case. In *Moore* the Supreme Court of California trying a preliminary point of law, decided that Moore had no property right over the tissue taken from his body. Although not expressed in such a way, if we impose the language that we have employed, the court appears to have found that Moore's consent to the operation entailed an abandonment of any claim to the removed tissue. Thus, he could not assert a claim in property as the basis either for objecting to the removal of his tissue or for having a share in whatever profit was gained through its use. The issue of the validity of the consent he gave to the operation and subsequent procedures then becomes the focus of the case.

9.13 It is not easy to predict whether an English court would adopt the Supreme Court of California's conclusion. Certainly the reasons advanced by the majority of the court for rejecting Moore's claim are somewhat unconvincing. The majority found that there were three 'reasons to doubt' Moore's claim, all of which Mosk J. sharply criticised in his dissenting judgment. The first was the absence of precedent. Mosk J.'s response was that the Supreme Court was there precisely to make law where necessary. The second was that the matter was more appropriately for the legislature, a view which Mosk J. said was out of place in a decision of the highest court, one of whose roles was to develop the law. The third was that the patent granted to the University of California preempted any claim Moore might have but the grant of the patent did not mean, according to Mosk J., that Moore could not share in any profits arising from it. Notwithstanding these weaknesses, the conclusion of the Supreme Court, if not the reasoning may recommend itself, not least because of the consequences of adopting the alternative. For, if the alternative approach were adopted and a potential property claim were recognised, the consequences could be far reaching. Consent to even the most minor procedures would have to refer to possible property rights in removed tissue and seek a waiver of such rights. Patients might be encouraged to bargain over tissue (if thought to be unusually valuable, for example, for research). Agencies to negotiate such bargains might appear and research may be impeded in a welter of contractual arrangements.

9.14 Of the various approaches referred to, therefore, it may be that a preferable approach for the English courts would be the following:

1. It will be entailed in any consent to treatment that tissue removed in the course of treatment will be regarded in law as having been abandoned by the person from whom it was removed.

2. tissue removed in circumstances other than treatment which is voluntarily donated will be regarded as a gift. Use for purposes other than those for which consent was given could give rise to a claim on the part of the person from whom the tissue was removed. Such a claim will depend upon the terms of the original consent;

3. where tissue is removed voluntarily but is intended to be kept for the donor, for example, autologous blood donations, the donor will be able to claim the tissue by virtue of the agreement under which it is kept. (The donation of gametes and embryos is subject to a specific statutory framework of consent regulating *inter alia* the giving and withdrawal of consent to use);

4. where tissue is removed without **explicit** knowledge and consent, any claim the person from whom it was removed may have as regards the subsequent use of that tissue will turn on the validity of any general consent which may have been given, i.e. as to whether removal and subsequent use of the tissue could legitimately be said to be implied.

9.15 From this summary it will be seen that, on the reasoning proposed legal claims may be open to persons from whom tissue is removed. It is suggested that they should properly proceed on the basis of consent given to the procedure which resulted in the removal, or its absence, rather than a claim in property . . .

The Report went on to consider the question of the claims of users of tissue.

10.1 In Chapter 9 we discussed whether or not the person from whom tissue is removed may have a property right in the tissue. Whatever view is taken, it does not follow that the user (broadly defined) has no such right. The tissue once removed comes into the possession of the remover and may then be passed to others. The nineteenth-century doctrine that a body may not be property would suggest, however, that no possessory or property right vests in the user of a body or, arguably, parts of a body. In this chapter we examine the claims users may have over human tissue . . .

10.3 The early twentieth-century Australian case of *Doodeward v. Spence* is cited as authority for the no property rule. "There can be no property in a human body dead or alive. I go further and say that if a limb or any portion of a body is removed that no person has a right of property in that portion of the body so removed", *per* Pring J. On appeal to the High Court of Australia the judgment of Griffiths C.J. in the New South Wales Court of Appeal decided that if some work was carried out on the body part, for example to preserve it, which changed the part, then it could acquire the characteristics of property and be subject to property rights.

10.4 By contrast to the view of Pring J. Stephen expressed the view that anatomical specimens could constitute personal property. More recently, as Magnusson points out, "there are a handful of English decisions in which human tissue has been treated as property". He cites criminal cases where a defendant was convicted of theft as well as assault when he cut a quantity of hair from a woman's head, where a defendant poured a urine sample he had given to establish his sobriety down the sink and was convicted of theft, and where the defendant was convicted of theft when he removed the blood sample, taken for the same reason, from the police station. The last two cases, albeit that the point was not directly discussed in either case, suggest that property vested in the police. Admittedly, two of these cases involve hair and urine, neither of which are, strictly speaking, tissue, but if they are treated as property, *a fortiori*, so would what we define as tissue by virtue of its identification as an organised collection of cells and the tangible quality such identification suggests. Finally, it must be recalled that Broussard J. in his dissenting opinion in the *Moore* case wrote that " . . . the majority's analysis cannot rest on the broad proposition that a removed part is not property, but . . . on the proposition that a patient retains no ownership interest in a body part once the body part has been removed."

. . .

10.6 The continued absence of clear legal authority admittedly leaves the law uncertain. It is suggested, however, that common sense as well as the common law require that the user of tissue acquires at least possessory rights and probably a right of ownership over tissue once removed. It cannot plausibly be argued that University College London does own not Bentham's skeleton. *Mutatis mutandis*, a hospital which has tissue in its possession, for example for transplant, has such property rights over the tissue as to exclude any claim of another to it, as does a coroner or pathologist who has carried out a post-mortem and retains body parts for examination. Equally, it would follow, they have the right to recover the tissue if it were taken without permission. The same must be true who operate a tissue bank or an archive of specimens used for research or teaching.

(The embalmed body of Jeremy Bentham is kept at University College London.)

NOTES:

1. The rejection of the property approach by the Nuffield Report has been criticised. Matthews argues that the earlier case law does not provide conclusive evidence of a "no-property" approach. He also sees inconsistencies in the Nuffield Report. For instance, he regards statements made later in the Report to the effect that defects in blood and bodily products may be actionable under the Consumer Protection Act 1987 as being at

variance with its earlier conclusions. (See P. Matthews, "The Man of Property" (1995) 3 *Medical Law Review* 251.)

2. Many of the assumptions made in the Report rely on the fact that the individual has consented to the removal of tissue. Difficulties may arise in relation to adults lacking mental capacity, as we noted above, with regard to the transplantation of organs. The Nuffield Report proposed that the courts should regard it as lawful to remove tissue from a mentally incompetent adult in the public interest where such use is a justifiable use (para. 9.17). This of course leaves open the question of what would constitute such a use.

3. The Report emphasises the concept of abandonment. However, again Matthews, *op. cit.* in Note 1, has questioned its reliance upon this approach. He notes that the doctrine has only been used in certain specific areas of law and that it is doubtful whether it could be said to be of general application. Furthermore he states that there is no authority in English law for treating property as *res nullis*. He also criticises the approach taken in the Nuffield Report to the *Moore* case. In that case abandonment was irrelevant because the court held that there were no rights to abandon.

4. It is likely that scientists will increasingly attempt to obtain intellectual property rights, such as patents, as a consequence of developments involving the use of bodily products with the aim of profiting from their invention. (See further G. Laurie, "Patenting and the Human Body" in A. Grubb (edn), *Principles of Medical Law* (2nd edn), Oxford: OUP, 2004.) Some would oppose the granting of such rights on the basis that it may inhibit future research in the area. One consideration which is taken into account when patents are granted are the ethics underlying the proposed development. Such elements are to be found in both the European Patent Convention and in the Patent Acts. Article 5(3) of the Convention provides that a patent should not be granted where the publication or exploitation of an invention would be contrary to public order or morality. The Patents Act (U.K.) 1977 provides in s.1(3)(a) that a patent would not be given in relation to "an invention, the publication or exploitation of which would be generally accepted to encourage offensive, immoral or anti-social behaviour". The Nuffield Report recommended that a protocol should be drawn up giving guidance to national courts who have to interpret the European Patent Convention and consider those exclusions under this convention which relate to immoral use (Article 53(a) EPC and s.1(3)(c) of the Patent Act (U.K.) 1977). The Nuffield Report concluded that rather than these issues being dealt with by the European Patent office they should instead be left to national courts. The Report leaves open what the protocol should contain. The Report was criticised for its failure to adequately address existing tensions in this area, particularly in relation to the need to promote research as against growing public controversy regarding the use of certain technologies. (See further on this issue L. Bentley and B. Sherman, "The Ethics of Patenting: Towards a Transgenic Patent System" (1995) 3 *Medical Law Review* 275.) The EU Directive on Biotechnology now provides for limitations on patenting. It is provided

that inventions "shall be considered unpatentable where their commercial exploitation would be contrary to ordre public or morality"—Directive EC 98/44 on the legal protection of biotechnological inventions ([1998] O.J. L213/13), Article 6(1). (For further discussion see T. Hervey and J. McHale, *Health Law and the European Union*, Cambridge: CUP 2004 at pp.258–274.)

5. The development of biotechnology has meant that it is possible to remove cells/tissue from a person and then later use them to produce a lucrative new cell line. The person may claim that s/he has a claim upon the profits made from that cell line, as in *Moore v Regents of the University of California* (1990) 13 P 2d 479, though the issue has not yet come before an English court. One possible claim is that such use amounts to the tort of conversion. Conversion is the term used to describe an "intentional dealing with goods which is seriously inconsistent with the possession/right to immediate possession" *(Caxton Publishing Co v Sutherland Ltd* [1939] A.C. 178 at p.202 as quoted by Brahams in "Bailment and Donation of Parts of the Human Body" (1989) N.L.J. 803). It is unclear as whether bodily products could be classed as "goods". Secondly, it is uncertain whether a person who has undergone an operation has any right to possession of tissue subsequently removed. Dworkin and Kennedy have suggested that an action for conversion may be possible if the individual expressly stipulates the manner in which he intends his tissue to be used after it was removed from him. Alternatively, it may be the case that the use to which the tissue was put was different from the use that the patient had been given to understand and that the information given could be regarded as a deception, thus vitiating the patient's consent regarding removal of that tissue. Nevertheless, even if a court were to accept such a claim, the measure of damages available would be uncertain. (See G. Dworkin and I. Kennedy, "Human Tissue" [1993] 1 *Medical Law Review* 291.)

6. The Nuffield Report suggested that where work is undertaken on a body or tissue, then a person acquires proprietory rights. Matthews *op. cit.* in Note 1 disagreed with this approach and noted that at common law unauthorised work on another's goods gives no rights to those goods.

The question of property in the body and its parts was explored in the Court of Appeal in *R v Kelly.*

R v Kelly [1998] 3 All E.R. 741

In 1997 an artist Anthony-Noel Kelly, was prosecuted for theft of body part. Along with a junior laboratory technician he had smuggled anatomical specimens from the Royal College of Surgeons in black bin bags. As press reports noted, these amounted to "an "alphabet" of body parts: a head and torso, two more heads, part of a brain and a collection of arms, hands, legs and feet" (reported in *The Guardian*, April 4, 1998.) The removal was not discovered by the college authorities. The artist made casts from the body parts and exhibited them at the London Contemporary Art Fair in Islington. The theft was only brought to the attention of the authorities when Her Majesty's Inspector of Anatomy spotted a mention of it in a article in a Sunday paper, where a reviewer noted that one particular cast, that of a silver-coated head and upper torso of an old man, was such that it could have only have been cast from, as the press report said, "an expertly dissected body part". The artists and the technician were prosecuted for theft from the Royal College of Surgeons. We consider there the issue raised in the case of ownership of the human material.

ROSE L.J.

"We return to the first question, that is to say whether or not a corpse or part of a corpse is property. We accept that, however questionable the historical origins of the principle, it has now been the common law for 150 years at least that neither a corpse nor parts of a corpse are in themselves and without more capable of being property protected by rights: see, for example, Erle J., delivering the judgment of a powerful Court for Crown Cases Reserved in *Reg. v. Sharpe* (1857) Dears. & B. 160, 163, where he said: 'Our law recognises no property in a corpse, and the protection of the grave at common law as contradistinguished from ecclesiastic protection to consecrated ground depends on this form of indictment.' He was there referring to an indictment which charged not theft of a corpse but removal of a corpse from a grave.

If that principle is now to be changed, in our view, it must be by Parliament, because it has been express or implicit in all the subsequent authorities and writings to which we have been referred that a corpse or part of it cannot be stolen.

To address the point as it was addressed before the trial judge and to which his certificate relates, in our judgment, parts of a corpse are capable of being property within section 4 of the Theft Act 1968 if they have acquired different attributes by virtue of the application of skill, such as dissection or preservation techniques, for exhibition or teaching purposes: see *Doodeward v. Spence,* 6 C.L.R. 406, 413, 414 in the judgment of Griffith C.J. to which we have already referred and *Dobson v. North Tyneside Health Authority* [1997] 1 W.L.R. 596, 601 where this proposition is not dissented from and appears, in the judgment of this court, to have been accepted by Peter Gibson L.J.; otherwise, his analysis of the facts of *Dobson's* case, which appears at that page in the judgment, would have been, as it seems to us, otiose. Accordingly the trial judge was correct to rule as he did.

Furthermore, the common law does not stand still. It may be that if, on some future occasion, the question arises, the courts will hold that human body parts are capable of being property for the purposes of section 4, even without the acquisition of different attributes, if they have a use or significance beyond their mere existence. This may be so if, for example, they are intended for use in an organ transplant operation, for the extraction of DNA or, for that matter, as an exhibit in a trial. It is to be noted that in *Dobson's* case, there was no legal or other requirement for the brain, which was then the subject of litigation, to be preserved: see the judgment of Peter Gibson L.J., at p. 601."

NOTES:

1. In the *Kelly* case it was proposed that body parts which have a use/ significance beyond their mere existence may constitute property. In *Kelly* Rose L.J. gave the examples of those body parts which were intended for use in organ transplant operation, sample for DNA extraction, or as an exhibit to be used at trial. This broader interpretation has itself come under some criticism. Grubb has suggested that "This would however, in effect, be to re-write the 'no-property' rule itself." (See A. Grubb, "Theft of Body Parts: Property and Dead Bodies" [1998] 6 *Medical Law Review* 247).

2. While it appears that there is no property interest in a corpse as such, the courts have held that a person under a duty to dispose of the body has a right of possession for that purpose. There are a number of possible actions which could be brought by such a person if organs are removed contrary to his wishes. It has been suggested that any unauthorised intereference with the right to possession of a dead body, for example, an unauthorised post mortem, will constitute a trespass to the person. Such an action could be brought without having to show actual damage (see P.D.K. Skegg, "Liability for the unauthorised regard of Cadaveric Transplant Material" (1974) *Medicine, Science and Law* 53). An action may be brought for the tort of intentional infliction of nervous shock (*Wilkinson v Downton* [1897] 2 Q.B. 57; *Janvier v Sweeney* [1919] 2 K.B. 316). However, it appears that in practice establishing such a claim would be exceedingly difficult. This is because one element of this tort—the necessary intention to inflict harm—would be almost impossible to prove. A spouse or other close relative may bring an action in negligence claiming damages for psychiatric injury caused due to the mutilation of the body by transplantation. In principle such an action may succeed if it could be shown that some recognisable psychiatric illness has been caused. However, the law in this area is unclear. While the courts have stated that they are prepared to recognise a bystander's claim for psychiatric injury if they are sufficiently closely connected (*Alcock v Chief Constable of South Yorkshire Police* [1991] 4 All E.R. 907), in a later case (*McFadden v EE Caledonian* [1994] 2 All E.R. 1) the court stated that such a claim cannot be made (see further J. Murphy, "A Reappraisal of Negligently Inflicted Psychiatric Harm" [1995] *Legal Studies* 415).

The issue of liability in the law of tort in relation to the unauthorised retention of human material came under consideration in the case of *AB v Leeds Teaching Hospital NHS Trust*. A number of actions were brought consequent upon the retention of human materials post Alder Hey. Application was made to the High Court by the Alder Hey families for a group litigation order. In January 2003 it was announced that the majority of the claims had been settled with a settlement of £5 million, an apology, the announcement that a commemorative plaque would be erected at Alder Hey hospital and a donation to charity. However families of children whose organs had been retained in other hospitals were offered lower sums.

This resulted in litigation in *AB v Leeds Teaching Hospital NHS Trust* [2004] EWHC 644. A number of possible causes of action were rejected. On the issue as to what amounted to property in human material Gage J. commented that:

"In my judgment the principle that part of a body may acquire the character of property which can be the subject of rights of possession and ownership is now part of our law. In particular, in my opinion, *R v Kelly and Another* establishes the exception to the rule that there is no property in a corpse where part of the body has been the subject of the application of skill such as dissection or preservation techniques. The evidence in the lead cases shows that to dissect and fix an organ from a child's body requires work and great deal of skill, the more so in the case of a very small baby such as Rosina. The subsequent production of blocks and slides is also a skilful operation requiring work and expertise of trained scientists."

In this case as the post mortems had been undertaken lawfully initial possession and retention by the pathologists was lawful. It was suggested that here retention constituted an infringement of the tort of wrongful interference with the body, drawing upon Scottish, Canadian and US case law. The basis for the alleged action was that there was a duty upon a parent to bury a child, and that the defendants interfered with that duty by retaining or disposing of the body parts without authority. Gage J. rejected this on the grounds that no such cause of action was currently part of English law. However Gage J. held that alongside the statutory requirements under the 1961 Act, there was a duty of care in the law of negligence to inform the parents of the nature of retention. The duty of care involved some explanation of the nature of the procedures of the post-mortem of which the removal and retention is a relevant part. He commented that the "practice of not warning parents and in particular the mother that a post-mortem right involved removal and subsequent retention of an organ cannot be justified". He found that consequent upon such a breach of duty, an action could be brought by the claimants as primary victims. Here one of the lead claimants successfully established that psychiatric harm had resulted from the breach of duty. On the application of the Human Rights Act 1998 and in particular Article 8 he commented that the decision to use the child's human material did engage Article 8 and it would be rare circumstances that infringement of Article 8 could be supported under Article 8(2). As the litigation concerned events which had taken place prior to the 1998 Act coming into force, this issue was not further explored although Gage J. commented intriguingly that "claimants were in his view more likely that defendants to succeed in such cases". Although not determinative in this case, Gage J. also indicated that there was the prospect of a future action in the tort of conversion.

(d) Legal Regulation of Human Material: the Human Tissue Act 2004

As noted above (at p.1102), following the inquiry reports into organ retention the Government finally published the Human Tissue Bill in 2003. This Bill, which eventually received Royal Assent in November 2004, is a broad piece of legislation. It governs the use of human material from both the dead and living subjects (subject to limitations discussed below). It also operates alongside the common law where applicable. So, for example, common law consent principles in relation to the performance of surgical procedures to remove tissue discussed above as in the context of transplantation are still applicable. In addition the common law position regarding property in human materials is not addressed directly in the legislation. This gives rise to the prospect that unauthorised use of human material may lead not only to criminal penalties (as discussed below) but may also to additional legal proceedings at common law. It is rooted in the principle of consent to use of human material as opposed to, for example, the "opt-out" approach taken to the use of organs for transplantation taken in other jurisdictions. The Bill led to considerable controversy. Some in the scientific community suggested that the Bill would have had the effect of severely inhibiting research (see, for example, S. Pinnock, "Human Tissue Bill Could Jeopardise Research: Scientists Warn" (2004) 328 B.M.J. 1034; P. Furness, "The Human Tissue Bill: Criminal Sanctions Linked to Opaque Legislation Threaten Research" (2004) 228 B.M.J. 533; and see K. Liddell and A. Hall, "The Future Regulation of Human Tissue" (2005) 13 *Medical Law Review* 170 at pp.172–173). As will be seen below, following much lobbying a number of notable amendments were made to the legislation during its passage through Parliament (see further D. Price, "The Human Tissue Act 2004" (2005) 68 *Modern Law Review* 798).

The Human Tissue Act 2004 covers a wide range of uses of human material for treatment and research purposes. So, for example, as regards the provisions setting out who can give consent, sections 2 and 3 apply both in the context of organ transplantation and in relation to research purposes. Specific additional provisions also provide regulation in the context of organ transplantation from living donors. It establishes a new licensing body, the Human Tissue Authority (see below at p.1156). The Act will operate alongside a number of related statutory instruments and Codes of Practice produced by the Human Tissue Authority. In the following pages, we consider first what constitutes "appropriate" consent. Secondly, who can consent in the context of adults with capacity, children and adults lacking capacity and also who can consent in relation to the deceased through provision for consent by a person in a "qualifying relationship" or as a "nominated representative". Thirdly, we consider a number of explicit exceptions to the consent principle set out in the legislation which are applicable notably in relation to the use of "spare" material for research purposes and where the person from whom material has been obtained cannot be traced. Next, as with the previous legislation, specific additional provision is made in the Human Tissue Act 2004 for the regulation of transplantation procedures concerning living donors over and above the standard consent provisions. The section goes on to consider the trafficking of human materials and some of the specific criminal penalties which are attached to non-compliance with the legislation, which provide a notable contrast with the position which existed under the Human Tissue Act 1961.

Finally, the role of the new statutory regulator, the Human Tissue Authority, is considered, together with the codes of practice.

(i) The Scope of the Legislation: "Appropriate Consent"

When is consent needed?

Human Tissue Act 2004, s.1(1–6)(11–13)

Authorisation of activities for scheduled purposes

    1.—(1) The following activities shall be lawful if done with appropriate consent—

    (a) the storage of the body of a deceased person for use for a purpose specified in Schedule 1, other than anatomical examination;

(b) the use of the body of a deceased person for a purpose so specified, other than anatomical examination;

(c) the removal from the body of a deceased person, for use for a purpose specified in Schedule 1, of any relevant material of which the body consists or which it contains;

(d) the storage for use for a purpose specified in Part 1 of Schedule 1 of any relevant material which has come from a human body;

(e) the storage for use for a purpose specified in Part 2 of Schedule 1 of any relevant material which has come from the body of a deceased person;

(f) the use for a purpose specified in Part 1 of Schedule 1 of any relevant material which has come from a human body;

(g) the use for a purpose specified in Part 2 of Schedule 1 of any relevant material which has come from the body of a deceased person.

(2) The storage of the body of a deceased person for use for the purpose of anatomical examination shall be lawful if done—

(a) with appropriate consent, and
(b) after the signing of a certificate—
   (i) under section 22(1) of the Births and Deaths Registration Act 1953 (c. 20), or . . .

(3) The use of the body of a deceased person for the purpose of anatomical examination shall be lawful if done—

(a) with appropriate consent, and
(b) after the death of the person has been registered—
   (i) under section 15 of the Births and Deaths Registration Act 1953 . . .

(4) Subsections (1) to (3) do not apply to an activity of a kind mentioned there if it is done in relation to—

(a) a body to which subsection (5) applies, or
(b) relevant material to which subsection (6) applies.

(5) This subsection applies to a body if—

(a) it has been imported, or
(b) it is the body of a person who died before the day on which this section comes into force and at least one hundred years have elapsed since the date of the person's death.

(6) This subsection applies to relevant material if—

(a) it has been imported,
(b) it has come from a body which has been imported, or
(c) it is material which has come from the body of a person who died before the day on which this section comes into force and at least one hundred years have elapsed since the date of the person's death.

. . .
(11) The Secretary of State may by order—

(a) vary or omit any of the purposes specified in Part 1 or 2 of Schedule 1, or
(b) add to the purposes specified in Part 1 or 2 of that Schedule.

(12) Nothing in this section applies to—

(a) the use of relevant material in connection with a device to which Directive 98/79/EC of the European Parliament and of the Council on in vitro diagnostic medical devices applies, where the use falls within the Directive, or
(b) the storage of relevant material for use falling within paragraph (a).

(13) In this section, the references to a body or material which has been imported do not include a body or material which has been imported after having been exported with a view to its subsequently being re-imported.

NOTES:

1. The Act regulates the use of "relevant material". This is defined in s.53 as being any material consisting of, or including, human cells, with the exception of gametes, embryos outside the body (as defined in, and separately regulated by, the Human Fertilisation and Embryology Act 1990), and hair and nail from a living person (called "discardables" in the Parliamentary debates). This is considerably broader than the Human Organs Transplant Act 1989 or the Human Tissue Act 1961. It accords more closely with the recommendation in the Bristol Interim Inquiry report of the use of the term "human material".

2. The Act excludes human cell lines. Section 54(7) excludes material created outside the human body. This exception, it has been argued, is inconsistent with the policy approach across the legislation. It has been suggested that "The longevity of cell lines and the public controversy regarding the commercialisation of certain cell lines is an obvious indication that they warrant as much protection as other cells. It is arguable that this exemption was actually the result of a disproportionate focus on industry interests" (see further K. Liddell and A. Hall, "The Future Regulation of Human Tissue" (2005) 13 *Medical Law Review* 170 at p.202.)

3. The Human Tissue Act Code of Practice on Consent (2006) makes specific provision for foetal tissue.

> "66. The law does not distinguish between fetal tissue and other tissue from the living—fetal tissue is regarded as the mother's tissue. However, because of the sensitivity attached to this subject, consent should be obtained for the examination of fetal tissue and for its use for all scheduled purposes, regardless of gestational age. REC approval is always required for the use of fetal tissue and the products of conception use in research."

See further Chapter 10.

4. The Act excludes medical devices regulated under the EU Directive 98/79 (s.1(12)).

5. In contrast to the previous law, the law is "consent-based". The legislation is rooted in "appropriate consent" but that term is left undefined and the legislation leaves much of the detail of appropriate consent to be subsequently resolved. Schedule 1 sets out those things for which consent is required. They are listed as being:

"PURPOSES REQUIRING CONSENT: GENERAL
Anatomical examination.

Determining the cause of death.

Establishing after a person's death the efficacy of any drug or other treatment administered to him.

Obtaining scientific or medical information about a living or deceased person which may be relevant to any other person (including a future person).

Public display.

Research in connection with disorders, or the functioning, of the human body.

Transplantation.

PURPOSES REQUIRING CONSENT: DECEASED PERSONS
Clinical audit.
Education or training relating to human health.
Performance assessment.
Public health monitoring.
Quality assurance."

6. As can be seen the Act covers use of human material for a very wide range of purposes, teaching, research, clinical and administrative. However, there are broader exceptions to the need for consent in the case of the living person. Some of these, such as clinical audit and performance monitoring, can be seen as legacies of the Bristol Inquiry into the infant mortality at the cardiac paediatric unit at Bristol Royal Infirmary. (See K. Liddell and A. Hall, "The Future Regulation of Human Tissue" (2005) 13 *Medical Law Review* 170 at p.195.) Public health monitoring for the purposes of ascertaining disease prevelance, spread and pattern is again seen as an exception in the general public interest.

7. The Act does not deal with the issue of when consent is required in order to bury a corpse (see Liddell and Hall, *op. cit.* at p.182).

Further guidance on the process of consent has now been given in the Human Tissue Act Code of Practice which was produced by the Human Tissue Authority in 2006.

The form of consent

Human Tissue Authority Code of Practice on Consent (Code 1, July 2006)

Form of consent

90. The guidance in the code is based on these key principles:

- as a first step, a willingness to discuss the question of consent should be established
- full information about the consent process should be provided where possible and in a variety of formats
- consent must be based on an understanding of what the procedure involves
- consent need not always be given in writing to be appropriate and informed
- consent should be generic i.e. consent should be obtained for all scheduled purposes where appropriate.

91. The validity of the consent does not depend on the form in which it is given except for anatomical examination and public display. The information required and the manner in which consent is taken and recorded can vary depending on the particular circumstances.

92. Seeking consent is a process which involves listening, discussing, and questioning so as to arrive at a shared understanding—a signed form is not necessarily an indication that such an understanding has been reached. For consent to be valid it must be given voluntarily, by an appropriately informed person who has the capacity to agree to the activity in question. If these elements have not been satisfied, a signature on a form will not make the consent valid.

93. The Act requires that consent must be in writing for anatomical examination and public display, but not for other scheduled purposes. Nevertheless, it is good practice to obtain written consent for significant procedures such as post mortem or organ donation.

94. Consent may be expressed verbally or non-verbally. An example of non-verbal consent would be where a patient, after receiving appropriate information, holds out an arm for blood to be taken.

95. When consent is obtained for future storage or use of samples, but the consent itself is not in writing, an appropriate note should be kept of the fact that consent has been given, and for what purpose(s). This could be entered in the patient record, the laboratory records, or both.

96. The process of seeking, gaining and recording consent should be appropriate and proportionate to the type of procedure for which it is being obtained, the sample required and its proposed use. Those involved in seeking consent should receive training and support in the implications and essential requirements of taking consent.

. . .

Multiple consents (e.g., post mortem examination/research)

101. When someone has died, it may be appropriate to seek consent for more than one of the scheduled purposes. For example, if a post mortem examination is to be carried out, some tissue samples could also usefully be taken for research purposes. In this case, it would be appropriate to seek the relevant consent to both activities.

102. Equally, if consent has been given to the use of tissue or organs post mortem for transplantation, it may be helpful to seek consent for storage and use for research purposes. In such cases, the necessary consents should ideally be sought in a single consent process and, where possible, on a single consent form.

103. In the case of post mortem tissue, all storage and use requires consent including all storage and use for scheduled purposes.

NOTES:

1. Further guidance in the form of model consent forms is to be given by the Human Tissue Authority.

The scope of consent

Human Tissue Authority Code of Practice on Consent (Code 1, July 2006)

Nature and duration of consent

104. When a person gives valid consent to an intervention, that consent usually remains valid unless the patient withdraws it.

105. Consent can be:

- general, i.e. if someone consents to the use of tissue for research, it need not be limited to a particular project
- specific, i.e. a patient limits their consent—a sample can only be used for research into a particular condition
- both general and specific, i.e. a general consent subject to specific exceptions.

106. When seeking consent, clinicians should ensure that it is appropriate to the intended purposes, and that the person understands this.

NOTES:

1. Further discussion of particular issues relating to consent in the context of live organ transplantation are discussed below at p.1143.
2. Whether consent is general (generic) or specific is an issue which is of considerable practical importance to researchers who intend to store and use materials in genetic databases over, for example, 10–20 years for a range of research purposes. If consent is specific for a particular use, this would mean that researchers would have to return to the person who had provided the material and gain fresh consent from them for the use of the material, perhaps several years on from when the original permission was given. The person who had given consent may be difficult to trace at that point and this may also give rise to costs. Generic consent gives the individual the option to make the decision at the start. However, some have argued that unduly generic consent can negate autonomous decision-making. Individuals may not fully appreciate the range of uses to which material may be put or indeed over time new potential research uses may be developed which could not have been foreseen at the start. There is also the possibility that individuals may have certain particular religious and cultural objections to such use (see further, for example, J.V. McHale, "Regulating Genetic Databases: Some Legal and Ethical Issues" (2004) 11(1) *Medical Law Review* 70).

QUESTIONS:

1. Is a consent-based approach legitimate in a situation in which there is a grave shortage of organs for transplantation? See further the discussion of alternatives to a consent-based approach, including the introduction of opt-out legislation in relation to organ transplantation at p.1164 below.
2. Is consent a necessary or sufficient criterion for the use of human material in the context of scientific research? See further K. Liddell and A. Hall, "The Future of Human Tissue" (2005) 13 *Medical Law Review* 170 at pp.197–201; and G. Laurie, *Genetic Privacy*, Cambridge: CUP, 2002; O. O'Neil, "Some Limits of Informed Consent" (2003) 29 *Journal of Medical Ethics*.
3. Instead of taking a consent-based approach, should the legislation have proceeded from a "property" perspective? See the discussion of the applicability of a property perspective prior to the 2004 Act in J.K. Mason and G. Laurie, "Consent or Property? Dealing with the Body and its Parts in the Shadow of Bristol and Alder Hey" (2001) *Modern Law Review* 710.
4. By consenting to the use of their material for research purposes, is it the case that individuals are "gifting" the material to researchers? (See further R. Tutton, "Person, Property and Gift: Exploring Languages of Tissue

Donation to Biomedical Researchers" in R. Tutton and O. Corrigan (eds), *Genetic Databases: Socio-Ethical Issues in the Collection and Use of DNA*, London: Routledge, 2004.)

Withdrawal of consent

Human Tissue Act Code of Practice on Consent (2006)

107. A competent person is entitled to withdraw consent at any time. However, if samples have already been used for a purpose such as research, the withdrawal of consent to any further use does not mean all existing information has to be withdrawn from the research project. Nevertheless, as set out in paragraph 29, it is generally good practice to meet the wishes of patients regarding the use to which their samples are put.

108. If someone withdraws consent to the storage or use of tissue for scheduled purposes such as research, this does not necessarily mean that the sample or samples have to be removed or destroyed. If samples from a living person are being stored for the purpose of maintaining a diagnostic record, or for other purposes such as audit or quality control, consent is not required.

109. But, if consent to the storage or use of post mortem samples by whoever originally consented to their storage or use is withdrawn, this must be respected for any samples that are still held. Clinicians should discuss with the person concerned how the samples should be returned to them or disposed of, and tell him/her about any samples that may have already been used or disposed of.

NOTE:

1. This provision of the Code of Practice has the effect of giving considerable discretion to the researchers in determining what constitutes withdrawal in practice. It is submitted that it would be advisable from the outset for researchers to state clearly to research subjects the circumstances in which consent may be withdrawn.

Should consent be conditional?

Considerable controversy arose in relation to the old law in the context of the Human Tissue Act 1961 regarding the donation of material subject to racially discriminatory conditions. In one incident, the family stated that they would only agree to organs being removed for subsequent use in transplantation if this was to a white recipient. This was considered in a Department of Health report on conditional organ donation which was published in 2001 (*Department of Health Investigation into Conditional Organ Donation* London: Department of Health, 2000). It was suggested that this may be in breach of the Race Relations Act 1976 (s.20(1) and s.31(1)). The report recommended that organs must not be accepted if the donor or family wish to attach conditions about the recipients. This view has been criticised. Wilkinson has argued that there is a distinction between attaching a condition to an offer and accepting that condition (T.M. Wilkinson, "What's not Wrong with Conditional Organ Donation?" (2003) 29 *Journal of Medical Ethics* 163.) He suggests that while there may indeed be unacceptable conditions, that does not mean that these should be accepted. He also suggests that some conditions such as a requirement that an organ is donated to a relative may indeed be seen as morally acceptable. While the DOH report was strongly condemnatory of the existing position, the law in this area has not been altered and much will depend upon the ultimate proposals for law reform in this area considered later. The new legislation is silent on the issue of conditional donation.

(ii) Who is Able to Give Consent?

Consent and children

Human Tissue Act 2004, s.2

"Appropriate consent": children

2.—(1) This section makes provision for the interpretation of "appropriate consent" in section 1 in relation to an activity involving the body, or material from the body, of a person who is a child or has died a child ("the child concerned").

(2) Subject to subsection (3), where the child concerned is alive, "appropriate consent" means his consent.

(3) Where—

(a) the child concerned is alive,
(b) neither a decision of his to consent to the activity, nor a decision of his not to consent to it, is in force, and
(c) either he is not competent to deal with the issue of consent in relation to the activity or, though he is competent to deal with that issue, he fails to do so,

"appropriate consent" means the consent of a person who has parental responsibility for him.

(4) Where the child concerned has died and the activity is one to which subsection (5) applies, "appropriate consent" means his consent in writing.

(5) This subsection applies to an activity involving storage for use, or use, for the purpose of—

(a) public display, or
(b) where the subject-matter of the activity is not excepted material, anatomical examination.

(6) Consent in writing for the purposes of subsection (4) is only valid if—

(a) it is signed by the child concerned in the presence of at least one witness who attests the signature, or
(b) it is signed at the direction of the child concerned, in his presence and in the presence of at least one witness who attests the signature.

(7) Where the child concerned has died and the activity is not one to which subsection (5) applies, "appropriate consent" means—

(a) if a decision of his to consent to the activity, or a decision of his not to consent to it, was in force immediately before he died, his consent;
(b) if paragraph (a) does not apply—
    (i) the consent of a person who had parental responsibility for him immediately before he died, or
    (ii) where no person had parental responsibility for him immediately before he died, the consent of a person who stood in a qualifying relationship to him at that time.

NOTES:

1. Section 3 is in contrast to the 1961 Act in relation to the deceased, as the 1961 Act did not make a specific reference to children. It means that for the first time children have a statutory right to consent to the use of their material for purposes such as transplantation and research.
2. The section does not define what constitutes "capacity". The Explanatory Notes to the Human Tissue Act 2004 suggest that this will be determined by reference to the common law test in *Gillick* and this is now confirmed in the Human Tissue Authority Code of Practice (2006) set out below.

CONSENT FROM THE LIVING CHILD: GENERAL

Human Tissue Authority Code of Practice on Consent (Code 1, July 2006)

Tissue from the living—children

41. Under the Act a child is defined as being under 18 years old.

42. Children may consent to a proposed medical procedure or the storage and use of their tissue if they are competent to do so. In the *Gillick* case, the court held that a child is considered to be competent to give valid consent to a proposed intervention if they have sufficient intelligence and understanding to enable them fully to understand what is involved . . .

43. A person who has parental responsibility for the child can consent on his/her behalf only if the child has not made a decision and:

- is not competent to do so; or
- chooses not to make that decision, although s/he is competent to do so.

A person who has parental responsibility will usually, but not always, be the child's parent.

44. However, it is good practice to consult the person who has parental responsibility for the child and to involve them in the process of the child making a decision. It is also important to make sure that a child has consented voluntarily and has not been unduly influenced by anyone else. Courts have identified certain important decisions which require court approval where one person with parental responsibility consents against the wishes of another. If there is any dispute between persons with parental responsibility or any doubt as to the child's best interests, the matter should be referred to court for approval.

NOTE:

1. It is likely that this provision will require considerable reconsideration of the consent process in relation to the use of human material from children. Researchers and clinicians will need to ascertain whether the child has capacity to make the decision regarding the use of material themselves or whether this is a decision which should be left to their parents.

CONSENT FROM THE LIVING CHILD: TRANSPLANTATION

Guidance is also given in the Codes of Practice regarding donation of organs and tissue for transplantation by the living child (*Donation of Organs, Tissues and*

Cells for Transplantation, HTA Code, July 2006, paras 27–36). This needs to be seen in conjunction with the requirements of the legislation in relation to transplantation from live donors. The common law provisions concerning consent will still apply (see above at p.1104) and in addition such transplantation procedures will need to have special approval from the Human Tissue Authority (see below at p.1143). The Code of Practice emphasises that donation from children will only be in "extremely rare circumstances" (para.30).

CONSENT FROM THE DECEASED CHILD

Here the Code of Practice (*Donation of Organs, Tissues and Cells for Transplantation*, (HTA Code 2, July 2006) notes that the position of a competent child is no different from that of an adult (see further below). If the child has not made a decision, then it will usually be made by the person in the qualifying relationship. However the Code of Practice does go on to suggest that:

43. Clearly, in any case where a child has given consent to donation, especially if the child has self-registered on the ODR, it is essential to discuss this with someone who has parental responsibility for the child and take their views and wishes into account before deciding how to proceed. In some cases it may also be advisable to discuss with the person who had parental responsibility for the deceased child whether the child was indeed competent to make the decision.

QUESTION:

1. Does this provision suggest that an autonomous decision of the child could be undermined?

Consent and adults

As with children general provision is made for adults to consent to the use of their material for a range of purposes, including research and organ transplantation, in s.3.

Human Tissue Act 2004, s.3

"Appropriate consent": adults

3.—(1) This section makes provision for the interpretation of "appropriate consent" in section 1 in relation to an activity involving the body, or material from the body, of a person who is an adult or has died an adult ("the person concerned").

(2) Where the person concerned is alive, "appropriate consent" means his consent.

(3) Where the person concerned has died and the activity is one to which subsection (4) applies, "appropriate consent" means his consent in writing.

(4) This subsection applies to an activity involving storage for use, or use, for the purpose of—

(a) public display, or
(b) where the subject-matter of the activity is not excepted material, anatomical examination.

(5) Consent in writing for the purposes of subsection (3) is only valid if—

(a) it is signed by the person concerned in the presence of at least one witness who attests the signature,
(b) it is signed at the direction of the person concerned, in his presence and in the presence of at least one witness who attests the signature, or
(c) it is contained in a will of the person concerned made in accordance with the requirements of—
    (i) section 9 of the Wills Act 1837 (c. 26), or
    (ii) Article 5 of the Wills and Administration Proceedings (Northern Ireland) Order 1994 (S.I. 1994/1899 (N.I. 13)).

(6) Where the person concerned has died and the activity is not one to which subsection (4) applies, "appropriate consent" means—

(a) if a decision of his to consent to the activity, or a decision of his not to consent to it, was in force immediately before he died, his consent;
(b) if—
    (i) paragraph (a) does not apply, and
    (ii) he has appointed a person or persons under section 4 to deal after his death with the issue of consent in relation to the activity, consent given under the appointment;
(c) if neither paragraph (a) nor paragraph (b) applies, the consent of a person who stood in a qualifying relationship to him immediately before he died.

(7) Where the person concerned has appointed a person or persons under section 4 to deal after his death with the issue of consent in relation to the activity, the appointment shall be disregarded for the purposes of subsection (6) if no one is able to give consent under it.

(8) If it is not reasonably practicable to communicate with a person appointed under section 4 within the time available if consent in relation to the activity is to be acted on, he shall be treated for the purposes of subsection (7) as not able to give consent under the appointment in relation to it.

NOTES:

1. Again the Act makes reference to the need for consent in relation to live and cadaver donors. Although there were attempts during the passage of the Human Tissue Act to amend it to enable "opt-out" legislation to be introduced in relation to transplantation these were unsuccessful. See further the discussion of "opt-out" legislation at p.1164 below.
2. Where an individual has not made a decision prior to death or appointed a decision-maker under s.4 (discussed below), s.3(6) provides that the decision is referred to a person who falls under the category of "qualifying relationship". This is a much broader category than that contained in the 1961 Act, recognising the changing nature of "family" relationships. Thos persons who are included in the category of qualifying relationships are considered below at p.1134.

One issue under the Human Tissue Act 1961 was that there was concern that relatives' objections were leading to organs not being used, despite the deceased having clearly opted in. In relation to cadavar donation of organs for transplantation under the Human Tissue Act 2004, guidance is given to address this issue.

Human Tissue Authority Code of Practice on Consent (Code 2, 2006)

Donation of Organs, Tissues and Cells for Transplantation

40. If the family or those close to the deceased person object to the donation, for whatever purpose, when the deceased person (or their nominated representative—see below) has explicitly consented, clinicians should seek to discuss the matter sensitively with them. They should be encouraged to accept the deceased person's wishes and it should be made clear that they do not have the legal right to veto or overrule those wishes. There may nevertheless be cases in which donation is inappropriate and each case should be considered individually.

41. If the deceased person's wishes are not known and the deceased has nominated a person to deal with the use of their body after death, then consent can be given by that nominated representative. If the deceased person has not indicated their consent (or refusal) to the removal, storage or use of their tissue for transplantation, nor appointed a nominated representative (or the nomination has been disregarded in accordance with paragraph 49 below), consent can be given by a person who was in a "qualifying relationship" immediately before the death of the deceased person (see paragraph 50 below).

Provision for proxy consent: the nominated representative

A new provision contained in the Human Tissue Act 2004 enables a person to appoint another person to give consent to the use of their material after their death.

Human Tissue Act 2004, s.4

Nominated representatives

4.—(1) An adult may appoint one or more persons to represent him after his death in relation to consent for the purposes of section 1.

(2) An appointment under this section may be general or limited to consent in relation to such one or more activities as may be specified in the appointment.

(3) An appointment under this section may be made orally or in writing.

(4) An oral appointment under this section is only valid if made in the presence of at least two witnesses present at the same time.

(5) A written appointment under this section is only valid if—

(a) it is signed by the person making it in the presence of at least one witness who attests the signature,

(b) it is signed at the direction of the person making it, in his presence and in the presence of at least one witness who attests the signature, or

(c) it is contained in a will of the person making it, being a will which is made in accordance with the requirements of—
 (i) section 9 of the Wills Act 1837 (c. 26), or
 (ii) Article 5 of the Wills and Administration Proceedings (Northern Ireland) Order 1994 (S.I. 1994/1899 (N.I. 13)).

(6) Where a person appoints two or more persons under this section in relation to the same activity, they shall be regarded as appointed to act jointly and severally unless the appointment provides that they are appointed to act jointly.

(7) An appointment under this section may be revoked at any time.

(8) Subsections (3) to (5) apply to the revocation of an appointment under this section as they apply to the making of such an appointment.

(9) A person appointed under this section may at any time renounce his appointment.

(10) A person may not act under an appointment under this section if—

(a) he is not an adult, or
(b) he is of a description prescribed for the purposes of this provision by regulations made by the Secretary of State.

NOTES:

1. Section 4 enables an individual to give a proxy decision-making power to another person. Use of this provision may be particularly appropriate to ensure that a decision is made by a preferred decision-maker such as a close friend rather than family members from whom the individual may have become estranged.
2. Section 3(8) indicates that where permission cannot be obtained from a "nominated person" under s.4 because it is not " reasonably practicable" to contact the nominated person, then they may be treated as not able to give consent. This gives discretion to the clinical practitioner. It remains to be seen whether this will have the effect of resultant uncertainty as to who to approach and when which hampered transplantation practice under the Human Tissue Act 1961.

Tissue and the deceased: consent from the person in the qualifying relationship

As noted above, one of the differences between the Human Tissue Act 1961 and the new Act is that the 2004 Act provides for a much broader category of persons who can give consent in the case of the deceased for the use of material for transplantation or for research.

Human Tissue Act 2004, s.27(4–8)

27.—(4) The qualifying relationships for the purpose of sections 2(7)(b)(ii) and 3(6)(c) should be ranked in the following order—

(a) spouse or partner;
(b) parent or child;
(c) brother or sister;
(d) grandparent or grandchild;
(e) child of a person falling within paragraph (c);
(f) stepfather or stepmother;
(g) half-brother or half-sister;
(h) friend of longstanding.

(5) Relationships in the same paragraph of subsection (4) should be accorded equal ranking.

(6) Consent should be obtained from the person whose relationship to the person concerned is accorded the highest ranking in accordance with subsections (4) and (5).

(7) If the relationship of each of two or more persons to the person concerned is accorded equal highest ranking in accordance with subsections (4) and (5), it is sufficient to obtain the consent of any of them.

(8) In applying the principles set out above, a person's relationship shall be left out of account if—

(a) he does not wish to deal with the issue of consent,
(b) he is not able to deal with that issue, or
(c) having regard to the activity in relation to which consent is sought, it is not reasonably practicable to communicate with him within the time available if consent in relation to the activity is to be acted on.

NOTES:

1. One difficulty may arise if there is a disagreement between those who fall under this category. The legislation appears to make no provision for such dispute resolution. If an individual consents, then it appears that one such consent will be sufficient. Whether this is the case in practice, however, remains to be seen. It may be that health care professionals are unwilling to proceed in the face of objections from family members. (See further discussion in D. Price, "The Human Tissue Act 2004" (2005) 68 *Modern Law Review* 798.)
2. As the section notes, a person may be left out of consideration in a number of situations, including those where it is not reasonably practical to communicate with them (s.27(8)).

Adults lacking mental capacity

At common law the position concerning adults lacking mental capacity was unclear and there was no specific statutory regulation of the position concerning adults lacking mental capacity, whether for transplantation or for research. This situation is now clarified in the Human Tissue Act 2004 and consequent statutory instruments and guidance.

Human Tissue Act 2004, s.6

Activities involving material from adults who lack capacity to consent

6. Where—

(a) an activity of a kind mentioned in section 1(1)(d) or (f) involves material from the body of a person who—
    (i) is an adult, and
    (ii) lacks capacity to consent to the activity, and
(b) neither a decision of his to consent to the activity, nor a decision of his not to consent to it, is in force, there shall for the purposes of this Part be deemed to be consent of his to the activity if it is done in circumstances of a kind specified by regulations made by the Secretary of State.

NOTES:

1. As noted above at p.1105, the common law the position on this issue was fundamentally unclear. While there was judicial confirmation that an adult

lacking capacity could act as a bone marrow donor for a close relative, the precise legitimacy of such an adult acting as a donor more generally was questionable. (See further p.1105 above, *Re Y* (1996) F.L.R. 791 and A. Grubb, "Adult Incompetent: Legality of Non-Therapeutic Procedure" (1996) 4 *Medical Law Review* 204.

2. Originally, no provision was made for adults lacking capacity in the legislation, as it was envisaged that this would be dealt with in the Mental Capacity Act. However, as this legislation was not due to come into force until a considerable period of time after the Human Tissue Bill, an amendment was made to the Human Tissue Bill during its passage. (See further K. Liddell and A. Hall, "The Future Regulation of Human Tissue" (2005) 13 *Medical Law Review* 170 at pp.193–194). Nonetheless, the position concerning adults lacking mental capacity has been still largely left to regulations.

Human Tissue Authority Code of Practice on Consent (Code 1, 2006)

Tissue from the living—adults who lack capacity

35. Adults are deemed competent to consent if they can:

- understand the nature and purpose of the proposed procedure
- understand and retain information relevant to the decision
- weigh the necessary information to arrive at a choice.

36. The Act does not specify the criteria for considering whether an adult has capacity. This should be approached on the same basis as considerations of competency to consent to medical procedures. (While the basis for considering whether an adult has capacity will be the same, the conclusion could differ, as some people might have the capacity to make some decisions, but not others). Guidance is available from the Department of Health's Reference guide to consent for examination and treatment. In addition, regard must be had to the provisions of the Mental Capacity Act 2005 (MCA 2005). The MCA 2005, which comes into force in 2007, governs decision-making on behalf of adults who lack capacity including adults who lose mental capacity during their lifetime and those with an incapacitating condition from birth. MCA 2005 defines persons who lack capacity and contains a set of key principles and a checklist to be used in ascertaining best interests.

37. It should be assumed that a person is competent to make a decision unless there is reason to believe otherwise. Individuals affected by trauma, illness, shock, etc., are sometimes temporarily unable to make a decision. Some adults may be competent to make decisions about some matters, but not others. Care should be taken to ensure that patients are given every opportunity, and support where needed, to understand what is proposed.

38. The ability of adults with learning difficulties, or with limited capacity, to understand should not be underestimated. Where appropriate, someone who knows the individual well, such as a family member or carer, should be consulted as he/she may be able to advise or assist with communication.

39. Storage or use of tissue from adults who lack capacity, other than in accordance with the regulations under the HT Act, is unlawful and could be an offence under the HT Act.

The Government also published regulations consequent upon these provisions in summer 2006.

The Human Tissue Act 2004 (Persons who Lack Capacity to Consent and Transplants) Regulations 2006 (SI 2006/1659)

PERSONS WHO LACK CAPACITY TO CONSENT

Deemed consent to storage and use of relevant material: England and Wales

3.—(1) This regulation applies in any case falling within paragraphs (a) and (b) of section 6 of the Act (storage and use involving material from adults who lack capacity to consent).

(2) An adult ("P") who lacks capacity to consent to an activity of a kind mentioned in section 1(1)(d) or (f) of the Act (storage or use of material for purposes specified in Schedule 1) which involves material from P's body, is deemed to have consented to the activity where—

(a) the activity is done for a purpose specified in paragraph 4 or 7 of Part 1 of Schedule 1 to the Act (the purposes of obtaining information relevant to another person and of transplantation) by a person who is acting in what he reasonably believes to be P's best interests;

(b) the activity is done for the purpose of a clinical trial which is authorised and conducted in accordance with the clinical trials regulations;

(c) the activity is done on or after the relevant commencement date for the purpose of intrusive research which is carried out in accordance with the requirements of section 30(1)(a) and (b) of the Mental Capacity Act 2005 (approval by appropriate body and compliance with sections 32 and 33 of that Act);

(d) the activity is done on or after the relevant commencement date for the purpose of intrusive research—

    (i) section 34 of the Mental Capacity Act 2005 (loss of capacity during research project) applies in relation to that research, and

    (ii) the activity is carried out in accordance with regulations made under section 34(2) of that Act; or

(e) the activity is done before the relevant commencement date for the purpose of research which, before that date, is ethically approved within the meaning of regulation 8.

    . . .

Ethical approval for the purposes of regulations 3 to 6

8.—(1) Research is ethically approved within the meaning of this regulation if approval is given by a research ethics authority in the circumstances specified in paragraph (2).

(2) The circumstances are that—

(a) the research is in connection with disorders, or the functioning, of the human body,

(b) there are reasonable grounds for believing that research of comparable effectiveness cannot be carried out if the research has to be confined to, or relate only to, persons who have capacity to consent to taking part in it, and

(c) there are reasonable grounds for believing that research of comparable effectiveness cannot be carried out in circumstances such that the person carrying out the research is not in possession, and not likely to come into possession, of information from which the person from whose body the defined material has come can be identified.

(3) "Defined material"—

(a) in relation to ethical approval for the purposes of regulations 3(2)(e) and 4(2)(c), means the relevant material involved in an activity of a kind mentioned in section 1(1)(d) or (f) of the Act, . . .

(4) "Research ethics authority" has the meaning given by regulation 2 of the Human Tissue Act 2004 (Ethical Approval, Exceptions from Licensing and Supply of Information about Transplants) Regulations 2006.

NOTES:

1. Like many of the provisions of the Human Tissue Act 2004, this provision has application across a number of areas. It applies in relation to storage and use of material in the context of clinical procedures such as transplantation and also for research.

2. The regulations make use of the "best interests" test in relation to transplantation and obtaining information regarding a third party. At present this will be the common law test set out in *Re F* [1990] 2 A.C. 1 and this will then be affected by the Mental Capacity Act 2005 when this comes into force in 2007 (see further Chapter 5 above).

3. Specific provision is also made under the regulations for the use of tissue from adults lacking mental capacity in the context of research. As we noted in our consideration of research and the adult lacking capacity in Chapter 9 above, the law in this area needs to be seen in relation to the provisions of the Mental Capacity Act 2005 and the Medicines for Human Use (Clinical Trials) Regulations 2004 which concern the conduct of drug trials (see further Chapter 9 at p.703). These regulations also cover the use of material for research purposes when the Mental Capacity Act 2005 comes into force in 2007. It also applies in relation to use of human material from adults lacking mental capacity where this is required for research regulated by the Clinical Trials Directive and consequent Medicines for Human Use (Clinical Trials) Regulations 2004.

4. The Regulations also make specific provision to enable research to be conducted before the Mental Capacity Act 2005 comes into force (reg.3(2)(e) and 8).

5. Additional provision is also made in the statutory instrument in relation to the analysis of DNA which comes from a person who lacks mental capacity (reg.5).

QUESTION:

1. Should material be obtained from adults lacking mental capacity be used in treatment or research?

(iii) Exceptions to the Consent Principle

The consent principle is not absolute and not situations require the use of human material to be subject to consent. As noted at pp.1124–1125 above there is a difference in the approach taken in relation to use of material from the deceased and the living in schedule 1 as to when consent is required. In addition there are specific exceptions provided for in the legislation in sections 1(7–9) in relation to the use of material for research purposes where anonymised and approved by a research ethics committee and in section 7 in situations in which the person cannot be traced . In addition the legislation also enables existing holding of human material created prior to the legislation coming into force to be retained in s.10.

Use of anonymised material for research purposes

Human Tissue Act 2004, s.1(7–10)

1.—(7) Subsection (1)(d) does not apply to the storage of relevant material for use for the purpose of research in connection with disorders, or the functioning, of the human body if—

(a) the material has come from the body of a living person, and
(b) the research falls within subsection (9).

(8) Subsection (1)(f) does not apply to the use of relevant material for the purpose of research in connection with disorders, or the functioning, of the human body if—

(a) the material has come from the body of a living person, and
(b) the research falls within subsection (9).

(9) Research falls within this subsection if—

(a) it is ethically approved in accordance with regulations made by the Secretary of State, and
(b) it is to be, or is, carried out in circumstances such that the person carrying it out is not in possession, and not likely to come into possession, of information from which the person from whose body the material has come can be identified.

(10) The following activities shall be lawful—

(a) the storage for use for a purpose specified in Part 2 of Schedule 1 of any relevant material which has come from the body of a living person;
(b) the use for such a purpose of any relevant material which has come from the body of a living person;
(c) an activity in relation to which subsection (4), (7) or (8) has effect.

NOTES:

1. Section 1(7) was introduced as an amendment to the legislation during its passage through Parliament in response to concerns expressed by the scientific community as to the consequences of requiring explicit consent for the use of "spare" material left over following diagnostic procedures or tissue left after operation. It was argued that this would be practically impossible due to the costs of such a process. For discussion of these issues in relation to the passage of the legislation see further K. Liddell, "The Future Regulation of Human Tissue" (2005) 13 *Medical Law Review* 170 at pp.194–201 and for critical commentary see J.V. McHale, "The Human

Tissue Act 2004: Innovative Legislation, Missed Opportunity or Fundamentally Flawed " [2005] 26 *Liverpool Law Review* 169). The provision itself is dependent upon regulations being introduced by the Secretary of State in relation to the ethical review of the proposed use. The use of material which has been anonymised may be seen as not infringing the individual's privacy rights and following the approach taken by the Court of Appeal in *Source Informatics* ([2001] QB 424 and see Chapter 9 at p.579) which held that the use of anonymised patient prescribing data without consent did not constitute an invasion of privacy; nonetheless, question marks remain as to the legitimacy of the decision of the court in that case and to attempt to extrapolate this in relation to the use of material may be questionable. In addition it is not envisaged that this material would be totally anonymised simply that the prospect of identification would be reduced.

2. The Human Tissue Act 2004 (Ethical Approval, Exceptions from Licensing and Supply of Information about Transplants) Regulations 2006 (SI 2006/1260) now provide that

> "2. Research is ethically approved for the purposes of section 1(9)(a) and paragraph 10(b) of Schedule 4 to the Act where it is approved by a research ethics authority."

Powers to sanction use of material where individuals cannot be traced

Human Tissue Act 2004, s.7

Powers to dispense with need for consent

7.—(1) If the Authority is satisfied—

(a) that relevant material has come from the body of a living person,
(b) that it is not reasonably possible to trace the person from whose body the material has come ("the donor"),
(c) that it is desirable in the interests of another person (including a future person) that the material be used for the purpose of obtaining scientific or medical information about the donor, and
(d) that there is no reason to believe—
  (i) that the donor has died,
  (ii) that a decision of the donor to refuse to consent to the use of the material for that purpose is in force, or
  (iii) that the donor lacks capacity to consent to the use of the material for that purpose,
it may direct that subsection (3) apply to the material for the benefit of the other person.

(2) If the Authority is satisfied—

(a) that relevant material has come from the body of a living person,
(b) that it is desirable in the interests of another person (including a future person) that the material be used for the purpose of obtaining scientific or medical information about the person from whose body the material has come ("the donor"),
(c) that reasonable efforts have been made to get the donor to decide whether to consent to the use of the material for that purpose,

(d) that there is no reason to believe—
    (i) that the donor has died,
    (ii) that a decision of the donor to refuse to consent to the use of the material for that purpose is in force, or
    (iii) that the donor lacks capacity to consent to the use of the material for that purpose, and
(e) that the donor has been given notice of the application for the exercise of the power conferred by this subsection,

it may direct that subsection (3) apply to the material for the benefit of the other person.

(3) Where material is the subject of a direction under subsection (1) or (2), there shall for the purposes of this Part be deemed to be consent of the donor to the use of the material for the purpose of obtaining scientific or medical information about him which may be relevant to the person for whose benefit the direction is given.

(4) The Secretary of State may by regulations enable the High Court, in such circumstances as the regulations may provide, to make an order deeming there for the purposes of this Part to be appropriate consent to an activity consisting of—

(a) the storage of the body of a deceased person for use for the purpose of research in connection with disorders, or the functioning, of the human body,
(b) the use of the body of a deceased person for that purpose,
(c) the removal from the body of a deceased person, for use for that purpose, of any relevant material of which the body consists or which it contains,
(d) the storage for use for that purpose of any relevant material which has come from a human body, or
(e) the use for that purpose of any relevant material which has come from a human body.

Existing holdings

Human Tissue Act 2004, s.9

Existing holdings

9.—(1) In its application to the following activities, section 1(1) shall have effect with the omission of the words "if done with appropriate consent"—

(a) the storage of an existing holding for use for a purpose specified in Schedule 1;
(b) the use of an existing holding for a purpose so specified.

(2) Subsection (1) does not apply where the existing holding is a body, or separated part of a body, in relation to which section 10(3) or (5) has effect.

(3) Section 5(1) and (2) shall have effect as if the activities mentioned in subsection (1) were not activities to which section 1(1) applies.

(4) In this section, "existing holding" means—

(a) the body of a deceased person, or
(b) relevant material which has come from a human body,

held, immediately before the day on which section 1(1) comes into force, for use for a purpose specified in Schedule 1.

NOTE:

1. Section 9 addresses concerns regarding the legality of existing holdings of human material such as in genetic databases and their future. In the period

up until the Act came into force, there is some evidence that researchers were destroying existing holdings of human material because of their concerns regarding the legality of continued retention.

Further guidance in relation to this provision is provided in the Human Tissue Authority Code of Practice on Consent.

Human Tissue Authority Code of Practice on Consent (Code 1, 2006)

Existing Holdings

111. It is lawful to store and use for scheduled purposes, without consent, human tissue that is already held in storage for a scheduled purpose on 1 September 2006. However, where the views of the deceased person or of their relatives or friends are known, those views must be respected.

112. Collections of organs and tissue can make an important contribution to training, education, audit and public health monitoring. Computerised images and photographs are not always an adequate substitute. Some of these collections are irreplaceable and of national or international importance. The fact that there is no evidence of consent to their storage and use should not be a reason for destroying existing collections. Samples may be retained and used for these purposes without consent.

113. If the family of a deceased person asks for the return or disposal of tissue or organs, their request should be complied with unless the samples are retained under the authority of a coroner, or in connection with criminal justice purposes.

(iv) Coroners

As with the Human Tissue Act 1961, the 2004 Act is subject to the separate powers of the coroners to investigate unexpected or suspicious deaths.

Human Tissue Act 1961, s.11

Coroners

11.—(1) Nothing in this Part applies to anything done for purposes of functions of a coroner or under the authority of a coroner.

(2) Where a person knows, or has reason to believe, that—

(a) the body of a deceased person, or
(b) relevant material which has come from the body of a deceased person,

is, or may be, required for purposes of functions of a coroner, he shall not act on authority under section 1 in relation to the body, or material, except with the consent of the coroner.

NOTE:

1. The operation of the coroner system is currently under review following the Shipman inquiry. It should be noted that, as Liddell and Hall comment, coroners acting without authority may commit an offence under s.5(4) of the Act. In addition, coroners may need to have regard to codes which the Human Tissue Authority prepare. (See further K. Liddell and A. Hall, "The

Future Regulation of Human Tissue" (2005) 13 *Medical Law Review* 170 at p.209.)

(v) Transplantation from Living Donors

Like the earlier Human Organ Transplants Act 1989, the Human Tissue Act 2004 makes specific provision for the regulation of transplantation from living organ donors.

Human Tissue Act 2004, s.33

Restriction on transplants involving a live donor

33.—(1) Subject to subsections (3) and (5), a person commits an offence if—

(a) he removes any transplantable material from the body of a living person intending that the material be used for the purpose of transplantation, and
(b) when he removes the material, he knows, or might reasonably be expected to know, that the person from whose body he removes the material is alive.

(2) Subject to subsections (3) and (5), a person commits an offence if—

(a) he uses for the purpose of transplantation any transplantable material which has come from the body of a living person, and
(b) when he does so, he knows, or might reasonably be expected to know, that the transplantable material has come from the body of a living person.

(3) The Secretary of State may by regulations provide that subsection (1) or (2) shall not apply in a case where—

(a) the Authority is satisfied—
   (i) that no reward has been or is to be given in contravention of section 32, and
   (ii) that such other conditions as are specified in the regulations are satisfied, and
(b) such other requirements as are specified in the regulations are complied with.

(4) Regulations under subsection (3) shall include provision for decisions of the Authority in relation to matters which fall to be decided by it under the regulations to be subject, in such circumstances as the regulations may provide, to reconsideration in accordance with such procedure as the regulations may provide.

(5) Where under subsection (3) an exception from subsection (1) or (2) is in force, a person does not commit an offence under that subsection if he reasonably believes that the exception applies.

(6) A person guilty of an offence under this section is liable on summary conviction—

(a) to imprisonment for a term not exceeding 51 weeks, or
(b) to a fine not exceeding level 5 on the standard scale, or
(c) to both.

(7) In this section—

"reward" has the same meaning as in section 32;
"transplantable material" means material of a description specified by regulations made by the Secretary of State.

NOTES:

1. As with the Human Organ Transplants Act 1989, transplants between living donors is to be the subject of specific legal provisions. The 1989 Act, while not banning organ transplantation from genetically unrelated donors, did require that such transplantation should be subject to specific approval by a body established under that Act, the Unrelated Live Organ Transplants Regulatory Authority. In contrast, donation from genetically related donors was not subject to approval from ULTRA. One major change under the Human Tissue Act 2004 is that all donations are to be subject to the approval of the new regulatory body, the Human Tissue Authority. This is discussed further below at p.1156.
2. Section 34 also makes provision for information regarding transplant procedures to be submitted to the Human Tissue Authority.

Further guidance as to what constitutes the meaning of transplantable material for the purposes of s.33 of the Act is now given in the regulations.

The Human Tissue Act 2004 (Persons who Lack Capacity to Consent and Transplants) Regulations 2006 (SI 2006/1659)

10.—(1) Subject to paragraphs (2) and (3), for the purposes of section 33 of the Act (restriction on transplants involving a live donor), "transplantable material" means—

(a) an organ, or part of an organ if it is to be used for the same purpose as the entire organ in the human body,
(b) bone marrow, and
(c) peripheral blood stem cells,

where that material is removed from the body of a living person with the intention that it be transplanted into another person.

(2) The material referred to in paragraph (1)(a) is not transplantable material for the purposes of section 33 of the Act in a case where the primary purpose of removal of the material is the medical treatment of the person from whose body the material is removed.

(3) The material referred to in paragraph (1)(b) and (c) is transplantable material for the purposes of section 33 of the Act only in a case where the person from whose body the material is removed is—

(a) an adult who lacks the capacity, or
(b) a child who is not competent,

to consent to removal of the transplantable material.

Procedure for transplantation concerning live donors

Further guidance as to the procedure to be adopted in relation to live donors is now set out in the 2006 regulations.

The Human Tissue Act 2004 (Persons who Lack Capacity to Consent and Transplants) Regulations 2006 (SI 2006/1659)

Cases in which restriction on transplants involving a live donor is disapplied

11.—(1) Section 33(1) and (2) of the Act (offences relating to transplants involving a live donor) shall not apply in any case involving transplantable material from the body of a living person ("the donor") if the requirements of paragraphs (2) to (6) are met.

(2) A registered medical practitioner who has clinical responsibility for the donor must have caused the matter to be referred to the Authority.

(3) The Authority must be satisfied that—

(a) no reward has been or is to be given in contravention of section 32 of the Act (prohibition of commercial dealings in human material for transplantation), and

(b) when the transplantable material is removed—
   (i) consent for its removal for the purpose of transplantation has been given, or
   (ii) its removal for that purpose is otherwise lawful.

(4) The Authority must take the report referred to in paragraph (6) into account in making its decision under paragraph (3).

(5) The Authority shall give notice of its decision under paragraph (3) to—

(a) the donor of the transplantable material or any person acting on his behalf,

(b) the person to whom it is proposed to transplant the transplantable material ("the recipient") or any person acting on his behalf, and

(c) the registered medical practitioner who caused the matter to be referred to the Authority under paragraph (2).

(6) Subject to paragraph (7), one or more qualified persons must have conducted separate interviews with each of the following—

(a) the donor,

(b) if different from the donor, the person giving consent, and

(c) the recipient,

and reported to the Authority on the matters specified in paragraphs (8) and (9).

(7) Paragraph (6) does not apply in any case where the removal of the transplantable material for the purpose of transplantation is authorised by an order made in any legal proceedings before a court.

(8) The matters that must be covered in the report of each interview under paragraph (6) are—

(a) any evidence of duress or coercion affecting the decision to give consent,

(b) any evidence of an offer of a reward, and

(c) any difficulties of communication with the person interviewed and an explanation of how those difficulties were overcome.

(9) The following matters must be covered in the report of the interview with the donor and, where relevant, the other person giving consent—

(a) the information given to the person interviewed as to the nature of the medical procedure for, and the risk involved in, the removal of the transplantable material,

(b) the full name of the person who gave that information and his qualification to give it, and

(c) the capacity of the person interviewed to understand—

(i) the nature of the medical procedure and the risk involved, and

(ii) that the consent may be withdrawn at any time before the removal of the transplantable material.

(10) A person shall be taken to be qualified to conduct an interview under paragraph (6) if—

(a) he appears to the Authority to be suitably qualified to conduct the interview,

(b) he does not have any connection with any of the persons to be interviewed, or with a person who stands in a qualifying relationship to any of those persons, which the Authority considers to be of a kind that might raise doubts about his ability to act impartially, and

(c) in the case of an interview with the donor or other person giving consent, he is not the person who gave the information referred to in paragraph (9)(a).

Decisions of the Authority: procedure for certain cases

12.—(1) In any case to which paragraph (2), (3) or (4) applies, the Authority's decision as to the matters specified in regulation 11(3) shall be made by a panel of no fewer than 3 members of the Authority.

(2) A case falls within this paragraph if—

(a) the donor of the transplantable material is a child, and

(b) the material is an organ or part of an organ if it is to be used for the same purpose as an entire organ in the human body.

(3) A case falls within this paragraph if—

(a) the donor of the transplantable material is an adult who lacks capacity to consent to removal of the material, and

(b) the material is an organ or part of an organ if it is to be used for the same purpose as an entire organ in the human body.

(4) A case falls within this paragraph if—

(a) the donor of the transplantable material is an adult who has capacity to consent to removal of the material, and

(b) the case involves—

(i) paired donations,

(ii) pooled donations, or

(iii) a non-directed altruistic donation.

(5) In this regulation—

"non-directed altruistic donation" means the removal (in circumstances not amounting to a paired or pooled donation) of transplantable material from a donor for transplant to a person who is not genetically related to the donor or known to him;

"paired donations" means an arrangement under which—

(a) transplantable material is removed from a donor ("D") for transplant to a person who is not genetically related or known to D, and

(b) transplantable material is removed from another person for transplant to a person who is genetically related or known to D; and

"pooled donations" means a series of paired donations of transplantable material, each of which is linked to another in the same series (for example, transplantable material from D is transplanted to the wife of another person ("E"), transplantable material from

E is transplanted to the partner of a third person ("F") and transplantable material from F is transplanted to D's son).

Right to reconsideration of Authority's decision

13.—(1) The Authority may reconsider any decision made by it under regulation 11(3) if it is satisfied that—

(a)   any information given for the purpose of the decision was in any material respect false or misleading, or
(b)   there has been any material change of circumstances since the decision was made.

(2) A specified person may in any case require the Authority to reconsider any decision made by it under regulation 11(3).
(3) "Specified persons", in relation to such a decision, are—

(a)   the donor of the transplantable material or any person acting on his behalf,
(b)   the recipient of the material or any person acting on his behalf, and
(c)   the registered medical practitioner who caused the matter to be referred to the Authority under regulation 11(2).

(4) The right under paragraph (2) is exercisable by giving to the Authority, in such manner as it may direct, notice of exercise of the right.
(5) A notice under paragraph (4) shall contain or be accompanied by such other information as the Authority may reasonably require.
(6) On receipt of the information required by paragraph (5), the Authority shall provide to the person requiring the reconsideration—

(a)   a copy of each report made under regulation 11(6) of the interviews that were conducted in the case, and
(b)   a statement of the Authority's reasons for its decision.

(7) Paragraphs (1) to (6) do not apply to a decision made by the Authority on reconsideration in pursuance of a notice under this regulation.

Procedure on reconsideration

14.—(1) Reconsideration shall be by way of fresh decision made at a meeting of the Authority.
(2) The meeting shall take place as soon as reasonably practicable after the provision of the reports and statement required by regulation 13(6), having regard to the need to allow time for the information contained in that material to be taken into account.
(3) Where a member of the Authority has taken part in the making of a decision subject to reconsideration (whether under regulation 12 or otherwise), he is disqualified from participating in the Authority's reconsideration of it.
(4) On reconsideration under regulation 13(2)—

(a)   the person ("A") by whom the reconsideration is required under regulation 13(2) shall be entitled to require that he or his representative be given an opportunity to appear before and be heard at the meeting of the Authority at which the decision is reconsidered, and
(b)   the members of the Authority in attendance at the meeting at which the decision is reconsidered shall consider any such written representations and comments.

(5) The Authority shall give a notice of its decision to A.

(6) If on reconsideration the Authority upholds the previous decision, the notice under paragraph (5) shall include a statement of the reasons for the Authority's decision.

(7) "Reconsideration" means reconsideration in pursuance of a notice under regulation 13.

NOTES:

1. The regulations also provide for a specified person, whether donor, recipient or medical practitioner, to require the Authority's decision to be reconsidered (reg.5) and the procedure for reconsideration is set out in reg.6 of the regulations.

2. The Code of Practice indicates that assessment will usually be undertaken by independent assessors. Further guidance as to how they will operate is set out in the Code of Practice and discussed below (Human Tissue Authority Code of Practice, *Donation of Organs, Tissues and Cells for Transplantation*, Code 2, July 2006). Additional checks are provided in those situations set out in para.4 above, including children and adults lacking mental capacity, and paired, pooled or altruistic donations by a panel of at least three members of the Human Tissue Authority.

3. One criticism of the Human Organ Transplants Act 1989 is that while recognising that unrelated donors may be at risk of coercion, it did not properly address the issue that genetically related donors may equally be at risk of moral pressure from family members to donate. In contrast to the 1989 Act, specific provision is now made for genetically related donation to be subject to specific approval (Code of Practice, *op. cit.* in Note 2, para.93.)

4. Specific guidance is also given in relation to "paired donation" and "pooled" donation. Pairing matches donor and recipient with a similar donor and recipient in circumstances where a close relation can donate but their organ is not compatible. Pooled donation arises in an analogous situation but where there are more than two "pairs". At present the Code of Practice makes clear that because these are new systems of donation specific HTA approval is required for them to go ahead (HTA Code of Practice, 2, para.95).

5. There is also recognition for the first time of the situation in which a person donates an organ for altruistic reasons where there is not a designated recipient (Code of Practice, *op. cit.* in Note 2, paras 98–102). This practice is known as "non-directed altruistic organ donation". As it is a new procedure, it will require HTA approval. The Code of Practice makes clear that not only should there be an explanation of the procedure but in addition under no circumstances would the recipient and donor know the other's identity (para.100).

6. Reference is also made to "domino" transplantation in the Code of Practice (paras 103–104). This arises where a person receives a heart and lung transplant in a situation in which their lungs were failing. Their heart is removed but can be suitable for transplantation into another person. As this is an already established procedure, specific HTA approval will not be required.

Role of the independent assessor

Further guidance on the role of the independent assessor in the transplant approval process is provided by the Code of Practice.

HTA Donation of Organs, Tissues and Cells for Transplantation (Human Tissue Authority Code 2 July 2006)

The Assessor's roles and responsibilities

86 The role of the Independent Assessor is to act on the HTA's behalf in an independent capacity to carry out interviews and prepare a report for the HTA. Their report will assist the HTA in satisfying itself that the requirements of the Act and Regulations have been met, and in making its decision, on a case by case basis, as to whether or not to approve the donation.

87 The Assessor's responsibility is to interview the donor and recipient separately and to draw up a report on the proposed procedure. It may be appropriate and desirable in certain cases for the Assessor to also interview the donor and recipient together. There are two circumstances where the Assessor may not see the donor and recipient separately and together:

- When the recipient is a child, it is expected that the child and the person with parental responsibility for the child, would be seen together by the Assessor, even when the person with parental responsibility is the potential donor.
- In non-directed altruistic donation, the Assessor would only see the donor.

88 The Independent Assessor's report should show that they are satisfied that:

- a registered medical practitioner has explained to the donor the nature of the medical procedure in question, the risks involved and any other wider implications — for example, the risks to both donor and recipient and the effect upon children and any other dependent relatives. This report should include the information given as to the nature of the procedure and the risks involved, the full name of the registered medical practitioner and their qualification to give this information.
- the donor understands the nature of the medical procedure and the risks, as explained by the registered medical practitioner, has the capacity to consent, and consents to the removal of the organ or part-organ in question.
- the donor's consent was not obtained by duress or coercion or the offer of any other inducement.
- there is no evidence of an offer of reward.
- the donor understands that they are entitled to withdraw consent at any time and understands the consequences of withdrawal for the recipient.
- the donor–recipient relationship is as stated, where directed organ donation is involved. This will usually require appropriate supporting evidence.
- there were no difficulties in communicating with the donor and/or recipient, or other person interviewed.

If there were, an explanation of how those difficulties were overcome. Any translator used should have no personal connection to either the donor or the recipient, should have some understanding of medical matters and speak the donor's and recipient's language fluently. In the case of someone with a speech or hearing disability, a translator should be used with experience in signing.

89 The report should provide the Independent Assessor's assessment based on the points in paragraph 88 and should be accompanied by a covering letter, stating whether it is recommended that the HTA approve the transplantation or not. In the case of routine

transplantations, where the Independent Assessor's advice is that the transplant should proceed, the report should be submitted to the HTA Executive which will make the final decision on whether the proposed transplant can proceed. For all novel transplantations and cases involving children and incapacitated adults, these must be referred to the HTA panel to make the decision. In cases where the Independent Assessor is not in a position, and/or requires further guidance, to recommend approval, such cases may, at the discretion of the HTA, also be referred to the HTA panel.

90 This report is valid for six months. If the transplant does not happen within that time for whatever reason, a repeat report should be provided to the HTA to ensure circumstances have not changed and for a further decision. If the Independent Assessor needs further advice, s/he should consult with the HTA for assistance.

91 The Independent Assessor should be an NHS medical consultant or someone of equivalent senior professional status, who is not otherwise party to the transplantation process.

92 In order to become an Independent Assessor, a person must have completed the training required by the HTA and have been accredited by them to undertake the role. Independent Assessors can be accredited only if they attend an Authority-approved training course.

NOTE:

1. The independent assessors are to be "usually but not exclusively based in hospitals with transplant units".

QUESTION:

1. The Human Tissue Authority Code of Practice states that the independent assessors will act "both as a representative of the HTA and as an advocate for the donor" (para.68). Are these roles truly compatible?

(vi) Trafficking in Materials for Transplantation

There is no general ban upon commercial dealing in bodily products in this country. Nonetheless in certain areas there are statutory limitations upon the extent to which that commercial dealing may be undertaken. We noted in Chapter 11 above the ban on commercial surrogacy agreements. Similarly in other areas considerations of public policy have led to government action, largely as an ad hoc response to a particular incident. An excellent illustration of such a response is provided by the Turkish organ sale scandal. During the 1980s there was much public controversy regarding trading in organs. Persons brought to the United Kingdom from Turkey were paid to donate organs. This practice contravened the GMC guidelines which stated that doctors could not give treatment if organ donors were paid. Three doctors were found guilty of serious professional misconduct and one was struck off the Medical Register. Prior to the enactment of the 1989 Act, it was suggested that trading in organs was illegal at common law. Brahams suggested that the courts might have been prepared to hold that such contracts were unenforceable because that they were contrary to public policy. In addition if it is illegal to sell organs, then the courts would not uphold a contract to sell such organs on the basis that this was unlawful. (See D. Brahams, "Kidneys for Sale by Living Donors" (1989) *Lancet* 285 and "Kidneys for Sale" (1989) New L.J. 159.) The Human Organ Transplant Act 1989 banned commercial dealing in organs. This issue is now dealt with in s.32 of the Human Tissue Act 2004.

Human Tissue Act 2004, s.32

Prohibition of commercial dealings in human material for transplantation

32.—(1) A person commits an offence if he—

(a) gives or receives a reward for the supply of, or for an offer to supply, any controlled material;
(b) seeks to find a person willing to supply any controlled material for reward;
(c) offers to supply any controlled material for reward;
(d) initiates or negotiates any arrangement involving the giving of a reward for the supply of, or for an offer to supply, any controlled material;
(e) takes part in the management or control of a body of persons corporate or unincorporate whose activities consist of or include the initiation or negotiation of such arrangements.

(2) Without prejudice to subsection (1)(b) and (c), a person commits an offence if he causes to be published or distributed, or knowingly publishes or distributes, an advertisement—

(a) inviting persons to supply, or offering to supply, any controlled material for reward, or
(b) indicating that the advertiser is willing to initiate or negotiate any such arrangement as is mentioned in subsection (1)(d).

(3) A person who engages in an activity to which subsection (1) or (2) applies does not commit an offence under that subsection if he is designated by the Authority as a person who may lawfully engage in the activity.

(4) A person guilty of an offence under subsection (1) shall be liable—

(a) on summary conviction—
　(i) to imprisonment for a term not exceeding 12 months, or
　(ii) to a fine not exceeding the statutory maximum, or
　(iii) to both;
(b) on conviction on indictment—
　(i) to imprisonment for a term not exceeding 3 years, or
　(ii) to a fine, or
　(iii) to both.

(5) A person guilty of an offence under subsection (2) shall be liable on summary conviction—

(a) to imprisonment for a term not exceeding 51 weeks, or
(b) to a fine not exceeding level 5 on the standard scale, or
(c) to both.

(6) For the purposes of subsections (1) and (2), payment in money or money's worth to the holder of a licence shall be treated as not being a reward where—

(a) it is in consideration for transporting, removing, preparing, preserving or storing controlled material, and

(b) its receipt by the holder of the licence is not expressly prohibited by the terms of the licence.

(7) References in subsections (1) and (2) to reward, in relation to the supply of any controlled material, do not include payment in money or money's worth for defraying or reimbursing—

(a) any expenses incurred in, or in connection with, transporting, removing, preparing, preserving or storing the material,

(b) any liability incurred in respect of—
  (i) expenses incurred by a third party in, or in connection with, any of the activities mentioned in paragraph (a), or
  (ii) a payment in relation to which subsection (6) has effect, or

(c) any expenses or loss of earnings incurred by the person from whose body the material comes so far as reasonably and directly attributable to his supplying the material from his body.

(8) For the purposes of this section, controlled material is any material which—

(a) consists of or includes human cells,
(b) is, or is intended to be removed, from a human body,
(c) is intended to be used for the purpose of transplantation, and
(d) is not of a kind excepted under subsection (9).

(9) The following kinds of material are excepted—

(a) gametes,
(b) embryos, and
(c) material which is the subject of property because of an application of human skill.

(10) Where the body of a deceased person is intended to be used to provide material which—

(a) consists of or includes human cells, and
(b) is not of a kind excepted under subsection (9),

for use for the purpose of transplantation, the body shall be treated as controlled material for the purposes of this section.

(11) In this section—

"advertisement" includes any form of advertising whether to the public generally, to any section of the public or individually to selected persons;
"reward" means any description of financial or other material advantage.

NOTES:

1. The original provision included in the Human Tissue Bill 2003 was much broader and related more generally to trafficking in human material but was amended during the passage of the legislation to provide only for trafficking in the context of transplantation.

2. The ban on trafficking in human materials needs to be set in its international and European context. The Council of Europe took a robust stance against commercial dealing in human material. The Convention on Human Rights and Biomedicine provides that:

Article 21

"The human body and its parts shall not, as such, give rise to financial gain."

Article 22

"When in the course of an intervention any part of a human body is removed it may be stored and used for a purpose other than for which it was removed, only if this is done in conformity with appropriate information and consent procedures."

3. The EU Tissue Directive (Directive 2004/23 on setting standards of quality and safety for the donation, procurement, testing, processing, preservation, storage and distribution of human tissues and cells), discussed further in Chapter 11 above, also emphasises the need for voluntary and unpaid donation (Article 12), anonymity of both donor and recipient, altruism of the donor and solidarity between donor and recipient (Recital 13). Member States are urged to take steps to encourage a strong public and non-profit sector involvement in the provision of tissue and cell application services and related research development. The European Parliament has also called for a ban on organ trafficking, and for the introduction of a criminal offence applicable to EU citizens who travel abroad and buy organs. (See further Watson, "European Parliament tries to stamp out trafficking in human organs" (2003) 327 B.M.J. 1003; S. Wheeler, "EU plans organ trade crackdown", BBC news online, October 22, 2003.)

4. It should be noted that s.32(9) provides that tissue is excluded where "it is the subject of property because of an application of human skill" (see further p.1112 above for a discussion as to where human material becomes "property").

(vii) Criminal Sanctions

One of the criticisms levied at the Human Tissue Act 1961 was in relation to the lack of effective enforceability due to the lack of criminal offences included in the legislation. The 2004 Act now includes a number of specific criminal penalties.

Human Tissue Act 2004, ss.5 and 8

Prohibition of activities without consent etc.

5.—(1) A person commits an offence if, without appropriate consent, he does an activity to which subsection (1), (2) or (3) of section 1 applies, unless he reasonably believes—

   (a) that he does the activity with appropriate consent, or
   (b) that what he does is not an activity to which the subsection applies.

(2) A person commits an offence if—

   (a) he falsely represents to a person whom he knows or believes is going to, or may, do an activity to which subsection (1), (2) or (3) of section 1 applies—
      (i) that there is appropriate consent to the doing of the activity, or
      (ii) that the activity is not one to which the subsection applies, and
   (b) he knows that the representation is false or does not believe it to be true.

(3) Subject to subsection (4), a person commits an offence if, when he does an activity to which section 1(2) applies, neither of the following has been signed in relation to the cause of death of the person concerned—

(a) a certificate under section 22(1) of the Births and Deaths Registration Act 1953 (c. 20), and
(b) a certificate under Article 25(2) of the Births and Deaths Registration (Northern Ireland) Order 1976 (S.I. 1976/1041 (N.I. 14)).

(4) Subsection (3) does not apply—

(a) where the person reasonably believes—
  (i) that a certificate under either of those provisions has been signed in relation to the cause of death of the person concerned, or
  (ii) that what he does is not an activity to which section 1(2) applies, or
(b) where the person comes into lawful possession of the body immediately after death and stores it prior to its removal to a place where anatomical examination is to take place.

(5) Subject to subsection (6), a person commits an offence if, when he does an activity to which section 1(3) applies, the death of the person concerned has not been registered under either of the following provisions—

(a) section 15 of the Births and Deaths Registration Act 1953, and
(b) Article 21 of the Births and Deaths Registration (Northern Ireland) Order 1976.

(6) Subsection (5) does not apply where the person reasonably believes—

(a) that the death of the person concerned has been registered under either of those provisions, or
(b) that what he does is not an activity to which section 1(3) applies.

(7) A person guilty of an offence under this section shall be liable—

(a) on summary conviction to a fine not exceeding the statutory maximum;
(b) on conviction on indictment—
  (i) to imprisonment for a term not exceeding 3 years, or
  (ii) to a fine, or
  (iii) to both.

(8) In this section, "appropriate consent" has the same meaning as in section 1.

Restriction of activities in relation to donated material

8.—(1) Subject to subsection (2), a person commits an offence if he—

(a) uses donated material for a purpose which is not a qualifying purpose, or
(b) stores donated material for use for a purpose which is not a qualifying purpose.

(2) Subsection (1) does not apply where the person reasonably believes that what he uses, or stores, is not donated material.

(3) A person guilty of an offence under this section shall be liable—

(a) on summary conviction to a fine not exceeding the statutory maximum;
(b) on conviction on indictment—
  (i) to imprisonment for a term not exceeding 3 years, or
  (ii) to a fine, or

(iii) to both.

(4) In subsection (1), references to a qualifying purpose are to—

(a) a purpose specified in Schedule 1,
(b) the purpose of medical diagnosis or treatment,
(c) the purpose of decent disposal, or
(d) a purpose specified in regulations made by the Secretary of State.

(5) In this section, references to donated material are to—

(a) the body of a deceased person, or
(b) relevant material which has come from a human body,

which is, or has been, the subject of donation.

(6) For the purposes of subsection (5), a body, or material, is the subject of donation if authority under section 1(1) to (3) exists in relation to it.

NOTE:

1. Price notes the criminalisation contained in s.5 led to "considerable consternation" and comments "These were however perceived to be necessary to cater for flagrant and egregious breaches characterised by the activities of Professor Van Veltzen although intended almost exclusively as a deterrent" (see D. Price "The Human Tissue Act 2004" (2005) 68 M.L.R. 798).

There is in addition a new specific criminal offence in relation to the use of material for DNA analysis.

Non-consensual analysis of DNA

45.—(1) A person commits an offence if—

(a) he has any bodily material intending—
  (i) that any human DNA in the material be analysed without qualifying consent, and
  (ii) that the results of the analysis be used otherwise than for an excepted purpose,
(b) the material is not of a kind excepted under subsection (2), and
(c) he does not reasonably believe the material to be of a kind so excepted.

(2) Bodily material is excepted if—

(a) it is material which has come from the body of a person who died before the day on which this section comes into force and at least one hundred years have elapsed since the date of the person's death,
(b) it is an existing holding and the person who has it is not in possession, and not likely to come into possession, of information from which the individual from whose body the material has come can be identified, or
(c) it is an embryo outside the human body.

(3) A person guilty of an offence under this section—

(a) is liable on summary conviction to a fine not exceeding the statutory maximum;

(b) is liable on conviction on indictment—
　　　(i) to imprisonment for a term not exceeding 3 years, or
　　　(ii) to a fine, or
　　　(iii) to both.

(4) Schedule 4 (which makes provision for the interpretation of "qualifying consent" and "use for an excepted purpose" in subsection (1)(a)) has effect.
(5) In this section (and Schedule 4)—

"bodily material" means material which—

　　(a) has come from a human body, and
　　(b) consists of or includes human cells;

"existing holding" means bodily material held immediately before the day on which this section comes into force.

NOTE:

1. Section 45 was introduced following the recommendation made by the Human Genetics Commission in their report *Inside Information* in 2002 on the unauthorised use of genetic material, for example for paternity testing purposes (London: HGC, 2002) (see further Chapter 8). The HGC recommended that there should be a "new offence to cover particular cases where the wrongful obtaining or disclosure of genetic information for non-medical purposes amounts to a gross intrusion on the privacy of another" (at para.3.59). See further in K. Liddell, "Beyond Bristol and Alder Hey: the Future Regulation of Human Tissue" (2005) 13 *Medical Law Review* 170 at pp.184–189.
2. One implication of this provision is that if DNA is held for analysis which may help a relative of the person from whom the DNA has been taken, then clinicians cannot analyse it without the consent of that person. This may be seen as problematic given the fact that genetic information can be seen in terms of the interests of the family as a whole. (See further Liddell, *op. cit.* at pp.186–188.)

(viii) The Human Tissue Authority

The Human Tissue Act 2004 in many ways mirrors the Human Fertilisation and Embryology Act 1990. As with that legislation it will operate through a new specially designated regulatory authority and a licensing structure.

Human Tissue Act 2004, s.13, Sch.2(1)

The Human Tissue Authority

13.—(1) There shall be a body corporate to be known as the Human Tissue Authority (referred to in this Act as "the Authority").
(2) Schedule 2 (which makes further provision about the Authority) has effect.

Schedule 2 sets out the framework for the Authority.

Schedule 2

1.—(1) The Authority shall consist of—

(a) a chairman appointed by the Secretary of State,
(b) such number of other members appointed by the Secretary of State as the Secretary of State thinks fit,
(c) a member appointed by the National Assembly for Wales, and
(d) a member appointed by the relevant Northern Ireland department.

(2) The Secretary of State shall exercise his power to appoint members of the Authority to secure that at all times not less than half of the members are persons who do not have, and have not had, a professional interest in any of the kinds of activity within the remit of the Authority.

NOTES:

1. The establishment of the Human Tissue Authority as a regulatory body in this area can be compared with the creation of the Human Fertilisation and Embryology Authority under the Human Fertilisation and Embryology Act 1990 (discussed in Chapter 11 above). Regulatory bodies may be introduced to control and to facilitate. They have the advantage that a body with appropriate expertise can be involved in decision-making.
2. The Government has already announced that the existence of the Human Tissue Authority in its current form will only be for a very limited duration. The Government intends to combine the Human Tissue Authority with the Human Fertilisation and Embryology Authority under a new body the initially called the Regulatory Authority for Fertility and Tissue (RAFT) (*Reconfiguring the Department of Health's Arm's-Length Bodies*, London: Department of Health, 2004). The acronym was subsequently redrafted, as it potentially conflicted with an existing organisation, and it is now to be known as RATE (*Review of the Human Fertilisation and Embryology Act*, London: Department of Health, 2005 at p.72). This move—which the Government argues is mandated by the EU Tissue Directive (Directive 2004/23 on setting standards of quality and safety for the donation, procurement, testing, processing, preservation, storage and distribution of human tissues and cells)—has not been uncontroversial (see the discussion of the proposed reforms of the HFEA in Chapter 11 above). The EU Directive itself is also considered in Chapter 11 above.

Human Tissue Act 2004, ss.14–16

Remit

14.—(1) The following are the activities within the remit of the Authority—

(a) the removal from a human body, for use for a scheduled purpose, of any relevant material of which the body consists or which it contains;
(b) the use, for a scheduled purpose, of—
    (i) the body of a deceased person, or

(ii) relevant material which has come from a human body;
(c) the storage of an anatomical specimen or former anatomical specimen;
(d) the storage (in any case not falling within paragraph (c)) of—
  (i) the body of a deceased person, or
  (ii) relevant material which has come from a human body,
  for use for a scheduled purpose;
(e) the import or export of—
  (i) the body of a deceased person, or
  (ii) relevant material which has come from a human body, for use for a scheduled purpose;
(f) the disposal of the body of a deceased person which has been—
  (i) imported for use,
  (ii) stored for use, or
  (iii) used, for a scheduled purpose;
(g) the disposal of relevant material which—
  (i) has been removed from a person's body for the purposes of his medical treatment,
  (ii) has been removed from the body of a deceased person for the purposes of an anatomical, or post-mortem, examination,
  (iii) has been removed from a human body (otherwise than as mentioned in sub-paragraph (ii)) for use for a scheduled purpose,
  (iv) has come from a human body and been imported for use for a scheduled purpose, or
  (v) has come from the body of a deceased person which has been imported for use for a scheduled purpose.

(2) Without prejudice to the generality of subsection (1)(a) and (b), the activities within the remit of the Authority include, in particular—

(a) the carrying-out of an anatomical examination, and
(b) the making of a post-mortem examination.

(3) An activity is excluded from the remit of the Authority if—

(a) it relates to the body of a person who died before the day on which this section comes into force or to material which has come from the body of such a person, and
(b) at least one hundred years have elapsed since the date of the person's death.

(4) The Secretary of State may by order amend this section for the purpose of adding to the activities within the remit of the Authority.
(5) In this section, "relevant material", in relation to use for the scheduled purpose of transplantation, does not include blood or anything derived from blood.

General functions

15.—The Authority shall have the following general functions—

(a) maintaining a statement of the general principles which it considers should be followed—
  (i) in the carrying-on of activities within its remit, and
  (ii) in the carrying-out of its functions in relation to such activities;
(b) providing in relation to activities within its remit such general oversight and guidance as it considers appropriate;
(c) superintending, in relation to activities within its remit, compliance with—
  (i) requirements imposed by or under Part 1 or this Part, and
  (ii) codes of practice under this Act;

(d) providing to the public, and to persons carrying on activities within its remit, such information and advice as it considers appropriate about the nature and purpose of such activities;

(e) monitoring developments relating to activities within its remit and advising the Secretary of State, the National Assembly for Wales and the relevant Northern Ireland department on issues relating to such developments;

(f) advising the Secretary of State, the National Assembly for Wales or the relevant Northern Ireland department on such other issues relating to activities within its remit as he, the Assembly or the department may require.

Licensing

Licence requirement

16.—(1) No person shall do an activity to which this section applies otherwise than under the authority of a licence granted for the purposes of this section.

(2) This section applies to the following activities—

(a) the carrying-out of an anatomical examination;

(b) the making of a post-mortem examination;

(c) the removal from the body of a deceased person (otherwise than in the course of an activity mentioned in paragraph (a) or (b)) of relevant material of which the body consists or which it contains, for use for a scheduled purpose other than trans-plantation;

(d) the storage of an anatomical specimen;

(e) the storage (in any case not falling within paragraph (d)) of—
   (i) the body of a deceased person, or
   (ii) relevant material which has come from a human body,
   for use for a scheduled purpose;

(f) the use, for the purpose of public display, of—
   (i) the body of a deceased person, or
   (ii) relevant material which has come from the body of a deceased person.

(3) The Secretary of State may by regulations specify circumstances in which storage of relevant material by a person who intends to use it for a scheduled purpose is excepted from subsection (2)(e)(ii).

(4) An activity is excluded from subsection (2) if—

(a) it relates to the body of a person who died before the day on which this section comes into force or to material which has come from the body of such a person, and

(b) at least one hundred years have elapsed since the date of the person's death.

(5) The Secretary of State may by regulations amend this section for the purpose of—

(a) adding to the activities to which this section applies,

(b) removing an activity from the activities to which this section applies, or

(c) altering the description of an activity to which this section applies.

(6) Schedule 3 (which makes provision about licences for the purposes of this section) has effect.

(7) In subsection (2)—

(a) references to storage do not include storage which is incidental to transportation, and

(b) "relevant material", in relation to use for the scheduled purpose of transplantation, does not include blood or anything derived from blood.

Persons to whom licence applies

17.—The authority conferred by a licence extends to—

(a) the designated individual,
(b) any person who is designated as a person to whom the licence applies by a notice given to the Authority by the designated individual, and
(c) any person acting under the direction of—
(i) the designated individual, or
(ii) a person designated as mentioned in paragraph (b).

Duty of the designated individual

18.—It shall be the duty of the individual designated in a licence as the person under whose supervision the licensed activity is authorised to be carried on to secure—

(a) that the other persons to whom the licence applies are suitable persons to participate in the carrying-on of the licensed activity,
(b) that suitable practices are used in the course of carrying on that activity, and
(c) that the conditions of the licence are complied with.

Right to reconsideration of licensing decisions

19.—(1) If an application for the grant, revocation or variation of a licence is refused, the applicant may require the Authority to reconsider the decision.
(2) If a licence is—

(a) revoked under paragraph 7(2) of Schedule 3, or
(b) varied under paragraph 8(3) or (5) of that Schedule,

the holder of the licence, or the designated individual, may require the Authority to reconsider the decision.
(3) If an application for the grant, or revocation, of permission for the purposes of an authorisation condition is refused, the applicant may require the Authority to reconsider the decision.
(4) If permission for the purposes of an authorisation condition is revoked under paragraph 12(4)(b) of Schedule 3, any of—

(a) the individual concerned,
(b) the holder of the licence, and
(c) the designated individual,

may require the Authority to reconsider the decision.
(5) The right under subsection (1) or (2) is exercisable by giving the Authority notice of exercise of the right before the end of the period of 28 days beginning with the day on which notice of the decision concerned was given under paragraph 11 of Schedule 3.
(6) The right under subsection (3) or (4) is exercisable by giving the Authority notice of exercise of the right before the end of the period of 28 days beginning with the day on which notice of the decision concerned was given under paragraph 12 of Schedule 3.
(7) Subsections (1) to (4) do not apply to a decision on reconsideration.
(8) In this section, "authorisation condition" means a condition of a licence where—

(a) the licence is one to which paragraph 3 of Schedule 3 applies, and
(b) the condition is the one required in the licence by sub-paragraph (2) of that paragraph.

NOTE:

    1. The licensing approach is comparable to that taken by the HFEA under the 1990 Act (see Chapter 11 above).

There are some exemptions which are provided from the requirement to have a licence and these distinguish between tissue banks and the individual researcher contained in draft regulations published in summer 2005.

(ix) Codes of Practice

Human Tissue Act 2004, s.26, 28

Codes of practice

Preparation of codes

    26.—(1) The Authority may prepare and issue codes of practice for the purpose of—

  (a) giving practical guidance to persons carrying on activities within its remit, and
  (b) laying down the standards expected in relation to the carrying-on of such activities.

    (2) The Authority shall deal under subsection (1) with the following matters—

  (a) the carrying-out of anatomical examinations;
  (b) the storage of anatomical specimens;
  (c) the storage and disposal of former anatomical specimens;
  (d) the definition of death for the purposes of this Act;
  (e) communication with the family of the deceased in relation to the making of a post-mortem examination;
  (f) the making of post-mortem examinations;
  (g) communication with the family of the deceased in relation to the removal from the body of the deceased, for use for a scheduled purpose, of any relevant material of which the body consists or which it contains;
  (h) the removal from a human body, for use for a scheduled purpose, of any relevant material of which the body consists or which it contains;
  (i) the storage for use for a scheduled purpose, and the use for such a purpose, of—
      (i) the body of a deceased person, or
      (ii) relevant material which has come from a human body;
  (j) the storage for use for a scheduled purpose, and the use for such a purpose, of an existing holding within the meaning of section 9;
  (k) the import, and the export, of—
      (i) the body of a deceased person, or
      (ii) relevant material which has come from a human body,
    for use for a scheduled purpose;
  (l) the disposal of relevant material which—
      (i) has been removed from a human body for use for a scheduled purpose, or
      (ii) has come from a human body and is an existing holding for the purposes of section 9.

    (3) In dealing under subsection (1) with the matters mentioned in subsection (2)(h) and (i), the Authority shall, in particular, deal with consent.
    (4) The Authority shall—

(a) keep any code of practice under this section under review, and
(b) prepare a revised code of practice when appropriate.

(5) Before preparing a code of practice under this section, the Authority shall—

(a) consult such persons as it considers appropriate,
(b) if the code of practice relates to Wales, consult the National Assembly for Wales, and
(c) if the code of practice relates to Northern Ireland, consult the relevant Northern Ireland department.

(6) The Authority shall publish a code of practice issued under this section in such way as, in its opinion, is likely to bring it to the attention of those interested.

(7) A code of practice issued under this section shall come into effect on such day as may be appointed by directions.

(8) Codes of practice under this section may make different provision in relation to England, Wales and Northern Ireland respectively.

Effect of codes

28.—(1) A failure on the part of any person to observe any provision of a code of practice under s.26 shall not of itself render the person liable to any proceedings.

(2) The Authority may, in carrying out its functions with respect to licences, take into account any relevant observance of, or failure to observe, a code of practice under section 26, so far as dealing with a matter mentioned in any of paragraphs (a) to (c) and (e) to (j) of subsection (2) of that section.

NOTE:

1. The provisions regarding the codes of practice are yet another way in which the Human Tissue Act 2004 resembles the Human Fertilisation and Embryology Act 1990. The codes of practice will be a crucial part of the regulatory process. Several codes have now been produced: *Consent* (Code 1, July 2006), *Donation of Organs, Tissues and Cells for Transplantation* (Code 2, July 2006), *Post Mortem Examination* (Code 3, July 2006), *Anatomical Examination* (Code 4, July 2006), *Removal, storage and disposal of human organs and tissue* (Code 5, July 2006), *Donation of allogenic bone marrow and peripheral blood stem cells for transplantation* (Code 6, July 2006).

4. Increasing the Supply of Organs for Transplantation: Measures for Reform

We noted above the fact that there is a chronic shortage of organs available for transplantation. A number of suggestions have been put forward on how to alleviate the shortage. Some of these relate to improvements in medical practice, such as the methods for harvesting organs; others concern proposals for the reform of legislation. (See R. Hoffenberg, *Report of the Working Party on Supply of Donor Organs for Transportation*, London: DHSS, 1987; British Medical Association, *Organ Donation in the 21st Century: Time for a Consolidated Approach*, London: BMA, 2000.) We consider below a number of initiatives advanced which may increase the supply of donor organs for transplantation.

Transplantation in the UK is co-ordinated through NHS Blood and Transplant which is concerned to ensure that organs are distributed in a fair and ethical manner. This is a new body established through the combination of the previous bodies, UK Transplant and the National Blood Authority (National Blood Authority and UK Transplant (Abolition) Order 2005, SI 2005/2352.)

(a) Opting-in Registry

B. New, M. Soloman, R. Dingwall, J. McHale, *A Question of Give and Take: Improving the Supply of Donor Organs for Transplantation*, London: King's Fund Institute, 1994

An opting-in registry operates on the same principle as the donor card; it is an explicit statement of consent by a potential donor while he or she is still alive. Such an explicit statement is in accord with section 1(1) of the Human Tissue Act 1961, the difference being that it would take the form of a record on a centralised computer register to which all relevant hospital units could have instant access. Such a proposal is claimed to hold significant advantages over the donor card. Once the statement is made, it cannot be "lost" nor can the statement fail to be found simply because the donor did not have it about his or her person at the time of death. A computer register should be cheaper to administer, involving only electronically recorded information (although the publicity needed to achieve a substantial response may be expensive). And it would be extremely flexible with anyone able to add or to remove their name at any time.

NOTES:

1. In the conclusions to the report, the authors expressed the view that opting-in registers had not demonstrated their effectiveness. However, the Government did introduce an NHS Organ Donor Register in 1994. It is held by the United Kingdom Transplant Support Services in Bristol where the national database of patients who are waiting for organ transplants is kept. Transplant co-ordinators can contact the service 24 hours a day to identify the wishes of the deceased person and pass this information on to the relatives (*The Guardian*, October 7, 1994).
2. Persons can now also register their intention to become donors by ticking a box on their driving licence application form. This information is also registered with the NHS Organ Donor Registry.

(b) Altering Clinical Procedures to Facilitate Transplantation

Controversy surrounded a technique called "elective ventilation". This was a practice whereby patients who were brought into hospital suffering from intracranial haemorrhage and regarded as suitable as potential organ donors were moved from a general ward to the intensive care unit. Before they were moved to intensive care, the consent of the relatives was obtained. The patient was then placed on a ventilator until brain stem death is diagnosed. The practice was halted in 1994 after the view was expressed that it was illegal. First, the procedure could not be regarded as simply part of the process of transplantation in relation to cadavers because the patient had not been declared brain stem dead. In addition it was argued that it was a non-therapeutic procedure which could not be said to be in the patient's best interests. It appears also that the practice of elective ventilation conflicted with suggestions made by the House of Lords in the *Bland* case that it would be unlawful to prolong life where this not in the best interests of the patient (see J.V. McHale, "Elective Ventilation—Pragmatic Solution or Ethical Minefield?" (1995) 10 *Professional Negligence* 28; S. McLean, "Transplantation and the Nearly Dead: The Case of Elective Ventilation" in S. McLean (ed.), *Contemporary Issues in Law, Medicine and Ethics* (Dartmouth: Aldershot 1996)). For general discussion on clinical options, see further S.M. Gore, "Organ Donation from Intensive Care Units in England and Wales: Two Year Confidential Audit of Deaths in Intensive Care" (1992), 349 B.M.J. 304, and New, Soloman, Dingwall and McHale, *op. cit.* at pp.47–52.

(c) Presumed Consent

A more radical alternative would be the introduction of presumed consentor "opting-out" scheme. This is the reverse of the present system. It enables organs to be removed automatically subject to expressions to the contrary.

B. New, M. Soloman, R. Dingwall, J. McHale, *A Question of Give and Take: Improving the Supply of Donor Organs for Transplantation*, London: King's Fund Institute, 1994

Presumed consent schemes have been introduced into many countries, although attempts to enact such legislation in the United Kingdom have always failed, the latest being the Transplantation of Human Organs Bill 1993. The international legislation falls into several categories. The purest version of the law allows automatic removal except in a situation in which the deceased has expressed an objection during his or her lifetime. This "strict" type of presumed consent procedure applies in Austria where organs can be removed "provided in his or her life, the person concerned had not expressed an objection. The views of close relatives are not taken into account."

A slightly less strict version of presumed consent operates in Belgium where, if there is no explicit objection by the deceased, the relatives are allowed to object but the medical profession are under no obligation to seek their views. The relatives must initiate the process under these circumstances. ⁖

Other, still weaker, schemes allow removal unless the deceased has made an explicit or informal objection at any time. Such a formulation of the law effectively requires that the relatives are consulted in order to glean the wishes of the deceased. Although it is formally the views of the deceased whilst alive which are being sought, such schemes allow the relatives to object on the deceased's behalf. France and Spain operate presumed consent legislation of this kind.

Finally, a scheme in operation in Singapore provides for the automatic exclusion of certain categories of potential donor, including non-citizens and Muslims. Muslims can, however, donate their organs if they wish, by pledging their organs whilst alive or if their relatives consent . . .

Does presumed consent work? Belgium

Belgium enacted presumed consent legislation in June 1986 in the middle of a period of sustained and steady growth in kidney transplantation in Europe . . .

Belgium did increase the number of available kidneys by a significant margin during 1987, a rise of 37 per cent over the year before and this does not seem to be simply the continuation of an earlier trend. Furthermore neither the United Kingdom, Germany nor the Netherlands experienced a similar increase in the same year. On the other hand Austria did not introduce similar legislation in the same year having done so in 1982 formalising a 200 year tradition of routinely utilising the corpse for medical purposes). For instance the publicity devoted to the organ donation issue whilst the law was being debated could itself have promoted a greater willingness to donate on the part of the public and a more informed attitude on behalf of ICU staff. It has been noted that the number of transplant co-ordinators increased around this time, and that the law formalised systems of reimbursement so that donating hospitals could be sure that they would receive the appropriate payment for managing the donor.

These objections are inconclusive, however. One would expect a "publicity effect" to subside. The increase in the number of co-ordinators was likely to be as much a result of the increased number of donors as the cause of it. And the law merely formalised payment systems which operated successfully for the majority of hospitals beforehand.

It is clear that the influence of publicity, co-ordinators and payment systems had no effect in those centres where relatives' permission is always sought. It certainly seems as though the law had an independent effect on kidney retrieval where its provisions were adopted.

In any time series-analysis "concurrent interventions" such as those described above will make it difficult to prove the causal influence of the intervention of the intervention in question, in this case a law. On balance, though, the evidence suggests that the introduction of presumed consent in Belgium had a significant impact on the availability of organs.

Does presumed consent work? Singapore

Singapore also introduced presumed consent legislation after a long period of transplant activity under an "opting-in" system. The number of transplants undertaken in Singapore are relatively small and so were not included in the international analysis. Nevertheless, the development of kidney transplantation over time has some interesting features . . .

Between 1970 and 1982 only 30 cadaveric kidneys were transplanted, constituting an average of approximately 0.9 pmp per year, clearly inadequate by any international standards. In an attempt to increase this level of activity, kidneys were imported from Europe and North America . . . The initial success of this policy was short lived when it became clear that the one year graft survival of these kidneys was poor probably as a result of the prolonged "cold ischaemia times" involved.

In 1987, the Human Organ Transplant Act was introduced incorporating the provisions described above. The number of transplants undertaken in 1989–1990 increased significantly over the "non-import" totals of the previous years, imports being discontinued in 1988. Some analyses . . . have attempted to isolate exactly the number of kidneys procured under the new law compared with the number obtained under the old opting-in legislation, which still applied for those wishing to pledge their organs. However, such analysis will underestimate the number of voluntary pledges since it cannot be known for certain how many families would have consented given the chance. Nevertheless the evidence from Singapore adds to that of Belgium as to the efficacy of presumed consent legislation.

The King's Fund Report went on to consider the ethical issues relating to the introduction of opting out legislation.

The wishes of the individual

Most commonly, individuals are given the opportunity to "opt-out" under presumed consent legislation. Although less serious, the concern remains that individual wishes would be ignored. The Hoffenburg Committee commented that there was a danger that organs would be removed when this was not the wish of the person. Whilst alive persons may feel pressurised into not opting-out because it might be seen as socially unacceptable. Others may be ignorant of the law or unable to understand it—vulnerable groups would be most at risk. In a multi-cultural society, the risk of ignoring the implicit wish of individuals with strong religious beliefs is particularly serious. No presumed consent legislation can possibly guarantee that the wishes of all concerned will be respected.

The sensibilities of the relatives

If concern would be felt by those now living with strong beliefs about the proper procedure for their body after death, distress could certainly be caused to family members who wished to wished to grieve without the knowledge or suspicion that the body of the loved one was being "mutilated" particularly if donation was conducted only under a "presumption" that the deceased had given consent. The Committee of European Health Ministers commented that,

> "the role of the family in deciding on organ removal is much more important in cases of presumed consent than in cases of express consent. In the latter case the sentimental objections of the family have to be weighed against the legal rights of the deceased who has willed the organ donation. In the case of presumed consent the family's express objection weighs more heavily against the presumed consent of the deceased . . . In practice therefore whether consent is express or presumed, the final decision rests to a very large extent with the family of the deceased."

It is worth noting however that the sensibilities of the family are not taken into consideration in the case of a coroner's autopsy. In England in the early 1980s "some 20 per cent of persons dying . . . [were] subject to a medico-legal autopsy." In other words a large number of deceased individuals are subjected to invasive surgery, without the need for consent, to satisfy social imperatives. What is more, society sanctions such investigations only as a means of establishing cause of death or to help the solving of a crime — lives are not directly at stake. The ethical distinction which supports the coroner's autopsy but denies the donation of organs unless consent is provided, is by no means clear.

Trust in the medical profession

Both these possible consequences — ignoring individual rights and offending the family's feelings — could have an impact on trust and respect for the medical profession. Whilst presumed consent may, in the short run, furnish more organs for transplants, in the long run its systematic effect on the institutions of medical care, could be depressing and corrosive of that trust upon which the doctor–patient relationship depend. And, even in the short run, public controversy can adversely affect donation rates. Furthermore, doctors may be unwilling to override the wishes of nearest relatives regarding organ donation, blunting the impact of the schemes.

Good medical practice

There may also be certain risks in removal without consent. In October 1979 a woman who died suddenly in France had her corneas transplanted. Unfortunately the patient who received her eyes contracted rabies. It was later revealed that the donor had contracted rabies when bitten by a dog in Eygpt where she had been shortly before her death. Her family knew this and had they been asked they would have been able to pass on this information to the medical team.

Can presumed consent legislation be ethical?

If a presumed consent scheme were to be introduced certain questions would need to be addressed. Would all organs be covered by the presumed consent scheme? Should organs be made available simply for clinical transplant or also for experimentation purposes? Should certain vulnerable groups of patients be excluded from routine removal? The 1969 Renal Transplantation Bill, an attempt to introduce a limited form of opting out, provided exclusions for persons who, at the time of death were suffering from mental illness or mental handicap, minors, those over 65, prisoners and permanent residents in institutions for the aged, disabled or handicapped.

It may also be necessary for a statutory definition of death to be enacted. This would, as was noted earlier, prove a difficult and controversial task. Presumed consent would also have to be accompanied by massive publicity in order that members of the public are made aware of their opportunity to opt out. In addition the legislators would need to address themselves to the question of who should have ownership and control of the cadaver and of the organs.

However, it may be that many of these ethical objections can be overcome by sufficiently carefully drafted legislation . . . Individual rights can be safeguarded by means of computer registries and exclusions of certain categories of individual. The sensibilities of the relatives can be safeguarded by allowing them to initiate an objection which must be respected. The position of the medical profession is protected by allowing the individual clinician to decide how and when to utilise the laws provisions. Such a law would also allow for donation under circumstances whereby the relatives at a moment of grief, do not wish to discuss the possibility, but would otherwise normally be in favour of donation.

Nevertheless, unless the medical profession broadly supports the implementation of presumed consent legislation there is a serious danger that transplantation will be brought into disrepute by the controversy which would ensue. This in turn may corrode the public's trust in doctors and medicine. The best way forward is for the debate to continue until those who would have to work within a new law are satisfied that those reservations have been addressed.

NOTES:

1. The Report did not finally recommend that opting-out legislation should be introduced into this country, although it was suggested that there should be continued debate regarding the concerns which were caused by presumed consent legislation. A number of attempts have been made to introduce presumed consent legislation into the UK and support has been given to this approach by the British Medical Association, but it has been consistently resisted by the UK Government (British Medical Association, *Organ Donation in the 21st Century: Time for a Consolidated Approach*, London: BMA, 2000, and *Briefing Organ Donation: Presumed Consent for Organ Donation*, London: BMA, 2005).

2. Some commentators would regard organs from the cadaver as a public resource for transplantation purposes and indeed that consent itself is not required at all. (See, for example, H.E. Emson, "It is Immoral to Require Consent for Cadaver Organ Donation" (2003) 29 *Journal of Medical Ethics* 125; J. Harris, "Organ Procurement: Dead Interests; Living Needs" (2003) 29 *Journal of Medical Ethics* 125). For further discussion of opting-out see I. Kennedy, "The Donation and Transplantation of Kidneys: Should the Law be Changed?" in I. Kennedy, *Treat Me Right*, Oxford: OUP, 1989; I. Kennedy *et al.*, "The Case for Presumed Consent in Organ Donation" (1998) 351 *The Lancet* 1650; and in opposition to such a scheme R.A. Sells, "Let's Not Opt-out: Kidney Donation and Transplantation" (1979) 5 *Journal of Medical Ethics* 165. Though note the change in approach by Sells, a leading surgeon, in I. Kennedy, R. Sells, A. Daar *et al.*, "The Case for Presumed Consent in Organ Donation" (1998) *Lancet* 1650).

3. There is a divergence of opinion among certain religious and cultural groups, for example, certain parts of the Jewish community (see R.P. Bulka, "Jewish Perspectives on Organ Transplantation" (1990) 22(3) *Transplantation Proceedings* 945), as to the removal of organs without consent having been obtained from the deceased and as to a definition of brain stem death. These concerns would need to be addressed before any change in the law was introduced to allow opting-out. (See further New, Solomon, Dingwall and McHale, *op. cit.* at pp.35–37). This is particularly the case today in the light of Article 9 of the European Convention of Human Rights which provides for respect for freedom of faith, conscience and belief.

4. Consistent with the King's Fund Report, a recent study indicated that presumed consent legislation was only one of four variables across European countries in determining organ donation rates (see further R.W. Gimbel, M.A. Strosberg, S.E. Lehrman, E. Gefence, F. Taft, "Presumed Consent and Other Predictors of Cadaveric Organ Transplantation in Europe (2003) 13 *Progress in Transplantation* 17).

(d) Required Request and Routine Enquiry

An alternative approach to the opting-out legislation commonly adopted in Europe is routine enquiry/required request, an approach which has been taken in the United States.

B. New, M. Solomon, R. Dingwall, J. McHale, *A Question of Give and Take: Improving the Supply of Donor Organs for Transplantation*, London: King's Fund Institute, 1994

Required request and routine enquiry are used extensively in the United States with the aim of increasing the supply of organs. The Uniform Anatomical Gift Act 1987 which forms the model for many state statutes makes provision for required request and routine enquiry. The development of required request policies by hospitals was encouraged by the Omnibus (Budget) Reconciliation Act 1986. This Act provides that failure on the part of hospitals to adopt routine enquiry or required request policies will lead to the denial of Medicare and Medicaid reimbursements from the Health Care Finance Authority.

Required request is a procedure in which enquiries are made of the families of potential donors to see whether they would allow their relatives' organs to be used. Twenty six U.S. states have this type of policy. The legislation in some states incorporates exceptions to the general duty of enquiry where for example, the wishes of the deceased are already known the medical staff are unable to locate the family in a timely manner and where enquiry would exacerbate mental or emotional distress.

Routine enquiry is the procedure of informing individuals and families of the option of organ donation. Eighteen states have legislation on this question. Some states do not require hospitals to directly approach families but stipulate that they must establish organ and tissue donation committees to design policies which would result in prompt identification of donors and prompt referral to the Organ Procurement Agency.

How successful have the required request and routine enquiry schemes been? While there was an initial increase in the availability of organs over time the schemes do not appear to have had a major impact. One reason for this, it is suggested, is the lack of institutional commitment to ensuring that the required request procedures are followed.

The United States experience illustrates that simply to enact required request legislation is not enough. It is vital to have adequately trained and qualified personnel.

"As one organ procurement official observed 'if you simply ask relatives about organ donation by simply citing the law the consent rate is zero.'"

Another reason suggested for the lack of dramatic impact of required request is that doctors find organ procurement time consuming and emotionally demanding. It is perhaps questionable as to whether statutory enactment of required request would have a significant impact. The national audit found that only 6 per cent of relatives in the U.K. are not approached when an otherwise potential donor is on a ventilator, and many of these would probably have communicated their unwillingness to consider donation by other means.

The Report also considers the ethics of this procedure:

A. L. Caplan has been one of the strongest advocates of the required request procedure. He argues that institutional required request means that opportunities for obtaining consent will not be missed. Required request standardises enquiry and thus places less strain on health care professionals and family members at a time of great stress and emotional upheaval. It also preserves the right of the individual to refuse consent since voluntary choice remains the ethical foundation upon which required request is based.

However others disagree, making a number of criticisms of the required request procedure. Doctors and relatives may find the system distressing, though for rather different reasons than those relating to presumed consent. Doctors may be put under pressure to find that donors are suitable candidates for donation with implications for the diagnosis of brain stem death. Unlike presumed consent legislation, required request prescribes actions. It does not in general allow for the doctor to decide on a case by case basis the proper approach. In some circumstances it may be quite clear that requesting organ donation may be insensitive to the needs of the family. To suggest to relatives that organ donation is a gift of life is to play upon their emotions and guilt feelings at the time of their loved one's death.

There is also a danger that respect for donors may be eroded in the constant search for organs and this may have long term implications for public confidence in the medical team and the organ donation process. In general it seems clear that required request's prescriptive nature, and the associated problems of enforceability, mean that it is ethically unsustainable. There is also little evidence that it would be effective in improving the supply.

NOTE:

1. A variant on such approach is the notion of mandated choice where individuals are required to make a decision prior to their death as to the use of their organs for transplantation (see further P. Chouhan and H. Draper, "Modified Mandated Choice for Organ Procurement" (2003) 29 *Journal of Medical Ethics* 157).

(e) A Market in Organs

A further option is to remove the statutory ban on commercial dealing in organs and tissue for the purposes of transplantation. There has been considerable debate internationally as to whether individuals should be allowed to trade in bodily products, in particular in organs/tissue. (See, for example, Lori Andrews, "My Body My Property" (1986) *Hastings Centre Report* 28; J. Stacey Taylor, *Stakes and Kidneys: Why Markets in Human Body Parts are Morally Imperative*,

Aldershot: Ashgate, 2005: D. Price, *Organ Transplants and Ethics*, Cambridge: Cambridge University Press, 2000; S. Wilkinson, *Bodies for Sale: Ethics and Exploitation in the Human Body Trade*, London: Routledge, 2003; J. Salvescue, "Is the Sale of Body Parts Wrong?" (2003) 29 *Journal of Medical Ethics* 138.) In the context of organs and tissue, it has been suggested that creation of a market may facilitate an increase in supply, with individuals being more willing to donate organs if given payment (J. Radcliffe-Richards *et al.*, "The Case for Allowing Kidney Sales" (1998) 351 *The Lancet* 1950). It can be seen as part of individual autonomy. As an alternative to a general free market it has been suggested that a regulated market could be adopted with donors selling to a state agency which would have the advantage of controlling the safety of clinical procedures. (See further C. Errin and J. Harris, "A Monopsonistic Market; or How to Buy and Sell Human Organs, Tissues and Cells Ethically" in I. Robinson (ed.), *Life and Death under High Technology Medicine*, Manchester: MUP, 1994 and C.A. Errin and J. Harris, "An Ethical Market in Human Organs" (2003) 29 *Journal of Medical Ethics* 137):

Against this it is argued that individuals do not have an unfettered ability to deal with their body as they choose and that there is a weighty public policy argument that may be deployed against the commercialisation of bodily products in such a situation. It has also been argued that commercialisation degrades humanity. (see J. Harris, *Wonderwoman and Superman: the Ethics of Human Biotechnology*, London: Routledge, 1992, p.118, and N. Duxbury, "Law, Markets and Valuation" [1995] *Brooklyn Law Review* 657; N. Duxbury, "Do Markets Degrade?" (1996) 6 59 *Modern Law Review* 33.) Some see it as a "slippery slope" and that undue pressure may be placed upon the poor and disadvantaged to donate. Particular concern has been expressed that rich nations may prey upon poor nations to obtain donors. It has also been suggested that the existence of a market may actively discourage some persons who would otherwise come forward to make a voluntary donation. (See generally D. Lamb, *Organ Transplants and Ethics*, London: Routledge, 1990 at pp.133–140.) The legalisation of a market in organs seems unlikely at least in the near future. A variant could be the provision of increased non-financial incentives. This was discussed in Pennsylvania in 1999 where it was suggested that families would be given $300 to the cost of funeral expenses where they consented to the donation of their relatives organs for transplantation.

(f) Xenotransplantation

It has been proposed that an alternative method of meeting the current organ shortage would be to use organs and tissues from animal sources (see generally M. Fox and J. McHale, "Xenotransplantation: the Ethical and Legal Ramifications" (1998) *Medical Law Review* 43; S. McLean and L. Williamson, *Xenotransplantation: Law and Ethics* Aldershot: Ashgate, 2005). Researchers have developed transgenic and other technologies which enable the transplantation of pig organs and tissue into primate recipients, with a view to ultimately transferring this technique to humans (see D. Lyons, *Dairies of Despair: the Secret History of Pig-to-Primate Organ Transplant Experiments*, Sheffield: Uncaged

Campaigns, 2000). While the use of animal bodies does offer a potential solution to the organ shortage, the technology poses numerous difficulties. The first is scientific. Human immune systems are programmed to reject the introduction of animal substances. At present, this limits the use of xeno technologies, although scientists have for many years used pig heart valves in transplantation, and animal genetic engineering has the potential to overcome the auto immune response of the human body (see Chapter 10). Secondly, there is considerable concern about the potential for cross-species infection which such technologies pose, especially in the wake of the current concerns about cross-species transmission of HN51 flu virus (see F. Morgan, "Babe the Magnificent Organ Donor: the Perils and Promises Surrounding Xenotransplantation" (1997) 14 *Journal of Contemporary Health Law and Policy* 127–165; S. Fovargue, "A Leap of Faith? Sanctioning Xenotransplant Clinical Trials" (2005) 26 *Liverpool Law Review* 125–148). Thirdly, some commentators focus on the ethical objections to using animals for human ends (see A. Capron, "Is Xenografting Morally Wrong?" (1992) 24 *Transplantation Proceedings* 722; see M. Fox, "Reconfiguring the Animal/ Human Boundary: the Impact of Xenotechnologies" (2005) 26 *Liverpool Law Review* 149–167).

(i) Ethical Issues

In 1996 the Nuffield Council on Bioethics issued a report on xenotransplantation (hereafter "the Nuffield Report"), which was also the subject of an inquiry the following year by the Department of Health under the chairmanship of Professor Ian Kennedy, *A Report by the Advisory Group on the Ethics of Xenotransplantation* (London: Department of Health, 1997, hereafter "the Kennedy Report").

Nuffield Council on Bioethics, *Animal to Human Transplants: the Ethics of Xenotransplantation*, London 1996

Animal concerns: principles

10.7 One line of thought holds that when judging whether it is acceptable to use animals for medical purposes it is necessary to consider whether the pain and suffering of the animals is justified by the potential benefit to human beings. Another line of thought suggests that animals, like human beings, have rights that must be respected when considering their use for such purposes. Whether the argument is framed in terms of the interests or the rights of animals, the crucial point is the extent to which animals share the features supposed to be important to human interests and rights. The feature to which most importance has generally been attached is that of self-awareness. To be self-aware requires a high degree of intelligence, the capacity to make comparisons and judgments, and a language with which to articulate them. It has been argued that suffering and death are uniquely painful to a self-aware being who not only senses pain but can also perceive the damage being done to his or her self and future.

10.8 The Working Party accepted that some use of animals for medical purposes is "an undesirable but avoidable necessity" and that "in the absence of any scientifically and morally acceptable alternative, some uses of animals . . . can be justified as necessary to safeguard and improve the health and alleviate the suffering of human beings". Not every benefit to human beings will justify the use of animals, and in some cases, the adverse effects on the animals will be so serious as to preclude their use. This conclusion drew on the position set out by the Institute of Medical Ethics towards biomedical research using animals.

The use of primates for xenotransplantation

10.9 Even if some use of animals for medical purposes can be justified in principle, their use for xenotransplantation raises specific issues that need further consideration. Particular concerns are raised by the use of primates, such as baboons. The high degree of evolutionary relatedness between human beings and primates both suggests that xeno-transplantation of primate organs and tissue might be successful and also raises questions about whether it is ethical to use primates in ways that it is not considered acceptable to use human beings. Certainly, any harm suffered by primates should be given great weight. This position is reflected in the principles underlying current practice in the U.K. The Working Party endorses the special protection afforded to primates used for medical and scientific purposes.

10.10 The Working Party would accept the use of very small numbers of primates as recipients of organs during research to develop xenotransplantation of organs and tissue from non-primates. In this case, using a small number of primates for research, while undesirable, can be justified by the potential benefits if xenotransplantation were to become a successful procedure.

10.11 The routine use of higher primates to supply organs for xenotransplantation on a scale sufficient to meet the organ shortage would represent a new use of primates in the U.K. In addition to the special harm suffered by primates other considerations must be taken into account. The endangered status of chimpanzees rules out their use for xenotransplantation. The potential risk of extinction, even to a specis like the baboon that is not currently endangered, must be taken seriously. Xenotransplantation using primate organs or tissue may pose particular risks of disease transmission.

10.12 Given the ethical concerns raised by the use of primates for xenotransplantation attention has turned to developing the pig as an alternative source of organs and tissue. As discussed below, in the view of the Working Party, the use of pigs for xenotransplantation raises fewer ethical concerns. To develop the use of primates for xenotransplantation, when there is an ethically acceptable alternative, would not be justifiable. The Working Party recommends that non-primate species should be regarded as the source animals of choice for xenotransplantation. However, possibilities for alleviating the organ shortage which do not involve the use of animals, such as increased donation of human organs, and the development of artificial organs and tissue, should be actively pursued.

10.13 The Working Party considered the possibility that, after a number of years of research, it might be found that pig organs and tissue could not be used for xeno-transplantation. Would it then be ethically acceptable to use primate organs and tissue for xenotransplantation? The members of the Working Party were agreed that the use of primates would be ethically unacceptable if any of the following conditions obtained:

- improving the supply of human organs and the use of alternative methods of organ replacement such as mechanical organs and tissue replacement could meet the organ shortage;
- the use of higher primates would result in them becoming an endangered species;
- concerns about the possible transmission of disease from higher primates to human beings could not be met; or
- the welfare of animals could not be maintained to a high standard.

These conditions would rule out all use of chimpanzees on conservation grounds. When considering the hypothetical situation in which the conditions might be satisfied for a species such as a baboon, some members of the Working Party felt that the use of primates for xenotransplantation would never be acceptable. Other members of the Working Party felt that, should these circumstances come to prevail, it would be appropriate to reconsider the use of higher primates to supply organs for xenotransplantation.

The use of pigs for xenotransplantation

10.14 While the pig is an animal of sufficient intelligence and sociability to make welfare considerations paramount, there is less evidence that is shares capacities with human beings to the extent that primates do. As such, the adverse effects suffered by pigs used to supply organs for transplantation would not outweigh the potential benefits to human beings. It is also difficult to see how, in a society in which the breeding of pigs for food and clothing is accepted, their use for life-saving medical procedures such as xenotransplantation could not be acceptable. The Working Party concluded that the use of pigs for the routine supply of organs for xenotransplantation was ethically acceptable.

10.15 If pigs are used for xenotransplantation they are likely to have been genetically modified so the human response to pig organs and tissue is reduced. The production of transgenic pigs for xenotransplantation is likely to involve the transfer of a gene or a few genes of human origin. This is a very small and specific change. It is only in combination with all the other genes that make up the human genome that a particular gene contributes to the specification of the characteristics of the human species. Thus, inserting these genes into a transgenic pig would not destroy the integrity of either species. Species boundaries in any case, are not inviolable but change through a number of other processes. The Working Party concluded that the use of transgenic pigs that have been genetically modified to reduce the human immune response to pig organs was ethically acceptable . . .

Animal Concerns: practice

10.18 In the U.K., animals used for scientific purposes are protected by the Animals (Scientific Procedures) Act 1986 (the 1986 Act). Before the use of animals is permitted, the likely effects on the animals must be weighed against the benefits likely to accrue from their use. The Home Office Inspectorate grants licences, in consultation where necessary with the Animals Procedures Committee. The use of animals for xenotransplantation raises questions about their breeding, especially if they are genetically modified, the welfare implications of producing animals free of infectious organisms, and their slaughter. The Working Party recommends that the convention by which the Animal Procedures Committee advises on project licences in difficult areas should extend to applications for the use of animals for xenotransplantation.

10.19 Xenotransplantation research may require the use of limited numbers of primates as xenograft recipients. Primates are afforded special protection by the 1986 Act. Project applications involving primates are examined by the Animals Procedures Committee and the Home Office sets standards for the care and welfare of primates involved in research. The Working Party recommended that non-primate species should be regarded as the source animals of choice for xenotransplantation. What follows, therefore, refers to the welfare implications of the use of non-primate animals, notably transgenic pigs, to supply organs and tissue for xenotransplantation.

10.20 The breeding of transgenic animals is under the control of the 1986 Act. Transgenic animals can, in principle, be released from the control of the 1986 Act if there is no significant effect on the animals' welfare after two generations. If they are released welfare concerns would be covered by the less demanding standards regulating agricultural practice and animal husbandry.

10.21 Animals used to provide organs and tissue will need to be free, as far as possible, from infectious organisms in order to reduce the risk that xenotransplantation will lead to the transmission of diseases into the human population. Repeated testing of animals and other procedures may adversely effect animal welfare. The Working Party recommends that, when decisions are made about the acceptability of using animals for xenotransplantation, particular attention is paid to reducing the adverse effects associated with the need to produce animals free from infectious organisms.

10.22 Removal of organs or tissue from anaesthetised animals will come under the control of the 1986 Act. It is possible, however, that killing animals and removing their organs without the use of anaesthetic would not come under the control of the 1986 Act. It would be possible, in principle, to remove non-vital organs, or tissues that regenerate, sequentially from animals. This could well result in an increase in animal suffering. The Home Office has stated that the provisions of the 1986 Act regarding re-use of animals would preclude the sequential removal of organs or tissue. The Working Party recommends that the Animals (Scientific Procedures) Act should continue to be interpreted as prohibiting sequential removal from animals of tissue and organs for transplantation.

10.23 Important welfare considerations are raised by the breeding of transgenic animals; producing animals free from infectious organisms; and removing organs and tissue from animals used for xenotransplantation. There is some uncertainty about whether, in practice, all these aspects would be covered by the 1986 Act. In view of the important welfare implications raised by xenotransplantation, the Working Party recommends that the Home Office should require that all animals used for xenotransplantation are protected under the Animals (Scientific Procedure) Act 1986. Any reputable company producing animals in order to supply organs and tissue for xenotransplantation would, in any case, wish to be licensed under the 1986 Act in order to reassure the public that their activities were meeting the highest standards of animal welfare. The Working Party recommends that the standards set by the 1986 Act become the minimum for the industry.

Transmission of infectious diseases

10.24 Xenotransplantation of animal organs and tissue carries with it the potential risk that diseases will be transmitted from animals to xenograft recipients and to the wider human population. It is difficult to assess this risk, since it is impossible to predict whether infectious organisms that are harmless in their animal host will cause disease in human xenograph recipients or whether the disease will spread into the wider human population. There are certain to be infectious organisms of both primates and pigs that are currently unknown, and some of these might cause disease in human beings. There is evidence that there are infectious organisms of both primates and pigs that are currently unknown, and some of these might cause disease in human beings. There is evidence that infectious organisms of primates, notably viruses, can pass into the human population and cause disease. This supports the recommendation that non-primate species should be regarded as the source animals of choice for xenotransplantation. The possible risk of disease transmission from pigs, however, also requires careful consideration.

10.25 It is not possible to predict or quantify the risk that xenotransplantation will result in the emergence of new human diseases. But in the worst case, the consequences could be far reaching and difficult to control. The principle of precaution required that action is taken to avoid risks in advance of certainty about their nature. It suggests that the burden of proof should lie with those developing the technology to demonstrate that it will not cause serious harm. The Working Party concluded that the risks associated with possible transmission of infectious diseases as a consequence of xenotransplantation have not been adequately dealt with. It would not be ethical therefore to begin clinical trials of xenotransplantation involving human beings . . . .

The Report recommends that a new body an Advisory Committee on Xenotransplantation should be established. It takes the view that before initial transplantation procedures are undertaken on human subjects the approval of both this committee and the local research ethics committee should be obtained.

Early patients

10.34 Even where the results from animal experiments suggest that xenotransplantation involving human recipients is justifiable, the early clinical trials will involve unknown and unpredictable risks. The question then becomes how best to protect early patients' welfare and interests. It is of the utmost importance that potential patients give free and properly informed consent to participation in the first xenotransplantation trials. The Working Party recommends that the consent of patients to participation in xenotransplantation trials is sought by appropriately trained professionals who are independent of the xenotransplantation team. The information given to prospective recipients should include an estimation of likely success, attendant risks and subsequent quality of life. Patients consenting to xenotransplantation should be informed that post-operative monitoring for infectious organisms is an integral part of the procedure and that their consent to the operation includes consent to this monitoring.

10.35 Teams conducting experimental trials on patients are under a scientific and ethical obligation to research and report the subsequent quality of life of the recipients. The Working Party recommends that no protocol to conduct a trial should be accepted unless it contains a commitment to a robust description and assessment of the patient's pre-operative and post operative quality of life . . .

10.36 Special issues arise in the case of children. Xenotransplantation has been proposed as a method of reducing the especially acute shortage of organs for babies and children. Early clinical trials of xenotransplantation will be a form of therapeutic research. Therapeutic research must offer some prospect of genuine benefit for the patient, but it involves greater uncertainties than treatment, and therefore greater caution must be exercised. The British Paediatric Association and the Medical Research Council have advised that therapeutic research should not involve children if it could equally well be performed with adults. It would be difficult to justify the involvement of children in major and risky xenotransplantation trials before some of the uncertainties have been eliminated in trials involving adults. The Working Party therefore recommend that the first xenotransplantation trials involve adults rather than children.

10.37 Similar issues arise for adults who are considered incapable of consenting to participation in therapeutic research because they are mentally incapacitated. The law would appear to be that incapacitated adults may be involved in therapeutic research if this is in their best interests. It would be difficult to justify the involvement of incapacitated adults in the first xenotransplantation trials before some of the major uncertainties have been eliminated in trials involving adults who are capable of weighing the benefits and risks on their own behalf. The Working Party recommends that the first xenotransplantation trials should not involve adults incapable of consenting to participation on their own behalf.

NOTES:

1. On all the recommendations above, the Kennedy Report reached the same conclusions.
2. For discussion of the Animal (Scientific Procedures) Act 1986, see Chapter 10 at p.737.

QUESTIONS:

1. Are the grounds on which the Nuffield and Kennedy Reports distinguished between primates and pigs as acceptable sources of organs and tissues ethically defensible? (See M. Fox, "Re-thinking Kinship: Law's Construction of the Animal Body" (2004) 57 *Current Legal Problems* 469–493.)
2. Would it ever be acceptable to enrol a mentally incapacitated patient in a xenotransplant clinical trial given the enactment of the Mental Capacity Act 2005.

(ii) Xenotransplantation Interim Regulatory Authority

In January 1997 the Government announced a moratorium on xenotransplantation in view of the risks involved, but did establish a non-statutory regulatory body to oversee the procedure (see M. Fox and J. McHale, "Regulating Xenotransplantation" (1997) 147 *New Law Journal* 139). The terms of reference of the Xenotransplantation Interim Regulatory Authority (UKIXRA) (*http://www.doh.gov.uk/ukxira*) are:

"To advise the Secretaries of State for Health, Northern Ireland, Scotland and Wales on the action necessary to regulate xenotransplantation, taking into account the principles outline in 'Animal Tissues into Humans' [the Kennedy Report] and worldwide developments in xenotransplantation. In particular, to advise:

> (a) on safety, efficacy and considerations of animal welfare in liaison with the Home Office, and any other pre-conditions for xeno-transplantation for human use, and whether these have been met;
> (b) on research required to assess safety and efficacy factors in xeno-transplantation procedures;
> (c) on the acceptability of specific applications to proceed with xeno-transplantation in humans; and
> (d) to provide a focal point on xenotransplantation issues within Government."

NOTES:

1. To date no clinical trials in humans have been sanctioned because of concerns about safety, and it must be doubted whether the UK Government will allow the technology to be used in humans given concerns about BSE/CJD and the H5NI (bird flu) virus. Moreover, arguably the technology is being superseded by stem cell research (see Chapter 10 at p.725).
2. In any event, it is questionable whether the transplantation of animal organs into human subjects is lawful and could validly be consented to given the likelihood of rejection (see J.K. Mason, "Organ Donation and Transplantation" in C. Dyer (ed.), *Doctors, Patients and the Law,* Oxford: Blackwell, 1992). Furthermore, given the potential global implications of virus transmission, some commentators have proposed that such risks may require some kind of community or public consent, as well as the consent of the individual recipient (see S. Fovargue, "Consenting to Bio-Risk" (2005) 26 *Legal Studies* 404.)
3. Serious questions concerning the erosion of civil liberties are raised by the surveillance and monitoring of future xenotransplant recipients, which would be required as a result of the threat of infection. UXIRA advocates a policy which would mandate acceptance of certain lifelong restrictions (some of them applicable to relatives and close contacts as well as the recipients themselves). This could require state regulation of lifestyle

choices, such as a condition that they use barrier contraception and refrain from having children (see *Draft Report of the Infection Surveillance Steering Group of the UKIXRA*). The biosecure conditions in which animal donor's have to be kept to reduce these infection risks also has significant implications for animal welfare (see UKIXRA, *Guidance Notes on Biosecurity Considerations in Relation to Xenotransplantation* (year).

4. For a comparative survey of approaches to xenotransplantation in other jurisdictions, see S. McLean and L. Williamson, *Xenotransplantation: Law and Ethics*, Aldershot: Ashgate, 2005, Chapter 5.

QUESTIONS:

1. What are the advantages and disadvantages of the moratorium on xenotransplant trials proceeding in human beings?
2. Would the restrictions on lifestyle proposed by UKIXRA breach the European Convention on Human Rights? Would such requirements be legally enforceable? For instance, as McLean and Williamson ask, "what would be the state's authority should an individual xenotransplant recipient or the partner of one become pregnant. Could the state compel a pregnancy termination, and if so on what grounds—ethical or legal?" (S. McLean and L. Williamson, "Xenoptransplantation: A Pig in a Poke?" (2004) 57 *Current Legal Problems* 468).
3. Do xenotranplantation and the genetic engineering of animals with human genes which is necessary for the procedure compromise the notion of human identity? (see M. Fox, "Reconfiguring the Animal/Human Boundary: the Impact of Xenotechnologies" (2005) 26 *Liverpool Law Review* 149–167).
4. Should there be a statutory right of conscientious objection to protect health care professionals who did not want to participate should the procedure ever be authorised for use on human beings? (See M. Fox and J. McHale, "Xenotransplantation: the Ethical and Legal Ramifications" (1998) *Medical Law Review* 43.)
5. At the present time it is questionable as to whether transplantation of animal organs into human subjects is lawful. As noted above an individual cannot consent to the infliction of any harm (see Chapter 6 above at p.355). Would it be lawful to accept an organ realising that there would be a high probability of rejection? (See J.K. Mason, "Organ Donation and Transplantation" in C. Dyer (ed.), *Doctors, Patients and the Law*, Oxford: Blackwell, 1992.)

5. ACCOUNTABILITY FOR DEFECTIVE ORGANS OR TISSUE

An action in negligence may be brought by a person who has received a defective organ or defective tissue during a transplant operation. A claim may be brought on the basis of negligence at common law or strict liability under the Consumer Protection Act 1987. In some situations an action may be brought for breach of statutory duty. An example of such an action brought in relation to defective bodily products was in *Re Haemophiliac Litigation* [1990] N.L.J.R. 1349. The plaintiffs were haemophiliacs who had been infected with HIV after they had been given a clotting agent—"Factor 8"—contaminated with the virus which had been imported from the United States. The hearing was an application for discovery of documents (this is discussed further in Chapter 1 above). In determining whether to order disclosure, the Court of Appeal considered the substantive merits of the plaintiff's case. The court said that there was an arguable case both in negligence and for breach of statutory duty. As far as the action for breach of statutory duty was concerned the plaintiffs had relied upon s.1 of the National Health Service Act 1977. However, both at first instance and in the Court of Appeal, the judges noted that bringing such an action involved considerable practical difficulties. Ralph Gibson L.J. stated that the duties under the 1977 Act did not clearly demonstrate that Parliament had intended to impose a duty enforceable by civil action. The action in negligence may have met with more success. The basis for the claim was that the Department of Health was negligent in not ensuring adequate provision of blood supplies in England and Wales which had resulted in the importation of contaminated blood from the United States. The Court of Appeal stated that such an action was sustainable in principle.

This case illustrates the difficulties in establishing an action where the courts are faced with a dilemma which involves policy-making and the allocation of medical resources. (See Chapter 1 at p.45.) The case was settled prior to trial. It is questionable whether the plaintiffs would have succeeded at the full hearing of the action.

The supply of a defective organ may lead to an action being brought under the Consumer Protection Act 1987 (discussed in Chapter 3 above at p.203). The difficulty facing the claimant will be to establish that the organ/tissue is a product for the purposes of the legislation. There are defences under the Act, for example, the state of scientific and technical knowledge at the time (s.4). An action may also be brought against a donor where a donee was affected by diseased organs/ tissue. Nonetheless establishment of such an action may be difficult. Even were a duty of care to be established in that the donor should have made the donee aware of the prospect of disease transmission, causation may not be established because the organ would be subject to screening prior to transplantation.

SELECT BIBLIOGRAPHY

M.R. Brazier, *Medicine, Patients and the Law* (3rd edn), Harmondsworth: Penguin, 2002, Chapter 18.

R. Chadwick, "Corpses, Recycling and Therapeutic Purposes" in R. Lee and D. Morgan (eds), *Death Rights: Law and Ethics at the End of Life*, London: Routledge (1994).

J. Dukeminier, "Supplying Organs for Transplantation" (1970) 68 Mich. L.R. 811.

G. Dworkin, "The Law Relating to Organ Transplantation in England" (1970) 33 M.L.R. 35.

G. Dworkin and I. Kennedy, "Human Tissue: Rights in the Body and Its Parts" (1993) 1 *Medical Law Review* 291.

D. Lamb, *Death, Brain Death & Ethics*, Beckenham: Croom Helm, 1985.

D. Lamb, *Organ Transplants and Ethics*, London: Routledge, 1990.

D. Lanham, "Transplants and the Human Tissue Act 1961" (1971) 11 Med. Sci. and the Law 16.

N. Machado, *Using the Bodies of the Dead: Legal, Ethical and Organisational Dimensions of Organ Transplantation*, Aldershot: Dartmouth, 1998.

J.K. Mason, "Organ Donation and Transportation" in C. Dyer (edn) "*Doctors, Patients and the Law*" Oxford: Blackwell, 1992.

J.K. Mason and G. Laurie, *Mason and McCall Smith's Law and Medical Ethics* (7th edn), London: Butterworths, 2005, Chapters 14 and 15.

P. McCullagh, *Brain Dead, Brain Absent, Brain Donors*, Chichester: John Wiley, 1993.

G. Northoff, "Do Brain Tissue Transplants Alter Personal Identity? Inadequacies of Some 'Standard Arguments'" (1996) 22 *Journal of Medical Ethics* 174.

C. Pallis, *The ABC of Brain Stem Death* (2nd edn), London: BMJ, 1996.

D. Price, *Organ Transplants and Ethics*, Cambridge: Cambridge University Press 2000.

P. Singer, *Rethinking Life and Death: the Collapse of Our Traditional Ethics*, Oxford: OUP, 1995, Chapters 2 and 3.

P.D.G. Skegg, *Law Ethics and Medicine*, Oxford: OUP, 1988, Chapter 10.

P.D.G. Skegg, "Liability for the Unauthorised Removal of Cadaveric Transplant Material" (1974) Med. Sci. and Law 53; (1977) *Med. Sci. and Law* 123.

L. Skeane, "Property Rights in Human Bodies, Body Parts and Tissue: Regulatory Contexts and Proposals for New Laws" (2002) *Legal Studies* 102.

R.F. Weir and R.S. Olick, *The Stored Tissue Issue*, Oxford: Oxford University Press, 2004.

S.J. Younger, M. Anderson and R. Schapiro, *Transplanting Human Tissue: Ethics Policy and Practice*, Oxford: Oxford University Press 2003.

Index

(all references are to page number)

Abortion
bibliography, 923–924
certification, 886–891
childbirth, and, 875–876
children, and, 471–473
conscientious objection, 919–922
criminal prohibition, 874–878
death during birth, 875–876
emergency situations, 898–899
ethics, 869–874
grounds for lawful termination, 878–886
interests of different parties
  foetus, 902–911
  incompetent pregnant woman, 901–902
  introduction, 899–900
  parents of underage girl, 919
  pregnant woman, 900–901
  putative father, 912–919
introduction, 859–860
lawful termination, 878–886
legal framework
  criminal prohibition, 874–878
  introduction, 874
medical treatment to children, and, 471–473
methods of treatment
  anti progession termination, 892–894
  aspiration termination, 892
  chemical abortion, 892–895
  generally, 891–898
  prostaglandin termination, 892
  surgical abortion, 892
place of treatment, 886
post-coital contraception, and, 894–898
procuring a miscarriage, 874–878
status of the foetus, 870–872
Access to health records
common law, at, 660–664
Data Protection Act 1998, under, 647–652
Access to health services
allocation of resources
  clinical judgment, 51–57
  disability discrimination, 68–69
  EU law, 69–79
  free movement principles, 69–79
  human rights, and, 57–68
  procedural irregularities, 68
community care, 43–44
compensation claims, 79–86
duties to provide
  community care, 43–44
  enforcement, 45–86
  generally, 41

Access to health services—*cont.*
duties to provide—*cont.*
  obligation of NHS, 41–43
enforcement of duties to provide
  allocation of resources, 57–79
  clinical judgment, 51–57
  compensation claims, 79–86
  human rights, and, 57–68
  introduction, 45
  judicial review, 45–79
  resource allocation, 51–79
introduction, 41
judicial review
  allocation of resources, 57–79
  clinical judgment, 51–57
  introduction, 45–51
obligation of NHS, 41–43
Access to medical records
legal proceedings, and, 658–660
Access to medical reports
generally, 654–664
Access to Justice **(1996)**
reform of fault-based liability, and, 215
Accountability
see **Complaints processes**
Acts-omissions doctrine
ethics, and, 136–141
Active termination of life
defence to those prosecuted, 1076–1077
generally, 1072–1076
Actual bodily harm
consent to treatment, and, 352–353
Admission to hospital
compulsory admission
  applications, 521–522
  arrival at hospital, 522–524
  criteria, 510–520
  degree of mental disorder, 517
  discretion of doctor, 524–525
  doctor's recommendations, 522
  emergencies, in, 526
  general provisions, 502–504
  holding powers, 526–528
  "hospital", 502
  informal resident, of, 526–528
  introduction, 502
  least restrictive alternative, 517
  mental disorder, 504–510
  mental illness, 504–507
  mental impairment, 504
  nature of mental disorder, 517
  need for treatment, 511–515

Admission to hospital—*cont.*
  compulsory admission—*cont.*
    prior arrangements, 522–524
    procedure, 520–526
    psychopathic disorder, 504, 508
    reform proposals, 517–520, 525–526
    severe mental impairment, 504, 507
    treatability, 515–517
    voluntary resident, of, 526–528
  control of patient activity, 529–531
  correspondence, 547
  detention, 528
  discipline, 529–531
  in hospital treatment
    control of patient activity, 529–531
    correspondence, 547
    detention, 528
    discipline, 529–531
    introduction, 528
    leave of absence, 528–529
    medical treatment, 531–547
    MHC's role, 547–548
    patient information, 547
    review, 547–548
  informal admission, 492–501
  leave of absence, 528–529
  medical treatment
    electro-convulsive therapy, 534–542
    emergencies, 542
    hormone implantation, 532–533
    introduction, 531–532
    medication, 533–534
    other, 543–547
    psychosurgery, 532–533
    reduction of male sexual drive, 532–533
    reforms, 547
  Mental Health Commission's role, 547–548
  patient information, 547
  reforms
    compulsory admission to hospital,
        517–520, 525–526
    medical treatment, 547
  review of detention, 547–548
  voluntary admission, 492
Advance directives
  generally, 1078–1082
After-care under supervision
  community care, and, 555–561
Alcohol consumption
  pregnancy, and, 949
Alder Hey inquiry
  human tissue, and, 1102–1103
Allocation of resources
  clinical judgment, 51–57
  disability discrimination, 68–69
  EU law, 69–79
  free movement principles, 69–79
  human rights, and, 57–68
  procedural irregularities, 68
Amniocentesis
  pregnancy, and, 948

Anencephalic infant
  human tissue, and, 1111–1112
Animal research
  generally, 734–742
Anonymised information
  breach of confidence claims, and, 579–581
  data protection, and, 645–647
  human tissue, and, 1139–1140
Anorexics
  force feeding, and, 370–371
Anti progestion termination
  abortion, and, 892–894
Appropriate consent
  adults, 1131–1133
  children, 1129–1131
  conditions, 1128–1129
  deceased's tissue, for, 1134–1135
  exceptions to principle
    anonymised material, 1139–1140
    existing holdings, 1141–1142
    generally, 1138–1139
    untraceable persons, 1140–1141
  form, 1125–1126
  incompetent adults, 1135–1138
  nominated representative, 1133–1134
  person able to give, 1129–1138
  scope, 1126–1128
  timing, 1122–1125
  withdrawal, 1128
Artificial transplants
  human tissue, and, 1101
Aspiration termination
  abortion, and, 892
Assault and battery
  consent to treatment, and, 351–352
Assisted insemination
  Blood decision, 765–768
  generally, 759–763
  HFEA Code, 768–772
  payment, 772–775
  statutory provisions, 763–764
  Warnock Committee Report, 760–761
Assisted reproduction
  access to reproductive technologies,
      802–812
  assisted insemination
    Blood decision, 765–768
    generally, 759–763
    HFEA Code, 768–772
    payment, 772–775
    statutory provisions, 763–764
    Warnock Committee Report, 760–761
  bibliography, 856–857
  child's rights, 828–835
  cloning, 850–853
  conscientious objection, 812
  donation of embryos, 835–841
  donor anonymity, 832–835
  donor insemination, 759
  egg sharing, 775–776
  embryo donation and storage, 835–841

Assisted reproduction—*cont.*
ethics, and
generally, 752–753
introduction, 87
gamete donation
Blood decision, 765–768
generally, 759–763
HFEA Code, 768–772
payment, 772–775
statutory provisions, 763–764
Warnock Committee Report, 760–761
Human Fertilisation and Embryology
Authority
constitution, 754–755
introduction, 753
legislative framework, 755–758
human rights, and, 814–817
impact of technologies on the family
children, 828–835
fathers, 819–828
introduction, 817–818
mothers, 818–819
in vitro fertilisation
definitions, 777
generally, 777–781
Warnock Committee Report, 777–778
infertility treatment
introduction, 751–752
resource allocation, 812–814
techniques for alleviating, 758–802
welfare of child, 802–812
introduction, 751–753
limits on choice
cloning, 850–853
introduction, 841
saviour siblings, 841–848
sex selection, 848–850
negligence in provision, 855–856
pre-implantation diagnosis (PGD), 851
procreative tourism, 853–854
resource allocation
generally, 812–814
NICE guideline, 813
rights to reproduce, 814–817
saviour siblings, 841–848
sex selection, 848–850
sibling selection, 841–848
sperm donation
Blood decision, 765–768
generally, 759–763
HFEA Code, 768–772
payment, 772–775
statutory provisions, 763–764
Warnock Committee Report, 760–761
storage of embryos, 835–841
surrogacy
definitions, 781–782
dispute resolution, 793–796
generally, 781–783
judicial attitudes, 784–787
legislative approach, 787–793
reforms, 797–802

Assisted reproduction—*cont.*
surrogacy—*cont.*
terms of arrangement, 796–797
Warnock Committee Report, 782–783
techniques for alleviating infertility
gamete donation, 759–776
in vitro fertilisation, 777–781
introduction, 758
surrogacy, 781–802
welfare of child
generally, 802–812
HFEA Code, 807–809
judicial review, 804–806
statutory provision, 806–807
Warnock Committee Report, 803
Assisted suicide
generally, 1001
overview, 997
Pretty decision, 1001–1014
Autonomy
abortion, and, 859
capacity to consent to treatment, and, 298
consent to treatment, and, 349
contraception, and, 859
end of life, and, 994
ethics, and, 121–123
medical treatment, and, 291–293
medical treatment for children, and, 406

Balance of probabilities
clinical negligence actions, and, 179
Battery
consent to treatment, and, 351–352
Beginning of life
see also **End of life**
acts-omissions doctrine, 136–141
double effect doctrine, 136–141
euthanasia, 141–144
introduction, 128
reproductive ethics, 130–136
sanctity of life, 128–130
Best interests test
children, and
bibliography, 477–478
Gillick competence, 439–470
introduction, 405–407
limits to parental power of consent,
470–477
older child, 439–451
young child, 407–439
common law, at, 320–327
end of life, and, 993–994
Mental Capacity Act 2005, under, 327–247
Bilary artesia
medical treatment for children, and, 420–422
***Bolam* test**
generally, 158–159
impact on causation, 201–203
introduction, 149
medical treatment, and, 292
reaction to, 167–174

Bournewood **safeguards**
mental health system, and, 492–498
Brain damaged baby
medical treatment for children, and, 413–415
Breach of confidence claims
anonymised information, 579–581
applicants, 581–596
basis for action, 571–573
children, by, 581–592
consent to disclosure, 596–598
damages, 622–623
deceased patient, by, 595–596
doctors with dual responsibilities, 621–622
ethics, and, 87
grounds for disclosure
consent, 596–598
public interest, 598–621
incompetent adult, by, 592–595
injunctions, 622
public interest, and
freedom of expression, 598–607
introduction, 598
risk to public, 607–619
serious communicable diseases, 619–621
relationship with privacy, 573–579
remedies for breach, 622–623
Burden of proof
clinical negligence actions, and, 179–183

Cadaver material
and see **Human tissue**
generally, 1100
Capacity to consent to treatment
autonomy, and, 298
best interests test
common law, at, 320–327
Mental Capacity Act 2005, under,
327–247
bibliography, 347–248
challenge of, 302–307
common law, at
best interests test, 320–327
generally, 308–314
introduction, 295–296
Law Commission reports, 298–302
legal presumptions, 295
Mental Capacity Act 2005, under
background, 296–298
best interests test, 327–247
care and treatment matters, 331–334
court-based jurisdiction, 338–347
decisions made on behalf of incapable
adult, 330–331
generally, 314–320
independent consultees, 334–338
Mental Incapacity (Law Com, 1995)
best interests test, 328–329
capacity test, 314–318
care and treatment matters, 331
court-based jurisdiction, 339–342
introduction, 296
principles, 301–302

Capacity to consent to treatment—*cont.*
overview, 292
principles, 298–302
reforms, 296–298
refusal of treatment, 302–307
Care in the community
after-care under supervision, 555–561
guardianship, 553–555
introduction, 552–553
Causation
failure to act, and, 201–203
childbirth, and, 977–978
generally, 183–203
loss of a chance, 193–201
standard of care, 188–193
Certification
abortion, and, 886–891
Chemical termination
abortion, and, 892–895
Childbirth
abortion, and, 875–876
bibliography, 988–989
breach of contract claims, 971–976
child born dead, 962
choice of place and method, 952–954
congenital disabilities, 962–967
enforced Caesareans, 954–961
method, 952–954
negligence claims
basis, 976–977
causation, 977–978
child, by or on behalf of, 962–971
child born dead, 962
congenital disabilities, 962–967
damages, 978–988
introduction, 961–962
parents, by, 977–988
wrongful life, 967–971
place, 952–954
wrongful life action, 967–971
Children
assisted reproduction, and, 828–835
breach of confidence claims, and, 581–592
human tissue, and, 1108–1111
medical treatment, and
and see **Children (medical treatment)**
bibliography, 477–478
Gillick competence, 439–470
introduction, 405–407
limits to parental power of consent,
470–477
older child, 439–451
young child, 407–439
medicinal product trials, and, 709–711
research subject consent, and, 688–692
Children (medical treatment)
abortion, 471–473
autonomy, and, 406
best interests
compelling treatment contrary to best
interests, 423–434
conjoined twins, 434–439

Children (medical treatment)—*cont.*
best interests—*cont.*
 withdrawal of medical treatment, 408–423
 withholding of medical treatment,
  408–423
bibliography, 477–478
bilary artesia, 420–422
brain damaged baby, 413–415
compelling treatment contrary to best
 interests, 423–434
conjoined twins, 434–439
Down's syndrome, 409–410
Gillick competence
 generally, 440–451
 overview, 405
 refusal of treatment, 451–463
 religious belief, 463–470
 retreat from original position, 451–470
HIV testing, 473–475
hydrocephalus, 411–412
International Convention on the Rights of
 the Child, 406
introduction, 405–407
Jehovah's Witnesses, and, 417–418
life-saving treatment, 408
limits to parental power of consent, 470–477
male circumcision, 475–477
older child
 common law power of consent, 440–470
 statutory power of consent, 439–440
refusal of treatment
 generally, 451–463
 religious belief, 463–470
reproductive choice, 471
severe disablement, 415–417
sterilisation, 470–471
withdrawal of medical treatment, 408–423
withholding of medical treatment, 408–423
young child
 compelling treatment contrary to best
  interests, 423–434
 conjoined twins, 434–439
 introduction, 407–408
 withdrawal of medical treatment, 408–423
 withholding of medical treatment,
  408–423
Chorus villus sampling
pregnancy, and, 948
Cigarettes
see **Smoking**
Circumcision
female, 356–358
male, 475–477
"Claims consciousness"
clinical negligence actions, and, 151
Clinical judgment
resource allocation, and, 51–57
Clinical negligence claims
balance of probabilities, 179
Bolam test
 generally, 158–159
 impact on causation, 201–203

Clinical negligence claims—*cont.*
Bolam test—*cont.*
 reaction to, 167–174
burden of proof, 179–183
causation
 failure to act, and, 201–203
 generally, 183–203
 loss of a chance, 193–201
 standard of care, 188–193
"claims consciousness", 151
"defensive medicine", and, 150
divergence of professional opinion, 163–167
duty of care, 153–156
inexperienced practitioners, 174–179
introduction, 152–153
overview, 149–150
reform of fault-based liability, and
 difficulties with system, 215–217
 NHS redress scheme, 233–236
 no-fault compensation, 217–224
 strict liability, 224–225
res ipsa loquitur, 179–183
standard of care
 Bolam test, 158–159
 Bolitho decision, 167–173
 divergence of professional opinion,
  163–167
 generally, 157–162
 inexperienced practitioners, 174–179
 Marriott decision, 173–174
Clinical research
animal research, 734–742
approval of trials
 challenging decision, 718
 role of Research Ethics Committee,
  670–682
 scrutiny, 718–719
bibliography, 742–743
cloning, 725–734
compensation for harm, 719–721
confidentiality of participants' information,
 714–717
Declaration of Helsinki, 667
embryo research
 cloning, 725–734
 general, 721–725
 HFEA 1990, under, 724
 stem cell research, 725–734
 Warnock Committee Report, 721–723
ethics, and, 667–668
ethics committees, 670
Ethics Committees Authority, 669–670
fraudulent researchers, 717–718
GMC guidance
 confidentiality of participants'
  information, 714–716
 research subject consent, 684–686
incompetent adults
 general issues, 692
 non-therapeutic research, 693–696
 statutory provisions, 696–702
introduction, 667–669

Clinical research—*cont.*
  medicinal product trials
    children, 709–711
    incompetent adults, 711–714
    informed consent, 709
    introduction, 703–704
    Regulations, 705–707
    scrutiny by REC, 707–709
  multi-centred research, 675–676
  national oversight, 669–670
  overview, 292
  regulation, 669–670
  Research Ethics Committee
    approval of multi-centred research,
        675–676
    consent of research subject, 683
    follow-up, 702–703
    introduction, 670
    liability of members for injuries, 719
    membership, 673–675
    procedure for review of trials, 676–680
    reform of system, 681–682
    remit, 670–673
  research subject consent
    child subjects, 688–692
    follow-up by REC, 702–703
    generally, 682–686
    GMC guidance, 684–686
    incompetent adults, 692–702
    randomised clinical trials, 686–688
    REC guidance, 683
  scrutiny of clinical trial approvals, 718–719
  stem cell research, 725–734
  Warnock Committee Report, 721–723
Cloning
  embryo research, and, 725–734
Codes of practice
  human tissue, and, 1161–1162
Communicable diseases
  consent to treatment, and, 368–370
  patient confidentiality, and, 630–631
Community care
  after-care under supervision, 555–561
  guardianship, 553–555
  introduction, 552–553
Community supervision orders
  mental health system, and, 557–558
Community treatment orders
  mental health system, and, 557
Compelling medical treatment
  children, and, 423–434
Compensation
  clinical research, and, 719–721
  duties to provide health services, and, 79–86
Complaints processes
  bibliography, 287–288
  Council for Healthcare Regulatory
      Excellence, 239–240
  disciplinary action against health care
      professionals, 258–260
  General Medical Council
    "fitness to practice" review, 270–2780

Complaints processes—*cont.*
  General Medical Council—*cont.*
    introduction, 269
    overview, 239
    reform, 280–287
    regulatory role, 269–270
  Health Service Commissioner, 260–268
  Healthcare Commission
    annual reports, 258
    decision on handling of complaint, 255
    introduction, 252–253
    investigation, 255–256
    monitoring, 257–258
    panels, 256
    remit, 253–254
    report of investigation, 257
  introduction, 239–240
  NHS complaints
    acknowledgement, 250–251
    aims, 241–242
    Being Heard (DOH, 1994) 241–242
    complainants, 248–249
    complaints manager, 245
    consideration, 244–245
    excluded matters, 246–247
    form and content, 249
    handling arrangements, 244–245
    independent review, 252–258
    introduction, 240–241
    investigation, 251
    local resolution, 244–252
    Making Things Right (DOH, 2003) 243
    NHS bodies, to, 246
    process, 243–258
    records, 250–251
    response, 252
    responsibility for arrangements, 245
    time limits, 249–250
  NHS disciplinary procedures, 258–260
  Nursing and Midwifery Council, 239
  Ombudsman, and, 239
  self-regulation by professions
    General Medical Council, 269–287
    introduction, 268
Compulsory admission to hospital
  applications, 521–522
  arrival at hospital, 522–524
  criteria
    degree of mental disorder, 517
    generally, 510–511
    least restrictive alternative, 517
    nature of mental disorder, 517
    need for treatment, 511–515
    reform proposals, 517–520
    treatability, 515–517
  degree of mental disorder, 517
  discretion of doctor, 524–525
  doctor's recommendations, 522
  emergencies, in, 526
  general provisions, 502–504
  holding powers, 526–528
  "hospital", 502

Compulsory admission to hospital—*cont.*
in hospital treatment
control of patient activity, 529–531
correspondence, 547
detention, 528
discipline, 529–531
introduction, 528
leave of absence, 528–529
medical treatment, 531–547
MHC's role, 547–548
patient information, 547
review, 547–548
informal resident, of, 526–528
introduction, 502
least restrictive alternative, 517
medical treatment
electro-convulsive therapy, 534–542
emergencies, 542
hormone implantation, 532–533
introduction, 531–532
medication, 533–534
other, 543–547
psychosurgery, 532–533
reduction of male sexual drive, 532–533
reforms, 547
mental disorder, 504–510
mental illness, 504–507
mental impairment, 504
nature of mental disorder, 517
need for treatment, 511–515
prior arrangements, 522–524
procedure, 520–526
psychopathic disorder, 504, 508
reform proposals
criteria, 517–520
procedure, 525–526
severe mental impairment, 504, 507
treatability, 515–517
voluntary resident, of, 526–528
Compulsory care
generally, 22
Mental Health Act, under, 22
National Assistance Acts, under, 22–24
Condoms
contraception, and, 862
Confidentiality
access to health records
common law, at, 660–664
Data Protection Act 1998, under, 647–652
access to medical records in legal
proceedings, 658–660
access to medical reports, 654–664
anonymised information, 579–581
bibliography, 664–665
breach of confidence claims
anonymised information, 579–581
applicants, 581–596
basis for action, 571–573
children, by, 581–592
damages, 622–623
deceased patient, by, 595–596

Confidentiality—*cont.*
breach of confidence claims—*cont.*
doctors with dual responsibilities,
621–622
grounds for disclosure, 596–621
incompetent adult, by, 592–595
injunctions, 622
relationship with privacy, 573–579
remedies for breach, 622–623
clinical research, and, 714–717
communicable diseases, 630–631
consent to disclosure, 596–598
criminal investigations, 633–634
data protection
access to health records, 647–652
anonymisation, 645–647
conditions for processing, 642–644
damages, and, 653
data protection principles, 641
exceptions, 644–645
"health professional", 640–641
"health records", 640
introduction, 637–638
legal proceedings, 645
overview, 566
processing, 639–640
rectification of data, 653–654
remedies, 652–654
research, history and statistics, 644–645
scope of provisions, 639–641
sensitive personal data, 640
statutory provision, 638–654
employment contracts, 568–571
ethics, and
GMC guidance, 567–568
introduction, 567
NMC code, 568
overview, 566
European Convention on Human Rights,
and, 565–566
freedom of expression, 598–607
GMC guidance
doctors with dual responsibilities,
621–622
ethics, 567–568
serious communicable diseases, 619–621
grounds for disclosure
consent, 596–598
public interest, 598–621
health care professionals with HIV/AIDS,
598–607
infertility treatment, 623–627
introduction, 565–567
judicial proceedings, 634–637
neoplasia, 630
non-statutory protection, 571–623
overview, 292–293
Patient Information Advisory Group, 629
privacy, and, 573–579
professional obligations and codes, 567–568
public health risks, 630–631

Confidentiality—*cont.*
 public interest, and
  freedom of expression, 598–607
  introduction, 598
  risk to public, 607–619
  serious communicable diseases, 619–621
 right to respect for private and family life,
  565
 risk to public, 607–619
 serious communicable diseases, 619–621
 statutory exceptions, 627–632
 statutory protection
  infertility treatment, 623–627
  introduction, 623
  veneral disease, 623
 veneral disease, 623
Congenital disabilities
 childbirth, and, 962–967
Conjoined twins
 medical treatment for children, and, 434–439
Conscientious objection
 abortion, and, 919–922
 assisted reproduction, and, 812
Consent
 organ donation, and, 1164–1168
Consent to disclosure
 patient confidentiality, and, 596–598
Consent to treatment
 actual bodily harm, and, 352–353
 anorexics, 370–371
 assault and battery, and, 351–352
 autonomy, and, 349
 bibliography, 402–403
 capacity
  and see **Capacity to consent**
  best interests test, 320–347
  bibliography, 347–248
  common law, at, 308–314
  introduction, 295–296
  Mental Capacity Act 2005, under,
   314–320
  principles, 298–302
  reform process, 296–298
  refusal of treatment, 302–307
 children
  and see **Children (medical treatment)**
  bibliography, 477–478
  Gillick competence, 439–470
  introduction, 405–407
  limits to parental power of consent,
   470–477
  older child, 439–451
  young child, 407–439
 civil liability, 358–360
 cosmetic treatment, 370–371
 criminal liability
  actual bodily harm, 352–353
  female circumcision, 356–358
  grievous bodily harm, 353–356
  introduction, 352
  wounding, 353–356

Consent to treatment—*cont.*
 disclosure to patient
  doctors, by, 372–396
  introduction, 372
  non-therapeutic cases, 384–385
  nurses, by, 396–397
  paternalism, and, 387
  pro-patient trend, 387–396
  questions by patient, 385–387
  therapeutic cases, 372–383
 ethics, and, 126–128
 false imprisonment, and, 352
 female circumcision, and, 356–358
 force feeding, 370–371
 grievous bodily harm, and, 353–356
 HIV tests, 368–370
 human rights, and, 349
 introduction, 349–351
 meaning
  introduction, 360
  "real consent", 360–365
 need
  civil liability, 358–360
  criminal liability, 352–358
  introduction, 351–352
 overview, 292
 "real consent", 360–365
 right to bodily integrity, 351
 self-determination, and, 349
 serious communicable diseases, 368–370
 treatment by whom, 365–368
 trespass against the person, and, 358–359
 vitiation, 397–402
 wounding, and, 353–356
Consequentialism
 ethics, and, 97–102
Contagious disease control
 right to health care, and, 11–22
Contraception
 condoms, 862
 diaphragm, 862
 generally, 860–869
 hysterectomy, 862
 intrauterine device, 863
 introduction, 859–860
 negligence, and, 865–868
 non-surgical techniques, 862–863
 oral contraceptive pill, 863–864
 patches, 863
 sexually transmitted diseases, and, 862–863
 side effects, 865
 sterilisation, 862
 vasectomy, 862
Control of patient activity
 mental health system, and, 529–531
Coroners
 human tissue, and, 1142–1143
Correspondence
 compulsory admission to hospital, and, 547
Cosmetic treatment
 consent to treatment, and, 370–371

Council for Healthcare Regulatory Excellence
complaints processes, and, 239–240
Criminal investigations
patient confidentiality, and, 633–634
Criminal liability
abortion, and, 874–878
assisted suicide
generally, 1001
overview, 997
Pretty decision, 1001–1014
consent to treatment, and
actual bodily harm, 352–353
female circumcision, 356–358
grievous bodily harm, 353–356
introduction, 352
wounding, 353–356
end of life, and
murder, 1014–1021
suicide, 998–1014
euthanasia
ethics, and, 141–144
generally, 1001
overview, 997
Pretty decision, 1001–1014
gross negligence, and, 209–213
human tissue, and, 1153–1156
mercy killing, 1077–1078
murder/manslaughter
basic principles, 1014–1016
failure to provide care, 1018–1021
infanticide, 1017–1018
pain-killing drugs, 1016–1017
suicide
aiding and abetting, 999–1001
assisted suicide, 1001–1014
general prohibition, 998
Pretty decision, 1001–1014

Damages
breach of confidence claims, and, 622–623
childbirth, and, 978–988
data protection, and, 653
Data protection
access to health records, 647–652
anonymisation, 645–647
conditions for processing, 642–644
damages, and, 653
data protection principles, 641
exceptions, 644–645
"health professional", 640–641
"health records", 640
introduction, 637–638
legal proceedings, 645
overview, 566
processing, 639–640
rectification of data, 653–654
remedies, 652–654
research, history and statistics, 644–645
scope of provisions, 639–641
sensitive personal data, 640
statutory provision, 638–654

Death
brain stem death, 1092–1096
cognitive death, 1099–1100
criminal liability, and, 209–213
definition, 1090–1092
determining point of death
common law, 1096–1098
statute, under, 1098
diagnosis, 1092–1096
generally, 1090–1092
introduction, 1089–1090
Declaration of Helsinki
clinical research, and, 667
Defective medicinal products and drugs
professional accountability, and, 203–209
Defensive medicine
clinical negligence actions, and, 150
Deontology
ethics, and, 102–104
Descriptive relativism
ethics, and, 88
Detention
compulsory admission to hospital, and, 528
Diaphragm
contraception, and, 862
Disability discrimination
resource allocation, and, 68–69
Discharge
compulsory admission to hospital, and, 548–549
Disciplinary action
compulsory admission to hospital, and, 529–531
health care professionals, and, 258–260
Disclosure to patients
doctors, by, 372–396
introduction, 372
non-therapeutic cases, 384–385
nurses, by, 396–397
paternalism, and, 387
pro-patient trend, 387–396
questions by patient, 385–387
therapeutic cases, 372–383
Discretion
compulsory admission to hospital, and, 524–52
Divergence of professional opinion
clinical negligence actions, and, 163–167
DNA sampling
human tissue, and, 1155–1156
Do not resuscitate orders
generally, 1044–1049
Donation of embryos
assisted reproduction, and, 835–841
Donor anonymity
assisted reproduction, and, 832–835
Donor insemination
assisted reproduction, and, 759
Double effect doctrine
ethics, and, 136–141
murder, and, 1017

Down's syndrome
  medical treatment for children, and, 409–410
  pregnancy, and, 948
Drugs and medicines
  product liability, and, 203–209
Dual responsibilities, doctors with
  breach of confidence claims, and, 621–622
Duty of care
  clinical negligence actions, and, 153–156

EC treaty
  resource allocation, and, 69–70
  right to health care, and, 11
Egg sharing
  assisted reproduction, and, 775–776
Elective ventilation
  organ donation, and, 1163–1164
Electro-convulsive therapy
  medical treatment for mental patient, and,
    534–542
Embryo donation and storage
  assisted reproduction, and, 835–841
Embryo research
  cloning, 725–734
  general, 721–725
  HFEA 1990, under, 724
  stem cell research, 725–734
  Warnock Committee Report, 721–723
Emergencies
  abortion, and, 898–899
  compulsory admission to hospital, and, 526
  medical treatment for mental patient, and,
    542
Employment contracts
  patient confidentiality, and, 568–571
End of life
  active termination of life
    defence to those prosecuted, 1076–1077
    generally, 1072–1076
  advance directives, 1078–1082
  assisted suicide
    generally, 1001
    overview, 997
    Pretty decision, 1001–1014
  autonomy, and, 994
  best interests, and, 993–994
  bibliography, 1087–1088
  criminal law
    murder, 1014–1021
    suicide, 998–1014
  death
    cognitive death, 1099–1100
    determining point of death, 1096–1098
    diagnosis, 1092–1096
    generally, 1090–1092
    introduction, 1089–1090
  do not resuscitate orders, 1044–1049
  double effect doctrine
    ethics, and, 136–141
    murder, 1017
  ethics, and
    acts-omissions doctrine, 136–141

End of life—*cont.*
  ethics, and—*cont.*
    double effect doctrine, 136–141
    euthanasia, 141–144
    introduction, 128
    reproductive ethics, 130–136
    sanctity of life, 128–130
  euthanasia
    ethics, and, 141–144
    generally, 1001
    overview, 997
    Pretty decision, 1001–1014
  failure to provide care, 1018–1021
  human tissue
    bibliography, 1178–1179
    introduction, 1100–1103
    legal regulation, 1121–1162
    negligence claims, 1177–1178
    ownership, 1112–1121
    trafficking, 1150–1153
    transplantation, 1143–1150
    use from living person, 1103–1112
  infanticide, 1017–1018
  introduction, 997–998
  lasting powers of attorney, 1082–1087
  law reform
    active termination of life, 1072–1076
    advance directives, 1078–1082
    defence to those prosecuted, 1076–1077
    mercy killing, 1077–1078
    powers of attorney, 1082–1087
  mercy killing, 1077–1078
  murder/manslaughter
    basic principles, 1014–1016
    failure to provide care, 1018–1021
    infanticide, 1017–1018
    pain-killing drugs, 1016–1017
  organ donation
    bibliography, 1178–1179
    increasing supply, 1162–1177
    introduction, 1100–1103
    negligence claims, 1177–1178
    opting-in registry, 1163–1169
    ownership, 1112–1121
    xenotransplantation, 1170–1177
  overview, 993–995
  pain-killing drugs, 1016–1017
  "passive" euthanasia, 1021
  persistent vegetative state, 1021
  powers of attorney, 1082–1087
  refusal of treatment, 993
  removal of life support systems
    adult patients, 1021–1037
    competent patients, 1058–1060
    conflicts over continuation of treatment,
      1049–1057
    do not resuscitate orders, 1044–1049
    GMC guidance, 1060–1071
    human rights, and, 1037–1044
    introduction, 1021
    overview, 993
  right to die, and, 993

End of life—*cont.*
right to live, 1060–1071
sanctity of life, and, 993
suicide
aiding and abetting, 999–1001
assisted suicide, 1001–1014
general prohibition, 998
Pretty decision, 1001–1014
withdrawal of treatment
adult patients, 1021–1037
competent patients, 1058–1060
conflicts over continuation of treatment,
1049–1057
do not resuscitate orders, 1044–1049
GMC guidance, 1060–1071
human rights, and, 1037–1044
overview, 993
Enforcement
duties to provide health services, of
allocation of resources, 57–79
clinical judgment, 51–57
compensation claims, 79–86
human rights, and, 57–68
introduction, 45
judicial review, 45–79
resource allocation, 51–79
Ethics
abortion, and, 869–874
acts-omissions doctrine, 136–141
assisted reproduction, and
generally, 752–753
introduction, 87
autonomy, 121–123
beginning of life, at
acts-omissions doctrine, 136–141
double effect doctrine, 136–141
euthanasia, 141–144
introduction, 128
reproductive ethics, 130–136
sanctity of life, 128–130
bibliography, 145
breach of confidence, and, 87
clinical research, and, 667–668
consent to treatment, 126–128
consequentialism, 97–102
deontology, 102–104
descriptive relativism, 88
double effect doctrine, 136–141
end of life, at
acts-omissions doctrine, 136–141
double effect doctrine, 136–141
euthanasia, 141–144
introduction, 128
reproductive ethics, 130–136
sanctity of life, 128–130
euthanasia, 141–144
feminist ethics, 111–119
"four principles" approach, 108–111
"harm principle", 92–93
introduction, 87
law and morality, 92–97
meta-ethical relativism, 88

Ethics—*cont.*
moral relativism, 88–92
moral rights, 104–108
nursing ethics, 119–121
paternalism, 124–126
patient confidentiality, and
GMC guidance, 567–568
introduction, 567
NMC code, 568
overview, 566
pregnancy, and, 87
principlism, 108–111
reproductive ethics, 130–136
rights, 104–108
sanctity of life, 128–130
utilitarianism, 101–102
valid consent, 126–128
value of life, 128–130
virtue ethics, 111–119
Ethics committees
clinical research, and, 670
Ethics Committees Authority
clinical research, and, 669–670
**EU Charter of Fundamental Rights and
Freedoms**
resource allocation, and, 69
right to health, and, 9
EU law
resource allocation, and, 69–79
European Convention on Human Rights
contagious disease control, and, 17
patient confidentiality, and, 565–566
European Social Charter
right to health, and, 8–9
Euthanasia
ethics, and, 141–144
generally, 1001
overview, 997
Pretty decision, 1001–1014

Failure to act
causation, and, 201–203
Failure to provide care
criminal liability, and, 1018–1021
False imprisonment
consent to treatment, and, 352
Fault-based liability, reform of
Access to Justice (1996), 215
available options
combination of approaches, 225–233
no-fault compensation, 217–224
redress scheme, 233–236
strict liability, 224–225
clinical negligence claims
difficulties with system, 215–217
reforms to system, 217–225
difficulties with tort system, 213–215
introduction, 213
Making Amends (2003)
consultation paper, 217–220, 223–224
recommendations, 225–232
NHS redress scheme, 233–236

Fault-based liability, reform of—*cont.*
no-fault compensation, 217–224
strict liability, 224–225
vaccine damage payments, 221–223
Female circumcision
consent to treatment, and, 356–358
Feminist ethics
ethics, and, 111–119
Foetus
general interests, 902–911
pregnancy, and, 949
status, 870–872
Food
health promotion, and, 25
Force feeding
consent to treatment, and, 370–371
Forced donations
human tissue, and, 1111
Foundation trust hospitals
provision of health services, and, 37–40
"Four principles" approach
ethics, and, 108–111
Fraudulent researchers
clinical research, and, 717–718
Free movement principles
resource allocation, and, 69–79
Freedom of expression
patient confidentiality, and, 598–607

Gamete donation
Blood decision, 765–768
generally, 759–763
HFEA Code, 768–772
payment, 772–775
statutory provisions, 763–764
Warnock Committee Report, 760–761
General Medical Council
clinical research, and
confidentiality of participants'
information, 714–716
research subject consent, 684–686
"fitness to practice" review, 270–2780
introduction, 269
overview, 239
patient confidentiality, and
doctors with dual responsibilities,
621–622
ethics, 567–568
serious communicable diseases, 619–621
reform, 280–287
regulatory role, 269–270
Gillick **competence**
generally, 440–451
overview, 405
refusal of treatment, 451–463
religious belief, 463–470
retreat from original position, 451–470
Grievous bodily harm
consent to treatment, and, 353–356
Gross negligence
criminal liability, and, 209–213

Guardianship
community care, and, 553–555

"Harm principle"
ethics, and, 92–93
Health, right to
bibliography, 86
EU Charter of Fundamental Rights and
Freedoms, 9
European Social Charter, 8–9
International Covenant on Economic, Social
and Cultural Rights, 8
introduction, 7
scope, 8–11
UN Convention on Rights of Child, 9–10
Health care ethics
acts-omissions doctrine, 136–141
assisted reproduction, and, 87
autonomy, 121–123
beginning of life, at
acts-omissions doctrine, 136–141
double effect doctrine, 136–141
euthanasia, 141–144
introduction, 128
reproductive ethics, 130–136
sanctity of life, 128–130
bibliography, 145
breach of confidence, and, 87
consent to treatment, 126–128
consequentialism, 97–102
deontology, 102–104
descriptive relativism, 88
double effect doctrine, 136–141
end of life, at
acts-omissions doctrine, 136–141
double effect doctrine, 136–141
euthanasia, 141–144
introduction, 128
reproductive ethics, 130–136
sanctity of life, 128–130
euthanasia, 141–144
feminist ethics, 111–119
"four principles" approach, 108–111
"harm principle", 92–93
introduction, 87
law and morality, 92–97
meta-ethical relativism, 88
moral relativism, 88–92
moral rights, 104–108
nursing ethics, 119–121
paternalism, 124–126
pregnancy, and, 87
principlism, 108–111
reproductive ethics, 130–136
rights, 104–108
sanctity of life, 128–130
utilitarianism, 101–102
valid consent, 126–128
value of life, 128–130
virtue ethics, 111–119

Health care, right to
access to health services
community care, 43–44
duties to provide, 41–44
enforcement of duties to provide, 45–86
introduction, 41
obligation of NHS, 41–43
allocation of resources
clinical judgment, 51–57
disability discrimination, 68–69
EU law, 69–79
free movement principles, 69–79
human rights, and, 57–68
procedural irregularities, 68
bibliography, 86
compensation claims, 79–86
compulsory care
generally, 22
Mental Health Act, under, 22
National Assistance Acts, under, 22–24
contagious disease control, 11–22
duties to provide health services
community care, 43–44
enforcement, 45–86
generally, 41
obligation of NHS, 41–43
EC Treaty, 11
enforcement of duties to provide health
services
allocation of resources, 57–79
clinical judgment, 51–57
compensation claims, 79–86
human rights, and, 57–68
introduction, 45
judicial review, 45–79
resource allocation, 51–79
food, and, 25
foundation trust hospitals, 37–40
health promotion, 24–30
human rights, and
introduction, 7
scope, 8–11
introduction, 7
judicial review
allocation of resources, 57–79
clinical judgment, 51–57
introduction, 45–51
NHS contracts, 35–37
NHS trusts, 33–35
primary care, 30–33
provision of health services
foundation trust hospitals, 37–40
introduction, 30
NHS contracts, 35–37
NHS trusts, 33–35
primary care, 30–33
secondary care, 33–40
resource allocation
clinical judgment, 51–57
disability discrimination, 68–69
EU law, 69–79
free movement principles, 69–79

Health care, right to—*cont.*
resource allocation—*cont.*
human rights, and, 57–68
procedural irregularities, 68
right to be ill, 22–24
role of the state
compulsory care, 22–24
contagious disease control, 11–22
health promotion, 24–30
introduction, 11
overview, 7
right to be ill, 22–24
scope, 8–11
secondary care
foundation trust hospitals, 37–40
NHS contracts, 35–37
NHS trusts, 33–35
smoking, and, 25–30
Health promotion
pregnancy, and, 949
right to health care, and, 24–30
Health Service Commissioner
complaints processes, and, 260–268
Health service provision
foundation trust hospitals, 37–40
introduction, 30
NHS contracts, 35–37
NHS trusts, 33–35
primary care, 30–33
secondary care, 33–40
Healthcare Commission
annual reports, 258
decision on handling of complaint, 255
introduction, 252–253
investigation, 255–256
monitoring, 257–258
panels, 256
remit, 253–254
report of investigation, 257
HIV tests
breach of confidence claims, and, 598–607
consent to treatment, and, 368–370
medical treatment for children, and, 473–475
Holding powers
compulsory admission to hospital, and,
526–528
Hormone implantation
medical treatment for mental patient, and,
532–533
**Human Fertilisation and Embryology
Authority**
constitution, 754–755
introduction, 753
Human rights
assisted reproduction, and, 814–817
consent to treatment, and, 349
mental health system, and
informal admission to hospital, 498–501
introduction, 479
safeguards, 489–491
removal of life support systems, and,
1037–1044

Human rights—*cont.*
resource allocation, and, 57–68
right to health care, and
introduction, 7
resource allocation, 57–68
scope, 8–11
Human tissue
Alder Hey inquiry, 1102–1103
anonymised material, 1139–1140
appropriate consent
adults, 1131–1133
children, 1129–1131
conditions, 1128–1129
deceased's tissue, for, 1134–1135
exceptions to principle, 1138–1142
form, 1125–1126
incompetent adults, 1135–1138
nominated representative, 1133–1134
person able to give, 1129–1138
scope, 1126–1128
timing, 1122–1125
withdrawal, 1128
artificial transplants, and, 1101
bibliography, 1178–1179
codes of practice, 1161–1162
Coroners, 1142–1143
criminal sanctions, 1153–1156
DNA sampling, and, 1155–1156
exceptions to consent principle
anonymised material, 1139–1140
existing holdings, 1141–1142
generally, 1138–1139
untraceable persons, 1140–1141
existing holdings, 1141–1142
forced donations, 1111
Human Tissue Act 2004
appropriate consent, 1122–1129
background, 1101–1102
codes of practice, 1161–1162
Coroners, 1142–1143
criminal sanctions, 1153–1156
exceptions to consent principle,
1138–1142
generally, 1121–1122
Human Tissue Authority, 1156–1161
person able to consent, 1129–1138
scope, 1122–1129
trafficking in materials, 1150–1153
transplantation from living donors,
1143–1150
Human Tissue Authority
functions, 1158–1159
generally, 1156–1157
licensing, 1159–1161
remit, 1157–1158
introduction, 1100–1103
legislative history, 1101–1102
living person, from
anencephalic infant, 1111–1112
children, 1108–1111
competent adults, 1104
force, by, 1111

Human tissue—*cont.*
living person, from—*cont.*
incompetent adults, 1105–1108
introduction, 1103
negligence claims, 1177–1178
ownership, 1112–1121
person able to consent, 1129–1138
research purposes, 1139–1140
trafficking, 1150–1153
transplantation from live donor
generally, 1143–1144
increasing supply of organs, 1162–1176
independent assessor's role, 1149–1150
procedure, 1144–1148
trafficking in materials, 1150–1153
untraceable persons, and, 1140–1141
use from living person, 1103–1112
xenographs, and, 1101
Human Tissue Authority
functions, 1158–1159
generally, 1156–1157
licensing, 1159–1161
remit, 1157–1158
Hydrocephalus
medical treatment for children, and, 411–412
Hysterectomy
contraception, and, 862

Implantable contraception
reproductive choice, and, 751
In vitro **fertilisation**
definitions, 777
generally, 777–781
Warnock Committee Report, 777–778
Incompetent adults
abortion, and, 901–902
breach of confidence claims, and, 592–595
clinical research, and
general issues, 692
non-therapeutic research, 693–696
statutory provisions, 696–702
human tissue, and, 1105–1108
medicinal product trials, and, 711–714
removal of life support systems, and
adult patients, 1021–1037
conflicts over continuation of treatment,
1049–1057
do not resuscitate orders, 1044–1049
human rights, and, 1037–1044
introduction, 1021
sterilisation, and
adult men, 938–941
adult women, 941–947
adults, 933–947
best interests, 926
Bolam test, 938
case law, 927–938
eugenics, and, 926
general principles, 926–927
minors, 927–933
new approach, 938–947

Inexperienced practitioners
clinical negligence actions, and, 174 —179
Infanticide
criminal liability, and, 1017–1018
Infertility treatment
assisted insemination
Blood decision, 765–768
generally, 759–763
HFEA Code, 768–772
payment, 772–775
statutory provisions, 763–764
Warnock Committee Report, 760–761
bibliography, 856–857
cloning, 850–853
conscientious objection, 812
donation of embryos, 835–841
donor anonymity, 832–835
donor insemination, 759
egg sharing, 775–776
embryo donation and storage, 835–841
ethics, and
generally, 752–753
introduction, 87
gamete donation
Blood decision, 765–768
generally, 759–763
HFEA Code, 768–772
payment, 772–775
statutory provisions, 763–764
Warnock Committee Report, 760–761
Human Fertilisation and Embryology
Authority
constitution, 754–755
introduction, 753
legislative framework, 755–758
human rights, and, 814–817
impact of technologies on the family
children, 828–835
fathers, 819–828
introduction, 817–818
mothers, 818–819
in vitro fertilisation
definitions, 777
generally, 777–781
Warnock Committee Report, 777–778
introduction, 751–753
limits on choice
cloning, 850–853
introduction, 841
saviour siblings, 841–848
sex selection, 848–850
negligence in provision, 855–856
patient confidentiality, and, 623–627
pre-implantation diagnosis (PGD), 851
procreative tourism, 853–854
resource allocation
generally, 812–814
NICE guideline, 813
rights to reproduce, 814–817
saviour siblings, 841–848
sex selection, 848–850
sibling selection, 841–848

Infertility treatment—*cont.*
sperm donation
Blood decision, 765–768
generally, 759–763
HFEA Code, 768–772
payment, 772–775
statutory provisions, 763–764
Warnock Committee Report, 760–761
storage of embryos, 835–841
surrogacy
definitions, 781–782
dispute resolution, 793–796
generally, 781–783
judicial attitudes, 784–787
legislative approach, 787–793
reforms, 797–802
terms of arrangement, 796–797
Warnock Committee Report, 782–783
techniques for alleviating
gamete donation, 759–776
in vitro fertilisation, 777–781
introduction, 758
surrogacy, 781–802
welfare of child
generally, 802–812
HFEA Code, 807–809
judicial review, 804–806
statutory provision, 806–807
Warnock Committee Report, 803
Informal admission to hospital
mental health system, and, 492–501
Informed consent
and see **Consent to treatment**
generally, 350
Injunctions
breach of confidence claims, and, 622
**International Convention on the Rights of
the Child**
medical treatment for children, and, 406
**International Covenant on Economic, Social
and Cultural Rights**
right to health, and, 8
Intrauterine device (IUD)
contraception, and, 863
reproductive choice, and, 751

Jehovah's Witnesses
medical treatment for children, and, 417–418
Judicial proceedings
patient confidentiality, and, 634–637
Judicial review
duties to provide health services, of
allocation of resources, 57–79
clinical judgment, 51–57
introduction, 45–51

Lasting powers of attorney
end of life, and, 1082–1087
Least restrictive alternative
compulsory admission to hospital, and, 517

Leave of absence
compulsory admission to hospital, and,
    528–529
Life-saving treatment
medical treatment for children, and, 408

Making Amends **(DoH, 2003)**
consultation paper, 217–220, 223–224
recommendations, 225–232
Male circumcision
medical treatment for children, and, 475–477
Male sexual drive
medical treatment for mental patient, and,
    532–533
Malpractice claims
and see **Medical negligence claims**
generally, 152–203
Manslaughter
criminal liability, and, 209–213
Medical negligence claims
balance of probabilities, 179
Bolam test
    generally, 158–159
    impact on causation, 201–203
    reaction to, 167–174
burden of proof, 179–183
causation
    failure to act, and, 201–203
    generally, 183–203
    loss of a chance, 193–201
    standard of care, 188–193
"claims consciousness", 151
"defensive medicine", and, 150
divergence of professional opinion, 163–167
duty of care, 153–156
inexperienced practitioners, 174–179
introduction, 152–153
overview, 149–150
reform of fault-based liability, and
    difficulties with system, 215–217
    NHS redress scheme, 233–236
    no-fault compensation, 217–224
    strict liability, 224–225
res ipsa loquitur, 179–183
standard of care
    Bolam test, 158–159
    Bolitho decision, 167–173
    divergence of professional opinion,
        163–167
    generally, 157–162
    inexperienced practitioners, 174–179
    Marriott decision, 173–174
Medical treatment
autonomy, and, 291–293
Bolam test, and, 292
capacity to consent
    and see **Capacity to consent to
        treatment**
    best interests test, 320–347
    bibliography, 347–248
    common law, at, 308–314
    introduction, 295–296

Medical treatment—*cont.*
capacity to consent—*cont.*
    Mental Capacity Act 2005, under,
        314–320
    overview, 292
    principles, 298–302
    reform process, 296–298
    refusal of treatment, 302–307
children
    bibliography, 477–478
    Gillick competence, 439–470
    introduction, 405–407
    limits to parental power of consent,
        470–477
    older child, 439–451
    young child, 407–439
clinical research
    and see **Clinical research**
    animal research, 734–742
    approval of trials, 670–682
    bibliography, 742–743
    compensation for harm, 719–721
    confidentiality of participants'
        information, 714–717
    embryo research, 721–734
    fraudulent researchers, 717–718
    introduction, 667–669
    medicinal product trials, 703–714
    national oversight, 669–670
    overview, 292
    regulation, 669–670
    Research Ethics Committee, 670–682
    research subject consent, 682–703
    scrutiny of clinical trial approvals,
        718–719
compulsory admission to hospital, and
    electro-convulsive therapy, 534–542
    emergencies, 542
    hormone implantation, 532–533
    introduction, 531–532
    medication, 533–534
    other, 543–547
    psychosurgery, 532–533
    reduction of male sexual drive, 532–533
    reforms, 547
consent
    and see **Consent to treatment**
    bibliography, 402–403
    introduction, 349–351
    meaning, 360–397
    need, 351–360
    overview, 292
    vitiation, 397–402
introduction, 291–293
mental patients
    admission to hospital, 492–501
    bibliography, 561–564
    community care, 552–561
    compulsory admission to hospital,
        502–528
    discharge, 548–549
    in hospital treatment, 528–548

Medical treatment—*cont.*
mental patients—*cont.*
introduction, 479
Mental Health Review Tribunals, 549–552
principles, 482–488
reforms, 479–482
safeguards, 488–492
patient confidentiality
and see **Patient confidentiality**
access to medical reports, 654–664
bibliography, 664–665
breach of confidence, 571–623
criminal investigations, 633–634
data protection, 637–654
employment contracts, 568–571
introduction, 565–567
judicial proceedings, 634–637
non-statutory protection, 571–623
overview, 292–293
professional obligations and codes, 567–568
statutory exceptions, 627–632
statutory protection, 623–627
self-determination, and, 292
Medication
medical treatment for mental patient, and, 533–534
Medicinal product trials
children, 709–711
incompetent adults, 711–714
informed consent, 709
introduction, 703–704
Regulations, 705–707
scrutiny by REC, 707–709
Medicines and drugs
product liability, and, 203–209
Mental Health Commission
compulsory admission to hospital, and, 547–548
Mental Health Review Tribunals
compulsory admission to hospital, and, 549–552
Mental health system
admission to hospital, 492–501
after-care under supervision, 555–561
bibliography, 561–564
Bournewood safeguards, 492–498
community care
after-care under supervision, 555–561
guardianship, 553–555
introduction, 552–553
community supervision orders, 557–558
community treatment orders, 557
compulsory admission to hospital
applications, 521–522
arrival at hospital, 522–524
criteria, 510–520
degree of mental disorder, 517
discretion of doctor, 524–525
doctor's recommendations, 522
emergencies, in, 526
general provisions, 502–504

Mental health system—*cont.*
compulsory admission to hospital—*cont.*
holding powers, 526–528
"hospital", 502
informal resident, of, 526–528
introduction, 502
least restrictive alternative, 517
mental disorder, 504–510
mental illness, 504–507
mental impairment, 504
nature of mental disorder, 517
need for treatment, 511–515
prior arrangements, 522–524
procedure, 520–526
psychopathic disorder, 504, 508
reform proposals, 517–520, 525–526
severe mental impairment, 504, 507
treatability, 515–517
voluntary resident, of, 526–528
control of patient activity, 529–531
correspondence, 547
criminal justice system, and, 479
detention, 528
discharge, 548–549
discipline, 529–531
guardianship, 553–555
human rights, and
informal admission to hospital, 498–501
introduction, 479
safeguards, 489–491
in hospital treatment
control of patient activity, 529–531
correspondence, 547
detention, 528
discipline, 529–531
introduction, 528
leave of absence, 528–529
medical treatment, 531–547
MHC's role, 547–548
patient information, 547
review, 547–548
informal admission to hospital, 492–501
introduction, 479
leave of absence, 528–529
medical treatment
electro-convulsive therapy, 534–542
emergencies, 542
hormone implantation, 532–533
introduction, 531–532
medication, 533–534
other, 543–547
psychosurgery, 532–533
reduction of male sexual drive, 532–533
reforms, 547
Mental Health Commission's role, 547–548
Mental Health Review Tribunals, 549–552
parens patriae, 482–483
patient information, 547
principles, 482–488
reforms
compulsory admission to hospital, 517–520, 525–526

Mental health system—*cont.*
  reforms—*cont.*
    medical treatment, 547
    MHA 1993, of, 479–482
  review of detention, 547–548
  Richardson report, 480
  safeguards, 488–492
  supervised community treatment, 560–561
  voluntary admission to hospital, 492
Mercy killing
  end of life, and, 1077–1078
Meta-ethical relativism
  ethics, and, 88
Moral relativism
  ethics, and, 88–92
Moral rights
  ethics, and, 104–108
Morality
  ethics, and, 92–97
Multi-centred research
  clinical research, and, 675–676
Murder/manslaughter
  basic principles, 1014–1016
  failure to provide care, 1018–1021
  infanticide, 1017–1018
  pain-killing drugs, 1016–1017

National health service provision
  foundation trust hospitals, 37–40
  introduction, 30
  NHS contracts, 35–37
  NHS trusts, 33–35
  primary care, 30–33
  secondary care, 33–40
Negligence
  assisted reproduction, and, 855–856
  childbirth, and
    basis, 976–977
    causation, 977–978
    child, by or on behalf of, 962–971
    child born dead, 962
    congenital disabilities, 962–967
    damages, 978–988
    introduction, 961–962
    parents, by, 977–988
    wrongful life, 967–971
  contraception, and, 865–868
  human tissue, and, 1177–1178
  malpractice actions
    and see **Clinical negligence actions**
    burden of proof, 179–183
    causation, 183–203
    duty of care, 153–156
    introduction, 152–153
    standard of care, 157–179
  organ donation, and, 1177–1178
  Interim Regulatory Authority, 1176–1177
  introduction, 1170–1171
  pregnancy, and, 961–988
  sterilisation, and
    basis, 976–977
    causation, 977–978

Negligence—*cont.*
  sterilisation, and—*cont.*
    child, by or on behalf of, 962–971
    child born dead, 962
    congenital disabilities, 962–967
    damages, 978–988
    introduction, 961–962
    parents, by, 977–988
    wrongful life, 967–971
Neoplasia
  patient confidentiality, and, 630
NHS complaints
  acknowledgement, 250–251
  aims, 241–242
  Being Heard (DOH, 1994) 241–242
  complainants, 248–249
  complaints manager, 245
  consideration, 244–245
  excluded matters, 246–247
  form and content, 249
  handling arrangements, 244–245
  independent review, 252–258
  introduction, 240–241
  investigation, 251
  local resolution, 244–252
  Making Things Right (DOH, 2003) 243
  NHS bodies, to, 246
  process, 243–258
  records, 250–251
  response, 252
  responsibility for arrangements, 245
  time limits, 249–250
NHS contracts
  provision of health services, and, 35–37
NHS disciplinary procedures
  health care professionals, and, 258–260
NHS redress scheme
  reform of fault-based liability, and, 233–236
NHS trusts
  provision of health services, and, 33–35
No-fault compensation
  reform of fault-based liability, and, 217–224
Nuffield Council on Bioethics
  animal research, and, 738–741
  human tissue, and, 1113–1116
  smoking, and, 26–27
  xenotransplantation, and, 1171–1175
Nursing and Midwifery Council
  complaints processes, and, 239
Nursing ethics
  ethics, and, 119–121

Ombudsman
  complaints processes, and, 239
Opting-in registry
  organ donation, and, 1163
Opting-out scheme
  organ donation, and, 1164–1168
Oral contraception
  generally, 863–864
  reproductive choice, and, 751

Organ donation
altering clinical procedures, 1163–1164
bibliography, 1178–1179
commercial dealings, and, 1169–1170
elective ventilation, 1163–1164
increasing supply, 1162–1163
introduction, 1100–1103
negligence claims, 1177–1178
opting-in registry, 1163
opting-out scheme, 1164–1168
ownership, 1112–1121
presumed consent, 1164–1168
required request/routine enquiry, 1168–1169
xenotransplantation
    ethical issues, 1171–1175
    Interim Regulatory Authority, 1176–1177
    introduction, 1170–1171

Pain-killing drugs
end of life, and, 1016–1017
Parens patriae
mental health system, and, 482–483
"Passive" euthanasia
end of life, and, 1021
Patches
contraception, and, 863
Paternalism
consent to treatment, and, 387
ethics, and, 124–126
Patient confidentiality
access to health records
    common law, at, 660–664
    Data Protection Act 1998, under, 647–652
access to medical records in legal
    proceedings, 658–660
access to medical reports, 654–664
anonymised information, 579–581
bibliography, 664–665
breach of confidence claims
    anonymised information, 579–581
    applicants, 581–596
    basis for action, 571–573
    children, by, 581–592
    damages, 622–623
    deceased patient, by, 595–596
    doctors with dual responsibilities,
        621–622
    grounds for disclosure, 596–621
    incompetent adult, by, 592–595
    injunctions, 622
    relationship with privacy, 573–579
    remedies for breach, 622–623
communicable diseases, 630–631
consent to disclosure, 596–598
criminal investigations, 633–634
data protection
    access to health records, 647–652
    anonymisation, 645–647
    conditions for processing, 642–644
    damages, and, 653
    data protection principles, 641
    exceptions, 644–645

Patient confidentiality—*cont.*
data protection—*cont.*
    "health professional", 640–641
    "health records", 640
    introduction, 637–638
    legal proceedings, 645
    overview, 566
    processing, 639–640
    rectification of data, 653–654
    remedies, 652–654
    research, history and statistics, 644–645
    scope of provisions, 639–641
    sensitive personal data, 640
    statutory provision, 638–654
employment contracts, 568–571
ethics, and
    GMC guidance, 567–568
    introduction, 567
    NMC code, 568
    overview, 566
European Convention on Human Rights,
    and, 565–566
freedom of expression, 598–607
GMC guidance
    doctors with dual responsibilities,
        621–622
    ethics, 567–568
    serious communicable diseases, 619–621
grounds for disclosure
    consent, 596–598
    public interest, 598–621
health care professionals with HIV/AIDS,
    598–607
infertility treatment, 623–627
introduction, 565–567
judicial proceedings, 634–637
neoplasia, 630
non-statutory protection, 571–623
overview, 292–293
Patient Information Advisory Group, 629
privacy, and, 573–579
professional obligations and codes, 567–568
public health risks, 630–631
public interest, and
    freedom of expression, 598–607
    introduction, 598
    risk to public, 607–619
    serious communicable diseases, 619–621
right to respect for private and family life,
    565
risk to public, 607–619
serious communicable diseases, 619–621
statutory exceptions, 627–632
statutory protection
    infertility treatment, 623–627
    introduction, 623
    veneral disease, 623
veneral disease, 623
Patient information
compulsory admission to hospital, and, 547
doctors, by, 372–396
introduction, 372

Patient information—*cont.*
non-therapeutic cases, 384–385
nurses, by, 396–397
paternalism, and, 387
pro-patient trend, 387–396
questions by patient, 385–387
therapeutic cases, 372–383
Patient Information Advisory Group
patient confidentiality, and, 629
Persistent vegetative state
end of life, and, 1021
Post-coital contraception
abortion, and, 894–898
Powers of attorney
end of life, and, 1082–1087
Pregnancy
alcohol consumption, 949
amniocentesis, 948
bibliography, 988–989
chorus villus sampling, 948
Down's syndrome, and, 948
ethics, and, 87
health promotion, 949
management, 948–952
negligence claims, 961–988
pre-natal genetic diagnosis, 948
smoking, 949
status of foetus, 949
ultrasound, 948–949
Pre-implantation diagnosis (PGD)
assisted reproduction, and, 851
Pre-natal genetic diagnosis
pregnancy, and, 948
Primary care
provision of health services, and, 30–33
Principlism
ethics, and, 108–111
Privacy
patient confidentiality, and, 573–579
Procedural irregularities
resource allocation, and, 68
Procreative tourism
assisted reproduction, and, 853–854
Product liability
drugs and medicines, and, 203–209
Professional accountability
bibliography, 236–237
Bolam test, 149
clinical negligence actions
burden of proof, 179–183
causation, 183–203
duty of care, 153–156
introduction, 152–153
standard of care, 157–179
complaints processes
bibliography, 287–288
Health Service Commissioner, 260–268
introduction, 239–240
NHS complaints, 240–258
NHS disciplinary procedures, 258–260
self-regulation by professions, 268–277
criminal liability, 209–213

Professional accountability—*cont.*
defective medicinal products and drugs,
203–209
defensive medicine, 149
gross negligence, 209–213
introduction, 151–152
overview, 149–150
reform of fault-based liability
available options, 217–236
difficulties with clinical negligence
litigation, 215–217
difficulties with tort system, 213–215
introduction, 213
no-fault compensation, 217–224
strict liability, 224–225
risk management, 149
self-regulation, 150
Prostaglandin termination
abortion, and, 892
Psychosurgery
medical treatment for mental patient, and,
532–533
Public health risks
patient confidentiality, and, 630–631
Public interest
patient confidentiality, and
freedom of expression, 598–607
introduction, 598
risk to public, 607–619
serious communicable diseases, 619–621

Randomised clinical trials
research subject consent, and, 686–688
"Real consent"
consent to treatment, and, 360–365
Reform of fault-based liability
Access to Justice (1996), 215
available options
combination of approaches, 225–233
no-fault compensation, 217–224
redress scheme, 233–236
strict liability, 224–225
clinical negligence claims
difficulties with system, 215–217
reforms to system, 217–225
difficulties with tort system, 213–215
introduction, 213
Making Amends (2003)
consultation paper, 217–220, 223–224
recommendations, 225–232
NHS redress scheme, 233–236
no-fault compensation, 217–224
strict liability, 224–225
vaccine damage payments, 221–223
Refusal of treatment
capacity to consent to treatment, and,
302–307
children, and
generally, 451–463
religious belief, 463–470
end of life, and, 993

Religious belief
medical treatment for children, and, 463–470
Removal of life support systems
adult patients, 1021–1037
competent patients, 1058–1060
conflicts over continuation of treatment, 1049–1057
do not resuscitate orders, 1044–1049
GMC guidance, 1060–1071
human rights, and, 1037–1044
introduction, 1021
overview, 993
Reproductive choice
and see under individual headings
abortion
bibliography, 923–924
certification, 886–891
conscientious objection, 919–922
criminal prohibition, 874–878
emergency situations, 898–899
ethics, 869–874
interests of different parties, 899–919
introduction, 859–860
lawful termination, 878–886
legal framework, 874–899
methods of treatment, 891–898
places of treatment, 886
status of the foetus, 870–872
assisted conception
access to reproductive technologies, 802–812
bibliography, 856–857
cloning, 850–853
conscientious objection, 812
donation of embryos, 835–841
gamete donation, 759–776
HFEA, 753–758
impact of technologies on the family, 817–835
in vitro fertilisation, 777–781
introduction, 751–753
limits on choice, 841–853
negligence in provision, 855–856
procreative tourism, 853–854
resource allocation, 812–814
rights to reproduce, 814–817
sex selection, 848–850
sibling selection, 841–848
storage of embryos, 835–841
surrogacy, 781–802
techniques for alleviating infertility, 758–802
welfare of child, 802–812
childbirth
bibliography, 988–989
choice of place and method, 952–954
enforced Caesareans, 954–961
negligence claims, 961–988
contraception
generally, 860–869
introduction, 859–860
ethics, and, 130–136

Reproductive choice—*cont.*
introduction, 747–750
medical treatment for children, and, 471
pregnancy
bibliography, 988–989
management, 948–952
negligence claims, 961–988
sterilisation
authorisation on incompetent patient, 926–948
bibliography, 988–989
introduction, 925–926
negligence claims, 961–988
Required request/routine enquiry
organ donation, and, 1168–1169
Res ipsa loquitur
clinical negligence actions, and, 179–183
Research
human tissue, and, 1139–1140
Research (clinical trials)
animal research, 734–742
approval of trials
challenging decision, 718
role of Research Ethics Committee, 670–682
scrutiny, 718–719
bibliography, 742–743
cloning, 725–734
compensation for harm, 719–721
confidentiality of participants' information, 714–717
Declaration of Helsinki, 667
embryo research
cloning, 725–734
general, 721–725
HFEA 1990, under, 724
stem cell research, 725–734
Warnock Committee Report, 721–723
ethics, and, 667–668
ethics committees, 670
Ethics Committees Authority, 669–670
fraudulent researchers, 717–718
GMC guidance
confidentiality of participants' information, 714–716
research subject consent, 684–686
incompetent adults
general issues, 692
non-therapeutic research, 693–696
statutory provisions, 696–702
introduction, 667–669
medicinal product trials
children, 709–711
incompetent adults, 711–714
informed consent, 709
introduction, 703–704
Regulations, 705–707
scrutiny by REC, 707–709
multi-centred research, 675–676
national oversight, 669–670
overview, 292
regulation, 669–670

Research (clinical trials)—*cont.*
  Research Ethics Committee
    approval of multi-centred research,
      675–676
    consent of research subject, 683
    follow-up, 702–703
    introduction, 670
    liability of members for injuries, 719
    membership, 673–675
    procedure for review of trials, 676–680
    reform of system, 681–682
    remit, 670–673
  research subject consent
    child subjects, 688–692
    follow-up by REC, 702–703
    generally, 682–686
    GMC guidance, 684–686
    incompetent adults, 692–702
    randomised clinical trials, 686–688
    REC guidance, 683
  scrutiny of clinical trial approvals, 718–719
  stem cell research, 725–734
  Warnock Committee Report, 721–723
Research Ethics Committee
  approval of multi-centred research, 675–676
  consent of research subject, 683
  follow-up, 702–703
  introduction, 670
  liability of members for injuries, 719
  membership, 673–675
  procedure for review of trials, 676–680
  reform of system, 681–682
  remit, 670–673
Research subject consent
  child subjects, 688–692
  follow-up by REC, 702–703
  generally, 682–686
  GMC guidance, 684–686
  incompetent adults, 692–702
  randomised clinical trials, 686–688
  REC guidance, 683
Resource allocation
  assisted reproduction, and
    generally, 812–814
    NICE guideline, 813
  clinical judgment, 51–57
  disability discrimination, 68–69
  EU law, 69–79
  free movement principles, 69–79
  human rights, and, 57–68
  procedural irregularities, 68
Review of detention
  compulsory admission to hospital, and,
    547–548
Richardson report
  mental health system, and, 480
Right to be ill
  compulsory care, and, 22–24
Right to bodily integrity
  consent to treatment, and, 351
Right to die
  end of life, and, 993

Right to health
  bibliography, 86
  EU Charter of Fundamental Rights and
    Freedoms, 9
  European Social Charter, 8–9
  International Covenant on Economic, Social
    and Cultural Rights, 8
  introduction, 7
  scope, 8–11
  UN Convention on Rights of Child, 9–10
Right to health care
  access to health services
    community care, 43–44
    duties to provide, 41–44
    enforcement of duties to provide, 45–86
    introduction, 41
    obligation of NHS, 41–43
  allocation of resources
    clinical judgment, 51–57
    disability discrimination, 68–69
    EU law, 69–79
    free movement principles, 69–79
    human rights, and, 57–68
    procedural irregularities, 68
  bibliography, 86
  compensation claims, 79–86
  compulsory care
    generally, 22
    Mental Health Act, under, 22
    National Assistance Acts, under, 22–24
  contagious disease control, 11–22
  duties to provide health services
    community care, 43–44
    enforcement, 45–86
    generally, 41
    obligation of NHS, 41–43
  EC Treaty, 11
  enforcement of duties to provide health
    services
    allocation of resources, 57–79
    clinical judgment, 51–57
    compensation claims, 79–86
    human rights, and, 57–68
    introduction, 45
    judicial review, 45–79
    resource allocation, 51–79
  food, and, 25
  foundation trust hospitals, 37–40
  health promotion, 24–30
  human rights, and
    introduction, 7
    scope, 8–11
  introduction, 7
  judicial review
    allocation of resources, 57–79
    clinical judgment, 51–57
    introduction, 45–51
  NHS contracts, 35–37
  NHS trusts, 33–35
  primary care, 30–33
  provision of health services
    foundation trust hospitals, 37–40

Right to health care—*cont.*
provision of health services—*cont.*
introduction, 30
NHS contracts, 35–37
NHS trusts, 33–35
primary care, 30–33
secondary care, 33–40
resource allocation
clinical judgment, 51–57
disability discrimination, 68–69
EU law, 69–79
free movement principles, 69–79
human rights, and, 57–68
procedural irregularities, 68
right to be ill, 22–24
role of the state
compulsory care, 22–24
contagious disease control, 11–22
health promotion, 24–30
introduction, 11
overview, 7
right to be ill, 22–24
scope, 8–11
secondary care
foundation trust hospitals, 37–40
NHS contracts, 35–37
NHS trusts, 33–35
smoking, and, 25–30
Right to live
end of life, and, 1060–1071
Right to reproduce
assisted reproduction, and, 814–817
Right to respect for private and family life
patient confidentiality, and, 565
Rights
ethics, and, 104–108
Risk management
professional accountability, and, 149
Risk to public
patient confidentiality, and, 607–619
Routine enquiry/required request
organ donation, and, 1168–1169

Sanctity of life
end of life, and, 993
ethics, and, 128–130
Saviour siblings
assisted reproduction, and, 841–848
Secondary care
foundation trust hospitals, 37–40
NHS contracts, 35–37
NHS trusts, 33–35
Self-determination
consent to treatment, and, 349
medical treatment, and, 292
Self-regulation by professions
General Medical Council
"fitness to practice" review, 270–2780
introduction, 269
overview, 239
reform, 280–287
regulatory role, 269–270

Self-regulation by professions—*cont.*
introduction, 268
overview, 150
Serious communicable diseases
consent to treatment, and, 368–370
patient confidentiality, and, 619–621
Severe disablement
medical treatment for children, and, 415–417
Sex selection
assisted reproduction, and, 848–850
Sexually transmitted diseases
contraception, and, 862–863
Sibling selection
assisted reproduction, and, 841–848
Smoking
health promotion, and, 25–30
pregnancy, and, 949
Sperm donation
Blood decision, 765–768
generally, 759–763
HFEA Code, 768–772
payment, 772–775
statutory provisions, 763–764
Warnock Committee Report, 760–761
Standard of care
Bolam test
generally, 158–159
impact on causation, 201–203
reaction to, 167–174
Bolitho decision, 167–173
divergence of professional opinion, 163–167
generally, 157–162
inexperienced practitioners, 174–179
Marriott decision, 173–174
Stem cell research
embryo research, and, 725–734
Sterilisation
authorisation on incompetent patient
adult men, 938–941
adult women, 941–947
adults, 933–947
best interests, 926
Bolam test, 938
case law, 927–938
eugenics, and, 926
general principles, 926–927
minors, 927–933
new approach, 938–947
bibliography, 988–989
contraception, and, 862
introduction, 925–926
medical treatment for children, and, 470–471
negligence claims
basis, 976–977
causation, 977–978
child, by or on behalf of, 962–971
child born dead, 962
congenital disabilities, 962–967
damages, 978–988
introduction, 961–962
parents, by, 977–988
wrongful life, 967–971

Storage of embryos
assisted reproduction, and, 835–841
Strict liability
reform of fault-based liability, and, 224–225
Suicide
aiding and abetting, 999–1001
assisted suicide, 1001–1014
general prohibition, 998
Pretty decision, 1001–1014
Supervised community treatment
mental health system, and, 560–561
Surgical termination
abortion, and, 892
Surrogacy
definitions, 781–782
dispute resolution, 793–796
generally, 781–783
judicial attitudes, 784–787
legislative approach, 787–793
reforms, 797–802
terms of arrangement, 796–797
Warnock Committee Report, 782–783

Trafficking
human tissue, and, 1150–1153
Transplantation from live donor
generally, 1143–1144
increasing supply or organs, 1162–1176
independent assessor's role, 1149–1150
procedure, 1144–1148
trafficking in materials, 1150–1153
Treatability
compulsory admission to hospital, and,
515–517
Trespass against the person
consent to treatment, and, 358–359

Ultrasound
pregnancy, and, 948–949
UN Convention on Rights of Child
right to health, and, 9–10
Untraceable persons
human tissue, and, 1140–1141
Utilitarianism
ethics, and, 101–102

Vaccine damage payments
reform of fault-based liability, and, 221–223
Valid consent
ethics, and, 126–128
Value of life
ethics, and, 128–130

Vasectomy
contraception, and, 862
Veneral disease
patient confidentiality, and, 623
Virtue ethics
ethics, and, 111–119
Vitiation
consent to treatment, and, 397–402
Voluntary admission to hospital
mental health system, and, 492

Warnock Committee Report
assisted insemination, 760–761
embryo research, 721–723
gamete donation, 760–761
in vitro fertilisation, 777–778
sperm donation, 760–761
surrogacy, 782–783
welfare of child, 803
Welfare of child
assisted reproduction, and
generally, 802–812
HFEA Code, 807–809
judicial review, 804–806
statutory provision, 806–807
Warnock Committee Report, 803
Withdrawal of medical treatment
adult patients, 1021–1037
children, 408–423
competent adult patients, 1058–1060
conflicts over continuation of treatment,
1049–1057
do not resuscitate orders, 1044–1049
GMC guidance, 1060–1071
human rights, and, 1037–1044
overview, 993
Withholding of medical treatment
medical treatment for children, and, 408–423
Wounding
consent to treatment, and, 353–356
Wrongful life
sterilisation, and, 967–971

Xenographs
human tissue, and, 1101
Xenotransplantation
ethical issues, 1171–1175
Interim Regulatory Authority, 1176–1177
introduction, 1170–1171